CRIMINAL LAW

CRIMINAL LAW
Case Studies & Controversies

Successor Edition to

Robinson, Fundamentals of Criminal Law
Second Edition

Paul H. Robinson
University of Pennsylvania Law School

ASPEN

PUBLISHERS

1185 Avenue of the Americas, New York, NY 10036
www.aspenpublishers.com

Permissions
Aspen Publishers
1185 Avenue of the Americas
New York, NY 10036

Printed in the United States of America.

2 3 4 5 6 7 8 9 0

ISBN 0-7355-5075-1

Library of Congress Cataloging-in-Publication Data

Robinson, Paul H.
    Criminal law : case studies & controversies / Paul H. Robinson.
       p.   cm.
    Rev. ed. of: Fundamentals of criminal law / Paul H. Robinson. 2nd ed. 1995.
    Includes index.
    ISBN 0-7355-5075-1
    1. Criminal law—United States—Cases.   I. Robinson, Paul H. Fundamentals of criminal law. II. Title.
KF9218.R63 2004
345.73—dc22

2004057488

About Aspen Publishers

Aspen Publishers, headquartered in New York City, is a leading information provider for attorneys, business professionals, and law students. Written by preeminent authorities, our products consist of analytical and practical information covering both U.S. and international topics. We publish in the full range of formats, including updated manuals, books, periodicals, CDs, and online products.

Our proprietary content is complemented by 2,500 legal databases, containing over 11 million documents, available through our Loislaw division. Aspen Publishers also offers a wide range of topical legal and business databases linked to Loislaw's primary material. Our mission is to provide accurate, timely, and authoritative content in easily accessible formats, supported by unmatched customer care.

To order any Aspen Publishers title, go to *www.aspenpublishers.com* or call 1-800-638-8437.

To reinstate your manual update service, call 1-800-638-8437.

For more information on Loislaw products, go to *www.loislaw.com* or call 1-800-364-2512.

For Customer Care issues, e-mail *CustomerCare@aspenpublishers.com*; call 1-800-234-1660; or fax 1-800-901-9075.

Aspen Publishers
A Wolters Kluwer Company

To Sarah, Mac, Harry, and Atticus

Summary of Contents

Contents

List of Charts and Tables

ABBREVIATION KEY

SCJS: *Sourcebook of Criminal Justice Statistics* (2000); Online at http://www. albany.edu/sourcebook/

JLB: Paul H. Robinson & John M. Darley, *Justice, Liability & Blame* (1995)

N.C.L.Rev.:   Paul H. Robinson & John M. Darley, Testing Competing Theories of Justification, 76 North Carolina Law Review 1095 (1998)

Callahan: Lisa Callahan, et al., Insanity Defense Reform in the United States— Post-*Hinckley,* 11 Mental and Physical Disability Law Reporter 54 (1987)

Preface

Criminal Law: Case Studies & Controversies differs significantly from other criminal law coursebooks in several respects. These differences arise from an effort to achieve three goals:

First, the materials seek to harness for educational purposes the natural interest inherent in criminal law cases. Perhaps more than any other course in the first-year curriculum, criminal law has great potential to engage but commonly fails to live up to that potential. *CS&C* uses the case studies method to put what might otherwise be dry or abstract issues in a context that shows their practical importance. Each of the twenty-six Sections typically begins with a principal case for which the full "story" is given of the people and events leading up to commission of the offense.

Second, *CS&C* offers a more efficient means of conveying an understanding of the operation and diversity of the legal rules in the United States, including an appreciation of how reliant criminal law is upon statutes, in contrast to the case-dominated subjects that otherwise populate the first-year curriculum. Each principal case is followed by the statutes that existed in that jurisdiction at the time of the offense. (And Appendix B contains Parts I & II of the Model Penal Code.) The process of applying these statutes to the case facts develops important lawyering skills, including statutory analysis and interpretation. Over the course of the twenty-six Sections, that application process also helps students accumulate considerable familiarity with criminal law and its diversity.

A second source for learning the legal rules comes from the "Overview" portion in each Section, in which the full range of rules on the specific subject are summarized in a treatise-like form. These materials also give a sense of the rationale for the rules and introduces the more important underlying theoretical issues. A third and final way of gaining familiarity with the rules is the hypothetical Problem case contained in each Section, which gives an opportunity to test one's knowledge of the rules.

A third *CS&C* goal, and another major difference from other current coursebooks, is its in-depth examination of the most important criminal law controversies. Each Section presents at least one important issue of controversy in that subject area as a "discussion question," providing on each side of the issue excerpts from the legal literature, case opinions, and sometimes the social science literature. The analytic and argument exercise that these materials offer not only develops a sophisticated understanding of the competing interests that shape modern criminal law but also trains the student on important lawyering skills.

Typical Structure. To summarize, most of the twenty-six Sections of the coursebook have the following structure:

Principal Case. The text gives two or three pages of factual detail about the people and events leading to the offense, enough to allow a three-dimensional view that will trigger one's own intuitions about an appropriate case disposition. (A "liability scale" at the conclusion of each case asks you to provide your own intuitive judgement about what punishment, if any, the offender deserves. The scale is aimed at putting your own analytic wheels in motion. Your teacher may report how other students as a group have responded.)

The Law. The relevant statutes as they existed in the applicable jurisdiction at the time of the offense are then presented. Where the criminal code is incomplete, as is often the case in non-Model Penal Code jurisdictions, the statutes are supplemented with one-paragraph summaries of the controlling cases that provide the legal rule that is missing from the statutes. The cases are drawn from a wide range of jurisdictions, including Alaska, Arizona, California, Indiana, Kansas, Maine, Maryland, Massachusetts, Michigan, Mississippi, Nevada, New York, Tennessee, Texas, Washington, Wisconsin, Wyoming, the federal system, as well as Israel.

Overview. What follows is a treatise-like presentation of the law and the underlying issues. It puts the law of the principal case in the context of the larger legal picture, so one can know whether the statutes applied above the Overviews represent a majority or minority position. (The format of the paragraph's heading signals the paragraph's importance in relation to other paragraphs. In descending order of superiority the signals are **HEADING, Heading,** *Heading,* Heading.) The theoretical and policy portions of the Overview set up the Discussion Materials later in the Section.

Problem Case(s). Following the Overview is a hypothetical Problem, which is short and straightforward. These Problems provide an opportunity to check your comprehension of the Overview material.

Discussion Question and Literature Excerpts. Next, the most important controversy in the topic area is presented, with excerpts discussing each side of the issue from the legal literature, and sometimes case opinions and social science literature. (In most Sections, the excerpts are divided into core and collateral materials by the heading "Other Discussion Materials." Your instructor will advise you whether you should read only the core materials.)

Appendix A: Advanced Issues. The main volume sticks to the basic issues. A professor may wish to explore more advanced issues using readings contained in this Appendix. Advanced Problems also are included.

Appendix B: Model Penal Code. This reproduces Parts I and II of the Model Penal Code, which serves as the foundation for the majority of American criminal codes and therefore is a useful point of comparison to the statutes appearing after each principal case.

Have a great time with these materials! Criminal law is a wonderful and special subject that has the potential to tell us much about law, our society, and ourselves.

Paul H. Robinson

October 2004

Acknowledgments

This project was made possible by the contributions of many people, in particular the research assistance of Phillip Bullard, Joseph Wheatley, Stephen Valdes, Itia Roth, Leila Fusfeld, Michael Areinoff, and Danielle Estrada, of the University of Pennsylvania Law School, Megan Bell, Elizabeth Black, and Amanda E. Adrian, of Northwestern University School of Law.

Many other people have helped with research into the case facts:*

Regarding the case of Sara Jane Olson, we thank Wanda Queen, of the Federal Bureau of Investigation, for photographs.

Regarding the case of Raymond Lennard Garnett, we thank Deborah St. Jean, Garnett's attorney, formerly with the public defender's office, for an interview; Catherine McAlpine for photographs.

Regarding the case of Thomas Fungwe, we thank prosecutor John O'Hair (retired), for an interview and photograph; Nancy Brown, Director of Communications for the State Bar of Michigan, for photographs; Nancy Diehl, Wayne County Prosecutor's Office, for research leads.

Regarding the case of Thomas Laseter, we thank Paul Canarsky, Laseter's attorney with the public defender's office, for an interview.

Regarding the case of Sabine Davidson, we thank James Hurla, of the Kansas State Collegian, for photographs; Luana Osmani, of the Guard Dog Training Center, for photographs of proper dog training; Anton Strauss, of AVP Productions, for photographs.

Regarding the case of John Gounagias, we thank the Camas-Washougal Historical Society for photographs; and Lanny Weaver, of the Washington State Archives, for court records and documents.

Regarding the case of Joe Paul Govan, we thank Shelly Stevens for photos; Bertha Yanaz, of the Superior Court of Arizona exhibits department, for photographs and research assistance.

Regarding the case of Robert Jackson, we thank Michael Cahill, of Brooklyn Law School, for photographs; W. H. Gilbert, owner, Delaware Auto Consultants, *www.DelawareAutoConsultantLLC.com,* for photographs.

Regarding the case of John Henry Ivy, we thank Joyce R. Loftin, Lee County Circuit Court Clerk, for photographs; Rowland Geddie, Jr., District Attorney in Ivy prosecution, for an interview; Dr. J. Purvis, Professor of Educational Administration, University of Southern Mississippi, Director, Southern Education Consortium, for an interview and insights into occult voodoo practices; Betty Cagle, of the Lee County Library, for research assistance and newspaper articles; Charlie Langford, of the Northeast Mississippi Daily Journal, for photographs; and the Memphis Commercial Review for photographs.

---

* N.B.—The facts recounted in these stories are true as best as we can determine from our research of court documents, newspaper articles, personal interviews, and other available sources. In some places, we have added what we think are reasonable speculations about a person's motivation or state of mind as it appears from the person's conduct and circumstances.

Regarding the case of Sheik Omar Abdel Rahman, we thank Dr. Hesham El Nakib, Director of the Egyptian Press & Information Office, for photographs; Daniel E. Beards for photographs; and Craig Nevill-Manning for photographs.

Regarding the case of Jordan Weaver, we thank Jordan Weaver for an interview; Joyce Perry, Office of County Clerk of Court, Marion County Superior Court, for documents and photographs; Marcell Pratt, trial defense counsel, for an interview; and Dawn Mitchell, of the Indianapolis Star, for research.

Regarding the case of Cardinal Bernard Law, we thank Menachem and Itia Roth for photographs and newspaper articles; the Reverend James F. Rafferty, Pastor of St. Paul's Church, for photographs; and Andy Murphy, of the Columbus Dispatch, for photographs.

Regarding the case of David Cash, we thank Joe Maguire, of the University of Michigan Law Library, for newspaper articles; Frank Reynolds for photographs; and R. Marsh Starks, of the Las Vegas Sun, for photographs.

Regarding the case of Ford Motor Company, we thank Patty Walsh, of And Books, for photographs; Wes Mills, of WNDU-TV, South Bend, Indiana, for photographs; Marion Stilley, assistant to Lee Strobel, for photograph leads; Scott Hamilton, of FordPinto.com, for photographs.

Regarding the case of the Israeli General Security Service, we thank the Palestinian Information Center for photographs; David Gerstein for drawings; and Tom Rose, of the Jerusalem Post, for photographs.

Regarding the case of Elton Hymon, we thank Lt. Elton Hymon, of the Memphis Police Department, for interviews; Julia Davis, of the United States District Court for the Western District of Tennessee, for photographs; Henry L. Klein, attorney for the Memphis Police Department in *Tennessee v. Garner*, for research leads; Steven L. Winter, attorney for Cleamtee Garner, for research leads; Mike Hues, of the Memphis Police Department, for research leads; and Ron Hackett for photographs.

Regarding the case of Andrew Goldstein, we thank Samuel Robinson for photographs.

Regarding the case of Patty Hearst, we thank Florence Fang, owner of the San Francisco Examiner, for photographs; and John Gollin, of the San Francisco Examiner, for photographs.

Regarding the case of Eric Steven Carlson, we thank Greg Babbitt, prosecuting attorney, for an interview.

Regarding the case of Todd Mitchell, we thank Kathy Bach, of the Kenosha Joint Service, for photographs; Michelle Laycock, of the Kenosha Daily News, for photographs; John Sorenson, of Kenosha News Photo, for photographs.

Thanks are also in order for permission to reprint the following material:

Ager, Susan, The Incident Detroit Free Press Magazine 17 (March 22, 1992). Reprinted by permission of the author.

American Law Institute, Model Penal Code Sections 1.01-251.4, Commentary for Sections 2.02, 2.04, 2.06, 210.2, 210.3, 2.13, 3.04, 3.06, 3.09(2), 5.01, and 5.03. Copyright 1985 by the American Law Institute. Reprinted with permission.

Andenaes, Johannes, The General Preventive Effects of Punishment, 114 University of Pennsylvania Law Review 949, 981-983 (1966). Reprinted with permission of the University of Pennsylvania Law Review.

Anderson, Douglas S., Corporate Homicide: The Stark Realities of Artificial Beings and Legal Fictions, 8 Pepperdine Law Review 367, 404-409 (1981). Reprinted with permission of the Pepperdine Law Review.

Ashworth, Andrew, A New Form of Corporate Liability? Principles of Criminal Law 86-88 (1991). Reprinted by permission of the author.

Ashworth, Andrew, Criminal Attempts and the Role of Resulting Harm under the Code and in the Common Law, 19 Rutgers Law Journal 725, 750-753 (1988). Reprinted by permission of the author.

Ashworth, Andrew J., Defences of General Application: The Law Commission's Report No. 83: (3) Entrapment, [1978] Criminal Law Review 137-138. Reprinted by permission of the author.

Bauer, Steven M., & Eckerstrom, Peter J., The State Made Me Do It: The Applicability of the Necessity Defense to Civil Disobedience, 39 Stanford Law Review 1173, 1184-1189 (1987). Reprinted with permission of the Stanford Law Review.

Bedau, Hugo A., Arguments For and Against Capital Punishment, Encyclopedia of Crime and Justice 138-141 (S. Kadish ed., 1983). Reprinted by permission of the author.

Bedau, Hugo A., Innocence and the Death Penalty, The Death Penalty in America: Current Controversies 344, 345, 350-359 (H. Bedau ed., 1997). Reprinted by permission of the author.

Bryden, David P., Redefining Rape, 3 Buffalo Criminal Law Review 317, 373-385 (2000). Reprinted by permission of the author.

Callahan, Lisa, et al., Insanity Defense Reform in the United States — Post-*Hinckley,* 11 Mental and Physical Disability Law Reporter 54-60 (1987). Reprinted by permission of the author.

Coffee, John, Corporate Criminal Responsibility, 1 Encyclopedia of Crime and Justice 253, 256-261 (S. Kadish ed., 1983). Reprinted by permission of the author.

Crocker, Lawrence, Justice in Criminal Liability: Decriminalizing Harmless Attempts, 53 Ohio State Law Journal 1057, 1069-1072 (1992). Originally published in 53 Ohio St. L.J. 1057, 1069-1072 (1972).

Crump & Crump, In Defense of Felony Murder, 8 Harvard Journal of Law and Public Policy 359, 362-364, 367-371 (1985). Reprinted with permission of Harvard Journal of Law and Public Policy.

Delgado, Richard, Ascription of Criminal States of Mind: Toward a Defense Theory for the Coercively Persuaded ("Brainwashed") Defendant, 63 Minnesota Law Review 1, 1-11 (1978). Reprinted by permission of the author.

Delgado, Richard, A Response to Professor Dressler, 63 Minnesota Law Review 361-365 (1979). Reprinted by permission of the author.

Dressler, Joshua, Professor Delgado's "Brainwashing" Defense: Courting a Determinist Legal System, 63 Minnesota Law Review 335, 335-336, 339-340, 351-360 (1979). Reprinted with permission of the author.

Dressler, Joshua, Some Brief Thoughts (Mostly Negative) About "Bad Samaritan" Laws, 40 Santa Clara Law Review 971-975, 980-988 (2000). Reprinted by permission of the author.

Dressler, Joshua, Where We Have Been, and Where We Might be Going: Some Cautionary Reflections on Rape Law Reform, 46 Cleveland State Law Review 409, 430-439 (1998). Reprinted by permission of the author.

Harvard Law Review, Developments in the Law: Criminal Conspiracy, 72 Harvard Law Review 920, 922-925 (1959). Reprinted with permission of the Harvard Law Review.

English, Jodie, The Light Between Twilight and Dusk: Federal Criminal Law and the Volitional Insanity Defense, 40 Hastings Law Journal 1, 45-52 (1988). Reprinted with permission of the Hastings Law Journal.

Epps, Garrett, Any Which Way But Loose: Interpretive Strategies and Attitudes Toward Violence in the Evolution of the Anglo-American "Retreat Rule," 55 Law and Contemporary Problems 303-305, 327-331 (1992). Reprinted by permission of the author.

Estrich, Susan, Rape, 95 Yale Law Journal 1087, 1096-1097, 1098-1101, 1102-1105 (1986). Reprinted by permission of the author.

Filvaroff, David B., Conspiracy and the First Amendment, 121 University of Pennsylvania Law Review 189-193 (1972). Reprinted by permission of the author.

Fletcher, George P., Arguments for Strict Liability: Mistakes of Law, Rethinking Criminal Law 731-736 (1978). Reprinted by permission of the author.

Fletcher, George P., A Crime of Self-Defense: Bernhard Goetz and the Law on Trial 64-67 (1988). Reprinted by permission of the author.

Fletcher, George P., Proportionality and the Psychotic Aggressor: A Vignette in Comparative Criminal Theory, 8 Israel Law Review 367, 367-370, 376, 379-382 (1973). Reprinted by permission of the author.

Fletcher, George P., Provocation Rethinking Criminal Law 246-250 (1978). Reprinted by permission of the author.

Fletcher, George P., The Theory of Criminal Negligence: A Comparative Analysis, 119 University of Pennsylvania Law Review 401, 426-427, 429-430, 433-434 (1971). Reprinted by permission of the author.

Gellman, Susan, Hate Crime Laws Are Thought Crime Laws, 1992/1993 Annual Survey of American Law 509, 509-513, 518-520, 528-531. Reprinted by permission of the author.

Gordon, Margaret T., & Stephanie Riger, The Female Fear: The Social Cost of Rape 2, 26-28, 32-36 (1991). Reprinted by permission of the authors.

Greenawalt, Kent, Conflicts of Law and Morality — Instructions of Amelioration, 67 Virginia Law Review 177, 194-200 (1981). Reprinted by permission of the author.

Hart, H.L.A., Punishment and Responsibility 153-154 (1968). Reprinted with permission of Clarendon Press (imprint of Oxford University Press).

Hart, Henry M., Jr., The Aims of the Criminal Law, 23 Law and Contemporary Problems 401-402 (1958). Reprinted by permission of Law and Contemporary Problems.

Henderson, Lynne N., Review Essay: What Makes Rape a Crime? Review of Estrich, Real Rape, 3 Berkeley Woman's Law Journal 193, 211-219 (1987-88). Reprinted by permission of the author.

Jacobs, James B., & Kimberly Potter, Hate Crime Laws, Hate Crimes: Criminal Law & Identity Politics 29-44 (1998). Reprinted by permission of the authors.

Johnson, Philip E., The Unnecessary Crime of Conspiracy, 61 California Law Review 1137-1141 (1973). Reprinted by permission of the author.

Kadish, Sanford H., The Criminal Law and the Luck of the Draw, 84 Journal of Criminal Law and Criminology 679, 679-690 (1994). Reprinted with permission of the author.

Kahan, Dan M., Ignorance of the Law Is an Excuse — But Only for the Virtuous, 96 Michigan Law Review 127, 131, 133, 141-142 (1997). Reprinted by permission of the author.

Keiter, Mitchell, Just Say No Excuse: The Rise and Fall of the Intoxication Defense, 87 Journal of Criminal Law and Criminology 482, 482-483, 518-519 (1997). Reprinted with permission of the Journal of Criminal Law and Criminology.

LaFave, Wayne R., & Austin W. Scott, Accomplice Liability — Acts and Mental State, 2 Substantive Criminal Law § 13.2(d) (2d ed. 2003). Reprinted with permission of West, a Thomson Business.

LaFave, Wayne, Jerold Israel & Nancy King, An Overview of the Criminal Justice Process: The Steps in the Process, Criminal Procedure § 1.3 (3d ed. 2000). Reprinted with permission of West, a Thomson Business.

LaFave, Wayne R., Rape — Overview; Act and Mental State Substantive Criminal Law § 7.18 (2d ed. 2003). Reprinted with permission of West, a Thomson Business.

LaFond, John Q., The Case for Liberalizing the Use of Deadly Force in Self-Defense, 6 University of Puget sound Law Review 237, 237-238, 274-284 (1983). Reprinted by permission of the author.

Lawrence, Frederick M., Punishing Hate: Bias Crimes Under American Law 58-63, 161-163, 167-169 (1999). Reprinted by permission of the author.

Levenson, Laurie L., Good Faith Defenses: Reshaping Strict Liability Crimes, 78 Cornell Law Review 401, 419-427 (1993). Reprinted by permission of the author.

MacKinnon, Catharine, A Rally Against Rape Feminism Unmodified 81-83 (1987). Reprinted by permission of the author.

Moore, Michael S., The Moral Worth of Retribution, Responsibility, Character and Emotions 179-182 (F. Schoeman ed., 1987). Reprinted by permission of the author.

Morse, Stephen J., Fear of Danger, Flight From Culpability, 4 Psychology, Public Policy, and the Law 250, 253-256 (1998). Reprinted by permission of the author.

Murphy, Jeffrie G., Three Mistakes About Retributivism, 31 Analysis 166-169 (1971). Reprinted by permission of the author.

National Law Journal, People v. Mentry: "Mother Says She Was Told To Sit on Child, Who Died," March 14, 1983. Reprinted with permission of the National Law Journal.

New York Times, 37 Who Saw Murder Didn't Call Police, N.Y. Times, March 27, 1964. Reprinted with permission of the N.Y. Times.

Pillsbury, Samuel H., Crimes of Indifference, 49 Rutgers Law Review 105, 106, 150-151 (1996). Reprinted by permission of the author.

Rapaport, Elizabeth, The Death Penalty and Gender Discrimination, 25 Law and Society Review 367-368, 369, 377-382 (1991). Reprinted by permission of the author.

Remick, Lani Anne, Read Her Lips: An Argument for a Verbal Consent Standard in Rape, 141 University of Pennsylvania Law Review 1103-1105 (1993). Reprinted with permission of the University of Pennsylvania Law Review.

San Francisco Chronicle, "A 'Cultural Defense' at Issue in Trial." Reprinted with permission of the San Francisco Chronicle.

Sayre, Francis B., Criminal Attempts, 41 Harvard Law Review 821, 845-847 (1928). Reprinted with permission of the Harvard Law Review.

Schulhofer, Stephen J., Rape: Legal Aspects, Encyclopedia of Crime and Justice 1306-1309 (2d ed. 2002). Reprinted by permission of the author.

Schwartz, Louis B., Reform of the Federal Criminal Laws: Issues, Tactics and Prospects, 1977 Duke Law Journal 171, 216. Reprinted with permission of the Duke Law Journal.

Seidman, Louis Michael, The Supreme Court, Entrapment, and Our Criminal Justice Dilemma, 5 The Supreme Court Review 111, 127-133, 135-137, 139-142, 145-146 (1981). Reprinted by permission of the author.

Tennenbaum, Abraham N., The Influence of the *Garner* Decision on Police Use of Deadly Force, 85 Journal of Criminal Law & Criminology 241-242, 257-260 (1994). Reprinted with permission of the Journal of Criminal Law & Criminology.

van den Haag, Ernest, Punishing Criminals 219-220 (1975). Reprinted with permission of Perseus Books Group.

von Hirsch, Andrew, Incapacitation in Principled Sentencing 101-108 (von Hirsch & Ashworth eds., 1992). Reprinted by permission of the author.

Wechsler, Herbert, & Jerome Michael, The Rationale of the Law of Homicide, 37 Columbia Law Review 701, 736 (1937). Reprinted with permission of the Columbia Law Review.

Weisberg, Robert, Deregulating Death, The Supreme Court Review 303, 386-387 (1983). Reprinted by permission of the author.

White, Thomas W., Reliance on Apparent Authority as a Defense to Criminal Prosecutions, 77 Columbia Law Review 775, 779, 801 (1977). Reprinted with permission of the Columbia Law Review.

Wilson, James Q., Thinking About Crime 145-258 (rev. ed. 1983). Reprinted by permission of the author.

Yeager, Daniel B., A Radical Community of Aid: A Rejoinder to Opponents of Affirmative Duties to Help Strangers, 71 Washington University Law Quarterly 1-8, 13-38 (1993). Reprinted by permission of the author.

CRIMINAL LAW

INTRODUCTORY MATERIALS

**An Overview of the Criminal Justice Process:
The Steps in the Process**
Wayne LaFave, Jerold Israel & Nancy King, Criminal Procedure
§ 1.3 (3d ed. 2000)

The overview presented in this section follows the sequence of the procedure in a typical felony case. . . .

(c) Step 1: The Reported Crime. Descriptions of the sequence of events in the criminal justice process commonly start with the commission of a crime. Our focus, however, is on the major steps taken in the administration of the process. From that perspective, the starting point ordinarily is the event that brings to the attention of the police the possible commission of a crime, for that event commonly triggers those series of administrative steps that may lead to the eventual enforcement of the criminal law against the offender. Quantitatively, there is a vast difference between the number of instances in which crimes are committed and the number in which the commission of a crime is brought to the attention of the police. The best available studies indicate that substantially less than half of all crimes are brought to the attention of the police.

Police may learn about crimes that have been committed from reports of citizens (usually victims), discovery in the field (usually observation on patrol), or from investigative and intelligence work. Where the police conclude that a crime may well have been committed, it will be recorded as a "reported crime" or "known offense." This record-keeping function has no legal significance with respect to further police action; police are not required to investigate further because a crime is recorded as a "known offense" and they are not prevented from seeking to obtain information where they do not have knowledge of an offense. The long-standing tradition of police departments, however, is to devote the vast bulk of their investigative efforts to solving "known offenses" and to at least initially attempt to investigate the vast majority of such offenses.

Accordingly, the distribution of "known offenses" provides a fairly accurate general picture of the types of crimes that are investigated (albeit sometimes minimally) by police. The dominant offenses among the reported crimes are those involving the taking or destruction of property (likely to approximate 50%), offenses relating to the use of alcohol or drugs, and assaults of various types. The most serious violent offenses (e.g., robbery, rape, aggravated assault, and homicide) are likely to constitute as a group no more than 7% of all reported crimes.

(d) Step 2: Prearrest Investigation. Various distinctions are used in grouping prearrest investigatory procedures, but the most common are the agency involved (distinguishing primarily between the investigative activities of the police and the prosecutor) and the focus of the procedure (distinguishing primarily between activities aimed at solving past crimes and activities aimed at anticipated crimes). Those distinctions create three basic groups of prearrest investigative procedures: (1) police procedures that are aimed at solving specific past crimes known to the police (commonly described as "reactive" procedures), (2) police procedures that are aimed at anticipated ongoing and future criminal activity (commonly described as "proactive" procedures), and (3) prosecutorial and other non-police investigations conducted primarily through the use of subpoena authority. . . .

(e) Step 3: Arrest. Once a police officer has obtained sufficient information to justify arresting a suspect (i.e., probable cause to believe the person has committed a crime), the arrest ordinarily becomes the next step in the criminal justice process. The term "arrest" is defined differently for different purposes. We refer here only to the act of taking a person into custody for the purpose of charging him with a crime (the standard commonly used in collecting statistics on the reporting of arrest statistics). This involves the detention of the suspect (by force if necessary) for the purpose of first transporting him to a police facility and then requesting that charges be filed against him. As an alternative to such a "full custody" arrest, many jurisdictions authorize the officer in some situations to briefly detain the suspect and then release him upon issuance of an official document (commonly titled a "citation," "notice to appear" or "appearance ticket") which directs the suspect to appear in court on a set date to respond to the charge specified in the document. This release-on-citation alternative commonly is authorized only for minor offenses, with the choice between the release procedure and the custodial arrest then lying in the discretion of the individual officer. In many localities, the standard practice is to use the citation alternative, rather than the arrest, for a wide range of minor offenses (including such offenses as disorderly conduct, vandalism, and petty shoplifting). In others, police generally prefer arrests and largely confine their regular use of the citation alternative to a few minor offenses, primarily regulatory in character. Where citations regularly are used for even a handful of the more common minor offenses, the number of citations issued can readily equal a quarter or a third of the total number of misdemeanor arrests.

Where there is no immediate need to arrest a suspect, an officer may seek to obtain an arrest warrant (a court order authorizing the arrest) prior to taking the person into custody. Arrest warrants in most jurisdictions are issued by magistrates. To obtain a warrant, the police must establish, to the satisfaction of the magistrate, that there exists probable cause to believe that the prospective arrestee committed the crime for which he will be arrested. The showing of probable cause may be made by affidavits or live testimony of either the investigating officer or a witness (usually the victim). Where a warrant is issued, it ordinarily will authorize the arrest to be made by any police officer in the state, not simply the officer seeking the warrant.

Arrests also can be made without a warrant, and that is the predominant practice in all localities. Of course, in a large percentage of all arrests (including, for example, "on scene" arrests), the police officer will make the arrest immediately after he has obtained probable cause for believing the person committed a crime. Yet, even where the investigating officer, after establishing probable cause, expects a lapse of a day or more before making an arrest, the common practice in most jurisdictions is not to use that opportunity to obtain an arrest warrant. Officers here will seek to obtain a warrant, rather than rely on a warrantless arrest, only where the special setting makes a warrant legally necessary or otherwise advantageous. The most common of those settings are: (1) cases in which the offender is located in another jurisdiction (as a warrant is needed to utilize procedures for having the person arrested by officers of another state and later extradited); (2) cases in which the person cannot be found and his name therefore will be entered into the computerized state or local law enforcement information network as someone who is subject to an arrest on the basis of an outstanding warrant; (3) cases in which there will probably be a need to enter into a dwelling without consent in order to make the arrest (a situation that requires a warrant); (4) cases in which the offense was a misdemeanor not committed in the officer's presence (a situation requiring a warrant in some states); and (5) cases in which the police have sought the advice of the prosecutor before deciding to proceed (where the prosecutor responds affirmatively, a complaint typically will be filed immediately, with a warrant then obtained prior to the arrest).

As noted in subsection (d), many offenses that come to the attention of the police cannot be solved. Hence, the number of arrests made will be substantially less than the number of offenses recorded as a known offense. The proportion of known offenses that are "cleared" by an arrest varies substantially with the nature of the crime. For those eight "Index" offenses on which national data is collected by the F.B.I., the overall clearance rate is roughly 21%, ranging from a high of 65% for homicide to a low of 13% for burglary.

The vast majority of arrests (60-80%) will be for misdemeanors, with more arrests made for driving-under-the-influence than for any other offense. Among felony arrests, property offenses will account for roughly a third, and drug offenses for 25-30%, and crimes of violence for another 25%. A substantial percentage of all of the persons arrested (e.g., 10-20%) will be juveniles, with that percentage varying considerably with the offense. Ordinarily, juvenile arrestees will be separated from adult arrestees shortly after they are taken into custody, and will be processed through the juvenile justice system, although some will later be returned to the regular criminal justice process and be prosecuted as adults. From this point on, we will assume the arrestee is an adult or a juvenile treated as an adult.

(f) Step 4: Booking. Immediately after making an arrest, the arresting officer usually will search the arrestee's person and remove any weapons, contraband, or evidence relating to a crime. If the arrested person was driving a vehicle, the officer

may also search the passenger compartment of the vehicle for the same items. The arrestee will then be taken, either by the arresting officer or other officers called to the scene, to the police station, a centrally located jail, or some similar "holding" facility. It is at this facility that the arrestee will be taken through a process known as "booking." Initially, the arrestee's name, the time of his arrival, and the offense for which he was arrested are noted in the police "blotter" or "log." This is strictly a clerical procedure, and it does not control whether the arrestee will be charged or what charge might be brought. As part of the booking process, the arrestee also will be photographed and fingerprinted.

Once the booking process is completed, the arrestee ordinarily will be allowed to make at least one telephone call. In many jurisdictions, an arrestee booked on a minor misdemeanor will be given the opportunity to obtain his immediate release by posting what is described as "stationhouse bail." This involves posting a specified amount of cash, as prescribed for the particular offense in a judicially approved bail schedule, and agreeing to appear in court on a specified date. Persons arrested for more serious offenses and those eligible to post stationhouse bail but lacking the resources will remain at the holding facility until presented before a magistrate (see step 9). Ordinarily they will be placed in a "lockup," which usually is some kind of cell. Before entering the lockup, they will be subjected to another search, more thorough than that conducted at the point of arrest. This search is designed primarily to inventory the arrestee's personal belongings and to prevent the introduction of contraband into the lockup.

(g) Step 5: Post-Arrest Investigation. The initial post-arrest investigation by the police consists of the search of the person (and possibly the interior of the automobile) as discussed above. The extent of any further post-arrest investigation will vary with the fact situation. In some cases, such as where the arrestee was caught "red-handed," there will be little left to be done. In others, police will utilize many of the same kinds of investigative procedures as are used before arrest (e.g., interviewing witnesses, searching the suspect's home, and viewing the scene of the crime). Post-arrest investigation does offer one important investigative source, however, that ordinarily is not available prior to the arrest—the person of the arrestee. Thus, the police may seek to obtain an eyewitness identification of the arrestee by placing him in a lineup, having the witness view him individually (a "showup"), or taking his picture and showing it to the witness (usually with the photographs of several other persons in a "photographic lineup"). They may also require the arrestee to provide handwriting or hair samples that can be compared with evidence the police have found at the scene of the crime. The arrest similarly facilitates questioning the arrestee at length about either the crime for which he was arrested or other crimes thought to be related (although warnings must be given prior to the custodial interrogation).

Although we do not have precise data on the use of these post-arrest procedures involving the arrestee, the best available estimates indicate they are not utilized in the vast majority of cases. In most communities, they are used almost exclusively in the investigation of felony cases and even then their use is tied to need and likelihood of success. Eyewitness identification, for example, is not sought where there were no eyewitnesses, where an eyewitness was well acquainted with the arrestee, or where the officer observed the crime and immediately thereafter made the arrest. Police more frequently seek to engage felony arrestees in sustained interrogation, but a substantial portion of those arrestees are either never questioned or simply given warnings and asked if they desire to make a statement.

(h) *Step 6: The Decision to Charge.* The initial decision to charge a suspect with the commission of a crime ordinarily comes with the decision of a police officer to arrest the suspect. That decision will subsequently be reviewed, first by the police and then by the prosecutor. As discussed in subsection (k), the arrestee must be brought before a magistrate within a relatively short period (typically 24 or 48 hours), and prior to that point, the charges against the arrestee must be filed with the magistrate. It is during this period that the police will review the arresting officer's initial decision to charge. The prosecutor's review of the decision to charge often occurs during this same period, but prosecutorial review is, in any event, an ongoing process. Whether or not the initial filing of charges comes after review of the prosecutor, the filed charges remain subject to reconsideration by the prosecutor up to and through the trial.

The decision to charge a person with a crime thus may be seen as having four ✷ components: (1) the decision of the investigating officer to arrest and charge; (2) the police review of that decision prior to filing charges; (3) prosecutorial review prior to filing; and (4) ongoing prosecutorial review after the filing. The first component has already been noted in step (3) (the arrest), and we consider here the remaining three. The third component, prosecutorial post-filing screening, is treated here, rather than at the later points in the process where it occurs chronologically, because of its close relationship to the pre-filing screening of the prosecutor.

Pre-Filing Police Screening   Sometime between the booking of the arrestee and the point at which the arrestee is to be taken before the magistrate, there will be an internal police review of a warrantless arrest. Ordinarily that occurs shortly after the booking, when the arresting officer prepares an arrest report to be given to his or her supervisor. The supervisor may approve the bringing of charges at the level recommended in the police report, raise or reduce the level of the recommended charges, or decide against bringing charges. A decision not to bring charges ordinarily will be based on the supervisor's conclusion either that the evidence is insufficient to charge or that the offense can more appropriately be handled by a "stationhouse adjustment" (e.g., in the case of a fight among acquaintances, a warning and lecture may be deemed sufficient). If the supervising officer decides against prosecution, the arrestee will be released from the lockup on the officer's direction (with some departments following the practice of seeking prosecutor approval before releasing felony arrestees). Studies that track the ultimate disposition of arrests have typically been limited to felony arrests. They report police decisions to release arrestees and forego prosecution in the range of 4% to 10%. Since police are more likely to utilize stationhouse adjustments for misdemeanor arrests, the percentage of misdemeanor arrestees released by the police without charging is likely to be somewhat higher.

Pre-Filing Prosecutor Screening   Prosecutors' offices vary substantially in their approach to pre-filing review of the decision to charge. In many jurisdictions, all arrests, both for misdemeanors and felonies, will be screened, and no charges will be filed except upon approval of the prosecutor. In many others, however, particularly in urban districts, police often file charges on their own initiative for at least some types of offenses. Typically, prosecutors here will screen the vast majority of the felony charges, but there will be districts in which prosecutors review only the most serious felony charges before they are filed. In those districts, the initial prosecutorial screening of most felony charges occurs sometime between the first appearance and the preliminary hearing or grand jury review (see steps 9 and 10 infra). Prosecutors are more likely to permit police to file misdemeanor charges without advance prosecutorial screening. When that occurs, prosecutors may not review a misdemeanor charge until it is scheduled for trial (and thus may never screen those charges that result in a guilty plea at the first appearance)....

A prosecutorial decision not to proceed commonly is described as a "rejection," "declination" or "no-paper" decision. The leading statistical studies on pre-charge prosecutor review have sorted out six major grounds for that decision. These are: (1) insufficient evidence; (2) witness difficulties (e.g., where the victim was acquainted with the offender and does not desire to proceed, the victim fears reprisal and is reluctant to pursue prosecution, or the victim cannot be located); (3) due process problems (e.g., critical evidence was obtained illegally and will not be admissible at trial); (4) adequate disposition will be provided by other criminal proceedings (e.g., prosecution by another jurisdiction, probation revocation, or prosecution for another offense); (5) the "interests of justice"; and (6) anticipated use of a diversion program. Among these factors, the two most frequently cited are the first two (evidence insufficiency and witness difficulty); while rejections based on the "interest of justice" attract the greatest attention, they are far less significant statistically.

As one might expect from the differences among prosecutors' offices in the proportion of arrests reviewed pre-filing, the differences in the depth of such review, and the subjective nature of many of the grounds for declining prosecution, studies reveal considerable variation from one community to another in the impact of pre-filing prosecutorial screening. Thus, a study of 13 urban prosecutorial districts found that the percentage of felony arrests that did not result in charges ranged from a low of 0% (in a jurisdiction which apparently did no pre-filing screening) to a high of 38%. Even higher rates of pre-filing rejections have been reported for other urban districts. On the other hand, the most comprehensive study, covering all districts within six states, found a pre-filing prosecutorial rejection rate of only 11%, reflecting perhaps, fewer rejections influenced by caseload pressures where the sample includes both urban and rural districts. Within the individual district, the rejection rate is likely to show considerable variation across the range of felony offenses, with the rate of rejections for some felony offenses being as much as twice that for others....

Post-Filing Prosecutorial Screening   Post-filing prosecutorial review of the charging decision is inherent in the many post-filing procedures that require the prosecutor to review the facts of the case. If the prosecutor should determine that the charge is not justified, a dismissal can be obtained through a nolle prosequi motion (noting the prosecutor's desire to relinquish prosecution), which ordinarily will be granted in a perfunctory fashion by the court. Similarly, if the prosecutor considers the charge to be too high, a motion can be entered to reduce the charges. In deciding whether to make such motions, the prosecutor will look to basically the same grounds that might justify a pre-filing rejection or reduction of the charge recommended by the police. Even where a charge was carefully screened and approved prior to filing, post-filing review can readily lead to a contrary conclusion as circumstances change (e.g., evidence becomes unavailable) or the prosecutor learns more about the facts of the case. Of course, where the charge was not previously screened or was screened only on a skimpy arrest report, post-filing review is even more likely to lead to a decision to drop or reduce the charges.

Although post-filing review is an ongoing process, the most critical point, particularly where there has been no pre-filing review, is the first instance at which the prosecutor must carefully review the facts of the case. In felony cases, that will usually come in the preparation of the case for the preliminary hearing or grand jury review (see steps 10 and 11), although it may even come before that. Accordingly, dismissals and reductions based on post-filing prosecutorial screening of the charging decision are most likely to come before the felony case reaches the general trial court, but even after that point, changed circumstances or additional information can lead to a significant portion of the post-filing dismissals occurring at the trial court level.

Available statistics make it difficult to measure the precise impact of post-filing prosecutorial screening. In categorizing the disposition of felony charges by both magistrate and general trial courts, many states use a single category of dismissal that includes both dismissals on a prosecutor's nolle prosequi motion and dismissals by the court on a challenge to the charge by the defense. Only a small group of states keep separate statistics on dismissals on the motion of the prosecutor. These states attribute to such dismissals a range of 19% to 37% of all final dispositions of felony cases. That range is consistent with a study of adjudication outcomes for felony defendants in the nation's 75 largest counties, which found an average rate of disposition of felony defendants by dismissals (of all types) of 26% (varying for offense groupings from a low of 20% for drug offenses to a high of 37% for violent offenses).

Of course, the prosecutorial-screening dismissal rate for felony charges builds upon the earlier pre-filing screening which determined the number of felony arrests that were converted into felony charges. Two jurisdictions may have identical dismissal rates, but their dismissal numbers, and the significance of that rate, will be quite different if one reduced its number of charges by 20% through pre-filing screening and the other reduced its number by only 2%. Thus, to evaluate the true impact of dismissals upon prosecutorial screening, they are best judged by reference to the disposition of felony arrests. The studies that measure dismissals in this fashion have shown that, as a general rule, the higher the percentage of arrests rejected in pre-filing screening, the lower the percentage of arrests as to which charges once filed are subsequently dismissed (although the jurisdiction with more extensive initial screening is likely to have an even higher dismissal rate measured by reference to charge dispositions). In other words, the greater the number of felony arrests rejected, the smaller the number of felony charges that will be dismissed on post-filing screening. A similar pattern is indicated for charge reductions, as jurisdictions with limited pre-filing screening tend to be more active in post-filing reductions of felonies to misdemeanors.

What is the end product of the combined pre-filing screening by police and prosecutor and post-filing screening by the prosecutor? The best source on that question is a series of studies on the attrition of felony arrests. A 1988 study, using a dozen urban prosecutorial districts, found that those districts screened out of the criminal justice system from 31% to 46% of all felony arrests, with a jurisdictional mean of 39%. When diversions were added, no jurisdiction removed from prosecution less than 33% of their felony arrests, all but three removed in excess of 40%, and one removed 50%. A 1992 study, drawing information from 11 states, provides data suggesting removal by screening (including diversion) fell in the range of 31-36% for those states as a group. California provides arrest-disposition data over the longest period, dating back to 1975. The California data show the potential for a substantial variation over a period of years in the proportion of felony arrests removed from the process through police and prosecutorial screening. While the California removal rate for 1994 was no higher than 32.5%, it had been close to 50% in 1975. A study of convictions as compared to felony arrests over a six year period in the nation's 75 largest counties suggests that substantial variations are possible over even a shorter period of time. . . .

(i) *Step 7: Filing the Complaint.* Assuming that the pre-charge screening results in a decision to prosecute, the next step is the filing of charges with the magistrate court. Typically, the initial charging instrument will be called a "complaint." In misdemeanor cases, which are triable before the magistrate court, the complaint will serve as the charging instrument throughout the proceedings. In felony cases, on the other hand, the complaint serves to set forth the charges only before the magistrate court; an information or indictment will replace the complaint as the charging instrument when the case reaches the general trial court.

For most offenses, the complaint will be a fairly brief document. Its basic function is to set forth concisely the allegation that the accused, at a particular time and place, committed specified acts constituting a violation of a particular criminal statute. The complaint will be signed by a "complainant," a person who swears under oath that he or she believes the factual allegations of the complaint to be true. The complainant usually will be either the victim or the investigating officer. When an officer-complainant did not observe the offense being committed, but relied on information received from the victim or other witnesses, the officer ordinarily will note that the allegations in the complaint are based on "information and belief."

With the filing of the complaint, the person accused in the complaint will have become a "defendant" in a criminal proceeding. The formal charge initiates a judicial record keeping procedure that puts his case on the docket and follows it through to its termination. Ordinarily that termination will come in a dismissal, a conviction, or an acquittal. However, some cases will either be transferred to an "inactive" docket, or dismissed with the prosecution specifically given authority to later reinstate the charge. These are the cases in which the defendant is "unavailable"—usually because he has absconded, but occasionally because he is incarcerated elsewhere or is outside the jurisdiction. The portion of the docket handled in this fashion depends in part on how long a state is willing to wait for the apprehension of a defendant before the charge against him will be "written off" as a disposition. In some jurisdictions, that portion will exceed 10%, while in others, it may not even amount to 1%. For misdemeanors, the portion tends to be somewhat larger; more cases were initiated by summons rather than arrest, and more arrestees obtained their pretrial release (commonly without posting bond or other financial security), so there tends to be a higher percentage of "no shows."

Just as the mix of offenses for which arrests were made differed from the mix of offenses known to police, the mix of offenses charged by complaint will differ from the mix of those arrest offenses. The differences here will not be nearly so striking as between arrests and known offenses, but the pre-filing decisions by police and prosecutor — including juvenile arrestees transferred to juvenile court, arrestees not charged, arrestees placed in diversion programs, and the reduction of charges — make the mix of offenses charged somewhat different than the mix of arrest offenses. Most significant will be the reduced proportion of felonies. While felony arrests might account for 20-40% of all arrests in a particular jurisdiction, felony complaints are likely to constitute only 10-20% of all complaints. Among felony complaints, the mix of offenses by general category is similar to that for arrests. Property offenses are likely to account for slightly over a third of the complaints, drug offenses for roughly 30%, and crimes of violence for roughly 25%. Within these general categories, however, there will be some shifts, as arrests for particular offenses (e.g., motor vehicle theft in the property category) are more likely to result in a decision not to prosecute or in a reduction of the offense when the charge is brought.

(j) Step 8: Magistrate Review of the Arrest. Following the filing of the complaint and prior to or at the start of the first appearance (see step 9), the magistrate must undertake what is often described as the "Gerstein review." As prescribed by the Supreme Court's decision in Gerstein v. Pugh, if the accused was arrested without a warrant and remains in custody, the magistrate must determine that there exists probable cause for the continued detention of the arrestee for the offense charged in the complaint. This ordinarily is an ex parte determination, similar to that made in the issuance of an arrest warrant and relying on the same sources of information. Where the arrest was made pursuant to a warrant, the judicial probable cause determination has already been made and a Gerstein review is not required. If the magistrate finds that probable cause has not been established, he will direct the prosecution to promptly produce more information or release the arrested person. Such instances are exceedingly rare, however.

(k) Step 9: The First Appearance. Once the complaint is filed, the case is before the magistrate court, and the accused must appear before the court within a specified period. This appearance of the accused is usually described as the "first appearance," although the terminology varies, with jurisdictions also using "preliminary appearance," "initial presentment," "preliminary arraignment," "arraignment on the warrant," and "arraignment on the complaint." The timing of the first appearance varies with the custodial status of the accused. Where the accused was not taken into custody, but was released on issuance of a citation, there is likely to be a gap of at least several days between the issuance of the citation and the first appearance date as specified in the citation. The same is often true also of the first appearance set for the arrestee who gained his release by posting stationhouse bail.

Almost all felony arrestees and many misdemeanor arrestees will have been held in custody following their arrest, however, and here the time span between the arrest and the first appearance is much shorter. All jurisdictions require that an arrestee held in custody be brought before the magistrate court in a fairly prompt fashion. Ordinarily, the time consumed in booking, transportation, limited post-arrest investigation, reviewing the decision to charge, and preparing and filing the complaint makes it unlikely that the arrestee will be presented before the magistrate until at least several hours after his arrest. Thus, if the magistrate court does not have an evening session, a person arrested in the afternoon or evening will not be presented before the magistrate until the next day. Many jurisdictions do not allow much longer detention than this, as they impose a 24 hour limit on pre-appearance detention, requiring both the filing of the complaint and the presentation of the detained arrestee within that period. Others, desiring to limit weekend sessions of the court, allow up to 48 hours of pre-appearance detention.

The first appearance often is a quite brief proceeding. Initially, the magistrate will make certain that the person before him is the person named in the complaint. The magistrate then will inform the defendant of the charge in the complaint and will note various rights that the defendant may have in further proceedings. The range of rights mentioned will vary from one jurisdiction to another. Commonly, the magistrate will inform the defendant of his right to remain silent and warn him that anything he says in court or to the police may be used against him at trial. Further advice as to rights may depend upon whether the defendant is charged with a felony or misdemeanor. In felony cases, the magistrate will advise the defendant of the next step in the process, the preliminary hearing, and will set a date for that hearing unless the defendant desires to waive it. If the defendant is charged with a misdemeanor, he will not be entitled to a preliminary hearing or a subsequent grand jury review (see steps 10 and 11).

At least where the defendant is not represented by counsel at the first appearance, the magistrate will inform the defendant of his right to be represented by retained counsel, and, if indigent, his right to court appointed counsel. The scope of the right to appointed counsel may vary with the level of the offense. In some jurisdictions, appointed counsel will not be available for defendants who are charged with low-level misdemeanors if they will not be sentenced to incarceration if convicted. Where there is a right to appointed counsel, which will be the case in all jurisdictions for indigent defendants charged with felonies and serious misdemeanors, the magistrate usually will have the responsibility for at least initiating the appointment process. This involves first determining that the defendant is indigent and that he desires the assistance of counsel. The magistrate then will either directly appoint counsel or notify a judge in charge of appointments that an appointment should be made. . . .

One of the most important first-appearance functions of the magistrate is to set bail (i.e., the conditions under which the defendant can obtain his release from custody pending the final disposition of the charges against him). In many misdemeanor cases, there will be no need to set bail. The defendant will already have been released on the police issuance of a citation or on the posting of stationhouse bail or the defendant will enter a guilty plea at the first appearance and be promptly sentenced. However, a bail determination ordinarily must be made in all felony and serious misdemeanor cases and in a substantial portion of the lesser misdemeanor cases.

At one time, bail was limited almost entirely to the posting of cash or a secured bond purchased from a professional bondsman. Today, those are only two of several alternatives available to the magistrate. Others are: (1) release upon a promise to appear (release on "personal recognizance"); (2) release on making a personal promise to forfeit a specified dollar amount upon a failure to appear (an "unsecured" personal bond); (3) release upon the imposition of one or more nonfinancial conditions (e.g., restrictions on defendant's associations or travel); and (4) the posting with the court of a percentage of the bail forfeiture amount (commonly 10%), which will be returned to the defendant if he appears as scheduled. In a few states, the 10% alternative has basically replaced the secured bond, resulting in the elimination of professional bondsmen.

In general, the magistrate is directed to impose such bail conditions as appear reasonably needed to assure that the defendant will make court appearances as scheduled throughout the proceedings. In making that determination, the magistrate looks to a variety of factors that might indicate a likelihood of flight (e.g., severity of possible punishment if convicted). Most jurisdictions also direct the magistrate to consider community safety in setting bail conditions, and approximately half of our fifty-two jurisdictions authorize preventive detention—a procedure under which the magistrate orders that the accused be detained because no bail condition will provide satisfactory assurance against his commission of an offense posing danger to the community.

In misdemeanor cases, magistrates most commonly utilize release on personal recognizance or personal bonds, and even where a secured bond is required, the amount is sufficiently low so that only a small percentage of defendants fail to gain their release. As a result, studies that cover both misdemeanor and felony arrestees report overall release rates of 85% or higher, with the vast majority of defendants released on nonfinancial conditions. However, when felony defendants alone are considered, the picture changes dramatically, especially for the more serious felony offenses. Thus, a study of the nation's 75 largest counties found that 37% of all felony defendants were detained until the final disposition of their charges, and that percentage rose to 50% or above for those charged with murder, rape, and robbery. As for the defendants who were released, more were released on non-financial conditions than on financial conditions. However, for the group released, a non-appearance rate of 25% and a rearrest rate of 14% for new offenses led to revocation of bail for a significant number. Also, at the end of a year, 8% of those released were unapprehended fugitives.

(l) Step 10: Preliminary Hearing. Following the first appearance, the next scheduled step in a felony case ordinarily is the preliminary hearing (sometimes called a preliminary "examination"). All but a few of our fifty-two jurisdictions grant the felony defendant a right to a preliminary hearing, to be held within a specified period (typically, within a week or two if the defendant does not gain pretrial release and within a few weeks if released). This hardly means, however, that the preliminary hearing will be held in almost all or even most cases. Initially, as mentioned previously, the critical stage for post-arrest prosecutorial screening of charges is in the period prior to the scheduled preliminary hearing, and a

prosecution can readily dismiss 15-30% of the felony cases before the scheduled hearing (the high percentage coming in those jurisdictions in which there is little or no pre-filing screening). Where the charges are not dismissed, two additional decisions—one by the prosecutor and one by the defense—can sharply reduce the number of preliminary hearings.

In almost all jurisdictions, if the prosecutor obtains a grand jury indictment prior to the scheduled preliminary hearing, the preliminary hearing will not be held, as the grand jury's finding of probable cause has rendered irrelevant any contrary finding that the magistrate might make at the preliminary hearing. Prosecutorial bypassing of the preliminary hearing by immediately obtaining a grand jury indictment is most likely to occur in those twenty jurisdictions that require prosecution by indictment (see step 11 infra). In some of these jurisdictions, prosecutors make such frequent use of the bypass option as to preclude preliminary hearings in 50-80% of the felony cases that reach the felony trial court. In many others, however, the bypass procedure is used sparingly, precluding no more than 10% of the potential preliminary hearings. Such sparing use (or no use) of the bypass procedure also tends to be the norm in jurisdictions that ordinarily prosecute by information (see step 12), although an occasional prosecutor in an information state may prefer grand jury indictments and bypass the preliminary hearing as a regular practice.

Finally, where the preliminary hearing is made available to the defendant, there nonetheless may not be a preliminary hearing because the defendant prefers to waive the hearing and move directly to the trial court. That is often the strategy employed where the defendant intends to plead guilty. Thus, a number of jurisdictions report a waiver rate exceeding 50%, although there also are jurisdictions in which defendants ask for the hearing in the vast majority of cases.

Where the preliminary hearing is held, it will provide, like grand jury review, a screening of the decision to charge by a neutral body. In the preliminary hearing, that neutral body is the magistrate, who must determine whether, on the evidence presented, there is probable cause to believe that defendant committed the crime charged. Ordinarily, the magistrate will already have determined that probable cause exists as part of the ex parte screening of the complaint (see step 8). The preliminary hearing, however, provides screening in an adversary proceeding in which both sides are represented by counsel. Jurisdictions vary in the evidentiary rules applicable to the preliminary hearing, but most require that the parties rely primarily on live witnesses rather than affidavits. Typically, the prosecution will present its key witnesses and the defense will limit its response to the cross-examination of those witnesses. The defendant has the right to present his own evidence at the hearing, but traditional defense strategy advises against subjecting defense witnesses to prosecution cross-examination in any pretrial proceeding.

If the magistrate concludes that the evidence presented establishes probable cause, he will "bind the case over" to the next stage in the proceedings. In an indictment jurisdiction (see step 11), the case is bound over to the grand jury, and in a jurisdiction that permits the direct filing of an information (see step 12), the case is bound over directly to the general trial court. If the magistrate finds that the probable cause supports only a misdemeanor charge, he will reject the felony charge and allow the prosecutor to substitute the lower charge, which will then be set for trial in the magistrate court. If the magistrate finds that the prosecution's evidence does not support any charge, he will order that the defendant be released. The rate of dismissals at the preliminary hearing quite naturally varies with the degree of previous screening exercised by the prosecutor. In a jurisdiction with fairly extensive screening, the percentage of dismissals is likely to fall in the range of 5-10% of the cases heard. However, other jurisdictions (usually those in which hearings are more sparingly utilized) report a much higher dismissal rate. In either type of jurisdiction, the preliminary hearing dismissal is likely to account for the disposition of less than 5% of all felony complaints.

   (m) Step 11: Grand Jury Review. Although almost all fifty-two jurisdictions still have provisions authorizing grand jury screening of felony charges, such screening is mandatory only in those jurisdictions requiring felony prosecutions to be instituted by an indictment, a charging instrument issued by the grand jury. In a majority of the states, the prosecution is now allowed to proceed either by grand jury indictment or by information at its option. Because prosecutors in these states most often choose to prosecute by information, the states providing this option commonly are referred to as "information" states. Eighteen states, the federal system, and the District of Columbia currently require grand jury indictments for all felony prosecutions. These jurisdictions commonly are described as "indictment" jurisdictions. Four additional states are "limited indictment" jurisdictions, requiring prosecution by indictment only for their most severely punished offenses (capital, life imprisonment, or both).

   Indictment and limited indictment jurisdictions commonly make prosecution by indictment an absolute mandate only for capital offenses. As to other offenses, the defendant may waive the right to be proceeded against by indictment, thereby allowing the prosecution to proceed by information. As in the case of preliminary hearing, defendants may prefer to waive when intending to plead guilty. Waiver rates vary from one jurisdiction to another but waivers are likely to be made by at least 10% of all felony defendants. Where a potential charge is brought to the grand jury for its possible issuance of an indictment, the grand jury is in no way bound by any prior ruling at a preliminary hearing on that charge. The grand jury may indict even though the magistrate dismissed the charge at the preliminary hearing, and may refuse to indict even though the magistrate bound over to the grand jury.

   The grand jury is composed of a group of private citizens who are selected to review cases presented over a term that may range from one to several months. Traditionally the grand jury consisted of 23 persons with the favorable vote of a majority needed to indict. Today, many states use a somewhat smaller grand jury (e.g., 12) and some require more than a simple majority to indict. As in the case of the magistrate at the preliminary hearing, the primary function of the grand jury is to determine whether there is sufficient evidence to justify a trial on the charge sought by the prosecution. The grand jury, however, participates in a screening process quite different from the preliminary hearing. It meets in a closed session and hears only the evidence presented by the prosecution. The defendant has no right to offer his own evidence or to be present during grand jury proceedings. If a majority of the grand jurors conclude that the prosecution's evidence is sufficient, the grand jury will issue the indictment requested by the prosecutor. The indictment will set forth a brief description of the offense charged, and the grand jury's approval of that charge will be indicated by its designation of the indictment as a "true bill." If the grand jury majority refuses to approve a proposed indictment, the charges against the defendant will be dismissed. In indictment jurisdictions, grand juries typically refuse to indict in less than 10% of the cases presented before them.

(n) *Step 12: The Filing of the Indictment or Information.* If an indictment is issued, it will be filed with the general trial court and will replace the complaint as the accusatory instrument in the case. Where grand jury review either is not required or has been waived, an information will be filed with the trial court. Like the indictment, the information is a charging instrument which replaces the complaint, but it is issued by the prosecutor rather than the grand jury. In most information states, the charge in the information must be supported by a preliminary hearing bindover (unless the preliminary hearing was waived).

(o) *Step 13: Arraignment on the Information or Indictment.* After the indictment or information has been filed, the defendant is arraigned—i.e., he is brought before the trial court, informed of the charges against him, and asked to enter a plea of guilty, not guilty, or, as is permitted under some circumstances, nolo contendere. In the end, most of those felony defendants whose cases reach the trial court will plead guilty. At the arraignment, however, they are likely to enter a plea of not guilty. Where there has not been a preliminary hearing, defense counsel probably will not be fully apprised of the strength of the prosecution's case at this point in the proceedings. Also, in most jurisdictions, guilty pleas in felony cases are the product of plea negotiations with the prosecution, and in many places, that process does not start until after the arraignment. When the defendant enters a plea of not guilty at the arraignment, the judge will set a trial date, but the expectation generally is that the trial will not be held.

Between the arraignment and the scheduled trial date, three possible dispositions can result in the termination of the case without trial. Although there will have been extensive prosecutorial screening by this point, changed circumstances and new information typically will lead to dismissals on a prosecutor's nolle prosequi motion in roughly 5-15% of the cases. A smaller percentage of the informations or indictments will be dismissed on motion of the defense, as discussed in step 14. The vast majority of the dispositions without trial will be the product of guilty pleas.

Guilty pleas in felony cases commonly will be entered in response to a plea agreement under which the prosecution offers certain concessions in return for the defendant's entry of the plea. Those concessions may take the form of a reduction of the charges (sometimes to a misdemeanor and sometimes to a lesser felony charge), a dismissal of related charges where the defendant faces multiple charges, a recommendation on sentence, or a specific sentence (when agreed to by the trial court). Prosecutors' offices vary in the concessions they offer and their willingness to bargain over concessions (as opposed to presenting a take-it-or-leave-it offer). Prosecutors also vary as to the types of cases in which they will offer concessions, with some generally refusing to do so on the most serious charges. Indeed, there are jurisdictions in which prosecutors will not plea bargain, although defendants here may still find an inducement to plead guilty in a general policy of trial judges to give favorable weight in sentencing to the defendant's willingness to plead guilty.

Although the guilty plea remains the primary mode of disposition for felony indictments and informations in all jurisdictions, considerable variation exists in the percentage of defendants who enter guilty pleas. Most jurisdictions appear to fall within the range of 60-85%. Of course when dismissals and other dispositions are excluded, and only guilty pleas and trials are compared, the rate of guilty pleas is much higher. Thus, a leading study of 14 communities found a median ratio of 11 pleas for every trial, with one jurisdiction having as many as 37 pleas for each trial. . . .

(p) *Step 14: Pretrial Motions.* In most jurisdictions, a broad range of objections must be raised by a pretrial motion. Those motions commonly present challenges to the institution of the prosecution (e.g., claims regarding the grand jury indictment process), attacks upon the sufficiency of the charging instrument, requests for disclosure of evidence within the government's possession that has not been made available through discovery, and requests for the suppression of evidence allegedly obtained through a constitutional violation. While some pretrial motions are made only by defendants who intend to go to trial, other motions (e.g., discovery) may benefit as well defendants who expect in the end to plead guilty. Nevertheless, pretrial motions are likely to be made in only a small portion of the felony cases that reach the trial court. Their use does vary considerably, however, with the nature of the case. In narcotics cases, for example, motions to suppress are quite common. In the typical forgery case, on the other, pretrial motions of any type are quite rare.

As a group, pretrial motions are unlikely to result in the dismissal of more than 5% of the felony cases before the trial court, and quite often will produce a dismissal rate of less than 2.5%. The pretrial motion most likely to produce a dismissal is the motion to suppress. Quite frequently, if the defendant gains suppression of unconstitutionally obtained evidence, there will be insufficient remaining evidence to continue with the prosecution. In misdemeanor cases before the magistrate court, motions tend to be made only in cases slated for trial and even there, they are uncommon. Thus, the percentage of cases dismissed on the basis of a successful defense motion probably will fall below two percent.

(q) *Step 15: The Trial.* Assuming that there has not been a dismissal and the defendant has not entered a guilty plea (or a nolle contendere plea), the next step in the criminal process is the trial. In most respects, the criminal trial resembles the civil trial. There are, however, several distinguishing features that are either unique to criminal trials or of special importance in such trials. These include (1) the presumption of defendant's innocence, (2) the requirement of proof beyond a reasonable doubt, (3) the right of the defendant not to take the stand, (4) the exclusion of evidence obtained by the state in an illegal manner, and (5) the more frequent use of incriminating statements of defendants. In most jurisdictions, the misdemeanor trial will be almost indistinguishable from a felony trial. In some jurisdictions, however, misdemeanor trials tend to be less formal, with rules of evidence applied in a rather loose fashion.

As noted previously, most felony and misdemeanor cases are likely to be disposed of either by a guilty plea or by a dismissal. Typically, only 4% to 8% of all felony complaints are resolved by a trial. Because a substantial portion of felony complaints are likely to be resolved at the magistrate level, the percentage of trials will be somewhat higher for the disposition of the smaller group of felony informations or indictments filed in the general trial court, but even so, that percentage will not ordinarily exceed 15% — although there are some exceptional jurisdictions in which the percentage is over 30%. For misdemeanor cases resolved at the magistrate level (including both cases originally filed as misdemeanors and felony complaints reduced to misdemeanors) the percentage of trials is likely to fall in the range of 3% to 7% on a statewide basis. However, individual judicial districts, particularly in urban areas, not uncommonly have trials in less than 1% of their misdemeanor dispositions — although, as with felonies, there also are very unusual districts in which the trial rate is in the neighborhood of 20-30%.

The median time frame from the arrest of the defendant to the start of the felony trial can exceed a year in judicial districts with slow moving dockets, but for most judicial districts, it is likely to fall within the range of 5-8 months. The median will be influenced, in particular, by the mix of jury and bench trials, as the time frame tends to be considerably longer for jury trials. While most jurisdictions have speedy trials requirements that impose time limits of 6 months or less, there are various excludable time periods (for factors such as witness unavailability and the processing of motions) which commonly extend the time limit by at least a few months.

The trial itself tends to be relatively short. Misdemeanor trials typically last less than a day. Felony jury trials are somewhat longer, but most will be completed within 2-3 days. One variable will be the local practice governing voir dire (the questioning of prospective jurors, either by judge or counsel), as some jurisdictions tend to spend considerably more time on jury selection than others. Another will be the type of case, as certain types of offense (e.g., complex white collar offenses and capital homicide cases) produce trials substantially longer than the typical felony. In general trials to the bench are considerably shorter, and unlikely to last more than a day.

In all fifty-two jurisdictions, the defendant will have a right to a jury trial for all felony offenses and for misdemeanors punishable by more than 6 months imprisonment. Most states also provide a jury trial for lesser misdemeanors as well (although that right may exist only through the opportunity to seek a trial de novo in the general trial court after an initial bench trial before the magistrate court). Juries traditionally were composed of 12 persons, but most states now utilize 6 person juries in misdemeanor cases and several use the smaller juries in non-capital felony cases as well. Of course, the right to a jury trial can be waived, and in most jurisdictions, a significant number of defendants will waive the jury in favor of a bench trial. Over the country as a whole, roughly 70% of all felony trials are tried to a jury, but in various individual judicial districts, as well as some states, bench trials actually outnumber jury trials. In misdemeanor cases, in contrast, bench trials typically predominate (often accounting for 95% or more of all trials), even in jurisdictions that extend the defendant's jury trial right to all misdemeanors. In all but a few jurisdictions, the jury verdict in both misdemeanor and felony cases, whether for acquittal or conviction, must be unanimous. Where the jurors cannot agree, no verdict is entered and the case may be retried. For most communities, such "hung juries" occur in only a very small percentage of all jury trials (e.g., 3-6%, but there are large urban districts in which juries cannot reach a verdict in as many as 10-15% of all jury trials).

Whether a criminal case is tried to the bench or the jury, the odds favor conviction over acquittal. A fairly typical ratio for felony charges will be 3 convictions for every acquittal. That ratio may vary significantly, however, with the nature of the offense. In some jurisdictions, the rate of conviction at trial tends to be substantially lower (though still well above 50%) for some crimes (e.g., rape and murder) than for others (e.g., drug trafficking).

With the end of the trial stage, the criminal justice process will have produced a disposition as to all persons who originally entered the process through an arrest or the issuance of citation. As for those who were arrested on felony charges, only one out of a hundred will have had the case against him carried through to a trial that resulted in an acquittal.

A much larger portion of the felony arrestees, anywhere from 30-50%, also will not have been convicted, but the dispositions in their favor will have come before the filing of the complaint, through pre-charge police and prosecutor screening, or before the trial, either through nolle prosequi motions or judicial and grand jury screening procedures. Because of the high percentage of cases disposed of through these procedures, as well as the high percentage of convictions obtained through guilty pleas, the median time from arrest to final adjudication (including sentencing for those convicted) is much shorter for the total body of arrests than is the time from arrest to trial. Indeed, more than half of all arrests are likely to have reached a final adjudication within 100 days.

Of the 50-70% of the felony arrestees who will have been convicted, many will not have been convicted of felonies. Depending upon the plea negotiation practices followed in the particular jurisdiction, anywhere from 10-30% of those felony arrestees convicted are likely to be convicted of misdemeanors. The mix of offenses for which felony convictions are obtained will differ somewhat from the mix of felony offenses first charged by complaint. The most significant difference by general category will be in the "violent crime" grouping. Because those offenses as group are less likely to produce convictions (although one of the offenses in that group — murder — has one of the highest conviction rates), they experience a substantial reduction (to roughly 18% from 25%) in their portion of felony convictions as compared to their portion of felony complaints. The other major categories retain their relative positions, with property offenses slightly ahead of drug offenses in their respective proportions of all felony convictions. Within categories, the portions for individual offenses tend to be altered here and there as one or two offenses in the category will produce comparatively a much lower rate on convictions or a higher percentage of convictions that are for misdemeanors rather than felonies.

(r) Step 16: Sentencing. Following conviction, the next step in the process is the determination of the sentence. In all but a few jurisdictions (which allow for jury sentencing, even apart from capital punishment), the sentence determination is the function of the court. Basically three different types of sentences may be used: financial sanctions (e.g., fines, restitution orders); some form of release into the community (e.g., probation, unsupervised release, house arrest); and incarceration in a jail (for lesser sentences) or prison (for longer sentences). The process

applied in determining the sentence is shaped in considerable part by the sentencing options made available to the court by the legislature. For a particular offense, the court may have no choice. The legislature may have prescribed that conviction automatically carries with it a certain sentence and there is nothing left for the court to do except impose that sentence. Most frequently, however, legislative narrowing of options on a particular offense does not go beyond eliminating the community release option (by requiring incarceration) and setting maximums (and sometimes mandatory minimums) for incarceration and financial sanctions.

The sentence of incarceration for a felony offense probably presents the widest diversity of approach to judicial sentencing authority. Initially, jurisdictions divide on the use of determinate and indeterminate sentences. In states utilizing indeterminate sentences, the sentencing structure calls for a maximum and minimum term of imprisonment, with the parole board determining the actual release date within the span set by the two terms. The legislature always sets the outer limit for the maximum term, but beyond that point, division of sentencing authority between the court and the legislature varies with the jurisdiction and the offense. Possibilities include: judicial authority to set both the maximum term (within the legislatively prescribed outer-limit) and the minimum term; judicial authority to set only the minimum (with the maximum and sometimes a mandatory minimum prescribed by the legislature); and judicial authority to set only a maximum within the prescribed outer-limit (with the minimum then set by law as certain percentage of the judicially set maximum).

The federal system and roughly a dozen states largely utilize determinate sentences. Those jurisdictions have eliminated for all or most offenses the discretionary release authority of the parole board. The sentence imposed by the court sets a fixed term which the prisoner will serve (subject to gaining earlier release through credits earned for "good time"). In all determinate sentencing jurisdictions, as in all indeterminate sentencing jurisdictions, the legislature sets the maximum sentence possible. In a few, the legislature sets a presumptive prison term (or narrow range of terms) which the sentencing judge is directed to use for the typical offense of a particular character (e.g., burglary), absent a finding of specific aggravating or mitigating factors calling for upward and downward adjustments. Typically, however, the setting of the specific sentence within the maximum is left either to unfettered judicial discretion or to judicial discretion operating within the restraints of guidelines formulated by a sentencing commission.

A second major division in felony sentencing structures relates to the use of legislatively mandated penalties. The legislature may mandate a specific penalty, as where it specifies that conviction for a specific crime automatically carries a sentence of life imprisonment. More frequently, however, the mandatory penalty consists of a mandated sentence of at least a certain term of incarceration. The judge in an indeterminate sentencing jurisdiction then must set a minimum term at least equal to the mandatory penalty and the judge in a determinate sentencing jurisdiction must set a fixed term at least equal to the mandatory penalty. All fifty-two jurisdictions make some use of mandatory penalties, but there is substantial variation in the frequency of their use. Some jurisdictions use mandatory penalties for a wide range of offenses and wide range of special circumstances (e.g., recidivist offenders, offenders who utilized weapons) and some use them in connection with offenses that account for only a small portion of a court's docket (e.g., murder).

Where mandatory sentences are widely available (and utilized by prosecutors in their charging decisions), a significant portion of judicial sentencing in felony cases will follow automatically from those mandates.

Insofar as the legislature leaves the judge authority to choose, a third major division is found in felony sentencing structures. Most states do not seek to direct the trial court in its choice of a sentence that would fit within statutorily prescribed limits, but the federal system and a growing number of states are relying on sentencing guidelines promulgated by a sentencing commission to channel the exercise of such discretion. Those guidelines serve to establish a presumptively correct sentence of incarceration for a particular offense in accordance with the circumstances of the offense and the criminal history of the offender. Where the jurisdiction utilizes determinate sentences, the guideline presumption sets the fixed sentence; where the jurisdiction uses indeterminate sentences, the guideline ordinarily sets the minimum sentence. Typically, the guidelines also specify where a sentence other than incarceration would be appropriate, although they do not direct that such a sentence be used. In some states, the guidelines are "voluntary," and the court is free to disregard them. In most guideline jurisdictions, however, the court can depart from the guidelines only if it finds good reason to do so. Jurisdictions vary in their toleration of "departures" from the guidelines, but even where most lenient in this regard, a substantial majority of the sentences (e.g., in excess of 80%) are likely to fit within the guidelines.

The process utilized in felony sentencing varies to some extent according to whether judicial discretion is broad or is channeled or limited by guideline or legislative reference to specific sentencing circumstances. In all jurisdictions, the process is designed to obtain for the court information beyond that which will have come to its attention in the course of trial or in the acceptance of a guilty plea. The primary vehicle here is the presentence report prepared by the probation department, although the prosecution and defense commonly will be allowed to present additional information and to challenge the information contained in the presentence report. The presentation of this information is not subject to the rules governing the presentation of information at trial. The rules of evidence do not apply, and neither the prosecution nor the defense has a right to call witnesses or to cross-examine the sources of adverse information presented in the presentence report or in any additional documentation presented by the opposing side. However, where the sentencing authority of the judge is restricted by guidelines or legislatively set presumptive sentences that require findings of fact as to specific factors, the sentencing process tends to be more formal. Here, the court often will find it necessary to hold an evidentiary hearing and utilize trial-type procedures if the presence of a critical factor is controverted. . . .

Sentences that are not automatically mandated, at least as to felony convictions and serious misdemeanor convictions, will be geared to a wide range of factors in addition to the basic elements of the crime of conviction. In choosing among allowable alternatives, the judge may consider, and often under guidelines will be required to consider, such factors as aggravating and mitigating circumstances relating to the particular offense, past criminal convictions, criminal behavior that did not result in a conviction, and the defendant's acceptance of responsibility. The end result is that it became very difficult without close analysis of individual cases to compare sentences even where convictions were for the same offense. Nonetheless, some general patterns emerge by reference to the level of the offense for which the sentence is imposed. . . .

As for felony convictions, the level of the offense and prior criminal history are the keys to the choice between incarceration and non-incarceration and the location of the incarceration. Defendants convicted of low level felony offenses more often than not receive a sentence of incarceration, but a substantial portion (e.g., 30-45%) will receive a sentence of nonincarceration (most often including probation). Among defendants sentenced to incarceration for such offenses, a majority tend to be sentenced to prison, but a substantial minority (35-45%) are sentenced to jail, receiving terms less than a year. Where the defendant convicted of such a felony has one or more prior felony convictions, however, there will be a substantial drop in the percentage receiving a sentence of nonincarceration and a substantial increase in those sentenced to prison rather than to jail. For more serious felonies which do not involve violence, such as burglary and drug trafficking, the proportion of defendants sentenced to prison terms is likely to approach or exceed 50%, with the remainder about equally divided between jail sentences (often combined with probation) and straight probation. Serious violent crimes, such as murder, rape, and robbery, have the highest rate of prison sentences, ranging from above 90% for the murder category (which includes non-negligent manslaughter) to close to 70% for the rape category (which includes forcible rapes and attempted forcible rapes).

Although the length of the prison sentence set by the court has quite different significance in different sentencing structures, nationwide sentence lengths are usually assessed by reference to the maximum term that can be served under the court's sentence. Under this standard, in 1992, the nationwide mean prison sentence was 164 months for persons convicted in state courts of rape, 117 months for persons convicted of robbery, 76 months for persons convicted of burglary, 53 months for persons convicted of larceny, and 55 months for persons convicted of drug possession. Since most of those terms merely set the maximum length in an indeterminate sentencing structure, the more important measurement is the minimum term that determines when the individual becomes eligible for parole. Moreover, many jurisdictions provide for extensive "good time credits" that will reduce that minimum term or the fixed term of a determinate sentence. As a result, prisoners nationwide tend to serve between 40% and 60% of the mean maximum sentence, with the percentage varying with the nature of the offense. Thus, while the mean term for rape is 164 months, the mean time actually served is likely to be in the range of 91 months, and while the mean term for larceny is 53 months, the mean time actually to be served will be about 17 months.

(s) Step 17: Appeals. For criminal cases disposed of in the general trial court, the initial appeal is to the intermediate appellate court. If the state has no intermediate appellate court, then the initial and final appeal within the state system is to the state's court of last resort. Initial appeals in cases disposed of by the magistrate court will be to the general trial court. In some jurisdictions, the appeal procedure from a conviction in the magistrate court is a trial de novo before the general trial court, rather than that court exercising appellate review of the lower court record.

Although all convicted defendants are entitled to appeal their convictions, appeals are taken predominantly by convicted defendants who were sentenced to imprisonment on a felony conviction. Imprisoned defendants convicted pursuant to a guilty plea are included in this group, but they account for only a narrow slice of all appeals. Though the trial court's acceptance of a guilty plea may be challenged on appeal, such appellate challenges are limited to exceptional cases, so that appeals by guilty plea defendants tend to be sentencing challenges, which usually are significant only in jurisdictions that use sentencing guidelines or legislatively mandated presumptive sentences. In those jurisdictions, challenges to the sentence can constitute a substantial portion (e.g., 15-30%) of all appeals.

Appeals challenging the conviction itself come primarily from imprisoned defendants who are seeking review of a trial conviction. Indeed, in some jurisdictions, as many as 90% of the defendants who were convicted after trial and sentenced to prison will appeal their convictions. Even with almost automatic appeal by this group, however, the total number of appeals to the intermediate appeals court is likely to amount to less than 10% of all convictions entered by the state's general trial court. Of course, where the jurisdiction provides for extensive appellate review of sentencing, the overall percentage of appeals is likely to be somewhat higher. Appeals from misdemeanor convictions before the magistrate courts, on the other hand, can very well amount to less than 1% of the number of convictions entered in the magistrate courts.

Appeals challenging convictions raise a wide range of issues, usually relating to some action or inaction of the trial judge. The court's admission of evidence challenged as unconstitutionally obtained stands out in several jurisdictions as by far the most frequently raised appellate objection, but in others, that objection is raised no more frequently than several other claims, such as the alleged insufficiency of the evidence and incompetency of counsel. Defense success on appeal varies with the particular appellate court. Among the federal Courts of Appeals, for example, for criminal appeals terminated on the merits in 1990, the percentage of reversals ranged from a high of 15% in the District of Columbia Circuit to a low of 7.4% in the First Circuit, with an overall rate of 10.4% for all circuits. State intermediate appellate courts commonly have a reversal rate on defense appeals of right in the 5-10% range, although those rates will be somewhat higher when reversals in part are included. Courts of last resort, with discretionary jurisdiction, may have a substantially higher rate of reversals than the intermediate appellate courts in the same state.

(t) Step 18: Postconviction Remedies. After the appellate process is exhausted, imprisoned defendants may be able to use postconviction remedies to challenge their convictions on limited grounds. In particular, federal postconviction remedies are available to state as well as federal prisoners to challenge their convictions in the federal courts on most constitutional grounds. The federal district courts currently receive roughly 18,000 such postconviction applications. Relief is granted on less than 3 percent of these petitions, however, and the relief often is limited to requiring a further hearing. In the state system, annual postconviction challenges typically fall below 5% of all felony filings.

The Nature of Criminal Law
and Its Analytic Structure

How is criminal law different from other kinds of law? What does society seek to achieve by imposing punishment through its criminal justice system? How is the criminal law organized to achieve this purpose? How are the sources and the form of criminal law different from that of other kinds of law? These are the questions addressed in this Section.

● OVERVIEW OF THE SOURCES OF CRIMINAL LAW

Two hundred years ago in England, criminal law was generally uncodified. This "common law" was developed by and embodied in judicial opinions. The American colonies adopted this common law of England as it existed at the time of their independence. The most popular treatise of the time, Blackstone's *Commentaries on the Laws of England,* became a highly influential work in America not because of anything particularly distinguished about the four volumes but rather because its popularity coincided with American independence. Volume 4 provided a useful summary of then-existing English common law criminal law.[1] American courts then took on the role of further refining and developing the law, thereby creating differences with English law. Today, courts generally no longer have this role with respect to criminal law. The function has been taken over by the legislatures. Nearly every state has a criminal code as its primary source of criminal law. Courts interpret the code but generally have no authority to create new

---

1. W. Blackstone, Commentaries on the Laws of England (1803, reprinted in 1969).

crimes or change the definitions of existing crimes. The reasons for the shift from common law's judicially defined offenses to criminal codes are found chiefly in the rationales for what is called the Legality Principle, the subject of Section 2. Even after codification, the power of courts to interpret criminal statutes can have significant effect.

Common Law Defined   When lawyers speak of "common law," they may mean either the law as it existed during the Common Law period in England or law that is derived from a process of judicial development. The intended meaning frequently is evident from the context. For example, the "common law *process*" typically refers to the process of judicial law-making, whether or not it occurs during the Common Law *period*. "*The* Common Law rule" usually refers to the legal rule that existed in England during the eighteenth century. On the other hand, a minority of states continue to rely upon judicially modified variations of the original Common Law rule. Such rules may be referred to as "common law" rules even if they are significantly different from the rule described by Blackstone.[1]

Current Role of Common Law   While no state continues to permit judges to create crimes, the common law continues to be important for several reasons. Some state criminal codes incorporate common law offenses by name without defining them. Under so-called "reception" statutes, judicial decisions must be relied upon to determine the requirements of a common law offense. In addition, because some codes are simply codifications of the previously existing common law doctrine, ambiguity in code language that calls for an examination of the drafters' intent may require review of the cases in which the doctrine was developed. Similarly, the common law cases may be consulted because they tend to explain the rationale behind the original rule if the legislative history of the rule does not. An attorney seeking to persuade a court of the wisdom, or folly, of the policy behind a particular interpretation of a statute may look to common law cases to establish and explain the policy. The rules and techniques of statutory interpretation are discussed further in Section 2, concerning the Legality Principle.

Modern Criminal Code Reform   While there were some heroic efforts, little criminal code reform occurred in the United States before the 1960s. Most codes at the time were less like codes and more a collection of ad hoc statutory enactments, each enactment triggered by a crime or a crime problem that gained public interest.[2] A major contribution of early codifiers frequently was to put the offenses in alphabetical order. The greatest catalyst of modern American criminal law codification has been the Model Penal Code, which was promulgated by the American Law Institute. Beginning even before its formal adoption in 1962, the Model Penal Code served and continues to serve as a basis for wholesale replacement of existing criminal codes in over two-thirds of the states. Some states have adopted the Code with only minor revision, while others, especially those that

---

1. If "Common Law" is capitalized it typically is meant to refer to the Common Law period, but most writers, including this one, are not consistent in following this convention.

2. See, e.g., 18 U.S.C. §§1201-1202 (the so-called Lindbergh Law), enacted in 1932, making kidnaping a federal crime when the victim is transported across state lines. The statute was an immediate response to the kidnaping of Charles Lindbergh, Jr., on March 1, 1932.

adopted it early, tended to redraft their existing doctrine, borrowing only pieces of the Model Penal Code language but most of its style and form.

The Model Penal Code   The American Law Institute, which drafted the Code, is a nongovernmental broad-based highly regarded group of lawyers, judges, professors, and others who undertake research and drafting projects designed to bring rationality and enlightenment to American law. The Institute's Restatements of the Law have been influential in bringing clarity and uniformity to many fields. When a criminal law project was undertaken in 1953, it was concluded that the criminal law of the various states had become too disparate to permit a "restatement" and, in any case, the existing law was seen as too unsound and ill-considered to merit restating. What was needed instead was a model criminal code. After nine years of work and a series of Tentative Drafts, the Institute approved an Official Draft in 1962. The original commentary, which was contained in the various Tentative Drafts, was consolidated, revised, and republished with the 1962 text in 1980 and 1985 as a seven-volume set.[1]

Federal Criminal Code Reform   Of the third or less of the jurisdictions that have not yet adopted a modern criminal code, the federal system is the most unfortunate example of frustrated reform. The Congress has been engaged in an effort to reform the federal criminal code since 1966.[2] Several modern code bills passed the Senate but did not pass the House. Criminal code reform is always difficult because it touches highly political issues, but the lack of a modern federal criminal code is a matter of some embarrassment in a country whose states lead the world in enlightened criminal codification. The present federal criminal code is not significantly different in form from the alphabetical listing of offenses that was typical of the original American codes in the 1800s.

Format of Modern Codes   Modern criminal codes have several hallmarks: a General Part that contains general provisions, affecting all or many of the specific offenses defined in the Special Part of the code. General provisions include such things as the general rules concerning omission liability, complicity, and voluntary intoxication; general defenses such as self-defense, insanity, and time limitations; general rules for the definition and interpretation of offenses; and a collection of definitions for commonly used terms. In the Special Part of a code, offenses are defined and organized as conceptually related groups and are consolidated and revised to avoid overlaps and gaps. Thus, the offenses against property work together to define all prohibited harms involving property, etc. A significant practical effect of reform is that code sections can no longer be read in isolation. To fully understand each offense definition in the Special Part, several General Part provisions must be consulted. The largely successful goal of modern criminal code reform is a code that provides clarity in defining a sophisticated and rational set of rules for distributing liability and punishment.

---

1. Three volumes containing Part II of the Model Penal Code, Definition of Specific Crimes with revised comments, were published in 1980. Three additional volumes containing Part I of the Code, General Provisions, with revised Comments, were published in 1985. An official version of the completed text of the Model Penal Code was published in 1985.

2. These efforts began with the establishment of the "Brown Commission" (Act of Nov. 8, 1966, Pub. L. No. 89-801, 80 Stat. 1516) followed by that Commission's Final Report on Reform of Federal Criminal Laws presented in 1971. See also Ronald C. Gainer, Report to the Attorney General on Federal Criminal Code Reform, 1 Crim. L. Forum 99 (1989) (a comprehensive critique of the federal criminal code).

▲ PROBLEM
Fear of the Daggers

Box lives next door to the Golden Daggers' clubhouse. As he walks by on this morning, on his way home from his night shift at the Tower Grill, two gang members grab him and drag him inside. "I hear you're friendly with Bet Peppe," one spits, with his face an inch from Box's. "No, not really," Box says, shaking. "I used to see her around, hanging with you guys. I'm not really a friend of hers." The man responds, "Then you won't mind doing me a favor. You'll cut her face for me." Box isn't thrilled about the idea. He says nothing. "Look, it's either your face or hers," the man says as he pricks a knife in Box's face an inch below his eye. "OK. OK. I'll do it." The Dagger stares, "If I don't see cuts on her face tomorrow, we'll be looking for you."

Box goes to his apartment and pours himself a drink, spilling much of it because his hands are shaking. Yes, he is scared of those guys, he admits to himself. Hurting Bet would be a bad thing, but what's the alternative, especially if the Daggers find out that he and Bet have been dating? After several more hours of anxious drinking, Box gets a butcher knife from the kitchen and heads for Bet's, bottle in hand. By the time he gets there, he is staggering badly and barely coherent. Bet opens the door. "Hi Box." Box lurches forward, stumbling into the back of the sofa. "What's wrong with you?" Box does not respond. He staggers around the apartment, knocking over furniture. "This is your own fault," he screams at her, and babbles on about blood, knives, and eyes. When he has worked himself into a frenzy, he pulls his knife and begins flailing at everything around him, curtains, lamps, pictures on the wall. Bet gets caught by several of his swings and is badly cut. She runs from the apartment, screaming for the police. Box also runs. He takes the subway to his brother's place on the other side of town where he spends the night.

After reflecting on his situation, Box decides not to return to his apartment but rather to take a job in a small town in the southern part of the state. Unaware that Box has left town, Bet does not disclose his identity to the police for fear of reprisals by Box. Bet's shoulder heals but a cut to her hand has permanently damaged the muscles. She is no longer able to write with that hand and becomes increasingly bitter about the episode.

Several years later Box returns to town. Bet chances to see him on the subway one day and, after much stewing, decides to report him to the police. His arrest comes three years after the incident.

Is Box liable for aggravated assault under the Model Penal Code?

● OVERVIEW OF THE OPERATIONAL STRUCTURE OF CRIMINAL LAW

Operational Structure　Let us use Box's case to examine how the doctrines of criminal law operate. Each rule typically does one of three things. A doctrine may define what constitutes an *offense*. A doctrine may define the conditions under which an actor will be acquitted even though he satisfies the elements of an offense. Such a doctrine commonly is termed a *defense*. Or a doctrine may define the conditions under which an actor will be held liable even though he does not satisfy the elements of an offense. Such a doctrine may be called a doctrine of *imputation*. This coursebook is organized around this three-part doctrinal structure. Their interaction in the analysis of criminal cases might be summarized as the flow chart illustrates.

Figure 1 **Structure of criminal law's liability decision**

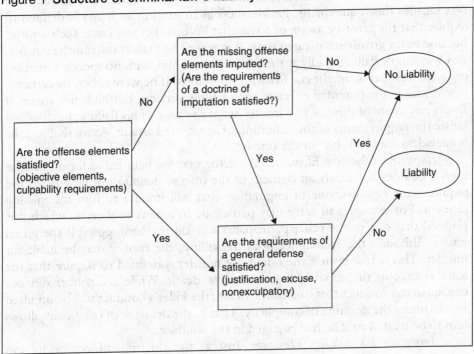

Offense Definitions　The definition of an offense typically is comprised of objective elements — for example, conduct, its attendant circumstances, and, sometimes, its results — and culpability elements — for example, purpose, knowledge, recklessness, or negligence — as to each objective element. Thus, the objective elements of murder might require that an actor engage in *conduct* that causes the *death* of *another human being*. The culpability elements might require that the actor *know* the nature of his conduct, that it will cause a death, and that the death caused is that of a human being (e.g., not that of a non-viable fetus). The culpability requirements may be different for different elements of the same offense. A jurisdiction might, for example, require that an actor *know* the nature of his conduct and that it will cause a death but only require that the actor be *reckless* as to whether the death is that of a human being.

Special vs. General Part of Code Part II of this coursebook examines the general principles governing objective and culpability elements of the offense definitions. Part III examines the elements of the most important offense, homicide. The definitions of specific offenses make up what is called the Special Part of a criminal code. The general rules governing the definition of the offenses, together with the doctrines of imputation and defense, make up the General Part of a code and typically apply to many or all specific offenses. Look at the table of contents of the Model Penal Code in Appendix B to see the distinction between the General Part and Special Part in the organization of a criminal code.

Box and Elements of Aggravated Assault In Box's case, aggravated assault might be defined to require, as an objective elements, that the actor engage in conduct that causes serious bodily injury to another.[1] Box has done that. The offense also might require, as culpability elements, that the actor be at least reckless as to causing such injury, at the time of his conduct. It is unclear that Box satisfies this requirement. Recklessness as to causing an injury is defined to require that the actor be aware of a risk that his conduct will cause such injury.[2] Because of his grossly intoxicated state, it may well be that, at the time he cut Bet, Box was simply flailing madly at the world around him, with no specific intention or awareness that he might cut Bet with his swings. If he were sober, he certainly would realize the potential effect of such knife-swinging, but he is not sober. If Box is not aware of this risk of harm to Bet at the time of his flailing, he does not satisfy the requirements of the definition of aggravated assault. As we shall see, he nonetheless may be liable for the offense.

Imputing Objective Elements An actor may be held liable for an offense even if he does not satisfy an element of the offense definition if he satisfies the requirements of a doctrine of imputation that will impute to him the missing element. For example, an actor may participate in a bank robbery in which it is planned that one of the other participants will kill the bank guard if the guard resists. Although the accomplice does the killing, the robber may be liable for murder. This is true even if the offense of murder is defined to require that the actor engage in the conduct that causes the death. While the robber did not engage in the conduct that caused the death, the killer's conduct will be imputed to him under the doctrine of complicity. That is, the doctrine of complicity allows him to be treated *as if* he had engaged in the conduct.

Imputing Culpability Elements Just as the doctrine of complicity can impute to the defendant an objective element — another's conduct — the doctrine of voluntary intoxication can impute a culpability element. An actor who voluntarily intoxicates herself and in that drunken state strikes and kills a pedestrian with her car in fact may lack the culpability as to causing death required for

---

1. Model Penal Code §§211.1(2), 210.0(3).
2. Model Penal Code §§2.02(2)(c).

the offense of manslaughter—for example an awareness of a substantial risk that her conduct will cause the death of another human being. Yet, such awareness of a risk of causing a death (i.e., recklessness as to causing death) may be imputed to the actor under the doctrine of voluntary intoxication. That is, because of her voluntary intoxication, she may be treated *as if* she satisfies the required element of recklessness as to causing death, and therefore may be convicted of manslaughter. Box would fall under the application of this doctrine. Because his intoxication was voluntary, recklessness as to causing serious bodily injury, required for aggravated assault liability, will be imputed to him.[1] Part V of this coursebook takes up the doctrines of imputation.

Doctrines of Defense Where an actor satisfies all of the elements of an offense, actually or through imputation, he nonetheless may be acquitted of the offense if he satisfies the conditions of a defense. Box has several claims of defense that he might make, although some are more promising than others. He might claim that his conduct was justified by his need to protect himself from the Golden Daggers. He might claim that he should be excused because the Daggers coerced him into doing what he did. Or, he might claim that the period of limitation has run and that he can no longer be prosecuted for the offense.

Failure of Proof Defenses Some doctrines that are called "defenses" are nothing more than the absence of a required offense element. When I take your umbrella believing it to be my own, I may claim a *mistake defense*. Yet my defense derives not from a special defense doctrine about mistake as to ownership but rather from the elements of the theft offense. The definition of theft includes a requirement that the actor know that the property taken is property owned by another. If I mistakenly believe that the umbrella I take is my own, I do not satisfy that required element of knowledge. Such a mistake "defense" is called a *failure of proof defense* because it derives from the inability of the state to prove a required element. When Box claimed that he did not have the required recklessness as to causing serious bodily injury to Bet, he is claiming such a failure of proof defense. He is claiming that the prosecution cannot prove all of the elements of the offense. In casual usage, such claims are called "defenses," but they are simply another way of talking about the requirements of an offense definition.

Offense Modification Defenses Some defenses are indeed independent of the offense elements but in fact concern criminalization issues closely related to the definition of the offense. They typically refine or qualify the definition of a particular offense or group of offenses. Voluntary renunciation, for example, can provide a defense to inchoate offenses like attempt or conspiracy. Consent is recognized as a defense to some kinds of assault. The consent defense helps to define what we mean by the offense of assault (as including minor injury when it is not consented to), just as renunciation helps refine the definition of inchoate offenses (as including only unrenounced criminal plans). Indeed, assault frequently is defined as an *unconsented to* touching. That is, the absence of consent sometimes is included as an element of the offense. As this illustrates, the difference between failure of proof defenses and offense modification defenses is one of

---

1. Model Penal Code §2.08(2).

form more than substance. An offense modification *defense* can as easily be drafted as a *negative element* of the offense.

Criminalization Defenses vs. General Defenses Because both failure of proof and offense modification defenses serve to refine the offense definition (and therefore might be called "criminalization" defenses), they tend to apply to a single offense or group of offenses. Justifications, excuses, and nonexculpatory defenses, in contrast, are unrelated to a particular offense; they theoretically apply to all offenses and therefore are called *general defenses*. The recognition of each general defense rests upon reasons extraneous to the criminalization goals and policies of the offense. A general defense is provided not because there is no criminal wrong, but rather despite the occurrence of a legally recognized harm or evil. The offense harm or evil may have occurred but the special conditions establishing the defense suggest that the violator ought not to be punished for the offense harm or evil.

Justification Defenses An actor may satisfy all of the elements of an offense and his or her conduct may clearly be a legally recognized harm or evil of the sort that generally is prohibited, yet the circumstances of the offense may suggest that, because of special justifying circumstances, this particular offense conduct ought to be tolerated or even encouraged under the circumstances. An unconsented-to striking of another constitutes assault and generally is prohibited, yet it ought not result in liability if done in self-defense against an aggressor to protect one's life. Burning another's farm constitutes arson, yet it ought to be tolerated and even encouraged if it creates a firebreak that saves a town from a raging forest fire. Providing a justification defense in such cases is not meant to lessen the general prohibition against assault and arson but only to recognize that the harm or evil of even such serious offenses as these can be outweighed by a greater good that flows from the commission of the offense under the special justifying circumstances.

Justification for Box? Box might claim a justification defense, arguing that the cuts to Bet were a less serious harm than the injury he was likely to suffer at the hands of the Daggers. But his conduct is not likely to be deemed justified. The defensive force justifications authorize injury to aggressors, but Bet is an innocent person.[1] Justification defenses also typically require that no other less harmful means of avoiding the harm be available.[2] Box could have reported the incident to police, gone into hiding, as he did, or both. Cutting Bet was not the least harmful means of avoiding the harm. Justification defenses are examined in Sections 17 through 19.

Excuse Defenses Even if an actor's conduct is harmful or evil in itself and is not justified by special circumstances, an acquittal nonetheless may be appropriate. The criminal law has a special commitment to punishing only the blameworthy. An actor who is acting involuntarily, who is insane, involuntarily intoxicated, or immature, or who is acting under duress or under a reasonable mistake of law or mistake as to a justification may be blameless. That is, we may feel that such an actor in such a situation could not reasonably have been expected to remain

---

1. Model Penal Code §3.04.
2. See, e.g., Model Penal Code §3.02.

law-abiding. The excuse defenses are designed to exculpate such blameless offenders. Excuse defenses are the subject of Sections 20 through 23.

Excuse for Box? Box might claim an excuse of some sort. Because his intoxication was voluntary, the law does not permit it to be the basis for an excuse.[1] He might do better to claim a duress defense based on the coercion from the Daggers. But many states make the duress defense unavailable for offenses of violence against another person. And, where it is not expressly barred in such cases, as in the Model Penal Code, a duress defense is available only where a person of reasonable firmness would have been unable to resist the coercion to commit the offense.[2] It seems unlikely that a jury could be persuaded that, faced with threats like those from the Daggers, a person of reasonable firmness would slash Bet the way Box did. In other words, a jury is likely to find that, despite the Daggers' threats, Box is blameworthy and ought to be held liable for his offense.

Nonexculpatory Defenses Even blameworthy actors may be acquitted if they satisfy the requirements of a nonexculpatory defense. Such defenses are disfavored yet recognized because they each further an important societal interest, judged to be more important than punishing the offender at hand. Diplomatic immunity, for example, is allowed to shield criminal offenders because by recognizing such a defense we protect our diplomats abroad, and this in turn allows the establishment of diplomatic relations between nations. That a societal benefit is derived from the defense may seem to make nonexculpatory defenses similar to justifications, but note that the benefit in nonexculpatory offenses flows not from the actor's offense conduct, as is the case with justifications, but rather from forgoing his conviction despite the undesirability of his conduct and his blameworthiness.

Nonexculpatory Defense for Box? Box may claim a nonexculpatory defense in the statute of limitations.[3] The passage of three years, during which he has been in the jurisdiction, may well bar his prosecution for the offense. The defense is not based on any lack of harm or blame but rather is recognized, despite the presence of both, because such a limitation period is said to avoid a counterproductive preoccupation with the past. At some point, the argument goes, society is better off letting go of the past and moving ahead to deal with the problems and challenges of today. In most jurisdictions, if the arrest warrant for Box is issued more than three years after the assault, prosecution will be barred. Section 24 examines nonexculpatory defenses.

Liability Assignment vs. Sentencing All of these criminal law doctrines — offense definitions, doctrines of imputation, and general defenses — serve only to assign criminal liability. Such liability suggests that some punishment is appropriate and gives a general classification of the offense — for example, third-degree felony, first-degree misdemeanor — that serves as a starting point for determining how much punishment is appropriate. The specific amount and nature of the

---

1. Model Penal Code §2.08(4).
2. Model Penal Code §2.09.
3. Model Penal Code §1.06.

punishment, however, is determined during the sentencing process, which frequently is entirely discretionary with the sentencing judge. In that sense, the criminal law, for all its intricacy and for all the resources devoted to its adjudication of an individual case, has a limited effect in determining the ultimate sanction. It has the important role of determining *who* shall be punished but it leaves to the sentencing process most of the determination of *how much* or *what kind* of punishment will be imposed.

Criminal Law Principles in Sentencing   This state of affairs may seem peculiar. The criminal law is drafted with great care to make the assignment of liability a matter of rules rather than discretion. As Section 2 details, this commitment to the articulation of liability rules, called the principle of legality, has always been a foundation of Anglo-American criminal law. Yet the highly articulated criminal law has a limited effect in determining the punishment imposed. Instead, the highly discretionary sentencing process determines the punishment. If unguided discretion is carefully avoided in the liability assignment process, why is it tolerated in sentencing, where the punishment is in large part determined? In part because of legality concerns, the trend in modern sentencing systems is toward more articulated sentencing rules. As one might expect, these articulations typically draw upon and extend principles of criminal law. Thus, while the rules of liability assignment are only a stop on the way to determining punishment, the principles behind those rules are likely to play an increasingly larger role in the formulation of sentencing rules and guidelines.

Practical Importance of Criminal Law Theory   The articulation of sentencing rules is but one example of the value of understanding the principles behind criminal law and not just its rules. The effective advocate and the informed judge are at their best when they understand the theory of the rules, why the doctrine is the way it is. Only then can they interpret code provisions to give them proper effect or criticize interpretations that would frustrate the purpose of a provision. In addition, lawyers inevitably play a large role in the law-making process, in which criminal codes are drafted and enacted. Therefore, a rational, effective, and just criminal law depends on an informed bar. The structure for criminal law described above is an example of a conceptualization that can have significant practical value. Lawyers and judges, not just academics, benefit from a sense of this larger conceptual framework of criminal law, for it is through such a structure that they can appreciate the role that each doctrine plays within the larger whole.

▲ PROBLEM
Fear, Pain, and Bubble Gum

Ike has decided to join ZBT fraternity. During "hell week" the aspiring "pledges" are on call at all times to provide labor, entertainment, or anything else that a brother of ZBT might desire. School policy prevents skipping classes during hell week, a godsend for the pledges. Classes provide the only opportunity to sleep. With the altered function of classes, books are unnecessary. Instead, pledges carry hardwood pledge paddles and the favorite candy of each brother. After a very restful hour of thermodynamics, Ike meets Brother Constin. "Cherry bubble gum, pledge." Ike's mouth drops and his heart stops. "Aaaah.... I thought you liked strawberry, Mr. Constin." "You have five minutes to compensate for your incompetence, pledge." Ike scrambles. He spots Ed Begley, another ZBT pledge, 100 yards away. "Ed, have you got cherry bubble gum for Constin?" Ed's eyebrows pop up. "I thought he liked strawberry." Ike bolts for the local convenience store, with Ed close behind. He spots cherry in the bubble gum box. "Yes!" The moment sours as they realize that neither has any money. Ike grabs two pieces and heads for the door. "I'll be back later to pay for this," he shouts over his shoulder to the shopkeeper, who is unimpressed. "Come back here. You can't take that without paying for it."

Ed explains their situation to the shopkeeper. After some discussion, the shopkeeper lets Ed have two pieces free, but notes that he still considers Ike a thief. Ed dashes out the front and around the back of the store. He thinks he can make up for lost time by taking a shortcut that he knows. But as he squeezes between two cars parked in the alley behind the store, he loses his footing. As he falls, he cuts his leg badly and becomes wedged between the two cars. His struggles only wedge him tighter and his cries for help go unheard. He feels himself getting faint from loss of blood and decides that he must break the window of one of the cars to get maneuvering room to extricate himself. He gets free and limps back into the store, where the owner calls an ambulance and puts a tourniquet on his bleeding leg.

Ike wonders where Ed is and concludes that Ed may be having second thoughts about pledging ZBT. Brother Constin is waiting at the edge of campus. "That was six minutes, pledge." Ike's watch says four minutes but he decides protestation would not be useful. Brother Constin pronounces sentence. "Three whacks." Ike hands Brother Constin his paddle and bends over. All three are stingers. He responds, "Thank you sir, you have helped me in my quest to reach the perfection of brotherhood." "You are welcome." Ike expects to have permanent scarring, as do all of the current brothers of ZBT.

While "hazing" is technically unlawful, it has been generally ignored in the past. But the incident at the convenience store, in particular, draws University ire. The fraternity's pledge privileges are suspended for a year. To show its concern for lawless conduct during pledge week, the University insists that both civil claims and criminal charges be filed against Brother Constin for assault, against Ike for theft of the bubble gum, and against Ed for damage to the car. The civil assault claims against Constin are dismissed on the ground that Ike consented, he knew the effects of the paddling he was consenting to, and he is an adult who can make an informed decision to consent to the injury. In the civil action for taking the gum without permission, Ike concedes his civil liability and pays the minor damages sought by the store owner. Ed similarly concedes and compensates the car owner.

What liability, if any, under the Model Penal Code, which is reproduced in Appendix B? Consider the following Model Penal Code sections for what they say about the nature of criminal law.

■ THE LAW

Model Penal Code
(Official Draft 1962)

Section 2.02. General Requirements of Culpability

(1) Minimum Requirements of Culpability. Except as provided in Section 2.05, a person is not guilty of an offense unless he acted purposely, knowingly, recklessly or negligently, as the law may require, with respect to each material element of the offense....

(3) Culpability Required Unless Otherwise Provided. When the culpability sufficient to establish a material element of an offense is not prescribed by law, such element is established if a person acts purposely, knowingly or recklessly with respect thereto....

Section 2.11. Consent

(1) In General. The consent of the victim to conduct charged to constitute an offense or to the result thereof is a defense if such consent negatives an element of the offense or precludes the infliction of the harm or evil sought to be prevented by the law defining the offense.

(2) Consent to Bodily Injury. When conduct is charged to constitute an offense because it causes or threatens bodily injury, consent to such conduct or to the infliction of such injury is a defense if:

(a) the bodily injury consented to or threatened by the conduct consented to is not serious; or

(b) the conduct and the injury are reasonably foreseeable hazards of joint participation in a lawful athletic contest or competitive sport or other concerted activity not forbidden by law; or

(c) the consent establishes a justification for the conduct under Article 3 of the Code.

(3) Ineffective Consent. Unless otherwise provided by the Code or by the law defining the offense, assent does not constitute consent if:

(a) it is given by a person who is legally incompetent to authorize the conduct charged to constitute the offense; or

(b) it is given by a person who by reason of youth, mental disease or defect or intoxication is manifestly unable or known by the actor to be unable to make a reasonable judgment as to the nature or harmfulness of the conduct charged to constitute the offense; or

(c) it is given by a person whose improvident consent is sought to be prevented by the law defining the offense; or

(d) it is induced by force, duress or deception of a kind sought to be prevented by the law defining the offense.

Section 2.12. De Minimis Infractions

The Court shall dismiss a prosecution if, having regard to the nature of the conduct charged to constitute an offense and the nature of the attendant circumstances, it finds that the defendant's conduct:

(1) was within a customary license or tolerance, neither expressly negatived by the person whose interest was infringed nor inconsistent with the purpose of the law defining the offense; or

(2) did not actually cause or threaten the harm or evil sought to be prevented by the law defining the offense or did so only to an extent too trivial to warrant the condemnation of conviction; or

(3) presents such other extenuations that it cannot reasonably be regarded as envisaged by the legislature in forbidding the offense. The Court shall not dismiss a prosecution under Subsection (3) of this Section without filing a written statement of its reasons.

Section 3.02. Justification Generally: Choice of Evils

(1) Conduct which the actor believes to be necessary to avoid a harm or evil to himself or to another is justifiable, provided that:

(a) the harm or evil sought to be avoided by such conduct is greater than that sought to be prevented by the law defining the offense charged; and

(b) neither the Code nor other law defining the offense provides exceptions or defenses dealing with the specific situation involved; and

(c) a legislative purpose to exclude the justification claimed does not otherwise plainly appear.

(2) When the actor was reckless or negligent in bringing about the situation requiring a choice of harms or evils or in appraising the necessity for his conduct, the justification afforded by this Section is unavailable in a prosecution for any offense for which recklessness or negligence, as the case may be, suffices to establish culpability.

● OVERVIEW OF THE NATURE OF CRIMINAL LAW

Criminal-Civil Similarities Criminal law is not unique in the conduct it punishes; some conduct violates criminal and civil law. Striking another person without her consent may be both a crime and a tort. Nor is criminal law unique in the deprivations that it imposes; civil commitment, tort law, and a variety of other civil measures can deprive a person of his or her liberty, put restrictions on what a person can do, and compel the payment of money. Criminal cases do typically have procedural characteristics different from civil cases. Crimes are prosecuted by the state rather than by the victim, while civil cases have a private "plaintiff" who brings the action. On the other hand, state prosecution is not unique to criminal actions; civil actions sometimes are brought by the state, as when the state sues for breach of a contract. If criminal law is not unique in either the conduct it prohibits, the deprivations it dispenses, or the party that brings the action, why is it kept distinct? Its existence must have an explanation apart from its prohibitions, deprivations, or procedures.

Criminal Conviction as Moral Condemnation The conventional wisdom holds that criminal liability and criminal commitment are different from civil liability and civil commitment in that the former generally are thought to reflect moral blameworthiness deserving condemnation and punishment. "An act or omission and its accompanying state of mind which, if duly proven to have taken place, will incur a formal and solemn pronouncement of the moral condemnation of the community."[1] This notion that the distinctiveness of criminal law is its focus on moral blameworthiness is supported by the traditional requirements for criminal liability, which as a group are not characteristic of civil liability.

Culpability Requirement Characteristic of criminal law is a requirement that the actor have a culpable state of mind as to the offense elements. Bringing about a prohibited harm or evil, even wrongfully, is not itself sufficient for criminal liability. Generally, a minimum culpability of recklessness is required as to every offense element;[2] that is, an actor must have some degree of awareness of the facts that make her conduct criminal. Still higher culpability levels, knowledge or purpose, commonly are required as to one or more offense elements. Lower culpability than recklessness, criminal negligence, is used infrequently; strict liability — liability in the absence of culpability — generally is limited to "violations,"[3] which are distinguished from "crimes." Civil liability, in contrast, frequently requires no culpable state of mind. When culpability is required, commonly only negligence need be shown.

---

1. H.L.A. Hart, The Aims of the Criminal Law, 23 Law & Contemp. Probs. 401, 405 (1958).

2. Model Penal Code §2.02(3).

3. Id. §2.05(2). The most notorious exception to this is the common law's use of strict liability in statutory rape, a serious offense. See, e.g., Model Penal Code §§213.1(1)(d), 213.3(1)(a), 213.6(1); id. §213.6(1) comment (1980).

De Minimis Defense   Another point of contrast is found in the fact that criminal law addresses only harms of a sufficient seriousness; situations analogous to civil law's liability-with-nominal-damages typically do not support criminal liability. Under the Model Penal Code's "de minimis infraction" defense, for example: "The Court shall dismiss a prosecution if . . . it finds that the defendant's conduct . . . did not actually cause or threaten the harm or evil sought to be prevented by the law defining the offense or did so only to an extent *too trivial to warrant the condemnation of conviction* . . . ."[1] Consider the person who leaves a restaurant with an apple from a buffet after paying for the buffet but in violation of the establishment's rule against removal of food. This violates the terms of the theft prohibition — taking property of another without consent — yet one might conclude, as the court did, that such a violation is too trivial to generate community condemnation and therefore is not properly dealt with by the criminal law.[2] At civil law, in contrast, the extent of the harm is important to assessment of the amount of the award but generally does not affect liability. Thus, the shopkeeper from whom Ike took the gum will not recover much in tort, but he does have a right to liability and compensation from Ike for the extent of his injury. Criminal law, on the other hand, generally limits liability to cases where the conduct is sufficiently serious to merit the condemnation of criminal conviction.

Crimes vs. Violations   In the same vein, the Code distinguishes "crimes" from "violations": "A violation does not constitute a crime and conviction of a violation shall not give rise to any disability or legal disadvantage based on conviction of a criminal offense." Thus, illegal parking, motor vehicle violations, and other such prohibitions generally are not "crimes," even though they are enforced by the same officers who enforce the criminal law.

Consent as a Defense   Consent similarly has a different effect in the criminal and civil contexts. It generally is a complete defense to a civil action. A plaintiff generally has no right to recover for a harm to which he or she consented. It was for this reason that Brother Constin was able to successfully defend the civil suit for assault. In contrast, a victim's consent is rarely a defense to a criminal charge. It is allowed as a defense only if it *vitiates the harm or evil of the offense*. That is, consent is a defense to criminal liability only if the presence of consent means that there no longer is a harm. That Ed got the shopkeeper's permission to take the bubble gum without paying for it means that the taking is not theft. Similarly, where valid consent is present, sexual intercourse is not rape.

Denying Consent Defense to Crime   In most criminal offenses, however, consent is not a defense. Assault occurs if one "purposely, knowingly, or recklessly causes bodily injury to another."[3] The criminal law generally does not allow consent of the victim to bodily injury as a defense.[4] Criminal conduct is seen as

---

1. Model Penal Code §2.12(2) (1962) (emphasis added). Where the damage is minor under civil law, in contrast, liability nonetheless is imposed but only nominal damages are awarded.

2. See State v. Nevens, 197 N.J. Super. 531, 485 A.2d 345 (1984) (conviction reversed and complaint dismissed as a de minimis infraction).

3. Model Penal Code §211.1(1)(a).

4. See, e.g., Model Penal Code §2.11(1). As is common in civil law, assent might not necessarily provide effective consent. See Model Penal Code §2.11(3).

a harm against the community. While it may be an individual who suffers the immediate injury, it is the breach of the society's rules of conduct prohibiting the act that serves to justify punishment. If the law prohibits the conduct without exception, it is not within the power of an individual to revoke the law's prohibition. The law may give an individual the authority to consent to minor injury, just as it gives individuals the authority to give away their property, as the shopkeeper gave Ed free bubble gum. But causing more than minor injury is an offense, no matter that the victim consents.

Justification and Excuse Defenses   Even if the actor has the required culpable state of mind for the offense, criminal liability is barred if the actor's conduct is justified because it avoids a greater societal harm. Such an actor is exculpated under a justification defense. Thus, one has a justification defense to theft if one breaks into a cabin to avoid starvation and exposure while lost in the woods. Even if the actor is not justified, criminal liability also is barred if the person commits the offense because of circumstances or conditions that render the person blameless for the offense, as is frequently the case with one who is insane or who commits the offense because coerced to do so by another. Such an actor is exculpated under an excuse defense. Criminal codes recognize a wide range of justification and excuse defenses, such as lesser evils, law enforcement authority, insanity, immaturity, involuntary intoxication, duress, and reasonable mistake as to a justification.[1] Civil liability, such as tort, typically recognizes neither justification nor excuse defenses. If you tie up to my dock in a storm in order to save your ship and those aboard, you will have a justification defense to criminal liability but nonetheless may be liable in tort to pay me for the damage you caused to my dock. Similarly, an insane person may gain an insanity defense to criminal liability but the person or his guardian nonetheless must compensate another for harm caused. The difference logically follows from the difference in the criteria for criminal and civil liability. Rather than the moral blameworthiness of the actor, the criterion for civil liability is frequently said to be the fair or efficient allocation of the loss, or some other nonblameworthiness criteria.

"Condemnation as Criminal"   Some aspects of civil law may recognize some doctrines similar to these, but criminal law is unique in reliance on such a collection of doctrines: the requirement of conscious culpability, rejection of consent as a general defense, recognition of a defense for de minimis violations, justification, and excuse. This is as one would expect. For, taken together, these doctrines serve "to safeguard conduct that is without fault from condemnation as criminal,"[2] and it is moral condemnation that distinguishes criminal law from all other law.

---

1. E.g., Model Penal Code §§3.02, 3.07, 4.01, 4.10, 2.08(4), 2.09.
2. Id. §1.02(1)(c).

2

The Legality Principle

The wide-spread codification of criminal law in the 1960s and 1970s, discussed in the previous Section, makes American criminal law primarily a statutory creature. Why should this be so? What prompted the enactment of these comprehensive criminal codes? The answer lies in what is called the "legality principle," a concept that expresses interests and values with special application to criminal law.

◆ THE CASE OF RAY BRENT MARSH

Noble, Georgia, is a small unincorporated cluster of houses and businesses off Highway 27, about 20 miles outside Chattanooga. Though people tend to live here for decades, they are not as close as they might be in the typical small town. "We come here and we stay here, but a lot of people don't know who their neighbors are," explains the video store owner, who has been living here for 47 years. "It's a place where you don't need to worry about what's in your backyard."

One prominent family in town is the Marsh family, descendants of Willie Marsh, who in the 19th century was the first African-American child in Walker County. In a county that is almost 94% white, the Marshes have become one of the more prominent families in town. Members of the family served in both World Wars and in Vietnam. During World War I, one of the Marshes got into the lumber business. Many of his thirteen children (nine of them boys) worked in the mill, where their father hired whites and blacks. His motto, passed down through the family, was "you don't look up, you don't look down, you look 'em straight in the eye." Several generations of Marshes are buried in the family graveyard a few blocks from the Tri-State Crematory, a family business started by Tommy Ray Marsh in 1982.

Tommy Ray had been a postal worker, but also worked digging septic tanks with a backhoe. In the mid-1970s, a family friend, William J. Willis, Sr., who now runs Willis Funeral Home, called Tommy Ray because he needed a grave digger. Realizing the business potential, Tommy Ray started his own burial vault.

After a decade of digging graves, he bought a $20,000 cremation unit from Industrial Equipment & Engineering in Apopka, Florida, and opened Tri-State Crematory. Local newspapers reported that it was the first minority-owned crematory in the country.

When he started the business, cremations were rare in that part of Georgia, but starting in the late 1980s they have become increasingly common, partly because they are less expensive than the alternatives. Tommy Ray's family now owns and rents out a fair amount of land in Noble. He is a member of the Rotary Club. His wife also is active in the community. After working as a school teacher for 30 years, she was Walker County Citizen of the Year, and was both president of the Walker County Association of Educators and the first African American to serve as chair of Walker County Democratic Committee.

In 1996, Tommy Ray has a stroke, which confines him to a wheelchair. His son Ray Brent Marsh now runs his father's cremation business. Like the rest of his family, Ray Marsh is well regarded in the community. He was a star sprinter at LaFayette High School, co-captain of the football team, and a linebacker at the University of Tennessee at Chattanooga. He is the treasurer at New Home Missionary Baptist Church, which his family helped start 93 years earlier. His mother sings in the choir. He and his wife Venessa recently had a baby girl. Like his parents, Marsh lives on the crematory grounds.

More than 30 funeral homes in the area use Tri-State Crematory, which is the only independent crematory. The Marshes charge as little as $250, where other such companies tend to start at $600. The Marshes have never really needed to advertise. One funeral director who did business with them noticed that there wasn't really any paperwork or tracking system, and the business, which is just in a shed, seemed a bit unprofessionally run.

In Georgia, the cremation industry was unregulated until 1990. Even when regulation began, there were only two inspectors. Recently, Georgia's Funeral Service Board has been trying to close down Tri-State. After an investigation that resulted in charges of operating without a state license, Marsh was granted exemption from some of the newer regulations, such as that requiring that a funeral director run the facilities; the Marshes argued that their daughter needed time to get certified as a funeral director. When the two-year exemption ended, the Board tried again to enforce the regulations and close the business. Marsh lobbied State Representative Mike Snow for another exemption, but Snow refused. The Marshes' attorney successfully argued, however, that the Marshes' facility did not fall within the regulatory definition of a crematory, defined as a place where cremations are done that is run by a funeral director and "open to the public."

Revised regulations are proposed for the industry, but language to close the loophole that the Marshes exploited have not made the final draft. The Board eventually gives up, thinking that the Marshes would get tired of the business and close it down after a short time or that people wouldn't want to do business with an unlicensed crematory. "We felt he would be out of our hair in a short while," James Neal, a member of Georgia's Funeral Services Board, would later say.

Yet, for now, Tri-State remains busy. For the most part, funeral directors are happy to let Marsh continue his father's business. They know that there is sometimes abuse in the industry, and that they should visit facilities or make unannounced inspections, but they never do because Tri-State has such prompt service and the family has a good reputation. The Marshes have never really had any trouble with the law; the only run-in arose when Tommy Ray received a citation for letting his son, Ray, drive without a license in 1988. Although in the past few years Ray's parents and sister have broken regulations by signing papers as if they were licensed funeral directors, people have either not noticed or not cared.

The community mainly tries to ignore the crematory tucked into the corner of their county. Neighbors don't go down to the nearby woods much. "We didn't like to be over there [because of] the fact that they were supposed to be burning bodies," explains Jessica Johnson, 22, a neighbor and niece of Ray Marsh.

After running the business for a year, Marsh has been having financial problems with the crematory. In 1997 a vault company filed suit against Marsh for nonpayment of about $2,000. In August, the cremation machine stops working. Marsh orders a $152 starter motor part for the crematorium. For the past thirteen years, the family has declined service visits from the equipment company, so the service representatives are not surprised when Marsh says that no one needs to come to install the new part.

After receiving the part, Marsh determines that he cannot fix the machine. Given the financial pressures on him, he decides nonetheless to keep accepting bodies for cremation but starts hiding bodies in the grove behind the crematory. He does not abuse them. He simply dumps them on the property in whatever condition he gets them. The grove is already littered with dryers, broken chairs, and a house trailer. There are six rusty cars abandoned there, stuffed with rusted tools and other trash. Among the debris, hundreds of corpses start piling up. A baby is stuffed in a box in the back of a rusty hearse. Dozens of bodies are stacked like cordwood in sheds or half-buried around the grove.

While Marsh lives among the bodies, he acts as if everything is normal. Unlike the smoke that can carry the smell of a crematory, the localized smell of a body takes just two weeks to stop, so it isn't very surprising that the neighbors haven't noticed what has been going on. For each new customer, Marsh continues to be prompt in arriving to pick up the body, the transit permit, the family's authorization, and the $200 check. He always insists on doing pickups and returning the "ashes" himself, often returning the next day. But in fact, Marsh often delivers a box of cement chips and limestone rather then cremated remains.

Marsh continues to be disorganized with his paperwork. He lets notices, bills, and papers, often unopened, pile up in the office and tucks them into corners and around his home. Still, from the outside things seem normal, though the locals later comment that they have not seen any smoke in a long time. In fact, although Marsh seems to exhibit no concern for the bodies once he has them, in some ways he has become more careful about the industry regulations. In the Fall of 2001, Neva Mason calls him to arrange service for her father-in-law. Marsh explains that even though her family had arranged the cremation and burial directly with Tri-State when her mother died a few years before, the rules have changed and she now must go through a funeral home. She does so and calls him later to make sure that Marsh received her father-in-law's body. Marsh tells her that he is taking care of him. Marsh adds Mason's body to the piles rotting in the grove.

In November 2001, the Atlanta office of the EPA receives an anonymous call reporting that someone has seen "body parts" on Tri-State's property. The EPA turns the tip over to the Sheriff's office, which briefly investigates, but as the investigators have no search warrant, they leave after a cursory look that fails to reveal anything.

By the beginning of 2002, Marsh has hidden bodies all over the property. His indifference may be rooted in depression or some other psychological disorder; a former FBI profiler comments later that Marsh's behavior is like those who have a hoarding obsessive-compulsive disorder. He hoards all his papers, and stacks all the bodies, perhaps hoping to deal with them later. He doesn't make decisions about what to do about the problem, and as it gets harder to decide, everything just piles up in a disordered and haphazard fashion.

By now, the result looks like something out of a Stephen King novel. After five years, some of the bodies look like they have been there for decades and now seem almost skeletal. Others, once quasi-buried and embalmed are now half disinterred, possibly to make them easier to stack later. Some are dumped still dressed in formal wear, others are wrapped in hospital sheets and wearing a toe tag. More than 20 bodies are stuffed into a single cement vault that is designed to hold one coffin. Four other vaults are just as full. Some cremated remains are mixed among it all. In all, there are more than three hundred and forty bodies in the grove. The bodies now outnumber Noble's living population.

Figure 2 **Police en route to the crematory**

(Reuters/Corbis)

In February 2002, the Atlanta EPA gets another call. This time they come to town to investigate. The next morning, February 15, a woman walking a dog finds a human skull, spurring a full investigation. As the first bodies are discovered, the county is horrified. Soon Dr. Kris Sperry, the state's chief medical examiner, is obliged to call in the Federal Disaster Mortuary Team, the group usually called when a cemetery is disrupted by a natural disaster. Dr. Sperry has performed more than 5,000 autopsies and viewed more than 30,000 bodies but is not prepared for what he sees around the crematory. He is most horrified by the lack of reverence for the dead. During the first week of the recovery effort, he has nightmares.

By Saturday, February 16, the Governor has declared "the Walker County incident" a state of emergency, making state funds available for the recovery efforts. He meets with a hundred families who dealt with Tri-State, and agrees to pay the cost of identifying bodies to give the families closure. He vows to use the full powers of the State to investigate and prosecute. The sheriff says the Marshes are "good folks. I don't know what went wrong."

The Marshes turn over their company records and generally cooperate with the authorities. The legislative loophole that protected Tri-State is quickly closed, and other states begin to review their licensing schemes.

On Sunday, a prayer service is held, while county employees comb the woods for bodies. Meanwhile, Marsh's sister puts up her house as a bond for $25,000 bail, and Marsh is released. His mother goes to church, and reports that he is doing nicely. She refuses to talk about the case. "I don't have anything to say about the charges, if that's what they are. I'm just surrounding myself in the Lord and the people who support me."

After the investigators clear away the bodies in plain view, they find the bodies stacked in the concrete burial vaults. Seeing the other vaults around the property, the crew stops trying to estimate numbers. At this point in the investigation, only 16 bodies have been identified. Investigators set up a makeshift morgue on the site to process the bodies and help the families identify them. People are asked to bring in photographs. Meanwhile, the Georgia Bureau of Investigation (GBI) urges people to bring in the remains they were given so they can be checked. At the Walker State Community Center, people line up holding "ashes" of loved ones received from Tri-State. Many turn out to be just dirt and cement chips.

On Thursday, February 21, underwater cameras spot a torso and skull in the lake behind the crematory. They begin to test the water for contamination, to see if it is safe for divers. Local residents are warned not to drink tap water.

By February 24, almost 300 bodies have been found. Investigators don't know when it will end. The families are devastated. Some tell GBI director Buddy Nix that their loved ones had asked to be cremated because "they were frightfully afraid of being buried or frightfully afraid of insects." When Pat Higdon's husband died of lung cancer, she couldn't afford a burial, so she chose to cremate him. "He looked like a corpse for two months before he died. He just laid

Figure 3 **Investigators collecting bodies in the woods on February 20, 2002**

(Reuters/Corbis)

there with his mouth open and his eyes open," she says. "I can't bear to think he still looks like that, only he's lying in a shed or a creek somewhere." Ellen West, on learning that the body of her mother, author Emmy Govan West, was among those discarded at the crematory, says, "When they called me and told me, it was worse news than her dying. I couldn't function." The Cash family moves the urn of Mrs. Cash's mother, Norma, from its prominent place at the end table in their front room. "The urn they gave us is nothing," says Mr. Cash. "If it is somebody, it is not my somebody. We put it in the garage."

The funeral directors who trusted the Marshes are also reeling. One director sent more than one hundred bodies there, including his brother Clyde. He says, "I don't sleep. It's a bad deal." He has tried to comfort the families, who have told him they are praying for him and aren't blaming him. Other funeral homes have had civil suits brought against them.

Figure 4 Investigators collecting bodies in the woods on February 20, 2002

(AP)

On Tuesday morning, February 25, Marsh's bail is set at $100,000. By that afternoon, 102 more charges of theft by deception are brought against him, requiring another bond hearing before he goes anywhere. The GBI tells a family member that there have been 260 threats against Marsh and his family. The prosecution is concerned for his safety if Marsh were to be released.

The last body on land is found on February 26. The next Monday, March 4, agents start draining the three-acre lake, which is eight feet deep at its deepest point. The potentially contaminated water is carted away in tankers, to keep it from affecting the local water supply. Eventually, using flat-bottomed boats, investigators probe the few feet of water that remain. No more bodies are found. Georgia has had to add $8.5 million to the state budget to cover the expenses of the excavation.

The excavation and search finish on March 6, 2002. Investigators determine that over the course of more than five years, Marsh dumped 339 bodies on his property.

Figure 5 **Women yelling at Marsh outside the courthouse**

(Reuters/Corbis)

1. Relying only on your own intuitions of justice, what liability and punishment, if any, does Ray Brent Marsh deserve **for his offensive treatment of the dead bodies?** (Assume that any fraud charges — based on his taking payment for services not performed — have been dropped pursuant to a civil settlement.)*

---

*N.B. — Throughout this coursebook, you will be asked to give your views of the liability and punishment deserved, if any, by the defendant in the principal case. In doing this, ignore what you know or think you know about criminal law. Also ignore any utilitarian considerations, such as the need or lack of need for deterrence of others or concern for future public safety from a dangerous person. Indicate simply what your own intuitive sense of justice tells you is the criminal liability and punishment deserved, if any, by the defendant. There are no right or wrong answers. Do not work with others. (There will be plenty of time for that during the course.) Give your own personal judgment of what is deserved.

If you decide that some punishment is deserved, you are asked to give a sentence of imprisonment that reflects the appropriate amount of punishment. In some cases, you may think punishment would best be imposed through a sentence other than imprisonment, such as supervised probation, fine, or community service. For the purposes of this question, translate any such non-imprisonment sentence into a term of imprisonment of the same punishment "bite." (This makes it possible to compare the amount of punishment imposed by different persons.)

This process of your forming your own independent intuition about what the defendant deserves in the case is important because, without having formed a view, it may be more difficult for you to evaluate the propriety of the legal rules that in practice determine the outcome of the case. Also, as we will see, a community's shared intuitions of justice can have an important influence on the effectiveness of a criminal rule. Even a utilitarian who prefers a distribution of liability other than desert — a subject we will discuss in the next Section — will want to know when a rule conflicts with the community's shared intuitions of justice, if for no other reason than to plan some compensation strategy to take account of the perceived injustices or failures of justice that the rule will inspire.

N	0	1	2	3	4	5	6	7	8	9	10	11
☐	☐	☐	☐	☐	☐	☐	☐	☐	☐	☐	☐	☐
no liability	liability but no punishment	1 day	2 wks	2 mo	6 mo	1 yr	3 yrs	7 yrs	15 yrs	30 yrs	life imprison- ment	death

2. What liability, if any, under the then-existing statutes?
3. What liability, if any, under the Model Penal Code?
4. What liability, if any, under the following statute?

Abuse of Corpse A person commits a misdemeanor if, knowing others would be offended by his conduct, he dismembers, disfigures, injures, or otherwise abuses any corpse, or he disturbs a buried corpse in any way.

■ THE LAW

Code of Georgia Annotated
(2002)

Title 16. Crimes and Offenses
Chapter 1. General Provisions

Section 16-1-4. Code Governs Crimes

No conduct constitutes a crime unless it is described as a crime in this title or in another statute of this state. However, this Code section does not affect the power of a court to punish for contempt or to employ any sanction authorized by law for the enforcement of an order, civil judgment, or decree.

Title 31. Health

Chapter 21. Dead Bodies
Article 3. Offenses

Section 31-21-44.1. Abuse of a Dead Body

(a) (1) A person commits the offense of abuse of a dead body if, prior to interment and except as otherwise authorized by law, such person willfully defaces a dead body while the dead body is lying in state or is prepared for burial, showing, or cremation whether in a funeral establishment, place of worship, home, or other facility for lying in state or at a grave site. The lawful presence of the offender at a place where the dead body is abused shall not be a defense to a prosecution under this Code section.

(2) A person who is providing care to another person, other than in a hospital, either on a permanent or temporary basis, shall, upon the death of such person while in such person's care, be required to notify a local law enforcement agency or coroner or a relative of such deceased person within six hours of the discovery of the death of such person. Any person who intentionally violates the provisions of this paragraph shall commit the offense of abuse of a dead body.

(b) Any person who violates subsection (a) of this Code section shall be guilty of a felony and shall be punished by imprisonment for not less than one nor more than three years.

Model Penal Code
(Official Draft 1962)

Section 1.05. All Offenses Defined by Statute; Application of General Provisions of the Code

(1) No conduct constitutes an offense unless it is a crime or violation under this Code or another statute of this State.

(2) The provisions of Part I of the Code are applicable to offenses defined by other statutes, unless the Code otherwise provides.

(3) This Section does not affect the power of a court to punish for contempt or to employ any sanction authorized by law for the enforcement of an order or a civil judgment or decree.

Section 250.10. Abuse of Corpse

Except as authorized by law, a person who treats a corpse in a way that he knows would outrage ordinary family sensibilities commits a misdemeanor.

● OVERVIEW OF THE LEGALITY PRINCIPLE

In its original Latin dress, the legality principle was expressed as *nullum crimen sine lege, nulla poena sine lege*, meaning roughly no crime without law, nor punishment without law. In its modern form it means that criminal liability and punishment can be based only upon a prior legislative enactment of a prohibition that is expressed with adequate precision and clarity. The principle is not a legal rule, but rather a legal concept embodied in a series of legal rules and doctrines.

THE DOCTRINES

Two of the doctrines that make up the "legality principle" are noted in the previous Section. Modern American criminal law abolishes common law crimes and prohibits the judicial creation of offenses. In 1962, the English House of Lords (equivalent to our Supreme Court) approved prosecution of a common law offense of "conspiracy to corrupt public morals."[1] American jurisdictions typically would bar prosecution for such an offense because it is uncodified (and probably too vague).[2] In addition, the legality principle is embodied in the constitutional prohibition against vague statutes, the rule requiring strict construction of penal statutes, and the constitutional prohibition against application of *ex post facto* laws.

1) *Void for Vagueness*   The vagueness prohibition is rooted in the Due Process Clause. The prohibition requires that a statute give "sufficient warning that men may conform their conduct so as to avoid that which is forbidden."[3] It has been used to invalidate so-called "vagrancy" statutes, which commonly provided for the arrest and conviction of persons such as "rogues and vagabonds,... common night walkers,... wanton and lascivious persons,... common railers and brawlers,... habitual loafers, disorderly persons...."[4] As one court explains, such a provision "fail[s] to give a person of ordinary intelligence fair notice that his contemplated conduct is forbidden by statute."[5] (An excerpt of this case, *Papachristou*, appears in the Discussion Materials below.) Similarly, a common law offense that is incorporated into a code by reference, without a definition of its elements, is likely to be void for vagueness. Thus, a conviction for the common law offense of being a "Common Scold" was invalidated. When the prosecution sought to rely on a statute that sought to criminalize all conduct that was indictable at common law,[6] the court explained, "One can scarcely conceive of anything more vague or indefinite. To know the criminal risks he might run, the average citizen would be obliged to carry a pocket edition of Blackstone with him." However, a statute is not unconstitutionally vague merely because one of its elements calls for a matter of judgement.

2 *Vague vs. Ambiguous*   An offense provision is _vague_ if it does not adequately define the prohibited conduct. If a provision defines the conduct with some specificity yet is subject to two or more interpretations, then it is termed _ambiguous_, which is not necessarily unconstitutional. In *People v. Nunez*, the prisoner injured a guard during an escape while awaiting transport to a state prison to serve a life sentence.[7] He was charged with an offense that punishes assault by a "person

---

1. Shaw v. Director of Public Prosecutions, [1962] A.C. 220 (H.L.) (defendant published "Ladies Directory" that contained names, addresses, and phone numbers of prostitutes).

2. Under Model Penal Code §1.05(1), for example: "No conduct constitutes an offense unless it is a crime or violation under this Code or another statute of this State."

3. Rose v. Locke, 423 U.S. 48, 50, 96 S. Ct. 243, 244, 46 L. Ed. 2d 185, 188 (1975) (statutory phrase "crime against nature" gave adequate notice that forced cunnilingus was prohibited).

4. Jacksonville, Florida Ordinance Code §26-57, invalidated in *Papachristou*, infra.

5. Papachristou v. City of Jacksonville, 405 U.S. 156, 162, 92 S. Ct. 839, 843, 31 L. Ed. 2d 110, 115 (1972), quoting United States v. Harris, 347 U.S. 612, 617, 74 S. Ct. 808, 812, 98 L. Ed. 989 (1954).

6. State v. Palendrano, 120 N.J. Super. 336, 293 A.2d 747 (Law Div. 1972). The court explains that a Common Scold is "a troublesome and angry woman, who, by brawling and wrangling among her neighbors, breaks the public peace, increases discord, and becomes a nuisance to the neighborhood."

7. 162 Cal. App. 3d 280, 283, 208 Cal. Rptr. 450, 451 (1984). The court in *People v. Nunez* considered whether the defendant had violated the California Penal Code, which provides: "Every person

undergoing a life sentence in a state prison." Must the person physically be "in a state prison" or is it enough that he is a person who is undergoing "a life sentence in a state prison"? Do we give the word "undergoing" a physical or legal meaning? There is nothing vague about the prohibited conduct, but the provision is ambiguous because it is subject to either of two interpretations.

3) Rule of Strict Construction   When faced with an ambiguity, the law traditionally applies a special rule for interpreting criminal statutes. The rule of strict construction, as it is called, directs that an ambiguity in a penal statute be resolved against the state and in favor of the defendant.[1] For this reason, it also is called the *rule of lenity*. Nunez was not yet physically in a state prison; he was awaiting transport to it. Therefore, the rule of strict construction would hold that the statutes be interpreted to require that the prisoner be physically located in a state prison at the time of the offense.[2] The modern trend is to ameliorate the strictness of the rule of strict construction by replacing it with a *rule of fair import*. Such rules of statutory interpretation are discussed later in this Section.

4) Ex Post Facto Laws   One final aspect of the legality principle is embodied in the constitutional prohibition against *ex post facto* laws.[3] This has been interpreted to invalidate:

> Every law that makes an action done before the passing of the law, and which was innocent when done, criminal; and punishes such action. 2d. Every law that aggravates a crime, or makes it greater than it was, when committed. 3d. Every law that changes the punishment, and inflicts a greater punishment, than the law annexed to the crime, when committed.[4]

For example, the prohibition bars liability for past use of a drug that is now a controlled substance but which was not at the time it was used. It similarly would bar application of a statute that changes an offense's punishment from life imprisonment or death to a mandatory death penalty, where the offense is committed before the statutory change.[5]

THE RATIONALES

The basis for the legality principle does not lie in the actor's blamelessness, but rather in non-blameworthiness rationales. While not all of the rationales may be applicable in all situations, the rationales most commonly offered in support of the legality principle include the following:

1) Procedural Fairness   Fairness requires that an actor have at least an opportunity to find out what the criminal law prohibits. Actual notice is not required for

---

undergoing a life sentence in a state prison of this state, who, with malice aforethought, commits an assault upon the person of another . . . is punishable with death or life imprisonment without possibility of parole." Cal. Penal Code §4500 (West 1982).

1. Rewis v. United States, 401 U.S. 808, 91 S. Ct. 1056, 28 L. Ed. 2d 493 (1971) (ambiguity in statute prohibiting interstate travel with intent to "promote, manage, establish . . . certain kinds of illegal activity," could not be construed to extend to operation of illegal establishment frequented by out of state customers).

2. The *Nunez* court concluded that the statute, which applied to a life-term prisoner "physically situated in state prison," so clearly required physical presence in prison at the time of the offense, and not just legal commitment to prison, that there was no reason to look to legislative history to determine the legislative intent. 162 Cal. App. 3d. at 284, 208 Cal. Rptr. at 452.

3. U.S. Const. art. I, §9, cl. 3 ("No bill of attainder or *ex post facto* law shall be passed"); U.S. Const. art I, §10, cl. 1 ("No State shall . . . pass any bill of attainder, *ex post facto* law . . .").

4. Calder v. Bull, 3 U.S. (3 Dall.) 386, 390, 1 L. Ed. 648, 650 (1798) (emphasis omitted).

5. See, e.g., Flaherty v. Thomas, 94 Mass. 428 (1866).

liability; it is enough that the prohibition has been lawfully enacted. By the same token, an actor's actual knowledge that the conduct is sought to be prohibited and punished does not vitiate a legality-based defense. The concern of the legality principle is procedural fairness, not blamelessness.

2) *Effective Deterrence and Improper Over-Deterrence*   Effective deterrence requires that the prohibited conduct be clearly defined. A reverse effect also can occur: Persons may refrain from engaging in lawful conduct that they mistakenly assume is included within the prohibition. Such forbearance may not be a problem in most cases, but it can be in some. The same danger exists whenever a vague prohibition may be interpreted to prohibit speech protected by the First Amendment.

3) *Criminalization as a Legislative Function*   In a democracy, the legislature, which is the most representative branch of government, is generally thought to be the proper body to exercise the criminalization decision. This rationale directly supports the prohibition of judicial creation of offenses and the abolition of judicially created offenses. It also has application in less obvious ways to support the invalidation of vague statutes, because vague statutes are *de facto* delegations of criminalization authority to the courts. Courts, applying the statutes, provide the specificity the legislature has not.

4) *Rules of Conduct and Principles of Adjudication*   All of the rationales noted so far — procedural fairness, effective deterrence, the danger of over-deterrence, and preserving the criminalization function for the legislature — concern the rule articulation function of the criminal law, its obligation to communicate the governing rules to all members of society. The rationales reflect our preference for how that rule articulation function ought to be performed: The legislature should set the rules, and the formulations should be calculated to give adequate notice to deter effectively and properly and to condemn a violation fairly. But the criminal law also serves an adjudication function, and there are rationales for the legality principle associated with that function as well.

5) *Avoiding Disparity in Application and Abuse of Discretion*   Consistency in the treatment of similar cases is possible only with a sufficiently clear and precise definition of an offense, one that does not call for discretionary judgments. With individual discretion inevitably comes disparity based on the inherent differences among decision makers. The exercise of discretion also can allow the operation of malevolent influences of racism, sexism, and the like. An unclear prohibition, therefore, can create a potential for abuse of discretion by police officers, prosecutors, and others with decision-making authority.[1] In *Papachristou v. City of Jacksonville*, for example, police officers arrested "mixed" (black and white) couples and charged them with a variety of vague offenses, such as "vagrancy," "loitering," and "disorderly loitering on street." The Court reversed the convictions, finding that the vagueness of the statutes encouraged arbitrary convictions as well as arbitrary arrests.[2] (An excerpt of this case appears in the Discussion Materials below.)

---

1. See, e.g., Smith v. Goguen, 415 U.S. 566, 572-573 (1974) (statute prohibiting contemptuous treatment of American flag declared void for vagueness under Fourteenth Amendment, because Constitution requires legislatures to set "reasonably clear guidelines for law enforcement officials and triers of fact in order to prevent 'arbitrary and discriminatory enforcement'" of criminal statutes).

2. 405 U.S. 156, 162 (1972).

COUNTERVAILING INTERESTS

Unfortunately, the virtues of the legality principle create their own vices. While precise prior written rules make liability decisions more predictable and uniform, such rules also tend to leave decisionmakers less able to adapt the law as needed to deal with new or unusual problems, create the potential for criminal law adjudication to be caught up in technicalities that undercut the moral credibility of the law, and make it more difficult for the law to incorporate the normative judgments of the community. This tension is the focus of the Discussion Materials below.

1) *Fostering Inflexibility* Fixed rules can leave the criminal law unable to punish new forms of criminal conduct. A precise listing of what constitutes a prohibited weapon, for example, may serve legality interests well, but may disallow the conviction and punishment of persons who develop new, "creative" weapons. The fact is, the legislature may not be able to keep up with what one court called "the malicious ingenuity of mankind."[1] Precise prior written rules also make it difficult for the law to account for unusual offenses,[2] common offenses committed in unusual contexts,[3] and the infinite combinations of factors that may be relevant in determining liability and its degree.

2) *Promoting Technicalities* The constraints dictated by the legality principle burden courts even in simple, commonplace cases. Precision tends to spawn technicalities that frustrate effective justice. For example, in the *Nunez* case, discussed previously, the court read the statute literally and held that it did not apply to the defendant because, although he assaulted someone while he was sentenced to serve a life sentence in state prison, he was at the time of the assault still physically located in county jail.[4] While the statute was subsequently amended to more explicitly cover such cases,[5] many would regard the result as a frustration of the legislature's will as to defendant Nunez. Legality also frequently makes proving guilt more difficult and costly.

3) *Excluding Normative Judgments* Another effect of the precision demanded by the legality principle is its tendency to exclude moral judgments, which typically cannot be expressed in precise language. The more intricate the rules, the greater the predictability and consistency, but also the greater the possibility that some cases will give results inconsistent with the community's moral assessment. The call for a normative judgment is sometimes codified, as with a *de minimis* defense for conduct "too trivial to warrant the condemnation of conviction" or the causation requirement that the result be "not too remote or accidental." But such codification only makes clear that the vagueness is intended; it does not avoid

---

1. Commonwealth v. Taylor, 5 Binn. 277, 281 (Pa. 1812).
2. See, e.g., Baker v. State, 215 Ark. 851, 223 S.W.2d 809 (1949) (posing corpse to make it appear alive found to be criminally indecent treatment of dead body); State v. Bradbury, 136 Me. 347, 9 A.2d 657 (1939) (cremation of corpse in house furnace).
3. For example, while fraud does not normally endanger human life, it may be committed by a person who purports to provide medical treatment. See, e.g., People v. Phillips, 64 Cal. 2d 574, 414 P.2d 353, 51 Cal. Rptr. 225 (1966) (in order to induce eight-year-old girl who suffered from eye cancer to accept treatment from him, chiropractor advised her to forgo medical treatment that might have cured her or prolonged her life).
4. Nunez, supra, at 283, 208 Cal. Rptr. at 452.
5. Cal. Penal Code §4500 (1989) (amendment effective January 1, 1987).

the vagueness challenge.[1] Finally, because fixed rules can accommodate only a limited degree of factual detail, they tend to group meaningfully different cases into a single factual category and treat them as if they were identical.[2]

4) *Principle of Analogy* Many of these difficulties of precise written rules can be avoided by affording discretion to decisionmakers. Discretion to expand the definition or interpretation of an offense to include conduct analogous to that expressly prohibited is sometimes described as application of the *principle of analogy*. In *Lewis v. Commonwealth*, for example, the prosecutor argued that defendant's conviction for riotous and disorderly conduct on a bus should be upheld because, even though the statute, which was enacted before buses were invented, referred only to disorderly conduct on a "railroad or street passenger railway," it could logically be assumed that the legislature wanted the same statute to apply to all similar forms of transportation.[3] A principle of analogy would allow such an expansion of the literal language of the statute to allow it to be applied to disorderly conduct on a bus. (The *Lewis* court applied the legality principle and reversed the conviction.) The difficulty with a principle of analogy is that it may be used to extend liability without prior notice in situations more serious and less analogous than the streetcar-bus dispute in *Lewis*.

5) *Legality in Liability vs. Sentencing* Given the competing interests of legality and discretion, one might expect the legal system to strike a balance between the two. This is essentially what occurs in the rules governing the interpretation of criminal statutes, discussed below. But with that exception, current practice creates a dichotomy rather than a compromise. In assessing whether to impose liability, and what grade of liability to impose, the criminal law follows fixed and specific rules that allow little discretion; the legality principle is well respected. But in the determination of an offender's sentence it is common to have few or no rules and broad judicial discretion. It is unclear whether this dramatic difference is justifiable. Determination of liability and grade is, after all, only the first of two necessary steps in the distribution of criminal punishment. As the traditional statement of the legality principle provides, "nullum *crimen* sine lege, nulla *poena* sine lege."[4] The rationales that support precise written rules to govern the assignment of liability and its degree apply as well to criminal sentencing. Indeed, beyond the formal finding of conviction, the determination of criminal liability and its degree means little without the imposition of punishment. The two are interdependent stages in a single process. There is little reason to insist that decisionmakers strictly adhere to legality when they determine whether a particular offender is liable for a Grade C felony or a Grade A misdemeanor, for

---

1. Compare La. Rev. Stat. Ann. §14:19 (1986) (reasonable and apparently necessary force is justified to prevent a forcible offense against person) with N.J. Stat. Ann. §2C:3-4 (1982), amended by A.B. Nos. 498323 and 297, Pub. L. 1987, ch. 120 (effective May 19, 1987) (detailed listing of circumstances that justify use of force and deadly force in self-defense).

2. For examples of such over-inclusive categories, see, e.g., N.J. Stat. Ann. §2C:3-7(b)(2)(d) (1982) (law enforcement officer justified in using deadly force to effect arrest for burglary of dwelling); Tennessee v. Garner, 471 U.S. 1, 105 S. Ct. 1694, 85 L. Ed. 2d 1 (1985) (deadly force not justified to prevent escape of all burglars).

3. 184 Va. 69, 34 S.E.2d 389 (1945).

4. "[N]o conduct may be held criminal unless it is precisely described in a penal law....[N]o person may be punished except in pursuance of a statute which prescribes a penalty." See generally Jerome Hall, General Principles of Criminal Law 28 (2d ed. 1960).

example, if there is then nearly complete discretion to give the same sentence no matter which grade of the offense is assigned. If the distribution of punishment is to be discretionary at the sentencing stage, society has benefitted little from the strict adherence to legality at the liability assignment stage. It is in part for this reason that the recent wave of sentencing reform introduced articulated rules and significantly reduced sentencing discretion.

(6) *Legality and Function* One can distinguish, on grounds other than liability versus sentencing, instances where the legality interests operate differently. Different legality rationales apply to different criminal law functions. The fair notice and deterrence rationales apply primarily to the criminal law's rule articulation function — defining and announcing the rules of conduct — and to the doctrines that serve that function. The uniformity and abuse of discretion rationales, on the other hand, apply primarily to the adjudication functions of liability assignment and grading, and to the doctrines that serve them. This suggests differential application of the legality principle depending on the function of the doctrine to which it is applied.

7) *Legality in Rule Articulation vs. Adjudication* The rationales of the legality principle would have the rules of conduct formulated to maximize procedural fairness and effective deterrence and to minimize over-deterrence of protected activities. For example, objective and simple criteria might be much preferred in the rules of conduct, for these are directed to the general public, who have no special training or background and who must apply the rules in the course of their everyday lives. Thus, one might tolerate imprecision if it contributes to simplicity. On the other hand, the rationales of the legality principle would have the doctrines of adjudication — that assess the minimum conditions of liability and set the range of punishment — formulated to maximize uniformity in application to similar cases and to minimize the potential for abuse of discretion. For example, a high degree of specificity might be desirable even if it creates a degree of complexity that would be unreasonable to expect the public to master. The special training of decisionmakers and the more contemplative pace of the adjudication process means that greater complexity can be tolerated.

▲ PROBLEM
The CG-PLA at the UN

Growing United Nations involvement in peace-keeping military activities has spawned a rash of terroristic acts against United Nation representatives and employees in New York. The Command Group of the Popular Liberation Army (CG-PLA) is suspected of much of the violence and is alleged to have received help in selecting targets and coordinating attacks from the United Nations representatives of several countries that oppose the United Nations involvement and that see terrorism as a legitimate political device. In response to this wave of violence, a United Nations resolution is proposed that would call upon the United States to enact legislation to criminalize entering United Nations headquarters in New

York City with a terroristic purpose.[1] No such offense currently exists. Also recommended are increased penalties for all existing violent offenses when those offenses are against United Nations delegates or employees, and the withdrawal of diplomatic immunity as a defense for all violent offenses against such persons. The United States Congress unanimously passes a resolution in support of the United Nations proposal and begins processing a bill that would implement the resolution's call for new offenses and penalties. At the direction of the President, the United States delegate votes in support of the resolution, as do the delegates of nearly all member states.

To show its defiance of the United Nations and its recent resolution, the CG-PLA undertakes a new campaign of terror against United Nations delegates and employees in New York. Surveillance set in place because of earlier suspicions of Ahmed Modafi, the Libyan representative to the United Nations, reveals that he is helping the CG-PLA in its campaign. The CG-PLA times its campaign to end just minutes before the President signs into law the United States legislation implementing the resolution, The United Nations Personnel Protection Act (UNPPA). One week later, federal and state prosecutors in New York indict Modafi and others for acts and threats of violence against UN victims under both UNPPA and previously existing statutes. The evidence of his involvement in the terror campaign is overwhelming. Can Modafi be convicted of anything?

● OVERVIEW OF STATUTORY INTERPRETATION

Vagueness, Ambiguity, and Conflict Because words are not perfect representations of ideas and because unanticipated situations inevitably arise, criminal statutes, like all other statutes, frequently are unclear. As previously noted, vague language may invalidate a statute as unconstitutional. If a statute's language is ambiguous — that is, if it is subject to two or more meanings — a court will be required to "interpret" the statute, to decide which of the possible meanings should be adopted. Interpretation problems also may arise where two or more statutes give conflicting rules, in which case the court must determine which of the two statutes is controlling.

Legislative Intent, Notice, and Analogy In such situations, courts are not free to choose the interpretation that they think results in the best rule or result. Recall that a central rationale of the legality principle is to reserve the criminalization decision to the legislative branch. It follows that a court's role in interpreting a criminal statute is to determine and follow the legislative intent. On the other hand, the legislature frequently will not have addressed, or even thought about, some of the issues that give rise to an ambiguity. It may be complete speculation as

---

1. More specifically, the proposal creates an offense of leaving United States property around the United Nations to enter United Nations property with a terroristic purpose. The drafters do not wish to create United States jurisdiction over United Nations property.

to what the legislative view on the issue would have been. Further, the average person bound by the law has little access to or familiarity with "legislative intent," thus deference to it may undercut fair notice. What, then, should a court do when faced with an ambiguous statute? Several rules of construction have been developed as guides.

Plain Meaning Rule　Reaffirming the limited role of courts in interpreting statutes is the *plain meaning rule*. It provides that the inquiry into legislative intent and related interpretive strategies are to be used only if a clear ambiguity exists in the statutory language. No inquiry beyond the face of the statute is appropriate "[w]here the language is plain and admits of no more than one meaning."[1] Even the limited discretion inherent in some rules of construction is not available if a statute is unambiguous. The court must apply the plain meaning of the statute even if it disagrees strongly with the wisdom of the underlying policy.

Drafting Errors and Implied Exceptions　On the other hand, it is said that a court need not mindlessly follow the literal language of a statute that clearly does not represent the legislative intent. A court may take note of an obvious drafting error. A court may recognize logically implied exceptions. But in each case, the court must conclude that *the legislature* would see the statute as obviously containing a drafting error or implied exception. And the conclusion that the legislature would want to correct the obviously mistaken language cannot come simply from the fact that *the court* strongly believes the language as written reflects a bad policy.

Rules of Construction　Some standard rules have been recognized by courts as being useful in resolving ambiguous language. The rules are of three sorts: rules for interpreting the language within a statute, rules directing where a court may look outside of the statutory language, and, in criminal cases, a special rule setting the standard of interpretation, usually either the rule of strict construction or the rule of fair import.

Interpreting the Language of a Statute　At least five rules have been recognized for interpreting ambiguous language on the face of a statute:

1) *Different language implies a different meaning.*　Where a document uses different language in different parts, there is a presumption that the legislature intended different meanings by the different language.

2) *A catch-all phrase is limited by the common factor of the items in the list.* Where a list of things ends in a catch-all phrase, such as "or other . . . ," the phrase must be interpreted to be limited to the theme or common factor of the specific entries in the list. This is called the rule of *ejusdem generis.*

3) *The expression of one thing excludes implication of another.*　Where a statute sets forth a list of exceptions, for example, other exceptions are by implication excluded. This is the rule of *expressio unius; exclusio alterius.*

4) *The special controls the general.*　Two statutes may each apply to the same fact situation and may generate different results. Where this occurs, the rules of

---

1. Caminetti v. United States, 242 U.S. 470, 485, 37 S. Ct. 192, 194, 61 L. Ed. 442, 453 (1917) (Mann Act prohibits transportation of female from one state to another "for the purpose of prostitution, debauchery or for other *immoral* purpose;" defendant transported willing girl to another state to have sexual relations with her; majority held that his purpose plainly fell within the intended meaning of "other immoral purpose").

construction provide that the more specific statute has priority over the more general.

5) *The later controls the earlier.*   Where two statutes enacted at different times conflict, the rules of construction give priority to the later enactment over the earlier.

Going Beyond the Language of the Statute   If a conflict or ambiguity remains unresolved after applying these rules to the language on the face of a statute, a court may look beyond the literal language of the statute. Legislatures sometimes keep records, even transcripts, of their deliberations and sometimes even the deliberations of their committees. The United States Congress is particularly good in this regard. Some state legislatures are particularly bad. These records of the *legislative history* of a statute may be examined to see whether they reveal the interpretation intended by the legislature. Where the statute was borrowed from another jurisdiction, the legislative history of that jurisdiction may be enlightening, although not as persuasive as that of the home jurisdiction itself. It is in this regard that the extensive Model Penal Code commentaries are particularly important and influential. Because the Code has been so widely adopted, its commentaries provide what is sometimes the only source of legislative history for many state code provisions. Finally, an authoritative interpretation of a statute sometimes may be available from an agency or official empowered by the legislature to issue such interpretations.

Special Status of Criminal Statutes   Because they are held to a higher standard of precision and clarity than civil statutes, criminal statutes are subject to special rules of statutory interpretation. One might argue that, if the rules of construction described above must be brought to bear to determine the proper interpretation of a criminal statute, the goals of the legality principle already have been frustrated. Only lawyers and judges are likely to know these rules for interpreting ambiguous language on the face of a statute or to have access to legislative history and authoritative agency interpretations. Thus, while the general rules for construction of statutes described above are adequate for civil statutes, they sometimes are ignored in favor of a special rule of construction for criminal statutes: the rule of strict construction. Some writers, however, suggest that the special rule of strict construction should be applied only if an ambiguity is not resolved by one of the standard rules of construction described above. Many modern codes reject the rule of strict construction altogether, preferring the rule of fair import discussed below.

Rule of Strict Construction   Under the rule of strict construction, "ambiguity concerning the ambit of criminal statutes should be resolved in favor of lenity."[1] This Rule of Lenity, as it also is called, suggests that while the terms of a prohibition are to be strictly construed, the same does not apply to the terms of a defense. In this respect the "rule of strict construction" label is potentially misleading, and the "rule of lenity" is preferable. The former label survives because many courts refuse to apply the rule to defenses. Their reluctance here, and with the rule generally, may stem from the potential of the rule to give absurd results if too literally applied.

---

1. See, e.g., Bell v. United States, 349 U.S. 81, 83, 75 S. Ct. 620, 99 L. Ed. 905 (1955).

Strengths and Weaknesses of Strict Construction Given that the rule of strict construction is one aspect of the legality principle, it should be no surprise that it shares the virtues and vices of the principle. Most important, it furthers the interest of fair notice by barring application of an offense provision against a defendant if, under one interpretation of the provision, the defendant's conduct is not in violation. The rule also serves to preserve the criminalization authority to the legislature by preventing a court from expanding an offense by adopting a broad interpretation of its language. On the other hand, the rule can frustrate a legislature's obvious intent on what may be an important issue and risks bringing the criminal justice system into disrepute, as a game governed by technicalities having little relation to fairness or justice. A literal application of the rule of strict construction to the abuse of corpse statute would leave people free to do anything to or with a dead body except literally dismember, disfigure, injure, or abuse it (in the narrow, physical harm sense). Dead bodies as hood ornaments would be legal as long as the restraining device was adequate.

Rule of Fair Import Because of the dangers of the rule of strict construction and in recognition of the greater attention that has been given to clarity and precision when modern criminal codes are drafted, most current codes abrogate the rule of strict construction and adopt instead a rule of fair import.

> The rule of the common law, that penal statutes are to be strictly construed, has no application to this Code. All its provisions are to be construed according to the fair import of their terms, with a view to effect its objects and to promote justice.[1]

The fair import rule gives courts the authority to interpret statutes in a way that does not frustrate the legislative purpose; yet, by relying upon the *fair import of the terms*, the rule seeks to ensure that some reasonable notice of the offense is possible. In that sense, the rule of fair import attempts a compromise between the virtues of legality and its countervailing interests (found in the principle of analogy).

Judicial Discretion Under the Rule of Strict Construction Despite appearances, it is unclear just how different the two rules are in application. An appearance of difference may come from the tendency to overestimate the literalness with which judges apply the rule of strict construction. If the rule of strict construction were applied literally, it would require no exercise of discretion: If an interpretation more favorable to the defendant is offered it must be adopted. But courts rarely apply the rule in mindless disregard for the intended meaning of its language. First, the rule of strict construction only applies if there is an ambiguity, and it is for the court to decide whether an ambiguity exists. An absurd and farfetched interpretation may simply be ignored by a court as not raising an ambiguity. Where an interpretation is opposed by the defendant as constituting a judicial expansion of criminal liability in violation of the prohibition against judicial legislation, the interpretation can be defended on the ground that it simply represents the first-time application of previously existing legislative criminalization. It is for the court to decide which characterization to adopt, even under a rule of strict construction.

---

1. Cal. Penal Code §4.

Exceptions to Strict Construction   Further, the rule of strict construction has been tempered with the exception that a statute is "not to be construed so strictly as to defeat the obvious intention of the legislature," or "to override common sense." Nor is it necessary that a statute be given its "narrowest meaning" or a "forced, narrow or overstrict construction." In other words, in practice, courts exercise considerable discretion in determining whether a "legitimate" ambiguity exists and in choosing among interpretations, even under the apparently mechanical rule of strict construction.

Practical Significance of Strict Construction vs. Fair Import   Once it is admitted that strict construction admits judicial discretion in interpretation, much as the fair import test more explicitly calls for such discretion, it is less clear that the rules generate a significant difference in application. In judging whether to recognize a defendant's claimed alternative interpretation under a rule of strict construction, a court is likely to look at such things as the common or fair meaning of the terms and the legislative purpose of the provision. Of course, this is precisely what a court is directed to consider under the fair import test. One might argue that the tests retain a significant difference in application because a fair import rule is more likely to induce a court to follow legislative intent that conflicts with a literal reading. That is, judges will be more hesitant to deviate from a strict reading under a rule of strict construction that does not on its face appear to permit such deviation. But the validity of such psychological speculations are difficult to assess. The primary difference between the tests may be the *admission* that judicial discretion is at work under fair import and the apparent denial of such discretion under strict construction. Some courts may prefer the strict construction test for just this reason. The rule permits discretion yet appears mechanical and thereby leaves the court's decision less open to criticism.

Effect of De Minimis Defense   In addition to explicitly adopting a rule of fair import, many modern codes follow the lead of the Model Penal Code in providing a defense for what it calls "de minimis infractions." In reality, the provision has a broader effect than simply providing a defense for trivial harms, such as taking a piece of bubble gum. It directs a court to exempt from liability conduct that, for any of a variety of reasons, was not meant to be covered by the offense. It calls on a judge to dismiss a prosecution if the defendant's conduct did not cause or threaten "the harm or evil sought to be prevented by the law defining the offense" or if it occurred under such conditions that "it cannot reasonably be regarded as envisaged by the legislature in forbidding the offense."[1] The provision explicitly directs the court to do what the rules of construction are designed to achieve: to dismiss a prosecution if, in the judge's view, the case at hand was not intended by the legislature to be punished by conviction for the offense charged. For the sake of clarity, these two distinct aspects of the "de minimis" defense might best be segregated into a defense for trivial harms and a defense for "conduct not envisioned by the offense."

An Unresolvable Tension?   In the end, none of these rules of construction gives a clear or easy answer to the range of ambiguities that can arise. The absence

---

1. See Model Penal Code §2.12. The section also directs the court to dismiss the prosecution if the conduct is within customary license or tolerance, and is not inconsistent with the purpose of the law, another instance in which the legislature presumably would not intend the offense to apply.

of clear rules with clean results may be inevitable. In one sense, ambiguities in statutes create an unresolvable conflict among interests that are each important to us; they are the points of tension within the legality principle and between that principle and the principle of analogy. We prefer to apply statutes as they read, for this is the best way to assure fair notice. We also prefer to interpret statutes to give rational results consistent with the legislative intent. But, in reality, applying a statute as written can give irrational results contrary to the legislative intent. We prefer that the legislature rather than judges make the criminalization decisions. Yet, if a statute is ambiguous, we must either turn to judges to fix it or suffer the legislative purpose to be frustrated. There are no obvious means of resolving the conflict among these interests — rational and effective criminalization, fair notice, and preservation of the legislative criminalization power. The conflict does not arise if every statute is perfectly clear and anticipates every possible form of violation but, even if legislative drafting is perfect, language is not. There seems little alternative other than to have judges continue to balance the competing interests as each case arises.

▲ PROBLEM
United States v. Gray

Defendant James Edward Gray was tried before a jury on March 24, 1986 and convicted of knowingly and willfully threatening to murder a United States district judge with the intent to intimidate or retaliate against such judicial officer on account of the performance of his official duties. Defendant subsequently filed a timely motion renewing his motion for judgment of acquittal which he made at the commencement of trial, immediately following impaneling of the jury. The pending motion does not appear to challenge the sufficiency of the evidence. Rather, defendant contends the indictment filed against him does not charge an offense....

The indictment charges:

> "That on or about the 12th day of August 1985, at Deer Lodge, in the state and District of Montana, James Edward Gray did knowingly and willfully threaten to murder the Honorable Paul G. Hatfield, a duly appointed United States District Judge for the District of Montana, with intent to intimidate or retaliate against Judge Hatfield on account of the performance of his official duties, in violation of Title 18 U.S.C. §115(a)."...

...Section 115 provides in part:

> "Whoever assaults, kidnaps, or murders, or attempts to kidnap or murder, or threatens to assault, kidnap or murder a <u>member of the immediate family of a United States official, judge or law enforcement officer</u> while he is engaged in or on account of the performance of his official duties, shall be punished as provided in subsection (b)."

[Defendant interprets the statute as making it a crime to threaten only family members of federal officials, not the federal officials themselves.]
    ... Section 1114 provides in part:

> "Whoever kills or attempts to kill any judge of the United States .... shall be punished as provided under Sections 1111 and 1112 of this title, except that any such person who is found guilty of attempted murder shall be imprisoned for not more than twenty years."

[On its face the statute does not appear to punish mere threats to a federal judge.]

✸ DISCUSSION MATERIALS

Should the Criminal Law Provide the Precision in Formulation That the Legality Principle Demands? Isn't There Sometimes Value in Permitting Prohibitions to Be Vague?

In his capacity as Chief of Counsel for the United States in the prosecution of Axis war criminals, Justice Robert Jackson argues in the excerpt below in favor of flexibility in determining what should be considered illegal. The cases of *City of Chicago v. Jesus Morales* and *Papachristou v. City of Jacksonville* deal with vagueness in a loitering statute and a vagrancy statute, respectively. The cases explore both sides of this debate but ultimately side with the legality principle.

Report to the President from Justice Robert H. Jackson, Chief of Counsel for the United States in the Prosecution of Axis War Criminals
Reprinted in 39 American Journal of International Law 178-190 (Supp. 1945)

My dear Mr. President:

    I have the honor to report accomplishments during the month since you named me as Chief of Counsel for the United States in prosecuting the principal Axis War Criminals. ...
    ... What specifically are the crimes with which these individuals and organizations should be charged, and what marks their conduct as criminal?
    There is, of course, real danger that trials of this character will become enmeshed in voluminous particulars of wrongs committed by individual Germans throughout the course of the war, and in the multitude of doctrinal disputes which are part of a lawyer's paraphernalia. We can save ourselves from those pitfalls if our test of what legally is crime gives recognition to those things which fundamentally outraged the conscience of the American people and brought them finally to the conviction that their own liberty and civilization could not persist in the same world with the Nazi power.
    Those acts which offended the conscience of our people were criminal by standards generally accepted in all civilized countries, and I believe that we may

proceed to punish those responsible in full accord with both our own traditions of fairness and with standards of just conduct which have been internationally accepted. I think also that through these trials we should be able to establish that a process of retribution by law awaits those who in the future similarly attack civilization. . . .

I believe that those instincts of our people, [that the Nazis were a "band of brigands,"] were right and that they should guide us as the fundamental tests of criminality. We propose to punish acts which have been regarded as criminal since the time of Cain. . . . *fundamenta principles*

In arranging these trials we must also bear in mind the aspirations with which our people have faced the sacrifices of war. After we entered the war, and as we expended our men and our wealth to stamp out these wrongs, it was the universal feeling of our people that out of this war should come unmistakable rules and workable machinery from which any who might contemplate another era of brigandage would know that they would be held personally responsible and would be personally punished. Our people have been waiting for these trials in the spirit of Woodrow Wilson, who hoped to "give to international law the kind of vitality which it can only have if it is a real expression of our moral judgment." *gives int'l law legitimacy*

Against this background it may be useful to restate in more technical lawyer's terms the legal charges against the top Nazi leaders and those voluntary associations such as the S.S. and Gestapo which clustered about them and were ever the prime instrumentalities, first, in capturing the German state, and then, in directing the German state to its spoliations against the rest of the world:

(a) Atrocities and offenses against persons or property constituting violations of International Law, including the laws, rules, and customs of land and naval warfare. The rules of warfare are well established and generally accepted by the nations. They make offenses of such conduct as killing of the wounded, refusal of quarter, ill treatment of prisoners of war, firing on undefended localities, poisoning of wells and streams, pillage and wanton destruction, and ill treatment of inhabitants in occupied territory. *customary int'l law*

(b) Atrocities and offenses, including atrocities and persecutions on racial or religious grounds, committed since 1933. This is only to recognize the principles of criminal law as they are generally observed in civilized states. These principles have been assimilated as a part of International Law at least since 1907. The Fourth Hague Convention provided that inhabitants and belligerents shall remain under the protection and the rule of "the principles of the law of nations, as they result from the usage established among civilized peoples, from the laws of humanity and the dictates of the public conscience."

(c) Invasions of other countries and initiation of wars of aggression in violation of International Law or treaties.

The persons to be reached by these charges will be determined by the rule of liability, common to all legal systems, that all who participate in the formulation or execution of a criminal plan involving multiple crimes are liable for each of the offenses committed and responsible for the acts of each other. All are liable who have incited, ordered, procured, or counselled the commission of such acts, or who have taken what the Moscow Declaration describes as "a consenting part" therein.

The legal position which the United States will maintain, being thus based on the common sense of justice, is relatively simple and non-technical. We must not permit it to be complicated or obscured by sterile legalisms developed in the age of imperialism to make war respectable.

Doubtless what appeals to men of good will and common sense as the crime which comprehends all lesser crimes, is the crime of making unjustifiable war. War necessarily is a calculated series of killings, of destructions of property, or oppressions. Such acts unquestionably would be criminal except that International Law throws a mantle of protection around acts which otherwise would be crimes, when committed in pursuit of legitimate warfare. In this they are distinguished from the same acts in the pursuit of piracy or brigandage which have been considered punishable wherever and by whomever the guilty are caught. But International Law as taught in the Nineteenth and the early part of the Twentieth Century generally declared that war-making was not illegal and is no crime at law. Summarized by a standard authority, its attitude was that "both parties to every war are regarded as being in an identical legal position, and consequently as being possessed of equal rights." This, however, was a departure from the doctrine taught by Grotius, the father of International Law, that there is a distinction between the just and the unjust war—the war of defense and the war of aggression.

International law is more than a scholarly collection of abstract and immutable principles. It is an outgrowth of treaties or agreements between nations and of accepted customs. But every custom has its origin in some single act, and every agreement has to be initiated by the action of some state. Unless we are prepared to abandon every principle of growth for International Law, we cannot deny that our own day has its right to institute customs and to conclude agreements that will themselves become sources of a newer and strengthened International Law. International Law is not capable of development by legislation, for there is no continuously sitting international legislature. Innovations and revisions in International Law are brought about by the action of governments designed to meet a change in circumstances. It grows, as did the Common-law, through decisions reached from time to time in adapting settled principles to new situations. Hence I am not disturbed by the lack of precedent for the inquiry we propose to conduct. After the shock to civilization of the last World War, however, a marked reversion to the earlier and sounder doctrines of International Law took place. By the time the Nazis came to power it was thoroughly established that launching an aggressive war or the institution of war by treachery was illegal and that the defense of legitimate warfare was no longer available to those who engaged in such an enterprise. It is high time that we act on the juridical principle that aggressive war-making is illegal and criminal . . . .

Respectfully yours,
*(s) Robert H. Jackson**

---

*Editor's Note.—In his closing argument for the Nazi war crime trials, Justice Jackson argued that the principle of analogy was one of the mechanisms that the Nazis used to seize power.

The doctrine of punishment by analogy was introduced to enable conviction for acts which no statute forbade. [They] considered every violation of the goals of life which the community set up for itself to be a wrong per se, and that the act could be punished even though it was not contrary to existing "formal law."

Jackson, Closing Arguments for Conviction of Nazi War Criminals, 20 Temp. L.Q. 85-87 (1946).

Other Discussion Materials

City of Chicago v. Jesus Morales, et al.
Supreme Court of the United States
527 U.S. 41; 119 S. Ct. 1849; 144 L. Ed. 2d 67; 1999 U.S. LEXIS 4005; 67 U.S.L.W. 4415 (1999)

Justice Stevens announced the judgment of the Court...

In 1992, the Chicago City Council enacted the Gang Congregation Ordinance, which prohibits "criminal street gang members" from "loitering" with one another or with other persons in any public place. The question presented is whether the Supreme Court of Illinois correctly held that the ordinance violates the Due Process Clause of the Fourteenth Amendment to the Federal Constitution.

I

Before the ordinance was adopted, the city council's Committee on Police and Fire conducted hearings to explore the problems created by the city's street gangs, and more particularly, the consequences of public loitering by gang members. Witnesses included residents of the neighborhoods where gang members are most active, as well as some of the aldermen who represent those areas. Based on that evidence, the council made a series of findings that are included in the text of the ordinance and explain the reasons for its enactment....

The ordinance creates a criminal offense punishable by a fine of up to $500, imprisonment for not more than six months, and a requirement to perform up to 120 hours of community service. Commission of the offense involves four predicates. First, the police officer must reasonably believe that at least one of the two or more persons present in a "public place" is a "criminal street gang member." Second, the persons must be "loitering," which the ordinance defines as "remaining in any one place with no apparent purpose." Third, the officer must then order "all" of the persons to disperse and remove themselves "from the area." Fourth, a person must disobey the officer's order. If any person, whether a gang member or not, disobeys the officer's order, that person is guilty of violating the ordinance.

Two months after the ordinance was adopted, the Chicago Police Department promulgated General Order 92-4 to provide guidelines to govern its enforcement. That order purported to establish limitations on the enforcement discretion of police officers "to ensure that the anti-gang loitering ordinance is not enforced in an arbitrary or discriminatory way." Chicago Police Department, General Order 92-4, reprinted in App. to Pet. for Cert. 65a....

II

During the three years of its enforcement, the police issued over 89,000 dispersal orders and arrested over 42,000 people for violating the ordinance....

The city believes that the ordinance resulted in a significant decline in gang-related homicides....

Given the myriad factors that influence levels of violence, it is difficult to evaluate the probative value of this statistical evidence, or to reach any firm conclusion about the ordinance's efficacy....

The Illinois Supreme Court...held "that the gang loitering ordinance violates due process of law in that it is impermissibly vague on its face and an arbitrary restriction on personal liberties."...

Like the Illinois Supreme Court, we conclude that the ordinance enacted by the city of Chicago is unconstitutionally vague.

III

The basic factual predicate for the city's ordinance is not in dispute. As the city argues in its brief, "the very presence of a large collection of obviously brazen, insistent, and lawless gang members and hangers-on on the public ways intimidates residents, who become afraid even to leave their homes and go about their business. That, in turn, imperils community residents' sense of safety and security, detracts from property values, and can ultimately destabilize entire neighborhoods." The findings in the ordinance explain that it was motivated by these concerns. We have no doubt that a law that directly prohibited such intimidating conduct would be constitutional, but this ordinance broadly covers a significant amount of additional activity. Uncertainty about the scope of that additional coverage provides the basis for respondents' claim that the ordinance is too vague....

Vagueness may invalidate a criminal law for either of two independent reasons. First, it may fail to provide the kind of notice that will enable ordinary people to understand what conduct it prohibits; second, it may authorize and even encourage arbitrary and discriminatory enforcement....

The Illinois Supreme Court recognized that the term "loiter" may have a common and accepted meaning, 177 Ill. 2d at 451, 687 N.E.2d at 61, but the definition of that term in this ordinance — "to remain in any one place with no apparent purpose" — does not. It is difficult to imagine how any citizen of the city of Chicago standing in a public place with a group of people would know if he or she had an "apparent purpose." If she were talking to another person, would she have an apparent purpose? If she were frequently checking her watch and looking expectantly down the street, would she have an apparent purpose?

Since the city cannot conceivably have meant to criminalize each instance a citizen stands in public with a gang member, the vagueness that dooms this ordinance is not the product of uncertainty about the normal meaning of "loitering," but rather about what loitering is covered by the ordinance and what is not. The Illinois Supreme Court emphasized the law's failure to distinguish between innocent conduct and conduct threatening harm....

The city's principal response to this concern about adequate notice is that loiterers are not subject to sanction until after they have failed to comply with an officer's order to disperse....

We find this response unpersuasive for at least two reasons. First, the purpose of the fair notice requirement is to enable the ordinary citizen to conform his or her conduct to the law. "No one may be required at peril of life, liberty or property to speculate as to the meaning of penal statutes." Lanzetta v. New Jersey, 306 U.S. 451, 453, 83 L. Ed. 888, 59 S. Ct. 618 (1939). Although it is true that a loiterer is not subject to criminal sanctions unless he or she disobeys a dispersal order, the loitering is the conduct that the ordinance is designed to prohibit. If the loitering is in fact harmless and innocent, the dispersal order itself is an unjustified impairment of liberty. If the police are able to decide arbitrarily which members of the public they will order to disperse, then the Chicago ordinance becomes indistinguishable from the law we held invalid in Shuttlesworth v. Birmingham, 382 U.S. 87, 90, 15 L. Ed. 2d 176, 86 S. Ct. 211 (1965). Because an officer may issue an order only after prohibited conduct has already occurred, it cannot provide the kind of advance notice that will protect the putative loiterer from being ordered to disperse. Such an order cannot retroactively give adequate warning of the boundary between the permissible and the impermissible applications of the law. . . .

Lack of clarity in the description of the loiterer's duty to obey a dispersal order might not render the ordinance unconstitutionally vague if the definition of the forbidden conduct were clear, but it does buttress our conclusion that the entire ordinance fails to give the ordinary citizen adequate notice of what is forbidden and what is permitted. . . .

The broad sweep of the ordinance also violates "'the requirement that a legislature establish minimal guidelines to govern law enforcement.'" Kolender v. Lawson, 461 U.S. at 358. There are no such guidelines in the ordinance. In any public place in the city of Chicago, persons who stand or sit in the company of a gang member may be ordered to disperse unless their purpose is apparent. The mandatory language in the enactment directs the police to issue an order without first making any inquiry about their possible purposes. It matters not whether the reason that a gang member and his father, for example, might loiter near Wrigley Field is to rob an unsuspecting fan or just to get a glimpse of Sammy Sosa leaving the ballpark; in either event, if their purpose is not apparent to a nearby police officer, she may — indeed, she "shall" — order them to disperse. . . .

It is true, as the city argues, that the requirement that the officer reasonably believe that a group of loiterers contains a gang member does place a limit on the authority to order dispersal. That limitation would no doubt be sufficient if the ordinance only applied to loitering that had an apparently harmful purpose or effect, or possibly if it only applied to loitering by persons reasonably believed to be criminal gang members. But this ordinance, for reasons that are not explained in the findings of the city council, requires no harmful purpose and applies to non-gang members as well as suspected gang members. It applies to everyone in the city who may remain in one place with one suspected gang member as long as their purpose is not apparent to an officer observing them. Friends, relatives, teachers, counselors, or even total strangers might unwittingly engage in forbidden loitering if they happen to engage in idle conversation with a gang member.

Ironically, the definition of loitering in the Chicago ordinance not only extends its scope to encompass harmless conduct, but also has the perverse consequence of excluding from its coverage much of the intimidating conduct that motivated its enactment. As the city council's findings demonstrate, the most harmful gang loitering is motivated either by an apparent purpose to publicize the gang's dominance of certain territory, thereby intimidating nonmembers, or by an equally apparent purpose to conceal ongoing commerce in illegal drugs. As the Illinois Supreme Court has not placed any limiting construction on the language in the ordinance, we must assume that the ordinance means what it says and that it has no application to loiterers whose purpose is apparent. The relative importance of its application to harmless loitering is magnified by its inapplicability to loitering that has an obviously threatening or illicit purpose....

In our judgment, the Illinois Supreme Court correctly concluded that the ordinance does not provide sufficiently specific limits on the enforcement discretion of the police "to meet constitutional standards for definiteness and clarity." We recognize the serious and difficult problems testified to by the citizens of Chicago that led to the enactment of this ordinance. "We are mindful that the preservation of liberty depends in part on the maintenance of social order." Houston v. Hill, 482 U.S. 451, 471-472, 96 L. Ed. 2d 398, 107 S. Ct. 2502 (1987). However, in this instance the city has enacted an ordinance that affords too much discretion to the police and too little notice to citizens who wish to use the public streets.

Accordingly, the judgment of the Supreme Court of Illinois is Affirmed....

Justice Thomas, with whom the Chief Justice and Justice Scalia join, dissenting.

The duly elected members of the Chicago City Council enacted the ordinance at issue as part of a larger effort to prevent gangs from establishing dominion over the public streets. By invalidating Chicago's ordinance, I fear that the Court has unnecessarily sentenced law-abiding citizens to lives of terror and misery. The ordinance is not vague. "Any fool would know that a particular category of conduct would be within [its] reach." Kolender v. Lawson, 461 U.S. 352, 370, 75 L. Ed. 2d 903, 103 S. Ct. 1855 (1983) (White, J., dissenting)....

The human costs exacted by criminal street gangs are inestimable. In many of our Nation's cities, gangs have "virtually overtaken certain neighborhoods, contributing to the economic and social decline of these areas and causing fear and lifestyle changes among law-abiding residents." U.S. Dept. of Justice, Office of Justice Programs, Bureau of Justice Assistance, Monograph: Urban Street Gang Enforcement 3 (1997). Gangs fill the daily lives of many of our poorest and most vulnerable citizens with a terror that the Court does not give sufficient consideration, often relegating them to the status of prisoners in their own homes. See U.S. Dept. of Justice, Attorney General's Report to the President, Coordinated Approach to the Challenge of Gang Violence: A Progress Report 1 (Apr. 1996) ("From the small business owner who is literally crippled because he refuses to pay 'protection' money to the neighborhood gang, to the families who are hostages within their homes, living in neighborhoods ruled by predatory drug trafficking gangs, the harmful impact of gang violence...is both physically and psychologically debilitating").

The city of Chicago has suffered the devastation wrought by this national tragedy. Last year, in an effort to curb plummeting attendance, the Chicago Public Schools hired dozens of adults to escort children to school. The youngsters had become too terrified of gang violence to leave their homes alone. Martinez, Parents Paid to Walk Line Between Gangs and School, Chicago Tribune, Jan. 21, 1998, p. 1. The children's fears were not unfounded. In 1996, the Chicago Police Department estimated that there were 132 criminal street gangs in the city. Illinois Criminal Justice Information Authority, Research Bulletin: Street Gangs and Crime 4 (Sept. 1996). Between 1987 and 1994, these gangs were involved in 63,141 criminal incidents, including 21,689 nonlethal violent crimes and 894 homicides. Many of these criminal incidents and homicides result from gang "turf battles," which take place on the public streets and place innocent residents in grave danger....

Before enacting its ordinance, the Chicago City Council held extensive hearings on the problems of gang loitering. Concerned citizens appeared to testify poignantly as to how gangs disrupt their daily lives. Ordinary citizens like Ms. D'Ivory Gordon explained that she struggled just to walk to work:

> "When I walk out my door, these guys are out there....
> "They watch you.... They know where you live. They know what time you leave, what time you come home. I am afraid of them. I have even come to the point now that I carry a meat cleaver to work with me....

At the outset, it is important to note that the ordinance does not criminalize loitering per se. Rather, it penalizes loiterers' failure to obey a police officer's order to move along. A majority of the Court believes that this scheme vests too much discretion in police officers. Nothing could be further from the truth. Far from according officers too much discretion, the ordinance merely enables police officers to fulfill one of their traditional functions....

In order to perform their peace-keeping responsibilities satisfactorily, the police inevitably must exercise discretion. Indeed, by empowering them to act as peace officers, the law assumes that the police will exercise that discretion responsibly and with sound judgment. That is not to say that the law should not provide objective guidelines for the police, but simply that it cannot rigidly constrain their every action. By directing a police officer not to issue a dispersal order unless he "observes a person whom he reasonably believes to be a criminal street gang member loitering in any public place," Chicago's ordinance strikes an appropriate balance between those two extremes. Just as we trust officers to rely on their experience and expertise in order to make spur-of-the-moment determinations about amorphous legal standards such as "probable cause" and "reasonable suspicion," so we must trust them to determine whether a group of loiterers contains individuals (in this case members of criminal street gangs) whom the city has determined threaten the public peace....

"They are commonsense, nontechnical conceptions that deal with the factual and practical considerations of everyday life on which reasonable and prudent men, not legal technicians, act.... Our cases have recognized that a police officer may draw inferences based on his own experience in deciding whether probable cause exists") (citations and internal quotation marks omitted). In sum, the Court's conclusion that the ordinance is impermissibly vague because it "'necessarily entrusts lawmaking to the moment-to-moment judgment of the policeman on his beat,'" cannot be reconciled with common sense, longstanding police practice, or this Court's Fourth Amendment jurisprudence....

In concluding that the ordinance adequately channels police discretion, I do not suggest that a police officer enforcing the Gang Congregation Ordinance will never make a mistake. Nor do I overlook the possibility that a police officer, acting in bad faith, might enforce the ordinance in an arbitrary or discriminatory way. But our decisions should not turn on the proposition that such an event will be anything but rare. Instances of arbitrary or discriminatory enforcement of the ordinance, like any other law, are best addressed when (and if) they arise, rather than prophylactically through the disfavored mechanism of a facial challenge on vagueness grounds. . . .

The plurality's conclusion that the ordinance "fails to give the ordinary citizen adequate notice of what is forbidden and what is permitted," is similarly untenable. There is nothing "vague" about an order to disperse. While "we can never expect mathematical certainty from our language," Grayned v. City of Rockford, 408 U.S. 104, 110, 33 L. Ed. 2d 222, 92 S. Ct. 2294 (1972), it is safe to assume that the vast majority of people who are ordered by the police to "disperse and remove themselves from the area" will have little difficulty understanding how to comply.

Assuming that we are also obligated to consider whether the ordinance places individuals on notice of what conduct might subject them to such an order, respondents in this facial challenge bear the weighty burden of establishing that the statute is vague in all its applications, "in the sense that no standard of conduct is specified at all." Coates v. Cincinnati, 402 U.S. 611, 614, 29 L. Ed. 2d 214, 91 S. Ct. 1686 (1971). I subscribe to the view of retired Justice White — "If any fool would know that a particular category of conduct would be within the reach of the statute, if there is an unmistakable core that a reasonable person would know is forbidden by the law, the enactment is not unconstitutional on its face." Kolender, 461 U.S. at 370-371 (dissenting opinion). This is certainly such a case. As the Illinois Supreme Court recognized, "persons of ordinary intelligence may maintain a common and accepted meaning of the word 'loiter.'" . . .

The plurality also concludes that the definition of the term loiter — "to remain in any one place with no apparent purpose" — fails to provide adequate notice. "It is difficult to imagine," the plurality posits, "how any citizen of the city of Chicago standing in a public place . . . would know if he or she had an 'apparent purpose.'" The plurality underestimates the intellectual capacity of the citizens of Chicago. Persons of ordinary intelligence are perfectly capable of evaluating how outsiders perceive their conduct, and here "it is self-evident that there is a whole range of conduct that anyone with at least a semblance of common sense would know is [loitering] and that would be covered by the statute." . . .

Members of a group standing on the corner staring blankly into space, for example, are likely well aware that passersby would conclude that they have "no apparent purpose." . . .

Today, the Court focuses extensively on the "rights" of gang members and their companions. It can safely do so — the people who will have to live with the consequences of today's opinion do not live in our neighborhoods. Rather, the people who will suffer from our lofty pronouncements are people like Ms. Susan Mary Jackson; people who have seen their neighborhoods literally destroyed by gangs and violence and drugs. They are good, decent people who must struggle to overcome their desperate situation, against all odds, in order to raise their families, earn a living, and remain good citizens. As one resident described, "There is only about maybe one or two percent of the people in the city causing these problems maybe, but it's keeping 98 percent of us in our houses and off the streets and afraid to shop." By focusing exclusively on the imagined "rights" of the two percent, the Court today has denied our most vulnerable citizens the very thing that

Justice Stevens, elevates above all else — the "freedom of movement." And that is a shame.

I respectfully dissent.

Papachristou v. City of Jacksonville
Supreme Court of the United States
405 U.S. 156, 92 S. Ct. 839, 31 L. Ed. 2d 110 (1972)

Douglas, J.

This case involves eight defendants who were convicted in a Florida municipal court of violating a Jacksonville, Florida, vagrancy ordinance.[1] . . .

At issue are five consolidated cases. Margaret Papachristou, Betty Calloway, Eugene Eddie Melton, and Leonard Johnson were all arrested early on a Sunday morning, and charged with vagrancy — "prowling by auto."

Jimmy Lee Smith and Milton Henry were charged with vagrancy — "vagabonds."

Henry Edward Heath and a codefendant were arrested for vagrancy — "loitering" and "common thief."

Thomas Owen Campbell was charged with vagrancy — "common thief."

Hugh Brown was charged with vagrancy — "disorderly loitering on street" and "disorderly conduct — resisting arrest with violence."

The facts are stipulated. Papachristou and Calloway are white females. Melton and Johnson are black males. Papachristou was enrolled in a job-training program sponsored by the State Employment Service at Florida Junior College in Jacksonville. Calloway was a typing and shorthand teacher at a state mental institution located near Jacksonville. She was the owner of the automobile in which the four defendants were arrested. Melton was a Vietnam war veteran who had been released from the Navy after nine months in a veterans' hospital. On the date of his arrest he was a part-time computer helper while attending college as a full-time student in Jacksonville. Johnson was a tow-motor operator in a grocery chain warehouse and was a lifelong resident of Jacksonville.

At the time of their arrest the four of them were riding in Calloway's car on the main thoroughfare in Jacksonville. They had left a restaurant owned by Johnson's uncle where they had eaten and were on their way to a nightclub. The arresting officers denied that the racial mixture in the car played any part in the decision to make the arrest. The arrest, they said, was made because the defendants had stopped near a used-car lot which had been broken into several times. There was, however, no evidence of any breaking and entering on the night in question.

---

1. Jacksonville Ordinance Code §26-57 provided at the time of these arrests and convictions as follows: "Rogues and vagabonds, or dissolute persons who go about begging, common gamblers, persons who use juggling or unlawful games or plays, common drunkards, common night walkers, thieves, pilferers or pickpockets, traders in stolen property, lewd, wanton and lascivious persons, keepers of gambling places, common railers and brawlers, persons wandering or strolling around from place to place without any lawful purpose or object, habitual loafers, disorderly persons, persons neglecting all lawful business and habitually spending their time by frequenting houses of ill fame, gaming houses, or places where alcoholic beverages are sold or served, persons able to work but habitually living upon the earnings of their wives or minor children shall be deemed vagrants and, upon conviction in the Municipal Court shall be punished as provided for Class D offenses."

Of these four charged with "prowling by auto" none had been previously arrested except Papachristou who had once been convicted of a municipal offense.

Jacksonville's ordinance and Florida's statute were "derived from early English law," and employ "archaic language" in their definitions of vagrants. The history is an often told tale. The breakup of feudal estates in England led to labor shortages which in turn resulted in the Statutes of Laborers, designed to stabilize the labor force by prohibiting increases in wages and prohibiting the movement of workers from their home areas in search of improved conditions. Later vagrancy laws became criminal aspects of the poor laws. The series of laws passed in England on the subject became increasingly severe. But "the theory of the Elizabethan poor laws no longer fits the facts,".... The conditions which spawned these laws may be gone, but the archaic classifications remain.

This ordinance is void for vagueness, both in the sense that it "fails to give a person of ordinary intelligence fair notice that his contemplated conduct is forbidden by the statute," . . . and because it encourages arbitrary and erratic arrests and convictions. . . .

Living under a rule of law entails various suppositions, one of which is that "[all persons] are entitled to be informed as to what the State commands or forbids." Lanzetta v. New Jersey, 306 U.S. 451, 453.

Lanzetta is one of a well-recognized group of cases insisting that the law give fair notice of the offending conduct. . . .

The Jacksonville ordinance makes criminal activities which by modern standards are normally innocent. "Nightwalking" is one. Florida construes the ordinance not to make criminal one night's wandering, only the "habitual" wanderer or, as the ordinance describes it, "common night walkers." We know, however, from experience that sleepless people often walk at night, perhaps hopeful that sleep-inducing relaxation will result.

"[P]ersons able to work but habitually living upon the earnings of their wives or minor children" — like habitually living "without visible means of support" — might implicate unemployed pillars of the community who have married rich wives.

"[P]ersons able to work but habitually living upon the earnings of their wives or minor children" may also embrace unemployed people out of the labor market, by reason of a recession or disemployed by reason of technological or so-called structural displacements.

Persons "wandering or strolling" from place to place have been extolled by Walt Whitman and Vachel Lindsay. The qualification "without any lawful purpose or object" may be a trap for innocent acts. Persons "neglecting all lawful business and habitually spending their time by frequenting . . . places where alcoholic beverages are sold or served" would literally embrace many members of golf clubs and city clubs.

Walkers and strollers and wanderers may be going to or coming from a burglary. Loafers or loiterers may be "casing" a place for a holdup. Letting one's wife support him is an intra-family matter, and normally of no concern to the police. Yet it may, of course, be the setting for numerous crimes.

The difficulty is that these activities are historically part of the amenities of life as we have known them. They are not mentioned in the Constitution or in the Bill of Rights. These unwritten amenities have been in part responsible for giving our people the feeling of independence and self-confidence, the feeling of creativity. These amenities have dignified the right of dissent and have honored the right to be nonconformists and the right to defy submissiveness. They have encouraged lives of high spirits rather than hushed, suffocating silence.

They are embedded in Walt Whitman's writings, especially in his "Song of the Open Road." They are reflected, too, in the spirit of Vachel Lindsay's "I Want to Go Wandering," and by Henry D. Thoreau.

This aspect of the vagrancy ordinance before us is suggested by what this Court said in 1876 about a broad criminal statute enacted by Congress: "It would certainly be dangerous if the legislature could set a net large enough to catch all possible offenders, and leave it to the courts to step inside and say who could be rightfully detained, and who should be set at large." United States v. Reese, 92 U.S. 214, 221.

While that was a federal case, the due process implications are equally applicable to the States and to this vagrancy ordinance. Here the net cast is large, not to give the courts the power to pick and choose but to increase the arsenal of the police. In Winters v. New York, 333 U.S. 507, the Court struck down a New York statute that made criminal the distribution of a magazine made up principally of items of criminal deeds of bloodshed or lust so massed as to become vehicles for inciting violent and depraved crimes against the person. The infirmity the Court found was vagueness — the absence of "ascertainable standards of guilt" in the sensitive First Amendment area. Mr. Justice Frankfurter dissented. But concerned as he, and many others, had been over the vagrancy laws, he added:

> "Only a word needs to be said regarding Lanzetta v. New Jersey, 306 U.S. 451. The case involved a New Jersey statute of the type that seek to control 'vagrancy.' These statutes are in a class by themselves, in view of the familiar abuses to which they are put. . . . Definiteness is designedly avoided so as to allow the net to be cast at large, to enable men to be caught who are vaguely undesirable in the eyes of police and prosecution, although not chargeable with any particular offense. In short, these 'vagrancy statutes' and laws against 'gangs' are not fenced in by the text of the statute or by the subject matter so as to give notice of conduct to be avoided."

Where the list of crimes is so all-inclusive and generalized as the one in this ordinance, those convicted may be punished for no more than vindicating affronts to police authority:

> "The common ground which brings such a motley assortment of human troubles before the magistrates in vagrancy-type proceedings is the procedural laxity which permits 'conviction' for almost any kind of conduct and the existence of the House of Correction as an easy and convenient dumping-ground for problems that appear to have no other immediate solution." Foote, Vagrancy-Type Law and Its Administration, 104 U. Pa. L. Rev. 603, 631.

Another aspect of the ordinance's vagueness appears when we focus, not on the lack of notice given a potential offender, but on the effect of the unfettered discretion it places in the hands of the Jacksonville police. Caleb Foote, an early student of this subject, has called the vagrancy-type as offering "punishment by analogy." Such crimes, though long common in Russia, are not compatible with our constitutional system. We allow our police to make arrests only on "probable cause," a Fourth and Fourteenth Amendment standard applicable to the States as well as to the Federal Government. Arresting a person on suspicion, like arresting a person for investigation, is foreign to our system, even when the arrest is for past criminality. Future criminality, however, is the common justification for the presence of vagrancy statutes. . . .

A direction by a legislature to the police to arrest all "suspicious" persons would not pass constitutional muster. A vagrancy prosecution may be merely the cloak for a conviction which could not be obtained on the real but undisclosed grounds for the arrest. . . .

Those generally implicated by the imprecise terms of the ordinance — poor people, nonconformists, dissenters, idlers — may be required to comport themselves according to the lifestyle deemed appropriate by the Jacksonville police and the courts. Where, as here, there are no standards governing the exercise of the discretion granted by the ordinance, the scheme permits and encourages an arbitrary and discriminatory enforcement of the law. It furnishes a convenient tool for "harsh and discriminatory enforcement by local prosecuting officials, against particular groups deemed to merit their displeasure." Thornhill v. Alabama, 310 U.S. 88, 97-98. It results in a regime in which the poor and the unpopular are permitted to "stand on a public sidewalk . . . only at the whim of any police officer." Shuttlesworth v. Birmingham, 382 U.S. 87, 90. Under this ordinance,

> "[I]f some carefree type of fellow is satisfied to work just so much, and no more, as will pay for one square meal, some wine, and a flophouse daily, but a court thinks this kind of living subhuman, the fellow can be forced to raise his sights or go to jail as a vagrant." Amsterdam, Federal Constitutional Restrictions on the Punishment of Crimes of Status, Crimes of General Obnoxiousness, Crimes of Displeasing Police Officers, and the Like, 3 Crim. L. Bull. 205, 226 (1967).

A presumption that people who might walk or loaf or loiter or stroll or frequent houses where liquor is sold, or who are supported by their wives or who look suspicious to the police are to become future criminals is too precarious for a rule of law. The implicit presumption in these generalized vagrancy standards — that crime is being nipped in the bud — is too extravagant to deserve extended treatment. Of course, vagrancy statutes are useful to the police. Of course, they are nets making easy the roundup of so-called undesirables. But the rule of law implies equality and justice in its application. Vagrancy laws of the Jacksonville type teach that the scales of justice are so tipped that even-handed administration of the law is not possible. The rule of law, evenly applied to minorities as well as majorities, to the poor as well as the rich, is the great mucilage that holds society together.

The Jacksonville ordinance cannot be squared with our constitutional standards and is plainly unconstitutional.

Reversed.

Theories of Punishment

Having a criminal justice system that imposes punishment can be justified on a variety of grounds: it can give offenders the punishment they deserve; it can deter future violations; and it can take control over dangerous persons to rehabilitate or incapacitate them. Once it is decided to have a criminal justice system, as all civilized societies have, there arises the question of how to distribute liability and punishment within that system. That is the central question in criminal law, an examination of which is begun in this Section.

◆ THE CASE OF SARA JANE OLSON

Sarah Jane Olson, then Kathleen Soliah, is born in 1947 into a comfortable middle class family in Fargo, North Dakota. Kathy, as she is known, is followed by two brothers and two sisters. While still a young child, her family moves to Palmdale, California, a desert town an hour northeast of Los Angeles, where her father teaches high school English and her mother stays home with the children. The family is close-knit and active, often camping in the mountains and going to the beach together. As a child, Kathy is involved in everything — Girl Scouts, the Rainbows, Sunday School. In high school, her upbeat and energetic personality makes her the president of the Pep Club, while still graduating with honors. She attends the University of California at Santa Barbara and falls in love with an economics graduate student, James Kilgore.

In 1971, Kathy and James move to San Francisco, where they become involved with groups in the counterculture movement. It is a time of social upheaval — many are even pushing for revolution. One group of particular notoriety is the Symbionese Liberation Army (SLA), which is led by a career criminal and comprised of mostly white, college-educated twenty-somethings who have

Figure 6 **Soliah at SLA rally in Berkeley, 1974**

(AP)

aligned themselves with society's "oppressed." They commit acts of murder, kidnaping, and robbery in an effort to topple the "establishment." The SLA is both well organized and disciplined, and has become well versed in surveillance, security, field operations, explosives, and political indoctrination techniques. Their motto is, "Death to the fascist insect that preys upon the life of the people." Kathy is not a full-fledged revolutionary but believes strongly in the movement for social equality, and has friends who are intimately involved in more radical politics.

While working as an actress, she meets Angela Atwood, a fellow actress and New Jersey native. Atwood is a graduate of the University of Indiana, where she majored in speech and earned honors in Theater. They become close friends and take waitressing jobs together at the same San Francisco cocktail lounge to make ends meet. They are fired, however, when they start a campaign to unionize employees in response to being forced to wear revealing outfits. Because they share a similar political orientation Atwood, a member of the SLA, introduces Kathy to her comrades. By this time, the SLA is connected to both the murder of the Oakland Schools' Superintendent and the kidnapping of Patty Hearst. Kathy claims her ties to the SLA are only through Atwood. Atwood then disappears. When Kathy returns to San Francisco from vacationing in Mexico, she learns that Atwood was one of six SLA members who were killed during a shootout with more than 400 police on May 17, 1974. Kathy organizes a public memorial service for June 2 in Berkeley's Ho Chi Minh Park and, distraught over her friend's death, takes the stage. Introducing herself as a close friend of Angela, calls her "a truly revolutionary woman" who was murdered by "500 pigs." She ends her speech with a pledge to the surviving SLA members, "Tania [Patty Hearst's alias], Emily, and Bill, your message—you have made your message clear. Keep fighting. We are with you. I am with you."

A few days after the memorial service, SLA member Emily Harris approaches Kathy at the bookstore where she works and pleads for help. The surviving SLA revolutionaries are on the run from the police and need food, new identities, and a hideout. Kathy helps by renting them cars and apartments under false names, creating aliases from the names of dead infants, and giving them money from time to time. She also becomes a SLA spokeswoman, attempting to explain its philosophy to the underground press in the Bay Area.

A little more than a year after Atwood's death, on August 20, 1975, Kathy ~Link to~ accompanies a solidly built white male, approximately six feet tall with short blond ~Pipe Bombs~ hair, to Larsen Supply Company in Southgate, California. The man purchases pipe fittings — two 3-inch by 12-inch galvanized nipples and one 3-inch galvanized cap, paying $16.53 in cash.

The next day, Officer James J. Bryan of the Los Angeles Police Department, Hollywood Division, and his partner, John David Hall, are on patrol duty. Around 11:15 p.m., they park their car in the parking lot of the International House of Pancakes at 7006 Sunset Boulevard, go inside, and have something to eat. The officers exit the restaurant around midnight and resume their patrol. About thirty minutes later, Bryan and Hall return to the IHOP in response to a request from another patrol unit to help block traffic on Sunset Blvd. Subsequently, they receive a robbery call and move their car to Sunset and LeBrea. They then receive information that police still at IHOP found a pipe bomb in the parking space where they had parked earlier that night. Bryan and Hall hurriedly check underneath their car and find a U-shaped magnet attached to a length of fishing line and a wooden wedge on the frame of the car. That same day, an identical pipe bomb is found underneath a police car parked near the Hollenbeck Police Station in Los Angeles. Both bombs were made from materials similar to those that Kathy and the unidentified white male had bought two days earlier.

The F.B.I. had placed Kathy and other SLA associates under surveillance in hopes that they would lead agents to Patty Hearst and Emily and Bill Harris, who were wanted for crimes previously linked to the SLA. On September 18, 1975, between 9 and 10 a.m., F.B.I. Agent Frank R. Doyle, Jr., sees Kathy leaving an apartment at 288 Precita in San Francisco, which is already known to the F.B.I. as an SLA safehouse, with her sister, Josephine Soliah, and brother, Steven Soliah. Around 1 or 2 p.m., Doyle observes Bill and Emily Harris exiting the apartment. The Harrises are arrested shortly thereafter and the apartment is searched. The F.B.I. discovers numerous weapons, a standing carbine, knapsacks,

Figure 7 **Weapons and SLA literature found in safehouse**
(Los Angeles Police Department)

gas masks, Browning Hi-Power publications (including "Carbines" and "The Browning Hi-Power Pistols"), blank checks, and bomb-making materials (wiring, knife switches, batteries, endpipe caps, pipe nipples, a wooden wedge, blasting caps with wires attached, magnets, epoxy, fishing line, clothespins, black tape, nails, plastic garbage bags). The F.B.I. identifies fingerprints lifted from two gun manuals found in the apartment as belonging to Kathleen Soliah, Patricia Hearst, James Kilgore, Emily Harris, Wendy Yoshimura, Steven Soliah, William Harris, Josephine Soliah, and Bonnie Wilder. F.B.I. explosives expert Frederick T. Smith, Jr., also matches the bomb-making materials found in the apartment to the bomb components found in the IHOP parking space and underneath the police car driven by Officers Bryan and Hall.

On February 18, 1976, a grand jury is convened to inquire into Kathy's participation in a conspiracy with William and Emily Harris to murder the police officers during their shoot-out, to possess destructive devices, and to place bombs under police cars. After hearing three days of testimony, during which 26 witnesses testify and numerous exhibits are presented, Kathy Soliah is indicted on February 26, 1976, for one count of Conspiracy to Commit Murder, two counts of Possession of a Destructive Device in a Specified Area for the two pipe bombs, and two counts of Possession of a Destructive Device with Intent to Commit Murder. An arrest warrant is issued for her that day.

Figure 8 **F.B.I. Identification Order, June 20, 1978**
(F.B.I.)

Figure 9 **St. Paul, Minnesota, home, June 1999**
(King Andy/Corbis)

Before she can be arrested, Kathy flees to her home state of Minnesota and takes the last name Olson because it is common, the first name Sara from a Bob Dylan song, and her sister's name, Jane, as her middle name.

She soon begins dating a young, socially conscious doctor named Fred Peterson. They join a local anti-apartheid group and work with African refugees in Minneapolis. In 1980, they marry and a few years later, after having their first child, Emily, move to rural Zimbabwe where Peterson sets up a free clinic and Olson teaches English. Olson gives birth to their second daughter, Sophia, while still in Zimbabwe. They return to Minnesota in 1982 and have their third daughter, Leila, in 1987. Olson stays at home to raise the children. She remains an active volunteer in political causes, and her home becomes a gathering place for "the larger peace and justice community in the Twin Cities." She also involves herself in the Twin Cities' theater scene, winning praise from the local press for many of her performances.

Figure 10 **Olson in community theater production of Great Expectations, 1997**

(Act One/Corbis Sygma)

Olson maintains limited contact with her parents, who are often visited by F.B.I. agents searching for their daughter. In a February 1984 interview with detectives from the Los Angeles Police Department's Criminal Conspiracy Section, they indicate that their daughter no longer lives in California, has assumed a new identity, and is married with children.

In 1989, Kathleen secretly attempts a surrender through her attorney, but the negotiations fail because of the government's unwillingness to grant her blanket immunity on all charges. In 1999, L.A.P.D. detective Tom King, whose father, Mervin, had been in charge of the deadly 1974 shoot-out with the SLA, decides to reopen the case. In June, Olson is on her way to teach a citizenship class to immigrants in suburban St. Paul when a swarm of police, acting on a tip from a viewer who saw her photograph during a broadcast of "America's Most Wanted," surround her minivan and take her into custody pursuant to the still outstanding 1976 warrant.

Olson insists that she is innocent and hires famed anti-establishment lawyer J. Tony Serra, known for defending members of the Black Panthers, Hells Angels, and New World Liberation Front, as well as a professional fire-eater. Within days, nearly 250 friends, many putting their homes up as collateral, raise one million dollars for her bail. Many friends also form a defense committee and publish a fund-raising cookbook of Olson's favorite recipes entitled, "Serving Time: America's Most Wanted Recipes." It features provocative imagery that includes allusions to SLA symbols and Olson mocking the trial proceeding by posing with a picture frame around her face. Olson demands a plea agreement with no jail time, but the district attorney refuses.

Figure 11 **Olson cookbook**

(Sara Olson Defense Fund Committee)

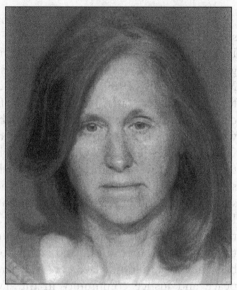

Figure 12 **Arrest photo, June 1999**

(AP)

At trial, Olson maintains her innocence, claiming she was motivated by compassion for her friends, whom she believed would be killed by police if ever found. "Though it seems misguided now, I thought that giving [Emily Harris] money [in support of the SLA] would help save their lives and I thought that was an honorable and Christian thing to do." She also attributes her actions in part to the turmoil of the era. "Like many who participated in the activities of the 1960s and 1970s to bring about change in our country, to make it what I thought would be a better country, I have, for many years, realized that my zeal led to some bad decisions."

1. Relying only upon your own intuitions of justice, what liability and punishment, if any, does Sara Jane Olson deserve?

N	0	1	2	3	4	5	6	7	8	9	10	11
☐	☐	☐	☐	☐	☐	☐	☐	☐	☐	☐	☐	☐
no liability	liability but no punishment	1 day	2 wks	2 mo	6 mo	1 yr	3 yrs	7 yrs	15 yrs	30 yrs	life imprison- ment	death

2. What liability, if any, under the then-existing statutes?
3. What liability, if any, under the Model Penal Code?

■ THE LAW

Deering's California Penal Code Annotated
(1975)

Title 7. Of Crimes Against Public Justice

Chapter 8. Conspiracy

Section 182. Definition; Punishment; Venue

If two or more persons conspire:

> ✓ (1) To commit a crime.

> (2) Falsely and maliciously to indict another for any crime, or to procure another to be charged or arrested for any crime.

> (3) Falsely to move or maintain any suit, action or proceeding.

> (4) To cheat and defraud any person of any property, by any means which are in themselves criminal, or to obtain money or property by false pretenses or by false promises with fraudulent intent not to perform such promises.

> (5) To commit an act injurious to the public health, to public morals, or to pervert or obstruct justice, or the due administration of the laws.

> (6) To commit any crime against the person of the President or Vice President of the United States, the governor of any state or territory, any United States justice or judge, or the secretary of any of the executive departments of the United States.

They are punishable as follows:

When they conspire to commit any crime against the person of any official specified in subdivision 6, they are guilty of a felony and are punishable by imprisonment in the state prison for not less than 10 years.

When they conspire to commit any other felony, they shall be punishable in the same manner and to the same extent as is provided for the punishment of the said felony. If the felony is one for which different punishments are prescribed for different degrees, the jury or court which finds the defendant guilty thereof shall determine the degree of the felony defendant conspired to commit. If the degree is not determined, the punishment for conspiracy to commit such felony shall be that prescribed for the lesser degree, except in the case of conspiracy to commit murder, in which case the punishment shall be that prescribed for murder in the first degree.

If the felony is conspiracy to commit two or more felonies which have different punishments and the commission of such felonies constitute but one offense of conspiracy, the penalty shall be that prescribed for the felony which has the greater maximum term.

When they conspire to do an act described in subdivison 4 of this section, they shall be punishable by imprisonment in the county jail for not more than 1 year, or by a fine not exceeding five thousand dollars ($5,000), or both.

When they conspire to do any of the other acts described in this section they shall be punishable by imprisonment in the county jail for not more than one year, or in the state prison for not more than three years, or by a fine not exceeding five thousand dollars ($5,000) or both.

All cases of conspiracy may be prosecuted and tried in the superior court of any county in which any overt act tending to effect such conspiracy shall be done.

Section 183. Non-Criminal Conspiracies; No Criminal Punishment

No other conspiracies punishable criminally. No conspiracies, other than those enumerated in the preceding section, are punishable criminally.

Section 184. Overt Act; Venue

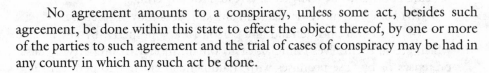

No agreement amounts to a conspiracy, unless some act, besides such agreement, be done within this state to effect the object thereof, by one or more of the parties to such agreement and the trial of cases of conspiracy may be had in any county in which any such act be done.

Title 8. Of Crimes Against the Person

Chapter 1. Homicide

Section 187. Murder Defined

(a) Murder is the unlawful killing of a human being, or a fetus, with malice aforethought.

(b) This section shall not apply to any person who commits an act that results in the death of a fetus if any of the following apply:

(1) The act complied with the Therapeutic Abortion Act, Chapter 11 (commencing with Section 25950) of Division 20 of the Health and Safety Code.

(2) The act was committed by a holder of a physician's and surgeon's certificate, as defined in the Business and Professions Code, in a case where, to a medical certainty, the result of childbirth would be death of the mother of the fetus or where her death from childbirth, although not medically certain, would be substantially certain or more likely than not.

(3) The act was solicited, aided, abetted, or consented to by the mother of the fetus.

(c) Subdivision (b) shall not be construed to prohibit the prosecution of any person under any other provision of law.

Section 188. Malice, Express Malice, and Implied Malice Defined

Such malice may be express or implied. It is express when there is manifested a deliberate intention unlawfully to take away the life of a fellow creature. It is implied, when no considerable provocation appears, or when the circumstances attending the killing show an abandoned malignant heart.

Section 189. Murder; Degrees

All murder which is perpetrated by means of a destructive device or explosive, poison, lying in wait, torture, or by any other kind of willful deliberate, and premeditated killing, or which is committed in the perpetration of, or attempt to perpetrate, arson, rape, robbery, burglary, mayhem, or any act punishable under Section 288, is murder of the first degree; and all other kinds of murders are of the second degree.

As used in this section, "destructive device" shall mean any destructive device as defined in Section 12301, and "explosive" shall mean any explosive as defined in Section 12000 of the Health and Safety Code.

Section 190. Murder, Punishment, Discretion of Jury

Every person guilty of murder in the first degree shall suffer death, confinement in the state prison for life without the possibility of parole, or confinement in the state prison for a term of 25 years to life....

Every person guilty of murder in the second degree shall suffer confinement in the state prison for a term of 15 years to life.

The provisions of Article 2.5 (commencing with Section 2930) of Chapter 7 of Title 1 of Part 3 of the Penal Code shall apply to reduce any minimum term of 25 years to 15 years in a state prison imposed pursuant to this section, but such a person shall not otherwise be released on parole prior to such time.

Title 2. Control of Deadly Weapons
Chapter 2.5

Section 12303.2. Possession of a Destructive Device

Every person who recklessly or maliciously has in his possession any destructive device or any explosive on a public street or highway, in or near any theater, hall, school, college, church, hotel, other public building, or private habitation, in, on, or near any aircraft, railway passenger train, car, cable road or cable car, vessel engaged in carrying passengers for hire, or other public place ordinarily passed by human beings is guilty of a felony, and shall be punishable by imprisonment in the state prison for a period of not less than five years.

Section 12308. Attempted Explosion of a Destructive Device with Intent to Murder

Every person who explodes, ignites, or attempts to explode or ignite any destructive device or any explosive with intent to commit murder is guilty of a felony, and shall be punished by imprisonment in the state prison for a period of not less than 10 years.

▲ PROBLEM
Daughters' Mustard

Devon receives a call from the doctor who has been caring for her mother and her sister, Erie, back home. The doctor asks Devon to return home as soon as possible, explaining that the effects of Erie's mental illness have become more severe and have made her difficult to handle. The doctor strongly recommends civil commitment. Mother has been painfully ill for several years and as a result has been unable to care for troubled Erie. Devon takes the first train home. She is met at the station by Fina, her other sister, who also was called by the doctor. Devon considers Fina deceitful and untrustworthy. She believes Fina's primary interest in the family is in trying to get as much inheritance as possible from her mother's sizeable fortune.

Soon after they arrive at the house, it becomes apparent why Erie's condition has worsened. Mother is in constant pain, unabated by the massive doses of painkillers prescribed by the doctor. She is frequently screaming and crying, asking to be killed. Devon feels that it is her mother's condition, rather than Erie's, that presents the emergency. The nurse who cares for both Mother and Erie reveals that, in her demented condition, Erie has concluded that screaming Mother is a wild dog, which will kill Erie if she does not kill it first. Erie has tried to poison Mother several times, but to date has given her harmless substances—peanut butter, chicken bones—that she thinks may kill what she thinks is a dog.

After a week at the house, Devon can no longer bear her mother's suffering. She concludes that Mother's death would be a blessing. Erie's constant mumblings indicate that she next intends to poison Mother with the "yellow poison," by which she apparently means the hot mustard in the refrigerator. Devon throws out the mustard and substitutes a jar laced with arsenic. Erie feeds it to Mother and Mother dies within hours. Both Devon and Erie are taken into custody after investigators piece together what happened. To Devon's surprise, Fina also is taken into custody. It turns out that, in order to inherit her share of the estate more quickly, Fina came up with the same mustard-substitution plan. When Devon threw away the mustard jar in the refrigerator, she was throwing away a jar that Fina had laced with arsenic.

What liability, if any, would be imposed on each daughter under each of the alternative principles discussed below for distributing liability and punishment—general deterrence, special deterrence, rehabilitation, incapacitation, just deserts—if each, in turn, were considered the sole distributive principle?

● OVERVIEW OF THEORIES OF PUNISHMENT

Why Punish? Punish Whom?   Why have a criminal justice system to punish crimes? The question may seem less than serious because not having a criminal justice system seems inconceivable. But there may be value nonetheless in answering such a question if for no other reason than to articulate why we assume a criminal justice system to be necessary. Note that this question, "why punish?," is different from the question "punish whom?" The first asks why punish anyone; the second asks, if we are to have a system for the infliction of punishment, how is punishment to be distributed within that system? What follows is a discussion of the theories that justify a system of punishment. We will see that each theory leads to a different answer to the second question. (This issue is also the focus of the Discussion Materials.) Traditionally, two sorts of justifications for imposing punishment are given: utilitarian and retributivist.

A. UTILITARIAN JUSTIFICATION

The utilitarian justification for the creation of a system of criminal justice derives from the system's ability to prevent or reduce future crime. This avoids harm to the individual victims and avoids the societal costs of crime. Such prevention frequently is possible at a cost of less than the cost of the crime to the society and thus can be justified on pure cost-efficiency grounds.[1] Such consequentialist theories (so-called because they use the consequences of liability and punishment to justify the same) can take any and all of the following forms. That is, each of the following is a mechanism by which crime might be efficiently prevented.

1) *General Deterrence* Punishment of offenders can create a societal benefit by demonstrating to potential offenders the sanctions they will suffer for a violation, and thereby deterring subsequent violations by others. Imprisoning a tax evader, for example, may deter other people from evading taxes. To be deterred, other potential offenders must know of the threatened punishment and must, in some general way, calculate the costs and benefits of engaging in the prohibited conduct. Persons who do not or cannot take account of the consequences of a violation cannot be deterred by the threat of sanctions. But punishment of such a person can deter others. Although Erie was unaware of the nature of her conduct—she thought she was killing a wild dog and therefore may have thought the prohibition of killing another person did not apply to her conduct—her punishment nonetheless might deter others from killing. Indeed, one might argue that the failure to punish her, or anyone who causes a death, undermines the effectiveness of the prohibition against killing, for it shows potential offenders that there is the possibility that they can kill, be caught, yet not be punished.[2]

2) *Generalization of a Deterrent Threat* Punishment of one kind of offense can have a generalized deterrent effect for other offenses as well. Thus, punishment of the daughters for homicide will deter other homicides in similar situations but also may provide some general reminder of criminal law sanctions and therefore help deter other homicides in general. The closer the contemplated offense to the conduct punished, all other things being equal, the more likely the punishment will have a deterrent effect. Punishment for homicide, for example, will have a greater deterrent effect on assaults than on tax evasion.

---

1. See generally Jeremy Bentham, An Introduction to the Principles of Morals and Legislation 178-188 (1789).

2. See generally Johannes Andenaes, Punishment and Deterrence (1974); Andrew von Hirsch, Doing Justice ch. 5 (1976); Franklin E. Zimring & Gordon Hawkins, Deterrence: The Legal Threat in Crime Control (1973).

3)   *Special Deterrence*   Deterrence also can operate on the offender who is punished — so-called special or specific deterrence. Special deterrence can have a more direct effect than general deterrence, for the offender has learned first-hand that a violation can lead to punishment. Because the effectiveness of deterrence depends on the offender calculating the costs and benefits of his or her planned criminal conduct, at least in some general way, there is no special deterrent value in punishing a person who does not or cannot do so. Thus, punishing Erie may reinforce her appreciation for the fact that killing another is prohibited (if someone is able to explain to her why she is being punished), but it is not likely to deter her from future killings if she is unable to identify the situations in which the prohibition applies because she is unable to distinguish persons from dogs).

4)   *Deterrence Through Stigmatization*   The punishment of an offender tends to stigmatize and condemn the offender and his or her conduct. This stigmatization can be a form of deterrence to potential offenders, but also can have an effect on law-abiding citizens. Such punishment reaffirms for law-abiding citizens that they are doing right and are good people, thereby encouraging them to continue to comply with the law. It also educates and instructs others as to the societal norms. If others see a moral dilemma in alleviating the excruciating pain of a loved one, as Devon did, conviction and punishment of Devon tells them society's view of the proper response; moreover, if the criminal law has moral credibility, conviction and punishment can encourage persons to resist the temptation to kill their suffering loved one. Thus, deterrence through stigmatization requires communication of the results of criminal adjudications to the general public.[1] It also requires that the criminal law have moral credibility with those sought to be deterred.

5)   *Incapacitation*   The most direct means of preventing future offenses is through incapacitation of persons who may commit offenses by imprisoning, executing, or in some other way making a subsequent offense impossible. For example, castrating a potential rapist or cutting off the hand of a potential pickpocket could prevent an offense. A failed attempt, such as Fina's, may indicate that the actor is as dangerous as one who perpetrates a successful attempt, such as Devon. If the dangerousness of two people is the same, the degree of punishment justified under a purely incapacitative rationale would be the same. Thus, under a distributive principle of incapacitation, attempts would generally be punished the same as the completed offense. Also under such a principle, punishment would not need to wait until after the commission of an offense; a reliable prediction of future criminality would provide adequate justification.[2] Indeed, if the circumstances stimulating the offense are unique or even rare, incapacitation is a persuasive justification for punishment only before the offense occurs. For example, if Devon was brought to the point of killing only because of her special love for her mother, and if there is no danger that she will develop such love for another person similarly in pain, there is no danger of future criminality and thus no incapacitative justification for sanctioning her. The same may be true for Fina. If

---

1. See generally Johannes Andenaes, Punishment and Deterrence ch. 4 (1974); Franklin E. Zimring & Gordon Hawkins, Deterrence: The Legal Threat in Crime Control 77-87 (1973).

2. See generally Marc Ancel, Social Defense: A Modern Guide to Criminal Problems (1965); Andrew von Hirsch, Doing Justice ch. 3 (1976); Contemporary Punishment ch. 4 (R. Gerber & P. McAnany eds., 1972).

she never again will have an opportunity for great financial gain by killing another and if this is her only trigger for homicide, sanctioning her for incapacitative purposes may be unjustified. Erie, because of her mental illness, seems the person most likely to cause injury or death to another; thus, she provides the strongest case for incapacitative sanction. Unlike deterence, the effectiveness of this crime prevention mechanism does not depend on either communication of the threatened sanction to potential offenders or the potential offenders' calculations of a cost-benefit analysis in governing their conduct. It does, however, require that the system have an ability to identify dangerous persons before they act, preferably with a minimum of "false positives" (that is, people indicated by the test mechanism to be dangerous but who in fact would not commit an offense). The behavioral sciences presently have only a limited ability to make such predictions accurately.[1]

6) _Rehabilitation_   Rehabilitating or reforming an offender is another means by which future offenses may be avoided. Rehabilitation takes away the offender's desire or need to engage in criminal conduct. Medical treatment, psychological counseling, and education and training programs are the most common forms of rehabilitation. However, anything that is designed to minimize the actor's wish to commit future crimes, other than intimidation by a deterrent threat, typically is included under the label of rehabilitation. Rehabilitation regimes frequently are seen as making the actor a better person. Nothing in this crime prevention mechanism requires that the potential offender agree with or approve of the changes that are made to him. Effectiveness of this mechanism requires the ability to accurately identify people who need rehabilitation (that is, people in danger of committing an offense in the future), the ability to find treatment regimes that will rehabilitate, and the ability to determine when a person under treatment is rehabilitated. As with incapacitation, the behavioral sciences presently have a limited ability to perform these functions.[2] Also, as with incapacitation, the effectiveness of this mechanism does not require that rehabilitative treatments wait until after the potential offender has committed an offense.

JUST DESERT

An alternative to these utilitarian means of justifying punishment is the claim that just punishment is a desirable end in itself. This justification for punishment is referred to as the retributivist or just desert theory. Whereas utilitarian theory is consequentialist, focusing on the beneficial social consequences of punishment, retributivist theory is nonconsequentialist. The theory urges that liability and punishment should be imposed because the offender deserves it, whether or not such liability and punishment would help avoid future offenses. Punishment is not justified by its effects; rather, it is justified by the notion that the person to be punished deserves it. A striking illustration of this theory is provided by Kant's

---

1. See generally Jacqueline Cohen, Selective Incapacitation: An Assessment, 1984 U. Ill. L. Rev. 253, 267-275; Marc Miller & Norval Morris, Predictions of Dangerousness: An Argument for Limited Use, 3 Violence & Victims 263, 268-271 (1988); Andrew von Hirsch, Prediction of Criminal Conduct and Preventative Confinement of Convicted Persons, 21 Buffalo L. Rev. 717, 730-739 (1972); Franklin E. Zimring & Gordon Hawkins, Dangerousness and Criminal Justice, 85 Mich. L. Rev. 481, 488-491 (1986).

2. See generally Francis A. Allen, Legal Values and the Rehabilitative Ideal, 50 J. Crim. L.C. & P.S. 226 (1959); Livingston Hall & Sheldon Glueck, Criminal Law and Its Enforcement 18 (2d ed. 1958); P. Bean, Punishment 194 (1981); Herbert L. Packer, The Practical Limits of Deterrence in Contemporary Punishment 102, 105 (R. Gerber & P. McAnany eds., 1972).

argument that an island society ought to execute its convicted murderers before disbanding, even if no one would be present to be threatened by them.[1] Under retributivist theory, the sole criterion for punishment is the actor's moral desert. An actor is punished if and only if he or she is blameworthy and is punished according to the degree of his or her blameworthiness, no more and no less. The degree of an offender's blameworthiness, in turn, depends on both the seriousness of the violation and the extent of the actor's moral accountability for it.

Unfair Advantage and Right to Punishment An additional non-consequentialist justification for imposing punishment focuses on what the law-abiding citizen deserves. By breaking the law, the offender has gained an unfair advantage over citizens who have suffered the burden of abiding by the law. Fairness to the law-abiding requires that the offender suffer the burden of punishment to nullify the unfair advantage.[2] One final theory of non-consequentialist justification for punishment is stated in terms of an offender's right to punishment, rather than his desert of punishment. To fail to punish is to fail to recognize the offender as a rational being capable of choice; punishment is the recognition of the offender's status as a moral being.[3]

C. UNANIMITY OF JUSTIFICATORY PURPOSES

One need not decide whether a utilitarian or a just desert (retributive) justification is the correct or the most attractive justification of punishment in order to answer the question of whether society should impose punishment. Each of these justifications leads to the same conclusion: We ought to have a system of criminal justice that punishes offenders. The imposition of sanctions on offenders can serve each of the purposes noted. It can prevent crime by deterring the offender or others, by encouraging the law-abiding, and by incapacitating or rehabilitating a potential offender. The same conviction can give the punishment the offender deserves, take away any unfair advantage gained over the law-abiding, and reaffirm the offender's status as a rational being whose freedom to make decisions must be acknowledged through punishment.

Justificatory Purposes vs. Distributive Principles The differences among the theories, especially between utilitarian and just desert theories, are important in answering a different question: If punishment is to be inflicted, *how should it be distributed?*[4] The above discussions of each of the theories of punishment touch on both justificatory and distributive issues. It is the distributive issue to which the doctrines of criminal law address themselves. They answer the question, who should be punished for what and how much punishment should be imposed for a given violation by a given offender?

D. DIFFERENT DISTRIBUTION FOR EACH THEORY

While both utilitarian and non-consequentialist (retributivist) rationales justify having a criminal justice system, within such a system they each would distribute liability and punishment in a different manner. Each utilitarian rationale, when used as the principle for the distribution of punishment, would distribute punishment differently from each other utilitarian rationale. More

---

1. Immanuel Kant, The Metaphysical Elements of Justice 102 (J. Ladd trans., 1965).
2. See Kent Greenawalt, Punishment, 74 J. Crim. L. & Crim. 343, 349-350 (1983).
3. See generally Georg Hegel, Hegel's Philosophy of Right 70-71 (T.M. Knox trans., 1965).
4. See H.L.A. Hart, Punishment and Responsibility 3-13 (1968). Hart distinguishes between theories for justifying punishment and for distributing punishment.

important, a distribution that would most effectively deter or incapacitate or rehabilitate potential offenders is not the distribution that would provide punishment to offenders who deserve it in an amount that they deserve. That the different rationales distribute liability and punishment differently logically follows from the fact each rationale relies on different criteria.

Ɛ. UTILITARIAN DISTRIBUTION IN CONFLICT WITH DESERT

A utilitarian distribution has the potential to conflict with a distribution of punishment according to desert. Some of the points of conflict are noted above. Deterrence as a distributive principle might justify punishment of an innocent person if the deterrent benefit of such punishment is greater than the cost of the punishment. Less dramatic but more likely is a deterrence principle's infliction of punishment that is disproportionate in relation to the seriousness of the offense or the moral accountability of the offender. That is, it may well be cost-effective in preventing crime to impose more or less punishment than is deserved. Incapacitation and rehabilitation have a similar potential for conflict with desert. Even if an offender's crime is minor, a long term of imprisonment might be justified under an incapacitation or rehabilitation theory if the offender is seen as likely to commit another offense in the future. Indeed, at the extreme, distributive principles based on either incapacitation or rehabilitation do not require commission of an offense. If reliable predictive judgments could be made as to an offender's future dangerousness, a criminal justice system under these distributive principles could "convict" an "offender" who has not, but who is predicted to commit, an offense and "punish" him in order to incapacitate or rehabilitate him. While some writers have proposed something close to this, no purely utilitarian system for the distribution of liability and punishment has ever been adopted. This is the case, in all likelihood, because such a system, built on purely utilitarian distributive principles, would generate results too inconsistent with society's notions of just punishment and thus would run afoul of the popular desire to impose punishment proportionate to an offender's blameworthiness.

Absolute and Relative Assessments of Desert   Some writers suggest that desert theory gives only broad ranges of punishment, outside of which a sanction will be seen as *un*just. Admittedly, as an absolute matter, it is difficult to establish the amount of punishment an offender might deserve. It has been observed, however, that it is possible to reliably establish the *relative* blameworthiness of offenders. And, given the natural ceiling for punishment—the death penalty or life imprisonment—the rank ordering of offenders ultimately sets each on a specific point or within a narrow range on the continuum of punishment. Because the utilitarian distributive principles look to factors extraneous to an actor's blameworthiness—for example, the newsworthiness of a case, which may increase the general deterrent effect of punishment; the reliability or lack thereof of the device predicting future dangerousness; the clinical success or failure of a particular rehabilitative program for a particular kind of offender—offenders committing similar offenses and having similar blameworthiness may receive different punishments under a utilitarian system. Thus, utilitarian distributive principles may create not only absolute but also relative injustices.

Disutility of Desert Distribution   On the other hand, a desert distribution of liability and punishment can be criticized for failing to avoid avoidable crimes. Such a distribution fails to maximize the crime reduction potential of the criminal justice system, as could be achieved by the utilitarian mechanisms of deterrence, incapacitation, and rehabilitation. While citizens might prefer that justice be done, it is argued, there is nothing so compelling as being hit over the head by a mugger or having one's house burglarized or vandalized to clarify one's priorities. Preventing crime continues to be one of the most important, if not the most important function that a citizen asks of government. Therefore, it would not be surprising if citizens might compromise their demand for a just distribution of liability and punishment if, by doing so, they could reduce crime.

Crime Reduction Through Other Mechanisms While the desire to reduce crime is understandable, it is not true that manipulation of the rules governing assignment of criminal liability and punishment is the only means or even the most efficient means of reducing crime. If another systemic reform can reduce crime more effectively or has the same crime reduction effect but without the resulting injustice that comes with deviation from a distributive principle of just desert, then such a reform ought to be implemented instead of, or at least before, deviation from just desert. For example, one might argue that a relaxation of the rules limiting search and seizure by police might hurt privacy interests, but it also might both reduce crime and increase the just distribution of punishment. Given the choice, a community might trade less privacy for less crime and more justice. The larger point is that in the utilitarian calculus for reducing crime, there are many systemic changes possible other than deviating from a distribution of liability based on just desert. The utility of any unjust distribution must be judged from the larger perspective, taking into account both the cost of the injustice and the comparative benefit of alternative crime control reforms.

F. UTILITY OF DESERT

One interesting aspect of the conflict between desert and utilitarian crime control is the recent claim that even a utilitarian analysis suggests a distribution of liability according to just desert. The utility of desert is said to arise from the greater compliance power of a criminal law that sets desert as its sole criterion and thereby earns a reputation for doing justice that gives it greater moral credibility with the community. Greater compliance would come from greater cooperation and acquiescence, the added deterrent effect of the law's increased capacity to stigmatize, the law's increased moral authority in declaring conduct morally condemnable, and the law's increased ability to influence the creation and reinforcement of shared norms.[1]

1) *Eliciting Cooperation and Acquiescence* Increasing the system's reputation for doing justice, it is argued, would elicit greater cooperation and acquiescence of those persons involved in the process (offenders, potential offenders, witnesses, jurors, etc.). Greatest cooperation is elicited where the criminal law's liability rules mirror the community's perceptions of the rules (those that most accurately give the punishment the offender deserves). Conflict between the law's rules and the community's views undercuts the moral credibility of the system and thereby engenders resistance and subversion.[2]

---

1. For a more detailed discussion of this point, see Paul H. Robinson & John M. Darley, The Utility of Desert, 91 Nw. U.L. Rev. 453 (1997).

2. See, e.g., Louis Michael Seidman, Soldiers, Martyrs, and Criminals: Utilitarian Theory and the Problem of Crime Control, 94 Yale L.J. 315, 319 (1984); Saul M. Kassin & L.S. Wrightsman, The American Jury on Trial, 158-159 (1988), Alan W. Scheflin & Jon Van Dyke, Jury Nullification: The contours of a controversy, 43 Law & Contemp. Probs. 52, 71-75 (1980); Mortimer R. Kadish & Sanford H. Kadish, Discretion to Disobey 32-33 (1973).

2) Moral Condemnation as Deterrence Increasing the law's moral credibility also increases its power to bring moral condemnation on an offender. People will take a criminal's conviction as a reliable signal that condemnation is deserved if the system has earned moral credibility. The law earns such credibility through a history of publicly committing itself to imposing punishment that is morally deserved; no more, no less. From the utilitarian's perspective, this mechanism is attractive because moral condemnation is an inexpensive yet powerful form of deterrent threat. It demands none of the costs that attend imprisonment or even supervised probation yet, for many persons, it is a powerful sanction that ought to be avoided. The more important social acceptance is to the person, the more terrible this threatened sanction. This marvelously cost-efficient sanction is available, however, only if the system has earned moral credibility. Each time the system is seen to convict where no community condemnation is appropriate, the condemnation for subsequent convictions is weakened.

3) Law as Moral Authority in Unsettled or Borderline Cases If the criminal law earns a reputation as a reliable statement of what the community perceives as condemnable, people are more likely to defer to its commands as morally authoritative and as appropriate to follow in those borderline cases where the actor is unsure about the propriety of certain conduct. This role should not be underestimated; in a society characterized by complex interdependencies, as ours is, apparently harmless actions can have destructive consequences (such as with insider trading). Sometimes these actions will be criminalized by the legal system, and one would want citizens to respect the law in that particular instance, even though they did not immediately intuit why that action was banned. This will be facilitated if the citizens are disposed to believe that the law is an accurate guide to appropriate prudential and moral behavior.

4) Law's Influence in Shaping Society's Norms The real power in shaping people's conduct lies in the networks of interpersonal relationships in which people find themselves, the social norms and prohibitions shared among those relationships and transmitted through those social networks, and the internalized representations of those norms and moral precepts. But law is not irrelevant to these forces. Criminal law, in particular, plays a central role in creating and maintaining the social consensus on morality necessary to sustain norms. In fact, in a society as diverse as ours, the criminal law may be the only mechanism that is society-wide, transcending cultural and ethnic differences. Thus, the criminal law's most important real-world effect can be its ability to assist in building, shaping, and maintaining these norms and moral principles. A central mechanism by which criminal law has a long-term crime-reducing effect therefore, is to contribute to and harness the compliance-producing power of interpersonal relationships and personal morality.

5) Compliance Power as Function of Moral Credibility The extent of the criminal law's effectiveness in both these respects — in facilitating and communicating societal consensus on what is and is not condemnable and in gaining compliance in borderline cases through deference to its moral authority — is to a great extent dependent on the degree of moral credibility that the criminal law has achieved in the minds of the citizens.[1] Thus, the criminal law's moral credibility is

---

1. See, e.g., Tom R. Tyler, Why People Obey the Law (1990); Austin Sarat, Studying American Legal Cultures: An Assessment of Survey Evidence, 11 L. & Socy. Rev. 427 (1977); Charles R. Tittle, Sanction and Social Deviance: A Question of Deterrence (1980).

essential, and it is enhanced if it mandates a distribution of liability that the community perceives as "doing justice"; that is, if it assigns liability and punishment in specific cases in ways that the community perceives as consistent with its sense of appropriate liability and punishment. Conversely, a distribution of liability that deviates from community perceptions of desert undermines the moral credibility of the criminal law.[1]

6) *Community's vs. Moral Philosophy's Conception of Desert* Note that the retributivists have not exactly won their argument with the utilitarians here. First, the arguments above are utilitarian in nature: They argue for use of a desert distribution because it has the *consequence* of reducing crime. Further, and perhaps more distressing to the retributivists, these arguments suggest a distribution of liability and punishment according to *public perceptions* of desert principles, not according to moral philosophy's notions. In a moral philospher's view, the community might be entirely wrong about the rules that generate desert. One can think of any number of societies that at one time accepted norms on liability and punishment that are now viewed as immoral. Community perceptions of desert may change while, at least theoretically, the principles of desert derived by moral philosophy do not.

7) *Community's Shared Intuitions of Justice* Following shared community intuitions of justice does not mean resolving individual cases as the public or the press desires in the heat of the moment. We know that the public and the press can lose perspective when buffeted by the biases and prejudices inspired by the facts of any particular case. The tendency of people to be more sympathetic to defendants and witnesses more like themselves is well documented.[2] In the long run, the criminal justice system will earn its moral credibility by relying not on public opinion of a case, but instead on the community's perception of just *principles* for determining liability and punishment. One ought not underestimate how complex a task it is to determine liability rules that will capture such shared community intuitions of justice. But recent empirical studies show that it is a feasible undertaking given the state of current social science methodology.[3]

---

1. See generally Paul H. Robinson & John M. Darley, Justice, Liability, and Blame: Community Views and the Criminal Law, chs. 1 & 7 (1995); Paul H. Robinson & John M. Darley, The Utility of Desert, 91 Nw. U.L. Rev. 453 (1997).

2. See, e.g., Jeffrey T. Frederick, The Psychology of the American Jury 166 (1987).

3. See, e.g., Paul H. Robinson & John M. Darley, Justice, Liability, and Blame: Community Views and the Criminal Law (1995). The authors suggest that there is a surprising amount of agreement on the principles of justice, across nearly all demographics. That will seem an odd claim as the school term continues and we see the wide variety of sentences that students impose on the defendants in the principal cases in this coursebook. But there are several reasons for this apparent disagreement, which do not necessarily undercut the above claim. First, the empirical studies suggest that there is a surprising amount of agreement about *the principles of justice.* There remain widely different views, however, about generally how harsh sentences should be; some students are harsh in their sentencing, others are lenient. What there is agreement on, the studies suggest, is in the factors that are seen as relevant to blameworthiness, the extent of their influence, and in the resulting rank-ordering of cases according to blameworthiness. That is, while some students will sentence high and some will sentence low, the *pattern* of liability among different cases is likely to be similar among even the high and the low students.

One other source of disagreement arises from the nature of the cases selected for this coursebook, which are a result of mining all of criminal law for the most difficult and interesting cases. As the title of the coursebook suggests, part of its mission is to focus on issues of controversy, and its selection of cases is meant to further that end.

◆ CASE STUDY
Sara Jane Olson

What liability, if any, would be imposed on Sara Jane Olson under each of the alternative principles discussed above for distributing liability and punishment — general deterrence, special deterrence, rehabilitation, incapacitation, just deserts — if each, in turn, were considered the sole distributive principle?

◉ DISCUSSION MATERIALS

Should Criminal Law Rules Be Formulated to Optimize Deterrence Through a Threatened Sanction?

The following excerpts explore the issues arising in the use of deterrence doctrine as a distributive principle. The criteria for an incapacitative distributive principle — dangerousness — and for a just deserts principle — moral blameworthiness — may be self-evident, at least in a general sense. But the criteria for a deterrence distributive principle may not be. As background, then, the Bentham excerpt gives some guidance. Johannes Andenaes speaks primarily to the inherent ethical obstacles of using the deterrence rationale, specifically with regard to "exemplary" punishments. Robinson and Darley use empirical evidence to critically explore the implementation and overall effectiveness of the doctrine in its current application.

Jeremy Bentham, The Theory of Legislation
322-324, 325-326, 336 (1931 ed.)

The Utility Principle as a Limit on Punishment

The cases in which punishment ought not be inflicted may be reduced to four heads; when punishment would be — 1st, Misapplied; 2nd, Inefficacious; 3rd, Superfluous; 4th, too expensive.

I. Punishments Misapplied. — Punishments are misapplied wherever there is no real offence, no evil of the first order or of the second order; or where the evil is more than compensated by an attendant good, as in the exercise of political or domestic authority, in the repulsion of a weightier evil, in self-defence, &c....

II. Inefficacious Punishments. — I call those punishments inefficacious which have no power to produce an effect upon the will, and which, in consequence, have no tendency towards the prevention of like acts.

Punishments are inefficacious when directed against individuals who could not know the law, who have acted without intention, who have done the evil innocently, under an erroneous supposition, or by irresistible constraint. Children, imbeciles, idiots, though they may be influenced, to a certain extent, by rewards and threats, have not a sufficient idea of futurity to be restrained by punishments. In their case laws have no efficacy. . . .

III. Superfluous Punishments. — Punishments are superfluous in cases where the same end may be obtained by means more mild — instruction, example, invitations, delays, rewards. A man spreads abroad pernicious opinions: shall the magistrate therefore seize the sword and punish him? No; if it is the interest of one individual to give currency to bad maxims, it is the interest of a thousand others to refute him.

IV. Punishments Too Expensive. — If the evil of the punishment exceeds the evil of the offence, the legislator will produce more suffering than he prevents. He will purchase exemption from a lesser evil at the expense of a greater evil. . . .

Punishments

First Rule. — The evil of the punishment must be made to exceed the advantage of the offence.

[E]rror is committed whenever a punishment is decreed which can only reach a certain point, while the advantage of the offence may go much beyond.

Some celebrated authors have attempted to establish a contrary maxim. They say that punishment ought to be diminished in proportion to the strength of temptation; that temptation diminishes the fault; and that the more potent seduction is, the less evidence we have of the offender's depravity.

This may be true; but it does not contravene the rule above laid down: for to prevent an offence, it is necessary that the repressive motive should be stronger than the seductive motive. The punishment must be more an object of dread than the offence is an object of desire. An insufficient punishment is a greater evil than an excess of rigour; for an insufficient punishment is an evil wholly thrown away. No good results from it, either to the public, who are left exposed to like offences, nor to the offender, whom it makes no better. What would be said of a surgeon, who, to spare a sick man a degree of pain, should leave the cure unfinished? Would it be a piece of enlightened humanity to add to the pains of the disorder the torment of a useless operation?

Second Rule. — The more deficient in certainty a punishment is, the severer it should be.

No man engages in a career of crime, except in the hope of impunity. If punishment consisted merely in taking from the guilty the fruits of his offence, and if that punishment were inevitable, no offence would be committed; for what man is so foolish as to run the risk of committing an offence with certainty of nothing but the shame of an unsuccessful attempt? In all cases of offence there is a calculation of the chances for and against; and it is necessary to give a much greater weight to the punishment, in order to counterbalance the chances of impunity.

It is true, then, that the more certain punishment is, the less severe it need be. . . . For the same reason it is desirable that punishment should follow offence as closely as possible; for its impression upon the minds of men is weakened by distance, and, besides, distance adds to the uncertainty of punishment, by affording new chances of escape.

Third Rule. — Where two offences are in conjunction, the greater offence ought to be subjected to severer punishment, in order that the delinquent may have a motive to stop at the lesser.

Two offences may be said to be in conjunction when a man has the power and the will to commit both of them. A highwayman may content himself with robbing, or he may begin with murder, and finish with robbery. The murder should be punished more severely than the robbery, in order to deter him from the greater offence....

Fourth Rule.—The greater an offence is, the greater reason there is to hazard a severe punishment for the chance of preventing it.

We must not forget that the infliction of punishment is a certain expense for the purchase of an uncertain advantage. To apply great punishments to small offences is to pay very dearly for the chance of escaping a slight evil....

In order that a punishment may adapt itself to the rules of proposition above laid down, it should...be susceptible of more or less, or divisible, in order to conform itself to variations in the gravity of offences. Chronic punishments, such as imprisonment and banishment, possess this quality in an eminent degree.

Johannes Andenaes, The General Preventive Effects of Punishment
114 University of Pennsylvania Law Review 949, 981-983 (1966)

Ethical Problems Connected with General Prevention

The use of any coercive measure raises ethical problems. This is so even when the motive rests upon the need to treat the person in question. To what extent are we justified in imposing upon someone a cure which he does not desire, and how are we to balance considerations in favor of his liberty against the need to eliminate the hazards he inflicts on society? Such problems are encountered in the public health services as well as in the exercise of criminal justice.

The conflict, however, assumes special proportions in connection with general prevention. It has often been said that punishment, in this context, is used not to prevent future violations on the part of the criminal, but in order to instill lawful behavior in others. The individual criminal is merely an instrument; he is sacrificed in a manner which is contrary to our ethical principles. This objection carries least weight in relation to general preventive notions connected with legislation. The law provides, for example, that whoever is found guilty of murder is liable to life imprisonment or that whoever drives a car when he is intoxicated is to be given a prison sentence of thirty days. Such penal provisions have been laid down with an aim to preventing *anyone* from performing the prohibited acts. If we accept the provisions as ethically defensible, we also have to accept the punishment prescribed in each individual case. As H.L.A. Hart has stated:

> The primary operation of criminal punishment consists simply in announcing certain standards of behavior and attaching penalties for deviation, making it less eligible, and then leaving individuals to choose. This is a method of social control which maximizes individual freedom within the coercive framework of law in a number of different ways.

The question, however, comes to a head when the individual penalty is decided by general preventions considerations, in other words, exemplary penalties. I have previously mentioned the sentences given in connection with the race riots in London in 1958. According to the newspaper bulletins, the penalties assessed in the earlier cases were lenient, ranging from six weeks to three months. As the riots continued, the courts introduced heavy penalties of four years imprisonment. "A groan of surprise came from the audience when the judgments were read," a correspondent reported. "On the galleries were seated the mothers of several of the boys, and they were led outside, weeping. Two of the boys were themselves totally paralyzed by the sentences and had to be helped out of the dock to their cells below the courtroom." The reporter continues: "After the encounters in West London, however, the race riots have waned away just as quickly as they started. The reason why they came to an end is undoubtedly the strong public reaction against racial persecution together with the resolute intervention of the police and the courts."

If the correspondent is right, the unusually heavy penalties in this case had a desirable effect, but the judgment is nevertheless felt to be ethically problematic. There is an element of ex post facto law involved in such sentences. Although the judge operates within the framework of the law, such sentences are not, in fact, applications of previously established norms. The judge establishes a norm to suit the situation. Nor does the result square with the ideal of equality before the law. The procedure calls to mind a practice which—at least according to historical novels—was commonly used in former times when a number of soldiers committed mutiny or similar grave violations: the commanding officer would have a suitable number of soldiers shot in order to instill fear and give warning, and the remaining soldiers were readmitted to service without penalty.

Such ethical doubts become even stronger if the individual sentence depends upon the kind of publicity—and hence the kind of preventive effect—which is expected. Suppose a judge is faced with two similar cases within a short interval. In the first case, the courtroom is filled with journalists, and the outcome of the trial is likely to become known to millions of readers. In the second case, the listener's benches are empty and, in all probability, the verdict will not spread far beyond the circles of those who are present in the courtroom. Is it defensible for the judge to pass heavy judgment in the first instance because the sentence is likely to gain much publicity and consequently bring about strong general preventive effects, while the defendant in the second case is merely given a warning because punishment in his case would only mean personal suffering, and would not yield results from a social point of view? Such speculation upon the general preventive effects of the individual sentence easily become tinged with cynicism and for ethical reasons this approach is only acceptable within very narrow limits.

Paul H. Robinson & John M. Darley, The Role of Deterrence in the Formulation of Criminal Law Rules: At Its Worst When Doing Its Best
91 Georgetown Law Journal 949, 950-956 (2003)

For the past several decades, the deterrence of crime has been a centerpiece of criminal law reform. Law-givers have sought to optimize the control of crime by devising a penalty-setting system that assigns criminal punishments of a magnitude sufficient to deter a thinking individual from committing a crime. Although this seems initially an intuitively compelling strategy, we are going to suggest that it is a poor one; poor for two reasons. First, its effectiveness rests on a set of assumptions that on examination cannot be sustained. Second, the attempt to employ the strategy generates a good many crimogenic costs that are hidden if one is functioning within a deterrence paradigm.

Experience has taught us to be precise about exactly what we are saying about the effectiveness of a deterrence strategy. There seems little doubt that having a criminal justice system that punishes violators, as every organized society has, does have an general effect in influencing the conduct of potential offenders. This we concede: having a punishment system does deter. But there is growing evidence to suggest skepticism about the criminal law's deterrent effect — that is, skepticism about the ability to deter crime through the manipulation of criminal law rules and penalties. The general existence of the system may well deter prohibited conduct but the formulation of criminal law rules within the system according to a deterrence-optimizing analysis may have a limited effect or even no effect beyond the system's broad deterrent warning that has already been achieved. We will suggest that it may be true that criminal law manipulation can influence behavior, but the conditions under which this can happen are unusual, rather than typical, in criminal justice systems of modern societies. By contrast, criminal law makers and adjudicators formulate and apply criminal law rules on the assumption that they always influence conduct. And it is this taken-for-granted assumption that we find so disturbing and so dangerous.

Let us briefly sketch our line of argument and conclusions: [T]he social science literature . . . suggests a skeptical view of criminal law deterrence. There is reason to think that potential offenders do not know the law, do not make rational choices, and/or do not perceive an expected cost for a violation that outweighs the expected gain.

In sharp contrast, criminal law has been formulated on the assumption that those legal formulation decisions will have a direct deterrent effect on conduct, and that assumption has been used in formulating nearly every aspect of criminal law, from defining the rules of conduct, to formulating principles of liability, to determining offense grades, to setting sentencing rules and practice.

Even if one concludes that deterrence skepticism overstates its case, there remain reasons for serious concern. We argue that even on the most cautious reading of the available studies enough is known to urge an end to the past practice of formulating criminal law based on a deterrence-optimizing analysis. [W]e offer four primary arguments.

First, a disabling problem for deterrence as a distributive principle is its need for information that is not available and not likely to be available any time in the foreseeable future. Formulating criminal law rules according to a deterrence analysis can produce erroneous results if based upon missing or unreliable data. In fact, inadequately informed analyses could produce criminal law rules that reduce rather than increase the possibility of deterrence. In such an informational void, we argue, it makes sense to follow a distributive principle that at the very least can achieve its objectives.

Further, even if full and perfect information were available, we argue that the dynamics of deterrence are dramatically more complex than has been supposed. The deterrent process involves complex interactions, like substitution effects, that make deterrent predictions enormously difficult. And the deterrent process is a dynamic rather than a static one. A criminal law rule manipulation may well increase deterrent effect as hoped, but that effect can itself change the existing conditions and require a new and different deterrence calculation....

Second, once it is recognized that any distributive principle for criminal liability and punishment will produce some deterrent effect (if any is to be had). A deterrence-based distribution makes sense only if it can provide meaningfully greater deterrent effect than that already inherent in competing distributions that advance other valuable goals, such as doing justice.

So, and third, there is an important implication here. Deterrence can only do better than another distribution—such as a justice distribution (by "justice distribution" we mean a distribution according to the shared intuitions of justice of the community bound by the law)—only if and where it deviates from it. Thus, a deterrence-based distribution can deter better than a justice-based distribution only if and where it deviates from a just result. But it is just these instances of deviation from justice in which it is most difficult to get a deterrent effect. People assume the law is as they think it should be, which is according to their own collective notions of justice. Thus, the simple prerequisite of making the deterrence-based rule now becomes a serious task. Further, it is these deviation-from-justice cases in which the system's deterrence-based rules are least likely to be followed. Because people commonly think of criminal liability and punishment in terms of justice, rather than deterrence, the exercise of police, prosecutorial, and judicial discretion, as well as jury nullification, commonly subvert application of deterrence-based deviation rules, thus subverting the deterrence program and confusing the deterrence message.

Fourth, even if one assumes for the sake of argument that a deterrence-based distribution produces a greater deterrent effect than a justice-based distribution despite its special deviation problems, there is reason to be concerned that the deterrence-based distribution simultaneously produces crime, because its deviation from the community's shared intuitions of justice can undercut the criminal law's moral credibility, lessening its crime-control power as a moral authority, a dynamic that we suspect can have significant crimogenic effect. Thus, even if a deterrence-based distribution did successfully produce a greater deterrent effect than a justice-based distribution, that greater deterrent effect might be offset by its greater crimogenic effect in undercutting the moral authority of the criminal law. These are the potential costs that we referred to above, that are incurred by a deterrence-based system.

We believe that optimizing deterrence through doctrinal manipulation is possible, but only under narrow conditions not typical in American criminal justice. There are possibilities for reform that might broaden these conditions, but also serious limitations, due in large part to the sacrifices such reforms would demand: in greater financial cost, in infringing interests of privacy and freedom from governmental intrusion, in compromising basic notions of procedural fairness, and in doing injustice and failing to do justice. Our conclusion is that if one takes a realistic view of deterrence, even after plausible reforms are made, little increase in the deterrent effect of doctrinal manipulation would be produced, and not enough to justify its continued use as the standard mechanism of criminal law-making....

I. Growing Reasons to Be Skeptical of Criminal Law Deterrence

If a criminal law rule is to deter violators, three prerequisites must be satisfied: the potential offender must know of the rule, he must perceive the cost of violation as greater than the perceived benefit, and he must be able and willing to bring such knowledge to bear on his conduct decision at the time of the offense. But typically, one or more of these three hurdles block any material deterrent effect of doctrinal manipulation. The social science literature suggests that potential offenders commonly do not know the law, do not perceive an expected cost for a violation that outweighs the expected gain, and do not make rational self-interest choices. Let us summarize the central conclusions of the literature that are relevant to our current inquiry.

The available studies suggest that most people do not know the law, that even career criminals who have a special incentive to know it do not, and that even when people think they know the law they frequently are wrong. Potential offenders typically do not read law books and their ability to learn the law even indirectly through hearing or reading of particular cases is limited by the fact that the legal rule is just one of hundreds of variables that have play in a case disposition. To devine the operative liability rule, hidden under the effects of all the other variables, would require both a higher number of reported cases than potential offenders are exposed to and a mind for complex calculation beyond that which is reasonable to expect.

As to the perceived net-cost hurdle, the possibilities of deterrent effect are weakened by the difficulties in establishing a punishment rate that would be meaningful to potential offenders, the difficulties in avoiding the delay in imposition of punishment that seriously erodes its deterrent effect, and the difficulties in establishing and modulating the amount of punishment imposed, as an effective deterrence distribution of punishment must do.

Establishing some base expectation of a meaningful chance of punishment is also a necessary condition to any deterrent effect. Yet, the perceived probability of punishment is low, to the point where the threatened punishment commonly is not thought to be relevant to the potential offender.

A delay between violation and punishment can dramatically reduce the perceived cost of the violation. Even if the punishment is certain, the more distant it is, the more its weight as a threat will be discounted. Further, the strength of the punishment memory — that is, its recalled punitive "bite" as a perceived threat for a future violation — is dramatically reduced as the length of delay increases. Unfortunately, in modern criminal justice such delay is substantial.

As to amount of punishment, there is no question that any system that can impose punishment can produce a credible deterrent "bite". The challenge for a deterrence-based system is to modulate the threatened punishment bite as the program for optimum deterrence requires. Lawmakers assume they have the greatest control over this aspect of the cost-benefit calculus in that they can modulate bite by simply altering the length of prison term. But in reality, the studies suggest that this aspect of the cost-benefit balance is neither simple nor predictable. The forces at work in determining the perceived amount of punishment are complex. For example, the "hedonic adaptation" and "subjective well-being" studies suggest that one's standard for judging perceived punitive effect changes over time and conditions. (Both paraplegics and lottery winners return to their original state of well-being despite their dramatically changed circumstances.) Thus, as a prison term continues, it can become increasingly less painful in effect, although its cost per unit time remains constant, making it increasingly less cost effective.

Further, it appears that it is the intensity of the punishment experience, rather than its duration, that is of significant effect. Indeed, because the remembered intensity is highly influenced by the end-point intensity, which we note above decreases over time, it is possible that the overall remembered "bite" of a prison term decreases as it gets longer! The point here is that, while legislatures (and judges) believe they can reliably manipulate the amount of punishment threatened by simply manipulating the length of the prison term, such manipulation does not provide the punishment bite they assume.

As to the rational decision-making hurdle, there are a host of conditions that interfere with the rational calculation of self-interest by potential offenders: drug or alcohol use, personality types inclined toward impulsiveness and toward discounting consequences, and social influences such as the arousal effect of group action and the tendency of group members to calculate in terms of group rather than individual interests. Further, these conditions are disproportionately high among deterrence's primary target group: those persons for whom criminal conduct is not already ruled out by their own internalized norms or by those of their family or peers. This bodes ill for effective deterrence because it precludes, or at least diminishes, a rule's deterrent effect even if the rule is known and is backed by what is perceived as a meaningful threat of punishment. We can expect greater deterrent possibilities when dealing with more rational target audiences, such as white collar offenders. Unfortunately, the more serious and the more common offenses tend to be committed by persons less likely to exercise rationality.

The most serious problems for deterrent effect stem from the combined effect of all three of these hurdles. A well known rule carrying a credible threat of punishment that exceeds the benefit of the offense will be ineffective nonetheless in deterring a person caught up in rage, group arousal, and drug effects, as in many gang-related offenses. A rational calculator who fears any form of punishment even if the likelihood of it is slight, nonetheless will not be deterred by a rule that he does not know, as where a homeowner shoots to protect his home, unaware that the law does not allow deadly force in protection of property alone. And a rule well known by a rational calculator as carrying a meaningful penalty nonetheless will not deter if the chance of getting caught is seen as trivial, as with rampant tax cheating.

● DISCUSSION MATERIALS

Should Criminal Law Rules Be Formulated to Optimize Rehabilitation or, Failing That, the Incapacitation of Dangerous Persons?

In these materials Andrew von Hirsch traces the development of the incapacitation and rehabilitation rationales while James Wilson evaluates some of the scientific research done to implement an effective incapacitation system. Finally, Robinson offers a conceptual look at the relationship between prevention and punishment, at the conflict that inheres, and at its broad effects on the criminal justice system.

James Q. Wilson, Thinking About Crime
145-158 (rev. ed. 1983)

When criminals are deprived of their liberty, as by imprisonment . . . , their ability to commit offenses against citizens is ended. We say these persons have been "incapacitated," and we try to estimate the amount by which crime is reduced by this incapacitation.

. . . [T]here is one great advantage to incapacitation as a crime control strategy — namely, it does not require us to make any assumptions about human nature. By contrast, deterrence works only if people take into account the costs and benefits of alternative courses of action and choose that which confers the largest net benefit (or the smallest net cost). . . . Rehabilitation works only if the values, preferences, or time-horizon of criminals can be altered by plan. . . .

Incapacitation, on the other hand, works by definition: Its effects result from the physical restraint of the offender and not from his subjective state. More accurately, it works provided at least three conditions are met: Some offenders must be repeaters; offenders taken off the streets must not be immediately and completely replaced by new recruits; and prison must not sufficiently increase the post-release criminal activity of those who have been incarcerated sufficiently to offset the crimes prevented by their stay in prison.

The first condition is surely true. Every study of prison inmates shows that a large fraction (recently, about two-thirds) of them had prior criminal records before their current incarceration; every study of ex-convicts shows that a significant fraction (estimates vary from a quarter to a half) are rearrested for new offenses within a relatively brief period. In short, the great majority of persons in prison are repeat offenders, and thus prison, whatever else it may do, protects society from the offenses these persons would commit if they were free.

The second condition — that incarcerating one robber does not lead automatically to the recruitment of a new robber to replace him — seems plausible. Although some persons, such as Ernest van den Haag, have argued that new offenders will step forward to take the place vacated by the imprisoned offenders, they have presented no evidence that this is the case, except, perhaps, for certain crimes (such as narcotics trafficking or prostitution), which are organized along business lines. For . . . predatory street crimes . . . — robbery, burglary, auto theft, larceny — there are no barriers to entry and no scarcity of criminal opportunities. . . . In general, the earnings of street criminals are not affected by how many "competitors" they have.

The third condition that must be met if incapacitation is to work is that prisons must not be such successful "schools for crime" that the crimes prevented by incarceration are outnumbered by the increased crimes committed after release attributable to what was learned in prison. It is doubtless the case that for some offenders prison is a school; it is also doubtless that for other offenders prison is a deterrent. The former group will commit more, or more skillful, crimes after release; the latter will commit fewer crimes after release. The question, therefore, is whether the net effect of these two offsetting tendencies is positive or negative.... In general, there is no evidence that the prison experience makes offenders as a whole more criminal, and there is some evidence that certain kinds of offenders (especially certain younger ones) may be deterred by a prison experience....

To determine the amount of crime that is prevented by incarcerating a given number of offenders for a given length of time, the key estimate we must make is the number of offenses a criminal commits per year free on the street. If a community experiences one thousand robberies a year, it obviously makes a great deal of difference whether these robberies are the work of ten robbers, each of whom commits one hundred robberies per year, or the work of one thousand robbers, each of whom commits only one robbery per year. In the first case, locking up only five robbers will cut the number of robberies in half; in the second case, locking up one hundred robbers will only reduce the number of robberies by 10 percent.

...Working with individual adult criminal records of all those persons arrested in Washington, D.C., during 1973 for any one of six major crimes (over five thousand persons in all), Alfred Blumstein and Jacqueline Cohen suggested that the individual offense rate varied significantly for different kinds of offenders. For example, it was highest for larceny and lowest for aggravated assault. But they also found, as had other scholars before them, that there was not a great deal of specialization among criminals—a person arrested today for robbery might be arrested next time for burglary. The major contribution of their study was the ingenious method they developed for converting the number of times persons were arrested into an estimate of the number of crimes they actually committed, a method that took into account the fact that many crimes are not reported to the police, that most crimes known to the police do not result in arrest, and that some crimes are likely to be committed by groups of persons rather than by single offenders. Combining all the individual crimes rates, the offenders in this study (a group of adults who had been arrested at least twice in Washington, D.C.) committed between nine and seventeen serious offenses per year free.

...[C]onfidence in the Blumstein-Cohen estimates was increased when the results of a major study at the Rand Corporation became known. Researchers there had been interviewing prisoners... to find out directly from known offenders how much crime they were committing while free.... [T]he Rand researchers cross-checked the information against arrest records and looked for evidence of internal consistency in the self-reports. Moreover, the inmates volunteered information about crimes they had committed but for which they had not been arrested....

The Rand group found that the average California prisoner had committed about fourteen serious crimes per year during each of the three years he was free.... To state the California findings in slightly different terms, if no one was confined in state prison, the number of armed robberies in California would be about 22 percent higher than it is now....

But the Rand group learned something else which would turn out to be even more important. The "average" individual offense rate was virtually a meaningless term because the inmates they interviewed differed so sharply in how many crimes they committed. A large number of offenders committed a small number of offenses while free and a small number of offenders committed a very large number of offenses. In statistical language, the distribution of offenses was highly skewed. For example, the median number of burglaries committed by the inmates in the three states was about 5 a year, but the 10 percent of the inmates who were the highest-rate offenders committed an average of 232 burglaries a year. The median number of robberies was also about 5 a year, but the top 10 percent of offenders committed an average of 87 a year. As Peter W. Greenwood, one of the members of the Rand group, put it, incarcerating one robber who was among the top 10 percent in offense rates would prevent more robberies than incarcerating eighteen offenders who were at or below the median. . . .

[A]ll the evidence we have implies that, for crime-reduction purposes, the most rational way to use the incapacitative powers of our prisons would be to do so selectively. Instead of longer sentences for everyone, or for persons who have prior records, or for persons whose present crime is especially grave, longer sentences would be given primarily to those who, when free, commit the most crimes. . . .

But how do we know who these high-rate, repeat criminals are? Knowing the nature of the present offense is not a good clue. The reason for this is quite simple — most street criminals do not specialize. Today's robber can be tomorrow's burglar and the next day's car thief. When the police happen to arrest him, the crime for which he is arrested is determined by a kind of lottery — he happened to be caught red-handed, or as the result of a tip, committing a particular crime that may or may not be the same as either his previous crime or his next one. If judges give sentences based entirely on the gravity of the present offense, then a high-rate offender may get off lightly because on this occasion he happened to be caught snatching a purse. The low-rate offender may get a long sentence because he was unlucky enough to be caught robbing a liquor store with a gun. . . . [W]hile society's legitimate desire for retribution must set the outer bounds of any sentencing policy, there is still room for flexibility within those bounds. We can, for example, act so that all robbers are punished with prison terms, but give, within certain relatively narrow ranges, longer sentences to those robbers who commit the most crimes.

If knowing the nature of the present offense and even knowing the prior record of the offender are not accurate guides to identifying high-rate offenders, what is? . . . In the Rand study, Greenwood and his colleagues discovered . . . that the following seven factors, taken together, were highly predictive of a convicted person being a high-rate offender: he (1) was convicted of a crime while a juvenile (that is, before age sixteen), (2) used illegal drugs as a juvenile, (3) used illegal drugs during the previous two years, (4) was employed less than 50 percent of the time during the previous two years, (5) served time in a juvenile facility, (6) was incarcerated in prison more than 50 percent of the previous two years, and (7) was previously convicted for the present offense.

Using this scale, Greenwood found that 82 percent of those predicted to be low-rate offenders in fact were, and 82 percent of those predicted to be medium- or high-rate offenders also were. To understand how big these differences are, the median California prison inmate who is predicted to be a low-rate offender will in fact commit slightly more than one burglary and slightly less than one robbery per year free. By contrast, the median California inmate who is predicted to be a high-rate offender will commit ninety-three burglaries and thirteen robberies per year free....

Andrew von Hirsch, Incapacitation
In von Hirsch & Ashworth eds., Principled Sentencing 101-108 (1992)

Incapacitation is the idea of simple restraint: rendering the convicted offender incapable, for a period of time, of offending again. Whereas rehabilitation involves changing the person's habits or attitudes so he or she becomes less criminally inclined, incapacitation presupposes no such change. Instead, obstacles are interposed to impede the person's carrying out whatever criminal inclinations he or she may have. Usually, the obstacle is the walls of a prison, but other incapacitative techniques are possible—such as exile or house arrest.

Incapacitation has, usually, been sought through predicting the offender's likelihood of reoffending. Those deemed more likely to reoffend are to be restrained, for example, by imposition of a term of imprisonment—or of a prison term of longer duration than they otherwise would receive....

Who, then, is likely to reoffend? Prediction research in criminology has had a more than sixty-year history.... The basic research technique has been straightforward enough. Various facts about convicted criminals are recorded: previous arrests and convictions, social and employment history, prior drug use, and so forth; and those factors that are, statistically, more strongly associated with recidivism are identified. The prediction instrument, based on these factors, is then constructed and tested. The studies suggest that a limited capacity to predict does exist. Certain facts about offenders—principally, their previous criminal records, drug habits, and histories of unemployment—are(albeit only to a modest extent) indicative of increased likelihood of recidivism.

Incapacitation was an important (although often less visible) element in the traditional rehabilitative penal ethic. Sentencing judges and correctional officials were supposed to gauge not only offenders' treatment needs but their likelihood of recidivism. "Curable" offenders were to be treated (in the community, if possible), but those judged bad risks were to be restrained. The traditional view had its appeal precisely because it thus offered both therapy and restraint. One did not have to assume that all criminals really were treatable, but merely that some might be. Therapy could be tried on the potentially responsive, but always with a fail-safe: the offender who seemed unsuitable for treatment could be separated from the community....

In the early 1970s, some penologists began raising doubts about predictive restraint in sentencing.... [Critics noted] that prediction in sentencing does not have to be left to judge's personal judgment. Before a defendant is incarcerated on incapacitative grounds, the degree of harmfulness of the predicted conduct, and its required degree of likelihood, could be specified in advance. The predictions could also rely, not on someone's intuitive sense of who is a bad risk, but on statistically tested forecasting methods. The question asked is whether—once these threshold requirements are met—it is fair to rely on forecasts of dangerousness in deciding the sentence.

In this connection, [commentators pointed] to the tendency of forecasts of criminality to overpredict. Although statistical forecasting methods can identify groups of offenders having higher than average probabilities of recidivism, these methods show a disturbing incidence of "false positives." Many of those classified as potential recidivists will, in fact, not be found to offend again. The rate of false positive is particularly high when forecasting serious criminality — for example, violence. The majority of those designated as dangerous turn out — when the predictions are followed up — to be persons who are not found to commit the predicted acts of violence when allowed to remain at large. . . .

False positives put the justice of predictive sentencing into question. Ostensibly, the offender classified as dangerous is confined to prevent him or her from infringing the rights of others. But to the extent the classification is mistaken, the offender would not have committed the infringement. The person's liberty is lost merely because people *like* him or her will offend again, and we cannot specify which of them will actually do so. . . .

[Some defenders of predictive sentencing concede the false positive problem and admit that in predicting dangerousness] at least half of those classified as risks will mistakenly be so classified. With such a high incidence of error, how then can sentencing on the basis of dangerousness be justified? It can only be [justified, these defenders suggest,] by the idea of shifting the burden of risk. An unconvicted dangerous person is entitled to remain at large, and any risk to potential victims must be borne by them. Once the person acts on the dangerous inclinations and is convicted for seriously harming others, however, we become entitled to shift the risk of victimization (in this case, of mistaken confinement) to the offender. Error is unavoidable, and the question is, who should bear its costs? . . .

[Such views raise a number of questions.] [E]ven if restraining the dangerous were justifiable on . . . such . . . "shifting of risk" [grounds,] one still has not explained why an offender's *punishment* should be extended on that ground. Punishment, [for many commentators,] involves not only deprivation but blame — so that increasing punishment implies the offender to be more blameworthy. . . . There is nothing about a convicted offender's dangerousness — that is, the mere likelihood of offending again as contrasted with the degree of culpability for crimes already committed — which renders him or her more to blame. Thus if confining offenders beyond their deserved term of punishment were justifiable at all, that confinement would be civil, not criminal. . . .

In the early 1980s, a number of studies, based mainly on interviews with incarcerated offenders, suggested that offense patterns are highly skewed, even among those individuals who recidivate after being convicted. While some recidivists reoffended only occasionally, others appeared to revert to serious criminality frequently. If incapacitative techniques could be targeted to the latter group — to the frequent, serious violators — might these techniques not offer hope, after all, for reducing crime?

It was during this period that Peter Greenwood, a Rand Corporation researcher, published a report on a prediction technique which he termed "selective incapacitation." The technique, derived from interviews with confined offenders, made use of a few simple indicia of dangerousness, concerned mainly with the offender's criminal, unemployment, and drug-use histories. It was designed to identify "high-rate" predators — those who would commit violent offenses (such as robbery) frequently. Because so many robberies were being committed by a small group of active predators, he argued, identifying and isolating these persons could considerably reduce the incidence of such crimes. Greenwood devised a method of projecting the resulting crime reduction effect. He estimated that imposing longer prison terms for the high-rate offenders could reduce the robbery rate by as much as 15 to 20 percent, without even any significant increase in prison populations.

Greenwood's suggestions generated considerable interest among criminologists and policymakers [who argued, among other things, that selective incapacitation is] not unfair or undeserved...because desert sets merely the broadest outer limits on permissible punishments. Reliance on status factors such as employment is no serious problem, because such factors are used by the criminal justice system in other contexts. The possible inaccuracies of the prediction technique should be no bar to use, because the technique is superior to the informal predictive judgments that judges and prosecutors make today....

The optimism...about selective incapacitation was soon challenged, however. Objections were raised both about the empirical soundness of the technique and about its ethics....

The empirical objections [questioned] whether Greenwood's factors can identify high-rate offenders, once official data that courts must rely upon are utilized, instead of offenders' self-reports of their own criminal activities. The projections of large crime-reduction effects are also suspect. Those projections rely on questionable extrapolations, from the criminal activity of *incarcerated* offenders to the activity of offenders generally. The projections also appear to make unrealistic estimates of such important factors as the anticipated length of offenders' criminal careers. In 1986, a research panel of the National Academy of Science examined these issues, and concluded that selective incapacitation at least today, has a much more modest crime-reduction potential than Greenwood ... claim[s].

The ethical objection to selective incapacitation...consists chiefly in the strategy's conflict with the requirements of proportionality. Selective incapacitation relies upon factors (e.g. early criminal history, drug use, and so forth) that have little bearing on the blameworthiness of the criminal conduct for which the offender stands convicted. The strategy can have significant crime prevention effects by its own proponents' reckoning, moreover, only if disparities among those convicted of comparable offenses are very large: the prison sentences visited on "high-risk" felons must be *much* longer than those visited on lower-risk felons convicted of the same offense. To sustain such large disparities, proportionality must either be disregarded or be treated as only marginal constraint.

Paul H. Robinson, Punishing Dangerousness: Cloaking Preventive Detention as Criminal Justice

114 Harvard Law Review 1429-1432, 1434-1439, 1444-1446, 1450-1454 (2001)

Laypersons have traditionally thought of the criminal justice system as being in the business of doing justice: punishing offenders for the crimes they commit. Yet during the past several decades, the justice system's focus has shifted from punishing past crimes to preventing future violations through the incarceration and control of dangerous offenders. Habitual offender statutes, such as "three strikes" laws, authorize life sentences for repeat offenders. Jurisdictional reforms have decreased the age at which juveniles may be tried as adults. Gang membership and recruitment are now punished. "Megan's Law" statutes require community notification of convicted sex offenders. "Sexual predator" statutes provide for the civil detention of sexual offenders who remain dangerous at the conclusion of their criminal commitment. New sentencing guidelines increase the sentence of offenders with criminal histories because these offenders are seen as the most likely to commit future crimes. These reforms boast as their common denominator greater official control over dangerous persons, a rationale readily apparent from each reform's legislative history.

Although the individual legislative histories make clear that a preventive rationale has motivated each of these reforms, the system's general shift from punishment toward prevention has not been accompanied by a corresponding shift in how the system presents itself. While increasingly designed to prevent dangerous persons from committing future crimes, the system still alleges that it is doing criminal "justice" and imposing "punishment." Yet it is impossible to "punish dangerousness." To "punish" is "to cause (a person) to undergo pain, loss, or suffering for a crime or wrongdoing" — therefore, punishment can only exist in relation to a past wrong. "Dangerous" means "likely to cause injury, pain, etc." — that is, dangerousness describes a threat of future harm. One can "restrain," "detain," or "incapacitate" a dangerous person, but one cannot logically "punish" dangerousness.

Why the shift to preventive detention? Why the wish to keep the old criminal "punishment" facade? These are the starting points of inquiry in this Commentary. It concludes that the trend of the last decade — the shifting of the criminal justice system toward the detention of dangerous offenders — is a move in the wrong direction. The difficulty lies not in the laudable attempt to prevent future crime but rather in the use of the criminal justice system as the vehicle to achieve that goal. The approach perverts the justice process and undercuts the criminal justice system's long-term effectiveness in controlling crime. At the same time, the basic features of the criminal justice system make it a costly yet ineffective preventive detention system.

Segregation of the punishment and prevention functions offers a superior alternative. Punishment and prevention are fundamentally different; they rely on different criteria and call for different procedures. Punishment, especially through imprisonment, happily produces a beneficial collateral effect of incapacitation. If preventive detention is needed beyond the prison term of deserved punishment, it ought to be provided by a system that is open about its preventive purpose and is specifically designed to perform that function.

The Justice Problems

From this perspective, it is understandable that today's citizens are demanding greater protection and that legislators are seeking new ways to provide it. But the use of the criminal justice system as the primary mechanism for preventing future crimes seriously perverts the goals of our institutions of justice.

Lowering the age for adult prosecution, with its longer terms of imprisonment, is likely to increase societal protection. Juveniles are committing an increasing number of serious crimes. But decreasing the age at which a juvenile can be prosecuted as an adult increases the number of cases in which a young offender lacking the capacity for moral choice is nonetheless held criminally liable.

There is little dispute that many young offenders, especially those below the age of fifteen, lack the cognitive and control capacities of normal adults. Some may not appreciate the enormity of the consequences of their acts and others may lack normal behavior control mechanisms. If an adult offender is similarly dysfunctional, due to insanity or involuntary intoxication for example, an excuse defense is generally available. Yet a young offender impaired in a similar way by immaturity has no defense or mitigation, because adult courts traditionally have not recognized an immaturity excuse. Courts have had no need to make such an excuse available in the past for the obvious reason that juvenile courts dealt with the cases involving youthful offenders. The recent trend toward trying youths in adult courts has created the need for such an excuse defense, but none has been developed, perhaps because the defense would interfere with the goal of gaining control over dangerous offenders without regard to their blamelessness.

A more common and more damaging distortion of justice derives from the use of "three strikes" and other habitual offender statutes, and the use of prevention-oriented sentencing guidelines that dramatically increase sentences for offenders with prior criminal records. These reforms affect nearly every case in which an offender has a prior criminal record.

Shocking cases of long-term imprisonment for minor offenses are well known. In Rummel v. Estelle, for example, the defendant took $129.75 from a bar owner to fix the bar's air conditioner with no intention of actually doing so. His conviction for fraud was his third, qualifying him for a term of life imprisonment without the possibility of parole under an early "three strikes" statute.

But problems are inherent not only in the shocking cases but in every case in which a habitual offender statute or prior-record-based sentencing guideline applies. In these cases, the sentence imposed exceeds the deserved punishment, albeit to a less dramatic extent than life imprisonment for minor check fraud. The imposition of that excess punishment is, of course, the motivating goal of such statutes: they significantly increase the sentence beyond the level deserved for the crime because a prior record may predict future offenses. But the effect of such a policy is that the criminal justice system regularly imposes sentences that exceed the punishment deserved. Sentencing guidelines that give great weight to prior criminal records and "three strikes" and related habitual offender provisions commonly double, triple, or quadruple the punishment imposed on repeat offenders. An initial portion of the sentence may well be deserved, but what follows is a purely preventive detention portion that cannot be justified as deserved punishment.

One can construct a theory that makes a prior criminal record relevant to deserved punishment, as Andrew von Hirsch has done. By committing an offense after a previous conviction, an offender might be seen as "thumbing his nose" at the justice system. Such disregard may justify some incremental increase in punishment over that deserved by a first-time offender, but it seems difficult to justify the doubling, tripling, or quadrupling of punishment because of nose-thumbing.

The recidivist nature of a second robbery is only one of many characteristics that determine blameworthiness. Lay intuitions may see the nose-thumbing as making the second robbery more condemnable than the first but not more condemnable than the second robbery itself, and certainly not twice as condemnable as the second robbery. But note that, although nose-thumbing may justify a minor portion of the dramatic increases imposed for a prior record, the theory allows proponents of preventive detention to implement their program unobtrusively within a system of criminal punishment.

Further, if such disrespect for law provided the impetus for these statutes, the aggravation of blameworthiness and increased punishment would apply to all offenses. That is, if nose-thumbing is itself condemnable, then it ought to be condemnable in every context, not just in selected contexts. Nose-thumbing through a second violent offense might be more condemnable than nose-thumbing through a second theft offense, but nose-thumbing through a second theft would hardly be irrelevant. Yet the three strikes provisions typically apply only to a limited class of offenses—commonly violent offenses—and typically account for only certain kinds of criminal history—again, commonly a history of violent offenses. It seems difficult to construct a desert theory of nose-thumbing disrespect that allows for such selective increases in punishment. But note that applying habitual-offender schemes only to violent offenses does make sense under a prevention rationale, however, because these offenses most demand prevention.

The criminal justice system's focus on dangerousness also causes, albeit less frequently, distortions of the reverse sort: failures of justice in which a person fails to receive the punishment he or she deserves. This kind of error can occur both in the assignment of liability and in the assessment of the proper amount of punishment. For example, the Model Penal Code provides a defense to inchoate liability if a person "presents [no] public danger" and the person's attempt was "inherently unlikely" to succeed. Such a defense may make sense for a system designed to incapacitate the dangerous person because incarcerating the nondangerous attempter is a waste of preventive resources. But if the person believes his conduct will cause a criminal harm, the person deserves punishment whether or not the chosen method is likely to succeed. For example, the HIV-positive son who attempts to kill his long-hated father by spitting on him can escape liability if the killing method is impossible and he is not otherwise dangerous. But if the son's intention to kill his father unjustifiably is real and he has shown a willingness to carry out the intention fully, his blameworthiness is clear.

Such failures of justice are more common in sentencing, at least in the discretionary systems that abounded two decades ago and that still exist in many jurisdictions. The judge who focuses on prevention instead of desert will give a minor sentence for a serious offense if the offender is no longer dangerous. Thus, the recently discovered, elderly former Nazi concentration camp official can escape the punishment he deserves.

These conflicts between pursuing justice and incapacitating dangerous persons should come as no surprise. Dangerousness and desert are distinct criteria that commonly diverge. Desert arises from a past wrong, whereas dangerousness arises from the prediction of a future wrong. A person may be dangerous but not blameworthy, or vice versa. Consider, for example, a mentally ill offender. A desert distributive principle acquits the dysfunctional person of all criminal liability because the person is not to blame for the offense; he deserves no punishment. But an incapacitation principle would impose liability and require incapacitation because the offender is dangerous.

In a reverse set of cases, an incapacitation principle does not call for punishment of an offender even though the desert principle calls for conviction, as with the elderly Nazi official and the HIV-positive spitter. Because the person's conduct is harmless and the person is not otherwise dangerous, an incapacitation principle suggests that imposing criminal sanctions is a waste of resources. The desert principle, in contrast, takes the person's attempt to kill as evidence of blameworthiness deserving punishment.

Cloaking Preventive Detention as Criminal Justice

It is ironic that the perversions of justice suffered in the name of prevention actually produce a seriously flawed prevention system. These prevention difficulties arise primarily because of the perceived need to cloak preventive measures as doctrines of criminal punishment to make them appear consistent with a criminal justice system that imposes punishment.

Why should this be so? If reformers want to detain dangerous offenders, why not adopt a system that is open about its preventive detention nature and its intention to fill any preventive need remaining after criminal justice incarceration? Most jurisdictions allow civil commitment of persons who are dangerous because of mental illness, drug dependency, or contagious disease. Why is there reluctance to detain preventively offenders who remain dangerous at the conclusion of their deserved criminal terms of imprisonment?

The intense controversy surrounding the preventive detention legislation of the 1960s may help to explain this reluctance. Critics denounced the legislation as "Clockwork Orange" and "'Alice in Wonderland' justice" in which the punishment precedes the offense and as introducing a "police state" and "fostering tyranny." Opponents described it as "intellectually dishonest," characterized it as "one of the most tragic mistakes we as a society could make," and feared that it "would change the complexion of American justice." Preventive detention was "simply not the American way."

A large part of the perceived problem with the 1960s preventive detention legislation was that it provided pretrial preventive detention. In contrast, most current reforms provide preventive detention only after trial and conviction, an important difference.

Yet the primary criticism of pretrial preventive detention — that the sentence precedes the trial — can also be applied to the postconviction preventive detention reforms. Detention for longer than the deserved term of imprisonment is justified as preventing predicted future crimes. Such detention not only punishes an offense for which the detainee has not yet been convicted, but also punishes an offense that he has not yet committed.

But the ability to punish the uncommitted crime, and thereby prevent it, is the genius of the current system's cloaking of preventive detention as criminal justice. By obscuring the preventive nature of the liability and sentence, by making it appear not so entirely different from a criminal justice system of deserved punishment, the preventive detention controversy can be avoided entirely.

The Preventive Detention Problems

It is evident, then, that there are various ways in which the current criminal justice system surreptitiously provides preventive detention at the expense of just punishment. Ironically, such cloaked preventive detention also seriously impedes the system's preventive effectiveness. For example, instead of examining each offender to determine the person's actual present dangerousness, the current system uses prior criminal record as a proxy for dangerousness. Prior record has some correlation with dangerousness and, with the assertion of the "nose-thumbing" theory, has plausible deniability as to its perverting justice. But prior record is only a rough approximation of actual dangerousness, and its use in preventive detention guarantees errors of both inclusion and exclusion.

A scientist's ability to predict future criminality using all available data is poor; using just the proxy of prior criminal history, a scientist's prediction is even less accurate. It is often true that a person who has committed an offense will do so again. But it is also frequently false — many offenders do not commit another offense. An explicit assessment of dangerousness would reveal that many second-time offenders are no longer dangerous, yet these offenders receive long preventive terms under three strikes statutes and criminal-history-based guidelines. At the same time, an explicit assessment of dangerousness would reveal that many first-time offenders are dangerous; yet these offenders are not preventively detained under three strikes statutes and criminal-history-based guidelines.

Indeed, this particular cloaking device stands good prevention on its head. Evidence suggests that criminality is highly age-related. Whether due to changes in testosterone levels or something else, the offending rate drops off steadily for individuals beyond their twenties. The prior-record cloak leads us to ignore younger offenders' future crimes when they are running wild, and to begin long-term imprisonment, often life imprisonment under "three strikes," just when the natural forces of aging would often rein in the offenders. Offenders with their criminal careers before them are not detained because they have not yet compiled their criminal resumes, whereas offenders with their criminal careers behind them are detained because they have the requisite criminal records. Such a scheme produces a costly prevention system of prisons full of geriatric life-termers. Simultaneously, the scheme leads to ineffective prevention, because the system does little during the period in a criminal's life when the need for preventive detention is greatest. A rational and cost-effective preventive detention system would more readily detain young offenders during their crime-prone years and release them for their crime-free older years. Yet the need to cloak preventive detention with deserved punishment prompts the use of prior record as a substitute for actual dangerousness.

An equally counterproductive aspect of the cloaked system is its mandating of fixed ("determinate") sentences immediately following a guilty verdict. In determining the length of a deserved sentence, all of the relevant information is known at the time of sentencing — the nature of the offense and the personal culpability and capacities of the offender. Thus, sentencing judges determining deserved punishment have little reason to impose any sentence other than a fully determinate one (that is, one that sets the actual release date) immediately after trial. A system that instead allows a subsequent reduction of sentence, as by a parole board, undercuts deserved punishment. Citizens become cynical that a just sentence will be undermined by early release. It is this cynicism that gives rise to demands for "truth in sentencing" and to the legislative response of establishing determinate terms and abolishing early release on parole.

Therefore, to maintain its justice cloak, the preventive system must follow this practice of imposing determinate sentences soon after trial. But this practice is highly inappropriate for effective prevention. It is difficult enough to determine a person's present dangerousness—whether he would commit an offense if released today. It is much more difficult to predict an offender's future dangerousness—whether he would commit an offense if released at the end of the deserved punishment term in the future. It is still more difficult, if not impossible, to predict today precisely how long the future preventive detention will need to last. Yet that is what determinate sentencing demands: the imposition now of a fixed term that predicts preventive needs far in the future.

A sentencing judge or guideline drafter is left to the grossest sort of speculation, inevitably doomed to setting either a term too long—thus unfairly detaining a nondangerous offender and wasting preventive resources—or a term too short—thus failing to provide adequate prevention. In deciding between these two bad choices, decisionmakers commonly opt for errors of the first sort rather than the second, resulting in the recent increases in the terms of imprisonment.

A rational preventive detention system would do what current civil commitment systems do: make a determination of present dangerousness in setting detention for a limited period, commonly six months, and then periodically revisit the decision to determine whether the need for detention continues.

Other inefficiencies resulting from the use of the cloak are found in the method of restraint. A rational preventive detention system would follow a principle of minimum intrusion: a detainee would be held at the minimum level of restraint necessary for community safety. If house arrest or regular medication would provide the same level of community safety as imprisonment, then the former choices would be preferred as less intrusive to the offender and less costly to society. Implementing deserved punishment, in contrast, may often require a prison term to reaffirm the community's strong condemnation of the offense. House arrest or regular medication may be unacceptable substitutes if they are perceived as trivializing the offense. If preventive detention must operate under the cloak of criminal justice, it too often must follow the punishment preference for imprisonment even in situations in which prevention would be satisfied with less intrusive restraint.

The preventive detention system hidden behind the cloak of criminal justice not only fails to protect the community efficiently but also fails to deal fairly with those being preventively detained. As noted above, the inaccuracies created by the use of prior record as a substitute for actual dangerousness result in the unnecessary detention of a greater number of nondangerous offenders. The inaccuracies created by the use of determinate sentences can have the same effect. In cases in which a nonincarcerative sentence would provide adequate protection, the use of a prison term provides one more example of needless restraint.

But the unfairness generated by the cloak of criminal justice extends to other aspects of the preventive detention system, such as the conditions of detention.

Punitive conditions are entirely consistent with a punishment rationale for the incarceration. But if an offender has served the portion of his sentence justified by deserved punishment and continues to be detained for entirely preventive reasons, punitive conditions become inappropriate.

Similarly, an offender being preventively detained should logically have a right to treatment, especially if such treatment can reduce the length or intrusiveness of the preventive detention — this constitutes a specialized application of the principle of minimum restraint. If treatment can reduce the necessary individual sacrifice, the offender ought to receive it.

✸ DISCUSSION MATERIALS

Should Criminal Law Rules Be Formulated to Give Offenders the Punishment They Deserve; No More, No Less?

The following excerpts begin with a classic article by Immanuel Kant, arguing from a philosophical and ethical perspective in favor of using only the just desert doctrine in determining punishment. In the subsequent excerpt, Jeffrie Murphy opposes retributivism given the reality of today's society. The principle of retributivism as a doctrine distinct from utilitarianism is then discussed by Michael Moore, followed by a Robinson and Darley article suggesting that the doctrines are, and should be, closely linked.

Immanuel Kant, The Philosophy of Law
194-197 (W. Hastie trans. 1887)

The right of administering punishment is the right of the sovereign as the supreme power to inflict pain upon a subject on account of a crime committed by him. . . .

Judicial or juridical punishment (*poena forensis*) is to be distinguished from natural punishment (*poena naturalis*), in which crime as vice punishes itself, and does not as such come within the cognizance of the legislator. Juridical punishment can never be administered merely as a means of promoting another good either with regard to the criminal himself or to civil society, but must in all cases be imposed only because the individual on whom it is inflicted has committed a crime. For one man ought never to be dealt with merely as a means subservient to the purpose of another, nor be (treated as though he were subject to the law of property). Against such treatment his inborn personality has a right to protect him, even though he may be condemned to lose his civil personality. He must first be found guilty and *punishable*, before there can be any thought of drawing from his punishment any benefit for himself or his fellow-citizens. The penal law is a categorical imperative; and woe to him who creeps through the serpent windings of utilitarianism to discover some advantage that may discharge him from the justice of punishment, or even from the due measure of it, according to the Pharisaic maxim: "It is better that *one* man should die than the whole people should perish." For if justice and righteousness perish, human life would no longer have any value in the world. What, then, is to be said of such a proposal as to keep a criminal alive who has been condemned to death, on his being given to understand that if he agreed to certain dangerous experiments being performed upon him, he would be allowed to survive if he came happily through them? It is argued that physicians might thus obtain new information that would be of value to the commonweal. But a court of justice would repudiate with scorn any proposal of this kind if made to it by the medical faculty; for justice would cease to be justice if it were bartered away for any consideration whatever.

But what is the mode and measure of punishment which public justice takes as its principle and standard? It is just the principle of equality, by which the pointer of the scale of justice is made to incline no more to the one side than the other. It may be rendered by saying that the undeserved evil which any one commits on another is to be regarded as perpetrated on himself. Hence it may be said: "If you slander another you slander yourself; if you steal from another, you steal from yourself; if you strike another, you strike yourself; if you kill another, you kill yourself." This is the right of retaliation (*jus talionis*): and properly understood, it is the only principle which in regulating a public court, as distinguished from more private judgement, can definitely assign both the quality and the quantity of a just penalty. All other standards are wavering and uncertain; and on account of other consideration involved in them, they contain no principle conformable to the sentence of pure and strict justice....

But how then would we render the statement: "If you *steal* from another, you steal from yourself?" In this way, that whoever steals anything makes the property of all insecure; he therefore robs himself of all security in property, according to the right of retaliation. Such a one has nothing, and can acquire nothing, but he has the will to live; and this is only possible by others supporting him. But as the state should not do this gratuitously, he must for this purpose yield his powers to the state to be used in penal labour; and thus he falls for a time, or it may be life, into a condition of slavery. But whoever has committed murder must *die*. There is, in this case, no juridical substitute or surrogate that can be given or taken for the satisfaction of justice. There is no *likeness* or proportion between life, however painful, and death; and therefore there is no equality between the crime of murder and the retaliation of it but what is judicially accomplished by the execution of the criminal. His death, however, must be kept free from all mal-treatment that would make the humanity suffering in his person loathsome or abominable. Even if a civil society resolved to dissolve itself with the consent of all its members — as might be supposed in the case of a people inhabiting an island resolving to separate and scatter themselves through the whole world — the last murderer lying in the prison ought to be executed before the resolution was carried out. This ought to be done in order that everyone may realize the desert of his deeds, and that blood guiltiness may not remain upon the people; for otherwise they might all be regarded as participators in the murder as a public violation of justice.

Jeffrie G. Murphy, Three Mistakes About Retributivism
31 Analysis 166-169 (1971)

Retributive theories of punishment maintain that criminal guilt merits or deserves punishment, regardless of considerations of social utility. Such theories may be put forth for either of two reasons: (1) It could be argued (e.g. by a Moral Sense theorist) that the claim is a primitive and unanalyzed proposition which is morally ultimate. Every ethical theory necessarily involves at least one such primitive (e.g. "happiness is good", "freedom is to be respected", *etc.*) and the retributivist may be offering this as his candidate. We can, he may argue, just intend the "fittingness" of guilt and punishment. (2) It might be maintained (as it was, I believe, by both Kant and Hegel) that the retributivist claim is demanded by a general theory of political obligation which is more plausible than any alternative theory. Such a theory will typically provide a technical *analysis* of such notions as crime and punishment and will thus not regard the retributivist claim as an indisputable primitive. It will be argued for as a kind of theorem within the system.

The objection to the first sort of theory is obvious: the retributivist may be able to intuit the fittingness of guilt and punishment, but most of us cannot — not, at any rate, in a sense strong enough to make us want to appeal to the notion in justifying punishment. Thus the first theory is subject to all the classical objections to intuitionism, and these do not have to be repeated here. Let us, then, try to make sense of a theory of the second sort. What sort of theory of political obligation would render it plausible?

Consider a quasi-contractual model (found in Kant and John Rawls) that seeks to analyze political obligation in terms of *reciprocity*. Such a model will proceed as follows: In order to enjoy the benefits that a legal system makes possible, each man must be prepared to make an important sacrifice — namely, the sacrifice of obeying the law even when he does not desire to do so. Each man calls on others to do this, and it is only just or fair that he bear a comparable burden when his turn comes. Now if the system is to remain just, it is important to guarantee that those who disobey will not thereby gain an unfair advantage over those who obey voluntarily. Criminal punishment thus attempts to maintain the proper balance between benefit and obedience by insuring that there is no profit in criminal wrongdoing. This is at least one point behind the *jus talionis* (return like for like) principle and was no doubt at least part of what Kant had in mind when he spoke, in a misleading idiom, of the criminal as owing a *debt* to the law-abiding members of his community. (The idiom of owing and paying a debt is misleading in that it tends to obscure the fact that (i) criminal "debts" differ from ordinary debts in that we have an antecedent moral obligation not to incur them and (ii) undergoing punishment for (say) murder, unlike paying the final installment on a loan, can hardly be said to make things all right again, to make the world morally the same as it was before.)

Now the above theory is one possible form retributivism might take and is, at least, not absurd on its face. What I want to do now is to show how retributivism, at least of this variety, does not fall to three stock objections which are frequently put forth to "demonstrate" that no reasonable man could be a retributivist.

1. Retributivism as Necessarily Involving Utilitarianism and as Being Obviously Unacceptable Without It

Rule utilitarians often maintain that retributivism, to be coherent, must involve a tacit appeal to utility—*i.e.* must tacitly presuppose that the principle "Do not allow men to profit from their criminal wrongdoing" has more desirable social consequences than any alternative principle. But I should argue that Kant's theory, for example, is (i) perfectly coherent and (ii) quite independent of utilitarian considerations. His principle is that no man should profit from his own wrongdoing, and retribution attempts to keep this from happening. If a man does profit from his own wrongdoing, from his disobedience, this is *unfair* or *unjust*, not merely to his victim, but to all those who have been obedient. Now it may be, as the utilitarian might argue, that such unfairness—if widespread—would have socially undesirable consequences. But this is not Kant's argument. His argument is that the *injustice* of *unfairness itself,* regardless of consequences, demands retribution. As H.L.A. Hart has argued, "a theory of punishment which disregarded these moral convictions (about justice) or viewed them simply as factors, frustration of which made for socially undesirable excitement is a different kind of theory from one which *out of deference to those convictions themselves* (justifies) punishment...." ("Murder and Principles of Punishment," in *Punishment and Responsibility,* Oxford, 1968, p.79). Kant's theory is clearly of the latter sort.

But if this line is taken, the utilitarian may argue, retributivism becomes obviously unreasonable—a bit of primitive, unenlightened and barbaric emotionalism. But why is retributivism so condemned? Typically the charge is that infliction of punishment, with no attention to utility, is pointless vengeance. But what is meant by the claim that the activity in question is pointless? If "pointless" is to be analyzed as "disutilitarian," then the whole question is being begged. One cannot refute a retributive theory merely by noting that it is a retributive theory and not a utilitarian theory. This is to confuse refutation with redescription. That the maximization of social utility is important is no more *obviously* true than that a man should not unfairly profit from his own criminal wrongdoing; and, if the utilitarian proposes simply to dig in his heels on the former, it is important to note that the charge of emotionalism cuts both ways.

2. The Inapplicability of *Jus Talionis*

Perhaps the most common criticism of Kant's theory is the claim that the principle *jus talionis* (return like to like) cannot with sense be taken literally. As Hegel observes, "it is easy enough...to exhibit the retributive character of punishment as an absurdity (theft for theft, robbery for robbery, an eye for an eye, a tooth for a tooth—and then you can go on to suppose that the criminal has only one eye or no teeth)" (*Philosophy of Right,* translated by T.M. Knox, Oxford, 1952, p.72).

But this objection, as Hegel rightly sees, is superficial. Surely the principle *jus talionis,* thought requiring likeness of punishment, does not require exact likeness in all respects. There is no reason *in principle* (though there are practical difficulties against trying to specify in a general way what the costs in life and labour of certain kinds of crime might be, and how the costs of punishments might be calculated, so that retribution could be understood as preventing criminal profit.

3. The Gap Between Theory and Practice

Another common criticism against the Kantian theory may be regarded as Marxist in character. Kant's theory, it may be argued, involves an ideal utopian model of society which is in fact so utterly different from the actual character of society as to render it useless in understanding or evaluating any existing practice of criminal punishment. Indeed, the theory is dangerous. For it allows us to hide from ourselves the vicious character of actual social arrangements and thereby perpetuate gross injustice.

Let me elaborate: Punishment as retribution (paying a kind of "debt") to one's fellow-citizens) makes good sense with respect to a community of responsible individuals, of approximate equality, bound together by freely adopted and commonly accepted rules which benefit everyone. This is an ideal community, approximating what Kant would call a kingdom of ends. In such a community, punishment would be justly retributive in that it would flow as an accepted consequence of accepted rules which benefitted everyone (including, as citizen, the criminal). But surely existing human societies are not in fact like this at all. Many people neither benefit nor participate but rather operate at a built-in economic or racial disadvantage which is *in fact,* if not in theory, permanent. The majority of criminals who are in fact punished are drawn from these classes, and they utterly fail to correspond to the model which underlies the retributive theory. Surely we delude ourselves in appealing to the retributive theory to justify their punishment.

The moral doubts raised here are extremely important. However, they may be doubts which testify to *strengths* rather than weaknesses in a retributive theory of the Kantian variety. Decent men surely want to object to the wanton handing out of punishments to those who, in a socially uneven community, always get the short end of the stick. But does not Kant's theory explain (or at least give one good reason) *why* we do want to object? Just punishment rests upon reciprocity; and is not one of the most serious moral problems confronting most existing communities the absence of such reciprocity, the absence of a balance between benefit and burden? Punishment is unjust in such a setting because it involves pretending (contrary to fact) that the conditions of justified punishment are met. Thus could not Kant, given his theory, easily share the Marxist scepticism about punishing in certain actual states? I believe that he could.

Michael S. Moore, The Moral Worth of Retribution
Responsibility, Character and Emotions 179-182 (F. Schoeman ed., 1987)

Retributivism is the view that punishment is justified by the moral culpability of those who receive it. A retributivist punishes because, and only because, the offender deserves it. Retributivism thus stands in stark contrast to utilitarian views that justify punishment of past offenses by the greater good of preventing future offenses. It also contrasts sharply with rehabilitative views, according to which punishment is justified by the reforming good it does the criminal.

Less clearly, retributivism also differs from a variety of views that are often paraded as retributivist, but that in fact are not. . . . The leading confusions seem to me to be [several].

1. First, retributivism is sometimes identified with a particular measure of punishment such as *lex talionis,* an eye for an eye, or with a kind of punishment such as the death penalty. Yet retributivism answers a question prior to the questions to which these could be answers. True enough, retributivists at some point have to answer the "how much" and "what type" questions for specific offenses, and they are committed to the principle that punishment should be graded in proportion to desert; but they are not committed to any particular penalty scheme nor to any particular penalty as being deserved. Separate argument is needed to answer these "how much" and "what" questions, *after* one has described why one is punishing at all. It is quite possible to be a retributivist and to be against both the death penalty and *lex talionis,* the idea that crimes should be punished by like acts being done to the criminal.

2.... [R]etributivism is *not* "the view that only the guilty are to be punished." A retributivist will subscribe to such a view, but that is not what is distinctive about retributivism. The distinctive aspect of retributivism is that the moral desert of an offender is a *sufficient* reason to punish him or her; the principle (that only the guilty may be punished) makes such moral desert only a *necessary* condition of punishment. Other reasons — typically, crime prevention reasons — must be added to moral desert, in this view, for punishment to be justified. Retributivism has no room for such additional reasons. That future crime might also be presented by punishment is a happy surplus for a retributivist, but not part of the justification for punishing.

3. Retributivism is not the view that punishment of offenders satisfies the desires for vengeance of their victims.... A retributivist can justify punishment as deserved even if the criminal's victims are indifferent (or even opposed) to punishing the one who hurt them. Indeed, a retributivist should urge punishment on all offenders who deserve it, even if *no* victims wanted it.

4. [R]etributivism is not the view that the preferences of all citizens (not just crime victims) should be satisfied. A preference utilitarian might well believe, as did Sir James Fitzjames Stephen, that punishment should be exacted "for the sake of gratifying the feeling of hatred — call it revenge, resentment, or what you will — which the contemplation of such (criminal) conduct excites in healthily constituted minds...," or that "the feeling of hatred and the desire of vengeance... are important elements of human nature which ought... to be satisfied in a regular public and legal manner." Yet a retributivist need not believe such things, but only that morally culpable persons should be punished, irrespective of what other citizens feel, desire, or prefer.

5. [R]etributivism is not the view that punishment is justified because without it vengeful citizens would take the law into their own hands.... Punishment for a retributivist is not justified by the need to prevent private violence, which is an essentially utilitarian justification. Even in the most well-mannered state, those criminals who deserve punishment should get it, according to retributivism.

6. Nor is retributivism to be confused with denunciatory theories of punishment. In this latter view punishment is justified because punishment is the vehicle through which society can express its condemnation of the criminal's behavior. This is a utilitarian theory, not a retributive one, for punishment is in this view to be justified by the good consequences it achieves — either the psychological satisfactions denunciation achieve, or the prevention of private violence, or the

prevention of future crimes through the education benefits of such denunciation. A retributivist justified punishment by none of these supposed good consequences of punishing. . . .

Retributivism is a very straightforward theory of punishment: We are justified in punishing because and only because offenders deserve it. Moral culpability ("desert") is in such a view both a sufficient as well as a necessary condition of liability to punitive sanctions. Such justification gives society more than merely a right to punish culpable offenders. It does this, making it not unfair to punish them, but retributivism justifies more than this. For a retributivist, the moral culpability of an offender also gives society the *duty* to punish. Retributivism, in other words, is truly a theory of justice such that, if it is true, we have an obligation to set up institutions so that retribution is achieved.

Paul H. Robinson & John M. Darley, The Utility of Desert
91 Northwestern University Law Review 454-458, 497-499 (1997)

Criminal punishment can be justified on two broad grounds. The first is utilitarian (sometimes called "consequentialist"): Punishment for a past offense is justified by the future benefits it provides. Characteristically, the future benefit is to avoid, or at least to reduce, future crimes. The other ground of justification is anchored in the past: Punishment that gives an offender what he or she deserves for a past crime is a valuable end in itself and needs no further justification (such as a showing of a future benefit). This is typically referred to as the "retributivist" or "just deserts" view. The arguments of these two positions are generally considered irreconcilable: Consequentialist grounds are justified on the basis of utility, desert grounds on the basis of fulfilling a deontological moral mandate. In this Article, we argue that, while the underlying rationales of the two views may be irreconcilable, their practical applications, properly done, suggest similar distributions of liability and punishment. More specifically, while we argue that society ought to assign criminal punishments on essentially just desert grounds, our arguments are based on purely utilitarian considerations. We argue that, because it promotes forces that lead to a law-abiding society, a criminal law based on the community's perceptions of just desert is, from a utilitarian perspective, the more effective strategy for reducing crime. While much empirical work remains before we fully understand the dynamics of the forces that we cite as suggesting this conclusion, we can say, at the very least, that utilitarians must include in their policy calculations the likelihood of a significant cost to crime control in any deviations from a desert distribution.

The debate over the justification for punishing criminals has been deeply confused, and the confusion has a long and honorable history. In the late eighteenth century, Jeremy Bentham argued that "general prevention ought to be the chief end of punishment, as it is its real justification." From this, Bentham went on to develop the classic formulation of the deterrence rationale for punishment. Thus, tautologically to him (but not tautologically to utilitarians who think rehabilitation could minimize crime, for example) an offender's punishment ought to be set not according to the amount deserved, but rather according to the amount needed to deter future instances of the offense. "If the apparent magnitude, or rather value of [the] pain be greater than the apparent magnitude or value of the pleasure or good he expects to be the consequence of the act, he will be absolutely prevented from performing it." Immanuel Kant, a contemporary of Bentham, summarized an opposing "just deserts" rationale. "[P]unishment can never be administered merely as a means for promoting another good . . . ." Punishment ought to be "pronounced over all criminals proportionate to their internal wickedness . . . ." Of course, the history of justifications goes back further; Kant was giving a particular formulation of the Aristotelian view that criminals should be given punishments and penalties, not rehabilitation. Plato weighed in with a justification for punishment that foreshadows the modern rehabilitation justification, arguing that punishment ought not be inflicted for vengeance, but rather to make the offender a better person. The debate between the desert justification and the various utilitarian justifications such as deterrence, incapacitation, and rehabilitation has continued to divide criminal law thinkers to this day. Perhaps more importantly, it has divided practitioners. In the history of incarceration in this country we have seen repeated confusions in what we might call the "public philosophy of punishment," the reasons claimed for the justification of criminal sanctions by policy-makers and legislators.

Recently, the confusion has seemed to accelerate; the last decades have seen a rapid oscillation among these rationales for the distribution of criminal liability. The rehabilitationist approach, popular in the 1960s, has lost credibility. Deterrence, grounded in a theory of rational conduct, has ceased to command much confidence among thoughtful criminologists, for a number of reasons that we shall show. Incapacitation, currently popular in the form of "three strikes and you're out" laws, can also be expected to run into difficulties for reasons we shall explain. Part I of this article details the limitations of the standard utilitarian theories. Those limitations mean that policy-makers and legislators, not just academics, should be interested in examining our claim that the greatest utility in controlling crime is found in doing justice.

As we signaled, we argue for a just desert allocation of liability, although a particular and unusual form of desert-based liability: one based upon the community's shared principles of justice rather than on those developed by moral philosophers. Our arguments for this system are, as far as we know, unique: The major claim for our desert-based liability assignment system lies in its advantages in promoting future law-abiding behavior. We give, in other words, a utilitarian justification for the only non-utilitarian system for allocating punishment.

The desert-based liability system that we advocate is one that normally assigns liability and punishment according to the principles of justice that the community intuitively uses to assign liability and blame. We ought to mark here that this is a sufficiently heretical variation on desert theory that it is likely that those who argue for a more standard desert theory, Kantians and others working from philosophical perspectives, will find it repugnant, first because it derives liability assignments from community sentiments rather than a reasoned logical system, and second because our arguments for a desert-based system are blatantly utilitarian.

Our goal then is to persuade those who determine rules of criminal liability and punishment — criminal law theorists, code drafters, legislators, and judges — that a criminal law that assigns punishment in ways that closely reflects the community's intuitions about appropriate condemnation and punishment has a number of hitherto unrecognized advantages over alternative systems. Specifically, a distributive theory that tracks the community's perceived principles of justice has a greater power to gain compliance with society's rules of lawful conduct. Therefore, we suggest, those who base criminal liability on the traditional utilitarian considerations — whether deterrence-based, rehabilitationist, or incapacitationist — run the considerable risk of causing a net drop in the law's effectiveness in controlling crime.

Here is a brief summary of our argument as detailed in Part II of this Article: The real power to gain compliance with society's rules of prescribed conduct lies not in the threat or reality of official criminal sanction, but in the power of the intertwined forces of social and individual moral control. The networks of interpersonal relationships in which people find themselves, the social norms and prohibitions shared among those relationships and transmitted through those social networks, and the internalized representations of those norms and moral precepts cause people to obey the law.

Next, the core of our argument, set out in Part III: The law is not irrelevant to these social and personal forces. Criminal law, in particular, plays a central role in creating and maintaining the social consensus necessary for sustaining moral norms. In fact, in a society as diverse as ours, the criminal law may be the only society-wide mechanism that transcends cultural and ethnic differences. Thus, the criminal law's most important real-world effect may be its ability to assist in the building, shaping, and maintaining of these norms and moral principles. It can contribute to and harness the compliance-producing power of interpersonal relationships and personal morality.

The criminal law can have a second effect in gaining compliance with its commands. If it earns a reputation as a reliable statement of what the community, given sufficient information and time to reflect, would perceive as condemnable, people are more likely to defer to its commands as morally authoritative and as appropriate to follow in those borderline cases in which the propriety of certain conduct is unsettled or ambiguous in the mind of the actor. The importance of this role should not be underestimated; in a society with the complex interdependencies characteristic of ours, an apparently harmless action can have destructive consequences. When the action is criminalized by the legal system, one would want the citizen to "respect the law" in such an instance even though he or she does not immediately intuit why that action is banned. Such deference will be facilitated if citizens are disposed to believe that the law is an accurate guide to appropriate prudential and moral behavior.

The extent of the criminal law's effectiveness in both these respects — in facilitating and communicating societal consensus on what is and is not condemnable, and in gaining compliance in borderline cases through deference to its moral authority — we argue is to a great extent dependent on the degree of moral credibility that the criminal law has achieved in the minds of the citizens governed by it. Thus, we assert, the criminal law's moral credibility is essential to effective crime control, and is enhanced if the distribution of criminal liability is perceived as "doing justice," that is, if it assigns liability and punishment in ways that the community perceives as consistent with the community's principles of appropriate liability and punishment. Conversely, the system's moral credibility, and therefore its crime control effectiveness, is undermined by a distribution of liability that deviates from community perceptions of just desert. In Parts IV, V, and VI, we discuss how past reforms have hurt the criminal law's moral credibility, and we propose reforms by which its moral credibility might be enhanced.

We begin the argument for our position by criticizing all of the alternatives. That is, before we detail the case for enhancing the criminal law's moral credibility, we comment on the other utilitarian theories for distributing criminal liability and the difficulties that each face. Our conclusion is not that these standard utilitarian mechanisms for controlling crime have no effect in reducing crime, but rather that they have only a limited benefit that is outweighed by their cost in undercutting the law's crime control power by reducing its moral credibility. Remember that sentences based upon desert do provide the opportunity for rehabilitation, incapacitation, and deterrence. In arguing for a desert distribution, then, we need show only that the additional crime control benefit that the standard utilitarian analysis claims by deviating from a desert distribution is outweighed by the additional cost that such deviation incurs as it inevitably undercuts the criminal law's moral credibility. The optimum distributive principle, we argue, is one that rehabilitates, incapacitates, and deters, but only through the use of liability and punishment that tracks the community's principles of perceived desert.

Summary and Conclusion

The evidence is reasonably clear that the power of interpersonal relationships and internalized norms to prevent crime is dramatically greater than that of official sanctions. The ability of the law to harness these forces is less clear. Studies suggest that increasing the law's moral credibility can enhance its compliance power, but the studies are preliminary and many important questions remain unanswered. Will research confirm our speculations about the mechanisms by which a morally credible criminal law can increase compliance? Will research confirm our speculations about the practices that most undercut the system's moral credibility and those that would most enhance it?

It will take some time for social scientists to answer these questions, but we need not wait for those answers before we make some changes in what we do. Most importantly, it is clear that a utilitarian calculus in determining the rules for the distribution of criminal liability and punishment must take account of real-world costs that come from deviating from the community's principles of deserved punishment. The costs and benefits of moral credibility may be more difficult to measure than those of the factors typically taken into account by utilitarian calculations in the past, but if they are more powerful in their effect than the other factors, to ignore them risks rendering the calculation meaningless.

While we do not know with any certainty the degree of importance of the criminal law's moral credibility, we can be reasonably sure that it has some. Thus, a corollary to the above is that we ought not tolerate any deviation from desert, or any other measure that may undercut moral credibility, without a clear and significant benefit. And even then, we counsel a close examination of long-term as well as short-term effects. This suggests a number of reforms, which we have mentioned.

Where have we left the long-running debate between desert and utilitarian justifications for punishment? We have used essentially utilitarian reasoning to argue for a desert-based system of criminal law. More specifically, we have argued that people obey the law not so much because they are fearful of being apprehended by the criminal justice system, but because they care about what their social group thinks of them and because they regard obedience as morally appropriate. Criminal laws based on community standards of deserved punishment enhance this obedience. We conclude that desert distribution of liability happens to be the distribution that has the greatest utility, in the sense of avoiding crime. Thus, utility theorists ought to support liabilities assigned according to such a desert-based system.

If our arguments are accepted, we have, in some sense, united two groups of criminal justice philosophers that have characteristically been thought to be at hopeless odds. Desert-based punishment proponents assert that what matters in liability and sentencing is doing justice; utilitarians require an analysis of the consequences of a liability assignment system to justify it, characteristically a showing of how the system is maximally effective in avoiding crimes in the future. We suggest that while these two sides do not agree on the reasons for imposing punishment, if they agree with our analysis, they can, incredibly enough, agree on how punishment should be distributed.

We have, perhaps, united utilitarians and just desert thinkers, but we may have united them in opposition to our recommendations. Liability and punishment should be distributed according to a desert-based distribution system, but the advocate for desert-based punishment systems may not be greatly pleased by this. Our desert-based system is importantly different from the standard one. In the standard desert-based system, what a criminal actually deserves is derived from some underlying systematization of moral principles; in our analysis, desert is not derived from any philosophically-based, coherently-reasoned systematization, but rather is patterned on the principles the community uses in assessing blameworthiness.

Has the utilitarian won the battle if our recommendations are accepted? In one sense, yes; we have used utilitarian arguments to justify our desert-based liability and sentencing scheme. However, the results of that analysis install the kind of liability distribution system that the utilitarians have argued against for decades. Worse, from their point of view, they cannot reject our arguments on principle, as they have rejected desert arguments in the past. If future investigations support the power we claim for the law's moral credibility, there is a powerful utilitarian argument for the adoption of a desert-based criminal law.

If our recommendations are adopted, the utilitarian criminal justice system is in some ways constrained in its distribution of liability, but it is freed from another constraint. During the past decades of the standard utilitarian approach, some criminal justice systems and institutions have had their charters set to a strictly utilitarian purpose, which seemed to exclude considerations of desert. Our thesis suggests that a charge to prevent crime is, as a practical matter, a charge primarily to do justice — to consider just desert — for that will reduce crime more than distributive criteria that ignore desert. Thus, our thesis not only allows these systems and institutions to take account of desert but in fact demands it.

The central point that we seek to make is this — there is practical value, not just "philosophical" value, in maintaining the criminal law's focus on moral blameworthiness. What we have in the past taken to be instances of injustice imposed by the criminal justice system on some individual, when the just desert principle is violated, we ought to understand now as instances of injustice imposed on us all, since each such instance erodes the criminal law's moral credibility and, thus, its power to protect us all.

⬤ DISCUSSION MATERIALS

If Criminal Law Rules Are to Be Formulated to Advance Two or More of the Traditional Purposes of Punishment — Deterrence, Rehabilitation/Incapacitation, and Desert — What Should Be the Interrelation Among Those Distributive Principles?

The Model Penal Code is excerpted here as an illustration of the competing distributive principles used in a single criminal justice system. Hart argues that having a multi-faceted system as such is beneficial, while Robinson speaks to its difficulties and urges a definition of the interrelation among distributive principles.

Model Penal Code
(Official Draft 1962)

Section 1.02. Purposes; Principles of Construction

(1) The general purposes of the provisions governing the definition of offenses are:

(a) to forbid and prevent conduct that unjustifiably and inexcusably inflicts or threatens substantial harm to individual or public interests;

(b) to subject to public control persons whose conduct indicates that they are disposed to commit crimes;

(c) to safeguard conduct that is without fault from condemnation as criminal;

(d) to give fair warning of the nature of the conduct declared to constitute an offense;

(e) to differentiate on reasonable grounds between serious and minor offenses.

(2) The general purposes of the provisions governing the sentencing and treatment of offenders are:

(a) to prevent the commission of offenses;

(b) to promote the correction and rehabilitation of offenders;

(c) to safeguard offenders against excessive, disproportionate or arbitrary punishment;

(d) to give fair warning of the nature of the sentences that may be imposed on conviction of an offense;

(e) to differentiate among offenders with a view to a just individualization in their treatment;

(f) to define, coordinate and harmonize the powers, duties and functions of the courts and of administrative officers and agencies responsible for dealing with offenders;

(g) to advance the use of generally accepted scientific methods and knowledge in the sentencing and treatment of offenders;

(h) to integrate responsibility for the administration of the correctional system in a State Department of Correction [or other single department or agency].

(3) The provisions of the Code shall be construed according to the fair import of their terms but when the language is susceptible of differing constructions it shall be interpreted to further the general purposes stated in this Section and the special purposes of the particular provision involved. The discretionary powers conferred by the Code shall be exercised in accordance with the criteria stated in the Code and, insofar as such criteria are not decisive, to further the general purposes stated in this Section.

Henry M. Hart, Jr., The Aims of the Criminal Law
23 Law and Contemporary Problems 401-402 (1958)

In trying to formulate the aims of the criminal law, it is important to be aware both of the reasons for making the effort and of the nature of the problem it poses.

The statement has been made, as if in complaint, that "there is hardly a penal code that can be said to have a single basic principle running through it." But it needs to be clearly seen that this is simply a fact, not a misfortune. A penal code that reflected only a single basic principle would be a very bad one. Social purposes can never be single or simple, or held unqualifiedly to the exclusion of all other social purposes; and an effort to make them can result only in the sacrifice of other values which also are important. Thus, to take only one example, the purpose of preventing any particular kind of crime, or crimes generally, is qualified always by the purposes of avoiding the conviction of the innocent and of enhancing that sense of security throughout the society which is one of the prime functions of the manifold safeguards of American criminal procedure. And the same thing would be true even if the dominant purpose of the criminal law were thought to be the rehabilitation of offenders rather than the prevention of offences.

Examination of the purposes commonly suggested for the criminal law will show that each of them is complex and that none may be thought of as wholly excluding the others. Suppose, for example, that the deterrence of offenses is taken to be the chief end. It will still be necessary to recognize that the rehabilitation of offenders, the disablement of offenders, the sharpening of the community's sense of right and wrong, and the satisfaction of the community's sense of just retribution may all serve this end by contributing to an ultimate reduction in the number of crimes. Even socialized vengeance may be accorded a marginal role, if it is understood as the provision of an orderly alternative to mob violence.

The problem, accordingly, is one of the priority and relationship of purposes as well as of their legitimacy — of multivalued rather than of single-valued thinking. There is still another range of complications which are ignored if an effort is made to formulate any single "theory" or set of "principles" of criminal law. The purpose of having principles and theories is to help in organizing thought. In the law, the ultimate purpose of thought is to help in deciding upon a course of action. In the criminal law, as in all law, questions about the action to be taken do not present themselves for decision in an institutional vacuum. They arise rather in the context of some established and specific procedure of decision: in a constitutional convention; in a legislature; in a prosecuting attorney's office; in a court charged with the determination of guilt or innocence; in a sentencing court; before a parole board; and so on. This means that each agency of decision must take account always of its own place in the institutional system and of what is necessary to maintain the integrity and workability of the system as a whole. A complex of institutional ends must be served, in other words, as well as a complex of substantive social ends.

The principal levels of decision in the criminal law are numerous. The institutional considerations involved at the various levels differ so markedly that it seems worth while to discuss the question of aims separately, from the point of view of each of the major agencies of decision.

Paul H. Robinson, Hybrid Principles for the Distribution of Criminal Sanctions
82 Northwestern University Law Review 19, 19-22, 28-35 (1987)

Most criminal codes, and criminal law courses, begin with the "familiar litany" of the purposes of criminal law sanctions — just punishment, deterrence, incapacitation of the dangerous, and rehabilitation. We train and direct our lawyers, judges, and legislators to use these purposes as guiding principles for the distribution of criminal sanctions. The purposes are thus to guide both the drafting and interpretation of criminal statutes and the imposition of criminal sanctions in individual cases.

The purposes frequently conflict, however, ... Conflicts arise because each purpose requires consideration of different criteria; in some cases a particular fact suggests different sentences or statutory formulations under different purposes. Ultimately, a choice must be made to follow one purpose at the expense of another. Yet, when faced with conflicting purposes, judges, legislators, and sentencing-guideline drafters have no principle to guide that decision.

In the absence of a guiding principle, the choices made are at best inconsistent. For example, most state criminal codes maintain an insanity defense because it exculpates the blameless (and thus furthers just punishment), even though abolishing the defense might more effectively incapacitate the dangerous. Yet, the same codes sacrifice just punishment, in favor of increasing deterrence, when they recognize strict liability. At the same time, rather than increasing the threatened sanction when the temptation or inclination is greater, as a deterrence principle suggests, the same codes frequently decrease the deterrent threat — as, for example, in cases of provocation — because of the offender's reduced blameworthiness. Code drafters are choosing to further different purposes in different contexts.

At worst, the absence of a guiding principle fosters arbitrariness or prejudice. This happens when the inconsistency in choice of distributive principles occurs in individual sentencing decisions. For instance, while rehabilitation might be the best means of avoiding future crime by a young addict who is caught selling drugs to support his habit, a judge rationally might decide to impose a long prison term in order to further general deterrent interests. When faced with a young bank teller who embezzled money from her cash drawer, the same judge might decide to sacrifice the general deterrent value of a long prison term and put the offender on probation, under an incapacitative theory — she is no longer dangerous because she will never again be placed in a position of trust. The judge has chosen to follow one distributive principle in one case but another principle in another case, but we do not know the grounds for the selection. Such unguided and hidden discretion creates the opportunity for arbitrary or biased decisionmaking, although each of the sentences will appear to have a social justification. Without a principle governing when one sentencing purpose is to be followed at the expense of another, judges and guideline drafters are free to choose whatever purpose justifies the sentence that they may desire for other, unspoken, reasons.

Why do we not insist that code and sentencing-guideline drafters adopt, and that judges follow, a statement of the interrelation among purposes that will guide the choice among conflicting purposes? A cynic may conclude that the use of "the purposes" to justify a particular code formulation or sentence is a convenient means of rationalizing results for which the decision-maker has another undisclosed reason. This suspicion — that "the purposes" are popular as a method of justification precisely *because* they offer hidden flexibility — is fueled by the almost universal failure to articulate a guiding principle. The Model Penal Code, for example, lists the traditional purposes, directs judges to use them in interpreting the provisions of the Code and in fashioning sentences under the Code; but the Code provides no more guidance in cases of conflict than to urge, in commentary, that the purposes be "just[ly] harmonize[d]." Other writers suggest that the competing interests are to be "balance[d]," "blend[ed]," "accommodate[d]," "taken account of," or "deal[t] with [such that] the public interest will be served."

Is it, as some suggest, simply a failure of the theorists? That is, "we would love to articulate a governing principle, but we cannot figure out how one feasibly can be fashioned." If so, then all will be greatly heartened by . . . this essay, which demonstrates several mechanisms for constructing a workable distributive principle embodying multiple purposes — a "hybrid distributive principle" — and . . . which illustrates how several of these mechanisms can be combined, creating hundreds of possible hybrid distributive principles, one of which is likely to be suitable to every decision-maker. On the other hand, [this essay] may be bad news to some. Identification of a principled basis for fashioning sentences and statutes will underscore the arbitrariness and personal bias of those who continue to adhere to ad hoc decision making.

Whether the flexibility of rationalization offered by "the purposes" has been used for conscious manipulation or is the result of inadvertent vagueness, a rational and principled system for the distribution of criminal sanctions is needed. if multiple principles are to be relied upon, a principled system must define the interrelation among the principles; that is, it must fully articulate a hybrid distributive principle. . . .

Conflict Points Among Alternative Purposes

1. Desert vs. — Desert can conflict with deterrence and incapacitation in two sorts of cases. First, the desert principle gives rise to doctrines like the insanity defense and the voluntary act requirement, which acquit blameless offenders even though they may be dangerous and even though their punishment might serve a general deterrent function. Conversely, in another set of cases, desert is sacrificed to deterrence and incapacitation. For example, the defense for inherently unlikely attempts acquits blameworthy offenders because the inherent harmlessness of the conduct suggests that both incapacitation and deterrence are unnecessary. In both sets of cases, a conflict arises: desert leads to one result while deterrence and incapacitation lead to another.

2. Deterrence vs. — Deterrence frequently conflicts with desert and incapacitation where some abnormal condition external to the actor, such as duress, coercion, or nonjustified necessity, contributes to the actor's criminal conduct. Because the conditions rather than the actor are judged responsible for the conduct, the actor is held blameless and nondangerous and thus is acquitted or receives a reduced sentence. On the other hand, the same coercive conditions can create the need for a greater rather than lesser deterrent threat. Greater sanctions would provide a needed additional deterrent in the face of unusual pressure to commit the offense.

If the pressure to commit the offense is so great as to be essentially irresistible, the "special deterrence" rationale (that is, punishment of the offender at hand so that he or she will not commit the same offense in a similar situation in the future) may disappear. In such a situation, any sanction would be futile and thus an inefficient expenditure. There may remain, however, a "general deterrent" purpose in imposing a significant sanction. In *Regina v. Dudley & Stephens*, for example, the sailors who killed the sick cabin boy to stay alive until they could be rescued were hardly shown to be dangerous people (as long as they stayed off boats that would be adrift for weeks) and their blameworthiness was significantly reduced because of the life-threatening conditions. Furthermore, people in their situation, or they again in the same situation, cannot be effectively deterred, because, as is assumed, the pressure they encountered was irresistible. However, there may remain nonetheless some general deterrent value in imposing a significant sanction to reaffirm the strong prohibition against the killing of innocent non-aggressors.

The same conflict arises in applying mitigating principles, like heat of passion, provocation, and mistake as to self-defense by battered wives and abused children. In these cases, an otherwise normal actor reacts less than admirably when confronted with a difficult situation. Such an actor is not as dangerous or blameworthy as an actor who kills absent the mitigating conditions, but, as with instances of duress, coercion, and nonjustified necessity, the need for a deterrent sanction to oppose the tendency and temptation is as great, if not greater.

A similar conflict between purposes arises under many strict liability doctrines when an offender, who is neither blameworthy nor dangerous, is sanctioned as a means of deterring similar violations by other potential offenders. Whenever these sorts of cases arise, a conflict arises in which principles of desert and incapacitation would support a reduction of the degree or scope of liability while deterrence principles would oppose reduction.

3. Incapacitation vs. — Incapacitation conflicts with deterrence and desert in setting the grade and sentences for attempted, as compared to completed, offenses, and in the related issue of defining the required causal relationship between an offender's conduct and a prohibited result. Reducing liability for unsuccessful attempts and requiring a strong causal connection between acts and results reflect two judgments: that an offender is less blameworthy when he or she creates no harm, and that efficient deterrence can justify greater sanctions where the offense has occurred than where it has not. The absence of a completed offense does not, however, alter the offender's dangerousness. Thus, whenever cases arise under doctrines giving significance to resulting harm, a conflict arises in which desert and deterrence will take account of resulting harm while incapacitation will not.

PART II

OFFENSE REQUIREMENTS

This coursebook is structured around the operational distinctions described in Section 1: offense definitions, doctrines of imputation, and general defenses. This Part takes up the first of these, the definition of offenses. Offense definitions commonly contain both objective elements—which include conduct, circumstance, or result elements—and culpability requirements. It is the latter that are most problematic and of greatest interest, and the subjects of the two Sections in this Part.

The particular requirements of offenses of special interest are examined in Part III, concerning homicide, Part IV, concerning inchoate offenses (such as attempt and conspiracy), and Part VII, concerning offenses of current reform attention, specifically rape and hate crimes.

Culpability
Requirements

Perhaps the central distinguishing feature of criminal law is its requirement that the offender not only have brought about some harm or evil but that he or she have some personal culpability as to the offense conduct. What "culpability" should be required, exactly, and why?

◆ THE CASE OF THOMAS FUNGWE

It is Wednesday, July 14, 1999, in Southfield, Michigan, one of Detroit's quiet northern suburbs. Thomas V. Fungwe is an assistant professor in the Department of Nutrition and Food Science at Wayne State University in downtown Detroit. He studies the effects that diet and certain enzymes have on cholesterol regulation. He is part of a team that investigates major contributors to excess morbidity within specific communities.

Fungwe is forty-seven years old and lives with his thirty-seven-year old wife, Florence. They are viewed as friendly, good neighbors. (When two brothers recently moved in next door, they stopped in to visit and welcome the men.) Their youngest son, Thorence, is five months old and is usually the center of attention. The Fungwes are loving parents, and talk about their children constantly.

Figure 13 **Wayne State University College of Science**

(Wayne State University)

Figure 14 **Thomas V. Fungwe**
(Wayne State University)

On this morning, Fungwe loads his children into the family's Chevy Venture minivan. He is to drop off his sons before going to teach summer session classes, which have just begun. First, he heads to his sons' day camp, where he drops off the two older boys. He then stops on Woodward Avenue to get gas, then parks his car in the faculty school parking lot on Putnam near Warren and Cass and makes his way to his campus office.

Fungwe does not yet realize it, but he has left his youngest son, five-month old Thorence, trapped in the locked car. It is a typical summer day. The temperature will rise to 88 degrees by three in the afternoon, but it feels much worse with the 33% humidity. Generally, babies cannot manage heat stress well because they do not have an effective mechanism to cool themselves.

Figure 15 **1998 Chevrolet Venture**

Locked in the Chevy Venture with the windows closed, Thorence soon feels uncomfortable and begins to cry. After an hour or so, the temperature continues to rise and he begins screaming. Soon he is beyond screaming. He begins having seizures, and his jaw starts to clamp shut. He finally passes out.

A passerby notices that he is motionless with his eyes rolled back. Someone calls the university police to report an abandoned baby. Thorence has now been in the van for almost five hours.

Meanwhile, Mrs. Fungwe picks up her older sons at day camp and goes to day care to pick up Thorence. When she finds that he is not there, she calls her husband.

As soon as his wife calls, Fungwe realizes what he has done. He runs out of his office and over to his car, just as a crowd is gathering around. The university police soon arrive. Thorence is pale and unconscious. Fungwe screams in anguish, "I killed my baby! I killed my baby!"

Thorence is rushed to the Michigan Children's Hospital and found to have a severe case of hyperthermia. The doctors try to resuscitate him but because his jaw is locked tightly, they have difficulty intubating him. He dies soon after reaching the hospital.

A Detroit Police Department spokesman later reports that the baby's body temperature was at least 108 degrees. The doctors are sure Thorence's temperature was higher than that, but "the thermometer would go no higher."

1. Relying only on your own intuitions of justice, what liability and punishment, if any, does Thomas Fungwe deserve?

N	0	1	2	3	4	5	6	7	8	9	10	11
☐	☐	☐	☐	☐	☐	☐	☐	☐	☐	☐	☐	☐
no liability	liability but no punishment	1 day	2 wks	2 mo	6 mo	1 yr	3 yrs	7 yrs	15 yrs	30 yrs	life imprisonment	death

2. What liability, if any, under the then-existing statutes?
3. What liability, if any, under the Model Penal Code?

■ THE LAW

Michigan Statutes Annotated
(1999)

Title 28. Crimes, Part Two. Substantive Criminal Law

Chapter 286a. Penal Code

Chapter XLV. Homicide

Section 28.548. First-Degree Murder; Penalty; Definitions

Sec. 316. (1) A person who commits any of the following is guilty of first degree murder and shall be punished by imprisonment for life:

(a) Murder perpetrated by means of poison, lying in wait, or any other willful, deliberate, and premeditated killing.

(b) Murder committed in the perpetration of, or attempt to perpetrate, arson, criminal sexual conduct in the first, second, or third degree, child abuse in the first degree, a major controlled substance offense, robbery, carjacking, breaking and entering of a dwelling, home invasion in the first or second degree, larceny of any kind, extortion, or kidnapping.

(c) A murder of a peace officer or a corrections officer committed while the peace officer or corrections officer is lawfully engaged in the performance of any of his or her duties as a peace officer or corrections officer, knowing that the peace officer or corrections officer is a peace officer or corrections officer engaged in the performance of his or her duty as a peace officer or corrections officer.

(2) As used in this section:

(a) "Arson" means a felony violation of chapter X.

(b) "Corrections officer" means any of the following:

(i) A prison or jail guard or other prison or jail personnel.

(ii) Any of the personnel of a boot camp, special alternative incarceration unit, or other minimum security correctional facility.

(iii) A parole or probation officer.

(c) "Major controlled substance offense" means any of the following:

(i) A violation of section 7401(2)(a)(i) to (iii) of the public health code, MCL 333.7401.

(ii) A violation of section 7403(2)(a)(i) to (iii) of the public health code, MCL 333.7403.

(iii) A conspiracy to commit an offense listed in subparagraph (i) or (ii).

(d) "Peace officer" means any of the following:

(i) A police or conservation officer of this state or a political subdivision of this state.

(ii) A police or conservation officer of the United States.

(iii) A police or conservation officer of another state or a political subdivision of another state.

Section 28.549. Murder; Second Degree

Sec. 317. All other kinds of murder shall be murder of the second [2nd] degree, and shall be punished by imprisonment in the state prison for life, or any term of years, in the discretion of the court trying the same.

Section 28.553. Manslaughter; Penalties

Sec. 321. Any person who shall commit the crime of manslaughter shall be guilty of a felony punishable by imprisonment in the state prison, not more than fifteen [15] years or by fine of not more than seven thousand five hundred [7,500] dollars, or both, at the discretion of the court.

Section 28.556. Negligent Homicide; Penalty

Sec. 324. Any person who, by the operation of any vehicle upon any highway or upon any other property, public or private, at an immoderate rate of speed or in a careless, reckless or negligent manner, but not wilfully or wantonly, shall cause the death of another, shall be guilty of a misdemeanor, punishable by imprisonment in the state prison not more than 2 years or by a fine of not more than $2,000.00, or by both such fine and imprisonment.

Section 28.557. Negligent Homicide; Inclusion in Manslaughter; Verdict of Guilty

Sec. 325. The crime of negligent homicide shall be deemed to be included within every crime of manslaughter charge to have been committed in the operation of any vehicle, and in any case where a defendant is charged with manslaughter committed in the operation of any vehicle, if the jury shall find the defendant not guilty of the crime of manslaughter, it may render a verdict of guilty of negligent homicide.

Section 28.330. Exposing Child with Intent to Injure or Abandon

Sec. 135. Any father or mother of a child under the age of six [6] years, or any other person who shall expose such child in any street, field, house or other place, with intent to injure or wholly to abandon it, shall be guilty of a felony, punishable by imprisonment in the state prison not more than ten [10] years.

Section 28.331(2). Definitions; Child Abuse

Sec. 136b. (1) As used in this section:

(a) "Child" means a person who is less than 18 years of age and is not emancipated by operation of law as provided in section 4 of MCL 722.4.

(b) "Cruel" means brutal, inhuman, sadistic, or that which torments.

(c) "Omission" means a willful failure to provide the food, clothing, or shelter necessary for a child's welfare or the willful abandonment of a child.

(d) "Person" means a child's parent or guardian or any other person who cares for, has custody of, or has authority over a child regardless of the length of time that a child is cared for, in the custody of, or subject to the authority of that person.

(e) "Physical harm" means any injury to a child's physical condition.

(f) "Serious physical harm" means any physical injury to a child that seriously impairs the child's health or physical well-being, including, but not limited to, brain damage, a skull or bone fracture, subdural hemorrhage or hematoma, dislocation, sprain, internal injury, poisoning, burn or scald, or severe cut.

(g) "Serious mental harm" means an injury to a child's mental condition or welfare that is not necessarily permanent but results in visibly demonstrable manifestations of a substantial disorder of thought or mood which significantly impairs judgment, behavior, capacity to recognize reality, or ability to cope with the ordinary demands of life.

(2) A person is guilty of child abuse in the first degree if the person knowingly or intentionally causes serious physical or serious mental harm to a child. Child abuse in the first degree is a felony punishable by imprisonment for not more than 15 years.

(3) A person is guilty of child abuse in the second degree if any of the following apply:

(a) The person's omission causes serious physical harm or serious mental harm to a child or if the person's reckless act causes serious physical harm to a child.

(b) The person knowingly or intentionally commits an act likely to cause serious physical or mental harm to a child regardless of whether harm results.

(c) The person knowingly or intentionally commits an act that is cruel to a child regardless of whether harm results.

(4) Child abuse in the second degree is a felony punishable by imprisonment for not more than 4 years.

(5) A person is guilty of child abuse in the third degree if the person knowingly or intentionally causes physical harm to a child. Child abuse in the third degree is a misdemeanor punishable by imprisonment for not more than 2 years.

(6) A person is guilty of child abuse in the fourth degree if the person's omission or reckless act causes physical harm to a child. Child abuse in the fourth degree is a misdemeanor punishable by imprisonment for not more than 1 year.

(7) This section does not prohibit a parent or guardian, or other person permitted by law or authorized by the parent or guardian, from taking steps to reasonably discipline a child, including the use of reasonable force.

People v. Richardson
293 N.W.2d 332 (Mich. 1980)

Defendant was convicted of first-degree murder, and appealed on the contention that the jury was not instructed on the definition of involuntary manslaughter, a crime for which his evidence provided support. The court held the judge's refusal to instruct on the lesser crimes to be in error, and noted that Michigan's "manslaughter statute does not define that offense [involuntary manslaughter], but instead incorporates the common-law definition."

People v. Ryczek
194 N.W. 609 (Mich. 1923)

Defendant was convicted of involuntary manslaughter for colliding with a boy pushing his baby sister in a cart, which resulted in the baby's death. The court affirmed his conviction and applied the common law definition that involuntary manslaughter is "the killing of another without malice and unintentionally, but in doing some unlawful act not amounting to a felony nor naturally tending to cause death or great bodily harm, or in negligently doing some act lawful in itself, or by the negligent omission to perform a legal duty.... [Here, the defendant] while doing a lawful act in driving his automobile, ... did it in such a negligent manner that it amounted to gross negligence on his part." The court found that if the "defendant [had] given the most casual glance ahead of him, he would have observed the children approaching." Consequently, the jury was "well within their province in finding that such conduct was gross negligence," deserving of conviction.

People v. Clark
556 N.W.2d 820 (Mich. 1996)

Defendant was convicted of involuntary manslaughter for the death of her four-year-old son. She was suspected of child abuse. The court adopted the common law definition of the crime, and added that "[t]he kind of negligence required for manslaughter is ... often described as ... 'gross negligence,' [for which] three elements must be satisfied. These elements are embodied in CJI2d 16.18 that expressed the people's theory of the defendant's guilt.... These elements are: (1) Knowledge of a situation requiring the exercise of ordinary care and diligence to avert injury to another. (2) Ability to avoid the resulting harm by ordinary care and diligence in the use of the means at hand. (3) The omission to use such care and diligence to avert the threatened danger when to the ordinary mind it must be apparent that the result is likely to prove disastrous to another."

People v. Clark
431 N.W.2d 88 (Mich. App. 1988)

Defendant was convicted of negligent homicide after he drove his semitrailer truck through a red light and struck an oncoming car. The court stated that "the crime of negligent homicide is the killing of a person through an act of ordinary negligence, an act which is otherwise noncriminal, which becomes criminal because the victim dies."

People v. Traughber
439 N.W.2d 231 (Mich. 1989)

Defendant was convicted of negligent homicide for causing a fatal crash when he swerved into another lane of traffic. On appeal, the defendant challenged the jury instructions as prejudicial by requiring more than a reasonable standard of care. The court held the trial judge's instructions were correct, and stated that "[t]here is no question that the applicable standard of care in negligent homicide cases is that of a reasonable person. CJI 16:5:02(1) states: 'For negligent homicide the prosecution must prove beyond a reasonable doubt that the defendant was guilty of ordinary negligence.' This instruction goes on to explain that '[o]rdinary negligence is defined as want of reasonable care; that is, failing to do what an ordinarily sensible person would have done under the conditions and circumstances then existing....' CJI 16:5:02(4)." However, the court reversed the conviction because the defendant had reacted to an emergency situation in a manner that was not contrary to that of a reasonably prudent man under similar circumstances.

◆ THE CASE OF RAYMOND LENNARD GARNETT

Raymond Lennard Garnett is a twenty-year old man living in Silver Spring, Maryland, a Washington, D.C., suburb. Garnett is average height (5' 8") and weight, but is legally mentally retarded, with an I.Q. of 52. (The Supreme Court recently held that an I.Q. of 70 or lower qualifies as mentally retarded.) Garnett reads at about a third-grade level and his math skills put him on a fifth-grade level. He attended special education classes, but recently left school for a short time when the other students teased him so mercilessly that he became too scared to return to class. He was home-schooled for a time but eventually returned to public school. He cannot complete many of the required tasks, because he does not understand the vocational assignments. He is often confused and sometimes gets lost. He does not pass any of the state's graduation tests and so receives only a certificate of attendance rather than a diploma. He presently interacts with others and processes things much as an eleven- or twelve-year old would.

In November of 1990, Garnett's friend introduces him to Erica Frazier. They both tell Garnett that Erica is sixteen years old, a fact later confirmed by her friends. In reality, Erica is only thirteen. Garnett is surprised that she is interested in talking to him. He likes her and enjoys talking with someone who does not make fun of him. Erica and Garnett talk on the phone off and on over the next several months.

On the evening of February 28, 1991, Garnett is stranded. He needs a ride home and notices that Erica's house is nearby. He approaches her house on

Figure 16 **Frazier's house (with tree)**
(Catherine McAlpine)

Liberty Heights Lane at about 9 p.m. Erica opens her bedroom window and invites him in. She tells him to get a ladder and to climb up to her window so as not to disturb her parents. He enters her room and the two sit and talk for a while. One thing leads to another and they eventually end up having consensual sex. Afterwards, Garnett and Erica lie for hours talking. Finally, at 4:30 a.m., Garnett leaves.

Eight and a half months after their encounter, on November 19, 1991, Erica gives birth to a baby girl at Shady Grove Adventist Hospital. Her mother, Brenda Freeman, had not been aware of the pregnancy. Erica explains that Garnett had visited once and that it was her only sexual experience. The next day, Ms. Freeman contacts the Youth Division of the police to report the rape of her daughter. Garnett is subsequently arrested for statutory rape after being determined to be the biological father.

1. Relying only on your own intuitions of justice, what liability and punishment, if any, does Raymond Lennard Garnett deserve?

N	0	1	2	3	4	5	6	7	8	9	10	11
☐	☐	☐	☐	☐	☐	☐	☐	☐	☐	☐	☐	☐
no liability	liability but no punishment	1 day	2 wks	2 mo	6 mo	1 yr	3 yrs	7 yrs	15 yrs	30 yrs	life imprisonment	death

2. What liability, if any, under the then-existing statutes?
3. What liability, if any, under the Model Penal Code?

■ THE LAW

Annotated Code of Maryland
(1990)

Article 27. Crimes and Punishments
I. Sexual Offenses

Section 461. Definitions

(a) In general. — In this subheading, the following words have the meanings indicated.

(b) Mentally defective. — "Mentally defective" means (1) a victim who suffers from mental retardation, or (2) a victim who suffers from a mental disorder, either of which temporarily or permanently renders the victim substantially incapable of appraising the nature of his or her conduct, or resisting the act of vaginal intercourse, a sexual act, or sexual contact, or of communicating unwillingness to submit to the act of vaginal intercourse, a sexual act, or sexual contact.

(c) Mentally incapacitated. — "Mentally incapacitated" means a victim who, due to the influence of a drug, narcotic or intoxicating substance, or due to any act committed upon the victim without the victim's consent or awareness, is rendered substantially incapable of either appraising the nature of his or her conduct, or resisting the act of vaginal intercourse, a sexual act, or sexual contact.

(d) Physically helpless. — "Physically helpless" means (1) a victim who is unconscious; or (2) a victim who does not consent to an act of vaginal intercourse, a sexual act, or sexual contact, and is physically unable to resist an act of vaginal intercourse, a sexual act, or sexual contact or communicate unwillingness to submit to an act of vaginal intercourse, a sexual act, or sexual contact.

(e) Sexual act. — "Sexual act" means cunnilingus, fellatio, analingus, or anal intercourse, but does not include vaginal intercourse. Emission of semen is not required. Penetration, however slight, is evidence of anal intercourse. Sexual act also means the penetration, however slight, by any object into the genital or anal opening of another person's body if the penetration can be reasonably construed as being for the purposes of sexual arousal or gratification or for abuse of either party and if the penetration is not for accepted medical purposes.

(f) Sexual contact. — "Sexual contact," as used in §§464B and 464C, means the intentional touching of any part of the victim's or actor's anal or genital areas or other intimate parts for the purposes of sexual arousal or gratification or for abuse of either party and includes the penetration, however slight, by any part of a person's body, other than the penis, mouth, or tongue, into the genital or anal opening of another person's body if that penetration can be reasonably construed as being for the purposes of sexual arousal or gratification or for abuse of either party. It does not include acts commonly expressive of familial or friendly affection, or acts for accepted medical purposes.

(g) Vaginal intercourse. — "Vaginal intercourse" has its ordinary meaning of genital copulation. Penetration, however slight, is evidence of vaginal intercourse. Emission of semen is not required.

Section 461A. Admissibility of Evidence in Rape Cases

(a) Evidence relating to victim's chastity. — Evidence relating to a victim's reputation for chastity and opinion evidence relating to a victim's chastity are not admissible in any prosecution for commission of a rape or sexual offense in the first or second degree. Evidence of specific instances of the victim's prior sexual conduct may be admitted only if the judge finds the evidence is relevant and is material to a fact in issue in the case and that its inflammatory or prejudicial nature does not outweigh its probative value, and if the evidence is:

(1) Evidence of the victim's past sexual conduct with the defendant; or

(2) Evidence of specific instances of sexual activity showing the source or origin of semen, pregnancy, disease, or trauma; or

(3) Evidence which supports a claim that the victim has an ulterior motive in accusing the defendant of the crime; or

(4) Evidence offered for the purpose of impeachment when the prosecutor puts the victim's prior sexual conduct in issue.

(b) In camera hearing. — Any evidence described in subsection (a) of this section may not be referred to in any statements to a jury nor introduced at trial without the court holding a prior in camera hearing to determine the admissibility of the evidence. If new information is discovered during the course of the trial that may make the evidence described in subsection (a) admissible, the court may order an in camera hearing to determine the admissibility of the proposed evidence under subsection (a).

Section 461B. Instructions

In any criminal prosecution for rape, attempted rape, assault with intent to commit a rape, assault with intent to commit a sexual offense, or any other sexual offense, the jury may not be instructed:

(1) To examine with caution the testimony of the prosecuting witness, solely because of the nature of the charge;

(2) That the charge is easily made or difficult to disprove, solely because of the nature of the charge; or

(3) As to any other similar instruction, solely because of the nature of the charge.

Section 462. First Degree Rape

(a) What constitutes. — A person is guilty of rape in the first degree if the person engages in vaginal intercourse with another person by force or threat of force against the will and without the consent of the other person and:

(1) Employs or displays a dangerous or deadly weapon or an article which the other person reasonably concludes is a dangerous or deadly weapon; or

(2) Inflicts suffocation, strangulation, disfigurement, or serious physical injury upon the other person or upon anyone else in the course of committing the offense; or

(3) Threatens or places the victim in fear that the victim or any person known to the victim will be imminently subjected to death, suffocation, strangulation, disfigurement, serious physical injury, or kidnaping; or

(4) The person commits the offense aided and abetted by one or more other persons; or

(5) The person commits the offense in connection with the breaking and entering of a dwelling house.

(b) Penalty. — Any person violating the provisions of this section is guilty of a felony and upon conviction is subject to imprisonment for no more than the period of his natural life.

Section 463. Second Degree Rape

(a) What constitutes. — A person is guilty of rape in the second degree if the person engages in vaginal intercourse with another person:

(1) By force or threat of force against the will and without the consent of the other person; or

(2) Who is mentally defective, mentally incapacitated, or physically helpless, and the person performing the act knows or should reasonably know the other person is mentally defective, mentally incapacitated, or physically helpless; or

(3) Who is under 14 years of age and the person performing the act is at least four years older than the victim.

(b) Penalty. — Any person violating the provisions of this section is guilty of a felony and upon conviction is subject to imprisonment for a period of not more than 20 years.

Section 464. First Degree Sexual Offense

(a) What constitutes. — A person is guilty of a sexual offense in the first degree if the person engages in a sexual act:

(1) With another person by force or threat of force against the will and without the consent of the other person, and:

(i) Employs or displays a dangerous or deadly weapon or an article which the other person reasonably concludes is a dangerous or deadly weapon; or

(ii) Inflicts suffocation, strangulation, disfigurement, or serious physical injury upon the other person or upon anyone else in the course of committing the offense; or

(iii) Threatens or places the victim in fear that the victim or any person known to the victim will be imminently subjected to death, suffocation, strangulation, disfigurement, serious physical injury, or kidnaping; or

(iv) The person commits the offense aided and abetted by one or more other persons; or

(v) The person commits the offense in connection with the breaking and entering of a dwelling house.

(b) Penalty. — Any person violating the provisions of this section is guilty of a felony and upon conviction is subject to imprisonment for no more than the period of his natural life.

Section 464A. Second Degree Sexual Offense

(a) What constitutes. — A person is guilty of a sexual offense in the second degree if the person engages in a sexual act with another person:

(1) By force or threat of force against the will and without the consent of the other person; or

(2) Who is mentally defective, mentally incapacitated, or physically helpless, and the person performing the act knows or should reasonably know the other person is mentally defective, mentally incapacitated, or physically helpless; or

(3) Under 14 years of age and the person performing the sexual act is four or more years older than the victim.

(b) Penalty. — Any person violating the provisions of this section is guilty of a felony and upon conviction is subject to imprisonment for a period of not more than 20 years.

Section 464B. Third Degree Sexual Offense

(a) What constitutes. — A person is guilty of a sexual offense in the third degree if the person engages in sexual contact:

(1) With another person against the will and without the consent of the other person, and:

(i) Employs or displays a dangerous or deadly weapon or an article which the other person reasonably concludes is a dangerous or deadly weapon; or

(ii) Inflicts suffocation, strangulation, disfigurement or serious physical injury upon the other person or upon anyone else in the course of committing that offense; or

(iii) Threatens or places the victim in fear that the victim or any person known to the victim will be imminently subjected to death, suffocation, strangulation, disfigurement, serious physical injury, or kidnaping; or

(iv) Commits the offense aided and abetted by one or more other persons; or

(2) With another person who is mentally defective, mentally incapacitated, or physically helpless, and the person knows or should reasonably know the other person is mentally defective, mentally incapacitated, or physically helpless; or

(3) With another person who is under 14 years of age and the person performing the sexual contact is four or more years older than the victim.

(b) Penalty. — Any person violating the provisions of this section is guilty of a felony and upon conviction is subject to imprisonment for a period of not more than 10 years.

Section 464C. Fourth Degree Sexual Offense

(a) What constitutes. — A person is guilty of a sexual offense in the fourth degree if the person engages:

(1) In sexual contact with another person against the will and without the consent of the other person; or

(2) In a sexual act with another person who is 14 or 15 years of age and the person performing the sexual act is four or more years older than the other person; or

(3) In vaginal intercourse with another person who is 14 or 15 years of age and the person performing the act is four or more years older than the other person.

(b) Penalty. — Any person violating the provisions of this section is guilty of a misdemeanor and upon conviction is subject to imprisonment for a period of not more than one year, or a fine of not more than $1,000, or both fine and imprisonment.

Eggleston v. State
241 A.2d 433, 434 (Md. Ct. Spec. App. 1968)

Defendant was charged with statutory rape. On appeal, he argued that the statute's language describing the crime as "feloniously" committed meant that a specific intent was required. However, the court rejected his argument, and held that the state's statutory rape provision did not permit a mens rea requirement and the term "feloniously" was merely a description used to classify the offense. The court applied the "generally accepted state of the law as set out in Wharton's Criminal Law, [which] fail[ed] to vindicate appellant's proposition: 'It is no defense that the defendant did not know that the female was under the statutory age of consent. It is immaterial that the defendant in good faith believed that the female was above the prohibited age; that his belief, though erroneous, was reasonable; or that the defendant had been misled by the appearance or statements of the female. The defendant acts at his peril that the female may in fact be under the age of consent. The fact that the defendant cannot assert as a defense his bona fide belief in the victim's age does not make unconstitutional the statutes under consideration.' "

Michael M. v. Superior Court of Sonoma County
450 U.S. 464, 465 (1981)

The defendant was convicted of statutory rape under the California Penal Code §261.5. He appealed his conviction on the grounds that the statute violated the Equal Protection Clause of the Fourteenth Amendment by defining unlawful sexual intercourse as "an act of sexual intercourse accomplished with a female not the wife of the perpetrator, where the female is under the age of 18 years." Thus, the statute made men alone criminally liable. However, the Court overturned the California Supreme Court's ruling and upheld the statute as not being invidious, and instead found it "realistically reflect[ed] the fact that the sexes are not similarly situated in certain circumstances." The Court recognized the state's interest in making the crime of statutory rape a strict liability offense, and held that California's interest of preventing teenage pregnancy to be a valid interest.

Model Penal Code
(Official Draft 1962)

Section 1.13. General Definitions

In this Code, unless a different meaning plainly is required: ...
    (9) "element of an offense" means (i) such conduct or (ii) such attendant circumstances or (iii) such a result of conduct as
        (a) is included in the description of the forbidden conduct in the definition of the offense; or
        (b) establishes the required kind of culpability; or
        (c) negatives an excuse or justification for such conduct; or
        (d) negatives a defense under the statute of limitations; or
        (e) establishes jurisdiction or venue;

(10) "material element of an offense" means an element that does not relate exclusively to the statute of limitations, jurisdiction, venue or to any other matter similarly unconnected with (i) the harm or evil, incident to conduct, sought to be prevented by the law defining the offense, or (ii) the existence of a justification or excuse for such conduct; . . .

Section 2.02. General Requirements of Culpability

(1) Minimum Requirements of Culpability. Except as provided in Section 2.05, a person is not guilty of an offense unless he acted purposely, knowingly, recklessly or negligently, as the law may require, with respect to each material element of the offense.

(2) Kinds of Culpability Defined.

(a) Purposely. A person acts purposely with respect to a material element of an offense when:

(i) if the element involves the nature of his conduct or a result thereof, it is his conscious object to engage in conduct of that nature or to cause such a result; and

(ii) if the element involves the attendant circumstances, he is aware of the existence of such circumstances or he believes or hopes that they exist.

(b) Knowingly. A person acts knowingly with respect to a material element of an offense when:

(i) if the element involves the nature of his conduct or the attendant circumstances, he is aware that his conduct is of that nature or that such circumstances exist; and

(ii) if the element involves a result of his conduct, he is aware that it is practically certain that his conduct will cause such a result.

(c) Recklessly. A person acts recklessly with respect to a material element of an offense when he consciously disregards a substantial and unjustifiable risk that the material element exists or will result from his conduct. The risk must be of such a nature and degree that, considering the nature and purpose of the actor's conduct and the circumstances known to him, its disregard involves a gross deviation from the standard of conduct that a law-abiding person would observe in the actor's situation.

(d) Negligently. A person acts negligently with respect to a material element of an offense when he should be aware of a substantial and unjustifiable risk that the material element exists or will result from his conduct. The risk must be of such a nature and degree that the actor's failure to perceive it, considering the nature and purpose of his conduct and the circumstances known to him, involves a gross deviation from the standard of care that a reasonable person would observe in the actor's situation.

(3) Culpability Required Unless Otherwise Provided. When the culpability sufficient to establish a material element of an offense is not prescribed by law, such element is established if a person acts purposely, knowingly or recklessly with respect thereto.

(4) Prescribed Culpability Requirement Applies to All Material Elements. When the law defining an offense prescribes the kind of culpability that is sufficient for the commission of an offense, without distinguishing among the material elements thereof, such provision shall apply to all the material elements of the offense, unless a contrary purpose plainly appears.

(5) Substitutes for Negligence, Recklessness and Knowledge. When the law provides that negligence suffices to establish an element of an offense, such element also is established if a person acts purposely, knowingly or recklessly. When recklessness suffices to establish an element, such element also is established if a person acts purposely or knowingly. When acting knowingly suffices to establish an element, such element also is established if a person acts purposely.

(6) Requirement of Purpose Satisfied if Purpose Is Conditional. When a particular purpose is an element of an offense, the element is established although such purpose is conditional, unless the condition negatives the harm or evil sought to be prevented by the law defining the offense.

(7) Requirement of Knowledge Satisfied by Knowledge of High Probability. When knowledge of the existence of a particular fact is an element of an offense, such knowledge is established if a person is aware of a high probability of its existence, unless he actually believes that it does not exist.

(8) Requirement of Wilfulness Satisfied by Acting Knowingly. A requirement that an offense be committed wilfully is satisfied if a person acts knowingly with respect to the material elements of the offense, unless a purpose to impose further requirements appears.

(9) Culpability as to Illegality of Conduct. Neither knowledge nor recklessness or negligence as to whether conduct constitutes an offense or as to the existence, meaning or application of the law determining the elements of an offense is an element of such offense, unless the definition of the offense or the Code so provides.

(10) Culpability as Determinant of Grade of Offense. When the grade or degree of an offense depends on whether the offense is committed purposely, knowingly, recklessly or negligently, its grade or degree shall be the lowest for which the determinative kind of culpability is established with respect to any material element of the offense.

● OVERVIEW OF CULPABILITY REQUIREMENTS

Notes on Culpability Requirements*

Significance of Mens Rea The requirement of culpability distinguishes the criminal law from other bodies of law. Without mens rea, the common law expression, there is little justification for condemning or punishing an actor. An

---

*N.B. — Remember that the formatting of paragraph titles signal descending superiority of paragraphs as follows: HEADING, **Heading**, *Heading*, Heading.

actor's conduct may be harmful; the victim may have a claim in tort; and fairness and utility both may suggest that the actor rather than the victim should bear the loss for the injury. But without culpability in the actor, causing the injury may be seen lacking in sufficient blameworthiness to deserve the condemnation and reprobation of criminal conviction.

Early Notions of Mens Rea   The law did not always require culpability of an actor. Early Germanic tribes, it is suggested, imposed liability upon the causing of an injury, without regard to culpability. But this was during a period before tort law and criminal law were divided. It seems likely that as the distinction between tort and crime appeared — that is, as the function of compensating victims became distinguished from the function of imposing punishment — the requirement of culpability took on increasing importance.[1] Early notions of mens rea requirements are seen in *Regina v. Prince*.[2] The defendant had taken an underage girl "out of the possession" of her father, reasonably believing she was over the age of consent. That the defendant's conduct was generally immoral was sufficient for Lord Bramwell to find that the defendant had the mens rea necessary for the crime. Lord Brett, on the other hand, would require that Prince at least have intended to do something (anything) that was criminal, not just immoral. A somewhat more demanding requirement is expressed in *Regina v. Faulkner*.[3] In the process of stealing rum from the hold of a ship, Faulkner accidentally set the ship afire, destroying it. Lords Fitzgerald and Palles conclude that the mens rea requirement means that Faulkner must have at least intended to do something criminal that might reasonably have been expected to have led to the actual harm caused and charged. Thus, Faulkner ought not be liable for the offense of burning a ship when he intended only to steal rum from it, and by that conduct could not reasonably have foreseen its destruction.

From Mens Rea to Mentes Reae   This last shift in the notion of mens rea meant not only a dramatic increase in the demand of the requirement, but also a significant qualitative change. No longer did there exist a single mens rea requirement for all offenses — the intention to do something immoral or, later, something criminal. Now each offense had a different mens rea requirement — the mens rea required for the offense of burning a ship was different from the mens rea required for theft. Now an actor had to intend to do something that might reasonably be expected to lead to the harm of the particular offense. As some have expressed it, there was no longer a mens rea for criminal liability but rather mentes reae.

From Offense Analysis to Element Analysis   The Model Penal Code carries this refinement another step. In section 2.02(1), the Code requires culpability "with respect to each material element of the offense." Even the notion of mentes reae conceives of each offense as having a single culpability requirement.

---

1. For centuries, admittedly, tort law remained tied to notions of fault, generally negligence, but the nature of the fault required for tort recovery was never set at the level that would justify condemnation of the actor, as was and is generally required at criminal law. Nor, admittedly, has criminal law completely forsaken the imposition of liability in the absence of subjective awareness of wrongdoing. Criminal liability sometimes is still permitted for "gross negligence" or a "gross deviation" from the standard of care of a reasonable person. See, e.g., Model Penal Code §2.02(2)(d).

2. 13 Cox's Crim. Cases 138 (1875).

3. 13 Cox's Crim. Cases 550 (1877).

Indeed, legal doctrine of that day grouped offenses according to the type of culpability that the offense required: There were said to be general intent offenses, specific intent offenses, and offenses of strict liability. In what may be described as a shift from *offense analysis* to *element analysis*, the Model Penal Code introduced the requirement of culpability as to each element of an offense. Moreover, under the Code, the level of culpability required may be different for different elements of the same offense.

Element Analysis as Comprehensive   This element analysis approach provides, for the first time, a comprehensive statement of the culpability required for an offense. The early conceptions of mens rea were not simply undemanding, they were hopelessly vague and incomplete. They failed to tell courts enough about the required culpability for an offense to enable the courts to resolve the cases that commonly arose. The vague conceptualizations left it for courts to fill in the culpability requirements that the statutes did not provide. Element analysis permits legislatures to reclaim from the courts the authority to define the conditions of criminal liability and, for the first time, to provide a comprehensive statement of the culpability required for an offense.

Misconceptions That Permitted Offense Analysis   The shift to element analysis did not come from a determination by the Model Penal Code drafters to change the traditional offense requirements. Rather, the drafters believed that element analysis was necessary to describe accurately an offense's culpability requirements, even requirements that had been recognized during the Common Law period. That is, Common Law lawyers and judges were wrong to think that their offense-analysis view of offense culpability requirements was adequate to describe the culpability that the Common Law required. Their misconception stemmed in part from their conceptualization of an independent "law of mistake," which they saw as supplementing the culpability requirements of an offense definition. Thus, an actor might satisfy the requirements of theft, yet have a defense if the "law of mistake" allowed a defense in the situation. The Model Penal Code drafters, in contrast, recognized that a mistake defense and a culpability requirement are one and the same: they are simply two ways of describing the same thing. Thus, the Model Code provides that mistake gives a defense if it negates an offense culpability requirement.[1] Mistakes negating an offense element are discussed further in Section 5.

Culpability Levels under Model Penal Code   Aside from their insight into the relation between mistake defenses and culpability requirements, the Code drafters' greatest contribution in this area is their use of a limited number of carefully defined deculpability terms. In place of the plethora of common law terms—wantonly, heedlessly, maliciously, and so on[2]—the Code defines four levels of culpability: purposely, knowingly, recklessly, and negligently. Ideally, all offenses are defined by designating one of these four levels of culpability as to each objective element. If the objective elements of an offense require that an actor take

---

1. See Model Penal Code §2.04(1).

2. The current federal criminal law, which has never undergone the modernization via the Model Penal Code that a majority of state codes have, uses 78 different culpability terms. "Present federal criminal law is composed of a bewildering array of terms used to describe the mental element of an offense." S. Rep. No. 605, 95th Cong., 1st Sess., pt.1, at 55.

the property of another, the culpability elements might require, for example, that the actor know that he is taking property and that he be at least reckless as to it being someone else's property. Modern codes give detailed definitions of each of the four culpability levels.

> The purpose of articulating these distinctions in detail is to advance the clarity of draftsmanship in the delineation of the definitions of specific crimes, to provide a distinct framework against which those definitions may be tested, and to dispel the obscurity with which the culpability requirement is often treated when such concepts as "general criminal intent," "mens rea," "presumed intent," "malice," "wilfulness," "scienter" and the like have been employed. What Justice Jackson called "the variety, disparity and confusion" of judicial definitions of "the requisite but elusive mental element" in crime should, insofar as possible, be rationalized by a criminal code.[1]

(The Code's culpability levels are defined slightly differently as to each of the kinds of objective elements of an offense — conduct, circumstance, and result. See the Advanced Issues materials in the Appendix. For this discussion, let us focus on the definition of culpability as to causing a result.)

Purpose Under the Code, a person acts "purposely" with respect to a result if his or her conscious object is to cause such a result.[2] Notice that, while the criminal law generally treats an actor's motive as irrelevant, the requirement of "purpose" is a requirement that the actor have a particular motive for acting, such as to cause a particular result. This is a demanding requirement that often is difficult to prove. The offense of indecent exposure, for example, requires more than showing that the actor "flashed" another, knowing that it would alarm the person; it must be proven that the conduct was motivated by a desire to gain sexual gratification or arousal by the conduct. Doing it just to annoy or alarm the victim would not satisfy the offense's special purpose requirement.[3]

Purposely vs. Knowingly A person acts "purposely" as to a result if it is his conscious object to cause the result. A person acts "knowingly" with respect to a result if it is not his conscious object, yet he is practically certain that the conduct will cause that result.[4] The anti-war activist who sets a bomb to destroy the draft board offices may be practically certain that the bomb will kill the night watchman yet wish that the watchman would go on a coffee break so that he will not be killed. The essence of the narrow distinction between these two culpability levels is the presence or absence of a *positive desire* to cause the result; purpose requires a culpability beyond the knowledge of a result's near certainty. In the broader sense, this distinction divides the vague notion of "callousness" from the more offensive "maliciousness" or "viciousness." The latter may simply be an aggressively ruthless form of the former.

Knowingly vs. Recklessly A person acts "knowingly" with respect to a result if she is nearly certain that her conduct will cause the result. If she is aware only of a substantial risk, she acts "recklessly" with respect to the result.[5] The

---

1. Model Penal Code §2.02 comment at 230 (1985).
2. Model Penal Code §2.02(2)(a)(i).
3. See, e.g., Model Penal Code §213.5 (requiring "purpose of arousing or gratifying sexual desire").
4. Model Penal Code §2.02(2)(b)(ii).
5. Model Penal Code §2.02(2)(c).

narrow distinction between knowledge and recklessness lies in the *degree of risk*—"practically certain" versus "substantial risk"—of which the actor is aware. The distinction between recklessness (and lower levels of culpability) and the two higher levels of culpability (purposely and knowingly) is that we tend to scold a reckless actor for being "careless," while we condemn an offender who falls within one of the higher culpability categories for "intentional" conduct.

Purpose as Independent of Likelihood   While knowing and reckless culpability focus on the likelihood of causing the result—"practically certain" versus "substantial risk"—purposeful culpability pays no regard to the likelihood of the result. This characteristic of the purpose requirement reflects an instinct that *trying* to cause the harm, whatever the likelihood, is more condemnable than acting with the belief that the harm will or might result without desiring it. The practical effect of this is that reckless conduct, as manifested in risk-taking, can be elevated to purposeful conduct if the actor hopes that the risk will come to fruition. This characteristic of purpose also illustrates how specially demanding it is. A requirement of a particular belief is something a jury might logically deduce from other facts: The actor "must have known" the certainty or the risk of harm if he knew this fact or that. A purpose requirement requires the jury to determine an actor's objective or goal, a somewhat more complex psychological state. To find this, a jury may have to dig deeper into the actor's psyche, his general desires and motivations, to reach a conclusion. If a jury is conscientious in adhering to the proof-beyond-a-reasonable-doubt standard constitutionally required for offense elements, this may be a difficult conclusion to reach.

Wilful Blindness   Most common law courts and modern codes make clear that an actor's deliberate blindness to a fact does not protect him from being treated as "knowing" that fact. For example, one who drives across the border in a car with a secret compartment but carefully avoids actually knowing that marijuana is hidden in the secret compartment can be held liable for knowingly transporting marijuana if it can be shown that "his ignorance in this regard was solely and entirely the result of his having made a conscious purpose to disregard the nature of that which was in the vehicle, with a conscious purpose to avoid learning the truth." The Model Penal Code resolves the problem of wilful blindness in a slightly different way. Section 2.02(7) provides:

> Requirement of Knowledge Satisfied by Knowledge of High Probability. When knowledge of the existence of a particular fact is an element of an offense, such knowledge is established if a person is aware of a high probability of its existence, unless he actually believes that it does not exist.

Thus, the smuggler is held to "know" of the marijuana if he is aware of a high probability that it is there. (Note that this standard requires something less than the "practically certain" standard that the Code uses when defining "knowingly" as to causing a result.[1])

Recklessly vs. Negligently   A person acts "recklessly" with respect to a result if she consciously disregards a substantial risk that her conduct will cause the result; she acts only "negligently" if she is unaware of the substantial risk but

---

1. Compare Model Penal Code §2.02(7) to §2.02(2)(b)(ii).

should have perceived it.[1] The recklessness issue focuses not on whether she should have been aware of the risk, but instead on whether she was in fact aware (and whether she was culpable in disregarding such a risk).

Recklessness as Conscious Wrongdoing The narrow distinction between recklessness and negligence lies in the actor's *awareness of risk*. The distinction between negligence and the three higher levels of culpability is one of the most critical to criminal law. A person who acts purposely, knowingly, or recklessly is aware of the circumstances that make his or her conduct criminal or is aware that harmful consequences may result and is therefore both blameworthy and deterrable. A defendant who acts negligently, in contrast, is unaware of the circumstances or consequences and therefore, some writers argue, is neither blameworthy nor deterrable. While writers disagree over whether negligence ought to be adequate to support criminal liability, it is agreed that negligence represents a lower level of culpability than, and is qualitatively different from, recklessness, in that the negligent actor fails to recognize, rather than consciously disregards, the risk. For this reason, recklessness is considered the norm for criminal culpability, while negligence is punished only in exceptional circumstances, as when a death is caused. The issue of what culpability level should constitute the minimum for criminal liability is the first of the two Discussion Materials questions below.

Negligence as Normative Assessment A person who fails to appreciate the risk that her conduct will cause a result is "negligent" as to the result if the failure "involves a gross deviation from the standard of care that a reasonable person would observe in the actor's situation."[2] Thus, unless she grossly deviates from the standard of care that a reasonable person would observe, she is not negligent and, at least in the eyes of the criminal law, is without cognizable fault. Would a reasonable person in her situation have been aware that a risk of death existed? Was her failure to perceive the risk a gross deviation from the attentiveness to the possibility of risk that the reasonable person in her situation would have had? These are the issues that the jury would consider in assessing whether she is negligent. They are not factual but normative issues. The jury is asked to judge whether her failure to perceive the risk was, under the circumstances, a blameworthy failure. Whether negligence should be assessed against a purely objective standard or a partially individualized standard is the second of the Discussion Materials questions below.

Negligently vs. Faultlessly Liability imposed for faultless conduct is termed "absolute" or "strict" liability. The narrow distinction between negligence and strict liability focuses on whether the defendant's unawareness of the risk is a *failure to meet the standard of the reasonable person* in the actor's situation. The broader distinction between the four categories of culpability, on the one hand, and faultlessness, on the other, is the distinction between a blameworthy and a blameless actor. Theoretical objections to strict liability understandably stem from a reluctance to punish conduct that is not unreasonable.

---

1. Model Penal Code §2.02(2)(d).

2. Model Penal Code §2.02(2)(d). Parallel language appears in the definition of recklessness, in §2.02(2)(c). In that context, however, the language concerns whether a "law-abiding" person would have consciously disregarded the risk that the actor disregarded.

Negligence and Omissions   One might think that "negligence" has something to do with omissions because of the common usage of the term; one "neglects" to act. Older cases sometimes suggested or assumed such a connection, but it has long since been agreed that "negligence," when used to refer to a level of culpability, can apply as easily to a commission as to an omission. The crux of negligent culpability is the failure to perceive a risk of which one should be aware, a risk from either an act or an omission to perform a legal duty. It is equally clear that one can have any level of culpability as to an omission, not just negligence. Where a parent fails to obtain needed medical care for a child and as a result the child dies, the actor may have been purposeful, knowing, reckless, negligent, or faultless as to allowing the resulting death. The parent may have failed to get medical care because she desired to cause the child's death; or she may not have desired to cause the death, but she may have been practically certain that her omission to get care would result in the death; or she may have been aware only of a substantial risk that her omission would result in the death; or she may have been unaware of a substantial risk but should have been aware (the reasonable person would have been aware); or she may have been unaware and a reasonable person similarly would have been unaware. Generally, culpability requirements apply to omissions in the same way that they do to commissions.

Concurrence Requirement   When an offense definition requires a particular level of culpability as to a particular element, it means that the required culpability as to the element must exist at the time of the conduct constituting the offense. This concurrence requirement, as it is called, reflects the law's interest in judging the culpability of the act rather than the general character of the actor. The required concurrence between act and culpability is implicit in the Model Penal Code culpability definitions in section 2.02(2), discussed above.[1] In *State v. Hopple*, for example, Hopple took possession of a neighbor's sheep in order to protect his land from their unauthorized trampling of his cattle feed. Without the neighbor's permission, he subsequently attempted to sell the sheep.[2] Citing the "concurrence requirement," the court held that if the defendant had formed his intention to deprive the owner permanently of the sheep only after gaining possession, there was no concurrence between the taking and the intent to deprive permanently, as is required for theft. (Hopple might be liable nonetheless for an offense other than theft, such as unlawful "conversion" of another's property.) Note that the concurrence requirement applies to the time of the offense conduct, not to the time of the result. It is neither necessary nor sufficient that the culpability exists at the later time of the result of the conduct. Changing one's mind after setting a bomb does not bar liability for deaths caused by the blast, even if the intent to kill no longer exists at the time the bomb explodes or the victims die.

Subverting Concurrence Requirement   In *Thabo Meli and Others v. The Queen*, the defendants struck the victim over the head, intending to kill him. They believed they were successful and rolled his body off a cliff to make the killing appear to be an accident. The victim, however, was alive after the beating but died later when they rolled him off the cliff.[3] Strict application of the concurrence

---

1. See Model Penal Code comment 1 at 229 (1985).
2. 357 P.2d 656 (Idaho 1960).
3. [1954] 1 W.L.R. 228, 1 ALL E.R. 373. See also Regina v. Church, [1965] 2 W.L.R. 1220 (defendant knocked victim unconscious, then threw her into river, thinking she was dead).

requirement would find liability for attempted murder for the beating and would find reckless or negligent homicide for rolling the body off the cliff (assuming it is reckless or negligent as to causing death to treat apparently dead bodies in this manner). However, the court chose to treat the two events as one "transaction" and, therefore, affirmed the conviction for murder.

Dangers of "Transaction" Analysis Even if one finds the result in *Thabo Meli* to be intuitively appealing, such "transaction" analysis has the potential to undermine the concurrence requirement's purpose. There seems little to distinguish the events in *Thabo Meli* from many other instances of related but distinct acts. Would it matter if the attackers went home after their deed and only happened upon the apparently dead body two days later, then thought it prudent to shove it off the cliff? Would this still be one transaction? What if the victim had recovered from his injuries during the intervening two days and, on this occasion, was simply lying in a drunken stupor when found, mistaken for a dead body, and tossed over the cliff? If a transaction approach were to be taken, as in *Thabo Meli*, it is unclear how the law is to define the bounds of such an analysis.

Model Penal Code Section 2.02 Commentary
Official Draft and Revised Comments 244-247, 250-251 (1985)

[Model Penal Code §2.02, the subject here, is reproduced at the end of the *Garnett* case "Law" section.]

5. *Offense Silent as to Culpability.* Subsection (3) provides that unless the kind of culpability sufficient to establish a material element of an offense has been prescribed by law, it is established if a person acted purposely, knowingly or recklessly with respect thereto. This accepts as the basic norm what usually is regarded as the common law position. More importantly, it represents the most convenient norm for drafting purposes. When purpose or knowledge is required, it is conventional to be explicit. And since negligence is an exceptional basis of liability, it should be excluded as a basis unless explicitly prescribed.

Some recent revisions and proposals have substantially similar provisions.

6. *Ambiguous Culpability Requirements.* Subsection (4) seeks to assist in the resolution of a common ambiguity in penal legislation, the statement of a particular culpability requirement in the definition of an offense in such a way that it is unclear whether the requirement applies to all the elements of the offense or only to the element that it immediately introduces. The draftsmen of the Wisconsin revision posed the problem in these terms: "When, for example, a statute says that it is unlawful to 'wilfully, maliciously, or wantonly destroy, remove, throw down or injure any [property] upon the land of another,' do the words denoting the requirement of intent apply only to the doing of the damage or do they also modify the phrase 'upon the land of another,' thus requiring knowledge or belief that the property is located upon land which belongs to another?" The Model Penal Code agrees with their view that these "problems can and should be taken care of in the definition of criminal intent."

The Code proceeds in the view that if a particular kind of culpability has been articulated at all by the legislature as sufficient with respect to any element of the offense, the assumption is that it was meant to apply to all material elements. Hence this construction is required, unless a "contrary purpose plainly appear." When a distinction is intended, as it often is, proper drafting ought to make it clear.

Two examples may help to clarify the intended scope of the provision and to illustrate its relationship with Subsection 3. False imprisonment is defined by Section 212.3 of the Model Code to include one who "knowingly restrains another unlawfully so as to interfere substantially with his liberty." Plainly, the word "knowingly" is intended to modify the restraint, so that the actor must, in order to be convicted under this section, know that he is restraining his victim. The question whether "knowingly" also qualifies the unlawful character of the restraint is not clearly answered by the definition of the offense, but is answered in the affirmative by the subsection under discussion.

To be contrasted with this illustration is the case of burglary, as defined in Section 221.1. The offense includes one who "enters a building...with purpose to commit a crime therein. . . ." The grading provisions make burglary a felony of the second degree if the offense is perpetrated "in the dwelling of another at night." Since an actor must have a "purpose" to commit a crime within a building, the definition of the offense might be thought ambiguous as to what culpability level applies to elements like "dwelling house" and "night." Must the actor know that he is entering a dwelling house in order to be convicted of a second degree felony, or is some lesser culpability level sufficient?

Section 2.02(3) should control elements of this character, and therefore recklessness should suffice in the absence of special provision to the contrary. Subsection (4) does not produce a contrary result, since it is designed to apply, as noted above, only to offenses where a particular culpability requirement is stated in such a way as to make it unclear whether the requirement applies to all of the material elements of an offense or only to the material element it introduces. In the burglary illustration, the phrase "with purpose to commit a crime therein" plainly does not make purpose the required level of culpability with respect to all material elements of the offense.

Most of the recently enacted and proposed revisions are in substantial agreement with the Model Code's formulation in this subsection.

7. Substitutes for Prescribed Culpability Levels. Subsection (5) establishes that when negligence suffices for liability, *a fortiori* purpose, knowledge or recklessness are sufficient; that purpose and knowledge similarly are sufficient for recklessness; and that purpose is sufficient for knowledge. Thus it is only necessary to articulate the minimal basis of liability in drafting specific offenses for the more serious bases to be implied. Many recent revisions and proposals contain similar provisions.

8. Conditional Purposes. Subsection (6) provides that a requirement of purpose is satisfied when purpose is conditional, unless the condition negatives the harm or evil sought to be prevented by the law defining the offense. Thus, it is no less a burglary if the defendant's purpose was to steal only if no one was at home or if he found the object he sought. The condition does not negative the evil that the law defining burglary is designed to control, irrespective of whether the condition is fulfilled or fails. But it would not be an assault with the intent to rape, if the defendant's purpose was to accomplish the sexual relation only if the mature victim consented; the condition negatives the evil with which the law has been framed to deal. If his purpose was to overcome her will *if* she resisted, he would of course be guilty of the crime. This is believed to be a statement and rationalization of the present law. Some recent revisions contain similar language. . . .

11. Culpability as to Illegality of Conduct. Subsection (9) states the conventional position that knowledge of the existence, meaning or application of the law determining the elements of an offense is not an element of that offense, except in the unusual situations where the law defining the offense or the Code so provides.

It should be noted that the general principle that ignorance or mistake of law is no excuse is greatly overstated; it has no application, for example, when the circumstances made material by the definition of the offense include a legal element. Thus it is immaterial in theft, when claim of right is adduced in defense, that the claim involves a legal judgment as to the right of property. Claim of right is a defense because the property must belong to someone else for the theft to occur and the defendant must have culpable awareness of that fact. Insofar as this point is involved, there is no need to state a special principle; the legal element involved is simply an aspect of the attendant circumstances, with respect to which knowledge, recklessness or negligence, as the case may be, is required for culpability by Subsections (1) and (3). The law involved is not the law defining the offense; it is some other legal rule that characterizes the attendant circumstances that are material to the offense.

The proper arena for the principle that ignorance or mistake of law does not afford an excuse is thus with respect to the particular law that sets forth the definition of the crime in question. It is knowledge of *that* law that is normally not a part of the crime, and it is ignorance or mistake as to *that* law that is denied defensive significance by this subsection of the Code and by the traditional common law approach to the issue.

It needs to be recognized, however, that there may be special cases where knowledge of the law defining the offense should be part of the culpability requirement for its commission, i.e., where a belief that one's conduct is not a violation of the law or, at least, such a belief based on reasonable grounds, ought to engender a defense. Such a result might be brought about directly by the definition of the crime, e.g., by explicitly requiring awareness of a regulation, violation of which is denominated as an offense. It also may be brought about by a general provision in the Code indicating circumstances in which mistakes about the law defining an offense will constitute a defense. In either case, the result is exceptional and arises only when the governing law "so provides."

Many recent revisions and proposals have provisions similar to Subsection (9) in their definitions of culpability. . . .

▲ PROBLEM
Babies and Ditches

Geets and Carrie find Anver intolerable. He struts about the club, being pompous beyond belief, expecting that he will be elected the next president. They concoct a practical joke to bring him down to earth. A winding road leading down the hill from the club runs by a playground. They plan to buy a baby carriage and two life-like dolls and to place them in the middle of the road near the playground. As Anver comes around the turn, he will be surprised by the carriage. If he pulls his precious Jaguar off the road into the high grass, he may get stuck in the soft ground. If he fails to pull off, he will blast through the carriage and the "babies." Either way, Geets and Carrie will have a tale to tell, either about Anver's humorous slide or his apparent indifference to killing babies. Either one will serve Carrie's purpose.

Geets has a slightly different goal in playing the practical joke: to kill Anver. While he jokes with Carrie about what a buffoon Anver is, the truth is Anver is likely to be elected the next president, a position that Geets covets for himself. He knows that the tall grass adjacent to the stretch of road by the playground hides a drainage ditch. If Anver swerves to miss the baby carriage and if he is unable to keep his car on the road and if he slides in the direction of the ditch, he may get injured and possibly even killed. Geets sees the chances of successfully killing Anver through this scheme as something less than 10% but he is hoping for the best. Carrie is unaware that their joke creates any risk of killing Anver.

The next day is perfect for the scheme, overcast with a light rain. Geets and Carrie put the carriage and dolls in the road just before Anver is scheduled to leave the club. Without telling Carrie about the ditch, Geets selects the location that he thinks maximizes the chance that Anver will slide into it. Anver's car approaches, swerves before hitting the carriage, hits the ditch, and sends Anver through the windshield. When he sees Anver's serious injuries, Geets has second thoughts about whether his scheme was such a good idea. He feels bad about Anver's injuries and hopes he will survive. Unfortunately, Anver dies two days later from injuries sustained in the accident. Are Geets and Carrie liable for homicide? If so, for which homicide offense?

▲ PROBLEM
Oatmeal for Ian

Dad usually leaves for work before two-year old Ian is up, but today Mom has an early meeting and Dad has none until 9:15 a.m. He will feed Ian his breakfast of choice, cooked oatmeal with applesauce, drop him at day care, and make it to work just in time for his 9:15. Dad puts the oatmeal on the stove while he gets dressed. Several minutes later, Ian comes screaming into the bedroom with a burned hand. The burn looks horrible, and Dad is very upset. He knows that ointment and bandages must be in the house somewhere but he cannot find them so he puts Ian into the car and drives quickly to the pharmacy. Too quickly, however; he fails to keep an eye on his speedometer and is stopped and ticketed for speeding. The ointment seems to work well and the pharmacist assures him that the burn is not as serious as he thought. Ian will be fine. Dad has missed his 9:15 meeting but nonetheless is relieved, until he arrives back at the apartment to find the fire department at work and angry neighbors in pajamas and robes. Apparently he had left the stove on, and the oatmeal had caught fire, setting the kitchen on fire. The fire spread to the adjoining apartments, destroying that part of the building and the personal effects of his neighbors. Luckily, no one was injured, but his neighbors are demanding that Dad be criminally charged for his carelessness in starting the fire. Criminal liability for Dad for property destruction? For speeding? The answer depends on the level of culpability required by these offenses as compared to Dad's culpability. What is Dad's level of culpability with respect to causing the property destruction? With respect to exceeding the speed limit?

● DISCUSSION MATERIALS

What Is the Minimum Culpability, If Any, That Should Be Required for Criminal Liability?

The Glanville Williams and Model Penal Code excerpts that follow explore the arguments for and against using negligence as a standard of criminal liability, and call for its limited use. Samuel Pillsbury argues that negligence liability is appropriate where the failure to be aware of a risk reflects a blameworthy indifference to others' interests, while Laurie Levensen discusses the justifications and counter-arguments for using strict liability.

Glanville Williams, Reasons for Punishing Negligence
Criminal Law: The General Part 122-124 (2d ed. 1961)

The use of the criminal law to punish negligence has been challenged. An American writer expressed the objection as follows:

> If the defendant, being mistaken as to material facts, is to be punished because his mistake is one which an average man would not make, punishment will sometimes be inflicted when the criminal mind does not exist. Such a result is contrary to fundamental principles, and is plainly unjust, for a man should not be held criminal because of lack of intelligence.

The retributive theory of punishment is open to many objections, which are of even greater force when applied to inadvertent negligence than in crimes requiring mens rea. Some people are born reckless, clumsy, thoughtless, inattentive, irresponsible, with a bad memory and a slow "reaction time." With the best will in the world, we all of us at some times in our lives make negligent mistakes. It is hard to see how justice (as distinct from some utilitarian reason) requires mistakes to be punished.

[T]he deterrent theory, which is normally accepted as a justification for criminal punishment, finds itself in some difficulty when applied to negligence. At best the deterrent effect of the legal sanction is a matter of faith rather than of proved scientific fact; but there is no department in which this faith is less firmly grounded than that of negligence.... Even if a person admits that he occasionally makes a negligent mistake, how, in the nature of things, can punishment for inadvertence serve to deter? . . .

The argument in favour of punishment is that, just as it is possible for punishment to cause a person to exercise greater control over his acts in view of the known dangers, so it is possible for punishment to bring about greater foresight, by causing the subject to stop and think before committing himself to a course of conduct. . . .

A supporting consideration is that punishment may deter in respect of some subsidiary rule of prudence the breach of which is intentional. Although the harmful result of careless driving is not intended, there is often an element in the careless driving that is intended (e.g., pulling out on a blind corner), and the punishment, coupled with a recollection of the circumstances of the accident, may "condition" the driver not to repeat his mistake, and may even cause him to be more careful in other respects. Conceivably it may also improve the conduct of others who come to know of the mistake that was made. In the same way, although the threat of punishment may not be able to make me remember something that I have already forgotten, it may cause me so to impress a fact on my mind that I do not forget.

This justification for the punishment of inadvertence does not go very far, and the law acts wisely in making such punishment exceptional. Even where punishment is imposed, it best takes the form of a fine, operating as a warning for the future rather than as a substantial punishment for the past. Loss of liberty is not a necessary measure for those who cause harm inadvertently. If the offender is so incompetent as to be a social danger in his present occupation, the remedy is not to incarcerate him but (if milder methods of correction fail) to exclude him from the activity in which he is a danger.

The chief problem concerns negligent driving, and this has been partly solved by turning some jury rules of prudence into rules of law, as by the imposition of speed limits and by the requirement of halting at major roads. The intentional breach of such rules can be punished without enquiry into negligence. In 1930 Parliament took the new step of allowing the negligent driver to be disqualified from driving; and this, regarded not as a punishment but as society's method of removing a source of danger, is certainly the most fitting way of dealing with accident-prone motorists.

Model Penal Code Section 2.02 Commentary
Official Draft and Revised Comments 243-244 (1985)

No one has doubted that purpose, knowledge, and recklessness are properly the basis for criminal liability, but some critics have opposed any penal consequences for negligent behavior. Since the actor is inadvertent by hypothesis, it has been argued that the "threat of punishment for negligence must pass him by, because he does not realize that it is addressed to him." So too, it has been urged that education or corrective treatment, not punishment, is the proper social method for dealing with persons with inadequate awareness, since what is implied is not a moral defect. This analysis, however, oversimplifies the issue. When people have knowledge that conviction and sentence, not to speak of punishment, may follow conduct that inadvertently creates improper risk, they are supplied with an additional motive to take care before acting, to use their faculties and draw on their experience in gauging the potentialities of contemplated conduct. To some extent, at least, this motive may promote awareness and thus be effective as a measure of control. Moreover, moral defect can properly be imputed to instances where the defendant acts out of insensitivity to the interests of other people, and not merely out of an intellectual failure to grasp them. In any event legislators act on these assumptions in a host of situations, and it would be dogmatic to assert that they are wholly wrong. Accordingly, negligence, as here defined, should not be wholly rejected as a ground of culpability that they may suffice for purposes of penal law, though it should properly not generally be deemed sufficient in the definition of specific crimes and it should often be differentiated from conduct involving higher culpability for the purposes of sentence. . . .

Most recent legislative revisions and proposals have adopted definitions of negligence similar to that of the Model Code. . . .

Samuel H. Pillsbury, Crimes of Indifference
49 Rutgers Law Review 105, 106, 150-151 (1996)

[T]he modern trend to require that the defendant have actual awareness of fatal risks for either or both of these offenses is a mistake, based on a misconception of responsible choice. . . .

We may blame persons for failing to perceive risks to others when we can trace their lack of awareness to bad perception priorities. In such a case, we judge the person guilty of a bad choice. In setting his or her perception priorities, the individual assigned too low a priority to the value of other human beings. The key to culpability for failure to perceive is why the person failed to perceive. Assume two cases in which a driver runs a red light and fatally injures a pedestrian in the cross-walk. One case involves a father rushing his severely injured child to the hospital. Another involves a teenager showing off for his friends. Assume that in both cases the driver saw neither the light nor the pedestrian. Culpability should depend on the drivers' reasons for perceptive failure, not on the failure itself. The father's lack of perception may be attributed to his overriding and morally worthy desire to help his child. The teenager's failure to perceive may be attributed to morally blameworthy perception priorities. The teenager placed a higher value on winning the admiration of friends than on attending to the risks of fast driving. The teenager's conduct demonstrates an attitude of indifference toward others, a morally culpable state to which society should forcefully respond by conviction and punishment. Meanwhile, the father's conduct demonstrates a tragic conflict between valuing his child and valuing others.

Individuals deserve punishment for all acts displaying serious disregard for the moral worth of other human beings. Such acts involve many different levels of awareness. . . . In all cases we should judge the actor's choices: what she has chosen to care about and perceive, and what she has chosen not to care about and perceive. These choices give the individual's conduct a distinct moral meaning.

Laurie L. Levenson, Good Faith Defenses: Reshaping Strict Liability Crimes
78 Cornell Law Review 401, 419-427 (1993)

Justifications for Strict Liability Crimes

1. Public Welfare Offenses

The strict liability doctrine often applies to so-called "public welfare" offenses or regulatory crimes promulgated to address the dangers brought about by the advent of the industrial revolution. Public welfare offenses include the sale of impure or adulterated foods or drugs, driving faster than the speed limit, the sale of intoxicating liquor to minors, and improper handling of dangerous chemicals or nuclear wastes. Defendants violate these laws regardless of their intent or absence of negligent conduct.

There are several reasons the strict liability doctrine is used to redress invasions of the public welfare. First, the doctrine is employed for these offenses because it shifts the risks of dangerous activity to those best able to prevent a mishap. For example, a pharmaceutical manufacturer is liable if that product becomes contaminated for any reason. The risk of mishap is shifted to the manufacturer, who can be assured of avoiding liability only by not engaging in the particular high risk activity.

Yet, this reason alone cannot justify the doctrine. The strict liability doctrine is not the only possible method for shifting risk onto the manufacturer. A criminal negligence standard also shifts the risk to the party engaging in the activity and punishes those who act carelessly. Under a negligence standard, a defendant is liable for failure to act as a reasonable person would have under the circumstances, even if he did not intend or appreciate the risks of his activities. Under a negligence standard, if the defendant acts reasonably and harm results, no punishment follows. Nonetheless, the burden to learn and operate within society's standards rests with the defendant.

The strict liability doctrine operates in a fundamentally different way. While both negligence and strict liability shift the burden of risk avoidance to the defendant, only under strict liability are individuals imprisoned even if they take all possible precaution to act reasonably. The sole question for the trier of fact is whether the defendant committed the proscribed act. The jury may not decide whether the defendant could have done anything else to prevent the unlawful act.

Thus, there must be additional reasons for selecting the strict liability doctrine over the negligence standard. Among these reasons is the need by the legislature to assure that juries will treat like cases alike when judging conduct involving public welfare. Juries may be ill-suited to decide what is reasonable in complex high risk activities. For example, in order for juries to decide what is reasonable conduct when dealing with nuclear waste, they would have to be educated on the nuclear industry, the risks posed by it, and the safeguards that might be taken. Legislatures prefer to make this assessment themselves, rather than relying on the competence of juries. Moreover, jurors may be swayed by sympathies or prejudices of a particular case. By dictating what is *per se* unreasonable, an individual jury cannot reassess the standard of reasonableness.

Accordingly, a second reason for using the strict liability doctrine is that it assures uniform treatment of particular, high risk conduct.

A third justification often offered for the strict liability doctrine is that it eases the burden on the prosecution to prove intent in difficult cases. Strict liability is based largely on the assumption that an accident occurs because the defendant did not take care to prevent it. No showing of intent or negligence is required, because the fact that a prohibited act occurred demonstrates the defendant's negligence. As with most irrefutable presumptions, the legislature believes individual inquiries are unnecessary because the overwhelming majority of cases will show that the defendant acted at least negligently. Seen in this light, strict liability is a procedural shortcut to punish those who would be culpable under traditional theories of criminal law.

Fourth, even if the presumption is incorrect in a particular case, legislatures determine that this risk is outweighed by the need for additional protection of society and expeditious prosecution of certain cases. For example, driving in excess of a posted speed limit is typically a strict liability crime. With nearly 398,000 annual traffic cases in one state alone, processing these cases as quickly as possible is important. The most efficient way to process such cases is to presume defendants drive carelessly when exceeding speed limits. The presumption is generally accurate and, even when it is not, the need for public safety and the relatively minor punishment minimizes any concern about injustice.

Finally, the strict liability doctrine is attractive as a powerful public statement of legislative intolerance for certain behavior. By labeling an offense as strict liability, the legislature can claim to provide the utmost protection from certain public harms. By affording no leniency for defendants causing harm, the legislature affirms society's interest in being protected from certain conduct. In this sense, strict liability expresses emphatically that such conduct will not be tolerated regardless of the actor's intent.

2. Morality Offenses

Similar justifications have been offered for the application of the strict liability doctrine to "morality crimes," offenses involving transgressions of society's sexual and social norms. Examples of these crimes are statutory rape, adultery, and bigamy.

Consider the classic case of *Regina v. Prince*. In *Prince,* the defendant was convicted for eloping with a minor without her father's permission. Although the jury accepted the defendant's claim that he did not know the girl was underage, the court denied a defense, finding "[t]he act forbidden is wrong in itself, . . . not . . . illegal, but wrong."

The court in *Prince* did not require that defendant know the age of the girl with whom he eloped. Eloping with any young woman without her father's permission was considered morally wrong. Because of this, the court felt it appropriate to impose punishment regardless of defendant's knowledge of the girl's age. The defendant bore the risk that his borderline conduct would violate a provision of the law.

As with the public welfare offenses, the less comfortable society is with certain types of behavior, the more likely the legislature will turn to the strict liability doctrine to transfer the risks of the behavior to the defendant. These risks include the possibility of physical or moral harm, and the possibility that a culpable defendant would escape punishment by feigning ignorance or mistake.

To assure that all juries assess the risks of a particular activity uniformly, the legislature designates an offense as a strict liability crime. By not allowing evidence as to why the defendant transgressed, the legislature can avoid the whims of any particular jury. Rather than having an individual jury decide what conduct is reasonable, the legislature decides for all strict liability cases. In this manner, firm social and moral lines are clearly drawn.

Application of the strict liability doctrine to morality offenses offers an additional justification for the doctrine. As already discussed, in strict liability offenses it is presumed that the defendant took an unjustifiable risk in his conduct and was therefore at least negligent. When the defendant's conduct is already morally questionable — "borderline" conduct — concern for punishing an innocent person decreases. Society does not approve of the defendant's conduct, although the limits of the law may seem to permit it. If the defendant crosses those limits, intentionally or unintentionally, society will seek to punish the defendant's behavior. The strict liability doctrine thereby serves an important function of setting firm limits on conduct that society is loath to tolerate. The interests in efficient punishment and maximum deterrence of certain conduct is seen as outweighing the risk that a nonculpable person will be punished.

Thus, for both public welfare and morality offenses, relieving the prosecution of the burden of proving a culpable mens rea is justified by the presumption that the defendant engaging in marginal and/or highly risky conduct deserves some punishment. Moreover, even if that presumption is incorrect in a given case, society receives valuable protection from such conduct.

3. Opposition to the Strict Liability Doctrine

Opponents of the strict liability doctrine argue that its justifications are inconsistent with both utilitarian and retributivist theories of punishment. Under utilitarian theory, punishment is justified if it deters unlawful behavior. If punishing those who commit prohibited acts will deter others from acting similarly, punishment is justified. Under the retributivist approach, an individual should be punished for choosing to violate the law. Punishment reflects respect for an individual's autonomy to choose to do "wrong." If an individual chooses to transgress the boundaries established to protect society, he "deserves" punishment.

The strict liability doctrine, especially when applied to defendants misled into committing an unlawful act, is not supported by either theory of punishment. Under retributivist theory, criminal law should hold individuals responsible for only those acts for which they are blameworthy. An individual is blameworthy, not because of accidental conduct, but because of a conscious and knowing breach of the law. At a minimum, the defendant must have acted below the standard of care that a reasonable person would have exercised under the same conditions. A strict liability defendant punished for an act that he has been misled into committing has not consciously decided to violate society's norms. Accordingly, under classic retributivist theory, this defendant does not "deserve" to be punished.

Additionally, the strict liability doctrine conflicts with utilitarian theories of punishment. Strict liability laws are inefficient because they tend to over deter individuals' behavior. If the strict liability defendant can be punished for *any* conduct crossing a certain proscribed line, the defendant will be inclined to abstain from *all* activities that could conceivably result in illegal behavior. In some situations, certain individuals might abstain from entering a high risk industry. [I]ndividuals may be deterred from engaging in constitutionally protected activity. Thus, strict liability may deter individuals from engaging in activities that are socially necessary or desirable, constitutionally protected, or both. In this manner, strict liability over deters conduct.

More fundamentally, the strict liability doctrine violates utilitarian theories of criminal punishment because an individual who has no basis for believing he is engaging in unlawful conduct will not be deterred from engaging in that behavior. If an individual has no indication that he is doing anything wrong until the harmful act is completed, then he has no reason to alter his conduct.

Given the conflicts with both the retributivist and utilitarian theories of punishment, it is understandable why opponents of strict liability do not want to use the doctrine against defendants who have made an affirmative effort to comply with the law but have been misled into committing a violation. Classic Anglo-American legal philosophy is that "[I]t is better that ten guilty persons escape than one innocent suffer." Strict liability theory operates from the opposite perspective. Under the strict liability doctrine, an occasional innocent may be punished to assure the safety of the majority. Thus, the prosecution of good faith defendants under strict liability laws appears to conflict with the most fundamental principles of just punishment.

● DISCUSSION MATERIALS

Should a Person's Negligence (and Recklessness) Be Judged Against an Objective or an Individualized Standard?

In the readings below, H.L.A. Hart examines the role of a partially individualized standard in negligence and of absolute liability. The Model Penal Code Commentary excerpt recognizes the existence of both standards in assessing liability, approving of the partially individualized standard but only in a somewhat confined manner that remains largely at the court's discretion. George Fletcher argues for the use of the partially individualized standard in a broader way.

H.L.A. Hart, Punishment and Responsibility
154-155 (1984)

When negligence is made criminally punishable, this...leaves open the question: whether, before we punish, both or only the first of the following two questions must be answered affirmatively:

> (i) Did the accused fail to take those precautions which any reasonable man with normal capacities would in the circumstances have taken?

(ii) Could the accused, given his mental and physical capacities, have taken those precautions?

One use of the dangerous expressions "objective" and "subjective" is to make the distinction between these two questions: given the ambiguities of those expressions, this distinction would have been more aptly expressed by the expressions "invariant" standard of care, and "individualized conditions of liability." It may well be that, even if the "standard of care" is pitched very low so that individuals are liable only if they fail to take very elementary precautions against harm, there will still be some unfortunate individuals who, through lack of intelligence, powers of concentration or memory, or through clumsiness, could not attain even this low standard. If our conditions of liability are invariant and not flexible, i.e., if they are not adjusted to the capacities of the accused, then some individuals will be held liable for negligence though they could not have helped their failure to comply with the standard. In such cases, indeed, criminal responsibility will be made independent of any "subjective element," since the accused could not have conformed to the required standard. But this result is nothing to do with negligence being taken as a basis for criminal liability....."Absolute liability" results, not from the admission of the principle that one who has been grossly negligent is criminally responsible for the consequent harm even if "he had no idea in his mind of harm to anyone," but from the refusal in the application of this principle to consider the capacities of an individual who has fallen below the standard of care.

Model Penal Code Section 2.02 Commentary
Official Draft and Revised Comments 240-242 (1985)

Negligence. The fourth kind of culpability is negligence. It is distinguished from purposeful, knowing or reckless action in that it does not involve a state of awareness. A person acts negligently under this subsection when he inadvertently creates a substantial and unjustifiable risk of which he ought to be aware. He is liable if given the nature and degree of the risk, his failure to perceive it is, considering the nature and purpose of the actor's conduct and the circumstances known to him, a gross deviation from the care that would be exercised by a reasonable person in his situation. As in the case of recklessness, both the substantiality of the risk and the elements of justification in the situation form the relevant standards of judgment. And again it is quite impossible to avoid tautological articulation of the final question. The tribunal must evaluate the actor's failure of perception and determine whether, under all the circumstances, it was serious enough to be condemned. The jury must find fault, and must find that it was substantial and unjustified; that is the heart of what can be said in legislative terms.

As with recklessness, the jury is asked to perform two distinct functions. First, it is to examine the risk and the factors that are relevant to its substantiality and justifiability. In the case of negligence, these questions are asked not in terms of what the actor's perceptions actually were, but in terms of an objective view of the situation as it actually existed. Second, the jury is to make the culpability judgment, this time in terms of whether the failure of the defendant to perceive the risk justifies condemnation. Considering the nature and purpose of his conduct and the circumstances known to him, the question is whether the defendant's failure to perceive a risk involves a gross deviation from the standard of care that a reasonable person would observe in the actor's situation.

Formulation of the standard in these terms is believed to be a substantial improvement over the traditional approach to defining negligence for purposes of criminal liability....

A further point in the Code's concept of negligence merits attention. The standard for ultimate judgment invites consideration of the "care that a reasonable person would observe in the actor's situation." There is an inevitable ambiguity in "situation." If the actor were blind or if he had just suffered a blow or experienced a heart attack, these would certainly be facts to be considered in a judgment involving criminal liability, as they would be under traditional law. But the heredity, intelligence or temperament of the actor would not be held material in judging negligence, and could not be without depriving the criterion of all its objectivity. The Code is not intended to displace discriminations of this kind, but rather to leave the issue to the courts....

George P. Fletcher, The Theory of Criminal Negligence: A Comparative Analysis

119 University of Pennsylvania Law Review 401, 426-427, 429-430, 433-434 (1971)

Is Negligence Invariably Measured Against an Objective Standard?

In the preceding section, we explored one sense in which negligence is conceptually objective or external and argued that this kind of externality — the absence of a subjective mental state — does not denigrate negligence as a basis for criminal liability. Despite this kind of externality or objectivity, there are good reasons to regard negligence as culpable, to regard it therefore as a form of *mens rea,* and to subject negligent conduct to criminal sanctions. A totally different argument, however, asserts that negligence is suspect because it is objective, not subjective. This argument holds that a subjective standard of negligence is conceptually untenable because it would take each individual as the measure of the propriety of his own conduct, thus rendering evaluation impossible by merging the standard of evaluation with the conduct to be evaluated.

This point is nicely captured in Tindal's famous admonition to avoid a standard of negligence that would be "as variable as the length of the foot of each individual." And again by Holmes: The standards of the law are standards of general application. The law takes no account of the infinite varieties of temperament, intellect, and education which make the internal character of a given act so different in different men.

The argument is undoubtedly sound — as far as it goes. It is true that legal rules, like all other rules, must apply to a range of cases. It follows that if liability for negligence is to be based on legal rules, the standard of liability must transcend individual differences; in this sense, the standard of liability is general, abstract, and objective. With this much we can agree.

It is the next step that provokes disagreement. On the basis of the invariable objectivity of the standard of negligence, common law analysts are inclined to view negligence as significantly different from intentional conduct. Their reasoning would run like this: A man's intentions are gauged by an individualized, subjective standard; it is his intention we try to establish, not that of an average man. But this is not the case with negligence where the issue is the behavior of an average member of the community. Therefore, the standard of negligence is less sensitive to individual culpability than the standard of intentional conduct; and accordingly, it should be used sparingly, if at all, as a ground for liability.

Although this line of reasoning may seem plausible, it derives from the false premise that standards of liability must be either subjective or objective, but not both. . . .

[T]he standard for negligence [is,] at once, objective and subjective. The objective issue is whether the risk is justified under the circumstances; the subjective issue is whether the actor's taking an unjustified risk is excusable on the ground of duress, insanity, or some other condition rendering his conduct involuntary and thus blameless. German theorists have recently come to conceptualize negligence as consisting of dimensions both of legality and culpability. There is also considerable evidence that common law analysts have long flirted with the same basic insight about the nature of negligence. For example, Holmes stresses that negligence is an objective standard; yet he concedes that conditions like blindness, infancy, and insanity should constitute excuses from liability. It seems contradictory for Holmes to admit the relevance of individualized excuses in the same passage in which he postulates that the "standards of the law are standards of general application. . . [taking] no account of the infinite varieties of temperament, intellect, and education. . . ." . . . In emphasizing the generality of standards, he acknowledged the dimension of legality in the structure of negligence. This interpretation establishes the consistency of Holmes' views by providing an account of how the standards of negligence can, at once, be of general application and yet accommodate excuses based on individual incapacities.

The Model Penal Code also displays an appreciation for the distinction between the dimensions of legality and culpability in the structure of negligence. Its definition of negligence specifies first that the risk in question be "substantial and unjustifiable." Secondly, it provides that "the actor's failure to perceive [the risk] . . . involves a gross deviation from the standard of care that a reasonable person would observe in the actor's situation." The first prong of the definition focuses on the justification and the legality of the risk; the second, on the culpability of the actor's ignorance of the risk. This definition invites criticism for its obvious circularity: it seeks to define negligence as a "kind of culpability," yet the key factor in the definition is whether the actor was culpable in failing to perceive particular risk. This duplicative reliance on the concept of culpability derives from the Code's confused use of the concept to refer sometimes to mental states, as in the definition of "purposely," — and sometimes to the blameworthiness of inadvertence, as in the definition of negligence. Thus negligence emerges as a "kind of culpability" that requires a special finding of culpability. . . .

Culpability and Difference Among Individuals

Although we have stressed the symmetry of liability for negligent and intentional criminality, we have yet to explain the frequent irrelevance of individual differences of "temperament, intellect, and education" in assessing liability for negligence. This characteristic of negligence inspired much of Holmes' analysis in *The Common Law*. It is another line of defense for those who insist that negligent criminality is significantly different from intentional criminality.

Individual differences are ignored in determining the legality of risks; the point of distinguishing between permissible and impermissible risks is to formulate a rule applicable to all men in the same situation. But many individual differences are also ignored in specifying the excuses bearing on culpability. Insanity is an excuse, but not awkwardness. If it is impossible for an actor to appreciate the illegality of the risk that he is running, he ought to be excused; if it is merely difficult for him to appreciate what others readily understand, his ignorance is not excusable. That differences among men are not always manifested in the criteria of excuses requires explanation.

It is important to note first that the practice of disregarding individual differences also prevails in assessing liability for intentional offenses. Duress is a defense to theft, but greediness is not. An irascible man, one easily provoked into fights, has a more difficult time avoiding liability for battery and homicide than does a man of even temperament. Legal systems inevitably impose greater burdens of compliance on some than on others. Norms of legal conduct cut across a wide range of human inclinations and capacities. Some men have an easier time than others in complying with prohibitions against negligent and intentional conduct; those for whom compliance is relatively easy are, to that degree, more culpable than others transgressing the law. Although this excess of culpability may be relevant in sentencing, it has no bearing on the issue of liability.

The point of excusing conditions is not to gauge degrees of culpability, but to determine when the actor's culpability falls below the threshold required for a fair conviction. Some men may be more culpable than is necessary for conviction; others may barely pass the required threshold. So long as the minimum threshold of culpability requires a finding that the defendant has a fair chance to avoid liability, it is immaterial whether some violators are more culpable than he. The goal of justly distributing sanctions is not one of finding the most culpable offenders, but one of assessing whether each alleged violator is sufficiently culpable to forfeit his freedom from sanctions.

Culpability and Mistake

The previous section described the meaning and use of offense culpability requirements. How are these related to mistake defenses? When will an offender's mistake provide a defense?

◆ THE CASE OF THOMAS LASETER

Fairbanks (named after Charles Fairbanks, a senator from Indiana who went on to become Vice President) is located in the heart of Alaska. It is the hub-town connecting Anchorage to Canada, which then leads to the only road passage to the continental United States. Athabascans have been living in this area for thousands of years, but when gold was discovered in the area in 1902, it suddenly boomed with new peoples, getting a court, a jail, a post office, and electricity. With the construction of the Alcan Highway (connecting Alaska to Canada to the United States) and the even more dramatic oil boom, Fairbanks got another boost. By 1982, it had the second largest population in Alaska.

Fairbanks is a land of extremes — and the climate affects the personality, culture, and lifestyle of the region. It goes from a bright, scorching flatland surrounded by looming mountains in the summer,

Figure 17 **Downtown Fairbanks, circa 1970-1990s**

(Joel Rogers/Corbis)

with highs in the 90s, to a dark wasteland with lows of −70s (without factoring in the wind chill) in the winter. The summer months yield 21 hours of daylight, with people then slammed by the adjustment to four hours of daylight in the winter. As a result of these extremes and other factors, Fairbanks has a large drug and alcohol problem. It also has high incidences of domestic violence, incest, and alcohol-related crimes. Many people become depressed from the weather, lack of daylight, and isolation, and turn to drugs and alcohol for release. There are also great disparities in lifestyle and wealth. More than 10% of the population live below the poverty line. Of the 30,000 residents, more than 200 families still lack plumbing. More than a third of the adults are not in the workforce.

Fairbanks also serves as a hub for people coming in from surrounding villages. Mixed in with the savvy city people are people who have what is called "village innocence." These differences lead to strong rural-urban cultural tensions.

The tensions are further accentuated by the military's presence in Fairbanks. As with many city-military base interactions, there are often striking differences between the two cultures. Many of the people in Fairbanks were born and raised there, often having never been farther than 50 miles out of town. They have their own understandings of rules for how people behave. The people brought in by the military are from many different regions, none quite like Fairbanks. They are typically far from home and from everything familiar to them. Faced with the cultural differences, plus the peculiar darkness and cold, many military personnel become homesick and depressed. Some try to fit in with the local culture, venturing into town for drinks, dates, and conversation.

On the evening of April 18, 1982, just as there is a glimmer of hope that Spring will come (even though snow will be on the ground until early June), Thomas Laseter leaves the Fort Wainwright Army base and heads into downtown Fairbanks. He is about 6′1″, 215 pounds and is a 21-year old career soldier. He has to work the next morning, but decides nonetheless to go to the French Quarter, a local bar on the strip. He is not necessarily trying to pick up a girl; he just wants to have some fun. When he gets to the bar, he notices a Native American woman with long dark hair drinking beer and playing pool. LP is a 23-year old Fairbanks native. She has a boyfriend, Bill, but he has been working up north for about two weeks, so tonight she is out with a girlfriend. After she has finished three or four games, Laseter walks over and asks LP if she would be willing to play one round with him. She agrees. They play and talk, and Laseter buys her four or

Figure 18 **U.S. Army Fort Wainwright**
(William Gossweiler/U.S.Army Alaska)

five drinks. He notices that she looks a little bit pregnant and asks her about it. She says that she is not, although in reality she is more than five months along. Laseter can tell that she is, but drops the subject. The French Quarter is winding down, and Laseter is interested in going to another bar. LP is still pretty sober. She declines his invitation to go to the Stampede, a bar just down the street. The Quarter closes at 2 a.m.

Later, both Laseter and LP somehow separately end up at the Stampede. When he sees her there he sits down next to her at the bar. They talk until early in the morning, discussing, among other things, her boyfriend and her pregnancy. They keep chatting, and he buys her another four or five drinks. At this point, Laseter has consumed about fifteen beers and LP has had about twelve. They listen to the jukebox until the bartender shuts things down.

By now, LP is tired and a little drunk. She has had problems with alcohol in the past and sometimes suffers from blackouts. She begins to fade in and out. Meanwhile Laseter notices that it is getting late. He also realizes that if he is going to give LP a ride and still make it to work on time, he needs to get going. He offers her a ride, but she says she wants to stay. He tells her he is leaving and heads out to the parking lot. As he is unlocking his door, he sees her walking past the passenger side on the way to her friend's house. Again, he asks her if she would like a ride. His car is filthy, but this time she accepts.

Laseter is pretty drunk and still not very familiar with the layout of Fairbanks. He tells LP she will have to give him directions. She explains where to go but then falls asleep (or passes out). Laseter ends up in an area of town that is far from where he thinks he should be. LP wakes up frightened and confused, and tells him to turn around. He says he will, but then she passes out and he turns down the wrong street. At one point she wakes up as the car is starting to slow down at a stop sign. She seems scared and starts fumbling with the door handle and tries to get out. Laseter reaches over, grabs her arm, and pulls her back into the car. He keeps driving and she passes out again. It is now about five in the morning and Laseter feels completely lost. He starts to shake LP to try to wake her up. The car hits some ice and slides into Bradford Gustin's fence.

Laseter gets out and gives Gustin his name and license plate number and explains that he is taking his date home. Gustin can tell Laseter has been drinking, but decides he is sober enough to drive. Gustin sees LP sitting up in the front seat. Laseter returns to the car and starts to drive down the road but does not get very far. As he takes a left to drive down an alley, the car gets stuck in a huge mud slick. Laseter gets out and tries to rock and push the car out of the hole but cannot. He asks Bill Hoople, who is passing by on his way to work, for assistance. Hoople cannot help and suggests that he wait for a tow truck. Hearing it will be at least half an hour until a truck arrives, Laseter returns to the car. He shakes LP to wake her up. He does not think she knows where she is. After waiting a little, he leans in and he starts to kiss her. She still seems a little out of it and does not say anything, but she seems to respond, and thinking that she is enjoying herself, he keeps kissing her. He starts taking their clothes off. He pulls down her pants and underwear, but before he gets any further he ejaculates. Embarrassed, he quickly puts his clothes back on and climbs out of the car to try to find someone to help him get his car out of the hole. He soon finds a man who offers him a tow with a rope. Meanwhile, LP, still tired and disoriented, is now extremely upset. She works her way out of the car and, stumbling a little, pounds on the door of a nearby apartment building. By the time Laseter returns, she is gone. The woman who lets her in later reports that LP seems badly shaken and says that a man raped her. The next thing LP remembers is a doctor examining her.

The police arrive as Laseter is hooking up the tow strap to his car. He is arrested and charged with sexual assault.

1. Relying only on your own intuitions of justice, what liability and punishment, if any, does Thomas Laseter deserve?

N	0	1	2	3	4	5	6	7	8	9	10	11
☐	☐	☐	☐	☐	☐	☐	☐	☐	☐	☐	☐	☐
no liability	liability but no punishment	1 day	2 wks	2 mo	6 mo	1 yr	3 yrs	7 yrs	15 yrs	30 yrs	life imprison-ment	death

2. What liability for Laseter, if any, under the then-existing statutes?
3. What liability for Laseter, if any, under the Model Penal Code?
4. *Jury Instructions.* The defense in *Laseter* proposed two instructions, which read:

"Without Consent." In order to find the defendant guilty of sexual assault in the first degree, you must find that he was subjectively aware that [LP] did not consent to sexual penetration. If from all the evidence you have a reasonable doubt as to the question whether the defendant believed that [LP] consented to sexual penetration, you must give the defendant the benefit of that doubt and find him not guilty.

"Recklessly." With respect to the circumstance of consent, a person acts recklessly with respect to a circumstance described by the law when he is aware of and consciously disregards a substantial and unjustifiable risk that the circumstance exists. The risk must be of such a nature and such a degree that disregard of it constitutes a gross deviation from the standard of conduct that a reasonable person would observe in the situation. A person who is unaware of a risk of which he would have been aware had he not been intoxicated acts recklessly with respect to that risk.

The state objected to both instructions, and would have the court substitute the following instruction as to "reasonable belief."

If from all the evidence you find that the defendant had a reasonable belief that L.P. consented to sexual penetration, you shall find the defendant not guilty as to the crime of sexual assault in the first degree. If the defendant's belief as to L.P.'s consent was induced by his state of intoxication, you shall find it is not a reasonable belief.

Given the statutes below, which, if either, of these proposed instructions should the court have given?

■ THE LAW

Alaska Statutes
(1982)

Article 4. Sexual Offenses

Section 11.41.410. Sexual Assault in the First Degree

(a) A person commits the crime of sexual assault in the first degree if,

    (1) being any age, he engages in sexual penetration with another person without the consent of that person;

    (2) being of any age, he attempts to engage in sexual penetration with another person without the consent of that person and causes serious physical injury to that person;

    (3) being 16 years or older, he engages in sexual penetration with another person under 13 years of age or aids, induces, causes or encourages a person under 13 years of age to engage in sexual penetration with another person; or

    (4) being 18 years of age or older, he engages in sexual penetration with another person who is under 18 years of age and who

        (A) is entrusted to his care by authority of law; or

        (B) is his son or daughter, whether adopted, illegitimate, or stepchild.

(b) Sexual assault in the first degree is a class A felony.

Section 11.41.420. Sexual Assault in the Second Degree

(a) A person commits the crime of sexual assault in the second degree if he coerces another person to engage in sexual contact by the express or implied threat of imminent death, imminent physical injury, or imminent kidnapping to be inflicted on anyone or by causing physical injury to any person, regardless of whether the victim resists.

(b) Sexual assault in the second degree is a class B felony.

Section 11.41.430. Sexual Assault in the Third Degree

(a) A person commits the crime of sexual assault in the third degree if he engages in sexual penetration with a person who he knows

    (1) is suffering from a mental disorder or defect which rendered him incapable of appraising the nature of the conduct under the circumstances in which a person who is capable of appraising the nature of the conduct would not engage in sexual penetration; or

    (2) is incapacitated.

(b) Sexual assault in the third degree is a class C felony.

Section 11.41.445. General Provisions

(a) In a prosecution under secs. 410-440 of this chapter, it is an affirmative defense that, at the time of the alleged offense, the victim was the legal spouse of the defendant unless
     (1) the spouses were living apart; or
     (2) the defendant caused physical injury to the victim.
(b) In the prosecution under secs. 410-440 of this chapter, whenever a provision of law defining an offense depends upon a victim's being under a certain age, it is an affirmative defense that, at the time of the alleged offense, the defendant reasonably believed the victim to be that age or older, unless the victim was under 13 years of age at the time of the alleged offense.

Section 11.41.470. Definitions

For purposes of secs. 410-470 of this chapter, unless the context requires otherwise,
     (1) "incapacitated" means that a person is temporarily incapable of appraising the nature of his conduct and is physically unable to express unwillingness to act;
     (2) "victim" means the person alleged to have been subject to sexual assault in any degree or sexual abuse of a minor;
     (3) "without consent" means that the person
         (A) with or without resisting, is coerced by the use of force against a person or property, or by the express or implied threat of imminent death, imminent physical injury, or imminent kidnapping to be inflicted on anyone; or
         (B) is incapacitated as a result of an act of the defendant.

Article 3. Kidnapping and Custodial Interference

Section 11.41.300. Kidnapping

(a) A person commits the crime of kidnapping if
     (1) he restrains another person with intent to
         (A) hold him for ransom, reward, or other payment;
         (B) use him as a shield or hostage;
         (C) inflict physical injury upon him or sexually assault him or place him or a third person in apprehension that any person will be subjected to serious physical injury or sexually assault;
         (D) interfere with the performance of a governmental or political function;
         (E) facilitate the commission of a felony or flight after commission of a felony; or

(2) he restrains another person

    (A) by secreting and holding him in a place where he is not likely to be found; or

    (B) under circumstances which expose him to a substantial risk of serious injury.

(b) In prosecution under (a)(2)(A) of this section, it is an affirmative defense that

    (1) the defendant was a relative of the victim;

    (2) the victim was a child under 18 years of age or an incompetent person; and

    (3) the primary intent of the defendant was to assume custody of the victim.

(c) Except as provided in (d) of this section, kidnapping is an unclassified felony and is punishable as provided in AS 12.55.

(d) In a prosecution for kidnapping, it is an affirmative defense which reduces the crime to a class A felony that the defendant voluntarily caused the release of the victim alive in a safe place before arrest, or within 24 hours after arrest, without having engaged in conduct described in sec. 410(a)(1) or (2) or 420 of this chapter.

Section 11.41.370. Definitions

In secs. 300-370 of this chapter, unless the context requires otherwise, . . .

    (2) "relative" means a parent, stepparent, ancestor, descendant, sibling, uncle, or aunt, including a relative of the same degree through marriage or adoption. . . .

    (3) "restrain" means to restrict a person's movements unlawfully and without consent, so as to interfere substantially with his liberty by moving him from one place to another or by confining him either in the place where the restriction commences or in a place to which he has been moved; a restraint is "without consent" if it is accomplished

    (A) by acquiescence of the victim, if the victim is under 16 years of age or is an incompetent person and his lawful custodian has not acquiesced in the movement or confinement; or

    (B) by force, threat, or deception.

Chapter 31. Attempt and Solicitation

Section 11.31.100. Attempt

(a) A person is guilty of an attempt to commit a crime if, with intent to commit a crime, he engages in conduct which constitutes a substantial step toward the commission of that crime.

(b) in a prosecution under this section, it is not a defense that it was factually or legally impossible to commit the crime which was the object of the attempt if the conduct engaged in by the defendant would be a crime had the circumstances been as he believed them to be.

(c) In a prosecution under this section, it is an affirmative defense that the defendant, under circumstances manifesting a voluntary and complete renunciation of his criminal intent, prevented the commission of the attempted crime.

(d) An attempt is a

(1) class A felony if the crime attempted is murder in any degree or kidnapping;

(2) class B felony if the crime attempted is a class A felony;

(3) class C felony if the crime attempted is a class B felony;

(4) class A misdemeanor if the crime attempted is a class C felony;

(5) class B misdemeanor if the crime attempted is a class A or class B misdemeanor.

Section 11.31.140. Multiple Convictions Barred

(a) It is not a defense to a prosecution under sec. 100 [attempt] or 110 [solicitation] of this chapter that the crime that is the object of the attempt or solicitation was actually committed pursuant to the attempt or solicitation.

(b) A person may not be convicted of more than one crime defined by sec. 100 or 110 of this chapter for conduct designed to commit or culminate in commission of the same crime.

(c) A person may not be convicted on the basis of the same course of conduct of both (1) a crime defined by sec. 100 or 110 of this chapter; and (2) the crime that is the object of the attempt or solicitation.

(d) This section does not bar inclusion of multiple counts in a single indictment or information charging commission of a crime defined by sec. 100 or 110 of this chapter and commission of the crime that is the object of the attempt of solicitation.

Section 11.31.150. Substantive Crimes Involving Attempt or Solicitation

Notwithstanding sec. 140(d) of this chapter,

(1) a person may not be charged under sec. 100 of this chapter if the crime allegedly attempted by the defendant is defined in such a way that an attempt to engage in the proscribed conduct constitutes commission of the crime itself; . . .

Section 11.81.610. Construction of Statutes with Respect to Culpability

(a) . . .

(b) Except as provided in AS 11.81.600(b), if a provision of law defining an offense does not prescribe a culpable mental state, the culpable mental state that must be proved with respect to

(1) conduct is "knowingly"; and

(2) a circumstance or a result is "recklessly."

(c) When a provision of law provides that criminal negligence suffices to establish an element of an offense, that element is also established if a person acts intentionally, knowingly, or recklessly. If acting recklessly suffices to establish an element, that element also is established if a person acts intentionally or knowingly. If acting knowingly suffices to establish an element, that element is also established if a person acts intentionally.

Section 11.81.620. Effect of Ignorance or Mistake upon Liability

(a) Knowledge, recklessness, or criminal negligence as to whether conduct constitutes an offense, or knowledge, recklessness, or criminal negligence as to the existence, meaning, or application of the provision of law defining an offense, is not an element of an offense unless the provision clearly so provides. Use of the phrase "intent to commit a crime", "intent to promote or facilitate the commission of a crime", or like terminology in a provision of law does not require that the defendant act with a culpable mental state as to the criminality of the conduct that is the object of the defendant's intent.

(b) A person is not relieved of criminal liability for conduct because the person engages in the conduct under a mistaken belief of fact, unless

(1) the factual mistake is a reasonable one that negates the culpable mental state required for the commission of the offense;

(2) the provision of law defining the offense or a related provision of law expressly provides that the factual mistake constitutes a defense or exemption; or

(3) the factual mistake is a reasonable one that supports a defense of justification as provided in AS 11.81.320-11.81.430.

Section 11.81.630. Intoxication as a Defense

Voluntary intoxication is not a defense to prosecution for an offense, but evidence that the defendant was intoxicated may be offered whenever it is relevant to negate an element of the offense that requires that the defendant intentionally cause a result.

Section 11.81.900. Definitions

(a) For purposes of this title, unless the context requires otherwise,

(1) a person acts "intentionally" with respect to a result described by a provision of law defining an offense when his conscious objective is to cause that result;

(2) a person acts "knowingly" with respect to conduct or to a circumstance described by a provision of law defining an offense when he is aware that his conduct is of that nature or that the circumstance exists; when knowledge of the existence of a particular fact is an element of an offense, that knowledge is established if a person is aware of a substantial probability

of its existence, unless he actually believes it does not exist; a person who is unaware of conduct or a circumstance of which he would have been aware had he not been intoxicated acts knowingly with respect to that conduct or circumstance;

(3) a person acts "recklessly" with response to a result or to a circumstance described by provision of law defining an offense when he is aware of and consciously disregards a substantial and unjustifiable risk that the result will occur or that the circumstance exists; the risk must be of such a nature and degree that disregard of it constitutes a gross deviation from the standard of conduct that a reasonable person would observe in the situation; a person who is unaware of a risk of which he would have been aware had he not been intoxicated acts recklessly with respect to that risk;

(4) a person acts with "criminal negligence" with respect to a result or to a circumstance described by a provision of law defining an offense when he fails to perceive a substantial and unjustifiable risk that the result will occur or that the circumstance exists; the risk must be of such a nature and degree that the failure to perceive constitutes a gross deviation from the standard of care that a reasonable person would observe in the situation;

(b) As used in this title, unless otherwise specified or unless the context requires otherwise,

(1) "affirmative defense" means that

(A) some evidence must be admitted which places in issue the defense; and

(B) the defendant has the burden of establishing the defense by a preponderance of the evidence; . . .

(5) "conduct" means an act or omission and its accompanying mental state; . . .

(9) "crime" means an offense for which a sentence of imprisonment is authorized: a crime is either a felony or a misdemeanor;

(10) "culpable mental state" means "intentionally", "knowingly", "recklessly" and with "criminal negligence", as those terms are defined in (a) of this section; . . .

(15) "defense", other than an affirmative defense, means that

(A) some evidence must be admitted which places in issue the defense; and

(B) the state then has the burden of disproving the existence of the defense beyond a reasonable doubt; . . .

(19) "felony" means a crime for which a sentence of imprisonment for a term of more then one year is authorized; . . .

(22) "force" means any bodily impact, restraint, or confinement or the threat of imminent bodily impact, restraint, or confinement; force includes deadly and nondeadly force;

(23) "government" means the United States, and state of any municipality or other political subdivision within the United States or its territories; any department, agency, or subdivision of any of the foregoing; any agency carrying out the functions of government; or any corporation or agency formed under interstate compact or international treaty; . . .

(25) "includes" means "includes but is not limited to";

(26) "incompetent person" means a person who is impaired by reason of mental illness or mental deficiency to the extent that he lacks sufficient understanding or capacity to make or communicate decisions concerning his person;

(27) "intoxicated" means intoxicated from the use of a drug or alcohol;

(28) "law" includes statutes and regulations; . . .

(31) "misdemeanor" means a crime for which a sentence of imprisonment for a term of more than one year may not be imposed; . . .

(33) "offense" means conduct for which a sentence of imprisonment or fine is authorized; an offense is either a crime or a violation; . . .

(39) "person" means a natural person and, when appropriate, an organization, government, or governmental instrumentality;

(40) "physical injury" means physical pain or an impairment of physical condition; . . .

(44) "property" means any article, substance, or thing of value, including money, tangible and intangible personal property, real property, a credit card, choses-in-action, and evidence of debt or of contract, a commodity of a public utility such as gas, electricity, steam, or water constitutes property but the supplying of such commodity to premises from an outside source by means of wires, pipes, conduits, or other equipment is considered a rendition of a service rather than a sale of delivery of property; . . .

(48) a "renunciation" is not "voluntary and complete" if it is substantially motivated, in whole or in part, by

(A) a belief that circumstances exist which increase the probability of detection or apprehension of the defendant or another participant in the criminal enterprise, or which render more difficult the accomplishment of the criminal purpose; or

(B) a decision to postpone the criminal conduct until another time or to transfer the criminal effort to another victim on another but similar objective;

(49) "serious physical injury" means physical injury which creates a substantial risk of death or which causes serious and protracted disfigurement, protracted impairment of health, or protracted loss or impairment of the function of a body member or bodily organ, or physical injury which unlawfully terminates a pregnancy;

(50) "services" includes labor, professional services, transportation, telephone or other communications service, entertainment, the supplying of food, lodging, or other accommodations in hotels, restaurants, or elsewhere, admission to exhibitions, and the supplying of equipment for use;

(51) "sexual contact" means

(A) the intentional touching, directly or through clothing, by the defendant of the victim's genitals, anus, or female breast; or

(B) the defendant's intentionally causing the victim to touch, directly or through clothing, the defendant's or victim's genitals, anus, or female breast;

(52) "sexual penetration" means genital intercourse, cunnilingus, fellatio, anal intercourse, or an intrusion, however slight, of an object or any part of a person's body into the genital or anal opening of another person's body; each party to any of the acts defined as "sexual penetration" is considered to be engaged in sexual penetration; ...

(54) "threat" means a menace, however communicated, to engage in conduct described in (1)-(7) of AS 11.41.520(a) but under (1) of that subsection includes all threat to inflict physical injury on anyone.

Model Penal Code
(Official Draft 1962)

Section 2.04. Ignorance or Mistake

(1) Ignorance or mistake as to a matter of fact or law is a defense if:

(a) the ignorance or mistake negatives the purpose, knowledge, belief, recklessness or negligence required to establish a material element of the offense; or

(b) the law provides that the state of mind established by such ignorance or mistake constitutes a defense.

(2) Although ignorance or mistake would otherwise afford a defense to the offense charged, the defense is not available if the defendant would be guilty of another offense had the situation been as he supposed. In such case, however, the ignorance or mistake of the defendant shall reduce the grade and degree of the offense of which he may be convicted to those of the offense of which he would be guilty had the situation been as he supposed.

(3) A belief that conduct does not legally constitute an offense is a defense to a prosecution for that offense based upon such conduct when:

(a) the statute or other enactment defining the offense is not known to the actor and has not been published or otherwise reasonably made available prior to the conduct alleged; or

(b) he acts in reasonable reliance upon an official statement of the law, afterward determined to be invalid or erroneous, contained in (i) a statute or other enactment; (ii) a judicial decision, opinion or judgment; (iii) an administrative order or grant of permission; or (iv) an official interpretation of the public officer or body charged by law with responsibility for the interpretation, administration or enforcement of the law defining the offense.

(4) The defendant must prove a defense arising under Subsection (3) of this Section by a preponderance of evidence.

● OVERVIEW OF CULPABILITY REQUIREMENTS & MISTAKE DEFENSES

Umbrella Crimes   When leaving a restaurant, you take the wrong umbrella from the coatroom by mistake. While you may satisfy the objective elements of theft (an unlicensed taking of another's property), your mistake (mistaken belief that the umbrella you take is your own) means that you do not have the culpable state of mind required for theft; you do not intend to take "property of another." Mistakes that provide a defense in this way, by negating a culpability requirement, are the topic of this Section. A mistake can provide a defense in other ways as well, sketched below and in greater detail in Sections 20 and 21.

Mistakes vs. Accidents   Your mistake in taking another's umbrella concerns what we called a "circumstance" element — the ownership of the umbrella. One can also make mistakes as to result elements. Under common language usage, we call these "accidents." While you were *mistaken* as to whose umbrella you took, you *accidentally* drop it under a street-sweeping machine (that is, you claim you have no culpability as to the result of property destruction).

General Mistake Defenses   You have just finished reading in the newspaper about a diplomat who is stabbed in the leg with a poison-tipped umbrella. The suspicious-looking man carrying the umbrella at your bus stop looks exactly like the man in the newspaper picture who is sought in the diplomat's death. Just as he seems to be about to stab the distinguished-looking woman in front of him in line, you strike him over the head with your umbrella in an effort to protect her. It turns out that your imagination has been a bit overactive. The "suspect" is entirely innocent; no attack was imminent. Your mistaken belief in an imminent umbrella attack does not negate a culpability element of assault; you *did* intend to hit the suspected attacker without consent. Nonetheless, you may have a defense if your mistake satisfies the conditions of a general defense, such as mistaken defense of another, one of the mistakes as to justification defenses, the subject of Section 20. A mistake also may provide a general defense if you commit an offense but are unaware that your conduct is criminal, because you relied upon an official misstatement of law or because the law you violated was not made reasonably available. Again, such ignorance or mistake of law does not negate an offense element. It provides a defense because it satisfies the conditions of one of the general mistake defenses discussed in Section 21.

Exculpatory Mistakes vs. Inculpatory Mistakes   Mistaken umbrella thefts and mistaken killings are both instances of an actor mistakenly believing that his conduct is not an offense. The reverse sort of mistakes also are possible. An actor may believe that he *is* committing an offense when, because of a mistake, he really is not. A downpour starts just as you are leaving the restaurant. Because you lost your umbrella last week, you steal someone else's from the coatroom. When you get outside you find that the umbrella you have "stolen" is your own, apparently "lost" in the coatroom the week before. You satisfy the culpability elements of theft (you have the intention to take the property of another), but you do not satisfy the objective elements (you did not take the property of another). Such instances of mistaken belief that one *is* committing an offense frequently are punished as an *attempt* to commit an offense, examined in Section 10.

Mistake at Common Law   With this general orientation to the various roles of mistake, let us turn to a closer examination of mistake negating a circumstance element of an offense. The Common Law did not recognize a defense of mistake negating an offense element. Rather than seeing mistake defenses as logical corollaries of culpability requirements, courts conceived of mistake defenses as independent doctrines. Thus, while each offense had a culpability requirement—a specific intent or a general intent, or strict liability—a court nonetheless would commonly analyze the public policy arguments for and against recognizing a particular kind of mistake defense and announce an appropriate rule. This was done even by courts that eagerly confirmed that the legality principle forbade the judicial creation or redefinition of offenses. In the courts' view, mistakes concerned independent matters of exculpation and, therefore, like other *defenses,* could be created and refined by the courts. They did not see that the definition of a mistake defense necessarily had the effect of defining the offense culpability that would be adequate for liability.

Mistake and General vs. Specific Intent Offenses   In time, some courts saw a connection between mistake defenses and culpability requirements. A general principle developed in these courts that defined the mistake defense in terms of the culpability requirements of the offense, albeit in an "offense analysis" form: An honest mistake provided a defense to a specific intent offense; only a reasonable mistake provided a defense to a general intent offense; no mistake could provide a defense to an offense of strict liability. While courts felt free to deviate from this general rule *ad hoc,* it nonetheless was of central importance to the development of the modern view. At the very least, the principle recognized some logical connection between culpability requirements and mistake defenses.

Rule of Logical Relevance   Model Penal Code section 2.04(1)(a) states the modern view:

> Ignorance or mistake as to a matter of fact or law is a defense if the ignorance or mistake negatives the purpose, knowledge, belief, recklessness or negligence required to establish a material element of the offense. . . .

In other words, a mistake is a defense if it negates a required culpability element. This is sometimes called the "rule of logical relevance"; mistake evidence is relevant if it is logically related to an offense culpability requirement. While the principle is simple, its application sometimes is difficult because it is not always easy to determine the culpability requirements of an offense. Nonetheless, determination of an offense's culpability elements is the only means in a modern code by which one can determine the kind of mistake, if any, that will provide a defense.

Negating Recklessness   Where recklessness is required, the defendant will have a defense if his mistake is reasonable or only negligent. In *Laseter v. State,*[1] for example, a general provision similar to Model Penal Code section 2.02(3) read in a requirement of "recklessness" as to lack of consent in a rape. The defendant claimed that he believed the victim consented. The jury was instructed that to get a defense the defendant's mistake as to the victim's consent had to be reasonable. But if recklessness as to lack of consent is required, either a reasonable (non-negligent) *or a negligent mistake* should provide a defense; either would show the absence of the required recklessness. The instruction given, requiring a reasonable mistake, gave too narrow a mistake defense. Laseter's conviction was reversed. (The defendant had requested an instruction that would have required the state to

---

1. 684 P.2d 139 (Alaska Ct. App. 1984).

show that the defendant "was subjectively aware" that the victim did not consent, but this would have essentially required "knowing" as to lack of consent, and therefore would have given too liberal a mistake defense.) The role of mistake as to consent in rape cases is the focus of this Section's Discussion Materials.

Negating Negligence   Where negligence is required, a reasonable mistake will provide a defense. In *State v. Elton*,[1] for example, a general provision was used to read in "negligence" as to the age of the underage partner in statutory rape. The trial court excluded the defendant's proffered evidence that his mistake as to age was reasonable. The reasonableness (non-negligence) of his belief would have negated the negligence as to age required for liability. The conviction was reversed.

Mistake and Strict Liability   Where no culpability is required, no mistake, even a reasonable mistake, will provide a defense. In a Pennsylvania statutory rape case, *Commonwealth v. Robinson*,[2] for example, a special code provision imposed strict liability as to age for certain sex offenses. The court held that the special provision preempted application of a general provision, which would have required at least negligence as to age.[3] Thus, even a reasonable mistake as to age was no defense. The point here is that the culpability required by the offense definition, whatever it may be, determines the kind of mistakes that will provide a defense.

"Reasonable" and "Unreasonable" Mistakes   A carryover from the Common Law period is our tendency to speak of "reasonable" and "unreasonable" mistakes. This terminology was adequate when an honest, albeit "unreasonable," mistake provided a defense to a specific intent offense, but only a "reasonable" mistake provided a defense to a general intent offense. With the advent of the Model Penal Code's culpability scheme and its provision that mistake is a defense when it negates a required culpability element, the terms "reasonable" and "unreasonable" became inadequate to recognize the relevant distinctions. A "reasonable" mistake can be accurately translated into modern code terms as a "non-negligent" mistake. But an "unreasonable" mistake has an ambiguous meaning in modern terms. A mistake might be unreasonable either because it is a negligent mistake or because it is a reckless mistake, and the difference can be significant.

Negligent and Reckless Mistakes   A *negligent mistake* occurs when an actor is unaware of a substantial risk that the required circumstance exists and a reasonable person would have been aware — for example, it never occurs to him that the umbrella he takes is not his own, but a reasonable person would be aware of this possibility. A *reckless mistake* occurs when an actor is aware of a substantial risk that the required circumstance exists — for example, he is aware of a substantial risk that the umbrella might not be his, although he thinks it probably is. The reckless mistake will provide a defense only when the offense requires purpose or

---

1. 680 P.2d 727 (Utah 1984).
2. 264 Pa. Super. 345, 399 A.2d 1084 (1979), aff'd, 497 Pa. 49, 438 A.2d 964 (1981).
3. The Model Penal Code has a similar special provision that imposes strict liability as to age in certain sex offenses. Model Penal Code §213.6(1).

knowledge as to the circumstance. The negligent mistake will provide a defense whenever purpose, knowledge, or recklessness is required.

Ambiguity of "Unreasonable" Mistake The ambiguity of the term "unreasonable" mistake in including both negligent and reckless mistakes is particularly problematic because it makes it impossible to describe the kind of mistake that will provide a defense in the most common situation: where recklessness is required. Recall that recklessness typically is the minimum culpability required and is the culpability read in by Model Penal Code section 2.02(3) whenever the required culpability is not stated. Where recklessness is required, a negligent mistake will provide a defense, but a reckless mistake will not. Thus, the distinction between reckless and negligent mistakes describes the borderline of criminality, but the term "unreasonable" mistake includes both kinds of mistakes and makes it impossible accurately to describe the borderline. To give a defense for an "unreasonable" mistake is improperly to give a defense to a reckless mistake (recklessness satisfies the required culpability); to deny a defense for an "unreasonable" mistake is to improperly deny a defense for a negligent mistake (negligence falls short of the required culpability of recklessness). A better course is to avoid use of the term "unreasonable" mistake and to use the more specific terms "reckless mistake" and "negligent mistake."

Culpability Requirements and Mistake Defenses The relation between culpability requirements and mistake defenses, in Model Penal Code culpability terms and in the common law terms of "reasonable" and "unreasonable," may be summarized as follows:

Table 5.1 Translation Between Culpability Requirements and Mistake Defenses

1. Culpability requirement:	2. May be negated by (i.e., actor may get defense for):	3. In language of "reasonable" and "unreasonable" mistake, may be negated by (i.e., actor may get defense for):
"purposely"	any mistake	any mistake
"knowingly"	any mistake (i.e., reckless, negligent, or faultless)	any mistake (i.e., reasonable or unreasonable)
"recklessly"	a negligent or faultless mistake	an unreasonable (in the sense of a "negligent"*) or a reasonable mistake
"negligently"	a faultless mistake	a reasonable mistake
None (strict liability)	no mistake (not even faultless)	no mistake (not even reasonable)

*N.B.—There is no defense, however, for an unreasonable, in the sense of a "reckless," mistake. It is this point at which the reasonable-unreasonable terminology breaks down in its translation to modern culpability terms. This is a particularly serious problem given that "recklessness" is the norm, the most common culpability required as to circumstance elements.

Common Law's Rejection of Mistake of Law Defense   At common law, mistake or ignorance as to a matter of fact might have provided a defense, as described above, but mistake or ignorance as to a matter of law did not. All persons were presumed by the law to know the law. In *State v. Woods*,[1] for example, the defendant was charged with violation of Vermont's "Blanket Act," which, among other things, punished "a woman [if she is found in bed together] *with another woman's husband*... under circumstances affording presumption of an illicit intention."[2] Defendant Woods had married a man from Vermont after the man's divorce in Reno, Nevada. She contended that her honest belief in the validity of the Reno divorce and of her subsequent marriage provided a defense. The court held, however, that even if her belief were reasonable it could not be a defense because it was "a mistake of law rather than a mistake of fact," citing the maxim "*Ignorantia legis non excusat*" (ignorance of the law does not excuse) and "the corresponding presumption that everyone is conclusively presumed to know the law."[3] Any other rule, it was feared, would encourage people to remain ignorant of the law and, in any case, was thought to allow defendants to raise frivolous yet hard-to-disprove claims in every case.

Mistake of Law in Modern Codes   The concern to avoid a flood of mistake of law claims might have been justified at a time when "the law of mistake" was seen as independent of an offense's defined culpability requirements. Presumably, it was within the power of the court to recognize a defense for any mistake in any case. Under modern codes, however, where the potential for a mistake defense is defined and therefore limited by the requirements of the legislature's offense definition, no such danger exists. A mistake of law provides a defense under modern codes *if it negates a required culpability element*. In practice, this does not frequently occur because most circumstance elements concern factual rather than legal matters.

Mistake of Law Negating Element   In the *Woods* case described above, one circumstance element of the offense requires that the defendant be in bed with "another woman's husband." Therefore, under normal rules of modern codes, some culpability is required as to the partner being "another woman's husband." (Recklessness would be read in by Model Penal Code section 2.02(3).) A reasonable belief in the validity of the man's divorce and remarriage would mean lack of culpability as to the man being "another woman's husband" and would provide a defense. In some common law cases, Woods' mistake might have been called a factual mistake as to a legal matter, sometimes called a "mixed fact-law mistake."

Mixed Fact-Law Mistake   Whether the man in *Woods* is single or married might be described as a fact, but admittedly it is an issue that depends upon legal matters: Marriage and divorce are legal concepts. Many circumstance elements of offenses are in some part legal concepts: ownership of property, privilege to enter, status as a fiduciary. Under modern codes, however, the fact-law distinction is irrelevant and such categorization issues are avoided. Any mistake, fact or law, will provide a defense if it negates an offense element.

---

1. 107 Vt. 354, 179 A. 1 (1935).
2. Vt. Pub. L. §8602 (1933).
3. 107 Vt. at 2, 179 A. at 356-357.

Mistake as to Criminality of Conduct An actor frequently may wish to claim a mistake as to whether the offense conduct was in fact a crime. That is, while the actor knew the circumstances that in fact constitute the offense — for example, he knew he was entering the United States and he knew he possessed certain vegetables — the actor may claim that he or she did not realize such conduct constituted an offense under the Customs laws. The same principle — mistake of law or fact is a defense if it negates an element — can work to provide a defense for a mistake as to whether one's conduct is criminal. This application of the defense is more rare, however, because culpability as to the unlawfulness of one's conduct is rarely an element of an offense. Model Penal Code section 2.02(9) expressly provides that such culpability as to the criminality of one's conduct is never to be "read in" or assumed to be an element; it must be explicitly provided by the offense definition.[1] Nevertheless, some offense definitions do explicitly or implicitly require culpability as to the criminality of the conduct. In *People v. Weiss,* for example, the defendants "arrested" one Paul H. Wendel, believing him to be the kidnapper of the Lindbergh baby.[2] He was not. Defendants were charged with kidnapping: "A person who wilfully seizes, confines, [etc., another], with intent to cause him, *without authority of law,* to be . . . in any way held . . . against his will . . . is guilty of kidnapping."[3] Defendants claimed that they had been deputized by the New Jersey Secret Service, or so they believed, and therefore believed they had authority to make the "arrest." On appeal, the court held that their mistaken belief that their conduct was lawful provided a defense because the statute required that they intend to act "without authority of law." Their conviction was reversed. Indeed, the Supreme Court has held that a "wilfully" requirement in federal criminal statutes often should be interpreted to require proof of a "voluntary, intentional violation of a known legal duty."

◉ DISCUSSION MATERIALS

What Kind of Mistake as to Consent, If Any, Should Be Permitted to Provide a Defense to Rape?

Susan Estrich, in an article calling for criminal liability for the negligent rapist, examines the American system's limited mistake defense for rape and argues that the current formulation has an adverse effect on victims. Lynne Henderson's review of the Estrich article purports to uncover various flaws in argument, and rejects her conclusions. Joshua Dressler explores the various dangers of rejecting the mens rea requirement, advocated by many rape law reformers, while Lani

---

1. Neither knowledge nor recklessness or negligence as to whether conduct constitutes an offense or as to the existence, meaning or application of the law determining the elements of an offense is an element of such offense, unless the definition of the offense or the code so provides.
Model Penal Code §2.02(9).
   2. 276 N.Y. 384, 12 N.E.2d 514 (1938).
   3. 276 N.Y. 384, 385, 12 N.E.2d 514, 514 (1938) (emphasis added).

Anne Remick advocates an overhaul of the consent requirement, and supports instead an affirmative verbal consent standard.

Susan Estrich, Rape
95 Yale Law Journal 1087, 1096-1097, 1098-1101, 1102-1105 (1986)

It is difficult to imagine any man engaging in intercourse accidentally or mistakenly. It is just as difficult to imagine an accidental or mistaken use of force, at least as force is conventionally defined. But it is not at all difficult to imagine cases in which a man might claim that he did not realize that the woman was not consenting to sex. He may have been mistaken in assuming that no meant yes. He may not have bothered to inquire. He may have ignored signs that would have told him that the woman did not welcome his forceful penetration.

In doctrinal terms, such a man could argue that his mistake of fact should exculpate him because he lacked the requisite intent or *mens rea* as to the woman's required nonconsent. American courts have altogether eschewed the *mens rea* or mistake inquiry as to consent, opting instead for a definition of the crime of rape that is so limited that it leaves little room for men to be mistaken, reasonably or unreasonably, as to consent. The House of Lords, by contrast, has confronted the question explicitly and, in its leading case, has formally restricted the crime of rape to men who act recklessly, a state of mind defined to allow even the unreasonably mistaken man to avoid conviction.

This Section argues that the American courts' refusal to confront the *mens rea* problem works to the detriment of the victim. In order to protect men from unfair convictions, American courts end up defining rape with undue restrictiveness. The English approach, while doctrinally clearer, also tends toward an unduly restricted definition of the crime of rape.

While the defendant's attitude toward consent may be considered either an issue of *mens rea* or a mistake of fact, the key question remains the same. In *mens rea* terms, the question is whether negligence suffices, that is, whether the defendant should be convicted who claims that he thought the woman was consenting, or didn't think about it, in situations where a "reasonable man" would have known that there was not consent. In mistake of fact terms, the question is whether a mistake as to consent must be reasonable in order to exculpate the defendant. . . .

To treat what the defendant intended or knew or even should have known about the victim's consent as irrelevant to his liability sounds like a result favorable to both prosecution and women as victims. But experience makes all too clear that it is not. To refuse to inquire into *mens rea* leaves two possibilities: turning rape into a strict liability offense where, in the absence of consent, the man is guilty of rape regardless of whether he (or anyone) would have recognized nonconsent in the circumstances; or defining the crime of rape in a fashion that is so limited that it would be virtually impossible for any man to be convicted where he was truly unaware or mistaken as to nonconsent. In fact, it is the latter approach which has characterized all of the older, and many of the newer, American cases. In practice, abandoning *mens rea* produces the worst of all possible worlds: The trial emerges not as an inquiry into the guilt of the defendant (is he a rapist?) but of the victim (was she really raped? did she consent?). The perspective that governs is therefore not that of the woman, nor even of the particular man, but of a judicial system intent upon protecting against unjust conviction, regardless of the dangers of injustice to the woman in the particular case.

The requirement that sexual intercourse be accompanied by force or threat of force to constitute rape provides a man with some protection against mistakes as to consent. A man who uses a gun or knife against his victim is not likely to be in serious doubt as to her lack of consent, and the more narrowly force is defined, the more implausible the claim that he was unaware of nonconsent.

But the law's protection of men is not limited to a requirement of force. Rather than inquire whether the man believed (reasonably or unreasonably) that his victim was consenting, the courts have demanded that the victim demonstrate her nonconsent by engaging in resistance that will leave no doubt as to nonconsent. The definition of nonconsent as resistance — in the older cases, as utmost resistance, while in some more recent ones, as "reasonable" physical resistance — functions as a substitute for *mens rea* to ensure that the man has notice of the woman's nonconsent.

The choice between focusing on the man's intent or focusing on the woman's is not simply a doctrinal flip of the coin.

First, the inquiry into the victim's nonconsent puts the woman, not the man, on trial. Her intent, not his, is disputed; and because her state of mind is key, her sexual history may be considered relevant (even though utterly unknown to the man). Considering consent from *his* perspective, by contrast, substantially undermines the relevance of the woman's sexual history where it was unknown to the man.

Second, the issue for determination shifts from whether the man is a rapist to whether the woman was raped. A verdict of acquittal thus does more than signal that the prosecution has failed to prove the defendant guilty beyond a reasonable doubt; it signals that the prosecution has failed to prove the woman's sexual violation — her innocence — beyond a reasonable doubt. Thus, as one dissenter put it in disagreeing with the affirmance of a conviction of rape: "The majority today . . . declares the innocence of an at best distraught young woman." Presumably, the dissenter thought the young woman guilty.

Third, the resistance requirement is not only ill-conceived as a definition of nonconsent, but is an overbroad substitute for *mens rea* in any event. Both the resistance requirement and the *mens rea* requirement can be used to enforce a male perspective on the crime, but while *mens rea* might be justified as protecting the individual defendant who has not made a blameworthy choice, the resistance standard requires women to risk injury to themselves in cases where there may be no doubt as to the man's intent or blameworthiness. The application of the resistance requirement has not been limited to cases in which there was uncertainty as to what the man thought, knew or intended; it has been fully applied in cases where there can be no question that the man knew that intercourse was without consent. Indeed, most of the cases that have dismissed claims that *mens rea* ought to be required have been cases where both force and resistance were present, and where there was no danger of any unfairness.

Finally, by ignoring *mens rea*, American courts and legislators have imposed limits on the fair expansion of our understanding of rape. As long as the law holds that *mens rea* is not required, and that no instructions on intent need be given, pressure will exist to retain some form of resistance requirement and to insist on force as conventionally defined in order to protect men against conviction for "sex." Using resistance as a substitute for *mens rea* unnecessarily and unfairly immunizes those men whose victims are afraid enough, or intimidated enough, or, frankly, smart enough, not to take the risk of resisting physically. In doing so, the resistance test may declare the blameworthy man innocent and the raped woman guilty. . . .

My view is that . . . a "negligent rapist" should be punished, albeit — as in murder — less severely than the man who acts with purpose or knowledge, or even knowledge of the risk. First, he is sufficiently blameworthy for it to be just to punish him. Second, the injury he inflicts is sufficiently grave to deserve the law's prohibition.

The traditional argument against negligence liability is that punishment should be limited to cases of choice, because to punish a man for his stupidity is unjust and, in deterrence terms, ineffective. Under this view, a man should only be held responsible for what he does knowingly or purposely, or at least while aware of the risks involved. As one of *Morgan*'s most respected defenders put it:

> To convict the stupid man would be to convict him for what lawyers call inadvertent negligence — honest conduct which may be the best that this man can do but that does not come up to the standard of the so-called reasonable man. People ought not to be punished for negligence except in some minor offences established by statute. Rape carries a possible sentence of imprisonment for life, and it would be wrong to have a law of negligent rape.

If inaccuracy or indifference to consent is "the best that this man can do" because he lacks the capacity to act reasonably, then it might well be unjust and ineffective to punish him for it. But such men will be rare, and there was no evidence that the men in *Morgan* were among them, at least as long as voluntary drunkenness is not equated with inherent lack of capacity. More common is the case of the man who could have done better but didn't; could have paid attention, but didn't; heard her say no, or saw her tears, but decided to ignore them. Neither justice nor deterrence argues against punishing this man.

Certainly, if the "reasonable" attitude to which a male defendant is held is defined according to a "no means yes" philosophy that celebrates male aggressiveness and female passivity, there is little potential for unfairness in holding men who fall below *that* standard criminally liable. Under such a low standard of reasonableness, only a very drunk man could honestly be mistaken as to a woman's consent, and a man who voluntarily sheds his capacity to act and perceive reasonably should not be heard to complain here — any more than with respect to other crimes — that he is being punished in the absence of choice.

But even if reasonableness is defined — as I argue it should be — according to a rule that "no means no," it is not unfair to hold those men who violate the rule criminally responsible, provided that there is fair warning of the rule. I understand that some men in our society have honestly believed in a different reality of sexual relations, and that many may honestly view such situations differently than women. But, it is precisely because men and women may perceive these situations differently, and because the injury to women stemming from the different male perception may be grave, that it is necessary and appropriate for the law to impose a duty upon men to act with reason, and to punish them when they violate that duty.

In holding a man to such a standard of reasonableness, the law signifies that it considers a woman's consent to sex to be significant enough to merit a man's reasoned attention. In effect, the law imposes a duty on men to open their eyes and use their heads before engaging in sex — not to read a woman's mind, but to give her credit for knowing her own mind when she speaks it. The man who has the inherent capacity to act reasonably, but fails to do so, has made the blame-worthy choice to violate this duty. While the injury caused by purposeful conduct may be greater than that caused by negligent acts, being negligently sexually penetrated without one's consent remains a grave harm, and being treated like an object whose words or actions are not even worthy of consideration adds insult to injury. This dehumanization exacerbates the denial of dignity and autonomy which is so much a part of the injury of rape, and it is equally present in both the purposeful and negligent rape.

By holding out the prospect of punishment for negligence, the law provides an additional motive for men to "take care before acting, to use their faculties and draw on their experience in gauging the potentialities of contemplated conduct." We may not yet have reached the point where men are required to ask verbally. But if silence does not negate consent, at least the word "no" should, and those who ignore such an explicit sign of nonconsent should be subject to criminal liability.

Lynne N. Henderson, Review Essay: What Makes Rape a Crime?
Review of *Estrich, Real Rape*
3 Berkeley Woman's Law Journal 193, 211-219 (1987-1988)

Mens Rea as to Consent

Estrich thinks the focus of reform legislation should be on the offender, but that it should be done via a mens rea requirement as to consent rather than via an emphasis on force. She begins with a discussion of the English gang rape case *Director of Public Prosecutions v. Morgan*, a horrible case often taught in first year criminal law classes to illustrate mistake of fact. *Morgan* held that an honest but unreasonable belief, or negligence, as to a woman's consent was *not* a culpable mental state for the crime of rape. Although Estrich disagrees with the holding of *Morgan*, she agrees with its focus on consent and the defendant's intent. She then criticizes American courts for failing to discuss intent or mistake, because the resulting definition of rape effectively excludes the acquaintance or date rape situation: American courts, she claims, "have provided protection for men who find themselves in . . . potentially ambiguous situations through the doctrines of consent, defined as nonresistance, and force, measured by resistance." Estrich argues that this leads to an almost exclusive focus on the victim by making "her intent, not his" the issue in dispute.

Estrich's analysis has two flaws. First, her assertion that American courts ignore the issue of mens rea as to consent is wrong. Second, she is mistaken in thinking that shifting attention to the man's mental state about consent and reducing the mens rea requirement to negligence will relieve the victim of the burden of physical resistance and of having to "prove" she was raped. Estrich contends that absent a mens rea requirement for consent, the question becomes "was this woman raped?" rather than "is this man a rapist?" In fact, focusing on whether or not the man believed he had consent is no solution at all. First, it returns us to the dangers of the focus on consent of the nineteenth century. Second, the methods of proving mens rea will continue to focus attention on the woman and her credibility. . . .

. . . Absent a confession or an admission by the defendant, the prosecutor must introduce evidence of the circumstances surrounding the event to prove mens rea. Consequently, although the woman's subjective state may not be an issue, her behavior is certainly relevant to establishing whether the defendant "honestly and reasonably" believed that she consented. Thus, resistance . . . becomes an issue. As the court in *Barnes* noted, "Absence of resistance may . . . be probative of whether the accused honestly and reasonably believed he was engaging in consensual sexuality." It is likely that the victim would be scrutinized every bit as closely under Estrich's proposed standard as under prior standards. Thus, resistance once more becomes an issue. . . .

Concentrating on the defendant's mens rea as to consent may bring back another nightmare: the survivor's sexual history. As of this writing, forty-nine states have rape shield laws limiting the introduction and use of a rape survivor's sexual history in rape trials. These statutes do far more than prevent "humiliating questions" in rape trials—they block the introduction of highly prejudicial evidence having little or no relevance to a victim's credibility. Traditionally, the premise underlying the use of this type of evidence has been that unchaste women are liars and should not be believed. A more recent premise is that if a woman previously consented to sex, she likely consented this time. Because the defendant in a criminal prosecution has the sixth amendment right to confront his accuser, inquiries focusing on a defendant's mens rea as to consent are likely to reopen the door to more extensive explorations of a victim's sexual past. For example, Vivian Berger's article on rape shield laws specifically mentions an exception for a man's claim of reasonable mistake as to consent. According to Berger, if a man has heard a woman is "easy," or if she behaves in a "seductive" way, the man may reasonably believe she *is* consenting regardless of whether she says no. "Therefore, a wisely drafted statute will not prohibit proof of the woman's sexual history offered to show the defendant's honest (reasonable) belief that she yielded (sic) to him voluntarily." Indeed, Berger's "model" rape shield statute permits exceptions to general prohibitions on evidence of sexual history. . . .

Estrich's solution lies in her definition of consent and her opposition to the resistance requirement. Throughout the book, she argues that "no means no," not yes. Under Estrich's proposal, the "reasonable man" is presumed to know that no means no. Although verbal manifestations of non-consent certainly should be sufficient, concentrating on the rapist's mens rea is not necessary to accomplish this objective. If verbal non-consent is sufficient, Estrich's proposal for making negligence the culpable mens rea as to consent is unnecessary: a woman's "no" would put a man on notice and alert him to the risk of committing rape. For the man to continue his sexual advances would seem, at the very least, to constitute recklessness. Rather than get tied into mens rea knots that lead back to the consent-force-resistance conundrum, it might be better to define consent in unequivocal terms — "no means no" — and presume recklessness by imposing strict liability on men who continue. Of course, this approach raises problems under our culture's existing models of sexual interaction — it raises the questions did the victim really *mean* "no," and did she really *say* "no." This inevitably leads back to an examination of the victim's credibility.

Estrich dismisses strict liability as an answer to the consent issue. Her reluctance to impose strict liability on the element of consent, even after it is established that the woman did not consent, reflects the very male nightmare that she seeks to combat. Estrich states that strict liability regarding consent would result in punishment of men who engaged in intercourse when "no one would realize the woman was not consenting." Yet as Kelman has observed:

> [i]f . . . we view the decision to have intercourse where consent is ambiguous as a separate decision [from the negligent perception as to consent], we are prone to be less sympathetic to the defendant. It is not as if the defendant is "trapped" into criminality either unavoidably or in the course of doing perfectly ordinary or protected acts. By avoiding sexual intercourse with women who are not clearly consenting, the defendant can avoid criminality.

The question becomes whether, as a society, we wish to continue to allow aggressive unwanted male sexual advances.

Moreover, if the standard is "no means no," how can any man possibly claim not to have known of the woman's lack of consent? Such a belief can only be justified if one assumes that men need not accept a woman's "no," that male persistence pays off, and that such persistence is in fact what women desire. The survival of Byron's phrase "[a]nd saying she would n'er consent, consented" certainly captures a vision of how male-female relationships are perceived in this culture, and it does not carry entirely negative connotations.

If Estrich's rejection of strict liability reflects a concern about women engaging in sexual relations who fail to outwardly manifest their non-consent, that is a different problem. Sexual intercourse with an adult woman who has not indicated her subjective opposition may be beyond the scope of what modern society can or should punish. That is, we must accept the notion that men should not be punished for engaging in sexual activity when the woman does not convey her subjective state in any tangible way. But, once the woman has managed *some* manifestation of that subjective state, whether by verbal, physical, or emotional behavior, imposing strict liability if the man proceeds seems justified.

What about the woman who does not want intercourse but fails to say anything because she is frightened of the man? Estrich's solution, because it focuses solely on the *verbal* "no" — although one assumes crying would count — fails to address the problem of what constitutes sufficient fear and/or force to make it seem pointless for the woman to speak the word "no." By focusing solely on the defendant's mens rea as to consent, Estrich leaves unprotected the woman who, frozen with fear, neither cries nor says "no." Estrich also offers little protection to the woman who says "no" long before the actual event, but who finally, giving up, "consents," as did the victims in both *Mayberry* and *Barnes*. Further, when must the "no" be said? At "the crucial genital moment," as Susan Griffin put it, or at any time during the interaction? Traditionally, women were supposed to fight and resist until actual penetration occurred: this extremely narrow time frame remains a potential problem. In a situation where the victim says "no" early on and then becomes paralyzed, speechless with fear — does the focus on consent or the "reasonable man" standard help or hurt? What if she says no, he persists, and she decides to go along — under the male persistence paradigm the reasonable man would think he has consent.

The definition of fear should include consideration of differences in size, verbal threats including harassment ("you bitch," etc.) and, as the court in *Barnes* observed, the generally threatening circumstances created by a particular man. In this type of situation, focus on force may be superior to Estrich's focus on consent. When the victim has been frightened into passive silence, justice is better served by focusing on the victim's fear and the nature of the threatening situation created by the defendant than on his mens rea as to her consent, or on whether she consented. Weapons negate consent; fear should too.

If it seems I do not trust Estrich's "reasonable man" standard, it is for a reason: Indications are that the reasonable man would infer consent where the reasonable woman would not. A woman might think it is reasonable to engage in necking, or invite a date into her home for coffee, at the end of an evening, without inevitably having it signal consent to intercourse. The reasonable man may consider the same conduct as foreplay rather than a pleasant exercise in itself. The reasonable woman might believe a verbal "no," said breathlessly or placatingly, sufficiently conveys her non-consent. The reasonable man may believe he is justified in disregarding anything short of a firm "no" followed by an implicit threat to do him physical harm. Reasonable men have determined the law of rape all along, and it has not helped us much; so calling it "mens rea" and concentrating on consent seems only to promote stereotypical attitudes, not combat them. Estrich's "answer" to this problem is in reality an abandonment of the "reasonable man" standard in any event. She writes that the law should hold "a man to a higher standard of reasonableness" than it has in the past, presumably by redefining nonconsent to mean "no means no."

The focus on mens rea as to consent has theoretical as well as practical flaws. Arguably, women do not voluntarily consent to heterosexual sex in a society in which they are subordinate to male power. Some feminists go so far as to argue that heterosexual intercourse itself is the evil. While I disagree with this claim, I do think that women do not experience the same freedom and autonomy in heterosexual relations as men experience. Consensual sex is not an "arm's length bargain." No one reads women their rights before seeking "consent." Women may *hope* men will ask, but they do not take the initiative in sex unless they are "bad" girls, or incredibly lucky in their relationships. Women frequently consent because they are frightened, because they want to please men, or because they think it is their duty. (And, there is also the ironic consequence of the "sexual revolution": women are no longer virgins so how can they say no?). The word "consent," therefore, does not adequately encompass women's experience of unwanted sex.

The absence of an objective manifestation of non-consent does not necessarily mean consent; a woman may experience sex in such a situation as tantamount to rape. Yet, if women are regarded as absolutely choiceless in the face of male sexuality, women will always and forever be victims. Women must not only take responsibility for their sexuality, but use the law to empower themselves when their sexuality is expropriated. Estrich's proposal is one of two possible approaches to this problem. The other approach involves a statutory redefinition of consent as "words or overt actions by a person who is competent . . . indicating a freely given agreement to have sexual intercourse or sexual contact," or as "positive cooperation in act or attitude pursuant to an exercise of free will. . . . The person must act freely and voluntarily. . . ."

Estrich's definition of consent ("no means no") empowers women formally by offering them a method of expressing non-consent men must heed. Statutes requiring *positive* manifestations of consent minimize the relevance of resistance and protect women who are completely passive because of fear, even if those statutes embody *male* understandings of what constitutes consent. (An unsympathetic court could conceivably find that a woman who, out of fear, submits to sexual acts at the defendant's demand, has manifested "positive cooperation," I suppose.) Perhaps a combination of approaches, "no means no" and "positive cooperation," would adequately encompass the possible variations in women's experiences of and reactions to rape.

Joshua Dressler, Where We Have Been, and Where We Might Be Going: Some Cautionary Reflections on Rape Law Reform
46 Cleveland State Law Review 409, 430-439 (1998)

Mens Rea

It is a fundamental principle of the criminal law — "no provincial or transient notion" — that we do not send people to prison and stigmatize them as serious wrongdoers in the absence of culpability for their actions. No matter how serious the harm caused, the general rule is that a person is not guilty of a criminal offense in the absence of *mens rea*. Imagine for a moment that you are driving safely on the highway, under an overpass, when a piece of the bridge crumbles, strikes your windshield, and causes you to lose control of your car. As a consequence, your car strikes and kills another. You are likely to feel awful about what happened, and in criminal law terms, you have committed the *actus reus* of criminal homicide. That is, you have caused precisely the type of harm that the criminal law wishes to prevent, the death of another human being. But, of course, you are guilty of no crime. You did not kill the pedestrian intentionally, or even recklessly or negligently.

Increasingly, we are forgetting — or, at least, at risk of forgetting — this basic culpability principle in the context of rape. In one sense, this is understandable. The female who is the victim of undesired sexual contact is initially apt to feel just as violated, whether the male knew he was acting against her will or, at the other extreme, was understandably clueless. The harm to her, after all, is the same. But, of course, the harm to the dead person on the highway in the imagined overpass accident is the same whether you killed *him* purposely or innocently — nonetheless, the law will exculpate you for the death assuming non-culpability in causing the harm. Unfortunately, as obvious as this seems, some people find the notion of a *mens rea* requirement in the rape context silly. The principle that a male should not be convicted of rape if he reasonably (but incorrectly) believed that the female consented has been trivialized (or distorted) to mean that "a woman [was] raped but not by a rapist"?

Before rape law reform, the issue of *mens rea* rarely arose in rape trials. As a practical matter, the *actus reus* proved the *mens rea*. If a male used or threatened force to obtain intercourse, then it was evident that he purposely or knowingly had nonconsensual sexual relations. If his conduct was not forcible, the female had to resist, and this gave the male reasonable warning of her lack of consent: if he proceeded against her resistance, a jury could reasonably assume that he knew she did not want sexual relations. At a minimum, the resistance meant that the male acted recklessly or negligently in regard to her wishes. Thus, there was always some form of culpability proven.

With the abandonment or softening of the resistance requirement and the increased willingness of lawmakers to permit prosecutions for nonforcible forms of nonconsensual intercourse — an appropriate change, as I have suggested — the risk of conviction in the absence of *mens rea* is enhanced. A person who sincerely believes that his partner has consented to sexual intimacy should not be convicted of rape if his belief was one that a reasonable person in the same circumstances might hold. And, indeed, this has been the traditional rule for "general intent" offenses, such as rape.

It is too early to know where rape law is going in regard to *mens rea*, but there are some distressing signs. One concern I have is that courts may abandon altogether the requirement of *mens rea* in the rape context. Recently, the Supreme Judicial Council of Massachusetts, an historically liberal court, and thus one that might be expected to honor the requirement of culpability, held that even a reasonable (but incorrect) belief as to a female's consent, is not a defense in a rape prosecution. Thus, even if a reasonable person in the actor's situation would have believed that the female was consenting, the male is guilty of rape, although the victim did not physically or verbally resist his overtures, and although he did not use or threaten to use any force. It would be as if you were convicted as a murderer for killing accidentally when the bridgework crumbled.

An appellate court in Massachusetts explained that the no-defense rule was "in harmony with the analogous rule that a defendant in a statutory rape case is not entitled to an instruction that a reasonable mistake as to the victim's age is a defense." But, it is only in harmony if one ignores the basic point that statutory rape is *a grave exception to the general rule that mens rea matters*. Wisely or not, most (although not all) jurisdictions treat statutory rape as an exceptional strict liability offense, in order to protect young females from the effects of their own decisions. Ordinary rape, however, has not been viewed as strict liability in character. There is simply no more principled basis for dispensing with the *mens rea* requirement in rape cases than there is in regard to any other serious crime.

Massachusetts, of course, is just one state. I do not mean to cry wolf here, but certain other judicial decisions suggest that courts might be prepared to erode, if not abolish, the *mens rea* requirement. Even if a person is entitled to be acquitted on the ground of a reasonable mistake of fact, courts might impose special rules regarding mistake claims in rape prosecutions that would effectively strip the defendant of the claim. For example, consider Justice Frederick Brown's remarks in *Commonwealth v. Lefkowitz*:

> The essence of the offense of rape is lack of consent on the part of the victim. I am prepared to say that when a woman says "no" to someone any

implication other than a manifestation of non-consent that might arise in that person's psyche is legally irrelevant, and thus no defense. Any further action is unwarranted and the person proceeds at his peril. In effect, he assumes the risk. In 1985, I find no social utility in establishing a rule defining non-consensual intercourse on the basis of the subjective (and quite likely wishful) view of the more aggressive player in the sexual encounter.

In short, if a female says no (I assume he means in words or actions) to intercourse, not only does this prove the *actus reus* of the offense, but it automatically proves the *mens rea*. If the defendant asserts a mistake claim, Justice Brown would consider the mistake unreasonable *as a matter of law*. Thus, the issue would not go to the jury.

"No means no" is an excellent rule to teach men (and women) in our culture. And, it is an excellent starting point—initial premise—in rape trials. But, bright-line rules such as this can only result, at best, in the correct outcome *most* of the time. Such rules do not insure justice to the individual whose case might not fit the bright-line assumptions. As troubling as it is to acknowledge, no does *not* always—in one hundred percent of the cases—mean no in sexual relations, even today. If no does not always mean no, there can surely be cases in which a reasonable person could *believe* that no does not mean no in the specific incident, *even when it does*. Such cases will be relatively few in number, but it is improper to convict a person on the basis of the law of averages. It is wrong to use the bludgeon of the criminal law to impose rules intended to change cultural attitudes when this means punishing an individual for rape who made a mistake that the community, represented by the jurors, would characterize as reasonable. If the mistake was, indeed, unreasonable—or if the jurors don't believe the defendant's claim that he was mistaken—they can convict on the facts. The jury should not be deprived of the issue of *mens rea* through bright-line rules. Each case should be considered on its own merits.

Lani Anne Remick, Read Her Lips: An Argument for a Verbal Consent Standard in Rape

141 University of Pennsylvania Law Review 1103-1105 (1993)

Always take "no" for an answer. Always stop when asked to stop. Never assume "no" means "yes." If her lips tell you "no" but there's "yes" in her eyes, keep in mind that her words, not her eyes, will appear in the court transcript.

Violence against women has reached an all-time high. An estimated fifteen to forty percent of all women are victims of attempted or completed rapes at some point in their lifetimes. Most of their rapists are never criminally punished.

The criminal justice system's failure to bring most rapists to justice means that women's right to decide "who may touch their bodies, when, and under what circumstances" is often unenforceable. One of the causes of this problem is that the law of rape does not recognize women's right to sexual autonomy as absolute. Instead, rape law reflects the sexually coercive society in which it operates. Although frowning upon aggressive sexual behavior at the extremes, our male-dominated society accepts a certain amount of coercion, aggressiosn or violence against women as a normal, even desirable, part of sexual encounters. Similarly, the law of rape is founded on a paradigm of violent stranger rape which fails to clearly proscribe less violent rapes or rapes in which some elements of a consensual sexual encounter are present. An estimated sixty to eighty percent of all rapes fit this description. The inability of victims of these "nontraditional" rapes to vindicate their rights through use of the criminal system is thus one of the biggest impediments to the comprehensive protection of female sexual autonomy under the law of rape. If such protection is to be afforded, therefore, "[m]uch, much more needs to be done.... The message that should go out today is that rape is a crime, whether it be date rape, intrafamilial rape, acquaintance rape, stranger rape or spousal rape. Rape is rape."

This Comment suggests a change in the law of rape that would bring all instances of nontraditional rape clearly within the boundaries of the criminal law. Its chosen vehicle for change is a redefinition of the consent standard. In searching for a solution to the current legal system's inadequate protection of women, several commentators have concluded that "the road to that solution presents itself clearly enough as a need for a reformulation of the criterion of consent." Other reformers call for simplicity and clarity in a new criterion, noting that "[c]ontinuous juggling of the elements of the crime by courts and commentators reflects an urge toward administrative simplicity, a search for an external standard by which to measure the subjective element of nonconsent. [Yet]...this interplay reveals a conviction that the central substantive issue in rape is consent."

In answer to the call for a new, clearer consent standard, this Comment proposes a rape law based on a norm of *affirmative verbal consent*. Under this standard, "no" would mean "no," "yes" would mean "yes," and the lack of any verbal communication as to consent would be presumed to mean "no." In more specific terms, a "no" or its verbal equivalent would be dispositive of the issue of consent, as would a freely-given "yes" or its verbal equivalent. The lack of a "yes" or its verbal equivalent would raise a presumption of non-consent. Such a standard would criminalize even "nonaggravated sexual assault, [that is,] nonconsensual sex that does not involve physical injury, or the explicit threat of physical injury." By establishing the threshold for rape at this level, the suggested standard clearly incorporates all instances of nontraditional rape. It also underscores the gravity of the harm of more traditional violent stranger rape. Finally, rather than simply mirroring our sexually coercive society, such a law declares that a woman's right to sexual autonomy is absolute.

It is because rape law currently operates in the context of a sexually coercive society and because rape victims are overwhelmingly female that this Comment argues for a change in the law on the ground of assuring sexual autonomy for women....

● OVERVIEW OF THE FUNCTION OF CRIMINAL LAW DOCTRINE

Your Basement Burglar   You are awakened by an unfamiliar sound from the basement garage of your rowhouse. As you sit up in bed, the handgun in your hall closet comes to mind. Then you remember Earl Miller, a neighbor down the row who shot and killed a night burglar in his garage last year. The prosecutor said Earl had no right to kill the burglar. Earl's attorney claimed that Earl had the right and that even if Earl didn't — although he was sure Earl did — Earl honestly and reasonably believed he had the right. Earl was tried and acquitted. You aren't sure what that means for you. Can you or can't you lawfully shoot a burglar in your basement garage?

You grab your gun from the hall closet and head down to the first floor. The light switch is at the top of the basement stairs. You open the door quietly, flip the switch, and draw back into the dark hall. The sound of steps is followed by the shattering of glass, a muffled scream, then silence. On descending the stairs, you find the intruder standing by the back door. You quickly aim, squeeze ... blam! After recovering from the recoil of the handgun you realize that you missed the intruder. You are about to squeeze off another round, but it occurs to you that the intruder is motionless. A closer look shows him to be unconscious, hanging from the back door with his arm through the door's broken window. Blood is pouring from a cut in his neck.

You believe you can stop the bleeding by applying pressure, but you don't really want to help the man. After all, you think he might have intended to steal from you. And on top of that, the gushing blood and mess make you wince. Should you help him? Must you? You aren't sure. You remember a newspaper story about a motorist who stood and watched another motorist bleed to death after their cars collided. The prosecutor claimed that the motorist could have and should have stopped the bleeding, but he stood and watched, ... which is exactly what you are doing now. The motorist's attorney claimed that he had no legal duty to act and, in any case, was dazed from the accident and unable to think clearly. The man was tried and acquitted. What does that mean for you? If you can, must you help the intruder? Will you be a criminal if you just stand and do nothing?

You wish you weren't thinking so clearly. Perhaps it would have been better if you had fallen down the stairs and been dazed. Not a good time to be making jokes, you conclude.

Would it have been legal for you to have shot the burglar in your basement? Are you criminally liable for not helping?

Three Functions   Criminal law doctrine has three primary functions. First, it must define the conduct that is prohibited (or required) by the criminal law. Such "rules of conduct," as they have been called, provide *ex ante* direction to the members of the community as to the conduct that must be avoided (or that must be performed) upon pain of criminal sanction. This may be termed the *rule articulation function* of criminal law. Where a violation of the rules of conduct occurs, the criminal law must take on another role. It must decide whether the violation is sufficiently blameworthy to merit criminal liability. This second function, setting the minimum conditions for *liability,* is part of the adjudication process. It assesses *ex post* whether an actor who violates a rule of conduct is sufficiently blameworthy for the violation and therefore ought to be held criminally liable for it. Finally, where liability is to be imposed, criminal law must assess the relative seriousness of the violation and the blameworthiness of the offender in order to determine the general range of punishment appropriate, the "grade" of the offender's liability. While the first step in the adjudication process expresses a simple yes or no decision as to whether the minimum conditions for liability are satisfied, this second step, the *grading* function, expresses a judgment of degree.[1]

Functions Cut Across Doctrinal Distinctions   These three functions — rule articulation, liability, and grading — are the primary functions of criminal law doctrine, but they are not reflected in the current doctrinal structure. Some elements of offenses serve one function while other elements serve other functions. Nor are the different functions reflected in the traditional distinctions between offense elements, actus reus and mens rea or objective and culpability elements. Similarly, some defenses serve one function while other defenses serve other functions. To give a sense of which doctrines serve which functions requires a review of most aspects of the doctrine.

Rule Articulation Doctrines   As a group, the rule articulation doctrines define the criminal law's rules of conduct. The rules state both prohibitions and requirements:

> No person shall take, exercise control over, or transfer property of another without consent of the owner.

Presumably, your basement burglar was in the process of violating this prohibition, as well as one that prohibits entry without consent. The law's prohibitions concern not only conduct under certain circumstances — "without consent of the owner," "property of another" — but also conduct that creates a certain risk.

> No person shall engage in conduct that creates a risk of death to another person.

Thus, much of the criminal law's rule articulation function is performed by the conduct and circumstance elements of offenses.

Duties and Omissions   The law not only prohibits some conduct but also affirmatively requires other conduct.

> All legal custodians of a child must protect the child's health and safety.

Or,

> All persons over the age of 18 must register with the Selective Service System.

You may have a similar legal duty to save the life of the helpless bleeding burglar. The law creates many duties and punishes the failure to perform them. The law's statement of legal duties, then, serves part of the law's rule articulation function.

Secondary Prohibitions   In addition to these "primary violations" are what may be called "secondary violations." Secondary violations are not independent prohibitions but rather prohibitions defined by reference to the primary rules. Not only are persons bound to avoid conduct that would be a primary prohibition, but also:

> No person shall engage in conduct that assists another person in conduct that would be a violation [of the rules of conduct].

---

1. For a general discussion, see Paul H. Robinson, A Functional Analysis of Criminal Law, 88 Nw. U.L. Rev. 857 (1994); Paul H. Robinson, Rules of Conduct and Principles of Adjudication, 57 U. Chi. L. Rev. 729 (1990).

No person shall attempt to engage in conduct that would constitute a violation [of the rules of conduct].[1]

Thus, additional aspects of the criminal law's rule articulation function are performed by the conduct and circumstance elements of such secondary prohibitions as complicity and inchoate offenses.

Criminalization Culpability Elements Not all rule articulation doctrines are objective elements, like conduct and circumstance elements. Some mens rea requirements serve to define the rules of conduct. That is, they are necessary elements in describing the conduct that the criminal law prohibits. In the general attempt offense, for example, the conduct and circumstance elements of the offense provide some statement of the prohibition, but standing alone these objective elements do not fully define the prohibited conduct. The requirement that the conduct constitute a "substantial step toward commission of an offense," which is common in modern attempt definitions,[2] is inadequate in itself to define the conduct that is prohibited. As a purely objective matter, some conduct may constitute a "substantial step toward commission of an offense" but in fact may be entirely innocent and acceptable conduct and is not meant to be prohibited. Your shooting a target in your basement may not be an offense. Such conduct becomes unacceptable and a societal harm only when accompanied by an intention to violate the substantive rules of conduct. That is, your same shooting conduct is made potentially criminal if accompanied by an intention to shoot another person. Lighting one's pipe is not a violation of the rules of conduct, unless it is a step in a plan to ignite a neighbor's haystack. Giving a young girl a ride is not a violation of the rules of conduct, unless it is done with the intention of sexually assaulting her. Thus, to describe the minimum requirements of prohibited conduct, the definition of a criminal attempt must include a state of mind requirement — the intention to engage in conduct that would constitute a rule violation.

Criminalization Offense Modifications Also serving the rule articulation function are miscellaneous doctrines outside of offense definitions. These doctrines, such as the consent defense, further modify or refine the conduct rules. While the rules prohibit conduct that risks causing bodily harm, an exception to the prohibition is admitted where the victim consents to a risk of minor injury or where the risk arises from participation in a lawful sporting event.[3]

Justification Defenses Taken together, these rule articulation doctrines give a complete account of what a person must not do or must do in order to obey the criminal law. They are not, however, a complete statement of the rules of conduct. The law recognizes that in some instances a greater harm can be avoided or a greater good can be achieved by allowing a person to violate a prohibition. Burning another person's property is a violation but it is to be tolerated (even encouraged) if the burning acts as a firebreak to save a town. Striking another

---

1. Nor may one conspire with or solicit another to engage in conduct that would constitute a violation of the rules of conduct.

2. See Model Penal Code §5.01(1)(c).

3. See, e.g., Model Penal Code §2.11 (consent is a defense to conduct which causes or threatens bodily injury when the injury and conduct consented to are not serious or are reasonably foreseeable hazards of participation in an athletic contest or sport which is a lawful activity).

person without consent is a violation but is to be tolerated if done by a police officer if necessary to overcome resistance to a lawful arrest. These doctrines of justification are permissive only; they tell persons when they will be permitted to violate a rule of conduct.[1] While your attempt to shoot another person normally would be illegal, it may be justified if it serves to protect yourself and your house.

Confusion in Rules of Conduct   The rules of lawful conduct frequently are unclear even to actors who are intelligent, thoughtful, and informed. Can you lawfully shoot the intruding burglar? Does the law require that you aid the helpless burglar? In the situation described above, the actor knows the disposition of a recently litigated case closely analogous to each dilemma confronted and seeks to use that outcome to guide his own conduct, yet he is still unable to discern the applicable legal rules. Such uncertainty is not uncommon in our current system. Frequently, neither existing statements of the law nor our process of public adjudication effectively communicates the rules that define lawful conduct. Unfortunately, current criminal law doctrine does a poor job at one of its most important functions: telling people what they can, must, and must not do, under threat of criminal sanction.

Need for Clear Rules   Our condemnation and punishment of criminal law violators, as distinguished from civil violators, rests on an assumption that a criminal violation entails some consciousness of wrongdoing or at least a gross deviation from a clearly defined standard of conduct. But how can such an assumption be sustained if the demands of the law are unclear? How can we condemn and punish violations of the rules of conduct if the rules are not and cannot reasonably be known by the general public? One also may wonder how effective the criminal law can be in deterring criminal conduct if the law's demands are unclear.[2]

Doctrines of Liability   The liability function of criminal law doctrine arises from the special condemnatory nature of criminal law, which requires that inadvertent and unavoidable violations not be punished. If the actor's conduct is blameless, liability ought not be imposed, even though the actor may well have caused the harm or evil described by the rules of conduct.[3] Further, the moral base of the criminal law is such that liability properly is reserved for violations of sufficient seriousness committed with sufficient blameworthiness to justify the condemnation of criminal liability.

Offense Culpability Elements   To ensure this minimum level of blameworthiness, the law requires proof of an actor's culpability as to each rule articulation element of an offense.[4] Thus, the "burglar" in your basement is liable for burglary only if he knew it was another's house that he was entering without

---

1. For a further discussion of the doctrines of justification and their relation to the doctrines of criminalization, see Robinson, Rules, at 740-742.

2. For a discussion of the reasons for the law's failure in clearly communicating rules of conduct to the public, see Paul H. Robinson, A Functional Analysis of Criminal Law: Rule Articulation, Liability, and Grading, 88 Nw. U.L. Rev. 857 (1994); Paul H. Robinson, Are Criminal Codes Irrelevant?, 68 S. Cal. L. Rev. 159 (1994).

3. As the Model Penal Code suggests: "The general purposes of the provisions governing the definition of offenses are: . . . to safeguard conduct that is without fault from condemnation as criminal." Model Penal Code §1.02 (1985).

4. See Model Penal Code §2.02(1).

permission. If, because all of the rowhouses are identical and he just moved in next door, he had entered your garage honestly believing it to be his own, his trespass might be a violation of the rules of conduct but might not be a sufficiently culpable violation to merit criminal liability. Generally, at least recklessness as to each such objective element is required. Thus, an actor must be aware of a substantial risk that his conduct may cause another's death or obstruct a highway or that the property he is taking belongs to another. As we have seen, this preference for recklessness as the normal minimum culpability required is expressed by provisions like the Model Penal Code's, which "read in" recklessness whenever an offense definition is silent on the required culpability as to an offense element.[1]

Culpability Offense Modifications   Some of the requirements for ensuring an actor's blameworthiness are not contained in the offense definition. The de minimis defense, for example, bars liability if the actor's conduct caused the harm or evil prohibited by the offense "only to an extent too trivial to warrant the condemnation of conviction."[2] Other defenses, such as renunciation, similarly refine the normal blameworthiness requirements for inchoate offenses. (Renunciation undercuts the blame that otherwise would apply if the actor did not voluntarily renounce his intention to violate a rule of conduct.)

Voluntariness Doctrines   In addition, the minimum requirements of blameworthiness are set by such doctrines as the voluntariness requirement in commission offenses, the capacity requirement for omission liability, and the requirement in possession offenses that the actor know of the possession for a period of time sufficient to terminate possession. These requirements are designed to ensure that the actor could have avoided the violation. Only if this is true can the actor be blamed for not avoiding it. Thus, the motorist who fails to help an accident victim might be acquitted if his dazed condition made it impossible for him to help.

Doctrines of Excuse   The general excuse defenses — such as insanity, immaturity, involuntary intoxication, and duress — serve a function analogous to the voluntariness doctrines noted above. While our assumptions of sanity, maturity, sobriety, and absence of coercion normally are correct, in the unusual case an actor may suffer a disability — insanity, immaturity, intoxication, or coercion — and its effects may be such that he or she cannot reasonably be expected to have avoided the violation. The mistake excuses also are of this category, but their excusing conditions operate in a different way.

Culpability Elements vs. Voluntariness   The culpable state of mind requirements in the offense definitions noted above serve a purpose similar to these voluntariness and excuse doctrines, although they function in a slightly different way. We assume, from past experience, that most conduct is voluntary, most omitted conduct was possible, and most possession knowing. It is the unusual case, frequently where the actor suffers some disability, where an assumption of voluntariness, capacity to act, or knowledge of possession is not warranted. In contrast, it is common that an actor may be unaware of some characteristic or

---

1. See Model Penal Code §2.02(3).
2. Model Penal Code §2.12(2).

circumstance of his or her conduct—that is, it is common that an actor may not have the culpability required by an offense definition. People frequently make mistakes and inadvertently create risks. It is these common possibilities for non-culpable violations that the culpability requirements are designed to exclude.

Doctrines of Grading The doctrines containing the rules of conduct plus those that establish the minimum requirements for liability provide the starting point for the grading function. The rule articulation doctrines contain many of the most important factors in assessing the degree of punishment an actor deserves, for they define the harm or evil of the offense. Assessing the relative seriousness of an offense requires an assessment of the relative value of the full range of interests protected by the criminal law. Human safety is more valuable than the safety of property; intercourse with a 9-year-old is a more egregious wrong than inter-course with a 16-year-old; and so forth. Criminal law theorists have only recently attempted to formulate principles for determining the relative seriousness of violations.

Culpability Level In addition to the harm or evil of an offense, an actor's deserved punishment will depend on his other level of culpability. Culpability greater than the minimum required for liability frequently increases the actor's deserved punishment. Purposely causing a death is more culpable than recklessly doing the same, which is more culpable than negligently doing so. Thus, those culpability elements of offense definitions that require more than the minimum that is required for liability serve a grading function by distinguishing the case of greater culpability from the case of minimum culpability.

Result and Causation Requirements Result elements and causation re-quirements also serve a grading function. Most codes have a provision like the Model Penal Code's attempt offense, which provides in part:

> A person is guilty of an attempt to commit a crime if...when causing a particular result is an element of the crime, [he] does or omits to do anything with the purpose of causing or with the belief that it will cause such result without further conduct on his part;...[1]

Thus, where the elements of an offense definition are not satisfied only because of the absence of a required result, or the result is not attributable to the actor because of the absence of an adequate causal connection, the actor will be liable for an offense, specifically an attempt, even if the code defines no other lesser included offense.[2] Your shooting at the person in the basement may be an offense even though your bad aim causes you to miss him.

Result vs. Conduct and Circumstances Note that result elements are objective elements, like conduct and circumstance elements, but they are not necessary to define the prohibited conduct. It is an actor's conduct, not its results, that the criminal law prohibits; it is only the actor's conduct that the law can influence. The law may claim to prohibit a particular result but what it means by that is to direct actors not to engage in conduct that would bring about (or risk bringing about) that result. An actual resulting harm may make the violation more

---

1. Model Penal Code §5.01(1)(b).
2. Not everyone would agree that results ought to increase an actor's punishment. See Section 9 (Causation) & Section 10 (Inchoate Offenses).

serious, most people would argue, but the fortuity of whether the result actually occurs does not alter the nature of the conduct that constitutes the violation. The conduct remains objectionable notwithstanding the happenstance that the result does not occur.[1] If you had wounded or killed the person in your basement, your potential liability would be higher than otherwise, but even your miss may subject you to liability (assuming you have no general defense). Result elements, then, are like many culpability elements in this regard: They serve to aggravate an actor's blameworthiness, and thus the actor's liability. Given the role of the causation requirement, in defining the relation between an actor's conduct and a result that will give rise to an actor's accountability for the result, the causation requirement is similarly part of the doctrines serving the grading function, not those serving the criminalization function. Like the requirement of a result, the causation rules determine when an actor is more blameworthy, and thus when the actor's liability is to be aggravated.

Special Grading Doctrines   Special grading provisions also are recognized, including both doctrines of aggravation — such as the doctrines of felony murder and abandoned and malignant heart murder[2] — and doctrines of mitigation — such as the doctrines of provocation and extreme emotional disturbance.[3] These doctrines are drafted as offense elements but their actual effect is one of grading; their effect is to increase or decrease an actor's liability by shifting liability to a greater or lesser offense. Other special grading provisions are explicitly defined as grading provisions and vary the degree of liability within the same offense definition, such as varying the seriousness of a theft with the value of the property taken. In other words, like the rule articulation and liability functions, the grading function of criminal law doctrine is implemented through doctrines of many different sorts.

Cumulative Nature of Functions   In determining which doctrines perform which function, the previous discussion groups the doctrines as if a doctrine serves exclusively one function or another. In fact, the interrelation of the doctrines is slightly more complex than this. A complete description of the minimum requirements for liability requires not only reference to the doctrines serving the liability function but also to the doctrines serving the rule articulation function. In other words, one prerequisite of liability is violation of the rules of conduct. Similarly, the criminal law's grading function cannot be performed by reference to the doctrines of grading alone. The doctrines of liability are part of the grading function because they define the requirements for minimum grade. The doctrines serving different functions might best be thought of as having cumulative roles as the law's inquiry moves from rule articulation to liability to grading. Their interrelation might be described as:

---

1. In some instances, however, as when less serious harms are only risked, the societal harm of the conduct may be too small to justify criminal condemnation. Conduct creating a low risk of a less serious harm may fall below the line of minimum seriousness required for adequate blameworthiness, unless the harm actually occurs.

2. See, e.g., Cal. Penal Code §188 (1988) (abandoned and malignant heart murder); Pa. Stat. Ann. tit. 18, §2502(b) (1973) (felony murder); N.Y. Penal Law §125.25(3) (1987) (felony murder).

3. See, e.g., Pa. Stat. Ann. tit. 18, §2503(a) (1973) (provocation); N.Y. Penal Law §§125.20(2), 125.25(1)(a), 125.27(2)(a) (1987) (extreme emotional disturbance).

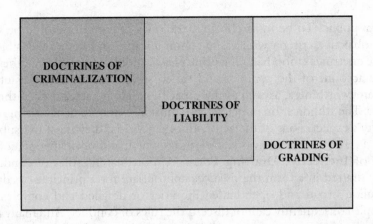

Communicative vs. Adjudicative Function   Current criminal law sometimes does poorly in its three primary functions, and this frequently is caused by the failure of the doctrine to distinguish the functions. For example, the criminal law frequently fails to communicate clear rules of conduct because it fails to distinguish its communicative from its adjudicative function. The failure derives in part from the ambiguity of acquittals and dismissals. Does the acquittal of the neighbor who shot the burglar mean that shooting burglars is lawful, that such a shooting is permitted by the rules of conduct? Or does the acquittal mean that such killing is *not* permitted but that the neighbor's mistake on the issue, given the difficult circumstances, was not blameworthy? The general "not guilty" acquittal does not tell us whether (1) the defendant's conduct was not a violation of the rules of conduct; or (2) it was a violation of the rules of conduct, but a blameless one. Thus, each case adjudication of acquittal serves only to blur the rule of conduct rather than to reinforce it. Similarly, does the acquittal of a motorist who lets an accident victim bleed to death mean that there is no legal duty to help the victim? Or, given the motorist's dazed condition and his decreased abilities, does the acquittal mean that he cannot be fairly blamed for his failure to perform what was his duty? The general "not guilty" acquittal alone, without explanation, only serves to raise questions about the rule of conduct.

Danger of Undercutting Rules of Conduct   Instead of restating, reinforcing, and refining society's rules of conduct, acquittals at public trials (as well as dismissals by courts and publicly reported decisions not to prosecute) frequently serve only to create ambiguity and confusion regarding those rules. Does the failure to condemn and punish follow from the *propriety* of the actor's conduct or from the actor's blamelessness for admittedly *improper* conduct? Only a system that distinguishes a no-violation-of-the-rules-of-conduct acquittal from a blameless-violation acquittal can avoid the ambiguity and resurrect the educational value of our public adjudication system.

Making Formulation Sensitive to Function   The failure to distinguish between these kinds of functions — articulating and communicating rules of conduct and adjudicating a violation of those rules (the liability and grading functions) — creates another kind of difficulty: The doctrines may be ineffectively formulated to serve their function. For example, rules of conduct need to communicate a legal standard that can be understood, remembered, and applied by the general public. To be most effective, the rules of conduct should be simple, based on objective criteria with easily communicable and comprehensible standards. The doctrines embodying the principles of adjudication, on the other hand, must take account of the complex and varied situational factors relevant to an actor's blameworthiness, as well as the capacities and characteristics of the particular actor. The adjudication principles also must incorporate or at least mirror the community's expectations of the actor. In other words, they must use subjective criteria and rely on more individualized, judgmental, and normative standards.

Use of Ineffective Drafting Form   Unfortunately, rules of conduct are frequently drafted in a form that is more appropriate for a principle of adjudication, entailing broad and open-ended inquiries or detailed and complex rules. Many people consequently cannot discern the rules of conduct. And many people who think they know the answers will be wrong. Can one lawfully shoot a basement burglar? Must one help him when he is bleeding and helpless? The rules governing the justification of force in the defense of one's property or premises and the rules defining one's affirmative duties to act are notoriously complex.[1] In other instances, principles of adjudication are drafted in a form that may be appropriate for a rule of conduct, which may be a form that does not accommodate the complex and multifaceted analyses that determine an actor's blameworthiness.

---

1. The lawfulness of your use of force against the burglar might require use of Model Penal Code §§3.04, 3.05, and 3.06, perhaps part of 3.07, each of which runs for more than a page of detail. See Sections 17 through 20 (Justifications). Understanding one's duties to act affirmatively requires an understanding of all of civil law. These civil duties, together with duties created by criminal law, may give rise to liability under the terms set out in Model Penal Code §2.01(1)&(3). See Section 13 (Omission Liability).

PART III

HOMICIDE AND RELATED ISSUES

To give us a point of reference in our discussion of offense requirements, let us examine the details of one particular offense: homicide. It is a useful illustration because, as the most serious offense, it is particularly nuanced and well-developed and raises many, if not most, of the issues that can arise in the definition of offenses. For these same reasons, however, it is a unique offense, and it would be wrong to assume that it is typical of other offense definitions.

Homicide grading schemes focus primarily on culpability level. In modern terms, this means grading the offense according to whether the defendant purposely or knowingly (murder), recklessly (manslaughter), or negligently (negligent homicide) caused the death. In other words, the grading schemes rely on the definitions and distinctions already closely examined in Sections 4 and 5. But most homicide schemes also recognize some exceptions to this pegging of homicide liability to culpability level; they create exceptions in both directions: aggravating reckless killings to murder, discussed in Section 6, and mitigating purposeful killings to manslaughter, the subject of Section 8.

Homicide: Doctrines of Aggravation

◆ THE CASE OF SABINE DAVIDSON

Sabine Davidson, a 26-year-old German citizen, lives with her husband, Jeffrey, 40, in Geary County, Kansas, a small community in the northeastern part of the State. They have three children, including Vicky, who is eight, and Ashley, who is two. For several years Mrs. Davidson has been buying and training dogs. She started with German shepherds and, in 1995, began purchasing rottweilers. At one point they had so many dogs and litters of puppies that one of their neighbors complained that they were unlawfully operating a kennel.

Her dogs are not well-behaved. One nipped the calf of a neighbor's three-year-old daughter. Mrs. Davidson laughs when told of it. One of the puppies tried to bite Ashley. Mr. Davidson threw it against a wall.

Ms. Bernardi, who has sold Mrs. Davidson three dogs, has begun insisting in subsequent sales that the dogs be socialized and trained in basic obedience. Bernardi also adds as a condition to further sales that the dogs not be allowed to run free. She has seen some of Davidsons' dogs get out of their yard. The Davidsons install a six-foot chain-link fence with a stirrup latch on the gate. Because the dogs still seem to get out quite often, they also discuss chaining them, but never begin to do so. Ms. Bernardi finally insists that they put

Figure 19 **Sabine Davidson, circa 1998**
(CourtTV.com)

209

a padlock through the gate latch to keep it horizontal, hoping it will stop the escapes.

Davidson has been trying to train her dogs in Schutzhund, "protection dog" training, a German dog sport that teaches the dogs tracking, obedience, retrieving,

and protection. Part of the protection training teaches the dog to attack an "agitator" and hang on, even when being hit, until the handler gives the command to let go. Experts say that once this training begins, dogs should be socialized extensively to humans and kenneled individually to keep them from developing pack behavior. The violence training makes it more important to use discipline to ensure that their natural "prey" drive does not overwhelm the control of the owner. Davidson has experience in the matter: she once had to destroy a German shepherd that was beyond control.

Figue 20 **Attack dog training**
(Guard Dog Training Center)

Her early attempts to train the dogs at one of the local dog clubs are not very successful. She attends meetings in Topeka for Schutzhund training for one of her dogs, but is eventually ejected for treating her dogs irresponsibly. At an Oklahoma Schutzhund club, the training director comments that her handling of her dogs is "very very poor." Another Schutzhund club official says "with a better dog, she'd be dangerous." Her application for the Schutzhund club in Salina is rejected because she does not get along well with club members and because her dogs are badly trained and dirty. She buys a video about "Bite Training Puppies" to try to train them herself. Experts say that such training can be dangerous unless combined with effective obedience training.

The dogs still sometimes escape from their enclosure and roam the neighborhood. In June 1996, at an intersection near the Davidsons' house, a Kansas

patrol trooper, Officer Van Buren, is in his front yard when he hears dogs barking. Three rottweilers have formed a semicircle around two children, remaining in the same formation as the children try to move away. When Van Buren runs toward them with a pistol and baseball bat, they run off toward the Davidsons' house. He rings their doorbell to no avail. His call to the Davidsons finds their phone disconnected. After

Figure 21 **Davidsons' home with 6-foot fence**
(Craig Hacker, Kansas State Collegian)

his wife calls the sheriff, an officer stops by the Davidsons' house but is unable to get in touch with them. She leaves her business card, but does not follow up further.

By April 1997, Sabine Davidson has four large rottweilers; the largest, a young male named Chance, is close to 80 pounds. Her dogs regularly fight each other inside the fence. A woman who often gives Mr. Davidson a ride to work has seen the dogs since they were puppies. She has grown more scared of them and now always stays in her car when she drives to the house because the dogs bark, growl, and sometimes get out and jump on her car. Mrs. Davidson explains that they are just playing.

Many neighbors feel terrorized by the rottweilers. They are alarmed that the dogs get agitated and bark aggressively whenever someone bikes or walks by the fence. The children in the neighborhood always bike by the yard quickly because the dogs jump and bark and seem like they want to attack. Mrs. Davidson is not sympathetic because she claims that some of the children, like the Wilson boys, who live a few houses away, tease the dogs when they come by her property.

On the morning of April 24, Mrs. Davidson lets the dogs out into the enclosure at 6:30 a.m. Still tired, she takes a sleeping pill and goes back to sleep on the living room couch. The rottweilers soon escape. Apparently, the dirt is loose around the post to which the latch hooks. The dogs can push the post and cause the latch to slip off.

Fifteen minutes later, a neighbor, Mary Smith, sees the three dogs sitting in a nearby yard. By 7 a.m., they have a neighbor's dog cornered on a porch. When the scared dog's owner comes out to see what is going on, the dogs start to advance on him. He goes back inside for his gun. When he returns, he sees them run off, and by the time he gets dressed and follows them it looks like they are back in the fenced enclosure.

But ten minutes later, the dogs race into the garage of another neighbor, Learie Thompson, just as he opens the door to go to work. They circle his pickup truck. He jumps up on his truck to avoid them. He knows the dogs are Mrs. Davidson's because he complained to the sheriff last year when the dogs were in his yard. His wife hears him yelling and activates the automatic door. Startled by the noise, the dogs run off. A few minutes later,

Figure 22 **An angry rottweiler**

(Antons Video Productions)

three rottweilers are seen crossing and recrossing the highway that runs by the Davidsons' subdivision.

A few minutes away, Mrs. Violet Wilson sets off for the Fort Riley PX to shop. Her husband, Brian, is an Army sergeant first class with the 1st Battalion 41st Infantry at Fort Riley, and is now stationed in Bosnia. She drops off her eleven-year old son, Chris, and eight-year old son, Tramel, at the bus stop about a block from the Davidsons' house. The bus stop is at the same intersection where the children were attacked the year before.

Figure 23 **Christopher Wilson, circa 1997**
(Kansas State Collegian)

The boys soon see the dogs coming at them. Panicked, they climb up the tree as fast as they can. The dogs circle, barking wildly. After a few minutes, the biggest dog leaves, and the other two follow. Soon the boys cannot see them anymore. Tramel wants to stay up in the tree until their school bus arrives, but Chris wants to go and see where the dogs went. Leaving his brother in the tree, Chris climbs down and starts to look around the nearby ravine. Then, in the distance he sees the dogs, circling back toward him. He starts running.

At that moment, the school bus approaches. As the bus slows down at the stop, the dogs catch Chris on the slope of the ravine. The bus driver, Kathy Roberge, does not see Tramel or Chris at first, but notices the boys' backpacks and musical instruments lying abandoned under the tree. As soon as Tramel sees the bus pull up, he climbs down from the tree and runs toward it. He gets on, out of breath, and tries to tell the bus driver what happened. She hears something incomprehensible about Chris and dogs. She waits a few minutes, then moves the bus around to signal Chris that he needs to hurry. From her side mirror she can now see three dogs fighting in the ravine. The seventeen children on the bus look over, curious. One says, "It looks like they have a rag doll." The driver realizes, horrified, that the pack of dogs have caught Chris in the ravine. She slams down on the horn to try to distract them and calls 911 on her radio. While they wait for the police, the driver tries to distract the children from the sight of the continuing attack. Another passing driver also calls 911 when he sees what is happening.

Chris is severely mauled by the dogs. The largest dog, Chance, tears Chris' carotid artery, and with a second bite breaks Chris' neck. The dogs' jaws engulf

Chris' neck; their back teeth leave marks. The dogs sever Chris' jugular vein, his esophagus, and crush his spinal cord. Bones are shattered. He dies within minutes, in sight of the school bus. The attack continues for almost ten minutes. (The County Sheriff, Bill Deppish, later reports that Chris had no blood in him when the deputy got to him. He tells reporters it is the worst incident he has witnessed in 27 years of law enforcement.)

As the neighbors gather near the scene to comfort each other, David Morrison, the Deputy Sheriff, arrives. The dogs head toward him as he moves toward the ravine. He shouts and gestures, but they continue toward him. As the lead dog gets closer, he can see blood in its jaws and on its legs. When it is 15 feet away, the officer shoots. The other dogs scatter as another officer shoots at them. As Deputy Shumate arrives, he is told that a wounded dog is running toward the Davidsons'. He heads in the direction of their house and shoots the dog. A Kansas highway patrol sharpshooter kills the third on Thursday. At the Davidson house, Deputy Shumate notices a fourth dog, Dunja, in a carrier. She strains wildly to get out and attack him. He can tell that the dog has been attack-trained. When the dog control officer later comes to take custody of the remaining dog, he tells Mrs. Davidson of the dog's aggressive behavior toward the officer. She laughs.

Deputy Shumate tells the Davidsons that their dogs attacked children and mauled one to death. Sabine Davidson says, "The dead one should be one of the Wilson boys," explaining that they waited at the nearby bus stop and sometimes teased the dogs.

Figure 24 **Neighbors visiting site of mauling, April 1997**
(Craig Hacker, Kansas State Collegian)

1. Relying only upon your own intuitions of justice, what liability and punishment, if any, does Sabine Davidson deserve?

N	0	1	2	3	4	5	6	7	8	9	10	11
☐	☐	☐	☐	☐	☐	☐	☐	☐	☐	☐	☐	☐
no liability	liability but no punishment	1 day	2 wks	2 mo	6 mo	1 yr	3 yrs	7 yrs	15 yrs	30 yrs	life imprisonment	death

2. What liability, if any, under the then-existing statutes?
3. What liability, if any, under the Model Penal Code?

■ THE LAW

Kansas Statutes Annotated
(1997)

Chapter 21. Crimes and Punishments

Section 21-3401. Murder in the First Degree

Murder in the first degree is the killing of a human being committed:

(a) Intentionally and with premeditation; or

(b) in the commission of, attempt to commit, or flight from an inherently dangerous felony as defined in K.S.A. 21-3436 and amendments thereto.

Murder in the first degree is an off-grid person felony.

Section 21-3402. Murder in the Second Degree

Murder in the second degree is the killing of a human being committed:

(a) Intentionally; or

(b) unintentionally but recklessly under circumstances manifesting extreme indifference to the value of human life.

Murder in the second degree as described in subsection (a) is an off-grid person felony.

Murder in the second degree as described in subsection (b) is a severity level 2, person felony.

Section 21-3403. Voluntary Manslaughter

Voluntary manslaughter is the intentional killing of a human being committed:

(a) Upon a sudden quarrel or in the heat of passion; or

(b) upon an unreasonable but honest belief that circumstances existed that justified deadly force under K.S.A. 21-3211, 21-3212 or 21-3213 and amendments thereto.

Voluntary manslaughter is a severity level 3, person felony.

Section 21-3404. Involuntary Manslaughter

Involuntary manslaughter is the unintentional killing of a human being committed:

(a) Recklessly;

(b) in the commission of, or attempt to commit, or flight from any felony, other than an inherently dangerous felony as defined in K.S.A.

21-3436 and amendments thereto, that is enacted for the protection of human life or safety or a misdemeanor that is enacted for the protection of human life or safety, including acts described in K.S.A. 8-1566 and 8-1568 and amendments thereto but excluding the acts described in K.S.A. 8-1567 and amendments thereto; or

(c) during the commission of a lawful act in an unlawful manner. Involuntary manslaughter is a severity level 5, person felony.

Section 21-3436. Inherently Dangerous Felony; Definition

(a) Any of the following felonies shall be deemed an inherently dangerous felony whether or not such felony is so distinct from the homicide alleged to be a violation of subsection (b) of K.S.A. 21-3401 and amendments thereto as not to be an ingredient of the homicide alleged to be a violation of subsection (b) of K.S.A. 21-3401 and amendments thereto:

(1) Kidnapping, as defined in K.S.A. 21-3420 and amendments thereto;

(2) aggravated kidnapping, as defined in K.S.A. 21-3421 and amendments thereto;

(3) robbery, as defined in K.S.A. 21-3426 and amendments thereto;

(4) aggravated robbery, as defined in K.S.A. 21-3427 and amendments thereto;

(5) rape, as defined in K.S.A. 21-3502 and amendments thereto;

(6) aggravated criminal sodomy, as defined in K.S.A. 21-3506 and amendments thereto;

(7) abuse of a child, as defined in K.S.A. 21-3609 and amendments thereto;

(8) felony theft under subsection (a) or (c) of K.S.A. 21-3701 and amendments thereto;

(9) burglary, as defined in K.S.A 21-3715 and amendments thereto;

(10) aggravated burglary, as defined in K.S.A. 21-3716 and amendments thereto;

(11) arson, as defined in K.S.A. 21-3718 and amendments thereto;

(12) aggravated arson, as defined in K.S.A. 21-3719 and amendments thereto;

(13) treason, as defined in K.S.A. 21-3801 and amendments thereto;

(14) any felony offense as provided in K.S.A. 65-4127a, 65-4127b or 65-4159 or K.S.A. 1995 Supp. 65-4160 through 65-4164 and amendments thereto; and

(15) any felony offense as provided in K.S.A. 21-4219 and amendments thereto.

(b) Any of the following felonies shall be deemed an inherently dangerous felony only when such felony is so distinct from the homicide alleged to be a violation of subsection (b) of K.S.A. 21-3401 and amendments thereto as to not be an ingredient of the homicide alleged to be a violation of subsection (b) of K.S.A. 21-3401 and amendments thereto:

(1) Murder in the first degree, as defined in subsection (a) of K.S.A. 21-3401 and amendments thereto;

(2) murder in the second degree, as defined in subsection (a) of K.S.A. 21-3402 and amendments thereto;

(3) voluntary manslaughter, as defined in subsection (a) of K.S.A. 21-3403 and amendments thereto;

(4) aggravated assault, as defined in K.S.A. 21-3410 and amendments thereto;

(5) aggravated assault of a law enforcement officer, as defined in K.S.A. 21-3411 and amendments thereto;

(6) aggravated battery, as defined in subsection (a)(1) of K.S.A. 21-3414 and amendments thereto; and

(7) aggravated battery against a law enforcement officer, as defined in K.S.A. 21-3415 and amendments thereto.

(c) This section shall be part of and supplemental to the Kansas criminal code.

Section 21-3608. Endangering a Child

(a) Endangering a child is intentionally and unreasonably causing or permitting a child under the age of 18 years to be placed in a situation in which the child's life, body or health may be injured or endangered.

(b) Nothing in this section shall be construed to mean a child is endangered for the sole reason the child's parent or guardian, in good faith, selects and depends upon spiritual means alone through prayer, in accordance with the tenets and practice of a recognized church or religious denomination, for the treatment or cure of disease or remedial care of such child.

(c) Endangering a child is a class A person misdemeanor.

Section 21-3201. Criminal Intent

(a) Except as otherwise provided, a criminal intent is an essential element of every crime defined by this code. Criminal intent may be established by proof that the conduct of the accused person was intentional or reckless. Proof of intentional conduct shall be required to establish criminal intent, unless the statute defining the crime expressly provides that the prohibited act is criminal if done in a reckless manner.

(b) Intentional conduct is conduct that is purposeful and willful and not accidental. As used in this code, the terms "knowing," "willful," "purposeful," and "on purpose" are included within the term "intentional."

(c) Reckless conduct is conduct done under circumstances that show a realization of the imminence of danger to the person of another and a conscious and unjustifiable disregard of that danger. The terms "gross negligence," "culpable negligence," "wanton negligence" and "wantonness" are included within the term "recklessness" as used in this code.

Section 21-3202. Criminal Intent; Exclusions

(1) Proof of criminal intent does not require proof of knowledge of the existence or constitutionality of the statute under which the accused is prosecuted, or the scope or meaning of the terms used in that statute.

(2) Proof of criminal intent does not require proof that the accused had knowledge of the age of a minor, even though age is a material element of the crime with which he is charged.

Section 21-3204. Guilt Without Criminal Intent, When

A person may be guilty of an offense without having criminal intent if the crime is a misdemeanor, cigarette or tobacco infraction or traffic infraction and the statute defining the offense clearly indicates a legislative purpose to impose absolute liability for the conduct described.

Section 21-3107. Multiple Prosecutions for Same Act

(1) When the same conduct of a defendant may establish the commission of more than one crime under the laws of this state, the defendant may be prosecuted for each of such crimes. Each of such crimes may be alleged as a separate count in a single complaint, information or indictment.

(2) Upon prosecution for a crime, the defendant may be convicted of either the crime charged or an included crime, but not both. An included crime may be any of the following:

    (a) A lesser degree of the same crime;

    (b) an attempt to commit the crime charged;

    (c) an attempt to commit a lesser degree of the crime charged; or

    (d) a crime necessarily proved if the crime charged were proved.

(3) In cases where the crime charged may include some lesser crime, it is the duty of the trial court to instruct the jury, not only as to the crime charged but as to all lesser crimes of which the accused might be found guilty under the information or indictment and upon the evidence adduced. If the defendant objects to the giving of the instructions, the defendant shall be considered to have waived objection to any error in the failure to give them, and the failure shall not be a basis for reversal of the case on appeal.

(4) Whenever charges are filed against a person, accusing the person of a crime which includes another crime of which the person has been convicted, the conviction of the included crime shall not bar prosecution or conviction of the crime charged if the crime charged was not consummated at the time of conviction of the included crime, but the conviction of the included crime shall be annulled upon the filing of such charges. Evidence of the person's plea or any admission or statement made by the person in connection therewith in any of the proceedings which resulted in the person's conviction of the included crime shall not be admissible at the trial of the crime charged. If the person is convicted of

the crime charged, or of an included crime, the person so convicted shall receive credit against any prison sentence imposed or fine to be paid for the period of confinement actually served or the amount of any fine actually paid under the sentence imposed for the annulled conviction.

Section 21-3110.   Definitions

The following definitions shall apply when the words and phrases defined are used in this code, except when a particular context clearly requires a different meaning.

(1) "Act" includes a failure or omission to take action.

(2) "Another" means a person or persons as defined in this code other than the person whose act is claimed to be criminal.

(3) "Conduct" means an act or a series of acts, and the accompanying mental state.

(4) "Conviction" includes a judgment of guilt entered upon a plea of guilty....

(14) "Person" means an individual, public or private corporation, government, partnership, or unincorporated association....

(17) "Prosecution" means all legal proceedings by which a person's liability for a crime is determined....

(22) "State" or "this state" means the state of Kansas and all land and water in respect to which the state of Kansas has either exclusive or concurrent jurisdiction, and the air space above such land and water. "Other state" means any state or territory of the United States, the District of Columbia and the Commonwealth of Puerto Rico.

The Kansas Sentencing Commission Desk Reference Manual
24-25, 28-33 (2003)

Sentencing Guidelines

The Kansas Sentencing Guidelines Act (KSGA) became effective July 1, 1993. Two grids, which contain the sentencing range for drug crimes and nondrug crimes, were developed for use as a tool in sentencing. The sentencing guidelines grids provide practitioners in the criminal justice system with an overview of presumptive felony sentences. The determination of a felony sentence is based on two factors: the current crime of conviction and the offender's prior criminal history. The sentence contained in the grid box at the juncture of the severity level of the crime of conviction and the offender's criminal history category is the presumed sentence. ...

Grid Boxes

Within each grid box are three numbers, representing months of imprisonment. The three numbers provide the sentencing court with a range for sentencing. The sentencing court has discretion to sentence at any place within the range. The middle number in the grid box is the standard number and is intended to be the appropriate sentence for typical cases. The upper and lower numbers should be used for cases involving aggravating or mitigating factors insufficient to warrant a departure.

The sentencing court may depart upward to increase the length of a sentence up to double the duration within the grid box. The court may also depart downward to lower the duration of a presumptive sentence to any extent. The court may also impose a dispositional departure when aggravating or mitigating circumstances exist that are substantial and compelling. . . .

CHAPTER III: CRIME SEVERITY LEVELS

General Rules for Determining Severity Levels

The severity levels range from severity level 1 to severity level 10 on the nondrug grid. Level 1 is used to categorize the most severe crimes, and level 10 is used to categorize the least severe crimes. Crimes listed within each level are considered relatively equal in severity.

The crime severity scale contained in the sentencing guidelines grid for drug crimes consist of 4 levels of crimes. Crimes listed within each level are also considered relatively equal in severity. Level 1 crimes are the most severe crimes and level 4 crimes are the least severe crimes. . . .

. . . The severity level designation of each felony crime is included in the statutory definition of the crime.

Some crimes include a broad range of conduct. In such circumstances, there may be a different severity level designated for violations of different subsections of the statute. All of the KSGA felonies are listed in Appendix E of this Manual in three versions: alphabetically by description; numerically by statute number; and by severity levels and then by statute numbers. . . .

CHAPTER IV: CRIMINAL HISTORY

Criminal History Rules

The horizontal axis, or top of the grid represents the criminal history categories. There are nine categories used to designate prior criminal history. Category A is used to categorize offenders having three (3) or more prior felony convictions designated as person crimes. Category I is used to categorize offenders having either no criminal record or a single conviction or juvenile adjudication for a misdemeanor. The criminal history categories classify an offender's criminal history in a quantitative as well as a qualitative manner. The categories between A and I reflect cumulative criminal history with an emphasis on whether prior convictions were for person crimes or nonperson crimes. Generally, person crimes are weighted more heavily than nonperson crimes. Within limits prior convictions for person crimes will result in a harsher sentence for the current crime of conviction.

The criminal history scale is represented in an abbreviated form on the horizontal axis of the sentencing guidelines grid for nondrug crimes and the sentencing guidelines grid for drug crimes. The relative severity of each Criminal History Category decreases from left to right on the grids, with Criminal History

Category A being the most serious classification and Criminal History Category I being the least serious classification.

Category	Descriptive Criminal History
A	The offender's criminal history includes three or more adult convictions or juvenile adjudications, in any combination, for person felonies.
B	The offender's criminal history includes two adult convictions or juvenile adjudications, in any combination, for person felonies.
C	The offender's criminal history includes one adult conviction or juvenile adjudication for a person felony, and one or more adult convictions or juvenile adjudications for nonperson felonies.
D	The offender's criminal history includes one adult conviction or juvenile adjudication for a person felony, but no adult conviction or juvenile adjudication for a nonperson felony.
E	The offender's criminal history includes three or more adult convictions or juvenile adjudications for nonperson felonies, but no adult conviction or juvenile adjudication for a person felony.
F	The offender's criminal history includes two adult convictions or juvenile adjudications for nonperson felonies, but no adult conviction or juvenile adjudication for a person felony.
G	The offender's criminal history includes one adult conviction or juvenile adjudication for a nonperson felony, but no adult conviction or juvenile adjudication for a person felony.
H	The offender's criminal history includes two or more adult convictions or juvenile adjudications for nonperson and/or select misdemeanors, and no more than two adult convictions or juvenile adjudications for person misdemeanors, but no adult conviction or juvenile adjudication for either a person or nonperson felony.
I	The offender's criminal history includes no prior record, or one adult conviction or juvenile adjudication for a person, nonperson, or a select misdemeanor, but no adult conviction or juvenile adjudication for either a person or a nonperson felony.

Table 6.1 1997 Sentencing Range — Nondrug Offenses

Category →	A	B	C	D	E	F	G	H	I
Severity Level ↓	3+ Person Felonies	2 Person Felonies	1 Person Nonperson Felonies	1 Person Felony	3+ Nonperson Felonies	2 Nonperson Felonies	1 Nonperson Felony	2+ Misdemeanor	1 Misdemeanor No Record
I	816 776 740	772 732 692	356 340 322	334 316 300	308 292 276	282 268 254	254 244 230	232 220 208	206 194 184
II	616 584 552	576 548 520	270 256 242	250 238 226	230 218 206	210 200 198	192 182 172	172 164 154	154 146 136
III	206 194 184	190 180 172	89 85 80	83 78 74	77 73 68	69 66 62	64 60 57	59 55 51	51 49 46
IV	172 162 154	162 154 144	75 71 68	69 66 62	64 60 57	59 56 52	52 50 47	48 45 42	43 41 38
V	136 130 122	128 120 114	60 57 53	55 52 50	51 49 46	47 44 41	43 41 38	38 36 34	34 32 31
VI	46 43 40	41 39 37	38 36 34	36 34 32	32 30 28	29 27 25	26 24 22	21 20 19	19 18 17
VII	34 32 30	31 29 27	29 27 25	26 24 22	23 21 19	19 18 17	17 16 15	14 13 12	13 12 11
VIII	23 21 19	20 19 18	19 18 17	17 16 15	15 14 13	13 12 11	11 10 9	11 10 9	9 8 7
IX	17 16 15	15 14 13	13 12 11	13 12 11	11 10 9	10 9 8	9 8 7	8 7 6	7 6 5
X	13 12 11	12 11 10	11 10 9	10 9 8	9 8 7	8 7 6	7 6 5	7 6 5	7 6 5

Recommended probation terms are:
  36 months for felonies classified in Severity Levels 1-5
  24 months for felonies classified in Severity Levels 6-10
Postrelease terms are:
For felonies committed on or after 4/20/95
  36 months for felonies classified in Severity Levels 1-6
  24 months for felonies classified in Severity Level 7-10
For felonies committed before 4/20/95
  24 months for felonies classified in Severity Levels 1-6
  12 months for felonies classified in Severity Levels 7-10

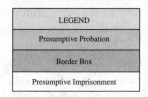

LEGEND
Presumptive Probation
Border Box
Presumptive Imprisonment

Model Penal Code
(Official Draft 1962)

Section 210.1. Criminal Homicide

(1) A person is guilty of criminal homicide if he purposely, knowingly, recklessly or negligently causes the death of another human being.

(2) Criminal homicide is murder, manslaughter or negligent homicide.

Section 210.2. Murder

(1) Except as provided in Section 210.3(1)(b), criminal homicide constitutes murder when:

(a) it is committed purposely or knowingly; or

(b) it is committed recklessly under circumstances manifesting extreme indifference to the value of human life. Such recklessness and indifference are presumed if the actor is engaged or is an accomplice in the commission of, or an attempt to commit, or flight after committing or attempting to commit robbery, rape or deviate sexual intercourse by force or threat of force, arson, burglary, kidnapping or felonious escape.

(2) Murder is a felony of the first degree [but a person convicted of murder may be sentenced to death, as provided in Section 210.6].

Section 210.3. Manslaughter

(1) Criminal homicide constitutes manslaughter when:

(a) it is committed recklessly; or

(b) a homicide which would otherwise be murder is committed under the influence of extreme mental or emotional disturbance for which there is reasonable explanation or excuse. The reasonableness of such explanation or excuse shall be determined from the viewpoint of a person in the actor's situation under the circumstances as he believes them to be.

(2) Manslaughter is a felony of the second degree.

Section 210.4. Negligent Homicide

(1) Criminal homicide constitutes negligent homicide when it is committed negligently.

(2) Negligent homicide is a felony of the third degree.

● OVERVIEW OF HOMICIDE AGGRAVATIONS

Model Penal Code Section 210.2 Commentary
Official Draft and Revised Comments 21-26 (1980)

Reckless Homicide Manifesting Extreme Indifference. Section 210.2(1)(b) also provides that criminal homicide constitutes murder when it is "committed recklessly under circumstances manifesting extreme indifference to the value of human life." This provision reflects the judgment that there is a kind of reckless homicide that cannot fairly be distinguished in grading terms from homicides committed purposely or knowingly.

Recklessness, as defined in Section 2.02(2)(c), presupposes an awareness of the creation of substantial homicidal risk, a risk too great to be deemed justifiable by any valid purpose that the actor's conduct serves. Since risk, however, is a matter of degree and the motives for risk creation may be infinite in variation, some formula is needed to identify the case where recklessness may be found and where it should be assimilated to purpose or knowledge for purposes of grading. Under the Model Code, this judgment must be made in terms of whether the actor's conscious disregard of the risk, given the circumstances of the case, so far departs from acceptable behavior that it constitutes a "gross deviation from the standard of conduct that a law-abiding person would observe in the actor's situation." Ordinary recklessness in this sense is made sufficient for a conviction of manslaughter under Section 210.3(1)(a). In a prosecution for murder, however, the Code calls for the further judgment whether the actor's conscious disregard of the risk, under the circumstances, manifests extreme indifference to the value of human life. The significance of purpose or knowledge as a standard of culpability is that, cases of provocation or other mitigation apart, purposeful or knowing homicide demonstrates precisely such indifference to the value of human life. Whether recklessness is so extreme that it demonstrates similar indifference is not a question, it is submitted, that can be further clarified. It must be left directly to the trier of fact under instructions which make it clear that recklessness that can fairly be assimilated to purpose or knowledge should be treated as murder and that less extreme recklessness should be punished as manslaughter.

Insofar as Subsection (1)(b) includes within the murder category cases of homicide caused by extreme recklessness, though without purpose to kill, it reflects both the common law and much pre-existing statutory treatment usually cast in terms of conduct evidencing a "depraved heart regardless of human life" or some similar words. Examples usually given include shooting into a crowd or into an occupied house or automobile, though they are not, of course, exhaustive.

Some indication of the content of this concept as a means of differentiating murder and manslaughter may be afforded by prior decisional law. One case involved a game of Russian roulette, where the defendant pointed a revolver loaded with a single cartridge at his friend. The weapon fired on the third try, and the fatal wound resulted. The court affirmed the conviction for murder, despite ample evidence that the defendant had not desired to kill his friend, with the statement that "malice in the sense of a wicked disposition is evidenced by the intentional doing of an uncalled-for act in callous disregard of its likely harmful effects on others." In another case, the defendant's claimed intention was to shoot over his victim's head in order to scare him. The court held that, even crediting this assertion, the jury could find the defendant guilty of murder on the ground that his act showed "such a reckless disregard for human life as was the equivalent of a specific intent to kill." A third illustration involved a defendant who fired several shots into a house which he knew to be occupied by several persons. The court affirmed his conviction of murder because the defendant's conduct was "imminently dangerous" and "evinced a wicked and depraved mind regardless of human life." Other acts held to show sufficient recklessness to justify a conviction of murder include shooting into a moving automobile and throwing a heavy beer glass at a woman carrying a lighted oil lamp. The Model Code formulation would permit a jury to reach the same conclusion in each of these cases.

At the time the Model Penal Code was under consideration, foreign codifiers had attempted to delineate the category of aggravated reckless homicide in various ways, illustrated by the codes in New Zealand,[45] Canada,[46] and Queensland.[47] The Indian Penal Code attempted a more precise articulation by including in the definition of culpable homicide cases where the actor committed the homicidal act "with the knowledge that he is likely by such act to cause death" and providing that the homicide was murder if "the person committing the act knows that it is so imminently dangerous that it must in all probability cause death, or such bodily injury as is likely to cause death." The difference between culpable homicide and murder was described as turning upon the degree of risk to human life: "If death is a likely result, it is culpable homicide; if it is the most probable result, it is murder."

European codes at this time seldom went into detail as to what constituted murder. They usually specified either intent to kill or willfulness as the required culpability. However, it appears that such provisions were construed to punish homicide as murder where there was realization that death was highly probable or even where there should have been such realization. . . .

Given the Model Code definition of recklessness, the point involved is put adequately and succinctly by asking whether the recklessness rises to the level of

---

45. The New Zealand statute provides:

Culpable homicide is murder . . . [i]f the offender for any unlawful object does an act that he knows or ought to have known to be likely to cause death, and thereby kills any person, though he may have desired that his object should be effected without hurting anyone.

Crimes Act 1908, §182(d).

46. The Canadian statute provides:

Culpable homicide is murder . . . where a person, for an unlawful object, does anything that he knows or ought to know is likely to cause death, and thereby causes death to a human being, notwithstanding that he desires to effect his object without causing death or bodily harm to any human being.

Criminal Code §201.

47. The Queensland statute provides:

[A] person who unlawfully kills another . . . [i]f death is caused by means of an act done in the prosecution of an unlawful purpose, which act is of such a nature as to be likely to endanger human life . . . is guilty of murder . . . [I]t is immaterial that the offender did not intend to hurt any person.

Criminal Code §302.

"extreme indifference to the value of human life." As has been observed, it seems undesirable to suggest a more specific formulation. The variations referred to above retain in some instances greater fidelity to the common-law phrasing but they do so at great cost in clarity. Equally obscure are the several attempts to depart from the common law to which reference has been made. The result of these formulations is that the method of defining reckless murder is impaired in its primary purpose of communicating to jurors in ordinary language the task expected of them. The virtue of the Model Penal Code language is that it is a simpler and more direct method by which this function can be performed.

At least 15 recently revised statutes have continued some version of reckless homicide as murder, and at least six proposed codes have done so. Moreover, at least four other revised statutes retain a residual category of second-degree murder that presumably includes extremely reckless homicide. Among those statutes that contain explicit provisions, there is considerable variation in the manner in which the recklessness formula is phrased. It is fair to say, however, that five of the 15 revised enactments base their formulation on the common-law language, whereas the remaining 10 have adopted language that either duplicates the Model Code or is substantially derived from it. Each of the six proposed codes is also substantially derived from the Model Code formulation. There are, however, a surprising number of recent enactments and proposals that apparently have omitted a category of murder based upon extreme recklessness.

Model Penal Code Section 210.2 Commentary
Official Draft and Revised Comments 29-30 (1980)

Felony Murder. . . . Section 210.2 advances a new approach to the problem of homicide occurring in the course of a felony. Such homicides will only constitute murder if they are committed purposely, knowingly, or recklessly under circumstances manifesting extreme indifference to the value of human life. Subsection (1)(b) creates a presumption of the required recklessness and extreme indifference, however, if a homicide occurs during the commission or attempted commission of a robbery, sexual attack, arson, burglary, kidnaping, or felonious escape. The presumption also arises if the defendant is in flight after such conduct or if he is an accomplice to the commission of one of the specified crimes when the killing takes place. Beyond the operation of this presumption, it is the submission of the Model Code that the felony-murder doctrine should be abandoned as an independent basis for establishing the criminality of homicide.

The presumption operates in the following manner. It applies only to the culpability for murder and in particular to the establishment of the extreme indifference required by Subsection (1)(b). In any circumstance, the actor must cause the death of another, except as general complicity principles provide otherwise. As Section 1.12(5) specifies, the presumption has the effect of leaving on the prosecution the burden of persuasion beyond a reasonable doubt that the defendant acted recklessly and with extreme indifference. The jury may, however, regard the facts giving rise to the presumption as sufficient evidence of the required culpability unless the court determines that the evidence as a whole clearly negatives that conclusion. The presumption may, of course, be rebutted by the defendant or may simply not be followed by the jury. In either of these cases, the defendant may be liable for manslaughter or negligent homicide, as these crimes are defined in Sections 210.3 and 210.4. If the presumption is not rebutted and if the jury finds with or without its aid, that the requisite extreme indifference in fact existed beyond a reasonable doubt, then the appropriate conviction is murder. The effect of the Model Code, therefore, is to abandon felony murder as a separate basis for establishing liability for homicide and to retain the presumption described above as a concession to the facilitation of proof.

◉ DISCUSSION MATERIALS

Should the Criminal Law Recognize a Felony-Murder Rule?

The materials begin with a Model Penal Code Commentary discussion of the conceptual problems facing the felony-murder rule and its relationship to the mens rea requirement. David Crump and Susan Waite Crump offer an opposing view, positing arguments in favor of the rule. In *People v. Washington,* the majority and dissenting opinions provide an analysis of the scope of the felony-murder rule and outline the arguments for and against its use. Finally, the Robinson and Darley study of lay intuitions of the felony-murder concept find that, while some variation of the rule is supported, the most common current formulations of the rule are too severe in their effect.

Model Penal Code Section 210.2 Commentary
Official Draft and Revised Comments 30 (1980)

The classic formulation of the felony-murder doctrine declares that one is guilty of murder if a death results from conduct during the commission or attempted commission of any felony. Some courts have made no effort to qualify the application of this doctrine, and a number of earlier English writers also articulated an unqualified rule. At the time the Model Code was drafted, a number of American legislatures, moreover, perpetuated the original statement of the rule by statute. As thus conceived, the rule operated to impose liability for murder based on the culpability required for the underlying felony without separate proof of any culpability with regard to the death. The homicide, as distinct from the underlying felony, was thus an offense of strict liability. This rule may have made sense under the conception of *mens rea* as something approaching a general criminal disposition rather than as a specific attitude of the defendant towards each element of a specific offense. Furthermore, it was hard to claim that the doctrine worked injustice in an age that recognized only a few felonies and that punished each as a capital offense.

In modern times, however, legislatures have created a wide range of statutory felonies. Many of these crimes concern relatively minor misconduct not inherently dangerous to life and carry maximum penalties far less severe than those authorized for murder. Application of the ancient rigor of the felony-murder rule to such crimes will yield startling results. For example, a seller of liquor in violation of a statutory felony becomes a murderer if his purchaser falls asleep on the way home and dies of exposure. And a person who communicates disease during felonious sexual intercourse is guilty of murder if his partner subsequently dies of the infection.

The prospect of such consequences has led to a demand for limitations on the felony-murder rule. American legislatures had responded to these demands at the time the Model Code was drafted primarily by dividing felony-homicides into two or more grades or by lowering the degree of murder for felony homicide. Only Ohio had abandoned the rule completely.

In addition, the courts had imposed restrictions, both overt and covert, on the reach of the felony-murder doctrine....

These limitations confine the scope of the felony-murder rule, but they do not resolve its essential illogic. This doctrine aside, the criminal law does not predicate liability simply on conduct causing the death of another. Punishment for homicide obtains only when the deed is done with a state of mind that makes it reprehensible as well as unfortunate. Murder is invariably punished as a heinous offense and is the principal crime for which the death penalty is authorized. Sanctions of such gravity demand justification, and their imposition must be premised on the confluence of conduct and culpability. Thus, under the Model Code, as at common law, murder occurs if a person kills purposely, knowingly, or with extreme recklessness. Lesser culpability yields lesser liability, and a person who inadvertently kills another under circumstances not amounting to negligence is guilty of no crime at all. The felony-murder rule contradicts this scheme. It bases conviction of murder not on any proven culpability with respect to homicide but on liability for another crime. The underlying felony carries its own penalty and the additional punishment for murder is therefore gratuitous—gratuitous, at least, in terms of what must have been proved at trial in a court of law.

It is true, of course, that the felony-murder rule is often invoked where liability for murder exists on another ground. One who kills in the course of armed robbery is almost certainly guilty of murder in the form of intentional or extremely reckless homicide without any need of special doctrine. Similarly, a man who burns another's house will scarcely be heard to complain that he lacks the culpability for murder if the blaze kills a sleeping occupant. For the vast majority of cases it is probably true that homicide occurring during the commission or attempted commission of a felony is murder independent of the felony-murder rule. At bottom, continued adherence to the doctrine may rest on assessments of this sort.

The problem is that criminal liability attaches to individuals, not generalities. It is a weak rejoinder to a complaint of unjust conviction to say that for most persons in the defendant's situation the result would have been appropriate. To be sure, limiting the rule to specified felonies increases the probability that conviction in a particular case will be warranted. Criminal punishment should be premised, however, on something more than a probability of guilt. Requiring that the defendant's conduct in committing the underlying felony create a foreseeable risk to human life is a roundabout way of limiting felony murder to cases of negligent homicide. This is a worthwhile reform, for it effectively excludes extreme applications of the rule to instances in which the actor would not otherwise be guilty of any homicide offense. Yet murder and negligent homicide are not interchangeable; they carry vastly different sanctions. Punishment for the greater offense, on proof that should suffice only for conviction of the lesser, works within reduced compass the same essential violence to the general principles of criminal liability as does the unqualified rule.

Principled argument in favor of the felony-murder doctrine is hard to find. The defense reduces to the explanation that Holmes gave for finding the law "intelligible as it stands":

> [I]f experience shows, or is deemed by the law-maker to show, that somehow or other deaths which the evidence makes accidental happen disproportionately often in connection with other felonies, or with resistance to officers, or if any other ground of policy it is deemed desirable to make special efforts for the prevention of such deaths, the law-maker may consistently treat acts which, under the known circumstances, are felonious, or constitute resistance to officers, as having a sufficiently dangerous tendency to be put under a special ban. The law may, therefore, throw on the actor the peril, not only of the consequences foreseen by him, but also of consequences which, although not predicted by common experience, the legislator apprehends.

The answer to such argument is twofold. First, there is no basis in experience for thinking that homicides *which the evidence makes accidental* occur with disproportionate frequency in connection with specified felonies. Second, it remains indefensible in principle to use the sanctions that the law employs to deal with murder unless there is at least a finding that the actor's conduct manifested an extreme indifference to the value of human life. The fact that the actor was engaged in a crime of the kind that is included in the usual first-degree felony-murder enumeration or was an accomplice in such crime, as has been observed, will frequently justify such a finding. Indeed, the probability that such a finding will be justified seems high enough to warrant the presumption of extreme indifference that Subsection (1)(b) creates. But liability depends, as plainly it should, upon the crucial finding. The result may not differ often under such a formulation from that which would be reached under some form of the felony-murder rule. But what is more important is that a conviction on this basis rests solidly upon principle.

David Crump & Susan Waite Crump, In Defense of Felony Murder
8 Harvard Journal of Law and Public Policy 359, 362-364, 367-371 (1985)

Such diverse philosophers and judges as Jeremy Bentham, H.L.A. Hart, Sir James Fitzjames Stephen, Joel Feinberg, and Chief Justice Warren Burger have noted the disrespect that the law engenders when its response is disproportionate to public evaluations of the severity of an alleged violation. Many penal codes declare proportionality to be among their major objectives. The classification and grading of offenses so that the entire scheme of defined crimes squares with societal perceptions of proportionality — of "just deserts" — is a fundamental goal of the law of crimes.

The felony murder doctrine serves this goal. . . . Felony murder reflects a societal judgement that an intentionally committed robbery that causes the death of a human being is qualitatively more serious than an identical robbery that does not. Perhaps this judgement could have been embodied in a newly defined offense called "robbery-resulting-in-death;" but while a similar approach has been adopted in some areas of the criminal law, such a proliferation of offense definitions is undesirable. Thus the felony murder doctrine reflects the conclusion that a robbery that causes death is more closely akin to murder than to robbery. If this conclusion accurately reflects societal attitudes, and if classification of crimes is to be influenced by such attitudes in order to avoid depreciation of the seriousness of the offense and to encourage respect for the law, then the felony murder doctrine is an appropriate classificatory device.

There is impressive empirical evidence that this classification does indeed reflect widely shared societal attitudes.... [C]haracterizing a robbery-homicide solely as robbery would have the undesirable effect of communicating to the citizenry that the law does not consider a crime that takes a human life to be different from one that does not — a message that would be indistinguishable, in the minds of many, from a devaluation of human life.

Another aspect of condemnation is the expression of solidarity with the victims of crime. If we as a society label a violent offense in a manner that depreciates its significance, we communicate to the victim by implication that we do not understand his suffering. He may be left with the impression that he is unprotected — or even that he is disoriented, having himself failed to understand the rules of the game. Felony murder is a useful doctrine because it reaffirms to the surviving family of a felony-homicide victim the kinship the society as a whole feels with him by denouncing in the strongest language of the law the intentional crime that produced his death.

Deterrence is often cited as one justification for the felony murder doctrine. ... Deterrence is the policy most often recognized in the cases. Scholars, however, tend to dismiss this rationale, using such arguments as the improbability that felons will know the law, the unlikelihood that a criminal who has formed the intent to commit a felony will refrain from acts likely to cause death, or the assertedly small number of felony-homicides.

The trouble with these criticisms is that they underestimate the complexity of deterrence. There may be more than a grain of truth in the proposition that felons, if considered as a class, evaluate risks and benefits differently than members of different classes in society. The conclusion does not follow, however, that felons cannot be deterred, or that criminals are so different from other citizens that they are impervious to inducements or deterrents that would affect people in general. There is mounting evidence that serious crime is subject to deterrence if consequences are adequately communicated. The felony murder rule is just the sort of simple, common sense, readily enforceable, and widely known principle that is likely to result in deterrence.

The argument against deterrence often proceeds on the additional assumption that felony murder is addressed only to accidental killings and cannot result in their deterrence. By facilitating proof and simplifying the concept of liability, however, felony murder may deter intentional killings as well. The robber who kills intentionally, but who might claim under oath to have acted accidentally, is thus told that he will be deprived of the benefit of this claim. By institutionalizing this effect and consistently condemning robbery homicides as qualitatively more blameworthy than robberies, the law leads the robber who kills intentionally to expect treatment for himself. Furthermore, the contrary argument proves too much even as to robbery-killings that are factually accidental. The proposition that accidental killings cannot be deterred is inconsistent with the widespread belief that the penalizing of negligence, and even the imposition of strict liability, may have deterrent consequences.

Other Discussion Materials

People v. James Edward Washington
Supreme Court of California
62 Cal. 2d 777, 402 P.2d 130, 1965 Cal. LEXIS 295, 44 Cal. Rptr. 442 (1965)

Defendant appeals from a judgment of conviction entered upon jury verdicts finding him guilty of first degree robbery (Pen. Code, §§211, 211a) and first degree murder and fixing the murder penalty at life imprisonment. (Pen. Code, §§187, 189, 190, 190.1.) He was convicted of murder for participating in a robbery in which his accomplice was killed by the victim of the robbery.

Shortly before 10 p.m., October 2, 1962, Johnnie Carpenter prepared to close his gasoline station. He was in his office computing the receipts and disbursements of the day while an attendant in an adjacent storage room deposited money in a vault. Upon hearing someone yell "robbery," Carpenter opened his desk and took out a revolver. A few moments later, James Ball entered the office and pointed a revolver directly at Carpenter, who fired immediately, mortally wounding Ball. Carpenter then hurried to the door and saw an unarmed man he later identified as defendant running from the vault with a moneybag in his right hand. He shouted "Stop." When his warning was not heeded, he fired and hit defendant, who fell wounded in front of the station....

The basic issue ... therefore is whether a robber can be convicted of murder for the killing of any person by another who is resisting the robbery.

"Murder is the unlawful killing of a human being, with malice aforethought." (Pen. Code, §187.) Except when the common-law-felony-murder doctrine is applicable, an essential element of murder is an intent to kill or an intent with conscious disregard for life to commit acts likely to kill. The felony-murder doctrine ascribes malice aforethought to the felon who kills in the perpetration of an inherently dangerous felony. That doctrine is incorporated in *section 189* of the Penal Code, which provides in part: "All murder ... committed in the perpetration or attempt to perpetrate ... robbery ... is murder of the first degree." Thus, even though section 189 speaks only of degrees of "murder," inadvertent or accidental killings are first degree murders when committed by felons in the perpetration of robbery.

When a killing is not committed by a robber or by his accomplice but by his victim, malice aforethought is not attributable to the robber, for the killing is not committed by him in the perpetration or attempt to perpetrate robbery. It is not enough that the killing was a risk reasonably to be foreseen and that the robbery might therefore be regarded as a proximate cause of the killing. Section 189 requires that the felon or his accomplice commit the killing, for if he does not, the killing is not committed to perpetrate the felony. Indeed, in the present case the killing was committed to thwart a felony. To include such killings within section 189 would expand the meaning of the words "murder . . . which is committed in the perpetration . . . [of] robbery . . ." beyond common understanding.

The purpose of the felony-murder rule is to deter felons from killing negligently or accidentally by holding them strictly responsible for killings they commit. This purpose is not served by punishing them for killings committed by their victims.

It is contended, however, that another purpose of the felony-murder rule is to prevent the commission of robberies. Neither the common-law rationale of the rule nor the Penal Code supports this contention. In every robbery there is a possibility that the victim will resist and kill. The robber has little control over such a killing once the robbery is undertaken, as this case demonstrates. To impose an additional penalty for the killing would discriminate between robbers, not on the basis of any difference in their own conduct, but solely on the basis of the response by others that the robber's conduct happened to induce. An additional penalty for a homicide committed by the victim would deter robbery haphazardly at best. To "prevent stealing, [the law] would do better to hang one thief in every thousand by lot." (Holmes, The Common Law, p. 58.) . . .

To invoke the felony-murder doctrine when the killing is not committed by the defendant or by his accomplice could lead to absurd results. Thus, two men rob a grocery store and flee in opposite directions. The owner of the store follows one of the robbers and kills him. Neither robber may have fired a shot. Neither robber may have been armed with a deadly weapon. If the felony-murder doctrine applied, however, the surviving robber could be convicted of first degree murder, even though he was captured by a policeman and placed under arrest at the time his accomplice was killed.

The felony-murder rule has been criticized on the grounds that in almost all cases in which it is applied it is unnecessary and that it erodes the relation between criminal liability and moral culpability. Although it is the law in this state (Pen. Code, §189), it should not be extended beyond any rational function that it is designed to serve. Accordingly, for a defendant to be guilty of murder under the felony-murder rule the act of killing must be committed by the defendant or by his accomplice acting in furtherance of their common design. Language in *People v. Harrison, 176 Cal. App. 2d 330,* inconsistent with this holding, is disapproved. . . .

The judgment is . . . reversed as to [defendant's] conviction of first degree murder.

Burke, J. I dissent. The unfortunate effect of the decision of the majority in this case is to advise felons:

> "Henceforth in committing certain crimes, including robbery, rape and burglary, you are free to arm yourselves with a gun and brandish it in the faces of your victims without fear of a murder conviction unless you or your accomplice pulls the trigger. If the menacing effect of your gun causes a victim or policeman to fire and kill an innocent person or a cofelon, you are absolved of responsibility for such killing unless you shoot first."

Obviously this advance judicial absolution removes one of the most meaningful deterrents to the commission of armed felonies.

Extreme examples may be imagined in which the application of a rule of criminal liability would appear manifestly unjust. However, when this court and others have been faced with such an example exceptions have been made to avoid an unconscionable result. To reject invocation of the felony-murder rule here, as do the majority, because of possible harshness in its application in other circumstances, for example, to fleeing robbers who are *not* armed, dilutes the enforcement of criminal responsibility. The case anticipated and the injustice sought to be protected against by the majority are not before us, and can best be dealt with when and if encountered. It may be observed, however, that robbers are not compelled to flee and thus to be shot at, endangering themselves and others. They need only surrender, as many have done, to avoid death, to themselves or others, and the awesome penalties which attach under the felony-murder law.

I agree with the majority that one purpose of the felony-murder rule is to deter felons from killing negligently or accidentally. However, another equally cogent purpose is to deter them from undertaking inherently dangerous felonies in which, as the majority state, a "killing was a risk reasonably to be foreseen. . . . In every robbery there is a possibility that the victim will resist and kill." As declared in *People v. Chavez (1951) 37 Cal.2d 656, 669,* "The statute [Pen. Code, *§189*] was adopted for the protection of the community and its residents, not for the benefit of the lawbreaker." Why a felon who has undertaken an *armed* robbery, which this court now expressly notifies him carries a "risk" and "a possibility that the victim will resist and kill," and which "might therefore be regarded as a proximate cause of the killing" should nevertheless be absolved because, fortuitously, the victim can and does shoot first and the lethal bullet comes from the victim's gun rather than from his own, will be beyond the comprehension of the average law-abiding citizen, to say nothing of that of victims of armed robbery. Nor is such a view compatible with the felony-murder doctrine.

But, say the majority, "The robber has little control over such a killing once the robbery is undertaken," and "To impose an additional penalty for the killing would discriminate between robbers, not on the basis of any difference in their own conduct, but solely on the basis of the response by others that the robber's conduct happened to induce." A robber has *no* control over a bullet sent on its way after he pulls the trigger. Certainly his inability to recall it before it kills does not cloak him with innocence of the homicide. The truth is, of course, that the robber may exercise various "controls over" a possible killing from his victim's bullet "once the robbery is undertaken." The robber can drop his own weapon, he can refrain from using it, or he can surrender. Other conduct can be suggested which would tend to reassure the victim and dissuade him from firing his own gun. Moreover, the response by one victim will lead to capture of the robbers, while that of another victim will permit their escape. Is the captured felon to be excused from responsibility for his crime, in order not to "discriminate between robbers . . . solely on the basis of the response by others that the robber's conduct happened to induce"?

The robber's conduct which forms the basis of his criminal responsibility is the undertaking of the *armed* felony, in which a "killing was a risk reasonably to be foreseen" including the "possibility that the victim will resist and kill." If that risk becomes reality and a killing occurs, the guilt for it is that of the felon. And when done, it is murder in the first degree — calling for death or life imprisonment. And to say that the knowledge that this awesome, sobering, terrifying responsibility of one contemplating the use of a deadly weapon in the perpetration of one of the listed offenses is not the strongest possible deterrent to the commission of such offenses belies what is being demonstrated day after day in the criminal departments of our trial courts.

I would hold, in accord with the rationale of *People v. Harrison, supra (1959) 176 Cal.App.2d 330,* that the killing is that of the felon whether or not the lethal bullet comes from his gun or that of his accomplice and whether or not one of them shoots first, and would affirm the judgment of conviction of murder in the instant case.

Paul H. Robinson & John M. Darley, Study 16: The Culpability of the Person — Felony Murder
Justice, Liability & Blame: Community Views and the Criminal Law 179 (1995)

This study confirms that subjects, like current legal doctrine, aggravate the liability of a person who kills during a felony over what it would be if not committed during a felony. They punish a person's negligent killing during a robbery at a liability level similar to a reckless killing in a non-felonious context. If one brandishes a gun during the course of a robbery, and it goes off accidently and kills an innocent, the subjects are not particularly sympathetic to the view that this is equivalent to accidentally discharging a gun and killing another. But according to our subjects, current doctrine goes too far, for it punishes such a negligent killing as if it were murder, while the subjects would prefer manslaughter. So, the subjects would support a "felony-manslaughter rule."

The complicity aspect of the felony-murder rule reflects similar differences. Like the doctrine, the subjects punish the accomplice for more than negligent homicide when the perpetrator kills during a felony. But while the doctrine treats the accomplice exactly like a murderer, the subjects impose liability somewhat less than they would for manslaughter. The lesser liability of the accomplice is significant. It reflects the view of the subjects, manifested in several studies, that the accomplice generally deserves less liability than the perpetrator, all other things being equal. If the code were to adopt a standard "accomplice discount," felony-murder accomplices could remain within the rule; the accomplice would be held at some level of liability less than that of the "felony-manslaughter" perpetrator.

The vicarious aspect of the felony-murder rule — holding a felon liable for murder for a killing by the intended victim of the felony or some other bystander — has even less support among the subjects than the aggravation and complicity aspects of the rule. Where the victim kills an accomplice, the liability imposed by the subjects on the surviving accomplice is not significantly more than that imposed for a negligent homicide, far from the murder liability imposed by the felony-murder rule in some jurisdictions. (Also, the state of mind of the accomplice as to planning to kill does not seem to matter.) Where an innocent person is killed by the robbery victim, the accomplice's liability is slightly more than that for negligent homicide but still nowhere near manslaughter liability. This result is likely under normal homicide grading; thus, the subjects would see no need for extension of the felony-murder rule to these cases.

To conclude, it is possible that a jury might reach the same conclusions as our subjects even without a felony-murder rule, by seeing culpability in the creation of a situation in which the likelihood of a killing is brought about. It may be, as we suggested earlier, that it is this perception of blame for creating the dangerous situation that generates the subjects' responses. Such increased liability is possible if not likely under the normal graded-homicide offenses, and its likelihood is increased if the Model Penal Code's evidentiary presumption approach is used. The Code, recall, uses the fact of the felony as grounds to create a presumption of "recklessness manifesting extreme indifference to the value of human life," which is defined as sufficient culpability for murder; the defendant can rebut this presumption. One might argue, then, that these results argue against the continuing need for a felony-murder rule. On the other hand, the results suggest that a form of a felony-murder rule might be unobjectionable — and, thus, if politically demanded, might be continued — if revised to better reflect the subjects' views, which call for lower liability levels.

A rule that mirrors the subjects' views would aggravate a negligent killing by a felon in the course of a felony to reckless homicide (manslaughter), not murder. No special complicity rule would be required; accomplices would receive the normal complicity discount, which varies with the level of the accomplice's culpability and degree of contribution. A felon might be liable for killings by an intended victim of the felony, at the level of negligent homicide, but not under a special rule for killings during a felony.

Death Penalty

The death penalty debate arises almost exclusively in the context of aggravated cases of homicide, the subject of the previous Section. This Section examines these basic issues: Under what circumstances is the death penalty imposed in current practice? Why is it imposed in those cases? Should it be imposed?

◆ THE CASE OF WILLIAM KING

Approximately 7,500 people live in the east Texas town of Jasper—a population almost equally divided between blacks and whites. As with many towns in the New South, Jasper's race relations record is mixed. Several prominent political and civic leaders are African-American, including the mayor, and the local country club admits African-American members. Nonetheless, racial epithets like "nigger" are still heard, and racial tensions clearly exist. For example, although the recent hanging death of a prominent African-American high school athlete who had been dating a white girl

Figure 25 James Byrd, Jr., 1997

(AP/Byrd Family)

was ruled a suicide, some Jasper residents believe it was a lynching. For the most part, however, racism in Jasper lives on only in words and resentment; there have been few acts of violence in recent years.

James Byrd, Jr., is the third of eight children born to James, Sr., a dry cleaner, and Stella, a homemaker. James, Jr., was an excellent student, graduating from high school in 1967, which was the final year of school segregation in Jasper. He does not follow his two older sisters to college, but he remains in Jasper and marries Thelma Adams, with whom he has three children, Renee, Ross, and Jamie. James leads a colorful life; sometimes selling vacuum cleaners door to door, in and out of jail on forgery and theft charges. He is noted for his musical talent, playing the piano and singing spirituals and hymns — his favorite is "Walk with Me, Lord."

Around the time James and Thelma are starting a family, Shawn Berry is born in Jasper. His mother divorces twice while he is very young and Berry experiences further trauma as a teenager when, having grown close to his mother's second husband, the man commits suicide by shooting himself in the chest with a shotgun. Berry is then raised by his paternal grandparents until they too divorce. Berry drops out of high school and becomes friends with John William ("Bill") King.

King, born in 1975, is adopted as an infant by a working class family from Jasper. He is the youngest of four children in his adoptive family; his adoptive father, Ronald King, describes Bill as "the most loved boy I knew." King grows up in an integrated neighborhood; his father has several black friends, and one of King's own closest childhood friends is black. Although he was diagnosed once as manic depressive, friends describe him as a low-key and unassuming kid.

King's adoptive mother dies when he is 15. In 1992, at the age of 17, he drops out of high school. Soon afterwards, he is arrested for burglary and placed on probation. A few months later, he and Berry are convicted of burglarizing a jukebox warehouse and receive ten-year prison sentences.

Figure 26 **John William King, circa 1999**
(R. Jaap/Beaumont Enterprises/Corbis Sygma)

They catch a break and are sent instead to a 90-day "boot camp" that is supposed to scare them away from a life of crime. The program seems to work on Berry, who returns to Jasper and settles into a normal life, first working at a tire dealership in exchange for a room in the boss's trailer home. He then moves on to a job at the local movie theater, where he meets future girlfriend Christie Marcontell, a local beauty who has twice been chosen to represent her region in the Miss Texas pageant. The two begin a relationship and she gives birth to their son, Montana, in 1997. Christie describes (Shawn) as a loving and attentive father, "Montana slept with his daddy the first three weeks of his life." Shawn and Christie set an August 1998 wedding date.

Unfortunately, boot camp seems to have little effect on Bill King, who violates his parole and is sent to Beto I, a maximum security prison near Houston in 1995. On his first day in prison, King is "pretty badly beaten" and raped by blacks, who are in the prison majority. King is approximately 5'7" and weighs only 140 pounds at the time. Like at many prisons, there are gangs that can make

Figure 27 **Berry and King, June 1998**
(Greg Smith/Corbis Saba)

life easier for their members, and, conversely, more difficult for enemies. King becomes immersed in a "thriving subculture" of racist hate groups and rises in the ranks to be known as an "exalted cyclops" of the Confederate Knights of America, a white supremacist gang. King is paroled in July 1997 and returns to Jasper a changed man. "When he came back, he was a person I'd never seen," said Shawn Berry's brother, Louis Berry. Once an avid guitar player in a rock band, King speaks only of his new racist beliefs. Among his many tattoos are a woodpecker (a term used in prison for whites) in a Ku Klux Klansman's uniform making an obscene gesture; a "patch" incorporating "KKK," a swastika, and the words "Aryan Pride"; and a black man with a noose around his neck hanging from a tree, of which he often remarks, "See my little nigger hanging from a tree." He entered prison a Baptist and leaves a believer in Odinism, a pagan creed that is popular among neo-Nazi groups, but friend Louis Berry maintains, "we always thought all that hatred Bill had would kind of wear down and go away." In the fall of 1997, Bill begins dating Kylie Greeney, a local 17-year old, who soon becomes pregnant with their child. Kylie concedes that Bill does not like Jews and most black people but she does not consider him a racist, claiming "...he did have some black friends." In May 1998, Shawn Berry moves into King's apartment, along with Russell Brewer, King's former cellmate from

Figure 28 **Shawn Berry, 1999**
(AP)

Beto I, who returns to Jasper after his own prison stay.

Lawrence Russell Brewer, Jr., is older than Shawn Berry and Bill King and has his own criminal tendencies. He was convicted of burglary, and sentenced to 15 years for drug possession in 1989. He is released in 1991 but violated parole in 1994 and was sent back to prison, where he too joined the Confederate Knights of America. There he met and befriended King. Oddly, Brewer is married to a Hispanic woman and, while in prison, he hides the fact of his marriage and their son from fellow gang members because he is afraid that they will hurt him.

King and Brewer sleep late on Saturday, June 6, 1998, and then drive to a nearby town to hang out with Berry and drink beer. When King and Brewer

Figure 29 **Lawrence Russell Brewer, 1999**
(AP)

arrive, Berry is having a heavy-metal jam session with some friends, one of whom is black. King gets angry that Berry has a black man over and refuses to come inside, saying he does not like black people. Berry tells him to leave, so he and Brewer take off. Later that night, King and Brewer go to the Twin Cinemas to meet up with Berry. While they are at the theater, Christie Marcontell comes by, trying to patch up an argument with Berry. Berry tells her he is going to go home and go to bed early but instead he, King, and Brewer drive around trying to find a party. They are unsuccessful and end up drinking beer and driving the country roads.

On that same afternoon, James Byrd attends a bridal shower for his niece, where he plays with his one-year old granddaughter and sees his sisters. His sisters give him a present after the shower and drop him off at a friend's house around 6 p.m. Byrd bids his sisters farewell, "I love ya'll both. I'll be all right from here on." Later that evening, Byrd goes to a party near the public housing development where he lives and around 1:30 a.m., unable to find a ride, sets out to walk home on Martin Luther King Boulevard. Byrd walks quite a bit because he cannot afford a car. He has acquired the nickname "Toe" because he walks with a limp due to a childhood accident in which he lost a toe.

While driving down Martin Luther King Boulevard, King, Berry, and Brewer come upon Byrd walking home. Berry recognizes Byrd because they had once shared a parole officer and offers him a ride over King's objections that they should not pick up a "f____ g n___r." Berry stops the truck and Byrd gets in the back, with the three white men in the cab. The foursome stop at a convenience store then drive off with King at the wheel.

King drives out of town to a secluded area and stops the truck in a clearing. He and Brewer drag Byrd from the back. They beat him viciously until he loses consciousness. Once he regains consciousness, they tie a chain used to haul lumber around Byrd's ankles and, with Berry driving, drag him behind the truck for 2 to 3 miles. Byrd experiences intense burning pain as his flesh is torn off by the pavement, down to the bone in places. Byrd tries to relieve the pain by rolling from side to side, swapping one part of his body for another and struggles to keep his head off the ground. He is in so much agony that each second feels like an eternity. He manages to stay alive until the truck passes over a large drainage culvert and his body hits it with such force that his head and right arm are ripped away from his body. Berry finally stops the truck in front of an African-American church on Huff Creek Road. They leave what remains of Byrd's mangled torso in the road in front of the church.

Almost all of Byrd's anterior ribs are fractured and he suffers "massive brush burn abrasions" over most of his body. Both testicles are missing and gravel is inside the scrotal sac. Byrd's knees and part of his feet are "ground down" and his left cheek is ground down to the jawbone, his buttocks down to the sacrum and lower spine. Some of his toes are missing, others fractured, and large lacerations expose muscle up and down his legs. However, his brain and skull are intact, suggesting, horrifically, that he maintained consciousness while being dragged. Byrd's heart was probably still beating when his body hit the culvert, tearing his head and right arm from his torso.

The next morning, June 7, police receive a phone call leading them to the church, where they find Byrd's torso with the remains of pants and underwear gathered around his ankles. "A trail of smeared

Figure 30 **Huff Creek Road in Jasper, Texas, where Byrd's body was found, June 12, 1998**

(Greg Smith/Corbis Saba)

blood and drag marks" lead from the torso down the road a mile and a half, where police find his head, neck, and right arm by a culvert. The gruesome trail continues another mile and a half down Huff Creek Road and onto a dirt logging road. At the end of the logging road police discover an area of matted-down grass where Byrd was beaten. The police mark the road where he was dragged with 81 orange spray-painted circles, designating his bodily remains and personal effects strewn along the way: "dentures," "keys," "head." Police can identify him only by his fingerprints. His sister Mylinda wonders, "What was going through his mind? What was he thinking while they were doing this to him?" The police also find a trail of personal effects of the suspects strewn down the road and at the fight scene: a wrench inscribed with the name "Berry," a cigarette lighter engraved with the words "Possum" (Bill King's nickname) and "KKK," three cigarette butts, a can of "fix-a-flat," a compact disk, a woman's watch, a can of black spray paint, a pack of Marlboro Lights, and beer bottles.

The wrench found at the murder scene makes Shawn Berry a suspect. The day after the murder, police spot his truck, notice that it has expired tags, and use that as an excuse to pull him over. They discover a set of tools matching the wrench found at the fight scene and bring him to the station for questioning. He says he was with King and Brewer on the night of the murder and that he knew James Byrd but offers nothing more. King and Brewer get word that Berry is in custody and worry that he will implicate them. King paces around the apartment, trying to come up with a plan. The police put the apartment under surveillance and when King and Brewer emerge at 2 a.m. Sunday for a trip to the Wal-Mart across the street, police ask the pair if they will come to the station. They agree and are taken in the squad car because neither King nor Brewer has a car of his own. During questioning, King appears smug and admits that on the night in question the three were driving around together looking for a party and picked up James Byrd, but claims that the last time he saw "Mr. Byrd" was when Berry drove off with Byrd after having dropped him and Brewer off at his apartment. Sheriff Rowles then asks King if they can search his apartment, to which he replies, "I've got nothing to hide; go ahead and search," and signs a voluntary consent-to-search form. By this time, it is almost 4 a.m. — Berry has been in the interrogation room for many hours and is losing his composure. Sheriff Rowles tells him that King and Brewer have been arrested and warns him that prison time will be much harder for him because he has never been there before. Rowles gives him an out: "Tell us what you know, and I will make sure the federal prosecutors I call down here come to your cell first. Otherwise, I may just start with King and Brewer, and there's no telling what they are going to say." Berry breaks down in tears and writes a statement confessing to the murder of James Byrd and detailing King's and Brewer's involvement. Soon thereafter, Rowles is on his way to a meeting with an F.B.I. hate crimes unit in Beaumont.

Figure 31 **Byrd's funeral, Jasper, Texas**
(Beaumont Enterprise/Corbis Sygma)

As news of the crime spreads, the people of Jasper are stunned and wonder how something so horrifying could happen in their town. Community meetings are held to discuss race relations — whites feel pangs of guilt; blacks are scared. Local African-American leaders struggle to prevent a violent response from angry black citizens. On Tuesday morning, two days after the body is found, yellow ribbons expressing solidarity begin appearing all over town. Thousands send cards and flowers expressing their sympathy and horror—so many that they cannot fit into the 300-seat Greater New Bethel Baptist Church for the funeral. National African-American leaders, including Jesse Jackson, U.S. Transportation Secretary Rodney Slater, Rep. Maxine Waters, and NAACP President Kweisi Mfume, attend the funeral. President Clinton calls to express his condolences, and Chicago Bull and Texas native Dennis Rodman pays for the funeral and gives Byrd's family $25,000. Fight promoter Don King gives Byrd's children $100,000 to be put toward their education expenses.

Figure 32 **King's tattoos, photograph released by DA's Office**

(Corbis Sygma)

Oddly, the trio of offenders did not attempt to hide the evidence. When police search the apartment, they find their bloody clothing. DNA analysis shows that the blood matches Byrd's DNA. DNA analysis also is performed on the cigarette butts found at the fight scene and along the logging road, revealing matches with the DNA of all three defendants. Further testing reveals that blood spatters underneath Berry's truck and on several of its tires match Byrd's DNA. The day after his arrest, Berry leads police and F.B.I. agents to the murder weapon buried in the woods behind his friend, Tommy Faulk's, trailer. He guides them to a large piece of plywood and kicks it up, revealing a large hole and inside, the 24-foot logging chain used to drag Byrd. The chain matches the rust imprint of a chain in the bed of Berry's truck. It does not take long for a grand jury to indict King, Brewer, and Berry for the capital murder of James Byrd.

While in jail awaiting trial, Bill King sends a letter to Russell Brewer celebrating the murder: "Reguardless [sic] of the outcome of this, we have made history and shall die proudly remembered if need be. Much Arayan Love, Respect, and Honor, my brother in arms. Sieg Heil, Possum." Unbeknownst to King and Brewer, jailers intercept many notes passed between them in which they all but admit to the murder. The notes are admitted at trial, and defense attorneys call them "the most damning evidence against their clients."

Bill King, Russell Brewer, and Shawn Berry are convicted of capital murder. Should King be executed for his crime?

1. Relying only upon your own intuitions of justice, what liability and punishment, if any, does Bill King deserve?

N	0	1	2	3	4	5	6	7	8	9	10	11
☐	☐	☐	☐	☐	☐	☐	☐	☐	☐	☐	☐	☐
no liability	liability but no punishment	1 day	2 wks	2 mo	6 mo	1 yr	3 yrs	7 yrs	15 yrs	30 yrs	life imprisonment	death

2. What liability, if any, under the then-existing statutes?
3. What liability, if any, under the Model Penal Code?

■ THE LAW

Texas Penal Code
(1998)

Title 5. Offenses Against the Person

Chapter 19. Criminal Homicide

Section 19.01. Types of Criminal Homicide

(a) A person commits criminal homicide if he intentionally, knowingly, recklessly, or with criminal negligence causes the death of an individual.

(b) Criminal homicide is murder, capital murder, manslaughter, or criminally negligent homicide.

Section 19.02. Murder

(a) In this section:

(1) "Adequate cause" means cause that would commonly produce a degree of anger, rage, resentment, or terror in a person of ordinary temper, sufficient to render the mind incapable of cool reflection.

(2) "Sudden passion" means passion directly caused by and arising out of provocation by the individual killed or another acting with the person killed which passion arises at the time of the offense and is not solely the result of former provocation.

(b) A person commits an offense if he:

(1) intentionally or knowingly causes the death of an individual;

(2) intends to cause serious bodily injury and commits an act clearly dangerous to human life that causes the death of an individual; or

(3) commits or attempts to commit a felony, other than manslaughter, and in the course of and in furtherance of the commission or attempt, or in immediate flight from the commission or attempt, he commits or attempts to commit an act clearly dangerous to human life that causes the death of an individual.

(c) Except as provided by Subsection (d), an offense under this section is a felony of the first degree.

(d) At the punishment stage of a trial, the defendant may raise the issue as to whether he caused the death under the immediate influence of sudden passion arising from an adequate cause. If the defendant proves the issue in the affirmative by a preponderance of the evidence, the offense is a felony of the second degree.

Section 19.03. Capital Murder

(a) A person commits an offense if he commits murder as defined under Section 19.02(b)(1) and:

(1) the person murders a peace officer or fireman who is acting in the lawful discharge of an official duty and who the person knows is a peace officer or fireman;

(2) the person intentionally commits the murder in the course of committing or attempting to commit kidnapping, burglary, robbery, aggravated sexual assault, arson, or obstruction or retaliation;

(3) the person commits the murder for remuneration or the promise of remuneration or employs another to commit the murder for remuneration or the promise of remuneration;

(4) the person commits the murder while escaping or attempting to escape from a penal institution;

(5) the person, while incarcerated in a penal institution, murders another:

(A) who is employed in the operation of the penal institution; or

(B) with the intent to establish, maintain, or participate in a combination or in the profits of a combination;

(6) the person:

(A) while incarcerated for an offense under this section or Section 19.02, murders another; or

(B) while serving a sentence of life imprisonment or a term of 99 years for an offense under Section 20.04, 22.021, or 29.03, murders another;

(7) the person murders more than one person:

(A) during the same criminal transaction; or

(B) during different criminal transactions but the murders are committed pursuant to the same scheme or course of conduct; or

(8) the person murders an individual under six years of age.

(b) An offense under this section is a capital felony.

(c) If the jury or, when authorized by law, the judge does not find beyond a reasonable doubt that the defendant is guilty of an offense under this section, he may be convicted of murder or of any other lesser included offense.

Chapter 20. Kidnapping and Unlawful Restraint

Section 20.03. Kidnapping

(a) A person commits an offense if he intentionally or knowingly abducts another person.

(b) It is an affirmative defense to prosecution under this section that:

(1) the abduction was not coupled with intent to use or to threaten to use deadly force;

(2) the actor was a relative of the person abducted; and

(3) the actor's sole intent was to assume lawful control of the victim.

(c) An offense under this section is a felony of the third degree.

Section 20.04. Aggravated Kidnapping

(a) A person commits an offense if he intentionally or knowingly abducts another person with the intent to:

(1) hold him for ransom or reward;

(2) use him as a shield or hostage;

(3) facilitate the commission of a felony or the flight after the attempt or commission of a felony;

(4) inflict bodily injury on him or violate or abuse him sexually;

(5) terrorize him or a third person; or

(6) interfere with the performance of any governmental or political function.

(b) A person commits an offense if the person intentionally or knowingly abducts another person and uses or exhibits a deadly weapon during the commission of the offense.

(c) Except as provided by Subsection (d), an offense under this section is a felony of the first degree.

(d) At the punishment stage of a trial, the defendant may raise the issue as to whether he voluntarily released the victim in a safe place. If the defendant proves the issue in the affirmative by a preponderance of the evidence, the offense is a felony of the second degree.

Title 2. General Principles of Criminal Responsibility
Chapter 6. Culpability Generally

Section 6.03. Definitions of Culpable Mental States

(a) A person acts intentionally, or with intent, with respect to the nature of his conduct or to a result of his conduct when it is his conscious objective or desire to engage in the conduct or cause the result.

(b) A person acts knowingly, or with knowledge, with respect to the nature of his conduct or to circumstances surrounding his conduct when he is aware of the nature of his conduct or that the circumstances exist. A person acts knowingly, or with knowledge, with respect to a result of his conduct when he is aware that his conduct is reasonably certain to cause the result.

Chapter 7. Criminal Responsibility for Conduct of Another
Subchapter A. Complicity

Section 7.01. Parties to Offenses

(a) A person is criminally responsible as a party to an offense if the offense is committed by his own conduct, by the conduct of another for which he is criminally responsible, or by both.

(b) Each party to an offense may be charged with commission of the offense.

(c) All traditional distinctions between accomplices and principals are abolished by this section, and each party to an offense may be charged and convicted without alleging that he acted as a principal or accomplice.

Section 7.02. Criminal Responsibility for Conduct of Another

(a) A person is criminally responsible for an offense committed by the conduct of another if:

(1) acting with the kind of culpability required for the offense, he causes or aids an innocent or nonresponsible person to engage in conduct prohibited by the definition of the offense;

(2) acting with intent to promote or assist the commission of the offense, he solicits, encourages, directs, aids, or attempts to aid the other person to commit the offense; or

(3) having a legal duty to prevent commission of the offense and acting with intent to promote or assist its commission, he fails to make a reasonable effort to prevent commission of the offense.

(b) If, in the attempt to carry out a conspiracy to commit one felony, another felony is committed by one of the conspirators, all conspirators are guilty of the felony actually committed, though having no intent to commit it, if the offense was committed in furtherance of the unlawful purpose and was one that should have been anticipated as a result of the carrying out of the conspiracy.

Section 7.03. Defenses Excluded

In a prosecution in which an actor's criminal responsibility is based on the conduct of another, the actor may be convicted on proof of commission of the offense and that he was a party to its commission, and it is no defense:

(1) that the actor belongs to a class of persons that by definition of the offense is legally incapable of committing the offense in an individual capacity; or

(2) that the person for whose conduct the actor is criminally responsible has been acquitted, has not been prosecuted or convicted, has been convicted of a different offense or of a different type or class of offense, or is immune from prosecution.

Title 1. Introductory Provisions

Chapter 1. General Provisions

Section 1.02. Objectives of Code

The general purposes of this code are to establish a system of prohibitions, penalties, and correctional measures to deal with conduct that unjustifiably and inexcusably causes or threatens harm to those individual or public interests for which state protection is appropriate. To this end, the provisions of this code are intended, and shall be construed, to achieve the following objectives:

(1) to insure the public safety through:

(A) the deterrent influence of the penalties hereinafter provided;

(B) the rehabilitation of those convicted of violations of this code; and

(C) such punishment as may be necessary to prevent likely recurrence of criminal behavior;

(2) by definition and grading of offenses to give fair warning of what is prohibited and of the consequences of violation;

(3) to prescribe penalties that are proportionate to the seriousness of offenses and that permit recognition of differences in rehabilitation possibilities among individual offenders;

(4) to safeguard conduct that is without guilt from condemnation as criminal;

(5) to guide and limit the exercise of official discretion in law enforcement to prevent arbitrary or oppressive treatment of persons suspected, accused, or convicted of offenses; and

(6) to define the scope of state interest in law enforcement against specific offenses and to systematize the exercise of state criminal jurisdiction.

Model Penal Code
(Official Draft 1962)

Section 210.6. Sentence of Death for Murder; Further Proceedings to Determine Sentence

(1) Death Sentence Excluded. When a defendant is found guilty of murder, the Court shall impose sentence for a felony of the first degree if it is satisfied that:

(a) none of the aggravating circumstances enumerated in Subsection (3) of this Section was established by the evidence at the trial or will be established if further proceedings are initiated under Subsection (2) of this Section; or

(b) substantial mitigating circumstances, established by the evidence at the trial, call for leniency; or

(c) the defendant, with the consent of the prosecuting attorney and the approval of the Court, pleaded guilty to murder as a felony of the first degree; or

(d) the defendant was under 18 years of age at the time of the commission of the crime; or

(e) the defendant's physical or mental condition calls for leniency; or

(f) although the evidence suffices to sustain the verdict, it does not foreclose all doubt respecting the defendant's guilt.

(2) Determination by Court or by Court and Jury. Unless the Court imposes sentence under Subsection (1) of this Section, it shall conduct a separate proceeding to determine whether the defendant should be sentenced for a felony of the first degree or sentenced to death. The proceeding shall be conducted before the Court alone if the defendant was convicted by a Court sitting without a jury or upon his plea of guilty or if the prosecuting attorney and the defendant waive a jury with respect to sentence. In other cases it shall be conducted before the Court sitting with the jury which determined the defendant's guilt or, if the Court for good cause shown discharges that jury, with a new jury empaneled for the purpose.

In the proceeding, evidence may be presented as to any matter that the Court deems relevant to sentence, including but not limited to the nature and circumstances of the crime, the defendant's character, background, history, mental and physical condition and any of the aggravating or mitigating circumstances enumerated in Subsections (3) and (4) of this Section. Any such evidence, not legally privileged, which the Court deems to have probative force, may be received, regardless of its admissibility under the exclusionary rules of evidence, provided that the defendant's counsel is accorded a fair opportunity to rebut such evidence. The prosecuting attorney and the defendant or his counsel shall be permitted to present argument for or against sentence of death.

The determination whether sentence of death shall be imposed shall be in the discretion of the Court, except that when the proceeding is conducted before the Court sitting with a jury, the Court shall not impose sentence of death unless it submits to the jury the issue whether the defendant should be sentenced to death or to imprisonment and the jury returns a verdict that the sentence should be death. If the jury is unable to reach a unanimous verdict, the Court shall dismiss the jury and impose sentence for a felony of the first degree.

The Court, in exercising its discretion as to sentence, and the jury, in determining upon its verdict, shall take into account the aggravating and mitigating circumstances enumerated in Subsections (3) and (4) and any other facts that it deems relevant, but it shall not impose or recommend sentence of death unless it finds one of the aggravating circumstances enumerated in Subsection (3) and further finds that there are no mitigating circumstances sufficiently substantial to call for leniency. When the issue is submitted to the jury, the Court shall so instruct and also shall inform the jury of the nature of the sentence of imprisonment that may be imposed, including its implication with respect to possible release upon parole, if the jury verdict is against sentence of death. . . .

(3) Aggravating Circumstances.

(a) The murder was committed by a convict under sentence of imprisonment.

(b) The defendant was previously convicted of another murder or of a felony involving the use or threat of violence to the person.

(c) At the time the murder was committed the defendant also committed another murder.

(d) The defendant knowingly created a great risk of death to many persons.

(e) The murder was committed while the defendant was engaged or was an accomplice in the commission of, or an attempt to commit, or flight after committing or attempting to commit robbery, rape or deviate sexual intercourse by force or threat of force, arson, burglary or kidnapping.

(f) The murder was committed for the purpose of avoiding or preventing a lawful arrest or effecting an escape from lawful custody.

(g) The murder was committed for pecuniary gain.

(h) The murder was especially heinous, atrocious or cruel, manifesting exceptional depravity.

(4) Mitigating Circumstances.

(a) The defendant has no significant history of prior criminal activity.

(b) The murder was committed while the defendant was under the influence of extreme mental or emotional disturbance.

(c) The victim was a participant in the defendant's homicidal conduct or consented to the homicidal act.

(d) The murder was committed under circumstances which the defendant believed to provide a moral justification or extenuation for his conduct.

(e) The defendant was an accomplice in a murder committed by another person and his participation in the homicidal act was relatively minor.

(f) The defendant acted under duress or under the domination of another person.

(g) At the time of the murder, the capacity of the defendant to appreciate the criminality [wrongfulness] of his conduct or to conform his conduct to the requirements of law was impaired as a result of mental disease or defect or intoxication.

(h) The youth of the defendant at the time of the crime.

● OVERVIEW OF THE DEATH PENALTY

The statistics below give an overview of the use of the death penalty in the United States. The debate over this controversial practice is the subject of the Discussion Materials below.

Sourcebook of Criminal Justice Statistics

(2000); online at http://www.albany.edu/sourcebook/

Table 7.1 **Prisoners executed under civil authority**
By race and offense, United States, 1930-97
(- represents zero)

	Total				White				Black				Other			
	Total	Murder	Rape	Other offenses[a]	Total	Murder	Rape	Other offenses	Total	Murder	Rape	Other offenses	Total	Murder	Rape	Other offenses
1997	74	74	-	-	45	45	-	-	27	27	-	-	2	2	-	-
1996	45	45	-	-	31	31	-	-	14	14	-	-	-	-	-	-
1995	56	56	-	-	33	33	-	-	22	22	-	-	1	1	-	-
1994	31	31	-	-	20	20	-	-	11	11	-	-	-	-	-	-
1993	38	38	-	-	23	23	-	-	14	14	-	-	1	1	-	-
1992	31	31	-	-	19	19	-	-	11	11	-	-	1	1	-	-
1991	14	14	-	-	7	7	-	-	7	7	-	-	-	-	-	-
1990	23	23	,	-	16	16	-	-	7	7	-	-	-	-	-	-
1989	16	16	-	-	8	8	-	-	8	8	-	-	-	-	-	-
1988	11	11	-	-	6	6	-	-	5	5	-	-	-	-	-	-
1987	25	25	-	-	13	13	-	-	12	12	-	-	-	-	-	-
1986	18	18	-	-	11	11	-	-	7	7	-	-	-	-	-	-
1985	18	18	-	-	11	11	-	-	7	7	-	-	-	-	-	-
1984	21	21	-	-	13	13	-	-	8	8	-	-	-	-	-	-
1983	5	5	-	-	4	4	-	-	1	1	-	-	-	-	-	-
1982	2	2	-	-	1	1	-	-	1	1	-	-	-	-	-	-
1981	1	1	-	-	1	1	-	-	-	-	-	-	-	-	-	-
1980	-	-	-	-	-	-	-	-	-	-	-	-	-	-	-	-
1979	2	2	-	-	2	2	-	-	-	-	-	-	-	-	-	-
1978	-	-	-	-	-	-	-	-	-	-	-	-	-	-	-	-
1977[b]	1	1	-	-	1	1	-	-	-	-	-	-	-	-	-	-
1967	2	2	-	-	1	1	-	-	1	1	-	-	-	-	-	-
1966	1	1	-	-	1	1	-	-	-	-	-	-	-	-	-	-
1965	7	7	-	-	6	6	-	-	1	1	-	-	-	-	-	-
1964	15	9	6	-	8	5	3	-	7	4	3	-	-	-	-	-
1963	21	18	2	1	13	12	-	1	8	6	2	-	-	-	-	-
1962	47	41	4	2	28	26	2	-	19	15	2	2	-	-	-	-
1961	42	33	8	1	20	18	1	1	22	15	7	-	-	-	-	-
1960	56	44	8	4	21	18	-	3	35	26	8	1	-	-	-	-
1959	49	41	8	-	16	15	1	-	33	26	7	-	-	-	-	-
1958	49	41	7	1	20	20	-	-	28	20	7	1	1	1	-	-
1957	65	54	10	1	34	32	2	-	31	22	8	1	-	-	-	-
1956	65	52	12	1	21	20	-	1	43	31	12	-	1	1	-	-
1955	76	65	7	4	44	41	1	2	32	24	6	2	-	-	-	-
1954	81	71	9	1	38	37	1	-	42	33	8	1	1	1	-	-
1953	62	51	7	4	30	25	1	4	31	25	6	-	1	1	-	-
1952	83	71	12	-	36	35	1	-	47	36	11	-	-	-	-	-
1951	105	87	17	1	57	55	2	-	47	31	15	1	1	1	-	-
1950	82	68	13	1	40	36	4	-	42	32	9	1	-	-	-	-
1949	119	107	10	2	50	49	-	1	67	56	10	1	2	2	-	-
1948	119	95	22	2	35	32	1	2	82	61	21	-	2	2	-	-
1947	153	129	23	1	42	40	2	-	111	89	21	1	-	-	-	-
1946	131	107	22	2	46	45	-	1	84	61	22	1	1	1	-	-
1945	117	90	26	1	41	37	4	-	75	52	22	1	1	1	-	-
1944	120	96	24	-	47	45	2	-	70	48	22	-	3	3	-	-
1943	131	118	13	-	54	54	-	-	74	63	11	-	3	1	2	-
1942	147	115	25	7	67	57	4	6	80	58	21	1	-	-	-	-
1941	123	102	20	1	59	55	4	-	63	46	16	1	1	1	-	-
1940	124	105	15	4	49	44	2	3	75	61	13	1	-	-	-	-
1939	160	145	12	3	80	79	-	1	77	63	12	2	3	3	-	-
1938	190	154	25	11	96	89	1	6	92	63	24	5	2	2	-	-
1937	147	133	13	1	69	67	2	-	74	62	11	1	4	4	-	-
1936	195	181	10	4	92	86	2	4	101	93	8	-	2	2	-	-
1935	199	184	13	2	119	115	2	2	77	66	11	-	3	3	-	-
1934	168	154	14	-	65	64	1	-	102	89	13	-	1	1	-	-
1933	160	151	7	2	77	75	1	1	81	74	6	1	2	2	-	-
1932	140	128	10	2	62	62	-	-	75	63	10	2	3	3	-	-
1931	153	137	15	1	77	76	1	-	72	57	14	1	4	4	-	-
1930	155	147	6	2	90	90	-	-	65	57	6	2	-	-	-	-
1930-97	4,291	3,666	455	70	2,016	1,929	48	39	2,228	1,792	405	31	47	45	2	-

[a]Includes 25 executed for armed robbery, 20 for kidnaping, 11 for burglary, 6 for sabotage, 6 for aggravated assault, and 2 for espionage.

[b]There were no executions from 1968 through 1976.

Source: U.S. Department of Justice, Bureau of Justice Statistics, *Correctional Populations in the United States, 1997*, NCJ 177613 (Washington, DC: U.S. Department of Justice, 2000), Table 7.26. Table adapted by SOURCEBOOK staff.

Table 7.2 **Prisoners under sentence of death**

By demographic characteristics, prior felony conviction history, and legal status, United States, on Dec. 31, 1996-2000[a]

	Percent of prisoners				
	1996	1997	1998	1999	2000
Sex					
Male	98.5%	98.7%	98.6%	98.6%	98.5%
Female	1.5	1.3	1.4	1.4	1.5
Race					
White	56.5	56.3	55.2	55.2	55.4
Black	41.9	42.2	43.0	42.9	42.7
Other	1.6	1.6	1.7	1.8	1.9
Hispanic origin					
Hispanic	8.8	9.2	10.0	10.2	10.6
Non-Hispanic	91.2	90.8	90.0	89.8	89.4
Age[b]					
17 years and younger	(c)	0	0	0	0
18 to 19 years	0.5	0.4	0.4	0.5	0.3
20 to 24 years	8.7	8.2	7.7	7.1	6.6
25 to 29 years	14.9	14.9	15.0	14.6	13.6
30 to 34 years	18.5	17.3	16.9	16.8	17.1
35 to 39 years	21.8	21.8	20.6	20.0	19.1
40 to 44 years	14.9	15.6	16.7	17.0	18.2
45 to 49 years	10.6	10.6	10.2	10.5	10.9
50 to 54 years	5.7	6.5	7.5	7.9	8.0
55 to 59 years	2.5	2.6	2.9	3.2	3.5
60 years and older	1.8	1.9	2.1	2.3	2.7
Education					
Grade 8 or less	14.4	14.2	14.3	13.9	14.4
Grades 9 to 11	37.5	37.6	37.6	37.7	37.3
High school graduate/GED	37.8	38.0	38.0	38.2	38.2
Any college	10.2	10.1	10.1	10.1	10.1
Marital status					
Married	24.9	24.5	24.0	22.9	22.6
Divorced or separated	21.3	21.3	20.8	21.2	21.0
Widowed	2.7	2.6	2.7	2.8	2.8
Never married	51.1	51.5	52.5	53.0	53.6
Prior felony conviction history					
Prior felony conviction	65.7	65.3	65.0	64.1	64.0
No prior felony conviction	34.3	34.7	35.0	35.9	36.0
Prior homicide conviction history					
Prior homicide conviction	8.6	8.6	8.6	8.4	8.1
No prior homicide conviction	91.4	91.4	91.4	91.6	91.9
Legal status at time of capital offense					
Charges pending	7.3	7.6	7.2	7.4	7.1
Probation	10.0	10.1	9.9	10.0	10.1
Parole	20.0	19.5	18.1	17.9	17.6
Prison escapee	1.4	1.3	1.3	1.3	1.2
Incarcerated	2.4	2.6	2.9	2.8	2.7
Other status	1.1	1.0	0.9	0.7	0.6
None	57.7	58.0	59.7	60.0	60.6

Note: Thirty-eight States and the Federal Government had death penalty statutes in effect at yearend 1996-2000. Percents are based on those cases for which data were reported. The U.S. military also has a death penalty provision, but the Bureau of Justice Statistics does not collect data for persons under military death sentence.

[a]Percents may not add to 100 because of rounding.

[b]The youngest person under sentence of death in 1996 was a black male in Nevada born in May 1979 and sentenced to death in June 1996; in 1997, a black male in Alabama born in November 1979 and sentenced to death in October 1997; in 1998, a black male in Alabama born in July 1980 and sentenced to death in December 1998; in 1999, a black male in Texas born in December 1981 and sentenced to death in November 1999; in 2000, a white male in Arizona born in April 1982 and sentenced to death in October 2000. The oldest person under sentence of death during the years 1996 to 2000 was a white male in Arizona born in September 1915 and sentenced to death in June 1983.

[c]Less than 0.1%.

Source: U.S. Department of Justice, Bureau of Justice Statistics, *Capital Punishment 1996*, Bulletin NCJ-167031, p. 8, Table 7; p. 9; p. 10, Table 9; *1997*, Bulletin NCJ-172881, p. 8, Table 7; p. 9; p. 10, Table 9; *1998*, Bulletin NCJ 179012, p. 8, Table 7; p. 9; p. 10, Table 9; *1999*, Bulletin NCJ 184795, p. 8, Table 7; p. 9; p. 10, Table 9; *2000*, Bulletin NCJ 190598, p. 8, Table 7; p. 9; p. 10, Table 9 (Washington, DC: U.S. Department of Justice). Table adapted by SOURCEBOOK staff.

Table 7.3 **Arrests**

By offense charged, age group, and race, United States, 2000

(9,017 agencies; 2000 estimated population 182,090,101)

| | Total arrests | | | | | Percent[a] | | | | |
Offense charged	Total	White	Black	American Indian or Alaskan Native	Asian or Pacific Islander	Total	White	Black	American Indian or Alaskan Native	Asian or Pacific Islander
Total	9,068,977	6,324,006	2,528,368	112,192	104,411	100.0%	69.7%	27.9%	1.2%	1.2%
Murder and nonnegligent manslaughter	8,683	4,231	4,238	87	127	100.0	48.7	48.8	1.0	1.5
Forcible rape	17,859	11,381	6,089	197	192	100.0	63.7	34.1	1.1	1.1
Robbery	72,149	31,921	38,897	445	886	100.0	44.2	53.9	0.6	1.2
Aggravated assault	315,729	200,634	107,494	3,542	4,059	100.0	63.5	34.0	1.1	1.3
Burglary	188,726	131,049	53,573	1,787	2,317	100.0	69.4	28.4	0.9	1.2
Larceny-theft	779,166	519,671	236,801	9,916	12,778	100.0	66.7	30.4	1.3	1.6
Motor vehicle theft	98,318	54,490	40,886	1,099	1,843	100.0	55.4	41.6	1.1	1.9
Arson	10,634	8,121	2,305	99	109	100.0	76.4	21.7	0.9	1.0
Violent crime[b]	414,420	248,167	156,718	4,271	5,264	100.0	59.9	37.8	1.0	1.3
Property crime[c]	1,076,844	713,331	333,565	12,901	17,047	100.0	66.2	31.0	1.2	1.6
Total Crime Index[d]	1,491,264	961,498	490,283	17,172	22,311	100.0	64.5	32.9	1.2	1.5
Other assaults	855,536	564,571	269,736	11,695	9,534	100.0	66.0	31.5	1.4	1.1
Forgery and counterfeiting	70,828	48,197	21,227	421	983	100.0	68.0	30.0	0.6	1.4
Fraud	211,984	142,684	66,672	1,173	1,455	100.0	67.3	31.5	0.6	0.7
Embezzlement	12,539	7,975	4,281	51	232	100.0	63.6	34.1	0.4	1.9
Stolen property; buying, receiving, possessing	78,429	46,233	30,690	579	927	100.0	58.9	39.1	0.7	1.2
Vandalism	184,010	139,662	39,779	2,573	1,996	100.0	75.9	21.6	1.4	1.1
Weapons; carrying, possessing, etc.	104,996	64,410	38,596	776	1,214	100.0	61.3	36.8	0.7	1.2
Prostitution and commercialized vice	61,347	35,567	24,222	514	1,044	100.0	58.0	39.5	0.8	1.7
Sex offenses (except forcible rape and prostitution)	60,936	45,317	14,149	668	802	100.0	74.4	23.2	1.1	1.3
Drug abuse violations	1,039,086	667,485	358,571	5,547	7,483	100.0	64.2	34.5	0.5	0.7
Gambling	7,149	2,195	4,607	29	318	100.0	30.7	64.4	0.4	4.4
Offenses against family and children	90,502	61,212	26,805	931	1,554	100.0	67.6	29.6	1.0	1.7
Driving under the influence	900,089	793,696	86,194	11,855	8,344	100.0	88.2	9.6	1.3	0.9
Liquor laws	433,637	371,186	46,107	13,091	3,253	100.0	85.6	10.6	3.0	0.8
Drunkenness	421,859	357,283	57,806	4,633	2,137	100.0	84.7	13.7	1.1	0.5
Disorderly conduct	419,408	273,884	136,573	6,030	2,921	100.0	65.3	32.6	1.4	0.7
Vagrancy	21,967	11,772	9,524	562	109	100.0	53.6	43.4	2.6	0.5
All other offenses (except traffic)	2,400,906	1,579,231	758,669	31,441	31,565	100.0	65.8	31.6	1.3	1.3
Suspicion	3,675	2,535	1,086	11	43	100.0	69.0	29.6	0.3	1.2
Curfew and loitering law violations	105,563	76,233	26,065	1,165	2,100	100.0	72.2	24.7	1.1	2.0
Runaways	93,267	71,180	16,726	1,275	4,086	100.0	76.3	17.9	1.4	4.4

Table 7.4 **Reported reasons for favoring the death penalty for persons convicted of murder**

United States, 2001

Question: "Why do you favor the death penalty for persons convicted of murder?"

Reason for favoring

An eye for an eye/they took a life/fits the crime	48%
Save taxpayers money/cost associated with prison	20
Deterrent for potential crimes/set an example	10
They deserve it	6
Support/believe in death penalty	6
Depends on the type of crime they commit	6
They will repeat their crime/keep them from repeating it	6
Biblical reasons	3
Relieves prison overcrowding	2
If there's no doubt the person committed the crime	2
Life sentences don't always mean life in prison	2
Don't believe they can be rehabilitated	2
Serve justice	1
Fair punishment	1
Would help/benefit families of victims	1
Other	3
No opinion	1

Note: This question was asked only of the respondents who answered "yes, in favor" to the question presented in table [2.64].

Source: The Gallup Organization, Inc., **The Gallup Poll** [Online]. Available: http://www.gallup.com/poll/releases/pr010302.asp [Mar. 2, 2001]. Table adapted by SOURCEBOOK staff. Reprinted by permission.

◉ DISCUSSION MATERIALS

Should Capital Punishment Be Allowed?

The following discussion materials begin with two articles by Hugo Bedau; the first summarizes the development of the capital punishment debate and identifies the key arguments among the distributive principles. Bedau then argues against capital punishment, pointing specifically to the racially skewed execution rate in the first excerpt and describing the problem of false positives in capital punishment in the second. In response, Ernest van den Haag offers a retributive justification for capital punishment even in the face of error. In examining the implementation of capital punishment, Elizabeth Rapaport offers a provocative feminist perspective, noting the disparity in men and women executed and the traditional rejection of domestic violence killings as capital murder cases. Finally, Robert Weisberg examines optimal execution rates to satisfy the criminal justice principles and comments on the current trend of sentencing many but executing few.

Hugo A. Bedau, Arguments For and Against Capital Punishment
Encyclopedia of Crime and Justice 138-141 (S. Kadish ed., 1983)

With the rise of rationalist thought in European culture during the Renaissance and Enlightenment (1550-1750), and the concurrent decline in an exclusively religious foundation for moral principles, philosophers and jurists increasingly lent their support to the doctrine of "the rights of man" as the foundation for constitutional law and public morality. The most influential continental, British, and American Enlightenment thinkers—John Locke, Jean-Jacques Rousseau, Cesare Beccaria, William Blackstone, Immanuel Kant, and Thomas Jefferson—all agreed that the first and foremost of these rights is "the right to life." Few of these thinkers, however, opposed the death penalty (Beccaria was the notable exception); most endorsed it explicitly. They argued, typically, that since each person is born with a "natural" right to life, murder must be viewed as a violation of that right; accordingly, executing the murderer is not wrong since the murderer has forfeited his own right to life by virtue of his crime.

Modern thinkers, under the influence of the human rights provisions advocated by the United Nations in various resolutions, declarations, and covenants, have sought to appeal to a more complex line of considerations embedded in other human rights, as well as in the idea of the right to life. This view was advocated most prominently in the 1970s by Amnesty International, the human rights organization awarded the Nobel Peace Prize in 1978 for its worldwide campaign against torture. On this view, the death penalty violates human rights because (1) its administration is inevitably surrounded by arbitrary practices and unreliable procedures that violate offenders' rights; (2) erroneous executions are an irrevocable and irremediable violation of the right to life; and (3) there are less severe and equally effective alternatives—notably, long-term imprisonment.

In the United States since the 1960s, these themes have been argued most vigorously by the American Civil Liberties Union and by attorneys for the NAACP Legal Defense and Educational Fund and the Southern Poverty Law Center on behalf of nonwhite and indigent clients accused of murder. Their basic argument has been that the death penalty as it is actually used in contemporary American criminal justice systems is inherently and irredeemably class- and race-biased, so that a self-respecting civilized society cannot afford to employ it.

Racism

The central evidence for the main criticism — racist administration of the death penalty — comes from research conducted in several states, particularly in the South, in which it has been shown that a person is more likely to be sentenced to death if the victim is white than if nonwhite. These results are consistent with the generally acknowledged results of earlier research on the death penalty for rape, in which it was shown that the overwhelming preponderance of death penalties for black offenders could be explained only by the race of the offender taken in conjunction with that of the victim: the death penalty was highly probable only if the victim was white.

Defenders of the death penalty have, or could have, replied as follows: (1) all current capital laws are color-blind and impose equal liability on all persons regardless of race, color, class, or sex of offender or of victim; (2) racism in the current administration of the death penalty cannot be inferred from evidence relating to the admittedly racist practices of the distant past; (3) the evidence tending to show that the race of the victim is the chief explanation for whether an offender is sentenced to death (white victim) or to prison (non-white victim) is incomplete and inconclusive; (4) since justice requires that all murderers be sentenced to death and executed, some racial bias (if there is any) in the day-to-day administration of capital punishment is merely another case of the regrettable but tolerable imperfect enforcement of a just law; and (5) the deterrent and incapacitating effects of executions provided by even a somewhat racially biased death penalty are better for society than are the results of a less potent (even if less biased racially) alternative mode of punishment.

Retribution

Many defenders of the death penalty rest their position on principles of retributive justice and the appropriateness of moral indignation at murder, which they believe can be expressed adequately only by punishing that crime (and others, if any, no less heinous) by death. Whether such retributive reasoning has its origins in a passion for vengeance is less important than whether the principles to which it appeals are sound. Most opponents of the death penalty do not dispute (1) the principle that convicted offenders deserve to be punished; (2) the principle that a suitable punishment is, like a crime itself, some form of harsh treatment; and (3) the principle that the severity of the punishment should be proportional to the gravity of the offense. What is disputed is whether the third principle *requires* the death penalty for murder (and other crimes) or whether this principle is merely *consistent* with such a punishment, so that the further step in favor of death as the ideally fitting penalty must be taken by reference to other (perhaps nonretributive) considerations. Making the punishment fit the crime in any literal sense is either impossible or morally unacceptable, given the horrible nature of many murders. Interpreting the third principle so that it entails, "a life for a life" thus verges on begging the question. As a result, the focus of controversy between proponents and opponents of the death penalty who agree in arguing the issue primarily on grounds of retributive justice is on how closely it is necessary and desirable to model a punishment on the crime for which it is meted out....

Utility and the Prevention of Crime

Quite apart from considerations rooted in principles of retributive justice or of constitutional law, arguments for and against the death penalty often proceed by reference to essentially utilitarian considerations, in which the consequences for overall social welfare—especially as this involves the reduction of crime—are the criteria to which both sides appeal. For example, defenders of the death penalty have argued that executions are a far less costly mode of punishment than any alternative. Abolitionists have replied that this is untrue if one takes into account the enormous cost to society of the extremely complex and lengthy litigation that surrounds a capital case, beginning with the search for an acceptable jury and culminating in postsentencing appeals and hearings in both state and federal courts. The chief issue of utilitarian concern, however, has always been whether the death penalty is an effective means of preventing crime and whether it is more effective than the alternative of imprisonment.

Incapacitation

Both sides concede that execution is a perfectly incapacitative punishment and that in this respect it is preferable to imprisonment. How much difference this makes to the crime rate is a matter of sharp dispute: the issue turns on (1) whether persons who have been executed would have committed further capital (or other) offenses if they had not been executed, and (2) whether persons convicted and imprisoned for capital crimes but not executed will commit further capital offenses when and if released. There is no direct evidence available regarding the first question. Evidence relevant to the second question from parole and recidivism records indicates that a very small number of capital offenders commit subsequent crimes. Roughly 1 convicted homicide offender out of every 340 such persons released from prison commits another homicide within the first year after release. Defenders of the death penalty often argue that it is inexcusable for society not to take measures guaranteeing that a convicted murderer is incapable of repeating his crime. Abolitionists argue that the alternatives open to society, if it abandons the present system of parole and release practices, are even worse: either society must execute *all* convicted murderers, at intolerable moral cost (these thousands of executions are unnecessary, since so few murderers recidivate), or society must imprison *all* convicted murderers until their natural death, also intolerable because of the prison management problems that such a policy would create.

General Deterrence

Still more important and controversial is the adequacy of the death penalty as a general deterrent. During the 1950s, evidence based on several different comparisons convinced most criminologists that there was no superior deterrent effect associated with the death penalty. The comparisons were between homicide rates in given states before, during, and after abolition; homicide rates in given jurisdictions before and after executions; homicide rates in adjacent states, some with and others without the use of capital punishment; and rates of police killings in abolitionist and death-penalty jurisdictions. In the 1970s, this conclusion was challenged by research which used new methods borrowed from econometrics and which asserted that each execution in the United States between 1930 and 1969 prevented between eight and twenty murders. Subsequent investigators, however, soon showed that the alleged deterrent effect was an artifact of arbitrary if not dubious statistical methods. A panel of the National Academy of Science (NAS) went even further and expressed extreme skepticism about the results of all available research studies; none, the panel said, provided any useful evidence on the deterrent effect of capital punishment. No reliable scientific investigations support the common sense inference that since the death penalty is more severe than long-term imprisonment, the death penalty must be a better deterrent.

It is difficult to say whether skepticism (as recommended by the NAS panel) or a more positive conclusion against the deterrent efficacy of the death penalty is justified by the totality of all research. Some research, based on the study of executions and homicides in New York, has even suggested the initially implausible hypothesis that executions may actually exert a "brutalizing" effect upon society and that instead of deterring murders it incites them. What does seem true is that any argument for the death penalty based primarily on the claim of its superior deterrent efficacy is untenable. It is worth noting that the Supreme Court, in its series of death-penalty decisions during the 1970s, skirted this controversy and never spoke with a clear and unanimous voice one way or the other. (The sole exception is its decision in *Gregg*, where the majority of the Court conjectured that in such cases as "calculated murders," for example, terrorist attacks, sanctions less severe than death may not be adequate.) How much evidence proponents of the death penalty should be expected to produce in favor of the superior deterrent power of executions is also unclear, and perhaps imponderable.

Hugo A. Bedau, Innocence and the Death Penalty
The Death Penalty in America: Current Controversies 344, 345, 350-359 (H. Bedau ed., 1997)

The most conclusive evidence that innocent people are condemned to death under modern death sentencing procedures comes from the surprisingly large number of people whose convictions have been overturned and who have been freed from death row. [In the period 1973-1992], at least 48 people have been released from prison after serving time on death row ... with significant evidence of their innocence. In 43 of these cases, the defendant was subsequently acquitted, pardoned, or charges were dropped. [O]ne defendant was released when the parole board became convinced of his innocence.

[Professor Bedau describes the circumstances for each of the 48 cases. Many involved complete factual innocence — definitive proof that the defendant was in no way involved in the offense. Some involved what might be termed "legal innocence" — the defendant was not definitively exonerated but there was prosecutorial misconduct and/or incompetent defense, together with insufficient evidence of actual guilt. In the latter cases, he notes, there may have been "a lingering doubt" about complete innocence, but the evidence fell far short of proving guilt beyond a reasonable doubt. Bedau then summarizes the factors that led to conviction and a death sentence in these cases.]

. . . The cases outlined above might convey a reassuring impression that although mistakes are made, the system of appeals and reviews will ferret out such cases prior to execution. In one sense that is occasionally true: the system of appeals sometimes allows for correction of factual errors. But there is another sense in which these cases illustrate the inadequacies of the system. [Many of t]hese men were found innocent *despite the system* and only as a result of [unusual media attention or other] extraordinary efforts not generally available to death row defendants.

Indeed, in some cases, these men were found innocent as a result of sheer luck. In the case of Walter McMillian, his volunteer outside counsel had obtained from the prosecutors an audio tape of one of the key witnesses' statements incriminating Mr. McMillian. After listening to the statement, the attorney flipped the tape over to see if anything was on the other side. It was only then that he heard the same witness complaining that he was being pressured to frame Mr. McMillian. With that fortuitous break, the whole case against McMillian began to fall apart. . . .

Most of the releases from death row over the past twenty years came only after many years and many failed appeals. . . . Too often, the reviews afforded death row inmates on appeal and habeas corpus do not offer a meaningful opportunity to present claims of innocence. . . . After trial, the legal system becomes locked in a battle over procedural issues rather than a re-examination of guilt. . . . Accounts which report that a particular case has been appealed numerous times before many judges may be misleading. [W]hen Roger Keith Coleman was executed in Virginia [in 1992,] it was reported that his last appeal to the Supreme Court "was Coleman's 16th round in court." However, the Supreme Court had earlier declared that Coleman's constitutional claims were barred because his prior attorneys had filed an appeal too late in 1986. His evidence was similarly excluded from review in state court as well. Instead, Coleman's innocence was debated only in the news media and considerable doubt concerning his guilt went with him to his execution. . . .

Investigation of innocence ends after execution. . . . Judging by past experience, a substantial number of death row inmates are innocent and there is a high risk that some of them will be executed. The danger is enhanced by the failure to provide adequate counsel and the narrowing of opportunities to raise the issue of innocence on appeal. Once an execution occurs, the error is final.

Ernest van den Haag, Punishing Criminals
219-220 (1975)

Errors would not justify the abolition of the death penalty for retributionists. Many social policies have unintended effects that are statistically certain, irrevocable, unjust and deadly. Automobile traffic unintentionally kills innocent victims; so does surgery (and most medicines); so does the death penalty. These activities are justified, nevertheless, because benefits (including justice) are felt to outweigh the statistical certainty of unintentionally killing innocents. The certain death of innocents argues for abolishing the death penalty no more than for abolishing surgery or automobiles. Injustice justifies abolition only if the losses to justice outweigh the gains—if more innocents are lost than saved by imposing the death penalty compared to whatever net result alternatives (such as no punishment or life imprisonment) would produce. If innocent victims of future murderers are saved by virtue of the death penalty imposed on convicted murderers, it must be retained, just as surgery is, even though some innocents will be lost through miscarriage of justice—as long as more innocent lives are saved than lost. More justice is done with than without the death penalty. . . .

Other Discussion Materials

Elizabeth Rapaport, The Death Penalty and Gender Discrimination
25 Law and Society Review 367-368, 369, 377-381 (1991)

. . . A gross comparison of the death-sentencing rates for men and women suggests that women convicted of murder are under-represented on death row. Two percent of men but only one tenth of 1 percent of women convicted of murder are condemned to die.

For a feminist to raise the issue of gender discrimination and capital punishment is not an altogether comfortable undertaking. At worst, it suggests a campaign to exterminate a few more wretched sisters. In my view, however, the issue is worth confronting. The reputed leniency that women receive with respect to death sentencing supports the view widely held in our society that women are incapable of achieving, nor are they in fact held to, the same standards of personal responsibility as are men. Although there may well be fields of endeavor in which the most profound forms of equality call for recognition of difference, equal democratic citizenship can proceed from no other premise than that of equal personal responsibility for decisions and actions. The chivalry from which women supposedly benefit is too costly: In ideological coin it is supposed to be repaid with tacit recognition of the moral inferiority of females and our lack of aptitude for full citizenship. As a matter of both logic and political necessity, then, feminists must embrace either gender-neutral evenhandedness or abolitionism. . . .

Does the sparseness of women on death row result from a chivalrous disinclination to mete out death to women under circumstances in which men would be consigned to this fate? Or does the apparent underrepresentation of women have an explanation other than gender discrimination in our favor?....

. . . The crimes whose prohibition we solemnize by treating as death eligible are those which, overwhelmingly, are predatory crimes committed by men against other men or against women and children not their own. The death penalty, therefore, is a dramatic symbol of the lesser dignity attached to the security and peace of the domestic sphere as compared with the realms of commerce and intercourse among nonintimates. . . .

Domestic crimes may . . . become capital cases if they are regarded as especially brutal crimes or if they are also pecuniary crimes. But the paradigmatic domestic killing, arising out of hot anger at someone who is capable, as it were by definition, of calling out painful and sudden emotion in his or her killer, is virtually the antithesis of a capital murder. Yet there are features of domestic homicides that could plausibly be regarded as among the most reprehensible crimes: They involve the betrayal of familial trust and responsibility on which not only domestic peace but presumably our civilization depends, as much it depends on honoring the law of mine and thine and respecting the authority of the state. They also have characteristics that could be read as inherent extreme brutality. The victims of family murders are typically especially vulnerable to their killers because of physical weakness and psychological dependency. Often the victims have been the objects of prior and habitual violence by their killers.

Whether or not one endorses or opposes capital punishment on moral or other grounds, and whether or not one would wish to see its domain enlarged for any purpose, there is, from a feminist point of view, an invidious subordination of the interests of women involved in the failure of the statutes to attach our society's most profound condemnation to crimes that destroy the domestic peace. These murders are also far more likely to have women and children as victims than are economic crimes. Our law reveals a disposition to regard killing a stranger for gain as more heinous than killing a spouse or child in anger. This hierarchy of opprobrium both privileges the interests of men over those of women and children and supports patriarchal values. . . .

The kinds of crimes that are most likely to result in death sentences — felony murders and other predatory murders — are most likely to be committed by men against other men and against women and children in other men's families. Of stranger murders, 96 percent are committed by males; 80 percent of the victims in stranger murders are also male. Women are much more likely to be victimized by family — especially current and former spouses and lovers — than are men. In 1988, 31 percent of female victims but only 5 percent of male victims were accounted for in this fashion. Children, especially young children, are even more likely to be murdered at home. Child abuse fatalities have been estimated to exceed 1,000 per year.

Although women are more likely to be victimized by intimates than men, they are also more likely to have intimates for victims. Indeed it is only in the domain of family murder that women kill nearly as many victims as do men. Nonetheless, it is in the interests of women that society treat domestic murder in its most aggravated forms as among the most heinous crimes.

Creating parity of opprobrium for the worst cases of domestic homicide — let us say by elevating serious and habitual abuse of a spouse or child to the status of a felony and including this felony among the enumerated felonies rendering a homicide eligible for capital sentencing — challenges directly the proposition that violence in the home, from which women and children suffer disproportionately, is less reprehensible than violence directed at a luckless clerk on night duty at a convenience store. The supposition that predatory violence is more reprehensible than domestic violence is a symptom or effect of the ancient family privacy doctrine that has supported male domestic authority, and the parental authority of both sexes, at the price of tolerating if not encouraging a culture of domestic violence. . . .

One piece of evidence that on the surface suggests social valuing of female victims is the finding that murderers of women are more likely to be death sentenced than murderers of men. We cannot, however, infer from this finding that the higher likelihood of a death sentence reflects a societal judgment that murders of female victims are in all circumstances more serious than murders of male victims. The greater likelihood that a female victim's killer will be death sentenced reflects, at least, the opprobrium with which we regard rape murder. Even if it proves to be the case that felony murderers of other types who kill female victims are at greater risk of a death sentence than those who kill males, we can conclude nothing from such a finding about the propensity of domestic killers of females to be death sentenced. The claim I am making here is that the capital statutes do not single out domestic killing as especially reprehensible; indeed, they single out crimes generally thought of as virtually opposite or complementary in type for that designation. If, however, it should prove to be the case that all predatory stranger killing of females, not merely rape murder, puts murderers at greater risk of a death sentence, the result would be compatible with the feminist analysis advanced here: It is congruent with patriarchal values, and offensive to feminist values, that violence against women belonging to others be more heavily sanctioned than violence against your own women.

Robert Weisberg, Deregulating Death
Supreme Court Review 303, 386-387 (1983)

There may never be a social consensus on the role of capital punishment, but a social engineer might try to identify a sort of culturally optimal number of executions that would best compromise among the competing demands made by the different constituencies of the criminal justice system.

The most obvious approach is to have some executions, but not very many. A small number of executions offers a logical, if crude, compromise between the extreme groups who want either no executions or as many as possible. It would also satisfy those who believe that execution is appropriate only for a small number of especially blameworthy killers, at least if the right ones are selected. It might further satisfy those who do not believe there is a discernible and small category of most blameworthy killers, but who believe that a small number of executions might adequately serve general deterrence and make a necessary political statement about society's attitude toward crime. But our hypothetical social engineer would want to consider other points of view or factors as well in designing his culturally optimal number. Too many executions might have the opposite effect of morally offending people with the spectacle of a blood-bath. On the other hand, if the number were too low in comparison with the number of murders, capital punishment might not serve general deterrence. Or if we execute too few people, we may not produce a big enough statistical sample to prove that the death penalty meets any tests of rationality and nondiscrimination.

We might therefore imagine a socially stabilizing design for the death penalty which leads to just the right number of executions to keep the art form alive, but not so many as to cause excessive social cost. It is, of course, fanciful to imagine any political institution having the will or authority to take a systematic approach to executions. Under the current capital punishment laws, judges have some opportunity to manipulate the rate of execution. Legislators theoretically can affect the execution rate by changing the substantive laws of murder and punishment. But between the constitutional restrictions on death sentencing and the voters' general demand for capital punishment, legislators in most states probably do not have a great deal of room to maneuver. A prosecutor can ensure that any given murder defendant will not face execution, but because he cannot control the jury or judges he can never guarantee that a defendant is executed. A juror can at best control the rate of execution in one case. But judges, especially appellate judges, have a good deal of freedom to control the number of executions within the pool of capital claimants who come before them.

Viewing the statistics of the last decade, one might imagine that in a rough, systematic way, judges have indeed manipulated death penalty doctrine to achieve a culturally optimal number of executions. That number is very close to zero, but it must be viewed in light of a very different number—the number of death sentences.

If we somewhat fancifully treat the judiciary as a single and calculating mind, we could say that it has conceived a fiendishly clever way of satisfying the competing demands on the death penalty: We will sentence vast numbers of murderers to death, but execute virtually none of them. Simply having many death sentences can satisfy many proponents of the death penalty who demand capital punishment, because in a vague way they want the law to make a statement of social authority and control. It will also satisfy jurors who want to make that statement in a specific case with the reassurance that the death sentence will never really be carried out. And we can at the same time avoid arousing great numbers of people who would vent their moral and political opposition to capital punishment only on the occasion of actual executions. Once a murderer enters the apparently endless appellate process, much of the public ceases to pay attention.

Homicide: Doctrines of Mitigation

Just as unintentional killings can sometimes be aggravated to murder, intentional killings can sometimes be mitigated to manslaughter. The common law doctrine of provocation can so mitigate, as can mental illness short of insanity. These older doctrines are carried forward in broader form in modern codes as the doctrine of extreme mental or emotional disturbance. The point of all this is to identify those cases in which the circumstances of the killing, while still deserving of serious punishment, are meaningfully different from cases of killings where no such mitigation is present. That is, the doctrines of mitigation serve as much to reinforce the greater condemnation deserved by non-mitigation cases as to reduce the condemnation in mitigation cases.

◆ THE CASE OF JOHN GOUNAGIAS

Like many Greek immigrants living in Camas, Washington, John Gounagias and Dionisios Grounas work at the local paper mill. They also room together and frequent a local coffeehouse, a popular gathering place for the Greek community. On April 18, 1914, the day before Greek Easter, Gounagias and two friends are leafing through a Greek magazine when they come across an ad for a thirty-two-caliber revolver and other miscellaneous articles. Gounagias thinks he sees a bargain and orders the gun.

The next day, on Greek Easter, both Gounagias and Grounas are at home. Gounagias is drinking beer and becomes extremely drunk, almost to the point of passing out. The two men get into an argument, during which Grounas insults Gounagias and his wife, who is still living in Greece. Later, when Gounagias is lying helplessly on the floor in a semiconscious state, Grounas forcibly sodomizes him with an object and leaves the house. After recovering his senses, Gounagias gathers his things and moves out, relocating to another house nearby. The following day, he

Figure 33 **Postcard of the Camas Mill, circa 1918.**
(Camas-Washougal Historical Society)

happens upon Grounas and confronts him. Grounas just laughs, "You're all right. It did not hurt you." Gounagias pleads with him not to tell their countrymen in order to avoid the humiliation that he knows it would bring. Grounas is unmoved. Wherever Gounagias goes in Camas during the next days, his countrymen suggest by lewd gestures and remarks that they have been told what happened. Under the constant and brutal ridicule, Gounagias develops severe, debilitating headaches.

About two weeks later, the revolver Gounagias ordered arrives. He buys ammunition for it and stores it in a slit in the underside of his mattress. Meanwhile, his countrymen, encouraged by Grounas, continue to taunt him about his being sodomized. A week after receiving the gun, Gounagias wakes up with such an excruciating headache that he cannot go to work. He tries to distract himself by going to the billiards hall, visiting the coffee house, and playing cards with the local baker. As the afternoon wears on though, he becomes so depressed that he goes to the river intending to commit suicide, but balks. He then visits some friends. Afterward, Gounagias meets a man from the old country and invites him back to his house, where they converse for quite some time. Around 11 p.m. he decides to return to the coffeehouse, but is barely inside before a group of rowdy Greeks publicly taunt him again about being sodomized. Gounagias finally snaps. He rushes out, enraged and full of vengeance, wishing to kill Grounas. Quickly returning home, he retrieves the gun, loads it, and runs up the hill to Grounas' house. Being dark inside, Gounagias lights a match to find his way, and discovers Grounas asleep in bed. Without hesitating, Gounagias shoots him in the head, firing five shots, emptying the revolver. He returns home, removing the empty shells on the way, and puts the gun back inside the mattress. He is arrested shortly after he gets into bed.

1. Relying only upon your own intuitions of justice, what liability and punishment, if any, does John Gounagias deserve?

N	0	1	2	3	4	5	6	7	8	9	10	11
☐	☐	☐	☐	☐	☐	☐	☐	☐	☐	☐	☐	☐
no liability	liability but no punishment	1 day	2 wks	2 mo	6 mo	1 yr	3 yrs	7 yrs	15 yrs	30 yrs	life imprisonment	death

2. What liability, if any, under the then-existing statutes?
3. What liability, if any, under the Model Penal Code?

■ THE LAW

Remington and Ballinger's Annotated Codes and Statutes of Washington
(1914)

Crimes and Punishments, Title XIV

Section 2390 Homicide — Defined and Classified

Homicide is the killing of a human being by the act, procurement or omission of another and is either (1) murder, (2) manslaughter, (3) excusable homicide or (4) justifiable homicide.

Section 2392 Murder in the First Degree

The killing of a human being, unless it is excusable or justifiable, is murder in the first degree when committed either —

(1) With a premeditated design to effect the death of the person killed, or of another; or

(2) By an act imminently dangerous to others and evincing a depraved mind, regardless of human life, without a premeditated design to effect the death of any individual; or

(3) Without a design to effect death, be a person engaged in the commission of, or in an attempt to commit, or in withdrawing from the scene of a robbery, rape, burglary, larceny or arson in the first degree; or

(4) By maliciously interfering or tampering with or obstructing any switch, frog, rail, roadbed, sleeper, viaduct, bridge, trestle, culvert, embankment, structure, or appliance pertaining to or connected with any railway, or any engine, motor or car of such railway.

Murder in the first degree shall be punishable by death or by imprisonment in the state penitentiary for life, in the discretion of the court.

Section 2393 Murder in the Second Degree

The killing of a human being, unless it is excusable or justifiable, is murder in the second degree when —

(1) Committed with the design to effect the death of the person killed or of another, but without premeditation; or

(2) When perpetrated by a person engaged in the commission of, or in an attempt to commit, or in withdrawing from the scene of, a felony other than those enumerated in section 2392.

Murder in the second degree shall be punished by imprisonment in the state penitentiary for not less than three years.

Section 2395 Manslaughter

In any case other than those specified in sections 2392, 2393 and 2394, homicide, not being excusable or justifiable, is manslaughter.

Manslaughter is punishable by imprisonment in the state penitentiary for not more than twenty years, or by imprisonment in the county jail for not more than one year, or by a fine of not more than one thousand dollars, or by both fine and imprisonment.

Section 2404 Homicide, When Excusable

Homicide is excusable when committed by accident or misfortune in doing any lawful act by lawful means, with ordinary caution and without any unlawful intent.

Section 2405 Justifiable Homicide by Public Officer

Homicide is justifiable when committed by a public officer, or person acting under his command and in his aid, in the following cases:

(1) In obedience to the judgment of a competent court.

(2) When necessary to overcome actual resistance to the execution of the legal process, mandate or order of a court or officer, or in the discharge of a legal duty.

(3) When necessary in retaking an escaped or rescued prisoner who has been committed, arrested for, or convicted of a felony; or in arresting a person who has committed a felony and is fleeing from justice; or in attempting, by lawful ways or means, to apprehend a person for a felony actually committed; or in lawfully suppressing a riot or preserving the peace.

Section 2406 Homicide by Other Person, When Justifiable

Homicide is also justifiable when committed either—

(1) In the lawful defense of the slayer, or his or her husband, wife, parent, child, brother or sister, or any other person in his presence or company, when there is reasonable ground to apprehend a design on the part of the person slain to commit a felony or to do some great personal injury to the slayer or to any such person, and there is imminent danger of such design being accomplished; or

(2) In the actual resistance of an attempt to commit a felony upon the slayer, in his presence, or upon or in a dwelling, or other place of abode, in which he is.

Section 2299 Common Law to Supplement Statute

The provisions of the common law relating to the commission of crime and the punishment thereof, in so far as not inconsistent with the institutions and statutes of this state, shall supplement all penal statutes of this state and all persons offending against the same shall be tried in the superior courts of the state.

Procedure in Criminal Actions, Title XIII

Section 2173 "Criminally Insane," Defined — Mental Irresponsibility

Any person who shall have committed a crime while insane, or in a condition of mental irresponsibility, and in whom such an insanity or mental irresponsibility continues to exist, shall be deemed criminally insane within the meaning of this act. No condition of mind induced by the voluntary act of a person charged with a crime shall be deemed mental irresponsibility within the meaning of this act.

Maher v. People

10 Mich. 212, 81 Am. Dec. 781 (1862)

The defendant appealed his conviction for assault with intent to murder another man, Patrick Hunt. During his trial, the defendant offered mitigating evidence to show that he was provoked by Hunt's adultery with the defendant's wife within half an hour of the assault, and consequently, his charges should be reduced to manslaughter. The defendant testified that he saw Hunt and his wife go into the woods together, which caused him to believe they were having an affair, and saw them return from the woods soon after. Additionally, he learned from a third party that they had been in the woods the day before. He followed Hunt into a bar in a state of excitement and assaulted him. The trial judge excluded this evidence, but the state supreme court reversed his judgment and remanded for a new trial because the evidence was admissible to show the defendant's nature and intent when committing the act. The supreme court held that in "determining whether the provocation is sufficient or reasonable, ordinary human nature, or the average of men recognized as men of fair average mind and disposition, should be taken as the standard." Further, it held that the question of adequate and reasonable provocation is generally a question for the jury, and "if [the jury] should find such provocation from the facts proved, and should further find that it did produce that effect in the particular instance, and that the homicide was the result of such provocation, it would give it the character of manslaughter."

Model Penal Code
(Official Draft 1962)

Section 210.2. Murder

(1) Except as provided in Section 210.3(1)(b), criminal homicide constitutes murder when:

(a) it is committed purposely or knowingly; or

(b) it is committed recklessly under circumstances manifesting extreme indifference to the value of human life. Such recklessness and indifference are presumed if the actor is engaged or is an accomplice in the commission of, or an attempt to commit, or flight after committing or attempting to commit robbery, rape or deviate sexual intercourse by force or threat of force, arson, burglary, kidnapping or felonious escape.

(2) Murder is a felony of the first degree [but a person convicted of murder may be sentenced to death, as provided in Section 210.6].

Section 210.3. Manslaughter

(1) Criminal homicide constitutes manslaughter when:

(a) it is committed recklessly; or

(b) a homicide which would otherwise be murder is committed under the influence of extreme mental or emotional disturbance for which there is reasonable explanation or excuse. The reasonableness of such explanation or excuse shall be determined from the viewpoint of a person in the actor's situation under the circumstances as he believes them to be.

(2) Manslaughter is a felony of the second degree.

● OVERVIEW OF HOMICIDE MITIGATIONS

Provocation at Common Law   One common exception to the paradigm of an intentional killing as murder is found in the common law doctrine of provocation, which mitigates an intentional killing from murder to manslaughter, in the same manner as its modern successor, the doctrine of extreme emotional disturbance. The common law mitigation arose from a recognition that passion frequently obscures reason and, in some limited way, renders the provoked intentional killer less blameworthy than the unprovoked intentional killer. In its common law form, the mitigation has very demanding standards, frequently requiring that the provocation be "reasonable" or that a reasonable person would have been similarly provoked:

The doctrine of mitigation is briefly this: That if the act of killing, though intentional, be committed under the influence of sudden, intense anger, or heat of blood, obscuring the reason, produced by an adequate or reasonable provocation, and before sufficient time has elapsed for the blood to cool and reason to reassert itself, so that the killing is the result of temporary excitement rather than of wickedness of heart or innate recklessness of disposition, then the law, recognizing the standard of human conduct as that of the ordinary or average man, regards the offense so committed as of less heinous character than premeditated or deliberate murder. Measured as it must be by the conduct of the average man, what constitutes adequate cause is incapable of exact definition.[1]

But the mitigation has severe limitations: For one, the actor loses the mitigation if sufficient time has passed for the reasonable person to cool off. Further, the person killed must be the person who provoked. Early forms of the mitigation required the provoking incident to have occurred in the presence of the defendant. Thus, the mitigation was typically available only in certain common situations: "extreme assault or battery upon the defendant; mutual combat; defendant's illegal arrest; injury or serious abuse of a close relative of the defendant's; on the sudden discovery of a spouse's adultery." Certain events were, as a matter of law, inadequate to trigger the provocation mitigation.

Difficulties with Common Law Test   One may wonder whether it is realistic or appropriate to apply a purely objective test, at least a test that seems to require that a reasonable person would have acted the same as the defendant. If such a test were satisfied — if the reasonable person would have acted the same as the defendant — ought not the defendant be held blameless? Perhaps what the common law mitigation means to assess is whether the actor's conduct is "reasonable" only in the sense that it is *understandable*. In other words, while the killing remains condemnable, the conditions of the killing suggest that the actor is noticeably less blameworthy than one who kills without such provocation. Many writers have criticized the limitations of the common law doctrine as failing to provide a mitigation to many actors of significantly reduced blameworthiness.

Extreme Emotional Disturbance   The Model Penal Code gives a broader mitigation than common law provocation. It gives a mitigation from murder to manslaughter where

> murder is committed under the influence of extreme mental or emotional disturbance for which there is reasonable explanation or excuse. The reasonableness of such explanation or excuse shall be determined from the viewpoint of a person in the actor's situation under the circumstances as he believes them to be.[2]

The mitigation has two components. First, the killing must in fact have been committed under the influence of extreme mental or emotional disturbance. If most people would have been provoked to violence by an incident, but the defendant in fact is not, he is not eligible for the mitigation. Second, if the actor is acting under the influence of extreme mental or emotional disturbance,

---

1. State v. Gounagias, 88 Wash. 304, 311-312, 153 P. 9, 12 (1915).
2. Model Penal Code §210.3(1)(b).

there must be a reasonable explanation or excuse for the disturbance. No mitigation is available if the disturbance is not reasonably explainable or is peculiar to the actor.

Broader Mitigation Under Model Penal Code   The Model Penal Code broadens the common law mitigation in several important respects. It makes no explicit exclusions, as the common law does; there are no conditions that are inadequate as a matter of law to provide a mitigation. It drops the common law rule that bars the mitigation if the killing occurs some period of time after the provoking event. In other words, the Code postulates that an actor's emotional disturbance may not necessarily decrease with time; indeed, it might increase.[1] Nothing in the Code's mitigation limits it to cases where the actor kills the source of the provocation, as the common law does. If the actor's killing is less blameworthy by virtue of the influencing conditions, the Code's argument is, such reduced blameworthiness exists no matter who is killed. This follows in part from the observation that the theory of the mitigation is not one of justification; this is not a defensive force defense, for example, where force may be justified against an aggressor but no other.[2] The mitigation's basis, rather, is more akin to excuse defenses, which are not conditioned on who the victim of the offense may be.

Individualized Objective Standard   The Model Penal Code mitigation uses an objective standard, as the common law doctrine does, but the objective standard is partially individualized through the requirement that the reasonableness of the explanation or excuse is to be determined "under the circumstances as [the actor] believes them to be" and "from the viewpoint of a person in the actor's situation." These two phrases provide significant opportunities for a court to endow the reasonable person with the belief and characteristics of the defendant and place that hypothetical person in the conditions under which the defendant acted. (Recall that the same two phrases are used in determining the criminality of risk-taking and risk-inattentiveness in the Code's definition of recklessness and negligence, respectively.[3]) The second phrase in particular — "in the actor's *situation*" — is intended by the drafters to permit a trial judge great leeway in individualizing the reasonable person standard.[4]

Difficulties in Individualizing Objective Standard   The most difficult aspect of applying the extreme emotional disturbance mitigation is the determination

---

1. Model Penal Code §210.3 comment at 48 (Tentative Draft No. 9, 1959).
2. In some provocation situations, of course, an actor may have a self-defense claim.
3. Model Penal Code §2.02(2)(c)&(d).
4. The Model Penal Code commentary explains that

> [t]here is an inevitable ambiguity in "situation." If the actor were blind or if he had just suffered a blow or experienced a heart attack, these would certainly be facts to be considered in a judgment involving criminal liability, as they would be under traditional law. But the heredity, intelligence or temperament of the actor would not be held material in judging negligence, and could not be without depriving the criterion of all its objectivity. The code is not intended to displace discriminations of this kind, but rather to leave the issue to the courts.

Model Penal Code §2.02 comment 4 at 242 (1985). See also id. at n.27 (noting that a similar problem exists with recklessness and that discriminations similar to those required by the negligence standard must be made).

of which characteristics of the defendant should be attributed to the reasonable person in judging the reasonableness of the explanation for the defendant's conduct. Clearly such things as an actor's age are relevant in assessing the reasonableness of his disturbance. But, presumably, a defendant's certifiably bad temper would not be taken into account to lower our expectations of him in resisting a provocation; he is not to be judged against the standard of the reasonable person with a similar bad temper. To individualize the objective standard fully would turn it into a purely subjective standard, which would give mitigations where the community would see no reduced blameworthiness. More difficult to deal with are factors like claimed genetic predisposition toward a violent reaction when provoked. If true, should it be used to alter the standard by which the defendant is to be judged? We are inclined to believe that people can control their temper if they choose to, but the claim of genetic predisposition clouds the issue by making it seem beyond the actor's control.[1] Unfortunately, criminal law theory has yet to develop a principle that will distinguish those characteristics to be included from those to be excluded. The Model Penal Code leaves the issue to the *ad hoc* determination of the trial judge. This issue is the focus of the Discussion Materials below.

Diminished Capacity Another doctrine that can reduce the degree of an intentional killing from murder to manslaughter, or to an even lesser offense, is the doctrine frequently called "diminished capacity" or "diminished responsibility." The name is misleading because it suggests a kind of partial insanity defense. In fact, the mitigation does not operate by finding that an actor suffers a degree of mental illness short of that required for a full insanity defense, hence it is a mitigation only. (The Code's extreme *mental* disturbance mitigation, described above, operates roughly in this way. That is, an extreme mental disturbance may mitigate murder to manslaughter even though the actor fully intended to cause the death — it was his "conscious object" or he was "practically certain" that his conduct would cause the death.) The diminished capacity defense, in contrast, gives a defense when an actor's mental illness negates a culpable state of mind required for the offense charged. In other words, it is neither more nor less than an absent element defense, like an actor's mistake negating an element. Depending on whether the offense charged has lesser included offenses with lower culpability requirements, and depending on the actual effect of an actor's mental illness, the doctrine may provide only a slight mitigation or a complete defense. In fact, the real purpose of the doctrine of diminished capacity at common law was to be a mechanism for *preventing* an actor from using evidence of mental illness to negate a required culpable state of mind. That is, it allowed evidence of mental illness to be used to negate an offense culpability requirement only under the conditions established in the diminished capacity doctrine. The trend is away from such restrictions on the use of mental illness to negate an offense element.

---

1. If genetics only create a *predisposition* toward violence, it would seem that the actor retains the ability to control his conduct. If genetics are to be relevant, the actor must show that the influence of genetics on his conduct is sufficiently strong that we should see him as less blameworthy. Note a similar discussion in the context of the requirements of excuse defenses in Sections 22 and 23.

Mental Illness Negating Offense Element — Survey   American jurisdictions take a variety of positions on the admission of mental disease or defect evidence that negates a required offense mental element. About 40% of the jurisdictions, typically those with modern criminal codes, admit any evidence of mental disease or defect that is relevant to negate any culpable state of mind offense element.[1] Another 30% allow such evidence to be admitted but purport to limit such admission to negating only a "specific intent"[2] — a concept that has little meaning in modern codes — or, even more restrictively, to negate only the malice or premeditation requirements in murder prosecutions.[3] The final 30% purport to exclude the admission of mental illness evidence to negate any offense element,[4] but some of these efforts have been held unconstitutional.[5]

---

1. See Alaska Stat. §12.47.020 (2002); Ark. Code Ann. §5-2-303 (2002); State v. Burge, 487 A.2d 532 (Conn. 1985); Colo. Rev. Stat. Ann. §18-1-803 (2003); Haw. Rev. Stat. Ann. §704-401 (2002); Idaho Code §18-207 (2002); Robinson v. Commonwealth, 569 S.W.2d 183 (Ky. Ct. App. 1978); Me. Rev. Stat. Ann. tit. 17-A, §38 (2003); Hoey v. State, 536 A.2d 622 (Md. 1988); Mo. Ann. Stat. §552.030 (2002); 2003 Mont. Sess. Laws ch. 452 (making minor revisions to Mont. Code Ann. §46-14-102 (2002)); Finger v. State, 27 P.3d 66 (Nev. 2001) (finding abolition of insanity defense unconstitutional and holding that evidence not meeting legal insanity standard may be admitted at trial to negate an offense element); Novosel v. Helgemoe, 384 A.2d 124 (N.H. 1978) (applying only in bifurcated trials); N.J. Stat. Ann. §2C:4-2 (2002); Or. Rev. Stat. §161-300 (2001); State v. Perry, 13 S.W.3d 724 (Tenn. Crim. App. 1999); 2003 Utah Laws ch. 11 (making minor revisions to Utah Code Ann. §76-2-305 (2002)); State v. Smith, 396 A.2d 126 (Vt. 1978); United States v. Pohlot, 827 F.2d 889 (3d Cir. 1987) (holding that in codifying an insanity excuse, 18 U.S.C.A. §17 (2003), Congress abolished defenses of "diminished capacity" and "partial responsibility" but did not intend to preclude admission of psychiatric evidence relevant to negate an element of the offense).

2. Cal. Penal Code §28 (2003); Veverka v. Cash, 318 N.W.2d 447 (Iowa 1982); State v. Dargatz, 614 P.2d 430 (Kan. 1980); People v. Atkins, 325 N.W.2d 38 (Mich. Ct. App. 1982); People v. Segal, 444 N.Y.S.2d 588 (N.Y. 1981); Commonwealth v. Walzack, 360 A.2d 914 (Pa. 1976); State v. Correra, 430 A.2d 1251 (R.I. 1981); State v. Huber, 356 N.W.2d 468 (S.D. 1984); State v. Bottrell 14 P.3d 164 (Wash. Ct. App. 2000).

3. People v. Leppert, 434 N.E.2d 21 (Ill. App. Ct. 1982) (considering defendant's claim that, due to mental defect, he lacked the requisite intent to attempt murder); Commonwealth v. Baldwin, 686 N.E.2d 1001 (Mass. 1997); Washington v. State, 85 N.W.2d 509 (Neb. 1957); State v. Beach, 699 P.2d 115 (N.M. 1985); State v. Shank, 367 S.E.2d 639 (N.C. 1988); LeVasseur v. Commonwealth, 304 S.E.2d 202 (Va. 1979).

4. Barnett v. State, 540 So. 2d 810 (Ala. Crim. App. 1988); State v. Schantz, 403 P.2d 521 (Ariz. 1965); Bates v. State, 386 A.2d 1139 (Del. 1978); Bethea v. United States, 365 A.2d 64 (D.C. 1976); Zamora v. State, 361 So. 2d 776 (Fla. Dist. Ct. App. 1978); Hudson v. State, 319 S.E.2d 28 (Ga. Ct. App. 1984); Brown v. State, 448 N.E.2d 10 (Ind. 1983); State v. Murray, 375 So. 2d 80 (La. 1979); State v. Bouwman, 328 N.W.2d 703 (Minn. 1982); Garcia v. State, 828 So. 2d 1279 (Miss. Ct. App. 2002); State v. Wilcox, 438 N.E.2d 523 (Ohio 1982); Gresham v. State, 489 P.2d 1355 (Okla. Crim. App. 1971); Gill v. State, 552 S.E.2d 26 (S.C. 2001); Warner v. State, 944 S.W.2d 812 (Tex. Crim. App. 1997); State v. Flint, 96 S.E.2d 677 (W.Va. 1957) (providing statement against diminished capacity defense that has since been questioned but not overruled, in State v. Simmon, 309 S.E.2d 89 (W.Va. 1983); Muench v. Israel, 715 F.2d 1124 (7th Cir. 1983) (finding that Wisconsin may constitutionally reject the diminished capacity defense and refuse to admit evidence proving defendant's inability to form requisite intent); Price v. State, 807 P.2d 909 (Wyo. 1991).
To date, North Dakota courts have not explicitly spoken to this issue — their position remains unclear.

5. See, e.g., Hendershott v. People, 653 P.2d 385 (Colo. 1982) (finding unconstitutional Colorado statute that barred evidence of mental illness to negate mens rea requirement for non-specific intent crimes) and Finger v. State, supra (holding Nevada statute unconstitutional); but see Muench v. Israel, supra (rejecting a constitutional challenge to Wisconsin's practice of excluding evidence of mental illness relevant to a mens rea requirement).

▲ **PROBLEM**

People v. Mentry: "Mother Says She Was Told to Sit on Child, Who Died"

San Jose, Calif.—A jury trial began last week over whether a 200-pound woman was grossly negligent, or reckless in following a counselor's alleged advice to discipline her 8-year old son by sitting on him.

Betty Mentry, 45, an electronics worker here, was charged with involuntary manslaughter after her son, Stephen, died last May 31 when she sat on him for the fourth time. People v. Mentry, 84637 (Santa Clara County Superior Court).

Meantime, Ms. Mentry is suing the Alum Rock Communications Center, a San Jose counseling service funded by the county with state money, for allegedly advising her to sit on her son. Her malpractice suit seeks $2.5 million. Mentry v. Alum Rock Communications Inc., 517164 (Santa Clara County Superior Court).

Police had suggested to Ms. Mentry to take her son to Alum Rock to break him of a stealing habit, said local lawyer Cyril R. Ash Jr., who represents her in both the civil and the criminal cases.

Mr. Ash claims that center counselor Jorge Sousa "insisted" that Ms. Mentry use a technique developed in the 1960s by Dr. Milton H. Erickson of New York. Mr. Sousa, the attorney said, threatened to advise the courts to remove Stephen from her custody if she refused to follow his advice.

The technique consisted, literally, of sitting on the child to make him understand who was in charge. Mr. Ash said Dr. Erickson detailed the case of a 27-year-old woman with an 8-year-old son who "refused to respond to punishment" until, as advised, his mother "threw him quickly to the floor on his stomach and sat her full weight upon him."

"I was to eat in front of him and I was to talk on the telephone [while sitting on Stephen]," Ms. Mentry testified at a preliminary examination in the criminal case last August. "I was supposed to act like I was having a gay old time. [Mr. Sousa] assured me that Stephen would yell, scream and cuss and carry on, and I was to ignore him. And when it was over, he said he was positive that Stephen would have the message that I was in charge."

Counselor's 'Assurances'

The woman said she sat her "full weight" on her son for eight hours the first time she used the technique. On the next two occasions, she said, she sat on him for a half hour and for 1-1/2 hours. The last time, she sat on him for two hours before she noticed he had stopped breathing. He died nine days later.

Mr. Ash claims the counselor failed in his duty to warn her of any danger. In fact, he said, "the counselor assured her no harm would come to the boy." And Ms. Mentry, he said, "is the type of individual who tends to follow such instructions explicitly."

The counselor's threat to strip her of custody, he said, also is enough to absolve her of any crime.

But the person is responsible for exercising a certain amount of common sense, said John F. Marshall, a Santa Clara County deputy district attorney.

"Even somebody who's less intelligent than normal, when a kid says, 'I can't breathe,' you do something about it," he said. "And if you don't, that's gross negligence."

Ms. Mentry's 11-year-old daughter, Sherry, testified at the preliminary hearing that she walked into the room and heard her brother say he couldn't breathe. Lawyers were expected to use her preliminary hearing testimony rather than bring her back to the stand at trial.

Alum Rock's director, George Doub, denied Ms. Mentry's allegations, saying his counselors never advised her to sit on her son. He called her claim a "unique shift of blame."

Mr. Sousa has been unavailable for comment.

Is Ms. Mentry liable for a homicide offense? If so, what grade?

❋ DISCUSSION MATERIALS

With What Characteristics of the Defendant, If Any, Should the Reasonable Person Standard Be Individualized?

The Model Penal Code Commentary excerpt concerning homicide's extreme-emotional-disturbance mitigation explains the Code's rationale for refining the reasonable person standard so the defendant is judged against a reasonable person "in the actor's situation." In *Director of Public Prosecutions v. Camplin,* the court examines the scope of the provocation doctrine and its reliance upon the "reasonable man" standard. George Fletcher's article further discusses the difficulties of the reasonable man concept in general, and its application to provocation in particular. Next, Robinson and Darley report on their study of community intuitions of a partially individualized reasonable person standard and compare the results to existing law. Finally, *People v. Wu* offers a case study of the difficulty in deciding whether a particular characteristic or circumstance ought to be introduced to individualize the standard by considering the proper effect, if any, the defendant's cultural background should be given.

Model Penal Code Section 210.3 Commentary
Official Draft and Revised Comments 62-63 (1980)

The critical element in the Model Code formulation is the clause requiring that reasonableness be assessed "from the viewpoint of a person in the actor's situation." The word "situation" is designedly ambiguous. On the other hand, it is clear that personal handicaps and some external circumstances must be taken into account. Thus, blindness, shock from traumatic injury, and extreme grief are all easily read into the term "situation." This result is sound, for it would be normally obtuse to appraise a crime for mitigation of punishment without reference to these factors. On the other hand, it is equally plain that idiosyncratic moral values are not part of the actor's situation. An assassin who kills a political leader because he believes it is right to do so cannot ask that he be judged by the standard of a reasonable extremist. Any other result would undermine the normative message of the criminal law. In between these two extremes, however, there are matters neither as clearly distinct from individual blameworthiness as blindness or handicap nor as integral a part of moral depravity as a belief in the rightness of killing. Perhaps the classic illustration is the unusual sensitivity to the epithet "bastard" of a person born illegitimate. An exceptionally punctilious sense of personal honor or an abnormally fearful temperament may also serve to differentiate an individual actor from the hypothetical reasonable man, yet none of these factors is wholly irrelevant to the ultimate issue of culpability. The proper role of such factors cannot be resolved satisfactorily by abstract definition of what may constitute adequate provocation. The Model Code endorses a formulation that affords sufficient flexibility to differentiate in particular cases between those special aspects of the actor's situation that should be deemed material for purposes of grading and those that should be ignored. There thus will be room for interpretation of the word "situation," and that is precisely the flexibility desired. There will be opportunity for argument about the reasonableness of explanation or excuse, and that too is a ground on which the argument is required. In the end, the question is whether the actor's loss of self-control can be understood in terms that arouse sympathy in the ordinary citizen. Section 210.3 faces this issue squarely and leaves the ultimate judgement to the ordinary citizen in the function of a juror assigned to resolve the specific case.

Director of Public Prosecutions v. Camplin
[1978] 2 All E.R. 168

Judge Diplock: . . .

My Lords, the doctrine of provocation in crimes of homicide has always represented an anomaly in English law. In crimes of violence which result in injury short of death, the fact that the act of violence was committed under provocation, which has caused the accused to lose his self-control, does not affect the nature of the offence of which he is guilty: it is merely a matter to be taken into consideration in determining the penalty which it is appropriate to impose: whereas in homicide provocation effects a change in the offence itself from murder, for which the penalty is fixed by law (formerly death and now imprisonment for life), to the lessor offence of manslaughter, for which the penalty is in the discretion of the judge. . . .

Section 3 of the 1957 Act is the following terms:

> 'Where on a charge of murder there is evidence on which the jury can find that the person charged was provoked (whether by things done or by things said or by both together) to lose his self-control, the question whether the provocation was enough to make a reasonable man do as he did shall be left to be determined by the jury; and in determining that question the jury shall take into account everything both done and said according to the effect which, in their opinion, it would have on a reasonable man.'

My Lords, this section was intended to mitigate in some degree the harshness of the common law of provocation as it had been developed by recent decisions in this House. It recognises and retains the dual test: the provocation must not only have caused the accused to lose his self-control but also be such as might cause a reasonable man to react to it as the accused did. Nevertheless it brings about two important changes in the law. The first is it abolishes all previous rules of law as to what can or cannot amount to provocation.... Secondly it makes it clear that if there was any evidence that the accused himself at the time of the act which caused the death in fact lost his self-control in consequence of some provocation however slight it might appear to the judge, he was bound to leave to the jury the question, which is one of opinion not of law, whether a reasonable man might have reacted to that provocation as the accused did....

The public policy that underlay the adoption of the 'reasonable man' test in the common law doctrine of provocation was to reduce the incidence of fatal violence by preventing a person relying on his own exceptional pugnacity or excitability as an excuse for loss of self-control. The rationale of the test may not be easy to reconcile in logic with more universal propositions as to the mental element in crime. Nevertheless it has been preserved by the 1957 Act but fails to be applied now in the context of a law of provocation that is significantly different from what it was before the Act was passed....

As I have already pointed out, for the purposes of the law of provocation the 'reasonable man' has never been confined to the adult male. It means an ordinary person of either sex, not exceptionally excitable or pugnacious, but possessed of such powers of self-control as everyone is entitled to expect that his fellow citizens will exercise in society as it is today. A crucial factor in the defence of provocation from earliest times has been the relationship between the gravity of provocation and the way in which the accused retaliated, both being judged by the social standards of the day. When Hale was writing in the 17th century pulling a man's nose was thought to justify retaliation with a sword; when Mancini was decided by this House, a blow with a fist would not justify retaliation with a deadly weapon. But so long as words unaccompanied by violence could not in common law amount to provocation the relevant proportionality between provocation and retaliation was primarily one of degrees of violence. Words spoken to the accused before the violence started were not normally to be included in the proportion sum. But now that the law has been changed so as to permit of words being treated as provocation, even though unaccompanied by any other acts, the gravity of verbal provocation may well depend on the particular characteristics or circum-stances of the person to whom a taunt or insult is addressed. To taunt a person because of his race, his physical infirmities or some shameful incident in his past may well be considered by the jury to be more offensive to the person addressed, however equable his temperament, if the facts on which the taunt is founded are true than it would be if they were not. It would stultify much of the mitigation of the previous harshness of the common law in ruling out verbal provocation as capable of reducing murder to manslaughter if the jury could not take into consideration all those factors which in their opinion would affect the gravity of taunts and insults when applied to the person to whom they are addressed. So to this extent at any rate the unqualified proposition accepted by this House in Bedder that for the purposes of the 'reasonable man' test any unusual physical characteristics of the accused must be ignored requires revision as a result of the passing of the 1957 Act....

Lord Morris of Borth-y-gest:

My Lords, for many years past in cases where murder has been charged, it has been recognised by courts that there can be circumstances in which the accused person was so provoked that this unlawful act was held to amount to manslaughter rather than to murder. Due and sensible regard to human nature and to human frailty and infirmity was being paid. In R v Hayward this result was said to be 'in compassion to human infirmity'. But courts were careful to ensure that a plea of provocation should involve more than some easy explanation as to how a death had been caused. What was involved was that the accused had acted in 'heat of blood' or in a 'transport of passion' or in other words had lost his self-control and that this was the result of the provocation. But in addition to this and by way of limitation, courts introduced certain tests of reasonableness....

Who then or what then was the 'reasonable man'? If a reasonable man is a man who normally acts reasonably, it becomes important to consider the mind of the accused person when considering his reactions to some provocation. To consider the mind of some different person, and to consider what his reactions would have been if comparably provoked, could involve an unreal test....

The original reasons in this branch of the law were largely reasons of the heart and of common sense, not the reasons of pure juristic logic. The potentiality of provocation to reduce murder to manslaughter was, as Tindal C.J. said in R v Hayward, 'in compassion to human infirmity'. But justice and common sense then demanded some limitation: it would be unjust that the drunk man or one exceptionally pugnacious or bad-tempered or over-sensitive should be able to claim that these matters rendered him peculiarly susceptible to the provocation offered, where the sober and even-tempered man would hang for his homicide. Hence, I think, the development of the concept of the reaction of a reasonable man to the provocation offered, even though it may have originally come into this branch of the law by way of testing the credibility of the claim of the accused (who could not at that time himself give evidence) that he had been so deprived of his self-control as to be incapable of forming the relevant intent. But it is one thing to invoke the reasonable man for the standard of self-control which the law requires; it is quite another to substitute some hypothetical being from whom all mental and physical attributes (except perhaps sex) have been abstracted.

Other Discussion Materials

George P. Fletcher, Provocation
Rethinking Criminal Law 246-250 (1978)

The primary source of difficulty in the analysis of provocation derives from the failure of the courts and commentators to face the underlying normative issue whether the accused may be fairly expected to control an impulse to kill under the circumstances. Obviously, there are some impulses such as anger and even mercy (as in the case of the father who killed his neglected child) that we do expect people to control. If they fail to control these impulses and they kill another intentionally, they are liable for unmitigated homicide or murder. The basic moral question in the law of homicide is distinguishing between those impulses to kill as to which we as a society demand self-control, and those as to which we relax our inhibitions.

Courts and commentators seek to evade this moral issue by trying the partial defense of provocation to the likely behavior of the "reasonable person." As a general matter, the invocation of this mythical standard of an exemplary person provides some assistance in analyzing the moral issues of criminal responsibility. By projecting our moral judgments into a prediction of what a reasonable person would do, we generate a standard for assessing the behavior of the accused. Yet in the context of provocation, the reasonable person is hardly at home. First, as everyone is prepared to admit, the reasonable person does not kill at all, even under provocation. Therefore it is difficult to assess whether his or her killing should be classified as manslaughter rather than murder. More serious than this conceptual anomaly is the danger that abnormal personal characteristics of the defendant will not be taken into consideration in assessing whether as to him, the provocation was adequate. Thus there are decisions holding that it is irrelevant that the defendant was suffering from a sunstroke or head injury at the time of the allegedly provocative incident. We certainly do not expect people to control the effects of a sunstroke, and therefore if this fact bore on the accused's excitability under the circumstances, it is irrational not to consider it in assessing whether his killing was at least partially beyond his control. In the most notorious case of this vein, the accused, one Bedder, killed a prostitute who was allegedly taunting and hitting him in a fracas about his inability to perform the negotiated sexual act. The claim was that the accused was impotent and particularly sensitive about his incapacity. Nonetheless, the House of Lords affirmed the instructions to the jury not to consider the impact of the accused's impotence on his reaction to the prostitute's taunting. It may be that the accused should have controlled himself whether he was impotent or not, yet this is a fact that should have been decided by the jury with full appreciation of all the pressures bearing on the event. One can hardly say that the jury passed judgment on Mr. Bedder if they did not even consider the most significant facts that influenced his loss of control.

It seems that decisions like *Bedder* derive from the court's losing sight of why one uses the test of the reasonable person to assess the mitigating effect of provocation. The underlying question is whether the accused should be able to control the particular impulse or emotion that issues in the killing. Yet the intrusion of this mythical standard sometimes induces judges and legislative draftsmen to think that the issue is whether if the average person would have killed under the circumstances, the killing should be partially excused. The test cannot be whether the average person *would have killed* under the circumstances, for that test should more plausibly generate a total excuse. Further, the average person is not impotent; nor does he have a sunstroke or head injury. Therefore these facts presumably should not bear on the question of provocation. This is a good example of the way in which a legal doctrine can become totally alienated from the moral sentiments that give rise to it.

Part of the problem, no doubt, is the general decline of moral thinking in the analysis of liability for homicide. Therefore, it does not generally occur to analysts of provocation that the central problem is determining those impulses that we expect people completely to control. Even the Royal Commission on Capital Punishment was confounded by the doctrine of the reasonable person; the commissioners recognized that the test was unfair and yet they were apparently persuaded by the judges who appeared before them that if physical disabilities and partial insanity were recognized as relevant, it would follow that a badtempered man should also receive special consideration under the law. This non sequitur is typical of the confusion that characterizes the decline of moral sensitivity in the analysis of culpability. Once we forget that the problem is the analysis of those impulses that we are fairly expected to control, it follows that judges would have difficulty distinguishing between a head injury and a bad temper.

Once the moral perspective on provocation is lost, the concern develops that the individuation of the standard might lead to its total collapse. Not knowing where to draw the line, judges would prefer not to include any unusual physical feature of the defendant. Thus the English Homicide Act of 1957 retains the rule that provocation should mitigate the homicide only if "it was enough to make a reasonable man do as he did . . . ." A few years later, the Model Penal Code broke from this pattern and boldly declared that the defense of provocation should be judged "from the viewpoint of a person in the actor's situation under the circumstances as he believes them to be." Lest anyone fear that individuation of the inquiry would lead to the indulgent mitigation of all provoked killings, the draftsmen added a proviso: there must be a "reasonable explanation or excuse" for the "extreme mental or emotional disturbance." Thus, for example, the moral issue whether insults should be sufficient to mitigate the killing is framed by the question whether the accused has a "reasonable explanation or excuse" for losing control and killing. The virtue of this shift in wording is that it discourages decisions like *Bedder*; the jury's assessment of his killing the taunting prostitute could not be short-circuited by a judicial determination that reasonable people are not impotent.

Paul H. Robinson & John M. Darley, Study 11: Individualization of the Objective Standard of Negligence
Justice, Liability and Blame: Community Views and the Criminal Law 121-123 (1995)

In the present study we sought to begin the inquiry into which attributes ought to be taken into account in judging a person's failure to be aware of or his conscious disregard of a risk. Because no existing literature or case law proposes a general theory or principal that can be tested, this study attempts the very preliminary step of identifying attributes that might be seen by people in the community as either mitigating or aggravating criminal negligence liability. From this initial sampling, it was hoped that the responses might show a pattern that could be used to develop hypotheses and that those hypotheses might then be tested in subsequent studies.

. . . Subjects were first asked to assign liability and punishment to each of three base scenarios, each of which presented a situation of risk: an omission resulting in property damage, an omission resulting in death, and a commission resulting in death. The omission resulting in property damage is depicted by an apartment house owner who does not maintain the property well, and thus it catches fire. This scenario . . . drew an average liability rating of 2.61, 5 to 6 weeks in jail. In the omission resulting in death case . . . a caretaker of a child pays insufficient attention to symptoms of the child's illness, and fails to seek medical attention for the child, who dies. This was assigned a liability of 4.92, between 10 and 11 months in jail. The commission resulting in death case . . . involves a hunter who, in a remote wilderness area, shoots into the bush at a noise he hears, and kills another hunter, earning a liability rating of 3.98, about 6 months in jail. . . .

Each subject then was asked to consider whether each of fourteen actor characteristics would make a difference in the liability they had assigned to the base scenarios. The fourteen actor characteristics were selected from those that were thought to be most likely to give some kind of reaction, either mitigating or aggravating. Frequently, the characteristics included the two extremes of a single continuum, for example, higher and lower than average intelligence, advanced and subnormal training, old age and youthfulness. Subjects were asked to indicate for each variation whether, if the person possessed this characteristic, they would alter the punishment assessment they gave in the base scenario. A nine point scale allowed subjects to indicate less liability (1), no change (5), or more liability (9). . . . A rating that hovers around 0 means that the respondents, on the average, did not think that characteristic either lowered or raised the liability assigned to the person in the original case. Ratings that differ from 0 by about 0.7 are reliably different from 0, meaning that a rating of −0.7 or lower indicates a tendency on the part of the respondents to want to lower the liability assigned to the negligent individual in that case, and a rating of +0.7 or higher indicates that the average respondent thinks that possession of that characteristic warrants an assignment of more liability.

Table 4.13 **Factors in Individualization of Negligence Standard**

Actor Characteristics	Scenarios		
	(a) Commission: Death	(b) Omission: Death	(c) Omission: Property Damage
1. Old age	−0.3	−0.4	0.0
2. Advanced experience	0.6	1.6*	1.8*
3. Genetic irregularity	−0.5	−0.9*	−0.7*
4. Upbringing (knowledge)	1.5*	−0.2	−0.3
5. Below-normal intelligence	−0.2	−1.4*	−0.7*
6. Religion (knowledge)	0.2	−0.2	0.0
7. Above-normal Intelligence	0.6	0.8*	0.6
8. Upbringing (environment)	0.7*	−0.3	−0.1
9. Lack of knowledge (culture)	−0.3	−1.7*	−1.0*
10. Substandard education	−0.4	−0.3	−0.2
11. Cultural norms	−0.8*	−0.1	−0.5
12. Recent upset	−0.4	−0.4	−0.5
13. Religion (norms)	0.2	0.0	−0.1

*These items are statistically significantly different ($p < .05$) from the liability assigned to the person who did not have the named condition.

Looking at Table 4.13, notice first that subjects do not often give ratings that deviate far from zero; that is, they rarely find that a particular characteristic is a reason to sharply increase or reduce the liability they assigned to the perpetrator of the original scenario. (We have starred those that are statistically significant in the table to call them to your attention.) Given that we created the stories in ways that we thought might make some claims on individuating, this is an interesting fact. Our respondents, like code drafters, seem cautious about individuating the objective standard of negligence.

However, in several instances the subjects do individuate. The results suggest that some actor characteristics do, in the subjects' view, affect a person's liability for inattention to risks. In each scenario, two or more characteristics showed statistically significant differences in each direction from the "no change" point on the scale, (0). In the hunter scenario, Table 4.13 column (a), an individual whose upbringing was such as to make him knowledgeable about hunting was judged more liable for shooting at a noise in the bushes. On the other hand, an individual whose cultural norms do not include care with guns is judged as less negligent. For the apartment house owner, Table 4.13 column (c), coming from a cultural background in which persons have little or no knowledge of the risks of particular materials catching fire, caused respondents to reduce liability, while having experience at building care increased it.

Our respondents saw a number of factors as increasing or mitigating liability in the case of the child caregiver who failed to take the child for medical attention, Table 4.13 column (b). This makes sense if we note that that case is a more complex one than the other two, involving recognizing complex cues of the infant's distress. Immaturity, below normal intelligence, genetic irregularity, and a lack of knowledge of children all decrease liability. Having above average intelligence or past experience with children, and still failing to get medical treatment for the infant, increases liability.

It is also possible to ask which individuating characteristics our respondents give weight to across the scenarios. This is a difficult generalization to make. We would tentatively suggest the following: in each of the cases, having relevant experience with the situation is seen as increasing liability for behaving negligently within it. Having a genetic defect or a culturally established lack of knowledge about the hazards often reduces liability. But the results suggest that the characteristics appropriate for individuating the reasonable person standard vary with the factual situation, confirming the code drafters' assessment that this is a complex problem and suggesting that perhaps they were right to leave this to the ad hoc determination of courts. Further study may reveal a pattern to the kind of characteristics judged influential on liability in different kinds of situations. Or perhaps the jurisprudential literature will develop a hypothesis that can be tested.

Summary

In several ways, the present results do give us some insights. They confirm that some individuation of the objective standard is consistent with the community view. Also, they suggest an answer to the question of whether individuation ought to increase as well as decrease our expectations of persons. Our subjects clearly believe that it is appropriate to elevate the standard of care required of an experienced person, and occasionally of a person who is above average in intelligence as well.

Furthermore, although the Code drafters in the [Model Penal Code] official commentary . . . specifically exclude the characteristics of sub-normal intelligence or genetic defect as reasons to lower the standard, our respondents occasionally use information about these characteristics to reduce the liability they assign. One might think that, within the legal system, given that it generally is left to the juries to decide on the particular ways that they will individuate the reasonable person standard, these cases of reduced liability can be accommodated. Unfortunately, this is not entirely true. It is the judge who decides whether evidence of a particular characteristic will be allowed to be introduced into evidence, so jury intuition on this point is not a safeguard, because the jury may never hear about relevant factors. The fact that the Code's official commentary specifically excludes low intelligence as an individuating factor is particularly troublesome for this reason. A judge may well feel bound to follow the commentary and exclude such evidence, while our respondents report that it is a factor on which they would individuate the standard. Were the court system willing to individualize the objective standard of negligence to the degree reflected in these results, it would be possible to call the jury's attention to the general possibilities of individuation, perhaps using these specific examples.

People v. Helen Wu

Court of Appeal of California, Fourth Appellate District, Division Two
235 Cal. App. 3d 614, 1991 Cal. App. LEXIS 1229, 286 Cal. Rptr. 868 (1991)

Timlin, Acting P. J.

I

Helen Wu, also known as Helen Hamg Ieng Chau (defendant), was convicted of the second degree murder of her son, Sidney Wu (Sidney), following trial by jury. . . .

The prosecution's theory seems to have been that defendant killed Sidney because of anger at Sidney's father, and to get revenge. The defense's theory was that defendant believed that Sidney, who lived with his father in the United States, was looked down upon and was ill-treated by everyone except his paternal grandmother because he had been borne out of wedlock, and that when she learned that the grandmother was dying of cancer, she felt trapped and, in an intense emotional upheaval, strangled Sidney and then attempted to kill herself so that she could take care of Sidney in the afterlife.

The only issues on appeal are whether the trial court committed prejudicial error by refusing to give two instructions requested by defendant, one related to the defense of unconsciousness, and one related to the effect her cultural background might have had on her state of mind when she killed Sidney.

When the issue is whether it was error to give an improper instruction, on appeal "we must assume that the jury might have believed the evidence upon which the instruction favorable to the losing party was predicated, and that if the correct instruction had been given upon that subject the jury might have rendered a verdict in favor of the losing party."

Therefore, for purposes of this appeal, we shall set forth the evidence, which the jury might have found credible and upon which defendant's requested instructions were predicated.

II

[Defendant was born in 1943 in Saigon, China. At the age of 19, in about 1962, she moved to Macau, married and had a daughter, who was 25 years old at the time of her mother's February 1990 trial. The defendant first met Gary Wu, the son of a friend, in 1963. That same year Wu moved to the United States and married another woman. He opened several restaurants in the Palm Springs area.

[In 1978 or 1979, after hearing that the defendant was divorced, Wu contacted her. He told her of his own marriage, which he said was unhappy because his wife could not bear children, and suggested that the defendant come to the United States and conceive a child with him. Defendant believed Wu would marry her after his divorce and agreed to come. Wu provided her with money for a joint bank account and $20,000 for a visa.

[In November 1979, defendant joined Wu in the United States and moved in with his mother. Wu told defendant his divorce proceedings would be completed soon and that he would marry her, but when his divorce was finalized in about December 1979, he did not reveal it to her. Defendant conceived a child, Sidney, by Wu in the early part of 1980, and she moved into her own apartment. Their son, Sidney, was born in November 1980, but defendant became depressed and wanted to leave because she didn't have a support system and could not drive or speak English. Wu did not stop her, and defendant returned to Macau in February 1981 without the baby because his out of wedlock birth would have been particularly shameful for both of them in the defendant's culture.

[From 1981 to 1988 defendant regularly asked Wu to bring Sidney to visit her. In 1984, Wu asked defendant to visit him, but defendant felt she could not bear the humiliation that her unmarried status would cause and declined to come until she had the dignity of married status. In January 1988, Wu finally brought Sidney, then seven years old, to visit defendant in Hong Kong. To lure Wu to Hong Kong, defendant had borrowed $100,000 cash and a receipt for a certificate of deposit of a million Hong Kong dollars. Wu did in fact propose marriage but defendant by then had concluded that it was only his belief in the money that had caused it and that once this was discovered she would again be humiliated. She declined the marriage proposal and attempted, unsuccessfully, to kill herself by jumping out of a window.

[In August 1989, the defendant learned that Wu's mother was terminally ill and visited her. While there, Wu's mother told her to that when she (the mother) died, Wu would not care for Sidney. She was given similar advice by Sandy, Wu's cousin. By September 1, Wu and the defendant were married, despite her reservations that Wu was doing so because he believed she had a lot of money. Her belief was reinforced by Wu's comments. When asked by the defendant whether the marriage was not worthwhile simply to legitimize Sidney, Wu replied that many people could give him children. Realizing the depth of Wu's indifference, she told him he would be sorry, and later explained her remark meant she was thinking of returning to Macau and committing suicide.

[Defendant gave Wu $6,300 and asked him to get her a plane ticket for September 16 so she could return to Macau, and asked him not to tell Sidney that she was leaving so she could have 10 last days of happiness with her son. On September 9, a week before the planned departure, defendant interceded when Wu attempted to hit Sidney for disobeying an instruction. Wu left the house to put on two birthday parties at his restaurant for his girlfriend, Rosemary. Defendant and Sidney played and talked, and defendant told Sidney she knew what he liked because of their special mother-child bond. During this time, Sidney confided that Wu had called the defendant "psychotic" and "very troublesome." Further, he said Wu often scolded and beat him, and that Wu loved Rosemary but not him. Defendant considered what Sidney's grandmother and Sandy said, and felt sick. She had heart palpitations and trouble breathing. Finally, beyond distress at the idea of leaving Sidney to a lonely and despised existence without her, she told him she wanted to die, and asked him to go with her to a better afterlife where she could care for him. He clung to her neck and cried. She left the bedroom where they had been playing, and obtained a rope by cutting the cord off a window blind. She returned to the bedroom and strangled Sidney with it. She did not later remember the strangling itself. She then wrote a note to Wu, and attempted to strangle herself, but failed. She then slashed her left wrist with a knife. She lay next to Sidney and placed a waste-paper basket under her bleeding wrist, so the floor would not be dirtied.

[Wu returned home several hours later and discovered defendant and Sidney. He called the police; the paramedics were also summoned. The police determined that Sidney was dead. The paramedics tested defendant's vital signs and found her alive. Her pulse was normal, but she exhibited a decreased level of consciousness.]

Defendant was charged with murder (*Pen. Code, §187*) and, following a trial by jury, was convicted of second degree murder.

III . . .

B. Upon Retrial, the Trial Court Should, If So Requested, Instruct the Jury on How Evidence of Defendant's Cultural Background Relates to Defendant's Theory of the Case

Defendant contends that the trial court erred by refusing to give an instruction which pinpointed a significant aspect of her theory of the case, i.e., an instruction which told the jury it could choose to consider the evidence of defendant's cultural background in determining the presence or absence of the various mental states which were elements of the crimes with which she was charged. Because we have already determined that the judgment must be reversed because of the failure to give an instruction on unconsciousness, we will address the issue of the propriety of an instruction pinpointing the cultural background theory of defendant's case for purposes of guiding the trial court on retrial.

Defendant requested the following instruction:

> You have received evidence of defendant's cultural background and the relationship of her culture to her mental state. You may, but are not required to, consider that the [sic] evidence in determining the presence or absence of the essential mental states of the crimes defined in these instructions, or in determining any other issue in this case.

At trial, the prosecutor objected to this instruction on the ground that

> it's real touchy, in a major case, to be messing around with non-pattern jury instructions.... People smarter than myself have put together all the pattern jury instructions. I think they have covered every conceivable type of crime, certainly in this case they have, and I don't think that we need to be giving the jury extra instructions.

In addition, the People stated the concern that there was no appellate law on the subject of instructions on "cultural defenses," and that

> the problem, apparently, to me, is that the jury has heard evidence about that, and whether we called it cultural defense, I don't know, but they certainly have heard the word "culture" probably a thousand times in this trial; maybe not a thousand, but hundreds....

The trial court expressed the concern that the instruction would be "telling [the jury] that is the law." Although defendant's attorney specifically pointed out that the instruction merely told the jury that it could either consider or not consider the evidence of cultural background in determining defendant's mental state at the time of the crime, the trial court disagreed that that was the instruction's effect.

Ultimately, the court refused to give the instruction, commenting that it did not want to put the "stamp of approval on [defendant's] actions in the United States, which would have been acceptable in China"....

The issue then is whether it was a correct statement of the law that the jury may consider evidence of defendant's cultural background in determining the presence or absence of the "essential mental states of the crimes defined in these instructions, or in determining any other issue in this case."

The essential mental states at issue here were (1) premeditation and deliberation, (2) malice aforethought, and (3) specific intent to kill. Generally speaking, all relevant evidence is admissible, and the trier of fact may consider any admitted evidence. Here, the admission of evidence of defendant's cultural background was never objected to by the People; there is no argument that the evidence was relevant. The question then is, on what issues was such evidence relevant? As discussed below, this evidence clearly related to certain mental states, which are elements of the charged offense.

First, the evidence of defendant's cultural background was clearly relevant on the issue of premeditation and deliberation. The prosecution's theory was that defendant's statements on days before the killing to Wu and other family members indicated that she had planned to take revenge on Wu by killing Sidney in a Medea-like gesture. The evidence of defendant's cultural background offered an alternative explanation for the statements (that defendant intended to kill herself) and also for motive behind the killing, that explanation being that the killing of Sidney (as opposed to defendant's own planned suicide) was not deliberate and premeditated, but instead occurred immediately after defendant learned from Sidney himself facts conclusively confirming, in defendant's mind, the statements by Gramma and Sandy, and her own observations, that Sidney was not loved by Wu and was badly treated.

Second, the evidence of defendant's cultural background was also relevant on the issue of malice aforethought and the existence of heat of passion at the time of the killing, which eliminates malice and reduces an intentional killing to voluntary manslaughter. The court recognized that "heat of passion" was an issue in this case because it instructed the jury regarding heat of passion negating malice and further instructed the jury regarding the lesser included offense of manslaughter.

...However, as this court stated in *Berry*, "there is no specific type of provocation required by [Penal Code] section 192 [defining manslaughter] and...verbal provocation may be sufficient."

In People v. Borchers (1958) 50 Cal.2d 321, 329... in the course of explaining the phrase "heat of passion" used in the statute defining manslaughter[,] we pointed out that "passion" need not mean "rage" or "anger" but may be any "[v]iolent, intense, high-wrought or enthusiastic emotion" and concluded there "that defendant was aroused to a heat of 'passion' by a series of events over a considerable period of time...."

Here, there was evidence that defendant had experienced a series of events for a 10-year period before and during her stay in late August and early September 1989 with Wu in California, from which the jury could have concluded that defendant was suffering from "pre-existing stress" at the time that Sidney told her things which confirmed her fear that Sidney, because he was not legitimate and because he had no mother to care for him, was not well-treated, and that things were going to get worse for him upon the death of his Gramma. The testimony related to defendant's cultural background was relevant to explain the source of such stress, as well to explain how Sidney's statements could have constituted "sufficient provocation" to cause defendant to kill Sidney in a "heat of passion."

The experts on transcultural psychology specifically testified that, in their opinion, defendant was acting while in an emotional crisis during the time that she obtained the knife and cord, strangled Sidney and then slashed her own wrist, and that her emotional state was intertwined with, and explainable by reference to, her cultural background. Specifically, the following testimony was given:

Dr. Chien testified:

A. So when all of this thought came up to her mind, all of a sudden she said she couldn't breathe. She almost got into some kind of state that she did not know what she was doing other than thinking that, "There's no way out other than bringing the son together with her to the other life."

After then describing the Chinese belief in an afterlife, he testified that:

A. She told me wondering that is a heaven, paradise. She thought the only way to find out a way out is to bring this Sidney to go together so the mother and son can finally live together in the other heaven, other world if that cannot be done in this realistic earth.

Dr. Chien further testified:

> And at that time, she said during the strangulation or that kind of emotional heat—obviously, she was under the heat of passion when she realized that her son was unwanted son, uncared by Gary, passed around from one woman to the other woman, and now the grandmother is dying and she was planning to leave, "What will happen to Sidney?"
>
> And all this information came up to her mind to stimulate all her guilt feeling which was probably more than ordinary guilt feeling that some depressive person would feel.
>
> I must say that guilt feeling is quite a common symptom in depressive patient, and for that many depressed person would commit suicide.
>
> But in this case, Helen had some realistic reason to be 200 percent or 300 percent more guilty in addition to her normal guilt feeling that came from depression. She would feel that she couldn't really do the duty to the son, so the only way to fulfill her duty when she realized her son was neglected and not to be cared by anybody in the future, she thought the way to go is to the heaven.
>
> So obviously, obviously she strangulated her son and she kind of start being after to breathe again after the strangulation and realize how quickly a boy who is not a small boy could be killed by her small stature.

Dr. Chien was asked about the significance of the "depression in [defendant's] thought processes" on her decision to strangle Sidney and he testified:

> A. It was very—in my expertise as a transcultural psychiatry, in my familiarity, with my familiarity with the Chinese culture translate and from the information interview I obtain from Helen, she thought she was doing that out from the mother's love, mother's responsibility to bring a child together with her when she realized that there was no hope for her or a way for her to survive in this country or in this earth.
>
> Q. Well, are you telling us that the death of Sidney was her act of love?
>
> A. Yes. It's a mother's altruism. This may be very difficult for the Westerner to understand because I have dealt with many other so-called children who are sent to me from the children bureau. Children can be easily taken away from the mother in our agencies' mind. Social worker, when they discovered child abuse case or whatever case, children can be easily taken away from the parents.
>
> But in the Asian culture when the mother commits suicide and leave the children alone, usually they'll be considered to be a totally irresponsible behavior, and the mother will usually worry what would happen if she died, "Who is going to take care of the children? Anybody [sic — "Nobody"?] can supply the real love that mother could provide," so and so....
>
> Q. Well, based upon what you heard from Helen and reviewed from the materials, was Helen in a fugue state when she strangled Sidney?
>
> A. Obviously.
>
> Q. Why is it obvious?
>
> A. Because that kind of emotion, mixed emotional of the despair, anger, disappointment, depression, sadness, hopelessness, everything all sudden come up to her mind that she thought the only way out is to go to the heaven together with the son. And that is not kind of comfortable thing for people to think long time ahead or to plan.
>
> So obviously, she was under a kind of heat of emotion or I call it heat of passion that went out like a dreamy state.

Dr. Terry Gock, a clinical psychologist who interviewed defendant for a total of nine and a half hours in three interview sessions and a witness for the defense, testified on direct examination that on the day Sidney was killed, defendant was experiencing a very high level of emotional turmoil, i.e., an emotional crisis, which he described as "when our, when our feelings are so conflicting, so confused and so, so distressful that we, that we don't perhaps know exactly how to plan a course of action, plan a solution in the most rational way." He testified that in his opinion, defendant's cultural background was very intertwined with her emotional state on the evening of the killing. Specifically, Dr. Gock testified:

> Is very difficult to divorce ourselves from our culture and act in a totally culturally different way. And so, you know, she in many ways is a product of her past experiences, including her culture. And also when she experience certain things, like some of the information that she, that she got from her son that evening, it was, it was very distressful for her. And in some sense the kind of alternatives that she, if you would perhaps, you know, it's not as rational as an alternative that the only way she saw out was perhaps — you know, maybe that's the best word is the way she saw how to get out of that situation was quite culturally determined....
>
> And then in terms of what are some of the alternatives then for her. In — perhaps in this country, even with a traditional woman may, may see other options. But in her culture, in her own mind, there are no other options but to, for her at that time, but to kill herself and take the son along with her so that they could sort of step over to the next world where she could devote herself, all of herself to the caring of the son, caring of Sidney.
>
> Q. Was that the motive for killing him?
> A. Motive, if you will, yes.
> Q. What was her purpose?
> A. Her purpose is to, is that she, is, in many ways is, is a benevolent one. It's a positive one where she believed — and this, this sounds sort of implausible to some, some of us whose, who are raised in another culture. That what she believed was that she was not exactly killing but, through death, both of them would be reunited in the next world where she could provide the kind of caring that Sidney did not get in this world....

Because the requested instruction was, for the most part, a correct statement of the law, and because it was applicable to the evidence and one of defendant's two basic defenses in this case, upon retrial defendant is entitled to have the jury instructed that it may consider evidence of defendant's cultural background in determining the existence or nonexistence of the relevant mental states....

The judgment is reversed.

Causation

The extent of an offender's liability can be dramatically different depending on whether he or she is held to be causally accountable for a result prohibited by an offense. Homicide is the most obvious example; the difference between murder and attempted murder can be the difference between the death penalty or a moderate term of imprisonment. When is an offender causally accountable for a result? Why should such a causal connection matter?

◆ THE CASE OF JOE PAUL GOVAN

It is April 5, 1980, in Phoenix, Arizona. For the past three years, Joe Paul Govan and his girlfriend, Sharon Keeble, have lived together. Sharon has three children, Kimberly, thirteen, Jimmy, twelve, and Christian, three. Both Govan and Keeble own guns. Govan is a five-foot, nine-inch African American weighing 160 pounds.

This afternoon Govan and Keeble have their guns out, cleaning them. As usual, they are arguing. Unwilling to continue fighting, Govan steps out to get some air. While he is out, Kimberly tells her mother that Govan was "messing" with her; she says that he kissed her on the neck. "Flipping out," Sharon immediately starts yelling at Govan as he returns. This time, however, yelling is not enough. She loads her gun and shoots at him but misses, as Govan quickly leaves. Sharon tells Kimberly that she was only trying to scare Govan. She has Kimberly take the other children to their friend Carrie Gray's apartment. (The children call her "Mama Carrie.")

Figure 34 **Crime scene, stairs leading up to porch and blood streaks along balcony on left**

(Superior Court of Arizona)

Later that day, Govan and Sharon meet at Gray's apartment. Before long, they are outside the apartment, again arguing loudly, this time over Sharon's attempt to call the police to report Govan's "messing around." Govan is desperately trying to convince her not to call. Finally, frustrated and angry, Govan decides it is time to walk away. Starting down the stairs, he pauses a moment, glances back over his shoulder, and sees Sharon reaching for her purse. He remembers that she sometimes keeps her gun in there, and takes his gun out of his pocket and says, "Well, I'll stop this." Without aiming, he shoots at her. A minute later, after hearing Kimberly yell, he realizes in horror that his shot has hit her. Govan panics and flees.

Figure 35 Crime scene, close-up of porch and blood
(Superior Court of Arizona)

The bullet has hit the left side of Keeble's neck. She is rushed to a Phoenix hospital, where doctors perform a tracheotomy to help her breathe, a procedure that requires inserting a tube into her throat. It is a medical necessity in this instance but, unfortunately, is likely to increase her susceptibility to future respiratory problems.

On May 1, 1985, authorities charge Govan with aggravated assault. Despite the charge, Govan visits Sharon frequently in the hospital. He expresses his remorse for the incident and wishes to care for her and help her recover. The continual courting works and they are eventually married.

Ten months later, on March 11, 1981, the assault charge is dropped without prejudice.

The incident has left Sharon a quadriplegic; she is unable to perform even the most basic activities to care for herself, and requires constant care, including keeping her trachea tube clear. For several months, Govan tries to care for Sharon, but by year's end feels obliged to place her in a convalescent home. Unhappy with the change, Sharon arranges to move to California, where her parents have her admitted to the medical center at the University of California at Irvine. She subsequently annuls her marriage to Govan. After a year in

Figure 36 Sharon Keeble after partially recovering from the shooting
(Superior Court of Arizona)

treatment, Sharon is able to leave the hospital and move into an apartment with a nursing assistant to care for her.

Sharon realizes that her life is not over. She begins taking classes at Coastline Community College, with hopes of becoming a counselor. Even her doctor, Dr. Edward Weir, notices that she is generally upbeat and excited about her studies. Nonetheless, Sharon is never free of the physical ailments connected with her quadriplegia; her trachea tube continues to be bothersome and she is frustrated with the efforts it takes to stay healthy.

In January 1985, Sharon develops pneumonia. After allowing it to go untreated for several weeks, her condition becomes quite serious. She finally seeks medical care and is admitted to the hospital on January 24, but dies the next day. Her doctor concludes that she died of "aspiration pneumonia due to tracheotomy problems due to the quadriplegia."

On May 13, 1985, Govan is charged with second degree murder for Sharon's death based upon the shooting five years earlier.

1. *Assuming the earlier assault has already been fully dealt with*, relying only upon your intuitions of justice, what *additional* liability and punishment, if any, does Joe Paul Govan deserve *because of Keeble's subsequent death*?

N	0	1	2	3	4	5	6	7	8	9	10	11
☐	☐	☐	☐	☐	☐	☐	☐	☐	☐	☐	☐	☐
no liability	liability but no punishment	1 day	2 wks	2 mo	6 mo	1 yr	3 yrs	7 yrs	15 yrs	30 yrs	life imprison- ment	death

2. Would Govan be causally accountable for Keeble's death under the causation provision reproduced in the questions immediately following the "Manny the Master" Problem later in this Section?

3. If there had been no death, what liability, if any, would be imposed under the then-existing statutes? After the death, what liability, if any?

4. If there had been no death, what liability, if any, would be imposed under the Model Penal Code? After the death, what liability, if any?

■ **THE LAW**

Arizona Revised Statutes
(1980)

Title 13. Criminal Code

Chapter 11. Homicide

Section 13-1101. Definitions

In this chapter, unless the context otherwise requires:

1. "Premeditation" means that the defendant acts with either the intention or the knowledge that he will kill another human being, when

such intention or knowledge precedes the killing by a length of time to permit reflection. An act is not done with premeditation if it is the instant effect of a sudden quarrel or heat of passion.

2. "Homicide" means first degree murder, second degree murder, manslaughter or negligent homicide.

3. "Person" means a human being.

4. "Adequate provocation" means conduct or circumstances sufficient to deprive a reasonable person of self-control.

Section 13-1102. Negligent Homicide; Classification

A. A person commits negligent homicide if with criminal negligence such person causes the death of another person.

B. Negligent homicide is a class 4 felony.

Section 13-1103. Manslaughter; Classification

A. A person commits manslaughter by:

1. Recklessly causing the death of another person; or

2. Committing second degree murder as defined in Section 13-1104, subsection A upon a sudden quarrel or heat of passion resulting from adequate provocation by the victim; or

3. Intentionally aiding another to commit suicide; or

4. Committing second degree murder as defined in Section 13-1104, subsection A, paragraph 3, while being coerced to do so by the use or threatened immediate use of unlawful deadly physical force upon such person or third person which a reasonable person in his situation would have been unable to resist.

B. Manslaughter is a class 3 felony.

Section 13-1104. Second Degree Murder; Classification

A. A person commits second degree murder if without premeditation:

1. Such person intentionally causes the death of another person; or

2. Knowing that his conduct will cause the death or serious physical injury, such person causes the death of another person; or

3. Under circumstances manifesting extreme indifference to human life, such person recklessly engages in conduct which creates a grave risk of death and thereby causes the death of another person.

B. Second degree murder is a class 2 felony.

Section 13-1105. First Degree Murder; Classification

A. A person commits first degree murder if:

1. Knowing that his conduct will cause death, such person causes the death of another with premeditation; or

2. Acting either alone or with one or more other persons such person commits or attempts to commit sexual assault under Section 13-1406, child molestation under Section 13-1410, narcotics offenses as provided in Section 36-1002.02, 36-1002.03 or 36-1002.04, kidnapping under Section 13-1304, burglary under Section 13-1506, 13-1507 or 13-1508, arson of an occupied structure under Section 13-1704, robbery under Section 13-1902, 13-1903 or 13-1904, escape under Section 13-2503 or 13-2504, and in the course of and in furtherance of such offense or immediate flight from such offense, such person or another person causes the death of any person.

B. Homicide, as defined in paragraph 2 of subsection A of this section, requires no specific mental state other than what is required for the commission of any of the enumerated felonies.

C. First degree murder is a class 1 felony and is punishable by death or life imprisonment as provided by Section 13-703.

Chapter 12. Assault and Related Offenses

Section 13-1201. Endangerment; Classification

A. A person commits endangerment by recklessly endangering another person with a substantial risk of imminent death or physical injury.

B. Endangerment involving a substantial risk of imminent death is a class 6 felony. In all other cases, it is a class 1 misdemeanor.

Section 13-1203. Assault; Classification

A. A person commits assault by:

1. Intentionally, knowingly or recklessly causing any physical injury to another person; or

2. Intentionally placing another person in reasonable apprehension of imminent physical injury; or

3. Knowingly touching another person with the intent to injure, insult or provoke such person.

B. Assault committed intentionally or knowingly pursuant to subsection A, paragraph 1 is a class 1 misdemeanor. Assault committed recklessly pursuant to subsection A, paragraph 1 or assault pursuant to subsection A, paragraph 2 is a class 2 misdemeanor. Assault committed pursuant to subsection A, paragraph 3 is a class 3 misdemeanor.

Section 13-1204. Aggravated Assault

A. A person commits aggravated assault if such person commits assault as defined in Section 13-1203 under any of the following circumstances:

    1. If such person causes serious physical injury to another.

    2. If such person uses a deadly weapon or dangerous instrument.

    3. If such person commits the assault after entering the private home of another person with the intent to commit the assault. . . .

B. Aggravated assault pursuant to subsection A, paragraph 1 or 2 of this section is a class 3 felony. Aggravated assault pursuant to subsection A, paragraphs 3, 4, 5, 6, 7 or 8 of this section is a class 6 felony.

Section 13-1001. [Attempt] Classifications . . .

C. Attempt is a:

    1. Class 2 felony if the offense attempted is a class 1 felony.

    2. Class 3 felony if the offense attempted is a class 2 felony.

    3. Class 4 felony if the offense attempted is a class 3 felony.

    4. Class 5 felony if the offense attempted is a class 4 felony.

    5. Class 6 felony if the offense attempted is a class 5 felony.

    6. Class 1 misdemeanor if the offense attempted is a class 6 felony.

    7. Class 2 misdemeanor if the offense attempted is a class 1 misdemeanor.

    8. Class 3 misdemeanor if the offense attempted is a class 2 misdemeanor.

    9. Petty offense if the offense attempted is a class 3 misdemeanor or petty offense.

Section 13-701. Sentence of Imprisonment for Felony; Presentence Report

A. A sentence of imprisonment for a felony shall be a definite term of years and the person sentenced, unless otherwise provided by law, shall be committed to the custody of the state department of corrections.

B. No prisoner may be transferred to the custody of the state department of corrections without a certified copy of the judgment and sentence, signed by the sentencing judge, and a copy of a recent presentence investigation report unless the court has waived preparation of the report.

C. Except as provided in §13-604 the term of imprisonment for a felony shall be determined as follows for a first offense:

    1. For a class 2 felony, seven years.

    2. For a class 3 felony, five years.

    3. For a class 4 felony, four years.

    4. For a class 5 felony, two years.

    5. For a class 6 felony, one and one-half years.

Chapter 1. General Provisions

Section 13-101. Purposes

It is declared that the public policy of this state and the general purposes of the provisions of this title are:

1. To proscribe conduct that unjustifiably and inexcusably causes or threatens substantial harm to individual or public interests;

2. To give fair warning of the nature of the conduct proscribed and of the sentences authorized upon conviction;

3. To define the act or omission and the accompanying mental state which constitute each offense and limit the condemnation of conduct as criminal when it does not fall within the purposes set forth;

4. To differentiate on reasonable grounds between serious and minor offenses and to prescribe proportionate penalties for each;

5. To insure the public safety by preventing the commission of offenses through the deterrent influence of the sentences authorized; and

6. To impose just and deserved punishment on those whose conduct threatens the public peace.

Section 13-103. Abolition of Common Law Offenses

All common law offenses are hereby abolished. No conduct or omission constitutes an offense unless it is an offense under this title or under another statute or ordinance.

Section 13-104. Rule of Construction

The general rule that a penal statute is to be strictly construed does not apply to this title, but the provisions herein must be construed according to the fair meaning of their terms to promote justice and effect the objects of the law, including the purposes stated in §13-101.

Section 13-105. Definitions

In this title, unless the context otherwise requires:

1. "Act" means a bodily movement.

2. "Benefit" means an act of value or advantage, present or prospective.

3. "Conduct" means an act or omission and its accompanying culpable state.

4. "Crime" means a misdemeanor or a felony.

5. "Culpable mental state" means intentionally, knowingly, recklessly or with criminal negligence as those are thusly defined:

    (a) "Intentionally" or "with the intent to" means, with respect to a result or to conduct described by a statute defining an offense, that a person's objective is to cause that result or to engage in that conduct.

(b) "Knowingly" means, with respect to conduct or to a circumstance described by a statute defining an offense, that a person is aware or believes that his or her conduct is of that nature or that the circumstance exists.

(c) "Recklessly" means, with respect to a result or to a circumstance described by a statute defining an offense, that a person is aware of and consciously disregards a substantial and unjustifiable risk that the result will occur or that the circumstance exists. The risk must be of such nature and degree that disregard of such risk constitutes a gross deviation from the standard of conduct that a reasonable person would observe in the situation. A person who creates such a risk but is unaware of such risk solely by reason of voluntary intoxication also acts recklessly with respect to such risk.

(d) "Criminal negligence" means, with respect to a result or to a circumstance described by a statute defining an offense, that a person fails to perceive a substantial and unjustifiable risk that the result will occur or that the circumstance exists. The risk must be of such nature and degree that the failure to perceive it constitutes a gross deviation from the standard of care that a reasonable person would observe in the situation. . . .

7. "Dangerous instrument" means anything that under the circumstance in which it is used, attempted to be used or threatened to be used is readily capable of causing death or serious physical injury.

8. "Deadly physical force" means force which is used with the purpose of causing death or serious physical injury or in the manner of its use or intended use is capable of creating a substantial risk of causing death or serious physical injury.

9. "Deadly weapon" means anything designed for lethal use. The term includes a firearm. . . .

11. "Felony" means an offense for which a sentence to a term of imprisonment to the custody of the department of corrections is authorized by any law of this state. . . .

15. "Intoxication" means any mental or physical incapacity resulting from the use of drugs, toxic vapors, or intoxicating liquors.

16. "Misdemeanor" means an offense for which a sentence to a term of imprisonment other than to the custody of the department of corrections is authorized by any law of this state.

17. "Narcotic drug" means narcotic drugs as defined by Section 36-1001.

18. "Offense" means conduct for which a sentence to a term of imprisonment or of a fine is provided by any law of this state or by any law, regulation or ordinance of a political subsection of this state.

19. "Omission" means the failure to perform an act as to which a duty of performance is imposed by law. . . .

22. "Petty offense" means an offense for which a sentence of a fine only is authorized by law.

23. "Physical force" means the impairment of physical condition. . . .

27. "Property" means anything of value, tangible or intangible....

29. "Serious physical injury" includes physical injury which created a reasonable risk of death, or which causes serious and permanent disfigurement, or serious impairment of health or loss or protracted impairment of the function of any bodily organ or limb.

30. "Unlawful" means contrary to law or, where the context so requires, not permitted by law....

32. "Voluntary act" means a bodily movement performed consciously and as a result of effort and determination.

33. "Voluntary intoxication" means intoxication caused by the knowing use of drugs, toxic vapors or intoxicating liquors by the defendant, the tendency of which to cause intoxication the defendant knows or ought to know, unless the defendant introduces them pursuant to medical advice or under duress as would afford a defense to an offense.

Chapter 2. General Principles of Criminal Liability

Section 13-201. Requirements for Criminal Liability

The minimum requirement for criminal liability is the performance by a person of conduct which includes a voluntary act or the omission to perform a duty imposed by law which the person is physically capable of performing.

Section 13-203. Causal Relationship Between Conduct and Result; Relationship to Mental Culpability

A. Conduct is the cause of a result when both of the following exist:

1. But for the conduct the result in question would not have occurred.

2. The relationship between the conduct and result satisfies any additional causal requirements imposed by the statute defining the offense.

B. If intentionally causing a particular result is an element of an offense, and the actual result is not within the intention or contemplation of the person, that element is established if:

1. The actual result differs from that intended or contemplated only in the respect that a different person or different property is injured or affected or that the injury or harm intended or contemplated would have been more serious or extensive than that caused; or

2. The actual result involves similar injury or harm as that intended or contemplated and occurs in a manner which the person knows or should know is rendered substantially more probable by such person's conduct.

C. If recklessly or negligently causing a particular result is an element of an offense, and the actual result is not within the risk of which the person is aware or in the case of criminal negligence, of which the person should be aware, that element is established if:

1. The actual result differs from the probable result only in the respect that a different person or different property is injured or affected or that the

injury or harm intended or contemplated would have been more serious or extensive than that caused; or

2. The actual result involves similar injury or harm as the probable result and occurs in a manner which the person knows or should know is rendered substantially more probable by such person's conduct.

Model Penal Code
(Official Draft 1962)

Section 2.03. Causal Relationship Between Conduct and Result; Divergence Between Result Designed or Contemplated and Actual Result or Between Probable and Actual Result

(1) Conduct is the cause of a result when:

(a) it is an antecedent but for which the result in question would not have occurred; and

(b) the relationship between the conduct and result satisfies any additional causal requirements imposed by the Code or by the law defining the offense.

(2) When purposely or knowingly causing a particular result is an element of an offense, the element is not established if the actual result is not within the purpose or the contemplation of the actor unless:

(a) the actual result differs from that designed or contemplated, as the case may be, only in the respect that a different person or different property is injured or affected or that the injury or harm designed or contemplated would have been more serious or more extensive than that caused; or

(b) the actual result involves the same kind of injury or harm as that designed or contemplated and is not too remote or accidental in its occurrence to have a [just] bearing on the actor's liability or on the gravity of his offense.

(3) When recklessly or negligently causing a particular result is an element of an offense, the element is not established if the actual result is not within the risk of which the actor is aware or, in the case of negligence, of which he should be aware unless:

(a) the actual result differs from the probable result only in the respect that a different person or different property is injured or affected or that the probable injury or harm would have been more serious or more extensive than that caused; or

(b) the actual result involves the same kind of injury or harm as the probable result and is not too remote or accidental in its occurrence to have a [just] bearing on the actor's liability or on the gravity of his offense.

(4) When causing a particular result is a material element of an offense for which absolute liability is imposed by law, the element is not established unless the actual result is a probable consequence of the actor's conduct.

Section 5.05. Grading of Criminal Attempt, Solicitation and Conspiracy; Mitigation in Cases of Lesser Danger; Multiple Convictions Barred

(1) Grading. Except as otherwise provided in this Section, attempt, solicitation and conspiracy are crimes of the same grade and degree as the most serious offense which is attempted or solicited or is an object of the conspiracy. An attempt, solicitation or conspiracy to commit a [capital crime or a] felony of the first degree is a felony of the second degree.

(2) Mitigation. If the particular conduct charged to constitute a criminal attempt, solicitation or conspiracy is so inherently unlikely to result or culminate in the commission of a crime that neither such conduct nor the actor presents a public danger warranting the grading of such offense under this Section, the Court shall exercise its power under Section 6.12 to enter judgment and impose sentence for a crime of lower grade or degree or, in extreme cases, may dismiss the prosecution.

(3) Multiple Convictions. A person may not be convicted of more than one offense defined by this Article for conduct designed to commit or to culminate in the commission of the same crime.

▲ PROBLEM
Manny the Master

An informant in the police department reports that Prosecutor Baylor is being investigated for taking bribes to forgo prosecutions. Kenny "The Hat," the local underworld boss, suspects that if Baylor is arrested he will reveal all to the authorities. Kenny decides to have Baylor killed. To be sure that the job gets done, he gives contracts to both Squeeze and Manny. Squeeze, who is somewhat brighter and more experienced than her competitor, Manny, arranges to poison Prosecutor Baylor at the corner hotdog stand where he frequently eats. Manny is tailing Baylor looking for an opportunity. When he sees Squeeze at the hotdog stand he suspects he has been outdone. Squeeze glides over with a smile. "He ate enough to kill an elephant," she tells Manny. "He'll be dead in 45 minutes. Better luck next time." Manny is not giving up so easily. He scurries after Baylor, who has finished his hotdog and is headed down to the subway. Manny spots Baylor at the edge of the platform and positions himself several feet behind him in the crowd. As the train approaches, he pushes another waiting passenger into Baylor, so that Baylor will be pushed in front of the train and be killed instantly. But as Manny pushes, the crowd surges and his push sends the wrong person off the platform. His push is also much too early. The fallen passenger scrambles back onto the platform before the train arrives. Manny turns to leave, angry and humiliated. Maybe he should go to computer school, he thinks, recalling an ad he saw on a matchbook cover. Screams from the track make him turn. People are milling about, peering under the train. He learns from others that a man straining to see the fallen passenger leaned out too far and was hit by the oncoming train. He presses forward to see the dead man. Could he be so lucky? They pull Prosecutor Baylor from under the train. Manny turns and heads for the exit, full of himself. Squeeze won't be making fun of him today.

Assume that the following statute is in force:

Section 11A-2-2. Causal Relationship Between Conduct and Result

Conduct is the cause of a result if:

(1) the conduct is an antecedent but for which the result in question would not have occurred; and

(2) the result is not too remote or too accidental in its manner of occurrence or too dependent upon another's volitional act to have a just bearing on the person's liability or on the gravity of his offense; and

(3) the relationship between the conduct and result satisfies any additional causal requirements imposed by the Code or by the law defining the offense.

(4) Concurrent Causes. Where the conduct of two or more persons each causally contributes to the result and each alone would have been sufficient to cause the result, the requirement of Subsection (1) of this section is satisfied as to both persons.[1]

Manny (and Squeeze and Kenny "The Hat") intended that Prosecutor Baylor be killed and acted upon that intention. Liability for at least attempted murder seems clear. Is Manny criminally liable for causing the death, thus liability for murder? Is Squeeze? Is Kenny "The Hat"?

● OVERVIEW OF CAUSATION

Causation Requirement Inherent in Result Elements Whenever an offense definition includes a result element, as, for example, homicide requires a death, a causation requirement also is implied. That is, it must be shown that the actor's offense conduct caused the prohibited result. This required relationship between the actor's conduct and the result derives from our notions of causal accountability. A result ought to affect an actor's liability only if it is a result for which the actor is causally accountable. Specifically, the law appears arbitrary and unfair if it increases an actor's liability because of a result for which the actor is not causally accountable. The rules of the causation doctrine are the means by which the law attempts to define the conditions under which such causal accountability exists.

---

1. Illinois Proposed Criminal Code §203; see also Rhode Island Proposed Criminal Code §11A-2-2; Kentucky Proposed Criminal Code §501.203.

REQUIREMENTS OF CAUSATION: FACTUAL AND PROXIMATE CAUSE

Current doctrine typically contains two independent requirements to establish a causal connection between an actor's conduct and a result. First, the conduct must be a "but for" cause of the result. That is, in the language of Model Penal Code section 2.03(1)(a), the conduct must be "an antecedent but for which the result in question would not have occurred." This is sometimes called the "factual cause" requirement. Second, the strength and nature of the causal connection between the conduct and the result must be sufficient. "Legal cause," or "proximate cause," as this is sometimes called, requires that the resulting harm be "not too remote or accidental in its occurrence to have a [just] bearing on the actor's liability or on the gravity of his offense." This language, from Model Penal Code section 2.03(2)(b) and (3)(b), is sometimes supplemented by states with an additional requirement that the resulting harm "not be too...dependent on another's volitional act."

Factual Cause Conduct is a factual ("but for") cause of a result if the result would not have occurred but for the conduct. In other words, the conduct is a factual cause if it was necessary for the result to occur. The factual cause inquiry is essentially a scientific and hypothetical one. It asks what the world would have been like had the actor not performed his conduct. Specifically, would the result still have occurred when it did? If the answer is no, then the actor's conduct was necessary for—was a "but for" cause of—the result. Manny's conduct is a necessary cause of Baylor's death. (But Squeeze's poisoning is not.)

Other Factual Cause Tests The *necessary*-cause test is not the only possible formulation of the factual cause requirement. Criticisms of some results of the necessary-cause test—such as Squeeze's escape from homicide liability for Baylor's death—may lead one to examine whether other formulations, such as a *sufficient*-cause test, might be preferable. A sufficient-cause test similarly presents a scientific and hypothetical inquiry, but a different inquiry: Would the actor's conduct have been sufficient by itself to cause the result?

Proximate (Legal) Cause In contrast to the scientific inquiry of the factual cause requirement, the proximate (legal) cause requirement presents essentially a normative inquiry. Deciding whether a result is "too remote or accidental in its occurrence" or "too dependent on another's volitional act" obviously calls for an exercise of intuitive judgment. The inquiry cannot be resolved by examining the facts more closely or having scientific experts analyze the situation. Ultimately, the decision maker must determine how much remoteness is "too remote" or how much dependence on another's volitional act is "too dependent" for the result to have a just bearing on the actor's liability.

Proximity Examples Some examples may help illustrate the concept. Consider a common hypothetical used to illustrate a result that is too remote: the actor who shoots at, but misses, his intended victim, who flees to escape the attack and four blocks later is struck and killed by a falling piano that has broken loose from its rope as it is being hoisted to a third-floor apartment. The actor's shot is a "but for" cause of the death; the deceased would not have been under the piano at the moment it fell *but for* the shot that caused him to flee. But the actor's missed shot would be judged by most people to be too remote and accidental a cause to have a just bearing on the actor's liability for the death caused by the piano. Compare this, however, to *People v. Acosta*, in which the jury concluded, and a majority of the appellate court agreed, that the defendant's conduct in trying to elude chasing police was a sufficiently proximate cause of the collision of two police helicopters.[1] Acosta was convicted of murder in the death of three officers who died in the crash, even though it appeared that the unusual crash occurred because one of the pilots flew recklessly and in violation of FAA regulations. Consider also *People v. Arzon.* In *Arzon*, the defendant's murder conviction was upheld on a finding that his setting fire to a couch was a sufficiently proximate cause of the death of a fireman, who while trying to escape the fire set by the defendant was enveloped in dense smoke from another arson fire of independent origin.[2]

Foreseeability as Factor in Determining Proximate Cause   The foreseeability of the result following from the actor's conduct is a highly influential factor in determinations of proximate cause. If Baylor had died from Squeeze's poisoning, there would be little dispute that the poisoning was sufficiently proximate even if the death had not occurred until a week, or a month, after the act. But foreseeability of the result itself is only one of the factors to which jurors look. Did Manny foresee Baylor's death when he did his pushing? Yes, but not quite in the way that Baylor's death came about. The foreseeability of the general manner in which the result came about also is relevant to jurors, but not every aspect of the way in which the result occurs need be foreseen. Squeeze (and most doctors) may expect that her poison would kill Baylor by slowly interfering with his respiratory system. But she is not likely to be judged less causally accountable if, instead, her poison induces uncontrollable vomiting and Baylor dies of extreme dehydration.

Vagueness in the Proximate Cause Standard   As is apparent from the statutory language, the standard for proximate cause is somewhat vague, in part because the judgement called for is complex. One might try to provide additional guidance by giving a decision maker a series of examples of what is and what is not "too remote" and "too dependent on another's volitional act." But it seems likely that "remoteness" and "dependence" are not judgements that can be conceived of as part of a single continuum along which a single point marks the point of "too remote" or "too dependent." Instead, the judgements appear to depend on the interaction of complex factors. Perhaps criminal law theorists will someday be able to articulate a standard with some greater guidance than is now available, but the project is an ambitious one. At present, the best we can do is to direct the decision maker's attention to certain general kinds of factors that seem highly relevant — the degree of "remoteness," the extent to which the result seems "accidental," the degree of dependence on "another's volitional act." We also can help the decision maker by making explicit, as the Model Penal Code does, that the inquiry is a normative one, and that the decision maker ought not look for a scientific solution, but rather ought to rely on his or her own judgement of what should and should not "have a [just] bearing on the actor's liability or on the gravity of his offense."[3]

---

1. 284 Cal. Rptr. 117 (1991).
2. 92 Misc. 2d 739, 401 N.Y.S.2d 156 (1978).
3. Model Penal Code §2.03(2)(b)&(3)(b).

CAUSING ANOTHER PERSON TO CAUSE RESULT

One actor causing another to cause the prohibited result, as with the informant and Kenny and Manny, is a common and somewhat special case of causation. Establishing causal accountability in the first of two serial causes frequently is troublesome. The potential for a remoteness problem appears in part because the presence of the second actor seems to remove the first actor further from the result. That is, an additional link exists in the causal chain between the first actor and the result. The remoteness problem is further exacerbated by the fact that the intermediate link is a human agent capable of independent volitional conduct. The fact is, one person cannot cause another person to act in the same way that a person can cause a chain of events that are governed by the laws of physics. The engineer can cause the train to accelerate to hit a person on the tracks by pushing the accelerator. We can reliably predict the physical chain of events that necessarily follow from pushing the accelerator. Kenny, in contrast, can only provide motivation to Manny. The issue is not just one of foreseeability or predictability. While Manny might in this instance be as predictable as the effect of pushing the accelerator, the fact remains that it is within Manny's ability to choose not to follow Kenny's wishes. No such possibility of volitional choice exists with the accelerator. And this possibility for independent action has a significant effect on the assessment of causal accountability under the proximate cause test.

Intervening Actor's Volition Breaks Chain In *Commonwealth v. Root*, the defendant was drag racing with another, who was killed when his car hit an oncoming truck as he was trying to pass the defendant.[1] The court found that while the defendant's conduct may have been a factual (necessary) cause of the death—the deceased would not have crashed but for the defendant's drag racing with him—defendant's conduct was not a proximate, legal cause because the deceased had voluntarily chosen to engage in the conduct that caused his own death. In *People v. Campbell*, the defendant was drinking with another man with whom he was angry for having had sex with the defendant's wife. He encouraged the man to kill himself. When the man responded that he had no weapon, the defendant offered to sell him his weapon and subsequently gave the man his gun. The man shot himself. The defendant's conviction for murder was reversed.[2]

Influencing Intervening Actor's Exercise of Volition An intervening actor's potential to act independently does not itself insulate the first actor from causal accountability for the result. The potential for independence must be sufficiently realized. In *State v. Lassiter*, for example, the defendant pimp was brutally beating one of his prostitutes when she jumped from an eleventh floor window to escape his attack.[3] While she chose to jump, the prostitute's choice was

---

1. 403 Pa. 571, 573, 170 A.2d 310, 310-311 (1961). But see *Commonwealth v. Atencio*, 345 Mass. 627, 189 N.E.2d 223 (1963), in which two defendants were held liable for manslaughter for the death of a co-participant in a game of "Russian roulette" in which each pointed a revolver with one cartridge at his own head and pulled the trigger. Compare to *Root* the case of *State v. McFadden*, 320 N.W.2d 608 (Iowa 1982), in which the defendant drag racer was held liable for involuntary manslaughter in the death of a six-year old passenger in a car with which his competitor collided.

2. 124 Mich. App. 333, 335 N.W.2d 27 (1983).

3. 197 N.J. Super. 2, 7-8, 484 A.2d 13, 15-16 (App. Div. 1984).

so highly influenced (coerced) by the defendant that it was close to no choice. Similarly, in *Stephenson v. State*, the defendant abducted and repeatedly performed sexual perversions, including inflicting bite wounds, on a woman who then secretly took poison because she was "distracted with the pain and shame so inflicted on her." The woman eventually received medical treatment but died of an infection. Defendant was held liable for second-degree murder.[1]

Continuum of Volition   In some cases, the intervening actor's potential for volitional conduct is altogether illusory. In *People v. Kibbe*, for example, the defendants robbed the victim and left him drunk and partially undressed on a dark, snowy rural road. Approximately 20-30 minutes later, a motorist struck and killed the victim.[2] Under the circumstances, one might conclude that the motorist was exercising little or no independent choice when he hit the victim. The court concluded that the defendants' conduct had caused the death despite the presence of a human agent in the causal chain. In *Lassiter*, the prostitute's decision to jump may be more akin to the lack of choice by the motorist in *Kibbe* than to the free choice exercised by the deceased drag racer in *Root*.[3] Root's drag racing tempted but did not compel the lethal conduct in the way that Lassiter's beating compelled the prostitute to jump. The point is that there is a continuum of voluntariness, and in each case the decision maker must determine whether the intervening actor's choice reaches that point on the continuum that extinguishes the primary actor's causal accountability for the result.

Proximate Cause and Complicity   To avoid such causation difficulties of the intervening actor where one actor induces another to commit an offense, most jurisdictions treat such conduct either as a form of complicity or as a special form of liability for causing crime by an innocent, depending on the status of the person induced to commit the offense.[4] This issue is taken up in Section 14.

● DISCUSSION MATERIALS

Should Resulting Harm Be Relevant to Criminal Liability? Should a Completed Offense Be Punished More than an Unsuccessful Attempt?

The issue that has been the focus of this Section — what constitutes an adequate causal connection between the actor's conduct and the resulting harm — is important only if the law alters the actor's liability based on a resulting

---

1. 205 Ind. 141, 179 N.E. 633 (1932).
2. 35 N.Y.2d 407, 321 N.E.2d 773, 362 N.Y.S.2d 848 (1974).
3. The *Lassiter* court seems to suggest that the chain is less likely to be broken if the deceased's conduct was "reasonable." By "reasonable" the court may mean "understandable in light of the highly coercive circumstances" rather than instinctive (and less calculated). The more "understandable" the deceased action, the more likely the subsequent actor's "choice" is likely to be judged *not* a break in the causal chain. Id. at 10-12, 484 A.2d at 17-19.
4. See, e.g., Model Penal Code §2.06(2)(a)&(3)(a)(ii).

harm. While the law traditionally takes into account resulting harm, not everyone agrees that it should. The dispute over whether resulting harm should be given significance is essentially the same dispute as to whether an unsuccessful attempt should be punished the same as an attempt that is successful in bringing about the contemplated harm: Should the actual occurrence of the resulting harm matter to criminal liability? The materials below introduce the competing arguments in these debates.

Sandy Kadish argues that, given the purposes of the criminal law, there is no rational defense for giving significance to resulting harm. George Fletcher, on the other hand, notes the arguments in support of the harm doctrine and places the dispute in the context of what he calls the competing "traditionalist" and "modernist" approaches to criminal law. After refining Fletcher's distinction (and shifting to an "objectivist" and "subjectivist" terminology), Robinson explores why most jurisdictions adopt an objectivist view and examines the Model Penal Code's inherent inconsistencies when it attempts to implement its stated preference for a subjectivist view.

Sanford H. Kadish, The Criminal Law and the Luck of the Draw

84 Journal of Criminal Law and Criminology 679, 679-690 (1994)

I propose to consider what to make of a doctrine of the criminal law that seems to me not rationally supportable notwithstanding its near universal acceptance in Western law, the support of many jurists and philosophers, and its resonance with the intuitions of lawyers and lay people alike. This is the doctrine—the harm doctrine, I'll call it—that reduces punishment for intentional wrongdoers (and often precludes punishment for negligent and reckless wrongdoers) if by chance the harm they intended or risked does not occur. I will also consider a corollary of the harm doctrine which offers a full defense if it so happens that, unbeknownst to the defendants, the harm they intended could not possibly have been done.

Whether the harm doctrine can be justified is, as George Fletcher has said, a "deep, unresolved issue in the theory of criminal liability." . . .

Of course our criminal law has for centuries included many irrational doctrines—whole Augean stables full. Some of them were that way from the start. Others got that way when changed conditions made them anomalous, like the murder rule requiring the victim to have died within a year and a day of the injury. But these differ from the harm doctrine in that they are widely recognized as insupportable, and their long persistence in the law is simply evidence that the law is slow to change. The harm doctrine is special (although, as we will see, not singular) in that large segments of the legal and lay community regard it as sound.

I will begin by setting out the law that most clearly exhibits the harm doctrine at work. This is the law governing the punishment of failed efforts to do some prohibited harm (the law of attempts) and of actions that create the risk of the harm without producing it (the law of culpable risk creation). These rules are well known and I will only sketch them briefly.

First, the law of attempts.* Consider the case of a man who stabbed his son in anger, pleaded guilty and was convicted of a crime equivalent for our purposes to attempted murder. After serving several months of a two year sentence he was paroled. However, three months later his son, who had been hospitalized since the attack, took a turn for the worse and died, whereupon the prosecutor, quite within the law, charged the father with murder, a crime punishable with life imprisonment or death.

What did the father do in jail or on parole that merited the greater punishment? Not a thing. If a good constitution or a good surgeon had saved the son, the father could not have been further punished. The occurrence of the resulting death alone raises the crime and the punishment. In most jurisdictions this same principle operates for all crimes, not just homicidal crimes. In California, for example, an attempt to commit a crime is punishable with half the punishment for the completed crime. Thus, the reward for failing, no matter how hard you try to succeed or how close you come, is a lesser punishment.

Now consider crimes of culpable risk creation — crimes in which a person is punished, not for attempting a harm, but for culpably risking it. The punishment of these crimes is also made to depend on chance. Take the case of Mr. Malone. He and his friend decided to play a game of Russian Roulette in which each took turns spinning the chamber of a revolver, with one round in it, and firing at the other. When Malone's turn came to pull the trigger the gun fired and killed his friend. Malone was convicted of second degree murder, based on the egregious risk to life he needlessly created.

That sounds fair enough. But suppose instead, that the bullet only inflicted a flesh wound, or that the bullet was not in the firing chamber when Malone pulled the trigger. Could Malone then have been convicted of any crime? Perhaps he could have been convicted of some ad hoc statutory offense concerning firearms, but such an offense would carry nothing like the penalty for murder. And if there had been no special statute of this kind, he could not be convicted of any crime at all, since traditionally just recklessly endangering another was itself not criminal — except in specific contexts, like driving a car. Some jurisdictions have in recent years made it criminal to recklessly endanger another person in all situations, but even these statutes treat the offense as a minor one.

Finally, I need to mention one more doctrine that exhibits the law's preoccupation with a resulting harm. It is the doctrine of impossibility, which takes the harm doctrine one step further.** The harm doctrine calls for a lesser punishment when no harm was done; the impossibility doctrine calls for no punishment at all when the harm could not possibly have been done. Though now a minority view, it still has its defenders, both on and off the bench.

The gist of this doctrine is that a serious effort to commit a crime, even one which includes what the actor thought was the last thing he needed to do to commit it, is not punishable if the crime could not have succeeded. . . . In another example a hunter, meaning to shoot a deer before the hunting season, shoots at a straw dummy the game warden erected, with reflectors for eyes to give it verisimilitude. Is this an attempt to take a deer out of season? No, said the court: "If the

---

*Editor's Note—Attempts are the subject of Section 10.
**Editor's Note—Impossibility is the subject of Section 11.

[s]tate's evidence showed an attempt to take the dummy, it fell far short of proving an attempt to take a deer." A final example: Professor Moriarty shoots at what he takes to be Sherlock Holmes, but which in reality is the shadow of Holmes' paper cutout profile that Holmes has set revolving on a phonograph in front of a lamp. Too clever by half, Mr. Holmes. Moriarty escapes again, this time thanks to the impossibility doctrine, since his action — shooting at a shadow — couldn't possibly kill Holmes.

Today, these impossibility cases would go the other way in most jurisdictions — though the attachment of courts to the doctrine is sometimes remarkable. But with the exception of the impossibility doctrine, all of the doctrines I have described are essentially still the law in most places. . . .

I. The Rational Indefensibility of the Harm Doctrine

To make my case that the harm doctrine cannot be rationally defended, I must establish two things: (a) that the doctrine cannot be justified in terms of the crime preventive purposes of criminal punishment; and (b) that neither can it be justified in terms of any convincing principle of justice.

A. The Argument from the Purposes of Punishment

Does the harm doctrine further the law's interest in crime prevention? There are two main ways in which criminal punishment is thought to reduce crime. One is by preventing further criminal acts by the offender. The other is by discouraging criminal acts by others. How far the law succeeds in particular times and places in attaining this goal is an empirical question I need not pursue here, for the question is whether, on the law's premise that punishment does work in this way, the distinction in punishment required by the harm doctrine is defensible. Let's first consider the goal of preventing further crime by the offender being punished.

Convicting offenders serves to identify those who have shown themselves to threaten further breaches of the law, and punishing them constitutes a response to the threat they constitute. The response may take the form of efforts to alter their criminal proclivities (reformation), or to teach them a lesson (special deterrence), or to physically keep them from doing harm for a while (incapacitation). The question is whether the actual occurrence of harm is relevant in assessing the dangerousness of the offenders and their suitability as subjects for reformation, special deterrence or incapacitation in the interest of public protection.

Consider in this light the attempt cases I presented a moment ago. Take the father who stabbed his son. He is now out on parole from his attempted murder conviction. Has he suddenly become more dangerous because the son finally succumbed? Or consider the Russian Roulette player, Mr. Malone. Would he have been less dangerous if the bullet had not fired because it was in another chamber? Of course not. And the same is surely true of the impossibility cases I just described. [W]hether the object the hunters shot at turns out to be a dummy or a live deer, whether the revolving shadow was really that of Holmes or only a cutout — in none of these cases does it make a whit of difference so far as identifying the actor as prima facie requiring protective measures or as indicating the length of time the actor should be held. It may be conceded that a different response may be called for if the impossibility would be obvious to any sane person — trying to open a safe with incantations, for example — or where the evidence of criminal intent is doubtful. But neither is true in any of my cases.

One might argue that we need the harm to happen in order to be sure of the dangerousness of the actors. Without it, the argument might go, we would have to speculate on whether they would actually go forward and do the harm, and thereby deprive actors of the freedom to make a final choice. This argument has no force, however, in cases where the defendants have done the last act they thought necessary to cause the harm — consider, for example, one who shoots to kill another but misses, or cases like those of Professor Moriarty and the hunters. Furthermore, even if the defendant has more to do, the law of attempts requires substantial acts — traditionally defined as acts that come proximately close to success — precisely to meet this concern. Finally, the argument is misdirected, for its logic leads not to punishing attempts less, but to not punishing them at all: freedom to make a final choice whether to take the last step or to desist is at stake whether the punishment is two years or four. . . .

Therefore, reducing punishment in all cases, just because luckily no harm occurs, makes no sense in terms of the purpose of punishment to identify danger-ous behavior and to prevent its perpetrators from repeating it. . . .

Now let's look at the second way criminal punishment may reduce crime, through general deterrence. This works not by protecting the public from the offender, but by providing others who might be tempted to commit a like crime with a warning of what may happen to them if they do. The question here is the same as before: whether it makes any sense to punish attempted and completed crimes differently, insofar as the goal of the law is to deter others from committing the crime.

It seems evident that in crimes of culpable risk creation, like that of my Russian Roulette player or my reckless driver, the lesser punishment for attempts reduces the deterrent efficacy of the law. Since the actors are not planning on doing the harm, the threat of punishment if they do is discounted for them by its improbability. The only way to maintain its full deterrent force is to threaten punishment whether or not the harm occurs. . . .

B. The Argument from the Principle of Desert

My argument to this point has been that attributing legal significance to the chance happening of harm either undercuts or is irrelevant to the crime prevention purposes of criminal punishment. Even so, as I said at the outset, a practice may be justified by some relevant principle of justice. Now I take the principle that limits punishment to what the offender deserves to be such a principle, and one which those subscribing to the harm doctrine would want to rely on. The question, then, is whether wrongdoers deserve less punishment (or none at all) because the harm they intended or culpably risked happens not to occur, or could not have occurred, for reasons unknown to them.

Isn't desert the same whether or not the harm occurs? It is commonly accepted that punishment is deserved if persons are at fault, and that fault depends on their choice to do the wrongful action, not on what is beyond their control. Reconsider my attempt cases. Would the father who stabbed his son deserve less punishment if a skillful doctor had been available to save the son's life? Would the

Russian Roulette player deserve less punishment if the bullet happened to be in another chamber when he fired? Or consider my impossibility cases. Do the hunters who shot the dummy believing it was a deer, or Professor Moriarty, who shot the shadow thinking it was Sherlock Holmes, deserve no punishment because they were mistaken?

While in principle it's difficult to find good reasons for making desert turn on chance, here's the rub: most of us do in fact make judgments precisely of this kind. Doesn't it seem natural for a parent to want to punish her child more for spilling his milk than for almost spilling it, more for running the family car into a wall than for almost doing so? That's the way our unexamined intuitions run. The sight of the harm arouses a degree of anger and resentment that far exceeds that aroused by apprehension of the harm....

What should we make of this paradox? Is there something to be said after all for the popular sentiment that fortuitous results do have a bearing on blame-worthiness, something that is missed by treating it simply as an irregularity? Can attributing punishment significance to the occurrence of harm be justified in terms of the desert principle?

Obviously, the foundation of my argument against making punishment turn on the chance happening of harm rests on the incompatibility of luck and desert. But perhaps this assumption is mistaken. A distinguished philosopher, Thomas Nagel, has advanced the paradoxical notion of "moral luck." His point is that we do commonly make and defend judgments of moral desert despite the presence of substantial elements of chance. So if the harm principle is irrational because it makes moral desert turn on chance, then so are many of our considered moral judgments.

Nagel instances four situations in which moral desert turns on chance. Two of the four are based on a determinist premise; namely, that you may be lucky or unlucky in the antecedent factors that determine the kind of person you turn out to be and in how you choose to exercise your will. True enough if one accepts determinism. But, first, that explanation of human action is highly contestable, and second, the criminal law, with its concepts of personal responsibility and desert, plainly rejects it.

A third instance Nagel gives of moral luck is that you may be lucky or not in whether circumstances present you with an occasion to make a moral choice that will reveal your moral shortcomings; for example, luck in whether you are ever presented with the need to choose to betray a friend or break a promise. But I don't believe that this threatens our sense of justice in blaming in the same way that luck in the fortuitous outcome of an action (the harm doctrine) threatens it. The settled moral understanding is that what you deserve is a function of what you choose. It may be that you would not have had occasion to make a choice that revealed your badness if you had better luck. Nonetheless, you did make a choice — nobody made you — and it is that choice for which you are blamed. It is a different matter, however, to say that chance occurrences that follow after you have made your choice determine what you deserve, for that is to rest desert upon factors other than what you chose to do. Fortuity prior to choice, therefore, may be accommodated to our notions of just desert; fortuity thereafter cannot. As I see it, that leaves the harm doctrine, Nagel's fourth instance of moral luck, as the one deep challenge to the desert principle, the singular paradox which Adam Smith early identified.

George P. Fletcher, A Crime of Self-Defense: Bernhard Goetz and the Law on Trial
64-67 (1988)

...Two conflicting schools of thought have emerged about the essential nature of criminal wrongdoing. A traditional approach emphasizes the victim's suffering and the actor's responsibility for bringing about irreversible damage. A modern approach to crime takes the act — the range of the actor's control over what happens — as the core of the crime. It is a matter of chance, the modernists say, whether a shot intended to kill actually hits its target....

The traditionalists root their case in the way we feel about crime and suffering. Modernists hold to arguments of rational and meaningful punishment. Despite what we might feel, the modernist insists, reason demands that we limit the criminal law to those factors that are within the control of the actor. The occurrence of harm is beyond his control and therefore ought not to have weight in the definition of crime and fitting punishment. The tension between these conflicting schools infects virtually all of our decisions in designing a system of crime and punishment.

Historically, it is hard to deny the relevance of actual harm and suffering in our thinking about crime. The criminal law would never have come into being unless people actually harmed each other. Our thinking about sin and crime begins with a change in the natural order, a human act that leaves a stain on the world. The sin of Eden was not looking at the apple, not possessing it, but eating it. Oedipus's offense against the gods was not lusting, but actually fornicating with his mother. Cain's crime was not endangering Abel, but spilling his blood. The notions of sin and crime are rooted in the harms that humans inflict on each other.

The classical conception of retributive punishment, the *lex talionis*, reenacts the crime on the person of the offender. This is expressed metaphorically in the biblical injunction to take any eye for an eye, a tooth for a tooth, and life for a life. In *Discipline and Punish*, the philosopher Michel Foucault argues that classically, punishment symbolically *expiated* the crime by replicating on the body of the criminal the harm he inflicted on another. It is hard even to think about punishment without perceiving the relationship between the harm wrought by the criminal and the harm he suffers in return....

This is not the way many or perhaps most policy makers think about crime in the modern world. Sometime in the last two or three centuries, our scientific thinking about crime began to shift from the harm done to the act that brings about the harm. The fortuitous connection between acts and their consequences did not trouble the great jurists of the past, but today, in the thinking of the moderns, a great divide separates the actor and his deed from the impact of his act on others. "There is many a slip 'twixt the cup and the lip." And all those slips, all those matters of chance, have undermined the unity we once felt between a homicidal act and the death of the victim.

The notions of risk, probability, and chance circumscribe the modern way of thinking about action and harm. Instead of seeing harm first and the action as the means for bringing about the harm, we are now inclined to see the action first and the harm as a contingent consequence of the action. And if we see the action first and the harm second, we invite the question, Why should we consider the harm at all . . . ? Many radical reformers hold that indeed the harm is totally irrelevant. If you shoot and miss, you should be punished as though you had killed someone. All that matter are the acts that you can control. And you cannot control the bullet after it leaves the barrel. Power may come from the barrel of a gun, as Chairman Mao said, but according to the modernists, you exhaust your power as soon as you fire the gun.

Modernists pride themselves on the rationality of their theory. If the purpose of punishment is *either* to punish wickedness *or* to influence and guide human behavior, the criminal law should limit its sights to conduct and circumstances within human control. There is nothing wicked about the way things fortuitously turn out. The actor's personal culpability is expressed in his actions — not in the accidents of nature that determine the consequences of his actions. And so far as the purpose of punishment is to set an example and deter future offenders, the only conduct that can be deterred is that within our control. The arguments of reason seem almost unbeatable.

The shift toward arresting and prosecuting those who merely attempt crimes reflects a practical concern as well. The legal system should arguably not only react to crimes already committed, but should intervene before the harm is done. The police should arrest the would-be offender before he has a chance to realize the harm his conduct bespeaks. Crimes should be defined and jail sentences inflicted not only to expiate previous wrongs and deter future offenders, but to prevent harm from occurring. This makes a good deal of sense in a world in which we try to manage the resources of government in order to maximize the welfare of all. This approach to punishment is typically called "preventive" as opposed to the traditional "retributive" practice of punishing past crimes, measure for measure.

The rationalists have held sway over English and American criminal law for most of the period since World War II. The prevailing view is that criminal law should serve social goals, rationally determined and efficiently pursued. Punishment should serve the goal of control either by rehabilitating offenders or, when we despair of changing criminals with doses of therapy, by deterring people in the future from choosing crime as a profitable career. The modern approach to crime dismisses as subrational the argument that people simply *feel* that actually killing someone is far worse than trying to kill. The Model Penal Code, a rationalist document that reflects the attitudes of reform-minded lawyers in the 1950s, goes so far as to recommend punishing attempted murder the same way we punish murder. Yet the concern for the suffering victims is too deep-seated to be rejected simply because the reformers have so limited a conception of fair and decent punishment.

We punish convicted criminals not only because as social planners we see a need to deter crime in the future, but because we recognize the irrepressible need of victims to restore their faith in themselves and in the society in which they live. The imperative to do justice requires that we heed the suffering of the victims, that we inquire at trial whether the defendant is responsible for that suffering, and we adjudge him guilty, if the facts warrant it, not for antiseptically violating the rules of the system, but for inflicting a wrong on the body and to the dignity of the victim. . . .

Whether the defendant actually causes the harm to the victim becomes, therefore, a pivotal question in every trial responding to the fact of suffering. . . .

Other Discussion Materials

Paul H. Robinson, The Role of Harm and Evil in Criminal Law: A Study in Legislative Deception?

5 Journal of Contemporary Legal Issues 304-322 (1994)

[The author argues that Fletcher oversimplifies when he portrays the disagreement as one between "traditionalists" and "modernists." The most common view of present codes and laypersons is to discount the significance of resulting harm in defining the minimum requirements of liability but to see it as highly relevant in issues of grading. To avoid confusion, the author suggests that use of the "objectivist" and "subjectivist" labels is preferable.]

Objectivist Versus Subjectivist View of Grading: The Arguments

Why do modern codes take what Fletcher calls the "traditionalist" (objectivist) view of harm and evil in grading? Why do they reject the modernist (subjectivist) view of grading? To set the stage for this discussion, let me review briefly the primary provisions that implement a subjectivist or objectivist view of grading. I will use the Model Penal Code as representative of the subjectivist view.

The most important provision is §5.05(1), which grades all inchoate offenses the same as the grade of substantive offense, with the exception that the inchoate form of a first degree felony (e.g., murder) is graded as a second degree felony. Thus, an unsuccessful conspiracy to commit arson is the same grade offense as if the arson occurs. An uncompleted plan to rape is graded the same as if the rape occurs. A solicitation to illegally dump toxic chemicals is graded the same as if the chemicals were dumped.

Subjectivist grading also is employed in the Code's complicity provision, which stipulates that an actor is as an accomplice if he "aids or agrees or attempts to aid" in the commission of an offense.* Thus, an unfulfilled agreement or unsuccessful attempt to assist or encourage is graded the same as the substantive offense that does not materialize. The actor who agrees to stand watch for a perpetrator bent on arson is liable for arson even if he gets the date confused and does not show. In other words, inchoate complicity is punished not as inchoate liability but as full substantive liability.

Adhering to an objectivist view of grading, a majority of jurisdictions reduce the grade of inchoate conduct below that of the corresponding substantive offense. Similarly, many jurisdictions require actual assistance or encouragement for full complicity; an unsuccessful attempt at complicity can only be punished as an attempt. Where the actor takes steps to burn a building but another arsonist

---

*Editor's Note—Complicity is the subject of Section 14.

gets to it first, the actor is liable only for attempted arson, graded less than the substantive offense. Where the actor tries but fails to aid an arsonist, unbeknownst to the arsonist, and therefore has no causal connection with the offense harm or evil, his liability similarly is attempt liability, not substantive offense liability, and accordingly graded less. These objectivist views are adopted even by jurisdictions that otherwise are heavily influenced by the Model Penal Code and generally accept its subjectivist view of the minimum requirements of liability.

Why these differences in perspective on the significance of harm and evil in grading? The objectivist's preference for increasing liability where the actor causes or contributes to the actual occurrence of the offense harm or evil may be explained in part by a strong intuitive sense.... The community's shared intuitive sense that resulting harm and evil increases blameworthiness is confirmed by recent empirical studies. [The author reviews the studies.] Assume, then, that a strong community intuition exists for increasing punishment where harm or evil actually occurs and is attributable to the actor. Why precisely should the community intuition be of interest to drafters of the community's criminal code? Code drafters typically are guided by either retributivist or utilitarian considerations (or a combination of the two) in determining the rules for the distribution of liability and punishment....

[The author reviews the arguments.]

To summarize, one can find both consequentialist and non-consequentialist arguments in support of giving significance to the occurrence of harm or evil in grading, but one also can find counterarguments of both sorts. If desert is the guiding principle, moral philosophers disagree over the significance of resulting harm or evil. If efficient crime prevention is the goal, the traditional arguments support the subjectivist view but more recent empirical data suggest there may be greater utility in following the community's sense of justice, which would take account of resulting harm and evil, the objectivist view.

Inconsistency in Application of the Subjective View of Grading

Given the arguments available to the subjectivist, one would expect to find a fairly consistent and complete execution of that view in the jurisdictions that adopt it. But no jurisdiction, even those that claim adherence to the principles of the subjectivist view of grading, is consistent or complete in its execution. The reasons for this failure are worth examining, but let me first demonstrate the inconsistencies and incompleteness, using the Model Penal Code again as an instructive subjectivist vehicle.

If the occurrence of the offense harm or evil should play no role in grading, one may wonder, for example, why the Code creates an exception for first degree felonies in grading inchoate offenses. If the arguments for grading inchoate conduct the same as the completed offense are sound, why should they not apply to first degree felonies as well? The Code's commentary offers a deterrent efficacy explanation:

> It is doubtful ... that the threat of punishment for the inchoate crime can add significantly to the net deterrent efficacy of the sanction threatened for the substantive offense that is the actor's object, which he, by hypothesis, ignores.

Hence, there is a basis for economizing in use of the heaviest and most afflictive sanctions by removing them from the inchoate crimes. The sentencing provisions for second degree felonies, including the provision for extended terms, should certainly suffice to meet whatever danger is presented by the actor.

Thus, the drafters seem to concede that deterrence arguments in support of their policy are unpersuasive; dangerousness is the key. Whether the harm or evil actually occurs does not affect the actor's dangerousness.

But then one may wonder why the Code, like all other modern codes, distinguishes between offenses that differ only in that one punishes an actor when harm or evil occurs and the other punishes an actor, at a lower grade, when the harm or evil does not occur. Note, for example, the dramatic difference in grading between manslaughter and endangerment. The Model Penal Code grading is typical: the former is a second degree felony, the latter, a misdemeanor. Yet, the actor's conduct and culpability may be the same under the two offenses; the sole distinguishing variable is existence of a resulting harm or evil. Similarly, recklessly causing a catastrophe is a third degree felony, while the same reckless- ness where the catastrophe does not occur is punished as a misdemeanor. The deterrent-efficiency arguments that the drafters give to explain the exception for grading inchoate first degree felonies does not apply to any of these offenses; in each instance, the no-harm offense is punished only as a misdemeanor, a grade that may not "suffice to meet whatever danger is presented by the actor." Perhaps because the drafters do not see the apparent contradiction in their position, the commentary gives no explanation for why the occurrence of harm or evil should not be relevant in the general grading of inchoate conduct but should be relevant when two substantive offenses are defined and graded disparately to take account of the occurrence of harm or evil.

Other incongruities in the standard implementation of the subjective view are equally mystifying. Recall that, under the subjectivist view, an attempt or agreement to aid in an offense results in full substantive liability for the attempted complicity, not merely inchoate liability. This is consistent with the subjectivist view that an actor's liability ought to be based on the actor's own conduct and attendant state of mind, rather than on subsequent events over which the actor has no control, such as whether the attempt to aid is successful. Yet, the standard subjectivist complicity formulation also provides that an accomplice may not be liable for full substantive liability unless the perpetrator actually commits the offense. For example, Model Penal Code §2.06 provides that, while a perpetra- tor's defense does not redound to the benefit of the accomplice, as it would have at common law, an accomplice cannot be liable for the substantive offense except upon "proof of the commission of the offense." It is unclear what exactly this requires; presumably, at the least, the objective harm or evil of the offense must have occurred. Consistent with this, the Code explicitly provides that complicity in a perpetrator's failed attempt can only be punished as an attempt.

But one might ask, 'If causing the occurrence of the offense harm or evil is immaterial to the grading inquiry, why should it matter to an accomplice's liability whether the perpetrator does or does not actually commit the offense?' To echo the subjectivist argument in support of full substantive liability for inchoate assistance, the accomplice is no less dangerous (or blameworthy) simply because the perpetrator subsequently fails to commit the offense. The accomplice has shown a willingness to aid such an offense. Similarly, if the unsuccessful accomplice is to be held for full substantive liability, based solely upon his or her subjective culpability, why should not the successful accomplice (to the unsuccessful perpetrator) be held to the same result? Indeed, one could argue that the successful accomplice (to the unsuccessful perpetrator) has more clearly demonstrated his dangerousness, by carrying through with all of his complicit conduct, than the unsuccessful accomplice. If subjective culpability is to be the sole criterion, is it not wrong to distinguish the two cases? And, if a distinction is to be made, does not the standard formulation have it backwards based on a subjectivist perspective?

The obvious difference between unsuccessful complicity in a complete offense and successful complicity in an unsuccessful offense is that the harm or evil of the offense has occurred only in the former, which is the only one for which the supposedly subjectivist Code imposes full substantive liability. But the subjectivist can hardly rely on this difference, at least not without renouncing the subjectivist view in grading that the occurrence of harm and evil ought to be irrelevant.

The care taken to distinguish unsuccessful complicity in a complete offense from successful complicity in an unsuccessful offense is all the more peculiar when one remembers that attempt liability, in the latter case, will be punished at the same grade as the substantive offense, the liability in the former case. If the grading ultimately is the same, what is the point of having such a carefully structured distinction within criminal law doctrine?

To make the same point more broadly, one may ask, 'Why would the subjectivist in grading have result elements in any offense definition?' Result elements are found in a variety of offenses, including such offenses as felonious restraint, sexual assault, and arson. In each instance, where all elements of an offense are proven except the result element, an actor is liable for an attempt to commit the offense. Yet, after the doctrine carefully distinguishes the presence and absence of the prohibited result, by including the result as a requirement of the substantive offense's definition, it then imposes the same grade of liability for both the inchoate and the completed conduct! What is the point of the exercise? If the result element is to be ignored in answering the grading inquiry, why not define the offense without it? Why define offenses to include elements that are supposedly irrelevant to the liability inquiry?

Similar observations can be made with regard to the standard subjectivist treatment of offenses other than those with result elements. If the actual occurrence of the evil conduct is irrelevant, why define offenses to distinguish the substantive offense and the attempt? Why not define each offense as "an actor is liable for [the offense] if he does or attempts to do . . . ?" (What constitutes an "attempt" could be defined just as it is now.) The Code's careful segregation of inchoate offenses from complete offenses is, again, peculiar in light of its general policy to punish the attempt at the same grade as the substantive offense.

Illogical Inconsistencies or Useful Deception? . . .

The most plausible explanation is that subjectivist drafters sought to create the appearance of doctrine that takes account of the occurrence of harm and evil because only that would give the doctrine the moral credibility with the community that it needs, while in reality making the occurrence of harm or evil insignificant because that is what the subjectivist drafters believed better serves the goal of crime prevention.

This grand illusion theory suggests another explanation for the inchoate grading exception for first degree felonies: these offenses, such as murder and kidnapping with serious bodily injury, are the most serious offenses and a failure to grade inchoate conduct lower in these cases would create the greatest and most obvious disparity between the community's intuitive judgment and the legal rules. A similar explanation exists for the subjectivists' giving only inchoate liability for complicity in an unsuccessful offense: full liability for such complicity would be too obvious a deviation from the community's expectations.

The concern for preserving the appearance of a code that mirrors community intuitions is illuminated in several other provisions of modern codes. . . .

The drafters' desire for a code that seems to take account of the occurrence of harm and evil, while generally seeking to ignore the same, may well have been a clever strategy, given the arguments presented above concerning the importance of criminal law mirroring community notions of justice. To deviate too conspicuously or too greatly is to risk the law's moral credibility and the cooperation, acquiescence, and coercion to compliance that moral credibility perpetuates. The drafters have every reason, then, to want the code to seem to mirror the community's moral intuitions, especially on matters such as the occurrence of harm and evil for which the intuitions are nearly universal and strongly held.

. . . If the community comes to understand the deception, the system may well lose more credibility than if the code simply overtly deviated from community views. Further, the deception may make it difficult for subsequent reform measures to regenerate credibility for the system. Once deceived, the community understandably may be suspicious and cynical about even genuine reforms meant to make grading more credible. They may understandably ask, another calculated deception? . . .

To put a more admirable gloss on the subjectivist structuring of the Model Penal Code, one might speculate that such was an attempt to make the Code a useful model even if its position on the insignificance of resulting harm and evil were rejected. Perhaps the drafters knew that their view on harm and evil was not shared by most members of the community and that in the political process surrounding adoption of a criminal code it was likely that many jurisdictions would seek to deviate from the Model Code to make harm and evil matter. To maximize the chance that other valuable contributions of the Code would be adopted, the drafters may have thought it best to make it easy to alter the Code into a document that takes account of harm and evil. Thus, by defining distinct substantive and inchoate offenses, and equating their grade in a single provision, a jurisdiction could simply alter that inchoate grading provision if it rejected the Code's view of the insignificance of resulting harm and evil.

If this was the drafters' strategy, they should be congratulated for their political acumen. In the United States, three-quarters of the jurisdictions reject the notion of grading inchoate offenses the same as the completed offense. Nearly two-thirds of American jurisdictions have adopted codes that have been heavily influenced by the Model Penal Code, but less than 30% of these have adopted the

Code's inchoate grading provision or something akin to it. To the many jurisdictions that disagree with the Code on the significance of harm and evil, the drafters' use of the inchoate grading provision, rather than defining all offenses in their inchoate form, no doubt seems a blessing. They can reverse the Code's position simply by altering the relevant grading provisions. The remainder of the Code, with result elements intact, provides many useful advances over prior law in many important respects.

But even this strategy of the Model Penal Code drafters, if that is what it was, can be deceptive, if perhaps inadvertently so. While it may seem that dropping the inchoate grading provision will purge the Code of its disregard for harm and evil, the truth is that the Code's indifference to harm and evil is more pervasive. Recall for example, that the Code's complicity provision requires only that the actor "aids *or agrees or attempts to aid*." If a jurisdiction rejects the subjectivist view of grading, it would want to delete the italicized language. Yet, of the States heavily influenced by the Model Penal Code that have dropped the Code's inchoate grading provision, more than a third have failed to drop the "agrees or attempts to aid" language from the complicity provision.

PART IV

INCHOATE LIABILITY

The previous Section, concerning causation, introduces the notion that the occurrence of results can make a difference to criminal liability. The causation requirements ensure that a defendant's liability and punishment are increased because of resulting harm only if the results are sufficiently causally attributable to the defendant. This Part continues the inquiry into the significance of results. Although there is controversy, in most American jurisdictions a person who unsuccessfully attempts murder might be as dangerous (or as much in need of deterrence and rehabilitation) as an identical person who succeeds in the killing, but the successful murderer is nonetheless assigned greater liability and punishment than the attempter. Why should this be so?

Inchoate liability also presents issues beyond the grading effect of resulting harm. It represents liability's very minimum requirements. The criminal law commonly punishes mere risk creation as well as "evil" conduct, such as cheating, incest between adults, or gambling. It should be no surprise, then, to find that the criminal law punishes inchoate offenses — that is, incomplete or unsuccessful offenses. Actors who plan or attempt offenses may well be blameworthy and dangerous and in need of deterrence and rehabilitation.

Inchoate offenses are consistent with the idea of liability in the absence of harmful results but such offenses go further: to impose liability even in the absence of the prohibited offense conduct. One can be liable for attempted cheating, attempted incest, or attempted gambling. It is enough for inchoate liability that the person in some way *sought* to commit an offense. In that sense, inchoate offenses are unique; they define the borderline of criminal conduct — the minimum that one can do to be criminally liable.

It is in part this role of defining the borderline of criminal liability that makes inchoate offenses so important and so interesting. Deciding on the minimum requirements for liability forces hard decisions, and the choices a society makes reveals much about its views of the nature of criminal liability generally. Principles and dilemmas that are part of the criminal liability landscape in many other areas come into sharp focus in this Part. If criminal liability does not require completed offense conduct, what does it require? If an intention to commit an offense is the gravamen of inchoate offenses, why require any act at all? It is in the definition of this liability borderline that the rationales underlying the criminal law's purposes and principles are revealed.

Attempt Liability

Where liability for a substantive offense fails because of lack of a prohibited result, or of a causal accountability for it, the offender nonetheless may be liable for an attempt. Indeed, attempt liability may attach even if the person never completes the required offense conduct. On the other hand, not every thought of committing an offense is itself a crime. The criminal law requires that the thought first mature into action. Why should this be? And exactly how much action is required to make conduct a criminal attempt?

◆ THE CASE OF ROBERT JACKSON

It is Thursday, June 10, 1976, in Brooklyn, New York. Vanessa Hodges is again explaining her plan to the enthusiastic Martin Allen, whom she met through her friend Rea Longhorne. Hodges has decided Allen trustworthy enough to be included in her plan to rob the Manufacturers Hanover Trust Company bank, on the corner of Flushing and Washington Avenues, in Brooklyn. The plan is simple—arrive at the bank around 7:30 a.m. Monday morning, when the weekend deposits are still there, and make an entrance just as the manager is opening the door. Allen quickly agrees to the plan, and tells Hodges that he has a shotgun and .38 caliber pistol they can use, if necessary.

On Monday morning, Allen meets Hodges at about 7:30 a.m. Robert Jackson, the third member of their team, then picks them up in Longhorne's brown Lincoln Continental. On the back seat is a red and black plaid suitcase containing their supplies—a sawed-off shotgun, shells, handcuffs, and some material for face masks.

Figure 37 **1976 Lincoln Continental**

(Earle K. Gould)

They reach the bank a bit late, a little past 8:00 a.m. The place seems busy. The manager has already opened the door, so they cannot force their way in with him as planned. Discouraged, the three decide to have some breakfast at a nearby restaurant and discuss whether to proceed. After about an hour, they elect to return to the bank to take another look. After getting out to assess the situation, Allen and Hodges decide it too risky to make an attempt now. They also decide they need another person because the night deposit bags are bigger and more bulky than Hodges had anticipated.

They drive to Coney Island to look for William Scott as the potential fourth member of their team. After hearing the plan, Scott immediately signs on. Allen stops to get the sawed-off shotgun and they head back to the bank. By the time they are there, however, it is well past noon and the bank is even more busy. Scott goes into the bank to assess the situation more closely. Trying to act casual, he pretends to be filling out a credit card application. Outside, Jackson covers the car's license plate with a fake one.

Inside, Scott observes that the tellers have begun to process the weekend deposits. He carefully notes that the lone surveillance camera is located over the door, and hurries back to the team. After he describes the layout, the group recognizes that they have missed their chance for the day. They agree to try again next Monday, June 21, at 7:30 a.m. sharp.

They head back to Coney Island. Hodges has decided that the facemask material they have is not right, and they buy some stockings to wear as masks. They also buy gloves for all members.

That Friday, June 18, the police arrest Hodges on an unrelated robbery charge. She tells them of the plan to rob the Flushing Avenue bank and to watch for a brown car with a cardboard license plate and three black men inside. The agents ask her to confirm the plan, so she calls Allen on Saturday to ask if he is still in. He tells her that he "is ready." Just to be sure, Hodges calls again on Sunday to finalize the details. At that time, Allen tells her he knows of her arrest and now thinks the bank job is a bad idea because the F.B.I. might be watching. Hodges suggests that they should proceed without her.

Monday, June 21, is a sunny, clear day. The F.B.I. begin their surveillance at 7:00 a.m. Ten agents are stationed around the bank — in the building across the street, in cars along the same block, and in a nearby parking lot. At a little past 7:00 a.m., they spot a brown Lincoln Continental approaching the bank from the west. The

Figure 38 **Chase Bank in Brooklyn, formerly the Manufacturers Hanover Trust Company**

(Michael Cahill)

three men are driving cautiously and pass the bank. Circling around, they park one block south of the bank, in front of a fire hydrant on Washington Avenue. Scott, wearing a denim hat, gets out and starts walking toward the bank. He walks past the bank on Washington, buys a cup of coffee, and then returns to the corner in front of the bank. He stands there for a few minutes, sipping his coffee and surveying the situation, before rejoining the men in the car. The car pulls out, makes a left and drives west, then makes a U-turn and stops a little west of the bank, on Flushing. After sitting for some time, they drive east toward the bank, continue two blocks past, then turn right and pull over. Jackson, wearing a maroon leisure suit, gets out, removes the front license plate, and throws it onto the floor of the car.

Turning around, they drive back toward the bank and pull over in the same spot where they had previously stopped, near the hydrant on Washington. They sit, debating what to do for almost thirty minutes. It is about 8:15 a.m. when they finally pull out again and drive east, away from the bank, having decided not to rob it. As they pass one of the F.B.I. cars, one of the men does a quick double take. The agents know they have been spotted. The Lincoln turns south onto Grand. Two blocks later, F.B.I. agents pull them over and arrest the three men. After having the defendants step out of their car, the arresting officers open the suitcase they find in the back. It contains two loaded shotguns — one is 24 inches, cut down to a 14-inch barrel, the other is 27 inches, cut down to a 15-inch barrel — and six additional rounds of ammunition, along with mask, a navy watch cap, and a nickel plate toy revolver.

1. Relying only on your intuitions of justice, what liability and punishment, if any, does Robert Jackson deserve?

N	0	1	2	3	4	5	6	7	8	9	10	11
☐	☐	☐	☐	☐	☐	☐	☐	☐	☐	☐	☐	☐
no liability	liability but no punishment	1 day	2 wks	2 mo	6 mo	1 yr	3 yrs	7 yrs	15 yrs	30 yrs	life imprisonment	death

2. What liability, if any, under the then-existing statutes?
3. What liability, if any, under the Model Penal Code?

■ THE LAW

United States Code
(1976)

Title 18
Part I. Crimes
Chapter 103. Robbery and Burglary

Section 2113. Bank Robbery and Incidental Crimes

(a) Whoever, by force and violence, or by intimidation, takes, or attempts to take, from the person or presence of another any property or money or anyother thing of value belonging to, or in the care, custody, control, management, or possession of, any bank, credit union, or any savings and loan association; (or)

Whoever enters or attempts to enter any bank, credit union, or any savings and loan association, or any building used in whole or in part as a bank, credit union, or as a savings and loan association, with intent to commit in such bank, credit union, or loan association, or building, or part thereof, so used, any felony affecting such bank, credit union, or such savings and loan association and in violation of any statute of the United States, or any larceny—

Shall be fined not more than $5,000 or imprisoned not more than twenty years, or both.

(b) Whoever takes and carries away, with intent to steal or purloin, any property or money or any other thing of value exceeding $100 belonging to, or in the care, custody, management, or possession of any bank, credit union, or any savings and loan association, shall be fined not more than $5,000 or imprisoned not more than ten years, or both; or

Whoever takes and carries away, with intent to steal or purloin, any property or money or any other thing of value not exceeding $100 belonging to, or in the care, custody, management, or possession of any bank, credit union, or any savings and loan association, shall be fined not more than $1,000 or imprisoned not more than one year, or both.

(c) Whoever receives, possesses, conceals, stores, barters, sells, or disposes of, any property or money or other thing knowing the same to have been taken from a bank, credit union, or any savings and loan association, in violation of subsection (b) of this section shall be subject to the punishment by said subsection (b) for the taker.

(d) Whoever, in committing, or in attempting to commit, any offense defined in subsections (a) and (b) of this section, assaults any person, or puts in jeopardy the life of any person by the use of a dangerous weapon or device, shall be fined not more than $10,000 or imprisoned not more than twenty-five years, or both.

(e) Whoever, in committing any offense defined in this section, or in avoiding or attempting to avoid apprehension for the commission of such offense, or in freeing himself or attempting to free himself from arrest or confinement for such offense, kills any person, or forces any person to accompany him without the consent of such person, shall be imprisoned not less than ten years, or punished by death if the verdict of the jury shall so direct.

(f) As used in this section the term "bank" means any member of the Federal Reserve System, and any bank, banking association, trust company, savings bank, or other banking institution organized or operating under the laws of the United States, and any bank the deposits of which are insured by the Federal Deposit Insurance Corporation.

(g) As used in this section the term "savings and loan association" means any federal savings and loan association and any "insured institution" as defined in section 401 of the National Housing Act, as amended, and any "Federal credit union" as defined in section 2 of the Federal Credit Union Act.

(h) As used in this section the term "credit union" means any federal credit union and any State-chartered credit union the accounts of which are insured by the Administrator of the National Credit Union Administration.

Chapter 19. Conspiracy

Section 371. Conspiracy to Commit Offense or to Defraud United States

If two or more persons conspire either to commit any offense against the United States, or to defraud the United States, or any agency thereof in any manner or for any purpose, and one or more of such persons do any act to effect the object of the conspiracy, each shall be fined not more than $10,000 or imprisoned not more than five years, or both. If, however, the offense, the commission of which is the object of the conspiracy, is a misdemeanor only, the punishment for such conspiracy shall not exceed the maximum punishment provided for such misdemeanor.

Title 26

Subtitle E. Alcohol, Tobacco and Certain Other Excise Taxes
Chapter 53. Machine Guns, Destructive Devices and Certain Other Firearms

Subchapter C. Prohibited Acts

Section 5861. Prohibited Acts

It shall be unlawful for any person—

(a) to engage in business as a manufacturer or importer or dealer in firearms without having paid the special (occupational) tax required by section 5801 for his business or having registered as required by section 5802; or

(b) to receive or possess a firearm transferred to him in violation of the provisions of this chapter; or

(c) to receive or possess a firearm made in violation of the provisions of this chapter; or

sawed off shot guns

(d) to receive or possess a firearm which is not registered to him in the National Firearms Registration and Transfer Record; or

(e) to transfer a firearm in violation of the provisions of this chapter; or

(f) to make a firearm in violation of the provisions of this chapter; or

(g) to obliterate, remove, change, or alter the serial number or other identification of a firearm required by this chapter; or

(h) to receive or possess a firearm having the serial number or other identification required by this chapter obliterated, removed, changed, or altered; or

(i) to receive or possess a firearm which is not identified by a serial number as required by this chapter; or

(j) to transport, deliver, or receive any firearm in interstate commerce which has been registered as required by this chapter; or

(k) to receive or possess a firearm which has been imported or brought into the United States in violation of section 5844; or

(l) to make, or cause the making of, a false entry on any application, return, or record required by this chapter, knowing such entry to be false.

United States v. Mandujano

499 F.2d 370 (5th Cir. 1974)

implementation
Attempt vs. preparation

Defendant appealed his conviction for attempted distribution of heroin. He had procured an ounce of heroin from a third party for an undercover narcotics agent. The Court affirmed his conviction, and defined the extent of action necessary to establish an attempt as "conduct which constitutes a substantial step toward commission of the crime." This substantial step must be "strongly corroborative of the firmness of the defendant's criminal intent. . . . [O]mission or possession, as well as positive acts, may in certain cases provide a basis for liability." The Court contrasted a substantial step, which would constitute an attempt, with mere preparation, which would not. The culpability required for an attempt was "the kind of culpability otherwise required for the commission of the crime which he is charged with attempting."

Model Penal Code
(Official Draft 1962)

Section 5.01. Criminal Attempt

(1) Definition of Attempt. A person is guilty of an attempt to commit a crime if, acting with the kind of culpability otherwise required for commission of the crime, he:

(a) purposely engages in conduct which would constitute the crime if the attendant circumstances were as he believes them to be; or

(b) when causing a particular result is an element of the crime, does or omits to do anything with the purpose of causing or with the belief that it will cause such result without further conduct on his part; or

(c) purposely does or omits to do anything which, under the circumstances as he believes them to be, is an act or omission constituting a substantial step in a course of conduct planned to culminate in his commission of the crime.

(2) Conduct Which May Be Held Substantial Step Under Subsection (1)(c). Conduct shall not be held to constitute a substantial step under Subsection (1)(c) of this Section unless it is strongly corroborative of the actor's criminal purpose. Without negativing the sufficiency of other conduct, the following, if strongly corroborative of the actor's criminal purpose, shall not be held insufficient as a matter of law:

(a) lying in wait, searching for or following the contemplated victim of the crime;

(b) enticing or seeking to entice the contemplated victim of the crime to go to the place contemplated for its commission;

(c) reconnoitering the place contemplated for the commission of the crime;

(d) unlawful entry of a structure, vehicle or enclosure in which it is contemplated that the crime will be committed;

(e) possession of materials to be employed in the commission of the crime, which are specially designed for such unlawful use or which can serve no lawful purpose of the actor under the circumstances;

(f) possession, collection or fabrication of materials to be employed in the commission of the crime, at or near the place contemplated for its commission, where such possession, collection or fabrication serves no lawful purpose of the actor under the circumstances;

(g) soliciting an innocent agent to engage in conduct constituting an element of the crime.

(3) Conduct Designed to Aid Another in Commission of a Crime. A person who engages in conduct designed to aid another to commit a crime which would establish his complicity under Section 2.06 if the crime were committed by such other person, is guilty of an attempt to commit the crime, although the crime is not committed or attempted by such other person.

(4) Renunciation of Criminal Purpose. When the actor's conduct would otherwise constitute an attempt under Subsection (1)(b) or (1)(c) of this Section, it is an affirmative defense that he abandoned his effort to commit the crime or otherwise prevented its commission, under circumstances manifesting a complete and voluntary renunciation of his criminal purpose. The establishment of such defense does not, however, affect the liability of an accomplice who did not join in such abandonment or prevention. Within the meaning of this Article, renunciation of criminal purpose is not voluntary if it is motivated, in whole or in part, by circumstances, not present or apparent at the inception of the actor's course of conduct, which increase the probability of detection or apprehension or which make more difficult the accomplishment of the criminal purpose. Renunciation is not complete if it is motivated by a decision to postpone the criminal conduct until

a more advantageous time or to transfer the criminal effort to another but similar objective or victim.

Section 5.05. Grading of Criminal Attempt, Solicitation and Conspiracy; Mitigation in Cases of Lesser Danger; Multiple Convictions Barred

(1) Grading. Except as otherwise provided in this Section, attempt, solicitation and conspiracy are crimes of the same grade and degree as the most serious offense which is attempted or solicited or is an object of the conspiracy. An attempt, solicitation or conspiracy to commit a [capital crime or a] felony of the first degree is a felony of the second degree.

(2) Mitigation. If the particular conduct charged to constitute a criminal attempt, solicitation or conspiracy is so inherently unlikely to result or culminate in the commission of a crime that neither such conduct nor the actor presents a public danger warranting the grading of such offense under this Section, the Court shall exercise its power under Section 6.12 to enter judgment and impose sentence for a crime of lower grade or degree or, in extreme cases, may dismiss the prosecution.

(3) Multiple Convictions. A person may not be convicted of more than one offense defined by this Article for conduct designed to commit or to culminate in the commission of the same crime.

▲ PROBLEM
A Plan to Kill

Xinchesi has had enough of the President's unfair trade policies toward his homeland. To save the hundreds of people who are suffering under the bad economic conditions there, he decides to kill the President. The Vice President is on record as supporting a change in policy that Xinchesi prefers.

Xinchesi knows several patriots who feel as he does and he believes they would be willing to help if asked. He works out a plan to assassinate the President as he leaves his hotel after a local speech scheduled for next week. After studying the layout each day as he passes the hotel on his way to work, Xinchesi decides that for the plot to be successful one of his friends must feign an attack from the opposite direction to divert Secret Service attention. Before he is able to raise the issue with his friends or to collect any of the needed material, his nosy cleaning woman finds his notes about his plan and reports him to the police. The evidence of his intention is overwhelming. He is charged with attempted murder.

Xinchesi's defense counsel does not deny Xinchesi's intention but argues that Xinchesi has done nothing toward actual commission of the offense and therefore cannot be held liable for an attempt. Is counsel correct?

● OVERVIEW OF ATTEMPT LIABILITY

Attempt vs. Mere Preparation At some point in the chain of events from thinking about committing an offense to completing it, an actor's conduct becomes criminal. The point typically is described as the point at which *mere preparation* becomes a *criminal attempt*. Defining the point is an important part of attempt liability, for it demarcates both when an actor becomes criminally liable and when authorities lawfully may intervene. Unlike other offenses, even after this point is reached and all the elements of attempt (or other inchoate offense) are satisfied, an actor may escape liability if he or she voluntarily and completely renounces the attempt. Absent such renunciation, the failure to complete an offense only avoids liability for the full offense; it does not relieve the actor from liability for the attempt. The Discussion Materials later in this Section consider the arguments in support of various alternative formulations for defining the conduct of attempt described below. Courts typically have adopted a preparation-versus-attempt test that fits into one of three groups.

① **Proximity Tests** Prevalent at common law were various *proximity* tests: the physical proximity doctrine,[1] the dangerous proximity doctrine,[2] the indispensable element approach,[3] and the probable desistance test.[4] The common characteristic of the proximity tests is that they each measure the point of attempt by the actor's closeness to commission of the substantive offense.[5] It is unlikely that Xinchesi has reached the point required by any of the proximity tests. The contemplated offense is a week or so off. Xinchesi has not collected any of the people or materials needed to carry it out. Of course, the issue is one for the jury, which might decide otherwise given the generality of the criteria of the proximity tests.

Objective View of Criminality One may argue, however, that attempt liability for Xinchesi ought to be imposed. He seems to present some danger. Apparently, he is willing to commit an offense, and a very serious one for that matter. He is not simply daydreaming; after all, he has made notes, and other preparations. He has externalized his intention. The evidence suggests not only that Xinchesi's intention exists but also that he is willing to act upon it. What, then, could be the reason for *not* imposing attempt liability on Xinchesi? What is

---

1. See, e.g., People v. Rizzo, 246 N.Y. 334, 158 N.E. 888 (1927) (defendant who intended to rob bank employee of company's payroll but could not find man before being arrested had conviction for attempted robbery reversed because acts were held not adequate for attempt).

2. See, e.g., Commonwealth v. Peaslee, 177 Mass. 267, 59 N.E. 55 (1901) ("mere collection and preparation of materials in room for purpose of setting fire to them, unaccompanied by any present intent to set fire, would be too remote," id. at 273, 59 N.E. at 57).

3. See, e.g., Model Penal Code §5.01 comment at 38-48 (Tentative Draft No. 10, 1960).

4. See, e.g., State v. Schwarzbach, 84 N.J.L. 268, 86 A. 423 (Ct. Err. & App. 1913) (defendant convicted of attempt to commit adultery after being caught, partially disrobed, in the bedroom of a married woman acts went beyond mere preparation).

5. One early test, which imposed attempt liability after the actor's last proximate act, was short-lived because it failed to allow time for intervention. Regina v. Eagleton, 6 Cox Crim. Cas. 559 (Crim. App. 1855) (defendant held guilty of attempt to defraud government where last act towards commission performed).

the rationale for taking as restrictive a view as the proximity tests do? Attempts are particularly interesting because they reveal some of the underlying principles in assessing liability. Some writers, such as George Fletcher in the Discussion Materials in the previous Section, would say that the proximity tests for preparation versus attempt simply reveal an *objectivist* view of criminality in general. According to this view, the gravamen of an offense is its harm or evil, tangible or intangible. The objectivist is not so foolish as to require the actual occurrence of the offense — no society could survive without the authority to intervene to prevent offenses. But where liability is to be imposed in the absence of the offense harm or evil, the objectivist view requires that the actor actually have come close to committing the offense. Some proximity tests explicitly require a real present danger that the offense will be committed.

(2) **Res Ipsa Loquitur Test** A different approach, taken by the *res ipsa loquitur* test, also called the unequivocality test, focuses not on how close the actor actually comes to committing the substantive offense, but rather on the actor's conduct manifestation of the actor's intent. Preparation becomes an attempt when an actor's intention to commit the offense is manifested in his or her conduct. Under any test of preparation versus attempt, liability requires proof (beyond a reasonable doubt) of the actor's intention to commit the substantive offense. The *res ipsa* test goes further, to require not only proof of this intent, but that the actor's conduct manifest this proof. Conduct in close proximity to completion will not necessarily manifest an actor's attempt intent. Lighting one's pipe next to a neighbor's haystack is equivocal as to intention, although it may be the last act in a plan to set the haystack on fire. Nothing in Xinchesi's public conduct suggests his intention to commit the offense. He examined the planned scene of crime on his normal trips to and from work. His incriminating planning notes are hidden in his room. Should he be liable under this test? It may depend on the reason for having a test like this. If the actor's intention to commit the offense is clear from other sources, why require that his intention be manifested in his conduct?

(a) *Desire for Clear Proof of Intent* Two explanations might be offered for the requirement that the attempt conduct manifest the attempt intent. First, unlike a substantive offense, where the gravamen of the offense is the harm or evil of the actor's conduct, attempt liability depends almost exclusively upon the actor's intention to commit the offense. Conduct otherwise innocent may be made criminal by virtue of an actor's culpable state of mind. Given this heavy reliance on state of mind, it is imperative that the actor's intention be clear, hence the *res ipsa* test requirement that the intention be manifested in his or her conduct. But this explanation for the *res ipsa* test is ultimately unpersuasive. If clear proof of the actor's intention is the goal, the *res ipsa* test is not the means that best achieves that goal. More reliable evidence of intent frequently exists independent of the attempt conduct. As in Xinchesi's case, a diary or an overheard discussion planning the offense may conclusively confirm an actor's criminal intention though his conduct, taken alone, does not. By its terms, the *res ipsa* test will bar attempt liability even if evidence of culpability is overwhelming, if that culpability does not show in the actor's conduct.[1]

v) *Punishing Provocative Conduct* An alternative explanation for the *res ipsa loquitur* test is that it reflects a view of attempt in which the harm of an attempt is not in coming close to completing the offense, as the proximity tests suggest, but rather in creating anxiety and disruption in society by openly manifesting an intention to commit an offense. For this reason, the *res ipsa loquitur* test has been said to reflect a view called *manifest criminality.*[2] This explanation seems persuasive in the limited context of the early blood feuds, where one tribe might be provoked to attack another if a member of one tribe manifested an intention to commit an offense against a member of another. If the central goal of law at that point was to do justice to the lawbreaker in order to avoid reprisals and the ensuing feuds, then the requirement that the intent be manifested in the attempt conduct played an important role. Certainly conduct that manifests a criminal intention disrupts society even today, but it is unclear why these are the only situations in which attempt liability is appropriate. In some instances, such as the farmer lighting his pipe near the haystack, the *res ipsa* test can be more restrictive than even the proximity tests.

3) **Substantial Step Test** The Model Penal Code's requirement that an actor take a "substantial step" toward commission of the offense illustrates a third kind of test.[3] Rather than focusing on *how close* to the end of the chain the actor has come, this approach focuses on how far *from the pure intention to commit the offense* the actor has gone. The Code gives seven illustrations of what "shall not be held insufficient as a matter of law" to constitute a substantial step:

> (a) lying in wait, searching for or following the contemplated victim of the crime;
> (b) enticing or seeking to entice the contemplated victim of the crime to go to the place contemplated for its commission;
> (c) reconnoitering the place contemplated for the commission of the crime;
> (d) unlawful entry of a structure, vehicle or enclosure in which it is contemplated that the crime will be committed;
> (e) possession of materials to be employed in the commission of the crime, which are specially designed for such unlawful use or which can serve no lawful purpose of the actor under the circumstances;
> (f) possession, collection or fabrication of materials to be employed in the commission of the crime, at or near the place contemplated for its commission, where such possession, collection or fabrication serves no lawful purpose of the actor under the circumstances;
> (g) soliciting an innocent agent to engage in conduct constituting an element of the crime.[4]

Note that most of these examples of conduct, without more, would fail most of the proximity tests. Xinchesi's conduct probably satisfies (c), reconnoitering.

---

1. One might argue that Xinchesi's "conduct" in making notes manifests his intention, but it is the content of his notes, not his conduct in making them, that is probative.
2. See George P. Fletcher, Rethinking Criminal Law 471-472 (1978).
3. Model Penal Code §5.01(1)(c).
4. Model Penal Code §5.01(2)(a)-(g).

"Strongly Corroborative of Purpose"   The Code adds to "substantial step" a requirement that the actor's conduct be "strongly corroborative of the actor's criminal purpose."[1] This is something less demanding than the *res ipsa* test.[2] Under the Code, the actor's intention need not be shown exclusively by his or her conduct. The actor's conduct need only *corroborate* his or her intent; that intention may be proven from independent sources. Thus the corroboration requirement is essentially an evidentiary requirement to help support in a modest way the existence of the alleged intent. This is appropriate given the increased importance of intent under the easily satisfied substantial-step formulation. Xinchesi's conduct appears to corroborate his intent. He has reconnoitered the place contemplated for the offense. He has made planning notes. The former may not be strongly corroborative of his purpose, given the way it was done (on his way to and from work), but the latter is.

Subjective View of Criminality   The substantial-step test reflects a shift in the justification for attempt liability, from coming close to committing an offense to intending to commit an offense. An actual danger of commission is not required. Indeed, the Model Penal Code imposes attempt liability even if commission of the offense is literally impossible (because, for example, the "illegal drugs" purchased are really powdered sugar).[3] The justification for attempt liability under the Code is, instead, the actor's intention to break the law and demonstrated willingness to act upon that intention, as shown by the externalization of intent into action—a "substantial step." Such persons are both blameworthy and dangerous and therefore are appropriate subjects of sanction. Note that this justification reflects a different view of what is required at a minimum to establish criminal liability. Under this *subjective* view of criminality, as it is called (again, recall the Discussion Materials at the end of Section 9, Causation), causing a harm or evil, or coming close to doing so, is not required; acting upon an intention to commit the offense is itself sufficient.

Culpability Requirements: Criminalizing Otherwise Innocent Conduct   What has been discussed so far are the objective requirements of attempt. But because it is an inchoate offense, it is the culpability requirements that are the core of the offense. The objective elements of attempt can be satisfied by conduct that otherwise would be lawful. That is, otherwise lawful conduct can be made criminal by virtue of the attempter's culpable state of mind. Entering a bank itself may be lawful, but it is made criminal if it is done with the purpose of robbing the bank. Driving another person to a remote cabin itself may be lawful, but it is made criminal if it is done with the intention forcibly to detain and demand a ransom. That one's intention can make otherwise innocent conduct criminal makes the

---

1. Model Penal Code §5.01(2).

2. The requirement of proving a substantial step generally will prove less of a hurdle for the prosecution than the res ipsa loquitur approach, which requires that the actor's conduct itself have manifested the criminal purpose.... Under the Model Code formulation, the two purposes to be served by the res ipsa loquitur test are, to a large extent, treated separately. Firmness of criminal purpose is intended to be shown by requiring a substantial step, while problems of proof are dealt with by the requirement of corroboration—although under the reasoning previously expressed the latter will also tend to establish firmness of purpose.

Model Penal Code §5.01 comment at 330 (Final Draft 1985).

3. Such impossibility is the subject of Section 11.

actor's culpability of central importance in assessing attempt liability and shows the necessity of requirements that will ensure proof of the actor's blameworthiness. There is some confusion, however, over just what culpability should be required.

Common Law's Specific Intent Requirement At common law, attempt was said to be a "specific intent offense,"[1] requiring a higher level of culpable state of mind than a "general intent" offense, where, it was thought, the actor's intention could be assumed from his or her conduct. Modern criminal law has some difficulty in determining exactly what is meant by "specific intent" and "general intent." Use of these two concepts is consistent with the common law's "offense analysis," where each offense was viewed as having a single culpability requirement, and where culpability concepts generally were vague and malleable. But when translated into a modern "element analysis" context, which requires a specifically defined culpability as to each offense element, the common law's concepts create confusion. The "specific intent" requirement of attempt typically is taken to require a *purpose* to commit the object offense. But what does this "purpose" requirement specifically require?

Purpose Requirement in Attempt Does the "purpose" requirement in attempt require simply a purpose to engage in the *conduct* constituting the substantive offense, or does it require that the actor be "purposeful" as to the elements of the offense? Under the latter interpretation, attempt liability would elevate the culpability required as to each element of the offense from that level in the substantive offense definition to the "purpose" level. That is, instead of the level of culpability required by the substantive offense, the latter interpretation would require elevated culpability as to each conduct, circumstance, and result in the offense definition. The holding in *People v. Trinkle* illustrates this view. After being refused further service, the resentful defendant fired a shot into a tavern, wounding a patron. Murder requires only that the actor "knew that his acts created a strong probability of causing death or great bodily harm." The attempt statute explicitly defines attempted murder to require this same culpability. Yet the court reverses the conviction, arguing that the common law rule that "attempt is a specific intent offense" means that attempt liability requires not only that the actor intend to engage in the conduct constituting the substantive offense,[2] but also that the actor *intend* (was "purposeful" as to) the prohibited result (death) and the required circumstances of the substantive offense.

Effect of Elevation to Purposeful Such elevation of culpability requirements has a fairly dramatic effect. In a prosecution for attempted statutory rape, for example, if the intercourse is completed, frequently little or no culpability as to the age of the victim is required; strict liability or negligence is sufficient. If the intercourse is frustrated at the last moment, would prosecution for attempted statutory rape require not only that the actor intended to have intercourse, but that he *intended* that the victim be underage?[3] If all culpability elements for attempt are elevated to require purpose, the answer is yes; the actor must intend

---

1. E.g., People v. Trinkle, 68 Ill. 2d 198, 204, 369N.E.2d 892 (1977).

2. In *Trinkle*, the defendant engaged in all of the conduct required to constitute the substantive offense; only the resulting harm — causing death — was missing from the requirements for the substantive offense.

3. In the context of circumstances, "purpose" is defined to require only awareness of circumstances, not a positive desire that they exist. See Model Penal Code §2.02(2)(a).

that the partner be underage. But that would exempt from liability much if not most attempt conduct. Similarly, where the offense has a result element — as in murder in *Trinkle* — elevation to *purposeful* means that there is no liability for attempted murder even if the actor *knew* (was practically certain) that his conduct would cause a death; for liability, it must be shown that causing a death was the actor's conscious objective. Many people would argue that these are inappropriate results, and that these violators deserve liability for attempt.

Model Penal Code Section 5.01 Consider how the Model Penal Code attempt provision, section 5.01, deals with the elevation issue. The section provides for attempt liability under any of three subsections. Subsection (1)(a) is intended to govern cases of impossible attempt, where the offense conduct is complete and where liability for the substantive offense would be imposed but for the absence of a required circumstance (for example, the white powder purchased is not a controlled drug, as was expected). Subsection (1)(b) is intended to govern cases where the actor's conduct constituting the offense is complete but a required result does not occur (for example, the shoot-and-miss cases). Subsection (1)(c) governs the cases of interrupted or incomplete conduct toward the substantive offense.

Culpability Requirements Under Code Section 5.01 might be interpreted as reflecting the common law view that attempt is a specific intent offense and the more demanding interpretation of what this requires. It imposes liability, in section 5.01(1)(a) and (1)(c), respectively, only if the actor "*purposely* engages in conduct which would constitute the crime . . ." or "*purposely* does or omits to do anything which [is] a substantial step. . . ." Section 5.01(1)(b) requires only that the actor act "with the purpose of causing or *with the belief*" that his conduct will cause the prohibited result, thus seeming to require elevation only to *knowing* rather than *purposeful* in completed conduct result-element cases. Yet these phrases leave the culpability requirements somewhat ambiguous. The introductory language of section 5.01(1) requires that the actor be "acting with the kind of culpability otherwise required for commission of the crime." That phrase alone would suggest that attempt liability requires no elevation of the normal culpability requirements of the substantive offense, but the purpose and belief requirements in the specific subsections might suggest that all elements are elevated.

Meaning of "Purposely" in Section 5.01(1) The question raised here — what is meant by the *purposeful* and *knowing* requirements that appear in the subsections of section 5.01(1) — is similar to that raised in the context of complicity (taken up more fully in Section 14), where Model Penal Code section 2.06(3)(a) requires that an accomplice have "the purpose of promoting or facilitating the commission of the offense." In that context, we will ask whether "purpose to promote or facilitate commission of the offense" requires that the actor be purposeful as to *assisting the perpetrator's conduct* constituting the offense or purposeful as to *all elements of the offense* (including the circumstances and results of the perpetrator's offense conduct constituting the offense). This same ambiguity between a narrow and a broad interpretation of "purposeful conduct" exists in the attempt section. The broad interpretation is reflected in decisions like *Trinkle*, which would interpret the "purpose" requirement of attempt to apply to all elements. It appears more likely, however, that here the narrow interpretation is the more sound position. (One may come to a similar conclusion in the context of complicity). This is the view taken in a number of modern codes and by a number of courts, such as the *Maestas* case under the Utah attempt statute.

> Regardless of any requirements which the common law may impose concerning [specific intent in] "attempt" crimes, Utah law requires only "the kind of culpability otherwise required for the commission of the [completed] offense." Thus, there can be no difference between the intent required as an element of the crime of attempted first degree murder and that required for first degree murder itself.[1]

Narrow Interpretation of Purpose Requirement   The narrow interpretation of the "purpose" requirement would require a showing that it was the actor's purpose to engage in all of the *conduct* required to constitute the substantive offense. It is not enough that he was thinking seriously about possibly engaging in the conduct that constitutes the offense. It must be proven beyond a reasonable doubt that he had made it his conscious object, his intention, to complete the conduct constituting the offense. However, it need not be shown that the actor was purposeful as to every *circumstance* and *result* of the substantive offense. The substantive offense's culpability requirements as to these elements will suffice. Thus, Trinkle would be liable for attempted murder if he was aware that it was practically certain that his conduct would cause a death.

● DISCUSSION MATERIALS
What Conduct Toward an Offense Should Be Sufficient to Constitute a Criminal Attempt?

The articles that follow urge different theories for determining the point at which one's conduct toward the commission of a crime becomes subject to criminal liability. The Model Penal Code Commentary compares the Code's proposed "substantial step" test to the other traditional tests, noting the benefits from its broadening of the scope of attempt liability. Andrew Ashworth compares the American and English approaches to attempt, posing the objectivist objections to England's subjectivist approach and concluding that although no test is precise, the "substantial step" test is the best available formulation. Francis Sayre argues that determining the point at which preparation becomes attempt ought to be case-dependent, with liability for more serious crimes attaching earlier in the process. Last, Robinson and Darley, in studying community views on the conduct requirement for attempt liability, find that the layperson tends to attach liability only when there is "dangerous proximity to completion of the offense" in contrast to the Model Penal Code's popular "substantial step" approach.

---

1. State v. Maestas, 652 P.2d 903, 904 (Utah 1982).

Model Penal Code Section 5.01 Commentary
Official Draft and Revised Comments 321, 329-330, 331 (1985)

General Distinction Between Preparation and Attempt. It is clear...that... liability should extend beyond the cases where the defendant has engaged in the "last proximate act." If, as is generally assumed, every act done with intent to commit a crime is not to be made criminal, it becomes necessary to establish a means of inclusion and exclusion. The formulation of a general standard for that purpose in Subsection (1)(c) [the "substantial-step provision"] presents the most difficult problem in defining criminal attempt....

(a) Requirements of "Substantial Step" and Corroboration of Purpose. Whether a particular act is a substantial step is obviously a matter of degree. To this extent, the Code retains the element of imprecision found in most of the other approaches to the preparation-attempt problem. There are, however, several differences to be noted:

First, this formulation shifts the emphasis from what remains to be done, the chief concern of the proximity tests, to what the actor has already done. That further major steps must be taken before the crime can be completed does not preclude a finding that the steps already undertaken are substantial. It is expected, in the normal case, that this approach will broaden the scope of attempt liability.

Second, although it is intended that the requirement of a substantial step will result in the imposition of attempt liability only in those instances in which some firmness of criminal purpose is shown, no finding is required as to whether the actor would probably have desisted prior to completing the crime. Potentially the probable desistance test could reach very early steps toward crime, depending on how one assesses the probabilities of desistance; but since in practice this test follows closely the proximity approaches, rejection of a test of probable desistance will not narrow the scope of attempt liability.

Finally, the requirement of proving a substantial step generally will prove less of a hurdle for the prosecution than the res ipsa loquitur approach, which requires that the actor's conduct itself have manifested the criminal purpose. The basic rationale of the requirement that the actor's conduct shall strongly corroborate his purpose to commit a crime is, of course, the same as that underlying the res ipsa loquitur view. But framed in terms of corroboration, the present formulation does not so narrowly circumscribe the scope of attempt liability. Rigorously applied, the res ipsa loquitur doctrine would provide immunity in many instances in which the actor had gone far toward the commission of an offense and had strongly indicated a criminal purpose....

Under the Model Code formulation, the two purposes to be served by the res ipsa loquitur test are, to a large extent, treated separately. Firmness of criminal purpose is intended to be shown by requiring a substantial step, while problems of proof are dealt with by the requirement of corroboration—although under the reasoning previously expressed the latter will also tend to establish firmness of purpose.

In addition to assuring firmness of purpose, the requirement of a substantial step will remove very remote preparatory acts from the ambit of attempt liability and the relatively stringent sanctions imposed for attempts. On the other hand, by broadening liability to the extent suggested, apprehension of dangerous persons will be facilitated and law enforcement officials and others will be able to stop the criminal effort at an earlier stage, thereby minimizing the risk of substantive harm, but without providing immunity for the offender.

A number of recent [criminal code] revisions have adopted the substantial step formula, some including the requirement that the actor's conduct strongly corroborate his criminal purpose....

Andrew Ashworth, Criminal Attempts and the Role of Resulting Harm under the Code, and in the Common Law
19 Rutgers Law Journal 725, 750-753 (1988)

The Conduct Element in Attempts

The English Court of Criminal Appeal has said that, if a person is charged with an attempt, "the intent becomes the principal ingredient of the crime." On the fully subjective principle . . . the paramountcy of the mens rea is assured. Does this dispense entirely with the need for proof of some conduct which might be described as an actus reus? Even in its most virulent form the fully subjective principle would not lead to this result: the theory turns on a "trying," which goes beyond a mere intention and requires some effort to put it into effect. Yet this is only a minimal actus reus, which might be satisfied by the doing of any overt act with the necessary intention. Those who might be described as "objectivists" in relation to the law of attempts would criticize this approach on two grounds: first, it would give too much power to law enforcement agents and would thus leave individuals vulnerable; second, it would leave insufficient room for an individual voluntarily to renounce a criminal endeavor.

The first objection is a qualifying principle which derives from a concern for individual rights and freedom from interference. One of the justifications for having a law of inchoate crimes . . . is to enable the police to intervene so as to prevent criminal activity before any harm is caused. But this police power should not be allowed to encroach upon individual rights and liberties. The English Law Commission referred to a need "to strike a balance in this context between individual freedom and the countervailing interests of the community" in other words, the justifications for penalising attempts must be tempered by considerations of individual liberty. If any overt act were to suffice as the actus reus, wrongful arrests might be more numerous; the police might be tempted to exert pressure in order to obtain a confession, since the mental element would be the overriding concern; miscarriages of justice might increase. The law should protect an individual's right not to be subjected to such treatment. Since an "overt act" test might in practice increase the risk of violation of that right, there is a strong argument for moving the actus reus somewhat further towards the substantive offence. The second objection is that, the earlier in the chain of events the actus reus of an attempt is placed, the less opportunity there is for the individual to change his mind before incurring criminal liability. This is particularly relevant to English law, which refuses to recognize any defense of abandonment and leaves its significance entirely to the courts' discretion when sentencing. It is perhaps less relevant when, as in the Model Penal Code, a defence of voluntary abandonment is available—partly on the reasoning that the voluntary renunciation negatives the inference of dangerousness and partly as an incentive to an attempter to desist even at the last moment.

Both these objections turn, to some extent, on judgements of degree which are also relevant in assessing other conceptions of the actus reus of an attempt. The "last act" or "final state" test might be thought to go too far in the direction of protecting the interests of would-be offenders. The English Law Commission rejected this approach, and rightly so. It would certainly maximize the defendant's opportunity to change his mind and abandon the attempt. However, if a defendant might exculpate himself from a charge of attempt by showing that he had not done the last act necessary to commit the crime, this would substantially reduce the preventive efficacy of the offence and would make it difficult for the police to intervene so as to forestall any harm.

A Working Party of the law Commission has earlier favored the concept of a "substantial step," following the Model Penal Code. In its final report, the Law Commission itself rejected the "substantial step" test for three reasons: first, they thought that it would be too imprecise; second, they disagreed with the Working Party's proposal that it should be for the judge to rule on whether certain conduct might amount to a substantial step; third, they believed that the test might extend the law of attempts so as to comprehend some acts of preparation. The Law Commission concluded that "the first element in a statutory test of proximity should be the drawing of the distinction between acts of preparation and acts which are sufficiently proximate to the offence." Their proposed test kept close to this rationale, and it is the test now embodied in Section 1 of the Criminal Attempts Act, 1981: "...an act which is more than merely preparatory to the commission of the offence." Yet, the first criticism which the Law Commission made against the "substantial step" test seems to have some application to the new test. Is it not an imprecise test, particularly if it is left for juries to determine in individual cases? Moreover, if the protection of individual rights and the confining of police discretion are regarded as important goals, does not its imprecision count against the test?

The fully subjective principle would be satisfied by the "overt act" test, but the objectivists are right to draw attention to the probable practical consequences of moving the threshold of criminal liability so far away from the last act in an attempt. It would be unworkable to require that the act should be unequivocally referable to the defendant's intent before liability for an attempt is established. Therefore, in order to strike an acceptable balance, there must be concrete discussion of specific examples based on experience of administering the law. The "substantial step" test classifies as an attempt certain forms of conduct which the new English test, "more than merely preparatory," is designed to exclude from the law of attempts. The American Law Institute, in proposing the "substantial step" test for the Model Penal Code, adopts the view that conduct such as reconnoitering and possession of incriminating equipment should amount to a criminal attempt (so long as they are strongly corroborative of the actor's criminal purpose); the English Law Commission disagreed, and believed that their new test would exclude these cases. Neither test is precise. And Sheriff Gordon's strictures on the Scots' distinction between preparation and perpetration might be applied to the English test:

> It has one inestimable advantage as a working authority, and that is its vagueness. It offers an impressive-sounding and apparently precise rationalization for doing justice in any particular case: if the jury think the accused should be punished for what he did they will characterize what he did as [more than merely preparatory]; if they do not, they will characterize it as [mere] preparation. What was a question of law related to how restricted the scope of the criminal law should be, becomes a value-judgment related to the jury's assessment of blameworthiness.

Tests of this kind are unduly vague, and purchase flexibility at much too high a cost in terms of insufficient guidance to the police and to courts and, therefore, inconsistences in the administration of justice.

In order to achieve a solution which maximizes both certainty and flexibility, it is necessary to seek a formulation which combines several specific examples with a generalized test. The illustrative and authoritative examples of the Model Penal Code follow this approach, and, since maximum certainty is one aim, it would be preferable to use legislation of this purpose rather than awaiting the gradual development of judicial authority. The courts would retain the important role of interpreting and applying the generalized test. The legislative scheme should be such as to make it proper to argue by analogy from the illustrative examples when interpreting the test. In choosing between the Model Penal Code's "substantial step" test and the "more than merely preparatory" test, the English Law Commission argues that the former was wider and unduly so, whereas the natural meaning of the two tests does not suggest any such simple division. My own preference remains with the "substantial step" test, with the insistence that neither test meets the requirements of a modern system of criminal law if it is not supported by authoritative examples.

Francis B. Sayre, Criminal Attempts
41 Harvard Law Review 821, 845-847 (1928)

The line between preparation and attempt, however, must at best depend largely upon the particular circumstances of each case — the seriousness of the crime attempted, and the danger to be apprehended from the defendant's conduct. Since the extent to which criminal law may justifiably encroach upon and restrict the freedom and liberties of the individual varies directly with the extent to which social and public interests are endangered, it follows that the more serious the crime attempted or the greater the menace to the social security from similar efforts on the part of the defendant or others, the further back in the series of acts leading up to the consummated crime should the criminal law reach in holding the defendant guilty for an attempt. For instance, the mere placing in joke of a substance known to be comparatively harmless in food which it is expected the victim will eat but which in fact he does not come near, might be held not to constitute an indictable attempt to commit a simple assault, whereas under an indictment for murder the same court might well hold that the placing of a harmless substance in the victim's food in the belief that it is poison and with the intent to kill does constitute an indictable attempt. In the language of Mr. Justice Holmes,

> As the aim of the law is not to punish sins, but is to present certain external results, the act done must come pretty near to accomplishing the result before the law will notice it. . . . Every question of proximity must be determined by its own circumstances, and analogy is too imperfect to give much help. Any unlawful application of poison is an evil which threatens death, according to common apprehension, and the gravity of the crime, the uncertainty of the result, and the seriousness of the apprehension, coupled with the great harm likely to result from poison even if not enough to kill, would warrant holding the liability for an attempt to begin at a point more remote from the possibility of accomplishing what is expected than might be the case with lighter crimes.

It is thus manifestly impossible to lay down any mechanical or hard and fast rule for the drawing of the line between preparation and indictable attempts; and such efforts in this direction as "the last proximate act" doctrine must be unhesitatingly rejected.

So far as the defendant's criminality is concerned, it would seem to make little or no difference whether the interruption of the defendant's intended acts is due to another's interference or to his own repentance or change of mind. Once the defendant's acts have gone far enough to make him liable for a criminal attempt, subsequent repentance or change of mind or abstention from further crime can possibly wipe away liability for the crime already committed. Genuine repentance may cause a reduction of sentence, but it cannot free from criminal liability. In the cases where the defendant voluntarily abandons his intended course of conduct, therefore, the problem reduces itself to whether or not the defendant's conduct before the abandonment had gone so far as to constitute an indictable attempt. The burglar who, while trying to force the lock on the front door, decides to abandon the attempt is equally guilty whether his change of mind is due to the voice of his own conscience or the voice of an approaching policeman. Present virtue never wipes away past crimes.

Other Discussion Materials

Paul H. Robinson & John M. Darley, Study 1: Objective Requirements of Attempt; Conflict Between Community Views and Criminal Codes
Justice, Liability & Blame 16-17, 27, 208-210 (1995)

We designed a study that sought to examine the community's views on the conduct requirements for attempt liability. To study these views, we presented subjects with a core scenario. Subjects were told that a locksmith, who is called to repair a safe in a coin dealer's store, notices that valuable coins are always kept in the safe. The locksmith decides to break in and rob the coin dealer by opening the safe and taking the contents. We then added to the core story various elements that created combinations of circumstances to which some common law and modern tests would assign attempt liability and others would not. For instance, in another scenario, we added the fact that the locksmith returns to the coin shop to make sure that the safe is still there, and is then charged with attempt. This variation satisfies the Model Penal Code's requirement, relied on in many jurisdictions, that the attempter need only take some "substantial step" in the direction of committing the offense. Our intent, by introducing these variations, was to determine where our respondents would assign liability and how this pattern of liability matched the various tests.

Therefore, in the design of the present study, each subject read eleven versions of the same core scenario to which various alterations had been made. Each scenario is identical to every other except for the facts describing how far the person progresses after forming his intention. Each scenario corresponds to one of the current legal tests. Table 2.1 outlines the eleven versions of the scenario, and the legal test to which each corresponds. The initial core scenario, in which the person only forms the intent to commit the crime, is shown in row (1). The substantial step scenario, in which the person returns to the shop to see if the safe is still there, is shown in row (2). Brief characterizations of the other scenarios are given in the "description" column of the table. The "summary" column of Table 2.1 gives a summary description of each scenario, and these are used to identify each scenario in subsequent tables. The "comment" column gives further explanation of the legal treatment of the case.

Table 2.1 Attempt Scenarios

Core Story: A locksmith, Ray, recalls working on a safe in a coin shop. The safe was kept in the back room and always contained valuable coins. Ray thinks about how easy it would be to "crack" the safe. Ray decides he will rob the safe in the coin shop.

Scenario Number, Description (and Abbreviation)	Summary	Comment
1. The actor only thinks about robbing the safe and decides to do so. He takes no action toward committing the crime. (TH)	Only *thinks* about offense	No test would assign liability.
2. After deciding to rob the shop, the actor goes to the coin shop to make sure the safe is still there. (SS)	*Substantial step test* satisfied	Actor is liable under this test, because "reconnoitering" (casing) the shop is a substantial step.
3. After deciding to rob the shop, the actor makes a special tool to crack the safe with. (EQ)	*Unequivocality test* satisfied	The actor is liable under this test because action manifests criminal intent.
3a. The actor cases the shop and meets the owner while he does so. Out of pity for the owner, he gives up his plan to rob the safe. (EQR)	*Renounces after* reaching point of *unequivocality*	The Model Penal Code (MPC) allows a defense if an actor's renunciation of criminal intent is "complete and voluntary." No liability if this defense is available.
4. Having told a friend he intends to rob the shop, the actor drives there. Before he can get to the shop he is stopped by police, who were informed of his intent by the actor's friend. (PD)	*Probable desistance test* satisfied	Without outside interruption the actor would have completed the offense. Actor is liable under this test.
5. The actor is in the process of cracking the safe in the coin shop when he is stopped by two undercover policemen. (PX)	*Dangerous proximity test* satisfied	Actor is liable because the offense is nearly completed.
5a. When he is in the shop and about to crack the safe, the actor feels pity for the shopowner and decides not to rob the safe. (PXR)	*Renounces* after reaching point of *dangerous proximity*	MPC allows a defense when actor renounces his criminal intent "completely and voluntarily." No liability if this defense is available.
5b. When he is in the shop and about to crack the safe, the actor stops because he sees a policeman in the front of the store and he fears getting caught. (FR)	*Desists* out of *fear* after *dangerous proximity*	Actor is allowed no renunciation defense because renunciation was not voluntary. Actor is liable for full attempt.
6. The actor completes the robbery and returns home with the coins. (CP)	*Offense complete, no renunciation*	The actor is liable for the completed offense.
6a. The actor completes the robbery and returns home. On the way home, he feels pity for the shopowner and returns the coins to the safe. (CPR)	*Renounces* after *offense* is *complete*	Actor is liable for completed offense because renunciation defense not available.
6b. The actor completes the offense, feels pity for the shopowner, tries to return the coins to the safe, but is caught by police. (UNR)	*Renounces, but is unsuccessful* at *"undoing"*	Actor is liable for completed offense because renunciation defense unavailable.

After reading each scenario, subjects indicated what criminal liability, if any, they would assign to the locksmith. The liability results of the study are reported in Table 2.2. Columns (d) and (e) summarize the liability that would be assigned to the scenario by the common law and the Model Penal Code, respectively.

We will first consider the different liabilities assigned to the various attempt scenarios, and later turn to examine the effects of renunciation of the crime and the related act of desisting out of fear of being apprehended.

Table 2.2 **Liability for Various Degrees of Conduct Toward a Completed Theft Offense**

Attempt Scenarios	(a) Liability	(b) % No Liability (N)	(c) % No Liability or No Punishment (N+0)	(d) Common Law Result	(e) Model Penal Code Result
1. Thought only (TH)	1.46	65	77	No liability	No liability
2. Substantial step (SS)	1.54	50	73	No liability	Attempt liability[a]
3. Unequivocality (EQ)	1.81	42	65	[b]	Attempt liability[a]
3a. Renounces	0.38	85	92	No defense	Complete defense
4. Probable desistance (PD)	1.88	27	62	[b]	Attempt liability[a]
5. Dangerous proximity (PX)	5.35	0	0	Attempt liability	Attempt liability[a]
5a. Renounces	0.69	46	85	No defense	Complete defense
5b. Desists out of fear	1.58	35	65	No defense	No defense
6. Completed offense (CP)	6.12	0	0	Full offense liability	Full offense liability
6a. Renounces and "undoes"	3.23	12	27	No defense	No defense
6b. Renounces but unable to "undo"	5.35	0	4	No defense	No defense

Liability Scale: N = No criminal liability, 0 = Liability but no punishment, 1 = 1 day, 2 = 2 weeks, 3 = 2 months, 4 = 6 months, 5 = 1 year, 6 = 3 years, 7 = 7 years, 8 = 15 years, 9 = 30 years, 10 = life, and 11 = death.

[a]An attempted theft under the Model Penal Code is graded the same as a completed theft.
[b]This depends upon which of the common-law tests is applicable in the jurisdiction.

Table 2.2 arrays the various scenarios from top to bottom in terms of the general progression of how close they come to the actual commission of the crime. In the first scenario, the individual develops an intention to commit the crime and does not progress farther. In the last scenario, row (6), the individual actually commits the crime.

Figure 2.3 **Liability for Various Degrees of Conduct Toward Theft**

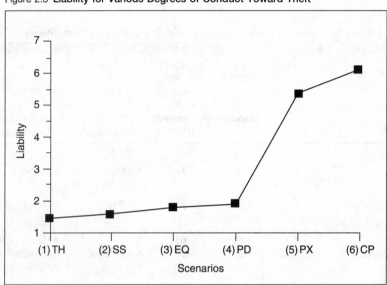

Figure 2.4 **Percentage of Subjects Assigning No Liability or Liability But No Punishment**

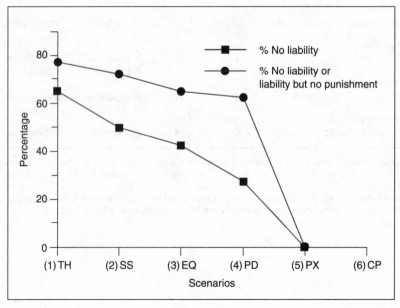

Summary

The liability results of the study might be summarized in psychological terms as follows. In the view of the subjects, punishment ought not be imposed until a person has reached a point of dangerous proximity to completion of the offense. Further, the level of punishment for attempt ought to be significantly less than that for the completed offense. Once the point of dangerous proximity is reached, punishment still may be avoided by complete and voluntary renunciation. Finally, when an offense is completed, a change of heart will only mitigate punishment, although undoing the offense will mitigate punishment still further.

With respect to legal implications, this study sought to determine which of the tests for the objective requirement of attempt best reflects the community's view. In the scenarios where the person has gone just far enough to satisfy the substantial step test, the unequivocality test, or the probable desistance test, a strong majority of subjects would impose either no liability or no punishment. But, in the scenarios where a person satisfies the common law's dangerous proximity test, a dramatic shift in opinion occurs: all of the subjects would impose both liability and punishment. This would seem to suggest that, if the community's view were to be the guiding principle in the definition of the offense, criminal codes should revert to the common law's dangerous proximity test. If early intervention by law enforcement is desired to increase the effectiveness of crime prevention, legislation could create authority to intervene without holding the person liable for an attempt to commit the substantive offense or holding the person liable only at a low level. Liability might be imposed at a fixed misdemeanor level, for an offense of "Preparing to Commit an Offense" or something of such nature. . . .

[In a concluding chapter, the authors discuss a more fundamental difference between criminal codes and the community's shared intuitions of justice, which is illustrated by the objective requirement for attempt as well as a variety of other issues, such as complicity, omission liability, and the grading of attempt.]

. . . Dichotomous Functions versus Continuous Functions

[T]he process by which subjects assess liability is different from the way in which current doctrine conceptualizes the issue. Where the doctrine treats a factor as setting a fixed minimum requirement for full liability, the subjects frequently see the same factor as aggravating or mitigating the degree of a person's liability and punishment.

For example, while the doctrine treats complicity as a means of establishing full liability for the substantive offense, the subjects generally consider an accomplice to be less blameworthy than the principal and reduce the accomplice's liability accordingly. A similar general "discount" in liability is seen in cases of omission. While the doctrine holds a person fully liable for the substantive offense if he satisfies the requirements of omission liability, the subjects significantly reduce a person's liability if he commits an offense by omission from what it would be if he committed the same offense by commission. Reacting intuitively, the community's views seem to us to be more rational than the code treatment here. In a failure to rescue case, the codes' assignment of no penalty to the person who fails to rescue, and assignment of a penalty equivalent to murder or manslaughter if certain complex conditions about the assumption of duty are met, seems initially too lenient and then too harsh.

The grading of attempt conduct further demonstrates this difference between the codes' and the respondents' treatment of liability. The codes define a particular point, during the preparation and conduct toward an offense, as the moment when liability attaches. The subjects, in contrast, see increasing liability as the person gets closer to committing the offense.

The code's tendency to dichotomize signals a serious and pervasive flaw in current law, from the subjects' perspective. The doctrine more often than not sees a fact as either establishing liability or not or as giving a mitigation (or aggravation) or not; the effect of a relevant fact typically is to trigger application of a particular rule or subrule. The subjects, in contrast, frequently see a continuum of blameworthiness and liability. A fact more frequently contributes to an increment or decrement in liability judgement than it produces a complete assignment of liability or total escape from liability.

The notion of a liability continuum for some factors is acknowledged by current doctrine in some contexts. Codes typically are structured to impose greater liability for greater harm done, all other things being equal. Codes sometimes — too rarely from the subjects' perspective — vary the degree of a person's liability with his level of culpability. The codes' culpability spectrum is not a strictly continuous one, at least as it is defined in modern codes, with four discrete levels of culpability. It is, however, a practical and useful approximation of a continuum.

In most other instances, however, current doctrine fails to acknowledge continuums that the subjects clearly support....

Obviously, a criminal code cannot take account of the infinite continuum over which many factors may range. It is not unrealistic, however, to expect a code to recognize that these factors are relevant to determining liability — i.e., to recognize some kind of discount — and to attempt a rough approximation of their varying effect. This can be done in the same way that modern codes approximate the harm and culpability continuums, by defining a few large categories for each of the most relevant factors. Such a rough approximation of a continuum generally is sufficient for the criminal code's role of indicating a range for the extent of punishment. More refined distinctions can be made in the sentencing process.

Isn't it the case that all such distinctions could be reserved for the sentencing process? We suggest that it would be a mistake to push over to the sentencing process the responsibility to make such rough approximations of highly relevant factors, especially when such determinations can effectively be made by a code. First, as a matter of principle, the purposes supporting the legality principle, as well as modern notions of due process, prefer that the most significant determinants of liability be considered at the liability stage, where the jury can make the determination under the normal rules of trial procedure. To leave such determinations to the more discretionary sentencing stage is to devalue legality, the jury system, and due process unnecessarily. Second, at the level of practice, jurors are more likely to abide by their legal instructions to the extent that those instructions reach results that they regard as fair outcomes. To fail to have verdicts that match the general range of punishment deserved is to invite jury dissatisfaction and resistance.

Impossibility

It is sometimes the case that the situation itself makes it impossible for a person to complete the offense contemplated. Should this impossibility of commission affect the person's liability for attempt? If so, how and why? If the underlying theory of attempt liability is coming close to causing a harm, such impossibility may undercut the offenses rationale. If the underlying theory is a manifested intention to break the law, then such impossibility may not be relevant. In other words, the impossibility cases force the underlying theory of attempt out into the open.

◆ **THE CASE OF JOHN HENRY IVY**

It is July 1988 in the Lee County seat of Tupelo, Mississippi, a small town of 28,000 that prides itself on being the birthplace of Elvis. John Henry Ivy is a twenty-five year old from Oxford, Mississippi, a small town about 60 miles west of Tupelo. He now stands before Judge Thomas Gardner III, awaiting sentencing for his latest armed robbery. This time he held up a gas station and made off with about $500. A hearty man, John Henry loves cracking jokes and tries not to take life too seriously. He is a little worried about his sentencing, however, because he has previous convictions for selling cocaine and armed robbery and might get the maximum penalty. Doing him no favors, Judge Gardner sentences him to 40 years in the state penitentiary.

A few months later, John Henry calls his half-brother, Leroy Ivy, from state prison. Leroy Ivy, thirty-three, is more quiet and serious than his half-brother and unlike him has not had any legal troubles, except minor scrapes when he was younger. Like his ten other siblings, he too lives in Oxford. John Henry is calling Leroy today to set up a three-way conference call between themselves and Emma Gates, Judge Gardner's housekeeper. His purpose for the call is to arrange a meeting between Leroy and Ms. Gates, so John Henry can buy some personal

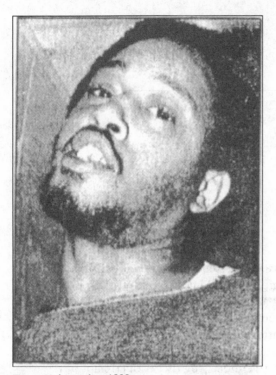

Figure 39 **Leroy Ivy, 1989**
(Northeast Mississippi Daily Journal)

items that belong to Judge Gardner, such as an old picture and a hairbrush with some of the judge's hair still in the bristles. Although slightly puzzled, Leroy does what his brother asks.

On the conference call, the brothers explain to Ms. Gates the items they want. They offer several hundred dollars for them. Gates refuses at first, but they continue to press her.

The items requested are commonly used in voodoo rituals. John Henry's plan is to send the items to a shaman contact in New Orleans, which is the center of the nation's voodoo activity. The items will be sent to a voodoo priestess in Jamaica, who will use them to put a death hex on Judge Gardner.

John Henry is familiar with voodoo practices from people in town and from other inmates. Although belief in voodoo is not particularly common in Mississippi, there is a community of those who believe in the West African religion, which combines aspects of Catholicism with worship of some African gods. Local law enforcement officials in Oxford say they have not heard of any voodoo activity there, although a few locals remember friends who bought voodoo gambling charms or who were hexed by an ex-wife. A University of Mississippi anthropologist estimates that there are about forty voodoo priests in Mississippi, and believes its practice is gathering support. For example, a local department store expects to sell about twenty-one tons of voodoo supplies, including candles, roots, and powder.

After hearing the request for a photo and hair, Ms. Gates immediately recognizes their possible use in a voodoo ritual. Fearful of what they might be planning, she tells the judge about the call. Not a believer in voodoo, Judge Gardner dismisses the death hex as a toothless threat. However, the housekeeper is frightened by the episode, and details of the plot are soon relayed to the authorities.

A team from the Mississippi Highway Patrol, headed by twenty-two-year-old Jerry Butler (he calls himself "Jailhouse Jerry") heads up the investigation and plans a sting operation to catch the brothers. Ms. Gates arranges to meet with Leroy at the J.C. Penney store on Main St. in Tupelo on October 14. The sheriff's office tapes a phone call between her and the Ivy brothers. The men have bargained a price of $500 for the items. The police intend to use an officer in disguise to meet Leroy, instead of Ms. Gates.

On October 14, Leroy drives to Tupelo to complete the purchase. At the appointed time, he exchanges a suitcase containing the money for a photograph and a lock of hair (which was taken from a detective on the case). After photographing the transaction, undercover officers from the Highway Patrol arrest Leroy. They later learn that the suitcase contained only $100; Leroy makes no attempt to explain why he is $400 short.

Both men are charged with planning "feloniously and with malice aforethought to kill and murder Judge Gardner."

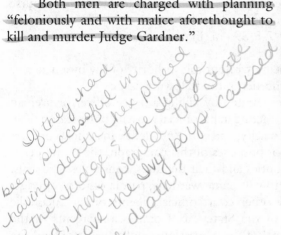

Figure 40 **Judge Gardner**
(Lee County Court)

1. Relying only on your own intuitions of justice, what liability and punishment, if any, does John Henry Ivy deserve?

N	0	1	2	3	4	5	6	7	8	9	10	11
☐	☐	☐	☐	☐	☐	☐	☐	☐	☐	☐	☐	☐
no liability	liability but no punishment	1 day	2 wks	2 mo	6 mo	1 yr	3 yrs	7 yrs	15 yrs	30 yrs	life imprison-ment	death

2. What liability, if any, under the then-existing statutes?
3. What liability, if any, under the Model Penal Code?

■ THE LAW

Mississippi Code Annotated
(1988)

Section 97-3-19. Homicide; Murder Defined; Capital Murder

(1) The killing of a human being without the authority of law by any means or in any manner shall be murder in the following cases:

(a) When done with deliberate design to effect the death of the person killed, or of any human being;

(b) When done in the commission of an act eminently dangerous to others and evincing a depraved heart, regardless of human life, although without any premeditated design to effect the death of any particular individual;

(c) When done without any design to effect death by any person engaged in the commission of any felony other than rape, kidnapping, burglary, arson, robbery, sexual battery, unnatural intercourse with any child under the age of twelve (12), or nonconsensual unnatural intercourse with mankind, or felonious abuse and/or battery of a child in violation of subsection (2) of Section 97-5-39, or in any attempt to commit such felonies.

(2) The killing of a human being without the authority of law by any means or in any manner shall be capital murder in the following cases:

(a) Murder which is perpetrated by killing a peace officer or fireman while such officer or fireman is acting in his official capacity or by reason of an act performed in his official capacity, and with knowledge that the victim was a peace officer or fireman. For purposes of this paragraph, the term "peace officer" means sheriffs of counties and their deputies, constables, marshals, and policemen of cities and towns, game wardens, parole officers, a judge, prosecuting attorney or any other court official, agents of the Alcoholic Beverage Control Division of the State Tax Commission, agents of the Bureau of Narcotics, personnel of the Mississippi Highway Patrol, and the superintendent and his deputies, guards, officers and other employees of the Mississippi State Penitentiary;

(b) Murder which is perpetrated by a person who is under sentence of life imprisonment;

(c) Murder which is perpetrated by use or detonation of a bomb or explosive device;

(d) Murder which is perpetrated by any person who has been offered or has received anything of value for committing the murder, and all parties to such a murder, are guilty as principals;

(e) When done with or without any design to effect death, by any person engaged in the commission of the crime of rape, burglary, kidnapping, arson, robbery, sexual battery, unnatural intercourse with any child under the age of twelve (12), or nonconsensual unnatural intercourse with mankind, or in any attempt to commit such felonies;

(f) When done with or without any design to effect death, by any person engaged in the commission of the crime of felonious abuse and/or battery of a child in violation of subsection (2) of Section 97-5-39, or in any attempt to commit such felony;

(g) Murder which is perpetrated by the killing of any elected official of a county, municipal, state or federal government with knowledge that the victim was such public official.

Section 1-3-4. Capital Case, Capital Offense, Capital Crime, and Capital Murder

The terms "capital case," "capital cases," "capital offense," "capital offenses," and "capital crime" when used in any statute shall denote criminal cases, offenses and crimes punishable by death or imprisonment for life in the state penitentiary. The term "capital murder" when used in any statute shall denote criminal cases, offenses and crimes punishable by death, or imprisonment for life in the state penitentiary.

Section 97-1-7. Attempt to Commit Offense; Punishment

Every person who shall design and endeavor to commit an offense, and shall do any overt act toward the commission thereof, but shall fail therein, or shall be prevented from committing the same, on conviction thereof, shall, where no provision is made by law for the punishment of such offense, be punished as follows: If the offense attempted to be committed be capital, such offense shall be punished by imprisonment in the penitentiary not exceeding ten years; if the offense attempted be punishable by imprisonment in the penitentiary, or by fine and imprisonment in the county jail, then the attempt to commit such offense shall be punished for a period or for an amount not greater than is prescribed for the actual commission of the offense so attempted.

Section 97-1-9. Attempt to Commit Offense; No Conviction If Offense Completed

A person shall not be convicted of an assault with intent to commit a crime, or of any other attempt to commit an offense, when it shall appear that the crime intended or the offense attempted was perpetrated by such person at the time of such assault or in pursuance of such attempt.

Section 97-1-1. Conspiracy

If two (2) or more persons conspire either:
(a) To commit a crime; or
(b) Falsely and maliciously to indict another for a crime, or to procure to be complained of or arrested for a crime; or
(c) Falsely to institute or maintain an action or suit of any kind; or
(d) To cheat and defraud another out of property by any means which are in themselves criminal, or which, if executed, would amount to a cheat, or to obtain money or any other property or thing by false pretense; or
(e) To prevent another from exercising a lawful trade or calling, or doing any other lawful act, by force, threats, intimidation, or by interfering

or threatening to interfere with tools, implements, or property belonging to or used by another, or with the use of employment thereof; or

(f) To commit any act injurious to the public health, to public morals, trade or commerce, or for the perversion or obstruction of justice, or of the due administration of the laws; or

(g) To overthrow or violate the laws of this state through force, violence, threats, intimidation, or otherwise; or

(h) To accomplish any unlawful purpose, or a lawful purpose by any unlawful means;

such persons, and each of them, shall be guilty of a felony and upon conviction may be punished by a fine of not more than five thousand dollars ($ 5,000.00) or by imprisonment for not more than five (5) years, or by both.

⟹ Provided, that where the crime conspired to be committed is capital murder..., the offense shall be punishable by a fine of not more than five hundred thousand dollars ($ 500,000.00) or by imprisonment for not more than twenty (20) years, or by both.

Provided, that where the crime conspired to be committed is a misdemeanor, then upon conviction said crime shall be punished as a misdemeanor as provided by law.

William Stokes v. State of Mississippi

Supreme Court of Mississippi
92 Miss. 415, 46 So. 627, 1908 Miss. LEXIS 245 (1908)

Will Stokes and Cora Lane, who were having an affair, hired Shorty Robertson to kill Lane's husband, Wallace Lane, for the proceeds of life insurance policies. They promised Robertson $1,000 and agreed that he would lay in wait for the husband on a particular night at a particular place to surprise the husband as he returned from a Lodge meeting. But Robertson reported his conversations to the police, who planned to hide themselves at the appointed place and time. The agreed upon night was rainy. Robertson went to Lane's house, where he found Stokes, and together they went to the planned location. Stokes produced a loaded gun and showed Robertson where he should wait. As Stokes was handing the gun to Robertson, the police intervened and arrested him. No money ever changed hands. In fact, the husband did not plan on taking his usual route home that night. Stokes was convicted of attempt to murder Wallace Lane. He appealed on the basis that the facts did not constitute an attempt.

... All the authorities hold, that, in order to constitute an attempt, the act attempted must be a possibility; and counsel for appellant argue from this that the appellant could not have committed this crime at the time he was arrested, because Lane was not even there, and therefore, they say, no conviction could be had. It was no fault of Stokes that the crime was not committed. He had the gun, and the testimony warrants the conclusion that it had been taken for the purpose of killing Lane. It only became impossible by reason of the extraneous circumstance that

Lane did not go that way, and, further, that defendant was arrested and prevented from committing the murder. [The impossibility defense] has application only to a case where it is inherently impossible to commit the crime. It has no application to a case where it becomes impossible for the crime to be committed, either by outside interference or because of miscalculation as to a supposed opportunity to commit the crime which fails to materialize; in short, it has no application to the case when the impossibility grows out of extraneous facts not within the control of the party....

... [T]he defendant's conviction of attempt to kill and murder Wallace Lane is affirmed.

Model Penal Code
(Official Draft 1962)

Section 5.01. Criminal Attempt

(1) Definition of Attempt. A person is guilty of an attempt to commit a crime if, acting with the kind of culpability otherwise required for commission of the crime, he:

(a) purposely engages in conduct which would constitute the crime if the attendant circumstances were as he believes them to be; or

(b) when causing a particular result is an element of the crime, does or omits to do anything with the purpose of causing or with the belief that it will cause such result without further conduct on his part; or

(c) purposely does or omits to do anything which, under the circumstances as he believes them to be, is an act or omission constituting a substantial step in a course of conduct planned to culminate in his commission of the crime....

Section 5.05. ...; Mitigation in Cases of Lesser Danger;...

(1)...

(2) Mitigation. If the particular conduct charged to constitute a criminal attempt, solicitation or conspiracy is so inherently unlikely to result or culminate in the commission of a crime that neither such conduct nor the actor presents a public danger warranting the grading of such offense under this Section, the Court shall exercise its power under Section 6.12 to enter judgment and impose sentence for a crime of lower grade or degree or, in extreme cases, may dismiss the prosecution....

● OVERVIEW OF IMPOSSIBILITY

People v. Rollino
Supreme Court of New York, Criminal Term, Queens County
37 Misc. 2d 14, 233 N.Y.S.2d 580 (1962)

J. Irwin Shapiro, Justice.

At the conclusion of his trial without a jury, under an indictment charging him with Grand Larceny, Second Degree, defendant has moved for its dismissal and thereby revived the question whether a would-be thief can be guilty of either a consummated or an attempted larceny when the coveted property is turned over to him with the knowledge and consent of the owner, by one of its agents, by pre-arrangement with the police, in order to supply a basis for the miscreant's criminal prosecution....

... [T]he question of "impossibility" was raised for the first time in *Regina v. McPherson*, Dears. & B. 197, 201 (1857), when Baron Bramwell said:

> ... The argument that a man putting his hand into an empty pocket might be convicted of an attempt to steal, appeared to me at first plausible; but suppose a man, believing a block of wood to be a man who was his deadly enemy, struck it a blow intending to murder, could he be convicted of attempting to murder the man he took it to be?

Subsequently, in *Regina v. Collins*, 9 Cox C.C. 497, 169 Eng. Rep. 1477 (1864) the court expressly held that attempted larceny was not made out by proof that the defendant pickpocket actually inserted his hand into the victim's empty pocket with intent to steal, Chief Justice Cockburn declaring:

> We think that an attempt to commit a felony can only be made out when, if no interruption had taken place, the attempt could have been carried out successfully, and the felony completed of the attempt to commit which the party is charged.

This very broad language, encompassing as it did all forms of "impossibility," was subsequently rejected by the English courts and it was held that the inability of the pickpocket to steal from an empty pocket did not preclude his conviction of an attempted larceny. Regina v. Ring, 17 Cox C.C. 491, 66 L.T.(N.S.) 300 (1892). The determination in that case, generally speaking, represents the existing state of the law in the United States.

In this country it is generally held that a defendant may be charged with an attempt where the crime was not completed because of "physical or factual impossibility" whereas a "legal impossibility" in the completion of the crime precludes prosecution for an attempt.

What is a "legal impossibility" as distinguished from a "physical or factual impossibility" has over a long period of time perplexed our courts and has resulted in many irreconcilable decisions and much philosophical discussion by legal scholars in numerous articles and papers in law school publications and by text-writers.

The reason for the "impossibility" of completing the substantive crime ordinarily falls into one of two categories: (1) where the act if completed would not be criminal, a situation which is usually described as a "legal impossibility" and (2) where the basic or substantive crime is impossible of completion, simply because of some physical or factual condition unknown to the defendant, a situation which is usually described as a "factual impossibility."

The authorities in the various States and the text-writers are in general agreement that where there is a "legal impossibility" of completing the substantive crime, the accused cannot be successfully charged with an attempt, whereas in those cases in which the "factual impossibility" situation is involved, the accused may be convicted of an attempt. Detailed discussion of the subject is unnecessary to make it clear that it is frequently most difficult to compartmentalize a particular set of facts as coming within one of the categories rather than the other. Examples of the so-called "legal impossibility" situations are:

(a) A person accepting goods which he believes to have been stolen, but which were not in fact stolen goods, is not guilty of an attempt to receive stolen goods. (People v. Jaffe, 185 N.Y. 497, 78 N.E. 169, 9 L.R.A., N.S., 263).

(b) It is not an attempt to commit subornation of perjury where the false testimony solicited, if given, would have been immaterial to the case at hand and hence not perjurious.

(c) An accused who offers a bribe to a person believed to be a juror, but who is not a juror, is not guilty of an attempt to bribe a juror.

(d) An official who contracts a debt which is unauthorized and a nullity, but which he believes to be valid, is not guilty of an attempt to illegally contract a valid debt.

(e) A hunter who shoots a stuffed deer believing it to be alive is not guilty of an attempt to shoot a deer out of season.

(f) [An attempt to unlawfully buy what one mistakenly believes is a controlled drug is an instance of legal impossibility.]*

Examples of cases in which *attempt* convictions have been sustained on the theory that all that prevented the consummation of the completed crime was a "factual impossibility" are:

(a) The picking of an empty pocket.

(b) An attempt to steal from an empty receptacle or an empty house.

(c) Where defendant shoots into the intended victim's bed, believing he is there, when in fact he is elsewhere.

(d) Where the defendant erroneously believing that the gun is loaded points it at his wife's head and pulls the trigger.

(e) Where the woman upon whom the abortion operation is performed is not in fact pregnant. . . .

---

*Editor's Note.—See, e.g., United States v. Everett, 700 F.2d 900 (1983); People v. Rosencrants, 89 Misc. 2d 721, 392 N.Y.S.2d 808 (1977).

The foregoing lines of demarcation laid down in the cases and by text writers as to when an attempt may and may not be successfully charged has been roundly criticized. Thus in Hall, General Principles of Criminal Law, the writer says:

> ...There are no degrees of impossibility and no sound basis for distinguishing among the conditions necessary for commission of the intended harm.

And we find Judge Thurman W. Arnold saying, with regard to the artificiality of the distinctions attempted to be made, the following:

> The distinctions...are ingenious, but...they lead us either to absurd results or else to no results.

In an exhaustive and extremely well considered opinion on this subject in *United States v. Thomas and McClellan*, we find the United States Court of Military Appeals dealing with this subject and saying:

> The lack of logic between some of the holdings; the inherent difficulty in assigning a given set of facts to a proper classification; the criticism of existing positions in this area; and, most importantly, the denial of true and substantial justice by these artificial holdings have led, quite naturally, to proposals for reform in the civilian legal concepts of criminal attempts.

> ...

Some Courts have by "heroic efforts" taken what I consider to be a progressive and more modern view on the subject than is permitted by the decisional law in this State. Thus, California has now abandoned the *People v. Jaffe* rationale that "a person accepting goods which he believes to have been stolen, but which was not in fact stolen goods, is not guilty of an attempt to receive stolen goods and imposes liability for the attempt."

Returning now from the discussion of "attempts" to the facts in this case...

Having determined that the defendant in this case may not be found guilty of the completed act of larceny because the drugs were not in fact taken from the owner without its consent, the next question is whether, under such circumstances, he may be found guilty of an attempt to commit larceny.

The answer would seem to be "no" for the very fact that prevents a conviction for the completed crime of larceny also precludes a conviction of an attempted larceny. "[I]n the present case, the act, which it was doubtless the intent of the defendant to commit would not have been a crime if it had been consummated" (People v. Jaffe, 185 N.Y. 497, 500, 78 N.E. 169) and "an unsuccessful attempt to do that which is not a crime, when effectuated, cannot be held to be an attempt to commit the crime specified." When the owner's agent offered the drugs to Rollino, to entrap him, defendant "succeeded in what he attempted, but what he did was not criminal." Since the completed act did not and could not as a *matter of law* constitute a larceny it is *legally impossible* for defendant to be guilty of an attempted larceny.

The *Jaffe* [case] has been the subject of analytic discussion and much criticism..., but that rule of law has never been modified or overruled in this state and it must, accordingly, be accepted and enforced by this Court.

The defendant's moral guilt is unquestionable. He intended to commit the crime of grand larceny and did everything that he could to implement and effectuate his criminal purpose and intent. That he cannot be adjudged legally guilty is due entirely to the existing state of the decisional and statutory law on the subject [in New York]. Clearly a modification of the law in this regard, to make it less favorable to criminal elements, is called for but this Court may only adjudicate; it may not legislate.

In this connection, attention is called to the proposal of The American Law Institute for the adoption of a "Model Penal Code" which in Article 5.01 defines "Criminal Attempts."

Tentative Draft No. 10 of the Model Penal Code makes obvious the reason and necessity for the adoption of the proposed Article 5.01 when it says:

> ...It should suffice, therefore, to indicate at this stage what we deem to be the major results of the draft. They are:
>
> (a) to extend the criminality of attempts by sweeping aside the defense of impossibility (including the distinction between so-called factual and legal impossibility) and by drawing the line between attempt and non-criminal preparation further away from the final act; the crime becomes essentially one of criminal purpose implemented by an overt act strongly corroborative of such purpose;...

The motion to dismiss the indictment is granted since an element essential to defendant's legal guilt of either a larceny or an attempted larceny of the kind here charged is entirely lacking.

Short form order signed and entered.

Notes on Impossibility

Reasons for Failure of Offense   Conduct toward a substantive offense may be unsuccessful for any number of reasons. The planned offense may be frustrated by the intervention of authorities, by the resistance of the intended victim or others, by the voluntary desistance of those planning the offense, or by the impossibility of completion of the offense. Incompletion because of intervention or resistance generally does not bar liability, although the result is inchoate liability rather than full liability for the object offense. Desistance and impossibility, on the other hand, may give rise to a complete defense in some jurisdictions, even a defense to inchoate liability. These notes examine the impossibility defense. A discussion of desistance — typically called abandonment, renunciation, or withdrawal — is provided in the Advanced Issues section of the Appendix. Much of the impossibility discussion in these Notes will focus on the context of attempt, where the issues are clearest and most common, but the principles governing impossibility apply equally to conspiracy and solicitation.

Impossibility as Revealing Rationale for Liability   Impossibility of completion is of special theoretical interest because the determination of whether or how impossibility should affect liability forces a determination of precisely why attempts are punished. If the danger of completion is the rationale for attempt liability — that is, coming close to committing an offense — then impossibility would seem to undercut the rationale. If, on the other hand, attempt liability is justified by the actor's intention to commit the offense and his demonstrated willingness to carry out that intention, then impossibility of completion that is unknown to the actor does not undercut the rationale for liability.

Difficulty in Applying Legal-Factual Impossibility Distinction As the *Rollino* case, reproduced above, makes clear, the common law rule was to provide a defense in cases of legal impossibility—where "the act if completed would not be criminal"—but not in cases of factual impossibility. But the legal-factual impossibility distinction is criticized as being difficult to apply and the results as being difficult to explain. Consider, for example, the actor who lights the fuse on what he mistakenly believes are dynamite sticks. Is it true that "the act if completed would not be criminal"? The completed conduct—lighting a fuse leading to wooden sticks—is not a substantive offense, thus one might conclude that the conduct constitutes a legally impossible attempt (for which there is a defense). Yet, in another sense, the case seems to be one of factual impossibility. How is lighting the dynamite sticks that in fact are wooden different from the factual impossibility case of the actor who performs an abortion on a woman who is not pregnant? Similarly, how is shooting a deer believing it to be alive (said to be legal impossibility) different from shooting at a bed believing that it contains the intended victim (said to be factual impossibility). (Would it matter if there were a stuffed dummy of the victim in the bed?) How is an actor's mistake as to whether goods are stolen (said to be legal impossibility) different from his mistake as to whether a woman is pregnant (said to be factual impossibility)?

Using Element Analysis to Distinguish In fact, the distinction's reputation for being notoriously difficult to apply may not be entirely deserved. The categorization in most of the cases can be predicted by the nature of the missing objective element: conduct, circumstance, or result. Remember that it is because of the absence of this objective element that the conduct is an attempt rather than a substantive offense. Where the missing offense element is a conduct or result element, the case is more likely to be characterized as one of factual impossibility. The actor cannot "take" (conduct) property from an empty pocket, receptacle, or house, as required by theft. The actor cannot cause "death" (result) where the victim is not in the bed or the gun is not loaded or the womb has no fetus, as required by homicide and abortion. Where the missing offense element is a circumstance, the case is more likely to be characterized as legal impossibility. The goods are not "stolen," the testimony is not "material," the intended bribee is not a "juror," the debt is not "valid," and the deer that is shot is not "alive." In each instance, the missing element is a circumstance element of the offense charged to have been attempted.[1]

Impossibility in Relation to Offense Charged This test for distinguishing factual and legal impossibility requires careful reference to the elements of the offense charged. In many instances, an actor's conduct cannot be judged factually or legally impossible in the abstract. Rather, an actor's conduct must be judged a factually or legally impossible attempt to commit *a specific offense*. Shooting

---

1. This method of distinction obviously requires definitions of what constitutes a conduct, a circumstance, and a result element. The Model Penal Code does not provide such definitions. Used here is this distinction: conduct is defined narrowly to include the physical movement, but to exclude the circumstances and results of the movement; a result is a circumstance changed by the conduct.

a stuffed deer out of season, for example, is a legally impossible attempt because *shooting a live deer* (conduct and circumstance) is the prohibition of the offense (and the missing element is a circumstance, *live* deer). If the offense were defined to prohibit *killing a deer,* the same shooting of a stuffed deer would be judged a factual impossibility because a required result is missing — namely, causing death. It is understandable, then, that before the more systematic analysis of offense elements came into being with the drafting of modern codes, the legal-factual impossibility distinction seemed somewhat unpredictable.

Confusion over Rationale for Distinction While the legal-factual impossibility distinction feasibly *can* be applied, the more important issue is whether the distinction *should* be applied. Why might the common law want to hold liable for attempt an actor whose attempt fails because he or she cannot perform the required conduct or cause the required result, yet exclude from liability, even from attempt liability, an actor whose attempt fails because, while the actor engages in the required conduct, unknown to him a required circumstance does not exist? In at least some respects, this common law position seems counterintuitive: Where the actor has completed his or her conduct and, unknown to the defendant, a circumstance is lacking, we are sure of the actor's willingness to carry the criminal intention to completion. Where the actor cannot complete the required conduct or cause the required result, we may not be quite as sure that he or she would have completed the conduct or caused the result if it had been possible. This is part of the point of Model Penal Code section 5.01(4), which gives a renunciation defense to an actor who stops before finishing the conduct that would complete the offense (from his mistaken view), but denies a voluntary renunciation defense to an actor who mistakenly believes that he or she has completed the offense (but, in fact, has not, because of a missing attendant circumstance).[1]

Impossibility Under Objectivist vs. Subjectivist View of Criminality But the common law position seems counterintuitive only if one assumes that attempt liability is designed primarily to punish subjective criminality — in other words, an actor's intention to commit an offense and his or her demonstrated willingness to carry out that intention. As discussed in previous Sections, the common law generally does not take this view; rather, it is said to reflect an objectivist view of criminality. Certainly an actor's culpable state of mind is an important prerequisite to liability even under an objectivist view of criminality, for this is the means by which innocent people are protected from mistaken convictions. But, under an objectivist view of criminality, the gravamen of all offenses, including inchoate offenses, is the actual harm or evil or danger that the offense conduct suggests. In an attempt, the actual harm, evil, or danger may not be as severe as in the completed offense, yet an attempt nonetheless can cause a danger of completion that disrupts the social order in a real way or, at the very least, appears to *come close*

---

1. Model Penal Code §5.01(4) denies a renunciation defense for an attempt under §5.01(1)(a), which imposes liability for an actor who has "engaged in conduct which would constitute the crime if the attendant circumstances were as he believes them to be...." One might argue that where the actor engages in all of the conduct required, but where the result does not occur, as in the case under §5.01(1)(b), he or she also should be excluded from the renunciation defense. The Code permits the defense for this person, however, because of its overriding commitment to crime control. It wishes to provide an incentive to stop more than it wishes to do justice.

to causing such a harm. This conflict between the objectivist and subjectivist approaches to impossibility is the focus of the Discussion Materials below.

Objectivist Rationale for Impossibility Defense From such an objectivist view of criminality, the factual-legal impossibility distinction may make good sense. If the missing element is a required circumstance that exists only in the actor's mind, in other words a legally impossible attempt, there may be less likelihood of any real danger of completion; moreover, because only the attempter may know of his mistake as to the circumstance, such conduct is less likely to be known by others and, therefore, less likely to be socially disruptive. The missing circumstance elements in the legal impossibility illustrations in *Rollino* include the status of property as "stolen," the status of a statement as "material," the status of a person as a "juror," and the status of a debt as "valid."[1] Conduct and result elements are rarely this abstract or intangible. An actor's frustrated attempt to engage in the *conduct* or cause the *result* required by the offense — picking an empty pocket, shooting with an unloaded gun, performing an abortion on a woman who is not pregnant — may be more potentially dangerous and more apparently criminal. The actor's conduct in missing-circumstance cases — instances of legal impossibility — may be judged to be less dangerous and may not as readily be seen as a criminal attempt. This analysis may not be entirely persuasive in arguing for a defense in legal impossibility cases, but it may at least give some sense of why the common law took this view.

Model Penal Code Position The Model Penal Code, having adopted a subjectivist view of criminality, denies a defense for both factual and legal impossibility. Section 5.01(1) holds an actor liable for attempt if he:

> (a) . . . engages in conduct which would constitute the crime *if the attendant circumstances were as he believes them to be*; or
>
> (b) . . . does or omits to do anything . . . *with the belief* that it will cause [a criminal result]; or
>
> (c) . . . does or omits to do anything which, *under the circumstances as he believes them to be*, is an act or omission constituting a substantial step [toward the offense].

The statute does not mention the terms "factual impossibility" or "legal impossibility" because, under the Code's approach, the distinction is not relevant. The actor will be held for an attempt to commit the offense that the actor believed he was committing, without regard to whether or why commission of the offense is impossible.

Impossibility Due to Mistake as to Offense Attempted Even if one adopts a subjectivist view of criminality and thus denies a defense for legal impossibility, as do the Model Penal Code and most of the states following its lead, one nonetheless may recognize two special forms of impossibility as defenses: These two might be called cases of "imaginary offenses" and cases of "inherently unlikely attempts." In the first, the impossibility arises from the absence or inapplicability of an offense prohibiting what the actor intends; the actor is mistaken in believing

---

1. This quality of circumstance elements is not universal. The status of a deer as a "live" deer is not so abstract.

that his intended conduct is an offense. The Bulgarian visitor who takes a picture of a military base may honestly believe that he is committing an offense because such an act is illegal in his native country. Under one interpretation of Model Penal Code section 5.01(1)(a), he might seem to satisfy the requirements for attempt: "if the attendant circumstances were as he believes them to be" (if taking pictures of a military installation were a crime), he would then have "engage[d] in conduct which would constitute the crime." From the view of subjectivist criminality, the Bulgarian has shown his intention to violate the law and his willingness to carry out that intention. One might argue, then, that liability for attempt is appropriate.

Impossibility and Legality Principle: Imaginary Offenses Yet, in such a situation, a defense to attempt liability generally is given[1] even by jurisdictions that adopt a subjectivist view of criminality. Despite the apparent moral blameworthiness and dangerousness of such an actor, who has demonstrated his willingness to break the law, the defense is given because of the demands of the legality principle (the subject of Section 2). That principle, and the legal doctrines implementing it, require a prior, written, specific statement of a prohibition before its violation can be punished. Most of the rationales of the principle do not concern matters of blameworthiness or dangerousness. They focus instead on such matters as satisfying the due process demands for prior notice, minimizing the potential for abuse of discretion in the administration of criminal justice, and ensuring allocation of the criminalization authority to the legislative branch.

Imaginary Offenses Under Model Penal Code The demands of the legality principle may be given expression even without a special defense provision for attempts to commit an imaginary offense. One need only interpret the Model Penal Code's impossibility language — "if the attendant circumstances were as he believes them to be" — to refer to "the attendant circumstances" *defined to be relevant by the definition of the offense charged.* In other words, the actor will be held liable for an offense only if the circumstances as the actor believes them to be are those defined as the circumstance elements of the charged offense. Even absent the legality principle, this would seem to be the better interpretation of the Code's language, because only the circumstances noted in the offense definition are relevant to determining liability, and because knowledge of the criminality of one's offense typically is not itself an element of an offense.[2]

Inherently Unlikely Attempt A second possibility for a defense under even the code's subjectivist view of criminality is that provided in Model Penal Code section 5.05(2):

> If the particular conduct charged to constitute a criminal attempt, solicitation or conspiracy is so inherently unlikely to result or culminate in the commission of a crime that neither such conduct nor the actor presents a public

---

1. See, e.g., Commonwealth v. Henley, 504 Pa. 408, 474 A.2d 1115 (1984) ("an intent to commit an act which is not characterized as a crime by the laws of the subject jurisdiction can not be the basis of a criminal charge and conviction, even though the actor believes or misapprehends the intended act to be proscribed by the criminal laws," but "in all other cases, the actor should be held responsible for his conduct"); R. v. Taaffe, [1984] 1 All E.R. 747 (H.L.) (defendant thought he was importing currency, which he mistakenly thought was offense; conviction for smuggling drugs reversed).

2. See Model Penal Code §2.02(9).

danger warranting the grading of such offense under this Section, the Court shall exercise its power . . . to enter judgment and impose sentence for a crime of lower grade or degree or, in extreme cases, may dismiss the prosecution.

Under this provision, the actor who tries to kill by sticking pins in a voodoo doll and who is judged to be not dangerous (that is, not likely to try a more effective method) might get a defense (or a mitigation) to a charge of attempted murder. The traditional example of this kind of case is the defendant who shakes his fist at a rain cloud, believing he can thereby destroy the world. (But, as this example suggests, where the actor's mistaken belief departs too far from reality, an insanity defense also may be available.)

▲ PROBLEM
The Smuggler's Deceit

Watson and So are surprised and pleased to find each other on the same flight from Panama to London. They are classmates from reform school and have years of stories to trade during the flight, most of which concern their criminal exploits during and since school. After an hour of catching up, the conversation turns to their current activities. To neither's surprise, each is on the flight to smuggle something into England. It is 1974, and Watson is smuggling in sugar concentrate, a profitable business because of England's current sugar shortage. So compliments Watson on his plan and explains with some pride that his trip is part of a just-developing drug-smuggling business operating with the unofficial help of certain Panamanian officials. Watson is deflated by the conversation. As was always the case in school, So has the better scheme and stands to make over 20 times as much for smuggling in a shipment of the same size. But Watson has become somewhat more crafty since his school days and, when So gets up to go to the bathroom, Watson switches their cases, which are similar in appearance. So does not notice until they are in line at customs. Instead of being angry with Watson, however, he just laughs.

Apparently having second thoughts about drug-smuggling, which he knows carries high penalties, Watson moves forward in the customs line without bringing his bag with him. So, who is farther back in the same line, speaks up helpfully, "Don't forget your bag, sir." Each man is stopped by the customs officers and taken with his bag for questioning. Each is at first cagey, but when things look bad, each turns the other in to ingratiate himself and then, under further questioning, confesses his own wrongdoing. Their accounts are somewhat different, however, for So was really on the plane to smuggle sugar and had only made up the story about the drugs to impress Watson.

It turns out that smuggling sugar is not in fact a crime, although it was widely thought to be so at the time.[1] What liability for Watson and for So, if any?

---

1. "Travellers trying to beat Britain's sugar shortage are smuggling more and more of it into [that] country. They do not know that importing sugar is legal. A woman filled a shoebox with sugar and wrapped it like a gift, with fancy ribbons and bright paper. Another woman had sugar in a can marked 'face powder.'" N.Y. Herald Tribune, Oct. 22, 1974, reprinted in Glanville Williams, Textbook of Criminal Law 398 (1978).

▲ PROBLEM

In re "The Nose . . ."

Dear Ann Landers:

I'm a 31-year-old bachelor, college-educated, church-going and normal in every way, except one. I love the smell of women's feet.

There is no fragrance more exciting than the sweet bouquet of an unshod feminine foot, provided it is not abnormally sweaty or just out of a tennis shoe. I have sniffed the toes of dozens of ladies and could identify any of them blindfolded.

Usually women I have dated a few times don't mind. Some even find this kinkiness amusing. Lately, however, my patience is waning and I don't care to go through the formality of getting to know a woman well before I take off her shoe and savor the heavenly aroma.

Some of these women are stunned, grossed out and afraid that I am trying to undress them. I have been called "a nut" and the evening has ended abruptly.

Questions: Could I be accused of attempted rape for suddenly taking off a woman's shoe? Am I the only man in the world who has this bizarre preference? Am I crazy? Please rush your reply.

— *The Nose Knows in Arizona*

Questions

If "The Nose" believes that the sexual satisfaction he receives by forcibly removing a woman's shoe is rape, could he be convicted of attempted rape if he successfully gains sexual satisfaction in this fashion? Why or why not?

Assume "The Nose" took a job in a women's shoe store in order to gratify his sexual desire. Could he be held liable for sexual assault under the following section (Model Penal Code Section 213.4)?

> A person who subjects another not his spouse to any sexual contact is guilty of sexual assault, a misdemeanor, if:
>
> (1) he knows that the contact is offensive to the other person; or . . .
>
> (3) he knows that the other person is unaware that a sexual act is being committed; . . .
>
> Sexual contact is any touching of the sexual or other intimate parts of the person of another for the purpose of arousing or gratifying sexual desire of either party.

Could "The Nose" be held liable for attempted sexual assault? Does it matter whether common law or the Model Penal Code is in force?

✽ DISCUSSION MATERIALS

If It Is Impossible for a Person to Commit the Offense Attempted, Should the Attempt Nonetheless Constitute a Crime? In Other Words, Should a Potential for Actual Commission Be Required, Or Is a Subjective Belief in the Potential for Commission Enough?

George Fletcher's article on the significance of resulting harm, which was excerpted in Section 9, is worth reexamining here to refresh your recollection of his distinction between the "objectivist view of criminality" and the "subjectivist view of criminality." The Model Penal Code Commentary excerpt discusses the strengths and weaknesses of the impossibility doctrine as it relates to punishing dangerousness, the purpose that guides the Code's formulation of the doctrine. Lawrence Crocker, taking an opposing objectivist view of criminality, challenges the Model Penal Code's subjectivist perspective, arguing that such a subjectivist view of criminality risks punishing without blameworthiness and that objectivist principles are and ought to be the core of many current criminal codes.

George P. Fletcher, A Crime of Self-Defense: Bernhard Goetz and the Law on Trial
64-67 (1988)

[Reread the Fletcher excerpt in the Section 9 (Causation) Discussion Materials.]

Model Penal Code Section 5.01 Commentary
Official Draft and Revised Comments 315-316 (1985)

Policy Considerations. Insofar as it has not rested on conceptual tangles that have been largely independent of policy considerations, the defense of impossibility seems to have been employed to serve a number of functions. First, it has been used to verify criminal purpose; if the means selected were absurd, there is good ground for doubting that the actor really planned to commit a crime. Similarly, if the defendant's conduct, objectively viewed, is ambiguous, there may be ground for doubting the firmness of his purpose to commit a criminal offense. A general defense of impossibility is, however, an inappropriate way of assuring that the actor has a true criminal purpose.

A second function that the defense of impossibility seems to have served in some cases is to supplement the defense of entrapment. In situations in which the technical entrapment rules do not exonerate the defendant, there is a temptation to find that the presence of traps and decoys makes the actor's endeavor impossible. The Model Code has a separate formulation on entrapment which is believed to state the appropriate considerations for a defense on this ground.

A third consideration that has been advanced in support of an impossibility defense is the view that the criminal law need not take notice of conduct that is innocuous, the element of impossibility preventing any dangerous proximity to the completed crime. The law of attempts, however, should be concerned with manifestations of dangerous character as well as with preventive arrests; the fact that particular conduct may not create an actual risk of harmful consequences, though it would if the circumstances were as the defendant believed them to be, should not therefore be conclusive. The innocuous character of the particular conduct becomes relevant only if the futile endeavor itself indicates a harmless personality, so that immunizing the conduct from liability would not result in exposing society to a dangerous person.

Using impossibility as a guide to dangerousness of personality presents serious difficulties. What is needed is a guideline that can inform judgment in particular cases, so that those that involve a danger to society can be successfully prosecuted while those that do not can be dismissed. Such a vehicle is provided in Section 5.05(2), which authorizes the court to reduce the grade of the offense, or dismiss the prosecution, in situations where the conduct charged to constitute an attempt is "so inherently unlikely to result or culminate in the commission of a crime that neither such conduct nor the actor presents a public danger warranting" the normal grading of the offense as an attempt. Section 5.05(2) thus takes account of those cases where neither the offender nor his conduct presents a serious threat to the public. There is also, of course, prosecutorial discretion, which seems to have eliminated most such cases from litigation in the past.

Lawrence Crocker, Justice in Criminal Liability: Decriminalizing Harmless Attempts

53 Ohio State Law Journal 1057, 1069-1072 (1992)

Among theories of criminal liability, two are polar opposites. On one theory, or more accurately family of theories, society's license to punish the offender derives from her dangerousness or wickedness. On pure versions of these theories wicked thoughts and plans unaccompanied by concrete acts fail to be punishable only because the trier of fact would have insufficient evidence to infer the appropriate level of personal dangerousness or depravity. Such theories are "subjective."

On the opposite theory, society's license to punish the offender derives from her commission of criminal acts that actually impose upon society. In the absence of these acts, we cannot justly punish the offender even if we know with certainty that she is desperately wicked and dreadfully dangerous. This is sometimes called an "objective" theory, but because that label can cover a great deal of ground, I will refer to this theory, which I endorse, by the more descriptive if less elegant phrase "imposition theory."

A theory is not "subjective" in the sense I have in mind merely because the mental state of the offender is an element of liability. In that weak sense we are all subjectivists — so long as we recognize the propriety of distinguishing among different degrees of homicide in terms of mental states. For the purposes of this Article a theory is "purely subjective" if an act is not a necessary condition of liability, and it is "subjective" if, for at least some offenses, an imposition upon discrete victims or society is not a necessary condition of liability.

I doubt that there is anyone who holds a pure version of a subjective theory. A purist would insist that the criminal act is only of evidentiary significance. In principle a machine that perfectly assessed subjective depravity or predicted future criminality could substitute for the criminal act as the predicate for criminal liability. Some may eschew this extreme view only because they believe such a machine to be impossible. Most would, I hope, concede that such a machine, even if it were possible, ought not be used for reasons of justice. In the end, this concession will take the modern subjectivist further than he may have anticipated. My present purpose, however, is only to avoid seeming to overstate my opponents' initial commitments.

Still, if there may be no "pure" subjectivists, the criminal justice community has taken on board a very heavy load of subjectivism. The Model Penal Code, for example, although it purports to forbid "conduct that unjustifiably and inexcusably inflicts or threatens substantial harm," apparently sees as the purpose of punishment "to subject to public control persons whose conduct indicates that they are disposed to commit crimes." Correspondingly, the official commentators concluded that "the primary purpose of punishing attempts is to neutralize dangerous individuals and not to deter dangerous acts."...

Commentators are so nearly unanimous that the key to criminal liability ought to be the dangerousness or depravity of the offender, rather than the extent of his actual imposition upon his victim or society, that this subjective theory is sometimes simply called the "modern" theory....

I want to emphasize, however, that what is at stake here is not simply a matter of theories of attempts, though harmless attempts — attempts that impose no risk — focus the dispute in a particularly sharp way. What is at stake is the general theory of criminal liability. Subjective theories and the imposition theory are fundamentally different ways of understanding what it is for conduct to be criminal. The imposition theory has its roots in retributive justice. Those of the subjective theories are primarily in utilitarianism.

The objective theory has differing consequences from subjective theories throughout the substantive criminal law including for such matters as punishment theory, victimless crimes, felony-murder, misdemeanor-manslaughter, conspiracy, possession offenses, and even criminal causation. Except for a brief excursion into punishment theory, this Article ignores these other matters to concentrate on the pivotal test case of attempts. My hope is thereby to show that there is some plausibility, after all, to an approach that has been all but universally rejected by academic commentators....

...I submit that there is nothing mysterious or terribly difficult about an imposition theory. It resonates with considerations that have long been staples of the jurisprudence of crime and punishment — legality, responsibility, autonomy, and "proportionality." There is surely some initial plausibility to the proposition that free people should not become criminally liable unless they trespass upon someone else's moral space, that is unless they impose in some way. Similarly, there is at least some intuitive support for the further proposition that free people ought not to acquire liability for serious crimes unless they have imposed in some serious way. The common sense appeal of the imposition theory is reflected in the old common law, for which there was no criminal liability for any unsuccessful attempt.

It will be the burden of . . . this Article to argue that the imposition theory's initial plausibility is, in fact, well founded. In large part I do this through arguing against subjective theories. Of course every argument against the class of subjective theories is simultaneously an argument for the imposition theory and vice versa inasmuch as I have defined the two to be mutually exclusive and jointly exhaustive. Everyone who rejects the requirement of an imposition for liability, and a sufficiently objective imposition at that, I stuff together into the subjectivist pigeonhole.

In fact, despite the obviousness of the imposition theory, I have identified no contemporary commentator who escapes consignment to the subjectivist pigeonhole. That is not to say that no one in the recent past has argued for any form of an imposition theory. But the few who have argued for a requirement of an imposition for criminal liability have slid back into subjectivism by watering down what would count as an imposition. . . .

Let me anticipate with a few examples. Lying in wait for a victim who is still some distance away is, I will argue, not yet an "attempt" at all, but even if it were, it would be a harmless attempt because there is no immediate risk imposed upon the victim until he comes within range. When he does come within range, and is fired upon with live ammunition, there is an attempt, and not a harmless one. Even if the shooter missed, the attempt was possible and properly gives rise to liability because it did impose immediate risk upon the intended victim. Firing a stage prop pistol and firing at a tree stump in the mistaken belief it is a person are harmless attempts. There is no immediate imposition. Similarly there is no risk, and hence ought not be attempt liability, for spooning what is in fact sugar out of an arsenic box into one's aunt's tea, for buying goods in the mistaken belief they are stolen, for the smuggling of lace in the mistaken belief it is dutiable, for picking an empty pocket, for shooting into a bed believed on good grounds to be occupied, or for trying to rape a deceased or secretly consenting victim. . . .

II. Arguments Against Subjectivism and for the Imposition Theory

I will here set out seven arguments in favor of the imposition theory of attempts and against the modern subjective theory.

The first argument is partially descriptive in character. It looks to the fact that existing criminal codes are built upon the concept of imposition. Most obvious is the fact that offenses are largely graded in terms of the seriousness of their effects. In particular, the seriousness of the offense increases with the size of the theft, the seriousness of the physical injury, and the degree of the sexual imposition. Moreover, successful attempts, despite the complaints of subjectivists, are almost always of higher grade than unsuccessful attempts. The incompatibility of the subjective theory with these basic features of criminal law is not just an apparent incompatibility.

My second argument is that the subjective theory is radically incomplete. There are fact situations in which subjectivism is committed to there being criminal liability, but for which it lacks the resources to specify the offense for which the offender is liable.

For my third argument I draw upon the fact that the concept of criminal liability is closely bound to that of criminal responsibility. There is no liability unless the offender is responsible for the creation of some condition. In the end, only impositions have enough substance to count as such conditions. [This argument is excerpted below, under the "C." heading.]

The fourth argument is linguistic. It turns on the fact that ordinary usage does not recognize as attempts two broad and important groups of cases that count as attempts on subjectivist theories.

Political philosophy is the heart of my rather more extended fifth argument, which deals with the first category of harmless attempts — those that have not gone far enough to impose immediate risk. The argument focuses on the value of individual autonomy and liberty. The imposition theory leaves more scope for individual liberty, and less for state coercion, than do its rivals. In the course of establishing this, I will argue that the imposition theory is to be preferred because the pure subjective theory is flatly and unquestionably unacceptable in its treatment of liberty and autonomy and because there is no tenable middle ground between the pure subjective theory and the pure imposition theory. In short, no satisfactory alternative to the imposition theory is available.

Moreover, even if there were such an alternative, it would encounter grave difficulties drawing the line between liability and nonliability. Just what step is it on the path from plan to executed crime that crosses the line? My sixth argument is that the criterial verbal formulae of subjective theories are inevitably far too vague to provide adequate notice. These theories, then, fall short of minimal conditions of legality and due process.

My final, and weightiest, argument is one of retributive justice or fairness. It would be fundamentally unfair for society to impose upon the individual in the dramatic, serious, and stigmatizing fashion of the criminal law unless the individual has done something that imposes upon society. . . .

C. The Conflict Between Subjective Theories and Criminal Responsibility

A defendant has committed a murder only if the victim died and only if the defendant's actions causally contributed to that death. If the latter condition fails, the defendant is not responsible for the death. If the former, then there is nothing for which the offender could be responsible. It is no accident or mere linguistic convention that there should be this connection between criminal liability and responsibility. The sanctions of the criminal law are among the most serious interferences that a state makes in the lives of individuals. Unchecked, these sanctions would be the stuff of social terrorism of the most threatening sort. Criminal law's chief internal protection against such excesses is the requirement that there be no criminal liability without criminal responsibility. The requirement of responsibility is what separates criminal justice from other forms of social protection. . . .

Consider three cases in turn. In the first, the defendant, with intent to kill, fires a bullet that strikes the victim in the head, killing her. In the second, with the same intent, the defendant fires a bullet that just misses the victim's head. In the third the defendant, again with the same intent, fires a pistol that is, unknown to him, a harmless stage prop.

In the first case, the defendant is unequivocally responsible for the death. In the second, it is not difficult to find something for which the defendant is responsible. Even in the absence of causing fright or the like, the defendant is responsible for the substantial risk to the victim's life that existed as the bullet sped through the air.

In the case of the stage pistol, one's first reaction ought, I think, to be that there is nothing here for which the defendant could be responsible. . . .

Does it properly describe the situation to say that we hold the defendant liable because he is responsible for this state of affairs? Such a description would be proper only if there is in this situation something that society takes to be an evil sufficiently great to sanction and if the offender is responsible for that evil. I will contend that, although there is something in this situation that society takes seriously and although there is something for which the defendant is responsible, the two are not the same.

In what does the seriousness of the situation consist? There would seem to be three possibilities: the defendant's evil character as evidenced by the act, the risk induced by the act, and the alarm actually caused by the act.

The last of these elements, of course, is perfectly at home in the imposition theory. If the victim was put in fear by the episode, then there was an imposition. Such lesser offenses as harassment or menacing are chargeable based on this imposition. This component of what the defendant did, however, clearly could not support a charge of attempted murder, as the subjective view would have it.

By contrast, the evil character evidenced is very different from an imposition. If we find in it the predicate for liability, then the imposition theory must be in error. Imposition would not be a necessary condition of liability.

It would be hard to deny that there is something that society regards as serious about so evil a state of mind. An evil state of mind is not, however, something that one can be said to be responsible for, in the sense of criminal responsibility. Under normal circumstances, we are not even causally responsible for our own desires or intents. We simply have this or that desire or intent.

More generally, when we are focusing upon the defendant's state of mind we are not really making use of the concept of moral responsibility at all. Moral assessment of character is a different and quite independent enterprise. Thus, insofar as the seriousness of the shooting with a stage prop is a matter of evidence of bad character, it falls outside the category of criminal responsibility. . . .

What follows from all this is that there is no account of such impossible attempts — as shooting with a stage pistol — on which what society finds worthy of condemning in them is comprehended under the concept of criminal responsibility. Indeed, a close look reveals that what tempts us to impose liability for such attempts comes down in the end to the wicked character of the defendant or to his future dangerousness. Now perhaps there is a corner of the criminal law in which criminal responsibility is unnecessary for criminal liability and in which bad character or dangerousness is sufficient to send to jail those who have done no harm. The concept of criminal responsibility, however, plays a crucial role in protecting us from overreaching in the name of public safety. For this reason, we should be cautious in accepting the proposition that there may be criminal liability without criminal responsibility. We should avoid this conclusion unless the moral force of arguments supporting it is overwhelming. In fact, the opposite turns out to be true.

Conspiracy

As attempt punishes conduct toward an offense, conspiracy punishes a specific kind of such conduct: an agreement with another that one of those agreeing will commit the offense. While this is just another form of inchoate conduct, albeit a very preliminary form, it is of special interest, for conspiracy has often been transformed into a different, and controversial, offense. This is so in part because conspiracy also represents a form of criminality arising from group conduct.

◆ THE CASE OF SHEIK OMAR ABDEL RAHMAN

Sheik Omar Abdel Rahman comes to the United States in 1990. He is an elderly blind cleric, sick with diabetes and other age-related health problems. He views the United States as Islam's main oppressor and thinks that America is helping Israel gain power in the Middle East because it is under the control of the Jewish lobby. Rahman comes to the U.S. nonetheless because he considers his homeland of Egypt to be no better. He is particularly dissatisfied with Egyptian President Hosni Mubarak, whom he views as another oppressor of Islam. Because of this oppression, Rahman believes that the Qur'an authorizes a jihad, or holy war, against the two countries.

In 1989, before Rahman arrives, his followers had already started organizing into small groups, cells, in New York City. They maintain contact with Rahman while he is still in Egypt, providing updates about their training and overall plans. The followers record their conversations with the Sheik and distribute them as inspirational propaganda to other cells in New York. By the time Rahman arrives in 1990 (after dropping his two sons off in Afghanistan to train in Osama bin Laden's Al Qaeda camps), several cells are fully operational.

Rahman is careful to avoid direct involvement with the particulars of any operation, but instead provides only general comment. For example, both before and after his arrival, Rahman issues fatwas, which are religious opinions on the

Figure 41 **Sheik Rahman, February 20, 1993**

(Reuters Newsmedia Inc./Corbis)

Figure 42 **Sheik Rahman with Emad Salem, May 1993**

(Elatab Said/Corbis-Sygma)

holiness of an act, condoning the proposed plans from the cells as furthering the jihad against the U.S. and Egypt. Meanwhile, the F.B.I. has been conducting surveillance against several of his followers and has photos of them firing AK-47s at a public range on Long Island, as well as recordings of their conversations with Rahman.

In 1990, an F.B.I. informant, Emad Salem, makes contact with Rahman's New York City group. He meets with Rahman and is successful in gaining the Sheik's immediate trust. A few days later, Salem accompanies Rahman to a conference in Detroit. En route, Salem attempts to further prove his loyalty by describing how he fought in the Egyptian military against Israel in 1973. Rahman is unimpressed, however, explaining to Salem that paid service does not count as jihad. Rahman suggests that a true act of jihad would be to assassinate the "loyal dog to the Americans" — Egyptian President Mubarak.

Salem continues to ingratiate himself with Rahman's group, including cultivating a friendship with another of Rahman's confidantes, El-Gabrowny. Eventually, El-Gabrowny invites Salem for dinner, but turns up the television before talking because he is paranoid of eavesdropping equipment. He regales Salem with talk of bombings and jihad, which during the course of their relationship will become the usual topic of conversation.

In July, Salem breaks with the F.B.I. and, shortly thereafter, withdraws as the New York group's paramilitary leader by leaving for Spain to allegedly sort out a jewelry deal. By late 1992, however, the group resumes paramilitary training under a new leader, Siddig Ali, who also reports regularly to Rahman.

Meanwhile, Hampton-El, another Rahman follower, tries purchasing guns and detonators from Garret Wilson. He also says he wants "train[ing] in commando tactics," including training techniques and bomb identification. Contemporaneously, Ramzi Yousef, who is later convicted for his involvement in the 1993 World Trade Center bombing, arrives in the United States. (When passing through the I.N.S. entry gate, Yousef shows multiple pieces of identification for different identities, but immigration officials, who are suspicious, are unable to detain him because the airport holding cells are full. They order him to appear in court, but he never shows and the I.N.S. takes no further action.)

In early 1993, Rahman attends a conference in Brooklyn. He tells the attendees that he supports a violent jihad and that the Qur'an condones terrorist acts if directed toward Islam's enemies, foremost of which are the United States and its allies.

In New York, Yousef joins Mohammed Salameh, and together they develop plans to attack the World Trade Center buildings. They continue to advise Rahman of their plans. After a month of careful planning, the details are finalized. On February 24, 1993, Salameh rents a van using a fake New York license that lists his name and El-Gabrowny's address. They will use the van to deliver the explosives into the World Trade Center. Simultaneously, Ayyad, another follower, arranges to purchase hydrogen gas for the bomb's construction.

Two days later, the World Trade Center is bombed, resulting in six deaths, thousands of injured, and massive destruction. Authorities arrest Salameh after he tries to demand his deposit back from the place where he rented the van to carry the bomb. Using the fake license he had presented as a lead, the police search El-Gabrowny's residence. They arrest him after he tries to assault them during the search. Yousef also is eventually caught. While being transported by helicopter, passing the twin towers of the World Trade Center, he says, "Next time we will take them both down." Meanwhile, Rahman remains untouched.

Figure 43 **Ramzi Yousef, 1995**

(Jeffrey Markowirz/Corbis-Sygma)

Figure 44 **Mohammed Salameh, circa 1993**

(Reuters NewsMedia Inc./Corbis)

Figure 45 **World Trade Center,
September 1999**

(Craig Nevill-Manning)

Figure 46 **Egyptian President
Hosni Mubarak**

(Egyptian Press and Information Office)

Figure 47 **United Nations
Headquarters in New York City**

(Daniel E. Beards)

In early March, President Mubarak schedules a visit to New York, which Rahman's followers see as a perfect opportunity to kill him. Needing funding for the operation, Ali, the training leader, contacts a man in the United Arab Emirates and asserts that Rahman will vouch for him. When Mubarak cancels his visit, the plan fades into the background.

The following month, Ali proposes an attack on the United Nations building. Rahman approves of the proposed attack as jihad. By now, Salem has made amends with the F.B.I. and has reestablished his connections with Rahman's group. Ali allows Salem to speak with Rahman about the proposed attack, but emphasizes that he must be careful because of surveillance. Ali instructs Salem to "phrase statements in a broad and general manner in order to assure that Rahman [is] insulated from active involvement in the plot."

Salem meets with Rahman in May and reaffirms his loyalty to him. When Salem tells Ali of the meeting, Ali informs him that Rahman has approved of the United Nations bombing plan by issuing an official fatwa, the issuance of which allows them to enjoy God's blessing to employ unlawful violence.

Ali and Salem then discuss plans to bomb the Lincoln and Holland Tunnels. They draft the plan on cardboard (later found in the safe house Rahman's group unknowingly rented from the F.B.I.) and decide that the attack requires three explosions spaced five minutes apart. They laugh at the thought of thousands of surprised commuters drowning on their way home. Ali and Amir drive to the tunnels, the United Nations building, and the Federal Building to observe the targets and check traffic patterns. During one reconnaissance trip, Amir suggests that they bomb Manhattan's diamond district, saying this would be like bombing Israel itself.

In June, the group meets to finalize the plan and to decide what additional preparations are necessary. Hampton-El says that he will find detonators. Saleh agrees to buy military equipment. They purchase timers for the bombs in Chinatown and buy stolen cars to use as a delivery vehicle and getaway car. In order to refine the plan, they meet with an engineer to discuss the plan's overall feasibility and determine where the tunnels' weak points are located.

On June 17, Rahman holds a press conference announcing that the United States will pay a tremendous price for supporting President Mubarak. Three days later, the group buys 55-gallon steel drums to hold the fuel for the explosions. They fill some of the drums at a gas station owned by a member of the group, Saleh. Even though Saleh has arranged for them not to pay for the fuel, his employee, Balhabri, makes out a receipt, which includes the license plate number of the van they are driving. The next day, they return to fill the remaining

Figure 48 **Sheik Rahman at a news conference in New Jersey**
(Najlah Feanny/Corbis Saba)

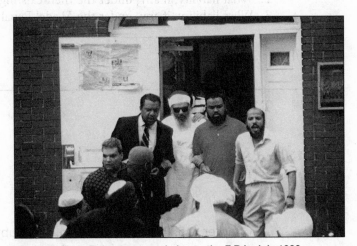

Figure 49 **Sheik Rahman surrendering to the F.B.I., July 1993**
(Les Stone/Corbis)

drums, but this time they chide Balhabri when he begins to write the plate number on the receipt. Elsewhere, Ali and Salem purchase the bombs' other principal component, fertilizer. About this time, Rahman, anticipating their success, tells followers that the bombing will "move Duane Street to Reade Street."

On the evening of June 23, Amir and Fadil bring the fuel to the safe house, and the operational group briefly meets to review the plan. After returning from prayers at a mosque, they begin mixing the fuel and fertilizer for the bombs, while also watching a video shot by Ali earlier in the day of the tunnels they plan to destroy.

Meanwhile, in Yonkers, the F.B.I. arrests Saleh. He denies selling the fuel, but says that Salem demanded it twice. He later calls an employee from prison and instructs him to tell Balhabri to burn the receipts. At 2:00 a.m., the F.B.I. raids the safe house, arrests the group, and seizes the fuel, fertilizer, and Ali's cardboard diagram illustrating the plan. Rahman is arrested shortly thereafter.

1. Relying only upon your own intuitions of justice, what liability and punishment, if any, does Sheik Rahman deserve?

N	0	1	2	3	4	5	6	7	8	9	10	11
☐	☐	☐	☐	☐	☐	☐	☐	☐	☐	☐	☐	☐
no liability	liability but no punishment	1 day	2 wks	2 mo	6 mo	1 yr	3 yrs	7 yrs	15 yrs	30 yrs	life imprison- ment	death

2. What liability, if any, under the then-existing statutes?
3. What liability, if any, under the Model Penal Code?

■ THE LAW

United States Code
Title 18 (1993)

Part I. Crimes

Chapter 115. Treason, Sedition, and Subversive Activities

Section 2384. Seditious Conspiracy

If two or more persons in any State or Territory, or in any place subject to the jurisdiction of the United States, conspire to overthrow, put down, or to destroy by force the Government of the United States, or to levy war against them, or to oppose by force the authority thereof, or by force to prevent, hinder, or delay the execution of any law of the United States, or by force to seize, take, or possess any property of the United States contrary to the authority thereof, they shall each be fined not more than $ 20,000 or imprisoned not more than twenty years, or both.

Section 2385. Advocating Overthrow of Government

Whoever knowingly or willfully advocates, abets, advises, or teaches the duty, necessity, desirability, or propriety of overthrowing or destroying the government of the United States or the government of any State, Territory, District or Possession thereof, or the government of any political subdivision therein, by force or violence, or by the assassination of any officer of any such government; or

Whoever, with intent to cause the overthrow or destruction of any such government, prints, publishes, edits, issues, circulates, sells, distributes, or publicly displays any written or printed matter advocating, advising, or teaching the duty, necessity, desirability, or propriety of overthrowing or destroying any government in the United States by force or violence, or attempts to do so; or

Whoever organizes or helps or attempts to organize any society, group, or assembly of persons who teach, advocate, or encourage the overthrow or destruction of any such government by force or violence; or becomes or is a member of, or affiliates with, any such society, group, or assembly of persons, knowing the purposes thereof—

Shall be fined not more than $ 20,000 or imprisoned not more than twenty years, or both, and shall be ineligible for employment by the United States or any department or agency thereof, for the five years next following his conviction.

If two or more persons conspire to commit any offense named in this section, each shall be fined not more than $ 20,000 or imprisoned not more than twenty years, or both, and shall be ineligible for employment by the United States or any department or agency thereof, for the five years next following his conviction.

As used in this section, the terms "organizes" and "organize", with respect to any society, group, or assembly of persons, include the recruiting of new members, the forming of new units, and the regrouping or expansion of existing clubs, classes, and other units of such society, group, or assembly of persons.

Section 2389. Recruiting for Service Against United States

Whoever recruits soldiers or sailors within the United States, or in any place subject to the jurisdiction thereof, to engage in armed hostility against the same; or

Whoever opens within the United States, or in any place subject to the jurisdiction thereof, a recruiting station for the enlistment of such soldiers or sailors to serve in any manner in armed hostility against the United States—

Shall be fined not more than $ 1,000 or imprisoned not more than five years, or both.

Section 2390. Enlistment to Serve Against United States

Whoever enlists or is engaged within the United States or in any place subject to the jurisdiction thereof, with intent to serve in armed hostility against the United States, shall be fined $ 100 or imprisoned not more than three years, or both.

Chapter 19. Conspiracy

Section 371. Conspiracy to Commit Offense or to Defraud United States

If two or more persons conspire either to commit any offense against the United States, or to defraud the United States, or any agency thereof in any manner or for any purpose, and one or more of such persons do any act to effect the object of the conspiracy, each shall be fined not more than $ 10,000 or imprisoned not more than five years, or both.

If, however, the offense, the commission of which is the object of the conspiracy, is a misdemeanor only, the punishment for such conspiracy shall not exceed the maximum punishment provided for such misdemeanor.

Section 373. Solicitation to Commit a Crime of Violence

(a) Whoever, with intent that another person engage in conduct constituting a felony that has as an element the use, attempted use, or threatened use of physical force against property or against the person of another in violation of the laws of the United States, and under circumstances strongly corroborative of that intent, solicits, commands, induces, or otherwise endeavors to persuade such other person to engage in such conduct, shall be imprisoned not more than one-half the maximum term of imprisonment or fined not more than one-half of the maximum fine prescribed for the punishment of the crime solicited, or both; or if the crime solicited is punishable by death, shall be imprisoned for not more than twenty years.

(b) It is an affirmative defense to a prosecution under this section that, under circumstances manifesting a voluntary and complete renunciation of his criminal intent, the defendant prevented the commission of the crime solicited. A renunciation is not "voluntary and complete" if it is motivated in whole or in part by a decision to postpone the commission of the crime until another time or to substitute another victim or another but similar objective. If the defendant raises the affirmative defense at trial, the defendant has the burden of proving the defense by a preponderance of the evidence.

(c) It is not a defense to a prosecution under this section that the person solicited could not be convicted of the crime because he lacked the state of mind required for its commission, because he was incompetent or irresponsible, or because he is immune from prosecution or is not subject to prosecution.

Chapter 40. Importation, Manufacture, Distribution and Storage of Explosive Materials

Section 842. Unlawful Acts

(a) It shall be unlawful for any person —

(1) to engage in the business of importing, manufacturing, or dealing in explosive materials without a license issued under this chapter;

(2) knowingly to withhold information or to make any false or fictitious oral or written statement or to furnish or exhibit any false, fictitious, or

misrepresented identification, intended or likely to deceive for the purpose of obtaining explosive materials, or a license, permit, exemption, or relief from disability under the provisions of this chapter; and

(3) other than a licensee or permittee knowingly —

(A) to transport, ship, cause to be transported, or receive in interstate or foreign commerce any explosive materials, except that a person who lawfully purchases explosive materials from a licensee in a State contiguous to the State in which the purchaser resides may ship, transport, or cause to be transported such explosive materials to the State in which he resides and may receive such explosive materials in the State in which he resides, if such transportation, shipment, or receipt is permitted by the law of the State in which he resides; or

(B) to distribute explosive materials to any person (other than a licensee or permittee) who the distributor knows or has reasonable cause to believe does not reside in the State in which the distributor resides.

(b) It shall be unlawful for any licensee knowingly to distribute any explosive materials to any person except —

(1) a licensee;

(2) a permittee; or

(3) a resident of the State where distribution is made and in which the licensee is licensed to do business or a State contiguous thereto if permitted by the law of the State of the purchaser's residence.

(c) It shall be unlawful for any licensee to distribute explosive materials to any person who the licensee has reason to believe intends to transport such explosive materials into a State where the purchase, possession, or use of explosive materials is prohibited or which does not permit its residents to transport or ship explosive materials into it or to receive explosive materials in it.

(d) It shall be unlawful for any licensee knowingly to distribute explosive materials to any individual who:

(1) is under twenty-one years of age;

(2) has been convicted in any court of a crime punishable by imprisonment for a term exceeding one year;

(3) is under indictment for a crime punishable by imprisonment for a term exceeding one year;

(4) is a fugitive from justice;

(5) is an unlawful user of or addicted to any controlled substance (as defined in section 102 of the Controlled Substances Act (21 U.S.C. 802)); or

(6) has been adjudicated a mental defective.

(e) It shall be unlawful for any licensee knowingly to distribute any explosive materials to any person in any State where the purchase, possession, or use by such person of such explosive materials would be in violation of any State law or any published ordinance applicable at the place of distribution.

(f) It shall be unlawful for any licensee or permittee willfully to manufacture, import, purchase, distribute, or receive explosive materials without making such records as the Secretary may by regulation require, including, but not limited to, a statement of intended use, the name, date, place of birth, social security number or taxpayer identification number, and place of residence of any natural person to whom explosive materials are distributed. If explosive materials are distributed to a corporation or other business entity, such records shall include the identity and principal and local places of business and the name, date, place of birth, and place of residence of the natural person acting as agent of the corporation or other business entity in arranging the distribution.

(g) It shall be unlawful for any licensee or permittee knowingly to make any false entry in any record which he is required to keep pursuant to this section or regulations promulgated under section 847 of this title [18 U.S.C.S §847].

(h) It shall be unlawful for any person to receive, conceal, transport, ship, store, barter, sell, or dispose of any explosive materials knowing or having reasonable cause to believe that such explosive materials were stolen.

(i) It shall be unlawful for any person —

(1) who is under indictment for, or who has been convicted in any court of, a crime punishable by imprisonment for a term exceeding one year;

(2) who is a fugitive from justice;

(3) who is an unlawful user of or addicted to any controlled substance (as defined in section 102 of the Controlled Substances Act (21 U.S.C. 802)); or

(4) who has been adjudicated as a mental defective or who has been committed to a mental institution;

to ship or transport any explosive in interstate or foreign commerce or to receive any explosive which has been shipped or transported in interstate or foreign commerce.

(j) It shall be unlawful for any person to store any explosive material in a manner not in conformity with regulations promulgated by the Secretary. In promulgating such regulations, the Secretary shall take into consideration the class, type, and quantity of explosive materials to be stored, as well as the standards of safety and security recognized in the explosives industry.

(k) It shall be unlawful for any person who has knowledge of the theft or loss of any explosive materials from his stock, to fail to report such theft or loss within twenty-four hours of discovery thereof, to the Secretary and to appropriate local authorities.

Section 844. Penalties

(a) Any person who violates subsections (a) through (i) of section 842 of this chapter [18 U.S.C.S. §842(a) through (i)] shall be fined not more than $ 10,000 or imprisoned not more than ten years, or both.

(b) Any person who violates any other provision of section 842 of this chapter [18 U.S.C.S. §842] shall be fined not more than $ 1,000 or imprisoned not more than one year, or both.

(c) Any explosive materials involved or used or intended to be used in any violation of the provisions of this chapter or any other rule or regulation promulgated thereunder or any violation of any criminal law of the United States shall be subject to seizure and forfeiture, and all provisions of the Internal Revenue Code of 1954 [26 U.S.C.S. §§1 et seq.] relating to the seizure, forfeiture, and disposition of firearms, as defined in section 5845(a) of that Code [26 U.S.C.S. §5845(a)], shall, so far as applicable, extend to seizures and forfeitures under the provisions of this chapter [18 U.S.C.S. §§841 et seq.].

(d) Whoever transports or receives, or attempts to transport or receive, in interstate or foreign commerce any explosive with the knowledge or intent that it will be used to kill, injure, or intimidate any individual or unlawfully to damage or destroy any building, vehicle, or other real or personal property, shall be imprisoned for not more than ten years, or fined not more than $ 10,000, or both; and if personal injury results to any person, including any public safety officer performing duties as a direct or proximate result of conduct prohibited by this subsection, shall be imprisoned for not more than twenty years or fined not more than $ 20,000, or both; and if death results to any person, including any public safety officer performing duties as a direct or proximate result of conduct prohibited by this subsection, shall be subject to imprisonment for any term of years, or to the death penalty or to life imprisonment as provided in section 34 of this title [18 U.S.C.S. §34].

(e) Whoever, through the use of the mail, telephone, telegraph, or other instrument of commerce, willfully makes any threat, or maliciously conveys false information knowing the same to be false, concerning an attempt or alleged attempt being made, or to be made, to kill, injure, or intimidate any individual or unlawfully to damage or destroy any building, vehicle, or other real or personal property by means of fire or an explosive shall be imprisoned for not more than five years or fined not more than $ 5,000, or both.

(f) Whoever maliciously damages, or destroys, or attempts to damage or destroy, by means of fire or an explosive, any building, vehicle, or other personal or real property in whole or in part owned, possessed, or used by, or leased to, the United States, any department or agency thereof, or any institution or organization receiving Federal financial assistance shall be imprisoned for not more than ten years, or fined not more than $ 10,000, or both; and if personal injury results to any person, including any public safety officer performing duties as a direct or proximate result of conduct prohibited by this subsection, shall be imprisoned for not more than twenty years, or fined not more than $ 20,000, or both; and if death results to any person, including any public safety officer performing duties as a direct or proximate result of conduct prohibited by this subsection, shall be subject to imprisonment for any term of years, or to the death penalty or to life imprisonment as provided in section 34 of this title [18 U.S.C.S. §34].

(g)(1) Except as provided in paragraph (2), whoever possesses an explosive in an airport that is subject to the regulatory authority of the Federal Aviation Administration, or in any building in whole or in part owned, possessed, or used by, or leased to, the United States or any department or agency thereof, except with the written consent of the agency, department, or other person responsible for the management of such building or airport, shall be imprisoned for not more than five years, or fined under this title, or both.

(2) The provisions of this subsection shall not be applicable to—

(A) the possession of ammunition (as that term is defined in regulations issued pursuant to this chapter [18 U.S.C.S. §§841 et seq.]) in an airport that is subject to the regulatory authority of the Federal Aviation Administration if such ammunition is either in checked baggage or in a closed container; or

(B) the possession of an explosive in an airport if the packaging and transportation of such explosive is exempt from, or subject to and in accordance with, regulations of the Research and Special Projects Administration for the handling of hazardous materials pursuant to the Hazardous Materials Transportation Act (49 App. U.S.C. 1801, et seq.).

(h) Whoever —

(1) uses fire or an explosive to commit any felony which may be prosecuted in a court of the United States, or

(2) carries an explosive during the commission of any felony which may be prosecuted in a court of the United States, including a felony which provides for an enhanced punishment if committed by the use of a deadly or dangerous weapon or device shall, in addition to the punishment provided for such felony, be sentenced to imprisonment for five years. In the case of a second or subsequent conviction under this subsection, such person shall be sentenced to imprisonment for ten years. Notwithstanding any other provision of law, the court shall not place on probation or suspend the sentence of any person convicted of a violation of this subsection, nor shall the term of imprisonment imposed under this subsection run concurrently with any other term of imprisonment including that imposed for the felony in which the explosive was used or carried.

(i) Whoever maliciously damages or destroys, or attempts to damage or destroy, by means of fire or an explosive, any building, vehicle, or other real or personal property used in interstate or foreign commerce or in any activity affecting interstate or foreign commerce shall be imprisoned for not more than ten years or fined not more than $ 10,000, or both; and if personal injury results to any person, including any public safety officer performing duties as a direct or proximate result of conduct prohibited by this subsection, shall be imprisoned for not more than twenty years or fined not more than $ 20,000, or both; and if death results to any person, including any public safety officer performing duties as a direct or proximate result of conduct prohibited by this subsection, shall also be subject to imprisonment for any term of years, or to the death penalty or to life imprisonment as provided in section 34 of this title [18 U.S.C.S. §34].

(j) For the purposes of subsections (d), (e), (f), (g), (h), and (i) of this section, the term "explosive" means gunpowders, powders used for blasting, all forms of high explosives, blasting materials, fuzes (other than electric circuit breakers), detonators, and other detonating agents, smokeless powders, other explosive or incendiary devices within the meaning of paragraph (5) of section 232 of this title [18 U.S.C.S. §232(5)], and any chemical compounds, mechanical mixture, or device that contains any oxidizing and combustible units, or other ingredients, in such proportions, quantities, or packing that ignition by fire, by friction, by concussion, by percussion, or by detonation of the compound, mixture, or device or any part thereof may cause an explosion.

Chapter 51. Homicide

Section 1111. Murder

(a) Murder is the unlawful killing of a human being with malice afore-thought. Every murder perpetrated by poison, lying in wait, or any other kind of willful, deliberate, malicious, and premeditated killing; or committed in the perpetration of, or attempt to perpetrate, any arson, escape, murder, kidnaping, treason, espionage, sabotage, aggravated sexual abuse or sexual abuse burglary, or robbery; or perpetrated from a premeditated design unlawfully and maliciously to effect the death of any human being other than him who is killed, is murder in the first degree. Any other murder is murder in the second degree.

(b) Within the special maritime and territorial jurisdiction of the United States, Whoever is guilty of murder in the first degree, shall suffer death unless the jury qualifies its verdict by adding thereto "without capital punishment", in which event he shall be sentenced to imprisonment for life; Whoever is guilty of murder in the second degree, shall be imprisoned for any term of years or for life.

Section 1112. Manslaughter

(a) Manslaughter is the unlawful killing of a human being without malice. It is of two kinds:

Voluntary — Upon a sudden quarrel or heat of passion.

Involuntary — In the commission of an unlawful act not amounting to a felony, or in the commission in an unlawful manner, or without due caution and circumspection, of a lawful act which might produce death.

(b) Within the special maritime and territorial jurisdiction of the United States,

Whoever is guilty of voluntary manslaughter, shall be imprisoned not more than ten years;

Whoever is guilty of involuntary manslaughter, shall be fined not more than $ 1,000 or imprisoned not more than three years, or both.

Section 1113. Attempt to Commit Murder or Manslaughter

Except as provided in section 113 of this title, whoever, within the special maritime and territorial jurisdiction of the United States, attempts to commit murder or manslaughter, shall, for an attempt to commit murder be imprisoned not more than twenty years or fined under this title, or both, and for an attempt to commit manslaughter be imprisoned not more than three years or fined under this title, or both.

Section 1116. Murder or Manslaughter of Foreign Officials, Official Guests, or Internationally Protected Persons

(a) Whoever kills or attempts to kill a foreign official, official guest, or inter-nationally protected person shall be punished as provided under sections 1111,

1112, and 1113 of this title [18 U.S.C.S. §§1111-1113], except that any such person who is found guilty of murder in the first degree shall be sentenced to imprisonment for life, and any such person who is found guilty of attempted murder shall be imprisoned for not more than twenty years.

(b) For the purposes of this section:

(1) "Family" includes (a) a spouse, parent, brother or sister, child, or person to whom the foreign official or internationally protected person stands in loco parentis, or (b) any other person living in his household and related to the foreign official or internationally protected person by blood or marriage.

(2) "Foreign government" means the government of a foreign country, irrespective of recognition by the United States.

(3) "Foreign official" means—

(A) a Chief of State or the political equivalent, President, Vice President, Prime Minister, Ambassador, Foreign Minister, or other officer of Cabinet rank or above of a foreign government or the chief executive officer of an international organization, or any person who has previously served in such capacity, and any member of his family, while in the United States; and

(B) any person of a foreign nationality who is duly notified to the United States as an officer or employee of a foreign government or international organization, and who is in the United States on official business, and any member of his family whose presence in the United States is in connection with the presence of such officer or employee.

(4) "Internationally protected person" means—

(A) a Chief of State or the political equivalent, head of government, or Foreign Minister whenever such person is in a country other than his own and any member of his family accompanying him; or

(B) any other representative, officer, employee, or agent of the United States Government, a foreign government, or international organization who at the time and place concerned is entitled pursuant to international law to special protection against attack upon his person, freedom, or dignity, and any member of his family then forming part of his household.

(5) "International organization" means a public international organization designated as such pursuant to section 1 of the International Organizations Immunities Act (22 U.S.C. 288) [22 U.S.C.S. §288] or a public organization created pursuant to treaty or other agreement under international law as an instrument through or by which two or more foreign governments engage in some aspect of their conduct of international affairs.

(6) "Official guest" means a citizen or national of a foreign country present in the United States as an official guest of the Government of the United States pursuant to designation as such by the Secretary of State.

(c) If the victim of an offense under subsection (a) is an internationally protected person, the United States may exercise jurisdiction over the offense if the alleged offender is present within the United States, irrespective of the place where the offense was committed or the nationality of the victim or the alleged offender. As used in this subsection, the United States includes all areas under the jurisdiction of the United States including any of the places within the provisions of sections 5 and 7 of this title [18 U.S.C.S. §§5 and 7] and section 101(38) of the Federal Aviation Act of 1958, as amended (49 U.S.C. 1301(38)) [49 U.S.C.S. Appx. §1301(38)].

(d) In the course of enforcement of this section and any other sections prohibiting a conspiracy or attempt to violate this section, the Attorney General may request assistance from any Federal, State, or local agency, including the Army, Navy, and Air Force, any statute, rule, or regulation to the contrary notwithstanding.

Section 1117. Conspiracy to Murder

If two or more persons conspire to violate section 1111, 1114, or 1116 of this title [18 U.S.C.S. §1111, 1114, or 1116], and one or more of such persons do any overt act to effect the object of the conspiracy, each shall be punished by imprisonment for any term of years or for life.

Yates v. United States
354 U.S. 298, 1 L. Ed. 2d 1356, 77 S. Ct. 1064 (1957)

The Smith Act [18 U.S.C.S. §2385] is aimed at the advocacy and teaching of concrete action for the forcible overthrow of the government, and not of principles divorced from action. In determining whether the advocacy of the forcible overthrow of government was directed to action to that end and hence punishable under Smith Act or was merely advocacy of abstract doctrines and hence not punishable under the Act, the essential distinction is that those to whom the advocacy is addressed must be urged to do something, now or in future, rather than merely to believe in something.

Scales v. United States
260 F.2d 21 (4th Cir. 1958)

In a prosecution under "membership clause" of 18 U.S.C. §2385, the trial judge must determine not only the relevancy and sufficiency of evidence as a whole, as in the ordinary case, but must also determine whether the facts proved constituted such a clear and present danger to the state as to overcome the prohibitions of constitutional amendments and to justify conviction under 18 U.S.C. §2385.

United States v. Sinclair
321 F. Supp. 1074, 1079 (E.D. Mich. 1971)

"In this turbulent time of unrest, it is often difficult for the established and contented members of our society to tolerate, much less try to understand, the contemporary challenges to our existing form of government. If democracy as we know it, and as our forefathers established it, is to stand, then 'attempts of domestic organizations to attack and subvert the existing structure of the Government' (see affidavit of Attorney General), cannot be, in and of themselves, a crime. Such attempts become criminal only where it can be shown that the activity was/is carried on through unlawful means, such as the invasion of the rights of others by use of force or violence."

Pinkerton v. United States

328 U.S. 640, 66 S. Ct. 1180, 90 L. Ed. 1489 (1946)

While the defendant was in jail, he was indicted for conspiring with his brother to evade taxes and for specific tax evasions. The jury was instructed that the defendant could be convicted of the substantive offenses if they found he had been engaged in a conspiracy and the specific offenses were in furtherance of the conspiracy. The Supreme Court affirmed, essentially holding that direct participation in the substantive offenses was not necessary for substantive liability, and that being a co-conspirator was sufficient for liability for a substantive offense in furtherance of the conspiracy.

United States v. Falcone

311 U.S. 205, 210, 61 S. Ct. 204, 207; 85 L. Ed. 128, 132 (1940)

The defendants sold sugar, yeast, and cans, with the knowledge that the materials would be used in illicit distilling operations, but without the knowledge that the buyers were parties to a conspiracy. The Court held that they could not be convicted as participants to the conspiracy, and that "[t]he gist of the offense of conspiracy as defined by [the federal statute] is agreement among the conspirators to commit an offense attended by an act of one or more of the conspirators to effect the object of the conspiracy." Here, the defendants were suppliers to an illicit distiller, and furthered the goal of the conspiracy, but they had not entered into an agreement. Thus, while they knew of the illicit use at the time they aided, that in itself was not enough to make them members of the conspiracy.

United States v. Feola

420 U.S. 671, 687, 95 S. Ct. 1255, 1265 43 L. Ed. 2d 541, 554 (1975)

Defendants were convicted for having assaulted federal officers in the performance of their official duties, and for conspiring to commit that offense. The defendants appealed, arguing that, unlike the requirements of the substantive crime, a conspiracy charge required the government to prove their actual knowledge of the victim's official identity. The Court rejected this argument, and held that "[a] natural reading of these words would be that since one can violate a criminal statute simply by engaging in the forbidden conduct, a conspiracy to commit that offense is nothing more than an agreement to engage in the prohibited conduct. Then where, as here, the substantive statute does not require that an assailant know the official status of his victim, there is nothing on the face of the conspiracy statute that would seem to require that those agreeing to the assault have a greater degree of knowledge."

Model Penal Code
(Official Draft 1962)
Section 5.03. Criminal Conspiracy

(1) Definition of Conspiracy. A person is guilty of conspiracy with another person or persons to commit a crime if with the purpose of promoting or facilitating its commission he:

(a) agrees with such other person or persons that they or one or more of them will engage in conduct which constitutes such crime or an attempt or solicitation to commit such crime; or

(b) agrees to aid such other person or persons in the planning or commission of such crime or of an attempt or solicitation to commit such crime.

(2) Scope of Conspiratorial Relationship. If a person guilty of conspiracy, as defined by Subsection (1) of this Section, knows that a person with whom he conspires to commit a crime has conspired with another person or persons to commit the same crime, he is guilty of conspiring with such other person or persons, whether or not he knows their identity, to commit such crime.

(3) Conspiracy With Multiple Criminal Objectives. If a person conspires to commit a number of crimes, he is guilty of only one conspiracy so long as such multiple crimes are the object of the same agreement or continuous conspiratorial relationship.

(4) Joinder and Venue in Conspiracy Prosecutions

(a) Subject to the provisions of paragraph (b) of this Subsection, two or more persons charged with criminal conspiracy may be prosecuted jointly if:

(i) they are charged with conspiring with one another; or

(ii) the conspiracies alleged, whether they have the same or different parties, are so related that they constitute different aspects of a scheme of organized criminal conduct.

(b) In any joint prosecution under paragraph (a) of this Subsection:

(i) no defendant shall be charged with a conspiracy in any county [parish, or district] other than one in which he entered into such conspiracy or in which an overt act pursuant to such conspiracy was done by him or by a person with whom he conspired; and

(ii) neither the liability of any defendant nor the admissibility against him of evidence of acts or declarations of another shall be enlarged by such joinder; and

(iii) the Court shall order a severance or take a special verdict as to any defendant who so requests, if it deems it necessary or appropriate to promote the fair determination of his guilt or innocence, and shall take any other proper measures to protect the fairness of the trial.

(5) Overt Act. No person may be convicted of conspiracy to commit a crime, other than a felony of the first or second degree, unless an overt act in pursuance of such conspiracy is alleged and proved to have been done by him or by a person with whom he conspired.

(6) *Renunciation of Criminal Purpose.* It is an affirmative defense that the actor, after conspiring to commit a crime, thwarted the success of the conspiracy, under circumstances manifesting a complete and voluntary renunciation of his criminal purpose.

(7) *Duration of Conspiracy.* For purposes of Section 1.06(4):

(a) conspiracy is a continuing course of conduct which terminates when the crime or crimes which are its object are committed or the agreement that they be committed is abandoned by the defendant and by those with whom he conspired; and

(b) such abandonment is presumed if neither the defendant nor anyone with whom he conspired does any overt act in pursuance of the conspiracy during the applicable period of limitation; and

(c) if an individual abandons the agreement, the conspiracy is terminated as to him only if and when he advises those with whom he conspired of his abandonment or he informs the law enforcement authorities of the existence of the conspiracy and of his participation therein.

Section 1.07. Method of Prosecution When Conduct Constitutes More Than One Offense

(1) *Prosecution for Multiple Offenses; Limitation on Convictions.* When the same conduct of a defendant may establish the commission of more than one offense, the defendant may be prosecuted for each such offense. He may not, however, be convicted of more than one offense if:

(a) one offense is included in the other, as defined in Subsection (4) of this Section; or

(b) one offense consists only of a conspiracy or other form of preparation to commit the other; or

(c) inconsistent findings of fact are required to establish the commission of the offenses; or

(d) the offenses differ only in that one is defined to prohibit a designated kind of conduct generally and the other to prohibit a specific instance of such conduct; or

(e) the offense is defined as a continuing course of conduct and the defendant's course of conduct was uninterrupted, unless the law provides that specific periods of such conduct constitute separate offenses....

(4) *Conviction of Included Offense Permitted.* A defendant may be convicted of an offense included in an offense charged in the indictment [or the information]. An offense is so included when:

(a) it is established by proof of the same or less than all the facts required to establish the commission of the offense charged; or

(b) it consists of an attempt or solicitation to commit the offense charged or to commit an offense otherwise included therein; or

(c) it differs from the offense charged only in the respect that a less serious injury or risk of injury to the same person, property or public interest or a lesser kind of culpability suffices to establish its commission....

Section 5.05....; Multiple Convictions Barred....

(3) Multiple Convictions. A person may not be convicted of more than one offense defined by this Article for conduct designed to commit or to culminate in the commission of the same crime.

● OVERVIEW OF CONSPIRACY

THREE ROLES OF CONSPIRACY

The offense of conspiracy serves two, and possibly three, distinct roles. One role, the most common modern form of the offense, is as an inchoate offense that punishes preparatory conduct; it operates in a way analogous to attempt. Another role, the common law view of conspiracy and currently the view in some jurisdictions without modern codes, is conspiracy as a harm in itself, or at least as a factor aggravating the seriousness of the object offense because of the special dangers inherent in group criminal activity. Finally, prosecutors frequently charge conspiracy not for the liability that it generates, either as an inchoate offense or as an aggravation for group criminality, but rather for the procedural advantages that it gives. Lack of clarity about which of these is the primary role of conspiracy accounts for much of the confusion surrounding the offense. Conspiracy's role and relevance in criminal law is the focus of the Discussion Materials later in this Section.

Conspiracy as Inchoate Offense   The Model Penal Code and the state codes following its lead treat conspiracy as an inchoate offense. Its placement in Article 5 of the Code, "Inchoate Crimes," formally signals this treatment, but other provisions confirm the role. Section 5.03(6) of the Code allows a renunciation defense to conspiracy, a defense that is unique to inchoate offenses. Section 1.07(1)(b) bars conviction for both conspiracy and the substantive offense that is its object, just as liability for an attempt would be subsumed in liability for the substantive offense that was the goal of the attempt. Section 5.05(3) bars conviction for both conspiracy and another inchoate offense toward the same crime, again suggesting that the drafters see conspiracy only as punishing inchoate conduct.

Inchoate Theory of Conspiracy   The underlying theory of conspiracy as an inchoate offense is the same as that for attempt: It punishes an actor who intends to commit an offense and externally manifests his willingness to carry out that intention. The agreement with another to commit an offense — the gist of conspiracy — is an externalization of what, until then, may have been simply a thought of the actor. The act of agreeing suggests that the actor has moved beyond mere fantasizing. It also provides some evidentiary confirmation of the actor's criminal intention. (The law frequently ensures further confirmation by requiring proof of an overt act.) The agreement with another to commit an offense often gives a more reliable, unambiguous indication of an actor's blameworthiness and dangerousness than does the "substantial step" toward commission required for attempt liability. In addition, conspiracy has the advantage of commonly allowing earlier intervention than the substantial step requirement of attempt allows. Thus, as an inchoate offense, conspiracy often is better than attempt not only at reliably identifying blameworthy offenders, but also at increasing the chances of crime prevention.

Conspiracy as Aggravation for Group Criminality   Alternatively, conspiracy has been viewed

> "as a curb to the immoderate power to do mischief which is gained by a combination of the means". Conspiracy as an offense recognizes increased public harm by group action. It seeks to strike at the special dangers incident to group activity.[1]

From this perspective, conspiracy serves as a substantive offense, one that takes account of the increased danger and harm that attends group criminality.[2] There is little reason to provide a renunciation defense for this version of conspiracy; renunciation generally is not a defense where the substantive harm or evil has occurred, which in this instance is the formation of a group for a criminal purpose. Also, under this view, there is no impropriety in convicting an offender for both the substantive offense and conspiracy to commit it. The latter is simply a means of properly aggravating liability for the former.

Wharton's Rule   Under the aggravation-for-group-criminality view of conspiracy, however, it would be appropriate to bar conviction for conspiracy if the defendant were convicted for the substantive offense and that offense necessarily involves the conduct of two or more actors and therefore already takes into account the added harm of group criminality. That is, what has traditionally been called Wharton's Rule, after the treatise writer who proposed it, bars conspiracy liability for offenses that necessarily involve a group, because conspiracy liability would "double-count" the group criminality harm. For example, if the offense of unlawful restraint of trade requires at least two persons to fix prices, Wharton's Rule will bar liability for the two offenders for both price fixing and conspiracy to price-fix. The Wharton's Rule rationale does not apply, however, if the actor is not convicted of the substantive offense. Thus, if the two only got so far as to agree to fix prices, and are not liable for the completed offense, they *can* be held liable for conspiracy to fix prices.[3] In other words, even when a jurisdiction uses conspiracy to aggravate for group criminality, it simultaneously will use it as an inchoate offense.

---

1. Archbold v. State, 397 N.E.2d 1071, 1073 (Ind. Ct. App. 1979).

2. Conspiracy as a substantive offense was the original form of the offense. It criminalized conduct by a group the object of which was unlawful but not criminal. Thus, although the objective was achieved, there was no offense (other than conspiracy) for which the conspirators could be held liable. See Andrew Ashworth, Principles of Criminal Law 453 (2d ed. 1995). It was not until 1977 that England required that the objective of a criminal conspiracy itself be a crime. See id. at 454.

3. *Wharton's Rule under inchoate theory of conspiracy*   The Model Penal Code drafters note that they explicitly adopt Wharton's Rule in section 5.04(2), incorporating by reference complicity subsection 2.06(6)(b), which provides a defense if the accomplice's conduct "is inevitably incident" to commission of the offense. One may question the Code's position. The Code uses conspiracy only as an inchoate offense, not as an aggravation for group criminality. Whether the actor's conduct is "inevitably incident" to commission of the substantive offense has no apparent relevance if the actor is not convicted of that substantive offense; there can be no "double-counting." And, consistent with the Code's inchoate approach, an actor can never be convicted of both conspiracy and the substantive offense. Thus, there is never a danger of "double-counting" under the Code and no need for Wharton's Rule.

AGREEMENT REQUIREMENT

Conspiracy typically requires an agreement between two or more conspirators that one of them will commit a substantive offense. The agreement need not be an act in a strict sense. Speaking, writing, or nodding can signal agreement, but one also can agree through silence where, under the circumstances or custom, silence is meant and understood to mean positive agreement. An agreement is shown whenever there is a tacit, mutual understanding. One can become a conspirator by agreeing to assist a person whom one knows to be a member of a conspiracy with others.[1] There is no special requirement that the actor's conduct corroborate his or her intent, as there is for attempt liability. The agreement to commit a criminal offense is taken as adequate proof that the actor's intention is not innocent.

Bilateral Agreement   At common law, and currently in some jurisdictions without modern codes, the agreement requirement is taken to require actual agreement on both sides, an actual "meeting of the minds." Thus, for the actor to be liable for conspiracy, *the other conspirator* must actually be agreeing, not just pretending to agree. An actor who conspires with an undercover police agent, for example, will get a defense under this so-called "bilateral agreement" requirement because the officer does not in fact intend that one of them will commit the substantive offense. Where an actor agrees with another true conspirator, in addition to the undercover agent, however, conspiracy liability can be imposed, for there does exist a real criminal group in such a case.

Unilateral Agreement   Modern codes have adopted a unilateral agreement requirement, which permits conspiracy liability as long as *the actor* agrees with another person. It does not require that the co-conspirator actually be agreeing back. The actor has demonstrated an intention to have one of the conspirators commit an offense. That the other apparent conspirator in fact is an undercover police officer does not undercut the blameworthiness and dangerousness demonstrated by the actor's intention to have the offense committed.

Objective vs. Subjective Views of Criminality   The difference between a bilateral and a unilateral agreement requirement is consistent with the difference between the objectivist and subjectivist views of criminality. Just as an objectivist view of criminality rejects liability for a legally impossible attempt because the actor never really comes close to committing an offense, so too would an objectivist view of criminality reject liability for an apparent agreement that never in fact exists. If there is no real agreement, there is no actual danger that the substantive offense will be committed. It is only from a subjectivist view of criminality that liability may be justified for a unilateral agreement: The actor *believes* that he is agreeing to the commission of an offense (or *believes* that he is engaging in the aggravated harm of group criminality).[2]

Overt Act   Perhaps because conspiracy's agreement requirement is so slim, a conduct requirement of an overt act typically is required of one of the

---

1. See United States v. Alvarez, 625 F.2d 1196 (5th Cir. 1980) (agreeing to be present at remote location to aid in unloading marijuana from plane rendered defendant member of conspiracy to illegally import).

2. Note that the substantive versus inchoate dispute is independent of the objectivist versus subjectivist criminality dispute. One can define objectivist and subjectivist forms of both the substantive and the inchoate offense of conspiracy.

conspirators in furtherance of the agreement.[1] The overt act requirement furthers many of the purposes for which the criminal law has an act requirement. An overt act helps confirm the actor's intention and the actor's willingness to carry through with his intention (to have the agreement carried out). The Model Penal Code drops the overt act requirement for conspiracies to commit a first or second degree felony, presumably on the theory that agreements to commit such serious offenses carry their own indicia of blameworthiness and dangerousness.[2]

CULPABILITY REQUIREMENTS

The culpability requirements for conspiracy follow a now familiar pattern. As with attempt, the common law viewed conspiracy as a specific intent offense. The Model Penal Code might be interpreted as following this view, to some extent, in that it requires that the actor have "the purpose of promoting or facilitating [the] commission" of the offense.[3] As in the analysis of the attempt requirements, the issue is: What is the meaning of this *purpose* requirement?

Elevation to Purposeful for All Elements A broad interpretation, adopting the apparent common law position, would take "purpose" to require that the actor be purposeful not only as to the conduct — making the agreement and performing the conduct that would constitute the offense — but also as to all circumstance and result elements of the object offense, no matter what culpability normally is required by the substantive offense definition. Under this broad interpretation, there can be no liability for conspiracy to commit an offense that requires less than purpose as to a result or circumstance element — no offense of conspiracy to commit reckless homicide or conspiracy to commit statutory rape, for example. (Or, more accurately, such offenses exist but their proof would require proof of purpose as to all elements, thus requiring proof of conspiracy to commit murder, for instance.) In *State v. Beccia*,[4] the owner of the Night Owl Cafe Club was convicted of conspiracy to commit third degree arson, which requires reckless damage or destruction of a building by intentionally starting a fire. Beccia agreed with another that one of them would intentionally start a fire, being aware of a substantial risk that the fire would destroy or damage the building. The court reversed the conviction, holding that, because "conspiracy is a specific intent crime," it must be shown that the conspirators "intended to commit the elements of the offense.... Since conspirators cannot agree to accomplish a result recklessly when that result is an essential element of the crime, they cannot conspire to commit this particular crime."

Culpability as to Result The Model Penal Code drafters explicitly adopt this broad interpretation of the purpose requirement with regard to result elements of the object offense in conspiracy — for example, the requirement of damage or destruction of the building in *Beccia*. No matter what culpability as

---

1. *Overt Act.* No person may be convicted of conspiracy to commit a crime, other than a felony of the first or second degree, unless an overt act in pursuance of such conspiracy is alleged and proved to have been done by him or by a person with whom he conspired.
Model Penal Code §5.03(5).
2. Model Penal Code §5.03 comment at 452-455 (1985).
3. Model Penal Code §5.03(1).
4. 199 Conn. 1, 505 A.2d 683 (1986).

to a result is required by the substantive offense, a purpose to cause that result must be shown for conspiracy to commit the offense. The drafters explain:

> While this result may seem unduly restrictive from the viewpoint of the completed crime, it is necessitated by the extremely preparatory behavior that may be involved in conspiracy.[1]

That is, the high culpability requirement is seen as necessary to counterbalance the minimal conduct requirement of conspiracy. The commentary distinguishes conspiracy, where the conduct may be very preliminary, from attempt, or complicity in a completed offense, where the conduct is more substantial. As the conduct progresses, the Commentary notes, the culpability requirement is reduced. Once the offense conduct is complete, only knowledge as to result is required for attempt liability.[2] Once the offense conduct is complete and the result occurs, the substantive offense and complicity doctrine govern, in which case there is no elevation of culpability.[3]

Culpability as to Circumstance While nothing on the face of the conspiracy provision would suggest that the purpose requirement should apply differently to a circumstance element than to a result element, the drafters apparently intend different treatment of the two. Regarding culpability as to a circumstance element, the drafters explain that

> The conspiracy provision in the code does not attempt to solve the problem [of culpability as to a circumstance] by explicit formulation, nor have the recent legislative revisions. Here, as in the section on complicity, it was believed that the matter is best left to judicial resolution as cases that present the question may arise, and that the formulations proposed afford sufficient flexibility for satisfactory decision.[4]

One may wonder whether this approach to code drafting fully satisfies the requirements or the spirit of the legality principle. One also may wonder how a court is to give different treatment to circumstance and result elements if the statute gives no hint on its face of such different treatment. There is no apparent statutory ambiguity that would authorize a court to examine the legislative history or official commentary, thus little opportunity for courts to engage in the kind of criminal law making that the Model Penal Code drafters contemplate. If a court gives the same treatment to both result and circumstance elements, it can either give a narrow interpretation to the purpose requirement — having it elevate neither result nor circumstance elements — or a broad interpretation — requiring purpose as to both result and circumstance elements. The latter would bar conspiracy liability for any offense where the conspirator is less than purposeful as to all circumstance elements, such as in sexual offenses as to the elements of consent or age.

No Elevation as to Circumstance The better view would seem to require only the culpability as to circumstance that is required for the substantive offense.

1. Model Penal Code §5.03 comment at 408 (1985).
2. Model Penal Code §5.01(1)(b).
3. Model Penal Code §2.06(4).
4. Model Penal Code §5.03 comment at 413 (1985).

Thus, two persons who conspired to have intercourse with a child that they know is nine years old could be liable for the conspiracy, although it is not proven that it was their "purpose" that the child be under ten. There is some case law support for this view. In *United States v. Feola*, for example, the Supreme Court concluded that defendants need not know that their victims were federal officers in order to be convicted of conspiracy to assault a federal officer.[1] Such culpability was not required by the substantive offense and, therefore, the court reasoned, would not be required for conspiracy to commit the substantive offense.

● DISCUSSION MATERIALS

Should the Criminal Law Recognize an Offense of Conspiracy?

The Harvard Law Review "Developments" excerpt traces the doctrinal development of the conspiracy offense, noting its procedural and theoretical shortcomings, but ultimately arguing in favor of its use. The Model Penal Code Commentary examines the Code's attempt to formulate the offense in a way that mitigates some of the major objections to it, exploring the ALI's rationale for attaching liability when it does (an agreement plus any overt act). Philip Johnson and David Filvaroff offer arguments against conspiracy, with Johnson summarizing the criticisms of the doctrine and calling for its complete abolition, rejecting reform of the offense as insufficient, while Filvaroff's article speaks specifically to the inadequacies of the American legal system in dealing with the procedural problems that the conspiracy doctrine raises.

Developments in the Law: Criminal Conspiracy
72 Harvard Law Review 920, 922–925 (1959)

With the growth of organized criminal activity the conspiracy indictment has become an increasingly important weapon in the prosecution's armory. In some cases this weapon serves to nullify the opportunities for escaping punishment that the defendant might otherwise obtain from the anonymity of his position within a group or from the difficulty of tracing his precise contribution to any given substantive offense. In other cases it facilitates the intervention of the law at a stage when antisocial consequences can still be prevented. However, the flexibility and formlessness — both procedural and substantive — which account for the effectiveness of conspiracy as a tool of enforcement also create a serious danger of unfairness to the defendant, and have consequently evoked widespread criticism from judicial and law-review commentators. By means of evidence inadmissible under usual rules the prosecutor can implicate the defendant not only in the conspiracy itself but also in the substantive crimes of his alleged coconspirators. In a large conspiracy trial the effect produced upon the jury by

---

1. 420 U.S. 671, 95 S. Ct. 1255, 43 L. Ed. 2d 541 (1975).

the introduction of evidence against some defendants may result in conviction for all of them, so that the fate of each may depend not on the merits of his own case but rather on his success in dissociating himself from his codefendants in the minds of the jury.

These and other procedural problems, however, are perhaps less basic than the conceptual difficulties involved in any attempt to explain the underlying theory of conspiracy and to relate this theory to generally applicable principles of criminal law. Conspiracy is usually defined as an agreement between two or more persons to achieve an unlawful object or to achieve a lawful object by unlawful means. The gist of the crime is the agreement itself rather than the action pursuant to it. . . . At this point it is enough to suggest a rationale for what might appear to be a somewhat inharmonious element in a system of criminal law which purports to punish intent only when objectively manifested by action resulting, or likely to result, in socially harmful consequences.

The history of conspiracy, as Mr. Justice Jackson has pointed out, exemplifies the "tendency of a principle to expand itself to the limit of its logic." Originating in a statute of 1305 which prohibited confederacies for the false and malicious procurement of indictments, conspiracy became a common-law crime only at the beginning of the seventeenth century. Whereas prior to that time the writ of conspiracy would not lie unless the victim had actually been indicted and acquitted, the Star Chamber, decided in the landmark *Poulterers Case* of 1611 that the agreement itself was punishable even if its purpose remained unexecuted. Once the focal point of the offense had shifted from the object of the agreement to the agreement itself, it was a short step to the proposition that an agreement to commit any crime was a criminal conspiracy. The eagerness of the courts, particularly the Star Chamber, to extend the scope of conspiracy was an aspect of the exceptionally vigorous growth of the criminal law generally during the seventeenth century and a reflection of the contemporary tendency to identify law with morality. The same factors probably account also for the widespread and permanent acceptance accorded a statement of Hawkins, doubtfully supported by previous case law, that the acts contemplated by a conspiracy need not themselves be criminal but need only be "wrongful" in order to make the conspiracy punishable.

Possibly the concept of conspiracy in such a highly generalized form could have been developed only within a system of judge-made law. In any event, a comparably broad doctrine of conspiracy has not emerged in civil-law countries. European penal codes frequently make concerted action a basis for aggravating the penalties for completed substantive crimes, but when no substantive offense has been completed, only certain types of conspiracies are proscribed—notably those directed against the security of the state, those involving many participants organized for the purpose of committing numerous crimes, and those contemplating particularly serious offenses. By applying the conspiracy doctrine only in situations involving a very great danger to society, continental legislators seem to have wisely limited the crime to the scope required by its underlying rationale.

The heart of this rationale lies in the fact—or at least the assumption—that collective action toward an antisocial end involves a greater risk to society than individual action toward the same end. Primarily, the state is concerned with punishing conduct that has actually resulted in antisocial consequences. It is reluctant to intervene as long as the actor can still withdraw and as long as his conduct is still consistent with the absence of any criminal intent. However, as action toward a criminal end nears execution, a point is reached at which the increasing risk to society is thought to outweigh the diminishing likelihood of a change of heart or of a misreading of intent, and at this point mere "preparation" become punishable as "attempt." When the defendant has chosen to act in concert with others, rather than to act alone, the point of justifiable intervention is reached at an earlier state. In this situation the reasons for which the law is reluctant to intervene are considerably weaker. The agreement itself, in theory at least, provides a substantially unambiguous manifestation of intent; it also reduces the probability that the defendant can stop the wheels he has set in motion, since to restore the status quo would now require the acquiescence and cooperation of other wills than his own. More important, the collaboration magnifies the risk to society both by increasing the likelihood that a given quantum of harm will be successfully produced and by increasing the amount of harm that can be inflicted. A conspirator who has committed himself to support his associates may be less likely to violate this commitment than he would be to revise a purely private decision. Moreover, encouragement and moral support of the group strengthen the perseverance of each member. Furthermore, the existence of numbers both facilitates a division of labor which promotes the efficiency with which a given object can be pursued, and makes possible the attainment of objects more elaborate and ambitious than would otherwise be attainable. The notion of increased social risk also provides a possible rationale for the punishment of agreements to engage in certain types of conduct that would not otherwise be criminal, since the absence of any specific prohibition against such conduct may be due to the fact that the likelihood that a single person will engage in it is small, or that its harmful impact when engaged in by a single person is slight. A further rationale may be that reliance on social pressure alone to deter certain forms of antisocial conduct becomes unwarranted when this pressure is countered by that of the conspiratorial group itself.

The antisocial potentialities of a conspiracy, unlike those of an attempt, are not confined to the objects specifically contemplated at any given time. The existence of a grouping for criminal purposes provides a continuing focal point for further crimes either related or unrelated to those immediately envisaged. Moreover, the uneasiness produced by the consciousness that such groupings exist is in itself an important antisocial effect. Consequently, the state has an interest in stamping out conspiracy above and beyond its interest in preventing the commission of any specific substantive offense. This additional interest may explain, for example, why some courts have imposed cumulative sentences for a conspiracy and for the crime which was its object....

A further distinction between the law of conspiracy and that of attempt emerges when each is regarded not as a means of enabling official intervention to prevent the fruition of the crime in a particular case, but rather as a means of deterring potential criminal conduct. In its deterrent function the law operates on the mechanism of choice, seeking to make the disadvantages of criminal activity appear to outweigh its advantages. Since one who has decided to commit a crime does not confront the further choice whether to attempt that crime, the deterrent function of the proscription against attempt is not additional to that of the proscription against the completed offense. By contrast, conspiracy is simply a route by which a given criminal object can be approached. Because the antisocial potentialities of this route are peculiarly great, it is arguable that even those who have not been deterred by the penalty for the completed offense should nevertheless be discouraged from embarking upon their criminal venture in concert with others. The role of conspiracy as a subordinate deterrent may provide further support for the imposition of cumulative sentences for conspiracy and the completed substantive offense.

Model Penal Code Section 5.03 Commentary
Official Draft and Revised Comments 386-393 (1985)

Though conspiracy has been an offense at common law as well as under statutes existing before the Model Code, there was only fragmentary legislative treatment of the scope and the components of the crime, and this was usually limited to statements of the conspiratorial objectives that suffice for criminality and the requirement, in some but not all cases, of an overt act. The law defining the offense and dealing with the many special problems in its prosecution has been, on the whole, the product of the courts.

This product has been a controversial one on many grounds. Putting aside such special grievances as those based on the early condemnation of the labor union as a criminal conspiracy and the use of the charge against political offenders, the general critique has pointed to the danger of a dragnet in the broad, uncertain ground of liability, the wholesale joinder of defendants, the imposition of vicarious responsibility, the relaxation of the rules of evidence, and some or all of these in combination.

The Model Penal Code attempts to meet or mitigate objections of this kind to the extent that it is feasible to do so in a legislative treatment of the crime.

It is worthwhile to note preliminarily that conspiracy as an offense has two different aspects, reflecting the different functions it serves in the legal system. In the first place, conspiracy is an inchoate crime, complementing the provisions dealing with attempt and solicitation in reaching preparatory conduct before it has matured into commission of a substantive offense. Second, it is a means of striking against the special danger incident to group activity, facilitating prosecution of the group, and yielding a basis for imposing added penalties when combination is involved.

As an inchoate crime, conspiracy fixes the point of legal intervention at agreement to commit a crime, or at agreement coupled with an overt act which may, however, be of very small significance. Conspiracy thus reaches further back into preparatory conduct than attempt, raising the question of whether this extension is desirable. The Institute believed it was, for the following reasons:

First: The act of agreeing with another to commit a crime, like the act of soliciting, is concrete and unambiguous; it does not present the infinite degrees and variations possible in the general category of attempts. The danger that truly equivocal behavior may be misinterpreted as preparation to commit a crime is minimized; purpose must be relatively firm before the commitment involved in agreement is assumed.

Second: If the agreement was to aid another to commit a crime or if it otherwise encouraged the crime's commission, complicity would be established in the commission of the substantive offense. It would be anomalous to hold that conduct that would suffice to establish criminality, if something else is done by someone else, is insufficient if the crime is never consummated. Although this reason covers less than all the cases of conspiracy, it is significant that it covers many others.

Third: In the course of preparation to commit a crime, the act of combining with another is significant both psychologically and practically, the former because it crosses a clear threshold in arousing expectations, the latter because it increases the likelihood that the offense will be committed. Sharing lends fortitude to purpose. The actor knows, moreover, that the future is no longer governed by this will alone; others may complete what he has had a hand in starting, even if he has a change of heart.

There is little doubt, therefore, that as a basis for preventive intervention by the agencies of law enforcement and for the corrective treatment of persons who reveal that they are disposed to criminality, a penal code properly provides that conspiracy to commit crime is itself a criminal offense.

In its aspect as a sanction against group activity, conspiracy presents quite different problems.

First: One function to be noted in this area is the use of conspiracy to proscribe agreements having objectives that would not be criminal if pursued or achieved by single individuals, on the ground that combination towards such ends presents a danger a lone actor could not create on his own. There are, of course, important areas of conduct in which such a delineation of the scope of criminality may be appropriate; it is commonplace, for instance, in the field of antitrust. But judgments of this kind must be made sparingly and in the context of the specific conduct that is involved, taking into consideration other weapons in the legal arsenal that may be brought to bear upon these acts. It is not a matter to be dealt with in a general provision on conspiracy and it is not so dealt with in the Model Code.

To the extent that earlier decisional and statutory law performed this function by defining conspiracy to embody condemnation of all combinations with objectives that are "unlawful," "malicious," "oppressive," or "injurious," as distinct from criminal, the approach was regarded as too vague for penal prohibitions and was rejected in the Code.

Second: Group prosecution is undoubtedly made easier by the procedural advantages enjoyed by the prosecution when conspiracy is charged. Acts and declarations of participants may be admissible against each other under an exception to the hearsay rule, and ordinarily will be received, subject to later ruling, even before the required basis has been laid. Vicarious responsibility may relax venue rules and the conception of conspiracy as a continuous offense extends the period of limitations. The presentation in the case of a full picture of the workings of a large and complex network of related criminal activities will often help the jury to grasp the part played by individuals who otherwise might be forgotten, but a strong case against some defendants may unduly blacken all; the need to work a root and branch extermination of the organized activity may overcome doubts that would otherwise prevail.

Not all the difficulties posed by these procedures are intrinsic to conspiracy as an offense, notwithstanding belief by prosecutors that it is by virtue of indictment for conspiracy that procedural advantages are gained. The same rules as to joinder and venue, and the same rules of evidence, will normally apply when the prosecution is for substantive offenses in which joint complicity is charged. Nevertheless, the Code makes some attempt to treat the problems that are raised, focusing separately upon the substantive conceptions that have bearing on procedure, as, for example, the scope of a conspiracy, and upon the strictly procedural issues that are involved.

Third: The older common law rule that conspiracy, like attempt, merges in the completed crime that is its object, with the result that conviction and sentence on both grounds are barred, has been superseded on the whole in modern law. The act of combination is regarded as "an independent crime condemned by the statute for the primary purpose of discouraging organized and concerted efforts by two or more people to violate the law." Indeed, the conspiracy is often said to be more dangerous than "the mere commission of the contemplated crime."

The Code embraces this conception in part and rejects it in part. When a conspiracy is declared criminal because its object is a crime, it is entirely meaningless to say that the preliminary combination is more dangerous than the forbidden consummation; the measure of its danger is the risk of such culmination. On the other hand, the combination may and often does have criminal objectives that transcend any particular offenses that have been committed in pursuance of its goals. In the latter case, cumulative sentences for conspiracy and substantive offenses ought to be permissible, subject to the general limits on cumulation that the Code prescribes. In the former case, when the preliminary agreement does not go beyond the consummation, double conviction and sentence are barred.

The barrier to double sentence thus erected does not, however, prevent taking due account of a combination when it has real bearing on the sentence that should be imposed. Such cases are, in the Institute's view, limited to situations in which organized, professional criminality is involved, and the sentencing provisions of the Code thus permit the use of an extended term. This seems a far better way to effect needed aggravation in the sentence than a cumulation based on an antecedent combination to commit a consummated crime.

It should be added that the Code rejects what was the usual sentencing provision for conspiracy, one that fixed sentence at a level unrelated to the sanction for the crime that is its object when the purpose is commission of a major crime. Under Section 5.05(1), conspiracy, like attempt and solicitation, is a crime of the same grade and degree as the most serious of its criminal objectives, except that it is never graded higher than a second degree felony. This is a further indication that the sentencing provisions do not suffer from weakness in dealing with the combinations incident to organized group crime.

Fourth: It was argued in the Advisory Committee that the Code should build on European models in shaping conspiracy explicitly as a crime of criminal organization, rather than as an inchoate crime. Under this approach, apart from exceptional provisions dealing with crimes against the state, whether and to what extent conspiratorial activity is criminal, or the gravity of the offense, has depended on such special factors as the size and continuity of the group involved, the number of its criminal objectives, and the character of the individual's participation. In the treatment of completed crimes by groups, the same factors have sometimes aggravated the sentence.

The Italian Code of 1930 afforded the best example of this treatment of the subject. As to inchoate activity, it declared that "whenever two or more persons agree for the purpose of committing an offence, and it is not committed, none of them is punishable for the sole fact of making the agreement," although in such cases the judge may apply a "police measure." It provided for penal servitude of from 3 to 7 years, however, for the leaders and promoters of an association of "*3 or more* persons . . . for the purpose of committing *more than one* crime . . ." and penal servitude of from 1 to 5 years for those who only participated in the association; the punishment is increased "if the number of persons associating is 10 or more." As to crimes that have been committed, the Italian Code provided for aggravation of the penalty "(1) [i]f the number of persons co-operating in the offence is 5 or more . . ." and "(2) [i]n the case of individuals who . . . have promoted or organised co-operation in the offence, or have directed the action of the persons who co-operated in that offence."

To the extent that legislation of this kind serves to immunize from liability conspiracies with only two participants or with a single criminal objective, the Institute perceived no solid case for limitation. The inchoate crime function sustains the broader scope of the offense that is traditional in our system. To the extent that these provisions permit sterner sanctions to suppress the more potent combinations, there is certainly no weakness in the sentencing provisions of the Code. For these reasons, the distinctive pattern of the continental codes was rejected.

Philip E. Johnson, The Unnecessary Crime of Conspiracy
61 California Law Review 1137-1141 (1973)

The literature on the subject of criminal conspiracy reflects a sort of rough consensus. Conspiracy, it is generally said, is a necessary doctrine in some respects, but also one that is overbroad and invites abuse. Conspiracy has been thought to be necessary for one or both of two reasons. First, it is said that a separate offense of conspiracy is useful to supplement the generally restrictive law of attempts. Plotters who are arrested before they can carry out their dangerous schemes may be convicted of conspiracy even though they did not go far enough towards completion of their criminal plan to be guilty of attempt. Second, conspiracy is said to be a vital legal weapon in the prosecution of "organized crime," however defined. . . . To deal with such dangerous criminal combinations the government must have the benefit of special legal doctrines which make conviction easier and punishment more severe.

The overbreadth of conspiracy and its potential for abuse have been extensively discussed in the literature. One principal theme of criticism, best illustrated by Mr. Justice Jackson's opinion in *Krulewitch v. United States,* emphasizes the difficulties which the ordinary criminal defendant may face when charged with conspiracy. The advantages which conspiracy provides the prosecution are seen as disadvantages for the defendant so serious that they may lead to unfair punishment unfairly determined. Critics taking this approach typically propose to trim conspiracy doctrine just enough to provide protection for defense interests without disturbing those rules deemed genuinely important for effective law enforcement. The leading reform proposal of this type is the conspiracy section of the American Law Institute's Model Penal Code, some of whose reforms were incorporated in the proposed Federal Criminal Code now before the Senate Subcommittee on Criminal Laws and Procedures of the United States.

The other major line of criticism stresses the dangers that conspiracy law raises for first amendment freedoms. Prosecutions of political dissidents, including labor organizers, Communist Party leaders, and contemporary radicals, typically have been conspiracy prosecutions. The law of conspiracy is intended, after all, to make it easier to impose criminal punishment on members of groups that plot forbidden activity. Insofar as it accomplishes this end, it unavoidably increases the likelihood that persons will be punished for what they say rather than for what they do, or for associating with others who are found culpable. Critics who are alarmed at the resulting threat to freedom of speech and freedom of association typically have proposed new constitutional doctrines derived from the first amendment to curtail the use of conspiracy charges in cases having some "political" element.

Unfortunately, the proposals for legislative or constitutional reforms of conspiracy law are inadequate. It will not do simply to reform conspiracy legislatively by removing its most widely deplored overextensions, or to reform it judicially by engrafting new doctrines derived from the first amendment. Such measures are appropriate for improving a doctrine that is basically sound, but in need of some adjustment at the edges. The law of criminal conspiracy is not basically sound. It should be abolished, not reformed.

The central fault of conspiracy law and the reason why any limited reform is bound to be inadequate can be briefly stated. What conspiracy adds to the law is simply confusion, and the confusion is inherent in the nature of the doctrine. The confusion stems from the fact that conspiracy is not only a substantive inchoate crime in itself, but the touchstone for invoking several independent procedural and substantive doctrines. We ask whether a defendant agreed with another person to commit a crime initially for the purpose of determining whether he may be convicted of the offense of conspiracy even when the crime itself has not yet been committed. If the answer to that question is in the affirmative, however, we find that we have also answered a number of other questions that would otherwise have to be considered independently. Where there is evidence of conspiracy, the defendant may be tried jointly with his criminal partners and possibly with many other persons whom he has never met or seen, the joint trial may be held in a place he may never have visited, and hearsay statements of other alleged members of the conspiracy may also be found guilty of any crime committed in furtherance of the conspiracy, whether or not he knew about the crime or aided in its commission.

Each of these issues involves a separate substantive or procedural area of the criminal law of considerable importance and complexity. The essential vice of conspiracy is that it inevitably distracts the courts from the policy questions or balancing of interests that ought to govern the decision of specific legal issues and leads them instead to decide those issues by reference to the conceptual framework of conspiracy. Instead of asking whether public policy or the interests of the parties requires a particular holding, the courts are led instead to consider whether the theory of conspiracy is broad enough to permit it. What is wrong with conspiracy, in other words, is much more basic than the overbreadth of a few rules. The problem is not with particular results, but with the use of a single abstract concept to decide numerous questions that deserve separate consideration in light of the various interests and policies they involve.

Although it is true that the confusion that conspiracy introduces into the law has an overall tendency to benefit the prosecution, sometimes it has the opposite effect. Occasionally, use of a conspiracy charge converts a relatively simple case into a monstrosity of conceptual complexity, giving the defense substantial grounds for an appeal. Furthermore, eliminating the substantive crime of conspiracy would not necessarily require the elimination of all the procedural rules that are now associated with it: at most it would require only that the rules be reconsidered on their own merits. In fact, many of these procedural rules are even now applicable in all criminal cases, whether conspiracy is charged or not.

Other Discussion Materials

David B. Filvaroff, Conspiracy and the First Amendment
121 University of Pennsylvania Law Review 189-193 (1972)

The American legal system has not always responded well in times of deep intellectual, social, and political unrest. From *Deb's*, to the *Japanese Relocation Cases*, to *Dennis*, the courts have often leaned with, rather than against, the winds of orthodoxy and popular prejudice; they have tended to vindicate officialdom, particularly at the federal level, in its response to dissent or potential disloyalty. There have been exceptions, to be sure, but renunciation of abuse has often come only belatedly.

One of the legal weapons used in the traditional unequal contest between government and dissent has been the doctrine of criminal conspiracy. While there has been much critical comment concerning the nature and uses of this historic crime, and while the literature surrounding the first amendment rights of free speech and association is certainly voluminous, relatively little careful study has been directed to the ways in which the two concepts converge and conflict when the government institutes prosecutions for conspiracy to commit speech or speech-related offenses, an American variant of the "political crime." Indeed it is only fairly recently that commentators have begun to focus on the analytical questions involved in the use, in first amendment areas, of conspiracy doctrine developed in other, non-speech contexts. Perhaps the lag should not be too surprising. The law of free speech itself is a comparatively recent development in our constitutional history, by and large evolving only within the past half-century; and, notwithstanding criticism of conspiracy doctrine and its use, the crime is supported by a long tradition which seems to have muted constitutional challenge....

Typically, when government acts against dissenters or the unorthodox, the rhetorical claims, if not the legal issues, are framed in terms of suppression of freedoms, particularly first amendment freedoms. By virtue of the very fact that the underlying issues are usually public, political, and controversial, they tend to generate responses founded on ideological, racial, or humanitarian ground, and lead to attempts at association designed to strengthen the sources of resistance. The very effectiveness of almost any social or political effort in our highly organized and complex society — particularly when it challenges government policy or power — may well depend on its success in enlisting the aid of others of like mind. Thus, the allegedly offending action is often of a collective nature, involving a group which finds its origin in a shared opposition to official action or inaction.

Predictably, then, a charge of conspiracy comes to the prosecutorial mind as a base for the institution of criminal proceedings. The crime is obviously well adapted to the political and ideological uses to which it has been put. History has produced an offense which is both vague in its substance and malleable in its procedures. Its elements can be stated with deceptive simplicity. Conviction requires agreement or combination, illegal means or illegal ends, and some sort of improper motive or intent. No overt act in furtherance of the agreement is necessary except as required by the particular statute under which the charge is laid, and even then there is confusion about its significance: whether as an element of the crime or as merely part of the evidence of conspiracy. It is the agreement itself which is the touchstone of illegality, irrespective of whether or not efforts have actually been made to implement prohibited objectives, and apparently without regard even to whether the combination is capable of achieving them. The very existence of group purpose is enough, without more, to support the presumption of societal danger warranting criminal punishment.

Reliance on conspiracy holds a number of familiar attractions for the prosecutor. The application of the conspiracy label serves to brand the opposing group with an image of secrecy and evil plotting that tends to exaggerate the threat of the challenged conduct and heightens apprehensions latent in the community. More directly, the charge of conspiracy gives the government substantive flexibility and ease of proof as well as specific procedural advantages which can operate to the substantial prejudice of the defendants....

There is substantial danger that any given defendant will become the victim of guilt by association. Not only does the very presence of all the defendants together in the courtroom itself suggest their combination and complicity, but there usually will be some evidence of illegality by someone and, given the lengthy trial and voluminous record typical of conspiracy proceedings, the jury will find it hard to sort out the individual merits of the case against each accused. The use of the conspiracy indictment in order to obtain prosecutorial advantage, even as applied to non-political cases, has met serious criticism from legal scholars: "[T]he general critique has pointed to the danger of a dragnet in the broad, uncertain ground of liability, the wholesale joinder of defendants, the imposition of vicarious responsibility, the relaxation of the rules of evidence, or some or all combined. Misuse of the conspiracy charge and the panoply of governmental advantages in conspiracy trials led Mr. Justice Jackson, in his noted concurrence in *Krulewitch v. United States,* to conclude that the "loose practice as to this offense constitutes a serious threat to fairness in our administration of justice."

The risk of prejudice at the trial is accentuated when the case involves dissenters whose views are in themselves likely to be distasteful to both judge and jury. The *threat* of conspiracy indictments in such cases also has an important effect which works outside the courtroom. While the danger of indictment for conspiracy, as an alternative or addition to an indictment for a substantive speech crime, may have little or no "chilling effect" on the first amendment rights of those who are determined to speak, it is a significant deterrent to the less hardy — those who would assist or aid others to speak. By virtue of an alleged "agreement" that a speech should be made, they may become indictable as co-conspirators with the speaker. Even if such third parties escape indictment, they run the risk that their words and actions will be used in the government's case against those who are defendants.

In such a setting — where the dragnet charge is so useful a tool to punish those who express critical, unorthodox, or unpopular views — it is crucial that the propriety of reliance on the charge of conspiracy to commit a speech crime be given the closest scrutiny. Peculiarly subject to abuse in even the run-of-the-mill criminal case, the conspiracy device — the "darling of the modern prosecutor's nursery" — demands heightened critical analysis when basic political rights may be at stake.

PART V

DOCTRINES OF IMPUTATION

Part II of this coursebook describes how offenses are defined. Typically, an actor is liable for an offense if and only if she satisfies the elements of an offense definition. There exist two kinds of exceptions to this paradigm of equivalency between satisfying an offense definition and exposure to criminal liability. An actor may be *liable* for an offense even though she does not satisfy all offense elements, if a rule or doctrine *imputes* the missing element. A second, and reverse, exception is found in general defenses, in which an actor *escapes liability* even though she *does* satisfy the elements of an offense if she satisfies the conditions of a *general defense*. General defenses are the subject of Part VI. This Part examines doctrines of imputation — voluntary intoxication, complicity, omission liability, and corporate criminality.

Notes on Imputation Generally

Criticisms of Imputation   Some writers have suggested that the imposition of liability absent a required element of the offense is illogical and immoral. In *Director of Public Prosecutions v. Majewski*,[1] for example, the defendant argued that it is both illogical and unethical to impute to a defendant a culpable state of mind (for assault) that he in fact did not have (because he was voluntarily intoxicated). The defendant relies on a passage from Lord Hailsham in *Director of Prosecutions v. Morgan*:

> [O]nce it be accepted that an intent of whatever description is an ingredient essential to the guilt of the accused I cannot myself see that any other direction [than requiring proof of the intent] can be logically acceptable. Otherwise a jury would in effect be told to find an intent where none existed or where none was proved to have existed. I cannot myself reconcile it with my conscience to sanction as part of the English law what I regard as logical impossibility, and, if there were any authority which, if accepted, would compel me to do so, I would feel constrained to declare that it was not to be followed.[2]

---

1. [1976] 2 All E.R. 142.
2. Morgan, [1975] 2 All E.R. 347, 360, quoted in Majewski, [1976] 2 All E.R. at 166.

Imputation as a Common and Accepted Basis of Liability   But just as many general defenses commonly are recognized—which exculpate despite satisfaction of the paradigm elements of the offense—many doctrines of imputation are common and well established. That is, many traditional doctrines inculpate an actor despite the absence of a "required" element of the offense definition. If, for example, an actor causes another person to engage in illegal conduct, the actor may be liable for an offense defined to require such conduct although in fact the actor has not performed the conduct that the offense requires. The actor is held liable despite this absent element because the conduct of the other person is imputed under the doctrine of complicity or causing crime by an innocent. Similarly, a requisite culpable state of mind commonly is imputed to an actor if he would have had the culpable state of mind but for his voluntary intoxication. These familiar results follow from special rules governing complicity and voluntary intoxication. There is no suggestion that the actor in fact satisfies the required element. In each instance, the special conditions required by the doctrine of imputation are said to justify treating the actor *as if* he or she satisfies the imputed element.

Imputation Principles as Independent of Offense   A legislature could conceivably include inculpatory (and exculpatory) exceptions to the offense paradigm within the offense definition.[1] Typically, this is not done, because a general provision defining the conditions of imputation (or defense) give ease and theoretical clarity. Like the general defenses, such as insanity, duress, and law enforcement authority, which are separate and apart from any offense definition, the rules of imputation represent principles of liability independent of any offense. Also like general defenses, most of the doctrines of imputed liability, at least theoretically, can impute a required element of any offense. Some may tend to apply to certain recurring factual situations: Transferred intent appears most commonly in bad-aim murder cases. But this is a factual rather than a theoretical limitation of the principles. The use of general imputation provisions also is efficient. Such general provisions can be stated once, in as much detail as is needed, yet can be applied to all offenses.

Scrutinizing Imputation Rationale Rather than Process   It is not the mechanism of imputation that deserves criticism but rather those doctrines of imputation in which the required special conditions do not fully justify the imputation that follows, that is, they do not justify treating the actor the same as if he satisfied the missing element. Defenses—exceptions to the offense paradigm that redound to the defendant's benefit—typically are supported by articulable, rational explanations. Can one articulate sound theoretical and practical reasons to support each inculpating exception? Many of the imputation doctrines described in this Part have a sound justification. In other doctrines, however, the justification for the imputation seems weak or unpersuasive. The crucial theoretical issue in each instance is: Do the special conditions of the doctrine justify treating the actor as if he satisfies the missing element?

---

1. Arson, for example, is defined in Tennessee to include complicity in arson: "Any person who willfully and maliciously sets fire to or burns, causes to be burned, *or who aids, counsels or procures* the burning of any house...shall be guilty of arson...." Tenn. Code Ann. §39-3-202 (1982) (emphasis added).

Doctrines Imputing Objective Elements   American criminal law permits the imputation of both objective and culpability elements of an offense. While the most obvious and common instances of imputing objective elements are found in the rules governing complicity,[1] such rules are only one of several doctrines that impose liability even though the defendant has not satisfied all of the objective elements of an offense. Where an actor exercises control over an innocent person's actions, the latter's satisfaction of an objective element of an offense may be imputed to the former as an instance of "causing crime by an innocent."[2] Various statutory and judicial presumptions permit the imposition of liability even though the evidence adduced at trial would not establish all the objective elements of the offense.[3] On occasion, the doctrines of "substituted culpability" and "transferred mens rea" have been formulated in reverse, to operate as doctrines of "substituted objective elements"[4] and "transferred actus reus,"[5] which would impute a missing objective element and thereby hold the actor liable for the offense intended. (Thus, an actor who commits statutory rape but who, because of his mistake as to the true identity of his partner, believes he is instead committing incest, can be held liable for the incest offense although he is not related to his partner. Modern codes more frequently adopt doctrines of "substituted culpability" and "transferred mens rea," which hold the actor liable for the offense he in fact commits, imputing to him the missing culpability requirements.) Finally, the rules imposing liability for omissions, when the offense charged is defined only in terms of affirmative conduct, also may be viewed as instances of imputed conduct.[6]

Doctrines Imputing Culpability Elements   Another group of doctrines impute a required culpability element. The most common of these doctrines shapes the law governing voluntary intoxication.[7] Also imputing a culpable state of mind, the doctrine of "transferred intent" imputes the required culpability to an actor who intends to harm one person but actually harms another. Imputation also is accomplished through a device that may be termed "substituted culpability." The doctrine uses an actor's culpability for the offense he thought he was committing as the basis for imputing to him the intention required for the offense that he in fact committed.[8] Courts that permit suspension of the requirement of concurrence between act and intent make a similar imputation: An actor's earlier intention to commit an act that he believes is the offense is relied on to impute to

---

1. See Model Penal Code §2.06(3), discussed in Section 14.

2. See Model Penal Code §2.06(2)(a).

3. See, e.g., Tenn. Code Ann. §39-1-507 (1982) (presumption of manufacture of moonshine from assembly of still).

4. For example, assume an actor believes he is burglarizing a store while he in fact is burglarizing a dwelling (a different offense), he may be convicted of the offense of burglarizing a store even though an element of the offense, "store," is not satisfied. The existence of a comparable objective element in the actual offense, "dwelling," is used as a justification for imputing the required objective element of the offense charged. This is one of the approaches originally proposed by the drafters of the Model Penal Code but ultimately rejected in favor of current Model Penal Code §2.04(2). See Model Penal Code §2.04(2) comment 2 at 137 (Tentative Draft No. 4, 1955). Kentucky and West Virginia have adopted this approach. See Ky. §501.070(2); W. Va. §61-2-7(b).

5. Where *A* shoots at *B* but hits *C,* the objective element of the death of *C* may be "transferred" to justify holding *A* liable for the intentional homicide of *B,* at whom he was shooting. See Mayweather v. State, 29 Ariz. 460, 462, 242 P. 864, 865 (1926).

6. This is the subject of Section 15.

7. This is the subject of Section 13.

8. See Model Penal Code §2.04(2).

him the required intention during his later conduct that actually constitutes the offense. Finally, as with objective elements, a variety of statutory and judicial presumptions effectively impute culpability elements, on proof of a logically related fact.

Doctrines Imputing Both Objective and Culpability Elements   Other rules impute both objective and culpability elements. If *A* and *B* conspire to rob a bank and *B* purposely kills a guard, both the killing and the purposeful culpability as to killing may be imputed to *A* under the *Pinkerton* doctrine. The common law's "natural and probable consequence" rule in complicity law analogously expands the liability of accomplices.[1] Similarly, the complicity aspect of the felony-murder rule imputes both objective and culpability elements to the accomplice. Finally, vicarious liability, and its special subclass governing the liability of officials of organizations, may impute offense elements to an actor because of the actor's relationship to another.[2] This is not an exhaustive list of the criminal law's instances of imputation.

---

1. Under this rule, "an accessory is liable for any criminal act which in the ordinary course of things was the natural or probable consequence of the crime that he advised or commanded, although such consequence may not have been intended by him." 22 C.J.S. Criminal Law §92 (1961).

2. The liability of corporate officials is the subject of Section 16.

Voluntary Intoxication

The effects of drugs or alcohol can block formation of a culpable mental state required by an offense definition, such as the awareness of risk required for recklessness. While this effect might normally bar criminal liability for an offense, the law takes account of an offender's role in voluntarily bringing about the effect by imputing a culpable mental state to the offender, usually recklessness, if the offender would have been aware of the risk had she been sober. Do the special conditions that trigger imputation under the voluntary intoxication rules justify the culpability imputed?

◆ THE CASE OF JORDAN WEAVER

It is late in the after-noon in Indianapolis on April 2, 1991, when Jordan Weaver takes two "triple-dipped" paper blotter "hits" of a particularly potent batch of lysergic acid diethylamide (LSD or "acid"). Toxicologists report that LSD can produce extremely disorienting effects. A "bad trip," or acute psychotic reaction to the drug, may cause irrational random violence and paranoia. During this "trip," Weaver will later report effects far beyond

Figure 50 **Jordan Weaver**

(Richard Miller, Indianapolis Star)

anything that he has previously experienced: "mold" growing in his head, people's faces melting, walls breathing, objects floating, being Jesus, being in a spaceship.

Later in the day, Weaver's girlfriend of fifteen months, seventeen-year old Wendy Waldman, picks him up to go out to eat. The two have planned a "special night" together at Renee's restaurant because she is leaving for a spring break trip to Florida.

Their relationship has been a stormy one, a type of "fatal attraction" affair. Friends and family question why the two stay together given that they have such dissimilar interests. Wendy's parents have tried to forbid her from seeing Jordan, but she continues to be drawn to his "exciting" personality. She is a serious student, deeply involved with her family, and "morally" disapproves of drug use and excessive drinking. In stark contrast, Weaver dropped out of high school during his junior year and is the product of a broken home. After they divorced, his parents both moved to Texas, in August 1990, so Weaver now lives with his twenty-year old sister, her husband, and their two young children. He has a long history of substance abuse, was first drunk at age 12, started smoking marijuana at 13, began taking hits of LSD at 15, and has experimented with a number of other drugs, including peyote, opium, cocaine, as well as "huffing" gasoline. In the last two years, he has "dropped acid" at least 15 times.

Before leaving for the restaurant, Weaver tells Wendy that he is tripping hard and is unsure about going out because he usually tries to "keep the trip under control" by remaining in a secluded space with close friends. On her insistence, however, they go anyway. Wendy later says that Weaver was "not acting like himself." At the restaurant, Weaver seems only loosely connected to the reality around him. He cannot read the menu. Weaver ends up handing the waitress some money before they have ordered anything and gets up to leave. Wendy makes up a story to explain the strange behavior. Outside, Weaver begins to say bizarre things: asking Wendy if he is dead and telling her he is Jesus Christ.

They end up going back to his sister's apartment. There he sees the walls breathing, closing in on him, objects floating in mid-air, and "tracers" of light following behind moving objects. He is also shocked to see his sister's face melting. Wendy arranges to meet some friends at Broad Ripple Park—Kris Hettle, Tracie Glanzman, Jessica Godley, and Kurt Steigerwald. At the park, Weaver's behavior becomes even more erratic; he now seems entirely in another world. He becomes fearful because his whole body has gone numb. "A slimy mold is crawling around" in his brain. Something is eating through his stomach. The group decides to take him to the deserted Alverna Retreat Center, a former Franciscan monastery, located on Indianapolis's quiet Northside. Kurt later observes that "It didn't seem to me like he had any idea of what was going on."

At the Center, Weaver only becomes increasingly agitated. He won't sit down on a blanket on the ground. He begins biting Wendy's hand and fingers, although it is not clear what it is that he thinks he is doing. Wendy offers to have sex with him as a means of calming him, but Weaver instead begins wrestling with Kurt and licking his neck. Kris intervenes but the episode escalates into violence as Weaver frantically escapes, hitting Kurt in the eye in the process. Weaver is now completely out of control and spasms into constant random violence. He then gets into Kurt's car and seizes Jessica by the throat. When she resists, Weaver begins strangling and shouting at her. Kurt and Kris grab a tire iron from the trunk and hit Weaver twice but the blows have no effect. They then throw a blanket over him and choke him, eventually getting him off Jessica. They try to put him in the car trunk but are unsuccessful. They briefly consider running him down with the car.

Weaver begins to attack Wendy, lifting her up and hurling her head-first into the pavement. While she is lying on the ground, he begins slamming her head and face into the concrete. He then pulls her head up by the hair and repeatedly punches her face, then kicks her limp body. At the end of the beating, Wendy's face is a "bloody pulp," with no distinguishable features — her nose is smashed in, her jaw is shattered, her ears are "inside her head," she is missing five teeth, her chin is partially torn off, her eyes are swollen shut, many of her facial bones are broken, and her brain is bruised. The state trooper who finds her will have to clear teeth and blood from her throat so she can breathe.

The others have vainly been trying to distract Weaver, who seems impervious to all assaults; indeed he is oblivious to them. They finally drive away to get help. When they leave, Wendy is comatose, lying face-down in a pool of blood.

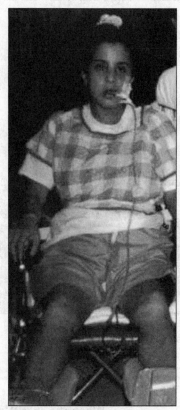

Figure 51 **Wendy Waldman three weeks after beating**

(Marion County Superior Court)

At some point, Weaver gets into Wendy's car, which he perceives to be a space ship, and drives off. But he quickly hits a tree and rolls the car over on its side. He thinks that with the crash of his spaceship he is out of air. Rather than using a door, he breaks through the car's "force field" — the windshield — to escape, and begins wandering into Indianapolis's Far Northside neighborhood, perhaps the quietest in the city. In the 8100 block of Round Hill Court, for reasons connected only to Weaver's

Figure 52 **Wendy Waldman's car after Weaver's wreck**

(Marion County Superior Court Records)

Figure 53 **Michael Blickman after his altercation with Weaver**

(Marion County Superior Court Records)

own reality, he crashes through the kitchen bay window of Barbara and Michael Blickman.

Michael, an attorney, races into the kitchen upon hearing the glass shatter and confronts Weaver, freshly bloodied by the glass. Fearing for his family's safety, Blickman smashes Weaver with a chair, and then tries to wrestle him out of the house. During the scuffle, which lasts several minutes, Weaver is thrusting his hand into Blickman's mouth. Blickman bites it, drawing blood. His wife, who has been screaming throughout the melee, beats Weaver with the leg of a broken chair. Mrs. Blickman later comments that Weaver had a "crazy look in his eye."

Next door, Jerome Sweeny, his wife, and their visiting adult son, Brian, rush outside at the sounds of Barbara's screams. Brian had earlier heard Wendy's screams from the Center and thought that a girl "was either being killed or raped." He had notified the sheriff's department.

When the sheriff's deputies arrive, Sweeny, a sixty-four-year old steel company representative, runs to show them a gap in the fence through which he thinks Weaver escaped. In the process, he suffers a heart attack and collapses in cardiac arrest. He had had a heart attack 15 years earlier and suffered from heart disease. The deputies administer CPR until paramedics arrive but Sweeney never recovers.

Meanwhile, Blickman and others finally manage to drag Weaver into the driveway, where five deputies subdue him. As he struggles with the officers, Weaver screams.

1. Relying only on your own intuitions of justice, what liability and punishment, if any, does Jordan Weaver deserve?

N	0	1	2	3	4	5	6	7	8	9	10	11
☐	☐	☐	☐	☐	☐	☐	☐	☐	☐	☐	☐	☐
no liability	liability but no punishment	1 day	2 wks	2 mo	6 mo	1 yr	3 yrs	7 yrs	15 yrs	30 yrs	life imprison-ment	death

2. What liability, if any, under the then-existing statutes?
3. What liability, if any, under the Model Penal Code?

■ THE LAW

West's Annotated Indiana Codes
(1991)

Title 35. Criminal Law and Procedure

Article 42. Offenses Against the Person
Chapter 1. Homicide

Section 35-42-1-1. Murder

A person who:
 (1) knowingly or intentionally kills another human being; [or]
 (2) kills another human being while committing or attempting to commit arson, burglary, child molesting, consumer product tampering, criminal deviate conduct, kidnaping, rape, robbery;...
commits murder, a felony.

Section 35-42-1-5. Reckless Homicide

A person who recklessly kills another human being commits reckless homicide, a Class C felony.

Section 35-42-1-4. Involuntary manslaughter

A person who kills another human being while committing or attempting to commit:
 (1) a Class C or Class D felony that inherently poses a risk of serious bodily injury;
 (2) a Class A misdemeanor that inherently poses a risk of serious bodily injury; or
 (3) battery;
commits involuntary manslaughter, a Class C felony. However, if the killing results from the operation of a vehicle, the offense is a Class D felony.

Chapter 2. Battery and Related Offenses

Section 35-42-2-1. Battery

(a) A person who knowingly or intentionally touches another person in a rude, insolent, or angry manner commits battery, a Class B misdemeanor.

However, the offense is:

(1) a Class A misdemeanor if it results in bodily injury to any other person, or if it is committed against a law enforcement officer or against a person summoned and directed by the officer while the officer is engaged in the execution of his official duty;

(2) a Class D felony if it results in bodily injury to:

(A) a law enforcement officer or a person summoned and directed by a law enforcement officer while the officer is engaged in the execution of his official duty;

(B) a person less than thirteen (13) years of age and is committed by a person at least eighteen (18) years of age;

(C) a person of any age who is mentally or physically disabled and is committed by a person having the care of the mentally or physically disabled person, whether the care is assumed voluntarily or because of a legal obligation;

(D) the other person and the person who commits the battery was previously convicted of a battery in which the victim was the other person;

(E) an endangered adult (as defined by IC 35-46-1-1); or

(F) an employee of the department of correction while the employee is engaged in the execution of the employee's official duty; and

(3) a Class C felony if it results in serious bodily injury to any other person or if it is committed by means of a deadly weapon.

Section 35-42-2-2. Criminal Recklessness; /...

(a) A person who recklessly, knowingly, or intentionally performs an act that creates a substantial risk of bodily injury to another person commits criminal recklessness, a Class B misdemeanor.

However, the offense is a:

(1) Class A misdemeanor if the conduct includes the use of a vehicle; or

(2) Class D felony if it is committed while armed with a deadly weapon.

(b) A person who recklessly, knowingly, or intentionally inflicts serious bodily injury on another person; or commits criminal recklessness, a Class D felony. However, the offense is a Class C felony if committed by means of a deadly weapon.

Article 41. General Substantive Provisions
Chapter 1. Jurisdiction; Definitions

Section 35-41-1-4. "Bodily Injury" Defined

"Bodily injury" means any impairment of physical, including physical pain.

Section 35-41-2-2. Culpability

(a) A person engages in conduct "intentionally" if, when he engages in the conduct, it is his conscious objective to do so.

(b) A person engages in conduct "knowingly" if, when he engages in the conduct, he is aware of a high probability that he is doing so.

(c) A person engages in conduct "recklessly" if he engages in the conduct in plain, conscious, and unjustifiable disregard of harm that might result and the disregard involves a substantial deviation from acceptable standards of conduct.

(d) Unless the statute defining the offense provides otherwise, if a kind of culpability is required for commission of an offense, it is required with respect to every material element of the prohibited conduct.

Chapter 3. Defenses Relating to Culpability

Section 35-41-3-5. Intoxication

(a) It is a defense that the person who engaged in the prohibited conduct did so while he was intoxicated, if the intoxication resulted from the introduction of a substance into his body:

(1) without his consent; or

(2) when he did not know that the substance might cause intoxication.

(b) Voluntary intoxication is a defense only to the extent that it negates an element of an offense referred to by the phrase "with intent to" or "with an intention to."

Chapter 5. Offenses of General Applicability

Section 35-41-5-1. Attempt

(a) A person attempts to commit a crime when, acting with the culpability required for commission of the crime, he engages in conduct that constitutes a substantial step toward commission of the crime. An attempt to commit a crime is a felony or misdemeanor of the same class as the crime attempted. However, an attempt to commit murder is a Class A felony.

(b) It is no defense that, because of a misapprehension of the circumstances, it would have been impossible for the accused person to commit the crime attempted.

Rhodes v. State

181 Ind. Ct. App. 265, 391 N.E.2d 666 (1979)

Indiana's attempt law, based on §35-41-5-1, does not permit an offense of "attempted reckless homicide." Citing Model Penal Code commentary, the Court ruled that, despite the attempt statute's language that only "the culpability required for the commission of the offense" is required, a "specific intent" must be proven, since the very definition of attempt is "to try."

Terry v. State of Indiana

465 N.E.2d 1085 (Ind. 1984)

Section 35-41-3-5(b) violates the state constitution and is therefore invalid, since "the attempt by the legislature to remove [voluntary intoxication as a defense] goes against [the] firmly ingrained principle [that] intoxication may be offered to negate capacity to formulate intent.... Any factor which serves as a denial of the existence of mens rea must be considered by a trier of fact before a guilty finding is entered." But the Court goes on to uphold the conviction, holding: "The potential of this defense should not be confused with the reality of the situation. It is difficult to envision a finding of not guilty by reason of intoxication when the acts committed require a significant degree of physical or intellectual skills. As a general proposition, a defendant should not be relieved of responsibility when he was able to devise a plan, operate equipment, instruct the behavior of others or carry out acts requiring physical skill."

Model Penal Code

(Official Draft 1962)

Section 2.08. Intoxication

(1) Except as provided in Subsection (4) of this Section, intoxication of the actor is not a defense unless it negatives an element of the offense.

(2) When recklessness establishes an element of the offense, if the actor, due to self-induced intoxication, is unaware of a risk of which he would have been aware had he been sober, such unawareness is immaterial.

(3) Intoxication does not, in itself, constitute mental disease within the meaning of Section 4.01.

(4) Intoxication which (a) is not self-induced or (b) is pathological is an affirmative defense if by reason of such intoxication the actor at the time of his conduct lacks substantial capacity either to appreciate its criminality [wrongfulness] or to conform his conduct to the requirements of law.

(5) Definitions. In this Section unless a different meaning plainly is required:

(a) "intoxication" means a disturbance of mental or physical capacities resulting from the introduction of substances into the body;

(b) "self-induced intoxication" means intoxication caused by substances which the actor knowingly introduces into his body, the tendency of which to cause intoxication he knows or ought to know, unless he introduces them pursuant to medical advice or under such circumstances as would afford a defense to a charge of crime;

(c) "pathological intoxication" means intoxication grossly excessive in degree, given the amount of the intoxicant, to which the actor does not know he is susceptible.

● OVERVIEW OF VOLUNTARY INTOXICATION

Notes on Voluntary Intoxication

Intoxication Negating Element   If, because of being involuntarily intoxicated, an actor does not have the culpable state of mind required for an offense — that is, if involuntary intoxication negates a required offense culpability element — the actor will have a defense, much as when ignorance or mistake negates a required culpability element.[1] If the intoxication is voluntary, however, the actor nonetheless may be criminally liable. Under the Model Penal Code, for example, if the intoxication is voluntary, recklessness as to an offense element may be imputed to an actor if the actor would have been aware of the risk had he or she been sober.[2] The nature and degree of the culpability that should be imputed is the subject of the Discussion Materials below.

Voluntary vs. Involuntary Intoxication   The case law typically recognizes four grounds which intoxication may be found involuntary: coerced intoxication, pathological intoxication, intoxication by innocent mistake, and unexpected intoxication resulting from the ingestion of a medically prescribed drug.[3] Under the Model Penal Code, and the many modern codes following its lead, intoxication is involuntary if it is not "self-induced," or if it is "pathological." These definitions appear to include all four of the categories recognized by the case law as well as several others:

> "self-induced intoxication" means intoxication caused by substances which the actor knowingly introduces into his body, the tendency of which to cause intoxication he knows or ought to know, unless he introduces them pursuant to medical advice or under such circumstances as would afford a defense to a charge of crime.[4]

This sets a negligence standard as to becoming intoxicated: intoxication is self-induced if the actor "knows or *ought to know*" the substance's tendency to intoxicate.

Voluntary Intoxication   Under the common law rule, voluntary intoxication was permitted as a defense to a specific intent offense but not to a general intent offense. The common law approach was problematic because of the difficulty in distinguishing specific intent offenses from general intent offenses. The Model Penal Code's treatment of voluntary intoxication is a somewhat more

---

1. See Model Penal Code §2.08(1). For a discussion of involuntary intoxication as a general excuse, see Section 23.

2. Model Penal Code §2.08(2).

3. See, e.g., Minneapolis v. Altimus, 306 Minn. 462, 238 N.W. 2d 851 (1976) (due to side effects of ingestion of medically prescribed valium, defendant became involved in car accident and assaulted police officer).

4. Model Penal Code §2.08(5)(b).

refined "element analysis" version of the common law's approach. Section 2.08 provides:

> (1) Except as provided [by the general excuse of intoxication], intoxication of the actor is not a defense unless it negatives an element of the offense.
>
> (2) When recklessness establishes an element of the offense, if the actor, due to self-induced intoxication, is unaware of a risk of which he would have been aware had he been sober, such unawareness is immaterial.

The first subsection confirms that, even if the intoxication is voluntary, it is permitted to provide a defense if it negates an actor's purpose or knowledge. The second subsection, however, prevents an actor from using self-induced intoxication as a defense even if it does in fact negate recklessness required by the offense definition. That is, even if the actor, because of self-induced intoxication, is in fact unaware of a risk, as recklessness requires, such awareness and recklessness are imputed to the actor because of his culpability in becoming intoxicated.

Problematic Compromise   Both the traditional common law and the Model Penal Code approaches create a legal fiction — that the defendant has a certain culpable state of mind that in fact he does not have — in an attempt to structure a compromise between the desire for some liability to protect society and to punish the actor's bringing about his intoxicated state, and the belief that a voluntarily intoxicated offender may be less culpable than an unintoxicated actor who commits the offense.[1] Unfortunately, the compromise frequently fails to achieve the desired result. The purposeful or knowing offense (or specific intent offense) for which a defense is given does not always have an included lesser offense of recklessness (or general intent) for which a defense will be denied. When voluntary intoxication negates the culpability required for attempted rape, for example, the defendant may escape all liability. On the other hand, voluntary intoxication may impute the required culpability in the case of a completed rape, so no mitigation in liability is provided to distinguish this actor from the rapist who is not intoxicated and is fully aware of the victim's lack of consent.[2]

Fixed Mitigation Proposal   The current law's poor performance in reaching compromise liability — less liability than is imposed on the unintoxicated offender, to reflect less blameworthiness, yet impose some liability, in order to protect the public and to punish the actor's blameworthiness in becoming intoxicated — may suggest that an alternative approach deserves consideration. As noted, the current approach frequently fails because many, if not most, offenses do not have increasing grades based on culpability level — a higher purpose-knowledge grade and a lower recklessness grade — in the way that homicide does. The doctrine could better ensure some reduced liability in all cases if it used the grading mechanism seen in most inchoate offenses, that of providing a standard mitigation reduction of one grade. Thus, where the actor lacks the culpability required for an offense because of voluntary intoxication, he would always be liable for an offense,

[margin handwritten note:] Rape Ex.

---

1. See, e.g., People v. Hood, 1 Cal. 3d 444, 462 P.2d 370 (1969).

2. See, e.g., United States v. Short, 4 U.S.C.M.A. 437, 446, 16 C.M.R. 11, 20 (1954) (J. Brosman, concurring in part, dissenting in part) (if drunken American soldier achieved intercourse with unwilling Japanese girl, drunkenness no defense because would not negative *mens rea* of rape; if drunkenness caused soldier to mistake Japanese girl for consenting prostitute, could negative intent to rape and give defense to offense of assault with intent to rape).

but an offense of one grade less than if he were sober. As we will see later in this Section, however, even this proposal may be criticized as "rough justice": The voluntarily intoxicated actor may have much less blameworthiness than that normally associated even with this reduced grade of liability, or in some cases much more.

Criticism of Imputation The more strenuous attacks on current law's voluntary intoxication doctrine are against not its awkward performance in attempting a rough compromise, but rather its fundamental operation. Treating an actor as if she has a culpable state of mind that in fact she does not have is said to be both illogical and unethical. As noted previously, such treatment is inconsistent with the general principles of criminal liability, it is argued, and unfair to the defendant. The House of Lords in *Director of Public Prosecutions v. Majewski*[1] (excerpted in the Discussion Materials) concedes these claims, but argues that public policy concerns require them to maintain the current rule. In rejecting the defendant's claim that his voluntary intoxication ought to be allowed to negate all culpable states of mind, even general intent (or recklessness), the Lords reason that allowing a defense for voluntary intoxication would endanger the community by frustrating the prosecution of offenses perpetrated by drug users. The danger from drug-induced or drug-assisted offenses, the court points out, is growing and requires sterner sanctions, not lighter ones. Indeed, some jurisdictions have taken such public policy arguments to their logical conclusion and have adopted a rule that would bar voluntary intoxication from negating nearly any culpable state of mind.[2] In *State v. Stasio*, for example, the court concludes that voluntary intoxication should be permitted only to negate the deliberation and premeditation required for first degree murder, not the intent for any other offense. The court's conclusion is based in part on the difficulty of the general intent-specific intent distinction, but primarily on the need to ensure public safety. The court specifically rejects the Model Penal Code approach that is urged by the dissent.[3]

Misguided Apologies for Imputation Though the *Majewski* court's public policy concerns are real, the court concedes too much when it admits its position to be illogical and unfair. The fact is, the law frequently treats an actor *as if* the actor satisfies an offense element when the actor in fact does not. As noted in the introduction to this Part, such "imputation" of an element occurs in a wide variety of doctrines, including complicity and omission liability. An offense definition may require that an actor have performed certain conduct, yet the actor may be liable for the offense — *treated as if* she performed the required conduct — if the actor is legally accountable through complicity for the conduct of another who did perform the conduct. In the context of omission liability, if the actor has a duty to act and also the capacity to act, yet fails to act and thereby causes a prohibited result, he will be held liable for the offense as if the actor had affirmatively acted to cause the prohibited result. In each instance, a doctrine of imputation — in

---

1. [1976] 2 All E.R. 142.

2. See Ga. Code Ann. §16-3-4(c) (1988); Del. Code Ann. tit. 11, §421 (1987); Mont. Code Ann. §45-2-203 (1989); Okla. Stat. Ann. tit. 21, §153 (1983); 18 Pa. Cons. Stat. Ann. §308 (1983).

3. 18 N.J. 467, 474-481, 396 A.2d 1129, 1132-1135 (1979). *Stasio* was effectively overruled when the new New Jersey Criminal Code took effect. The Code had been enacted and was awaiting its effective date at the time *Stasio* was decided.

complicity and omission liability, respectively — serves to treat the actor as if she satisfies a required offense element that she in fact does not possess. From this perspective, the Lords' apology for imputation seems misguided.

Need to Justify Imputation   Doctrines of imputation — such as the doctrine of voluntary intoxication — should be criticized not because they impute a required element, but rather because they often have inadequate justification for the imputation they provide. There seems to be general agreement that the conditions required by the doctrines of complicity and omission liability, and others as well, adequately justify the imputation of required conduct. The doctrine of voluntary intoxication, in contrast, can be criticized on this ground: It is not clear that the actor's culpability in becoming intoxicated justifies the imputation of recklessness (or general intent) as to all manner of offense elements — for example, recklessness as to causing death in manslaughter.

Negligent Intoxication as Inadequate to Impute Recklessness   The most common rationale for imputing recklessness in cases of voluntary intoxication is the actor's culpability in becoming intoxicated. Imputing such recklessness because of voluntary intoxication is troubling, however, for several reasons. The imputation of recklessness under the Model Penal Code, and of greater culpability under many other codes,[1] is triggered by a definition of "voluntariness" in becoming intoxicated that requires only negligence. As noted above, under the Model Penal Code, intoxication is "self-induced" if the actor "knows or *ought to know*" the tendency of the substance to intoxicate.

Culpability as to Intoxication Inadequate to Impute Offense Culpability   A second and more serious weakness in the justification for imputing recklessness concerns the object of the culpability. The notion that a person risks all manner of resulting harm when she voluntarily becomes intoxicated is common, but obviously incorrect.[2] Becoming intoxicated in itself is not an offense, or is at most a minor offense when done in public. It seems difficult to use a person's culpability as to becoming intoxicated as the grounds for imputing the required culpability for an offense as serious as recklessly causing a death.

Mitchell Keiter, Just Say No Excuse: The Rise and Fall of the Intoxication Defense

87 Journal of Criminal Law and Criminology 482, 482-483, 518-519 (1997)

On perhaps no other legal issue have courts so widely differed, or so often changed their views, as that of the legal responsibility of intoxicated offenders. The question contrasts the individual's right to avoid punishment for the unintended consequences of his acts with what then-New Hampshire Supreme Court Justice

---

1. Ark. Stat. Ann. §41-207 (1977); Del. Code Ann. tit. 11, §421 (1979); Ga. Code Ann. §16-3-4 (1982); Okla. Stat. Ann. tit. 21, §153 (1983).

2. Hawaii rejects the Model Penal Code provision for just this reason: "It equates the defendant's becoming drunk with the reckless disregard by him of risks created by his subsequent conduct and thereby forecloses the issue." Hawaii Rev. Stat. §702-230 comment (1976).

David Souter described as the individual's "responsibility...to stay sober if his intoxication will jeopardize the lives and safety of others." The issue presents the choice of whether the magnitude of an offense should be measured from the objective perspective of the community or the subjective perspective of the offender.

Prompted by myriad changes in social, political, medical and legal philosophies, nineteenth and early twentieth century courts greatly expanded the exculpatory effect of intoxication. Beginning in the 1980s and 1990s, however, the pendulum began to swing back toward a policy of accountability for acts committed while intoxicated. Throughout this process, the issue has been highlighted by the competing positions of courts and legislatures. For example, in 1994 both the California and Canada Supreme Courts issued decisions which protected or expanded a defendant's right to introduce evidence of his intoxication. Both decisions sparked public outrage, and were in effect reversed by new statutes in 1995.

The United States Supreme Court's decision in *Montana v. Egelhoff* will likely have a profound effect on the debate surrounding the intoxication defense. The Court upheld a Montana statute which holds intoxicated offenders fully responsible for the consequences of acts they commit while intoxicated. While the plurality, concurring, and various dissenting opinions reflected differing perspectives, none found it would be unconstitutional for a state to equate a severe state of intoxication with the requisite mens rea for any crime. The Court's approval will likely influence other states to adopt a full responsibility policy....

Appendix

The following states do not admit intoxication evidence as a defense to any crime: Arizona, Arkansas, Delaware, Georgia, Hawaii, Mississippi, Missouri, Montana, South Carolina, Texas.

The following states admit intoxication evidence as a defense only to first degree murder: Pennsylvania, Virginia.

The following states admit intoxication evidence as a defense only to crimes requiring purpose: Alaska, Colorado.

The following states follow the Model Penal Code and admit intoxication evidence as a defense only to crimes requiring purpose or knowledge: Alabama, Connecticut, Kentucky, Maine, New Hampshire, New Jersey, New York, North Dakota, Oregon, Tennessee, Utah, Wisconsin.

The following states admit intoxication as a defense only to crimes requiring a "specific intent": California, Florida, Idaho, Illinois, Iowa, Kansas, Louisiana, Maryland, Massachusetts, Michigan, Minnesota, Nebraska, Nevada, New Mexico, North Carolina, Oklahoma, Rhode Island, South Dakota, Vermont, West Virginia, Wyoming.

The following states admit intoxication as a defense to all crimes requiring purpose, knowledge or recklessness: Ohio, Washington.

The following state admits intoxication evidence as a defense to any crime: Indiana.

▲ PROBLEM
Food for Thought

Sharon and Buff have become very close as they have struggled together through their first year of law school. Buff is particularly appreciative of Sharon's support because Buff's husband, Peter, is so unsupportive. Buff is somewhat understanding about her husband's complaints. She knows she has been moody and, during the past exam week, even verbally and emotionally abusive. Sharon is less understanding. She thinks Peter is a worthless, whining leech who is taking gross advantage of her friend. She repeatedly urges Buff to "Kill the pig!", said only half in jest.

After their last exam, Sharon suggests that they stop at a local club for a few drinks to celebrate and unwind. Sharon's real plan is to get roaring drunk. She wants to kill Peter and knows that when she gets drunk she becomes violent toward people she does not like; the more drunk the more violent. She assumes that, while intoxicated, their conversation will turn to Peter and that he will become the focus of her drunken rage. In such a drunken state she knows she will not hesitate to kill him, but has learned from her criminal law outline that she will not be responsible for the killing because, if she is sufficiently intoxicated, she will not at the time be acting consciously. Sharon does not tell Buff of her plan. At the club Sharon orders two Bloody Marys. Buff orders a glass of white wine. Sharon wants Buff to help her in the killing and figures that white wine won't do the trick, so she adds a few pills to both of their drinks, telling Buff that the pills will give the drinks more zap: "It'll really make us fly." Buff is hesitant. She generally doesn't drink, but she reminds herself that she has just finished a tough year and she deserves to celebrate. She sips her glass of wine while Sharon has three more Bloody Marys, with the additive, in quick succession. Both women are now grossly intoxicated and barely coherent. Sharon is babbling incessantly about killing "Peter the Pig."

A friend of Buff's sees them at the club falling out of their chairs, and insists on taking Buff home. Sharon goes along. When they arrive, they stagger from the friend's car and sprawl on Buff's front yard. Buff discovers that she is lying on her law books, apparently thrown from the upstairs window by a disgusted Peter, who is angry at her exam week abuse. "My books!" "The pig!", Sharon responds. They storm into the house, rip pages from the books, and stuff them in sleeping Peter's mouth. Both break into a chant of "Eat, Pig, eat."

The next morning, Sharon and Buff awake in bed with Peter's body. Neither woman remembers anything after the first drink at the club. Peter is found to have died of asphyxiation. From witnesses, the police piece together the events, including Sharon's plan to kill Peter by making herself grossly intoxicated. What should be the extent of Sharon's and Buff's liability, if any? What will be their liability, if any, under the Model Penal Code?

DISCUSSION MATERIALS

What Level of Culpable Mental State, If Any, Should Be Imputed When It Is Absent Because the Offender Voluntarily Intoxicated Himself?

In *Director of Public Prosecutions v. Majewski* the House of Lords defends the traditional voluntary intoxication rule (which imputes recklessness or specific intent) against those who claim the rule to be illogical and immoral because it treats a defendant as if he has a culpable state of mind that he does not in fact have. The *Pennsylvania v. Graves* dissent argues for an even more severe position than the *Majewski* court—allowing voluntary intoxication to justify the imputation of all culpable mental states. Stephen Morse then offers objections to the full range of rules that impute offense culpability because of voluntary intoxication, including that of the Model Penal Code, arguing that all are based on an unreliable assumption that the culpability in becoming intoxicated is comparable to, and a justified basis for imputing, culpability as to committing an offense. Based on a study of community perspectives, Robinson and Darley conclude that lay intuitions differ from most code voluntary intoxication rules; laypersons tend to assign liability based on the pre-intoxication culpability toward committing the offense. Finally, Robinson proposes, on jurisprudential grounds, an alternative approach, which better tracks the community's shared intuitions.

Director of Public Prosecutions v. Majewski

House of Lords
[1976] 2 All E.R. 142

[Each of seven Law Lords prepared an address and each reached the same conclusion. Only the address of Lord Edmund-Davies is reproduced here.]

Lord Edmund-Davies. My Lords, during a brawl in a public house the appellant attacked the landlord and two others, injuring all three of them. When the police arrived, he assaulted the officer who arrested him. Another officer was struck by the appellant when he was being driven to the police station. The next morning in his cell he attacked a police inspector. As a result, he was indicted at the Chelmsford Crown Court on four counts of occasioning actual bodily harm and on three counts of assaulting a police constable in the execution of his duty. The appellant testified that he had no recollection of the greater part of what had transpired after he entered the public house, and that during the preceding 48 hours he had taken a substantial quantity of drugs and had ordered one drink at the public house. There was adduced a statement from a doctor who saw him the following morning and evidence by another doctor as to the possible effect of the ingestion of such drink and drugs as the appellant had spoken of. During the course of legal submissions, the attention of the learned judge was drawn to the short report of *Bolton v. Crawley* in which the Court of Appeal held that on a charge of assault occasioning actual bodily harm the consumption of drink or drugs was irrelevant to criminal responsibility. Accordingly, after telling the jury that an assault 'means some blow, not something which is purely accidental', the judge directed them that—

> ...the fact that [the appellant] may have taken drink and drugs is irrelevant, provided that you are satisfied that the state which he was in was a result of those drink and drugs [*sic*] or a combination of both was self-induced....

The jury convicted on six of the seven counts and the convictions were upheld by the Court of Appeal, who, however, granted leave to appeal, certifying that the following point of law of general importance was involved:

> Whether a defendant may properly be convicted of assault notwithstanding that, by reason of his self-induced intoxication, he did not intend to do the act alleged to constitute the assault.

...The argument advanced on behalf of the appellant can be summarized in the following propositions: (i) Save in relation to offenses of strict responsibility, no man is guilty of a crime unless he has a guilty mind. (ii) A person who, though not insane, commits what would in ordinary circumstances be a crime when he is in such a mental state (whether it be called 'automatism' or by any other name) that he does not know what he is doing, lacks a guilty mind and is therefore not criminally culpable for his actions. (iii) Such freedom from culpability exists regardless of (a) whether the offence charged is one involving a 'specific' (or 'ulterior') intent or one involving only a 'general' (or 'basic') intent; and (b) whether the automatism was due to causes beyond the control of the person charged or was self-induced by the voluntary taking of drink or drugs. (iv) Assaults being crimes involving a guilty mind, a man who in a state of automatism unlawfully assaults another must be treated as free from all blame and is accordingly entitled to be wholly acquitted: the certified question therefore demands a negative answer. (v) Not only is it logically and ethically indefensible to convict such a man of assault; it also constitutes a contravention of §8 of the Criminal Justice Act 1967. (vi) There accordingly having been a fatal misdirection the appeal should be allowed.

The basic submission of the Crown, on the other hand, may be far more shortly stated thus: a rule of law has been established that self-induced intoxication can provide a defence only to offenses requiring an 'ulterior' intent, and is therefore irrelevant to offenses of 'basic' intent such as assaults; the direction given was accordingly right, the certified question must be answered in the affirmative, and the appeal should be dismissed....

If logic is to be the sole guide, ...a man can never be regarded as committing an assault unless he is conscious of what he is doing. Whatever be the reason for its absence, if he in fact lacks such consciousness he cannot be said to act either intentionally or recklessly. It is submitted on the appellant's behalf that he was at all material times in a condition of 'non-insane automatism resulting from pathological intoxication.' In *Bratty v. Attorney General for Northern Ireland* Lord Kilmuir LC acceptably defined 'automatism' as—

> the state of a person who, though capable of action, "is not conscious of what he is doing.... It means unconscious involuntary action, and it is a defence because the mind does not go with what is being done."

In strict logic it may be that a physical action performed in such a state ought never to be punished as a criminal assault, no matter how grievous the injury thereby inflicted on the person attacked.

Then is it the case that a man is always to be absolved by the criminal law from the consequences of acts performed when in a state of automatism, regardless of how that state was brought about? The law is certainly clear and commendable in relation to cases where the actor is wholly free from fault in relation to the onset of such a mental state.

But a markedly different attitude has long been taken in respect of a state of automatism brought about by the *voluntary* act of the person charged with a crime.

... [T]he established law then was and is now that self-induced intoxication, however gross, cannot excuse crimes of basic intent such as that giving rise to this appeal.

Of recent years there has been increasing academic criticism of this virtually uniform judicial attitude. Such criticism is understandable, being based on what is advanced as the logical necessity of acquitting an accused who acted without mens rea, whatever be the reason for its absence. Thus Professor Glanville Williams comments: 'There is no reason why drunkenness should not negative a battery, if it tends to show that the accused did not intend to hit anyone.' The contrary view applied in our courts certainly presents problems. ...

The criticism by the academics of the law presently administered in this country is of a two-fold nature: (1) It is illogical and therefore inconsistent with legal principle to treat a person who of his own volition has taken drink or drugs any differently from a man suffering from some bodily or mental disorder of the kind earlier mentioned or whose beverage had, without his connivance, been 'laced' with intoxicants. (2) It is unethical to convict a man of a crime requiring a guilty state of mind when, ex hypothesi, he lacked it. I seek to say something about each of these two criticisms.

(1) Illogicality

The appellant's counsel places strong reliance on a passage in the speech of Lord Hailsham of St. Marylebone in *Director of Public Prosecutions v. Morgan* in which, alluding to criminal intent, he said:

> ...once it be accepted that an intent of whatever description is an ingredient essential to the guilt of the accused I cannot myself see that any other direction can be logically acceptable. Otherwise a jury would in effect be told to find an intent where none existed or where none was proved to have existed. I cannot myself reconcile it with my conscience to sanction as part of the English law what I regard as logical impossibility, and, if there were any authority which, if accepted, would compel me to do so, I would feel constrained to declare that it was not to be followed.

Well, I have respectfully to say that were such an attitude rigorously adopted and applied, it would involve the drastic revision of much of our established law. Many would say that this would not be a bad thing, but it is well to realize clearly that such would be the consequence, for the criminal law is unfortunately riddled with illogicalities.

So we find the Court of Appeal decision in *R v. Lipman* criticized because Widgery LJ justified the conviction for manslaughter on the basis of death being caused by what was described as the unlawful act of the accused in stuffing bedclothes down his companion's throat under the delusion (induced by the drugs he had taken) that he was dealing with snakes. . . . The undeviating application of logic leads inexorably to the conclusion that a man behaving even as Lipman unquestionably did must be completely discharged from all criminal liability for the dreadful consequences of his conduct. It was, as I recall, submissions of this startling character which led my noble and learned friend, Lord Simon of Glaisdale, to comment trenchantly to appellant's counsel: 'It is all right to say "Let justice be done though the heavens fall". But you ask us to say "Let logic be done even though public order be threatened", which is something very different.'

If such be the inescapable result of the strict application of logic in this branch of the law, it is indeed not surprising that illogicality has long reigned, and the prospect of its dethronement must be regarded as alarming.

(2) Lack of ethics

It is sometimes said in such cases as the present that it is morally wrong to convict of a crime involving a certain state of mind even where it be established that the charge is based on a man's behavior when he lacked that guilty mind. Rightly or wrongly, Coke was not of that view, for although he asserted that 'Actus non facit reum nisi mens sit rea'* he also said that, so far from gross intoxication excusing crime, it aggravated the culpability.

Your Lordships are presently concerned with a publichouse brawl, which is said to have been due to the ingestion of drugs rather than drink. Such a plea is becoming much more common, and those acting judicially or who have otherwise acquired any knowledge of addiction are familiar with such parlance of the drug scene as 'going on a trip' or 'blowing the mind', the avowed intention of the taker of hallucinatory drugs being to lose contact with reality. Irrationality is in truth the very essence of drug-induced phantasies.

Illogical though the present law may be, it represents a compromise between the imposition of liability on inebriates in complete disregard of their condition (on the alleged ground that it was brought on voluntarily), and the total exculpation required by the defendant's actual state of mind at the time he committed the harm in issue. It is at this point pertinent to pause to consider why legal systems exist. The universal object of a system of law is obvious — the establishment and maintenance of order. . . . The relevant quotations on the purpose of law are endless and they serve to explain (if, indeed, any explanation be necessary) the sense of outrage which would naturally be felt not only by the victims of such attacks as are alleged against the appellant — and still more against Lipman — were he to go scot free. And a law which permitted this would surely deserve and earn the contempt of most people. But not, it seems, of the joint authors of Smith and Hogan, who in the third edition of their valuable book write:

> While a policy of not allowing a man to escape the consequence of his voluntary drunkenness is understandable, it is submitted that the principle that

---

* Editor's Note — "An act does not make [the doer of it] guilty, unless the mind be guilty."

a man should not be held liable for an act over which he has no control is more important and should prevail.

They add that this is not to say that such a man should in all cases escape criminal liability but that, if he is to be held liable, it should be for the voluntary act of taking the drink or drug. Such a suggestion is far from new. Thus, it appears from Hale's Pleas of the Crown that some lawyers of his day thought that the formal cause of punishment ought to be the drink and not the crime committed under its influence. Edwards expressed concern in 1965 over the possible existence of this gateway to exemption from criminal responsibility and stressed the need for urgent attention to the provision of new statutory powers under which the courts may place such offenders on probation or commit them, as the case may require, to a hospital capable of treating them for the underlying cause of their propensity to automatism. Glanville Williams anticipated in 1961 the Butler Report on Mentally Abnormal Offenders by recommending the creation of an offence of being drunk and dangerous and the committee itself proposed that a new offence of 'dangerous intoxication' be punishable on indictment for one year for a first offence or for three years on a second or subsequent offence.

Such recommendations for law reform may receive Parliamentary consideration hereafter but this House is presently concerned with the law as it is. The merciful relaxation of the old rule that drunkenness was no defence appears to have worked reasonably well for 150 years. As to the complaint that it is unethical to punish a man for a crime when his physical behavior was not controlled by a conscious mind, I have long regarded as a convincing theory in support of penal liability for harms committed by voluntary inebriates, the view of Austin, who argued that a person who voluntarily became intoxicated is to be regarded as acting recklessly, for he made himself dangerous in disregard of public safety.

But, to my way of thinking, the nearest approach to a satisfactory refutation of charges of lack of both logic and ethics in punishing the most drunken man for actions which, were he sober, would call for his criminal conviction is that of Stroud, who wrote:

> [D]runkenness is not incompatible with *mens rea*, in the sense of ordinary culpable intentionality, because mere recklessness is sufficient to satisfy the definition of *mens rea*, and drunkenness is itself an act of recklessness. The law therefore establishes a conclusive presumption against the admission of proof of intoxication for the purpose of disproving *mens rea* in ordinary crimes. Where this presumption applies, it does not make "drunkenness itself" a crime, but the drunkenness is itself an integral part of the crime, as forming, together with the other unlawful conduct charged against the defendant, a complex act of criminal recklessness.
>
> This explanation affords at once a justification of the rule of law, and a reason for its inapplicability when drunkenness is pleaded by way of showing absence of full intent, or of some exceptional form of *mens rea* essential to a particular crime, according to its definition.

Reverting to the same topic immediately after the decision in *Beard*, Stroud added:

> ... His drunkenness can constitute a defence only in those exceptional cases where some additional mental element, of a more heinous and mischievous

description than ordinary *mens rea*, is required by the definition of the crime charged against him, and is shown to have been lacking in consequence of his drunken condition.

Professor Glanville Williams would probably condemn such an approach as savoring of 'judge-made fiction'. While generally sharing his dislike of such fictions, in my judgment little can properly be made out of the criticisms that a law which demands the conviction of such persons who behave as the appellant did is both illogical and unethical. It may be that Parliament should look at it, and devise a new way of dealing with drunken or drugged offenders. But, until it does, the continued application of the existing law is far better calculated to preserve order than the recommendation that he and all who act similarly should leave the dock as free men. . . .

For these reasons, I concur in holding that Yes is the proper answer to the certified question and that, there having been no misdirection, the appeal should be dismissed.

Commonwealth of Pennsylvania v. Daniel Lee Graves
Supreme Court of Pennsylvania
461 Pa. 118, 334 A.2d 661, 1975 Pa. LEXIS 729 (1975)

Eagen, Justice (dissenting).

In the past, this Court has never deviated from the position that voluntary intoxication, no matter how gross or long continued, neither exonerates nor excuses a person from his criminal acts. "If it were [so], all crimes would, in a great measure, depend for their criminality on the pleasure of their perpetrators, since they may pass into that state when they will." *Keenan v. Commonwealth, 44 Pa. 55, 58 (1862).* Today, however, the majority has adopted a new position which, in effect, will allow voluntary intoxication to serve as an excuse for criminal responsibility.

The rationale behind our long-standing rule as to voluntary ingestion of intoxicants and drugs is apparent. An individual who places himself in a position to have no control over his actions must be held to intend the consequences. Such a principle is absolutely essential to the protection of life and property. There is, in truth, no injustice in holding a person responsible for his acts committed in a state of voluntary intoxication. It is a duty which everyone owes to his fellowmen and to society, to preserve, so far as it lies in his own power, the inestimable gift of reason. If such reason is perverted or destroyed by fixed disease, though brought on by his own vices, the law holds him not accountable. But if by a voluntary act he temporarily casts off the restraints of reason and conscience, no wrong is done him if he is considered answerable for any injury which he, in that state, may do to others or to society.

While adhering to the above-mentioned rule, this Court has recognized there may be instances where an individual has voluntarily placed himself in a state of intoxication so as to be incapable of conceiving any intent. In those instances, we have permitted evidence of such intoxication to lower the *degree of guilt* within a crime, but only where the Legislature has specifically provided for varying degrees of guilt within a crime. Thus "[i]f the charge is *felonious* homicide, intoxication, which is so great as to render the accused incapable of forming a wilful, deliberate and premeditated design to kill or incapable of judging his acts and their consequences, may properly influence a finding by the trial court that no specific intent to kill existed, and hence to conclude the killing was murder in the second degree." [Emphasis in original.] *Commonwealth v. Tarver, 446 Pa. at 239, 284 A.2d at 762.* As the *Tarver* Court recognized, this exception to the general rule does not change the nature of the crime. Murder still remains murder. Only the degree of the crime has been affected. Because there exist no analogous degrees of robbery (and instantly burglary), the *Tarver* Court refused to extend this exception beyond the homicide area. To hold otherwise, and allow evidence of voluntary intoxication to negate the necessary specific intent required of both robbery and burglary, would permit an individual's voluntary intoxication to serve as a complete exoneration for all criminal acts committed while in that state. This cannot be tolerated.

The majority, while paying lip-service to the fundamental rule that voluntary intoxication is no defense to an individual's criminal acts, nevertheless sanctions such a defense. In ruling that evidence of voluntary intoxication can be offered for the purpose of negating the presence of the required specific intent in both robbery and burglary, the majority has, without good reason, discarded the traditional rule. It matters little that the majority regards such evidence as only bearing upon an element of the crime, the specific intent of the perpetrator, rather than serving as a defense to such crime. The end result is the same and no amount of legal jargon will make it otherwise. If a criminal defendant, charged with either robbery or burglary, is found by the jury, because of voluntary intoxication, not to have had the requisite specific intent, he must be found not guilty. Only a person blind to reality could fail to perceive that there is no practical difference between the admission of evidence to negate an element of the crime and the admission of evidence to constitute a defense. The end result is that human life and property would hardly be considered any longer as being under legal protection. An individual will, henceforth, be permitted to avail himself of his voluntary intoxication to exempt him from any legal responsibility which would attach to him, if sober. As one noted annotator said in speaking of voluntary intoxication as a defense to criminal responsibility, "... all that the crafty criminal would require for a well planned ... [robbery or burglary] would be a revolver in one hand to commit the deed, and a quart of intoxicating liquor in the other...."

Today, all too many murderers, robbers, burglars, rapists and other felons escape the imposition of justice for unsound and unrealistic reasons. The present ruling of this Court widens that avenue of escape.

I emphatically dissent.

Stephen J. Morse, Fear of Danger, Flight From Culpability
4 Psychology, Public Policy, and the Law 250, 253-256 (1998)

Montana's statute, which prohibits defendants from using evidence of voluntary intoxication to rebut an allegation that a crime was committed with a required, subjective mens rea, expresses moral condemnation of behaving badly when drunk. Aristotle, for example, thought that a person who did harm when drunk was undoubtedly culpable. But getting drunk is one wrong, and whatever else an agent does while drunk is another. With the notable exceptions of felony-murder and certain forms of accomplice liability, the common law does not allow the mens rea for one crime to substitute for the mens rea required for a second crime.... The exceptions to this rule already noted are highly controversial precisely because they permit strict liability....

The influential Model Penal Code tries to have it both ways about intoxication. While rejecting strict liability generally, the Code provides that a voluntarily intoxicated defendant may use evidence of such intoxication to negate purpose and knowledge but not to negate recklessness. The Code thus equates the culpability for becoming drunk with the conscious awareness of anything criminal that the agent might do while drunk. This "equation" permits the state to meet its burden of persuasion concerning recklessness without actually proving that the defendant was ever actually aware that getting drunk created a grave risk that the defendant would then commit the specific harm the statute prohibited. As an empirical matter, however, this equation is often preposterous. An agent will not be consciously aware while becoming drunk that there is a substantial and unjustifiable risk that he or she will commit a particular crime when drunk, unless the person has a previous history of becoming unconsciously involved when drunk in the creation of great risk of committing this specific crime. If such a prior history or other circumstances indicating previous conscious awareness exists, then the prosecution is capable of proving and should be required to prove the existence of previous awareness. The prosecution should not be able to rely on what is, in effect, the conclusive presumption that becoming drunk demonstrates the same culpability as the actual conscious awareness of a substantial and unjustifiable risk that the defendant would commit the specific harm.

The Montana statute goes even further toward strict liability than the Model Penal Code, of course, by providing that a defendant cannot use evidence of voluntary intoxication to negate purpose or knowledge. One interpretation of the statute — rejected by Montana's own Supreme Court, but adopted by Justice Ginsburg — is that the intoxication provision simply works to redefine the mental state element for murder to include an objective mens rea: negligence. Ever since the Court's opinion in Patterson v. New York, it has been clear that the states have the federal constitutional authority to effect such a redefinition, but this was not Montana's interpretation of its own law. More important for my analysis, this redefinition undermines the standard view that culpability is hierarchically arrayed depending on the blameworthiness of the various mental states. Our society's dominant morality simply does not accept, and with good reason, that negligent harmdoing is as blameworthy as committing the same harm purposely or with conscious awareness. The latter mental states indicate that the agent is consciously lacking in concern for the interests and well-being of an identifiable victim or class of victims, an attitude toward moral obligations that is more blameworthy than lack of awareness. Few except Oliver Wendell Holmes think that objective and subjective blameworthiness ought to be equated. Characterizing a negligent killer as a murderer does violence to our ordinary notions of culpability and desert.

With these observations in mind, consider Egelhoff's culpability again. First, assume that as the result of voluntary intoxication, James Allen Egelhoff was actually in a mental state that would meet the law's requirement of unconsciousness when he killed Pavola and Christenson. It is not unthinkable morally to condemn drinking oneself purposely or recklessly into a state of unconsciousness, but this behavior is not a crime per se. Criminal law theorists dispute the basis for the exculpatory effect of unconsciousness, but all agree that it does exculpate. Thus, if one believes Egelhoff's claim that he was legally unconscious, or to put it more accurately, if the prosecution were unable to prove beyond a reasonable doubt that he was legally conscious, then Egelhoff is not guilty of purposely or knowingly killing. Moreover, there is no evidence that Egelhoff was consciously aware when he was drinking that he would become homicidal when drunk. Thus, he did not kill recklessly, even if one looks back to his earlier mental states to find culpability. Once again, Egelhoff might be fully responsible for becoming unconscious, but without proof of the mental states usually required, it is a form of strict liability to hold him fully accountable for anything that he did while unconscious. He culpably caused the condition that would negate the prima facie case, but not with purpose, knowledge, or recklessness that he would be exculpated.

Egelhoff is a dangerous agent, and it is undeniable that the State might have great difficulty proving beyond a reasonable doubt on these facts that he was legally conscious and thus guilty of purposely or knowingly killing. If he was legally conscious at the time of the killings, of course, the precision of the executions suggests that the most sensible inference is that he killed purposely or knowingly, even if one believes his claim that he did not remember the homicides. Without the crutch of strict liability, however, the State might be able to convict only for negligent homicide, typically graded as involuntary manslaughter, which carries a substantially shorter term of years than murder. But our fear of Egelhoff and revulsion at his deeds should not be allowed to prove too much. The Constitution's requirement that in criminal cases the state must prove each element of the crime charged beyond a reasonable doubt almost always makes it more difficult for the prosecution to prove its most serious charge. Our society bears this risk because, except in a small number of inevitable cases, we believe that it is unacceptable to convict a legally innocent person. Concern with culpability thus almost always conflicts with concern for public safety.

Egelhoff signals weakened commitment to the importance of culpability. Negligent homicide is not the same as intentional killing, and the culpability of becoming drunk and unconscious is not the same as the culpability for murder. The Supreme Court's acceptance of the equation of these morally distinguishable cases is disquieting....

Other Discussion Materials

Paul H. Robinson & John M. Darley, Study 10: Voluntary Intoxication

Justice, Liability and Blame 114-115 (1995)

[The authors summarize as follows the findings of their empirical study of lay intuitions of justice with regard to offenses during which the offender is voluntarily intoxicated:]

In the subjects' view, the factor that is highly determinative of liability is the person's pre-intoxication culpability as to committing the offense. A person who becomes intoxicated — purposefully, recklessly, or negligently — and at the time of becoming intoxicated is purposeful as to causing death, is treated by the subjects as a murderer and . . . is seen as having a highly culpable state of mind as to the killing at the time he causes the death. A person who is reckless as to whether he will cause a death, as shown by his plans to severely beat another individual, becomes intoxicated either purposefully, recklessly, or negligently, and while intoxicated beats and kills the other, is assigned liability similar to one committing reckless homicide (manslaughter). In the faultless [pre-intoxication culpability] cases, [the killer] receives quite high sentences, although ones that are diminished from the reckless and purposeful cases.

These results suggest that the differences between our respondent's moral intuitions and most codes are occasionally different, but not as different as some other cases that we have considered. Certainly the codes' position is consistent with the subjects' view in the cases where a person culpably intoxicates himself and, before his intoxication, has no purpose as to causing another's death. He is treated as liable for manslaughter by most codes and nearly so by the subjects.

The major code-community difference arises in the consideration of the person's pre-intoxication degree of culpability as to causing death. It makes a great deal of difference to our respondents and none in the codes. For instance, when a person is purposeful as to causing death before he becomes intoxicated, the subjects would impose liability for murder while the codes' voluntary intoxication provision imposes liability only for manslaughter. That is, the codes, counterintuitively, do not discriminate the case of the individual who is purposeful about killing another beforehand, and then gets drunk and kills, from the individual who has no such pre-intoxication purpose. But . . . the codes do not prevent a prosecutor from using as the basis for homicide liability the person's conduct in becoming intoxicated and his culpable state of mind as to causing death at that time. Such a theory of prosecution would produce the murder liability that the subjects impose.

Higher culpability than negligence as to becoming intoxicated generally has some but not a major effect in increasing the liability assigned by our subjects, and is given no such effect in the legal codes. Apparently culpability as to getting intoxicated is only slightly a determinant of degree of liability but serves mainly to provide a fixed minimum requirement for liability. [To match lay intuitions,] codes could be altered to give a slightly higher degree of liability for greater culpability in becoming intoxicated, or such could be taken into account as a factor in sentencing.

Paul H. Robinson, Causing the Conditions of One's Own Defense: A Study in the Limits of Theory in Criminal Law Doctrine
71 Virginia Law Review 1, 14-17, 27, 30-31, 35-36, 51 (1985) (abridged)

Most jurisdictions allow a defense of voluntary intoxication negating an offense element for offenses requiring purpose or knowledge but deny it for other, lesser-included offenses. . . . The most common rationale given for this rule is that the actor's culpability in becoming intoxicated is an adequate basis on which to impute recklessness as to committing the offense.

Denying a failure of proof defense for voluntary intoxication that negates the recklessness required for manslaughter is troubling, however, for a number of reasons . . . . First, the imputation of culpability — recklessness under codes following the Model Penal Code, and greater culpability under many other codes — is generally triggered by a definition of "voluntariness" in becoming intoxicated that requires only negligence. . . .

Second, the imputation of recklessness is objectionable because even if the actor is reckless, or even purposeful, as to *getting intoxicated*, it does not follow that he is reckless as to *causing the death of the pedestrian*. The notion that a person risks all manner of resulting harm when he voluntarily becomes intoxicated is common, but is obviously incorrect.[50]

Finally, the imputation of a culpable state of mind when none truly exists seems particularly strange for the Model Penal Code drafters, who opposed placing the burden of persuasion on the defendant for most defenses. Yet as to intoxication, the drafters permit what is in essence an irrebuttable presumption as to the existence of an element of the offense.

Proposal: Maintaining the Defense for the Offense Conduct But Imposing Liability for Conduct in Causing the Defense Conditions

As has been illustrated above, the current treatment of an actor who is culpable in causing the conditions of his defense is problematic in several respects. An alternative approach suggested here would continue to allow the actor a defense for the immediate conduct constituting the offense, but would separately impose liability on the basis of the actor's earlier conduct in culpably causing the conditions of his or her defense.

This alternative "conduct-in-causing" analysis avoids the problems arising from current law treatment and has several advantages. It avoids the improper assumption that an actor who intends to cause (or risks causing) the conditions under which an offense is committed necessarily intends to commit (or risks committing) the offense. It also properly distinguishes among levels of culpability at the time of causing one's defense in determining the level of liability to be imposed. . . .

This analysis has several advantages. For example, it properly accounts for different levels of culpability as to causing the subsequent offense. Assume an actor knows that he always beats his wife uncontrollably after he returns from drinking with his buddies and that he knows that the severity of the beating is directly proportional to the extent of his drinking. He decides to kill his wife, goes to the bar intending to drink heavily to cause the desired beating, and returns homes and uncontrollably beats his wife to death. The evidence suggests that at the time of the beating, because of his gross intoxication, he was unaware of a risk that his conduct would kill his wife. He may not even have been aware of his conduct. The Model Penal Code would permit his intoxication to negate purpose or knowledge as to the death of his wife; it would impute recklessness

---

50. Hawaii rejects the Model Penal Code provision for just this reason: "[The Model Penal Code] equates the defendant's becoming drunk with the reckless disregard by him of risks created by his subsequent conduct and thereby forecloses the issue." Hawaii Rev. Stat. §702-230 commentary (1976).

and thereby convict him of reckless homicide (manslaughter). It seems clear, however, that a conviction for an intentional killing (murder) would be appropriate here. The proposed conduct-in-causing analysis would hold the actor liable for murder, based on his conduct in causing his intoxication and his then-existing intention to kill his wife.

Not only does the proposed analysis avoid treating such a grand schemer too leniently, but it also protects a less-culpable actor from being treated too harshly. The Model Penal Code would impute recklessness to the drinker who at the time of his imbibing is unaware of any risk that he may kill or even beat his wife, and thus would convict him of reckless homicide. The proposed analysis would avoid such an unwarranted result. The jury would examine his state of mind as to killing his wife at the time he began to drink and would probably conclude that at that time he was at most negligent as to causing his wife's death. He would thus be liable for, at most, negligent homicide. Indeed, a jury might conclude that a *reasonable person* under the same circumstances would have been unaware of a risk of causing his wife's death; thus, the actor might escape liability even for negligent homicide, [although he might be liable for some lesser offense about which he might have been reckless, such as reckless assault].

The theory...suggests reformulation of the doctrine [of] intoxication negating an offense element...:

> Intoxication Negating An Offense Element
>   (1) Evidence of intoxication, voluntary or involuntary, may be admitted into evidence to negate a culpability element of an offense.
>   (2) If an actor's intoxication negates a required culpability element at the time of the offense, such element is nonetheless established if:
>   (a) the actor satisfied such element immediately preceding or during the time that he was becoming intoxicated or at any time thereafter until commission of the offense, and
>   (b) the harm or evil intended, contemplated, or risked is brought about by the actor's subsequent conduct during intoxication....

Thus, the translation from theory to doctrine is relatively easy. Difficulties arise, however, in guaranteeing the feasibility or workability of the resulting doctrine....

SECTION **14**

Complicity

Offense definitions typically require certain conduct. But when offenders act in a group, only one of the group may satisfy the offense conduct requirement. The law takes account of the contribution of the accomplices in assisting the perpetrator by imputing that conduct to all of the accomplices. What exactly are the requirements for complicity liability, and do they justify such imputation?

◆ THE CASE OF CARDINAL BERNARD LAW

Father John Geoghan begins sexually abusing children at his first parish, Blessed Sacrament, in Saugus, a working-class community outside Boston. When victims from the parish later come forward, the archdiocese will quickly settle the lawsuits. In 1967, when more allegations of abuse surface, Geoghan's superiors become suspicious and transfer him to St. Paul's in Hingham, a southern suburb of Boston. At St. Paul's, another family accuses him of abuse. This time the parish priest assures them that "It will never happen again. He will never be a priest again."

Notwithstanding these assurances, the archdiocese again transfers Geoghan to another parish. In his new assignment, St. Andrews, in Boston's Forest Hills community, he supervises altar boys and a Boy Scout troop. In 1974, he lures a boy into the rectory and fondles him. A few days later, Geoghan attempts to do so again, but is interrupted when another priest enters yelling, "Jack, we told you not to do this up here....Are you nuts?" He does not stop, however, and over the next two years molests all seven of Maryette Dussourd's boys. When she learns what is happening, Dussourd contacts a pastor in a nearby parish, Reverend

Figure 54 **Blessed Sacrament Parish in Saugus, Massachusetts**

(Itia Roth)

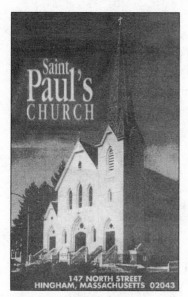

Figure 55 **St. Paul's Church,**
Hingham, Massachusetts

(St. Paul's Church)

Thomas. He confronts Geoghan, who then confesses, saying simply, "Yes, that's all true." Reverend Thomas immediately contacts the archdiocese, where Bishop Daily, an administrator, relieves Geoghan of his duties and sends him home. The archdiocese also prepares a memorandum, marked "personal and confidential," that notes the frequency and extent of Geoghan's abuse. Finally, Reverend Thomas informs Dussourd about Geoghan's confession, but urges her not to publicize the story.

In 1980 and 1981, the archdiocese places Geoghan on sick leave, and he lives at home with his sister in West Roxbury. During this period, he also undergoes church-mandated treatment, consisting of psychotherapy and psychoanalysis with, respectively, Dr. Mullins, his long-time physician and friend, and Dr. Brennan, a psychiatrist. Neither have specialized training in the treatment of sex offenders. The archdiocese eventually permits Geoghan to return to work based on the doctors' conclusion that "he [is] able to resume priestly duties."

In February 1982, the archdiocese assigns Geoghan to St. Brendan's in Dorchester, a diverse working-class neighborhood, without informing the parish priest, Father Lane, about his history. Geoghan again works with children, including supervising first communicants.

On August 16, 1982, Margaret Gallant, the Dussourd children's aunt, writes Cardinal Medeiros, asking why the archdiocese fails to deal with Geoghan. Specifically, she writes, "As you know, our family had a conference with Bishop Daly [sic] over two weeks ago. Since that priest is still in his parish, it appears that no action has been taken." Cardinal Medeiros quickly replies, in a letter dated August 20, thanking Gallant for her "candid expression of opinion concerning the priest...who has caused hardship to your family and most especially to several of the boys." He reassures her that the archdiocese is working to find the "most Christian way to deal with the problem with him and at the same time remove any source of scandal for the sake of the faithful."

Figure 56 **Chapel at Pontifical College**
Josephinum, June 2002

(Craig Holman, Columbus Dispatch)

That same month, Cardinal Medeiros informs Geoghan that funds have been provided to enable him to study in Rome. The Cardinal writes, "It is my hope that the three months will provide [the] renewal of mind, body and spirit that will enable you to return to parish work refreshed and strengthened in the Lord." Upon returning, Geoghan claims that he no longer is attracted to children and rejoins St. Brendan.

Bernard Francis Law follows his graduation from St. Joseph's Seminary in St. Benedict, Louisiana, with six years of rigorous study at Pontifical College Josephinum in Worthington, Ohio. Ordained a priest in 1961, he is initially assigned to St. Paul's Parish in Vicksburg, Mississippi. There he participates in the Civil Rights movement, helps to establish the state's first Human Rights Council, and supports adult literacy programs. Church leaders consider him bright and capable, with a strong future ahead. (Accusations of sexual abuse by a priest, and close friend of Law, have since arisen from that time in Mississippi, and Law has recently admitted in a deposition that he knew of the accusations in 1973. He has said he could not recall what he did, only that he left the diocese soon after that.)

In January 1984, Law fulfills those expectations when he is selected Boston's new archbishop. Quickly thereafter, he announces that his priorities are to crusade against abortion, contraception, divorce, and homosexuality. Meanwhile, he delegates to others the day-to-day operations of the diocese. He retains primary responsibility over all personal transfers and maintains ultimate possession of the diocese's confidential personnel files.

On September 6, 1984, Margaret Gallant again writes to the archdiocese, this time to inform the newly installed Archbishop Law about Geoghan's history of molestation:

> There is a priest at St. Brendan's in Dorchester who has been known in the past to molest boys. Cardinal [Medeiros] had sent father for treatment, and after returning to parish duties he maintained a low profile for quite a while. Lately, however, he has been seen in the company of many boys, to the extent of dropping them off at their homes as late as 9:30 p.m.

Law marks the envelope of Gallant's letter "Urgent, please follow through," and sends it to Bishop Daily. On September 18, Law terminates Geoghan's

Figure 57 **John Geoghan, 2002**
(AP)

assignment at St. Brendan's, in the process informing him that he is "in between assignments."

On September 21, Gallant receives a reply from Law thanking her for her "letter of September 6, 1984 concerning the priest at St. Brendan's Dorchester. . . . The matter of your concern is being investigated and appropriate pastoral decisions will be made for both the priest and God's people."

On October 31, however, Law assigns Geoghan to St. Julia's parish in Weston, a wealthy Boston suburb. He informs its parish priest, Monsigner Rossiter, of Geoghan's history. They inform no one else in the parish, however. Geoghan again supervises the altar boys, along with two other youth groups. Law later acknowledges that he knew of Geoghan's alleged abuse when he reassigned him.

In 1985, Reverend Thomas Doyle, a canon lawyer, and Michael Peterson, a psychiatrist at St. Luke's, which is a treatment facility in Maryland for abusive priests, publish a controversial study on the propensity of sexual abuse by clergy members. They report that the rate of repeat offenders is high among pedophiles, and controlled studies reveal that "traditional outpatient psychiatric or psychological treatment DOES NOT WORK" with this cohort of offenders. In addition, they observe that pedophilia is "a lifelong disease with NO HOPE AT THIS TIME FOR A CURE." Law initially supports the study's conclusions, but withdraws his support by the time the National Conference of Catholic Bishops convenes. The Conference, according to its general counsel, decides not to consider the study because it merely reiterates information that the bishops have already gathered.

Meanwhile, under Law's direction, the Boston Archdiocese begins paying out settlements on claims against more than seventy priests. Victims maintain their anonymity but are usually required to sign a confidentiality agreement as a condition of receiving their settlement. (Law was recently asked in a deposition for a pending trial why he did not institute policies to deal with the abuse when he became aware of complaints against the priests. "I'm not certain," Cardinal Law says, "that the judgment at that time would have been that we were facing a major, overwhelming problem.")

In February 1986, while Geoghan is still working at St. Julia's, the boyfriend of a ten-year old boy's mother contacts the Department of Social Services and Boston Police alleging Geoghan sexually abused the boy. While at the Boys and Girls Club swimming pool, Geoghan reached inside the boy's trunks and grabbed his buttocks. When the victim fails to testify, however, the authorities drop the

Figure 58 **Law speaking to a crowd in Boston after his elevation to Cardinal**

(Bettmann/Corbis)

matter entirely, lacking any additional evidence. Shortly thereafter, Geoghan abuses twelve-year old Patrick McSorley. While driving McSorley home, Geoghan puts his hands on the boy's genitals and starts masturbating McSorley while at the same time masturbating himself. (McSorley does not tell his parents about the abuse until 1999, when along with eighty-five other plaintiffs, he brings a civil suit against Geoghan.)

In 1989, Geoghan tells Bishop Banks, a deputy of Cardinal Law, that he had been accused of fondling a boy, but denies the allegations and says the matter was dropped because of discrepancies in the victim's story. Ten years later, the victim contacts the Suffolk County District Attorney, who investigates and brings criminal charges for two counts of rape against Geoghan on December 11, 1999. In March 2002, a Superior Court judge dismisses the charges, ruling that the statute of limitations has run.

Figure 59 **Patrick McSorley, December 2002**
(Reuters NewsMedia Inc./Corbis)

Later in 1989, Cardinal Law pulls Geoghan from service and sends him to St. Luke's, which has a program for priests who are sex offenders. After three weeks of observation, the psychiatrists classify him as a "high risk homosexual pedophile." Dr. Brennan, Geoghan's psychiatrist, recommends to Bishop Banks that the archdiocese clip his wings before there is an explosion. Banks informs Geoghan that he may not return to his parish and sends him to Hartford's Institute for Living, which treats priests who are sex offenders. After three months, doctors report that despite being "a high-risk-taker," he is an "atypical pedophile in *remission*."

So, on November 13, 1989, Law allows Geoghan to resume his duties as vicar at St. Julia's. He writes, "It is most heartening to know that things have gone well for you and that you are ready to resume your efforts with a renewed zeal and enthusiasm. I am confident that you will again render fine priestly service to the people of God in Saint Julia Parish." Banks obtains written confirmation from the Institute for Living that it was its recommendation that Geoghan was fit to return to parish work. Within a few weeks of his return, however, Geoghan is again abusing boys. (The lawsuits against Geoghan later include claims that he abused at least thirty boys during his time at St. Julia's.)

In 1992, the archdiocese passes over Geoghan in selecting a new pastor for St. Julia's. An administrator informs Geoghan, however, that he should not take this "in any negative way with reference to [him]self," and recommends contacting the archdiocese about any positions that interest him.

In January 1993, after new allegations surface, Law removes Geoghan from parish service and assigns him to the Office of Senior Priests at Regina Cleri. He also proposes several new policies, including a comprehensive review of old records, an offer to pay for victim counseling, and the appointment of a review board to consider allegations of abuse. Law makes it clear, however, that he will allow some priests treated for sexual disorders to return to parish work, and that the archdiocese's procedures will be the primary means of investigating allegations of abuse. He says that priests and other church officials will report allegations in accordance with state law, but at the time state law does not require them to do so, unlike other professionals such as teachers and physicians.

In May, Law and his staff meet with experts in the field of child sexual abuse to better understand how to treat the problem they face. The experts state forcefully that the archdiocese is mishandling the problem twofold: by permitting homosexual pedophiles, who have a high rate of repeat behavior, easy access to young boys, and by not reporting the allegations to authorities. However, the archdiocese politely declines the group's offer to help develop a policy to deal with the problem, and there is no subsequent follow-up.

By 1994, civil authorities are again investigating Geoghan. Law puts him on administrative leave, effective December 30, 1994, writing, "I realize this is a difficult time for you and for those close to you. If I can be of help to you in some way, please contact me. Be assured you are remembered in my prayers."

In 1995, Geoghan caresses the genitals of a ten-year old Weymouth boy while driving. Some months earlier, Geoghan had caressed the same boy's genitals while helping him into his altar boy's robe — in preparation for the christening of the boy's younger sister. Later, Geoghan is charged with indecent assault and battery of a child. This is the third set of criminal charges he faces.

On August 4, 1996, Law places Geoghan on sick leave. Two months later, Geoghan asks to retire. Law grants him senior priest retirement status on December 12, 1996, writing him, "Yours has been an effective life of ministry, sadly impaired by illness. On

Figure 60 **Cardinal Law, 2002**
(AP)

behalf of those you have served well, and in my own name, I would like to thank you.... God bless you, Jack."

1. Relying only on your own intuitions of justice, what liability and punishment, if any, does Cardinal Law deserve?

N	0	1	2	3	4	5	6	7	8	9	10	11
☐	☐	☐	☐	☐	☐	☐	☐	☐	☐	☐	☐	☐
no liability	liability but no punishment	1 day	2 wks	2 mo	6 mo	1 yr	3 yrs	7 yrs	15 yrs	30 yrs	life imprison- ment	death

2. What liability, if any, under the then-existing statutes?
3. What liability, if any, under the Model Penal Code?

■ THE LAW

Massachusetts General Laws Annotated
(1988)

Crimes and Punishments

Chapter 265. Crimes Against the Person

Section 13A. Assault or Assault and Battery; Punishment

Whoever commits an assault or an assault and battery upon another shall be punished by imprisonment for not more than two and one half years in a house of correction or by fine of not more than five hundred dollars....

Section 13B. Indecent Assault and Battery on Child Under Fourteen; Penalties; Subsequent Offenses; Eligibility for Parole, etc.

Whoever commits an indecent assault and battery on a child under the age of fourteen shall be punished by imprisonment in the state prison for not more than ten years, or by imprisonment in a jail or house of correction for not more than two and one-half years; and whoever commits a second or subsequent such offense shall be punished by imprisonment in the state prison for life or any term of years.

No person serving a sentence for a second or subsequent such offense shall be eligible for furlough, temporary release, or education, training or employment programs established outside a correctional facility until such person shall have served two-thirds of such minimum sentence or if such person has two or more sentences to be served otherwise than concurrently, two-thirds of the aggregate of the minimum terms of such several sentences.

In a prosecution under this section, a child under the age of fourteen years shall be deemed incapable of consenting to any conduct of the defendant for which said defendant is being prosecuted.

Section 13H. Indecent Assault and Battery on Child of Fourteen; Penalties

Whoever commits an indecent assault and battery on a person who has attained age fourteen shall be punished by imprisonment in the state prison for not more than five years, or by imprisonment for not more than two and one-half years in a jail or house of correction.

Section 22. Rape, Generally; Penalties; Eligibility for Parole, etc.

(a) Whoever has sexual intercourse or unnatural sexual intercourse with a person, and compels such person to submit by force and against his will, or compels such person to submit by threat of bodily injury and if either such sexual intercourse or unnatural sexual intercourse results in or is committed with acts resulting in serious bodily injury, or is committed by a joint enterprise, or is committed during the commission or attempted commission of an offense defined in section fifteen A, fifteen B, seventeen, nineteen or twenty-six of this chapter, section fourteen, fifteen, sixteen, seventeen or eighteen of chapter two hundred and sixty-six or section ten of chapter two hundred and sixty-nine shall be punished by imprisonment in the state prison for life or for any term of years.

No person serving a sentence for a second or subsequent such offense shall be eligible for furlough, temporary release, or education, training or employment programs established outside a correctional facility until such person shall have served two-thirds of such minimum sentence or if such person has two or more sentences to be served otherwise than concurrently, two-thirds of the aggregate of the minimum terms of such several sentences.

(b) Whoever has sexual intercourse or unnatural sexual intercourse with a person and compels such person to submit by force and against his will, or compels such person to submit by threat of bodily injury, shall be punished by imprisonment in the state prison for not more than twenty years; and whoever commits a second or subsequent such offense shall be punished by imprisonment in the state prison for life or for any term of years.

No person serving a sentence for a second or subsequent such offense shall be eligible for furlough, temporary release, or education, training or employment programs established outside a correctional facility until such person shall have served two-thirds of such minimum sentence or if such person has two or more sentences to be served otherwise than concurrently, two-thirds of the aggregate of the minimum terms of such several sentences.

For the purposes of prosecution, the offense described in subsection (b) shall be a lesser included offense to that described in subsection (a).

Section 22A. Rape of Child; Use of Force

Whoever has sexual intercourse or unnatural sexual intercourse with a child under sixteen, and compels said child to submit by force and against his will or compels said child to submit by threat of bodily injury, shall be punished by imprisonment in the state prison for life or for any term of years; and whoever over the age of eighteen commits a second or subsequent such offense shall be sentenced to the state prison for life or for any term of years, but not less than five years.

Section 23. Rape and Abuse of Child

Whoever unlawfully has sexual intercourse or unnatural sexual intercourse, and abuses a child under sixteen years of age shall, for the first offense, be punished by imprisonment in the state prison for life or for any term of years, or, except as otherwise provided, for any term in a jail or house of correction, and for the second or subsequent offense by imprisonment in the state prison for life or for any term of years, but not less than five years.

Section 24. Assault with Intent to Commit Rape; Penalties; Eligibility for Parole, etc.

Whoever assaults a person with intent to commit a rape shall be punished by imprisonment in the state prison for not more than twenty years or by imprisonment in a jail or house of correction for not more than two and one-half years; and whoever commits a second or subsequent such offense shall be punished by imprisonment in the state prison for life or for any term of years.

No person serving for a second or subsequent such offense shall be eligible for furlough, temporary release, or education, training or employment programs established outside a correctional facility until such person shall have served two-thirds of such minimum sentence or if such person has two or more sentences to be served otherwise than concurrently, two-thirds of the aggregate of the minimum terms of such several sentences.

Section 24B. Assault of Child; Intent to Commit Rape; Punishment

Whoever assaults a child under sixteen with intent to commit a rape, as defined in section thirty-nine of chapter two hundred and seventy-seven, shall be punished by imprisonment in the state prison for life or for any term of years; and whoever over the age of eighteen commits a subsequent such offense shall be punished by imprisonment in the state prison for life or for any term of years but not less than five years.

Chapter 274. Felonies, Accessories and Attempts to Commit Crimes

Section 2. Aiders; Accessories Before Fact; Punishment

Whoever aids in the commission of a felony, or is accessory thereto before the fact by counseling, hiring or otherwise procuring such felony to be committed, shall be punished in the manner provided for the punishment of the principal felon.

Section 3. Prosecution; Time; Joinder with Felon; Felon's Conviction or Amenability to Justice; . . .

Whoever counsels, hires or otherwise procures a felon to be committed may be indicted and convicted as an accessory before the fact, either with the principal felon or after his conviction; or may be indicted and convicted of the substantive felony, whether the principal felon has or has not been convicted, or is or is not amenable to justice; and in the last mentioned case may be punished in the same manner as if convicted of being an accessory before the fact. . . .

Section 4. Accessories After Fact; Punishment; Relationship As Defense; Cross Examination; Impeachment

Whoever, after the commission of a felony, harbors, conceals, maintains or assists the principal felon or accessory before the fact, or gives such offender any other aid, knowing that he has committed a felony or has been accessory thereto before the fact, with intent that he shall avoid or escape detention, arrest, trial or punishment, shall be an accessory after the fact, and, except as otherwise provided, be punished by imprisonment in the state prison for not more than seven years or in jail for not more than two and one half years or by fine of not more than one thousand dollars. The fact that the defendant is the husband or wife, or by consanguinity, affinity, or adoption, the parent or grandparent, child or grandchild, brother or sister of the offender, shall be a defense to a prosecution under this section. . . .

Chapter 277. Indictments and Proceedings Before Trial

Section 39. Construction of Words Used in Indictment

The words used in an indictment may, except as otherwise provided in this section, be construed according to their usual acceptation in common language; but if certain words and phrases are defined by law, they shall be used according to their legal meaning

The following words, when used in an indictment, shall be sufficient to convey the meaning herein attached to them: . . .

Rape. — Sexual intercourse or unnatural sexual intercourse by a person with another person who is compelled to submit by force and against his will or by threat of bodily injury, or sexual intercourse or unnatural sexual intercourse with a child under sixteen years of age. . . .

Commonwealth v. Morrow

363 Mass. 601, 296 N.E.2d 468 (1973)

Defendant was held liable for a rape of a woman committed by an accomplice during the armed robbery of two men at the house. The court held that being an accessory before the fact involves counseling, hiring, or otherwise procuring, which means something more than mere acquiescence, but does not require physical participation, if the defendant has associated himself with the criminal venture and in any significant way participated in it.

Commonwealth v. Stout

356 Mass. 237, 249 N.E.2d 12 (1969)

Defendant was held liable as an accessory before the fact for supplying guns employed in an attempted bank robbery. The court held that, in order for a person to be an accessory before the fact, the defendant must "in some way associate himself with the venture, that he participate in it as in something that he wishes to bring about, that he seek by his actions to make it succeed." (quoting U.S. v. Peoni, 100 F.2d 401 (2d Cir.)) Conviction affirmed.

Model Penal Code
(Official Draft 1962)

Section 2.06. Liability for Conduct of Another; Complicity

(1) A person is guilty of an offense if it is committed by his own conduct or by the conduct of another person for which he is legally accountable, or both.

(2) A person is legally accountable for the conduct of another person when:

(a) acting with the kind of culpability that is sufficient for the commission of the offense, he causes an innocent or irresponsible person to engage in such conduct; or

(b) he is made accountable for the conduct of such other person by the Code or by the law defining the offense; or

(c) he is an accomplice of such other person in the commission of the offense.

(3) A person is an accomplice of another person in the commission of an offense if:

(a) with the purpose of promoting or facilitating the commission of the offense, he

(i) solicits such other person to commit it; or

(ii) aids or agrees or attempts to aid such other person in planning or committing it; or

(iii) having a legal duty to prevent the commission of the offense, fails to make proper effort so to do; or

(b) his conduct is expressly declared by law to establish his complicity.

(4) When causing a particular result is an element of an offense, an accomplice in the conduct causing such result is an accomplice in the commission of that

offense, if he acts with the kind of culpability, if any, with respect to that result that is sufficient for the commission of the offense.

(5) A person who is legally incapable of committing a particular offense himself may be guilty thereof if it is committed by the conduct of another person for which he is legally accountable, unless such liability is inconsistent with the purpose of the provision establishing his incapacity.

(6) Unless otherwise provided by the Code or by the law defining the offense, a person is not an accomplice in an offense committed by another person if:

    (a) he is a victim of that offense; or

    (b) the offense is so defined that his conduct is inevitably incident to its commission; or

    (c) he terminates his complicity prior to the commission of the offense and

        (i) wholly deprives it of effectiveness in the commission of the offense; or

        (ii) gives timely warning to the law enforcement authorities or otherwise makes proper effort to prevent the commission of the offense.

(7) An accomplice may be convicted on proof of the commission of the offense and of his complicity therein, though the person claimed to have committed the offense has not been prosecuted or convicted or has been convicted of a different offense or degree of offense or has an immunity to prosecution or conviction or has been acquitted.

● OVERVIEW OF COMPLICITY

Complicity as Theory for Imputing Conduct Complicity is not an offense in itself, as are conspiracy and solicitation, for example. It is rather a theory of liability by which an accomplice is held liable for an offense committed by the perpetrator. An offense definition typically requires that the actor have performed certain conduct. Yet a person may be held liable for the offense, although the person has not performed the required conduct, if he is legally accountable for the perpetrator's conduct. The complicity doctrine thus *imputes* the perpetrator's conduct to the accomplices if the special requirements for complicity are satisfied. Complicity requires proof of both special objective and culpability requirements.

OBJECTIVE ELEMENTS

At Common Law At common law, complicity required that the accomplice *assist* the perpetrator in committing the offense. The assistance need not be necessary for successful commission of the offense, nor need it be substantial.

It is quite enough if the aid merely rendered it easier for the principal actor to accomplish the end intended by him and the aider and abettor, though in all human probability the end would have been attained without it.[1]

Indeed, the accomplice need not assist in a physical sense; encouragement is recognized as a form of assistance.

[I]t nerves [the principal actor] to the deed, and helps him execute it through a consciousness — a purely mental condition — that another is standing by in a position to help him.

Objective Elements Under Modern Codes   The Model Penal Code, in section 2.06(3)(a)(ii), goes beyond the common law and extends complicity liability to those instances in which the actor simply "agrees or attempts to aid" the principal. Actual assistance, even in the form of psychological assistance through encouragement, is not required. The drafters intend that what constitutes an adequate "attempt to aid" will be determined by reference to the definition of the general inchoate offense of attempt in Model Penal Code section 5.01. That is, the accomplice must take a "substantial step" toward providing assistance. Similarly, whether an actor "agrees to aid" another is determined by the general inchoate offense of conspiracy, defined in Code section 5.03 as a unilateral agreement requirement.

Derivative vs. Personal Liability   The difference in objective require-ments — actual assistance versus an attempt or agreement to assist — reflects different conceptualizations of complicity at common law and in modern codes. Common law viewed complicity as liability derivative from that of the principal; the principal's liability is extended to those who assist. The requirement of actual assistance, no matter how slight, served to tie the accomplice to the perpetrator and his deed. Under modern codes, on the other hand, complicity liability is viewed as personal to the accomplice. Liability is based on *the actor's* conduct and culpable state of mind, rather than that of the perpetrator. It follows from this view that a perpetrator's knowledge of, or actual assistance from, an accomplice is not determinative. The central question is whether the accomplice intended to assist and whether she externalized a willingness to act on that intention. (The derivative theory of the common law also supports a defense for the actor when the principal is unconvictable. Indeed, at early common law the accomplice was subject to prosecution only *after* the perpetrator's liability was established. Modern codes explicitly reject an unconvictable perpetrator defense.) The accom-plice's liability depends on *the accomplice's* conduct and culpable state of mind, regardless of the perpetrator's liability.[2]

Objectivist vs. Subjectivist Views of Criminality   The difference between derivative and personal views of complicity is one manifestation of the larger differ-ence in perspective between the common law and modern codes, a difference described previously as that between an objectivist and a subjectivist view of crimin-ality. The common law's objectivist view requires actual assistance because objective

---

1. State ex rel. Martin, Atty. v. Tally, Judge, 102 Ala. 25, 68-72, 15 So. 722, 738-739 (1894) (defendant guilty of complicity for sending telegram ordering receiving operator not to deliver message previously sent warning victim of ambush, although such warning was not possible).

2. See Model Penal Code §2.06(7).

harm or evil was viewed as essential to substantive criminality, and actual assistance causally tied the offender to the harm or evil of the offense. In contrast, the Model Penal Code's shift to a subjectivist view of criminality derives from its view that an actor's culpable state of mind, manifested in conduct, is itself a sufficient basis for criminality, even absent a causal connection with the harm of evil of an offense.

Objective Elements to Be Satisfied by Perpetrator In addition to proof of assistance or an attempt or agreement to assist, there is one final objective requirement of complicity: the perpetrator's commission of the offense. That is, in order for *the accomplice* to be held liable for an offense, *the perpetrator* must commit the offense. The Model Penal Code follows the common law on this point. Section 2.06(7) explicitly provides that accomplice liability requires "proof of the commission of the offense." Consistent with this, the Code states that complicity in a failed attempt is to be punished only as an attempt.[1]

CULPABILITY REQUIREMENTS

Purpose vs. Knowing It is common for courts to describe complicity as necessarily being intentional. One cannot, it is claimed, accidentally be an accomplice. This raises several issues. The first concerns whether the common law's "intention" requirement should be taken to mean, in modern code terms, "purposeful" or "knowing." In *United States v. Peoni*, Judge Learned Hand concludes that the accomplice must "in some sort associate himself with the venture, ... participate in it as in something that he wishes to bring about, ... seek by his action to make it succeed." He must have a "purposive attitude towards it."[2] In *Backun v. United States*, in contrast, Judge Parker concludes that knowing assistance is adequate for complicity liability. "[G]uilt as an accessory depends, not on ... 'having a stake' in the outcome of crime ... but on aiding and assisting the perpetrators.... [The actor] may not ignore" the aims of the perpetrator.[3] The Model Penal Code drafters initially proposed a knowing standard,[4] but in the final draft a purposeful requirement was adopted.[5] The appropriate culpability requirement is the subject of the Discussion Materials later in this Section.

Effect of Degree of Assistance and Offense Seriousness The preference for requiring only knowing assistance, as reflected by Judge Parker's opinion in *Backun* and in the Model Penal Code's Tentative Draft formulation (the commentary for which is excerpted in the Discussion Materials below), stems from a belief that an actor ought not be free to assist what he knows to be a criminal offense. The belief is particularly strong where the offense is serious and the assistance is substantial or necessary to its commission. Volunteering the where-

---

1. See Model Penal Code §5.01(3).

2. 100 F.2d 401, 402 (2d Cir. 1938) (knowledge purchaser of counterfeit bills would sell to another insufficient to charge original seller as accessory to third-party possession).

3. 112 F.2d 635, 637 (4th Cir. 1940) (seller of goods known to be stolen held liable for buyer transporting stolen property across state lines).

4. Model Penal Code §2.04(3)(b) (Tentative Draft No. 1, 1953) (subsequently revised and renumbered §2.06(3)(b)).

5. Model Penal Code §2.06(3)(a). Some jurisdictions continue to provide a form of complicity liability upon knowledge. See, e.g., New York Penal Law §115.00 ("A person is guilty of criminal facilitation ... when believing it probable that he is rendring aid to a person who intends to commit a crime, he engages in conduct which provides such person with means or opportunity for the commission thereof and which in fact aids such person to commit a felony....")

abouts of an intended victim for a fee, *knowing* that the questioner intends murder, would seem to many people to be adequate for complicity liability. But permitting accomplice liability on knowing assistance seems problematic in other cases, as reflected in Judge Hand's opinion in *Peoni*. While a knowing requirement would appropriately impose liability for identifying the person another is seeking in order to murder, such a requirement also would impose liability on persons who provide minor, nonessential assistance toward less serious offenses, such as selling cigarette papers to customers knowing they will use them to smoke marijuana. Many would balk at holding the tobacconist as an accomplice to each of the multitude of illegal uses of marijuana that follow the sale, even if the seller knows of the intended illegal use. Consistent with this concern for the degree of assistance, statutes that adopt a knowing standard frequently increase the degree of assistance required to that of "substantial facilitation" or something similar.[1] Other "knowing" complicity statutes impose reduced liability.[2]

Recklessly an Accomplice vs. Complicity to Recklessness   The purpose-versus-knowing issue is complicated by the common belief, held at common law and, unfortunately, in many modern cases, that there exists a single culpability requirement for complicity. This notion is typical of the "offense analysis" view prevalent at common law, discussed in Section 4. In this context, offense analysis confuses an accomplice's culpability as to assisting the perpetrator's conduct with the accomplice's culpability as to the elements of the object offense. One might intentionally assist an actor in the actor's conduct, yet have no culpability as to such conduct assisting a criminal objective. Or one might be only negligent or reckless as to assisting an actor's conduct (as in accidentally leaving car keys out where the perpetrator might take them, thereby allowing him to commit the offense), yet actually hope that the offense be committed. Even modern codes do not distinguish the two issues as clearly as they might, and, as a result, they often give no clear answer on whether the "purpose" required for complicity liability requires that it be the accomplice's purpose to assist the perpetrator's conduct, the accomplice's purpose to advance commission of the offense, or the accomplice's purpose to do both. (For a more in-depth discussion of this issue, see the Robinson & Darley excerpt in the Discussion Materials at the end of the Section.)

LIABILITY FOR CAUSING CRIME BY INNOCENT

Under complicity liability, an actor is held accountable for the conduct of another person whom the actor assists to commit an offense. Both parties typically are guilty of the offense, one as the perpetrator, the other as an accomplice. Where the other actor is not a confederate but is instead an innocent instrumentality, the person causing the innocent person to act may be held accountable for the

---

1. E.g., Model Penal Code §2.04(3)(b) (Tentative Draft No. 1, 1953) (establishes accomplice liability when "acting with knowldege that such other person was committing or had the purpose of committing the crime, he knowingly, substantially facilitates its commission"); Mich. S.B. 82 §415; Wash. Rev. Code Ann. §9A.08.020; U.S. S.1437, 95th Cong., 2d Sess. §401(a)(1) (Jan. 1978); Cal. S.B. 27 §2302; D.C. Code Ann. §22-110(a)(1) (1978).

2. New York Penal Law §115.00 (creates offense of criminal facilitation that adopts knowing standard but imposes liability for lesser offense). For similar provisions, see Ariz. Rev. Stat. Ann. §13-604; Ky. Rev. Stat. Ann. §§506.080 to 506.100; N.D. Cent. Code §12.1-06-02.

conduct of the innocent or irresponsible person through a doctrine analogous to, but different from, complicity. As the Model Penal Code states it,

> A person is legally accountable for the conduct of another person when, acting with the kind of culpability that is sufficient for the commission of the offense, he causes an innocent or irresponsible person to engage in such conduct.[1]

Need for Alternative Theory of Liability   Liability for "causing crime by an innocent" was provided at common law. Recognition of such a doctrine was made a practical necessity by the common law's recognition of an unconvictable perpetrator defense, which bars liability for an accomplice when the perpetrator is unconvictable. Absent a special rule, recognition of an unconvictable perpetrator defense made it impossible to convict an actor who caused an innocent or irresponsible person to commit an offense. Also influential in creating this alternative theory of liability was the difference in fact patterns between complicity and innocent-perpetrator cases. Rather than assisting the perpetrator, as an accomplice does, the third party generally is the moving force; the innocent or irresponsible actor is typically more an "instrument" of the actor than a "perpetrator." (The Advanced Issues Section in the Appendix examines the specific requirements for causing crime by an innocent and how they differ from those for complicity.)

▲ PROBLEM
Bib Tries to Help

Having failed to pass several grades in grammar school, Muscle and Bib are 21-year old seniors at K Street High School. Muscle is interested in dating a young freshman, Susan Rigg, but Susan's older brother, John, with whom she has lived since her parents died, has made it clear that he does not want Muscle associating with Susan. Susan nonetheless has encouraged Muscle's interest, and this has resulted in several confrontations between the two men. The latest has left Muscle steaming and only more determined than ever to pursue Susan.

Muscle arranges with Susan for a rendezvous at Susan and John's house while John is away at his night job, and asks Bib to come along as a lookout. "Goin' over there's not a good idea," Bib warns. "She's probably jail bait." "Let me worry about her age. You just keep your eyes open." "Yeh, and what if big brother shows up?" "He won't give me any trouble. I'll bring my. 45." Bib smiles, "You're a buster."

Muscle and Bib drive to Susan and John's house, where they find Susan waiting on the stoop. Muscle disappears upstairs with Susan. Bib settles in the car for a long wait but soon slips into a snooze. A rattle at the front door wakes him. John Rigg is back. Bib hits the horn to alert Muscle but it won't sound with the ignition off. As he heads for the house, he hears shouts and one shot from inside.

---

1. Model Penal Code §2.06(2)(a).

He finds John in a pool of blood just inside the front doorway. Muscle and Bib flee but are arrested within hours. Muscle is charged and convicted of the murder of John Rigg, who dies before police arrive, and of the statutory rape of Susan Rigg, who is 14 years old. Bib is charged as an accomplice to both offenses. Is Bib liable?

● DISCUSSION MATERIALS

Should Criminal Liability Be Imposed for Facilitating Conduct That One Knows Is a Crime, Even If Facilitating the Crime Is Not One's Purpose?

The first Model Penal Code Commentary excerpt comes from a proposed draft, subsequently rejected by the ALI, that attempts to justify imposing complicity liability on only "knowingly" assisting an offense (but also requires substantial facilitation of the crime). The second Commentary excerpt is taken from the final official Commentary and offers the Institute's reasons for adopting instead the more demanding "purposeful" assistance requirement. Robinson & Darley's study concludes that lay intuitions are more in line with the original Code proposal and would even assign liability for "reckless" assistance, although they also would provide an increasing liability discount as the culpability level diminishes. Finally, the Wayne LaFave & Austin Scott excerpt offers a proposal for alternative formulations of the complicity rule that would adjust for the various challenges it faces.

Model Penal Code Section 2.04 Tentative Draft No. 1 Commentary
11-12, 27-32 (1953)

§2.04 Liability based on behavior; Liability for behavior of another; Complicity

(1)...

(3) A person is an accomplice of promoting or facilitating the commission of the crime if:

    (a) with the purpose of promoting or facilitating the commission of the crime, he

        (1) commanded, requested, encouraged or provoked such other person to commit it; or

        (2) aided, agreed to aid or attempted to aid such other person in planning or committing it; or

        (3) having a legal duty to prevent the crime, failed to make proper effort so to do; or

    (b) acting with knowledge that such other person was committing or had the purpose of committing the crime, he knowingly, substantially facilitated its commission; or

[Alternate: (b) acting with knowledge that such other person was committing or had the purpose of committing the crime, he knowingly provided means or opportunity for the commission of the crime, substantially facilitating its commission; or]

(c) his behavior is expressly declared by law to establish his complicity. . . .

The draft does not confine [accomplice liability] to the case where there is a true purpose to promote or to facilitate commission of the crime. It also reaches those who, with knowledge that another is committing or has the purpose of committing an offense, knowingly facilitate its commission. In this event, however, it requires that the actor knowingly facilitate substantially. This is a median position on a much debated issue that requires explanation.

This issue is whether knowingly facilitating the commission of a crime ought to be sufficient for complicity, absent a true purpose to advance the criminal end. The problem, to be sure, is narrow in its focus: often, if not usually, aid rendered with guilty knowledge implies purpose since it has no other motivation. But there are many and important cases where this is the central question in determining liability. A lessor rents with knowledge that the premises will be used to establish a bordello. A vendor sells with knowledge that the subject of the sale will be used in commission of a crime. A doctor counsels against an abortion but, at the patient's insistence, refers her to a competent abortionist. A utility provides telephone or telegraph service, knowing it is used for book-making. An employee puts through a shipment in the course of his employment though he knows the shipment is illegal. A farm boy clears the ground for setting up a still, knowing that the venture is illicit. Such cases can be multiplied indefinitely; they have given the courts much difficulty when they have been brought, whether as prosecutions for conspiracy or for the substantive offense involved.

The problem has had most attention in the federal courts where there is division of opinion as to the criterion . . . [author reviews Learned Hand's opinion in *Peoni*, discussed in the Overview materials, which argues for a purposeful requirement in complicity].

The Supreme Court has quoted the *Peoni* formulation with approval and it has had some influence on other Circuits. Strong disagreement has, however, been expressed. Judge Parker, for example, has declared that guilt "as an accessory depends, not on 'having a stake' in the outcome of the crime . . . but on aiding and assisting the perpetrators . . . . The seller may not ignore the purpose for which the purchase is made if he is advised of that purpose, or wash his hands of the aid that he has given the perpetrator of a felony by the plea that he has merely made a sale of merchandise. One who sells a gun to another knowing that he is buying it to commit a murder, would hardly escape conviction as an accessory to the murder by showing that he received full price for the gun . . . ." Even the Second Circuit has been less than rigorous in application of the doctrine of *Peoni*, finding such factors as the contraband quality of the article supplied and failure to report the sale, as legally required, sufficient to meet its demands. Such factors seem, however, to have smaller bearing on the actor's purpose, which *Peoni* treats as crucial, than they have on the effects of his behavior, the extent to which it actually does facilitate commission of the crime.

The draft, it is submitted, should not embrace the *Peoni* limitation. Conduct which knowingly facilitates the commission of crimes is by hypothesis a proper object of preventive effort by the penal law, unless, of course, it is affirmatively justifiable. It is important in that effort to safeguard the innocent but the requirement of guilty knowledge adequately serves this end — knowledge both that there is a purpose to commit a crime and that one's own behavior renders aid. There are, however, infinite degrees of aid to be considered. This is the point, we think, at which distinctions should be drawn. Accordingly, when a true purpose to further the crime is lacking, the draft requires that the accessorial behavior substantially facilitate commission of the crime and that it does so to the knowledge of the actor. This qualification provides a basis for discrimination that should satisfy the common sense of justice. A vendor who supplies materials readily available upon the market arguably does not make substantial contribution to commission of the crime since the materials could have easily been gotten elsewhere. The minor employee may win exemption on this ground, though he minded his own business to preserve his job. What is required is to give the courts and juries a criterion for drawing lines that must be drawn. The formula proposed accomplishes this purpose by a standard that is relevant, it is submitted, to all the legal ends involved. There will, of course, be arguable cases; they should, we think, be argued in these terms.

It has been urged in criticism of section 3(b) that "substantially facilitates" lays down too vague a test of liability to guide a jury verdict and that the legislature should determine whether or not in specific types of situations aid with knowledge but without purpose to further the commission of a crime ought to suffice for criminality. Whether a vendor, for example, must forego a sale because he knows of the illegal purpose of his would-be customer requires, it is argued, resolution of competing interests: that of vendors in freedom to refrain from the policing of vendees and that of the community in reducing the incidence of behavior that facilitates the commission of crimes.

We readily concede the vagueness of "substantially facilitates" but defend the formula by the submission that no less vague alternative has been proposed that both affirms a liability without a purpose to facilitate the crime and gives the court and jury a discretion to avoid it when its imposition would be deemed extreme. This practical consideration, coupled with the requirement of *scienter*, serves to allay a constitutional problem upon this score.

We also agree that a problem of conflicting interests is presented but submit that, absent special grounds that constitute legal justification, it ought to be resolved in favor of a principle that regards crime prevention as the prior value to be served. The justification provisions (Article 3) must, of course, be adequate for this case as for others and, when they are submitted, should be studied with this case in mind. But when the only interest of the actor is his wish for freedom to forego concern about the criminal purposes of others, though he knowingly facilitates in a substantial measure the achievement of such purposes, it is an interest that, we think, is properly subordinated generally to the larger interest of preventing crime. . . .

Model Penal Code Section 2.06 Commentary
Official Draft and Revised Comments 318-319, 321-322 (1985) (footnote numbers altered)

Though the Chief Reporter favored a formulation that would broaden liability beyond merely purposive conduct, the Institute rejected that position, principally on the argument that the need for stating a general principle in this section pointed toward a narrow formulation in order not to include situations where liability was inappropriate. Many recent revisions and proposals reflect a similar judgment about accomplice liability.[1] The possibility that a broadened liability should obtain in particular contexts is one that can be, and has been dealt with in the drafting of the substantive offenses themselves,[2] a situation explicitly left open by Subsection (3)(b), as well as by Subsection (2)(b). There is thus still room for the judgment that when the only interest of the actor is his wish to forego concern about the criminal purposes of others, though he knowingly facilitates in a substantial measure the achievement of such purposes, his interest is properly subordinated generally to the larger interest of preventing crime.

Some states have gone further, following the lead of New York, and have adopted general facilitation provisions.[3] These extend accessorial liability to persons who engage in conduct with the awareness that it will aid others to commit serious crimes, but treat such facilitation as a less grave offense than the crimes that are aided. This approach may well constitute a sensible accommodation of the competing considerations advanced at the Institute meeting....

7. Result Elements. Subsection (4) makes it clear that complicity in conduct causing a particular criminal result entails accountability for that result so long as the accomplice is personally culpable with respect to the result to the extent demanded by the definition of the crime. Thus, if the accomplice recklessly

---

1. See Ala. §13A-2-23; Ariz. §13-301; Ark. §41-303(1); Colo. §18-1-603; Del. tit. 11, §271(2); Haw. §702-222(1); Ill. ch. 38, §5-2(c); Ky. §502.020(1); Mo. §562.041(1)(2); Mont. §94-2-107(3) (but see §94-2-107(1)); N.H. §626.8(III)(a); N.J. §2C:2-6(c)(1); N.D. §12.1-03-01(1)(b); Ore. §161.155(2); Pa. tit. 18, §306(c)(1); Tex. §7.02(a)(2); Alaska §11.16.110(2) (H.B. 661, Jan. 1978); S.C. §11.1; Tenn. §502(a)(2); W. Va. §61-2-13(a).

2. See Section 242.6(2): "Any person who knowingly causes or facilitates an escape commits an offense."

3. New York provided:

> A person is guilty of criminal facilitation in the second degree when, believing it probable that he is rendering aid to a person who intends to commit a crime, he engages in conduct which provides such person with means or opportunity for the commission thereof and which in fact aids such a person to commit a felony.
>
> Criminal facilitation in the second degree is a Class A misdemeanor.

N.Y.§115.00. Id. §115.05 defined criminal facilitation in the first degree, a class C felony, in the same language, except that the offense facilitated was either murder or kidnapping in the first degree (but following a 1972 amendment, any class A felony). These provisions were superseded in 1978 by a finer division of facilitation into four degrees. N.Y. §115.00 to .08 (Cum. Supp. 1978-79). There is also provision, in §115.10, denying defenses to the facilitator in three situations: (1) where the person facilitated is not guilty because he was irresponsible or lacked the mental state (the "innocent or irresponsible person" situation); (2) where the person facilitated has not been prosecuted or convicted or has been acquitted; and (3) where the defendant himself is not guilty of the facilitated offense because he lacked the mental state required therefor. Finally, §115.5 precludes conviction upon the uncorroborated testimony of the perpetrator of the offense.

For similar provisions, see Ariz. §13-604; Ky. §506.080 to .100; N.D. §12.1-06-02. See also Brown Comm'n Final Report §1002; Mass. ch. 263, §46; W. Va. §61-4-8 to 61-4-10.

endangers life by rendering assistance to another, he can be convicted of manslaughter if a death results,[1] even though the principal actor's liability is at a different level. In effect, therefore, the homicidal act is attributed to both participants, with the liability of each measured by his own degree of culpability toward the result.

The most common situation in which Subsection (4) will become relevant is where unanticipated results occur from conduct for which the actor is responsible under Subsection (3). His liability for unanticipated occurrences rests upon two factors: his complicity in the conduct that causes the result, and his culpability towards the result to the degree required by the law, that makes the result criminal. Accomplice liability in this event is thus assimilated to the liability of the principal actor; the principal actor's liability for unanticipated results, of course, would turn on the extent to which he was reckless or negligent, as required by the law defining the offense, toward the result in question. There is also room for application of Subsection (4) to the common felony-murder situation. An accomplice in a felony where one of the felons causes a death could be convicted for manslaughter or murder upon proof that, under Subsection (3), he was an accomplice in the conduct that caused the death and, under Subsection (4), he had the requisite culpability as to the death imposed by the relevant provision.[2]

This formulation combines the policy that accomplices are equally accountable within the range of their complicity with the policies underlying those crimes defined according to results. It is thus a desirable extension of accomplice liability beyond the principles stated in Subsection (3). A number of recent revisions have similar coverage.*

---

1. See Section 210.3.

2. A manslaughter prosecution could be brought on the theory that the defendant consciously disregarded a substantial and unjustifiable risk that death would result from the assisted conduct, the risk being of such a nature and degree that, considering the nature and purpose of the defendant's conduct and the circumstances known to him, its disregard involved a gross deviation from the standard of conduct that a law-abiding person would have observed in the defendant's situation. See Sections 2.02(2)(c); 210.3(1)(a). A murder prosecution could be brought on the theory that the defendant was reckless as described, and moreover that he was reckless under circumstances manifesting extreme indifference to the value of human life. See Section 210.2(1)(b). In addition, of course, and by the explicit terms of Section 210.2(1)(b), the presumption that the requisite recklessness and indifference to make out a case of murder exist is afforded by the fact that "the actor is...an accomplice in the commission of...robbery...."

* Editor's Note—The Model Penal Code drafters say this about the required culpability as to a circumstance element of the substantive offense:

> There is deliberate ambiguity as to whether the purpose requirement extends to circumstance elements of the contemplated offense or whether, as in the case of attempts, the policy of the substantive offense on this point should control. The reasoning is the same as in the case of conspiracy, which is set forth in some detail in Section 5.03 Comment 2(c)(ii). The result, therefore, is that the actor must have a purpose with respect to the proscribed conduct or the proscribed result, with his attitude towards the circumstances to be left to resolution by the courts. His attitude towards the criminality of the conduct, *see* Section 2.02(9), is irrelevant here as it is in the other cases, subject of course to the limitations in Section 2.04(3).

Model Penal Code Section 2.06 Commentary at n.37 (1985).

Other Discussion Materials

Paul H. Robinson & John M. Darley, Study 9: Culpability Requirements for Complicity

Justice, Liability & Blame 96-98, 103-105 (1995)

Just as criminal liability is inappropriate for an inadvertent commission of an offense, so too is liability inappropriate where one inadvertently assists another in the commission of an offense. Thus the Model Penal Code requires that, at the time of assisting the perpetrator, the accomplice must be acting "with the purpose of promoting or facilitating the commission of the offense." MPC §2.06(3)(a)....

The phrase "purpose to promote or facilitate the commission of the offense" is ambiguous on an important point, however. Does the very demanding "purpose" requirement apply only to the person's culpable state of mind as to assisting ("promoting or facilitating") the perpetrator's conduct, or does it apply as well to all elements of the substantive offense, such as "purposeful" with respect to the prohibited results of the person's conduct? If it applies to all elements of the substantive offense, the effect is dramatic, for it makes complicity very difficult to establish, essentially limiting it to cases where the accomplice wanted not only the offense conduct to occur but also wanted any required results to occur or circumstances to exist. For example, statutory rape typically requires no more than negligence as to the partner being underage. Where a person purposely assists conduct that in fact constitutes statutory rape, can he defend by saying that he only thought it probable (reckless) that his partner was underage but did not know or did not necessarily want or hope that she was underage? If complicity liability requires purpose as to all offense elements, anything less than purpose as to underage will provide a defense. For another example, relating to a result element, the offense of endangerment requires that the perpetrator be at least reckless as to creating a risk of death. Where a person purposely assists conduct that constitutes endangerment (dumping hazardous chemicals near a playground, for example), can he defend by saying that he knew that the conduct he was assisting would create a risk of death but he did not necessarily want it to? If complicity liability requires purpose as to all offense elements, anything less than purpose as to creating the risk of death will provide a defense.

This was the ambiguity at issue in *Etzweiler v. State*, for example, where the defendant was charged as an accomplice to a killing caused by a drunk driver. The defendant clearly had "purposely" assisted his drunk friend to engage in the conduct constituting the offense, driving; he gave his drunken friend the keys to his car. It was not clear, however, that Etzweiler was "purposeful" or even "knowing" as to his conduct creating a risk of death. At most, one might conclude that, by giving car keys to his obviously intoxicated friend, he was "reckless" as to the resulting death; that is, at the time of giving the keys, he was aware of a substantial risk that a death could result.

The justices of the New Hampshire Supreme Court in *Etzweiler* disagree over the proper interpretation of the state code's "purpose" requirement for complicity, which was modeled in large part on the Model Penal Code. A majority of the court holds that the purpose requirement has the effect of elevating all culpability requirements of the homicide definition to purposeful for the accomplice. Thus, while manslaughter normally requires only recklessness as to causing a death, complicity in manslaughter requires that the accomplice be purposeful as to causing the death. (Even murder liability requires only knowing as to causing death). Some common law cases came to a similar view that the culpability requirements for complicity in an offense are "elevated" over those of the substantive offense itself. Other common law cases essentially came to the view of the dissenting judges, a view that we now sketch.

The dissenting justices in *Etzweiler* conclude that complicity's purpose requirement only requires that the complicit individual be purposeful as to *assisting the perpetrator's conduct*—that is, purposely giving the friend the car keys with the purpose of allowing him to drive the car. The culpability requirements of the substantive offense—recklessness as to causing death, for manslaughter—are not elevated to purpose for complicity liability. Under this view, a person can be an accomplice to manslaughter by purposely assisting another to engage in conduct that the accomplice is aware creates a substantial risk of causing death (i.e., is reckless as to causing death). The Model Penal Code drafters make it relatively clear that they support this "no-elevation" view, at least with respect to result elements, as in *Etzweiler*. See MPC §2.06(4). The complicity culpability study sought to test the subjects' view on the importance to liability of an accomplice's culpability as to assisting and culpability as to the elements of the substantive offense.

Six scenarios presented variations on the *Etzweiler* situation. The study involved the same core description of an individual who makes his car keys available to an intoxicated friend. The two individuals arrive at the plant where they work. Because the friend is intoxicated, our individual is driving. The intoxicated friend announces his plan to borrow the car to race home to pick up something he needs for work. The area through which he will drive is crowded with workers arriving for their shift at the plant. In some cases, we describe the non-intoxicated individual as sure that the drunk will kill people if he drives; in the other cases, only aware of the possibility that the drunk might kill people. Thus we attempted to make clear that the state of mind of the complicit individual was knowing or reckless as to causing the death that we described as ensuing, an element that we intuited was likely to be an important one to our respondents. The drunk obtains access to the car keys, heads home, and kills two workers just coming to work through the factory gate.

We manipulated the description of the circumstances of the drunk's obtaining the car keys of his friend to create the perceptions that the accomplice is either purposeful, knowing, or reckless as to his drunk friend taking his car keys to drive while intoxicated. In the purposeful case, he willingly hands the friend the keys. In the knowing case, he first urges the friend not to drive, then reluctantly hands over the keys. In the reckless case, he refuses his friend but then leaves the keys in a place where his friend can find them, even though it crosses his mind that the friend might take them.

The results of the study are presented in [Table] 4.6.... In Table 4.6, we include the liability assigned to the accomplice.... [Liability as a function of accomplice culpability as to causing the resulting death is graphed in Figure 4.8.]

Table 4.6 Liability as Related to Culpability Requirements for Complicity

Scenarios	(a) Driver Liability	(b) Accomplice Liability	(c) % No Liability (N)	(d) % No Liability or No Punishment (N+0)	(e) Result Under MPC (& Etzweiler dissent)	(f) Result Under "Elevation" View (Etzweiler decision)
Purposeful as to assisting driving:						
1. Knowing as to causing death	7.76	4.50	8.8	29.4	Murder	No liability
2. Reckless as to causing death	7.65	3.56	8.8	44.1	Manslaughter	No liability
Knowing as to assisting driving:						
3. Knowing as to causing death	7.82	3.56	5.9	38.3	No liability	No liability
4. Reckless as to causing death	7.68	2.74	14.7	50.0	No liability	No liability
Reckless as to assisting driving:						
5. Knowing as to causing death	7.50	1.82	17.6	67.6	No liability	No liability
6. Reckless as to causing death	7.74	1.68	23.5	70.6	No liability	No liability

Liability Scale: N=No criminal liability, 0=Liability but no punishment, 1=1 day, 2=2 weeks, 3=2 months, 4=6 months, 5=1 year, 6=3 years, 7=7 years, 8=15 years, 9=30 years, 10=life, and 11=death.

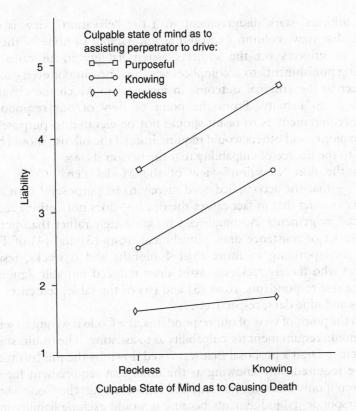

Liability Scale: N=No criminal liability, 0=Liability but no punishment,
1=1 day, 2=2 weeks, 3=2 months, 4=6 months, 5=1 year, 6=3 years, 7=7 years,
8=15 years, 9=30 years, 10=life, and 11=death.

Figure 4.8 **Liability as a Function of Accomplice's Culpability as to Resulting Death**

Summary First,... the respondents are making essentially continuous judgements when the code makes dichotomous ones. [That is, they vary the degree of liability with the level of culpability, rather than setting a single culpability level as a minimum for liability and ignoring any culpability higher than this minimum.] Next, our subjects can and do see the difference between the two culpability issues that this study presented to them [— culpability as to assisting and culpability as to causing the death —] and these two dimensions of culpability make a difference in their liability assignment. This suggests that both of these issues should be addressed within the legal provisions dealing with complicity liability.

Next, let us consider how our results bear on the various formulations of the doctrine. [O]ur respondents do not hold the interpretation that purposefulness with regard to causing death is essential for liability. In fact, they do not even require knowledge for liability; they assign significant although reduced criminal liability to an accomplice who is merely reckless, not even knowing, with respect to the death that eventuated. (See the bottom line of Figure 4.8.) However, notice also that the accomplice's state of mind about the death, when it is reduced from knowing to reckless, does cause respondents to assign considerably less punishment. (This is shown by the liability difference between the opposite ends of each of the three lines in Figure 4.8.)

The subjects' stark disagreement with the "elevation" view is shown in Table 4.6; that view (column *f*) would assign liability in none of the cases we presented to subjects yet the subjects assign liability in all cases. Subjects are assigning punishments to accomplices who are knowing or even only reckless with respect to the criminal outcome in instances in which the elevation view would assign no liability. From the point of view of our respondents, the culpability requirement as to result should not be elevated to purposeful as the *Etzweiler* majority and others would require; instead the offense should be graded according to the degree of culpability that the person shows.

Even the non-"elevation" view of the Model Penal Code, shown in column (e) — that the accomplice need merely to be purposeful with respect to *assisting the conduct* that in fact causes the death — does not entirely accord with our subjects' judgements. Accomplices who knowingly rather than purposefully commit the act of assistance draw punishment, rows (3) and (4) of Table 4.6, sentences corresponding to more than 4 months and 6 weeks, respectively. Accomplices who merely recklessly assist draw reduced but still significant sentences from our respondents, rows (5) and (6) of the table, sentences of about eleven days and nine days, respectively. . . .

From the point of view of our respondents, the Code is wrong to set purpose as the minimum requirement for culpability as to assisting. The results support the MPC Tentative Draft's proposal that was voted down by the full Institute, which would have required only knowing as the minimum requirement for assisting. Further, even if only knowing was required as to assisting, the Code would differ from our respondents' judgements because it would exclude liability in cases of recklessness as to assisting. Finally, our respondents would also view the Code deficient, as a grading matter, because it fails to adjust grade according to culpability level.

So our subjects assign liability, although reduced liability, in knowing and reckless cases of assistance, and the Code does not. What might explain this difference? One rather speculative possibility occurs to us. The legal code seems to begin by taking for granted that the central question is whether the accomplice should be regarded as committing the same offense as that with which the perpetrator is charged. In other words, is the crime committed by the "assister" the same as the crime committed by the perpetrator? Not surprisingly, the Code sets quite high standards for a "yes" answer to that question. Judging by the reduced liability ratings that they give, our subjects do not ask themselves the same question. They do not ask, in the present case, "Is the accomplice guilty of manslaughter?" They instead express the view that an individual who contributes to the commission of a crime by another deserves some punishment. The more purposeful that contribution, both in terms of facilitating the actions of the perpetrator and being aware of the perpetrator's criminal purposes, the higher the liability incurred. But, even when the accomplice is merely reckless in his or her contributions to the offense, some liability is incurred, although eventually it may result in nothing more than a condemnation rather than incarceration.

There are some hints that legal code drafters have recognized this point. Some states have created an offense called "criminal facilitation" that punishes at a lower level than is assigned to the perpetrator of the offense, but also requires less in the way of culpability. This would approximate the liability pattern assigned by our respondents.

Wayne R. LaFave & Austin W. Scott, Accomplice Liability — Acts and Mental State
2 Substantive Criminal Law §13.2(d) (2d ed. 2003)

Various compromises between the views expressed in *Backun* and *Peoni** have been suggested. One is that knowing aid should be deemed sufficient when the criminal scheme is serious in nature. Some of the decided cases may be reconciled on this basis; this would explain, for example, why liability has been imposed for knowing aid to a group planning the overthrow of the government or to one planning to burglarize a bank, but not for knowing aid to such crimes as gambling, prostitution, and unlawful sale of liquor. Taking into account the seriousness of the crime aided makes some sense, for it may be argued that in such a case the "inconvenience to legitimate trade of requiring a merchant to concern himself with the affairs of his customers" is a lesser consideration than the prevention of major crimes.

Another approach is to take into account the degree to which the accomplice knowingly aided in the criminal scheme. This was the recommendation of the draftsmen of the Model Penal Code, who proposed accomplice liability for a person if, "acting with knowledge that such other person was committing or had the purpose of committing the crime, he knowingly, substantially facilitated its commission." This, they explained, would avoid the imposition of liability upon the vendor who supplies materials readily available on the open market and the minor employee who minds his own business to keep his job, but at the same time provide a basis for conviction of those who were aware that they were giving substantial aid. The conflicting interests would be balanced by subordinating the "freedom to forego concern about the criminal purposes of others" to the interest in crime prevention when the supplier is aware that his contribution to the criminal enterprise would be a substantial one. However, this recommendation was voted down by the American Law Institute, perhaps because of its vagueness, and the Code thus limits accomplice liability to instances in which there exists "the purpose of promoting or facilitating the commission of an offense."

A somewhat different solution is to deal with knowing assistance or encouragement as a distinct criminal offense rather than as a basis for accomplice liability for the crime aided. This would have the advantage of providing means whereby such persons, clearly less culpable than those directly participating in the crime, could be subjected to lesser and different penalties, just as has long been the case for the accessory after the fact. This is the solution adopted in a few of the modern codes by adding "criminal facilitation" to the usual list of anticipatory crimes.

---

*Editor's Note — These cases are referred to in the Overview to this Section.

The Act Requirement and Liability for an Omission

Most offenses define prohibited conduct, such as engaging in conduct that causes a death. But a person sometimes can be criminally liable for failing to act if such failure is the violation of a legal duty. Thus, the effect of legal duties may be to treat offenders *as if they had* engaged in prohibited offense conduct—that is, to *impute* required offense conduct. What legal duties does the law create, and when should their violation lead to criminal liability?

◆ THE CASE OF DAVID CASH

It is Memorial Day weekend, 1997. Best friends Jeremy Strohmeyer and David Cash are seniors at Woodrow Wilson High School in Long Beach, California. Classmates consider Cash smart but socially awkward. He acts cool by spiking his hair and growing sideburns, but he is still baby-faced, short, and interested in subjects like engineering. In contrast, Strohmeyer is outgoing, wild, and worldly, after living in Singapore for several years while his mother was working there. He drinks, has a fake ID, and is very flirtatious. The two have a firm friendship, though, after meeting in computer class during their junior year, just after Strohmeyer returned to the States. Both have aspirations for after graduation. Strohmeyer wants to be an officer in the Air Force, like his adoptive father, and Cash a nuclear engineer.

Strohmeyer is responsible for introducing Cash to the wilder side of high school by taking him to parties and getting him drunk for the first time, even bringing a camcorder to tape the evening. Cash's parents, who are reconciling after being separated for years, are not terribly concerned. They treat Cash leniently because he has always been independent and trustworthy, and his grades remain good. Even when Cash returns home drunk with Strohmeyer, they do not get angry. Strohmeyer also shows off to Cash his upper-class lifestyle, which includes a maid, a jet, and four cars.

Figure 61 **Strohmeyer and Cash in Wilson High School senior class photo**

(Las Vegas Review Journal)

Strohmeyer's behavior is increasingly wild and erratic, and his grades have dropped since he returned from Singapore. For example, a teacher who once described him as one of the best students he ever taught has recently changed his mind; he now sees two different sides to Strohmeyer. In school, he is thought of as a hard partier with a violent temper. His Internet sign-in name is "Killer." He also has a secret interest in child pornography. Recently, he had an Internet chat, under the screename "flyboy1030," where he wrote that he fantasizes about sex with five- or six-year old girls. He even asked a girlfriend to dress up in a young girl's school uniform and put her hair in pigtails. (She refused.)

Over the past year, Strohmeyer has slowly spiraled into a destructive pattern. He uses drugs more often, drinks frequently, and is taking amphetamines, the combination of which explains his recent behavior at parties. At one, he spit in a jock's face and screamed profanities at a girl after she asked him to leave. On another occasion, he sneaked a kitten out of a host's house and threw it out of a car's window as he drove away. He even incited others to help him throw marshmallows, then books, and finally bottles down a hallway at a party, which he followed up by personally kicking holes in the walls. His parents think he is just going through a typical teenage rebellion stage, while classmates attribute his behavior to extreme senioritis.

Nonetheless, Cash still looks up to Strohmeyer. Strohmeyer is one of the "cool kids," and helps Cash overcome his struggles of trying to fit in by introducing him to people and giving him the chance to hang out with other "cool kids." Cash sometimes joins Strohmeyer in a big group when it goes cruising the town, which occasionally also includes harassing prostitutes and the homeless. Strohmeyer often brags about smashing eggs in the faces of prostitutes.

Strohmeyer also benefits from his friendship with Cash. As the more impressionable of the two, Cash helps Strohmeyer feel cool by laughing at all of Strohmeyer's jokes and pranks and defending his actions. Cash is also allowed to drive his mother's red Chevrolet convertible, while Strohmeyer's parents never allow him to drive their cars. The two recently used Cash's mother's car for a road trip to UC Berkeley, during which they got their tongues pierced. The university is Cash's top choice. A serious car crash ended their trip, but Strohmeyer's father bailed them out by purchasing them airline tickets back to Long Beach.

For the long Memorial Day weekend, Cash's father invites Strohmeyer along for a trip to Las Vegas as a thank-you to his parents for letting Cash stay with them for three weeks. Cash is looking forward to the trip.

On the evening of Saturday, May 24, 1997, they leave for Las Vegas. On the way, they stop at several towns for food and gas, reaching Primm, on the Nevada border, at midnight. There they visit the Primadonna Casino. Cash's father gives the two some money and tells them to meet up again at 3:00 a.m. He then goes to play poker. Cash and Strohmeyer want to ride Wild Bill's Roller Coaster, but cannot find the entrance. Instead, they end up at another casino and then an arcade. Neither place thrills them, and they eventually make their way back to the Primadonna.

Figure 62 **David Cash, May 1997**
(Las Vegas Review Journal)

Sitting by the pool, Strohmeyer uses his fake ID to order some drinks. He has a whiskey and Coke, while Cash goes for a strawberry daiquiri. As the night creeps on, they grow restless. At one point, Strohmeyer tries sneaking into the gambling section, but casino security promptly kicks him out. They order more drinks and play arcade games. Strohmeyer starts talking to a girl who he thinks has a nice body. He asks for her beeper number, but she refuses, recalling later that she thought he was creepy. Strohmeyer leaves to get more drinks, but when he returns he keeps trying to talk to her. He tries to impress her by showing off his nipple and tongue piercings. When her mother arrives, they quickly leave.

Figure 63 **Strohmeyer school yearbook photo**
(Las Vegas Review Journal)

Figure 64 **The Primadonna Resort in Primm, Nevada, which changed its name to the Primm Valley Resort in 1998**

(Frank Reynolds, www.vegasgallery.com)

Cash and Strohmeyer are tired of playing video games and decide to urinate on them to entertain themselves. They quickly become distracted, however, by two young children having a spitball fight. One of their wet paper towels hits Strohmeyer, and he throws it back. He then starts playing with the kids, and they run through the rows of video games.

One of the children is seven-year old Sherrice Iverson of South Central Los Angeles. Like them, she has grown tired of waiting for her father. Casino security has twice taken her back to her father, and she had already fallen asleep in the driver's seat of a video game. She is used to the long nights that the Nevada casinos trips bring, because her father, a diabetic on disability, has "gamblin' fever." While thinking it too dangerous to allow Sherrice to play in front of their house in South Central, he thinks the Primadonna is safe and lets her have the run of the place. Sherrice is generally well cared for; she always sports freshly pressed clothes and neatly braided hair. At age seven, she likes "The Little Mermaid," purple, and jump-roping, but is still afraid of the dark. When she grows up, she wants to be a "nurse, policewoman, model, or dancer." She is less than four feet tall and weighs about forty-six pounds. Her playmate on this night, Strohmeyer, is almost six feet tall and weighs about one hundred fifty pounds.

They continue playing in the arcade for another ten minutes or so, until Sherrice runs into the women's restroom. Strohmeyer gets a drink of water, takes a puff of his cigarette, and follows her in. A few seconds later, Cash follows after him. In the bathroom, Sherrice swings a plastic "Wet Floor" sign at Strohmeyer and he gets angry. He picks her up, placing one of his arms under her armpit with his hand over her mouth, while using

Figure 65

the other arm to lift her into the handicap stall, locking the door behind him. He chooses this one because it has more room.

Thinking that the game has gone too far, Cash becomes a little concerned. He tries to get Strohmeyer's attention by standing on the toilet in the stall adjacent to the handicap one. Cash tells him to let Sherrice go and tries to convince him to leave the bathroom. He then starts tapping on Strohmeyer's head to get his attention. Finally, Cash catches Strohmeyer's attention when he knocks off Strohmeyer's "Bruins" hat. Strohmeyer just stares back weirdly, like "he [doesn't] care what [Cash] is saying." After his unsuccessful attempts to get Strohmeyer to stop, Cash gives up. He leaves the arcade and waits for Strohmeyer and his father on a bench in the resort's courtyard.

Strohmeyer notices Cash's intervention, but quickly refocuses on Sherrice. He takes off her boots, followed by her pants and underwear. She screams when he "fingers" her a few times. He notices blood on his index finger. To quiet her down, he puts her on the floor, with her hands pulled around her neck. He holds her in this position for about ten minutes and then puts her on the toilet and begins to masturbate against her body. He thinks she is unconscious but alive.

When women suddenly come into the restroom, Strohmeyer quickly props her up on the toilet and sits on her, so that only his feet show under the stall's door. With people still there, he tries masturbating again, but cannot maintain an erection. Strohmeyer quickly covers her mouth when he hears Sherrice gasping for air.

After the restroom empties, Sherrice is limp. Strohmeyer thinks that it would be cruel to leave Sherrice as she is. He considers her future as a "vegetable" and decides to "put her out of her misery." He tries to break her neck. Despite hearing a loud pop, he sees her still moving, and uses all of his strength to do it again. This time he is convinced that she is dead.

Figure 66 **Iverson on Primmadonna Resort arcade surveillance camera**

(Las Vegas Sun/Ethan Miller)

Figure 67 **Surveillance tape of Strohmeyer outside the women's bathroom of the Primadonna Resort**

(Las Vegas Sun/Ethan Miller)

Figure 68 **Cash and Strohmeyer (in hat) on arcade surveillance camera**

(Las Vegas Metropolitan Police Department)

Strohmeyer cleans up by putting Sherrice's boots, pants, and underwear in the toilet. He then wipes his forearm clean of white foam and blood before finally putting Sherrice's legs in the toilet and propping her up so that none of her limbs are visible from under the stall door. Twenty-two minutes after following Sherrice in, Strohmeyer leaves.

As he walks out of the casino, he stays close to the walls of the arcade in an attempt to avoid the security cameras. He meets Cash. On their way to the car, they talk to a valet and show off their piercings. Cash asks Strohmeyer what went on in the bathroom after he left. Looking him straight in the eye, Strohmeyer answers, bluntly, "I killed her." Cash later recalls being shocked by the revelation and having no idea how to react. His only other question of Strohmeyer is whether she was "wet" when he digitally raped her.

Shortly afterwards, Cash's father arrives and they finish driving to Las Vegas, arriving there on the morning of Sunday, May 25. They check into the Holiday Inn at noon. Strohmeyer and Cash play slot machines, drink beer, ride a roller coaster, and check out all the casinos. During their explorations, they discuss what happened at the Primadonna. Cash is convinced they will be caught because of the video surveillance that was all over the resort. He is also worried that they made themselves conspicuous by showing off their piercings and saying they were from Long Beach. They make a pact not to tell anyone. If caught, they make up various excuses for Strohmeyer to use, ranging from sheer innocence to intoxication to insanity. Early Monday morning, the three arrive back in Long Beach. At the Primadonna, meanwhile, a female employee has found Sherrice's body and has informed the police and the girl's father.

On Tuesday, school is back in session, but Cash sleeps in and skips his classes. He hangs around the house all day and during the five o'clock news sees that there is a videotape of him and Strohmeyer entering and exiting the restroom. Realizing that they will certainly be found, the color drains from his face. He calls Strohmeyer to tell him about the video. Cash watches it again with Strohmeyer. To gain perspective, they decide they need to tell someone about the incident. They tell the whole story to a friend, James Trujillo, in a Kinko's parking lot. When Trujillo does not believe them, Cash tells another friend, Jeremy Phillips, who tells Cash to turn Strohmeyer in to the police.

The next day, a classmate, Melissa Ellis, sees the video on television before school. She immediately recognizes the pair, identifying Strohmeyer from his posture and walk and Cash by his sideburns and hair. Strohmeyer and Cash drive to school that day in Cash's mother's red convertible with an *LA Times* newspaper in the backseat. On the front page of the paper are pictures of the two (stills from the videotape). They talk with Justin Ware, whose mother called him at 10:00 p.m. the night before to see if he recognized the boys in the video. Ware asks them if they really did it; Strohmeyer says he did. Ware is speechless. The pair goes to class and Strohmeyer acts normally the entire day, goofing off and flashing his piercings.

Later, Ellis runs into her friend, Lisa Cota, and finds out that she too recognized Strohmeyer and Cash in the video. They talk to Carmela Rhmyer, who says that Strohmeyer just told her that he and Cash were in Las Vegas over the weekend, but that he was drunk and is innocent. Later, a girl in Ware's class says that the *LA Times* photo looks like Strohmeyer. Ware tells Strohmeyer about it and asks him what he is going to do. Strohmeyer says, "Nothing," and that another student has already confronted him. Strohmeyer and Cash go to Taco Bell for lunch and make "last supper" jokes throughout the meal. Cash thinks they will be arrested when they return to school. Acting on information from Ellis and Cota, Assistant Principal Greg Mendoza contacts Officer Birdsall about the video. Birdsall interviews the two students and arranges for surveillance on Strohmeyer's house.

Strohmeyer goes home after school, growing increasingly anxious. He calls an ex-girlfriend, Agnes Lee, and asks her to come over. Although she feels ill, she does not want to let him down and goes. They go to Jamba Juice, where she notices that he is nervous and fidgety. She drops him off at his house just as his older sister, Heather, is arriving. He runs back to Lee's car and asks her to stay because he has to tell her something—that he has done something horrible. He tells her that he strangled a young black girl and asks her to leave the country with him. He also says the girl was sexually molested, but (falsely) blames it on Cash. Lee refuses to flee with him and tells him he deserves to be punished. When she gets back to her house, she sees the video and recognizes Strohmeyer and Cash. Lee calls her father and recounts her conversation with Strohmeyer. Her father immediately calls the Long Beach police. They contact Lee, who warns them of Strohmeyer's temper and desire to leave the country.

By now, Cash has received a phone call from his father, instructing him to stay home. Cash is certain that his father is now aware of their involvement in the crime at the Primadonna. Cash calls Strohmeyer to explain that his father knows and he will probably be forced to talk to the police. Strohmeyer agrees and says that he understands the situation. He is now aware that he is being watched. He takes his ADD medication off the shelf, empties the bottle into his mouth, and writes a suicide note. He then goes out on the porch to smoke a cigarette while the police sit in their cars, watching patiently. Strohmeyer's sister drops their mother off at home, but he does not want her to see him in this state and scrambles out the door and down the street. He does not make it very far, however, before the police overtake him.

They take him to a community hospital, after his mother alerts them to his drug ingestion. Meanwhile, Cash's father asks Cash if he saw the video. They go to the police department. Cash is scared, thinking, "even though I didn't do anything, I could get into more trouble." The police take his picture and interview him, but do not charge him with a crime. Cash goes home to finish homework that is due the next day.

At the hospital, Strohmeyer tells the police he wants to talk and get things in the open. They inform him of his rights. He tells them that Cash had nothing to do with the murder. Strohmeyer "wanted to experience death." He describes that it was like a dream and he can only remember bits and pieces. After giving a full account of the evening, Strohmeyer adds that he hopes some good will come of his crime, in the form of parents keeping better watch over their children.

Figure 69 **Cash driving by prom that he was unable to attend, June 1997**
(Las Vegas Review Journal)

At school the next day, Cash is curious whether things will be different and what people's reactions will be. His day is cut short, however, when he is thrown out of class for his project—a collage of pictures of pierced female genitalia. When he finally returns to school, Cash is shocked to learn that he will not be allowed to participate in his class's graduation or its prom. He is told that his diploma will be sent to him and the cost of his prom tickets refunded.

The story is sensational and the media quickly descends on Cash. They interview him and even pay for the video of him getting drunk for the first time with Strohmeyer. He sells it for $1,500, keeping $500 for himself, and gives the rest to Philips for orchestrating the deal. Cash and Philips later show up outside the school prom, standing through the sunroof of a limo screaming, "I'm not going." The media cover the stunt heavily, and Cash later recalls that he enjoyed being in the limelight. He later goes with friends to watch a belly-dancing performance at a restaurant.

On Saturday, May 31, Sherrice's funeral is held at Paradise Baptist Church. Her parents are not speaking to each other and both are suing Strohmeyer and the Primadonna. (Sherrice's father is also involved in another lawsuit for slander, after a casino official told reporters that the father asked for $100, a six-pack, a hotel room, and payment for Sherrice's funeral, after learning of her death.) The Primadonna files cross-claims and third-party claims against Cash and Strohmeyer. Sherrice's mother says she still dreams about her daughter. Strohmeyer's parents are receiving death threats.

Figure 70 **Leroy Iverson at Sherrice's funeral**
(Las Vegas Review Journal)

In an interview with the *LA Times,* Cash says that "if anything, the case has made it easier for [me] to score with women." When asked whether he is angry with Strohmeyer, Cash says no, only that he misses his friend. When asked if he feels sorry for Sherrice Iverson, he says that the "situation sucks in general." He says he feels worse for Strohmeyer because he knows him.

> It is very tragic, okay? But the simple fact remains I do not know this little girl. I do not know starving children in Panama. I do not know people that die of disease in Egypt. The only person I knew in this event was Jeremy Strohmeyer, and I know as his best friend that he had potential. . . . I'm sad that I lost a best friend. . . . I'm not going to lose sleep over somebody else's problem.

1. Relying only on your own intuitions of justice, what liability and punishment, if any, does David Cash deserve?

N	0	1	2	3	4	5	6	7	8	9	10	11
☐	☐	☐	☐	☐	☐	☐	☐	☐	☐	☐	☐	☐
no liability	liability but no punishment	1 day	2 wks	2 mo	6 mo	1 yr	3 yrs	7 yrs	15 yrs	30 yrs	life imprison-ment	death

2. What liability, if any, under the then-existing statutes?
3. What liability, if any, under the Model Penal Code?

■ THE LAW

Nevada Revised Statutes Annotated
(1998)

Title 15. Crimes and Punishments
Chapter 200. Crimes Against the Person
Homicide

Section 200.010. "Murder" Defined

Murder is the unlawful killing of a human being, with malice aforethought, either express or implied, or caused by a controlled substance which was sold, given, traded or otherwise made available to a person in violation of chapter 453 of

NRS. The unlawful killing may be effected by any of the various means by which death may be occasioned.

Section 200.020. Malice: Express and Implied Defined

1. Express malice is that deliberate intention unlawfully to take away the life of a fellow creature, which is manifested by external circumstances capable of proof.

2. Malice shall be implied when no considerable provocation appears, or when all the circumstances of the killing show an abandoned and malignant heart.

Section 200.030. Degrees of Murder; Penalties

1. Murder of the first degree is murder which is:

(a) Perpetrated by means of poison, lying in wait, torture or child abuse, or by any other kind of willful, deliberate and premeditated killing;

(b) Committed in the perpetration or attempted perpetration of sexual assault, kidnaping, arson, robbery, burglary, invasion of the home, sexual abuse of a child or sexual molestation of a child under the age of 14 years; or

(c) Committed to avoid or prevent the lawful arrest of any person by a peace officer or to effect the escape of any person from legal custody.

2. Murder of the second degree is all other kinds of murder.

3. The jury before whom any person indicted for murder is tried shall, if they find him guilty thereof, designate by their verdict whether he is guilty of murder of the first or second degree.

4. A person convicted of murder of the first degree is guilty of a category A felony and shall be punished:

(a) By death, only if one or more aggravating circumstances are found and any mitigating circumstance or circumstances which are found do not outweigh the aggravating circumstance or circumstances; or

(b) By imprisonment in the state prison:

(1) For life without the possibility of parole;

(2) For life with the possibility of parole, with eligibility for parole beginning when a minimum of 20 years has been served; or

(3) For a definite term of 50 years, with eligibility for parole beginning when a minimum of 20 years has been served.

A determination of whether aggravating circumstances exist is not necessary to fix the penalty at imprisonment for life with or without the possibility of parole.

5. A person convicted of murder of the second degree is guilty of a category A felony and shall be punished by imprisonment in the state prison:

(a) For life with the possibility of parole, with eligibility for parole beginning when a minimum of 10 years has been served; or

(b) For a definite term of 25 years, with eligibility for parole beginning when a minimum of 10 years has been served.

6. As used in this section:

(a) "Child abuse" means physical injury of a nonaccidental nature to a child under the age of 18 years;

(b) "Sexual abuse of a child" means any of the acts described in NRS 432B.100; and

(c) "Sexual molestation" means any willful and lewd or lascivious act, other than acts constituting the crime of sexual assault, upon or with the body, or any part or member thereof, of a child under the age of 14 years, with the intent of arousing, appealing to, or gratifying the lust, passions or sexual desires of the perpetrator or of the child.

Section 200.040. "Manslaughter" Defined

1. Manslaughter is the unlawful killing of a human being, without malice express or implied, and without any mixture of deliberation.

2. Manslaughter must be voluntary, upon a sudden heat of passion, caused by a provocation apparently sufficient to make the passion irresistible, or, involuntary, in the commission of an unlawful act, or a lawful act without due caution or circumspection.

Section 200.070. "Involuntary Manslaughter" Defined

Except under the circumstances provided in NRS 484.348 and 484.377, involuntary manslaughter is the killing of a human being, without any intent to do so, in the commission of an unlawful act, or a lawful act which probably might produce such a consequence in an unlawful manner, but where the involuntary killing occurs in the commission of an unlawful act, which, in its consequences, naturally tends to destroy the life of a human being, or is committed in the prosecution of a felonious intent, the offense is murder.

Chapter 193. General Provisions

Section 193.0175. "Malice" and "Maliciously" Defined

"Malice" and "maliciously" import an evil intent, wish or design to vex, annoy or injure another person. Malice may be inferred from an act done in willful disregard of the rights of another, or an act wrongfully done without just cause or excuse, or an act or omission of duty betraying a willful disregard of social duty.

Chapter 200. Crimes Against the Person
Homicide

Section 200.033. Circumstances Aggravating First Degree Murder

The only circumstances by which murder of the first degree may be aggravated are:

1. The murder was committed by a person under sentence of imprisonment.

2. The murder was committed by a person who was previously convicted of another murder or of a felony involving the use or threat of violence to the person of another.

3. The murder was committed by a person who knowingly created a great risk of death to more than one person by means of a weapon, device or course of action which would normally be hazardous to the lives of more than one person.

4. The murder was committed while the person was engaged, alone or with others, in the commission of or an attempt to commit or flight after committing or attempting to commit, any robbery, sexual assault, arson in the first degree, burglary, invasion of the home or kidnaping in the first degree, and the person charged:

   (a) Killed or attempted to kill the person murdered; or

   (b) Knew or had reason to know that life would be taken or lethal force used.

5. The murder was committed to avoid or prevent a lawful arrest or to effect an escape from custody.

6. The murder was committed by a person, for himself or another, to receive money or any other thing of monetary value.

7. The murder was committed upon a peace officer or fireman who was killed while engaged in the performance of his official duty or because of an act performed in his official capacity, and the defendant knew or reasonably should have known that the victim was a peace officer or fireman. For the purposes of this subsection, "peace officer" means:

   (a) An employee of the department of prisons who does not exercise general control over offenders imprisoned within the institutions and facilities of the department but whose normal duties require him to come into contact with those offenders, when carrying out the duties prescribed by the director of the department.

   (b) Any person upon whom some or all of the powers of a peace officer are conferred pursuant to NRS 281.0311 to 281.0353, inclusive, when carrying out those powers.

8. The murder involved torture or the mutilation of the victim.

9. The murder was committed upon one or more persons at random and without apparent motive.

10. The murder was committed upon a person less than 14 years of age.

11. The murder was committed upon a person because of the actual or perceived race, color, religion, national origin, physical or mental disability or sexual orientation of that person.

12. The defendant has, in the immediate proceeding, been convicted of more than one offense of murder in the first or second degree. For the purposes of this subsection, a person shall be deemed to have been convicted of a murder at the time the jury verdict of guilt is rendered or upon pronouncement of guilt by a judge or judges sitting without a jury.

Section 200.035. Circumstances Mitigating First Degree Murder

Murder of the first degree may be mitigated by any of the following circumstances, even though the mitigating circumstance is not sufficient to constitute a defense or reduce the degree of the crime:

1. The defendant has no significant history of prior criminal activity.

2. The murder was committed while the defendant was under the influence of extreme mental or emotional disturbance.

3. The victim was a participant in the defendant's criminal conduct or consented to the act.

4. The defendant was an accomplice in a murder committed by another person and his participation in the murder was relatively minor.

5. The defendant acted under duress or under the domination of another person.

6. The youth of the defendant at the time of the crime.

7. Any other mitigating circumstance.

Chapter 200. Crimes Against the Person
Kidnaping

Section 200.310. Degrees

1. A person who willfully seizes, confines, inveigles, entices, decoys, abducts, conceals, kidnaps or carries away a person by any means whatsoever with the intent to hold or detain, or who holds or detains, the person for ransom, or reward, or for the purpose of committing sexual assault, extortion or robbery upon or from the person, or for the purpose of killing the person or inflicting substantial bodily harm upon him, or to exact from relatives, friends, or any other person any money or valuable thing for the return or disposition of the kidnaped person, and a person who leads, takes, entices, or carries away or detains any minor with the intent to keep, imprison, or confine him from his parents, guardians, or any other person having lawful custody of the minor, or with the intent to hold the minor to unlawful service, or perpetrate upon the person of the minor any unlawful act is guilty of kidnaping in the first degree, which is a category A felony.

2. A person who willfully and without authority of law seizes, inveigles, takes, carries away or kidnaps another person with the intent to keep the person secretly imprisoned within the state, or for the purpose of conveying the person out of the state without authority of law, or in any manner held to service or detained against his will, is guilty of kidnaping in the second degree, which is a category B felony.

200.320. Kidnaping in First Degree: Punishment

A person convicted of kidnaping in the first degree is guilty of a category A felony and shall be punished:

1. Where the kidnaped person suffers substantial bodily harm during the act of kidnaping or the subsequent detention and confinement or in attempted escape or escape therefrom, by imprisonment in the state prison:

(a) For life without the possibility of parole;

(b) For life with the possibility of parole, with eligibility for parole beginning when a minimum of 15 years has been served; or

(c) For a definite term of 40 years, with eligibility for parole beginning when a minimum of 15 years has been served.

2. Where the kidnaped person suffers no substantial bodily harm as a result of the kidnaping, by imprisonment in the state prison:

(a) For life with the possibility of parole, with eligibility for parole beginning when a minimum of 5 years has been served; or

(b) For a definite term of 15 years, with eligibility for parole beginning when a minimum of 5 years has been served.

Chapter 200. Crimes Against the Person
Sexual Assault and Seduction

Section 200.366. Sexual Assault: Definition; Penalties

1. A person who subjects another person to sexual penetration, or who forces another person to make a sexual penetration on himself or another, or on a beast, against the victim's will or under conditions in which the perpetrator knows or should know that the victim is mentally or physically incapable of resisting or understanding the nature of his conduct, is guilty of sexual assault.

2. Except as otherwise provided in subsection 3, a person who commits a sexual assault is guilty of a category A felony and shall be punished:

(a) If substantial bodily harm to the victim results from the actions of the defendant committed in connection with or as a part of the sexual assault, by imprisonment in the state prison:

(1) For life without the possibility of parole;

(2) For life with the possibility of parole, with eligibility for parole beginning when a minimum of 15 years has been served; or

(3) For a definite term of 40 years, with eligibility for parole beginning when a minimum of 15 years has been served.

(b) If no substantial bodily harm to the victim results:

(1) By imprisonment in the state prison for life, with the possibility of parole, with eligibility for parole beginning when a minimum of 10 years has been served; or

(2) By imprisonment in the state prison for a definite term of 25 years, with eligibility for parole beginning when a minimum of 10 years has been served.

3. A person who commits a sexual assault against a child under the age of 16 years is guilty of a category A felony and shall be punished:

(a) If the crime results in substantial bodily harm to the child, by imprisonment in the state prison for life without the possibility of parole.

(b) If the crime does not result in substantial bodily harm to the child, by imprisonment in the state prison for:

(1) Life with the possibility of parole, with eligibility for parole beginning when a minimum of 20 years has been served; or

(2) For a definite term of not less than 5 years nor more than 20 years, without the possibility of parole.

Section 200.364. Definitions

As used in this section and NRS 200.364 to 200.3774, inclusive, unless the context otherwise requires:

1. "Perpetrator" means a person who commits a sexual assault.

2. "Sexual penetration" means cunnilingus, fellatio, or any intrusion, however slight, of any part of a person's body or any object manipulated or inserted by a person into the genital or anal openings of the body of another, including sexual intercourse in its ordinary meaning.

3. "Statutory sexual seduction" means:

(a) Ordinary sexual intercourse, anal intercourse, cunnilingus or fellatio committed by a person 18 years of age or older with a person under the age of 16 years; or

(b) Any other sexual penetration committed by a person 18 years of age or older with a person under the age of 16 years with the intent of arousing, appealing to, or gratifying the lust or passions or sexual desires of either of the persons.

4. "Victim" means a person who is subjected to a sexual assault.

Chapter 195. Parties to Crimes

195.020. Principals

Every person concerned in the commission of a felony, gross misdemeanor or misdemeanor, whether he directly commits the act constituting the offense, or aids or abets in its commission, and whether present or absent; and every person who, directly or indirectly, counsels, encourages, hires, commands, induces or otherwise procures another to commit a felony, gross misdemeanor or misdemeanor is a principal, and shall be proceeded against and punished as such. The fact that the person aided, abetted, counseled, encouraged, hired, commanded, induced or procured, could not or did not entertain a criminal intent shall not be a defense to any person aiding, abetting, counseling, encouraging, hiring, commanding, inducing or procuring him.

Lee v. GNLV Corporation
22 P.3d 209, 212 (Nev. 2001)

Survivors of an intoxicated invitee who choked to death in restaurant sued the restaurant for negligence, alleging that it breached a duty of reasonable care owed to the invitee when its employees failed to administer the Heimlich maneuver to him. The trial court granted summary judgment for restaurant. The Supreme Court held that, "In Nevada, as under the common law, strangers are generally under no duty to aid those in peril. This court, however, has stated that, where a special relationship exists between the parties, such as with an innkeeper-guest, teacher-student or employer-employee, an affirmative duty to aid others in peril is imposed by law." The restaurant owed a duty to the invitee to act reasonably, but the restaurant had no duty to administer Heimlich maneuver to invitee.

Labastida v. State
112 Nev. 1502, 931 P.2d 1334 (1996)

The defendant's conviction for second-degree murder and child neglect charges were affirmed, upon the court holding that her failure to prevent severe and repeated abuse of her infant child by the child's father was sufficient to support the conviction. The seven-weeks-old infant was severely beaten and bitten by its father over the course of many weeks. Its bruises and bite marks were conspicuous and covered fifty to seventy-five percent of the baby's body. The court held that the statutes permitted the jury to find the defendant guilty of child abuse and first-degree murder on the grounds that she was responsible for the child, was aware of the abuse, could have taken preventive measures, but did nothing to stop it. By finding second-degree murder, the jury was simply being lenient.

Model Penal Code
(Official Draft 1962)

Section 2.01. Requirement of Voluntary Act; Omission As Basis of Liability; Possession As an Act

(1) A person is not guilty of an offense unless his liability is based on conduct which includes a voluntary act or the omission to perform an act of which he is physically capable....

(3) Liability for the commission of an offense may not be based on an omission unaccompanied by action unless:

 (a) the omission is expressly made sufficient by the law defining the offense; or

 (b) a duty to perform the omitted act is otherwise imposed by law.

(4) Possession is an act, within the meaning of this Section, if the possessor knowingly procured or received the thing possessed or was aware of his control thereof for a sufficient period to have been able to terminate his possession.

▲ **PROBLEM**
Dunning's Deal

Dunning's expenses for school are more than he can handle, so he decides to earn extra money by working as an escort. He is relatively good looking and can be very charming as the need arises. Mrs. Harrington, an elderly widow, particularly enjoys Dunning's company, so they agree that he will be an escort for her, exclusively, in exchange for a monthly salary. Both are pleased with the arrangement until Mrs. Harrington by chance sees Dunning with a young woman. When he arrives that evening at his usual time, she confronts him with her observation. "That's my girlfriend, not another customer," he insists. "We agreed that you would escort only me," she responds. They continue to argue. Concerned that Mrs. Harrington intends not to pay him what he has already earned, Dunning insists on getting paid for the past month. Mrs. Harrington snaps, "It's not due until tomorrow. Anyway, why should I pay you? You broke our agreement." She continues with a tirade on Dunning's breach of their agreement. As she gets more excited, Mrs. Harrington's face turns pale and she falls to the floor, gasping for air. She crawls toward her handbag, which contains her medicine, but is unable to get more than a few yards. Her breathing gets more labored and her color turns to chalk white. Dunning knows that she needs the medicine in her handbag but he turns and leaves. Mrs. Harrington dies several minutes later.

Is Dunning criminally liable under the following statute for his failure to aid Mrs. Harrington? Involuntary Manslaughter: "A person is guilty of involuntary manslaughter when as a direct result of the doing of an unlawful act in a reckless or grossly negligent manner, he causes the death of another person." (Pa. Stat. Ann. tit. 18, §2504)

● **OVERVIEW OF THE ACT REQUIREMENT AND LIABILITY FOR AN OMISSION**

Notes on the Act Requirement

Criminal liability typically requires an act. Model Penal Code section 2.01(1) provides in part that "[a] person is not guilty of an offense unless his liability is based on conduct which includes a voluntary act."[1] Offense definitions typically have a conduct element. Thus, proving the elements of the offense typically satisfies the act requirement. In other words, the act requirement has an effect only for offenses that do not expressly require an act. Homicide in the Model Penal Code, for example, does not expressly require an act; it only requires that an actor "cause the death of another human being." Thus, section 2.01(1) operates to require that liability for homicide, despite the lack of an explicit requirement of an act in the offense definition, nonetheless requires proof of some act. Even if the act requirement is satisfied, of course, liability does not follow unless all elements of the offense definition are satisfied; the act requirement is just the start of offense requirements. For homicide, the actor also must have the required culpability as to causing the death and there must be an adequate causal connection between his conduct and the resulting death.

Meaning of "Act"   Writers disagree as to the precise definition of an "act". Some writers define "act" as simply a muscular movement. This is the most common modern usage. Others define it as a willed movement. The disagreement is not of practical importance because the act requirement is nearly always drafted to require not only an act but a *voluntary* act, as in the Model Penal Code provision quoted above. (Where a *voluntary* act is required, the disagreement becomes a dispute over whether the requirement of a "willed" act is included in the requirement of an act or is added by the requirement that the act be voluntary. The voluntariness requirement is discussed at the end of these Notes and in Section 23.) Other writers define "act" to include the circumstances and consequences of the act. But this usage is not the modern view and, if it was adopted, it would undercut the modern offense definition system that divides the objective components of an offense into conduct, circumstance, and result elements.

Intangible Acts   In some instances, the law assumes that an act has occurred although the actor has performed no muscular movement. A legal or intangible act, for example, may occur where an actor shows his "agreement" or "command" in some way other than by movement. "Let me know if I shouldn't kill him like the rest, Boss," may allow the Mafia chief to direct a killing by doing nothing. Such can be the basis for criminal liability; a muscular movement typically is not required in such a case. Similarly, courts have found the "agreement" required for conspiracy to be satisfied by the acquiescence of a party. The argument in support of liability in such cases focuses on the special circumstances that express the actor's intention and willingness to carry out the act. The special circumstances are said to be adequate to serve the primary rationales of the act requirement (to be discussed in a moment) as effectively as an affirmative act does.

Punishing Thoughts   It is said that one cannot be held liable for thoughts alone, and it is in expression of this that an act requirement is needed. Properly construed, the maxim is accurate, but it can invite too broad an interpretation. Otherwise lawful conduct *can* be made criminal by an actor's accompanying state of mind. In that sense, one can be punished because of one's thoughts. (Recall the discussion of attempts in Section 10.) Lighting one's pipe is not itself

---

1. The provision goes on to allow, alternatively, liability for an omission to perform a legal duty of which one is physically capable of performing, the subject of the Notes on Liability for an Omission, immediately below.

an offense, but it becomes attempted arson if it is a step in a plan to ignite a neighbor's haystack. Giving a young girl a ride is not an offense, but it becomes attempted sexual assault if it is done with the intention of subsequently sexually assaulting her. Just thinking about committing an offense — arson or sexual assault — is not an offense; but once the actor externalizes his or her thoughts by performing an act toward the offense, even an otherwise innocent act, the actor may be subject to criminal liability. The act requirement is the criminal law's mechanism for requiring such externalization.

Why an Act Requirement? Why should criminal liability normally require an act? Several reasons are traditionally offered in support of the act requirement:

Excluding Fantasizing and Irresolute Intentions By requiring an act, the law excludes from liability those persons who only fantasize about committing an offense, as well as those persons who may indeed form an intention to commit an offense but whose intention is not sufficiently firm that it would ever be externalized. One might argue that such people are dangerous, at least more dangerous than persons without such fantasies or intentions, and perhaps the criminal law ought to take jurisdiction. But many people may fantasize or form irresolute intentions, and most never act, thus use of criminal sanctions in those cases is wasteful and unfair. More important, as long as the criminal law continues to concern itself with punishing bad acts, not bad character, there is little justification for punishing pure fantasizing or the forming of irresolute intentions. Further, because one cannot easily control one's thoughts, it is difficult to blame an actor for the same. Condemnation sufficient for criminal liability typically attaches only after the actor externalizes her criminal intention in action.

Objective Evidence of State of Mind Beyond barring punishment for unexternalized thoughts, the act requirement is thought to provide some minimal objective confirmation that an actor's intention does exist. That is, evidence of an actor's intention to commit an offense can gain additional confirmation from an act in furtherance of that intention. But the act requirement by itself performs this function poorly. Admittedly, some conduct may well manifest a mind unambiguously bent on crime, such as agreeing with another that one or the other will commit an offense. More frequently, however, conduct (especially that short of a substantive offense) does little by itself to indicate a culpable state of mind. The farmer lighting his pipe and the actor giving a ride to a young girl, to recall earlier examples, may in fact have no intention of committing arson or sexual assault.

Providing Time and Place of Occurrence The act requirement also is said to be useful in providing a time and place of occurrence for the offense. While one's intention may range over a long period of time and cover many places, the conduct constituting the offense can be identified with a particular time and place. This assists enforcement of the concurrence requirement — that is, ensuring that the required mens rea exists at the time of the conduct constituting the offense. An identifiable time and place also ease application of procedural rules governing jurisdiction, venue, and time limitations for prosecution. Even here, however, the act requirement cannot be relied on for too much. Many offenses require several acts, and some punish so-called "continuing acts" (such as concealment, criminal agreement, possession, or obstruction). The greater the number of acts or the longer "a continuing act," the messier the application of these procedural rules. In some cases, the rationale of the procedural rules may be undercut, such as where jurisdiction and venue are appropriate everywhere and the statute of limitations never begins to run.

Distinguishing Multiple Offenses Some states, such as California, have tried to use the act requirement as a basis for resolving the thorny issue of liability and punishment for multiple offenses. The California Penal Code purports to allow punishment for only one offense for a single act.[1] Even the California courts have rejected a strict application of this provision where one act causes two results, such as two deaths, or constitutes two violations of the same offense provision, such as two instances of attempted murder.[2] The California courts continue to give deference to the provision, however, where one act violates different provisions, such as arson and attempted murder. But even this narrow application seems problematic. If an actor sets a house on fire with two people in it, intending to burn the house and the people, why should the state have to elect to punish for arson or for attempted murder? Why is it not appropriate to punish both? To exclude punishment for one is to trivialize the other. One also may wonder about the logic of allowing multiple liability for the two instances of attempted murder arising from a single act, yet denying liability for the arson and attempted murder from the same act. Under what theory must the state choose between different kinds of harms from a single act, yet not need to choose between distinct but related harms from a single act? As the California experience illustrates, the act requirement is of minimal value in solving the difficult problem of multiple offenses. At best, it serves as a starting point for a more complex analysis.

Modest Demands of Act Requirement The goals of the act requirement are important, especially its exclusion from liability of fantasizing and forming irresolute intentions, but the effect of the doctrine in achieving those goals is modest. The act requirement is satisfied if the actor externalizes his intention to commit the offense in any way. It does not require that the actor perform the conduct element of a completed offense or *any* particular conduct. The attempt offense, such as that set out in Model Penal Code section 5.01(1), on the other hand, does provide some requirement, vague as it may be; it requires that conduct constitute "a substantial step" in a course of conduct planned to culminate in the substantive offense. Similarly, in the offense of conspiracy, under section 5.03(1), one's "agreement" with another person that one of the two will commit an offense satisfies the act requirement. Speaking — as in "I agree" — is an act. But there is nothing in *the act requirement* or in Model Penal Code section 2.01(1) that requires that the act performed be sufficiently close to the completed offense or sufficiently expressive of an actor's intention or willingness to act on the intention.

Is Act Requirement Needed? It appears, then, that it is not the act requirement, but rather the definition of offenses, including inchoate offenses, that ensures that conduct is sufficiently related to the offense to support liability.

---

1. Cal. Penal Code §654 provides:

> An act or omission which is made punishable in different ways by different provisions of this code may be punishable under either of such provisions, but in no case can it be punished under more than one.

2. See, e.g., Neal v. State, 9 Cal. Rptr. 607, 357 P.2d 839 (1960) (defendant convicted on two counts of attempted murder and one of arson; because both resulted from one act, defendant's conviction for arson dismissed, but not two convictions for attempted murder).

Why, then, have a requirement of an act in section 2.01(1)? Note that section 2.01(1) requires a "*voluntary* act." This "voluntariness requirement" is important. It is discussed in greater detail below in Section 23 (Disability Excuses). Is there value in the "*act* requirement" itself? Consider the doctrines of liability for possession and omission. Each has a set of special requirements, to be detailed in a moment. When is it that these special requirements are needed? Answer: when liability is not based on an act, as required by Model Penal Code section 2.01(1). In other words, *the primary practical function of the act requirement is to identify those cases where the special rules of possession and omission liability are triggered.*

Omission as "Negative Act" Liability frequently is imposed for an omission to perform an act that one has a legal duty to perform. An omission is sometimes called a "negative act," but this seems a dangerous practice, for it too easily permits an omission to be substituted for an act without requiring the special requirements for omission liability, such as a legal duty and the physical capacity to perform the act. This nearly universal exception to the act requirement is justified on the claim that an actor's failure to perform a legal duty of which she is capable satisfies the rationales of the act requirement as effectively as does an affirmative act. More on the subject of omission liability in the upcoming Notes.

Possession as Act Another almost universally recognized exception to the act requirement is the criminalization of possession. Rather than treating it as a formal exception to the act requirement, most codes simply define possession to be an act, similar to the way intangible acts are treated. Under the Model Penal Code, for example,

> Possession is an act, within the meaning of this Section [requiring that liability be based on a voluntary act,] if the possessor knowingly procured or received the thing possessed or was aware of his control thereof for a sufficient period to have been able to terminate his possession.[1]

With the addition of the special requirement—*knowing* receipt or control—the intent-based rationales of the act requirement are sought to be satisfied. That is, where the actor has knowledge of receipt or control but fails to terminate possession, he has made a conscious choice to keep possession. The intent rationales also are satisfied by the additional requirement that an actor have control "for a sufficient period to have been able to terminate his possession." This ensures that the actor could have terminated possession, thus his retention can be viewed again as the manifestation of a choice. In this respect, possession and other intangible acts are analogous. The Mafia chief's silence is judged an "act" because the chief *knows* that his silence will be taken as assent, has the *opportunity* to speak, yet *chooses* to have the killing performed.

Possession and Intangible Acts as Omissions One might view possession and other such intangible acts as forms of criminal omission, rather than as intangible acts. That is, the actor's liability flows from his failure to dispossess himself of contraband, as he has the legal duty and capacity to do. (His knowledge of his possession for a period of time needed to terminate possession demonstrates his capacity.) Note that the special requirements for liability for possession or for

---

1. Model Penal Code §2.01(4).

intangible acts mirror the special requirements for omission liability: a duty and the capacity to act.

Act Requirement for Code Drafters   What has been discussed so far is what might be called the act requirement in assessing liability. Criminal liability must be based on conduct that includes a voluntary act. If it is not, then the special requirements of possession or omission liability must be satisfied. A second kind of act requirement directs itself to the definition of offenses. Nothing in the act requirement in Model Penal Code section 2.01(1) requires that an offense defini-tion contain any act as an element of the offense. The provision is addressed to adjudicators, not code drafters. But several Supreme Court cases do set an "act requirement" of sorts for code drafters. These cases may be read as constitu-tionalizing a requirement that an offense definition must contain a requirement of an act on its face, or something analogous to it. The effect and the rationale of such a requirement is found in the need to limit governmental power to define criminal offenses.

Constitutionalization of Act Requirement   In *Scales v. United States,* for example, the Court bars the government from criminalizing pure membership in the Communist Party. It does, however, allow liability for "active" members.[1] Similarly, vagrancy offenses that punish "not having any visible means of support" have been invalidated. Also invalidated are statutes such as those criminalizing "keeping a place...with intent" to sell liquor unlawfully. In *Robinson v. California,* the Court invalidated a state statute that made it an offense to "be addicted to the use of narcotics."[2] Yet these cases limit governmental criminaliza-tion authority only in a modest way. It would not be a violation of this constitutional act requirement to criminalize using drugs or selling liquor. This act requirement may make the government's case more difficult to prove, but it only modestly limits what the government may criminalize.

Voluntariness Requirement and Its Rationales   In discussing the act requirement one tends to assume, often without noting, that it is a voluntary act to which one refers. An *in*voluntary act would not satisfy the primary purposes of the act requirement. Permitting liability to be based on an involuntary act would do little or nothing to protect from punishment fantasizing or forming irresolute intentions, and would provide little or no objective evidence of intention. For these reasons, the "act" requirement typically is meant to require a voluntary act, even if such is not expressly provided. Section 23 examines the issue of defenses to liability for conduct that is not voluntary.

---

1. 367 U.S. 203, 222, 81 S. Ct. 1469, 6 L. Ed. 2d 782 (1961).

2. 370 U.S. 660, 667, 82 S. Ct. 1417, 8 L. Ed. 2d 758 (1962). The holding in *Robinson* was modified, or at least more clearly explained, in *Powell v. Texas,* 392 U.S. 514, 88 S. Ct. 2145, 20 L. Ed. 2d 1254 (1968), but *Robinson* remains as a constitutionalization of an act requirement for offense definitions. The plurality in *Powell* explains:

> The entire thrust of *Robinson*'s interpretation of the Cruel and Unusual Punishment Cause is that criminal penalties may be inflicted only if the accused has committed some act, had engaged in some behavior, which society has an interest in preventing, or perhaps in historical common law terms, has committed some actus reus.

Id. at 533, 88 S. Ct. at 2154-2155, 20 L. Ed. 2d at 1268. What *Powell* does is call into question whether *Robinson* can be read to also constitutionalize the voluntariness requirement.

Notes on Liability for an Omission

Omission as Exception to Act Requirement / The previous Notes discuss the virtues of the act requirement, yet criminal liability for an omission is also well accepted where the actor has a legal duty and the capacity to act.[1] It is said that this rather fundamental exception to the act requirement is permitted because an actor's failure to perform a legal duty of which she is capable satisfies the purposes of the act requirement, or at least satisfies them as well as an act does.

Omission Satisfying Act Requirement Rationales / Specifically, the special requirements for omission liability — the requirements of (1) a legal duty (2) of which one is capable of performing — help to exclude from liability cases of fantasizing and irresolute intentions. A failure to act by itself does nothing to screen out mere fantasies. It is the actor's failure to act in light of her capacity to do so that suggests the actor's willingness to go beyond mere fantasizing and to have the harm or evil of the offense occur. Even then, however, the screening effect seems weak; "letting something happen" simply does not carry the same implication of resolute intention that is shown in causing something to happen by affirmative action. An actor's failure to perform a legal duty also provides some evidentiary support for the existence of an intention to have the harm or evil occur but, again, the force of the implication is weak. Inaction often carries no implication of intention unless it is shown that the actor knows of his duty to act and the opportunity to do so.

As to other rationales for the act requirement, an omission also does poorly in limiting governmental criminalization authority. The government need only create a legal duty in order to criminalize an omission. Nor are an omission and its special requirements helpful in providing an identifiable time and place of occurrence. An omission necessarily is a continuing state. On balance, then, while an omission itself serves none of the rationales of the act requirement, the special requirements of duty and capacity do something toward satisfying those rationales, but considerably less than even the poor performance of the act requirement itself. It should be no surprise, then, that omission liability traditionally is limited. Legal duties to act generally are few in number and narrow in scope.

Omission to Perform Duty a Substitute Only for Act Keep in mind that where an actor fails to perform a duty, though the actor has the capacity to do so, criminal liability does not necessarily follow. Satisfaction of the requirements for omission liability serves only to satisfy the act requirement. As always, liability requires proof of all elements of the offense — all objective elements (circumstance and result elements), a causal connection between the omission and any result element, and all culpability elements — as well as the absence of all general defenses. In Dunning's case, this means that even if Dunning had a legal duty and the capacity to get Mrs. Harrington her medicine, he is criminally liable for

---

1. Most modern codes state that crimes may be committed either by an act or an omission. See, e.g., Ala. Code 1975, §13A-2-3; Alaska Stat. §11.81.600; Ariz. Rev. Stat. Ann. §13-201; Ark. Stat. §41-202; Del. Code tit. 11, §242; Hawaii Rev. Stat. §702-200; Ky. Rev. Stat. Ann. §501.030; La. Rev. Stat. Ann. §14:18; Me. Rev. Stat. Ann. tit. 17-A, §31; Mo. Rev. Stat. §562.011; Mont. Code Ann. §45-2-202; N.H. Rev. Stat. Ann. §626:1; N.J. Stat. Ann. §2C:2-1; New York Penal Law §15.10; N.D. Cent. Code §12.1-02-01; Ohio Rev. Code Ann. §2901.21; Or. Rev. Stat. §161.095; 18 Pa. Cons. Stat. Ann. §301; Tex. Penal Code Ann. §6.01.

her death only if he also satisfies the requirements of the homicide offense: At the time of his omission, he must have had a culpable state of mind as to his omission that causes her death, and there must be an adequate causal connection between his omission and her death (including proof that, if he had acted, she would not have died).

Duty Requirement Inherent in Omission Offenses Liability for an omission requires a legal duty to act; a moral duty to act is not sufficient. The duty may arise either from the offense definition itself or from some other provision of criminal or civil law. A duty arises from the former when an offense is defined in terms of omission. This is the situation where the legislature has made it an offense, for example, to fail to file a tax return, for a parent to neglect to furnish medical care to a sick child, for a motorist to fail to stop after having an accident, or for a draftee to fail to report for induction. In each instance, the offense makes the omission criminal and thereby creates the duty to act.

Duty Requirement in Commission Offenses A legal duty to act also may be created by a provision of either criminal or civil law separate from the offense charged. For example, a municipal regulation requiring homeowners to shovel the sidewalk in front of their homes creates a legal duty to act and therefore ultimately might provide the basis for criminal liability if an actor's failure to shovel is accompanied by the required elements of a criminal offense. In *Commonwealth v. Howard*, for example, the defendant was held liable for involuntary manslaughter, which required causing death of another by "*the doing of an unlawful act* in a reckless or grossly negligent manner."[1] Yet liability was based on the defendant's omission, her "failure to protect her child from the...regular and severe beatings" by her boyfriend. The defendant's failure to perform her legal duty to protect her child, created by Pennsylvania case law, was treated as adequate to satisfy the requirement of the offense that the offender cause the death by "doing an unlawful act."

Authorization Needed for Omission Liability of Commission Offense This substitution of the failure to perform a legal duty for an offense definition's requirement of affirmative conduct, as seen in *Howard*, typically is authorized in modern codes by a general provision. Model Penal Code section 2.01(3) provides a poor model because it provides only that "liability...may *not* be based on an omission...*unless*...a duty to perform [is] imposed by law." The legality principle would disapprove assuming the converse to be true — that liability *may* be imposed for an omission *if* the actor fails to perform a duty. The preferable statutory form would affirmatively provide that an actor's failure to perform a legal duty may be used as a substitute for a required act — that is, may be a justification for *imputing* conduct required by an offense definition.[2] Such a provision also might be useful as a reminder that an omission to perform a legal duty is not itself enough to establish liability; all other offense elements also must be proven.

---

1. 265 Pa. Super. 535, 537, 402 A.2d 674, 676 (1979) (emphasis added).
2. The Model Penal Code formulation would be adequate if every offense definition were defined so as to allow liability for either an act or an omission. But, it is not uncommon even in the Model Penal Code for offenses to be defined as requiring affirmative conduct, such as "menace," "restrain," or "start a fire" (see §§211.1(1)(c), 212.2(a), 220.1(2)).

Civil Sources of Legal Duty Where an offense is defined in terms of an affirmative act, the legal duty required for omission liability must be found elsewhere than in the offense definition. A legal duty to act commonly is recognized in the following instances: (1) Landowners may have specific duties with regard to the condition of their property, as in the requirement that homeowners fence in their swimming pools; (2) a duty may arise from a relationship between the actor and the victim, as in the duty of a parent to protect a child, noted in *Howard;* (3) a contract between parties may create a legal duty to act, such as a hotel lifeguard's duty to save a drowning guest (this might be viewed as a form of relationship created by contract and thus a subset of (2) above); (4) tort law may create a continuing duty of care to an actor who voluntarily assumes responsibility for another; (5) also under tort law, an actor may have a duty to rescue if the actor has created the peril, even if such creation is neither tortuous nor criminal (for example, an actor who sets a legal trap for vermin may be liable for failing to immediately release a trapped dog). These are the general categories of duties recognized by case law. Civil statutes have created any number of other miscellaneous duties. For example, a special provision may give dog owners a duty to keep their dogs on leashes.

Duty and Legality Principle One may wonder whether this mechanism for defining the duties that may give rise to criminal liability — that is, by cross-reference to the entire body of civil law — is consistent with the spirit of the legality principle. The demands of the legality principle exist in part to ensure that citizens can know the law that they are obliged to follow on pain of criminal sanction. Yet no one would argue that it is realistic for a citizen to know the full breadth of civil (and criminal) law that might give rise to a duty to act. Indeed, this aspect of omission liability requires citizens not only to know all existing statutes and case law creating a duty, but also to be able to apply those statutes and case law at a moment's notice. Does Dunning have a duty to aid Mrs. Harrington? The answer depends on the nature of their contractual agreement. Does Dunning's escort duty extend to protecting Mrs. Harrington's health, getting her medicine? Does her refusal to confirm that Dunning will be paid give Dunning a right to declare an anticipatory breach? Has Dunning's "escorting" of his girlfriend breached his contract with Mrs. Harrington, thereby giving Mrs. Harrington a right to renegotiate that month's payment, making lawful her refusal to confirm full payment? Contract law no doubt has an answer to these questions, but it is unrealistic to think that Dunning would.

Knowledge of Duty Not Required The potential complexity in determining one's duty is all the more problematic because an actor's mistake as to the existence or extent of his duty typically is no defense. This is true of even a reasonable mistake as to one's legal duty. The absence of a knowledge-of-duty requirement follows from the rule that ignorance of the law is no excuse. But while that rule may have some justification in the context of affirmative acts, liability for omissions presents special problems and may justify a special rule. An actor's failure to know of her legal duty to act undercuts the moral implications that may be drawn from the actor's omission. One might urge adoption of a rule consistent with this by arguing in cases of omission liability that the duty to act is an element of the offense and therefore is subject to the standard requirement of proof of a minimum culpability, usually recklessness. While nothing in the Code suggests that this is intended by the drafters, nothing in the Code would seem to prevent such an interpretation.[1]

Constitutionalization of Knowledge-of-Duty Requirement   In *Lambert v. California*,[2] the Supreme Court seems to recognize the unfairness of imposing omission liability where an actor is unaware of a duty to act. The Court suggests the possibility of a constitutional requirement, under the Due Process Clause, that an actor have some awareness of, or at least a reasonable opportunity to become aware of, the duty to act. Lambert failed to register with the police, as all convicted felons were required to do by a Los Angeles ordinance. She won a reversal by arguing that she was unaware of her obligation to register and could not reasonably have been expected to be aware of it. But *Lambert* has been given the narrowest of readings, and its continuing significance is unclear. It can be argued that it applies only to cases of omission liability for minor offenses or regulatory offenses like the felon registration requirement, or only where the existence of a duty is not generally known and has not reasonably been made known, or only to cases where all of these special conditions are satisfied.

General Duty to Aid   Many writers have argued for a general duty to aid a stranger when the stranger is in danger of death or serious bodily injury. While such a duty is not uncommon in Europe, few states have adopted such a general duty to aid.[3] The opponents of such a general duty argue that it would create undue governmental intrusion into the affairs of the individual and, further, that any general duty necessarily would be susceptible to overbroad interpretations. They prefer liability for an omission only where the law already has created a specific duty to act. Proponents of a general duty to rescue argue that a limited general duty to rescue is morally required and legally feasible. They would create a duty to save life if it could be done without personal danger or pecuniary loss. The most dramatic illustrations of the need for a general duty are provided by cases like the stabbing of Catherine Genovese outside of her New York apartment building. This case and the issues surrounding a general duty to rescue are the focus of the following Discussion Materials.

● DISCUSSION MATERIALS

Should There Be a Criminal-Law-Enforced Duty to Protect, Rescue, or Assist a Stranger in Danger If One Can Do So Without Unreasonable Risk or Inconvenience?

In its portrayal of Catherine Genovese's murder in front of more than thirty witnesses, the *New York Times* article below offers a look at the disturbing outcome of not imposing a duty to rescue or to assist. The obvious moral concerns

---

1. The fact that the duty requirement is drafted in Model Penal Code §2.01(3)(b) as a defense does admittedly make the interpretation more difficult. It does not clearly fall within the definition of "element of an offense" contained in §1.13(9).

2. 355 U.S. 225, 78 S. Ct. 240, 2 L. Ed. 2d 228 (1957).

3. See, e.g., R.I. Gen. Law §§11-56-1; Vt. Stat. Ann. tit. 12 §519; Wis. Stat. Ann. §940.34(1), (2).

have inspired three state provisions creating a duty to assist — those adopted by Rhode Island, Vermont, and Wisconsin. Even in the face of cases like the Genovese murder, Joshua Dressler opposes enacting "Bad Samaritan" laws by appealing to retributive, utilitarian, practical, and liberty-oriented arguments. In support of rescue statutes, Daniel Yeager examines what personal and societal motivations lead people not to rescue and evaluates the duty-to-rescue laws in place in some states. As a counterpoint, the Indian Law Commissioners Report explains its rejection of broad liability for omission to act, in favor of a less imposing rule.

37 Who Saw Murder Didn't Call Police

N.Y. Times, March 27, 1964

For more than half an hour thirty-eight respectable, law-abiding citizens in Queens watched a killer stalk and stab a woman in three separate attacks in Kew Gardens. Twice the sound of their voices and the sudden glow of their bedroom lights interrupted him and frightened him off. Each time he returned, sought her out and stabbed her again. Not one person telephoned the police during the assault; one witness called after the woman was dead. That was two weeks ago today. But Assistant Chief Inspector Frederick M. Lussen, in charge of the borough's detectives and a veteran of twenty-five years of homicide investigations, is still shocked.

He can give a matter-of-fact recitation of many murders. But the Kew Gardens slaying baffles him — not because it is a murder, but because the "good people" failed to call the police. "As we have reconstructed the crime," he said, "the assailant had three chances to kill this woman during a thirty-five minute period. He returned twice to complete the job. If we had been called when he first attacked, the woman might not be dead now."

This is what the police say happened beginning at 3:20 a.m. in the staid, middle-class, tree-lined Austin Street area:

Twenty-eight-year-old Catherine Genovese, who was called Kitty by almost everyone in the neighborhood, was returning home from her job as manager of a bar in Hollis. She parked her red Fiat in a lot adjacent to the Kew Gardens Long Island Rail Road Station, facing Mowbray Place. Like many residents of the neighborhood, she had parked there day after day since her arrival from Connecticut a year ago, although the railroad frowns on the practice. She turned off the lights of her car, locked the door and started to walk the 100 feet to the entrance of her apartment at 82-70 Austin Street, which is in a Tudor building, with stores on the first floor and apartments on the second.

The entrance to the apartment is in the rear of the building because the front is rented to retail stores. At night the quiet neighborhood is shrouded in the slumbering darkness that marks most residential areas.

Miss Genovese noticed a man at the far end of the lot, near a seven-story apartment house at 82-40 Austin Street. She halted. Then, nervously, she headed up Austin Street toward Lefferts Boulevard, where there is a call box to the 102d Police Precinct in nearby Richmond Hill. She got as far as a street light in front of a bookstore before the man grabbed her. She screamed. Lights went on in the ten-story apartment house at 82-67 Austin Street, which faces the bookstore. Windows slip open and voices punctured the early-morning stillness. Miss Genovese screamed: "Oh, my God, he stabbed me! Please help me! Please help me!" From one of the upper windows in the apartment house, a man called down: "Let that girl alone!"

The assailant looked up at him, shrugged and walked down Austin Street toward a white sedan parked a short distance away. Miss Genovese struggled to her feet. Lights went out. The killer returned to Miss Genovese, now trying to make her way around the side of the building by the parking lot to get to her apartment. The assailant stabbed her again.

"I'm dying!" she shrieked. "I'm dying!"

Windows were opened again, and lights went on in many apartments. The assailant got into his car and drove away. Miss Genovese staggered to her feet. A city bus, Q-10, the Lefferts Boulevard line to Kennedy International Airport, passed. It was 3:35 a.m.

The assailant returned. By then, Miss Genovese had crawled to the back of the building, where the freshly painted brown doors to the apartment house held out hope of safety. The killer tried the first door; she wasn't there. At the second door, 82-62 Austin Street, he saw her slumped on the floor at the foot of the stairs. He stabbed her a third time — fatally.

It was 3:50 by the time the police received their first call from a man who was a neighbor of Miss Genovese. In two minutes they were at the scene. The neighbor, a seventy-year-old woman and another woman were the only persons on the street. Nobody else came forward. The man explained that he had called the police after much deliberation. He had phoned a friend in Nassau County for advice and then he had crossed the roof of the building to the apartment of the elderly woman to get her to make the call.

"I didn't want to get involved" he sheepishly told the police.

Six days later, the police arrested Winston Moseley, a twenty-nine-year-old business-machine operator, and charged him with the homicide. Moseley had no previous record. He is married, has two children and owns a home at 133-19 Sutter Avenue, South Ozone Park, Queens. On Wednesday, a court committed him to Kings County Hospital for psychiatric observation.

The police stressed how simple it would have been to have gotten in touch with them. "A phone call," said one of the detectives, "would have done it." The police may be reached by dialing "0" for operator or SPring 7-3100.

The question of whether the witness can be held legally responsible in any way for failure to report the crime was put to the Police Department's legal bureau. There, a spokesman said: "There is no legal responsibility, with few exceptions, for any citizen to report a crime."

Under the statutes of the city, he said, a witness to a suspicious or violent death must report it to the medical examiner. Under state law, a witness cannot withhold information in a kidnaping.

Today witnesses from the neighborhood, which is made up of one-family homes in the $35,000 to $60,000 range with the exception of the two apartment houses near the railroad station, find it difficult to explain why they didn't call the police.

Lieut. Bernard Jacobs, who handled the investigation by the detectives, said: "It is one of the better neighborhoods. There are few reports of crimes. You only get the usual complaints about boys playing or garbage cans being turned over."

The police said most persons had told them they had been afraid to call, but had given meaningless answers when asked what they had feared.

"We can understand the reticence of people to become involved in an area of violence," Lieutenant Jacobs said, "but where they are in their homes, near phones, why should they be afraid to call the police?"

He said his men were able to piece together what happened—and capture the suspect—because the residents furnished all the information when detectives rang doorbells during the days following the slaying.

"But why didn't someone call us that night?" he asked unbelievingly.

Witnesses—some of them unable to believe what they had allowed to happen—told a reporter why.

A housewife, knowingly if quite casually, said, "We thought it was a lover's quarrel." A husband and wife both said, "Frankly, we were afraid." They seemed aware of the fact that events might have been different. A distraught woman, wiping her hands in her apron, said, "I didn't want my husband to get involved."

One couple, now willing to talk about that night, said they heard the first screams. The husband looked thoughtfully at the bookstore where the killer first grabbed Miss Genovese. "We went to the window to see what was happening," he said, "but the light from our bedroom made it difficult to see the street." The wife, still apprehensive, added: "I put out the light and we were able to see better."

Asked why they hadn't called the police, she shrugged and replied: "I don't know."

A man peeked out from a slight opening in the doorway to his apartment and rattled off an account of the killer's second attack. Why hadn't he called the police at the time? "I was tired," he said without emotion. "I went back to bed."

It was 4:25 a.m. when the ambulance arrived for the body of Miss Genovese. It drove off. "Then," a solemn police detective said, "the people came out."

Rhode Island General Laws Section 11-56-1
Duty to Assist

Any person at the scene of an emergency who knows that another person is exposed to or has suffered grave physical harm shall, to the extent that he or she can do so without danger or peril to himself or herself or to others, give reasonable assistance to the exposed person. Any person violating the provisions of this section shall be guilty of a petty misdemeanor and shall be subject to imprisonment for a term not exceeding six (6) months or by a fine of not more than five hundred dollars ($500.00), or both.

Vermont Statutes Annotated, Title 12, Chapter 23, Section 519
Emergency Medical Care

(a) A person who knows that another is exposed to grave physical harm shall, to the extent that the same can be rendered without danger or peril to himself or without interference with important duties owed to others, give reasonable assistance to the exposed person unless that assistance or care is being provided by others.

(b) A person who provides reasonable assistance in compliance with subsection (a) of this section shall not be liable in civil damages unless his acts constitute gross negligence or unless he will receive or expects to receive remuneration. Nothing contained in this subsection shall alter existing law with respect to tort liability of a practitioner of the healing arts for acts committed in the ordinary course of his practice.

(c) A person who willfully violates subsection (a) of this section shall be fined not more than $ 100.00.

Wisconsin Statutes Annotated Section 940.34(1), (2)
Duty to Aid Endangered Crime Victim

(1) Whoever violates sub. (2) is guilty of a Class C misdemeanor.

(2) Any person who knows that a crime is being committed and that a victim is exposed to bodily harm shall summon law enforcement officers or other assistance or shall provide assistance to the victim. A person need not comply with this subsection if any of the following apply:

(a) Compliance would place him or her in danger.
(b) Compliance would interfere with duties the person owes to others.
(c) Assistance is being summoned or provided by others.

Joshua Dressler, Some Brief Thoughts (Mostly Negative) About "Bad Samaritan" Laws
40 Santa Clara Law Review, 971-975, 980-988 (2000)

"Soulless Individuals" in Our Midst? [The author recounts the events of the Cash-Strohmeyer-Iverson case and the events of the Kitty Genovese case.]

What is to be done with persons like David Cash? He violated no Nevada criminal law when he purportedly left Sherrice Iverson in the clutches of Strohmeyer. But if some legislators get their way, future David Cashes will not get away so easily. Legislators of all political stripes may find it hard to resist the opportunity to enact Bad Samaritan ("BS") criminal laws. After all, who would possibly want to defend the "soulless" David Cashes or "rabies-infected animals... disguised as... human beings" of this world?

I, too, have no intention of defending the indefensible.... But it is precisely because the case for punishing people like Cash seems so obvious and so comforting to our psyche — it allows us to express our moral revulsion and, perhaps less charitably, feel morally superior — that we should hesitate long and hard before enacting BS legislation. Although such laws are morally defensible, there are also powerful reasons for rejecting them....

Refuting the Justifications for Bad Samaritan Laws Although [some] retributive arguments support punishment of a Bad Samaritan, there are significant reasons — some retributive-based, some utilitarian, and some founded in political theory — that should give responsible lawmakers considerable pause before endorsing general duty-to-aid legislation.

Criticisms of BS laws begin with legalist concerns with retributive overtones. First, why is the offense called a "Bad Samaritan" law? The name suggests, I think, that we punish the bystander for being a bad person, i.e., for his "selfishness, callousness, or whatever it was" that caused him not to come to the aid of a person in need. However, the criminal law should not be (and, ordinarily, is not) used that way: criminal law punishes individuals for their culpable acts (or, perhaps here, culpable non-acts), but not generally for bad character. As mortals, we lack the capacity to evaluate another's soul. It is wrongful conduct, and not an individual's status as a bad person or even an individual's bad thoughts, that justify criminal intervention. BS laws may violate this principle. At a minimum, there is a serious risk that juries will inadvertently punish people for being (or seeming to be) evil or "soulless," rather than for what occurred on a specific occasion. One need only consider David Cash and the public's intense feelings of disgust and anger toward him to appreciate why jurors might convict Bad Samaritans less on the basis of the "technicalities" of a statute, and more on the basis of character evaluation.

Second, for retributivists, punishment of an innocent person is always morally wrong, and the risk of false positives — punishing an innocent person — is especially high with BS laws. . . .

Notice the inherent problem of punishing people for not-doings rather than wrongdoings. When a person points a loaded gun at another and intentionally pulls the trigger, it is reasonable to infer that the actor intended to cause harm. His mens rea is obvious. It is far harder to determine why a person does not act. . . .

[W]hy did the Genovese bystanders hear the woman scream but fail to act, if in fact that was the case? Is it at least possible that some of the bystanders did not know she was in dire jeopardy? A person who wakes up from a sleep often fails to appreciate her surroundings. Also, perhaps some of them — even all of them — believed that someone else had already called the police. It may be that, despite the condemnation directed at the Genovese bystanders, few, if any, of them were guilty of Bad Samaritanism. In view of the inherent ambiguities in such circumstances, if juries take their duties seriously — including the presumption of innocence — few, if any, BS convictions will result. If emotions and bad character attributions rule the day, however, innocent persons will be improperly convicted.

Third, the threat of convicting innocent persons points to a related danger. BS statutes are so rubbery in their drafting that they grant police and prosecutors too much discretion to determine whether and whom to prosecute. The due process clause prohibits the enforcement of penal laws that "fail to establish guidelines to prevent arbitrary and discriminatory enforcement of the law." However, even if the issue is seen as a non-constitutional matter, it is difficult to see how a prosecutor can fairly determine when charges are proper.

Again, the distinction between actions and non-actions demonstrates the vagueness problem. BS laws compel people to make the world (or, at least, a small part of it) better, rather than punish actors for actively making it worse. In the latter case, the identifiable conduct of the accused, and the demonstrable harm caused by those actions, serve to single out the actor as a plausible candidate for prosecution. With laws that punish for nothing, rather than something, there is a need for alternative objective criteria. At least with commission-by-omission liability, there are identifiable criteria, such as the status relationship of the parties, contractual understandings, or the suspect's personal connection to the emergency by having created the initial risk. In contrast, with BS laws, which impose a duty to aid strangers (potentially, anyone), criminal responsibility is based on imprecise factors (e.g., the duty to provide "reasonable assistance") and nearly unknowable circumstances (e.g., that the stranger is exposed to "grave" physical harm, and that assistance can be rendered without any "danger or peril" to the actor or others).

As the Genovese case demonstrates, these omission criteria are far less helpful in determining whether and against whom a prosecution should be initiated than are identifiable acts of commission. There is a significant risk with BS laws that the decision to prosecute will be based on a prosecutor's perceived need to respond to public outrage, which, in turn, may be based less on the merits of the case and more on media coverage (which, in turn, may be founded on inappropriate factors, such as race, background, or even the physical attractiveness of the victim and/or the supposed poor character of the bystander). Not only may persons guilty of Bad Samaritanism avoid conviction because of selective enforcement, but the process may result in prosecution of persons who, upon cooler reflection, we might realize are innocent of wrongful not-doing.

There are also utilitarian reasons to question the wisdom of BS legislation. First, if such laws are taken seriously, the costs of investigating and potentially prosecuting bystanders might be prohibitive. Imagine the investigation necessary to decide whether to prosecute any of the Genovese bystanders and, if the decision were to proceed, to determine which of them to prosecute. Second, to the extent that BS statutes are narrowly drafted to reduce the risk of unfairness, prosecutions are likely to be rare (and convictions even rarer). Therefore, it is unlikely that the threat of punishment will have the desired effect of inducing bystanders to help persons in peril. The muted threat of a misdemeanor conviction is less likely to promote good behavior than the threat of public scorn that follows the publicity of such cases, or a Samaritan's own conscience.

Third, to the extent that such laws do, in fact, compel "Good Samaritanism," there is a risk that the Samaritan will hurt the person she is trying to assist, hurt others in the process, or unforeseeably harm herself. Fourth, since BS statutes are not linked to any prevention-of-harm causal requirement (i.e., it is not necessary to successfully prevent the threatened harm from occurring; it is enough to give it "the old college try"), the costs of such laws may easily outweigh their limited practical benefits. Even supporters of BS legislation concede that the law only helps at the boundaries.

There is one final reason to question the wisdom of BS statutes. Not only are positive duties morally less powerful than negative ones, but they also restrict human liberty to a greater degree. A penal law that prohibits a person from doing X (e.g., unjustifiably killing another person) permits that individual to do anything other than X (assuming no other negative duty). In contrast, a law that requires a person to do Y (e.g., help a bystander) bars that person from doing anything other than Y....

What is the significance of this point? It is that the United States is a country that highly values individual liberty:

> Each person is regarded as an autonomous being, responsible for his or her own conduct. One aim of the law is to maximize individual liberty, so as to allow each individual to pursue a conception of the good life with as few constraints as possible. Constraints there must be, of course, in modern society: but freedom of action should be curtailed only so far as is necessary to restrain individuals from causing injury or loss to others.

Few people, except the most ardent libertarians, accept the latter statement in full. The point, however, is that in a society that generally values personal autonomy, we need to be exceptionally cautious about enacting laws that compel us to benefit others, rather than passing laws that simply require us not to harm others. The issue here, after all, is whether criminal law (as distinguished from tort law and religious, educational, and family institutions) should try to compel Good Samaritanism. Traditionally, Anglo-American criminal law sets only minimalist goals. The penal law does not seek to punish every morally bad act that we commit (aren't we glad of that?), and it leaves to other institutions the effort "to purify thoughts and perfect character."

Other Discussion Materials

Daniel B. Yeager, A Radical Community of Aid: A Rejoinder to Opponents of Affirmative Duties to Help Strangers
71 Washington University Law Quarterly 1-8, 13-38 (1993)

Introduction The use of law to coerce strangers to help one another always has been suspect in American legal thought. Laws that attempt to balance autonomy and a minimally acceptable level of neighborliness by imposing affirmative duties to help others are unpopular because they interfere with personal autonomy and the American "obsession with privacy." Even the most well-intentioned balance seems to prefer soulless individualism to creeping involuntary servitude and "unforeseen partnership." Our freedom to ignore those in need of immediate aid, however, may be a sign that we are "too free to consult the general good," or at least too free to acquiesce in our neighbors' misery.

This "crescendo of self-centeredness" downplays the cramped view of communal obligations that the rejection of a duty to aid others implies. By elevating rights over responsibilities, critics have argued, the law discourages the positive acts of communal solidarity that are part and parcel of citizenship. Adherents of the view that good citizenship entails communal obligations include Cicero, Plato, Mill, Bentham, Darwin, and Kant. Together they intimate that Jesus' admonition in the Good Samaritan parable, to go and do as the Samaritan did, should be perceived as duty, not charity. Because community membership inevitably involves dependency and vulnerability, these exceptional voices suggest that "the claim of each of us on the resources of the others is equal," even if we are not equally dependent in matters of strength, wealth or usefulness.

Contemporary sociologist Robert Wuthnow adds to this dialogue his studies, which challenge the assumption that individualism and altruism are antagonistic. . . . Wuthnow's studies support his conclusion that those who claim to be most intensely committed to self-realization and material pleasure are also most likely to value helping others.

Despite the arguments of many influential critics, the American reluctance to impose a legal duty to help others "shows remarkable staying power." Apparently fed up with a view so pessimistic and unsatisfying from an imperiled's standpoint (if not from that of a disinterested by-stander), Vermont, Rhode Island, and Wisconsin have adopted criminal statutes that impose an affirmative duty to help those in grave danger. Minnesota has imposed civil liability for failure to rescue under identical circumstances. Modeling their legislation on European precursors, this minority of states imposes liability for knowingly failing to undertake "easy rescue." Florida, Massachusetts, Ohio, Rhode Island, Washington, and Wisconsin have established slightly more stringent criminal penalties for the failure to report the commission of a serious crime. Although the laws are rarely invoked, they not only encourage a climate of increased personal security, but they also betray a view of community, solidarity, and humanity that is worth aspiring toward and expressing by law.

A Critique of the Majority Approach The majority view of duties among strangers is bleak. A passerby need not "warn a blind man of an open manhole, . . . lift the head of a sleeping drunk out of a puddle of water, . . . throw a rope from a bridge to a drowning swimmer, [or] rescue or even report the discovery of a small child wandering lost in a wood." The harshness of the law reflects that even if in a moral sense all men are brothers, they are not their brothers' keepers. Thus moral philosophy and theology, not law, govern beneficence among strangers. The problem is purely one of individual empathy, not one of social or legislative importance.

Several writers have suggested ways to bring brotherhood to law. Most suggestions resemble the Vermont statute, substantially duplicated by Minnesota and Rhode Island, which penalizes omitters who knowingly fail to undertake easy rescues. An easy rescue is one which involves no danger to the rescuer and does not interfere with important duties that the rescuer owes to others. Through these laws, "common humanity . . . forges between us a link, but a weak one," given that the rescuer may opt out at the first sign of danger. Realistically, the law cannot require much more, since each of us should be permitted to remain a live coward rather than a dead public servant. . . .

Why Bystanders Fail To Intervene Why those who see others in danger so often do nothing is unclear. In the case of witnesses to crimes, danger — real or imagined — and fear of retaliation account for some failures to intervene or notify authorities. In addition, because emergencies are, for most of us, exotic, a bystander's lack of opportunity for planning and rehearsal and the difficulty of quickly selecting the appropriate type of intervention might make her assistance less likely.

Some commentators, however, do not place the blame on individuals, but on urban conditions. Our "Cold Society" is a "fragmented," dispassionate "megalopolis" of crumbling morality, of "apathy" and "indifference," where "homo urbanis," charged by "T.V. sadism," "fear of police" and "unconscious sadistic impulses," ignores the suffering of others. Despite the deterioration of urban life, American cities remain densely populated because "few of us are attracted to the stifling small-town images of community we find championed in social-science textbooks."

The presence of other bystanders may reduce each potential rescuer's individual sense of responsibility to the imperiled, and increase the probability of free-riding. Each is lulled into a state of "pluralistic ignorance," which induces multiple bystanders to interpret others' nonaction as a sign of no danger. Despite the apparent incentive that risk-sharing would provide to potential co-intervenors, because of social inhibitions that arise in groups, people are more prone to respond to another's distress when alone than when accompanied by other witnesses.

Bystanders thus face a "choice of nightmares": fail to intervene and experience the empathic distress of watching another human being suffer, the guilt of failing to live up to a minimal threshold of decency, and the shame of having that failure witnessed by others; or, intervene and risk retaliation by an assailant, the ridicule and derision of nonintervening bystanders, and the threat of being mistaken for the cause of the harm. Moreover, the victim may spurn, attack, or become completely dependent on the rescuer, while the legal system may enlist the rescuer as a witness subject to innumerable encounters with police, lawyers, and judges. The nightmare then may be most easily resolved by convincing oneself that the victim is not imperiled.

Contradictory norms further complicate the bystander-imperiled episode and tend to produce inaction. Specifically, the controlling norm to "mind one's own business" clashes with the equally dominant norm to "do unto others." Even "do unto others" carries social baggage. Citizens may actively censor themselves to avoid the pejorative labels "bleeding heart," "do-gooder," and "goody two-shoes," perhaps because compassion and altruism are often explained as no more than masks for self-interest.

A duty to report clashes with settled concepts such as loyalty and privacy when, based on relational affinity among family, friends, or ethnic or other groups, one has agreed not to disclose an incriminating fact. For example, in *Roberts v. United States,* a drug defendant appealed his sentence, which the lower court had increased when he failed to name his suppliers. Affirming his sentence, the Supreme Court condemned his contumacy as "antisocial conduct." In dissent, Justice Marshall strongly disagreed with the majority's conclusion that the defendant had a duty to become an informer, explaining:

> ...The countervailing social values of loyalty and personal privacy have prevented us from imposing on the citizenry at large a duty to join in the business of crime detection. If the Court's view of social mores were accurate, it would be hard to understand how terms such as "stool pigeon," "snitch," "squealer," and "tattletale" have come to be the common description of those who engage in such behavior.

In its use of terms such as "stool pigeon" and "snitch," Justice Marshall's comment seems most apt when applied to an "informer," defined as "someone who betrays a comrade, i.e., a fellow member of a movement, a colleague, or a friend, to the authorities." His statement has less force, however, for a victim or stranger who witnesses a crime. Even the relationships among doctors, lawyers, or police officers, which are guided by institutionally imposed affirmative reporting requirements, also carry informal pressures to refuse to testify against a fellow member. The duty among strangers, however, involves no affinity-based obstacles, not even those endemic to the criminal milieu, such as the honor that is said to exist among thieves....

A Contemporary Illustration: "The Accused" In 1983, six patrons of "Big Dan's," a New Bedford, Massachusetts bar, raped and sodomized a twenty-two-year-old mother of two while other patrons cheered. The setting was a working-class tavern in a largely Portuguese, economically depressed waterfront town of 98,000. The victim initially entered the bar to buy cigarettes, ordered a "high-ball," and talked briefly both with a woman she recognized and with her future assailants. She was then "'dragged literally kicking and screaming' across the floor," and "'thrown' onto the pool table, where one assailant tried to pull her jeans off." After two of the attackers tried unsuccessfully to force the victim to perform fellatio, two others raped her. "I could hear yelling, laughing, down near the end of the bar," she said. "My head was hanging off the edge of the pool table....I was screaming, pleading, begging....One man held my head and pulled my hair. The more I screamed, the harder he pulled...." Finally, "clothed only in a shirt and one shoe, the victim escaped and ran into the street where she flagged down a passing truck."

In forty-three states, the nonfeasant witnesses committed no crime, although those who cheered on the assailants may have committed acts subjecting them to accomplice liability. No special relationship existed between the victim and the witnesses, with the possible exception of the bartender, who testified at trial but was not indicted. In these states, inaction in such a situation remains a matter of the passive witnesses' private morality, not law. In the substantial majority of states where the law is content to punish only active assailants, "rape is...a lawful spectator sport."

A Penal Code Prepared by the Indian Law Commissioners
Note M, 53-56 (1837)

Early in the progress of the Code it became necessary for us to consider the following question: When acts are made punishable on the ground that those acts produce, or are intended to produce, or are known to be likely to produce certain evil effects, to what extent ought omissions which produce, which are intended to produce, or which are known to be likely to produce the same evil effects be made punishable?

Two things we take to be evident; first, that some of these omissions ought to be punished in exactly the same manner in which acts are punished; secondly, that all these omissions ought not to be punished.... It is difficult to say whether a Penal Code which should put no omissions on the same footing with acts, or a Penal Code which should put all omissions on the same footing with acts would produce consequences more absurd and revolting. There is no country in which either of these principles is adopted. Indeed, it is hard to conceive how, if either were adopted, society could be held together.

It is plain, therefore, that a middle course must be taken. But it is not easy to determine what that middle course ought to be. The absurdity of the two extremes is obvious. But there are innumerable intermediate points; and wherever the line of demarcation may be drawn it will, we fear, include some cases which we might wish to exempt, and will exempt some which we might wish to include.

Mr. Livingston's Code provides, that a person shall be considered as guilty of homicide who omits to save life, which he could save "without personal danger, or pecuniary loss." This rule appears to us to be open to serious objection. There may be extreme inconvenience without the smallest personal danger, or the smallest risk of pecuniary loss, as in the case . . . of a surgeon summoned from Calcutta to Meerut, to perform an operation. He may be offered such a fee that he would be a gainer by going. He may have no ground to apprehend that he should run any greater personal risk by journeying to the Upper Provinces than by continuing to reside in Bengal. But he is about to proceed to Europe immediately, or he expects some members of his family by the next ship, and wishes to be at the residency to receive them. He, therefore, refuses to go. Surely, he ought not, for so refusing, to be treated as a murderer. It would be somewhat inconsistent to punish one man for not staying three months in India to save the life of another, and to leave wholly unpunished the man who, enjoying ample wealth, should refuse to disburse an anna to save the life of another. Again it appears to us that it may be fitting to punish a person as a murderer for causing death by omitting an act which cannot be performed without personal danger, or pecuniary loss. A parent may be unable to procure food for an infant without money. Yet the parent, if he has the means, is bound to furnish the infant with food, and if by omitting to do so he voluntarily causes its death he may with propriety be treated as a murderer. A nurse hired to attend a person suffering from an infectious disease cannot perform her duty without running some risk of infection. Yet if she deserts the sick person, and thus voluntarily causes his death, we should be disposed to treat her as a murderer.

We pronounce with confidence, therefore, that the line ought not to be drawn where Mr. Livingston has drawn it. But it is with great diffidence that we bring forward our own proposition. It is open to objections: cases may be put in which it will operate too severely, and cases in which it will operate too leniently: but we are unable to devise a better.

What we propose is this, that where acts are made punishable on the ground that they have caused, or have been intended to cause, or have been known to be likely to cause a certain evil effect, omissions which have caused, which have been intended to cause, or which have been known to be likely to cause the same effect shall be punishable in the same manner; provided that such omissions were, on other grounds, illegal. An omission is illegal . . . if it be an offence, if it be a breach of some direction of law, or if it be such a wrong as would be a good ground for a civil action. . . .

We are sensible that in some of the cases which we have put our rule may appear too lenient. But we do not think that it can be made more severe, without disturbing the whole order of society. . . .

It is, indeed, most highly desirable that men should not merely abstain from doing harm to their neighbors, but should render active services to their neighbors. In general however the penal law must content itself with keeping men from doing positive harm, and must leave to public opinion, and to the teachers of morality and religion, the office of furnishing men with motives for doing positive good. It is evident that to attempt to punish men by law for not rendering to others all the service which it is their duty to render to others would be preposterous. We must grant impunity to the vast majority of those omissions which a benevolent morality would pronounce reprehensible, and must content ourselves with punishing such omissions only when they are distinguished from the rest by some circumstance which marks them out as peculiarly fit objects of penal legislation. Now, no circumstance appears to us so well fitted to be the mark as the circumstance which we have selected. It will generally be found in the most atrocious cases of omission: it will scarcely ever be found in a venial case of omission: and it is more clear and certain than any other mark that has occurred to us. That there are objections to the line which we propose to draw, we have admitted. But there are objections to every line which can be drawn, and some line must be drawn.

Corporate Criminality

When a non-human legal fiction, such as a corporation, is charged with a criminal offense, all the offense elements must be imputed because, obviously, legal fictions cannot act or think except through the humans that serve as their agents. When and how, and whether, this should be done is the subject of this Section.

◆ THE CASE OF FORD MOTOR COMPANY

It is about 5:30, the evening of August 10, 1978, in Elkhart County, Indiana. Lyn Ulrich, 16, hops into the back of her sister Judy's 1973 Ford Pinto. The Ulrichs' cousin Donna, 18, who is visiting from Illinois, climbs in after her. With Judy behind the wheel, and they set off out of Osceolo down Highway 33 toward Elkhart. Elkhart County is a small conservative community in northern Indiana, east of South Bend. About 45,000 of the 125,000 residents live in the city of Elkhart itself. Many in the community share a common Amish or Mennonite heritage or, like the Ulrichs, a strong fundamentalist Christian faith. The girls are on their way to play volleyball at a Baptist church near Goshen, about 20 miles away.

The Pinto is Judy's first car. Her parents, Earl and Mattie, are helping with payments as a graduation present. Judy knows that Pintos have been popular for years, and has seen many on the road. Ford has sold almost two million, but recently they have become a major problem for the company.

Figure 71 **1973 Ford Pinto**

(FordPinto.com)

Figure 72 **Henry Ford II (right) announces restructuring of President Lee Iacocca's job, 1977**

(Bettmann/Corbis)

The development of the car in the early 1970s was rushed from the start. Lee Iacocca, then president of Ford, insisted that the car be under 2,000 pounds and less than $2,000, which did not leave the engineers a great deal of flexibility in design features. Although the first Pinto passed all federal regulations, it did not hold up well in rear-end collisions. Horrible accidents involving Pintos eventually lead to more than 50 civil suits against Ford. In one case in southern California, a new Pinto stalls and is hit from behind by a car going about 30 mph. The Pinto immediately catches fire. Richard Grimshaw, a 13-year old riding in the car, survives but is left with burns on 90% of his body. He loses his nose, left ear, and most of his left hand, and endures four months in the hospital and 65 surgeries. A jury awards him almost $128 million in punitive damages, in addition to $2.8 million in compensatory funds. At the time, it is the largest award ever made by a jury for a personal injury case, though the judge later reduces it to $6.6 million. There are several more accidents, and Ford soon learns to avoid jury trials.

Media attention increased dramatically when, in September 1977, Mark Dowie published an article in Mother Jones entitled "Pinto Madness." In the award-winning article, Dowie reports that Ford unquestionably knew the Pinto gas tank was unsafe. The car had failed every collision test when the gas tank was not altered using one of three relatively simple methods. A Ford engineer is quoted as saying that even though they knew it was not safe, no one would necessarily tell Lee Iacocca, who had personally pushed the development of the car to be completed in almost half the normal time. "That person would have been fired. Safety was not a popular subject around Ford in those days. With Lee it was taboo. Whenever a problem was raised that meant a delay in the Pinto, Lee would chomp on his cigar, look out the window, and say, 'Read the product objectives again and get back to work.'" At that time, safety was not one of the product objectives. Dowie went on to detail the internal Ford documents that used cost-benefit analysis to evaluate the costs of the Pinto casualties. The document showed that Ford rounded down the National Highway Traffic Safety Administration's (NHTSA) calculation that a human life is worth $200,275, and by estimating 180 fiery deaths, 180 serious burn injuries and 2,100 burned vehicles, determined that damages would be about $49.5 million. According to company calculations, it was therefore less expensive to leave the flawed gas tank alone than to spend the $137 million estimated for an $11 adjustment to each of the 11 million cars and 1.5 million light trucks. Dowie questions the calculations as well as the underlying process, arguing that crashes would result in many more injuries than the company allowed, and that the cost to make the car safer could have been as low as $5.08. Ford contests most aspects of Dowie's evaluation, arguing as well that their decisions were not based on such cost-benefit calculations.

Public announcement of the Dowie report at a D.C. press conference began a public outcry against the Pinto. The next day, the NHTSA began a formal investigation. On May 8, 1978, the NHTSA issued a report stating that the 1.9 million Ford Pintos and 30,000 Mercury Bobcats (a similar model) built between 1971 and 1976 have a system defect that could lead to fires in a rear-end collision. The Department of Transportation is then authorized to order a formal recall. Ford has thirty days to review the results before a public hearing set for June 14.

As a result of the bad publicity, on June 9, Ford recalls all Pintos made between 1971 and 1976, including Judy's car. The company reports that it will take a few months to get all the letters out; owners probably will not receive them until September. On this cool August evening, the girls are not thinking about any of these car troubles. Their family has not yet received word of the recall or the particular susceptibility of the gas tank to leaks during collisions.

Enjoying the sun and the cool evening breeze on their way, the Ulrichs chat with their cousin Donna. Born just a few days after Judy, Donna is president of her Mennonite church's youth group, and is thinking about doing a full-time volunteer program now that she has graduated. She tells her cousins about the volunteer trip in rural Kentucky that her group just completed.

Figure 73 **Judy Ulrich**
(And Books)

Judy has also just graduated from high school, and plans to study interior design in college in the Fall. She is working at an ice cream shop in South Bend to make money for college. Her younger sister, Lyn, is about to start her junior year at Penn High School, and is a straight-A student. She thinks that she might study mathematics in college, and works as a cashier at the local supermarket. She and Judy have become active in the youth group at church, and sometimes accompanies the hymns on the piano at evening services.

After they have driven for about half an hour, Judy notices that the gas is running low. She pulls into a Checker gas station and rests the gas cap on the roof of the car. After paying, she forgets to put the gas cap back on and starts driving with it still resting on the roof of the car. They do not notice until they have driven about a mile and a half and the cap suddenly flies off the roof and lands on the other side of the five-lane highway.

Figure 74 **Lyn Ulrich**
(And Books)

Traffic is not too bad. Judy waits until it seems safe, then carefully makes a U-turn and puts on her hazard flashers. She slowly drives westward toward the lost cap. There is an eight-inch curb along the side of the road that keeps her from pulling off the road.

At the same time, Robert Duggan is driving westward along Highway 33 in a gold van with "Peace Train" written across the hood. He is on his way to a friend's to get the van tuned up and ready for a vacation. He also needs to clean it up a bit; there are two Budweiser cans, the ends of two

Figure 75 **Donna Ulrich**
(And Books)

marijuana cigarettes, some rolling papers, and a baggie of what he thinks are amphetamines (actually, caffeine pills). He had just gotten his license back a few weeks before, after speeding, running a stop sign, and failing to yield enough times that the authorities suspended his driving privileges. He is trying to be more careful now, so when he sees a police car coming the other way, he checks his speedometer to make sure he is still driving under the 55 mph limit. Relieved that he is, he reaches down to grab his pack of cigarettes that has fallen to the floor of the van. When he looks up, he sees the Ulrich's Pinto about ten feet ahead. There is no time to stop.

Witnesses see Duggan's van slowing to what looks like about 30 mph before he hits the girls' car. The pine board bumper of the gold van slams into the back of the Pinto. The rear of the car is jammed into the highway and leaves three gouges in the road. Duggan is thrown forward but is not shaken too badly.

Rear steel sub-frames that might have protected the gas tank were rejected from the early Pinto design as too heavy and expensive to fit the self-imposed design requirements. The back bumper in these models can withstand a collision of only about five or ten mph. Ford, with other car manufacturers, successfully lobbied to hold off federal requirements for resisting even 20 mph rear-end collisions until 1977. Even in a 30 mph collision, the car's back half entirely crumples.

The gas tank of Judy's Pinto is about six inches away from the bumper. From the force of the crash, the tank slams into the differential housing, the block in the middle of the rear axle, and ruptures on one of the four sharp bolts that stick out from the housing. Gas spills from these holes all over the road. The impact also pulls out the tube leading from the gas tank, leaving a two and one-half inch hole. More gas spills out through this hole. Then the tank bursts along the seams, and the seam rips, leaving a six-inch gap. More gas pours out.

All of this happens in a moment. The passenger compartment of Judy's car is splashed with a sheet of gasoline. Duggan can smell it from the road. The impact sets steel scraping against steel as the car grinds along the road. As a spark ignites the gasoline, a long flame shoots out, then a huge explosion as the car bursts into flames.

Witnesses are shocked by the explosion and by the fire. For a 30 mph collision, they expected a mild fender bender; instead, the car looked "like a large napalm bomb." Bystanders can no longer see the girls in the back seat. It is "a solid mass of orange flame." Black smoke and flames billow out 20 feet into the air. The temperature in the back of the car reaches almost one thousand degrees. The plastic dashboard and steering wheel melt almost completely, and the vinyl seats are burnt down to the springs. Lyn's sunglasses melt around her eyes. Donna and Lyn die in less than a minute.

Judy is thrown from the car, still alive, but is burned over more than 95% of her body. Her right ankle is caught in the door, and as her sneaker melts on her foot she begins to call for help. Bystanders, stunned that she is still alive, run to try to help, and use a board to pry the door open. They pull her to the side of the road.

Duggan is on his knees, watching in horror and sobbing. When someone checks to see if he is all right, he beats the ground with his fists and cries for people to help the girls.

Figure 76 **The accident scene**

(And Books)

Bradley McCalim, one of the first EMTs to arrive, has not seen such a burn victim since Vietnam. He cannot believe Judy is still alive; in fact, until she speaks, he is sure she is dead. Judy asks him if the other girls are all right. A bystander, without looking into the burnt shell of the car, reassures her that they are.

The medics, thankful that Judy cannot feel the extent of her injuries because the nerve endings are burned, reassure her about her chances, telling her that she will make it, even though they know that there is no hope. She dies eight hours later.

Neil Graves, a six-and-a-half-year veteran state trooper is soon radioed to report to the scene. He has seen 987 accidents and does not expect this to be anything new. But the scene is not what he expects. He has seen only three car fires, and they were usually only after high-speed collisions. Here the cars do not look like they are from the same accident. One of the van's headlights is cracked, the grill is pushed in, and there are a few dents. The back of the Pinto is completely buckled, and only the burnt shell of the car remains.

Looking inside, he sees two charred bodies in the back seat, a gruesome sight he will never forget. Then he notices the smell of gasoline in the interior of the car. At some point, he remembers the article he read in Mother Jones the year before about the Pinto and starts wondering about the role the car might have played in the accident.

News of the accident gets out. After a local television station calls Terry Shewmaker, the county's assistant prosecutor, to ask him about the case, Shewmaker calls the sheriff to find out what happened. Then he calls his boss, Mike Consentino. Hearing of the severity of the death, injuries, and damage, Consentino tells Shewmaker to treat it as a potential homicide.

Mike Consentino is a hard-working Republican who ran for and won the elected position of county prosecutor on a "law and order" platform. He was raised by his mother and as a teenager earned an athletic scholarship to Beloit College, where he majored in philosophy. He briefly served in the military, then put himself through evening classes at the University of Wisconsin Law School. His job as prosecutor is only part-time; he spends the rest of his time in private practice, often defending corporations and others in the community. But he is proud of his record as a prosecutor; he has won convictions in every one of the 25 murder cases he has tried.

On Friday, Duggan is arrested for possession of an illegal drug when the pills are found in his van. They are later determined to be caffeine. Meanwhile, national media track down the state trooper, Graves, where he works at his part-time job. They ask about the car, not the drivers. Consentino calls "Pinto Madness" author Dowie and gets more details about Ford's development of the car and suggestions on whom to contact at the company.

Evidence from the accident site is collected and processed during the weekend. Consentino and Shewmaker meet with Graves and the rest of the staff to discuss the charges for the case. Pictures of the dead girls are passed around, leaving

Figure 75 **Close up view of the van and Pinto**
(And Books)

the men horrified and upset. No one should die that way, they think. Something must have gone wrong, and they feel that they need to find out who was responsible.

Lawyers with civil cases pending against Ford start calling Consentino offering corporate documents that would be damaging to Ford. The criminal case could have great influence over other Pinto civil suits. A verdict against Ford in a criminal case, which has a stricter burden of proof than in civil cases, would hurt Ford's position in civil trials and give civil lawyers an edge.

Seeing the volume of evidence against Ford that points to the company's knowledge of the Pinto's dangerousness, and the company's delay in acting

Figure 78 **Prosecutor Mike Consentino**

(And Books)

on a recall, Consentino concludes that the company had a role in the girls' deaths. Looking at the case as a prosecutor, he concludes that Ford's development of the Pinto makes the company criminally culpable, not just tangentially responsible. The company has done something morally wrong that resulted in three individuals' deaths, he reasons. It should be prosecuted. Mattie and Earl Ulrich strongly support the idea of going after Ford in a criminal prosecution.

Constentino files an indictment that charges Ford Motor Company, a corporation, with causing the Ulrichs' deaths "through the acts and omission of its agents acting within the scope of their authority with said corporation [when they] did recklessly design and manufacture a certain 1973 Pinto...in such a manner as would likely cause said automobile to flame and burn upon rear-end impact, ...[and such] reckless disregard for the safety of other persons [caused the girls] to languish and die by incineration."

It is the first time that a major corporation has been indicted on homicide charges for making an allegedly defective product that led to a consumer's death. The maximum penalty is a fine of $10,000 for each death. The van driver, Duggan, is not charged with an offense.

1. Relying only on your own intuitions of justice, what liability and punishment, if any, does the Ford Motor Company deserve? (Obviously a corporate defendant cannot be imprisoned. Use the scale below simply as a device by which to communicate the quantum of punishment you think is deserved. That punishment, if any, obviously would be imposed through a mechanism other than imprisonment.)

N	0	1	2	3	4	5	6	7	8	9	10	11
☐	☐	☐	☐	☐	☐	☐	☐	☐	☐	☐	☐	☐
no liability	liability but no punishment	1 day	2 wks	2 mo	6 mo	1 yr	3 yrs	7 yrs	15 yrs	30 yrs	life imprison- ment	death

2. What liability, if any, under the then-existing statutes?

3. What liability, if any, under the Model Penal Code?

■ THE LAW

Burns Indiana Statutes Annotated
(1978)

Division 5. Courts and Judicial Proceedings

Title 35, Book 2. Criminal Law and Procedure
Article 42. Offenses Against the Person

Section 35-42-1-1. Murder

A person who:

(1) Knowingly or intentionally kills another human being; or

(2) Kills another human being while committing or attempting to commit arson, burglary, child molesting, criminal deviate conduct, kidnapping, rape, or robbery;

commits murder, a felony.

Section 35-42-1-4. Involuntary Manslaughter

A person who kills another human being while committing or attempting to commit:

(1) A class C or class D felony that inherently poses a risk of serious bodily injury;

(2) A class A misdemeanor that inherently poses a risk of serious bodily injury; or

(3) Battery;

commits involuntary manslaughter, a class C felony. However, if the killing results from the operation of a vehicle, the offense is a class D felony.

Section 35-42-1-5. Reckless Homicide

A person who recklessly kills another human being commits reckless homicide, a Class C felony. However, if the killing results from the operation of a vehicle, the offense is a Class D felony.

Section 35-42-2-2. Recklessness

(a) A person who recklessly, knowingly, or intentionally performs an act that creates a substantial risk of bodily injury to another person commits criminal recklessness, a Class B misdemeanor. However, the offense is a Class A misdemeanor if the conduct includes the use of a vehicle or deadly weapon.

(b) A person who recklessly, knowingly, or intentionally inflicts serious bodily injury on another person commits criminal recklessness, a Class D felony.

Article 41. Crimes — General Substantive Provisions
Chapter 2. Basis of Liability

Section 35-41-2-1. Voluntary Conduct

(a) A person commits an offense only if he voluntarily engages in conduct in violation of the statute defining the offense. However, a person who omits to perform an act commits an offense only if he has a statutory, common law, or contractual duty to perform the act.

(b) If possession of property constitutes any part of the prohibited conduct, it is a defense that the person who possessed the property was not aware of his possession for a time sufficient for him to have terminated his possession.

Section 35-41-2-2. Culpability

(a) A person engages in conduct "intentionally" if, when he engages in the conduct, it is his conscious objective to do so.

(b) A person engages in conduct "knowingly" if, when he engages in the conduct, he is aware of a high probability that he is doing so.

(c) A person engages in conduct "recklessly" if he engages in the conduct in plain, conscious, and unjustifiable disregard of harm that might result and the disregard involves a substantial deviation from acceptable standards of conduct.

(d) Unless the statute defining the offense provides otherwise, if a kind of culpability is required for commission of an offense, it is required with respect to every material element of the prohibited conduct.

Section 35-41-2-3. Liability of a Corporation, Partnership or Unincorporated Association

(a) A corporation, partnership, or unincorporated association may be prosecuted for any offense; it may be convicted of an offense only if it is proved that the offense was committed by its agent acting within the scope of his authority.

(b) Recovery of a fine, costs, or forfeiture from a corporation, partnership, or unincorporated association is limited to the property of the corporation, partnership, or unincorporated association.

Howell v. State
200 Ind. 345, 163 N.E. 492, 1928 Ind. LEXIS 78 (1928)

Defendant drove an automobile along a paved road at an unlawful speed of thirty-five miles per hour and collided with a nine-year old girl, who, with two companions, was proceeding along the road facing the oncoming automobile, but on the opposite side of the road. When the car was within ten feet of her, the deceased suddenly darted in front of the automobile. The court held that the unlawful act of the defendant was not the proximate cause of her death.

Model Penal Code
(Official Draft 1962)

Section 2.07. Liability of Corporations, Unincorporated Associations and Persons Acting, or Under a Duty to Act, in Their Behalf

(1) A corporation may be convicted of the commission of an offense if:

(a) the offense is a violation or the offense is defined by a statute other than the Code in which a legislative purpose to impose liability on corporations plainly appears and the conduct is performed by an agent of the corporation acting in behalf of the corporation within the scope of his office or employment, except that if the law defining the offense designates the agents for whose conduct the corporation is accountable or the circumstances under which it is accountable, such provisions shall apply; or

(b) the offense consists of an omission to discharge a specific duty of affirmative performance imposed on corporations by law; or

(c) the commission of the offense was authorized, requested, commanded, performed or recklessly tolerated by the board of directors or by a high managerial agent acting in behalf of the corporation within the scope of his office or employment.

(2) When absolute liability is imposed for the commission of an offense, a legislative purpose to impose liability on a corporation shall be assumed, unless the contrary plainly appears.

(3) An unincorporated association may be convicted of the commission of an offense if:

(a) the offense is defined by a statute other than the Code which expressly provides for the liability of such an association and the conduct is performed by an agent of the association acting in behalf of the association within the scope of his office or employment, except that if the law defining the offense designates the agents for whose conduct the association is accountable or the circumstances under which it is accountable, such provisions shall apply; or

(b) the offense consists of an omission to discharge a specific duty of affirmative performance imposed on associations by law.

(4) As used in this Section:

(a) "corporation" does not include an entity organized as or by a governmental agency for the execution of a governmental program;

(b) "agent" means any director, officer, servant, employee or other person authorized to act in behalf of the corporation or association and, in the case of an unincorporated association, a member of such association;

(c) "high managerial agent" means an officer of a corporation or an unincorporated association, or, in the case of a partnership, a partner, or any other agent of a corporation or association having duties of such responsibility that his conduct may fairly be assumed to represent the policy of the corporation or association.

(5) In any prosecution of a corporation or an unincorporated association for the commission of an offense included within the terms of Subsection (1)(a) or Subsection (3)(a) of this Section, other than an offense for which absolute liability has been imposed, it shall be a defense if the defendant proves by a preponderance of evidence that the high managerial agent having supervisory responsibility over the subject matter of the offense employed due diligence to prevent its commission. This paragraph shall not apply if it is plainly inconsistent with the legislative purpose in defining the particular offense.

(6) (a) A person is legally accountable for any conduct he performs or causes to be performed in the name of the corporation or an unincorporated association or in its behalf to the same extent as if it were performed in his own name or behalf.

(b) Whenever a duty to act is imposed by law upon a corporation or an unincorporated association, any agent of the corporation or association having primary responsibility for the discharge of the duty is legally accountable for a reckless omission to perform the required act to the same extent as if the duty were imposed by law directly upon himself.

(c) When a person is convicted of an offense by reason of his legal accountability for the conduct of a corporation or an unincorporated association, he is subject to the sentence authorized by law when a natural person is convicted of an offense of the grade and the degree involved.

● OVERVIEW OF CORPORATE CRIMINALITY

Organizational Liability as Imputation Because an organization can neither act nor think except through its agents and officers, it cannot satisfy the elements of an offense except through imputation. Thus, if criminal liability of organizations is to be provided, the criminal law must specify the rules for imputation of conduct and culpability to an organization. Whether criminal liability for organizations, sometimes called "enterprise liability," is appropriate and useful is the subject of the Discussion Materials.

Common Law Reluctance Courts in the Common Law period were reluctant to impose criminal liability on corporations. The imposition of such liability seemed impossible: How could a legal entity have the mens rea required by criminal law? Many procedural requirements — such as the presence of the defendant at trial — also seemed to suggest that organizations were inappropriate subjects for criminal prosecutions. Finally, organizations cannot be imprisoned or executed, the most common forms of punishment. But growing industrialization and public pressure for more effective control of corporate behavior brought about a change of view. Prosecution of corporations was first allowed for strict liability offenses. Because such offenses required no mens rea and rarely involved a sentence of imprisonment, their use against a legal entity seemed less objectionable. The potential for corporate criminality then spread to general intent offenses. Common law rules often presumed a required "general intent" from the offense conduct. This made it possible to prosecute organizations without any special rules for imputing mens rea. Corporations could not be held liable for specific-intent offenses, however, because of the impossibility of proving the required specific intent. This last expansion of corporate liability to specific intent offenses is of modern origin. It is sometimes criticized as double vicarious liability — the shareholders being punished without regard to their ability to control the management, and the management being punished without regard to their ability to control the offending employee — but liability in many jurisdictions tends to avoid the most egregious instances of vicarious liability by imposing important limitations.

Offenses Authorized by Upper Management   Most jurisdictions today permit corporate liability for a traditional criminal offense, even an offense carrying a significant penalty and requiring culpability. In *State v. Christy Pontiac-GMC, Inc.*, for example, a salesman for the Christy Pontiac car dealership swindled two customers out of cash rebates and kept the money for the corporation. Under the rules of organizational liability used in *Christy,* the criminal acts of a corporation's agents are imputed to the corporation if they are (1) performed within the scope of employment; (2) in furtherance of the interests of the corporation; and (3) authorized, tolerated, or ratified by corporate management.[1] Because the corporation received the swindled funds and the conduct was ratified, if not authorized, by the corporation's president, the corporation was held liable for the employee's criminal act.

Offense Conduct "Recklessly Tolerated"   Some jurisdictions follow the Model Penal Code in extending liability beyond conduct authorized or ratified by corporate management to offense conduct "recklessly tolerated".[2] This seeks to prevent management from simply turning a blind eye to violations because the violations further the corporate interest. This approach, focusing on the acts or omissions of upper management, stems from a belief that punishing management misconduct is the most effective and fair means of controlling future corporate misconduct.

Liability for Unauthorized Regulatory Violations by Agent   Some jurisdictions, including the Model Penal Code, allow liability without a showing of authorization (or reckless toleration) by upper management for quasi-criminal offenses (often called "violations") and regulatory offenses (typically defined outside of the criminal code). As section 2.07(1)(a) provides:

> A corporation may be convicted of the commission of an offense if...the offense is a violation or the offense is defined by a statute other than the Code in which a legislative purpose to impose liability on corporations plainly appears and the conduct is performed *by an agent of the corporation acting in behalf of the corporation within the scope of his office or employment,* except that if the law defining the offense designates the agents for whose

---

1. 354 N.W.2d 17, 18-20 (Minn. 1984).
2. Model Penal Code §2.07(1)(c). This form of liability is not available under the Code for the prosecution of unincorporated associations. See §2.07(3). Many states have similar rules. See, e.g., Mo. Ann. Stat. §562.056(1)&(2) (1979); Pa. Stat. Ann. tit. 18, §307(a)(1) (1983).

conduct the corporation is accountable or the circumstances under which it is accountable, such provisions shall apply . . . .

As the italicized language makes clear, liability can arise from any conduct performed on behalf of the corporation, even if entirely unauthorized. But where such is the basis for liability, many jurisdictions follow the Model Penal Code in allowing a "due diligence defense," such as under section 2.07(5):

> [I]t shall be a defense if the defendant proves by a preponderance of evidence that the high managerial agent having supervisory responsibility over the subject matter of the offense employed due diligence to prevent its commission. This paragraph shall not apply if it is plainly inconsistent with the legislative purpose in defining the particular offense.[1]

Liability for Agent's Unauthorized Criminal Offense   Other jurisdictions, including the federal system, provide a still broader form of corporate liability. These jurisdictions simply impute the acts and omissions of agents within the scope of employment to the corporation, even for serious offenses; corporate liability is not limited to violations authorized by, or recklessly tolerated by, upper management. Nor do most of these jurisdictions provide a due diligence defense for upper management attempts to prevent the offense. Under this approach, criminal liability for corporations is not significantly different from tort liability under the doctrine of *respondeat superior*. In fact, some courts have put it in just those terms.[2] Thus, a corporation may be liable for a serious offense based on the acts of an agent that were expressly forbidden by management and that management diligently sought to prevent. In *United States v. Hilton Hotels Corp.*,[3] for example, a group of hotels, restaurants, and hotel and restaurant supply companies organized an association with other businesses in Portland, Oregon, to attract conventions to their city. Members were to contribute money to help fund the association. To aid collections, hotel members, including appellant, agreed to give preferential treatment to suppliers who paid their assessments and to curtail purchases from those who did not. The agreement was held by the court to be a violation of the Sherman Antitrust Act. Despite disapproval of such illegal actions by the hotel's president and manager, the purchasing agent abided by the agreement. The *Hilton* court concludes that there need be no official authorization or toleration of the criminal conduct of agents for imputation: the offense conduct will be imputed to the corporation even if management specifically prohibits the conduct. *Hilton* requires only that the conduct be within the scope of employment and that outsiders might reasonably assume that the agent's conduct was authorized.

Liability for Agent's Conduct Disapproved by Management   The *Hilton* court reasons that a corporation's express prohibition of the criminal conduct ought not protect the corporation from liability because, after issuing formal

---

1. Model Penal Code §2.07(5).

2. Judge Learned Hand concludes that "there is no distinction in essence between the civil and the criminal liability of corporations based upon the element of intent or wrongful purpose. Each is merely an imputation to the corporation of the mental condition of its agents." United States v. Nearing, 252 F. 223, 231 (D.N.Y. 1918).

3. 467 F.2d 1000, 1002 (9th Cir. 1972).

orders against a violation, the upper management nonetheless may create pressure for the violation in less visible ways. Further, the court believes that high management is likely to know about violations and thus ought to have the burden of doing whatever is necessary to prevent them. But these concerns may be satisfied by using a "reckless toleration" standard of liability, as the Model Penal Code does. One can argue, however, that the broader liability of the federal approach provides greater deterrence and that limiting potential liability to only the offending agent would be an ineffective deterrent. In a large corporation, the offending agent may be difficult to identify and, even if caught and punished, the agent is not in a position to change the practices of other corporate agents. Only high management has the opportunity and authority effectively to avoid violations. But this line of argument openly abandons any pretense that criminal liability for corporations rests upon the traditional blameworthiness criterion that governs criminal liability in non-organizational contexts and that distinguishes criminal liability from civil liability.

Relaxing Concurrence Requirement   For reasons similar to those offered by the *Hilton* court, many jurisdictions have done much to relax the normal rules of imputation and proof. Some hold that it need not be shown that any agent of the company satisfies both the actus reus and mens rea of the offense, although concurrence between the two normally would be required. Indeed, many courts do not require the identification of the agent who performed the actus reus. The requirement that the agent be acting within the scope of his employment has been similarly broadened to include nearly any job-related activity. Also, it need not be shown that the corporation actually received any benefit from the agent's offense, although conduct that is against the corporation's interest will not support liability for the corporation. The wisdom of these kinds of attempts to make corporate prosecution easier, and to broaden the scope of corporate liability, depends in large measure on why corporate criminality is imposed, the subject of the Discussion Materials.

▲ PROBLEM
Evergreen Greenbacks

Garden Centers Supply, Inc. (GCS) supplies independent retailers with plants, flowers, bushes, trees, and so forth. During the two months before Christmas, GCS hires additional help to handle the large increase in business generated by Christmas tree sales. Bob and Chester Turner have recently been hired to tour the many small tree farms. They are authorized to buy trees for up to $2.25 per foot. If they negotiate a lower price, they receive a bonus equal to 20% of any amount saved. Because demand is high this year, trees are harder to find and those available are bringing higher prices. As the first three weeks of hauling close, Bob and Chester find that they are far from the bonuses that they were counting on. Indeed, they have failed to meet their quota and are concerned that they may not be hired again next year. They hit on a plan that they think will improve their situation. A state forest within their territory has suitable trees. By adding state trees to their farm purchases and doctoring their transport slips, they can both fill their quota and reduce the per-foot cost of each load. The company handbook for drivers specifically prohibits such unauthorized cuttings, but Bob and Chester see little chance of being caught either by the state foresters or by the company. By week five, their record has improved dramatically and they are in line for big bonuses. Company officials are surprised by the dramatic improvement, especially given the poor condition of the market supply. When asked to explain their sudden success, Bob and Chester have no explanation other than "just lucky." Officials are puzzled and suspicious but see no way to effectively pursue the matter further. They remind Bob and Chester of the company's policy against unauthorized cuttings.

A state forester in Flemington is shocked to find a Z-type spruce on sale when she takes her children to buy their Christmas tree. Z-types are an experimental tree bred for their capacity to quickly absorb large amounts of water, an important characteristic for successful plantings in sandy soil. She relates her discovery to state investigators, who paper-trace the tree to a purchase by Bob and Chester from the Elliott farm, which has no Z-types. Interviews with the Elliotts reveal alterations in the transport slips. The illegal cuttings from the state forest are discovered. Bob and Chester are charged, but state officials also institute a prosecution against GCS for the actions of its employees. The officials cite their inability to effectively police the large stands of state evergreens found in unpopulated areas throughout the state and the special need for a high deterrent effect. By prosecuting GCS, they hope to motivate all wholesalers to more actively discourage illegal state cuttings. They also believe that the publicity surrounding the prosecution will discourage the traditional increase in state tree thefts immediately preceding Christmas. Is GCS liable for the thefts of state trees by Bob and Chester?

● DISCUSSION MATERIALS

Should Criminal Liability Be Imposed on a Legal Fiction, Such as a Corporation?

John Coffee proposes various utilitarian arguments in favor of imposing corporate criminal liability but also points to the potential efficacy of using the civil justice system instead. The excerpt from Douglas Anderson also advocates criminal liability for corporations and argues for legislative reform that would make clear their potential liability for homicide offenses where life-endangering products are concerned. Robinson & Cahill criticize the criminalization of regulatory violations, from a desert and moral condemnation perspective, and call for regulatory and corporate liability to be assessed via the civil system. Finally, Andrew Ashworth evaluates an alternative, prevention-seeking approach to corporate criminal liability, proposed by Fisse and Braithwaite, which would impose requirements on corporations that maintain the criminal label but are distinct from that which is required of individuals.

John Coffee, Corporate Criminal Responsibility

1 Encyclopedia of Crime and Justice 253, 256-261 (S. Kadish ed., 1983)

A Policy Appraisal: Is Corporate Criminal Liability Useful? "Corporations don't commit crimes; people do." This theme (borrowed, of course, from the opponents of gun control) has been implicit in a substantial body of legal commentary that has criticized the idea of corporate criminal liability. The criticism has had two quite different focal points: (1) the asserted injustice of vicarious criminal liability; and the alleged inefficiency of corporate liability. The following critiques have been repeatedly made. First, with respect to the rationale underlying corporate liability, it has been claimed that:

1. Vicarious liability is appropriate only as a principle of tort law since its justification lies in its allocation of the loss to the party more able to bear it (or at least more deserving of the burden), but it is unrelated to the purposes of retribution, deterrence, prevention, and rehabilitation that underlie the criminal law....

2. Vicarious liability is unjust because its burden falls on the innocent rather than the guilty — that is, the penalty is borne by stockholders and others having an interest in the corporation, rather than by the guilty individual....

3. Vicarious liability results in a disparity between businesses conducted in the corporate form and those run as a proprietorship, since the individual proprietor will not be criminally liable for the independent acts of his employees....

4. Vicarious liability for the corporation may in the future open the door to expanded vicarious criminal liability for individuals as well.

Second, a number of arguments have been advanced to claim that corporate punishment is inefficient or even counterproductive [detailed below]:

1. Corporations are largely undeterrable; fines are ineffective, and only the imprisonment of guilty individuals achieves real deterrence....

2. Prosecution of the corporation may lead courts, juries, and prosecutors to acquit or dismiss charges against individual defendants, and thus corporate liability serves as a shield behind which the truly guilty can hide....

3. Civil remedies are more flexible and potentially severe, and they also avoid the constitutional restrictions associated with a criminal prosecution....

Although none of these arguments is frivolous, each on closer examination seems seriously overbroad or at least unconfirmed by the relatively slim empirical evidence available....

The Utility of Corporate Punishment Some critics of corporate liability have doubted whether the corporation itself can be deterred. Such an evaluation seems premature, however, given another conclusion which virtually every commentator on the subject has reached: that corporations tend to receive very small fines in relation to their size, their earnings, or even their expected gain from the criminal transaction.... Thus, it is logically difficult to assert simultaneously that corporations are not punished and that they are not deterrable.

But here a problem noted earlier resurfaces: corporate punishment tends to fall on the innocent — not only on stockholders but also on employees (who may be laid off), creditors, the surrounding community, and, of course, the consumer, who may in effect indemnify the corporation if the fine can be passed on as a cost of doing business. Thus, an apparent paradox is reached: the economist's model asserts that only the imposition of severe fines in an amount well in excess of the expected gain will generate adequate deterrence, since it is necessary to compensate for a risk-of-apprehension factor that invariably falls well below 100 percent. But if corporate penalties are escalated in this fashion, the remedy may be worse than the disease, because layoffs, plant closings, and the threatened insolvency of major corporate institutions may be a more adverse result than the financial loss suffered by consumers or the government as a result of price-fixing or tax fraud....

This problem suggests the desirability of corporate penalties that minimize "overspill."...

An argument frequently made against corporate liability is that it may interfere with the assignment of individual liability. Here, anecdotal evidence does suggest that juries have sometimes compromised, acquitting all individual defendants while convicting the corporation.... The pervasiveness of this pattern cannot be estimated. Still, public-opinion surveys suggest that many white-collar crimes are no longer viewed as mere "regulatory" or technical violations but are ranked relatively high on a scale of seriousness, and consequently this pattern of jury reluctance to convict individual defendants for white-collar crimes may be a declining phenomenon. In any event, the prosecution always has the option of not prosecuting the corporation — or, at least, of not doing so in the same proceeding....

Still another perspective on the potential utility of corporate criminal liability begins from the much repeated observation that it is frequently difficult to identify the "true" culprit within a firm. Although the point is undoubtedly correct, its truth may lie less in the ability of the "true" culprit to hide his identity than in the absence of any such "true" offender in a broad range of cases. From a social-science perspective, it is virtually a truism that knowledge may exist collectively within an organization, even though it is not localized within any one individual.... [I]t is likely that information will exist at one level of an organization that would alter decisions at another, but no mechanism will necessarily force the transmission of this information to where it is needed. Some federal decisions appear to have responded already to such considerations by recognizing a "collective knowledge" doctrine, under which the corporation may be held liable even though no single individual had the requisite information....

These problems indicate one inadequacy of an exclusive focus on the individual decision maker: recurrently, it is unlikely that any single individual within the corporate hierarchy will have the requisite intent, and yet the firm as an entity may have knowledge of an unsafe design, a carcinogenic risk, or a dangerous side effect that its products can cause. In this light, the argument for corporate liability rests not only on the evidentiary problems of identifying the "true" culprit but on the organizational reality that there may be no actual individual culprit at all, because of the diffusion of responsibility within the corporate hierarchy. Moreover, an insistence on finding a responsible individual decision maker might produce a scapegoat system of criminal justice, in which lower-echelon operating officials would probably bear the primary responsibility and risk exposure.

The forgoing arguments focus on the problem of cognitive failures within the corporation's internal information processing as a justification for corporate liability. An alternative justification proceeds from the motivational failures that also accompany the corporate form. Almost inevitably, there is an incongruence between the interests of the manager and those of the firm as an entity: criminal behavior may be attractive to the pressured or ambitious manager, even if it is not to the corporation. Compounding this problem is the tendency for conflicting signals to issue from the senior levels of the corporate hierarchy to the middle echelons, which tend to be the locus of criminal behavior. Such signals may formally require obedience to law, but they also demand and reward short-term profit maximization. The implicit signal may thus be read by middle-level managers as meaning only "don't get caught." Of course, individual criminal liability may partially countervail this pressure on the middle manager. But even if the severity of the criminal sanction vastly exceeds that of the counterthreats the corporation can make, such as dismissal, demotion, or forgone promotion, the absolute severity of the sanction must be discounted by its probability of imposition. . . . This means that the discounted threat of apprehension and conviction by the state for a criminal offense may be less than that of the strong likelihood of internal discipline or dismissal by the corporation for failure to maximize profits. Thus, the manager faces both public and private sanction, and the latter, although lesser in gravity, tend[s] to be higher in probability, making the outcome uncertain and possibly dependent on the level of risk-aversion of the individual manager.

The Alternative of Civil Remedies Corporate sanctions may be necessary, but it's far from clear that such sanctions must be criminal in nature. Civil penalties are now utilized by many, if not most, administrative agencies. Moreover, a system of civil penalties offers some obvious advantages to the prosecutor. First, the corporation could not claim the protection of constitutional rights, such as the "reasonable doubt" standard or double jeopardy, that are applicable only to criminal proceedings. Second, the possibility of judicial or jury nullification is reduced because of the lesser stigma. Third, courts of equity traditionally have been more able than criminal courts to fashion flexible and novel forms of relief. Thus, from the standpoint of specific deterrence and incapacitation, some have concluded the civil penalties offer significant advantages over criminal law enforcement in the case of the corporation. . . .

In this light, what arguments remain for the use of the criminal law as a preferred legislative strategy? Little agreement exists here, but the following arguments deserve consideration. First, the criminal law has long been thought uniquely capable of performing an educative role in defining and reinforcing the boundaries of acceptable conduct. The civil law's quieter, less theatrical character limits its ability to perform this socializing function. Closely allied to this point is the criminal law's ability to stigmatize and employ publicity as a sanction. The highly publicized prosecution of the Ford Motor Company in 1979 for the allegedly unsafe design of the Pinto illustrates this capacity of the criminal process. Second, the criminal law characteristically moves at a faster pace than the civil law. Thus, to the extent that restitution is an authorized sentence, the criminal law can serve as the engine by which to obtain victim compensation more quickly. In addition, because the double jeopardy clause does not preclude a successive civil prosecution after an acquittal in a criminal trial, the prosecutor can in effect obtain a second chance by proceeding first criminally and then civilly.

Third, courts of equity have traditionally been barred from imposing penalties, and although this does not amount to a constitutional barrier, there may linger a reluctance on the part of courts when operating in a civil mode to pursue deterrent objectives. The basic format of the civil enforcement proceeding also has yet to be resolved, and the fairness and reliability of administratively determined civil penalties is a matter of serious dispute.

Finally, joint prosecutions of the corporation and its agents require a criminal forum if the threat of incarceration is to be used to deter individuals. From a law enforcement perspective, such joint trials are desirable both because they are less costly than separate prosecutions and because they permit one prosecutor to pursue the case in an integrated fashion; a separate prosecution, particularly if pursued in a different forum, might require a different prosecutor.

At most, these arguments suggest that corporate prosecutions for truly significant violations might best remain in a criminal courtroom, but they do not deny that corporate prosecutions for many regulatory and strict liability offenses, which today fit awkwardly at best within the criminal process, could be safely transferred to the civil process.

Douglas S. Anderson, Corporate Homicide: The Stark Realities of Artificial Beings and Legal Fictions

8 Pepperdine Law Review 367, 404-409 (1981)

Practical Considerations Opponents of corporate criminal liability advance several justifications for retaining the limited scope of this liability. One reason is the resulting inequity to innocent parties. Shareholders are one such group, who in the final analysis feel the sting of any verdict against a corporation. Yet they are most likely innocent of personal wrongdoing and incapable of exerting any effective control over actions of the corporate agents.

While innocent shareholders are similarly "stung" by civil damage awards, it is critical to understand that corporate liability is achieved by the concept of vicarious liability which arose in the civil arena. As such, a criminal liability theory that penalizes innocent shareholders is a "substantial departure from the ordinary rule that a principal is not answerable *criminally* for the acts of his agent without the principal's authorization, consent or knowledge."

In addition to the basic unfairness theory was the idea of an "historical quid pro quo." Since the investor already had to deal with the inherent economic risk, the courts did not choose to impose an additional legal risk as well, in fear that capital investments would be curtailed.

In actual practice, however, criminal liability may not be the substantial departure that was originally presumed. If it is true that decisions to market "defective products in flagrant disregard of excessive dangers spring from the intensity of the profit motive rather than from animus toward consumers," then such behavior could be impliedly consented to and authorized by the shareholder who seeks a high return on his investment. Moreover, any impact upon the shareholder is minimized in at least two ways. First, shareholder losses are limited only to the amount of individual capital investment. Secondly, it is believed by some that corporations often transfer the costs of fines to the consumer in the form of higher product prices.

Another concern is the impact of placing criminal liability on unknowing corporate directors, on the theory that the wrongful activity occurred as a result of the principal's failure to exercise due care and attention to corporate affairs. Directors, who are primarily concerned about long term planning and company goal setting, may never become aware that the product they recently marketed had failed all its safety tests or for some other reason is dangerously defective.... This expanded liability of directors has stopped many able businessmen from accepting directorships in large companies....

Even within the narrow scope of this article (the conscious disregard for human life resulting from an active effort to suppress the dangers of consumer products and services), indirect implication of directors remains a concern....

While there is validity to the claim that unknowing directors might become implicated by the stigma of a criminal fine, it is well to realize that an unsuspecting director usually will not suffer personal economic harm in the capacity of a director. Often fines assessed upon a corporation will be paid out of the corporate coffers.

Yet the fact remains that corporations do not commit crimes—people do, and thus it would seem to be more appropriate to proceed directly against the individual perpetrator than the corporation as a whole. While holding the entire corporate body criminally liable for acts of reckless disregard for human life would be a dramatic improvement over present liability schemes, punishment of the particular individual offenders by means of frequently imposed jail sentences would provide a better mechanism for deterrence. As compared to monetary fines assessed upon the corporation as a whole, even where the fine is correlated to the amount of economic wrongdoing, corporations will eventually pass the costs on to the consumers, thereby minimizing any deterrent impact there would have been otherwise. Additionally, concerns for the "innocent" shareholders would be removed.

Of major concern with the individual liability approach is the difficulty in identifying the guilty party. At common law, this was not such a problem given the corporation's limited size and complexity, and hence, courts found no reason to subject the corporation to liability. Today the corporate diversity and complexity has necessitated the expansion of corporate liability to the point where a court has held a corporation guilty of manslaughter. There is even scholarly support for the concept of corporate murder.

Yet even when the particular wrongdoers cannot be ascertained, there remains justification for criminal corporate liability as opposed to individual liability, which stems from the effects of the organization on individual behavior. Consider the following:

> What prevents most of us from committing murder is not a calculation based upon the threat of what the law will do, but mechanisms — guilt, shame, anxiety, conscience, superego — internalized within us through the forces of family, school, church, and peer group. When individuals are placed in an organizational structure, some of the ordinary internalized restraints seem to lose their hold.

Epilogue Our judicial system labels acts that are particularly offensive and repugnant to our sense of right and wrong as criminal. This labeling process has a two-pronged effect. First, it generally invokes more severe penalties as a means of deterring the offensive behavior, and secondly, a criminal charge attaches a stigma upon the convicted person or group which serves as an advertisement to all that this form of behavior will not be tolerated. Today, this stigma has not been placed on corporations who knowingly market life-endangering products, but as both primary and secondary authorities continue to carve out more and more exceptions to criminal corporate liability, it appears the courts are now at the brink of extending the analysis to acts of corporate homicide. However, courts are limited to interpreting the statutory language given them by the various state legislatures. Real reform must therefore come from the legislative branches to modify statutory definitions of "person" to encompass the corporate body. The "juristic" person must be held accountable along with its homo sapiens counterpart in those cases where there is: (1) a calculated and deliberate failure to correct a life-threatening product without warning those persons subjected to the danger, and (2) an active suppression or attempt to suppress such information of a product's dangerous defect.

Under present law, if an individual makes a conscious decision to act so as to subject others to a substantial certainty of death, it is considered a homicidal act *unless* that person does so while employed by acting on behalf of a corporation. It is time to judicially and legislatively recognize that the result is the same in either case, whether the actor is a corporate agent or a common street criminal, or whether the murder weapon is a dangerously designed fuel tank or a loaded pistol. The stark realities of "artificial beings" and "legal fictions" is that their impact is far from artificial or fictional.

The specter of the crumpled, ash-blackened 1973 Pinto strewn along the side of U.S. Highway 33 brought forth the ugly side of the profit motive, a motive which at times makes human life little more than another factor in the economic analysis of business. While this will likely continue, the human element needs to be made a more substantial factor than it is presently. If this attempt is to accomplish anything more than a quixotic chasing of windmills, jurists and legislators alike must recognize their reckless disregard for human life for what it really is — the crime of corporate homicide.

Paul H. Robinson & Michael Cahill, Law Without Justice: How and Why Criminal Law Deliberately Sacrifices Desert
(Oxford forthcoming 2005)

Criminalization of Regulatory Violations; Corporate Criminality Governmental regulation has shown an increasing, and disturbing, tendency to criminalize actions other than those the community would conceive of as morally condemn-able conduct. The trend toward the criminalization of regulatory offenses has led to an astounding 300,000 or so federal "crimes," extending criminalization beyond even the domain of traditional *malum prohibitum* offenses, to criminalize conduct that is "harmful" only in the sense that it causes inconvenience for bureaucrats.

As the *Lindsey* case illustrates, in which the defendants were charged with felony camping,[1] many federal regulations are now routinely converted to federal crimes for the sole purpose of giving regulators greater leverage in enforcement. But this criminalization of regulatory violations deviates from the goal of desert, for it punishes behavior that is morally neutral and frequently objectively trivial. Moreover, the heedless generation of regulatory crimes is counterproductive on its own terms. First, by imposing criminal liability in cases lacking in moral blameworthiness, the practice dilutes the condemnatory meaning of criminal liability, thereby damaging the very characteristic of crim-inal law that it attempts to exploit by expanding regulatory sanctions beyond civil liability. Additionally, the current trend toward blurring the criminal-civil distinction is particularly foolish because it can provide little or no long-term gain, even with respect to the very cases brought within the expansion.[2] *Criminal* penalties are thought desirable because they bring to bear the moral condemnation that civil liability does not, but as noted, using criminal sanctions in morally neutral cases only dilutes criminal liability's condemnatory effect over time, destroying the very characteristic of criminal law that regulatory-offense advocates seek to press into service.

Like regulatory crimes, imposition of criminal liability on corporations is often justified on the ground that it gives civil sanctions more teeth. Criminal prosecution of corporations, the argument goes, provides a deterrent that civil actions cannot: the stigmatization of criminal conviction. Proponents note that while some civil wrongs are condemnable, many are not; thus, civil liability at best sends an ambiguous message. Only criminal liability, it is argued, can bring moral condemnation to bear.

But such corporate criminal liability is inconsistent with desert, although here for a different reason than the deviations we have seen elsewhere: it is nonsensical in terms of desert to assign "blame" to a fictitious, conceptual entity. Because condemnation of a non-human entity has no apparent moral meaning, each such conviction creates ambiguity about the criminal law's distinguishing feature and primary concern: its focus on moral blameworthiness. To try to use that special characteristic where personal blameworthiness cannot exist is to risk destroying the criminal law's most important asset. The potential cost to the

---

1. See U.S. v. Lindsey, 595 F.2d 5 (9th Cir. 1979).

2. Regulatory offenses are cases for which the likelihood of a prison sentence is remote. The majority of regulatory offenses are misdemeanors, for which a serious prison term is not authorized. Even for the most egregious forms of these offenses, where danger to life or property is created, the likelihood of an incarcerative sentence is not high. In 1989, for example, the number of convicted federal regulatory violators sentenced to prison was: 37 agricultural, 22 antitrust, 2 labor, 24 food and drug. Bureau of Criminal Justice Statistics, Table 5.17, Sentences Imposed in Cases Terminated in U.S. District Courts, 1992 Sourcebook of Criminal Justice Statistics 488 (1993). Instead, the sentences for regulatory offenses typically are fines and restitution, the same sanctions that are available at civil law. Thus, by criminalizing these offenses, we do not effectively access more severe sanctions.

criminal law's credibility is all the more difficult to justify if civil prosecution of organizations would be, or could be made, as effective as criminal prosecution.[1]

Here again, it is also highly dubious whether present criminal sanctions on organizations achieve the compliance goal for which they sacrifice desert. In fact, some writers have argued that, on balance, civil liability is more effective than criminal liability in gaining organizational compliance.[2] The most serious criminal sanctions — deprivation of life or liberty — are not available against an organizational offender. The available sanctions are essentially the same as those available under civil law: fines, orders for restitution, and orders requiring or limiting future organizational action. Some features of criminal procedure, such as speedy trial, may be considered more appropriate than the comparable civil procedures, but the legislature could alter the civil procedures for organizations in these regards if doing so were thought necessary to exact greater compliance. In fact, *criminal* rules can limit effective prosecution of organizations in ways that legislatures cannot get around.[3] Civil actions thus can provide a greater possibility of liability for a greater number of offenses with less demanding elements of proof.

Both regulatory "crimes" and corporate "crimes," then, could be dealt with as effectively, and probably more effectively, through the civil rather than the criminal system. Further, civil mechanisms could tailor liability and enforcement to focus on issues other than the blameworthiness of past behavior.[4]

We argue . . . that a better approach for such quasi-crimes is to use administrative sanctions imposed by regulatory agencies.

---

1. That current American law allows criminal liability of organizations may indicate how much American criminal law has strayed from its traditional criterion of moral blameworthiness. European countries rarely permit such liability. *See* V.S. Khanna, *Corporate Criminal Liability: What Purpose Does It Serve?*, 109 Harv. L. Rev. 1477, 1488-1491 (1996) (comparing corporate criminal liability in the United States and Western Europe); John C. Coffee, Jr., *"No Soul to Damn, No Body to Kick": An Unscandalized Inquiry into the Problem of Corporate Punishment*, 79 Mich. L. Rev. 386 (1981). Great Britain traditionally has allowed such liability, but only to a limited extent. *See* Coffee, *Does "Unlawful" Mean "Criminal"?*, *supra*, at 230; Celia Wells, Corporations and Criminal Responsibility 95-107 (1993). There has been an increasing trend in Europe toward allowing corporate criminal liability, however.

2. See *Developments in the Law — Corporate Crime: Regulating Corporate Behavior Through Criminal Sanctions*, 92 Harv. L. Rev. 1227, 1365-1374 (1979).

3. Constitutional guarantees, such as those requiring proof beyond a reasonable doubt and barring double jeopardy, are available to an organization in defending a criminal action, but not in defending a civil action. *See* Laura J. Kerrigan et al., *Project: The Decriminalization of Administrative Law Penalties, Civil Remedies, Alternatives, Policy, and Constitutional Implications*, 45 Admin. L. Rev. 367, 374-75 (1993). In certain circumstances, however, constitutional criminal protections will apply to an enforcement action notwithstanding that the legislature has labeled it "civil" rather than criminal. *See id.* at 397–419. Further, criminal law's general disapproval of strict liability and negligence liability, *see generally* Paul H. Robinson, Criminal Law §4.3 (1997), may limit the prosecution of organizations when it ought not; many of the objections to such liability have little force in the context of corporate liability.

4. For example, imposition of civil fines and other remedies could incorporate consideration of post-offense internal reforms that will prevent future regulatory or other violations. *See* Coffee, *"No Soul to Damn,"* *supra*, at 430-32, 454-55.

Other Discussion Materials

Andrew Ashworth, A New Form of Corporate Liability?
Principles of Criminal Law 86-88 (1991)

The theoretical arguments in favor of corporate criminal liability seem strong, but developments at common law have made [such liability] possible only to a limited extent [in England]. An alternative strategy of placing the emphasis on individual liability would be unlikely to work. Any particular individual might be dispensable within a corporation (e.g. the "Company Vice-President responsible for going to [jail]"), allowing the company [to] continue on its course with minimal disruption; or it might be difficult to identify the individual responsible, not least because companies sometimes have convoluted lines of accountability. A further alternative strategy would be to rely even more on new offenses of strict liability to punish corporate harm-doing, but this might not be a sufficient response to some [disasters], or to other harm-doing on a broad scale.

Reasoning of this kind has led to Fisse and Braithwaite's entirely new approach to corporate criminal liability, using concepts not applicable to individuals.[1] Their strategy rests on three key elements: "enforced accountability"; a new concept of corporate fault; and a fresh approach to sanctions. The idea of "enforced accountability" is that the law should recognize the complexity of lines of accountability in some corporations, and, rather than expending prosecutorial energy and court time trying to disentangle them, should require a company which has caused or threatened a proscribed harm to take its own disciplinary and rectificatory measures. The State should order the company to activate its own private justice system, and a court should then assess the adequacy of the measures taken. As this suggests, the concept of fault would then become a *post hoc* phenomenon. Rather than struggling to establish some antecedent fault within the corporation, the prosecution would invite the court to infer fault from the nature and effectiveness of the company's remedial measures after it had been established that it was the author of a harm-causing or harm-threatening act or omission. The court would not find fault if it was persuaded that the company had taken realistic measures to prevent a recurrence, had ensured compensation to any victims, and had taken the event seriously in other respects. This "reactive corporate fault" is a far cry from the notions of *mens rea* and prior fault which dominate criminal-law doctrine. The third element in the scheme is that the courts should be able to impose new penalties, specially designed for application to companies. Under the present system, a company can hardly be imprisoned, moderate fines can be swallowed up as business overheads, and swingeing fines might have such drastic side-effects on the employment and livelihoods of innocent employees as to render them inappropriate. The proposal is for a range of special penalties, some

---

1. B. Fisse and J. Braithwaite, "The Allocation of Responsibility for Corporate Crime: Individualism, Collectivism and Accountability" (1988) 11 Sydney L.R. 468; see also L. H. Leight, "The Criminal Liability of Corporations and other Groups" (1977) 9 Ottawa L.R. 247; and J. Braithwaite, Corporate Crime in the Pharmaceutical Industry (1984).

of which are rehabilitative (putting corporations on probation to supervise their compliance with the law), some of which are deterrent (punitive injunctions to require resources to be devoted to the development of new preventive measures), and others of which have mixed aims (e.g. community service by companies).

Fisse and Braithwaite's proposals for a radically new legal regime for corporate crime are grounded in arguments of prevention. They emphasize the enormity of the harms which corporations both cause and risk causing, and contend that the primary search should be for a regime which ensures maximum prevention. This is inconsistent with an approach to liability and punishment based on "just deserts": the authors explicitly reject the idea of holding corporations criminally liable according to their culpability in causing the harms, not merely because it is difficult in practice to make such enquiries, but also because they believe that the prevention of future harm is of greater social importance in this sphere than any abstract notion of "justice" based on past events.[1] "Desert" theory would, however, make a clearer distinction between preventive measures and conviction and sentence. In principle, punishment for corporations, no less than for individuals, should be proportioned to culpability: if that proves impossible in practice, for the reasons given by Fisse and Braithwaite, then that is an argument for legal presumptions or other special doctrines, but not for abandoning the distinctive aims of the criminal law and punishment. Broader preventive measures, perhaps through regulatory mechanisms, should be put in hand in order to reduce the risk of further harms from similar sources.

---

1. See further John Braithwaite, "Challenging Just Deserts: Punishing White Collar Criminals" (1982) 73 *J. Crim. Law & Criminology* 723, and the reply by Andrew von Hirsch, "Desert and White Collar Criminality: A Reply to Dr. Braithwaite," id. at 1164.

PART VI

GENERAL DEFENSES

In casual language, anything that prevents conviction of a defendant is called a "defense," but this term includes doctrines that are very different from one another. An "alibi defense," for example, simply refers to the presentation of facts that suggest the defendant was somewhere else when the offense was committed and therefore cannot be the perpetrator. It is not a legal doctrine but a form of factual counterclaim. A defense of diplomatic immunity, on the other hand, may admit commission of the offense (although it need not), yet suggest that the jurisdiction nonetheless cannot legally prosecute the offense. The legal doctrines that we refer to as defenses typically are one of five sorts: absent element "defenses," offense modifications, justifications, excuses, or nonexculpatory defenses.

Absent Element "Defenses" Many defenses are simply facts that prevent proof of the requirements of the offense definition, such as mistake negating a culpability element, the subject of Section 5, and mental illness negating the culpability required for homicide ("diminished capacity"), taken up at the end of the Section 8 (Homicide Mitigations) Overview materials. In some cases these absent element doctrines do not provide complete defenses; they are only a reduction in liability, a "mitigation." In truth, such mitigations are simply instances where a fact—such as mistake or mental illness—negates a required culpable state of mind for one offense, but not that for a lesser included offense. It is true that the effect of an absent element may be to reduce liability, but this effect is not the specific dictate of the doctrine; rather, it is the result of applying the normal rules of proof to the elements of the relevant offense definitions.

Offense Modifications Other defenses and mitigations exist independent of offense definitions. They do more than simply describe the negation of an offense element; they introduce a new issue that refines our definition of the offense harm or evil. Many such doctrines apply only to a particular offense or group of offenses. For example, renunciation is a defense to inchoate liability, and "inevitably incident" conduct is a defense to complicity liability. While they are independent in form, the nature of these defenses suggests that they are, in essence, part of the definition of what constitutes the prohibited conduct. That is, what we mean by

527

conspiracy is an agreement that is not renounced. What we mean by complicity is assistance that is not "inevitably incident" to commission of the offense (such as a kidnapping victim's family paying ransom to a kidnapper.)

General Defenses   Other defenses, in contrast, have general application to all offenses. Such "general defenses" represent general principles of defense that are not dependent on or related to the definition of any particular offense or group of offenses. They exist to bar liability for reasons unrelated to the criminalization decision embodied in the offense definition. General defenses, the subject of this Part, are of three sorts: justifications, excuses, and nonexculpatory defenses.

Justifications   Justification defenses, such as lesser evils, self-defense, and law enforcement authority, exculpate on a theory that the actor's otherwise criminal conduct in fact avoided a greater harm or evil. While an actor satisfies the elements of an offense, his offense is tolerated or even encouraged because it does not cause a *net* societal harm. An actor who burns a firebreak on another's land may thereby commit arson, but also may have a justification defense (of lesser evils) because, by the burning, the actor saves innocent lives threatened by the fire. The three major groups of justification defenses are examined in Section 17, concerning the lesser evils defense, in Section 18, concerning defensive force justifications, and in Section 19, concerning public authority justifications.

Excuses   Excuse defenses, such as insanity and duress, exculpate under a different theory. The actor has admittedly acted improperly — has caused a net societal harm or evil — but is excused because she cannot properly be held responsible for her offense conduct. Note the difference in focus between justifications and excuses. An actor's *conduct* is justified; *an actor* is excused. The theory of excuses is introduced in Section 20. The major excuses are examined in Section 22, concerning insanity, Section 23, concerning other disability excuses, and Sections 20 and 21, concerning mistake excuses.

Nonexculpatory Defenses   A final group of general defenses, discussed in Section 24, does not exculpate an actor but does provide an escape from liability. Even if the actor's conduct is criminal and unjustified and the actor is fully responsible for the conduct, such "nonexculpatory defenses" are made available because in each instance the forgoing of prosecution or punishment is thought to advance some other important societal interest. Thus, diplomatic immunity may provide a defense, without regard to the guilt or innocence of the defendant, because by doing so a country's diplomats are protected from interference when abroad and diplomatic communications among nations can more easily be established and maintained.

JUSTIFICATION DEFENSES GENERALLY

● OVERVIEW OF JUSTIFICATION DEFENSES GENERALLY

Lesser Evils Defense   A forest fire rages toward a town of unsuspecting inhabitants. The actor burns a field of corn located between the fire and the town; the burned field serves as a firebreak, saving lives. The actor satisfies all elements of the offense of criminal mischief by setting fire to the field with the purpose of destroying it. The immediate harm he causes — the destruction of the field — is precisely the harm that the statute seeks to prevent and punish. Yet the actor is likely to have a complete defense, because his conduct and its harmful consequences are justified. His conduct is tolerated, even encouraged, by society.

Balancing Competing Harms   The forest fire case provides an example of the "lesser evils" or "choice of evils" justification (sometimes called "necessity"). This defense, though the least common in American criminal codes, most clearly reflects the general principle of justification. The defense explicitly requires that "the harm or evil sought to be avoided by such conduct is greater than that sought to be prevented by the law defining the offense charged."[1] As we shall see, the "defensive force" and "public authority" justifications, the subject of the next two Sections, have no such general balancing language but nonetheless are based on the same balancing principle. In those defenses, the legislature has undertaken to establish the balance of competing interests and has promulgated specific rules that embody its conclusions. Neither the defendant nor a jury is permitted to strike the balance differently.

Defensive Force Justifications   A prowler attempts to steal chickens from a chicken coop. May the owner use physical force against the prowler to prevent the theft? Some limited degree of force commonly is permitted, if it is necessary to

---

1. Model Penal Code §3.02(1)(a).

protect the property. It is not that society deems injury to a person as a less significant interest than the right to ownership of chickens. Rather, in weighing the interests at stake, the legislature considers not only the immediate physical harms — personal injury versus loss of a chicken — but also the intangible societal interest in maintaining a right to hold personal property. The threatened theft endangers not only the rightful possession by this owner, but also the stability and vitality of the rule of private possession generally. To state it negatively, society generally abhors unjustified aggressive takings because they undercut the security of private possession. Society therefore tolerates the injury that must be inflicted to stop the aggressor. The same reasoning applies when the aggression is toward the actor himself or toward another person. Society's interest in maintaining a right to bodily integrity when combined with the physical harm threatened, may outweigh the personal injury that must be inflicted to block the aggression.

Defending Against Unlawful Force   Such "defensive force" justifications are each triggered by a threat of unlawful force. They are distinguished from one another by the interest that is threatened: defense of self, defense of others, defense of property. Legislatures often wish to make special alterations or exceptions to the basic principle of defensive force, depending on the interest to be protected. For example, they may add a special provision to the defense of property to exclude the use of deadly force. They might permit the use of force to defend another person only if such other person would be justified in using such force.

Public Authority Justifications   A third category of justifications, "public authority" defenses, reflects a similar balancing of harms. When a deputy sheriff uses force in the execution of a judicial arrest warrant, his conduct may satisfy all the elements of assault. But his use of force furthers effective criminal justice, as well as the effective exercise of judicial authority. These intangible societal interests are said to justify the harm that the deputy causes in executing the warrant. Unlike defensive force defenses, public authority defenses need not be triggered by a threat from another. An actor may be justified if she affirmatively acts to further a legally recognized interest. For example, a bus driver might be authorized to be the aggressor in ejecting passengers who refuse to pay or who insist on playing their radios too loudly. On the other hand, the use of public authority justifications often is limited to certain persons whose position or training makes them particularly appropriate protectors of the interest at stake, whereas defensive force justifications are generally available to all citizens.

Furthering Public Interests   The interests to be furthered or protected by public authority justifications may be personal or societal. They include criminal law enforcement, child rearing and education, safety and order on public transportation vehicles or in public institutions, life or health (as in medical emergencies and suicide prevention), military operations, and effective exercise of judicial authority, to name the most prominent. In each instance, the interest gives rise to an authority for the appropriate persons to act in a way that otherwise would be criminal, if it furthers or protects the interest. Like defensive force justifications, public authority justifications are distinguished from one another according to the interest protected. Legislatures may refine the basic principle to provide a suitably limited justification defense for each interest and authority. Thus, the restrictions on law enforcement authority may be different from the restrictions on the authority of a bus driver to maintain safety and decorum.

17

Lesser Evils Defense

When should the law authorize conduct that would otherwise be an offense but that special circumstances would seem to justify? This Section begins the examination of this important group of general defenses: justifications.

◆ **THE CASE OF THE ISRAELI GENERAL SECURITY SERVICE**

For decades, Israelis and Palestinians have been locked in conflict. To force the Israeli government to compromise, Palestinian extremist groups regularly use car and suicide bombings against civilians. Over a recent two- and a half year period, these types of bombings have killed 121 and injured 707. For example, two bus bombings in April 1994 killed thirteen people in operations for which Hamas, a Palestinian militant extremist group, claimed responsibility. A few months later, another Hamas bus bombing kills 20 people and injured another 48. Yehuda Shloss, a witness to the explosion, describes how the explosion lofted the bus full of passengers a meter into the air, and crushes the bus as it falls back to the ground. Passengers' dismembered body parts flew out, crashing through the widows of nearby stores and apartment buildings. Looking at the remains, a teenage girl expresses the Israelis' despair, "How much can we take?" Hamas is just one of several Palestinian groups set on killing as many Israelis as they can.

To prevent these terrorist attacks, Israel established the General Security Service (GSS), which has had moderate success. In September 1995, state attorney Shai Nitzan reports that the GSS recently prevented ten attempted car bombings, seven attempts to kidnap soldiers, and several attempted murders. The GSS has also discovered a lab equipped to manufacture explosives and pipe bombs. In August 1995, Israel reports that the GSS has uncovered and arrested the commanders and planners of groups that attacked Jerusalem twice the previous year. Following those arrests, the GSS uncover more Hamas organizations throughout Judea and Samaria, including Eastern Jerusalem. The arrest of these members foil a number of planned attacks, including a suicide attack at the Jerusalem central bus station, a suicide attack on a civilian bus in Tel Aviv, the kidnaping of two Israeli soldiers, the killing of a settler in the Samaria region, the attempt to plant a bomb on a train in the Jerusalem area, and the killing of a settler in the Gaza Strip. In July 1995, Prime Minister Rabin reports that the GSS prevented a potentially devastating attack planned by Hamas for July 1, the date on which the Camp David Israel-Palestinian peace agreement was to be signed. In May 1998, it is revealed that the GSS foiled not only the usual suicide bombing attacks but also several attempts at kidnaping Israeli dignitaries.

The GSS commonly detains and questions alleged members of various radical or militant Palestinian groups. Ordinarily, the GSS does not formally charge the detainees; it holds them "administratively" to obtain information about planned or impending attacks. While the method has successfully yielded information, it often involves the GSS use of severe methods, including electrical shock, cold showers, and harsh beatings.

Figure 79 "Qas'at-a-Tawleh"
Method: forcing the interrogee to kneel or sit down with his back to a table, while the interrogator places his arms, bound and stretched behind him, on the table. In that position, the inter-rogator sometimes pushes the interrogee's body forward or pulls his legs

(B'Tselem)

Figure 80 "Qambaz"
Method: forcing the interogee to crouch on his toes with his hands tied behind him

(B'Tselem)

Figure 81 "Standing Shabeh"
Method: having the interrogee stand, with his hands tied and drawn upwards

(B'Tselem)

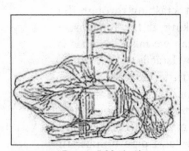

Figure 82 "Banana" Method: having the interrogee lie on his back on a high stool with his body arched backwards

(B'Tselem)

Figure 83 "Violent shaking"
Method: interrogator grasps and violently shakes the detainee

(B'Tselem)

Figure 84 "Regular Shabeh"
Method: tying the interrogee to a low chair, tilting forward

(B'Tselem)

In the 1990s, Hamas markedly increased its terrorist activities. Formed during the 1987 intifada, Hamas vehemently opposes the existence of Israel, and openly advocates the use of terrorist attacks against Israeli civilians. In April 1994, for example, Hamas claimed responsibility for separate suicide attacks that killed eight people on a bus in the center of Afula and five at the central bus station of Hadera. Later that year, Israel also linked Hamas to two more attacks in Jerusalem. GSS is thus highly suspicious of any person having an affiliation with Hamas.

Abdel Zamed Hassan Harizat is an educated, thirty-year old computer operator who still lives at home with his parents and a brother in Hebron. He is a diminutive man at four feet six inches but makes up for his lack of height with a pleasant personality. His employer is a Hebron publishing company, which is known for supporting fundamentalists. His boss, Manager Jewad Said, is pleased with Harizat's performance.

Figure 85 **Fatma Harizat holds a photo of her son, Abdel Samad Harizat, at her home in Hebron, Sept. 6, 1999**

(AP Photo/Nasser Shiyoukhi)

Two years ago, Harizat spent three months in an Israeli prison and was fined $1,350 for distributing Hamas leaflets. The GSS now believes him to be a senior member of Izzadin Kassam, the military wing of Hamas. He is also suspected of being involved in three fatal attacks on Jewish settlers in Hebron.

The GSS has recently learned that Taher Kapisha, a Hamas terrorist, is planning an imminent attack. They believe Harizat can lead them to Kapisha and to other members of the Izzadin Kassam. (Kapisha is tracked down and killed by security forces in June.)

On the night of Saturday, April 22, 1995, GSS agents come to Harizat's home. They drag him out blindfolded, while several beat him. Other agents lock the rest of his family in the room, before ransacking the house looking for intelligence and finding only Hamas leaflets. Meanwhile, other agents take Harizat to one of its facilities, the Russian Compound, in Jerusalem. A doctor who examines him concludes that he is in good health, despite his protestations that he has a medical problem. Agents begin the interrogation, which for the first one-half-hour involves beating him. They follow with banging his head against a wall and shaking him violently a dozen times by his shirt collar and shoulders. They stop when they notice he is having trouble breathing. Harizat is left in the interrogation room alone, bleeding, and eventually loses consciousness. Several hours later, agents take him to Jerusalem's Hadassah Hospital. He arrives still unconscious, and the doctors treat him for severe head injuries. There are also visible signs of bruising on his chest and indications that he has multiple concussions.

Later that day, GSS agents return to Harizat's house and ask his brother and mother to accompany them to the hospital. There they see his beaten, unconscious, shackled body. Two days later, he dies of his wounds. He is the fourth detainee to die in custody since January. The following week, Dr. Yehuda Hiss, an Israeli pathologist, performs an autopsy, despite Harizat's mother's initial opposition. At the family's request, an independent Scottish pathologist observes during the procedure. The autopsy confirms that Harizat died of traumatic causes.

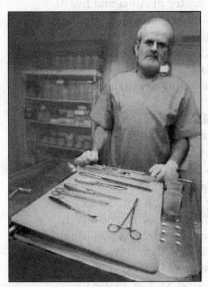

Figure 86 **Dr. Yehuda Hiss, who performed the autopsy of Harizat, 1999**

(Jonathan Bloom, Jerusalem Post)

In protest of Harizat's death, Hamas files a formal complaint with the International Committee of the Red Cross. It also issues a press release threatening that Israel "will pay a high price" for torturing Harizat to death. Palestinian Liberation Authority leader Yasser Arafat adds that "what happened to Harizat is an execution.... Israel is not only killing Palestinian prisoners... but the whole peace process." A chief Israeli government spokesman says that "there is no systemized torture in Israel. But since we are threatened with a huge ring of terror, the main duty of the government is to protect its citizens, and therefore we have to resort to methods that are not so nice." Meanwhile, the Israeli Justice Minister initiates an official investigation, while a senior defense official believes that deviation from standard procedures caused the death.

1. Relying only on your own intuitions of justice, what liability and punishment, if any, does the GSS official who authorized the interrogation techniques used on Harizat deserve?

N	0	1	2	3	4	5	6	7	8	9	10	11
☐	☐	☐	☐	☐	☐	☐	☐	☐	☐	☐	☐	☐
no liability	liability but no punishment	1 day	2 wks	2 mo	6 mo	1 yr	3 yrs	7 yrs	15 yrs	30 yrs	life imprisonment	death

2. What liability, if any, under the then-existing statutes?
3. What liability, if any, under the Model Penal Code?

■ THE LAW

Israeli Penal Law (1995)
(5737-1977, as amended in 5754-1994)

Chapter Ten. Offenses Against the Person

Article One. Causing Death

Section 298. Manslaughter

If a person — by an unlawful act or omission — causes the death of another, he is guilty of manslaughter and is liable to twenty years imprisonment.

Section 300. Murder

(a) If a person does one of the following, he is guilty of murder and is liable to life imprisonment, and only to that penalty:

(1) he willfully causes the death of his father or mother or grandfather or grandmother by an unlawful act or omission;

(2) he premeditatively causes the death of any person;

(3) in the commission of an offense or while preparing for or facilitating the commission of an offense, he willfully causes the death of a person;

(4) having committed another offense, he causes the death of a person in order to secure the escape or to avoid punishment of himself or of a person who participated in the commission of that offense.

(b) A person convicted of murder under section 2(f) of the Nazis and Nazi Collaborators (Punishment) Law 5710-1950, is liable to the death penalty.

Section 300A. Reduced Penalty

Notwithstanding the provisions of section 300, a penalty lighter than that set in it may be imposed, if the offense was committed in one of the following situations:

(a) when, because of a severe mental disturbance or because of his limited intellectual capability, the defendant's ability to do one of the following was severely reduced, even though not to the point of the complete incapacity said in section 34H:

(1) to understand what he was doing or that his act is wrong; or

(2) to refrain from committing the act;

(b) when, under the circumstances of the case, the defendant's act exceeded by little what would have been reasonable, as required under section 34P, for the application of the exceptions of self defense, necessity or duress under sections 34I, 34J and 34K can be applied;

(c) when the defendant was in a state of severe mental distress, because of severe or continued harassment of himself or of a member of his family by the person whose death the defendant caused.

Section 301. Premeditation

(a) For purposes of section 300, a person shall be deemed to have killed another person premeditatively, if he resolved to kill him and killed him in cold blood without immediate provocation, under circumstances in which he was able to think and understand the result of his actions, after having prepared to kill him or after having prepared the instrument with which he killed him.

(b) As regards the resolution and preparation to kill, it is immaterial whether the accused resolved to kill the other person or a particular member — or any member — of his family or race.

(c) To prove premeditation, it is not necessary to show that the accused was in any state of mind for any particular period before the offense was committed or that the instrument with which the offense was committed was prepared at any particular time before the act.

Section 304. Causing Death by Negligence

If a person causes another person's death by negligence, then he is liable to three years imprisonment.

Section 309. Definition of Causing Death

A person even though his act or omission is not the immediate or sole cause of death, shall be deemed to have caused the death of another person in any of the following cases:

(1) he inflicted bodily injury which necessitated medical or surgical treatment and the treatment caused the injured person's death; it is immaterial whether the treatment was mistaken, so long as it was given in good faith and with ordinary knowledge and skill; if it was not so given, the person who inflicted the injury shall not be deemed to have caused the injured person's death;

(2) he inflicted bodily injury which would not have caused the injured person's death, had he received proper medical or surgical treatment or had he observed proper precautions as to his way of life;

(3) he caused a person, by violence or threats of violence, to commit an act which caused his own death, if that act appeared to that person — under the circumstances — a natural way of avoiding the violence or threats;

(4) he hastened, by deed or by omission, the death of a person who suffers from a disease or injury, which — even without that deed or omission — would have caused death;

(5) the act or omission would not have caused death, unless accompanied by an act or omission of the person killed or of some other person.

Article Four. Endangering Life and Health

Section 329. Harm with Aggravating Intent

If a person does one of the following with intent to disable, disfigure or cause grievous harm to another, or with intent to resist or prevent the lawful arrest or detention of himself or of another, then he is liable to twenty years imprisonment:

(1) he unlawfully wounds or causes grievous harm to a person;

(2) he unlawfully attempts to strike a person with a projectile, knife or other dangerous or offensive weapon;

(3) he unlawfully causes an explosive substance to explode;

(4) he sends or delivers an explosive substance or other dangerous or noxious object to a person, or he causes a person to receive such a substance or object;

(5) he puts a destructive or explosive substance or a corrosive fluid in any place;

(6) he throws any substance or fluid said in paragraph (5) at a person or otherwise applies it to his body.

Section 333. Grievous Harm

If a person unlawfully does grievous harm to another person, he is liable to seven years imprisonment.

Section 334. Wounding

If a person unlawfully wounds another person, he is liable to three years imprisonment.

Section 341. Harm Through Negligence

If a person unlawfully commits any act, or omits anything which it is his duty to do, that act or omission not being one specified in sections 338 to 340, and if by that act or omission harm is caused to a person, then he is liable to one year imprisonment.

Article Eight. Assault

Section 378. Definition of Assault

If a person directly or indirectly strikes, touches, pushes or otherwise applies force to another without his consent or with his consent, which was obtained by fraud, he is said to commit assault; for this purpose, the application of force includes the application of heat, light, electricity, gas, smells or any other thing or substance, if it is applied to a degree that causes injury or discomfort.

Section 379. Common Assault

If a person unlawfully assaults another, he is liable to two years imprisonment, except to the extent that this Law provides a different punishment for the offense, in view of its circumstances.

Section 380. Assault that Causes Actual Bodily Harm

If a person commits assault that causes actual bodily harm, he is liable to three years imprisonment.

Section 381. Various Kinds of Assault

(a) If a person does one of the following, he is liable to three years imprisonment:
    (1) he assaults another in order to commit a felony;
    (2) he assaults another in order to steal anything;
    (3) he assaults another in order to resist or prevent the Lawful arrest or apprehension of himself or of another for any offense;

(b) If a person assaults a public servant, or a person who performs a duty or function assigned to him under law, or a person who renders a service to the public on behalf of a body that provides a service to the public—the assault being connected with the performance of the assaulted person's duty or function—he is liable to five years imprisonment.

Section 382. Assault Under Aggravating Circumstances

If any offense under sections 379, 380, or 381(a)(1) or (3) was committed in the presence of two or more persons, who combined for the commission of the act by one or some of them, each of them is liable to double the penalty prescribed for the offense.

Chapter Five. A Restrictions on Criminal Liability
Article Two. Restrictions on Criminal Nature of Act

Section 34J. Defensive Force

No person shall bear criminal responsibility for an act that was immediately necessary in order to repel an unlawful attack, which posed real danger to his own or another person's life, freedom, bodily welfare or property; however, a person is not acting in self defense when his own wrongful conduct caused the attack, the possibility of such a development having been foreseen by himself.

Section 34K. Necessity

No person shall bear criminal responsibility for an act that was immediately necessary in order to save his own or another person's life, freedom, bodily welfare or property from a real danger of severe injury, due to the conditions prevalent at the time the act was committed, there being no alternative but to commit the act.

Section 34M. Justification

No person shall bear criminal responsibility for an act that he committed under any of the following circumstances:

(1) he was lawfully obligated or authorized to commit it;

(2) he committed it under the order of a competent authority, which he lawfully was obligated to obey, unless the order is obviously unlawful;

(3) in respect of an act which lawfully requires consent, when the act was immediately necessary in order to save a person's life or his bodily welfare, or to prevent severe injury to his health, if, under the circumstances, he was not able to obtain the consent;

(4) he committed it on a person with lawful consent, in the course of a medical procedure or treatment, the objective of which was that person's or another person's benefit.

(5) he committed it in the course of a sports activity or of a sports game, such as are not prohibited by law and do not conflict with public order, in accordance with rules customary for them.

Section 34P. Unreasonableness

The provisions of sections 34J, 34K, and 34L shall not apply, if, under the circumstance, the act was not a reasonable one for the prevention of the injury.

Section 34R. Misinterpretation of Situation

(a) If a person commits an act, while imagining a situation that does not exist, he shall not bear criminal responsibility, except to the extent that he would have had to bear it, had the situation really been as he imagined it.

(b) Subsection (a) shall also apply to an offense of negligence, on condition that the mistake was reasonable, and to an offense of [strict liability]. . . .

Model Penal Code
(Official Draft 1962)

Section 3.02. Justification Generally. Choice of Evils

(1) Conduct which the actor believes to be necessary to avoid a harm or evil to himself or to another is justifiable, provided that:

(a) the harm or evil sought to be avoided by such conduct is greater than that sought to be prevented by the law defining the offense charged; and

(b) neither the Code nor other law defining the offense provides exceptions or defenses dealing with the specific situation involved; and

(c) a legislative purpose to exclude the justification claimed does not otherwise plainly appear.

(2) When the actor was reckless or negligent in bringing about the situation requiring a choice of harms or evils or in appraising the necessity for his conduct, the justification afforded by this Section is unavailable in a prosecution for any offense for which recklessness or negligence, as the case may be, suffices to establish culpability.

▲ PROBLEM
A Life-Saving Break-In

Burke and his two roommates, Tim and Henry, have AIDS. Burke as yet has few debilitating symptoms. He remains physically and mentally strong. Tim is in very poor health and is getting worse rapidly. Henry was in the same condition several months ago until he began participating in a research study using a drug called IIR. His health, like that of many others in the study, dramatically improved upon use of the drug. While Burke is thrilled with Henry's recovery, he is angry that the study's sponsors will not let him and Tim participate. He has urged government authorities in the Food and Drug Administration to make IIR generally available, but his requests have been denied on grounds that insufficient research has been done to justify FDA approval. Burke is convinced that the only way he can save his own life and Tim's is to break into the research study's offices and steal sufficient doses of IIR for them both. He breaks into the building but trips several silent alarms and is apprehended by police as he is leaving with the drug. He is charged with burglary and offers a lesser evils justification defense. Should Burke get the defense?

● OVERVIEW OF LESSER EVILS DEFENSE

General Principle of Justification   The lesser evils defense — sometimes called "choice of evils" or "necessity," or simply the "general justification" defense — is formally recognized in about half of the American jurisdictions. It illustrates the structure and operation of justification defenses generally by relying explicitly on the rationale inherent in all justifications: While the actor may have caused the harm or evil of an offense, the justifying circumstances suggest that his conduct avoided a greater harm or evil than it caused. In the language of the Model Penal Code, an actor is justified if his conduct is

> necessary to avoid a harm or evil to himself or to another . . . provided that: the harm or evil sought to be avoided by such conduct is greater than that sought to be prevented by the law defining the offense charged. . . . [1]

TRIGGERING CONDITIONS

The lesser evils defense was once limited to situations in which the threat was from natural forces, such as the threat of starvation to survivors in a drifting lifeboat. But modern codes follow the lead of the Model Penal Code in doing away with that limitation. The rationale for the defense — that the conduct avoided a greater harm than it caused — supports a defense no matter what the source of the threat. Modern defenses typically are interpreted, however, to require that the threat be to a legally protected interest and that the threat be unjustified. In application, these requirements are very broad and tend to exclude few cases.

Threat to Legally Protected Interest   Legally protected interests relevant to the defense include not only those interests given express sanction in the law, such as one's right to freedom of political or religious expression, but also interests that the community is willing to recognize that are not specifically denied recognition by the legal system. Impairing a convict's right to freedom of movement does not trigger a lesser evils justification for escape, for example, because the convict's right has been expressly limited by his conviction and commitment. At the same time, the deprivation of an actor's opportunity to see his dying mother might trigger the defense, although the law does not expressly recognize such a visitation as a legal right. The defendant might receive a general justification defense, then, if he violates a traffic law in his rush to the hospital, provided the jury decides that the evil avoided outweighs the evil of the offense committed. Burke should have little difficulty arguing that his life and Tim's are interests worth protecting and that both are in danger.

---

1. Model Penal Code §3.02(1)(a).

Opportunity to Further Interest   While the triggering condition of the lesser evils defense is typically expressed to require a threat — the offense conduct must be "necessary to avoid a harm or evil to himself or to another" — it is not difficult to argue that in fact the application of the defense is much broader, that the defense can be used to justify what might be viewed as taking an opportunity to further an interest. Conduct furthering a good frequently can be described as avoiding a harm that otherwise would result or persist in the absence of such conduct. Interfering with the selective service system to stop the Vietnam War might be described by protestors either as advancing the interests of peace or as averting the evils of war. Private use of marijuana in the treatment of glaucoma can be seen as furthering the interest of the defendant's good health or as combating the threat of impending blindness.

NECESSITY REQUIREMENT

The triggering of a lesser evils defense, like that of all other justifications, does not give an actor unlimited authority. His response must be both necessary and proportionate. The necessity requirement has two components: the conduct must be necessary in time and in the amount of harm caused. That is, the necessity requirement is not satisfied if the conduct would have been as effective if delayed or if a less harmful alternative is available and would suffice. The case law reveals a concern for both elements, though they typically are expressed in the statutes by the single requirement that the conduct be "necessary."

Necessary in Time   The famous case of *Regina v. Dudley and Stephens*[1] raises, among others, the issue of the temporal aspect of the necessity requirement. The court denied a necessity defense in some part because the defendants, who turned to murder and cannibalism after days at sea without food, *might* have survived until rescued if they had waited a few days more. Burke would have to clear a similar hurdle. He would have to show that he risked death or injury if he delayed the drugs. His ability to show this will depend in part on the operation of the drug. Is a patient's prognosis improved when he begins the treatment earlier? Certainly Burke's best position is to argue that Tim's life was in immediate danger because of his quickly deteriorating condition and, in any case, Tim's present suffering justified immediate action. He can argue that every moment of delay was an additional moment of suffering.

"Imminent" Threat   Many statutes require that the threat of harm must be "imminent" in order to entitle the actor to act under a lesser evils defense. Underlying this requirement is a presumption that, unless the danger is imminent, action is not yet necessary. But such a presumption is not always valid. Suppose, for example, a ship's crew discovers a slow leak soon after leaving port. The captain unreasonably refuses to return to shore. In order to save themselves and the passengers, the crew must mutiny. If the leak would not pose an actual danger of capsizing the vessel for several days, should the crew be forced to wait until the danger is imminent, even though this would mean that the ship would be too far out to sea to reach shore before it sinks? Or should the crew be able to act before it is too late, even though it may be several days before the danger of capsizing is imminent? To require that the harm be "imminent" sometimes may require the

---

1. 14 Q.B.D. 273 (1884).

actor to wait until it is too late. Since the lesser evils defense already requires that the actor engage in conduct only when it is necessary, such an "imminent" requirement is an unnecessary and potentially improper limitation.

"*Immediately Necessary*" Some necessity statutes require that the actor's conduct be "immediately necessary."[1] This formulation is less problematic. In the sinking ship hypothetical, for example, the actors could argue that as soon as they discover the leak, it is immediately necessary to act, even though the danger of capsizing is not yet imminent. There are other situations, however, where the "immediately necessary" language would force an actor to wait longer before acting than he would have to wait without the requirement. Commonly, the effect of such a requirement is to force an actor to delay his actions and thereby create a risk that the threatened harm will occur in order to maximize the chance that the justified conduct will not be necessary. Reasonable persons may disagree over whether it is appropriate to require such a delay, and one's views may vary with the situation. The "immediately necessary" requirement would seem always to force an actor to delay, rather than leaving it for a jury to decide whether it was reasonable under the circumstances to reduce the risk of the harm by acting earlier.[2]

Necessary Amount of Harm The amount-of-harm aspect of the necessity requirement bars the lesser evils defense where a lawful or a less harmful means exists to protect the threatened interest. Where prisoners escape or rebel in order to avoid or publicize life-threatening prison conditions, for example, courts frequently refuse the defense on grounds that less harmful, even lawful, alternatives are available, such as registering complaints with the prison authorities. The necessity requirement also implicitly requires that there be a causal connection between the actor's conduct and avoiding the threatened harm: If the threatened harm could not be prevented by conduct like the defendant's, then the conduct cannot be "necessary" to prevent the harm. Burke probably can show that no less harmful means of saving his life and Tim's is available. He has approached government officials to no avail. On the other hand, the implicit requirement that his conduct be effective in saving his life and Tim's requires a showing that IIR would have made a difference. If IIR would not have been an effective treatment for him or Tim, Burke can hardly argue that the theft of it was necessary to save their lives. (Section 20 takes up the issue of a mistaken belief as to a justification.)

PROPORTIONALITY REQUIREMENT

The lesser evils defense, like all other justifications, requires proportionality between the harm or evil caused by the actor's conduct and the harm or evil avoided. Indeed, the defense contains a more explicit proportionality requirement than any other justification, which require proportionality only through a general

---

1. See Tex. Penal Code Ann. § 9.22(1) (1974); accord Ala. Code § 13A-3-29(1) (1982) (repealed); Ark. Stat. Ann. § 41-504(1)(a) (1977); Colo. Rev. Stat. § 18-1-702(1) (1978); Del. Code Ann. tit. 11, § 463 (1979); Haw. Rev. Stat. § 703-302(1) (1976); Ky. Rev. Stat. Ann. § 503.030(1) (1975); Me. Rev. Stat. Ann. tit. 17-A, § 103(1) (1983); Mich. 2d Proposed Rev. § 605(1) (1979); N.Y. Penal Law § 35.05(2) (1975); Or. Rev. Stat. § 161.200(1)(a) (1981); Wis. Stat. Ann. § 939.47 (1982); Guam Crim. & Corr. Code § 7.80 (1977); P.R. Laws Ann. tit. 33, § 3096 (Cum. Supp. 1981).

2. The Model Penal Code does not adopt this formulation in lesser evils, although it does in other justifications (see, e.g., self-defense, § 3.04). In its lesser evils defense, the Code requires only that the conduct be "necessary."

requirement that the actor's conduct be "reasonable." The lesser evils requirement might be seen as being more demanding. It is not enough for the defense
that the harmfulness of the actor's conduct is generally proportionate to the harm
threatened or that the actor's conduct caused no more harm than it avoided. The
actor's conduct must be shown to have been *less harmful* than the harm threatened. Thus, in the case where two lives hang in conflict, neither actor could
lawfully take the other's, unless some tangible interest (such as the law's abhorrence of unjustified aggression) favored one over the other. Thus, one could kill an
unjustified aggressor to save oneself but could not kill an innocent non-aggressor
to save oneself (in order to take the only available life preserver, for example).
Burke no doubt will feel that he can easily persuade a jury that the harm threatened — two deaths, one of which is imminent — is greater than the harm he
caused — breaking in and stealing IIR (burglary). On the other hand, the prosecution may argue that important intangible interests also must be considered, not
the least of which is the dangerousness of the precedent of justifying burglaries of
researchers' offices. Any adverse effect on the operation of the research effort
ought to be included in the balancing.

Balancing Innocent Lives   One of the more difficult issues that arises in
lesser evils situations is whether to allow the taking of one innocent life in order to
save several innocent lives. The opinion of Lord Coleridge in *Queen v. Dudley and
Stephens,*[1] suggests a philosophy that the value of innocent human life is an
absolute that can never be outweighed, even in the interest of saving a greater
number of lives. This philosophy, consistent with the Kantian position that the
many must die in order to avoid killing a single innocent, is an alternative to the
more utilitarian approach that would permit the taking of an innocent life to bring
about a net saving of lives. But the situation in *Dudley and Stephens,* where one
innocent life is taken to save only two or three others, does not present the strongest
case for justifying the killing of an innocent. Where more than two or three lives are
at stake, it may be more difficult to hold to the absolutist position. This was the
situation in the leading American case, *United States v. Holmes,*[2] which approved
the jettison of some passengers of a sinking lifeboat in order to prevent the death of
all, but only if the selection for jettison is made by drawing lots. Consider the kind
of situation that occurred during the sinking of the ferry *Herald of Free Enterprise.*[3]
Several passengers were trying to reach safety by ascending a rope ladder, but the
ladder was blocked by a passenger petrified by fear and unable to move. After
shouting failed to get him to move, it was agreed that he should be pushed off the
ladder. He fell into the water and was not seen again. It seems unlikely that juries, at
least, would adhere to the strict Kantian position in such a situation and to insist
that the many must die in order to avoid killing the innocent one.

Supremacy of Community's Balance of Interests   In the balancing called
for by the proportionality requirement, no jurisdiction delegates to the individual
actor the right to determine authoritatively the relative value of the harm avoided
and the harm inflicted. It is the community's view, not the actor's, that matters.

---

1. L.R. 14 Q.B. 273 (1884).
2. 26 F. Cas. 360 (1842) (No. 15,383).
3. Reported in J.C. Smith, Justification and Excuse in the Criminal Law 73-79 (1989).

Where the community-view standard is not contained within the language of the defense provision, it is often judicially supplied. As a practical matter, the community's view is given supremacy because the balance of interests is left to the judgment of the jury.[1] Thus, it is of no consequence that the proper balance was clear to Burke; Burke's defense depends on persuading the jury that his calculations were correct.

Preemption by Legislative Balance   It is a corollary of representative government that the ultimate power to judge the relative values of competing interests rests with the legislature. If an actor balances the competing interests in a way that is different from the legislature's, the legislature's view must prevail. This limitation is expressed in part by a Model Penal Code provision that withdraws the lesser evils defense whenever "a legislative purpose to exclude the justification claimed" plainly appears.[2] Such superiority of legislative determinations explains the common refusal of courts to grant a justification for a prison inmate's escape to avoid unhealthy or dangerous, but common, prison conditions. The legislature presumably was aware of the conditions, the argument goes, when it authorized prison sentences. Apparently it was the legislature's view, the argument continues, that the harm of potential prison violence is more tolerable than the public fear and institutional disorder that would result from allowing prisoners lawfully to escape. This limitation on the lesser evils defense will give Burke some difficulty. That the FDA has expressly prohibited the use of IIR outside of the study reflects an authoritative governmental view. Presumably the agency's decision weighs the potential benefits and risks of such use. While the agency is not the legislature, the authority to make such decisions probably has been delegated to it by the legislature. As long as the terms of that delegation have been met, the agency's view would seem to be beyond challenge.

Civil Disobedience   It is because of this same limitation that the lesser evils defense generally is unavailable in cases of civil disobedience. A firm belief in the immorality of a particular national defense policy or abortion policy, for example, will not justify illegal interference with its execution if the policy is lawfully arrived at and implemented. Legitimately promulgated laws and administrative policies are conclusive evidence of the legislature's view and, through it, the community's view of the competing interests. The most controversial instances in which this issue arises are where a law is disobeyed in an exercise of civil disobedience to protest the immorality of the law. Examples include "sit-ins" to protest racial segregation policies and draft card burnings to protest draft registration laws. But the supremacy of legislative judgment means that the enforcement of the law that the actor is charged with violating can never be an alleged harm.

Transcendent Legal Norms   Some writers argue that while the individual may not substitute her own personal judgment, the legislative view ought not be taken as conclusive. There exist, it is argued, some fundamental moral precepts outside the written law that an individual and a court may rely on to justify

---

1. As the Model Penal Code Commentary explains: "The balancing of evils is not committed to the private judgment of the actor; it is an issue for determination at the trial." Model Penal Code §3.02 comment 2 (1985).

2. Model Penal Code §3.02(1)(c).

conduct without regard to contradictory legislative action. This is the point of conflict between a system of "positivist" jurisprudence and one that recognizes "transcendent legal norms," such as natural law. Reliance on transcendent legal norms is said to create the danger that either defendants or courts might seek to use the law to further their own moral convictions.[1] On the other hand, to give absolute authority to a legislature is to assume that legislatures will always behave in a way consistent with fundamental human rights. The lawfully enacted yet universally condemned legislative acts of the Third Reich is one illustration of the dangerousness of such an assumption.

Legislative Preemption Through Offense Exceptions The supremacy of legislative judgment also means that the lesser evils defense is not available where an offense definition addresses situations similar to those at issue. If the legislature exhaustively enumerates the situations where an offense shall not apply, a court may find that those exceptions are meant to be all-inclusive. The Model Penal Code lesser evils defense is expressly made unavailable when the "law defining the offense provides exceptions or defenses dealing with the specific situation involved."[2] This is no more than an accepted and obligatory rule of statutory construction. In *Bice v. State,* the defendant sought to justify violation of a law against bringing liquor to church, with a claim that his doctor deemed the liquor necessary for medicinal purposes.[3] The statute expressly provided that a practicing physician could bring liquor to church; thus, the court concluded, the legislature apparently intended to exclude anyone other than a doctor from doing so. By specifying certain exceptions, the lawmakers impliedly rejected others and foreclosed the issue of additional exceptions, at least exceptions that arguably are of the sort that the legislature might have included on its list. This limitation on justification defenses does not pertain exclusively to proportionality concerns, but may reflect a legislative predetermination to exclude the defense for a variety of reasons.

Superiority of More Specific Justification One means by which a legislature precludes use of the general justification defense is to provide another justification defense that specifically addresses the situation. Thus, more specific justification defenses are given superiority over more general defenses, such as lesser evils. In the language of the Model Penal Code, a lesser evils justification is not available if "the Code . . . provides . . . defenses dealing with the specific situation involved."[4] It is through the definition of more specific justifications that the legislature imposes the numerous restrictions on the triggering conditions, necessity, and proportionality requirements for particular situations. Thus, an actor cannot use

---

1. Perhaps because of these concerns, the New York lesser evils defense provides in part: "The necessity and justiciability of such conduct may not rest upon considerations pertaining only to the morality and advisability of the statute, either in its general application or with respect to its application to a particular class of cases arising thereunder." N.Y. Penal Law § 35.05(2) (1975).

2. Model Penal Code § 3.02(1)(b); accord Haw. Rev. Stat. § 703-302(1)(b) (1976); Neb. Rev. Stat. § 28-1407(1)(b) (1979); N.J. Stat. Ann. § 2C:3-2(a)(1982).

3. 109 Ga. 117, 34 S.E. 202 (1899).

4. Model Penal Code § 3.02(1)(c). A similar limitation on the general public authority defense appears in section 3.03. Together these provisions may cover the most common complications of this sort. One might prefer a single provision that states the general principle for the superiority of the more specific justification, whatever the context. See Proposed R.I. Gen. Laws § 11A-3-1 (1985).

lesser evil as a defense to the use of force to protect himself; the self-defense justification specifically addresses that situation. Special rules frequently are provided in the most common justification situations, where an actor is given a special public authority to act or when defensive force is needed to defend against an aggressor. For example, the legislature may wish to limit the use of deadly force in self-defense to instances in which the actor cannot retreat in safety. More detailed rules such as these help increase uniformity in the adjudication of justification cases and make the law's operation more predictable. Such special rules ought not be subject to circumvention by allowing a defendant to look to the general justification defense of lesser evils.

● DISCUSSION MATERIALS

What Limitations, If Any, Should Be Placed on the Lesser Evils Justification Defense? Should the Defense Even Be Recognized?

In denying a defense for trespass by nuclear power protestors, the court in *State v. Warshow* shows its concern that a lesser evils defense might have an overly broad reach and might improperly intrude on governmental decision making. The court in *State v. Green*, denying a lesser evils defense for a prison escape to avoid threatened gang rape, responds to similar concerns by adhering to a strict application of the traditional "imminent danger" requirement as a means of limiting the defense. In each instance, however, concurring and dissenting opinions reveal the tensions in the issues raised. The Greenawalt excerpt discusses the significance of the defense, exploring its potential misuse but supporting its current formulation on the grounds that no alternative formulation would do better. Finally, Steven Bauer and Peter Eckerstrom urge a new and broader application of the defense — a political necessity defense — and discuss the responsibility that would be on the jury in such cases.

State v. Warshow

Supreme Court of Vermont
410 A.2d 1000 (1980)

Barney, Chief Justice.

The defendants were part of a group of demonstrators that traveled to Vernon, Vermont to protest at the main gates of a nuclear power plant known as Vermont Yankee. The plant had been shut down for repairs and refueling, and these protestors had joined a rally designed to prevent workers from gaining access to the plant and placing it on-line.

They were requested to leave the private premises of the power plant by representatives of Vermont Yankee and officers of the law. The defendants were among those who refused, and they were arrested and charged with unlawful trespass.

The issue with which this appeal of their convictions is concerned relates to a doctrine referred to as the defense of necessity. At trial the defendants sought to present evidence relating to the hazards of nuclear power plant operation which, they argued, would establish that defense. After hearing the defendants' offer of proof the trial court excluded the proffered evidence and refused to grant compulsory process for the witnesses required to present the defense. The jury instruction requested on the issue of necessity was also refused, and properly preserved for appellate review.

In ruling below, the trial court determined that the defense was not available. It is on this basis that we must test the issue.

The defense of necessity is one that partakes of the classic defense of "confession and avoidance." It admits the criminal act, but claims justification. It has a counterpart in civil litigation, recognized in Vermont in the case of Ploof v. Putnam, 81 Vt. 471, 71 A. 188 (1908).

The doctrine is one of specific application insofar as it is a defense to criminal behavior. This is clear because if the qualifications for the defense of necessity are not closely delineated, the definition of criminal activity becomes uncertain and even whimsical. The difficulty arises when words of general and broad qualification are used to describe the special scope of this defense.

In the various definitions and examples recited as incorporating the concept of necessity, certain fundamental requirements stand out:

(1) there must be a situation of emergency arising without fault on the part of the actor concerned;

(2) this emergency must be so imminent and compelling as to raise a reasonable expectation of harm, either directly to the actor or upon those he was protecting;

(3) this emergency must present no reasonable opportunity to avoid the injury without doing the criminal act; and

(4) the injury impending from the emergency must be of sufficient seriousness to outmeasure the criminal wrong.

There is no doubt that the defendants wished to call attention to the dangers of low-level radiation, nuclear waste, and nuclear accident. But low-level radiation and nuclear waste are not the types of imminent danger classified as an emergency sufficient to justify criminal activity. To be imminent, a danger must be, or must reasonably appear to be, threatening to occur immediately, near at hand, and impending. . . . We do not understand the defendants to have taken the position in their offer of proof that the hazards of low-level radiation and nuclear waste buildup are immediate in nature. On the contrary, they cite long-range risks and dangers that do not presently threaten health and safety. Where the hazards are long term, the danger is not imminent, because the defendants have time to exercise options other than breaking the law. . . .

Nor does the specter of nuclear accident as presented by these defendants fulfill the imminent and compelling harm element of the defense. The offer does not take the position that they acted to prevent an impending accident. Rather, they claimed that they acted to foreclose the "chance" or "possibility" of accident. This defense cannot lightly be allowed to justify acts taken to foreclose speculative and uncertain dangers. Its application must be limited to acts directed to the prevention of harm that is reasonably certain to occur. . . .

These acts may be a method of making public statements about nuclear power and its dangers, but they are not a legal basis for invoking the defense of necessity. Nor can the defendants' sincerity of purpose excuse the criminal nature of their acts.

Judgment affirmed.

Hill, Justice, concurring . . .

Both the State of Vermont and the Federal government have given their imprimatur to the development and normal operation of nuclear energy and have established mechanisms for the regulation of nuclear power. . . . Implicit within these statutory enactments is the policy choice that the benefits of nuclear energy outweigh its dangers.

If we were to allow defendants to present the necessity defense in this case we would, in effect, be allowing a jury to redetermine questions of policy already decided by the legislative branches of the federal and state governments. This is not how our system of government was meant to operate. . . .

In my opinion the majority puts the cart before the horse. It measures the offer made against the requisite elements of the defense of necessity and concludes that the defendants failed to show a likelihood of imminent danger; yet it reserves judgment on the legislative policy exception to the defense. It is illogical to consider whether the necessary elements of a defense have been shown before determining whether the defense is even available in the particular situation.

The dissent, on the other hand, assumes that defendants' offer was sufficient to show not only imminent danger but also a failure of the regulatory scheme. I cannot agree with this assumption because the offer failed to show a danger not contemplated by the legislative scheme. The legislative framework was set up to deal with the very situation defendants offered to prove "might" happen. But because neither the state legislature nor Congress acted to shut down the power plant based on speculative possibilities does not, in my opinion, give rise to the questionable inference that there was an emergency which the regulatory scheme failed to avert. . . .

Since defendants' defense of necessity was foreclosed by a deliberate legislative policy choice, there was no error on the trial court's part in not allowing the defense to be presented.

Billings, Justice, dissenting . . .

The majority states that the danger of low-level radiation and nuclear waste, which the defendants offered to prove, are "not the types of imminent danger classified as an emergency sufficient to justify criminal activity." Furthermore, the majority dismisses those portions of the proof dealing with the threat of a nuclear accident by characterizing them as mere "speculative and uncertain dangers." In doing so the majority has decided to so read the evidence as to give credibility only to that evidence offered on the effects of low-level radiation. . . . The defendants also stated that "there was reasonable belief that it would have been an emergency had they started that reactor up. [T]here was a very good chance of an accident there for which there is no insurance coverage or very little." Specifically, the defendants offered to show by expert testimony that there were defects in the cooling system and other aspects of the power plant which they believed could and would result in a meltdown within seven seconds of failure on the start up of the plant. In addition, the defendants went to great lengths to base their defense on the imminent danger that would result from the hazardous radiation emitted from the plant and its wastes when the plant resumed operations.

While the offer made by the defendants was laced with statements about the dangers they saw in nuclear power generally, it is clear that they offered to show that the Vermont Yankee facility at which they were arrested was an imminent danger to the community on the day of the arrests; that, if it commenced operation, there was a danger of meltdown and severe radiation damage to persons and property....

Furthermore, the defendants offered to show that, in light of the imminent danger of an accident, they had exhausted all alternative means of preventing the start up of the plant and the immediate catastrophe it would bring. Under the circumstances of imminent danger arising from the start up of the plant, coupled with the resistance of Vermont Yankee and government officials, which the defendants offered to prove, nothing short of preventing the workers access to start up the plant would have averted the accident that the defendants expected....

I would also dissent from the concurring opinion in so far as it attempts to hide behind inferences that the legislature precluded the courts from hearing the defense of necessity in the instant case.... The defendants are entitled to show that although there is a comprehensive regulatory scheme it had failed to such an extent as to raise for them the choice between criminal trespass and the nuclear disaster which the regulatory scheme was created to prevent.

I am of the opinion that the defendants are entitled to present evidence on the defense of necessity as it exists at common law. To deny them this opportunity is to deny them a fair trial merely because they express unpopular political views....

State v. Green
Supreme Court of Missouri
470 S.W.2d 565 (1971)

Henley, Judge.

John Charles Green (hereinafter defendant) was charged by information with the offense of escape from a state institution in which he was lawfully confined, a felony. He waived a jury, was tried before the court, found guilty, and was sentenced to imprisonment for a term of three years. He appeals. We affirm.

[A few days after his arrival, on December 16, 1966, Green appears before the disciplinary board for fighting, the result of fending off sexual advances by other prisoners. On January 2, 1967, after lights out, two men pick the lock on Green's cell, an easy and common practice. One man is about Green's size. The other is approximately six feet tall and 200 pounds. Green yells for a guard, but the guard on duty is separated from the wing by a heavy door and does not respond.

Green tries to push the first man aside but the second man grabs him, holds a knife to his throat, and threatens to stab him if he does not "cooperate" with them. Green then submits to rape by both men.

[Several minutes after the assailants leave, Green slits his own arm in order to get removed from the inmate population, then goes for a guard. He is taken to the prison hospital where he is kept for several days. Green reports what happened to Donald Hartness, the Assistant Superintendent of Treatment, and asks to be moved to avoid further attacks. Green refuses to name his attackers for fear that he will be killed. Hartness tells him he must resolve his own problems and suggests that he go back and fight it out. Despite his objections, Green is returned to his old cell.

[Several days later, again after lights out, three men pick Green's lock and enter his cell. Green attempts to run but is knocked out. He wakes up later with anal pain and discovers "grease" in his anal area. Realizing he has been raped again, he feigns having swallowed glass so that he can talk to an official without the other inmates knowing, and asks a guard to hospitalize him.

[The next day, Green is brought before the disciplinary board and charged with self-destruction. The disciplinary board is composed of Mr. Baldwin (the Assistant Superintendent of Custody), Mr. Hartness, and a guard. Green describes the assaults and asks for protective custody. He again refuses to give his attackers' names. Mr. Baldwin tells Green the best that he can do is to arrange a wing change. He advises Green to "fight it out, submit to the assaults, or go over the fence." The Board assigns no punishment for the violation charged. The Superintendent of the center, Edward Hayes, reviews the hearing's record and approves Green's cell change to an adjoining wing.

[When Green is moved to the new wing, other prisoners taunt him. He also is propositioned for sex by a guard, named Petre. He reports this to Captain Chapman, and the guard is transferred. At noon on April 14, 1967, five inmates come to Green's cell and tell him they will come for him that night to gang-rape him, and that he will be their "punk" (the person who is penetrated in male same-sex intercourse) for the remainder of his time in prison. They threaten to seriously injure or to kill him if he does not cooperate.

[As before, the lock in Green's cell can easily be picked. Because his past reports have been futile, Green decides not to tell authorities of the threat of gang homosexual rape, but to escape instead. Around 6:00 p.m. that day, he quietly escapes. Green climbs over the fence near the powerhouse on the west side of the institution and walks down a railroad track for a short distance, across several fields, and along the highway. At the 10:00 p.m. bed check, he is discovered missing and a search begins. Early the next afternoon, Trooper Roy Robinson comes across Green sitting beside the road looking at a highway map. He takes Green into custody without incident and returns him to Moberly.]

The court ruled [in pre-trial motion] that the evidence did not constitute a legal defense. Immediately after this ruling, defendant waived a jury, evidence was offered by the state on the offense charged, and, as previously noted, the court found him guilty. . . .

Defendant says he has been unable to find any Missouri cases supporting his theory of "necessity" as a defense in this case. We find none. The state refers us to *People v. Richards*, 269 Cal. App. 2d 768, 75 Cal. Rptr. 597 (1969), for a concise definition of the defense of necessity. The California Court of Appeal said: "The principle of justification by necessity, if applicable, involves a determination that 'the harm or evil sought to be avoided by such conduct is greater than that sought to be prevented by the law defining the offense charged.' . . . The compulsion from the harm or evil which the actor seeks to avoid, should be present and impending. . . ."

This is not a case where defendant escaped while being closely pursued by those who sought by threat of death or bodily harm to have him submit to sodomy. Moreover, the threatened consequences of his refusal to submit could have been avoided that day by reporting the threats and the names of those making the threats to the authorities in charge of the Center. Defendant had several hours in which to consider and report these threats.

The defense of "necessity" was not available to defendant and the court did not err in excluding his offer of proof. Defendant's defense resolves itself into the simple proposition that the conditions of his confinement justified his escape. Generally, conditions of confinement do not justify escape and are not a defense.

The judgment is affirmed.

Seiler, Judge (dissenting). . .

I interpret the majority opinion to decide that the proposed defense is not available because (1) defendant did not delay his escape until his would-be assailants had him in close pursuit and (2) because he could have avoided his predicament had he only turned in their names earlier in the day.

As to the first, defendant knew from prior experience that if he waited until the band was close at hand, it would be too late. If escape were to save him, it had to be made earlier than the last minute. Five against one is hopeless odds. As to the second, this overlooks the evidence that to turn in the names to the prison authorities meant defendant was risking his life by being a "snitch".

Defendant had already been told by a high prison official that he had three alternatives: submit, defend himself, or escape. The majority opinion does not recommend submission, and as a practical matter, self defense was impossible. All that was left was escape, and under these circumstances, the coercion and necessity were not remote in time, but present and impending. Escape or submission (and I do not believe defendant was unreasonable in not being willing to submit to five-fold sodomy) were literally all this defendant had left. . . .

Other Discussion Materials

Kent Greenawalt, Conflicts of Law and Morality — Instructions of Amelioration
67 Virginia Law Review 177, 194-200 (1981)

One who wants to think intelligently about the desirable scope of a principle of general justification must understand its place among other rules and practices in the system of criminal justice. The defense is crucial in very few cases, both because of the range of more specific justifications and because of police and prosecutorial choices not to proceed in most cases covered by the defense. Further, when the defense reaches choices made under threats, as does the Model Code version, it overlaps substantially with the defense of duress, which excuses an actor who submits to coercion that a person of reasonable firmness would have been unable to resist. Finally, if the defense were abolished, instances of jury nullification and lenient sentencing would aid actors who might now claim its justification.

Thus, the defense of necessity does not have tremendous practical significance. Yet it fills important offices. It serves as a safeguard against prosecutorial abuse, and even if prosecutorial policy is enlightened, actors who are genuinely justified in what they do should have the satisfaction of thinking they have acted appropriately under the law rather than having to depend on the grace of the prosecutor or even the grudging acknowledgment, represented by a finding of duress, that their submission to pressure was excusable. Moreover, for those cases in which the asserted justifying facts are in doubt, the crime is very serious, or the balance of relevant values is extremely difficult, formal adjudication may well be preferable to placing on the prosecutor the great weight of deciding whether a possibly justified actor will be punished. Despite its limited impact, therefore, the defense belongs in the criminal law unless its drawbacks are too great.

It would certainly be a drawback if the existence of the defense encouraged actors to violate the law without sufficient assessment of whether their actions really were necessary to avoid greater evils. As far as private actors and ordinary circumstances are concerned, this possibility is implausible in the extreme, because such a rarely used defense is unlikely to have a significant effect on how private persons react to emergency situations. The concern, however, may have greater relevance for two situations discussed below. Another possible drawback is that the defense is too open-ended, failing to provide fair warning and lending itself to uneven administration. If we assume that the defense will infrequently be relied upon in advance (or otherwise lead actors to engage in behavior that they would not have engaged in but for the defense), actors will rarely be put in a worse position because of the defense, which provides immunity when none would otherwise exist. Thus, the fair warning point has much less force than it would in the context of basic definitions of criminal behavior. A degree of vagueness is tolerable and, indeed, necessary when a subject does not lend itself to more precise definition. Moreover, the answers to questions of general justification are not quite so uncertain as the open-ended phraseology might lead one to think. Many questions about necessity and relative values will, after all, appear relatively simple (although cases in which the actor's behavior is undeniably justified will not often get to court). Insofar as uneven administration remains a concern, that risk constitutes one argument for giving the application of the defense to judges rather than jurors. In any event, abolition of the defense on that ground would be largely self-defeating, since unevenness would remain for those cases in the exercise of prosecutorial discretion, jury nullification, and sentencing decisions.

In three special circumstances, the drawbacks of a defense as broad as the Model Code formulation may be more substantial. With respect to certain acts that, viewed individually, may seem justified, the damage to legal clarity and general deterrence that could be caused by successful employment of the defense may tell against its application. For example, if one is threatened with a serious assault by a fellow prisoner and authorities cannot provide adequate protection against such assaults, escape can perhaps be seen as a necessary lesser evil to prevent the assault. But if prisoners who escape are subsequently returned to the same institutions, the level of freedom from assault will not rise much if the defense is recognized. Because the closed community of fellow prisoners is likely to learn of such rulings, allowing the defense may well encourage more escapes, and the burden upon juries or judges assessing the adequacy of in-prison protection and the existence and credibility of purported threats of assault would be formidable. One might reasonably conclude that, although the evil of escape is less than the evil of assault and escape is sometimes necessary to avoid assault, the defense nevertheless should not be admitted for such situations. Ideally, the law-applier's endeavor to weigh evils could take into account the prospects for genuine relief from avoided evils, future administrative difficulties, and overall deterrent effects, but that is obviously a hard task for a judge and an inappropriate one for jurors. In any event, by focusing attention on the particular instance rather than on a general class of actions, the Model Code and other formulations do not explicitly encourage such a broader view.

A different problem arises when an actor claims that violation of one law (e.g., a traffic regulation) was warranted as a protest against another law or government policy. Courts have not been receptive to such claims, and perhaps the necessity requirement effectively precludes them, because the actor may have difficulty showing that his acts were necessary to avoid the evil to which he objects. It is not inconceivable, however, that a jury might be persuaded that such acts of disobedience by the defendant and others are required to stop some evil (e.g., the Vietnamese War); even the imminence requirement of many formulations need not be an absolute bar, for illegal acts of protest are usually addressed at what the actors consider to be continuing evil. Yet it hardly seems an appropriate task for judges or juries to determine whether the harm of one law or policy is so great that citizens are justified in causing the harm another law is aimed at preventing. Moreover, such a task conflicts with a conception of the defense as particularizing general legislative aims.

Illegal protest and even acts like escapes might be considered precluded from the defense on the ground that permitting a justification would not be consonant with the general purposes that the legislature seeks to pursue. Much can be said for some latitude of judicial interpretation to deal with these matters, but the Model Code formulation is not particularly well suited for it. It bars the defense only when the legislature has provided other explicit exceptions or defenses or when a legislative purpose to exclude the justification "otherwise plainly appear[s]." It would take a strained interpretation to say that a purpose to exclude "plainly appears" for illegal protests and an even more strained interpretation to reach that conclusion about escapes.

Probably the greatest danger with the defense is its possible use when officials or outraged citizens take action against unpopular minorities, a danger sharply evidenced by its submission to the jury in the *Bisbee Deportation* case. In that case, a posse had kidnaped over one thousand striking I.W.W. members and sympathizers and transported them out of the state, subsequently claiming necessity to protect the lives and property of local residents. Blatantly illegal actions by officials may, in a time of continuing national and international crisis, be defended as necessary to prevent grave harms to the country, and the officials who raise such defenses will not always be as tarnished as were the members of the Nixon administration by the time they got to trial. In contrast with use of the defense for isolated private acts, a prominent official's successful invocation of the defense, and even his employment of this theory in public claims that criticized actions were warranted, might affect the inclinations of other officials to observe legal limits.

The Model Code partly addresses this problem about public officials by barring the general justification when other justifications are relevant, but the apparent result is somewhat paradoxical. Official duty is a separate justification, so when the official is acting like an official, but oversteps the limits of his authority, he must do without the choice-of-evils argument. If his action is blatantly illegal, however, and if he lays no claim to official authority in the usual sense, despite having relied upon his position within the government when performing the action, then he may be free to claim choice of the lesser evil as would a private individual. It might be preferable to bar this defense altogether for officials who act under the color of authority in any sense, particularly because the official authority justification is sufficiently flexible to cover almost all defensible acts by officials.

This approach would not, of course, solve the problem of private mob action against feared minorities. Are there any principles that might be employed to preclude the defense in such situations? Conceivably the defense should not be allowed when private citizens take upon themselves the responsibilities of government officers, at least when the government has had time to act. Such a rule, however, would eliminate the defense not only when a private mob overreacts to some supposed danger, but also when private persons respond with minimum force to a real danger that officials refuse to recognize, are too frightened to meet, or are unable to contain. Moreover, if private persons were not allowed to do the things that public officials are supposed to do (such as confine a dangerous person), it would be anomalous to allow them to respond to a threat by harming the interests of an innocent person if prompt and effective official action could have stymied the person making the threat. Yet a broader principle that would bar the defense whenever a prompt plea to officials could have provided relief from feared dangers if officials had responded effectively would leave some persons who accurately perceive that officials cannot or will not protect them against serious threatened harms without the justification. In short, it is not easy to develop a sensible principle that would prevent misuse of the defense by those who take action against unpopular groups without also preventing its use by persons whose claim of justification is appealing.

These various difficulties do provide arguments against having the defense against choice of evils or for narrowing the defense more than the Model Code has done. They may also be used to support the position of the Brown Commission that the defense should be left to whatever common-law status it enjoys rather than reduced to codified form. My own view is that despite these problems the defense should be retained, that codification is desirable to supply reasonably clear guiding criteria, and that the difficulties can be largely met within the basic approach of the Model Code by a combination of moderate variations in the statutory language and sensitive judicial interpretation.

Steven M. Bauer & Peter J. Eckerstrom, The State Made Me Do It: The Applicability of the Necessity Defense to Civil Disobedience

39 Stanford Law Review 1173, 1184-1189 (1987)

Arguments for the Political Necessity Defense

The use of our courts as a forum for individualized challenges to laws raises fundamental issues about the shape of American political culture. A significant body of academic work points to the demise of the common citizen in American politics....

To the theorist or reformer who bemoans the shrinking role of the individual in our society, the political necessity defense makes possible a much needed infusion of individual expression and grassroots political activity. The defense promotes a more vibrant and empowered political culture by amplifying individual viewpoints, by empowering a cross section of the community (the jury), and by increasing the quantity and quality of public discourse. Even considering the arguments against the political necessity defense, one might find these ends alluring enough to permit its use.

1. The Necessity Defense as Amplifier of Individual Viewpoints

The political necessity defense empowers the individual primarily by presenting a forum in which stifled minority or unheeded majority viewpoints receive a public hearing and a governmental response. Civil disobedience as a form of public expression possesses its greatest utility and legitimacy when orthodox channels of democratic participation have failed. Only then is it needed; only then is it morally acceptable. For this reason, the political necessity defense will be used mainly by those individuals or factions most frustrated by the political system — those most in need of an officially sponsored hearing to renew faith in themselves as potent political units in the democracy.

The elements of the political necessity defense ensure its use by those parties most in need of a hearing. The necessity defense demands that the defendant lack any reasonable legal alternative to the unlawful act. To demonstrate that lawful forms of political protest did not present a reasonable means by which to change policy, the civil disobedient must convince the jury that, in his case, the orthodox political structure denied his opportunity to participate effectively in shaping the policies of his government....

The availability of an officially sanctioned hearing plays a significant role in remedying individual political discouragement. It conveys the symbolic message that our society highly values political input and gives special attention to apparent systemic failures in our form of democratic government. In particular, the hearing amplifies intensely held individual views: Since the civil disobedient risks criminal sanction to express his view, we can expect that view to be intensely held. Equally important, the political necessity defense presents a forum wherein an individual can demand a response from the government. While complaints directed at other governmental forums may be met with a form letter, shelved, or put off for study, the judicial process demands an immediate exploration and resolution of the issue involved. Here, the government must answer or dismiss its case. Broader acceptance of the political necessity defense is also consistent with recent legal literature that advocates granting individuals greater access to the judicial system.

2. Empowering the Jury

The political necessity defense places the jury in a position to acquit the defendant, nullifying the effect of the law that has been broken. In its factual determination, the jury is called upon to weigh controversial political issues. The wisdom of using the political necessity defense thus depends to some extent upon the wisdom of entrusting the jury with these decisions.

The idea of empowering a jury to make significant case-by-case political decisions is neither novel nor foreign to the American legal tradition. During the colonial period, the jury became an important source of indigent political power set in opposition to the unpopular laws of the mother country. Well into the nineteenth century, American juries retained the power to decide questions of law as well as fact. Today, juries can still acquit criminal defendants against the evidence and the judge's instructions. Empowering the jury thus conforms with a longstanding American willingness to use citizens as a buffer between the defendant and the harsh and sometimes arbitrary enforcement of the law. Historically, American juries have performed their duties in a "consistently responsible manner" even in the most politically inflammatory cases of the last century. The political necessity defense heightens that traditional role.

An empowered jury fulfills several positive legal roles. To the extent that moral condemnation forms the basis for criminal law, the jury is not simply a factfinder but a judge of moral culpability.... Arguably, common law necessity developed to protect just this class of defendants: those who have violated the letter of the law but lack true moral culpability. In short, necessity cases present precisely the sort of situation in which the jury's role as "conscience of the community" gains its greatest importance.

...Where prosecutorial discretion fails, jury discretion can succeed in molding definitions of deviance to conform to community standards of fairness. This function gains greater significance in political trials. Since prosecutors are often politically accountable to either the electorate or the executive branch, prosecutorial discretion "no longer acts as a buffer between the community and the laws and thus the ordinary restraint exercised to prevent unfair prosecutions can no longer be counted upon." Empowering the jury helps to provide a substitute for this lost buffer.

Juries are not, of course, representative conduits of popular political sentiment. However, a number of factors limit the jury's role and thus mitigate its inadequacy as a representative body. First, the acquittal of civil disobedients and the consequent nullification of the law are not automatic. The defendant must still convince the jury that the evil allegedly prevented by the act was great enough to warrant lawbreaking. More difficult yet, the civil disobedient must show a failure in the political process. Convincing a jury of the elements of political necessity will present defendants with quite a challenge.

Second, an acquittal nullifies the effect of a law only as applied on a case-by-case basis. While the jury may find the enforcement of a law in an individual case to be unjust, it possesses no power to invalidate the law. Authorities could continue to enforce laws regardless of the result of a particular political necessity trial. Nor would anything prevent the government from explaining to the jury the drawbacks of civil disobedience. One can envision an effective closing argument by the prosecution portraying the defendant as self-righteous egotist, too stubborn to accept his fair loss at the voting booth.

While the jury's limited power mitigates its possible defects as a representative body, the infusion of political interest and energy into the community through the jury can be significant. Each political necessity trial exposes twelve members of the community to a situation in which they must assess difficult political issues and consider arguments about the adequacy of our democratic processes. But the trial presents more than an extended civics lesson: It empowers the jury to make a legally binding decision. The jurors make a politically potent choice in a context where their individual judgment is not drowned out by thousands or millions of other electors. Moreover, the jury makes its decision after hearing a discussion of the issues that is considerably more thorough than the quick generalities, slogans, and encapsulated presentations that are routine in mass media politics. The judicial system demands that the complaint or defense be reduced to specific elements, fostering a more disciplined consideration of the issues.

Finally, the political necessity trial places the juror in a role where he must judge and actively discuss issues with other jurors. This experience might cause the citizen-juror to enlarge the scope of his political participation outside the courtroom, thereby providing more benefits for participatory democracy. Again, the message conveyed is positive: Our society feels comfortable granting legal and political authority to a small group of common citizens in a context where thorough discussion can occur. Political messages and political power flow from a collection of twelve citizens, and lawmakers are told when they are out of touch with citizens' preferences.

3. Improving the Quality and Quantity of Public Discourse

The airing of political necessity arguments generally improves the quality and quantity of public discussion. Outside the courtroom, the trial draws attention both to the discrete issue raised by the civil disobedient and to the health of the democratic political process. Inside the courtroom, the quality of discourse improves through the patience of the court in hearing all arguments, the concreteness of the discussion, and the specificity required by evidentiary rules. This may also stimulate a higher quality of discussion outside the courtroom as the media reports on the trial's progress.

The government is drawn into the discussion in several ways. Obviously, the trial itself requires the government to argue its position. Moreover, the litigation over the political necessity defense sends a message to legislators and other officials by bringing the law or policy under challenge to their attention. Thus, small-scale popular adjudication of law enforcement through the referendum of the jury may actually enhance the legislative function.

One can also expect the trial participants — the jury, attorneys, staff, and observers — to enlarge their own political interest and participation outside the courtroom. The quality and quantity of their interpersonal political dialogue will increase. Most of all, the political necessity defense opens an avenue by which laws and lawmakers are held accountable to the people they serve, and an avenue by which people affirm and enforce their role as citizen-participants in the democratic process.

Defensive Force Justifications

Perhaps the most common fact pattern that raises justification issues is that of a person using force in defense of person or property. Unlike the general justification defense of lesser evils, the law has developed explicit and detailed rules governing the case of defensive force, and typically these rules are embodied in modern criminal codes.

◆ THE CASE OF BERNHARD GOETZ

It is December 22, 1984. New York City faces problems of widespread drug use and rampant crime. Six hundred thousand crimes have already been committed this year. The steeply escalating rates of street and violent crime are linked to the introduction of crack cocaine. (The crime rate is more than twice what it is today: 8.397.1 per 100,000 compared to 3,293.3 per 100,000 in 2001.) On average, forty felonies are committed against subway riders every day.

The fear has caused people to change the way they live their lives. They have stopped wearing valuables. Some carry a wallet with enough cash to satisfy a mugger. Many stay indoors at night and plan their daily commutes and errands to avoid certain streets and subway routes thought to be dangerous. Women don't walk near buildings with shadows. Fewer tourists visit the Big Apple. People are moving to the suburbs in droves. Many feel that "the system" has let them down and no longer trust law enforcement to protect them.

One of three brothers, Bernhard (Bernie) Goetz was raised in upstate New York, the son of a Jewish mother and a German father. When Bernie was thirteen, his father was convicted of abusing two boys, an incident that brought the family closer. Goetz always believed in his father's innocence. It was a profound

Figure 87 **Bernhard Goetz at his home, 1985**
(Bettmann/Corbis)

experience for Goetz, and the first of many disappointments he has with the legal system.

Goetz left his hometown to study nuclear and electrical engineering at New York University. While there, he discovered he had a talent for fixing machines, and after graduation took a job as nuclear engineer for submarines. Never a team player, Goetz had trouble interacting with people in college, and his difficulties continued when he worked for private contractors. He often reported defects to the military when they would have preferred his silence. Goetz finally came to realize that his aversion to both authority and people generally would make it difficult for him to work in a corporate environment. He decided to become his own boss and today repairs electronics from his apartment, which is in New York City's rough Fourteenth Street neighborhood.

Goetz was recently victimized by crime, which makes his decision to stay in the City all the more surprising. In 1981, he was riding the subway home, carrying electronic equipment for his business, when he was mugged for the first time. Three young men jumped him by slamming him into a glass door, driving its handle into his chest, and then throwing him to the ground. With the help of a janitor, Goetz was able to grab hold of the ringleader, Fred Clark, until the police arrived.

The incident served only to solidify further Goetz's distrust of the criminal justice system. After the mugging, the police interrogated him for more than six hours, while apparently releasing the criminals after just a few hours. His assailants were charged only with criminal mischief—for ripping Goetz's jacket—when authorities concluded that there was insufficient evidence for an attempted robbery charge. Goetz was frustrated; the system seemed so focused on details that it ignored the real harm of the crime.

The mugging and the system's inability to protect him so disturbed Goetz that he spent more than $2,000 trying to obtain a concealed weapon permit. The police turned him down. When pressed for a reason, an officer explained simply that the department cannot give every person a permit. The system's concern with "technicalities" again frustrates Goetz.

Even now, the physical and emotional scars of the mugging remain; his knees are permanently injured and he is frightened of being "beaten to a pulp" by muggers. He likens himself to a caged rat that is continuously poked with red-hot needles. To feel safe, he now leaves his apartment only with a .38 caliber gun in a quick-draw holster. He also never wears gloves, even in the coldest weather, in order to be "fast on the draw." Despite Goetz's fears, he still engages in risky behavior. For example, one evening, he stays on the wrong subway, going toward Harlem, rather than getting off and switching directions. He exits at a stop near the northern edge of Central Park, an area notorious for muggings and assaults, and goes for a walk. While walking, Goetz scares off a mugger with his gun.

Today, feeling depressed about his father's recent death, Goetz leaves his apartment in the early afternoon to head downtown. He catches the No. 2 train at the corner of Seventh Avenue and Fourteenth Street, and sits in the first car, near four young African-American men, Darrell Cabey, Barry Allen, Troy Canty, and James Ramseur. They are all high school dropouts with criminal records. Earlier in the year, Cabey had been arrested for armed robbery. Shortly before the subway shooting, Cabey was accused of robbing three other men at gunpoint. He and Allen also menaced a woman on a train, asking for money. Allen has twice pled guilty to disorderly conduct. Ramseur and Canty have been convicted of petit larceny. Ramseur has been accused of being involved in the gang rape of a pregnant woman.

Their aggressive and somewhat threatening behavior causes the fifteen to twenty other passengers to move to the other end of the car. Canty, lying on the bench across the way, says to Goetz, "How are ya?" Along with Allen, he approaches Goetz and asks for five dollars. Canty and Allen stand to Goetz's left, between Goetz and the passengers who had distanced themselves from the situation. Goetz sees one of the other two men reach into his pocket, which appears to be bulging. (It is later determined that the men are carrying sharpened screwdrivers in their pockets, but at this point Goetz does not know what the bulge is.) Goetz asks them to repeat their request, later explaining that he wanted to be sure that they were "playing the game." They repeat themselves, saying, "Give us $5.00." Cabey later admits that they were intending to rob Goetz because "he looked like easy bait."

After their second request, Goetz pulls his gun and fires rapidly at them as they scatter. He hits each of them at least once. After some confusing moments,

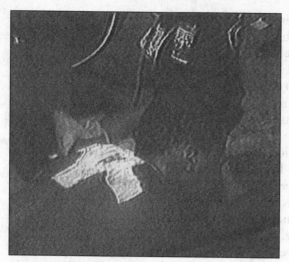

Figure 88 **Crime scene on the No. 2 train in New York City, 1984**

(CNN)

Figure 89 **Darrell Cabey entering Bronx State Supreme Court during civil suit against Goetz, April 12, 1996**

(CNN)

he sees Cabey sitting near the conductor's cab, grasping the seat. Goetz approaches him and says, "You seem to be doing all right. Here's another," and shoots him. Other passengers pull the emergency cord, jerking the train to a stop. Everyone exits, except two terrified women whom Goetz tries to comfort. When the conductor enters the car and asks Goetz if he is a police officer, Goetz says no, and explains that the young men were trying to rob him. Keeping his gun, Goetz walks off into the subway tunnel. He later describes his shooting the four men as wanting "to murder them, to hurt them, to make them suffer as much as possible." He was sick of being "played with . . . as a cat plays with a mouse."

The young men are left lying in pools of blood on the train car's floor. Canty, Allen, and Ramseur are all injured in the upper body, but eventually recover from their serious injuries. The shooting paralyzes Cabey and causes brain damage.

After Goetz surfaces from the tunnels, he rents a car and drives north to Vermont and New Hampshire. He thinks that the whole thing will blow over in a few days. Nine days later, he returns to New York and notices that things have quieted down for the most part. The police have left notes on his door and in his mailbox, requesting that he come in for questioning. They have not singled out Goetz as their prime suspect, but have information from a caller that he might be the shooter. Seeing the notes, he panics and returns to New Hampshire. Two days later, he walks into the Concord, New Hampshire, police station and gives a statement to police.

1. Relying only on your own intuitions of justice, what liability and punishment, if any, does Bernhard Goetz deserve?

N	0	1	2	3	4	5	6	7	8	9	10	11
☐	☐	☐	☐	☐	☐	☐	☐	☐	☐	☐	☐	☐
no liability	liability but no punishment	1 day	2 wks	2 mo	6 mo	1 yr	3 yrs	7 yrs	15 yrs	30 yrs	life imprison-ment	death

2. What liability, if any, under the then-existing statutes?

3. What liability, if any, under the Model Penal Code?

■ THE LAW

New York Penal Law
(1984)

Section 120.00. Assault in the Third Degree

A person is guilty of assault in the third degree when:

1. With intent to cause physical injury to another person, he causes such injury to such person or to a third person; or

2. He recklessly causes physical injury to another person; or

3. With criminal negligence, he causes physical injury to another person by means of a deadly weapon or a dangerous instrument. Assault in the third degree is a class A misdemeanor.

Section 120.05. Assault in the Second Degree

A person is guilty of assault in the second degree when:

1. With intent to cause serious physical injury to another person, he causes such injury to such person or to a third person; or

2. With intent to cause physical injury to another person, he causes such injury to such person or to a third person by means of a deadly weapon or a dangerous instrument; or . . .

4. He recklessly causes serious physical injury to another person by means of a deadly weapon or a dangerous instrument; . . . Assault in the second degree is a class D felony.

Section 120.10. Assault in the First Degree

A person is guilty of assault in the first degree when:

1. With intent to cause serious physical injury to another person, he causes such injury to such person or to a third person by means of a deadly weapon or a dangerous instrument; or . . .

3. Under circumstances evincing a depraved indifference to human life, he recklessly engages in conduct which creates a grave risk of death to another person, and thereby causes serious physical injury to another person; ...

Assault in the first degree is a class C felony.

Section 125.00. Homicide Defined

Homicide means conduct which causes the death of a person or an unborn child with which a female has been pregnant for more than twenty-four weeks under circumstances constituting murder, manslaughter in the first degree, manslaughter in the second degree, criminally negligent homicide, abortion in the first degree or self-abortion in the first degree.

Section 125.10. Criminally Negligent Homicide

A person is guilty of criminally negligent homicide when, with criminal negligence, he causes the death of another person.

Criminally negligent homicide is a class E felony.

Section 125.15. Manslaughter in the Second Degree

A person is guilty of manslaughter in the second degree when:

1. He recklessly causes the death of another person; or ...

3. He intentionally causes or aids another person to commit suicide.

Manslaughter in the second degree is a class C felony.

Section 125.20. Manslaughter in the First Degree

A person is guilty of manslaughter in the first degree when:

1. With intent to cause serious physical injury to another person, he causes the death of such person or of a third person; or

2. With intent to cause the death of another person, he causes the death of such person or of a third person under circumstances which do not constitute murder because he acts under the influence of extreme emotional disturbance, as defined in paragraph (a) of subdivision one of section 125.25. The fact that homicide was committed under the influence of extreme emotional disturbance constitutes a mitigating circumstance reducing murder to manslaughter in the first degree and need not be proved in any prosecution initiated under this subdivision; ...

Manslaughter in the first degree is a class B felony.

Section 125.25. Murder in the Second Degree

A person is guilty of murder in the second degree when:

1. With intent to cause the death of another person, he causes the death of such person or of a third person; except that in any prosecution under this subdivision, it is an affirmative defense that:

(a) The defendant acted under the influence of extreme emotional disturbance for which there was a reasonable explanation or excuse, the reasonableness of which is to be determined from the viewpoint of a person in the defendant's situation under the circumstances as the defendant believed them to be. Nothing contained in this paragraph shall constitute a defense to a prosecution for, or preclude a conviction of, manslaughter in the first degree or any other crime; or . . .

2. Under circumstances evincing a depraved indifference to human life, he recklessly engages in conduct which creates a grave risk of death to another person, and thereby causes the death of another person; . . .

Murder in the second degree is a class A-I felony.

Section 160.10. Robbery in the Second Degree

A person is guilty of robbery in the second degree when he forcibly steals property and when:

1. He is aided by another person actually present; or

2. In the course of the commission of the crime or of immediate flight therefrom, he or another participant in the crime:

(a) Causes physical injury to any person who is not a participant in the crime; or

(b) Displays what appears to be a pistol, revolver, rifle, shotgun, machine gun or other firearm.

Robbery in the second degree is a class C felony.

Section 160.15. Robbery in the First Degree

A person is guilty of robbery in the first degree when he forcibly steals property and when, in the course of the commission of the crime or of immediate flight therefrom, he or another participant in the crime:

1. Causes serious physical injury to any person who is not a participant in the crime; or

2. Is armed with a deadly weapon; or

3. Uses or threatens the immediate use of a dangerous instrument; or

4. Displays what appears to be a pistol, revolver, rifle, shotgun, machine gun or other firearm; except that in any prosecution under this subdivision, it is an affirmative defense that such pistol, revolver, rifle, shotgun, machine

gun or other firearm was not a loaded weapon from which a shot, readily capable of producing death or other serious physical injury, could be discharged. Nothing contained in this subdivision shall constitute a defense to a prosecution for, or preclude a conviction of, robbery in the second degree, robbery in the third degree or any other crime.

Robbery in the first degree is a class B felony.

Section 10.00. Definitions of Terms of General Use in This Chapter

Except where different meanings are expressly specified in subsequent provisions of this chapter, the following terms have the following meanings:

1. "Offense" means conduct for which a sentence to a term of imprisonment or to a fine is provided by any law of this state or by any law, local law or ordinance of a political subdivision of this state, or by any order, rule or regulation of any governmental instrumentality authorized by law to adopt the same....

4. "Misdemeanor" means an offense, other than a "traffic infraction," for which a sentence to a term of imprisonment in excess of fifteen days may be imposed, but for which a sentence to a term of imprisonment in excess of one year cannot be imposed.

5. "Felony" means an offense for which a sentence to a term of imprisonment in excess of one year may be imposed.

6. "Crime" means a misdemeanor or a felony....

8. "Possess" means to have physical possession or otherwise to exercise dominion or control over tangible property.

9. "Physical injury" means impairment of physical condition or substantial pain.

10. "Serious physical injury" means physical injury which creates a substantial risk of death, or which causes death or serious and protracted disfigurement, protracted impairment of health or protracted loss or impairment of the function of any bodily organ.

11. "Deadly physical force" means physical force which, under the circumstances in which it is used, is readily capable of causing death or other serious physical injury.

12. "Deadly weapon" means any loaded weapon from which a shot, readily capable of producing death or other serious physical injury, may be discharged, or a switchblade knife, gravity knife, dagger, billy, blackjack, or metal knuckles.

13. "Dangerous instrument" means any instrument, article or substance, including a "vehicle" as that term is defined in this section, which, under the circumstances in which it is used, attempted to be used or threatened to be used, is readily capable of causing death or other serious physical injury....

Section 15.00. Culpability; Definitions of Terms

The following definitions are applicable to this chapter:

1. "Act" means a bodily movement.

2. "Voluntary act" means a bodily movement performed consciously as a result of effort or determination, and includes the possession of property if the actor was aware of his physical possession or control thereof for a sufficient period to have been able to terminate it.

3. "Omission" means a failure to perform an act as to which a duty of performance is imposed by law.

4. "Conduct" means an act or omission and its accompanying mental state.

5. "To act" means either to perform an act or to omit to perform an act.

6. "Culpable mental state" means "intentionally" or "knowingly" or "recklessly" or with "criminal negligence," as these terms are defined in section 15.05.

Section 15.05. Culpability; Definitions of Culpable Mental States

The following definitions are applicable to this chapter:

1. "Intentionally." A person acts intentionally with respect to a result or to conduct described by a statute defining an offense when his conscious objective is to cause such result or to engage in such conduct.

2. "Knowingly." A person acts knowingly with respect to conduct or to a circumstance described by a statute defining an offense when he is aware that his conduct is of such nature or that such circumstance exists.

3. "Recklessly." A person acts recklessly with respect to a result or to a circumstance described by a statute defining an offense when he is aware of and consciously disregards a substantial and unjustifiable risk that such result will occur or that such circumstance exists. The risk must be of such nature and degree that disregard thereof constitutes a gross deviation from the standard of conduct that a reasonable person would observe in the situation. A person who creates such a risk but is unaware thereof solely by reason of voluntary intoxication also acts recklessly with respect thereto.

4. "Criminal negligence." A person acts with criminal negligence with respect to a result or to a circumstance described by a statute defining an offense when he fails to perceive a substantial and unjustifiable risk that such result will occur or that such circumstance exists. The risk must be of such nature and degree that the failure to perceive it constitutes a gross deviation from the standard of care that a reasonable person would observe in the situation.

Section 15.10. Requirements for Criminal Liability in General and for Offenses of Strict Liability and Mental Culpability

The minimal requirement for criminal liability is the performance by a person of conduct which includes a voluntary act or the omission to perform an act which he is physically capable of performing. If such conduct is all that is required for commission of a particular offense, or if an offense or some material element thereof does not require a culpable mental state on the part of the actor, such offense is one of "strict liability." If a culpable mental state on the part of the actor is required with respect to every material element of an offense, such offense is one of "mental culpability."

Section 15.15. Construction of Statutes with Respect to Culpability Requirements

1. When the commission of an offense defined in this chapter, or some element of an offense, requires a particular culpable mental state, such mental state is ordinarily designated in the statute defining the offense by use of the terms "intentionally," "knowingly," "recklessly" or "criminal negligence," or by use of terms, such as "with intent to defraud" and "knowing it to be false," describing a specific kind of intent or knowledge. When one and only one of such terms appears in a statute defining an offense, it is presumed to apply to every element of the offense unless an intent to limit its application clearly appears.

2. Although no culpable mental state is expressly designated in a statute defining an offense, a culpable mental state may nevertheless be required for the commission of such offense, or with respect to some or all of the material elements thereof, if the proscribed conduct necessarily involves such culpable mental state. A statute defining a crime, unless clearly indicating a legislative intent to impose strict liability, should be construed as defining a crime of mental culpability. This subdivision applies to offenses defined both in and outside this chapter.

Section 110.00. Attempt to Commit a Crime

A person is guilty of an attempt to commit a crime when, with intent to commit a crime, he engages in conduct which tends to effect the commission of such crime.

Section 110.05. Attempt to Commit a Crime; Punishment

An attempt to commit a crime is a:
1. Class A-I felony when the crime attempted is the A-I felony of murder in the first degree, criminal possession of a controlled substance in the first degree or criminal sale of a controlled substance in the first degree;
2. Class A-II felony when the crime attempted is a class A-II felony;
3. Class B felony when the crime attempted is a class A-I felony except as provided in subdivision one hereof;
4. Class C felony when the crime attempted is a class B felony;
5. Class D felony when the crime attempted is a class C felony;
6. Class E felony when the crime attempted is a class D felony;
7. Class A misdemeanor when the crime attempted is a class E felony;
8. Class B misdemeanor when the crime attempted is a misdemeanor.

Section 25.00. Defenses; Burden of Proof

1. When a "defense," other than an "affirmative defense," defined by statute is raised at a trial, the people have the burden of disproving such defense beyond a reasonable doubt.

2. When a defense declared by statute to be an "affirmative defense" is raised at a trial, the defendant has the burden of establishing such defense by a preponderance of the evidence.

Section 35.00. Justification; a Defense

In any prosecution for an offense, justification, as defined in sections 35.05 through 35.30, is a defense.

Section 35.05. Justification; Generally

Unless otherwise limited by the ensuing provisions of this article defining justifiable use of physical force, conduct which would otherwise constitute an offense is justifiable and not criminal when:

1. Such conduct is required or authorized by law or by a judicial decree, or is performed by a public servant in the reasonable exercise of his official powers, duties or functions; or

2. Such conduct is necessary as an emergency measure to avoid an imminent public or private injury which is about to occur by reason of a situation occasioned or developed through no fault of the actor, and which is of such gravity that, according to ordinary standards of intelligence and morality, the desirability and urgency of avoiding such injury clearly outweigh the desirability of avoiding the injury sought to be prevented by the statute defining the offense in issue. The necessity and justifiability of such conduct may not rest upon considerations pertaining only to the morality and advisability of the statute, either in its general application or with respect to its application to a particular class of cases arising thereunder. Whenever evidence relating to the defense of justification under this subdivision is offered by the defendant, the court shall rule as a matter of law whether the claimed facts and circumstances would, if established, constitute a defense.

Section 35.10. Justification; Use of Physical Force Generally

The use of physical force upon another person which would otherwise constitute an offense is justifiable and not criminal under any of the following circumstances:

1. A parent, guardian or other person entrusted with the care and supervision of a person under the age of twenty-one or an incompetent person, and a teacher or other person entrusted with the care and supervision

of a person under the age of twenty-one for a special purpose, may use physical force, but not deadly physical force, upon such person when and to the extent that he reasonably believes it necessary to maintain discipline or to promote the welfare of such person.

2. A warden or other authorized official of a jail, prison or correctional institution may, in order to maintain order and discipline, use such physical force as is authorized by the correction law.

3. A person responsible for the maintenance of order in a common carrier of passengers, or a person acting under his direction, may use physical force when and to the extent that he reasonably believes it necessary to maintain order, but he may use deadly physical force only when he reasonably believes it necessary to prevent death or serious physical injury.

4. A person acting under a reasonable belief that another person is about to commit suicide or to inflict serious physical injury upon himself may use physical force upon such person to the extent that he reasonably believes it necessary to thwart such result.

5. A duly licensed physician, or a person acting under his direction, may use physical force for the purpose of administering a recognized form of treatment which he reasonably believes to be adapted to promoting the physical or mental health of the patient if (a) the treatment is administered with the consent of the patient or, if the patient is under the age of eighteen years or an incompetent person, with the consent of his parent, guardian or other person entrusted with his care and supervision, or (b) the treatment is administered in an emergency when the physician reasonably believes that no one competent to consent can be consulted and that a reasonable person, wishing to safeguard the welfare of the patient, would consent.

6. A person may, pursuant to the ensuing provisions of this article, use physical force upon another person in defense of himself or a third person, or in defense of premises, or in order to prevent larceny of or criminal mischief to property, or in order to effect an arrest or prevent an escape from custody. Whenever a person is authorized by any such provision to use deadly physical force in any given circumstance, nothing contained in any other such provision may be deemed to negate or qualify such authorization.

Section 35.15. Justification; Use of Physical Force in Defense of a Person

1. A person may, subject to the provisions of subdivision [2], use physical force upon another person when and to the extent he reasonably believes such to be necessary to defend himself or a third person from what he reasonably believes to be the use or imminent use of unlawful physical force by such other person, unless:

(a) The latter's conduct was provoked by the actor himself with intent to cause physical injury to another person; or

(b) The actor was the initial aggressor; except that in such case his use of physical force is nevertheless justifiable if he has withdrawn from the encounter and effectively communicated such withdrawal to such other person but the latter persists in continuing the incident by the use or threatened imminent use of unlawful physical force; or

(c) The physical force involved is the product of a combat by agreement not specifically authorized by law.

2. A person may not use deadly physical force upon another person under circumstances specified in subdivision one unless:

(a) He reasonably believes that such other person is using or about to use deadly physical force. Even in such case, however, the actor may not use deadly physical force if he knows that he can with complete safety as to himself and others avoid the necessity of so doing by retreating; except that he is under no duty to retreat if he is:

(i) in his dwelling and not the initial aggressor; or

(ii) a police officer or peace officer or a person assisting a police officer or a peace officer at the latter's direction, acting pursuant to section 35.30; or

(b) He reasonably believes that such other person is committing or attempting to commit a kidnapping, forcible rape, forcible sodomy or robbery; or

(c) He reasonably believes that such other person is committing or attempting to commit a burglary, and the circumstances are such that the use of deadly physical force is authorized. . . .

Section 35.25. Justification; Use of Physical Force to Prevent or Terminate Larceny or Criminal Mischief

A person may use physical force, other than deadly physical force, upon another person when and to the extent that he reasonably believes such to be necessary to prevent or terminate what he reasonably believes to be the commission or attempted commission by such other person of larceny or of criminal mischief with respect to property other than premises.

Section 40.15. Mental Disease or Defect

In any prosecution for an offense, it is an affirmative defense that when the defendant engaged in the proscribed conduct, he lacked criminal responsibility by reason of mental disease or defect. Such lack of criminal responsibility means that at the time of such conduct, as a result of mental disease or defect, he lacked substantial capacity to know or appreciate either:

1. The nature and consequences of such conduct; or

2. That such conduct was wrong.

Section 70.00. Sentence of Imprisonment for Felony

1. Indeterminate sentence. Except as provided in subdivision four, a sentence of imprisonment for a felony shall be an indeterminate sentence. When such a sentence is imposed, the court shall impose a maximum term in accordance with the provisions of subdivision two of this section and the minimum period of imprisonment shall be as provided in subdivision three of this section.

2. Maximum term of sentence. The maximum term of an indeterminate sentence shall be at least three years and the term shall be fixed as follows:

(a) For a class A felony, the term shall be life imprisonment;

(b) For a class B felony, the term shall be fixed by the court, and shall not exceed twenty-five years;

(c) For a class C felony, the term shall be fixed by the court, and shall not exceed fifteen years;

(d) For a class D felony, the term shall be fixed by the court, and shall not exceed seven years; and

(e) For a class E felony, the term shall be fixed by the court, and shall not exceed four years.

3. Minimum period of imprisonment. The minimum period of imprisonment under an indeterminate sentence shall be at least one year and shall be fixed as follows:

(a) In the case of a class A felony, the minimum period shall be fixed by the court and specified in the sentence.

(i) For a class A-I felony, such minimum period shall not be less than fifteen years nor more than twenty-five years.

(ii) For a class A-II felony, such minimum period shall not be less than three years nor more than eight years four months.

(b) Where the sentence is for a class B or class C violent felony offense as defined in subdivision one of section 70.02, the minimum period shall be fixed by the court pursuant to subdivision four of section 70.02. Where the sentence is for any other felony, the minimum period shall be fixed by the court and specified in the sentence and shall be not less than one year nor more than one-third of the maximum term imposed.

(c) [Repealed]

4. Alternative definite sentence for class D, E, and certain class C felonies. When a person, other than a second or persistent felony offender, is sentenced for a class D or class E felony, or to a class C felony specified in article two hundred twenty or article two hundred twenty-one, and the court, having regard to the nature and circumstances of the crime and to the history and character of the defendant, is of the opinion that a sentence of imprisonment is necessary but that it would be unduly harsh to impose an indeterminate sentence, the court may impose a definite sentence of imprisonment and fix a term of one year or less.

Model Penal Code
(Official Draft 1962)

Section 3.04. Use of Force in Self-Protection

(1) Use of Force Justifiable for Protection of the Person. Subject to the provisions of this Section and of Section 3.09, the use of force upon or toward another person is justifiable when the actor believes that such force is immediately necessary for the purpose of protecting himself against the use of unlawful force by such other person on the present occasion.

(2) Limitations on Justifying Necessity for Use of Force

(a) The use of force is not justifiable under this Section:

(i) to resist an arrest which the actor knows is being made by a peace officer, although the arrest is unlawful; or

(ii) to resist force used by the occupier or possessor of property or by another person on his behalf, where the actor knows that the person using the force is doing so under a claim of right to protect the property, except that this limitation shall not apply if:

(1) the actor is a public officer acting in the performance of his duties or a person lawfully assisting him therein or a person making or assisting in a lawful arrest; or

(2) the actor has been unlawfully dispossessed of the property and is making a re-entry or recaption justified by Section 3.06; or

(3) the actor believes that such force is necessary to protect himself against death or serious bodily harm.

(b) The use of deadly force is not justifiable under this Section unless the actor believes that such force is necessary to protect himself against death, serious bodily harm, kidnapping or sexual intercourse compelled by force or threat; nor is it justifiable if:

(i) the actor, with the purpose of causing death or serious bodily harm, provoked the use of force against himself in the same encounter; or

(ii) the actor knows that he can avoid the necessity of using such force with complete safety by retreating or by surrendering possession of a thing to a person asserting a claim of right thereto or by complying with a demand that he abstain from any action which he has no duty to take, except that:

(1) the actor is not obliged to retreat from his dwelling or place of work, unless he was the initial aggressor or is assailed in his place of work by another person whose place of work the actor knows it to be; and

(2) a public officer justified in using force in the performance of his duties or a person justified in using force in his assistance or a person justified in using force in making an arrest or preventing an escape is not obliged to desist from efforts to

perform such duty, effect such arrest or prevent such escape because of resistance or threatened resistance by or on behalf of the person against whom such action is directed.

(c) Except as required by paragraphs (a) and (b) of this Subsection, a person employing protective force may estimate the necessity thereof under the circumstances as he believes them to be when the force is used, without retreating, surrendering possession, doing any other act which he has no legal duty to do or abstaining from any lawful action.

(3) Use of Confinement as Protective Force. The justification afforded by this Section extends to the use of confinement as protective force only if the actor takes all reasonable measures to terminate the confinement as soon as he knows that he safely can, unless the person confined has been arrested on a charge of crime.

Section 3.06. Use of Force for the Protection of Property

(1) Use of Force Justifiable for Protection of Property. Subject to the provisions of this Section and of Section 3.09, the use of force upon or toward the person of another is justifiable when the actor believes that such force is immediately necessary:

(a) to prevent or terminate an unlawful entry or other trespass upon land or a trespass against or the unlawful carrying away of tangible, movable property, provided that such land or movable property is, or is believed by the actor to be, in his possession or in the possession of another person for whose protection he acts; or

(b) to effect an entry or re-entry upon land or to retake tangible movable property, provided that the actor believes that he or the person by whose authority he acts or a person from whom he or such other person derives title was unlawfully dispossessed of such land or movable property and is entitled to possession, and provided, further, that:

(i) the force is used immediately or on fresh pursuit after such dispossession; or

(ii) the actor believes that the person against whom he uses force has no claim of right to the possession of the property and, in the case of land, the circumstances, as the actor believes them to be, are of such urgency that it would be an exceptional hardship to postpone the entry or re-entry until a court order is obtained.

(2) Meaning of Possession. For the Purposes of Subsection (1) of This Section:

(a) a person who has parted with the custody of property to another who refuses to restore it to him is no longer in possession, unless the property is movable and was and still is located on land in his possession;

(b) a person who has been dispossessed of land does not regain possession thereof merely by setting foot thereon;

(c) a person who has a license to use or occupy real property is deemed to be in possession thereof except against the licensor acting under claim of right.

(3) Limitations on Justifiable Use of Force.

(a) Request to Desist. The use of force is justifiable under this Section only if the actor first requests the person against whom such force is used to desist from his interference with the property, unless the actor believes that:

(i) such request would be useless; or

(ii) it would be dangerous to himself or another person to make the request; or

(iii) substantial harm will be done to the physical condition of the property which is sought to be protected before the request can effectively be made.

(b) Exclusion of Trespasser. The use of force to prevent or terminate a trespass is not justifiable under this Section if the actor knows that the exclusion of the trespasser will expose him to substantial danger of serious bodily harm.

(c) Resistance of Lawful Re-entry or Recaption. The use of force to prevent an entry or re-entry upon land or the recaption of movable property is not justifiable under this Section, although the actor believes that such re-entry or recaption is unlawful, if:

(i) the re-entry or recaption is made by or on behalf of a person who was actually dispossessed of the property; and

(ii) it is otherwise justifiable under paragraph (1)(b) of this Section.

(d) Use of Deadly Force. The use of deadly force is not justifiable under this Section unless the actor believes that:

(i) the person against whom the force is used is attempting to dispossess him of his dwelling otherwise than under a claim of right to its possession; or

(ii) the person against whom the force is used is attempting to commit or consummate arson, burglary, robbery or other felonious theft or property destruction and either:

(1) has employed or threatened deadly force against or in the presence of the actor; or

(2) the use of force other than deadly force to prevent the commission or the consummation of the crime would expose the actor or another in his presence to substantial danger of serious bodily harm.

(4) Use of Confinement as Protective Force. The justification afforded by this Section extends to the use of confinement as protective force only if the actor takes all reasonable measures to terminate the confinement as soon as he knows that he can do so with safety to the property, unless the person confined has been arrested on a charge of crime.

(5) Use of Device to Protect Property. The justification afforded by this Section extends to the use of a device for the purpose of protecting property only if:

(a) the device is not designed to cause or known to create a substantial risk of causing death or serious bodily harm; and

(b) the use of the particular device to protect the property from entry or trespass is reasonable under the circumstances, as the actor believes them to be; and

(c) the device is one customarily used for such a purpose or reasonable care is taken to make known to probable intruders the fact that it is used.

(6) Use of Force to Pass Wrongful Obstructor. The use of force to pass a person whom the actor believes to be purposely or knowingly and unjustifiably obstructing the actor from going to a place to which he may lawfully go is justifiable, provided that:

(a) the actor believes that the person against whom he uses force has no claim of right to obstruct the actor; and

(b) the actor is not being obstructed from entry or movement on land which he knows to be in the possession or custody of the person obstructing him, or in the possession or custody of another person by whose authority the obstructor acts, unless the circumstances, as the actor believes them to be, are of such urgency that it would not be reasonable to postpone the entry or movement on such land until a court order is obtained; and

(c) the force used is not greater than would be justifiable if the person obstructing the actor were using force against him to prevent his passage.

● OVERVIEW OF DEFENSIVE FORCE JUSTIFICATIONS

Defensive force justifications provide a defense for the use of force necessary to protect persons or property from unjustified aggression. Three such defenses traditionally are recognized: self-defense, defense of another, and defense of property. (Some jurisdictions recognize a special defense of premises and others combine self-defense and defense of another.) The defenses reflect the same internal structure as other justifications: *triggering conditions* authorizing responsive force that must be *necessary* to protect from and *proportional* to the harm threatened.

TRIGGERING CONDITIONS

A defensive force justification is triggered when an aggressor unjustifiably threatens harm to persons or property. The name of each defense identifies the interest threatened that triggers the defense: self-defense, defense of others, defense of property. The defensive force triggering conditions are considerably more specific than those of the lesser evils defense; defensive force requires an unlawful, aggressive use or threat of force. These triggering conditions also are more demanding than those for public authority defenses, which generally are triggered by any need to protect or further a public interest.

Requirement of Aggressor   That the person against whom the actor uses force is acting unlawfully is not sufficient to trigger a defensive force justification. Smoking on a bus or refusing to get out of the way of an emergency vehicle may be unlawful conduct that justifies the use of force against the violator, but a justification defense other than defensive force must be relied upon (probably a public authority justification). For defensive force, active physical aggression is required.

Distinguishing Aggression and Defense   The defensive character of an actor's conduct provides much of the rationale for these justifications. In practice, however, this critical distinction between defense and aggression may be unclear. Suppose *A* breaks into *B*'s house in order to steal his television. *B* discovers *A* in the act and wrestles with him, but *A* breaks loose and, still carrying the set, bolts for the door. Further action by *B* would, in a narrow sense, constitute aggressive rather than defensive action. *A* has physical possession of the television; *B*'s conduct would constitute an attempt to take it away from *A*. Even so, a strong argument can be made that, given the brief interval of actual possession by *A*, it is not inappropriate to view *B*'s conduct as still essentially defensive. If *B* tracks *A* for several days before attempting recapture, his conduct might be recharacterized as having become aggressive, and thus having fallen outside the scope of the defensive force justifications. Necessarily left unclear by current law is the precise point at which the struggle for repossession changes from defensive to offensive.

Unjustified Threat   In order to trigger a defensive force justification, the aggressor must unjustifiably threaten harm to the actor. Thus, when a police officer uses justified force to effect an arrest, the arrestee has no right of self-defense, and others may not lawfully use defensive force on his behalf. Similarly, where an actor unjustifiably attacks another and his victim then uses justified defensive force to repel the actor, the initial aggressor has no right of self-defense against the justified defensive response. On the other hand, where the intended victim uses unnecessary or disproportionate force in response, the initial aggressor regains a right to use defensive force. (The point is illustrated by the "Rosie's Homerun" Problem immediately following this Overview.)

"Unlawful Force"   A common formulation of defensive force triggering conditions permits an actor to defend only against "unlawful force." This is the language of the Model Penal Code.[1] There is the potential for confusion in this language, however, because some threats may be "lawful"—in the sense that the aggressor will have a defense to a criminal charge for the attack—yet the use of defensive force against such "lawful" force is nonetheless appropriate. Such is the case, for example, where the aggressor is not liable for the use of force because he lacks the required culpability for an offense (if the aggressor is mistaken about the facts of the situation) or because the aggressor has an excuse for the aggressive conduct (the aggressor is insane or acting under duress, for example). In these cases, the victim ought to be able lawfully to defend, even though the aggressor will have no liability for her attack. Unfortunately, the phrase "unlawful force," by itself, can be misleading on this point. What is needed is a clear description of the kinds of defenses an aggressor might have that nonetheless will allow a victim justifiably to defend and the kind of aggressor defenses that ought to bar a victim's defense. What kind of aggressor defenses should bar a victim's defensive force?

Resisting Conduct for Which Aggressor Has Defense   The short answer is that a victim ought to be able to defend against any attack except one where the

---

1. See, e.g., Model Penal Code §3.04(1) (Use of Force in Self-Protection); §3.06(1)(a) (Use of Force for the Protection of Property).

aggressor is justified, in an objective sense. Thus, where an actor has an absent element or offense modification defense that hinges on the absence of a required culpability element, the objective elements of the offense having been satisfied, the aggressor's attack properly may be resisted. Even though the attacker or apparent thief acts inadvertently due to mistake or intoxication, he properly is subject to defensive force. Of course, such an actor might be stopped with a simple, "excuse me, that is my umbrella," and when this is so, as we shall see in a moment, any attempt to use force would be unjustified because the use of force is unnecessary. An aggressor with an excuse defense similarly should be subject to lawful resistance. The victim of the psychotic attacker should be able lawfully to defend and to have others assist in such defense. While the aggressor ultimately may be judged blameless, the actor's conduct is clearly harmful and unjustified. When an attacker has only a nonexculpatory defense, such as diplomatic immunity, the case is clearest for permitting, indeed encouraging, resistance and interference. The conduct is harmful; the actor may be blameworthy. The immune diplomat may escape conviction for an unjustified and unexcused attack, but it hardly follows that the victim is bound to submit, or the observer to acquiesce. Where an aggressor has a justification defense, in contrast, the rule is different: Justified aggression cannot be lawfully subject to resistance or interference. When conduct is objectively justified, it is by definition conduct that follows the rules of conduct (conduct that does not create a net harm to society). The owner of a field should not be allowed to resist one who would burn the field to stop a spreading fire, and others should be encouraged to assist the burning and should not be permitted to interfere with it.[1]

Difficulties in the Model Penal Code Formulation   As noted above, the Model Penal Code authorizes defensive force only to defend against "unlawful" force. This provision, by itself, might seem too narrow, for it might be interpreted to bar a justification for resisting an attacker who has an excuse, a nonexculpatory defense, or an absent element or offense modification defense based on lack of culpability. But the Code drafters understand the distinctions that the law must make. Their "unlawful force" formulation does in fact give the results that it should, albeit through a rather awkward definition. Section 3.11(1) defines "unlawful force" to mean

> force, . . . the employment of which constitutes an offense or actionable tort or would constitute such offense or tort except for a defense (such as the absence of intent, negligence, or mental capacity; duress; youth; or diplomatic status) not amounting to a privilege to use force.

The language of the definition appears to be consistent with the conclusions of the analysis above as to what kinds of attacks the law ought to allow. It includes within "unlawful force" aggression for which the actor has a "defense . . . such as the absence of . . . mental capacity; duress; [or] youth" — that is, an excuse — or "a defense . . . such as . . . diplomatic status" — that is, a nonexculpatory defense — or "a defense . . . such as the absence of intent [or] negligence" — that is, an absent element or offense modification defense based on absence of

---

1. Of course, the owner may have an excuse for mistaken justification if he is unaware that those burning the field are justified in their actions. See Section 20.

culpability. By including such aggression within the definition of "unlawful force," the Model Penal Code formulation permits resistance to, and interference with, that aggression. Moreover, by including within the definition "a defense . . . not amounting to a privilege," the provision suggests by implication that force "amounting to a privilege" is not "unlawful force" and, therefore, cannot lawfully be resisted.

Criticisms of Code's Formulation. Several criticisms of the Code's provision may be made. First, such important distinctions as those defining the force that lawfully may be resisted ought not to be hidden in a definitional section, for many lawyers and courts will miss it there.[1] Second, as the previous discussion illustrates, even when discovered, the provision is a bit difficult to digest. Even several readings can lead to a misinterpretation. This is due in part to the provision's use of illustrations of the defenses that should be categorized as "unlawful force" but with a failure to provide a conceptual framework by which one can deduce the defense group of which each is an illustration. Without a conceptual framework the Code drafters leave us guessing as to which defenses are meant to be included and which excluded. Third, the Code never defines which defenses are those "amounting to a privilege," by which they apparently mean objective justifications.

Superiority of Formulation That Segregates Objective Justification and Subjective Mistake. It ought to be embarrassing to the Code drafters that they are compelled to rely on a tort concept, privilege, but they have made it impossible to use the term "justification" in this context because they have used that term in the Code to include both objective justification (what they call here "privilege") and subjective (that is, mistaken) justification: They have throughout Article 3 of the Code defined conduct as "justified" if the actor *believes* that it is justified.[2] This approach — subjectivizing the formulation of justification defenses to hold an actor "justified" even if he only mistakenly "believes" that he is justified — makes it impossible for the Code to easily distinguish the cases of objective (actual) justification and subjective (mistaken) justification, even though that distinction is of great practical importance: The former may not lawfully be resisted, the latter may. It seems a sadly inadequate criminal law that cannot define so central a concept as objective justification without reference to tort law. The better approach is to do what the Draft Code of the National Commission did: define justification defenses objectively and provide a separate mistake provision that recognizes an *excuse* for reasonable mistakes as to a justification.[3] Under such an approach, the triggering conditions of defensive force defenses may be defined simply: A right to use defensive force is triggered by an "unjustified" threat of force. The issue is discussed further in the Section 20 Overview.

---

1. And many drafters, not understanding the importance of such a definition, may omit it. See, e.g., Ala. Code §13A-3-20 (1982); Ill. Ann. Stat. ch. 38 (1972); N.H. Rev. Stat. Ann. §627.9 (1986); Tex. Penal Code Ann. §9.01 (1979); Wash. Rev. Code Ann. §9A.16.010 (1988).

2. See Section 20.

3. The National Commission's Draft Code formulated justifications objectively and provided a separate mistake excuse defense:

NECESSITY REQUIREMENT

Once the right to use defensive force is triggered by an unjustified threat, an actor may lawfully use force in defense, but only force that is necessary to protect the person or property threatened. A common formulation of the necessity requirement in self-defense, for example, gives the actor the right to act when "such force is necessary to defend himself." The formulation includes two essential parts of the necessity requirement: force may be used only (1) when necessary and (2) to the extent necessary. The actor may not use force when such force would be equally effective at a later time and the actor suffers no harm or risk by waiting. Nor may an actor use more force than is necessary for the defensive purpose. If the threat can be effectively defended against without force or with lesser force, the greater force is not justified.

Lesser Evils Compared   The defensive force justifications typically contain an explicit necessity requirement. The Model Penal Code, for example, requires that the force be "immediately necessary" to protect the person or property. (The common law and some codifications commonly require that the threat be "imminent.") Thus, the necessity requirement in defensive force apparently is meant to be stricter than it is in lesser evils where the conduct need only be "necessary."

PROPORTIONALITY CONCERN

The proportionality requirement also is apparent in defensive force justifications but of a different sort: It does not leave it to juries to determine the balance of conflicting interests but rather is seen in a legislative predetermination of such balancing, as expressed in a variety of special rules. This series of special restrictions on the use of defensive force contrasts with the open and explicit proportionality requirement of the lesser evils defense, and may help explain why many legislatures

---

§603. Self-Defense

A person is justified in using force upon another person in order to defend himself against danger of imminent unlawful bodily injury, sexual assault or detention by such other person, except that:

(a) a person is not justified in using force for the purpose of resisting arrest, execution of process, or other performance of duty by a public servant under color of law, but excessive force may be resisted; and

(b) a person is not justified in using force if (i) he intentionally provokes unlawful action by another person in order to cause bodily injury or death to such other person, or (ii) he has entered into a mutual combat with another person or is the initial aggressor unless he is resisting force which is clearly excessive in the circumstances. A person's use of defensive force after he withdraws from an encounter and indicates to the other person that he has done so is justified if the latter nevertheless continues or menaces unlawful action.

§608. Excuse

(1) Mistake. A person's conduct is excused if he believes that the factual situation is such that his conduct is necessary and appropriate for any of the purposes which would establish a justification or excuse under this Chapter, even though his belief is mistaken, except that, if his belief is negligently or recklessly held, it is not an excuse in a prosecution for an offense for which negligence or recklessness, as the cause may be, suffices to establish culpability. Excuse under this subsection is a defense or affirmative defense according to which type of defense would be established had the facts been as the person believed them to be.

(2) Marginal Transgression of Limit of Justification. A person's conduct is excused if it would otherwise be justified or excused under this Chapter but is marginally hasty or excessive because he was confronted with an emergency precluding adequate appraisal or measured reaction.

Final Report of the National Commission on Reform of Federal Criminal Laws 1971.

are hesitant to formally recognize the lesser evils defense for fear that it would give juries a power to balance interests that the legislature wishes to reserve for itself. Rather than allowing such *ad hoc* jury balancing of competing interests, the legislature has predetermined the proper balance in those special situations to which the rules apply. As is evident in the discussion that follows, the competing interests in defensive force cases typically include much more than the competing tangible harms. The legislative balancing has taken into account important intangible interests as well, in particular society's abhorrence of and interest in discouraging unjustified aggression. In the balance of interests, such aggression may be seen as discounting in the value of the aggressor's life or, in perhaps a better characterization of the analytic process, as adding to the evil of unjustified aggression.

Proportionality in Protection of Property   Legislative concern for proportionality is most obvious in the defense of property. The harm of physical injury to a thief is balanced against both the owner's interest in retaining the threatened property and society's interest in preserving a right of property ownership generally and in condemning unjustified aggression. As noted, the intangible societal interests may be more important in this balancing than the individual owner's interests. But even the weight of these important intangible societal interests has a limit, and that limit generally is exceeded when human life is taken in defense of property. A human life, even that of a thief, is seen as having greater value than protecting property and discouraging aggression against property. Thus, all codes bar the use of deadly force in defense of property.

Proportionality in Self-Defense   The same balancing principles apply when the actor kills another to save his own life. Self-defense, however, is unique among defensive force justifications and can be conceptually troublesome. By definition only one human life is at stake on the side of the actor relying on self-defense; if there are more, a defense of others is applicable. This presents a difficult situation: A balance of one life for one life demands complete reliance on intangible societal interests in order to break the deadlock. There is no reason, however, that the method of analysis should vary. The community generally gives due weight to the intangible interests — protecting personal autonomy and condemning and deterring unjustified aggression — to outweigh the life of the aggressor and thereby permit the killing of the aggressor.

Legislating Special Defense Rules   The legislative proportionality concern is reflected in a number of other special rules that limit defensive force justifications. For example, defense provisions typically require that one must give up one's right to be in a particular public place before one can use deadly force (called the "retreat rule"), and one must suffer an unlawful arrest rather than use force against a police officer. In some of these special rules, the legislature seeks only to make explicit what the requirements of proportionality and necessity normally would demand if properly applied. In other instances, the legislature's special rule alters the result that the general principles would otherwise generate. The role of the proportionality requirement is the focus of the Discussion Materials below.

▲ PROBLEM
Rosie's Home Run

Rosie is playing ball with her friends in a vacant lot. In the bottom of the third, she hits a home run off Spano's fastball. "I'm dangerous low and inside," she yells to Spano as she rounds first at full tilt. "I guess so," responds Spano with a smirk, "you just got Logan's window." Sure enough, the ball had gone through Logan's bathroom window. Worse yet, Mr. Logan is screaming out of the window, shaking a fist with one hand and holding his eye with the other. "Game's over," Rosie yells as she rounds second and heads for her house.

As she slips through the front door, her mother and her mother's new boyfriend, Frankie, quickly sit up on the couch, clearing their throats and arranging their clothes. "How's it going, Rosie?," Frankie asks, a little too loudly. "Game over so soon?" "Yeah. I hit the ball through Logan's window and I don't think he's in the mood to give it back." "You leave it to me, Kitten. I'll talk to the bum. I'll have you guys playing ball again in no time." "Not a good idea, Frankie; he's really pissed." "Yeah? We'll see how tough he is." He turns to Rosie's mom. "I'll take care of this for you, Poopsy."

Frankie, who is six feet tall and weighs 220 pounds, walks up on Logan's porch and pounds on the front door. "Let's have that ball, Logan," he bellows. Logan pulls open the door and rushes out. He is six feet, three inches tall, and weighs 230 pounds. "Get off my f __ porch. The only way you'll get this ball back is if I stick it up your a __." Frankie, who takes two steps back in surprise when Logan rushes out, is momentarily speechless. He looks behind him to see who is watching, and catches Rosie's eye. He looks back to Logan, "Give me that ball, m __ f __, or you're dead meat." Frankie grabs the ball from Logan's hands. Logan tries to wrestle the ball away. Frankie punches Logan in the face but Logan knees Frankie in the chest and smashes him on the back of the head with his two hands cupping the ball. Frankie goes down hard, hitting his head on the cinder block wall. He doesn't move. Someone calls an ambulance. Frankie dies at the hospital from head injuries suffered in the fall.[1] Logan is charged with manslaughter. Is he liable?

● DISCUSSION MATERIALS

Should the Criminal Law Give a Defense for the Use of Whatever Force Is Necessary to Defend Persons or Property Against an Unlawful Attack? Or Should the Law Deny a Defense If the Force, Even Though Necessary for Defense, Would Injure Interests Greater Than Those Injured by the Unlawful Attack?

In *Judgment of the German Supreme Court*, the Court provides its rationale for not requiring proportionality in self-defense and defense of property. John

---

1. The facts are a variation on State v. Griffith, 91 Wash. 2d 572, 589 P.2d 799 (1979).

LaFond's piece argues for dispensing with the proportionality requirement, for both practical and theoretical reasons. In two Model Penal Code Commentary excerpts, justification is offered for the necessity and proportional requirements as codified, elaborating on the debates that preceded the Code's current formulation and examining the scope of the rule. George Fletcher, in comparing the German approach to that of the United States and England and in discussing the rationales of each, posits that the different approaches taken are based on different theories of self defense: absolute autonomy and protection of one's liberty, as subscribed to by the German court, versus proportionality and balancing of competing interests, seen in the alternative system. In a rather provocative article, Garrett Epp advocates limitations on the use of defensive force, including, most dramatically, doing away with the right altogether. Robinson and Darley offer empirical evidence that society supports a defensive force doctrine, and examine community views on proportionality and the limits of defense of property.

Judgment of the German Supreme Court of September 20, 1920
55 Decisions of the Supreme Court in Criminal Matters 82

The defendant held watch during the night in a shed amidst his fruit trees; he was accompanied by his dog and armed with a loaded rifle. In the early morning, he noticed two men taking fruit from his trees. Upon hearing the defendant both thieves took flight with the fruit that they had picked; the defendant shouted to both of them to halt and he threatened to shoot. When they did not stop, the defendant fired buckshots in their direction and injured one of them, not insignificantly. One may surmise from the judgment below that this result was intended by the defendant. The defendant was charged with intentional battery and was acquitted on the ground that he acted in self-defense. The trial court assumed that the defendant justifiably used force to regain the fruit and that there was "no other means" except the firing of the shot to force the thieves to stop thereby to regain the property. In appealing the decision, the prosecutor argued that this was not justly to be considered a case of self-defense (*Notwehr*); for at the moment that the shot was fired the thieves had completed their attack upon the defendant's property and had begun to flee from the scene of the crime. This meant that the risk to the defendant's property was no longer "imminent." The prosecutor also argued that the defendant used excessive defensive force because the fruit in question was an insignificant interest and the defendant endangered lives and health of the fleeing persons, and thereby thought to sacrifice the higher interest to save the lower.

This appeal does not prevail [i.e., acquittal affirmed]....

If the defendant fired the shot in order to protect his property and the fruit, and if the defendant had no other equally effective means to this end, then this is a case of permissible defense against an imminent attack against property and possession. The legal conclusions of the trial court are therefore unexceptionable.

The attack of the thieves had not yet ended; and this would be true even if it is assumed that the act of theft had already been completed. So long as the thieves and the property they were stealing could be reached by the defendant, the defendant's act is to be construed as a defense against a continuing attack.... The use of defensive force against a continuing attack against property requires only that the force be fitted to the circumstances of the case, which means that no more force be used to achieve the permitted goal than is "necessary." Whether that requirement is satisfied is a question for the trier-of-fact.... The opinion is occasionally expressed that the degree of permissible force should be determined not only by the severity of the attack and the available defensive means, but also by the principle that to preserve a minor interest one may not force the assailant to sacrifice a valuable interest. If this were the case, defensive force involving attacks upon life and bodily integrity would simply not be available against thieves. So weighing the relative merit of competing interests could not possibly be justified where someone in the Right is locked in struggle against someone in the Wrong; it is not to be expected of the party exercising the defensive force that in protecting his rights against a [*wrongfully*] acting assailant, he limit the harm he causes to the amount that is threatened to him by the [unjustified] attack. If that were the law governing the case in which one had to protect one's property or possession by threatening the life or bodily security of the assailant, the decision to fight on behalf of a relatively insignificant interest would frequently depend upon moral views, sensibilities of justice, and other views held by the party under attack. Accordingly, men might frequently choose not to endanger the lives of others and suffer the loss of their rights and thereby tolerate [unlawfulness].... [The] statutory law does not provide any support for the view that the relative value of the conflicting interests imposes a limitation on the right of self-defense. The balancing of values may be justified where the conflict is between two rights, but not in a case in which balancing would serve to protect [unlawfulness] and would represent a limitation on the use of defensive force against attacks upon interests of a particular sort, and thus make the degree of defensive force dependent on the harm that might occur to the [wrongfully] acting assailant....

John Q. LaFond, The Case for Liberalizing the Use of Deadly Force in Self-Defense

6 University of Puget Sound Law Review 237, 237-238, 274-284 (1983)

Introduction

For at least a century the common law of Washington and of virtually every state in the United States has permitted a citizen to use deadly force in self-defense, but only if he was unlawfully threatened, or appeared to be threatened, with death or serious bodily harm. Despite growing public fear of violent crime and recent statistics which provide a strong empirical basis for that fear, almost no state has expanded the common law right to permit a citizen to use deadly force to resist unlawful violence to his person if he was not threatened with death or serious bodily harm. It is no longer clear that the common law's stringent rules limiting the use of deadly force to instances in which the victim's life may be at stake are in accord with a shifting public value system or are sufficiently protective of the individual in these increasingly violent times....

A Critique of the Law Governing the Use of Deadly Force in Self-Defense

. . . The law can thus be perceived as granting, in many violent confrontations not involving threatened deadly force, death or great bodily harm, an illusory right of self-defense; that is, as a practical matter, no right at all. The public may well react adversely to this hypocrisy in the law, considering it of minimal help at best and at worse debilitating.

Insisting that a citizen threatened "only" with physical force or a "mere" battery forego the immediate private right of effective self-defense in exchange for a deferred public remedy of criminal prosecution may have made more sense in an era in which subsequent arrest and successful prosecution of the aggressor were more likely. Given the increased violence of our times and the statistical likelihood that a majority of violent aggressors will in fact not be successfully apprehended and punished, many victims will be without any remedy, private or public. The better social policy is to recognize the extremely contingent nature of the public remedy and to increase the availability and efficacy of private remedies authorized by the law, lest unlawful violence continue without any effective restraint, private or public.

The present formulation of the law of self-defense, in its attempt to minimize social loss, has adopted a utilitarian scheme of justice without explicitly acknowledging its underlying philosophic premise. Adopting this premise condemns many individual victims to bear the primary cost of minimizing social loss. Maximizing the preservation of human life by inexorably distributing a significant personal burden of physical harm and psychic scarring to many innocent citizens chosen at random by violent aggressors may no longer accord with society's sense of social good. The abstract goal of preserving human life must be tempered with the recognition that the people whose lives are being protected by the law are frequently violent criminals who are thus free to prey again on society.

Even if one accepts this utilitarian premise, it is not clear that society currently agrees with the answer generated many years ago by the common law's reckoning on the utilitarian calculus. It is submitted that society today would not choose to preserve the lives of violent aggressors at the expense of physical and psychic harm to innocent victims. Interest balancing always contains a large degree of subjective value preference and courts may not be the institution best suited to gauge society's preferences. In any event, it seems quite clear that the legislature can reach a different conclusion in measuring the utilitarian preferences of society.

There are other cogent criticisms that can be made of the limitation on the use of deadly force in self-defense. As observed previously, limiting the right to use deadly force to instances in which deadly force is threatened may insure an ineffective response to violence. The victim may, once subjugated, only suffer physical harm together with the psychic scarring which usually accompanies such violence. It is also possible, however, that the aggressor will proceed to inflict even more serious damage on a victim once subjugation is complete and the possibility of resistance has been terminated. Indeed, the very helplessness of the victim may invite further aggression since there is virtually no present risk of resistance and harm to the aggressor. This fear is not unfounded. For it is precisely the random and unpredictable nature of violence, the possibility of unforeseen shifting aggressor objectives, and the escalation in the level of aggressor violence after the initial confrontation that are so bewildering today. It is not unusual to read about purse snatchings, muggings, and other crimes initially involving nondeadly force that result in appalling harm to the victim, including death. If initial aggressor threats of mere physical harm in fact frequently explode unpredictably into instances in which aggressors cause death or serious bodily harm, then even utilitarian objectives may not be furthered by the present law.

In its current formulation, the law of self-defense effectively creates a strong evidentiary presumption about the nature of the harm threatened to the victim based on the nature of the force threatened by the aggressor. As a practical matter most juries are unlikely to conclude that a victim reasonably feared death or serious bodily injury at the hands of the aggressor unless the aggressor was armed with a deadly weapon or other deadly force. This inference of fact seems both unnecessarily rigid and incongruent with experience.

Predicting violence is at best a difficult task. Predicting the level of violence or the outcome of a violent confrontation is no easier. Nor is there any necessary logical correlation between what harm an aggressor intends to inflict and the force he has at his disposal. Certainly, the actual threat or use of deadly force ought to permit the victim reasonably to fear that the aggressor intends to inflict death or serious bodily harm on him. It is not clear, however, that the presence of deadly force is a necessary factual predicate for such fear. Rather the presence, use, or threat of deadly force ought simply to be one fact among others for the jury to consider in determining what the victim reasonably feared.

Violent confrontations normally occur under conditions of uncertainty. Frequently they are of short duration and without warning. They may also occur in situations in which the victim may be at an extreme disadvantage in gauging the level of violence or harm threatened or the intention of the aggressor. . . . Requiring further factual inquiry on the part of the victim may well disadvantage him even more and shift the odds enormously in favor of the aggressor.

With the possible exception of the problem of mistakes, no compelling argument can be offered that would justify requiring the victim to bear the risk of uncertainty generated by the aggressor's unlawful conduct. The aggressor has initiated the violent confrontation and the concomitant uncertainty. It is difficult to accept the logic and value of rules which, most citizens probably believe, generate an intolerable allocation of risk to innocent citizens in such paradigmatic cases. It seems far more preferable that all disadvantages which flow from such uncertainty should be allocated to the person who has caused the situation to occur.

Finally, an organized police force and the other apparatus of public security are simply not adequate by themselves to the tasks of controlling violent crime and of protecting ordinary people. Enhancing the ability of the private citizen to engage in effective self-defense will help provide the means of assuring personal security that the state can no longer insure.

The Proper Formulation of the Right of Self-Defense

The private right of self-defense should be grounded primarily in the theory of personal autonomy. The utilitarian theory of self-defense as a form of necessity should continue to be relevant to the scope of the right but only as a subordinated principle of limitation.

Accordingly, the private right of self-defense should be carefully expanded in order to permit innocent victims to respond effectively to unlawful violence against their persons. At the very core of the proposed change is the premise that effectiveness of response should be the paramount principle of authorization rather than proportionality. This change will acknowledge that an innocent victim need not endure unlawful violence to his person (with all its attendant risk of unknown outcome, including his possible death) in exchange for the forlorn hope of subsequent arrest and successful prosecution of the aggressor at some unknown time in the future.

Model Penal Code Section 3.04 Commentary
Official Draft and Revised Comments 47-48, 52-55 (1985)

Limitations on Use of Deadly Force

Subsection (2)(b) adds ... limitations on the use of force, dealing with force that the actor uses with the purpose of causing or that he knows will create a substantial risk of causing death or serious bodily injury. As defined by Section 3.11(2), "deadly force" explicitly includes purposely firing a firearm in the direction of another person or at a vehicle in which another person is believed to be. Clearly, deadly force, as so conceived, should be privileged only in extreme situations. Subsection (2)(b) represents an effort to describe what those situations are.

Apprehension of Serious Injury. Subsection (2)(b) denies justification to the use of deadly force unless the actor believes that such force is necessary to protect himself against death, serious bodily injury, kidnaping or sexual intercourse compelled by force or threat. The formulation rests on the common law principle that the amount of force used by the actor must bear a reasonable relation to the magnitude of the harm that he seeks to avert. It is not reasonable "that for every assault ... a man should be banged with a cudgel."

To give the law a measure of precision, force is divided into two categories, deadly and moderate. Force threatening only moderate harm may be inflicted by way of defense against any harm apparently threatened, while deadly force may be employed only by way of defense against the type of serious harm noted above. The premise is, of course, that the discouragement of the infliction of death or serious bodily injury is so high on the scale of preferred societal values that such infliction cannot be justified by reference to the protection of an interest of any lesser pretensions, with the possible exception of dispossession from one's own dwelling. Since the actor's own concept of morality will normally indicate that he sacrifice a lesser interest rather than engage in such behavior, the limitation of the privilege can be expected to have substantial deterrent effect.

There is no complete agreement on the nature of the extreme harm against which it is permissible to defend oneself by the use of deadly force. All authorities agree that it includes death or serious bodily injury. The Restatement of Torts adds "ravishment," which is defined in its Comment to mean not only rape but "any form of carnal intercourse which is criminal in character as, for example, sodomy." As well as including these forms of harms, Subsection (2)(b) of the Code adds kidnaping to the enumeration. Whether that inclusion will be appropriate in a particular jurisdiction will depend largely on how kidnaping is defined. Deadly force is not an appropriate response when one parent attempts to abduct a beloved child from the custody of another parent; under the Model Code that act is not kidnaping but it is under the law of some states.

The harms to one's person for which deadly force may appropriately be used are similar to those specified in the Model Code in many states that have undertaken recent legislative revisions.

Model Penal Code Section 3.06 Commentary
Official Draft and Revised Comments 91-92, 94-97 (1985)

Deadly Force

Subsection (3)(d) deals with the occasions when more than moderate force can be used in contexts where the main objective is the protection of property. It follows the common law in limiting the force that may generally be used in the protection of property to moderate nondeadly force, reflecting a value judgment that in most situations surely is sound. The principle controls, moreover, even though the person against whom force is used is making such resistance to the protective force that the defender must either proceed to extreme measures or give up the use of protective force. For example, suppose a trespasser in being ejected so defends himself that the occupier cannot eject him except by shooting him. The occupier is not entitled to shoot, and should not be.

The difficulty, and the controversy, comes in deciding to what extent exceptions to this general principle should be admitted. As originally drafted, this section included only the exception that is now found in Subsection (3)(d)(i). The matter was hotly debated on the floor of the Institute, however, terminating in directions to the Reporter to draft a more expansive exception to encompass the most serious and potentially violent situations that are likely to arise. The result is Subsection (3)(d)(ii). . . .

Subsection (3)(d)(ii) permits the use of deadly force in a number of. . . situations where any danger to the life or well-being of the actor, though once existing, has passed. [It] permits the use of deadly force to prevent the commission or the consummation of the offense if the aggressor "has employed or threatened deadly force against or in the presence of the actor." It thus affords a privilege to kill even though drastic action may no longer be necessary in order to preserve the safety of the actor. For if the thief has once manifested or threatened deadly force in the attempt to commit or to consummate one of the enumerated property crimes, deadly force may be used in order to prevent him from capitalizing upon his offense. To give an illustration, one who commits robbery on the streets at gunpoint and who is in the course of fleeing from the offense may be shot by the victim if in the victim's judgment such force is immediately necessary in order to prevent the consummation of the offense.

The policy issues that such an extension exposes proved deeply divisive within the Institute. On the one hand is the basic value judgment, breached in this instance, that the protection of property interests should not justify the taking of life. On the other is the judgment that resort to deadly force in this context is a predictable response of reasonable people, and should not be met with condemnation by the criminal law. Moreover, since the use of deadly force is limited to situations where the aggressor has himself used or threatened deadly force, and his willingness to resort to such force on one occasion may be thought to indicate a willingness to do so again, the privilege afforded here may be thought to protect the bodily safety of potential future victims. In response to this point, however, one should note the deliberate judgment underlying Section 3.07(2)(b)(ii) that resort to deadly force in effecting an arrest should be limited to law enforcement officials or persons assisting them. Private citizens are not authorized to use deadly force to make an arrest of someone who has previously used deadly force and who may be thought likely to use it against future victims. Thus, to rely on the theory that prevention of harm to future victims justifies the use of deadly force by citizens to prevent successful commission of a crime against property would not be consonant with the judgment underlying Section 3.07.

It is clear, however, that the Institute determined to go beyond the use of deadly force for the prevention of the violent crime. It chose to permit actors to use deadly force to prevent escape with the fruits of such crimes by those who have used or threatened violence, as well as to permit the use of such force where the actor apprehends that the use of lesser force would expose him to danger. Hence, the Institute resolved the policy debate in favor of the broadened privilege, and the formulation could not well have been narrower than that presented in Subsection (3)(d)(ii) without nullifying those decisions.

Most recently enacted and proposed revised codes formulate justifications for the use of deadly force in defense of property, but they follow a variety of approaches.

Other Discussion Materials

George P. Fletcher, Proportionality and the Psychotic Aggressor: A Vignette in Comparative Criminal Theory
8 Israel Law Review 367, 367-370, 376, 379-382 (1973)

Western legal systems diverge radically in their approaches to setting limits on the privilege of self-defence. Some systems incline to the view that a person defending his or another life or property may use all the force necessary to stifle an aggressive attack. Taken to the extreme, this means that if there is no other way to apprehend a thief escaping with a petty bounty, one may shoot him — if necessary, shoot to kill. In contrast to this approach, which is adverse to limits on the use of necessary force, another set of western jurisdictions insists that the degree of force meet two desiderata: it must be both necessary and proportional to the interest protected. The requirement of proportionality or reasonableness means that there are some cases, like petty thievery, where the cost of protecting a threatened interest may be so great that one must surrender the interest rather than inflict grievous harm on the aggressor.

As examples of the tendency to reject the rule of proportionality, I shall focus . . . on the German Federal Republic and the Soviet Union and as examples of systems adopting the rule of proportionality, I shall take England and the United States. The breakdown among Western systems is not so simple as any neat cleavage between Continental and common law jurisdictions. It turns out that France numbers among the countries unhesitatingly adopting the rule of proportionality and thus is closer in this respect to the position taken in the common law tradition. Of course there are important differences between the Federal Republic of Germany and the Soviet Union; in both countries there have been marked efforts in recent years to move closer to the principle of proportionality. It would be difficult to say that today either jurisdiction flatly rejects all limits on the use of necessary force. Yet in both countries, the weight of authority opposes articulating a formal test for limiting the right of self-defence. This is the position of the 1960 RSFSR Code, as it is presently interpreted and it is the view reflected in the failure of the new West German Criminal Code, effective this year, to modify the traditional sweeping formula for self-defence.

This position of German and Soviet jurisprudence may come as a surprise to common law jurists, for at least since Blackstone, everyone in the common law tradition has assumed, almost without discussion, that use of force in self-defence must be both necessary and reasonable. The rule of reasonableness demands a constant weighting of competing interests. On the basis of detailed balancing, common law courts have worked out rules specifying the amount of force permissible to defend particular interests, such as life, habitation and chattels. Thus, in the common law tradition, there is no overarching conception of self-defence, rather a number of distinct defences, each hewn to protect a particular interest. The scope of each defence depends on the importance of the interest protected; the right to defend one's life obviously permits a greater degree of force than the distinct privilege applicable to the defence of chattels.

In Germany and the Soviet Union, in contrast, all defendable interests, from life to property and personal honor, receive the same degree of protection. There is but one privilege of necessary defence (*Notwehr, neobxodimaja oborona*); the only question is whether there is or is not a right to defend a particular interest. If there is, the cost of protecting that interest is, in principle, irrelevant. German and Soviet jurists do balance competing interests in analyzing the defence of necessity or lesser evils, but not in construing the privilege of self-defence.

One cannot but be puzzled. Are German and Soviet jurists inhumane? Why do they resist a rule so eminently "reasonable" as that requiring a balancing of competing interests? If the rule is appropriate in cases of necessity, why should it not apply in the related case of self-defence? . . . The thesis that I . . . develop is that differing attitudes toward the principle of proportionality derive from fundamentally different conceptions of self-defence, and these different concepts relate in an intriguing way to the demands placed on the overall theory of self-defence. . . .

Three Theories of Self-Defence

[O]ne can explicate at least three coherent models of the defence that interact in different ways in different legal systems. . . .

Self-defence III is the dominant theory of self-defence in German and Soviet criminal theory. It also found expression in early common law theory. Sir Edmond Coke insisted that no "man shall (ever) give way to a thief, etc., neither shall he forfeit anything". And John Locke supported the same theory of an absolute right to protect one's liberty and rights from encroachment by aggressors. Among the various accounts for Self-defence III one finds the common theme that the act of aggression puts the aggressor outside the protection of the law. Locke, for example, speaks of the aggressor's being in a "state of war" with the defender. The argument is that the aggression breaches an implicit contract among autonomous agents, according to which each person or country is bound to respect the living space of all others. The intrusion upon someone's living space itself triggers a justified response.

The same doctrine finds expression in the rhetoric of the American revolution. The slogan "Don't tread on me" expresses the claim that "treading" upon someone else in itself entails a justified response. It is irrelevant whether the country or person so "treading" is culpable for his deeds. When at war, one is concerned only about the enemy's aggression, not about its possible excuses. The roots of the right of defence are not in the culpability of the aggressor, but in the autonomy of the defender.

Self-defence III generates a paradoxical view of aggression. It treats the aggressor as a participant in the legal system, yet it views the aggression as a breakdown of the framework for compassion and solicitude. The aggressor is protected by the legal conditions for exercising defensive force and simultaneously treated as though his interests were irrelevant. He is at once inside and outside the legal community, simultaneously a colleague and an outlaw.

This paradoxical status is generated by a characteristic set of legal expressions. In the German idiom, each case of self-defence represents a conflict between *Recht* (Right) and *Unrecht* (Wrong); the victim stands for the Right; the aggressor for the Wrong — as though each instance of self-defence were an Everyman drama. Another central concept is that of the Legal Order (*die Rechtsrodnung*), which in the German view, is threatened by every breach of the law. Thus the autonomy of the defender is identified with the idea of Law itself, and every act of self-defence is a defence of the basic structure of legal relationships. This conceptual framework, much of which appears as well in the Soviet literature, thrusts the aggressor to the fringes of the legal system. Though he may be psychotic and morally innocent, he becomes an enemy of the Law itself.

Self-Defence and Proportionality

As one may imagine the doctrinal lens of Self-defence III filters out shades and nuances and transforms all situations into black and white relief. The only question is whether the aggressor has intruded upon the defender's sphere of autonomy; questions of degree are suppressed. This absolutist perspective proves to be hostile to the rule of proportionality, as confirmed by the German Supreme Court in 1920 in a classic case. An orchard owner shot a couple of thieves running away with fruit from his trees. He claimed that he shot in self-defence, namely in defence of his property. He was acquitted, the prosecutor appealed, and the Supreme Court affirmed, adding that if necessary the defendant could have shot with the intent to kill. The court recalled the basic premise of Self-defence III: Right need never yield to Wrong. Thus any intrusion upon a protected interest generates a right to use whatever force necessary to restore the victim's autonomy.

German and Soviet scholars have been anxious for generations about the problem of shooting petty thieves. Yet there are powerful pressures against recognizing the principle of proportionality. Both autonomy and proportionality are jealous standards; it seems that neither can accommodate the other without surrendering its primacy. If autonomy is protected only to the extent compatible with the rule of proportionality, then it is in fact the latter, and not autonomy, that determines the boundaries of the defence. Thus one must choose between the standards of autonomy and balancing interests. And it is clear that German and Russian theorists still adhere to centrality of autonomy in the theory of self-defence.

In addition, many Soviet and German writers object to an imprecise boundary to self-defence, for one cannot fairly expect someone in danger to reflect on the merits of competing interests. Thus the rule of proportionality invites excessive caution in order to avoid the risk of conviction. This caution results in undue deference to aggressors and encourages criminal conduct.

Garrett Epps, Any Which Way But Loose: Interpretive Strategies and Attitudes Toward Violence in the Evolution of the Anglo-American "Retreat Rule"
55 Law and Contemporary Problems 303–305, 327–331 (1992)

> If any one be in danger of receiving a buffet,* or the like evil, some hold that he has a right to protect himself by killing his enemy. If merely corrective justice be regarded, I do not dissent. For though a buffet and death are very unequal, yet he who is about to do me an injury thereby gives me a Right that is a moral claim against him, in infinitum, so far as I cannot otherwise repel the evil. And even benevolence per se does not appear to bind us to advantage of him who does us wrong. But the Gospel law has made every such act unlawful: for Christ commands us to take a buffet, rather than hurt our adversary; how much less may we kill him? . . . Hence it appears also that that is wrong which is delivered by most writers, that defense with slaying is lawful, that is by Divine law (for I do not dispute that it is by Natural Law,) when flight without danger is possible: namely, because flight is ignominious, especially in a man of noble family. In truth, there is, then, no ignominy, but a false opinion of ignominy, to be despised by those who follow virtue and wisdom. . . .
>
> *On the Right of War and Peace*
> Hugo Grotius

A traveler on a dark road is set upon by an armed stranger. The stranger's assault threatens death or atrocious physical harm. The traveler pulls out a knife or a gun and kills the assailant. Has the traveler done something wrong — or, more precisely, something for which the legal system should punish him or her? Most contemporary Americans, faced with the facts above, would likely say that the traveler has killed in self-defense and thus has committed no crime. Further, most would likely perceive the scene described above as an easy case. H. L. A. Hart writes,

---

* Editor's Note — A blow, stroke; now usually one given with the hand.

"Killing in self-defense is an exception to a general rule making killing punishable; it is admitted because the policy or aims which in general justify the punishment of killing (for example, protection of human life) *do not include cases such as this.*"

But easy cases may make bad law. Two problems arise in the analysis of the uncomplicated narrative above. First, the very ease of the case conceals a contradiction: If "protection of human life" is a paramount goal of the criminal law, the incident on the highway, so far from falling outside the policy, must fall squarely within its purview. An act of violence has been committed, human life has been taken by another human being, and a legal system sincerely concerned with protecting human life should explain the exception in more rigorous terms than Hart admits. The case above seems easy to contemporary thinkers only because considerable historical grappling has been done by the legal system over half a millennium.

Second, the case cited above, in its very archetypicality, has the potential to distort legal analysis of actual cases. Available evidence suggests that most killings, even those in which the killer successfully pleads self-defense, are not of the "pure variety cited above, in which an unknown assailant begins an unprovoked assault on a surprised victim. Instead, the majority of homicides take place after ambiguous confrontations between persons who know each other and have a history of involvement and conflict. The criminal justice system must assess the culpability of the survivor and decide what, if any, atonement is to be exacted for the act of killing. This complex investigation is powerfully shaped, and often distorted, by the belief of those in the system that are comparing the actual case before them with the archetype cited above. Our "intuition" about the "easy case," which is in fact a historically shaped perception about a troubling moral dilemma, leads us to view actual events as instances of that case. If there were different "easy cases" available... the outcome might often be different.

One aspect of the doctrine of self-defense has proved unusually problematic for theoreticians and courts. What if the traveler, menaced by the stranger's assault, could escape by dashing into a nearby house and closing a sturdy oaken door? To what extent should the law, if satisfied that the opportunity existed and that the traveler knew of it, penalize the traveler for using deadly force instead of running away?

The law's answer to this is most authoritatively stated by the Model Penal Code:

> The use of deadly force is not justifiable under this Section unless the actor believes that such force is necessary to protect himself against death, serious bodily injury, kidnaping or sexual intercourse compelled by force or threat; nor is it justifiable if... the actor knows that he can avoid the necessity of using such force with complete safety by retreating... except that... the actor is not obliged to retreat from his dwelling or place of work, unless he was the initial aggressor or is assailed in his place of work by another person whose place of work the actor knows it to be....

But at the time they adopted the "retreat rule," the drafters of the Code recognized that "American jurisdictions [are] divided on the question... with the preponderant position favoring the right to stand one's ground." In fact, the "retreat rule" has spawned a strong argument — one that has attained the status of law in many jurisdictions — for the contrary rule, a rule of "no retreat." ...

It would certainly be defensible to use the retreat cases as evidence for the proposition, advanced by legal realists, that courts do not use rules to decide cases, but simply to rationalize their own intuitive decisions; and by critical legal scholars, that "the law" as a construct is inherently incoherent, self-contradictory, and unprincipled, and that criminal-law rules cannot be drawn in a way that would successfully prevent courts from using their interpretive discretion to achieve results actually determined by class, race, or sexual bias.

. . . Much criminal doctrine remains grounded in largely obsolete nineteenth-century notions of free will and individualism. Legal analysis uses rights theory to analyze interactions between persons who are members of a social context and for whom largely unconscious reciprocal relationships are often more important determinants of behavior than are rational calculations about rights. Ideas and attitudes formulated during the sparsely populated, heavily rural, expanding frontier culture of nineteenth century America serve badly a crowded, multiracial, technological, urbanized society trembling on the lip of the twenty-first century. One of the chief needs of the evolving society of the United States is a reduction in the use of violence, whether expressed as crime, unprincipled law enforcement and corrections, or war and militarism. The law need not necessarily play a passive role in the attempt to wean our society from its uniquely violent mores; it could be used to restrict the tolerance and use of violence by all levels of society.

The law of self-defense is a logical place to begin this inquiry because contemporary thinkers tend to see the area of self-defense as one in which the general rules against violence simply do not apply. But if, as this note suggests, cases of "self-defense" represent a fragile, socially mediated interpretive construct, a determined effort to bring them more closely within a general proscription of violence might serve the purpose of awakening legal thinkers to the ways we use such "exceptions" to negate the rules we claim to live by.

Accordingly, I close with a few suggestions for change in the self-defense area. These are intended, at least at present, more as "thought experiments" than as formal proposals for statutory reform. . . .

[M]ost radically, the very idea of self-defense could be changed or negated altogether. Few things are more strange and threatening to the contemporary mind than a suggestion that the law should withdraw recognition of the "right" to use violence in any circumstances, even those historically recognized as self-defense. Self-defense is seen as a natural right, one that arises independently of the social context in which it is exercised and that can be recognized easily without reference to that context. I believe that what we call self-defense is in fact socially constructed and created by those who, after the fact, interpret events. And it is arguable that for every occasion on which the right of self-defense is invoked by a wronged party who has successfully resisted an aggressor, it is invoked at least once by an aggressive party seeking to justify unprovoked violence. Few aggressive wars are ever begun without a solemn declaration that the aggressor is defending itself against the weaker party;[1] in daily life, few violent acts are undertaken in which the

---

1. In the Persian Gulf War, Iraqi President Saddam Hussein justified his invasion of Kuwait on the grounds that Kuwait, by allegedly pumping oil from a disputed oil field on the Iraqi-Kuwaiti border and selling oil at a price lower than that at which he wanted to sell, had commenced "economic warfare" against

aggressor does not claim, and usually believe, that he or she was in some sense acting in self-defense. A world without a concept of permissible violent self-defense — in which all acts of violence are seen as culpable to some degree — is difficult to imagine. I have not successfully imagined it; I cannot confidently argue that it would be better or less violent than the world we currently live in. But contemporary ethical theories, and the traditions bequeathed to us by all the major world religions, uniformly reveal a deep ambivalence about the use of force in self-defense. The Judeo-Christian tradition is often unable to choose between "an eye for an eye" and "turn the other cheek." It might be useful to imagine what the law would be like if it began turning more cheeks and plucking fewer eyes.

Paul H. Robinson & John M. Darley, Study 6: Use of Force in Defense of Property
Justice, Liability & Blame 65, 66, 71-72 (1995)

In this defense of property study, we tested the current defense of property rules against our subjects' assignment of liability in analogous defense of property situations. Subjects were given seven scenarios in which the person uses force to defend against an attempt to steal his motorcycle. One scenario presented a baseline case in which necessary, nondeadly force is used, which would receive complete exculpation under current doctrine. The other six scenarios presented variations in which the person deviates from the baseline case in one or more ways, typically in violation of one of the limitations on the use of force to defend property. The liability results are shown in Table 3.5. Notice that column *e* contains the various liabilities assigned to the person who attempts the theft. As one would expect, the thief is assigned some liability, and it is roughly constant across the cases.

With respect to perceptions of the use of necessary nondeadly force (the baseline case results in row 1), our subjects agree that complete exculpation is appropriate. Of the respondents, 89 percent judge that no liability should be assigned to the property defender; the remaining 11 percent assign liability but no punishment. . . .

Iraq, which Iraq was justified in resisting by military force. "Some of the Gulf states, [Hussein] said, were keeping the price of oil too low by pumping too much of it. Since every dollar off the price of a barrel cost Iraq $1 billion a year in lost revenues, this was an 'economic war' on Iraq. . . . [In a note to the Arab League,] Iraq accused Kuwait of planting military posts inside Iraq and stealing from an Iraqi oilfield. Both Kuwait and the U[nited] A[rab] E[mirates] were indeed, said the note, part of an 'imperialist-Zionist plot against the Arab nation.'" *Kuwait: How the West Blundered*, The Economist (Sept 29, 1990), reprinted in Micah L. Sifry & Christopher Cerf, eds., *The Gulf War Reader* 99, 103, 104 (Times Books 1991). Saddam told the American ambassador to Iraq that "some brothers are fighting an economic war against us. And . . . not all wars use weapons. . . ." *The Glaspie Transcript: Saddam Meets the U.S. Ambassador*, reprinted in *The Gulf War Reader* at 122, 131. After the invasion, the United States then justified its organization and leadership of a multinational force that devastated Iraq on the grounds, inter alia, that Iraq represented an economic and military threat to the West. "Our country now imports nearly half the oil it consumes and could face a major threat to its economic independence." George Bush, *In Defense of Saudi Arabia* (Speech of Aug 8, 1990), reprinted in *The Gulf War Reader* at 197, 198. "While the world waited, Saddam sought to add to the chemical weapons he now possesses, an infinitely more dangerous weapon of mass destruction — a nuclear weapon." George Bush, *The Liberation of Kuwait Has Begun* (Speech of Jan 16, 1991), reprinted in *The Gulf War Reader* at 311, 312.

Table 3.5 Liability for the Use of Force in Protection of Property

Scenarios	(a) Liability	(b) % No Liability (N)	(c) % No Liability or No Punishment (N+0)	(d) Model Penal Code Result for Defender	(e) Liability for Thief	(f) Maximum Force That Should be Permitted
1. Necessary force	0.00	89	100	Complete defense	4.58	3.80
2. Questionably necessary force	0.00	77	98	Unclear[a]	4.70	3.91
3. Necessary force applied by device	0.19	77	93	Complete defense[b]	5.11	3.91
4. No imminent threat (perceived as not immediately necessary)	0.48	48	82	Unclear[c]	4.14	3.36
5. More than necessary force by choice	0.14	55	93	No defense: liable for simple assault, a misdemeanor	4.05	3.41
6. Deadly force, knowing not lawful	2.58	21	46	No defense; liable for aggravated assault, a second-degree felony	5.39	4.32
7. Deadly force, mistakenly believing it lawful	2.53	18	48		5.45	4.25

Liability Scale: N = No criminal liability, 0 = Liability but no punishment, 1 = 1 day, 2 = 2 weeks 3 = 2 months, 4 = 6 months, 5 = 1 year, 6 = 3 years, 7 = 7 years, 8 = 15 years, 9 = 30 years, 10 = life, and 11 = death.

Key to scenarios:

1. *Necessary force:* "Joe arrives home from work to find a man attempting to steal his motorcycle. Joe yells at him to get away and the thief ignores him. Joe then approaches him and grabs his arm, and the thief shrugs him off and continues hot wiring. Finally *Joe punches the thief, hitting him in the face. The thief runs off.*" In this, as well as in all the following scenarios, the thief is later apprehended by the police.

2. *Questionably necessary force:* "Joe punches the man, believing at the time that it is necessary. Joe's wife begins to yell at Joe that the man was small and not very muscular and Joe probably could have scared him off with a yell. Joe later realizes that his wife was right."

3. *Necessary force applied by device:* The owner of the motorcycle has "rigged a protective device to the garage door so that if anyone tried to break into the garage and steal the motorcycle, the device is triggered, firing a beanbag at the intruder." The thief breaks in and triggers the device, which breaks his nose.

4. *No imminent threat (perceived as not immediately necessary):* "The thief agrees to leave when Joe yells at him, but the thief makes it clear that he has an imprint of the keyhole and will return for the motorcycle. Joe resorts to force in order to retrieve the imprint."

5. *More than necessary by force of choice:* "Joe realizes that he can simply scare the man away by yelling at him. He nonetheless approaches the man and punches him in the face."

6. *Deadly force:* "A thief is detected attempting to steal a motorcycle and the owner attempts to get him to stop. The thief persists, and the owner gets a gun and shoots him." Respondents are told that the thief is wounded but not killed. The facts are manipulated slightly in scenarios 6 and 7 to create the knowing and mistaken belief scenarios.

Key to Column Heads:

(f) What is the maximum amount of force that someone should be permitted to use to protect his property in this situation? 0 = "no force," 2 = "risk of bodily injury," 4 = "bodily injury," 6 = "serious bodily injury," 8 = "serious bodily injury with risk of death," and 10 = "death."

[a] This scenario was intended to present the case of a mistaken actor. Such an actor might get a defense under current law, especially if his mistake was reasonable; he might only get a mitigation if his mistake was not reasonable. In fact, the scenario was perceived as a case of necessary force, for which the actor would have a defense under current doctrine.

[b] If the scenario had been perceived as the device creating a substantial risk of serious bodily injury, as was intended, there would be no defense. But no such risk was perceived by the subjects. See column d of Table 3.6. In a case of no risk of serious bodily injury, a complete defense is available.

[c] An "imminent threat" was required by common law; modern codes such as the Model Penal Code require only that the "force used be immediately necessary."

Study 6 Summary

Even where the force used in defense of property is unnecessary or dispro-portionate, according to legal codes, the vast majority of subjects impose no punishment. The subjects also show a tendency to interpret a person's conduct as necessary to defend his property even in instances where such a conclusion is difficult to support on the objective facts. As with self-defense, the defensive nature of the person's situation appears to have a significant effect on the subjects' judgement. Even where the person's defensive response is knowingly improper — i.e., he knows that the law does not justify his conduct — the subjects significantly reduce the person's liability. Again, the subjects appear to distinguish a person who improperly defends his property from a person who uses the same force in other than a defensive context. This argues in favor of providing reduced grades of liability for those who err in defending against an attack. It remains a question for further research as to whether the value of the property being defended enters into the respondents' calculus.

If the legal code were modeled after the subjects' responses, it would give a complete defense for non-deadly force, necessary or not, used in the defense of property. The use of deadly force would be disapproved of but would result in low liability and punishment if the force appeared to be necessary (and the thief is not actually killed). In further research it would be important to address the question of what "philosophies" lie behind the judgements of individuals. Are there some individuals who believe that even deadly force is allowable in the defense of property? Does this belief reflect the view that the criminal justice system has become ineffective in defending property? The results may well be consistent with a public that is angry with what they see as the criminal justice system's failure to protect. "At the very least," the argument might go, "if the system will not protect my property, I should be permitted to do what is necessary (and perhaps more) to protect it myself."

Public Authority Justifications

A person need not be acting defensively in order to be justified. It is common for situations to arise in which societal interests would be furthered by aggressive use of force, as when used to make an arrest or to maintain the order required for safety on public transportation.

◆ THE CASE OF OFFICER ELTON HYMON

Born in 1948, Elton Hymon grows up with two brothers and five sisters in a devout Christian family in Memphis, going to church and Sunday school each week. His father works at the Memphis Cemetery and his mother as a cook at Tall Trees, a center for troubled youths. His neighborhood forms a tight community, where people look out for one another; children go to neighbors for advice as if they were parents. Hymon enjoys basketball and plays on Geeter High School's A team. He wants to be a doctor until he sees the burned back of a cousin who gets scalded by water. He decides that he cannot deal with such things. After

Figure 90 **Officer Elton Hymon, circa 1984**
(NCJRS)

graduating from high school, Hymon begins studying business at Tennessee State University in Nashville, but switches to English in his sophomore year. He also plays on the Tennessee State basketball team until a back injury forces him to quit. He takes up judo and rises to become a brown belt. After graduating with a B.S. in 1970, Hymon takes a job as a treatment service counselor at Fort Pillow State Prison. The 65-mile commute to Fort Pillow from Memphis begins to wear on him, so Hymon begins to look for a job in his hometown. Though his parents are against it because they believe it too dangerous, Hymon joins the Memphis Police Department in July 1973, a month after getting married, and graduates as one of the top five in his class at the police academy.

Edward Garner is a fifteen-year old who lives with his father and five other siblings in Memphis. At five feet four inches and less than one hundred pounds, he is small for a teenager. His father, Cleamtee, works the second shift at the Memphis Defense Depot, and has trouble keeping an eye on Garner. Like other boys in the neighborhood, Garner has already had minor troubles with the law. Three years ago, he and some friends were caught after illegally sneaking into a house, and this past July Garner stole a jar of pennies from a neighbor's house. Although the neighbor thought it unnecessary to call the police, the neighbor's family insisted on reporting the incident. Garner receives one year of probation, and his father imposes a curfew. Police subsequently arrest him for violating his probation, but dismiss the matter when they learn he is working at a local store.

It is October 3, 1974, about 10:40 p.m., and Edward Garner is somewhat intoxicated as he walks toward 739 Vollintine Street, which is just a few blocks from his own house at 929 Tully Street. He pulls a garbage can beneath a window, climbs onto it, smashes the window, and climbs into the house. Inside the dark and empty house, he rummages around for valuables. Next door, at 737 Vollintine, Daisy Bell States thinks she hears a noise and calls the police to report what she thinks is a prowler. Her prudence is understandable because over the last three months her neighborhood has been plagued by a string of over one hundred and twenty burglaries and larcenies.

Officers Elton Hymon and Leslie B. Wright are at a nearby fire station when

Figure 91 **Edward Garner, age unknown**
(NCJRS)

they receive the call to investigate. It takes them about fifteen minutes to arrive. States, a middle-aged African-American woman, is standing on her porch in a housecoat. Hymon goes to the porch, and States explains to him quietly that she heard glass shatter next door. She also tells him that she thinks that a person is still inside the house. After conferring with Wright, both officers take flashlights and head to the back of the house from opposite sides. Wright calls in to report that they are investigating the scene, then circles around to the back of the house.

Figure 92 **Bedroom ransacked by Garner while looking for money and valuables**

(U.S. District Court, Western District Tennessee)

Hymon arrives first, with his .38 caliber revolver drawn. When he sees the broken window and a light on in the house, he thinks something is "wrong inside."

Inside, Garner, possibly hearing the officers outside, quickly glances around the room one last time and grabs a small purse with ten dollars. He heads to the back door and tries to make a run for it. Hymon hears the screen door slam and sees Garner sprint through a stream of light in the otherwise dark backyard. As Garner runs for the chain-link fence on the other side of the yard, he hears Hymon yell, "Police, Halt!" Garner freezes at the foot of the fence.

Scanning the backyard with his flashlight, Hymon sees a waist-high chicken-wire fence between him and Garner, as well as a clothesline and other clutter. Training his light on Garner, he sees the face of a young black man, who he thinks is about seventeen, crouching beside a six-foot-high chain-link fence. Although Hymon is about forty feet away, and despite seeing something unidentifiable in one of Garner's hands, Hymon believes that Garner is unarmed. When Wright arrives at the backyard, Hymon calls out to him to circle around the chain-link fence.

Hymon takes a step toward the fence, but Garner leaps up to climb over, almost making it to the top in a single jump. When he sees how fast Garner moves, Hymon is sure that Garner will escape because he cannot see beyond the fence and his boots and equipment will inevitably slow him down. Wright is too far away to catch up with Garner.

Figure 93 **The view Officer Hymon had of the backyard. Garner had accessed the house using the trash can in the front left.**

(U.S. District Court, Western District Tennessee)

Figure 94 **Daytime view of the backyard.**
Officer Hymon stood at the short fence in
the front left; Garner was along the fence in
the far right-hand corner.

(U.S. District Court, Western District Tennessee)

Figure 95 **Blood spot in corner where**
Garner was shot

(U.S. District Court, Western District Tennessee)

Hymon aims at Garner's torso, as he was trained to do, and fires one shot. Only when Hymon sees Garner slump over the fence does he realize that the shot hit him in the back of the head. This is the first time Hymon has fired at a suspect since joining the force.

Wright reaches Garner first and yells out that he is bleeding badly from the head. It is the most bleeding he has ever seen. They get him down from the fence and call an ambulance and their lieutenant. The ambulance arrives in minutes and rushes Garner to John Gaston Hospital, where he dies on the operating table. The news of Garner's death is devastating to Hymon, who had seen him alive and hoped he would survive. Hymon's supervisor later informs him that he faces a murder charge, despite apparently following department procedures.

1. Relying only on your own intuition of justice, what liability and punishment, if any, does Officer Hymon deserve?

N	0	1	2	3	4	5	6	7	8	9	10	11
☐	☐	☐	☐	☐	☐	☐	☐	☐	☐	☐	☐	☐
no liability	liability but no punishment	1 day	2 wks	2 mo	6 mo	1 yr	3 yrs	7 yrs	15 yrs	30 yrs	life imprisonment	death

2. What liability, if any, under the then-existing statutes?
3. What liability, if any, under the Model Penal Code?

■ THE LAW

Tennessee Code Annotated
(1974)

Title 39. Criminal Offenses

Chapter 2. Offenses Against the Person
Part 2. Homicide

Section 39-2401. Murder Generally

If any person of sound memory and discretion, unlawfully kills any reasonable creature in being, and under the peace of the state, with malice aforethought, either express or implied, such person shall be guilty of murder.

Section 39-2402. Murder in the First Degree

An individual commits murder in the first degree if:

(1) he commits a willful, deliberate, malicious and premeditated killing or murder;

(2) he commits a willful, deliberate, malicious killing or murder, and:

(a) the victim is an employee of the department of correction having custody of the actor,

(b) the victim is a prison inmate in custody with the actor,

(c) the victim is known to the actor to be a peace officer or fireman acting in the course of his employment,

(d) the victim is a judge acting in the course of his judicial duties,

(e) the victim is a popularly elected public official,

(f) the offense is committed for hire; or,

(g) the offense is committed while attempting to evade law enforcement officials;

(3) he hires another to commit willful, deliberate, malicious and premeditated killing or murder, and such hiring causes the death of the victim; or,

(4) he commits a willful, deliberate, and malicious killing or murder during the perpetration of any arson, rape, robbery, burglary, larceny, kidnapping, aircraft piracy, or unlawful throwing, placing, or discharging of a destructive device or bomb.

Section 39-2403. Murder in the Second Degree

All other kinds of murder shall be deemed murder in the second degree

Section 39-2404. Jury to Ascertain Degree

The jury before whom the offender is tried shall ascertain in their verdict whether it is murder in the first or second degree; and if the accused confess his guilt, the court shall proceed to determine the degree of crime by the verdict of a jury, upon the examination of testimony, and give sentence accordingly.

Section 39-2405. Punishment for Murder in the First Degree

Every person convicted of murder in the first degree, or as accessory before the fact to such crime, shall suffer death by electrocution.

Section 39-2406. Death Penalty Mandatory for Conviction of Murder in the First Degree

When a person is convicted of crime of murder in the first degree, or as an accessory before the fact of such crime, it shall be the duty of the jury convicting him in their verdict to fix his punishment at death as provided by law.

Section 39-2408. Punishment for Murder in the Second Degree

Every person convicted of murder in the second degree shall be imprisoned in the penitentiary for life or for a period of not less than ten (10) years.

Section 39-2409. Manslaughter

Manslaughter is the unlawful killing of another without malice, either express or implied, which may be either voluntary upon a sudden heat, or involuntary, but in the commission of some unlawful act.

Section 39-2410. Punishment for Voluntary Manslaughter

Whoever is convicted of the crime of voluntary manslaughter shall undergo confinement in the penitentiary not less than two (2) years nor more than ten (10) years.

Section 39-2411. Punishment for Involuntary Manslaughter

Whoever is convicted of involuntary manslaughter shall undergo confinement in the penitentiary for not less than one year nor more than five (5) years.

Title 39. Criminal Offenses

Chapter 6. Assaults, Attempts and Injuries to Persons

Section 39-601. Assault with Deadly Weapon — Penalty

If any person assaults and beats another with a cowhide, stick, or whip, having at the time in his possession a pistol or other deadly weapon, with intent to intimidate the persons assaulted, and prevent him from defending himself, he shall, on conviction, be imprisoned in the penitentiary not less than two (2) years nor more than ten (10) years.

Section 39-612. Shooting or Stabbing Without Malice — Assault and Battery

When any person is indicted for malicious stabbing or shooting, and the jury shall be of the opinion that the defendant is not guilty of the malice, they shall have the power to find the defendant guilty of an assault and battery.

Section 40-808. Resistance to Officer

If, after notice of the intention to arrest the defendant, he either flees or forcibly resists, the officer may use all the necessary means to effect the arrest.

Chapter 3. Offenses Against Property

Section 39-401. Burglary Generally

(a) Burglary is the breaking and entering into a dwelling house, or any other house, building, room or rooms therein used and occupied by any person or persons as a dwelling place or lodging either permanently or temporarily and whether as owner, renter, tenant, lessee or paying guest, by night, with intent to commit a felony.

(b) Every person convicted of this crime shall be imprisoned in the penitentiary not less than five (5) years nor more than fifteen (15) years.

(c) Provided, however, if the person convicted of this crime had in his possession a firearm at the time of the breaking and entering, he shall be imprisoned in the penitentiary not less than ten (10) nor more than fifteen (15) years.

Section 39-405. Treatment upon Conviction of Burglary or Safecracking

(a) . . .

(b)

(1) Upon conviction for a violation of §39-3-401, if the district attorney general, or his designee, introduces a certified document to the court showing that such person has been previously convicted of such offense, such person shall not be considered for or granted parole or otherwise released until such time as he has served at least five (5) calendar years of the sentence received for the second such conviction. . . .

(5) Notwithstanding any other provision of chapters 3 or 18 of title 41 to the contrary, no person serving a sentence for a second conviction of one (1) of the offenses specified in subsection (b)(1) or (b)(2) of this section shall be eligible for any program whereby he may be granted supervised or unsupervised release into the community.

(c)

(1) Upon conviction for a violation of §39-3-401, if the district attorney general, or his designee, introduces certified documents to the court showing that such person has been previously convicted of such offense two (2) or more times, such person shall not be considered for or granted

parole or otherwise released until such time as he has served at least five (5) calendar years of the sentence received for the third or subsequent such conviction....

(5) Notwithstanding any other provision of chapters 3 or 18 of title 41 to the contrary, no person serving a sentence for a third or subsequent conviction of one (1) of the offenses specified in subsection (c)(1) or (c)(2) of this section shall be eligible for any program whereby he may be granted supervised or unsupervised release into the community.

(d) For purposes of this section, convictions for multiple offenses occurring as part of a single criminal episode shall constitute only one (1) offense.

Morelock v. State
460 S.W.2d 861 (Tenn. Crim. App. 1970)

The defendant was engaged in an illicit affair with the victim, and they had planned to leave their partners and secretly marry. While drinking and driving, the couple engaged in an argument that was caused by the victim's alleged decision not to marry the defendant that day. When the defendant tossed a beer can out of the car window, he attracted police attention and was pulled over. He suddenly panicked and shot the victim four times in the head, then shot himself. The court upheld his conviction for first-degree murder, despite his defense that he had not shown malice, because the "settled law in this State is that all homicides are presumed to be malicious, in the absence of evidence which would rebut the implied presumption." Further, the court reasoned that "[i]t is also no longer debatable or open to question that if a weapon is handled in a manner so as to make the killing a natural or probable result of such conduct, malice will be presumed from the use of the weapon."

Leake v. State
29 Tenn. 144, 149 (1849)

The defendant, a young man of small stature and missing his right hand, went to the house of deceased, a strong woman of ill repute to harass her. They quarreled, and she attacked him with a skillet, whereupon he shot her with his pistol. The defendant appealed his conviction of second-degree murder on the basis that his case was devoid of malice and his self-defense reduced the offense to manslaughter. The court set aside his verdict, finding that the evidence did not support malice. The court held that "the presumption of malice arising in law from this killing, and from the deadly character of the weapon used, is rebutted by the proof of the suddenness of the rencounter [sic], the violence of the assault on the part of the deceased, and the dangerous nature of the weapon used by her." Further, the court held that "in the absence of proof of express malice, this killing must be held to have been the result of sudden heat and excited passion, and, therefore, not murder in either the first or second degree."

Copeland v. State
154 Tenn. 7, 285 S.W. 565 (1926)

"Plaintiff in error was convicted of involuntary manslaughter for causing the death of Robert Holland on the public highway at Saltillo, December 4, 1924, when he was struck and killed by an automobile driven by Copeland.

"... [I]nvoluntary manslaughter is not only an unintentional homicide occasioned by a person engaged at the time in an unlawful act. It may consist in doing a lawful act in an unlawful manner, as where one by his gross or culpable negligence causes the death of another. Or, ... if the homicide results from a criminal want of caution and circumspection, and not misadventure, it is involuntary and manslaughter.

"In a charge otherwise accurate the trial judge failed to instruct the jury that, to convict for homicide caused from a lawful act committed in an unlawful manner, it must appear that the death was not the result of misadventure, but the natural and probable result of a reckless or culpably negligent act.

"... Allowance must always be made for misadventure and accident, as distinguished from culpable negligence.

> While the kind of negligence required to impose criminal liability has been described in different terms, it is uniformly held that it must be of a higher degree than is required to establish negligence upon a mere civil issue, and it must be shown that a homicide was not improbable under the facts as they existed which should reasonably have influenced the conduct of accused.

"Reversed and remanded, for the failure of the trial court to charge that, if death did not result from Copeland's violation of the statute, there could be no conviction, unless the boy's death was the reasonable and probable result of Copeland's negligent or reckless act, and if he acted as a man of reasonable care in attempting to pass the wagons, and death was the result of an accident caused by the boy unexpectedly running from behind the wagon in front of the automobile, the homicide would not be unlawful."

Bouie v. City of Columbia
378 U.S. 347 (1964)

The defendants were two African-American college students who took seats in a booth in the restaurant department at an Eckerd's, which had a policy of excluding non-whites. While they waited to be served, the store called the police, who arrested the students for breach of the peace and trespass. They were convicted on both counts, and the state supreme court affirmed their trespass convictions, interpreting the trespass statute to "cover not only the act of entry on the premises of another after receiving notice not to enter, but also the act of remaining on the premises of another after receiving notice to leave." The defendants appealed their trespass convictions to the U.S. Supreme Court, and in a 6-3 decision, the Court reversed their convictions. Writing for the majority, Justice Brennan decided that "by applying such a construction of the statute to affirm their convictions in this case, the State has punished them for conduct that was not criminal at the time they committed it, and hence has violated the requirement of the Due Process Clause that a criminal statute give fair warning of the conduct which it prohibits." The South Carolina Supreme Court had construed the trespass statute to cover the defendants' actions a year after they committed them. This prevented the defendants from having fair warning of the offense. The Court limited its recognition of a defense to those extreme situations, like the case at bar, in which the state interprets a statute to hold other than its plain meaning, and in which prior judicial decisions would lead an individual to construe the statute in a different manner.

Model Penal Code
(Official Draft 1962)

Section 3.03. Execution of Public Duty

(1) Except as provided in Subsection (2) of this Section, conduct is justifiable when it is required or authorized by:

    (a) the law defining the duties or functions of a public officer or the assistance to be rendered to such officer in the performance of his duties; or

    (b) the law governing the execution of legal process; or

    (c) the judgment or order of a competent court or tribunal; or

    (d) the law governing the armed services or the lawful conduct of war; or

    (e) any other provision of law imposing a public duty.

(2) The other sections of this Article apply to:

    (a) the use of force upon or toward the person of another for any of the purposes dealt with in such sections; and

    (b) the use of deadly force for any purpose, unless the use of such force is otherwise expressly authorized by law or occurs in the lawful conduct of war.

(3) The justification afforded by Subsection (1) of this Section applies:

    (a) when the actor believes his conduct to be required or authorized by the judgment or direction of a competent court or tribunal or in the lawful execution of legal process, notwithstanding lack of jurisdiction of the court or defect in the legal process; and

    (b) when the actor believes his conduct to be required or authorized to assist a public officer in the performance of his duties, notwithstanding that the officer exceeded his legal authority.

Section 3.07. Use of Force in Law Enforcement

(1) Use of Force Justifiable to Effect an Arrest. Subject to the provisions of this Section and of Section 3.09, the use of force upon or toward the person of another is justifiable when the actor is making or assisting in making an arrest and the actor believes that such force is immediately necessary to effect a lawful arrest.

(2) Limitations on the Use of Force

(a) The use of force is not justifiable under this Section unless:

(i) the actor makes known the purpose of the arrest or believes that it is otherwise known by or cannot reasonably be made known to the person to be arrested; and

(ii) when the arrest is made under a warrant, the warrant is valid or believed by the actor to be valid.

(b) The use of deadly force is not justifiable under this Section unless:

(i) the arrest is for a felony; and

(ii) the person effecting the arrest is authorized to act as a peace officer or is assisting a person whom he believes to be authorized to act as a peace officer; and

(iii) the actor believes that the force employed creates no substantial risk of injury to innocent persons; and

(iv) the actor believes that:

(1) the crime for which the arrest is made involved conduct including the use or threatened use of deadly force; or

(2) there is a substantial risk that the person to be arrested will cause death or serious bodily harm if his apprehension is delayed.

(3) Use of Force to Prevent Escape from Custody. The use of force to prevent the escape of an arrested person from custody is justifiable when the force could justifiably have been employed to effect the arrest under which the person is in custody, except that a guard or other person authorized to act as a peace officer is justified in using any force, including deadly force, which he believes to be immediately necessary to prevent the escape of a person from a jail, prison, or other institution for the detention of persons charged with or convicted of a crime.

(4) Use of Force by Private Person Assisting an Unlawful Arrest

(a) A private person who is summoned by a peace officer to assist in effecting an unlawful arrest, is justified in using any force which he would be justified in using if the arrest were lawful, provided that he does not believe the arrest is unlawful.

(b) A private person who assists another private person in effecting an unlawful arrest, or who, not being summoned, assists a peace officer in effecting an unlawful arrest, is justified in using any force which he would be justified in using if the arrest were lawful, provided that (i) he believes the arrest is lawful, and (ii) the arrest would be lawful if the facts were as he believes them to be.

(5) Use of Force to Prevent Suicide or the Commission of a Crime

(a) The use of force upon or toward the person of another is justifiable when the actor believes that such force is immediately necessary to prevent such other person from committing suicide, inflicting serious bodily harm upon himself, committing or consummating the commission of a crime involving or threatening bodily harm, damage to or loss of property or a breach of the peace, except that:

(i) any limitations imposed by the other provisions of this Article on the justifiable use of force in self-protection, for the protection of others, the protection of property, the effectuation of an arrest or the prevention of an escape from custody shall apply notwithstanding the criminality of the conduct against which such force is used; and

(ii) the use of deadly force is not in any event justifiable under this Subsection unless:

(1) the actor believes that there is a substantial risk that the person whom he seeks to prevent from committing a crime will cause death or serious bodily harm to another unless the commission or the consummation of the crime is prevented and that the use of such force presents no substantial risk of injury to innocent persons; or

(2) the actor believes that the use of such force is necessary to suppress a riot or mutiny after the rioters or mutineers have been ordered to disperse and warned, in any particular manner that the law may require, that such force will be used if they do not obey.

(b) The justification afforded by this Subsection extends to the use of confinement as preventive force only if the actor takes all reasonable measures to terminate the confinement as soon as he knows that he safely can, unless the person confined has been arrested on a charge of crime.

Section 3.08. Use of Force by Persons with Special Responsibility for Care, Discipline or Safety of Others

The use of force upon or toward the person of another is justifiable if:

(1) the actor is the parent or guardian or other person similarly responsible for the general care and supervision of a minor or a person acting at the request of such parent, guardian or other responsible person and:

(a) the force is used for the purpose of safeguarding or promoting the welfare of the minor, including the prevention or punishment of his misconduct; and

(b) the force used is not designed to cause or known to create a substantial risk of causing death, serious bodily harm, disfigurement, extreme pain or mental distress or gross degradation; or

(2) the actor is a teacher or a person otherwise entrusted with the care or supervision for a special purpose of a minor and:

(a) the actor believes that the force used is necessary to further such special purpose, including the maintenance of reasonable discipline in a school, class or other group, and that the use of such force is consistent with the welfare of the minor; and

(b) the degree of force, if it had been used by the parent or guardian of the minor, would not be unjustifiable under Subsection (1)(b) of this Section; or

(3) the actor is the guardian or other person similarly responsible for the general care and supervision of an incompetent person; and:

(a) the force is used for the purpose of safeguarding or promoting the welfare of the incompetent person, including the prevention of his misconduct, or, when such incompetent person is in a hospital or other institution for his care and custody, for the maintenance of reasonable discipline in such institution; and

(b) the force used is not designed to cause or known to create a substantial risk of causing death, serious bodily harm, disfigurement, extreme or unnecessary pain, mental distress, or humiliation; or

(4) the actor is a doctor or other therapist or a person assisting him at his direction, and:

(a) the force is used for the purpose of administering a recognized form of treatment which the actor believes to be adapted to promoting the physical or mental health of the patient; and

(b) the treatment is administered with the consent of the patient or, if the patient is a minor or an incompetent person, with the consent of his parent or guardian or other person legally competent to consent in his behalf, or the treatment is administered in an emergency when the actor believes that no one competent to consent can be consulted and that a reasonable person, wishing to safeguard the welfare of the patient, would consent; or

(5) the actor is a warden or other authorized official of a correctional institution, and:

(a) he believes that the force used is necessary for the purpose of enforcing the lawful rules or procedures of the institution, unless his belief in the lawfulness of the rule or procedure sought to be enforced is erroneous and his error is due to ignorance or mistake as to the provisions of the Code, any other provision of the criminal law or the law governing the administration of the institution; and

(b) the nature or degree of force used is not forbidden by Article 303 or 304 of the Code; and

(c) if deadly force is used, its use is otherwise justifiable under this Article; or

(6) the actor is a person responsible for the safety of a vessel or an aircraft or a person acting at his direction, and

(a) he believes that the force used is necessary to prevent interference with the operation of the vessel or aircraft or obstruction of the execution of a lawful order, unless his belief in the lawfulness of the order is erroneous and his error is due to ignorance or mistake as to the law defining his authority; and

(b) if deadly force is used, its use is otherwise justifiable under this Article; or

(7) the actor is a person who is authorized or required by law to maintain order or decorum in a vehicle, train or other carrier or in a place where others are assembled, and:

(a) he believes that the force used is necessary for such purpose; and

(b) the force used is not designed to cause or known to create a substantial risk of causing death, bodily harm, or extreme mental distress.

● OVERVIEW OF PUBLIC AUTHORITY JUSTIFICATIONS

Public authority justifications are available to actors specially authorized, and usually specially trained, to engage in conduct otherwise constituting an offense that is necessary to protect or further a societal interest. Unlike defensive force justifications, the actor's authority is not limited to defensive action. She may act affirmatively to further a public interest, even one that is entirely intangible. These justification defenses are distinguished from one another according to the specific interests they foster; different defenses authorize the use of force for law enforcement purposes,[1] medical purposes, military purposes, judicial purposes, to maintain order and safety on public carriers or in other public places of assembly, or for use by parents or guardians.[2] A catch-all public authority justification commonly provides a defense for performing public duties.[3]

Broad Range of Interests The interests to be furthered or protected by these defenses include those of an individual (such as the child, patient, or potential suicide victim in parental, medical, or suicide prevention justification defenses, respectively), those of a class of citizens (such as the users of public facilities in authority to maintain order and safety), or those of society as a whole (as in law enforcement, judicial, military, and general public authority). The interests may be of immediate concern or of long-range effect. For example, not only are the personal interests of the child pertinent in parental authority, but also the more general societal interest in preserving the family structure. The interests to be furthered may be either physical or intangible or both. When a mother disciplines a child caught playing with matches, for example, such disciplinary conduct has the immediate effect of avoiding the child or others being burned, and the long-range effect of advancing the child's proper discipline and upbringing. The wide variety of interests at stake — individual, group, societal, immediate, long-range, physical, and intangible — is reflected in the large number and diversity of public authority justifications.

Common Internal Structure The general form of public authority justifications may be summarized as follows: *special authorization* and *evoking conditions* trigger an actor's right to use *necessary* and *proportional* force. The authorization and evocation elements, as triggering conditions, act together to describe the persons and circumstances that will trigger an authority to act. The necessity and proportionality requirements, the response elements, describe the nature of the conduct that is justified once the authority to act is triggered.

Authorization Requirement The authorization requirement is unique to public authority justifications; the defensive force and lesser evils justifications have no such requirement and generally are available to all persons. This does not conflict with the general rule that justified conduct is equally justified for all actors in similar circumstances. The circumstances here that give rise to the justifying societal interests simply include the fact that an actor has been specially authorized; an unauthorized person engaging in the same conduct might not be able to further the societal or personal interests at stake, or at least not to the same extent and with the same efficiency that an authorized person could.

Rationale of Authorization Requirement   Assume a death warrant has been issued for a person found guilty of murder. After hearing the sentence, the victim's

---

1. Model Penal Code § 3.07.
2. Model Penal Code § 3.08.
3. Model Penal Code § 3.03 (Execution of Public Duty); see also Model Panel Code § 2.10 (Military Orders).

vengeful brother enters the prison on the day of execution, confines the executioner, takes his place, and executes the prisoner at the appointed time and in the prescribed manner. The brother's conduct conforms to that mandated by the judicial order but he acts without the court's authority. The conduct furthers the immediate interest of causing the death, but not the similarly important societal interest in impartial punishment nor its interest in promoting the criminal justice system's reputation for impartial punishment.[1] For a more commonplace example, consider the authority given to train conductors or bus drivers to keep order on their vehicles. If a passenger becomes rowdy, another passenger might stop the disorder as effectively as the bus driver could. On the other hand, without special training and, more important, without special authority, typically signaled, as with a uniform, another passenger's attempts to maintain order may prompt resistance and escalation of hostilities. In addition, even if successful, the passenger's actions would not further the societal interest in fostering public respect for, and compliance with, the bus driver's commands in maintenance of order. It is the precedential value, the reaffirmation of a bus driver's authority, that will deter future disruption and encourage future cooperation when a driver seeks to exercise his authority.

Exceptions to Authorization Requirement   The rule that limits public authority justifications to a special class of persons has two exceptions: All persons are authorized to use force to prevent a suicide and, under certain circumstances, persons without special authority are authorized to use force against a person who is preparing to commit, or who has just committed, a crime. Limiting authority to persons specially authorized is not feasible in these two instances because averting the threatened harm may require immediate action by whoever is present. Recall that defensive force justifications do not require special authorization. It is significant that these two public authority justifications, suicide and crime prevention, are the two for which the threat evoking the defense is most similar to the threat that evokes defensive force justifications. In both situations there is an identifiable aggressor threatening physical harm to persons or property. If these two defenses had not been drafted as part of a public authority defense (a subsection of the law enforcement authority defense[2]), they might properly have been treated as defensive force justifications.[3]

Evocation Requirement   In addition to the requirement that the actor be authorized, public authority justifications typically require that the existing circumstances trigger the need for the actor to act. Public authority justifications do not require a threat of harm to persons or property, as defensive force justifications do. They are evoked whenever a recognized interest is endangered or an

---

1. It is not the brother's improper subjective motivation that disqualifies him from the defense but rather his absence of official authorization. As in all justifications, the defendant's personal motives should be irrelevant. If the victim's brother were the lawful executioner and carried out the death warrant as directed, but with vengeance and ill will, he nonetheless would be justified. The appointment of a relative of the victim as executioner may suggest a poor administrative choice, but the official appointment protects the executioner brother.

2. See, e.g., Model Penal Code § 3.07(5).

3. These two public authority justifications — law enforcement and suicide prevention authority — are distinguishable from defensive force justifications, however, because the suicide victim is an "aggressor" only in a purely objective sense, and law enforcement authority extends to preventing other than aggressive crimes and to arrest after completion of a crime.

opportunity to further an interest is presented. A violator may injure or endanger an interest without being an "aggressor" in the normal sense of that term. Neither the noisy bus passenger nor the escaping prisoner is an aggressor in the same way as a person who threatens physical injury for which defensive force is justified. Yet both threaten important interests: the former the decorum of the bus and health of its passengers and the latter the effective operation of the criminal justice and correctional systems, respectively. The specific conditions that will trigger a public authority defense frequently are set out in administrative regulations promulgated by an oversight body.

Necessity Requirement   Once the authorization and evocation requirements are satisfied, the actor has authority to act but must use the least harmful conduct necessary to protect or further the interests at stake, and the actor must act only when necessary. This limitation is analogous to the necessity requirement of other justifications.

"Purpose" as Substitute for Necessity   The necessity requirement frequently is explicit,[1] but sometimes is replaced by a requirement that the actor act with a proper "purpose."[2] Conduct motivated by the purpose to protect the interest at stake typically will be necessary for that purpose, thus satisfying a necessity requirement. But a "purpose" requirement does give an actor somewhat greater latitude than would a pure "necessity" requirement. The parent who acts with the proper purpose need not show that the conduct in fact was necessary in the sense that no less harmful means could have been used as effectively. It is enough for the defense that the conduct is intended and designed to serve the disciplinary purpose. This substitution of a purpose requirement for a necessity requirement is another example of the Model Penal Code's subjectivization of justification defenses, in which it includes within the meaning of "justified" conduct an actor who only mistakenly believes that she is justified. The parent gets the defense even if her conduct is not in fact necessary, as long as she acted for the proper purpose and therefore presumably believed that the conduct was necessary.

Proportionality Requirement   The proportionality requirement ensures that, no matter what force may be necessary to protect or further the interest at stake, no more force may be used than is justified by the importance of that interest. Like the defensive force justifications, the public authority justifications do not leave it to individual juries to determine the balance of conflicting interests. The legislature has predetermined the balance and promulgated a set of explicit limitations on the use of force. For example, public authority defenses rarely

---

1. This is the case in the Model Penal Code's public authority justifications for law enforcement authority, authority to prevent suicide or self-infliction of bodily injury, teacher's authority, jailer's authority, and authority to maintain order and safety on a vessel. See Model Penal Code §§ 3.07, 3.08(2), 3.08(5), 3.08(6).

2. This is the case in parental, benevolent custodial, and medical authority. See Model Penal Code §§ 3.08(1), 3.08(4). The Model Penal Code's general public authority defense requires only that the conduct be "required or authorized" by the actor's source of public authority. Model Penal Code § 3.03. This presumes that only necessary force would be so required or authorized, but such may not always be the case. For example, in the context of law enforcement authority, a statute may authorize an officer of the law to use a chokehold in order to prevent a violent felon from escaping custody. But there may be situations in which a chokehold, although "authorized," is not necessary. A similar situation may arise in other situations, including those that would be governed by Model Penal Code § 3.03.

authorize the use of force that risks serious injury, even if it is necessary to stop the violation. Under the Model Penal Code, for example, a bus driver's use of force to maintain order and decorum is limited to force that does not "create a substantial risk of causing death, bodily harm, or extreme mental distress."[1] (Greater force may be justified, of course, if the safety of the driver or a passenger is threatened, thereby triggering a defensive force justification.) As the bus driver limitation illustrates, the proportionality requirement, as expressed in statutes, typically does not permit *ad hoc* balancing, but rather is embodied in a series of specific limitations on the amount and kind of force that the justification will permit in a given situation.[2]

General Public Authority   Model Penal Code section 3.03 describes the broadest public authority justification. It provides a defense for otherwise criminal conduct that is specifically "required or authorized" by the actor's public duty. The provision sets no specific limits on the use of force but rather provides a defense to actors who do what they are told to do by higher authority. One might worry that this general public authority defense could be interpreted too broadly — perhaps to circumvent the many limitations placed upon the use of force in one of the more specific public authority defenses simply by having a governmental official authorize the conduct by the public officer — but the danger of abuse is reduced by section 3.03(2)(a), which gives superiority to all more specific justification provisions.[3] In other words, the general public authority defense is, like the lesser evils defense, only a catchall for the instances where the situation is not covered by one of the specific public authority defenses.

▲ PROBLEM
Docker's Box

Pacer (his real name is George Brooke) has been driving the same bus route for two years. He prides himself in providing safe, courteous, and on-time transportation for his riders, and believes that his service is an important part of their lives. His attitude is reflected in his nickname. Everyone calls him Pacer because, even when he is behind schedule, with bad traffic and people standing in the aisle, he is known to "maintain an even strain." Today is one of the bad days. He fears his regulars are going to be late for work and school but is making as much progress as he can in heavy traffic. At Tenth and Locust, Docker gets on. He is carrying a huge "boom box" that takes up an entire seat. He decides to demonstrate just how high he can pump up the volume. The passengers sitting near Docker do not protest. With most of his six feet and 240 pounds covered in black

---

1. Model Penal Code § 3.08(7)(b).
2. See, e.g., the subsection (b)s in Model Penal Code § 3.08.
3. This is similar to the limitation on the lesser evils provision, contained in Model Penal Code § 3.02(1)(b).

leather and chrome, Docker looks intimidating and carries himself in a way that makes the point. Pacer tries to ignore the ear-splitting sound, hoping the demonstration will be brief.

After a few minutes, it becomes apparent that the sound is here to stay. The passengers grow restless. The box drowns out Pacer's yells to turn it off. After several blocks, Pacer pulls the bus over and makes his way down the aisle to confront Docker. He signals Docker to turn off the box or get off the bus but is ignored. Pacer reaches over and flips the power switch off himself. The sudden silence brings a collective sigh from the bus. "Don't touch my box, man," Docker says, staring, as he flips the power back on and the box blares again. Pacer grabs the box, wrenching it from Docker's hands, and sprints for the front of the bus with Docker a half step behind. Docker catches up just as Pacer reaches the front. He reaches over Pacer's shoulder and gets a hand on the antenna. Pacer has been unable to flip the off switch so the box is still blaring, but when he jerks it from Docker's grasp it flies down the front steps, cracks open as it bounces off the bottom step, and falls to the pavement in pieces, terribly silent. With antenna in hand, Docker slowly steps down to the box, staring in disbelief. No one breathes. Docker bends over the pile but does not touch it. As he straightens, his face turns to a scowl. He fixes on Pacer. "I'm going to . . ." His words are lost as the doors close and the engine roars. He is seen running through the exhaust, antenna outstretched and waving, but the words are muffled. No one speaks for half a block. Finally a passenger in the last row yells up to Pacer, "I think he's saying that's not his stop." Does Pacer have a justification defense for his use of force against Docker in silencing Docker's box?

● DISCUSSION MATERIALS

Should the Criminal Law Allow the Shooting of a Fleeing Felon If It Is Necessary to Prevent Escape?

The readings begin with a Robinson and Darley study exploring community views on the citizen's law enforcement authority — specifically examining what liability the subjects would assign to a person who uses force (deadly and non-deadly) to apprehend a fleeing rapist or a person who damaged property — and comparing those views to the liability provided by the Model Penal Code. Next, in *Tennessee v. Garner*, the Supreme Court decision addressing the civil liability issues arising from the events of this Section's principal case, the Court evaluates the constitutionality of statutes authorizing police to use deadly force in the apprehension of fleeing, unarmed, non-violent felons. The majority and dissenting opinions provide the rationales on each side of the debate. In an interesting follow-up to the decision, Abraham Tennenbaum looks at the effects of the *Garner* case on police homicide rates and the benefits and cost of the changes in police procedure prompted by the decision.

Paul H. Robinson & John M. Darley, Study 7: Citizen's Law Enforcement Authority

Justice, Liability & Blame 72-73, 78-79 (1995)

Citizens sometimes seek to exercise the authority of a law enforcement officer, as when they attempt to apprehend a person who has committed a crime against them. If the use of force is defensive in any way—for example, an aggressor is attacking them or attempting to take their property—a citizen can rely on a defensive force defense, such as self-defense or defense of property, which frequently permits the use of greater force than would a citizen's law enforcement authority. If the use of force is not defensive, as when an offense is complete—for example, after a rape or after property damage has been caused—a citizen nonetheless has a right to use some degree of force to apprehend and restrain the offender. MPC §3.07(1).

Exercise of a citizen's law enforcement authority is subject to several limitations. A citizen is never justified in using deadly force to arrest an offender (unless he does so in assisting a peace officer and meets other special conditions). MPC §3.07(2)(b). A person may use non-deadly force only to the extent that it is immediately necessary to effect a lawful arrest. If he is mistaken in some respect, for instance about whether the person he is attempting to arrest is the actual perpetrator of the crime, he may nevertheless get a defense if his mistake is reasonable. If it is unreasonable, some jurisdictions deny any defense or mitigation while others permit a mitigation. In the latter jurisdictions, if the person recklessly or negligently injures an innocent person, for example, he may be liable for an offense of recklessness or negligence, as the case may be. MPC § 3.09(3). The Code does not alter the degree of non-deadly force permissible according to the seriousness of the offense for which the arrest is made; in all cases, the force must be just that which is necessary to effect the arrest.

The citizens' law enforcement authority study sought to test the current doctrine's rules on such authority against the community's views. Subjects were presented with scenarios involving the use of deadly and non-deadly force by the victim to restrain an offender after a rape and after a property damage offense (setting the victim's car on fire). Notice that in both cases the offense is already complete at the time force is used; thus we are not dealing with cases of self-defense or defense of property. The deadly force scenarios depict the victim as shooting the fleeing offender with a handgun and killing him; the non-deadly force scenarios involve the use of a stun gun, which would temporarily immobilize the offender but not inflict lasting injury on him. In some scenarios the person stuns or kills the offender and in others the person stuns or kills an innocent person that she mistakes for the offender. The subjects were asked . . . to determine how much liability the person should receive, if any. They were also asked how much force a person in such a situation should have been able to use, column (e) of Table 3.7, and whether the actual force used created a risk of death, column (f). The results are as follows:

Table 3.7 **Liability for Exercise of Citizens' Law Enforcement Authority**

Scenarios	(a) Liability	(b) % No Liability (N)	(c) % No Liability or No Punishment (N+Q)	(d) Model Panel Code Result	(e) Maximum Force That Should Be Permitted	(f) "Force Used Created Risk of Death"
Rape—Deadly force:						
1. Actual offender	0.21	65	90	Liable for murder	7.55	7.87
2. Mistaken identity	1.27	13	68	Liable for murder	6.87	7.82
Rape—Non-deadly force:						
3. Actual offender	0.00	83	100	Complete defense	6.85	2.92
4. Mistaken identity	0.35	30	83	Complete defense[a]	6.49	2.82
Property destructions— Deadly force:						
5. Actual offender	2.60	33	45	Liable for murder	4.39	8.08
6. Mistaken identity	3.27	8	43	Liable for murder	3.92	7.92
Property destruction— Nondeadly force:						
7. Actual offender	0.00	70	100	Complete defense	4.07	2.67
8. Mistaken identity	0.62	23	80	Complete defense[a]	4.00	2.90

Liability Scale: N = No criminal liability, 0 = Liability but no punishment, 1 = 1 day, 2 = 2 weeks, 3 = 2 months, 4 = 6 months, 5 = 1 year, 6 = 3 years, 7 = 7 years, 8 = 15 years, 9 = 30 years, 10 = life, and 11 = death.
Key to column heads:
(e) What is the maximum amount of force that a person should be permitted to use to detain an offender in this situation? 0 = no force, 2 = risk of bodily injury, 4 = bodily injury, 6 = serious bodily injury, 8 = serious bodily injury with risk of death, and 10 = death.
(f) The force used was likely to cause death or bodily injury: 1 = "strongly disagree," 5 = "unsure," and 9 = "strongly agree."
[a] This assumes that the individual was reckless. If the individual was reckless, the person could be liable for assault under MPC §§ 3.09(3) and 211.1(1).

Study 7: Summary

To summarize our general findings on force in citizen arrests: the subjects agree with the Code's defense for a citizen's use of non-deadly force to effect an arrest. They disagree, however, with the Code's position that a citizen may not, independent of an officer, use deadly force. Most would approve the use of deadly force to arrest a fleeing rapist. A large minority would take the same view even if the offender is fleeing from a property damage offense.

In general, the subjects are much more forgiving than the Code of a person's mistakes in using deadly force to affect a citizen's arrest. The Code imposes murder liability if the person kills an innocent person. A strong majority of the subjects, in contrast, impose no punishment even where the citizen kills an innocent person in trying to stop a fleeing rapist. Only where an innocent person is killed in an attempt to stop an offender fleeing from a property damage offense does a (bare) majority of subjects judge punishment to be appropriate and, there, liability is a few months rather than the murder liability that the Code provides. As the above discussion demonstrates, the difference in views between the rape and property damage cases reveals that many subjects take into account the seriousness of the offense in judging the amount of force permissible to make an arrest, while the Code does not.

We are surprised by these results. Although intuitively we expected that our respondents might judge the use of force by citizens to apprehend criminals more leniently than does the legal code, we did not expect the overwhelming magnitude of the differences we found. We had expected that the use of deadly force would be more widely condemned where, as here, the damage is already done and the force is being used aggressively (rather than defensively) to arrest the offender. This seems especially true where only damage to property is involved, but while our respondents do assign more liability to that case than to others, the liability assigned is very low.

Given these results, future research should test the generality of the leniency that the subjects display. Intuitively, one would expect that there must be limits on what sorts of mistake will generate these lenient patterns of liability. Surely one cannot egregiously mistake innocents for criminals and kill them with little or no liability. Furthermore, in the present scenarios, the respondents could believe that the person's primary goal in shooting the offender is to apprehend him rather than to kill him as deserved punishment. What if it were established instead that her primary purpose was otherwise? Would this receive such lenient treatment? Finally, our offenders were fleeing. Do people believe that the legal system would be successful in eventually apprehending the perpetrator? Do those people who believe that the police will not be able to apprehend the criminal believe that it is more acceptable for the victim to shoot the perpetrator as a kind of victim-administered vigilante justice? From the perspective of the legal code, whether the criminal justice system will catch the offender is an irrelevant factor, but it may not be to the community.

Tennessee v. Garner et al.

Supreme Court of the United States

471 U.S. 1, 105 S. Ct. 1694, 85 L. Ed. 2d 1, 1985 U.S. LEXIS 195, 53 U.S.L.W. 4410 (1985)

Justice White delivered the opinion of the Court.

This case requires us to determine the constitutionality of the use of deadly force to prevent the escape of an apparently unarmed suspected felon. We conclude that such force may not be used unless it is necessary to prevent the escape and the officer has probable cause to believe that the suspect poses a significant threat of death or serious physical injury to the officer or others. . . .

B

[N]otwithstanding probable cause to seize a suspect, an officer may not always do so by killing him. The intrusiveness of a seizure by means of deadly force is unmatched. The suspect's fundamental interest in his own life need not be elaborated upon. The use of deadly force also frustrates the interest of the individual, and of society, in judicial determination of guilt and punishment. Against these interests are ranged governmental interests in effective law enforcement. It is argued that overall violence will be reduced by encouraging the peaceful submission of suspects who know that they may be shot if they flee. Effectiveness in making arrests requires the resort to deadly force, or at least the meaningful threat thereof. "Being able to arrest such individuals is a condition precedent to the state's entire system of law enforcement." Brief for Petitioners 14.

In lamenting the inadequacy of later investigation, the dissent relies on the report of the President's Commission on Law Enforcement and Administration of Justice. It is worth noting that, notwithstanding its awareness of this problem, the Commission itself proposed a policy for use of deadly force arguably even more stringent than the formulation we adopt today. The Commission proposed that deadly force be used only to apprehend "perpetrators who, in the course of their crime threatened the use of deadly force, or if the officer believes there is a substantial risk that the person whose arrest is sought will cause death or serious bodily harm if his apprehension is delayed." In addition, the officer would have "to know, as a virtual certainty, that the suspect committed an offense for which the use of deadly force is permissible."

Without in any way disparaging the importance of these goals, we are not convinced that the use of deadly force is a sufficiently productive means of accomplishing them to justify the killing of nonviolent suspects. The use of deadly force is a self-defeating way of apprehending a suspect and so setting the criminal justice mechanism in motion. If successful, it guarantees that that mechanism will not be set in motion. And while the meaningful threat of deadly force might be thought to lead to the arrest of more live suspects by discouraging escape attempts, the presently available evidence does not support this thesis. The fact is that a majority of police departments in this country have forbidden the use of deadly force against nonviolent suspects. If those charged with the enforcement of the criminal law have abjured the use of deadly force in arresting nondangerous felons, there is a substantial basis for doubting that the use of such force is an essential attribute of the arrest power in all felony cases. Petitioners and appellant have not persuaded us that shooting nondangerous fleeing suspects is so vital as to outweigh the suspect's interest in his own life.

We note that the usual manner of deterring illegal conduct—through punishment—has been largely ignored in connection with flight from arrest. Arkansas, for example, specifically excepts flight from arrest from the offense of "obstruction of governmental operations." The commentary notes that this "reflects the basic policy judgment that, absent the use of force or violence, a mere attempt to avoid apprehension by a law enforcement officer does not give rise to an independent offense." In the few States that do outlaw flight from an arresting officer, the crime is only a misdemeanor. Even forceful resistance, though generally a separate offense, is classified as a misdemeanor.

This lenient approach does avoid the anomaly of automatically transforming every fleeing misdemeanant into a fleeing felon — subject, under the common-law rule, to apprehension by deadly force — solely by virtue of his flight. However, it is in real tension with the harsh consequences of flight in cases where deadly force is employed. For example, Tennessee does not outlaw fleeing from arrest. The Memphis City Code does, § 22-34.1 (Supp. 17, 1971), subjecting the offender to a maximum fine of $50, § 1-8 (1967). Thus, Garner's attempted escape subjected him to (a) a $50 fine, and (b) being shot.

The use of deadly force to prevent the escape of all felony suspects, whatever the circumstances, is constitutionally unreasonable. It is not better that all felony suspects die than that they escape. Where the suspect poses no immediate threat to the officer and no threat to others, the harm resulting from failing to apprehend him does not justify the use of deadly force to do so. It is no doubt unfortunate when a suspect who is in sight escapes, but the fact that the police arrive a little late or are a little slower afoot does not always justify killing the suspect. A police officer may not seize an unarmed, nondangerous suspect by shooting him dead. The Tennessee statute is unconstitutional insofar as it authorizes the use of deadly force against such fleeing suspects.

It is not, however, unconstitutional on its face. Where the officer has probable cause to believe that the suspect poses a threat of serious physical harm, either to the officer or to others, it is not constitutionally unreasonable to prevent escape by using deadly force. Thus, if the suspect threatens the officer with a weapon or there is probable cause to believe that he has committed a crime involving the infliction or threatened infliction of serious physical harm, deadly force may be used if necessary to prevent escape, and if, where feasible, some warning has been given. As applied in such circumstances, the Tennessee statute would pass constitutional muster. . . .

Justice O'Connor, with whom the Chief Justice and Justice Rehnquist join, dissenting.

The Court today holds that the Fourth Amendment prohibits a police officer from using deadly force as a last resort to apprehend a criminal suspect who refuses to halt when fleeing the scene of a nighttime burglary. This conclusion rests on the majority's balancing of the interests of the suspect and the public interest in effective law enforcement. Notwithstanding the venerable common-law rule authorizing the use of deadly force if necessary to apprehend a fleeing felon, and continued acceptance of this rule by nearly half the States, the majority concludes that Tennessee's statute is unconstitutional inasmuch as it allows the use of such force to apprehend a burglary suspect who is not obviously armed or otherwise dangerous. Although the circumstances of this case are unquestionably tragic and unfortunate, our constitutional holdings must be sensitive both to the history of the Fourth Amendment and to the general implications of the Court's reasoning. By disregarding the serious and dangerous nature of residential burglaries and the longstanding practice of many States, the Court effectively creates a Fourth Amendment right allowing a burglary suspect to flee unimpeded from a police officer who has probable cause to arrest, who has ordered the suspect to halt, and who has no means short of firing his weapon to prevent escape. I do not believe that the Fourth Amendment supports such a right, and I accordingly dissent. . . .

II

For purposes of Fourth Amendment analysis, I agree with the Court that Officer Hymon "seized" Garner by shooting him. Whether that seizure was reasonable and therefore permitted by the Fourth Amendment requires a careful balancing of the important public interest in crime prevention and detection and the nature and quality of the intrusion upon legitimate interests of the individual. In striking this balance here, it is crucial to acknowledge that police use of deadly force to apprehend a fleeing criminal suspect falls within the "rubric of police conduct . . . necessarily [involving] swift action predicated upon the on-the-spot observations of the officer on the beat." The clarity of hindsight cannot provide the standard for judging the reasonableness of police decisions made in uncertain and often dangerous circumstances. Moreover, I am far more reluctant than is the Court to conclude that the Fourth Amendment proscribes a police practice that was accepted at the time of the adoption of the Bill of Rights and has continued to receive the support of many state legislatures. Although the Court has recognized that the requirements of the Fourth Amendment must respond to the reality of social and technological change, fidelity to the notion of *constitutional*—as opposed to purely judicial—limits on governmental action requires us to impose a heavy burden on those who claim that practices accepted when the Fourth Amendment was adopted are now constitutionally impermissible.

The public interest involved in the use of deadly force as a last resort to apprehend a fleeing burglary suspect relates primarily to the serious nature of the crime. Household burglaries not only represent the illegal entry into a person's home, but also "[pose] real risk of serious harm to others." According to recent Department of Justice statistics, "[three-fifths] of all rapes in the home, three-fifths of all home robberies, and about a third of home aggravated and simple assaults are committed by burglars." During the period 1973-1982, 2.8 million such violent crimes were committed in the course of burglaries. Victims of a forcible intrusion into their home by a nighttime prowler will find little consolation in the majority's confident assertion that "burglaries only rarely involve physical violence." Moreover, even if a particular burglary, when viewed in retrospect, does not involve physical harm to others, the "harsh potentialities for violence" inherent in the forced entry into a home preclude characterization of the crime as "innocuous, inconsequential, minor, or 'nonviolent.'"

Because burglary is a serious and dangerous felony, the public interest in the prevention and detection of the crime is of compelling importance. Where a police officer has probable cause to arrest a suspected burglar, the use of deadly force as a last resort might well be the only means of apprehending the suspect. With respect to a particular burglary, subsequent investigation simply cannot represent a substitute for immediate apprehension of the criminal suspect at the scene. Indeed, the Captain of the Memphis Police Department testified that in his city, if apprehension is not immediate, it is likely that the suspect will not be caught. Although some law enforcement agencies may choose to assume the risk that a criminal will remain at large, the Tennessee statute reflects a legislative determination that the use of deadly force in prescribed circumstances will serve generally to protect the public. Such statutes assist the police in apprehending suspected perpetrators of serious crimes and provide notice that a lawful police order to stop and submit to arrest may not be ignored with impunity.

The Court unconvincingly dismisses the general deterrence effects by stating that "the presently available evidence does not support [the] thesis" that the threat of force discourages escape and that "there is a substantial basis for doubting that the use of such force is an essential attribute to the arrest power in all felony cases." There is no question that the effectiveness of police use of deadly force is arguable and that many States or individual police departments have decided not to authorize it in circumstances similar to those presented here. But it should go without saying that the effectiveness or popularity of a particular police practice does not determine its constitutionality. Moreover, the fact that police conduct pursuant to a state statute is challenged on constitutional grounds does not impose a burden on the State to produce social science statistics or to dispel any possible doubts about the necessity of the conduct. This observation, I believe, has particular force where the challenged practice both predates enactment of the Bill of Rights and continues to be accepted by a substantial number of the States.

Against the strong public interests justifying the conduct at issue here must be weighed the individual interests implicated in the use of deadly force by police officers. The majority declares that "[the] suspect's fundamental interest in his own life need not be elaborated upon." This blithe assertion hardly provides an adequate substitute for the majority's failure to acknowledge the distinctive manner in which the suspect's interest in his life is even exposed to risk. For purposes of this case, we must recall that the police officer, in the course of investigating a nighttime burglary, had reasonable cause to arrest the suspect and ordered him to halt. The officer's use of force resulted because the suspected burglar refused to heed this command and the officer reasonably believed that there was no means short of firing his weapon to apprehend the suspect. Without questioning the importance of a person's interest in his life, I do not think this interest encompasses a right to flee unimpeded from the scene of a burglary. The legitimate interests of the suspect in these circumstances are adequately accommodated by the Tennessee statute: to avoid the use of deadly force and the consequent risk to his life, the suspect need merely obey the valid order to halt.

A proper balancing of the interests involved suggests that use of deadly force as a last resort to apprehend a criminal suspect fleeing from the scene of a nighttime burglary is not unreasonable within the meaning of the Fourth Amendment. Admittedly, the events giving rise to this case are in retrospect deeply regrettable. No one can view the death of an unarmed and apparently nonviolent 15-year-old without sorrow, much less disapproval. Nonetheless, the reasonableness of Officer Hymon's conduct for purposes of the Fourth Amendment cannot be evaluated by what later appears to have been a preferable course of police action. The officer pursued a suspect in the darkened backyard of a house that from all indications had just been burglarized. The police officer was not certain whether the suspect was alone or unarmed; nor did he know what had transpired inside the house. He ordered the suspect to halt, and when the suspect refused to obey and attempted to flee into the night, the officer fired his weapon to prevent escape. The reasonableness of this action for purposes of the Fourth Amendment is not determined by the unfortunate nature of this particular case; instead, the question is whether it is constitutionally impermissible for police officers, as a last resort, to shoot a burglary suspect fleeing the scene of the crime.

Other Discussion Materials

Abraham N. Tennenbaum, The Influence of the *Garner* Decision on Police Use of Deadly Force

85 Journal of Criminal Law & Criminology 241-242, 257-260 (1994)

I. Introduction

People have criticized use of deadly force ever since police officers began carrying guns. . . .

In March of 1985, the United States Supreme Court, in *Tennessee v. Garner,* held that laws authorizing police use of deadly force to apprehend fleeing, unarmed, non-violent felony suspects violate the Fourth Amendment, and therefore states should eliminate them. This paper investigates the impact of the *Garner* decision on homicides committed by police nationwide. . . .

IV. Discussion

a. The Facts

Three conclusions seem to be self-evident from the data presented here. The first, and most important one is that *Garner* had a clear effect on justifiable police homicides. It reduced the total number of police homicides by approximately sixty homicides a year (more than sixteen percent). Second, *Garner* had an influence in both unconstitutional states and constitutional states. The magnitude of the reduction, however, was greater in unconstitutional states. Finally, *Garner* influenced not only a reduction in the number of police shootings of fleeing felons, but of all shootings, even those that are not correlated to defending life. This conclusion, however, needs more empirical support before it can be unequivocally accepted.

b. Why Did the Garner Decision Have Such an Impact?

The impact of *Garner* is surprising. Even before *Garner,* many police departments had already restricted their guidelines, and repealed the Any-Felony Rule. Accordingly, observers did not expect *Garner* to have such a dramatic impact.

A recent study on the influence of the *Garner* decision on the Memphis Police Department (MPD) may explain this phenomenon. Sparger & Giacopassi investigated MPD shootings in three different periods: 1969-1974; 1980-1984; 1985-1989. They concluded that *Garner* definitely reduced police shootings. Even though Memphis' policy before *Garner* was consistent with the Supreme Court's decision, the police restricted the policy even further after the decision. In fact, the policy after *Garner* emphasized "that deadly force should be used only as a last resort to protect life, not merely to apprehend fleeing dangerous felons."

... This tendency by police departments to restrict their shooting guidelines beyond legal requirements is not a new one. Kenneth Matulia, who conducted a survey among fifty-seven big city police departments, wrote that "the individual police department rules... generally place a more restrictive standard of conduct than permitted by law." Professors Geller and Scott also described a tendency in law enforcement agencies to move towards guidelines which were more restrictive than *Garner* required.

Thus, the adoption of more restricted policies by police departments nationwide after the Court's decision in *Garner* seems to have caused the reduction in police homicides. This is consistent with the evidence that restricted policies can reduce police shootings, and therefore police homicides. The magnitude of the change can explain the differences in reduction between the unconstitutional states (23.8% reduction in police homicides), and the constitutional states (12.96% reduction). The modifications which should have been made in department policies were higher in states that had the Any-Felony Rule than in states which did not. As a result, *Garner's* influence was more accentuated in the unconstitutional states.

The self-restrictions on police behavior concerning deadly force were not only the result of good will but were also a political necessity. Police shootings of civilians have huge social costs, including riots. This has happened not only in the United States but in other nations too, and it is almost anticipated in some neighborhoods. Aside from public disturbances, police use of deadly force often spawns civil lawsuits. The fear of riots and law suits may explain why mayors and police chiefs prefer to severely limit the instances in which their officers may use deadly force.

In sum, the *Garner* decision seems to have reduced police homicides directly (by reducing police shooting at fleeing felons), and indirectly (by influencing police departments to reduce and modify their guidelines beyond *Garner* to appear just and sensitive to the public). As a result, all police shooting unrelated to protecting life seems to be declining.

c. Some Undesirable Outcomes

Until the 1960s, the number of homicides in the United States was relatively stable. There were fewer homicides then [than] there are today, and the percentage of homicides which qualified as justifiable (by police or civilians) was much higher than today. As Professor Brearley wrote in 1932, "it may be safely concluded that justifiable homicides comprise from one-fourth to one-third of the total number of slayings."

These statistics suggest that the more society views police and civilian homicides as justifiable, the more criminals these homicides deter. Professor Cloninger investigated the connection between police homicides and the crime rate in fifty cities. He found that non-homicide violent crime rates are inversely related to the police's lethal response rate, and concluded that police use of deadly force has a deterrent effect on the crime rate.

Further, police officers believe that the threat of deadly force deters felony criminals, and that harsh statutory limitations on police discretion is dangerous. In fact, some officers have already complained that the *Garner* decision, and resulting restrictive practices, have made their work frustrating and more dangerous.

Arguably, Justice O'Connor recognized this concern in her dissenting opinion: "I cannot accept the majority's creation of a constitutional right to flight for burglary suspects seeking to avoid capture at the scene of the crime." The majority of the Court considered this concern, but decided that the deterrent effect does not justify the risk of unnecessary police homicides. While the data is not sufficient to answer the empirical questions, the possibility that the Court's decision in *Garner* eroded the deterrent effect of police homicide should be considered in any evaluation of *Garner*'s influence.

Mistake as to a Justification

The previous three Sections have addressed the conditions under which a person's conduct is actually, objectively justified — that is, the conditions under which the law would be happy to have (or at least tolerant of having) the person and other persons engage in the same conduct under the same circumstances in the future. But it is commonly the case that a person is mistaken in the belief that his or her conduct is justified, typically because he or she misperceives the actual situation. When should such mistaken justification be a defense and what kind of defense should it be — a justification or an excuse?

◆ THE CASE OF RICHARD JOHN JAHNKE, JR.

Richard Jahnke, Jr., is a 16-year old R.O.T.C. student in Laramie, Wyoming, a handsome, sensitive, all-American boy who has never been in trouble. Lately, however, Jahnke has been doing poorly in school. The problem is the cumulative effect of years of physical and mental abuse at the hands of his father. Himself a victim of child abuse, Richard Jahnke, Sr., is cruel and insensitive, and is a bully to his family and has been for years. As a result, his son is frequently on edge, and feels as though he lives in a state of near-constant danger.

The beatings are torturous. His father punches his back, slaps his head, and slams him into whatever surface is nearby. Jahnke has asthma, and his father commonly beats him to make him stop coughing. A beating also can be triggered by his not finishing his food. (The children eat with plastic forks because the father thinks metal ones are too loud.) Jahnke's mother recalls that her husband was once a caring young soldier. He is now an I.R.S. investigator, and things are quite different.

One of Jahnke's early memories is of his father breaking a toy boat when Jahnke was five. With the father screaming and chasing his young son, Jahnke's mother stepped in to shield him from the blows. The father then beat his mother, while calling her a "slut" and a "spic". Jahnke, beaten almost daily, felt that his father enjoyed it. His father would whip him with a belt simply for walking with his mouth open, and hit him even harder if he cried.

When Jahnke was ten, he found it particularly painful and difficult to watch his father beat his mother. His father would pin his mother to the ground and continually hit her while she pleaded and cried. Jahnke finally rallied to her defense. His father then beat him badly, pinning him to the ground, punching him on his head and back and whipping him with a belt.

As Jahnke grew up, the beatings came slightly less frequently, though they were still violent. His father had become preoccupied with his older sister, Deborah. He began watching her in the shower and rubbing her breasts and groping her as discipline. He also lay on top of her when she went to bed. Jahnke is disgusted with the abuse and has discussed it with his mother. She responds by getting angry at Deborah, telling her it is her own fault for wearing shorts. At the same time, his mother is afraid of her husband and fears that he may kill Jahnke if he voices dissent about his father's treatment of Deborah.

Jahnke knows his father always carries a gun — when answering the door, in the bathroom, sitting on the couch, even in the middle of the night. (On one occasion, Jahnke got up to get food at 10 p.m. and found himself staring down the barrel of the gun). He becomes increasingly scared for both his safety and that of his mother and sister. On a recent hunting trip, Jahnke's father tells him he is going to lose it one day and kill Jahnke. Jahnke is afraid to tell his teachers and friends about the rampant abuse, but his feelings of desperation are building.

On the afternoon of May 2, 1982, Jahnke's father gets irritated about something and begins to mercilessly beat Jahnke. When he is finished, he shoves him down the stairs and orders him to clean the basement, his usual chore. Jahnke obeys and begins to clean. He is startled, however, when he hears his father stomping down the stairs. Ever since he was little, Jahnke has associated his father's stomping with an imminent severe beating. Jahnke's fears are realized; his father starts punching him again. Jahnke begins to cry, overcome by pain and helplessness. He runs from the house and reports his father to the sheriff. The sheriff sets up a meeting with a police officer and a social worker and the rest of Jahnke's family. After a short discussion, everyone is sent home. As soon as they arrive at home, Jahnke's father says he will never forgive Jahnke for snitching on him.

Jahnke begins putting a chair in front of his bedroom door at night. His father does not beat him for a week, but then he starts again, increasing the frequency of the beatings to every day.

By Saturday, Jahnke has become desperate. That morning, his father beats Jahnke's sister for not combing her hair. After she is thoroughly battered, he puts his hands down her pants while Jahnke's mother is in the room. She ignores the scene and keeps cooking. Jahnke decides he needs to do something. As his father grabs his sister by the hair and starts to beat her again, Jahnke tells him to leave her alone. For a moment he feels a sense of pride for standing up for Deborah, but he soon pays the price. His father chases him and beats him instead. Later, badly hurt and upset, Jahnke begins to consider shooting his father as the only way to stop the brutality.

A few days later, Jahnke asks his mother for a ride to his school's open house. His mother gets angry with him. She tells Jahnke that she blames him for ruining her marriage. Jahnke, hurt and angered by the rebuke, tells her to shut up. His mother responds angrily by throwing a can of dog food at him, hitting him squarely on the head.

When Jahnke's father gets home, Jahnke's mother tells him that Jahnke sassed her. Cursing, the father starts to beat Jahnke, saying he is disgusted with the way Jahnke turned out and will find a way to get rid of him. His language is interspersed with cursing. His sister tries to intervene but the father screams at her to get out, calling her "a bitchy pimple face." Jahnke's father gets his gun, turns back to his son, punches him again, and warns Jahnke that he had better not be there when he returns. Jahnke's parents leave for dinner to celebrate the anniversary of the day they met.

Figure 96 **Richard John Jahnke, Jr., circa 1984**
(AP)

Jahnke is distraught. Deborah is hysterical. Jahnke feels he must do something to protect his sister and mother, but feels trapped. He thinks that the sheriff will not take his allegations seriously and that his teachers would leak the embarrassing information to his peers. He can think of no one who will help him. (At their celebration dinner, Jahnke's father is telling his mother how much he hates his children and is disappointed in them.)

Jahnke concludes that the only way to prevent a serious beating, perhaps to death, on his father's return is to kill his father first. (Jahnke's mother wonders during dinner whether her husband's threat might have meant more than simply kicking Jahnke out of the house.)

Jahnke changes his clothes to something less visible and places weapons throughout the house in case his initial attempt fails. In all, he has two shotguns, three rifles, a .38 caliber pistol, and a marine knife. He gives his sister a gun and quickly shows her how to use it. He feels it is important that she be protected even if his attempt fails. Jahnke puts the family pets into the basement so they will not be hurt. He goes to the garage, closes the door and waits, selecting a spot where he cannot be seen but can see the driveway. His parents return from their romantic dinner at 6:30 p.m. As his father steps out of the car, Jahnke experiences a moment of hesitation. Part of him wants to run to his father and tell him that he loves him. But he remembers past attempts at reconciliation, all of which ended in the same way—with a violent beating.

The sound of his father's heavy steps jars him back, reminding him of the prelude to countless incidents of violence. With his twelve-gauge shotgun in one hand and his R.O.T.C. whistle in the other, Jahnke musters his courage. He blows the whistle for strength and opens fire as soon as he sees his father's head. He fires six shots, hitting his father four times. Jahnke later recalls that every shot at his father pained him (Jahnke). The most damaging shot hits in the chest and passes through his rib cage, lungs, liver, heart, and esophagus before ending up embedded in his back. Jahnke leaves his mother screaming in the driveway and runs into the house to get his sister. They go out a back window and run for a while, then go their separate ways. Jahnke ends up at his girlfriend's house, where he tells her father that he killed his father for revenge. His sister goes to a local mall. His father is pronounced dead one hour after the encounter.

1. Relying only on your own intuitions of justice, what liability and punishment, if any, does Richard Jahnke, Jr., deserve?

N	0	1	2	3	4	5	6	7	8	9	10	11
☐	☐	☐	☐	☐	☐	☐	☐	☐	☐	☐	☐	☐
no liability	liability but no punishment	1 day	2 wks	2 mo	6 mo	1 yr	3 yrs	7 yrs	15 yrs	30 yrs	life imprison- ment	death

2. What liability, if any, under the then-existing statutes?
3. What liability, if any, under the Model Penal Code?

■ THE LAW

Wyoming Statutes
(1982)

Chapter 4. Offenses Against the Person

Article 1. Homicide

Section 6-4-101. Murder in the First Degree

(a) Whoever purposely and with premeditated malice, or in the perpetration of, or attempt to perpetrate any rape, sexual assault, arson, robbery or burglary, or by administering poison or causing the same to be done, kills any human being, or whoever purposely and with premeditated malice kills any peace officer, correction employee or fireman acting in the line of duty, is guilty of murder in the first degree.

(b) A person convicted of murder in the first degree shall be punished by death or life imprisonment according to the law.

Section 6-4-102. Presentence Hearing for Murder in the First Degree; Mitigating and Aggravating Circumstances

(a) Upon conviction of a person for murder in the first degree the judge shall conduct a separate sentencing hearing to determine whether the defendant should be sentenced to death or life imprisonment. The hearing shall be conducted before the judge alone if:

(i) The defendant was convicted by a judge sitting without a jury;

(ii) The defendant has pled guilty; or

(iii) The defendant waives a jury with respect to the sentence.

(b) In all other cases the sentencing hearing shall be conducted before the jury which determined the defendant's guilt or, if the judge for good cause shown discharges the jury, with a new jury impaneled for that purpose.

(c) The judge or jury shall hear evidence as to any matter that the court deems relevant to a determination of the sentence, and shall include matters relating to any of the aggravating or mitigating circumstances enumerated in subsections (h) and (j) of this section. Any evidence which the court deems to have probative value may be received regardless of its admissibility under the exclusionary rules of evidence, provided the defendant is accorded a fair opportunity to rebut any hearsay statements, and provided further that only such evidence in aggravation as the state has made known to the defendant or his counsel prior to his trial shall be admissible.

(d) Upon conclusion of the evidence and arguments the judge shall give the jury appropriate instructions, including instructions as to any aggravating or mitigating circumstances, as defined in subsections (h) and (j) of this section, or proceed as provided by paragraph (ii) of this subsection:

(i) After hearing all the evidence, the jury shall deliberate and render a recommendation of sentence to the judge, based upon the following:

(A) Whether one (1) or more sufficient aggravating circumstances exist as set forth in subsection (h) of this section;

(B) Whether sufficient mitigating circumstances exist as set forth in subsection (j) of this section which outweigh the aggravation circumstances found to exist; and

(C) Based upon these considerations, whether the defendant should be sentenced to death or life imprisonment.

(ii) In nonjury cases, the judge shall determine if any aggravating or mitigating circumstances exist and impose sentence within the limits prescribed by law, based upon the considerations enumerated in (A), (B), and (C) of this subsection.

(e) The death penalty shall not be imposed unless at least one (1) of the aggravating circumstances set forth in subsection (h) of this section is found. The jury, if its verdict is a recommendation of death, shall designate in writing signed by the foreman of the jury the aggravating circumstance or circumstances which it found beyond a reasonable doubt. In nonjury cases the judge shall make such a designation. If the jury cannot, within a reasonable time, agree on the punishment to be imposed, the judge shall impose a life sentence.

(f) Unless the jury trying the case recommends the death sentence in its verdict, the judge shall not sentence the defendant to death but shall sentence the defendant to life imprisonment as provided by law. Where a recommendation of death is made, the court shall sentence the defendant to death.

(g) If the trial court is reversed on appeal because of error only in the presentence hearing, the new trial which may be ordered shall apply only to the issue of punishment.

(h) Aggravating circumstances are limited to the following:

(i) The murder was committed by a person under sentence of imprisonment;

(ii) The defendant was previously convicted of another murder in the first degree or a felony involving the use or threat of violence to the person;

(iii) The defendant knowingly created a great risk of death to two (2) or more persons;

(iv) The murder was committed while the defendant was engaged, or was an accomplice, in the commission of, or an attempt to commit, or flight after committing or attempting to commit, robbery, rape, sexual assault, arson, burglary, kidnapping, or aircraft piracy or the unlawful throwing, placing, or discharging of a destructive device or bomb;

(v) The murder was committed for the purpose of avoiding or preventing a lawful arrest or effecting an escape from custody;

(vi) The murder was committed for pecuniary gain;

(vii) The murder was especially heinous, atrocious, or cruel;

(viii) The murder of a judicial officer, former judicial officer, district attorney, former district attorney, or former county and prosecuting attorney, during or because of the exercise of his official duty.

(j) Mitigating circumstances shall be the following:

(i) The defendant has no significant history of prior criminal activity;

(ii) The murder was committed while the defendant was under the influence of extreme mental or emotional disturbance;

(iii) The victim was a participant in the defendant's conduct or consented to the act;

(iv) The defendant was an accomplice in a murder committed by another person and his participation in the homicidal act was relatively minor;

(v) The defendant acted under extreme duress or under the substantial domination of another person;

(vi) The capacity of the defendant to appreciate the criminality of his conduct or to conform his conduct to the requirements of law was substantially impaired;

(vii) The age of the defendant at the time of the crime.

Section 6-4-104. Murder in the Second Degree

Whoever purposely and maliciously, but without premeditation, kills any human being, is guilty of murder in the second degree, and shall be imprisoned in the penitentiary for any term not less then twenty (20) years, or during life.

Section 6-4-107. Manslaughter

Whoever unlawfully kills any human being without malice, expressed or implied, either voluntarily, upon the sudden heat of passion, or involuntarily, but in commission of some unlawful act, except as provided in W.S. 31-5-1117 [Homicide by vehicle; aggravated homicide by vehicle; penalties], or by any culpable neglect or criminal carelessness, is guilty of manslaughter, and shall be imprisoned in the penitentiary not more than twenty (20) years.

Chapter 1. General Provisions
Article 2. Conspiracy

Section 6-1-203. Conspiracy

(a) A person is guilty of conspiracy to commit a crime if he agrees with one (1) or more persons to commit a crime and he or another person does an overt act to effect the object of the agreement.

(b) A person is not liable under this section if after conspiring he withdraws from the conspiracy under circumstances manifesting voluntary and complete renunciation of his criminal intention.

(c) A conspiracy may be prosecuted in the county where the agreement was entered into, or in any county where any act evidencing the conspiracy or furthering the purpose took place.

Section 6-1-204. Penalty

The penalty for attempt, solicitation, and conspiracy is the same as the penalty for the most serious offense which is attempted, solicited or is an object of the conspiracy except that an attempt, solicitation or conspiracy to commit a capital crime is not punishable by the death penalty if the capital crime is not committed.

Loy v. State
26 Wy. 381, 185 P. 796 (1919)

The defendant was convicted of murder in the first degree and sentenced to imprisonment in the penitentiary for life. The defendant was a white guest of a hotel in Laramie who shot an African-American porter during a brief altercation. The court approved the following jury instruction given to the jury regarding premeditation:

> The word "premeditated," as used in the information and in the statute, means to think beforehand. It implies an interval, however brief, between the formation of the intent or design and the commission of the act. To find the defendant guilty of murder in the first degree, you must find from the evidence beyond a reasonable doubt that he killed the deceased purposely and with premeditated malice as herein defined. But it is not necessary that such premeditation should have existed in the mind of the defendant for any particular length of time before the killing; it is sufficient if he has deliberately formed in his mind a determination to kill and has thought over it before the shot was fired.... It is the fixed, deliberate, premeditated intention to kill which characterizes the crime of murder in the first degree, and the premeditated malice mentioned in the information need only be such deliberation and thought as enable a person to appreciate and understand at the time the act is committed the nature of the act and its probable results.

The defendant claimed that the porter approached him in a threatening way while touching his coat pocket. In response, the defendant pulled out a gun and shot the victim, as he claimed, in self-defense. The court affirmed his conviction and held that self-defense was permitted as a justification for murder when the "Defendant...not only believe[s] he is in danger, but the circumstances must be such as to afford reasonable grounds for the belief." In this case, the circumstances did not afford such reasonable grounds for his belief.

Ross v. State
57 P. 924 (Wyo. 1899)

The defendant was charged with first-degree murder, but convicted of second-degree murder and sentenced to life imprisonment for the shooting death of a competitor saloon owner. While the facts were in dispute, it was clear that the defendant had attempted to provoke the decedent with insults and disparaging remarks, and that his actions resulted in either a gun battle between the men or the defendant's unprovoked shooting of the decedent. The state's evidence showed that the decedent was unarmed. The defendant appealed his conviction and charged that the trial court erred by permitting a jury instruction as to implied malice. The supreme court affirmed the lower court's decision and held that the instruction that "[t]hough there was no premeditation, a charge that 'malice is implied from any deliberate and cool act done against another, however sudden, which shows an abandoned and malignant heart, and where one person assaults another with a deadly weapon in such a manner as is likely to cause death, although he had no previous malice or ill will against the party assaulted, yet he is presumed, in law, to have such malice at the moment of the assault, and, if death result therefrom, it is murder,' was not erroneous, as authorizing a conviction of murder in the first degree."

State v. Helton
73 Wyo. 92, 115, 276 P.2d 434, 442 (1954)

In reversing a conviction for murder and entering a judgement for voluntary manslaughter for the defendant's shooting of her husband, the court explained the offense of voluntary manslaughter in this way:

> Our laws recognize an intermediate crime lying someplace between the excusable, justifiable or privileged killing of a human being, and the unlawful taking of a life with malice [i.e., murder]. [W]e find in our law, that the intentional (i.e., voluntary) doing of the wrongful act, "upon a sudden heat of passion," although completely free of express, implied, constructive or legal malice, but committed without legal excuse, privilege or justification, is a punishable crime which we call voluntary manslaughter. This simply recognizes that there may be circumstances surrounding a killing which...while not producing that degree of mental disturbance or aberration of the mind which is necessary in law to excuse the homicide, still leaves the mind devoid of that wicked, evil and unlawful purpose, or of that wilful disregard of the rights of others which is implied in the term "malice". Such circumstances mitigate or extenuate the act and make the homicide a crime of lesser degree. The "sudden heat of passion" contemplated by our voluntary manslaughter statute is descriptive of just such a state of mind, and it may occur from any emotional excitement of such intensity that it temporarily obscures reason, or leaves the mind bereft of reason.

Foley v. State
72 P. 627 (Wyo. 1903)

The defendant was convicted of second degree murder and appealed on an issue of error by the trial court for admitting hearsay testimony. Within its opinion, the court defined a defense for mistaken self-defense: "[h]omicide is justifiable on the ground of self-defense where the slayer, in the careful and proper use of his faculties, bona fide believes, and has reasonable ground to believe, that he is in imminent danger of death or great bodily harm, and that his only means of escape from such danger will be by taking the life of his assailant, although in fact he is mistaken as to the existence or imminence of the danger."

Harries v. State
650 P.2d 273 (Wyo. 1982)

The defendant was convicted of use of a weapon to commit assault and battery on another. He had been involved in a bar fight during which he was struck by an unknown assailant. He retaliated with a shot to the leg of a third party. He then went for a weapon in his friend's truck, pulled out a gun, and fired it when a third party tried to take the weapon from him. He claimed a reasonable belief that actions were justified as self-defense and defense of others based on the third party's movements toward him during the scuffle. The court dismissed his defense-of-others argument because it had not been raised at trial. It affirmed his conviction despite his self-defense claim because the defendant's belief was not one that an objectively reasonable person would hold. The court affirmed the trial court's jury instruction that the elements of self-defense required that the defendant have "reasonable grounds for believing and does believe that bodily injury is about to be inflicted upon him. In doing so he may use all force and means which he believes to be necessary and which would appear to a reasonable person, in the same or similar circumstances, to be necessary to prevent the injury which appears to be imminent." (Quoting Instruction No. 10; Wyoming Pattern Jury Instructions, Criminal, 5.208.) The court further held that "[t]o justify acting in self-defense, it is not necessary that the danger was real, or that the danger was impending and immediate, so long as the defendant had reasonable cause to believe and did believe these facts. If these two requirements are met, acting in self-defense was justified even though there was no intention on the part of the other person to do him harm, nor any impending and immediate danger, nor the actual necessity for acting in self-defense." (Quoting Instruction No. 11; Wyoming Pattern Jury Instructions Criminal, 5.210.)

Delaney v. State
14 Wyo. 1, 81 P. 792 (1905)

Defendant was found guilty of assault with intent to murder one Stark. Because he was in his own home at the time of the assault, he objected to the following jury instruction, on the ground that it violated his right not to have to retreat from his own house before using deadly force:

> If you find from the evidence that the defendant could have retired to a place of safety before Stark reached his gun, then it was his duty to have done so, and he was not justified in shooting Stark because he may have believed that Stark was going after his gun. To justify the use of a deadly weapon by the defendant when an assault has been made upon him, the circumstances must

appear to be such that there is no other reasonable means of escape from death or great bodily harm.

The court rejects the claim and affirms the conviction, saying:

> Having been the aggressor, the defendant placed himself in the attitude of one who assaults another on the highway, and upon whom the law imposes the duty of withdrawing in good faith from, and not for the purpose of renewing, the assault, before he can justify shooting his adversary on the ground of self-defense.

Model Penal Code
(Official Draft 1962)

Section 3.09. Mistake of Law as to Unlawfulness of Force or Legality of Arrest; Reckless or Negligent Use of Otherwise Justifiable Force; Reckless or Negligent Injury or Risk of Injury to Innocent Persons

(1) The justification afforded by Sections 3.04 to 3.07, inclusive, is unavailable when:

    (a) the actor's belief in the unlawfulness of the force or conduct against which he employs protective force or his belief in the lawfulness of an arrest which he endeavors to effect by force is erroneous; and

    (b) his error is due to ignorance or mistake as to the provisions of the Code, any other provision of the criminal law or the law governing the legality of an arrest or search.

(2) When the actor believes that the use of force upon or toward the person of another is necessary for any of the purposes for which such belief would establish a justification under Sections 3.03 to 3.08 but the actor is reckless or negligent in having such belief or in acquiring or failing to acquire any knowledge or belief which is material to the justiciability of his use of force, the justification afforded by those Sections is unavailable in a prosecution for an offense for which recklessness or negligence, as the case may be, suffices to establish culpability.

(3) When the actor is justified under Sections 3.03 to 3.08 in using force upon or toward the person of another but he recklessly or negligently injures or creates a risk of injury to innocent persons, the justification afforded by those Sections is unavailable in a prosecution for such recklessness or negligence towards innocent persons.

Section 2.10. Military Orders

It is an affirmative defense that the actor, in engaging in the conduct charged to constitute an offense, does no more than execute an order of his superior in the armed services which he does not know to be unlawful.

▲ PROBLEM
Moro's Mistake

Moro loves to play the horses. And "Snake," a local mobster, loves it when he does. Moro is so far in the hole to Snake that he can hardly cover the vig (the interest) each week. Snake has been less than happy as of late, however, because Moro has not been covering even the vig. Things have gotten out of hand. Snake has his reputation to think about. If Moro doesn't keep up, others will think they don't have to either. To help make his point, Snake gave Moro a severe beating last week with a warning that if Moro missed another payment, he would be killed. Nothing personal; general deterrence and all that.

The payment is due today but Moro doesn't have the money. He borrows a gun and hangs out at Joshua's Deli, the neighborhood grocery store, in the hopes that Snake will leave him alone in public. He is shocked when Snake comes in and walks straight at him. "I won't let you get me, Snake!" Moro says as he pulls his gun and aims. Just before he pulls the trigger, Joshua, the proprietor, who is directly across the counter from Moro, leans over and punches him. "That's not Snake. It's his brother, you moron." Joshua has made a point of learning to tell the look-alike brothers apart because Snake does not pay his bill. Joshua's punch deflects Moro's shot. Snake's brother is wounded but not killed.

At a preliminary hearing on an attempted murder charge, the court finds that, while Moro did intend to kill, he reasonably believed that he was in danger of being killed and acted in what he reasonably believed was self-defense. Moro is cleared of all charges. Moro then files assault charges against Joshua. Is Joshua criminally liable for striking Moro under the Model Penal Code? Is he criminally liable under the North Dakota provisions reproduced in the Overview section below?

● OVERVIEW OF MISTAKE AS TO A JUSTIFICATION

Mistake as to Offense Element vs. Mistake as to Justification An actor's mistake may exculpate the actor in any number of ways. Assume a hunter's companion violates basic safety rules by moving too far ahead of his partner and into the partner's line of fire. When the partner shoots the companion because he reasonably mistakes him for a deer, the partner is properly exculpated because his mistake negates the culpable state of mind required for murder; he lacks the required intention to kill another human being. No justification or excuse defense is required because the required elements of the offense have not been satisfied. In contrast, when Moro shoots Snake's brother, he does intend to cause his death. If Snake's brother had died, Moro would satisfy the requirements of murder. Moro nonetheless may have a defense if, had the circumstances been as he reasonably believed them to be, his shooting would have been justified. Because of a mistaken belief, neither the hunter nor Moro knows that his conduct is criminal, and their punishment would not serve the condemnatory function of the criminal law. In Moro's case, however, because the elements of murder are satisfied had Snake's brother died, a general defense is required if Moro is to be exculpated.

Mistake as to Justification Every jurisdiction recognizes a defense for some class of mistake as to a justification. The often unpredictable and confrontational nature of justifying circumstances make such mistakes particularly understandable. This is especially true for defensive force justifications, where the actor must make the decision to act under an impending threat of harm. To impose liability where an actor reasonably believes that he is justified is to punish a blameless actor, an actor who could not reasonably have been expected to have avoided the offense. Society encourages, or at least tolerates, justified conduct. Recognition of a defense for a reasonable mistake as to a justification is important to remove the fear of liability that may discourage some persons from engaging in justified conduct that society would want performed.

Justification for Actor Who "Believes" Conduct Justified Most jurisdictions provide a mistake as to a justification defense by including the word "believes" or "reasonably believes" in the definition of justification defenses: An actor will get the justification defense if she believes her conduct is justified, even if in fact it is not. This common formulation has two independent effects, both of which may be problematic. First, giving a justification defense to one who "believes" her conduct is justified treats as "justified" conduct that which is in fact not objectively justified. Giving the mistake defense is appropriate, even important, but to do it through this formulation is to confuse justification and excuse, which invites confusion and error. More on this below. Recall that this issue was raised at the end of the defensive force "triggering conditions" discussion in the Section 18 Overview. (Recall that an attack by one who mistakenly believes he is justified triggers a right of the victim to use defensive force; the objectively justified attack does not.) The second effect of defining justifications subjectively—giving a justification defense to one who "believes" she is justified—is to deny a justification defense to an actor whose conduct actually is justified but who does not "believe" that it is. This is the problem of the unknowingly justified actor, which is discussed in the Advanced Issues section of Section 18. An alternative means of providing an excuse for mistake as to a justification is to define justifications objectively, without the "believes" language, and to provide a separate general excuse defense for mistakes as to a justification. The National Commission recommended this approach. A sample of its formulations are provided in the footnotes of the Section 18 Overview noted above.

Reasons vs. Deeds Theory of Justification Defining justification defenses *subjectively* to require that an actor "believe" his conduct is justified, reflects what might be called the *reasons* theory of justification, where the rationale of the defense is the actor's proper motivation. Defining justification defenses *objectively,* to require that the actor's conduct actually follows the *ex ante* rules of conduct, reflects what might be called the *deeds* theory of justification, where the rationale of the defense is the justified character of the actor's deed, rather than his justificatory motivation. (These competing theories of justification and their relationship to mistake are discussed further in the Robinson & Darley excerpt in the Discussion Materials section below.)

Liability for Joshua? Should Joshua be liable for striking Moro? As the previous sections in this Part have described (objectively) justified conduct is conduct that the law tolerates and even encourages. It makes sense, then, that an actor ought not to be able lawfully to interfere or resist such justified conduct; society wants justified conduct to be performed. In Moro's case, however, his conduct only *appears* to him to be justified. Because he has mistaken Snake's brother for Snake, he is not in fact in danger and his use of force is not (objectively) justified. Once we determine that his shooting is not justified, it follows that Joshua ought to be able to intervene lawfully and justifiably in order to prevent it. Most people agree with this result — allowing a justification defense for Joshua's interference with Moro's shooting — but it is not always clear how it can be reached under current statutes. Recall that many statutes, including the Model Penal Code, give a justification defense if the actor "believes" that his conduct is justified. Under this approach, Moro's shooting of the wrong brother is "justified." How, then, can Joshua lawfully interfere with it?

Under the Model Penal Code Under the Model Code, Joshua is not justified in interfering to defend Snake's brother unless Snake's brother would be justified in using the same force in defense of himself.[1] The use of force against Moro by Snake's brother is justified only if Snake's brother satisfies the requirements of self-defense:

> *Use of Force in Self-Protection.* [T]he use of force upon or toward another person is justifiable when the actor believes that such force is immediately necessary for the purpose of protecting himself against the use of *unlawful* force by such other person on the present occasion.[2]

Thus Joshua and Snake's brother can lawfully resist the mistaken Moro only if Moro's force is "unlawful." But, because the Model Penal Code defines justifications subjectively, Moro's shooting is "justified" under the Model Penal Code; Moro "believes" that his shooting is immediately necessary to protect himself, as self-defense requires. If Joshua can only defend against "unlawful" force and if Moro's shooting is "justified," how can the Code reach the proper result of giving a justification defense to Joshua for his intervention?

"Privileged" vs. "Unprivileged" Justification One might normally assume that "justified" force is not "unlawful force." Therefore, if Moro's shooting of Snake's brother is "justified," it is not "unlawful"; thus Joshua has no right to resist or to interfere with the shooting. But the Code's definition of "unlawful force" gives a different result: It includes some kinds of "justified" force but excludes others. Section 3.11(1) defines "unlawful force" as:

> force . . . which . . . would constitute [an] offense . . . except for a defense . . . not amounting to a privilege to use the force.

In other words, under the Model Penal Code's scheme, two kinds of "justified" conduct exist: privileged and unprivileged. The former may not lawfully be resisted; the latter may. Therefore, assuming Moro's force is not "privileged"

---

1. See Model Penal Code §3.05(1).
2. Model Penal Code §3.04(1) (emphasis added).

(an undefined term in the Code), such force may be justified but nonetheless be "unlawful force"; therefore, Joshua can lawfully defend Snake's brother against it.

Treating Mistaken Justification as Justified While the Model Penal Code's approach — giving a justification defense to an actor who mistakenly *believes* his conduct is justified — may cause some confusion in application, its greatest problem is the conceptual confusion that it creates by characterizing mistaken conduct as "justified." The approach fails to distinguish clearly the important difference between a mistaken justification, which ought only be excused, and objectively justified conduct. Conduct that is actually, objectively justified — "privileged justification" — is consistent with the rules of conduct. Such conduct is to be publicly approved and encouraged (or at least tolerated) under similar circumstances in the future. Conduct that is not actually, objectively justified — mistaken justification or "unprivileged justification" — violates the rules of conduct and should be avoided by others under similar circumstances in the future, although the violator at hand may be excused if his reasonable mistake as to the justification of his conduct renders him blameless.

Ambiguity of Acquittals By treating mistaken conduct as "justified," current doctrine creates an ambiguity that risks distorting the true rules of conduct. An acquittal described as justified but actually based on a mistake as to a justification, sends an ambiguous message as to the rules of conduct: Do the rules permit what the actor actually did or just what he thought he was doing, or both? Giving the same "justification" defense to both the objectively justified actor and the mistaken actor leaves the ambiguity dangerously unresolved in every case. A case of mistaken justification might be misinterpreted as a case of true justification, thereby approving conduct that ought to be prohibited. Meanwhile, an actual justification — approved conduct; conduct consistent with the law's rules of conduct — might be misinterpreted to be only a mistaken justification — undesirable conduct that the law discourages — thereby distorting the rules in a way that may discourage desirable conduct.

Objective vs. Subjective Justifications The difficulty can be avoided by adopting an objective definition of "justification" and segregating a mistaken justification into a separate excuse, as is done in some justification statutes.[1] Under this approach, the doctrines of justification are defined in an objective rather than subjective form: An actor is "justified" only if her conduct is in fact objectively justified, not because the actor "believes" that it is justified. This distinguishes the two cases and permits a clear communication of the rules of conduct. Only objective justifications can provide the unambiguous and invariant rules needed to define the rules of conduct for all people.

Objectively Defined Justifications Objectively defined justifications might look something like the following. Consider Joshua's liability for striking Moro under the following provisions, taken from existing statutes:

Section 12.1-05-03. Self-Defense. A person is justified in using force upon another person to defend himself against danger of imminent unjustified bodily injury . . . by such other person. . . .

---

1. N.D. Cent. Code §§12.1-05-03 to -12; see Final Report of the National Commission on Reform of Federal Criminal Law ("Brown Commission") §§603 to 608 (1971) (quoted in the footnotes at the end of the Section 18 Overview discussion of defensive force triggering conditions).

Section 12.1-05-04. Defense of Others. A person is justified in using force upon another person in order to defend anyone else if:

1. The person defended would be justified in defending himself; and
2. The person coming to the defense has not, by provocation or otherwise, forfeited the right of self-defense.

Section 12.1-05-07. Limitations on the Use of Force — Excessive Force. A person is not justified in using more force than is necessary and appropriate under the circumstances.

Section 12.1-05-08. Excuse. A person's conduct is excused if he believes that the facts are such that his conduct is necessary and appropriate for any of the purposes which would establish a justification ... under this chapter, even though his belief is mistaken. However, if his belief is negligently or recklessly held, it is not an excuse in a prosecution for an offense for which negligence or recklessness, as the case may be, suffices to establish culpability....[1]

Mistake Under Objectively Defined Justification Does Joshua have a defense under these provisions for striking Moro? Joshua will have a defense-of-others justification, under section 12.1-05-04, for trying to defend Snake's brother, provided that Snake's brother would have a defense of self-defense under section 12.1-05-03. Self-defense is available if the threatened force by Moro is "unjustified." Moro's mistaken conduct is not *justified*; he is not in fact "using force upon another person to defend himself against danger...," as required by section 12.1-05-03. He does have an excuse under section 12.1-05-08, though, because he reasonably *believed* in the existence of circumstances that would justify his conduct.[2] Nonetheless, his conduct *is* "unjustified" force. Therefore, Joshua *is* justified under section 12.1-05-04 in using force against Moro to defend Snake's brother from the excused attack. These statutes differ from the Model Penal Code in that they segregate defenses of true justification from the excuse of mistake as to a justification. With this distinction, the statutes are better able to identify clearly and simply when one may and may not resist or interfere with an attack. The rule is simple: One may defend against an excused attack but not against a justified attack.

Case for Subjective Theory Many codes and some writers insist on defining justifications subjectively. That is, they argue that one ought to be justified if one (reasonably) believes that one's conduct is justified.[3] According to this argument, the actor has behaved properly; to convict the actor is to disapprove improperly of the conduct as the actor saw it. One writer gives the example of the *Young* case (the case opinion is excerpted in the Discussion Materials below), in which the actor bravely intervened to help defend a youth being beaten by two men, only to be charged with criminal assault for interfering with an arrest. The writer observes:

> Actions like Young's should not be the subject of criminal liability, but the
> question here is whether they should be labeled justified or excused. Young is

---

1. N.D. Cent. Code, supra.
2. Because his belief was reasonable, he is not liable even for a lesser degree of assault (e.g., reckless wounding).
3. See Model Penal Code §§3.02, 3.04-3.07.

> to be praised, not blamed, for what he did, and *members of society would wish*
> *that others faced with similar situations requiring instant judgment would act as*
> *Young did*. A moral assessment of Young's act would treat it as justified.[1]

The argument is, in part, that a justification defense must be given to Young because only in this way can the law (1) give the moral approval to his conduct that it deserves and (2) encourage others to intervene in similar situations in the future. But the logic of this subjective theory is flawed.

Counter-arguments to Subjective Theory   An excuse defense for Young, rather a justification defense, also would judge him blameless. The writer might respond, however, that it is Young's act that should be judged proper, not just Young. This is important because, as he explains, we want "others faced with similar situations [to] act as Young did." But this incorrectly assumes that we must label as "justified" Young's mistaken act in order to encourage others in the future to act as Young thought he was acting. In fact, the future actor who believes she has come upon the mugging of an innocent youth will be encouraged to act by a rule of conduct that allows as a (true) objective justification defense the right to defend another from an unjustified attack. The future actor will not be deterred by the absence of a justification for the mistaken actor, like Young, because the future actor believes that the circumstances are such that the intervention actually is justified. (If the actor is concerned about the possibility that he might be mistaken in his perception of the justifying circumstances—a concern that we might want to encourage in people—the actor can take comfort in the fact that a complete (excuse) defense is provided for a reasonable mistake as to a justification.) The rule of conduct need provide a justification defense for (objectively) justified conduct in order to encourage future actors to act in situations where intervention appears to them to be justified.[2]

Culpable Mistake as to Justification   For simplicity's sake, the discussion has so far assumed that Moro would get a complete defense—an excuse—because he reasonably believed that his conduct was justified. Would the results be different if Moro were negligent or reckless in believing that he was about to be killed? Both the objective-justification defense provisions quoted above and the Model Penal Code's subjective-justification provisions would allow an unreasonable mistake, such as a negligent or reckless mistake, to at least mitigate the degree of liability. Moro's reckless mistake would render him liable for reckless wounding, if such an offense

---

1. Kent Greenawalt, The Perplexing Borders of Justification and Excuse, 84 Colum. L. Rev. 1897, 1919-1920 (1984) (emphasis added).

2.   From the perspective of objective justification, it is entirely predictable that Greenawalt would conclude that the borders of justification and excuse are "perplexing," as the title of his article suggests. By defining justification to include reasonable mistake as to a justification, his attempt to distinguish justification and excuse is an attempt to distinguish mistaken justification from excuse, which cannot be done because a mistaken justification *is* an excuse. His conclusion that the doctrine ought not systematically embody the troublesome distinction between justification and excuse is defensible only if one adopts a subjective theory of justification, as Greenawalt does. But most, if not all, of his troublesome cases are clear and unproblematic under an objective theory of justification. In fact, one might conclude that the point he has demonstrated in his article is not the perplexing borders of justification and excuse but rather the perplexing borders created by the use of a subjective theory of justification. His article, then, is simply an advertisement for the comparative conceptual clarity of an objective theory of justification.

exists. A negligent mistake would render him liable for negligent wounding.[1] As happened with reasonable mistake, where Moro's mistake is culpable, his conduct is only excused, not justified, and thus triggers a defense-of-others justification for Joshua to assault Moro.

Requiring Reasonable Mistake   Some jurisdictions, however, permit no defense, justification or excuse, if an actor's mistake is unreasonable.[2] Thus a reckless or negligent mistake will bar any defense and leave the actor liable for an intentional assault or killing. To get any defense, the mistake must be reasonable. Some writers support such a reasonableness requirement:

> If a mistaken claim of justification functions as an excuse, then one can expect it to meet the standard applied to other excusing conditions—namely, that it actually excuse the actor from blame. As the claim of duress must satisfy normative criteria, so must the claim of mistake as an excuse satisfy normative criteria—namely, the requirement of reasonableness—in order effectively to excuse the wrongful act.[3]

This issue is the focus of the Discussion Materials below.

Standard of Reasonableness   "Reasonable" typically is defined as "non-negligent";[4] thus the reasonableness of a mistake is to be judged by the partially individualized objective standard used in the negligence concept.[5] But there can be confusion on this point. In *People v. Goetz* (discussed in Section 18, regarding Defensive Force), for example, the trial court determined that the defendant's belief need only be "reasonable as to him," which essentially amounted to a purely subjective standard.[6] Recall that the defendant shot several youths on a subway car after they had approached him in what he believed was an attempt to rob him. The court's interpretation of the "reasonable belief" requirement of the New York statute (an all-or-nothing scheme) was reversed on appeal, however, where the Court of Appeals made clear that the reasonableness of the defendant's belief was to be judged by an objective standard, albeit one individualized by certain characteristics of the defendant and his situation. This individualization allows the court to admit and the jury to consider evidence of factors that may distort the defendant's perception of what is reasonable. In *State v. Kelly*, for example, the court allowed expert testimony concerning battered woman's syndrome as relevant to establishing the reasonableness of the defendant's belief that she was in imminent danger of death.[7] The defendant in *Kelly* stabbed and killed her husband, believing that he was about to kill her but under circumstances where a reasonable person would not necessarily have come to such a conclusion. The testimony suggested that a pattern of past abuse tends to cause

---

1. See Model Penal Code § 3.09(2); N.D. Cent. Code § 12.1-05-08.

2. Both the New York and New Jersey codes, for example, exemplify this deviation from the Model Penal Code; they both require a reasonable belief for a defense of self-defense. N.Y. Penal Law § 35.15 (1987); N.J. Stat. Ann. § 2C:3-4 (1982). See People v. Goetz, 68 N.Y.2d 96, 497 N.E.2d 41, 506 N.Y.S.2d 18 (1986); State v. Kelly, 97 N.J. 178, 478 A.2d 364 (1984).

3. George P. Fletcher, Rethinking Criminal Law 696 (1978).

4. See, e.g., Model Penal Code § 1.13(16).

5. See, e.g., Model Penal Code § 2.02(2)(d).

6. 68 N.Y.2d 96, 497 N.E.2d 41 (1986).

7. 97 N.J. 178, 478 A.2d 364 (1984). But see State v. Norman, 324 N.C. 253, 378 S.E.2d 8 (1989) (severely battered wife not entitled to jury instruction on perfect or imperfect self-defense).

the abused to overestimate the extent and immediacy of the threat and to underestimate her ability to avoid the threat by retreat. On appeal, the court directed that such evidence of battering and its effects could be relevant to a determination of the reasonableness of Kelly's belief.

⦿ DISCUSSION MATERIALS

Should the Criminal Law Recognize a Defense or Mitigation for an Honest but Unreasonable Mistake as to a Justification?

Under the harshest view, when one believes one is acting justifiably, one acts at one's own peril; even a reasonable mistake gives no defense. The first article, by Herbert Wechsler and Jerome Michael, and the opinion in *People v. Young*, capture the earlier debate on this point and generally reject the harsh view in favor of granting a defense for a reasonable mistake. The Model Penal Code Commentary accepts as fundamental the need for a defense for a reasonable mistake as to a justification and goes a step farther, to provide a mitigation (but not a defense) for even an unreasonable mistake. While some modern state codes adopt the all-or-nothing approach — that is, giving a complete defense for a reasonable mistake but full liability for an unreasonable mistake — the Model Code rejects that approach and instead varies the degree of liability with the defendant's level of culpability in making the mistake. An empirical study by Robinson & Darley determines that community intuitions more closely track the Model Penal Code's graduated approach than the competing all-or-nothing approach.

Herbert Wechsler & Jerome Michael, The Rationale of the Law of Homicide
37 Columbia Law Review 701, 736 (1937)

The most obvious case of homicidal behavior that serves the end of preserving life is that of the victim of a wrongful attack who finds it necessary to kill his assailant to save his own life. We need not pause to reconsider the universal judgment that there is no social interest in preserving the lives of aggressors at the cost of those of their victims. Given the choice that must be made, the only defensible policy is one that will operate as a sanction against unlawful aggression. But here the simplicity of the matter ends. The initial problem arises from the fact that men sometimes believe that they are being attacked, that their lives are in immediate peril and that it is necessary to kill to save themselves when such is not the case. So long as the belief is reasonable, it seems quite clear, however, that the original policy still obtains. Men must act on the basis of what was known or could have been known to them at the moment of action, not at some later time. To concede a privilege to kill only in cases of actual necessity is to lay down a rule that must either be disregarded or else must operate to deny freedom of action even in cases where the necessity exists and not merely in those where it does not. On the other hand, no such onerous limitation on freedom of action is imposed by requiring that men exercise the degree of care to appraise the facts correctly which is appropriate to the situation. It is desirable to deter men from acting without exercising such care; unless such care is taken, death is not a justifiable means even to the preservation of their own lives.

People v. Young
Court of Appeals of New York
11 N.Y.2d 274, 183 N.E.2d 319, 229 N.Y.S.2d 1 (1962)

Per Curiam.

Whether one, who in good faith aggressively intervenes in a struggle between another person and a police officer in civilian dress attempting to effect the lawful arrest of the third person, may be properly convicted of assault in the third degree is a question of law of first impression here.

The opinions in the court below in the absence of precedents in this State carefully expound the opposing views found in other jurisdictions. The majority in the Appellate Division have adopted the minority rule in the other States that one who intervenes in a struggle between strangers under the mistaken but reasonable belief that he is protecting another who he assumes is being unlawfully beaten is thereby exonerated from criminal liability. The weight of authority holds with the dissenters below that one who goes to the aid of a third person does so at his own peril.

While the doctrine espoused by the majority of the court below may have support in some States, we feel that such a policy would not be conducive to an orderly society. We agree with the settled policy of law in most jurisdictions that the right of a person to defend another ordinarily should not be greater than such person's right to defend himself. Subdivision 3 of section 246 of the Penal Law, Consol. Laws, c. 40, [which authorizes the use of force in defense of another,] does not apply as no offense was being committed on the person of the one resisting the lawful arrest. Whatever may be the public policy where the felony charged requires proof of a specific intent and the issue is justifiable homicide, it is not relevant in a prosecution for assault in the third degree where it is only necessary to show that the defendant knowingly struck a blow.

In this case there can be no doubt that the defendant intended to assault the police officer in civilian dress. The resulting assault was forceful. Hence motive or mistake of fact is of no significance as the defendant was not charged with a crime requiring such intent or knowledge. To be guilty of third degree assault, "It is sufficient that the defendant voluntarily intended to commit the unlawful act of touching." Since in these circumstances the aggression was inexcusable the defendant was properly convicted.

Accordingly, the order of the Appellate Division should be reversed and the information reinstated.

Froessel, Judge (dissenting).

The law is clear that one may kill in defense of another when there is reasonable, though mistaken, ground for believing that the person slain is about to commit a felony or to do some great personal injury to the apparent victim (Penal Law § 1055); yet the majority now hold, for the first time, that in the event of a simple assault under similar circumstances, the mistaken belief, no matter how reasonable, is no defense.

Briefly, the relevant facts are these: On a Friday afternoon at about 3:40, Detectives Driscoll and Murphy, not in uniform, observed an argument taking place between a motorist and one McGriff in the street in front of premises 64 West 54th Street, in midtown Manhattan. Driscoll attempted to chase McGriff out of the roadway in order to allow traffic to pass, but McGriff refused to move back; his actions caused a crowd to collect. After identifying himself to McGriff, Driscoll placed him under arrest. As McGriff resisted, defendant "came out of the crowd" from Driscoll's rear and struck Murphy about the head with his fist. In the ensuing struggle Driscoll's right kneecap was injured when defendant fell on top of him. At the station house, defendant said he had not known or thought Driscoll and Murphy were police officers.

Defendant testified that while he was proceeding on 54th Street he observed two white men, who appeared to be 45 or 50 years old, pulling on a "colored boy" (McGriff), who appeared to be a lad about 18, whom he did not know. The men had nearly pulled McGriff's pants off, and he was crying. Defendant admitted he knew nothing of what had transpired between the officers and McGriff, and made no inquiry of anyone; he just came there and pulled the officer away from McGriff.

Defendant was convicted of assault third degree. In reversing upon the law and dismissing the information, the Appellate Division held that he is not "criminally liable for assault in the third degree if he goes to the aid of another who he mistakenly, but *reasonably,* believes is being unlawfully beaten, and thereby injures one of the apparent assaulters" (emphasis supplied). While in my opinion the majority below correctly stated the law, I would reverse here and remit so that the Appellate Division may pass on the question of whether or not defendant's conduct was reasonable in light of the circumstances presented at the trial.

As the majority below pointed out, assault is a crime derived from the common law. Basic to the imposition of criminal liability both at common law and under our statutory law is the existence in the one whom committed the prohibited act of what has been variously termed a guilty mind, a mens rea or a criminal intent.

Criminal intent requires an awareness of wrongdoing. When conduct is based upon mistake of fact reasonably entertained, there can be no such awareness and, therefore, no criminal culpability. . . .

It is undisputed that defendant did not know that Driscoll and Murphy were detectives in plain clothes engaged in lawfully apprehending an alleged disorderly person. If, therefore, defendant reasonably believed he was lawfully assisting another, he would not have been guilty of a crime. Subdivision 3 of section 246 of the Penal Law provides that it is not unlawful to use force "When committed either by the party about to be injured or *by another person in his aid or defense, in preventing or attempting to prevent an offense against his person,* . . . if the force or violence used is not more than sufficient to prevent such offense" (emphasis supplied). The law is thus clear that if defendant entertained an "honest and reasonable belief" that the facts were as he perceived them to be, he would be exonerated from criminal liability.

By ignoring one of the most basic principles of criminal law that crimes mala in se require proof of at least general criminal intent, the majority now hold that the defense of mistake of fact is "of no significance". We are not here dealing with one of "a narrow class of exceptions" where the Legislature has created crimes which do not depend on criminal intent but which are complete on the mere intentional doing of an act malum prohibitum.

There is no need, in my opinion, to consider the law of other States, for New York policy clearly supports the view that one may act on appearances reasonably ascertained, as does New Jersey. Our Penal Law (§ 1055), to which I have already alluded, is a statement of that policy. The same policy was expressed by this court in *People v. Maine,* 166 N.Y. 50, 59 N.E. 696. There, the defendant observed his brother fighting in the street with two other men; he stepped in and stabbed to death one of the latter. The defense was justifiable homicide under the predecessor of section 1055. The court held it reversible error to admit into evidence the declarations of the defendant's brother, made before defendant happened upon the scene, which tended to show that the brother was the aggressor. We said: "Of course, the acts and conduct of the defendant must be judged solely with reference to the situation as it was when he first and afterwards saw it." Mistake of relevant fact, reasonably entertained, is thus a defense to homicide under section 1055, and one who kills in defense of another and proffers this defense of justification is to be judged according to the circumstances as they appeared to him.

The mistaken belief, however, must be one which is reasonably entertained, and the question of reasonableness is for the trier of the facts. "The question is not, merely, what did the accused believe? but also, what did he have the right to believe?" Without passing on the facts of the instant case, the Appellate Division had no right to assume that defendant's conduct was reasonable, and to dismiss the information as a matter of law. Nor do we have the right to reinstate the verdict without giving the Appellate Division the opportunity to pass upon the facts.

Although the majority . . . are now purporting to fashion a policy "conducive to an orderly society," by their decision they have defeated their avowed purpose. What public interest is promoted by a principle which would deter one from coming to the aid of a fellow citizen who he has reasonable ground to apprehend is in imminent danger of personal injury at the hands of assailants? Is it reasonable to denominate, as justifiable homicide, a slaying committed under a mistaken but reasonably held belief, and deny this same defense of justification to one using less force? Logic, as well as historical background and related precedent, dictates that the rule and policy expressed by our Legislature in the case of homicide, which is an assault resulting in death, should likewise be applicable to a much less serious assault not resulting in death.

I would reverse the order appealed from and remit the case to the Appellate Division . . . for determination upon the questions of fact raised in that court.[*]

Model Penal Code Section 3.09(2) Commentary
Official Draft and Revised Comments 150-153 (1985)

Reckless or Negligent Belief. . . .

Against the requirement of reasonable belief in justification defenses, there has been little more than a thin line of academic criticism. Keedy argued against the rule that a mistake must be reasonable on the ground that "[i]f the mistake, whether reasonable or unreasonable, as judged by an external standard, does negative the criminal mind, there should be no conviction." He thought that negligence should establish mens rea only where the actor failed to use the care that appeared proper to him under the circumstances and that the proper test must be: "Did the defendant act up to his own standard?" This attempted "subjective" definition of negligence has not been followed.

It is, however, commonly agreed that negligence at common law means for criminal purposes something more gross than civil negligence in that it implies a wide departure from the reasonable standard. On this view, it might be said that for a mistake to preclude justification it must be not merely unreasonable but grossly unreasonable. Even with this qualification, however, a person should not be convicted of a crime of intention where he has labored under a mistake that, had the facts been as he supposed, would have left him free from guilt. The unreasonableness of an alleged belief quite properly is considered as evidence that it was not in fact held, but if the tribunal is satisfied that the belief was held, the defendant, in a prosecution for crime founded on wrongful purpose, should be entitled to be judged as if his belief was true. To convict for a belief arrived at on an unreasonable ground is to convict for negligence. Where the crime otherwise requires greater culpability for a conviction, it is neither fair nor logical to convict when there is only negligence as to the circumstances that would establish a justification.

The solution in this section, as indicated earlier, is that such situations should be taken out of the category of purposeful crime and dealt with as cases of recklessness or negligence. If the belief is recklessly arrived at, i.e., with awareness of the risk that it may be unfounded, then it is appropriate to assess the defendant as one would be assessed who had acted recklessly with respect to the material elements of the offense. In homicide, for example, the distinction between purposeful and reckless homicide has enormous import when it comes to the degree of the offense and to the sentence. And it makes more sense to assimilate the defendant who is reckless as to the existence of justifying circumstances to one who recklessly takes life than to assimilate him to one who purposefully does so.

---

[*] Editor's Note — New York courts have since determined that *Young* has been overruled by N.Y. Penal Law 35.15 and that "if the intervenor . . . reasonably should have known that the person being defended initiated the original conflict, then justification is not a defense" but that otherwise the mistake as to justification defense is available. People v. Melendez, 588 N.Y.S.2d 718, 722 (N.Y. Sup. Ct. 1992); see also People v. Wang, 625 N.Y.S.2d 413 (N.Y. Sup. Ct. 1995). (The New York Court of Appeals has not addressed the issue again since *Young*.)

Sections 3.03 to 3.08 accordingly provide that the actor's belief alone will qualify him for the justification. Subsection (2) imposes as a general qualification the principle that when the actor's belief in the necessity for using the force that he used was recklessly or negligently formed, or when he was reckless or negligent in acquiring or failing to acquire any knowledge that is otherwise material to the justification for his use of force, the justification is lost in a prosecution for an offense for which recklessness or negligence, as the case may be, suffices for conviction. By the same token, the justification is retained in a prosecution for an offense that can only be committed purposely or knowingly, irrespective of recklessness or negligence in assessing the grounds for the justification. Reckless-ness and negligence as to the factors that establish justification, in short, are treated on a parity with recklessness or negligence as to the other material elements of the offense involved.

This subsection rejects the views of those who would have gone even further and accepted any honest belief as to justification as exculpating an actor from conviction for crimes of negligence and recklessness as well as crimes of purpose. Glanville Williams, who urged this position, contended that the concept of negligence was not a useful legal one in this context. The judgment of the Institute was that although caution should be exercised in finding recklessness or negligence in forming the beliefs that are material to justification, nevertheless cases do arise where such judgments can fairly be made.

No jurisdiction has gone as far as Professor Williams suggested. A number of recently revised codes and proposals follow the approach of this subsection toward reckless and negligent beliefs about justifying circumstances; but many of them adopt the older principle that no justification exists if a belief in justifying circum-stances is unreasonable, thus permitting conviction for a crime of purpose when an actor has negligently concluded that a circumstance that would sustain a justifica-tion exists.

Other Discussion Materials

Paul H. Robinson & John M. Darley, Testing Competing Theories of Justification

76 North Carolina Law Review 1095, 1097-1104, 1115, 1123-1124, 1127-1129, 1131-1133 (1998)

Despite the universal recognition of justification defenses, there is disagree-ment over the underlying theory of the justificatory principle, and thus the proper legal formulation of such defenses. At the core of the debate about the principle is the following question: Are justification defenses given because the actor's deed avoids a greater harm, or because she acted for the right reason?

The *deeds theory* of justification justifies conduct that avoids a greater harm, and thus it is conduct that we would be happy to tolerate under similar circum-stances in the future. Justified conduct, under this theory, is conduct where the actor has done the right deed, hence, the "deeds" theory of justification. The *reasons theory* looks not to the deed but to the reason for the deed. The reasons theory, then, gives a defense when a person acts for the right reason, generally *trying* to avoid a greater harm. The issue between the two theories concerns the focus of justification. Is the focus of justification the nature of the *deed* or the actor's *reason* for acting?

The debate to date relies in large part upon legal and philosophical arguments. But frequently a third source of authority is brought into play. Each side buttresses its arguments with claims that its theory better tracks the community intuitions, a common claim in criminal law arguments. In this article we test those claims about the community's intuitions, using "policy capturing" social science research techniques designed for such inquiries. In the process, we learn about community views on the proper theory and formulation of justification defenses, as well as other criminal law doctrines, and about the value of social science research to criminal law formulation.

I. Competing Theories of Justification...

Most writers have signed on in support of the reasons theory and in opposition to the deeds theory, some suggesting that the latter is "absurd," unfair, or unduly burdensome. (It is worth noting that the first two of these objections are based on the moral intuitions of the writers, coupled with their certainty that others share their moral intuitions.) Taking the minority side, one of us has argued that a deeds theory of justification is better for a variety of reasons, including that it generates liability results that are more just and that better match our collective intuitions of what is just.

Most, but not all, state criminal law appears to follow the reasons theory, although there is often some ambiguity as to which theory of justification they actually adopt, despite the apparent clarity of first appearances. The Model Penal Code formulation is quoted above: An actor is justified if she *believes* that her conduct is necessary for defense.

Current English law also appears to adopt the reasons theory....

The contrasts between the two theories are illuminated when we consider how the deeds theory and the reasons theory suggest different results at each of their two conflict points: (1) where the actor mistakenly believes her conduct is not justified (the unknowingly justified actor), and (2) where the actor mistakenly believes her conduct is justified (mistake as to a justification)....

B. Mistake as to a Justification

[Consider this case]: A person's conduct is objectively unjustified but the person subjectively, mistakenly believes that it is justified. In such cases of mistaken justification, the actor believes that her conduct avoids a greater harm, when in fact it does not. The club-wielding attacker, when successfully overcome and dragged to the street light, turns out to be a jogger carrying a flashlight whose bulb is out. Whether beating the jogger-mistaken-for-an-attacker is justified depends again on whether the justification defense is given (1) because the conduct in fact is justified or (2) because the person acts for a justified reason.

Under a reasons theory, the force used against the jogger-mistaken-for-an-attacker is justified because it is used for the purpose of self-defense. The actor's reason is right even if the conduct is wrong.

Under the deeds theory, a person who mistakenly believes that the conduct is justified is not justified, although the person may gain an excuse defense if the mistake is reasonable or perhaps a mitigation even if it is not.

Note that . . . the result of the two theories is the same for the actor at hand. Both the deeds theory's excuse defense and the reasons theory's justification defense exculpate the actor who mistakenly believes she is justified. Yet, the different views of justification may show themselves in another aspect of defense formulations that has been the subject of much disagreement: the proper treatment of mistake as to a justification. All agree that a reasonable mistake as to a justification ought to fully exculpate. What is the proper treatment of an unreasonable mistake as to a justification?

A majority of jurisdictions permit a mistake as to a justification defense only if the actor's mistake is reasonable. An unreasonable mistake, reckless or negligent, gives no defense and hence generates full liability for the substantive offense. A minority of jurisdictions give a complete defense for reasonable mistake but also allow a mitigation for an honest but unreasonable mistake. The level of liability, that is, the extent of the mitigation given, typically is tied to the level of culpability of the mistake: A negligent mistake, being less culpable than a reckless mistake, gives a greater mitigation than does a reckless mistake.

The few jurisdictions that take the deeds approach in formulating their justification defenses objectively (e.g., North Dakota, the Proposed Federal Criminal Code) all give mitigations for unreasonable mistakes as to justification. In contrast, a majority of the jurisdictions that take a reasons approach and formulate their justification defenses subjectively take the all-or-nothing approach, giving no mitigation or defense for unreasonable mistakes as to a justification. This pattern suggests a connection between the deeds-reasons dispute and the dispute over the proper treatment of unreasonable mistakes as to a justification. But the fact is there is no logical reason why the reasons theory should demand an-all-or-nothing approach.

One could speculate about the source of the apparent correlation between the reasons theory and the all-or-nothing approach. If one views mistaken justification as a justification, it would be easy to conclude that an all-or-nothing approach is needed. After all, all-or-nothing is the way objective justification does operate. Either the actor's conduct avoids a greater harm and is to be encouraged or at least tolerated in the future, or it does not avoid a greater harm and is to be discouraged in the future. When the subjective reasons theory of justification combines objective justification and mistaken subjective justification under the same label, "justified," it should be no surprise that such creates the tendency to treat a mistaken justification as if it were a true objective justification. It should be no surprise to see mistake as to a justification treated, like all other justifications, as an all-or-nothing issue.

This same possibility for confusion does not exist under the deeds approach to formulating justifications. The deeds theory distinguishes true objective justifications from mistakes as to a justification, and treats the latter as excuses. Objective justifications are properly all-or-nothing matters. Mistake as to a justification, like other excuses, just as clearly is not an all-or-nothing matter. Excuses function as part of law's adjudication of an actor's blameworthiness for a violation. Blameworthiness exists on a continuum, as is evident by the doctrines that contribute to this function.

One of us has written about the different functions of criminal law, pointing out that objective justifications serve the ex ante rule articulation function, telling people the rules for future conduct, while the excuses, including mistaken justification, perform an ex post adjudication function, assessing the degree of liability and punishment for a violation of the rules of conduct.

In performing the adjudication function, doctrines commonly express degrees of liability and punishment. For example, criminal codes typically recognize levels of culpability: purpose, knowledge, recklessness, and negligence. The law also recognizes mitigations for partial excuses in both its definition of offenses — e.g., the extreme mental or emotional disturbance mitigation in homicide — and its sentencing rules — e.g., the federal sentencing guideline authorization for sentence reduction below the guidelines for offenders influenced by coercion, duress, or diminished capacity. Under the deeds theory, mistakes as to a justification are seen as excuses, and like other doctrines for the adjudication of an actor's blameworthiness, the resulting liability may reflect a continuum of liability. Reasonable mistakes may excuse entirely, while the culpability inherent in unreasonable mistakes may suggest something less, a mitigation rather than a defense. . . .

III. Liability Predictions

. . . We believe the community's views are more accurately reflected in doctrine based upon a deeds theory of justification. It matters to lay persons whether a net societal harm actually occurs or not, we think, just as it matters to them whether a prohibited result, such as a resulting death, occurs or not. [W]e think the community views unreasonable mistakes as to a justification as deserving mitigation, in contrast to the majority rule in the United States. We describe below exactly how these general claims translate into specific predictions with regard to the liability results of the scenarios used in the study.

The first six scenarios are contrast cases, the responses to which established benchmarks for each test subject. These scenarios provide the full range of possible liability, as well as a variety of intermediate points. Not only do they give us results of considerable intrinsic interest in their own right, but more importantly for the present purposes, they allow us to interpret the liability results of the last five scenarios, the test scenarios. For each test scenario, we used as a point of comparison the contrast scenario most relevant with respect to the competing theories, from a case of an intentional unjustified act to a completely justified act, or any one of the many possibilities between those two extremes on the continuum of liability. Taken together, the following six contrast cases represent all of the obvious variations of a non-justification case to which the subjects' responses might be compared. . . .

IV. Liability Results

The mean liability for each of the scenarios is set out in Table 3.

B. The Cases for Which the Theories of Justification Have Different Predictions . . .

Turn . . . to the three scenarios in which the perpetrator, mistakenly believing that the town was in danger of a fire, set his neighbor's fields on fire to provide a firebreak. The reasonableness of the mistake varied across these three scenarios.

Table 3. Liability Means

Scenario	Liability Mean	Imprisonment Equivalent
Contrast Cases		
1. Intentional (unjustified) burning	4.65	~10 months
2. Attempted (unjustified) burning	3.52	~ 4 months
3. Created risk of (unjustified) burning, realized	2.69	~ 6 weeks
4. Created risk of (unjustified) burning, unrealized	0.48	essentially no punishment
5. Attempted risk creation	0.42	essentially no punishment
6. Intentional justified burning	0.57	essentially no punishment
Test Cases		
7. Unknowingly justified burning	3.63	~4 months
8. Knowingly justified burning but with bad motive	2.10	~2 weeks
9. Mistake as to justification, reasonable	1.10	~2 days
10. Mistake as to justification, negligent	2.02	~2 weeks
11. Mistake as to justification, reckless	2.33	~4 weeks

Scenario 9 presents the case of a reasonable mistake as to a justification. Both reasons and deeds theories would give a complete defense. Our subjects give liability of 1.10 (2.3 days), which is higher than we expected. Further, only 17.3% gave the complete defense verdict of "not guilty." On the other hand, 42.3% gave liability but no punishment. Perhaps these subjects are concerned about the implications of giving a complete defense in a case where the conduct in fact is not justified in an objective sense. There is reason to think that they should be concerned, as discussed in Section V.C. below, which presents our proposal to revise acquittal verdicts.

Scenarios 10 and 11 are cases of unreasonable mistakes as to a justification. In scenario 10, the actor honestly believes his conduct is justified but is mistaken and his mistake is negligent rather than reasonable. That is, a reasonable person in the actor's situation would have been aware of a risk that the contemplated conduct was not justified. In scenario 11, the actor similarly honestly believes his conduct is justified and is similarly wrong. But here his mistake is more culpable; he is reckless. That is, he is aware of a risk that his conduct might not be justified, although, on balance, he concludes that it is justified. He disregards the risk (that the conduct might not be justified) and proceeds with the conduct. In other words, he makes a reckless mistake as to a justification.

As expected, the subjects impose greater liability in these two cases than in the case of the reasonable mistake. Further, liability is greater in the case of greater culpability in making the mistake: 2.02 (2 weeks) for the negligent mistake, 2.33 (about 4 weeks) for the reckless mistake. But this range of liability is considerably less than that imposed by current law's majority rule, which denies any defense or mitigation and imposes full substantive liability. In the context of this burning offense, current law's assignment of no defense would give the perpetrator 10 months imprisonment, as imposed in scenario 1, not the 2 weeks and 4 weeks that scenarios 10 and 11, respectively, actually received. We conclude that the subjects would very much support recognition of mitigations for unreasonable mistakes as to a justification. These results suggest that the Model Penal Code's mitigations of this sort should have not been so regularly rejected by state criminal code drafters.

EXCUSE DEFENSES GENERALLY

OVERVIEW OF THE NATURE OF EXCUSES

Justifications vs. Excuses Justifications and excuses may seem similar in that both are general defenses and both exculpate an actor because of his blamelessness. A distinction between the two was of practical importance at early common law, but it fell into disuse when both kinds of defenses came to acquit a defendant in the same fashion. The distinction remains one of conceptual importance, however. Justified conduct is correct behavior that is to be encouraged (or at least tolerated) in the future. In determining whether conduct is justified, the focus is on the *act* and its circumstances, not the actor. An excuse, in contrast, represents a legal conclusion that the conduct is wrong, undesirable, but that criminal liability is inappropriate because some characteristic of the actor or his situation undercuts his blameworthiness and, thereby, society's wish to punish him. Excuses do not suggest the absence of net harm, as do justifications, but rather shift blame for the harm from the actor to the disability or other cause of the excusing conditions. The focus in excuses is on the *actor*. Acts are justified; actors are excused.

Rationale for Recognizing Excuses Not every distributive principle for criminal liability would necessarily recognize excuses. A distributive principle based on just desert supports the recognition of excuses in order to exculpate blameless offenders. One also might argue that a utilitarian distributive principle based exclusively on special deterrence similarly would support the recognition of excuses. That is, there is little special deterrent value in sanctioning an offender if the offender is unable to appreciate the criminality of his conduct or to conform it to the requirements of law. On the other hand, there may well be *general* deterrent value—the deterrence of other potential offenders, who do not have an excuse—in sanctioning such a blameless offender. It would signal just how serious the law is about punishing such violations. And persons contemplating such violations in the hopes of claiming an excuse will now be discouraged. A distributive principle that looks only to incapacitation or rehabilitation of dangerous offenders similarly might deny an excuse to a blameless offender, at least where the source of the excuse continues or is likely to recur. The criminal law would want jurisdiction over such offenders in order to administer needed incapacitation or rehabilitation. That excuses are in fact recognized by current doctrine suggests that in this instance desert and possibly special deterrence are the guiding distributive principles rather than general deterrence, incapacitation, or rehabilitation.

Common Requirements of Excuses Many doctrines and defenses serve as excuses: the involuntary act requirement; and the defenses of insanity, subnormality, involuntary intoxication, immaturity, duress, mistake as to a justification, and certain mistake of law defenses. The common rationale of these excuses—to exculpate the blameless—gives rise to common requirements: a *disability* or *reasonable mistake* must cause an *excusing condition*. Under each doctrine, an actor is excused if, because of the special conditions of the defense, the actor could not reasonably have been expected to have avoided the violation. This conclusion may derive from either of two kinds of explanations. In all but the mistake excuses, the actor can point to abnormal circumstances or abnormal characteristics that make it too difficult for her to appreciate the criminality or wrongfulness of her conduct or too difficult to conform her conduct to the law. In the mistake excuses, no disabling abnormality exists, but the actor can claim that, because of a reasonable mistake, she did not realize that her conduct violated the law or was wrongful.

Disability vs. Mistake Excuses The disability and mistake excuses generate the same conclusion of blamelessness in different ways. In the disability excuses, the disabling abnormality sets the actor apart from the general population. The mistake excuses seem to do the opposite: They argue that the actor should not be punished because in fact he has acted in a way that anyone else would and should have acted in the same situation. That is, the actor's mistake is reasonable; any reasonable person would have made the same mistake. This path to blamelessness has complications, however, for no disabling abnormality exists to which the blame for the offense can be shifted. Further, with no disability to distinguish the actor from the general population, there is greater danger that acquitting the apparently normal actor will undercut the law's prohibition of the actor's conduct. More on this in a moment. The absence of a disabling abnormality may help explain why the law is more hesitant to recognize mistake excuses and, when they are recognized, why it severely restricts their reach. Objective appearances aside, however, the two mechanisms of excuse in fact are analogous. Both rely on a conclusion that the actor could not reasonably have been expected to avoid the violation. Where a disabling abnormality exists, the claim of excuse is essentially a claim that the reasonable person suffering a similar disability similarly would have been unable to avoid a violation.

Disability Requirement By *disability* is meant an abnormal condition of the actor at the time of the offense, such as insanity, intoxication, subnormality, or immaturity. Each such disability is a real-world condition with a variety of observable manifestations apart from the conduct constituting the offense. It may be a long-term or even permanent condition, such as subnormality, or a temporary state like intoxication, somnambulism, automatism, or hypnotism. Its cause may be internal, as in insanity, or external, as in coercion from another person (duress). The disability requirement serves to distinguish the actor from the general population; it provides an object to which the blame may be shifted; and it allows the law to acquit the actor because he is different, while continuing to condemn and prohibit the conduct for all others. The existence of a disability also provides some evidence that a resulting excusing condition does in fact exist. These purposes help explain why a disability typically must have confirmable manifestations beyond the criminal conduct at hand. The Model Penal Code intoxication defense, for example, requires "a disturbance of mental or physical capacities resulting from the introduction of substances into the body."[1] The insanity defense requires that the defendant be suffering from a "mental disease or defect,"[2] which is defined to exclude "an abnormality manifested only by repeated criminal or otherwise antisocial conduct."[3]

Excusing Conditions   Having a recognized disability does not itself qualify an actor for an excuse, for it is not the disability that is central to the reason for exculpating the actor. An actor is not excused because she is involuntarily intoxicated, but rather because the *effect* of the intoxication in the instant situation is to create a condition that renders the actor blameless for the conduct constituting the offense. The requirement of an *excusing condition,* then, is not an element independent of the actor's disability but rather a requirement that the actor's disability cause a particular result, a particular exculpating mental or emotional condition in relation to the conduct constituting the offense.

Four Types of Excusing Conditions   Society generally is willing to excuse an actor under any of four types of conditions. In descending order of severity, they include situations where:

(1) the conduct constituting the offense simply is not the product of the actor's voluntary effort or determination (e.g., the actor is having a seizure);

(2) the conduct is the product of the actor's voluntary effort or determination, but the actor does not accurately perceive the physical nature or consequences of the conduct (e.g., the actor hallucinates that what in fact is a gun is a paint brush, or accurately perceives the physical characteristics of the gun but does not know that guns shoot bullets that can injure people) and therefore does not know that the conduct is wrong or criminal;

(3) the actor accurately perceives and understands the physical nature of the conduct and its consequences, but does not know that the conduct is wrong or criminal (e.g., the actor thinks God has ordered him to sacrifice a neighbor for the good of mankind or believes, because of paranoid delusions, that the man waiting for a bus is about to attack him); or

---

1. Model Penal Code § 2.08(5).
2. Model Penal Code § 4.01(1).
3. Model Penal Code § 4.01(2).

(4) the actor accurately perceives the nature and consequences of the conduct and knows its wrongfulness and criminality but lacks the ability to control the conduct (e.g., because of an insane compulsion or duress) to such an extent that the actor can no longer reasonably be expected to conform his conduct to the requirements of law.

Involuntary Act The first excusing condition occurs where the conduct constituting an offense does not include a volitional act. Cases of this sort include "conduct" that is a reflex action or convulsion. This first excusing condition presents the clearest case of blamelessness. The absence of volition in the doing of a criminal act is only a step above the absence of a muscular contraction. Nearly any disability causing the excusing condition is recognized as adequate for a defense; the resulting dysfunction apparently is sufficiently gross that it establishes its own abnormality. Traditionally, such conditions bar conviction because they prevent satisfaction of the voluntary act requirement that is said to be an element of all offenses. However, there may be advantages to treating such cases as providing a general excuse defense rather than as negating a required element, as discussed later in this Subpart.

Ignorance of Nature of Act In an excusing condition of the second sort there is, admittedly, a voluntary act but the actor is exculpated because she is unaware of the nature of her act; that is, she is unaware of its physical nature or normal immediate consequences. Such is the case of an actor who, suffering from a delusion that she is squeezing an orange, strangles her spouse. The defect typically is one of perception[1] and commonly results from insanity or intoxication or from more exotic disabilities such as automatism or somnambulism.[2] When this second excusing condition is relied on, the law limits the excuse to specific disabilities, such as involuntary intoxication, insanity, somnambulism, which must be independently proved.

Ignorance of Criminality or Wrongfulness of Act In the third category of excusing condition, the actor engages in conduct voluntarily and knows the nature of the act but does not know that the act is wrong or criminal. The defect is one of knowledge rather than perception. It can result from a simple lack of information or from a lack of the intelligence or cognitive function necessary to use available information to determine wrongfulness or criminality. The law seems more suspicious of these claims for excuse. A normal person's plea for excuse based on ignorance of the law that proscribes his conduct generally is rejected. Because normal people can make such mistakes, presence of the excusing condition alone does little to distinguish the actor from the general population. Instances of this third excusing condition thus are more selectively excused, generally requiring either a disability with persuasive indications of abnormality or special circumstances suggesting a reasonable mistake and compelling a conclusion of blamelessness. This basis for exculpating an actor underlies the disability excuses of insanity, subnormality, involuntary intoxication, and immaturity. The few mistake excuses that are recognized also use the excusing condition of this third group.

---

1. However, where the excusing condition concerns ignorance of the probable *consequences* of the actor's conduct, it can be the result of a severe defect in knowledge rather than a defect in perception.

2. The latter are sometimes treated, inaccurately, as instances of involuntary conduct.

Mistake Excuses as Third Type of Excusing Condition   Four types of mistakes commonly are allowed as grounds for a general excuse defense (as distinguished from mistakes that provide a "failure of proof" defense by negating an element of the offense). Reliance on an official misstatement of law and mistake due to the unavailability of a law are two such general mistake excuses. A mistake as to whether one's conduct is justified also is commonly recognized as an excuse, as discussed in Section 20. In the latter instance, the actor does not know his conduct is wrong or criminal because, under the circumstances as he perceives and understands them, his actions are justified. A fourth commonly recognized mistake excuse, reliance on unlawful military orders, is essentially a special subclass of a mistake as to a justification excuse, where the justification is the public authority of lawful military orders.[1]

Impairment of Control   The fourth excusing condition exists where an actor engages in conduct voluntarily, correctly perceives the nature of his act, and is aware that it is wrong. The act is exculpated because she lacks the capacity to control her conduct and thus cannot justly be held accountable for it. For this fourth excusing condition, the law generally is unwilling to excuse unless there is a clear and confirmable disability that distinguishes the actor from others, a disability that explains the criminal conduct and takes responsibility for it. A loaded .357 Magnum pointed at the actor's head, for example, may provide the objective, confirmable criterion necessary to distinguish the actor's ability to control her conduct from that of the general population. Insanity and intoxication may cause this excusing condition, just as they may cause the previous two excusing conditions. The duress defense is based solely on this defect in control. Hypnotism sometimes is recognized as an excuse because it may cause this fourth excusing condition, although it often is incorrectly listed as an example of the involuntary act defense, the first excusing condition.

"Status Excuses"   To say that one of these excusing conditions must be satisfied is to say that a disability by itself will not excuse. It is not enough that the actor is intoxicated or subject to duress; his intoxication or duress must cause an excusing condition. This may seem rudimentary, especially in the case of duress or intoxication, but the implications for other excuses can be dramatic. The inadequacy of a disability by itself to excuse means that there ought to be no such thing as a "status excuse," as the common law recognized and some modern theorists appear to support. Being mentally ill is not itself enough. It is not that the law recognizes a class of mentally ill persons who are automatically free of criminal responsibility for whatever they might do. Rather, the insanity defense requires that the actor's mental illness be such that on this occasion it is of such a nature and effect that it excuses the offense at hand. One might well be seriously mentally ill yet be liable for an offense if the mental illness does not play a sufficient role in commission of the offense. In other words, the disability must cause an excusing condition *for the conduct constituting the offense charged.* If *A,* while preparing a knowingly false income tax return, hallucinates that a neighbor's barking dog has turned into an attacking tiger, he may be considered insane at the time of filing the false return, but he does not merit an insanity excuse if his hallucination plays no

---

1. The excuse and the justification of lawful military orders commonly are treated together under the "defense of military orders." See, e.g., Model Penal Code § 2.10.

part in the preparation and filing of the return. If he kills the dog/tiger in perceived self-defense, of course, he may be excused for the killing. In both cases, *A* may be suffering from insanity. Only in the case of the killing, however, can the disability be said to have created an excusing condition (type two) that undercuts *A*'s responsibility for the offense.[1]

Disability as "But For" Cause Is Insufficient   The importance of the excusing condition requirement is seen in the rule that an existing disability, without an adequate excusing condition, is insufficient to excuse *even if the disability is a "but for" cause of the offense.* The effect of this rule can be quite dramatic. Assume an elderly male, with no prior record of child abuse, is given a drug while in the hospital and, while under the influence of the drug, he goes to another room in the hospital and molests a young girl. Assume further that the evidence shows conclusively that the actor would not have committed the offense if he had not been given the drug. Should he be excused? One can appreciate the appeal of the defendant's claim that it was the drug, not his own free choice, that has caused the offense. Yet, current excuse formulations are not likely to provide a defense. It is not enough that the drug created an impulse that would not otherwise have existed or that it eroded a restraint that otherwise would have existed. Current excuses require that the compulsion be sufficiently overwhelming or that the actor's capacity to resist be sufficiently impaired that he could not reasonably have been expected to have avoided the offense. It is the excusing condition requirement that implements this normative standard in judging the adequacy of the compulsion or incapacity.

Disparate Burdens to Avoid Crime   The result of this principle may be a greater burden on one actor than on another. And the greater burden may be one for which the actor is not responsible, as is the case with the hospitalized molester. But then many people no doubt have naturally occurring greater burdens than others in conforming their conduct to the requirements of law, either because of the kind of place in which they live or grew up or the kinds of genes and physiology they have. The law generally does not take account of such differences in burden to conform unless the burden reaches a level of severity that is sufficiently gross and abnormal that compliance cannot reasonably be expected. When an actor's life circumstances or internal makeup cause a sufficiently severe burden to conform that it alters our expectations of the person's ability to avoid the offense, an excuse defense generally is available. But absent a clear abnormality causing an adequate excusing condition, each actor is obliged to resist the compulsions and overcome the incapacities tending toward crime. Thus, despite the fact that the elderly man in the hospital would not have committed the molestation but for the drug, he will not be given a defense unless the jury is persuaded that the effect of the drug was sufficiently overwhelming that he could not have been expected to have avoided the violation.

---

1. In practice, immaturity is formulated as a "status excuse" in many jurisdictions. That is, the defense requirements look only to whether the actor fits a defined class, without regard for whether he satisfies the excusing conditions for the offense at hand. But many other jurisdictions require a showing of actual immaturity or allow the state to rebut a presumption of immaturity that arises when the defendant is under a certain age. Even where a conclusive age cutoff is used, it is offered as an effective approximation for an immaturity assessment. That is, no one claims a defendant should be excused *because he is 13* but rather because being 13 suggests that *he is immature.*

Objective Limitation on Excuses To judge whether a person has sufficient capacity to avoid a violation, the law introduces objective standards into its excuses. While we may tend to think of excuses as being very subjective, the fact is that in principle all modern excuses hold an actor to some form of objective standard in judging her efforts to remain law-abiding. Several excuses have explicit objective standards as part of their criteria. Mistake defenses require that the actor's mistake be reasonable. The duress defense requires that the actor meet the standard of resistance of "the person of reasonable firmness."[1] Recall that reasonableness, non-negligence, is assessed through an individualized objective standard: the reasonable person in the actor's situation.[2] Such objective limitations are what one would expect, given the fact that excuses serve a normative blaming/excusing function. It simply is not the case that we intuitively excuse every person who can show pressure or temptation or a disadvantage in resisting the same. Our blaming/excusing judgments are more complex. We want to know: How strong was the pressure or temptation? How difficult was it for the actor to resist? Inevitably, we may try to put ourselves in the actor's situation and try to imagine whether we would have been able to resist the violation.

Presumed Satisfaction of Objective Standard Not every excuse defense includes in its legal formulation an objective standard. Involuntary act, insanity, and involuntary intoxication have no apparent requirement of this sort. It would be a mistake, however, to assume that these defenses excuse without regard for whether the actor has met our collective normative expectations for efforts to avoid a violation. These defenses assure compliance with our expectations by limiting each defense in other ways. In the involuntary act defense, for example, relying on the first type of excusing condition, the required dysfunction is sufficiently great that it assures that the burden of compliance was unattainable. The act constituting the offense simply was not the product of the actor's effort or determination.

Inviting Normative Assessment Without Use of Objective Standard The formulations of the insanity and involuntary intoxication defenses take a somewhat different approach. A person is excused if, as a result of either disability, "he lacks *substantial* capacity either to appreciate the criminality [wrongfulness] of his conduct or to conform his conduct to the requirements of law."[3] The formulation leaves it to the jury to determine how much loss of capacity is enough to render the actor's violation blameless. Instead of explicitly providing an individualized objective standard that calls for a normative assessment, the formulation uses an openly vague term, "substantial," knowing, indeed intending,[4] that the jury will use their collective intuitive judgments in deciding whether the loss of capacity was substantial enough to excuse. It seems likely that the analysis and the result will be the

---

1. Model Penal Code § 2.09(1).
2. Model Penal Code §§ 1.13(16) & 2.02(2)(d).
3. Model Penal Code §§ 2.08(4) & 4.01(1) (emphasis added).
4. It was recognized, of course, that 'substantial' is an open-ended concept, but its quantitative connotation was believed to be sufficiently precise for practical administration. The law is full of instances in which courts and juries are explicitly authorized to confront an issue of degree. Such an approach was deemed to be no less essential and appropriate in dealing with this issue....

Model Penal Code § 4.01 comment 3 (1985).

same as under the individualized reasonable person test used in the mistake and duress excuses. That is, an actor's loss of capacity to appreciate or control his conduct will be judged "substantial" only if "the reasonable person in the actor's situation" could not reasonably have been expected to have avoided the offense.

Disability as Distinguishing Among Excuses   Most excuses are defined and distinguished according to the disabilities to which they apply. Where a mental disease or defect is the cause of the excusing condition, the insanity defense is applicable. Even where the results of the defendant's disability are identical to those that may result from insanity — distortion in perception, ignorance of criminality, or impairment of ability to control one's conduct — if the disability is not mental disease or defect, a defendant will not be eligible for an insanity excuse. Thus, it is the excusing condition's cause — be it involuntary intoxication, immaturity, subnormality, hypnotism, duress, or some other disability — rather than the results, that determines which excuse is applicable. This practice of defining excuses by their disability elements may have evolved because the disability is an independently observable phenomenon, while the resulting excusing condition is not.

Special Rules for Specific Disabilities   Such a disability-organized system of excuses probably developed also because it has practical value. As with justification defenses, it frequently is appropriate to attach special rules to particular disabilities. For example, it may be more of a concern in practice that an actor voluntarily caused his own intoxication, than that he caused his own insanity. Thus, special rules relating to an actor's culpability in becoming intoxicated are added to the intoxication excuse. On the other hand, as a theoretical matter, it would seem that the same principles should apply, no matter what the disability. If it is appropriate to take account of an actor's causing his own disability, for example, there is no reason why the principle should not apply to all disabilities, whether the defendant causes his own intoxication, hypnotism, duress, or insanity.

Mistake Excuses

◆ THE CASE OF BERNARD BARKER

Bernard Barker was born March 17, 1917, in Havana, Cuba, to American parents. He attended the University of Havana and joined the United States Air Force. During World War II, the Germans held him as a prisoner of war for sixteen months. After the war, he returned to Cuba and worked for its police and for the C.I.A. When Castro rose to power, Barker fled to the United States, settled in Miami, and opened a real estate office. His formal relationship with the C.I.A. ended in 1966.

On April 17, 1971, ten years after the Bay of Pigs operation—the failed C.I.A. plan to invade Cuba and overthrow Castro—Barker returns home to find a note taped to his front door that asks him to call a number. Barker calls the number on the note and quickly recognizes the voice on the other end as Howard Hunt's, his former C.I.A. supervisor. Hunt was a C.I.A. agent for twenty-one years, but retired on May 1, 1970, a detail of which Barker is unaware. The Executive Office of the President subsequently

Figure 97 **Bernard Barker, 1973**

(Bettmann/Corbis)

Figure 98 **E. Howard Hunt, January 1973**
(Bettmann/Corbis)

hired Hunt as a consultant to work on covert special investigations, which is similar to what he had done while with the C.I.A. After an exchange of pleasantries, Hunt invites Barker to visit him at his hotel. Barker is curious as to why Hunt is in Miami and wonders whether a new operation may be in the works.

Barker and Hunt spend time catching up, then meet with some of their fellow operatives and former members of the Cuban Revolutionary Council. Later, the Barkers, the Hunts, a Mr. Martinez, and a friend of Barker have dinner together at a Cuban restaurant and spend the evening reminiscing.

In 1971, the *New York Times* publishes a story detailing aspects of a confidential Pentagon report on the United States' involvement in Vietnam. After its publication, the White House frantically scrambles to investigate the leak and to plug any future leaks by establishing a special unit known as the Plumbers. John Ehrlichman, Assistant to the President for domestic affairs, heads the group, which includes persons from the National Security Council, as well as G. Gordon Liddy, a former F.B.I. agent, and Hunt.

The group quickly concludes that Daniel Ellsberg was the source of the leaked Pentagon report. In an effort to gather information on Ellsberg, the F.B.I. tries, unsuccessfully, to obtain records from his psychiatrist, Dr. Lewis J. Fielding. The Plumbers want the records in the hope of finding information to discredit Ellsberg. They decide it is best to use a covert operation that does not require direct involvement by White House staff. Following Hunt's recommendation, they elect to use his ex-C.I.A. associates.

Hunt contacts Barker when he returns to Miami in August. Without providing details, Hunt explains that he is part of a White House group that is " a sort of superstructure," with greater jurisdiction than the F.B.I. and C.I.A., "because the F.B.I. was tied by Supreme Court decisions…and the Central Intelligence Agency didn't have jurisdiction in certain matters." He asks Barker to become "operational" again and to help them collect information about "a traitor to this country, who was passing…classified information to the Soviet Embassy." Finally, he asks Barker to also recruit two experienced men with C.I.A. training.

Having worked for Hunt, Barker assumes that the government has authorized the mission. He agrees to become operational. Barker loves America and considers it his duty to offer his services to protect national security. He also hopes that working with Hunt will lead the government to reciprocate the gesture in the form of future support to help liberate Cuba. He recruits two other men, Eugenio Martinez and Felipe de Diego. Like Barker, Martinez is a former covert agent for the C.I.A. He was born in Cuba and fled to Miami when Castro came into power. In 1970, he became a naturalized citizen and is still on C.I.A. retainer when Barker contacts him. De Diego also has intelligence experience in Cuba and as an intelligence officer in the United States Army. Both are dedicated to the cause of national security and hope to gain support for Cuban liberation. Barker provides them with the same minimal information that he was given about the operation. All three are accustomed to receiving operational information on a "need-to-know basis." Shortly after Hunt returns to Washington, he contacts Barker to inform him that Barker's new recruits have received clearance and that the operation is a go.

On August 25, 1971, Hunt and Liddy fly to Los Angeles to complete a "feasibility study and preliminary reconnaissance" for the mission. Eight days later, the group stops in Chicago on their way to Los Angeles to purchase four walkie-talkies and camera equipment. When they arrive in Los Angeles, Hunt completes follow-up reconnaissance to determine what tools they will need to enter Fielding's building. They purchase delivery-man's uniforms, a crowbar, glass cutters, masking tape, and other burglary-related

Figure 99 G. Gordon Liddy
(Bettmann/Corbis)

tools. Later they meet at the Beverly Hills Hilton, where Hunt gives the team a briefing of the mission plan — to enter Fielding's office without using force, look for a file (unspecified at this point), photograph it, and replace it. He also explains

that Fielding is not the target of the investigation. There is no discussion about obtaining a warrant or other judicial authorizations for the search. Barker is not concerned, however, because he sees the mission as a matter of national security, of high sensitivity, and typical by C.I.A. standards. He does not ask questions.

The next day, September 3, Hunt shows Barker and Martinez the disguises and identification papers. In the evening, he reveals to Barker that they are looking for any files on "Ellsberg." That night, disguised as delivery-men, Barker and de Diego go to Fielding's office building carrying a valise marked with delivery labels and containing the camera equipment. They leave it there for use during the search and confirm for themselves that the outside doors of the building are unlocked.

Later that night, Liddy and Hunt station themselves as lookouts outside Fielding's

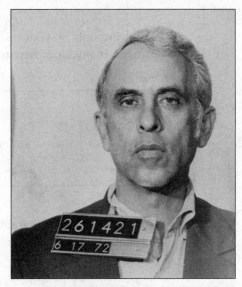

Figure 100 Mugshot of Eugenio Martinez, alias Jeane Valdes, June 18, 1972
(Bettmann/Corbis)

building and house, respectively. The other three proceed as "deliverymen" to his office to conduct the search. The plan originally was for them to just walk in, but they now find that both the front and back doors are locked. When using a glass cutter to open a window fails, they tape up the window (to avoid making too much noise) and smash it in. They climb through the shattered window and go to Fielding's second floor office.

It is impossible to avoid using force again; they must crowbar open Fielding's office door. Once inside, Barker tells the others that they are looking for any files on Ellsberg, "a great traitor to the United States." Wearing gloves, they pry open locked cabinets and flip through drawers of files. After almost forty-five minutes of searching, they find nothing except Ellsberg's name in an address book. They photograph the book and open file cabinets to show they made a good faith attempt to complete their mission. De Diego has taken photographs to help them know where things belong, but Barker tells them the mission is over before they have a chance to rearrange things. Since force was used to enter the office, they follow Hunt's instructions to make it look as if a drug addict had broken in to look for drugs by scattering some of the doctor's pills on the floor.

Figure 101 **During their trial at district court, the defendants stand outside with their attorney. From left to right: Virgilio Gonzales, Frank Sturgis, attorney Henry Rothblatt, Bernard Barker, and Eugenio Martinez, January 9, 1973**

(Wally McNamee/Corbis)

The next day, Barker and his men return to Miami. They are reimbursed for living expenses, the cost of travel, and one hundred dollars for lost income. No other payment is forthcoming, nor do they expect it.

On March 7, 1974, Barker is indicted for the break-in at Dr. Fielding's office.

1. Relying only on your own intuitions of justice, what liability and punishment, if any, does Bernard Barker deserve?

N	0	1	2	3	4	5	6	7	8	9	10	11
☐	☐	☐	☐	☐	☐	☐	☐	☐	☐	☐	☐	☐
no liability	liability but no punishment	1 day	2 wks	2 mo	6 mo	1 yr	3 yrs	7 yrs	15 yrs	30 yrs	life imprison-ment	death

2. What liability, if any, under the then-existing statutes?
3. What liability, if any, under the Model Penal Code?

■ THE LAW

United States Code
Title 18 (1971)

Section 241. Conspiracy Against Rights of Citizens

If two or more persons conspire to injure, oppress, threaten, or intimidate any citizen on the free exercise or enjoyment of any right or privilege secured to him by the Constitution or laws of the United States, or because of his having so exercised the same; or

If two or more persons go in disguise on the highway, or on the premises of another, with the intent to prevent or hinder his free exercise or enjoyment of any right or privilege so secured —

They shall be fined not more than $10,000 or imprisoned not more than ten years, or both; and if death results, they shall be subject to imprisonment for any term of years or for life.

United States v. Simpson
460 F.2d 515, 517-518 (9th Cir. 1972)

The defendant was prosecuted for burning Selective Service files in an attempt to disrupt the Vietnam War, which he believed to be illegal and immoral. The court recognized the existence of a general justification defense but held that it was not available in the case at hand.

> The theoretical basis of the justification defenses is the proposition that, in many instances, society benefits when one acts to prevent another from intentionally or negligently causing injury to people or property. That benefit is lost, however, and the theory fails when the person seeking to avert the anticipated harm does not act reasonably. Thus, it is commonly held, for example, that a person may not use excessive force in repelling an attacker or any force when the necessity therefor disappears.

United States v. Mancuso
139 F.2d 90 (3d Cir. 1943)

The defendant was convicted of failing to appear and present himself for induction into the army on order of his local draft board. He appealed the conviction on the ground that the draft board's order had been stayed by a judicial decree (although it was itself later held to be erroneous and subject to reversal). The court reversed the defendant's conviction, based on his reliance on the trial judge's ruling, and held that the defendant could not "be convicted for failing to obey an order, issuance of which [was] forbidden by the court's injunction. While it is true that men are, in general, held responsible for violations of the law, whether they know it or not, we do not think the layman participating in a law suit is required to know more law than the judge. If the litigant does something, or fails to do something, while under the protection of a court order he should not, therefore, be subject to criminal penalties for that act or omission."

Raley v. Ohio
360 U.S. 423 (1959)

The defendants were charged with contempt of court for refusal to answer questions put to them by the Ohio Un-American Activities Commission, established by the Ohio legislature. They had relied on information by the Commission that they had a right to rely on the privilege against self-incrimination. The Ohio Supreme Court, however, held that the appellants were presumed to know the law of Ohio — that an Ohio immunity statute deprived them of the protection of the privilege — and that they therefore had committed an offense by not answering the questions as to which they asserted the privilege. The United States Supreme Court reversed their convictions, holding that "in the circumstances of these cases . . . [a]fter the Commission, speaking for the State, acted as it did, to sustain the Ohio Supreme Court's judgment would be to sanction an indefensible sort of entrapment by the State — convicting a citizen for exercising a privilege which the State had clearly told him was available to him."

Cox v. Louisiana
379 U.S. 559 (1965)

The defendant was convicted of violating a state statute prohibiting picketing and parading near a courthouse. The Court reversed his conviction because the highest local police officials had told demonstrators that they could meet for a designated period of time across the street from courthouse. "In effect, [the defendant] was advised that a demonstration at the place it was held would not be one 'near' the courthouse within the terms of the statute. . . . As in *Raley* . . . to sustain [the defendant's] later conviction for demonstrating where they told him he could 'would be to sanction an indefensible sort of entrapment by the State — convicting a citizen for exercising a privilege which the State had clearly told him was available to him.' . . . The Due Process Clause does not permit convictions to be obtained under such circumstances."

Finn v. United States
219 F.2d 894 (9th Cir. 1955)

The defendants were brothers who were prosecuted for "wilfully and knowingly conspiring to prevent [the] United States Attorney from discharging his official duties by unlawfully causing his arrest and wilfully interfering with the performance of official duties." They believed the United States Attorney had illegally taken their airplane, so they performed a citizens' arrest, took him to the police station, at which point they were themselves arrested. Their defense was that "they thought when they 'arrested' [the United States Attorney] he had violated their civil rights; that specifically they thought he had violated Sections 241, 242 and 372 of Title 18 of the United States Code; and that having honestly thought so they lacked the specific requisite 'intent' to be guilty of the offenses with which they are charged." Summarizing their defense, the court stated that "[e]ssentially the defendants defended their conduct on the ground that ignorance and bad information as to what the law is constitute an excuse for them." The court rejected their claim for a mistake of law defense.

Model Penal Code
(Official Draft 1962)

Section 2.04. Ignorance or Mistake

(1) Ignorance or mistake as to a matter of fact or law is a defense if:

(a) the ignorance or mistake negatives the purpose, knowledge, belief, recklessness or negligence required to establish a material element of the offense; or

(b) the law provides that the state of mind established by such ignorance or mistake constitutes a defense.

(2) Although ignorance or mistake would otherwise afford a defense to the offense charged, the defense is not available if the defendant would be guilty of another offense had the situation been as he supposed. In such case, however, the ignorance or mistake of the defendant shall reduce the grade and degree of the offense of which he may be convicted to those of the offense of which he would be guilty had the situation been as he supposed.

(3) A belief that conduct does not legally constitute an offense is a defense to a prosecution for that offense based upon such conduct when:

(a) the statute or other enactment defining the offense is not known to the actor and has not been published or otherwise reasonably made available prior to the conduct alleged; or

(b) he acts in reasonable reliance upon an official statement of the law, afterward determined to be invalid or erroneous, contained in (i) a statute or other enactment; (ii) a judicial decision, opinion or judgment; (iii) an administrative order or grant of permission; or (iv) an official interpretation of the public officer or body charged by law with responsibility for the interpretation, administration or enforcement of the law defining the offense.

(4) The defendant must prove a defense arising under Subsection (3) of this Section by a preponderance of evidence.

● OVERVIEW OF GENERAL MISTAKE OF LAW EXCUSE

Variety of Mistake Defenses   When an actor mistakes another's umbrella for his own, his mistake will negate the culpable state of mind that is required for theft, as discussed in Section 5. Such a mistake is an example of mistake as an absent element defense. A mistake also may be the basis for a general defense, without regard to the elements of the offense charged. An actor who takes another's umbrella, mistakenly believing it to be a disguised terrorist bomb that is endangering a restaurant full of people, satisfies all the elements of theft, yet may have a general mistake excuse if the actor's belief is reasonable. His defense would be one of mistake as to justification, discussed in Section 20. If a new anti-terrorist law makes it an offense to carry a sharply pointed object in a public place, an actor may have a defense to a violation if the law has not yet reasonably been made available to the public or if a public official incorrectly advises the actor that the law does not apply to umbrellas. It is this latter kind of mistake, providing a general mistake defense unrelated to offense elements or to a belief in justification, that is the subject of this Section.

"Ignorance of Law Is No Excuse"   The common law adhered to a maxim that "ignorance or mistake of law is no excuse." The maxim frequently was applied even where the mistake of law negated an element required by the offense definition. This extreme form of adherence to the maxim is no longer common. A mistake that negates an offense element, even a mistake of law, is now typically recognized as a defense. The maxim continues to be given effect, however, in denying a defense where an actor erroneously believes that his conduct is lawful, but where the actor's mistake does not negate an offense element. In fact, few mistakes of law negate an offense element because few offenses have knowledge of criminality as an element.[1] Therefore, even under today's more limited application of the maxim, an actor's belief, even a reasonable belief, that her conduct is not criminal typically is not itself grounds for a defense. Whether criminal law should recognize a defense for a reasonable mistake of law is the focus of the Discussion Materials below.

Exceptions to Maxim   States following the lead of the Model Penal Code, and some court opinions, recognize two general-defense exceptions to the maxim. A general defense commonly is available to an actor whose ignorance or mistake of law results because the law she violated was not made reasonably available or because the actor reasonably relied on an official misstatement of the law.[2] But these exceptions may reflect less a concern for the rule's potential to punish blameless actors and more on an estoppel rationale independent of blameworthiness concerns.

Unavailable Law   The impropriety of convicting an offender where the law was not made reasonably available occasionally was recognized as an exception to the maxim even before the Model Penal Code. In *The Cotton Planter* case, for

---

1. See also Model Penal Code § 2.02(9).
2. See Model Penal Code § 2.04(3) & (4).

example, a ship set sail from St. Mary's in Georgia for Antigua in the West Indies. After the ship was beyond land communication, word was received at the port that sailing to Antigua had been made unlawful by a new statute that put an embargo on all ships and vessels in the ports and harbors of the United States.[1] The court reverses the lower court's judgment of forfeiture:

> A more abject state of slavery cannot easily be conceived than that the legislature should have the power of passing laws inflicting the highest penalties, without taking any measure to make them known to those whose property or lives may be affected by them. It is not only necessary, therefore, in a country governed by laws, that they be passed by the supreme or legislative power, but that they be notified to the people who are expected to obey them.

The defense is codified in Model Penal Code as follows:

> A belief that conduct does not legally constitute an offense is a defense to a prosecution for that offense based upon such conduct when: . . . the statute or other enactment defining the offense is not known to the actor and has not been published or otherwise reasonably made available prior to the conduct alleged; . . . .
>
> The defendant must prove a defense arising under [this] Subsection by a preponderance of evidence.[2]

Reliance on Official Misstatement Similar arguments can be made in support of a defense for an actor who reasonably relies on an official misstatement of law. But in *United States v. Anthony*,[3] where Susan B. Anthony relied on the opinion of the election inspectors that she had a right to vote even though the Constitution did not appear to permit women to do so, the court stuck to the maxim:

> One illegally voting was bound and was assumed to know the law, and that a belief that he had a right to vote gave no defense, if there was no mistake of fact. No system of criminal jurisprudence can be sustained upon any other principle.

On the other hand almost a century later, the Model Penal Code codifies such a defense:

> A belief that conduct does not legally constitute an offense is a defense to a prosecution for that offense based upon such conduct when:
>
> > [the defendant] acts in reasonable reliance upon an official statement of the law, afterward determined to be invalid or erroneous, contained in (i) a statute or other enactment; (ii) a judicial decision, opinion or judgment; (iii) an administrative order or grant of permission; or (iv) an official interpretation of the public officer or body charged by law with responsibility for the interpretation, administration or enforcement of the law defining the offense.

---

1. 6 F. Cas. 620, 620 (No. 3,270) (1810).
2. Model Penal Code § 2.04(3)(a) & (4).
3. 24 F. Cas. 829 (No. 14, 459) (1873).

The defendant must prove a defense arising under [this] Subsection by a preponderance of evidence.[1]

Estoppel Rationale   One may be tempted to see these two exceptions to the maxim as the spearhead in a move toward rejection of the maxim itself. After all, the maxim does seem to conflict with the law's general requirement of blame-worthiness as a precondition to criminal conviction: An actor who makes a reasonable mistake of law—a mistake that a reasonable person would have made—is blameless. Unfortunately, this is not the case. These two exceptions are explained instead by the presence of a governmental role in causing the mistake: the government's failure to make the law reasonably available and a government official's misstatement of law to the defendant. There is a special unfairness, it may be argued, if the government misleads a person as to the law or fails to make the law available and then tries to prosecute for the resulting violation. Aside from such estoppel-based exceptions, the maxim appears to continue to enjoy vigorous support. Note, for example, that it is no defense under the Model Penal Code that one reasonably relies upon a statement of law from a person who one reasonably believes is a government official; the person must in fact be such an official. [2] Yet a reasonable belief that one was relying on an official would seem to render the actor blameless, as one might argue is the case in *Barker*.

Reasonable Mistake of Law Defense   The maxim is clearly rejected, however, by a current New Jersey statute, which provides a true general excuse for a reasonable mistake of law, albeit in fairly restrictive form:

> A belief that conduct does not legally constitute an offense is a defense to a prosecution for that offense based upon such conduct when:...
>
> The actor...diligently pursues all means available to ascertain the meaning and application of the offense to his conduct and honestly and in good faith concludes his conduct is not an offense in circumstances in which a law-abiding and prudent person would also so conclude.
>
> The defendant must prove a defense arising under [this] subsection by clear and convincing evidence.[3]

The feared potential for abuse of a general mistake of law defense is minimized here in several ways. It is not enough that the actor reasonably believes the conduct is not criminal; the New Jersey provision explicitly requires that the actor affirmatively seek to ascertain the proper meaning and application of the law to the contemplated conduct. The provision also appears to take into account the difficulties of proving the defendant's state of mind by shifting the burden of proof to the defendant, thus making those proof problems the defendant's problems. The defendant must prove the defense by "clear and convincing" evidence, as compared to the Model Penal Code's less demanding "by a preponderance" of the evidence.

---

1. Model Penal Code § 2.04(3)(b) & (4).
2. See Model Penal Code § 2.04(3)(b): defense if "he acts in reasonable reliance upon an official statement of the law...."
3. N.J. Stat. Ann. § 2C:2-4(c)(3).

▲ PROBLEM
Sophie's Stand

Sophie is upset at the recent practice of "pro-life" groups in heckling women who enter the local Woman's Center, where abortions are performed. As an active member of a "pro-choice" group, she has joined in counter-demonstrations but is increasingly persuaded that they are ineffective at deterring or countering what she sees as unfair harassment. Because she is a law student, she is asked at a recent planning meeting of her group to investigate other methods for minimizing the effect of the pro-life picketing. All present agree that any course of action that they take as a group should not be unlawful. While visiting the scene of the demonstrations, Sophie notices that the only access to the Center for a large group is along the street from the park where the pro-life people now assemble their group. If pro-choice forces congregated on both sidewalks at some point on the street, the pro-life demonstrators would have to switch to much longer and more narrow routes, which would both delay their arrival at the Center and force them to break into small groups that might not be quite as emotionally charged as the large excited groups that have done the harassing.

Sophie reviews applicable law and concludes that the planned action would not be unlawful because the pro-life demonstrators would never be touched or detained in any way, they would have another means of access to where they wished to go, and the sidewalk-blocking would last only a short time and therefore would not interfere with normal public use. Her group likes her idea but asks that she check with officials to be sure that such congregation on the sidewalks would not be unlawful. In response to Sophie's inquiry, the local police advise against the proposed plan or any other such confrontational activity. When Sophie presses for a formal legal opinion, the police refer her to the State Attorney's office, pointing out that they are police officers, not lawyers. They repeat their advice against this or any other confrontation. The State Attorney's office responds to Sophie's inquiry by noting their long-standing policy against giving prior official interpretations of state law. Providing such legal advisory service, they note, would be impossible with their current legal staff, which is barely able to keep up with current court cases. Sophie reports her efforts to her group, together with her own research and her legal opinion that the planned conduct would not be a violation of law. The group accepts her recommendation.

The next day the pro-choice supporters congregate on the sidewalk in the path of the pro-life demonstrators. No contact is made. The pro-life marchers split up and take other routes to the Center. All members of Sophie's group are arrested for "Obstructing a Public Passageway," a county ordinance that does expressly criminalize their conduct. It turns out that her law school's library collection, where she had done her research, does not include county ordinances. Does Sophie have a defense? Do the members of her group have a defense?

⊛ DISCUSSION MATERIALS

Should the Criminal Law Recognize an Excuse Defense for a Reasonable Mistake of Law?

In commenting on the *Barker* case, the principal case of the Section, Thomas White discusses the rationale of the mistake of law defense and argues against its use. Louis Schwarz, on the other hand, advocates the defense's recognition particularly in situations involving law enforcement. George Fletcher's piece similarly argues in favor of the defense, based on what he perceives as the complexity of today's criminal law system. He rejects the utilitarian and conceptual counter-arguments and adopts a Kantian perspective. *People v. Marrero* illustrates the application of the defense and its potential for odd results (the defendant gets no defense for his reasonable mistake, even though almost half the judges thought his interpretation was actually correct!), with the dissent contrasting the pragmatic/utilitarian and blameworthiness arguments. Finally, Dan Kahan attempts to defend the result in *Marrero*, rejecting a reasonable mistake of law defense, by arguing that rejecting the defense makes sense as a device to prevent people from taking advantage of legal certainty in order to skate close to the line of legality and perhaps over the line of morality.

Thomas W. White, Reliance on Apparent Authority as a Defense to Criminal Prosecutions

77 Columbia Law Review 775, 779, 801 (1977)

[T]he values promoted by the general mistake of law rule do not obtain when the actor honestly and reasonably relies on what seems to be an authoritative statement of law. By seeking to inform himself of the law and then relying on it, the individual demonstrates his law-abiding nature; this exception to the rule advances, rather than hinders, the social value of making individuals know and obey the law.

Allowing the defense in the circumstances of the *Barker* cases does not serve to advance these policy interests. Reliance on a government official's apparent status as carrying with it all the legal authorization necessary for the operation is inconsistent with an affirmative effort to know the law. The burglars did not seek from Hunt an interpretation as to the legality of the break-in. Their reliance demonstrated not a law-abiding nature, but rather a failure to inquire into the law....

[T]he defense should be rejected on policy grounds: because of the societal interest in deterring conduct by government officials that infringes the civil rights of citizens, a person who purports to act on behalf of the government should be held to a high standard of knowledge of the important restrictions imposed by the law on governmental action. Only where such a person has made a reasonable effort to know the basis of legality of his actions, should he be granted a defense. An uninformed subjective belief in the legality of one's actions, unsupported by a reasonable basis for that belief, should not provide a defense.

Louis B. Schwartz, Reform of the Federal Criminal Laws: Issues, Tactics and Prospects
1977 Duke Law Journal 171, 216

There are hundreds of thousands of public servants whose duties involve arrest and search behavior ordinarily prohibited by law: customs officials, revenue agents, building guards, policemen, firemen, investigating officials and so on. The line between what is lawful for them to do and what is unlawful is notoriously vague, yet they are under pressure zealously to do all that is lawful in carrying out their responsibilities. Excesses of zeal must be corrected, and in cases of gross and wilful abuse of official authority, they must be prosecuted as crimes. But surely in a civilized society the correction of nonculpable transgressions of vaguely defined authority should not be accomplished by criminal prosecution where the servant acted in good faith obedience to seemingly lawful directions of high authorities. It is the errant high authorities who are shown to be at fault, and such correction as is required for too-obedient subordinates should take the form of better training and of civil disciplinary measures such as suspension or discharge from employment.... [I]t would amount to entrapment for society to train and arm men for law enforcement duties, place them in quasi-military subordination to superiors, and then prosecute them for conforming to plausible commands. Even if the mistake of law defense were narrowly defined for ordinary applications, it would have to be broadened for people placed in such circumstances. The ordinary citizen acts on his own initiative in complying or not complying with the law. He is not placed in a crossfire between official demand that he act aggressively and official threat of punishment if the aggressive act, though conforming to plausible particularization of society's demand through superior orders, is subsequently held to be unlawful.

George P. Fletcher, Arguments for Strict Liability: Mistakes of Law
Rethinking Criminal Law 731-736 (1978)

Various efforts have been made to defend the principle that even a reasonable mistake of law should not constitute an excuse for wrongdoing. In the early stages of the criminal law, when the range of offenses was limited to aggression against particular victims and other obvious moral wrongs, it was more plausible to assume that everyone knew the law. If someone did not realize that rape or homicide was wrong, one might properly expect a proof of mental illness in order to make out a believable claim. It is not surprising that the *M'Naghten* test of insanity is linked to the question whether, because of a mental disease or defect, the actor did not realize that the particular act was wrong.

The tight moral consensus that once supported the criminal law has obviously disappeared. This has happened as a result both of the vast expansion of the criminal law into regulatory offenses and the disintegration of the Judeo-Christian moral consensus. In a pluralistic society, saddled with criminal sanctions affecting every area of life, one cannot expect that everyone know what is criminal and what is not. The problem is compounded in some fields, such as abortion and obscenity, by constantly changing standards of permissible conduct. The "obscenity" that could send Ralph Ginzburg to jail for five years is now readily exhibited at adult theaters around the United States. Assuming that everyone who violates the law does so in disregard and disrespect of the law is obviously outdated. Maintaining that policy today verges on blindness to the problem of individual justice.

Oliver Wendell Holmes confronted the problem directly and found a harmonic consistency between disregarding mistakes of law and his favorite chord: "to admit the excuse at all would be to encourage ignorance . . . and justice to the individual is rightly outweighed by the larger interests on the other side of the scales." This utilitarian rationale for the traditional rule is hardly convincing to those who try to assess whether, in a particular case, the interests of society outweigh the interests of the individual. Surely, Holmes would not favor sacrificing the individual, however innocent, for the sake of the general good, however minimal. Therefore in a particular case, we have to assess whether or not the scales weigh more heavily on one side or on the other. If we wish to embark on this task of adjudication, how do we decide, and how should lawyers demonstrate, that one side of the scale outweighs the other? The problem with pursuing the general good is that the results of one instance of applying the criminal sanction are so speculative as to be chimerical. The problem with punishing a morally innocent person is that if one is willing to do that at all, the harm entailed is likely to appear either minimal or infinite: either because one does not perceive the evil of punishing the innocent, or because one does perceive the evil and regards it as so great as not to be worth any transient benefits. In either event, Holmes' proposal bears witness to his own famous aphorism about legal method: "General propositions do not decide concrete cases." The utilitarian calculus is too commodious a crucible for resolving concrete problems of mistakes of law.

Another rationale for disregarding mistakes of law is Jerome Hall's theory that there is a fundamental logical contradiction between deferring to the suspect's view of the law and the theory of legality. This argument merits consideration, for it illustrates the confusion engendered by a failure to recognize the distinction between wrongdoing and culpability. Hall's argument on mistake of law is best stated in his own words:

> If that plea [mistake of law] were valid, the consequence would be: whenever a defendant in a criminal case thought the law was thus and so, he is to be treated as though the law were thus and so, *i.e., the law actually is thus and so*. But such a doctrine would contradict the essential requisites of a legal system. . . .

The fallacy in this line of reasoning consists in shifting the meaning of the word "law" as we move from the premise to the conclusion. In the phrase, "whenever a defendant thought the law was thus and so," the word "law" refers to the norms about which the defendant might be mistaken. In the conclusion, "the law actually is thus and so," the word "law" no longer refers to a norm or a rule about which the defendant is mistaken, but to an empirical concept of the law equivalent to whether the court actually acquits in the particular case. These two concepts of law have little to do with each other. The norms of the law provide reasons for acting and reasons for convicting those who transgress the law. The empirical set of decisions — "what the courts do in fact" — does not provide a reason for convicting or acquitting anyone. The practice of the courts does not justify itself.

The norms of the law do not change when a jury finds that a particular suspect could not have been expected to know, say, that posting a particular sign violated the law against soliciting marriages. If the suspect violates the rule in reasonable reliance on advice of the attorney general, the conduct may be subject to an excuse, but it does not follow that the court has engrafted an exception onto the norm. The proof of that proposition is that if the suspect, acquitted on grounds of mistake, left the courthouse and posted exactly the same sign, he would obviously be guilty. Recognizing a mistake of law as an excuse does not alter the norm any more than recognizing insanity as an excuse alters the prohibition against the conduct in question.

The more general flaw in Jerome Hall's system of criminal law is the failure to recognize the profound significance of distinguishing between wrongdoing and accountability or culpability. Recognizing a claim of justification does in fact acknowledge an exception to the norm; but recognizing an excuse means merely that in the particular case, the actor cannot be fairly held accountable for his wrongdoing. Mistake of law is an excuse that leaves the norm intact. Its effect is merely to deny the attribution of the wrongdoing to the particular suspect.

If there were any doubts about this, we need only ask how the norms of the criminal law would read if a mistake of law precluded a finding that the norm was violated. Norms are designed to guide and influence conduct. The norm itself cannot include a condition about what should happen in the event that the norm was violated involuntarily or by mistake. If it is unlawful to possess brass knuckles, the norm could not be read to say: Thou shalt not possess brass knuckles unless thou art reasonably mistaken about whether it is legal to do so. Nor does it say: Thou shalt not do X unless thou art insane or under duress or involuntarily intoxicated. The norm only includes those elements about which the actor should make a decision in seeking to conform his conduct to the law. It is not up to the actor to decide whether he is insane, whether the duress of another is sufficient to excuse a violation, or whether he is reasonably mistaken about the legality of his conduct. It is impossible to give an account of excuses by referring to the content of the norm and the question whether the norm is violated. The question of excusing arises after it is established that the norm is violated. The grounds for excusing are extrinsic to the norm and reserved for assessment by the trier of fact.

These two arguments rejecting mistake of laws — one associated with Holmes and the other with Hall — correspond to the two themes that run through this section on disregarding mistakes. One general strategy for suppressing mistakes is utilitarian: It is socially beneficial to eliminate the possibility of acquittal on some claims of mistake. The other strategy is moral or conceptual: There is some reason in the nature of the things why the mistake ought to be irrelevant. . . .

Utilitarian arguments raise broader questions of moral philosophy and, therefore, they resist refutation by laying bare their premises. There is nothing hidden in Holmes' argument. "Public policy," he tells us, "sacrifices the individual to the common good." An assault on this explicit and coherent premise requires far more than the feeble claim that it is unjust to sacrifice the individual to the common good. Unjust it may be, but one needs to ground the imperative to do justice in a set of values at least as compelling as the value of furthering the social good. The most compelling argument offered to date is the Kantian thesis that the categorical imperative requires us to respect persons as ends in themselves, and we violate this imperative when we punish a person solely to further interests of other persons. The skeptic might wonder how the practice of punishing criminals can escape the charge of using persons as means to the end of deterrence and social order. The answer to this objection takes us back to the classical theory of punishment. If punishment is based on accountability for wrongdoing, then the punishing agency does not act in disregard for the wrongdoer's autonomy. On the contrary, the imposition of punishment — as contrasted with civil commitment — expresses respect for the wrongdoer's autonomy and his capacity to avoid liability under the law.

Other Discussion Materials

People v. Marrero
Court of Appeals of New York
69 N.Y.2d 382, 515 N.Y.S.2d 212, 507 N.E.2d 1068 (1987)

Bellacosa, Judge
[Defendant, a federal corrections officer, was arrested in a Manhattan social club for possession of a loaded .38 caliber automatic pistol. The statute under which he was charged exempted "peace officers," which another statute defined to include "correction officers of any state correction facility or of any penal correctional institution." The charge was dismissed on the ground that defendant fell within that definition, but on appeal the court ruled otherwise, and defendant was thereafter convicted at a trial where the judge refused to instruct that his reasonable belief that he fell within the statutory exemption would be a defense.]

The common-law rule on mistake of law was clearly articulated in *Gardner v People (62 NY 299)*. In *Gardner*, the defendants misread a statute and mistakenly believed that their conduct was legal. The court insisted, however, that the "mistake of law" did not relieve the defendants of criminal liability....

Subject to the mistake statute, the instant case ... falls within the *Gardner* rationale because the weapons possession statute violated by this defendant imposes liability irrespective of one's intent.

The desirability of the *Gardner*-type outcome, which was to encourage the societal benefit of individuals' knowledge of and respect for the law, is underscored by Justice Holmes' statement: "It is no doubt true that there are many cases in which the criminal could not have known that he was breaking the law, but to admit the excuse at all would be to encourage ignorance where the lawmaker has determined to make men know and obey, and justice to the individual is rightly outweighed by the larger interests on the other side of the scales."

The revisors of New York's Penal Law intended no fundamental departure from this common-law rule in Penal Law § 15.20, which provides in pertinent part:

§ **15.20. Effect of ignorance or mistake upon liability**....

2. A person is not relieved of criminal liability for conduct because he engages in such conduct under a mistaken belief that it does not, as a matter of law, constitute an offense, unless such mistaken belief is founded upon an official statement of the law contained in (a) a statute or other enactment ... (d) an interpretation of the statute or law relating to the offense,

officially made or issued by a public servant, agency, or body legally charged or empowered with the responsibility or privilege of administering, enforcing or interpreting such statute or law.

This section was added to the Penal Law as part of the wholesale revision of the Penal Law in 1965 (L 1965, ch 1030). When this provision was first proposed, commentators viewed the new language as codifying "the established common law maxim on mistake of law, while at the same time recognizing a defense when the erroneous belief is founded upon an 'official statement of the law.'"

The defendant claims as a first prong of his defense that he is entitled to raise the defense of mistake of law under section 15.20(2)(a) because his mistaken belief that his conduct was legal was founded upon an official statement of the law contained in the statute itself. Defendant argues that his mistaken interpretation of the statute was reasonable in view of the alleged ambiguous wording of the peace officer exemption statute, and that his "reasonable" interpretation of an "official statement" is enough to satisfy the requirements of subdivision (2)(a). However, the whole thrust of this exceptional exculpatory concept, in derogation of the traditional and common-law principle, was intended to be a very narrow escape valve. Application in this case would invert that thrust and make mistake of law a generally applied or available defense instead of an unusual exception. . . . The momentarily enticing argument by defendant that his view of the statute would only allow a defendant to get the issue generally before a jury further supports the contrary view because that consequence is precisely what would give the defense the unintended broad practical application.

The prosecution further counters defendant's argument by asserting that one cannot claim the protection of mistake of law under section 15.20(2)(a) simply by misconstruing the meaning of a statute but must instead establish that the statute relied on actually permitted the conduct in question and was only later found to be erroneous. To buttress that argument, the People analogize New York's official statement defense to the approach taken by the Model Penal Code (MPC) [§ 2.04(3)(b)]. . . .

Although the drafters of the New York statute did not adopt the precise language of the Model Penal Code provision . . . , it is evident and has long been believed that the Legislature intended the New York statute to be similarly construed. . . .

It was early recognized that the "official statement" mistake of law defense was a statutory protection against prosecution based on reliance of a statute that did *in fact* authorize certain conduct. "It seems obvious that society must rely on some statement of the law, and that conduct which *is in fact* 'authorized . . . should not be subsequently condemned. The threat of punishment under these circumstances can have no deterrent effect unless the actor doubts the validity of the official pronouncement — *a questioning of authority that is itself undesirable.*" While providing a narrow escape hatch, the idea was simultaneously to encourage the public to read and rely on official statements of the law, not to have individuals conveniently and personally question the validity and interpretation of the law and act on that basis. If later the statute was invalidated, one who mistakenly acted in reliance on the authorizing statute would be relieved of criminal liability. That makes sense and is fair. To go further does not make sense and would create a legal chaos based on individual selectivity.

In the case before us, the underlying statute never in fact authorized the defendant's conduct; the defendant only thought that the statutory exemptions permitted his conduct when, in fact, the primary statute clearly forbade his conduct. Moreover, by adjudication of the final court to speak on the subject in this very case, it turned out that even the exemption statute did not permit this defendant to possess the weapon. It would be ironic at best and an odd perversion at worst for this court now to declare that the same defendant is nevertheless free of criminal responsibility....

Strong public policy reasons underlie the legislative mandate and intent which we perceive in rejecting defendant's construction of New York's mistake of law defense statute. If defendant's argument were accepted, the exception would swallow the rule. Mistakes about the law would be encouraged, rather than respect for and adherence to law. There would be an infinite number of mistake of law defenses which could be devised from a good-faith, perhaps reasonable but mistaken, interpretation of criminal statutes, many of which are concededly complex. Even more troublesome are the opportunities for wrong-minded individuals to contrive in bad faith solely to get an exculpatory notion before the jury. These are not in terrorem arguments disrespectful of appropriate adjudicative procedures; rather, they are the realistic and practical consequences were the dissenters' views to prevail....

Accordingly, the order of the Appellate Division should be affirmed.

Hancock, Judge (dissenting).

The rule adopted by the majority prohibiting the defense of mistake of law under Penal Law § 15.20(2)(a) in the circumstances here is directly contrary to the plain dictates of the statute and a rejection of the jurisprudential reforms and legislative policies underlying its enactment. For these reasons, as more fully explained herein, we cannot agree with this decision....

...Various justifications have been offered for the rule [that mistake of law is no excuse], but all are frankly pragmatic and utilitarian—preferring the interests of society (e.g., in deterring criminal conduct, fostering orderly judicial adminis-tration, and preserving the primacy of the rule of law) to the interest of the individual in being free from punishment except for intentionally engaging in conduct which he knows is criminal.

Today there is widespread criticism of the common-law rule mandating categorical preclusion of the mistake of law defense. The utilitarian arguments for retaining the rule have been drawn into serious question, but the fundamental objection is that it is simply wrong to punish someone who, in good-faith reliance on the wording of a statute, believed that what he was doing was lawful. It is contrary to "the notion that punishment should be conditioned on a showing of subjective moral blameworthiness." ...

It is difficult to imagine a case more squarely within the wording of Penal Law § 15.20(2)(a) or one more fitted to what appears clearly to be the intended purpose of the statute than the one before us....

Nothing in the statutory language suggests the interpretation urged by the People and adopted by the majority: that Penal Law § 15.20(2)(a) is available to a defendant not when he has mistakenly read a statute but only when he has correctly read and relied on a statute which is later invalidated. Such a construction contravenes the general rule that penal statutes should be construed against the State and in favor of the accused and the Legislature's specific directive that the revised Penal Law should not be strictly construed but "must be construed according to the fair import of [its] terms to promote justice and effect the objects of the law."...

Any fair reading of the majority opinion, we submit, demonstrates that the decision to reject a mistake of law defense is based on considerations of public policy and on the conviction that such a defense would be bad, rather than on an analysis of CPL 15.20(2)(a) under the usual principles of statutory construction....

We believe that the concerns expressed by the majority are matters which properly should be and have been addressed by the Legislature....

It is no answer to protest that the defense may become a "false and diversionary stratagem", or that "wrongminded individuals [could] contrive" an "infinite number of mistake of law defenses"; for it is the very business of the courts to separate the true claims from the false....

We do not believe that permitting a defense in this case will produce the grievous consequences the majority predicts. The unusual facts of this case seem unlikely to be repeated.... Nor is there any reason to believe that courts will have more difficulty separating valid claims from "diversionary stratagem[s]" in making preliminary legal determinations as to the validity of the mistake of law defense than of justification or any other defense.

Dan M. Kahan, Ignorance of the Law Is an Excuse — But Only for the Virtuous

96 Michigan Law Review 127, 131, 133, 141-142 (1997)

> If you want to know the law and nothing else, you must look at it as a bad man, who cares only for the material consequences which such knowledge enables him to predict, not as a good one, who finds his reasons for conduct, whether inside the law or outside of it, in the vaguer sanctions of conscience.
>
> Oliver Wendell Holmes, Jr.

> It is no doubt true that there are many cases in which the criminal could not have known that he was breaking the law, but to admit [mistake of law as an] excuse at all would be to encourage ignorance where the law-maker has determined to make men know and obey, and justice to the individual is rightly outweighed by the larger interests on the other side of the scales.
>
> Oliver Wendell Holmes, Jr.

It's axiomatic that "ignorance of the law is no excuse." My aim in this essay is to examine what the "mistake of law doctrine" reveals about the relationship between criminal law and morality in general and about the law's understanding of moral responsibility in particular.

The conventional understanding of the mistake of law doctrine rests on two premises, which are encapsulated in the Holmesian epigrams with which I've started this essay. The first is liberal positivism. As a descriptive claim, liberal positivism holds that the content of the law can be identified without reference to morality: one needn't be a good man to perceive what's lawful, Holmes tells us; one need only understand the consequences in store if one should choose to act badly. The normative side of liberal positivism urges us to see the independence of law from morality as a good thing. In a pluralistic society, the law should aspire to be comprehensible to persons of diverse moral views. What's more, it should avoid embodying within itself a standard of culpability or blame that depends on an individual's acceptance of any such view as orthodox; in a liberal society, even the bad man can be a good citizen so long as he lives up to society's rules.

Liberal positivism supports denying a mistake of law defense when combined with a second premise; the utility of legal knowledge. Under the liberal positivist view, the law disclaims any reliance on the moral knowledge of citizens, as well as any ambition to make them value morality for its own sake. Accordingly, to promote good (that is, law-abiding) conduct, it becomes imperative that citizens be made aware of the content of the law and the consequences of breaking it. Hence, the law shows no mercy for those who claim to be ignorant of what the criminal law proscribes, a position that maximizes citizens' incentive to learn the rules that "the law-maker has determined to make men know and obey."

I want to challenge the accuracy of this account of why ignorance of law does not excuse. In its place, I'll suggest an alternative understanding, which rests on premises diametrically opposed to the Holmesian aphorisms that undergird the classic account.

The first premise of this anti-Holmesian conception is legal moralism. This principle asserts that law is suffused with morality and, as a result, can't ultimately be identified or applied to law without the making of moral judgments. It asserts, too, that individuals are appropriately judged by the law not only for the law-abiding quality of their actions but also for the moral quality of their values, motivations, and emotions—in a word, for the quality of their characters.

The second premise of the anti-Holmesian view can be called the prudence of obfuscation. Moral judgments are too rich and particular to be subdued by any set of abstract rules; as a result, law will always embody morality only imperfectly. That means that from the standpoint of legal moralism, private knowledge of the law isn't unambiguously good. The more readily individuals can discover the law's content, the more readily they'll be able to discern, and exploit, the gaps between what's immoral and what's illegal. The law must therefore employ strategies to discourage citizens from gaining knowledge for this purpose. One is to deny an excuse for ignorance of law. Punishing those who mistakenly believe their conduct to be legal promotes good (that is, moral) behavior less through encouraging citizens to learn the law—an objective that could in fact be more completely realized by excusing at least some mistakes—than by creating hazards for those who choose to rely on what they think they know about the law. By denying a mistake of law defense, the law is saying, contra Holmes, that if a citizen suspects the law fails to prohibit some species of immoral conduct, the only certain way to avoid criminal punishment is to be a good person rather than a bad one.

This anti-Holmesian account, I'll argue, not only offers a superior explanation of why ignorance of the law is not ordinarily regarded as an excuse; it also does a better job in explaining why it sometimes is. Sometimes it's a crime to engage in an act—for example, omitting to file a tax return or failing to report certain financial transactions—that wouldn't be viewed as immoral were it not for the existence of a legal duty. Crimes of this sort are often referred to as malum prohibitum—wrong because prohibited—and are distinguished from crimes that are malum in se—wrong in themselves independent of law. Malum prohibitum crimes are the ones most likely to be interpreted as permitting mistake of law defenses. This aspect of the doctrine defies both premises of the classic position: to distinguish malum prohibitum crimes from malum in se ones, courts must employ moral judgments of the sort that liberal positivism forbids; and by allowing a mistake of law defense for malum prohibitum crimes, courts relax citizens' incentives to learn the law. Excusing someone for ignorance of a malum prohibitum crime makes perfect sense, however, under the anti-Holmesian view: since morality abstracted from law has nothing to say about the underlying conduct, a person can't be expected to rely on her perception of morality rather than her understanding of what such laws prohibit; because even a good person could make that kind of mistake in such circumstances, the defendant is excused.

A final advantage associated with the anti-Holmesian understanding of mistake of law is that it more completely defends the doctrine from the standard criticism made of it. Denying a mistake of law defense, it is said, sanctions punishment of the morally blameless. The classic conception demurs: "[J]ustice to the individual is rightly outweighed by the larger interests on the other side of the scales." But the anti-Holmesian conception goes further, showing that the standard criticism rests on a truncated understanding of when punishment is just: a person is rightly condemned as a criminal wrongdoer not only for knowingly choosing to violate the law, but also for exhibiting the kind of character failing associated with insufficient commitment to the moral norms embodied in the community's criminal law....

This account makes it easier to see why *Marrero* came out the way it did. Marrero ignored the law's injunction to do what's right rather than what one thinks is legal. New York's restrictive gun possession law embodies its citizens' strong antipathy toward, and fear of, handguns. But rather than defer to those norms, Marrero decided to be strategic, availing himself of what must have appeared even to him to be a largely fortuitous gap in the law. That's the attitude that made the court see in Marrero's efforts to decode the law not an earnest and laudable attempt to obey but rather a "false and diversionary stratagem," a form of "game playing and evasion."

Other facts, not even mentioned by the court, also likely played a role: that the policy of the federal prison at which Marrero worked forbade guards to carry guns either on or off duty; that Marrero had supplied his girlfriend and another companion with guns, even though they clearly had no grounds for believing their possession to be lawful; and that Marrero menacingly reached for his weapon when the police approached him in the Manhattan club. These facts might not have been formally relevant to the court's disposition, but they no doubt helped the court to see Marrero as a Holmesian bad man. And in the eyes of the court, a Holmesian bad man is plenty bad enough to be designated a criminal.

SECTION 22

Insanity

Mistake excuses, the subject of the last two Sections, exculpate because the person has acted reasonably given what he knew. A second group of general excuses—disability excuses—exculpate on a very different ground: that the person's offense conduct was heavily influenced by serious cognitive or control dysfunction such that we could no longer reasonably have expected the person to remain law-abiding. This section takes up the highest profile disability excuse, insanity. The next Section examines the other disability excuses.

◆ THE CASE OF ANDREW GOLDSTEIN

It is January 3, 1999. Yesterday, Andrew Goldstein, a shy, average-looking 29-year old, was in the emergency room having his ankle examined. The doctors told him that he was fine; he returned home to his apartment in Howard Beach, Queens. Yesterday's trip to the hospital is just another reason to be sad this holiday season. His family does not want to have much to do with him. A few years ago, his parents divorced. His mother remains in New York, but his father moved to Delaware. Since he turned sixteen, Goldstein's relationship with his family (and the world) has been strained. Ten years ago, Goldstein was diagnosed with schizophrenia.

One of three brothers, Goldstein was raised in Queens and Little Neck and attended Yeshiva elementary school in central Queens. He graduated with honors and appeared to be on his way to a promising future. His classmates report that he is a loner. His solitariness did not impede his academic performance, however; he attended the elite Bronx High School of Science and then earned admission to SUNY Stony Brook. But just before he was applying to SUNY, while riding a bus, something clicked—he could no longer understand anything in the book he was reading. His family was concerned and sought medical and psychiatric care. Goldstein was eventually diagnosed as a paranoid schizophrenic, prone to violence. He tried to overcome the disease by staying in school, but its symptoms only intensified.

After he pushed his mother and accused her of poisoning his food, Goldstein was hospitalized at Creedmoor Psychiatric Center. He tried returning to college several times after his release, but found it too difficult to concentrate and comprehend what he read. In December 1992, he was recommitted for assaulting a nurse, and remained at Creedmoor until August 1993. He then lived in a community residence facility until he was discharged in November 1994. He later moved into the Leben Home for Adults in Elmhurst, New York, which provided him a place to live but did not offer any supervision or counseling.

Goldstein's disease has grown progressively worse. The frequency and duration of his hallucinations have increased, leading him to believe that aliens are sucking oxygen from the earth and that there is someone inside him controlling his behavior and movements. His medication can help control the symptoms, but Goldstein does not like that it causes drowsiness, dissociation, and stiffness.

He knows that there are newer medications without these side effects, but they are too expensive for him. He lives on $500 per month from welfare, and an occasional $50 from his father.

He reports to psychiatrists that he is turning purple, that his penis is enlarged because his food is contaminated, and that a gay man is stealing his excrement from the toilet (by way of "interpolation") and eating it with a fork and knife. Goldstein has also hit at least a dozen people without provocation in restaurants, stores, hospitals, and subways. When police arrive, he always admits to what he did and asks to be taken to a hospital. Reflecting on these incidents, Goldstein describes that each time it happened, it felt as if a spirit or ghost had overtaken him.

Goldstein is uncomfortable and frustrated. He

Figure 102 **Andrew Goldstein, circa 1990**

(Vern Lovic)

wants a normal life and on several occasions has requested to be placed in long-term care at a state hospital or given a bed at a group home. There are no vacancies, however, at either of these facilities, in part because of Governor Pataki's recent state budget cuts.

These days, Goldstein lives in a decrepit one-bedroom basement apartment for $300 a month. It has no lock, the bathroom does not work, and it smells of dead mice. Since he is prone to late-night walks, he does not often sleep there. He shares the apartment with two roommates who, at times, are kind to him. In November, one of them invited Goldstein to his family's Thanksgiving celebration, but the event turned out badly. After the visit, Goldstein was again hospitalized, at North General Hospital, from November 24 until December 15. When released, doctors advise him to seek counseling and provide him with a week's worth of medication. If unsupervised, Goldstein typically stops taking his medication, misses counseling appointments, and ignores letters requesting that he reschedule. With a lack of funding, the state mental health system is unable to do anything besides send a letter when patients fail to show for an appointment.

Today, Goldstein forgoes his medication again, before going into Manhattan for the day. It is his mother's birthday. He goes to a Virgin Records store and listens to Natalie Imbruglia's "Wishing I Was There" and Madonna's "Ray of Light." He enjoys listening to music because it allows him to draw pictures in his mind to go along with what he hears. He then watches scenes from "The Good, the Bad, and the Ugly," in the video section and thinks that he would like to be a director someday. Getting hungry, he goes to Dunkin' Donuts for an iced donut and a cup of water. He once worked at the donut chain, but lasted only a day. Still hungry, he gets a McRib sandwich and Coke at a McDonald's. Feeling stuffed, he goes to visit his brother at his optical shop, but finds he is not there. Goldstein then goes to another Virgin Records store and listens to Madonna again. It is now getting late, and, feeling hungry again, he stops at Wendy's for a steak burger and another Coke.

After he finishes eating, he walks nine blocks uptown to Twenty-third Street and enters the underground subway station. Dawn Lorenzino is walking behind him and sees that he is acting strangely and stumbling, "taking baby steps on his tip toes." She also hears him mumbling to himself. When they reach the platform, Goldstein stares intensely at Lorenzino, until she finally asks what he is looking at. Troubled, Goldstein backs away and starts pacing so furiously that a man on the platform says to him, "Yo, buddy, can you stop pacing, you're making us nervous." He stops and approaches another blond woman, Kendra Webdale.

Webdale is originally from Fredonia, a small town near Buffalo in western New York. She majored in communications at SUNY Buffalo. After graduation, she worked for a couple of small weekly alternative papers in Buffalo before moving to New York City looking for more excitement. When she arrived, she worked for a Queens newspaper and now is a receptionist for a recording company. She is wearing her favorite black boots, dressed up for an evening out.

Goldstein asks Webdale for the time. She replies and returns her attention to her magazine. He then steps back and leans on the wall just behind Webdale.

Soon the train is rumbling toward the station. As it arrives, Goldstein darts from the wall and, as a witness later describes, "lurk[s] right behind Webdale with his fingers extend[ing] toward her shoulders." He then pushes her hard enough under her shoulder blades for people on the platform to hear it over the roar of the train. Webdale struggles to regain her balance, but cannot, and falls directly into the train's path. The motorman, Jacqus Lewis, pulls the emergency brake and closes his eyes, hoping to avoid her somehow. The train decapitates Webdale, killing her instantly. Its first three cars run over her body.

After the train stops, Lewis jumps out and asks Goldstein if he killed Webdale. He replies that he did, but quickly asks for a doctor, explaining that he is a mental patient. Goldstein then begins to walk toward the north turnstile. Another commuter, Alston, screams "murderer" when she sees him walking off and orders him to stop where he is. She later recalls that he looked scared and "recoiled like a child, pulling his arms up to his chest with his fingers pointed downward and trembling." She wonders what is wrong with him. Some passengers stand guarding him, as another fetches the police.

When the police arrive, one officer yells that he sees a leg. Goldstein looks at the other officers, glances toward the train, and says, "I don't know the woman. I pushed her." Detective William Hamilton, who first questions Goldstein, notes that he appears alert and answers all of the detective's questions promptly. Twelve hours later, in a videotaped session, police again question Goldstein. He admits to knowing that Webdale might be killed if he pushed her off the platform. When asked if pushing Webdale was wrong, Goldstein says yes, but then adds, "Yeah, definitely. I would never do something like that." When they press the fact that he actually did push her, he says, "I know, but the thing is I would never do it on purpose." He explains that "I wasn't thinking about anything when I pushed her." Throughout the interview, Goldstein speaks with a "polite, chatty tone" and answers all of the questions posed. He becomes confused, however, whenever the conversation returns to him pushing Webdale. Trying to explain his actions and the spirits that overcame him, Goldstein says, "When it happens, I don't think, it just goes whoosh, whoosh, push, you know. It's like a random variable."

Figure 103 Andrew Goldstein being escorted by police the day after the attack, 1999

(AP)

Psychiatric examinations show that at the time of the offense Goldstein continued to suffer from schizophrenia of the paranoid type, a disorder with these symptoms:

> The essential feature of the Paranoid Type of Schizophrenia is the presence of prominent delusions or auditory hallucinations in the context of a relative preservation of cognitive functioning and affect.... Delusions are typically persecutory or grandiose, or both, but delusions with other themes (e.g., jealousy, religiosity, or somatization) may also occur. The delusions may be multiple, but are usually organized around a coherent theme. Hallucinations are also typically related to the content of the delusional theme. Associated features include anxiety, anger, aloofness, and argumentativeness. The individual may have a superior and patronizing manner and either a stilted, formal quality or extreme intensity in interpersonal interactions. The persecutory themes may predispose the individual to suicidal behavior, and the combination of persecutory and grandiose delusions with anger may predispose the individual to violence. Onset tends to be later in life than the other types of Schizophrenia, and the distinguishing characteristics may be more stable over time. These individuals usually show little or no impairment on neuropsychological or other cognitive testing. Some evidence suggests that the prognosis for the Paranoid Type may be considerably better than for the other types of Schizophrenia, particularly with regard to occupational functioning and capacity for independent living.[1]

1. Relying only on your own intuition of justice, what liability and punishment, if any, does Andrew Goldstein deserve?

N	0	1	2	3	4	5	6	7	8	9	10	11
☐	☐	☐	☐	☐	☐	☐	☐	☐	☐	☐	☐	☐
no liability	liability but no punishment	1 day	2 wks	2 mo	6 mo	1 yr	3 yrs	7 yrs	15 yrs	30 yrs	life imprisonment	No punishment but civil preventive detention for as long as he is dangerous

2. What liability, if any, under the then-existing statutes?
3. What liability, if any, under the Model Penal Code?

---

1. American Psychiatric Association, Diagnostic and Statistical Manual of Mental Disorders 313-314 (4th ed. text revision 2000).

■ THE LAW

New York Penal Code
(1999)

Part 3. Specific Offenses

Title H. Offenses Against the Person Involving Physical Injury, Sexual Conduct, Restraint and Intimidation
Article 125. Homicide, Abortion and Related Offenses

Section 125.00. Homicide Defined

Homicide means conduct which causes the death of a person or an unborn child with which a female has been pregnant for more than twenty-four weeks under circumstances constituting murder, manslaughter in the first degree, manslaughter in the second degree, criminally negligent homicide, abortion in the first degree or self-abortion in the first degree.

Section 125.10. Criminally Negligent Homicide

A person is guilty of criminally negligent homicide when, with criminal negligence, he causes the death of another person.

Criminally negligent homicide is a class E felony.

Section 125.15. Manslaughter in the Second Degree

A person is guilty of manslaughter in the second degree when:

1. He recklessly causes the death of another person; . . .

Manslaughter in the second degree is a class C felony.

Section 125.20. Manslaughter in the First Degree

A person is guilty of manslaughter in the first degree when:

1. With intent to cause serious physical injury to another person, he causes the death of such person or of a third person; or

2. With intent to cause the death of another person, he causes the death of such person or of a third person under circumstances which do not constitute murder because he acts under the influence of extreme emotional disturbance, as defined in paragraph (a) of subdivision one of section 125.25. The fact that homicide was committed under the influence of extreme emotional disturbance constitutes a mitigating circumstance reducing murder to manslaughter in the first degree and need not be proved in any prosecution initiated under this subdivision; . . .

Manslaughter in the first degree is a class B felony.

Section 125.25. Murder in the Second Degree

A person is guilty of murder in the second degree when:

1. With intent to cause the death of another person, he causes the death of such person or of a third person; except that in any prosecution under this subdivision, it is an affirmative defense that:

(a) The defendant acted under the influence of extreme emotional disturbance for which there was a reasonable explanation or excuse, the reasonableness of which is to be determined from the viewpoint of a person in the defendant's situation under the circumstances as the defendant believed them to be. Nothing contained in this paragraph shall constitute a defense to a prosecution for, or preclude a conviction of, manslaughter in the first degree or any other crime; or

(b) The defendant's conduct consisted of causing or aiding, without the use of duress or deception, another person to commit suicide. Nothing contained in this paragraph shall constitute a defense to a prosecution for, or preclude a conviction of, manslaughter in the second degree or any other crime; or

2. Under circumstances evincing a depraved indifference to human life, he recklessly engages in conduct which creates a grave risk of death to another person, and thereby causes the death of another person; or

3. Acting either alone or with one or more other persons, he commits or attempts to commit robbery, burglary, kidnapping, arson, rape in the first degree, sodomy in the first degree, sexual abuse in the first degree, aggravated sexual abuse, escape in the first degree, or escape in the second degree, and, in the course of and in furtherance of such crime or of immediate flight therefrom, he, or another participant, if there be any, causes the death of a person other than one of the participants; except that in any prosecution under this subdivision, in which the defendant was not the only participant in the underlying crime, it is an affirmative defense that the defendant:

(a) Did not commit the homicidal act or in any way solicit, request, command, importune, cause or aid the commission thereof; and

(b) Was not armed with a deadly weapon, or any instrument, article or substance readily capable of causing death or serious physical injury and of a sort not ordinarily carried in public places by law-abiding persons; and

(c) Had no reasonable ground to believe that any other participant was armed with such a weapon, instrument, article or substance; and

(d) Had no reasonable ground to believe that any other participant intended to engage in conduct likely to result in death or serious physical injury; or

4. Under circumstances evincing a depraved indifference to human life, and being eighteen years old or more the defendant recklessly engages in conduct which creates a grave risk of serious physical injury or death to another person less than eleven years old and thereby causes the death of such person.

Murder in the second degree is a class A-I felony.

Part 1. General Provisions

Title B. Principles of Criminal Liability
Article 15. Culpability

Section 15.00. Culpability; Definitions of Terms

The following definitions are applicable to this chapter:

1. "Act" means a bodily movement.

2. "Voluntary act" means a bodily movement performed consciously as a result of effort or determination, and includes the possession of property if the actor was aware of his physical possession or control thereof for a sufficient period to have been able to terminate it.

3. "Omission" means a failure to perform an act as to which a duty of performance is imposed by law.

4. "Conduct" means an act or omission and its accompanying mental state.

5. "To act" means either to perform an act or to omit to perform an act.

6. "Culpable mental state" means "intentionally" or "knowingly" or "recklessly" or with "criminal negligence," as these terms are defined in section 15.05.

Section 15.05. Culpability; Definitions of Culpable Mental States

The following definitions are applicable to this chapter:

1. "Intentionally." A person acts intentionally with respect to a result or to conduct described by a statute defining an offense when his conscious objective is to cause such result or to engage in such conduct.

2. "Knowingly." A person acts knowingly with respect to conduct or to a circumstance described by a statute defining an offense when he is aware that his conduct is of such nature or that such circumstance exists.

3. "Recklessly." A person acts recklessly with respect to a result or to a circumstance described by a statute defining an offense when he is aware of and consciously disregards a substantial and unjustifiable risk that such result will occur or that such circumstance exists. The risk must be of such nature and degree that disregard thereof constitutes a gross deviation from the standard of conduct that a reasonable person would observe in the situation. A person who creates such a risk but is unaware thereof solely by reason of voluntary intoxication also acts recklessly with respect thereto.

4. "Criminal negligence." A person acts with criminal negligence with respect to a result or to a circumstance described by a statute defining an offense when he fails to perceive a substantial and unjustifiable risk that such result will occur or that such circumstance exists. The risk must be of such nature and degree that the failure to perceive it constitutes a gross deviation from the standard of care that a reasonable person would observe in the situation.

Section 15.10. Requirements for Criminal Liability in General and for Offenses of Strict Liability and Mental Culpability

The minimal requirement for criminal liability is the performance by a person of conduct which includes a voluntary act or the omission to perform an act which he is physically capable of performing. If such conduct is all that is required for commission of a particular offense, or if an offense or some material element thereof does not require a culpable mental state on the part of the actor, such offense is one of "strict liability." If a culpable mental state on the part of the actor is required with respect to every material element of an offense, such offense is one of "mental culpability."

Section 15.15. Construction of Statutes with Respect to Culpability Requirements

1. When the commission of an offense defined in this chapter, or some element of an offense, requires a particular culpable mental state, such mental state is ordinarily designated in the statute defining the offense by use of the terms "intentionally," "knowingly," "recklessly" or "criminal negligence," or by use of terms, such as "with intent to defraud" and "knowing it to be false," describing a specific kind of intent or knowledge. When one and only one of such terms appears in a statute defining an offense, it is presumed to apply to every element of the offense unless an intent to limit its application clearly appears.

2. Although no culpable mental state is expressly designated in a statute defining an offense, a culpable mental state may nevertheless be required for the commission of such offense, or with respect to some or all of the material elements thereof, if the proscribed conduct necessarily involves such culpable mental state. A statute defining a crime, unless clearly indicating a legislative intent to impose strict liability, should be construed as defining a crime of mental culpability. This subdivision applies to offenses defined both in and outside this chapter.

Part 1. General Provisions

Title C. Defenses
Article 25. Defenses in General

Section 25.00. Defenses; Burden of Proof

1. When a "defense," other than an "affirmative defense," defined by statute is raised at a trial, the people have the burden of disproving such defense beyond a reasonable doubt.

2. When a defense declared by statute to be an "affirmative defense" is raised at a trial, the defendant has the burden of establishing such defense by a preponderance of the evidence.

Article 40. Other Defenses Involving Lack of Culpability

Section 40.15. Mental Disease or Defect

In any prosecution for an offense, it is an affirmative defense that when the defendant engaged in the proscribed conduct, he lacked criminal responsibility by reason of mental disease or defect. Such lack of criminal responsibility means that at the time of such conduct, as a result of mental disease or defect, he lacked substantial capacity to know or appreciate either:

1. The nature and consequences of such conduct; or

2. That such conduct was wrong.

Part 2. Sentences

Title E. Sentences
Article 70. Sentences of Imprisonment

Section 70.00. Sentence of Imprisonment for Felony

1. Indeterminate sentence. Except as provided in subdivisions four, five and six, a sentence of imprisonment for a felony shall be an indeterminate sentence. When such a sentence is imposed, the court shall impose a maximum term in accordance with the provisions of subdivision two of this section and the minimum period of imprisonment shall be as provided in subdivision three of this section.

2. Maximum term of sentence. The maximum term of an indeterminate sentence shall be at least three years and the term shall be fixed as follows:

(a) For a class A felony, the term shall be life imprisonment;

(b) For a class B felony, the term shall be fixed by the court, and shall not exceed twenty-five years; provided, however, that where the sentence is for a class B felony offense specified in subdivision two of section 220.44, the maximum term must be at least six years and must not exceed twenty-five years;

(c) For a class C felony, the term shall be fixed by the court, and shall not exceed fifteen years;

(d) For a class D felony, the term shall be fixed by the court, and shall not exceed seven years; and

(e) For a class E felony, the term shall be fixed by the court, and shall not exceed four years.

3. Minimum period of imprisonment. The minimum period of imprisonment under an indeterminate sentence shall be at least one year and shall be fixed as follows:

(a) In the case of a class A felony, the minimum period shall be fixed by the court and specified in the sentence.

(i) For a class A-I felony, such minimum period shall not be less than fifteen years nor more than twenty-five years; provided that where a sentence, other than a sentence of death or life imprisonment without parole, is imposed upon a defendant convicted of murder in the first degree as defined in section 125.27 of this chapter, such minimum period shall be not less than twenty years nor more than twenty-five years.

(ii) For a class A-II felony, such minimum period shall not be less than three years nor more than eight years four months.

(b) Where the sentence is for a class B felony offense specified in subdivision two of section 220.44, the minimum period must be fixed by the court at one-third of the maximum term imposed and must be specified in the sentence. Where the sentence is for any other felony, the minimum period shall be fixed by the court and specified in the sentence and shall be not less than one year nor more than one-third of the maximum term imposed.

4. Alternative definite sentence for class D, E, and certain class C felonies. When a person, other than a second or persistent felony offender, is sentenced for a class D or class E felony, or to a class C felony specified in article two hundred twenty or article two hundred twenty-one, and the court, having regard to the nature and circumstances of the crime and to the history and character of the defendant, is of the opinion that a sentence of imprisonment is necessary but that it would be unduly harsh to impose an indeterminate or determinate sentence, the court may impose a definite sentence of imprisonment and fix a term of one year or less.

5. Life imprisonment without parole. Notwithstanding any other provision of law, a defendant sentenced to life imprisonment without parole shall not be or become eligible for parole or conditional release. For purposes of commitment and custody, other than parole and conditional release, such sentence shall be deemed to be an indeterminate sentence. A defendant may be sentenced to life imprisonment without parole only upon conviction for the crime of murder in the first degree as defined in section 125.27 of this chapter and in accordance with the procedures provided by law for imposing a sentence for such crime.

6. Determinate sentence. Except as provided in subdivision four of this section and subdivisions two and four of section 70.02, when a person is sentenced as a violent felony offender pursuant to section 70.02 or as a second violent felony offender pursuant to section 70.04 or as a second felony offender on a conviction for a violent felony offense pursuant to section 70.06, the court must impose a determinate sentence of imprisonment in accordance with the provisions of such sections and such sentence shall include, as a part thereof, a period of post-release supervision in accordance with section 70.45.

People v. Segal
444 N.Y.S.2d 588, 591-592 (1981)

At a criminal trial the People bear the burden of proof, not only with respect to ordinary defenses which have been codified but more fundamentally they must prove every element of the crime, including intent whenever relevant. Although proof of a mental defect other than insanity may not have acquired the status of a statutory defense, and will not constitute a "complete" defense in the sense that it would relieve the defendant of responsibility for all his acts, it may in a particular case negate a specific intent necessary to establish guilt.

Model Penal Code
(Official Draft 1962)

Section 4.01. Mental Disease or Defect Excluding Responsibility

(1) A person is not responsible for criminal conduct if at the time of such conduct as a result of mental disease or defect he lacks substantial capacity either to appreciate the criminality [wrongfulness] of his conduct or to conform his conduct to the requirements of law.

(2) As used in this Article, the terms "mental disease or defect" do not include an abnormality manifested only by repeated criminal or otherwise anti-social conduct.

Section 4.02. Evidence of Mental Disease or Defect Admissible When Relevant to Element of the Offense; [Mental Disease or Defect Impairing Capacity as Ground for Mitigation of Punishment in Capital Cases]

(1) Evidence that the defendant suffered from a mental disease or defect is admissible whenever it is relevant to prove that the defendant did or did not have a state of mind which is an element of the offense.

[(2) Whenever the jury or the Court is authorized to determine or to recommend whether or not the defendant shall be sentenced to death or imprisonment upon conviction, evidence that the capacity of the defendant to appreciate the criminality [wrongfulness] of his conduct or to conform his conduct to the requirements of law was impaired as a result of mental disease or defect is admissible in favor of sentence of imprisonment.]

● OVERVIEW OF INSANITY

Notes on the Insanity Defense

Negating an Element vs. General Excuse   The effects of mental illness can sometimes make it impossible for the state to prove the culpability requirements for an offense. (Recall the discussion at the end of the Section 8 (Homicide Mitigations) Overview materials.) For example, an actor who hallucinates that a knife is a clothes brush may not have the required culpability for homicide if he kills someone thinking that he is brushing lint from the victim's suit. Similarly, mental illness can mitigate murder to manslaughter if the actor killed during an "extreme *mental* or emotional disturbance," as was also discussed in Section 8. In contrast to these doctrines, the insanity defense provides a defense without regard to (that is, despite the defendant's satisfaction of) the elements of the offense definition. To get the insanity defense the actor need only satisfy the conditions set out in the defense provision. As one of the traditional disability excuses, it reflects the excuses' traditional structure: the requirements that a *disability* (in this instance, mental disease or defect) cause an *excusing condition*. (More on the internal structure of disability excuses in the next Section, Disability Excuses.)

Mental Disease or Defect as Disability The disability requirement of the insanity defense is a mental disease or defect. What constitutes a mental disease or defect is a question for the jury. It is a legal concept, not a medical one, but the jury will no doubt be influenced by the expert witnesses they hear. Many experts called to testify as to whether the defendant suffers from a mental disease or defect will rely on the classification system contained in the *Diagnostic and Statistical Manual* of the American Psychiatric Association, now in its fourth edition (DSM-IV-TR). The APA gives the following definition of "mental disorder":

> In DSM-IV, each of the mental disorders is conceptualized as a clinically significant behavioral or psychological syndrome or pattern that occurs in an individual and that is associated with present distress (e.g., a painful symptom) or disability (i.e., impairment in one or more important areas of functioning) or with a significantly increased risk of suffering death, pain, disability, or an important loss of freedom. In addition, this syndrome or pattern must not be merely an expectable and culturally sanctioned response to a particular event, for example, the death of a loved one. Whatever its original cause, it must currently be considered a manifestation of a behavioral, psychological, or biological dysfunction in the individual. Neither deviant behavior (e.g., political, religious, or sexual) nor conflicts that are primarily between the individual and society are mental disorders unless the deviance or conflict is a symptom of a dysfunction in the individual, as described above[1].

Intoxication Excluded Intoxication may cause mental dysfunction, but it is excluded as a basis for the insanity defense because it is not a form of mental disease or defect.[2] It is dealt with instead under the law's special intoxication defense. The habitual and excessive use of intoxicants, however, may cause a mental disease with resulting dysfunction apart from the intoxication, and this mental disease can be the basis for an insanity defense. Addiction, for example, has been recognized as a mental disease.[3]

Psychopathy Excluded Also excluded as a disability from the insanity defense is "an abnormality manifested only by repeated criminal or otherwise anti-social conduct."[4] In other words, being a habitual criminal is not in itself a sufficient

---

1. American Psychiatric Association, Diagnostic and Statistical Manual of Mental Disorders (4th ed. text revision 2000) (hereinafter DSM-IV-TR) at xxxi.

2. Model Penal Code § 2.08(3).

3. See DSM-IV-TR, supra, at 199-200. Some cases, however, expressly reject the notion that addiction can qualify an actor for an insanity defense. See, e.g., United States v. Moore, 486 F.2d 1139 (D.C. Cir. 1973).

4. Model Penal Code § 4.01(2).

indication of a cognizable abnormality. Such an abnormality may be a mental disease for clinical purposes, but to recognize it as a mental disease for the purposes of the insanity defense would generate results inconsistent with the theory of excuses as serving to exculpate blameless offenders. As DSM-IV-TR describes the disorder:

> The essential feature of Antisocial Personality Disorder is a pervasive pattern of disregard for, and violation of, the rights of others that begins in childhood or early adolescence and continues into adulthood.
>
> This pattern has also been referred to as psychopathy, sociopathy, or dyssocial personality disorder. . . .
>
> . . . The specific behaviors characteristic of Conduct Disorder fall into one of four categories: aggression to people and animals, destruction of property, deceitfulness or theft, or serious violation of rules. . . .
>
> The pattern of antisocial behavior continues into adulthood. Individuals with AntiSocial Personality Disorder fail to conform to social norms with respect to lawful behavior. They may repeatedly perform acts that are grounds for arrest (whether they are arrested or not), such as destroying property, harassing others, stealing, or pursuing illegal occupations. Persons with this disorder disregard the wishes, rights, or feelings of others. They are frequently deceitful and manipulative in order to gain personal profit or pleasure (e.g., to obtain money, sex, or power). The may repeatedly lie, use an alias, con others, or malinger. A pattern of impulsivity may be manifested by a failure to plan ahead. Decisions are made on the spur of the moment, without forethought, and without consideration for the consequences to self or others; this may lead to sudden changes of jobs, residences, or relationships. Individuals with Antisocial Personality Disorder tend to be irritable and aggressive and may repeatedly get into physical fights or commit acts of physical assault (including spouse beating or child beating). Aggressive acts that are required to defend oneself or someone else are not considered to be evidence for this item. These individuals also display a reckless disregard for the safety of themselves or others. This may be evidenced in their driving behavior (recurrent speeding, driving while intoxicated, multiple accidents). They may engage in sexual behavior or substance use that has a high risk for harmful consequences. They may neglect or fail to care for a child in a way that puts the child in danger.
>
> Individuals with Antisocial Personality Disorder also tend to be consistently and extremely irresponsible. Irresponsible work behavior may be indicated by significant periods of unemployment despite available job opportunities, or by abandonment of several jobs without a realistic plan for getting another job. There may also be a pattern of repeated absences from work that are not explained by illness either in themselves or in their family. Financial irresponsibility is indicated by acts such as defaulting on debts, failing to provide child support, or failing to support other dependents on a regular basis. Individuals with Antisocial Personality Disorder show little remorse for the consequences of their acts. They may be indifferent to, or provide a superficial rationalization for, having hurt, mistreated, or stolen from someone (e.g., "life's unfair," "losers deserve to lose," or "he had it coming anyway"). These individuals may blame the victims for being foolish, helpless, or deserving their fate; they may minimize the harmful consequences of their actions; or they may simply indicate complete indifference. They generally fail to compensate or make amends for their behavior. They may believe that

everyone is out to "help number one" and that one should stop at nothing to avoid being pushed around.[1]

Such habitual criminality by itself may be fully volitional conduct and thus fully blameworthy.

Excusing Conditions It is not enough for an excuse that an actor suffers some abnormality, even one that causes dysfunction. To be held blameless, the actor must have a disability with such an effect as to make it no longer reasonable to expect the actor to have avoided the violation. This required effect of the disability, or "excusing condition," has been formulated in several different ways for the insanity defense. The most significant tests include the McNaghten test, the McNaghten test plus the "irresistible impulse" test, the Durham "product" test, the A.L.I. test, and the more recent federal insanity test.

McNaghten Test In *McNaghten's Case*, the House of Lords held that an actor has a defense of insanity if, "at the time of committing the act, the party accused was laboring under such a defect of reason, from disease of the mind, as not to know the nature and quality of the act he was doing, or, if he did know it, [he] did not know he was doing what was wrong."[2] The test was an advance over prior case law, which set the standard for the defense as having no more understanding than "an infant, a brute, or a wild beast."[3] It gave the jury specific criteria to focus on rather than vague analogies. The test is in use in many American jurisdictions today, and remains the test for the insanity defense in England.

"Irresistible Impulse" Test As early as 1887, the McNaghten test was criticized as failing to reflect the advances in the behavioral sciences. Mental illness, it was observed, can take away the *power to choose* as effectively as it does the *knowledge* of what is right and what is wrong.[4] To permit a defense in cases of such loss of the power to choose, a "control prong" was introduced by adding the "irresistible impulse" test[5] to McNaghten. Under this modification, an actor is given an insanity defense if he or she satisfies the requirements of the McNaghten defense or:

> (1) if, by reason of the duress of such mental disease, he had so far lost the *power to choose* between the right and wrong, and to avoid doing the act in question, as that his free agency was at the time destroyed; (2) and if, at the same time, the alleged crime was so connected with such mental disease, in the relation of cause and effect, as to have been the product of it *solely*.

Durham "Product" Test The McNaghten-plus-irresistible-impulse test was criticized in turn by the court in *Durham v. United States* as not fully reflecting the more recent advances in the behavioral sciences.[6] Mental dysfunctions, both cognitive and control type, it was observed, always are a matter of degree and are not, as was previously thought, absolute in their effect. Further, it was argued,

---

1. DSM-IV-TR, supra, at 701-703.
2. McNaghten's Case, 8 Eng. Rep. 718, 722 (1843) (emphasis added).
3. Arnold's Case, 16 How. State Tr. 695, 765 (1724).
4. Parsons v. State, 81 Ala. 577, 2 So. 854 (1887).
5. The term "irresistible impulse" is something of a misnomer. As the quotation in the text illustrates, nothing in the defense requires that the "duress of mental illness" be impulsive. It may be, and frequently is, a long process that both creates the mental illness and has the mental illness cause the criminal conduct.
6. Durham v. United States, 214 F.2d 862 (D.C. Cir. 1954).

McNaghten and the irresistible-impulse tests improperly focus on particular symptoms rather than on the key question of whether the mental illness, whatever its nature, *had the effect of causing the offense.* Under the *Durham* "product" test, in contrast, an accused "is not criminally responsible if his unlawful act was the product of mental disease or mental defect." The product test was adopted in only a few jurisdictions and only arguably remains in use in one.[1] *Durham* was criticized as overstating what are adequate grounds of exculpation. It is not enough, the critics of *Durham* argued, that the mental illness is a "but for" cause of the offense; the mental illness must cause a certain minimum degree of impairment of capacity sufficient to render the defendant blameless for the offense.

only used in NH

4) *ALI Test*   In *United States v. Brawner,*[2] the Court of Appeals for the District of Columbia Circuit overruled their earlier decision in *Durham* and adopted the American Law Institute test, contained in Model Penal Code section 4.01(1):

1972 MPC, also v. popular

> A person is not responsible for criminal conduct if at the time of such conduct as a result of mental disease or defect he *lacks substantial capacity either to appreciate the criminality [wrongfulness] of his conduct or to conform his conduct to the requirements of law.*

This formulation concedes that there are *degrees* of impairment, as *Durham* had sought to provide, but requires a minimum degree of impairment: the actor must "lack substantial capacity...." The ALI test reverts to the structure of the McNaghten-plus-irresistible-impulse test in specifically noting that the dysfunction may affect either cognitive or control capacities. It differs from McNaghten-plus-irresistible-impulse test, however, in that those two tests appear to require absolute dysfunction: the absence of knowledge of criminality or the loss of power to choose.[3] The ALI test, in contrast, requires only that the actor lack "substantial capacity" to "appreciate" the criminality or to conform her conduct to the requirements of the law. The test has gained wide acceptance, rivaling the popularity of McNaghten and McNaghten-plus-irresistible-impulse formulations.

5) *Cannot Be "Justly Held Responsible"*   Another formulation of the insanity defense, which was considered but rejected by the ALI, calls for a jury's general assessment of an actor's responsibility and blameworthiness for the offense. It would provide the defense if the actor, because of mental disease or defect, lacked sufficient capacity to be "justly held responsible" for his conduct. The approach is similar to the Model Penal Code's approach in other contexts where an admittedly normative judgment is called for. An actor is not responsible for causing a result,

---

1. State v. Shackford, 127 N.H. 695, 506 A.2d 315 (1986) (holding that insanity test is matter "to be weighed by the jury upon the question whether the act was the offspring of insanity," quoting State v. Jones, 50 N.H. 369, 398-399 (1871)); State v. Pike, 49 N.H. 399 (1870).

2. 471 F.2d 969 (D.C. Cir. 1972).

3. Some writers have observed that the irresistible impulse test may not be as absolute in application as it appears. By requiring that the actor have no power to choose, it certainly urges the jury to be demanding in the level of dysfunction that they will require, but it seems unusual, if not impossible, that an actor would lose all power to choose. Typically, control impairments make an actor's decisions to remain law-abiding more difficult, but rarely take away all decision. See Model Penal Code § 4.01 comment 3 (1985) (explaining that workable test calling for complete loss of ability to know or control is not possible and that such test would impose unrealistic restriction on scope of proper inquiry).

for example, if the result's occurrence is too remote or accidental "to have a [just] bearing on the actor's liability or on the gravity of his offense."[1] Such an open formulation was rejected in the insanity context, because it was judged as failing to provide adequate guidance to the jury. The specific reference to cognitive or control dysfunction in the version of the test adopted by the ALI was thought useful to focus the jury's attention on the nature and effect of the dysfunction and to avoid having a jury wander into considerations of general sympathy or bias that they might think permissible under the broader "justice" standard.

Federal Insanity Test Some jurisdictions that previously adopted the ALI test have cut back on it. The new federal insanity statute, for example, uses the "appreciates" language of the ALI, rather than the *McNaghten* "know" language, and thereby concedes that there are degrees of cognitive dysfunction short of complete loss that nonetheless may exculpate.[2] On the other hand, the new federal statute drops the "lacks substantial capacity" language, which makes it closer to the apparently absolute requirement of *McNaghten*. Most important, the federal formulation drops the control prong of the defense; it reverts to the single cognitive prong, adopting a position that was criticized one hundred years before. This reflects a recent skepticism as to whether behavioral scientists can measure an actor's degree of self-control or impairment of capacity to control and as to whether jurors can understand what they are being asked to determine in judging a defendant's impairment of control. Whether a control prong should be recognized as part of an insanity test is the subject of the Discussion Materials below.

Abolition of Insanity Defense A few jurisdictions have abolished their insanity defense, although each continues to allow mental disease or defect to provide a defense if it negates a required offense element.[3] A constitutional challenge to abolition has been successful in some cases,[4] but not in others.[5] Whether or not the federal or state constitutions bar abolition, it is a questionable policy. To the extent that the criminal law claims to express conclusions about an actor's blameworthiness (the characteristic that traditionally has distinguished criminal law from civil law) it cannot impose criminal liability and punishment on clearly insane offenders without destroying its moral credibility. If society has a need to protect itself against dangerous persons who are predicted to commit future crimes, it can and should do so. Typically, dangerous persons are blameworthy offenders. In the unusual case where an offender is dangerous yet blameless, incarceration must be civil in nature if the criminal law is to protect its moral credibility.

---

1. Model Penal Code § 2.03(2)(b) & (3)(b). Similar instances of broad language calling for a normative judgment can be found in Model Penal Code §§ 2.02(2)(c) & (d) (defining recklessness and negligence), § 2.12(2) (defining *de minimis* infraction), § 3.02(1)(a) (defining less evils defense), § 2.09(1) (defining duress defense).

2. See the excerpt from the legislative history of the federal Insanity Defense Reform Act of 1983 in the Discussion Materials section, infra.

3. See Idaho Code § 18-207; Kan. Stat. Ann. § 22-3220 (2002); Mont. Code Ann. § 46-14-102; Utah Code Ann. § 76-2-305(1). See generally 2 Paul H. Robinson, Criminal Law Defenses § 173(a) n.5 (1984).

4. See, e.g., State v. Strasburg, 60 Wash. 106, 110 P. 1020 (1910).

5. See, e.g., State v. Korell, 213 Mont. 316, 690 P.2d 992 (1984).

Insanity Defense in the United States — Survey   All of the alternative approaches to the insanity defense are reflected in one or another of the American jurisdictions. Almost half of the jurisdictions apply the traditional McNaghten test,[1] with one jurisdiction adding the irresistible-impulse element.[2] Most of the jurisdictions that have adopted a control prong have done so by shifting to the somewhat broader ALI formulation; close to 30% of the states have adopted the Model Penal Code's ALI formulation in its entirety.[3] Another 20% have adopted the ALI formulation but only its cognitive prong.[4] Four jurisdictions purport to abolish the insanity defense altogether, though they continue to allow mental illness to negate an offense's mens rea requirement.[5] One state adopts what appears to be close to the *Durham* product test.[6] The Callahan Study excerpted below details the extent to which the current constellation of defense formulations is a product of the recent insanity reform wave prompted by John Hinckley's insanity acquittal for his attempted assassination of the late President Reagan.

"Guilty But Mentally Ill"   Several jurisdictions have adopted a new ver-dict of "guilty but mentally ill" (GBMI). The verdict replaces the insanity defense in only a few states. More frequently, it provides the trier of fact with an additional verdict in cases where mental illness is an issue. The special verdict may be returned where a defendant is mentally ill but where his mental illness is insufficient to provide either an insanity defense or a defense of mental illness negating an offense element. Upon a verdict of "guilty but mentally ill," the court typically may impose the same sentence that would have been imposed had the defendant been found guilty of the offense charged. However, the defendant must be examined by psychiatrists before beginning to serve the sentence and, if the

---

1. Ariz. Rev. Stat. Ann. § 13-502 (2003); Cal. Penal Code § 25 (2003); Colo. Rev. Stat. Ann. § 16-8-101 (2003); Fla. Stat. Ann. § 775.027 (2003); Ga. Code Ann. § 16-3-2 (2002); Iowa Code Ann. § 701.4 (2003); La. Rev. Stat. Ann. § 14 (2003); Minn. Stat. Ann. § 611.026 (2003); Roundtree v. State, 568 So. 2d 1173 (Miss. 1990); Mo. Ann. Stat. § 552.030 (2002) (modifying the standard language slightly to "incapable of knowing *and appreciating*"); State v. Harms, 650 N.W.2d 481 (Neb. 2002); N.J. Stat. Ann. § 2C:4-1 (2003); Finger v. State, 27 P.3d 66 (Nev. 2001) (finding unconstitutional the legislator's attempt to abolish the insanity defense and applying the McNaghten test instead); State v. Vickers, 291 S.E.2d 599 (N.C. 1982); Ohio Rev. Code Ann. § 2901.01 (2003); Okla. Stat. Ann. tit. 21 § 152 (2003); 18 Pa. Cons. Stat. Ann. § 314 (2003); S.C. Code Ann. § 17-24-10 (2002); S.D. Codified Laws § 22-1-2 (2003); Tex. Penal Code Ann. § 8.01 (2003); Price v. Commonwealth, 323 S.E.2d 106 (Va. 1984); Wash. Rev. Code Ann. § 9A.12.010 (2003).

2. State v. White, 270 P.2d 727 (N.M. 1954).

3. Ark. Code Ann. § 5-2-312 (2002); Conn. Gen. Stat. Ann. § 53a-13 (2003); Patton v. United States, 782 A.2d 305 (D.C. 2001); Haw. Rev. Stat. Ann. § 704-400 (2002); Ky. Rev. Stat. Ann. § 504.020 (2003); Md. Code Ann., Crim. Proc. § 3-109 (2002); Commonwealth v. Brown, 434 N.E.2d 973 (Mass. 1982); Mich. Comp. Laws Ann. § 768.21a (2003); Or. Rev. Stat. § 161.295 (2001); State v. Johnson, 399 A.2d 469 (R.I. 1979); Vt. Stat. Ann. tit. 13 § 4801 (2002); State v. Samples, 328 S.E.2d 191 (W. Va. 1985); Wis. Stat. Ann. § 971.15 (2003); Wyo. Stat. Ann. § 7-11-304 (2002).

4. Ala. Code § 13A-3-1 (2003); Alaska Stat. § 12.47.010 (2002); Del. Code Ann. tit. 11, § 401 (2002); 720 Ill. Comp. Stat. Ann. 5/6-2 (2003); Ind. Code Ann. § 35-41-3-6 (2002); Me. Rev. Stat. Ann. tit. 14, § 14 (2003); N.Y. Penal Law § 40.15 (2003); N.D. Cent. Code § 12.1-04.1-01 (2001) (requiring also that "an essential element of the crime charged [is] that the individual act willfully"); Tenn. Code Ann. § 39-11-501 (2002).

5. Idaho Code § 18-207 (2002); Kan. Stat. Ann. § 22-3220 (2002); Mont. Code Ann. § 45-2-101 (2002); 2003 Utah Sessions Laws Ch. 11 (making slight revisions to Utah Code Ann. § 76-2-305 (2002)).

6. State v. Shackford, 127 N.H. 695, 506 A.2d 315 (1986) (holding that insanity test is matter "to be weighed by the jury upon the question whether the act was the offspring of insanity," quoting State v. Jones, 50 N.H. 369, 398-399 (1871)).

defendant is found to be in need of treatment, she will then be imprisoned in a criminal mental health facility.

Asking Jury to Judge Need for Treatment The "guilty but mentally ill" verdict raises some significant concerns. First, one must question why the fact finder in a criminal trial is an appropriate body to determine whether an offender is in need of a psychiatric examination. The expertise of the jury is in finding the facts of past events and in applying that community's notion of blameworthiness. The issue of the need for a psychiatric treatment is a clinical one, appropriate for prison psychiatrists, for example. It is not within the lay judgment of the jury,[1] and asking the jury to undertake such an inquiry can mislead it from its task of assessing blameworthiness.

Collateral Effects of GBMI Verdict A second concern arises from an analysis of the legislative history for the "guilty but mentally ill" verdict. The history suggests that the verdict was not designed to perform a psychiatric screening function, which clinicians can do more reliably, but rather arose as a response to constitutionally mandated limitations on the use of civil commitment. The limitations were thought to risk imprudently the release of dangerously insane acquittees back into the community. The operation of the verdict against the perceived danger is indirect in achieving its goal. It works not by loosening civil commitment standards but by diverting mentally ill offenders from civil commitment to the criminal justice system. A jury that is given a choice between rendering a verdict of "not guilty by reason of insanity" and a verdict of "guilty but mentally ill" may select the latter not because the jury finds the defendant blameworthy, but because the latter verdict guarantees what may be the obvious need for treatment and confinement. The difficulty with the verdict is that it invites jurors to consider matters unrelated to guilt at a time when guilt and guilt alone ought to be the issue before them. (In addition to inviting an improper verdict, the "guilty but mentally ill" verdict poses a risk of a mistaken verdict. The jury may inadvertently confuse the statutory definition of "mental illness" relevant to the "guilty but mentally ill" verdict and the definition of legal "insanity.") The use of such an improper compromise verdict may do as much to undermine the insanity defense as a total abolition would. If effective abolition is the objective, abolishing the insanity test openly would better further the interests of informed debate and reform.

Incapacitating Dangerous but Blameless Offenders as Civil Function Protecting the public from potentially violent offenders, sane or insane, is an important, irreproachable goal. The "guilty but mentally ill" verdict may be effective at protecting the public from some dangerously insane offenders, but it does so not through rational reform of civil commitment, but rather by subverting the insanity defense and thereby perverting the criminal justice system to condemn through criminal conviction violators who may be blameless. Such condemnation of blameless offenders may have the long-term effect of weakening the condemnatory force of criminal conviction generally—weakening the criminal law's

---

1. Referrals for such professional evaluation of offenders who may need treatment can be done more effectively and efficiently by the court after receiving the pre-sentence report. Indeed, several jurisdictions have established specific post-trial procedures to provide treatment for mentally ill offenders who are sentenced to prison.

"moral credibility" — and may thereby reduce the effectiveness of the system and increase the danger to the public. The answer to the problem of dangerous but insane offenders lies not in the perversion of the insanity defense, but rather in the adoption of civil commitment standards and procedures that will adequately protect the public. While there exist some serious constitutional limitations on civil commitment, the Supreme Court has held that the same limitations do not apply to commitment after an acquittal based on an insanity defense. Civil commitment after an insanity defense is made easier in part because the insanity acquittee's past offense is taken as evidence of dangerousness that may not exist in the normal civil commitment case.

Lisa Callahan, et al., Insanity Defense Reform in the United States — Post-*Hinckley*

11 Mental and Physical Disability Law Reporter 54-60 (1987)

Study Design

To assess the types of insanity defense reform made following John Hinckley's shooting of President Ronald Reagan, we examined all insanity defense reforms in the 51 U.S. jurisdictions from 1978 through 1985....

January 1978 through March 1981 is referred to as the "pre-Hinckley" time period. Reforms that occurred during this time are clearly not related to the shooting and subsequent acquittal. Analyzing the time period from the shooting to the acquittal, April 1981 through June 1982, is of questionable value as it is unclear if those reforms were in the process prior to Hinckley's actions and acquittal. The time from July 1982 through September 1985 is referred to as the "post-Hinckley" period. We have approximately 3 years of "pre-Hinckley" reforms and 3 years of "post-Hinckley" reforms. The reforms are categorized as follows: (1) changes in the test of insanity or in the entering of the plea; (2) addition of the GBMI [guilty but mentally ill] option; (3) changes in the burden and/or standard of proof; (4) changes in trial procedures; and (5) changes in commitment and release procedures. Clearly each state's reforms are idiosyncratic to its legal system. However, our classification system permits comparisons of the general types of reforms that have occurred after the Hinckley case.

Findings

First, it should be noted that 13 states made no changes in the insanity defense during our 6-year study period. It is acknowledged that some changes may have occurred in other systems (e.g., civil commitment) that affect insanity acquittees, but these 13 states had no change in law that speaks directly to NGRI [not guilty by reason of insanity] procedures. We have identified 38 states that made significant reforms at some point between 1978 and 1985.

During the pre-Hinckley period, 11 states made changes in their insanity defense laws; two of the states made multiple changes. Five of these states made changes in the commitment/release procedures; in three of those states, this was the only change made. The two states that made multiple changes involved a change in commitment/release rules and a change in the test of insanity. Other

Table 2: Instances of Insanity Defense Reforms

State	Test Used	Locus of Burden of Proof	Standard of Proof	GBMI	Trial Procedures	Release/ Commitment
Alabama						
Alaska				3		
Arizona		3	3			3
Arkansas						3
California	1, 2, 3					1
Colorado	3	3				3
Connecticut	3	3	3			3
Delaware				3	3	3
District of Columbia						
Florida						1, 3
Georgia		1	1	3		3
Hawaii		2, 3	2		1	3
Idaho	3					3
Illinois		3	3	2		3
Indiana	3			2		2, 3
Iowa		3	3			3
Kansas						
Kentucky				3		
Louisiana						
Maine						
Maryland		3	3		3	3
Massachusetts						
Michigan						
Minnesota		3				3
Mississippi						
Missouri						3
Montana	1					
Nebraska		3	3			1, 2
Nevada						
New Hampshire		1	1			2, 3
New Jersey						
New Mexico				2		
New York		3	3			3
North Carolina					1	2, 3
North Dakota	3	3	3		3	3
Ohio						1
Oklahoma					3	3
Oregon	3					1
Pennsylvania		3	3	3		
Rhode Island	1					
South Carolina				3		
South Dakota		3	3			3
Tennessee						3
Texas	3					3
Utah		3	3	3		3
Vermont		3	3			
Virginia						
Washington						3
Wisconsin					1	
Wyoming		3	3			

Key

1 = Pre-Hinckley (1/78-3/81)
2 = During Hinckley (4/81-6/82)
3 = Post-Hinckley (7/82-9/85)

single reforms were in three states that changed trial procedures — two that changed the burden and standard of proof, and one that changed the test of insanity (see Table 2).

Eight states made changes in their laws "during" Hinckley, the time between the shooting and the acquittal. One state made two reforms — adding the GBMI option and a change in commitment/release. The remaining seven states made single reforms: Three in commitment/release, two additions of GBMI, one in the test of insanity and one in the burden and standard of proof (see Table 2).

Twenty-five states that made no changes during or pre-Hinckley did make changes in the post-Hinckley period (see Table 2). Additionally, nine states made changes both pre- and post-Hinckley. Many states made multiple reforms during this period: 64 reforms occurred in 34 states. The most common reform made was in commitment/release (27 reforms in 26 states). Changes in the burden and standard of proof were made in 16 states. Eight states changed the test for insanity; eight states added the guilty but mentally ill option, and four states changed trial procedures.

Reforms that were made in the commitment process for persons acquitted by reason of insanity generally mandate some period of commitment for all such persons. This mandatory commitment is generally temporary "for evaluation," requiring court review at the end of a stated period of time. Distinctions are sometimes made among acquittees by the type of offense of which they were acquitted. Defendants acquitted of more serious crimes involving bodily injury may be automatically and indefinitely committed, while defendants convicted of less serious offenses may be entitled to a hearing to determine whether commitment is proper.

Reforms addressing release of persons acquitted by reason of insanity most often include mandatory court review prior to release of the person. Furthermore, some jurisdictions added provisions for conditional release, a program similar to parole. Only one of these changes could be interpreted outright as allowing more "due process" for insanity acquittees: in Florida the hearing for revocation of conditional release now must occur within seven days instead of "within a reasonable time" as the prior law provided.

In all reform jurisdictions but one (Utah) in which the burden of proof was changed, the burden was shifted from the state to the defendant. In conjunction with this reform, the standard of proof was changed from "beyond a reasonable doubt" to either the preponderance test or to "clear and convincing evidence."

In jurisdictions that altered the test of insanity, seven made changes that restricted the definition and use of insanity as a defense. Four jurisdictions changed from the American Law Institute (A.L.I.) or M'Naughten plus irresistible impulse tests to the simple M'Naughten test; two jurisdictions restricted the use of the insanity defense so that it could not be utilized to negate mens rea as a defense to certain types of offenses; and one jurisdiction repealed the plea and the test of insanity altogether. Two jurisdictions, however, expanded the test for insanity by repealing the M'Naughten test and adopting the A.L.I. test.

Discussion

There have clearly been more reforms in the insanity defense during the post-Hinckley time than during a comparable period prior to the shooting and acquittal. While this may reinforce a conclusion that this increased activity resulted from the "notorious" case, there is at least one other plausible conclusion. Although our data cannot directly address the issue of causality, it seems plausible that a 1983 U.S. Supreme Court decision, *Jones v. U.S.*, accounts for much of the observed change being attributed to Hinckley.

The *Jones* decision requires that in states that have an automatic, indefinite commitment of persons acquitted by reason of insanity, the burden of proof must be on the defendant to demonstrate insanity by a preponderance of the evidence. Thus, states that wish to have an automatic, indefinite commitment retained or created must change the burden and standard of proof to comply with *Jones*. Such legal changes in reference to *Jones* could be attributed to states responding to public pressures to make sure "Hinckley couldn't happen in our state." In fact, the precipitant was case law, which at best, was an indirect result of Hinckley.

It is just as likely that these reforms were enacted in compliance with *Jones*. Twelve of 14 changes in the burden of proof at trial occurred in the period following *Jones*. Before attributing causality to the *Jones* decision, however, we must recognize that the legislative process is slow, and that changes occurring on the heels of the *Jones* decision nevertheless may have been initiated in response to *Hinckley* but not finalized until after *Jones*.

Most insanity defense reforms in recent years have been in the area of commitment and release. Historically, commitment as "not guilty by reason of insanity" was indefinite, with no procedure obligating the state to review the commitment. As a result, such persons often languished in institutions long after they were no longer a danger to themselves or others. The release of persons criminally committed as well as civilly committed patients was historically based on unilateral discretionary power of the hospital director. As Wexler observes, NGRI individuals have "had an easier route into and a more difficult route out of the institutions than have their civilly committed counterparts." This in large part reflects the desire to protect the public from the release of these individuals without assurance that they are no longer a danger. The trend toward more due process protections for persons acquitted due to insanity and the public's demand for protection has led to a similar result. Many jurisdictions either require (for protection) or permit (for due process) court review of the commitment at various intervals. The result is more court involvement in the disposition and supervision of persons acquitted by reason of insanity.

▲ PROBLEM
Michael's Madness

Michael Monte was discharged from the Navy at the age of 18 after a psychiatric examination concluded that he suffered from "a profound personality disorder that renders him unfit for Naval service." He now lives alone in a boarding house and, because of repeated outbursts of temper, has no close friends. He has not held a job for more than two weeks at a time and is always on the verge of being evicted from his room for his unpredictable behavior. His landlady is tolerant of his minor misconduct because she feels sorry for him, believing that he is not always in control of himself. "He is as sweet as can be for a while, then will turn to a very black mood and blow up at whoever happens to be around," she explains. "He is always very sorry immediately after and makes a nuisance of himself trying to apologize." On this particular day, when Michael leaves the building in the morning, his landlady notices that he is in one of his black moods. He seems to be even more distressed when he returns that afternoon. She asks him if he is "ok" as he passes her door. He does not respond. Twenty minutes later one of the other tenants knocks on Michael's door and demands that the music be turned down. Getting no response, he continues to pound on the door for several minutes. Michael suddenly opens the door swinging a baseball bat. He strikes the surprised tenant in the head, killing him instantly. When the landlady reaches the landing, she finds Michael standing over the body, as if frozen. She checks the body and tells Michael that the man is dead. Michael gasps and falls to his knees. "Why did I do that? I knew I shouldn't have hit him."

Court-appointed psychiatrists testify that at the time of the killing Michael knew what he was doing and knew that it was wrong, but that he suffers from a severe anger control disorder and, as a result, has great difficulty in controlling his conduct. Will Michael receive an insanity defense?

⬤ DISCUSSION MATERIALS

Should the Criminal Law Recognize an Excuse Defense for an Offender Who, Because of Mental Illness, Knows His Conduct Constituting the Offense Is Wrong But Lacks the Capacity to Control It?

In limiting the insanity defense to exclude a control prong, the majority in *United States v. Lyons* and the excerpted legislative history to the Insanity Defense Reform Act of 1983 justify their rejection of the earlier Model Penal Code's formulation. The dissenting *Lyons* opinion and Jodie English, in arguing against this rejection, question the motivations and sources used by the court and Congress and offer alternative approaches that would restrict the control prong without abolishing it. Robinson and Darley's empirical research provides insights into community intuitions regarding the insanity defense and finds that the subjects deem control-dysfunction to be relevant to assessing blameworthiness and legitimate grounds for an insanity defense.

United States v. Robert Lyons
United States Court of Appeals, Fifth Circuit
731 F.2d 243, 739 F.2d 994 (1984)

Gee, Circuit Judge:

Defendant Robert Lyons was indicted on twelve counts of knowingly and intentionally securing controlled narcotics by misrepresentation, fraud, deception and subterfuge in violation of *21 U.S.C. § 843(a)(3) (1976)* and *18 U.S.C.*

§ 2 (1976). Before trial Lyons informed the Assistant United States Attorney that he intended to rely on a defense of insanity: that he had lacked substantial capacity to conform his conduct to the requirements of the law because of drug addiction. Lyons proffered evidence that in 1978 he began to suffer from several painful ailments, that various narcotics were prescribed to be taken as needed for his pain, and that he became addicted to these drugs. He also offered to present expert witnesses who would testify that his drug addiction affected his brain both physiologically and psychologically and that as a result he lacked substantial capacity to conform his conduct to the requirements of the law.

In response to the government's motion *in limine*, the district court excluded any evidence of Lyon's drug addiction, apparently on the ground that such an addiction could not constitute a mental disease or defect sufficient to support an insanity defense. A panel of this Court reversed, holding that it was the jury's responsibility to decide whether involuntary drug addiction could constitute a mental disease or defect depriving Lyons of substantial capacity to conform his conduct to the requirements of the law. *United States v. Lyons, 704 F.2d 743 (5th Cir. 1983)*. We agreed to rehear the case en banc.

I.

For the greater part of two decades our Circuit has followed the rule that a defendant is not to be held criminally responsible for conduct if, at the time of that conduct and as a result of mental disease or defect, he lacked substantial capacity either to appreciate the wrongfulness of his conduct *or to conform his conduct to the requirements of the law*.

II.

Because the concept of criminal responsibility in the federal courts is a congeries of judicially-made rules of decision based on common law concepts, it is usually appropriate for us to reexamine and reappraise these rules in the light of new policy considerations. We last examined the insanity defense in *Blake v. United States, 407 F.2d 908 (5th Cir. 1969)* (en banc), where we adopted the A.L.I. Model Penal Code definition of insanity: that a person is not responsible for criminal conduct if, at the time of such conduct and as a result of mental disease or defect, he lacks substantial capacity either to appreciate the wrongfulness of his conduct or to conform his conduct to the requirements of the law. Following the example of sister circuits, we embraced this standard in lieu of our former one, defined in *Howard v. United States, 232 F.2d 274, 275 (5th Cir. 1956)* (en banc), because we concluded that then current knowledge in the field of behavioral science supported such a result. Unfortunately, it now appears our conclusion was premature — that the brave new world that we foresaw has not arrived.

Reexamining the *Blake* standard today, we conclude that the volitional prong of the insanity defense — a lack of capacity to conform one's conduct to the requirements of the law — does not comport with current medical and scientific knowledge, which has retreated from its earlier, sanguine expectations. Consequently, we now hold that a person is not responsible for criminal conduct on the grounds of insanity only if at the time of that conduct, as a result of a mental disease or defect, he is unable to appreciate the wrongfulness of that conduct.

We do so for several reasons. First, as we have mentioned, a majority of psychiatrists now believe that they do not possess sufficient accurate scientific bases for measuring a person's capacity for self-control or for calibrating the impairment of that capacity. "The line between an irresistible impulse and an impulse not resisted is probably no sharper than between twilight and dusk." *American Psychiatric Association Statement on the Insanity Defense*, 11 (1982) [APA Statement]....

In addition, the risks of fabrication and "moral mistakes" in administering the insanity defense are greatest "when the experts and the jury are asked to speculate whether the defendant had the capacity to 'control' himself or whether he could have 'resisted' the criminal impulse." Moreover, psychiatric testimony about volition is more likely to produce confusion for jurors than is psychiatric testimony concerning a defendant's appreciation of the wrongfulness of his act. It appears, moreover, that there is considerable overlap between a psychotic person's inability to understand and his ability to control his behavior. Most psychotic persons who fail a volitional test would also fail a cognitive test, thus rendering the volitional test superfluous for them. Finally, Supreme Court authority requires that such proof be made by the federal prosecutor beyond a reasonable doubt, an all but impossible task in view of the present murky state of medical knowledge. Davis v. United States, 160 U.S. 469, 16 S. Ct. 353, 40 L. Ed. 499 (1895).*

One need not disbelieve in the existence of Angels in order to conclude that the present state of our knowledge regarding them is not such as to support confident conclusions about how many can dance on the head of a pin. In like vein, it may be that some day tools will be discovered with which reliable conclusions about human volition can be fashioned. It appears to be all but a certainty, however, that despite earlier hopes they do not lie in our hands today. When and if they do, it will be time to consider again to what degree the law should adopt the sort of conclusions that they produce. But until then, we see no prudent course for the law to follow but to treat all criminal impulses—including those not resisted—as resistible....

III.

Thus, Lyons' claim that he lacked substantial capacity to conform his conduct to the requirements of the law will not raise the insanity defense. It would be unfair, however, to remit him retroactively to our newly restricted insanity defense without allowing him the opportunity to plan a defense bearing its contours in mind. Consequently, we vacate his conviction and remand for a new trial in accordance with our new insanity standard....

Vacated and Remanded.

Alvin B. Rubin, Circuit Judge, with whom Tate, Circuit Judge, joins dissenting....

---

*Editor's Note—In *Rivera v. Delaware*, 429 U.S. 877 (1976), the Supreme Court dismissed, and consequently sustained, the constitutionality of a Delaware statute that required a criminal defendant raising an insanity defense to prove his or her mental illness or defect by a preponderance of the evidence.

The majority offers several reasons for its decision both to reexamine and to change the method by which we determine who is criminally responsible....

The first is the potential threat to society created by the volitional prong of the insanity defense. Public opposition to any insanity-grounded defense is often based, either explicitly or implicitly, on the view that the plea is frequently invoked by violent criminals who fraudulently use it to evade just punishment....

Despite the prodigious volume of writing devoted to the plea, the empirical data that are available provide little or no support for these fearsome perceptions and in many respects directly refute them....

Another set of objections to the plea is based on the thesis that factfinders — especially juries — are confused and manipulated by the vagueness of the legal standards of insanity and the notorious "battle of the experts" who present conclusory, superficial, and misleading testimony. These conditions, the argument runs, conspire to produce inconsistent and "inaccurate" verdicts....

The manipulated-jury argument is supported largely by declamation, not data.... [O]ne major study ... found that jurors responsibly and carefully consider the evidence presented, do recognize that the final responsibility for the defendant's fate rests with them, do appreciate the limits and proper use of expert testimony, and do grasp the instructions given them. Although the evidence does not warrant the conclusion that juries function better in insanity trials than in other criminal cases, it certainly does not appear that they function *less* effectively. And no source has been cited to the court to support the conclusion that, as an empirical matter, pleas based upon the volitional prong present an especially problematic task for the jury.

Indeed, the majority opinion does not assert that the insanity defense, particularly the control test, *doesn't* work; it contends that the defense *can't* work. The principal basis for this contention is the belief, held by "a majority of psychiatrists," that they lack "sufficient accurate scientific bases for measuring a person's capacity for self-control or for calibrating the impairment of that capacity." This argument raises practical and important questions regarding the usefulness of expert testimony in determining whether a person has the ability to conform his conduct to law; but the absence of useful expert evidence, if indeed there is none, does not obviate the need for resolving the question whether the defendant ought to be held accountable for his criminal behavior....

The relevant inquiry under either branch of the insanity test is a subjective one that focuses on the defendant's actual state of mind. Our duty to undertake that inquiry is not based on confidence in the testimony of expert witnesses, but on the ethical precept that the defendant's mental state is a crucial aspect of his blameworthiness.... The availability of expert testimony and the probative value of such testimony are basically evidentiary problems that can be accommodated within the existing test.

A recent Second Circuit case demonstrates that the volitional test can be reasonably cabined to prevent abuse. In *United States v. Torniero*, the court ... established two guidelines: (1) a defendant seeking to rely on a newly recognized disorder to meet the volitional test must show "that respected authorities in the field share the view that the disorder is a disease or defect that could have impaired the defendant's ability to desist from the offense charged ...", and (2) the alleged disease or defect must be relevant to the crime charged....

Even the few cases in which the trial develops into a battle of experts provide no basis for the majority's conclusion that the prosecution faces an "all but impossible task." The prosecution appears to be able to locate experts as readily as the defense. Indeed, a defendant pleading insanity typically faces both a judge and a jury who are skeptical about psychiatry in general and the insanity plea in particular. Sharply adversarial presentation of conflicting psychiatric testimony may increase this skepticism, and thus make acquittal more unlikely. Usually the defendant will have been adjudicated sane enough to understand the proceedings against him and to assist in his defense; otherwise he would be incompetent to stand trial. The formal allocation of the persuasion burden notwithstanding, the defendant to prevail must convince the doubting factfinder that, despite present outward appearances, he was insane at the time he committed the crime.

The majority's fear that the present test invites "moral mistakes" is difficult to understand. The majority opinion concedes that some individuals cannot conform their conduct to the law's requirements. . . . Without citing any data that verdicts in insanity cases decided under a control test are frequently inaccurate, the majority embraces a rule certain to result in the conviction of at least some who are not morally responsible and the punishment of those for whom retributive, deterrent, and rehabilitative penal goals are inappropriate. A decision that virtually ensures undeserved, and therefore unjust, punishment in the name of avoiding moral mistakes rests on a peculiar notion of morality. . . .

The majority opinion is a radical departure from the established jurisprudence of every federal circuit that has spoken on the issue. It is based only on intuitive reactions and the published recommendations, to which no one has testified, of a few professional groups. We would permit no jury to decide even an unimportant issue on such hearsay. The purposes to be served by this innovation are unclear. . . . Its effect will be felt by only two small groups: a few who otherwise might have made a case for the jury but who will be deprived of a plea that in any event would likely have been bootless, and those few unfortunate persons so afflicted by mental disease that they knew what the law forbade but couldn't control their actions sufficiently to avoid violating it. . . .

In sum, I cannot join in a decision that, without supporting data, overturns a widely used rule that has not been shown to be working badly in order to adopt a change that will likely produce little or no practical benefit to society as a whole, conflicts with the fundamental moral predicates of our criminal justice system, and may inflict undeserved punishment on a few hapless individuals.

Legislative History to Public Law 98-473, Title IV, Insanity Defense Reform Act of 1983

225-228, reprinted in U.S. Code Congressional and Administrative News 3407-3410 (1984)

Provisions of the bill, as reported . . .

Section 402 adds a new section 20 to title 18 of the United States Code to define the scope of the insanity defense for Federal offenses and to shift the burden of proof to the defendant. In its entirety the new section would provide:

§20. Insanity defense

(a) Affirmative Defense — It is an affirmative defense to a prosecution under any Federal statute that, at the time of the commission of the acts constituting the offense, the defendant, as a result of a severe mental disease or defect, was unable to appreciate the nature and quality or the wrongfulness of his acts. Mental disease or defect does not otherwise constitute a defense.

(b) Burden of Proof — The defendant has the burden of proving the defense of insanity by clear and convincing evidence.

The principal difference between the statement of the defense in S. 1762 and that presently employed in the Federal courts is that the volitional portion of the cognitive-volitional test of the A.L.I. Model Penal Code is eliminated. The Committee, after extensive hearings, concluded that it was appropriate to eliminate the volitional portion of the test.

While there has been criticism of the "right-wrong" *M'Naghten* test, the "irresistible impulse" part of the current Federal insanity defense has received particularly strong criticism in recent years. Conceptually, there is some appeal to a defense predicated on lack of power to avoid criminal conduct. If one conceives the major purpose of the insanity defense to be the exclusion of the nondeterrables from criminal responsibility, a control test seems designed to meet that objective. Furthermore, notions of retributive punishment seem particularly inappropriate with respect to one powerless to do otherwise than he did.

A strong criticism of the control test, however, is associated with a determinism which seems dominant in the thinking of many expert witnesses. As noted by [Professor] David Robinson of George Washington University, "[m]odern psychiatry has tended to view man as controlled by antecedent hereditary and environmental factors." [The Report goes on to support this position with quotes from Freud and a psychiatric text.]

Such a view is consistent with a conclusion that *all* criminal conduct is evidence of lack of power to conform behavior to the requirements of law. The control tests and volitional standards thus acutely raise the problem of what is *meant* by lack of power to avoid conduct or to conform to the requirements of law which leads to the most fundamental objection to the control tests — their lack of determinate meaning.

Richard J. Bonnie, Professor of Law and Director of the Institute of Law, Psychiatry and Public Policy at the University of Virginia, while accepting the moral predicate for a control test, explained the fundamental difficulty involved:

> Unfortunately, however, there is no scientific basis for measuring a person's capacity for self-control or for calibrating the impairment of such capacity. There is, in short, no objective basis for distinguishing between offenders who were undeterrable and those who were merely undeterred, between the impulse that was irresistible and the impulse not resisted, or between substantial impairment of capacity and some lesser impairment. Whatever the precise terms of the volitional test, the question is unanswerable — or can be answered only by "moral guesses." To ask it at all, in my opinion, invites fabricated claims, undermines equal administration of the penal law, and compromises its deterrent effect.

Professor Robinson states the same idea as follows:

> No test is available to distinguish between those who cannot and those who will not conform to legal requirements. The result is an invitation to semantic justice, metaphysical speculation and intuitive moral judgments masked as factual determinations.

Similarly, The Royal Commission on Capital Punishment stated:

> Most lawyers have consistently maintained that the concept of an "irresistible" or "uncontrollable" impulse is a dangerous one, since it is impracticable to distinguish between those impulses which are the product of mental disease and those which are the product of ordinary passion, or, where mental disease exists, between impulses that may be genuinely irresistible and those which are merely not resisted.

A brief but perceptive discussion of the problem is contained in the concurring opinion of Mr. Justice Black, joined by Mr. Justice Harlan, in *Powell v. Texas*, upholding the constitutionality of criminal penalties applied to alcoholics whose public drunkenness is alleged to be beyond volitional control:

> When we say that appellant's appearance in public is caused not by "his own" volition but rather by some other force, we are clearly thinking of a force which is nevertheless his except in some special sense. The accused undoubtedly commits the proscribed act and the only question is wither the act can be attributed to a part of "his" personality that should not be regarded as criminally responsible. . . . [T]he question whether an act is "involuntary" is, as I have already indicated, an inherently elusive question, and one which the State may, for good reasons wish to regard as irrelevant.

The American Psychiatric Association also has commented on the ability of expert witnesses to provide adequate information to resolve issues inherent in the current insanity test:

> The above commentary [concerning the legal standards for an insanity defense] does not mean that given the present state of psychiatric knowledge psychiatrists cannot present meaningful testimony relevant to determining a defendant's understanding or appreciation of his act. Many psychiatrists, however, believe that psychiatric information relevant to determining whether a defendant understood the nature of his act, and whether he appreciated its wrongfulness, is more reliable and has a stronger scientific basis than, for example, does psychiatric information relevant to whether a defendant was able to control his behavior. The line between an irresistible impulse and an impulse not resisted is probably no sharper than that between twilight and dusk.

Jodie English, The Light Between Twilight and Dusk: Federal Criminal Law and the Volitional Insanity Defense
40 Hastings Law Journal 1, 45-52 (1988)

The Policy Perspective

If not unconstitutional, Congress' complete omission of a volitional insanity defense is bad policy. The abolition of this defense constitutes a radical departure from widely held federal and state understandings of the scope of a proper insanity defense. Prior to *Hinckley*, all of the federal courts that had considered the matter favored inclusion of a volitional test. . . .

The NMHA convened a National Commission on the Insanity Defense that explicitly considered the ABA's proposal to eliminate the control test. The Commission rejected the proposal in favor of a formulation including both cognitive and volitional elements, comporting with "the modern view of the mind as a unified entity whose functioning may be impaired in numerous ways." In the aftermath of the *Hinckley* acquittal, however, what was once viewed as proper policy-making has drastically changed.

By abolishing the volitional prong and recasting the cognitive prong in language requiring absolute rather than substantial incapacitation, and by mandating that the potential class of exculpating mental diseases be restricted to those denominated as "severe," the Act has turned back the jurisprudential clocks to the unenlightened days of *M'Naghten*. . . .

M'Naghten terminology is based on an antiquated perception of human psychology that defines reason as the sole determinant of human behavior. This view ignores contemporary psychiatric understandings of man as an integrated personality and is, consequently, an inadequate yardstick by which to assess responsibility. . . . In short, the *M'Naghten* test is both bad psychiatry and bad law.

The arguments in favor of a return to *M'Naghten* and, concomitantly, an abolition of a federal control test are few. In *United States v. Lyons*, the arguments are distilled to their critical essence. The criticisms are directed at a professed inability of psychiatry to scientifically calibrate human incapacity for control and a concern that jurors, cast "adrift upon a sea of unfounded scientific speculation," will end up making the "moral mistake" of wrongfully acquitting. The allegations regarding inadequacies in current psychiatric discernment are only skeletally supported. The same conclusory record undergirded the congressional debate, which relied upon APA and ABA position papers to support an abolitionist posture toward volitional insanity. None of these sources presented any empirical analysis to justify their conclusions. Moreover, no contrary positions were either referred to or summarized. . . .

[Richard] Rogers' work on the development of empirical scales to objectively measure both cognitive and volitional impairment has been widely respected. Contemporaneously with the congressional debate, Rogers perfected clinical tests to calibrate both defects of reason and defects of control. These tests exhibited near perfect interexaminer reliability (ninety-seven percent), a high concordance rate with subsequent legal disposition (eighty-eight percent), and theoretically consistent and statistically significant differences between sane and insane subjects. Neither this research, nor any like it, ever informed the congressional debate.

Concededly, even if statistical reality rather than rhetoric characterized the legislative colloquy, there was not a perfect clinical measure for assessment of either cognitive or volitional impairment, nor will there ever be one. Yet, as was acknowledged in response to like concern over problems of proving volitional defects in *Parsons v. State*, "[i]t is no satisfactory objection to say that the rule above announced by us is of difficult application. The rule in *McNaghten's Case* is equally obnoxious to a like criticism. The difficulty does not lie in the rule, but is inherent in the subject of insanity itself."

These matters are simply not amenable to absolute psychiatric certitude. Even if they were, the resolution of the dividing line between responsibility and non-responsibility is the purview of the jury, not the medical expert. . . .

The second concern which dominated the congressional debate, and the *Lyons* majority opinion, centered on a fear that moral mistakes would result from juror speculation regarding the defendant's capacity for self-control. Such a concern is sorely misplaced. The existence of persons who cannot conform their conduct to the requirements of the law is fully conceded. Neither Congress nor the *Lyons* court, however, provide for the exculpation of such mentally infirm individuals. By eliminating the volitional prong altogether, Congress implied that the law "would achieve morally correct results more often. The objective of the law, however, should not be to achieve morally correct results more often, but rather to avoid morally incorrect results at all times." . . .

. . . Congress should have considered less restrictive measures rather than completely abdicate its obligation to fairly administer the criminal justice system on behalf of this population. . . .

In *United States v. Torniero*, for example, the Second Circuit declined invitations to abolish the insanity defense generally and the volitional prong specifically, but did adopt a narrowing of the A.L.I. volitional standard. Under *Torniero*, a defendant had to establish that his mental infirmity was widely understood by respected authorities in the field as being a mental disease or defect that impairs behavioral controls, and that there was a relevant connection between this condition and the defendant's incapacity to control his conduct. . . . Professor Bonnie also acknowledges a middle ground: "The volitional inquiry probably would be manageable if the insanity defense were permitted only in cases involving psychotic disorders." Since Congress adopted such a compromise position by limiting the availability of the insanity defense to those suffering from "severe" mental diseases or defects, abolition of the volitional prong was unnecessary from a policy perspective.

Similarly, Professor Morse has suggested that retention of a volitional test could be upheld if it were narrowly proscribed so as to "excuse only those who were utterly overwhelmed by their impulses." Again, while the Act overrides the A.L.I.'s provision for exculpation based on "substantial" incapacitation by requiring total impairment, it is readily apparent that avenues existed by which perceived abuses could be minimized, while still perpetuating a federal insanity test based on defects of control.

An intermediate position was also proposed by the Pennsylvania Supreme Court in the 1846 decision of *Commonwealth v. Mosler*. In *Mosler*, a control test was upheld subject to express conditions that the offender's alleged volitional impairment must clearly exist and have evidenced itself on more than the occasion for which the volitional insanity plea was interposed.

Conclusion

Congress' decision to jettison all provisions for volitional exculpation from the federal insanity formulation is contrary to historical precedent, constitutionally infirm, and impeachable from a policy perspective. The Act denies mentally impaired offenders the right to be held blameless for conduct that is beyond their power to control and leaves them defenseless against criminal accusations. A law with such grim consequences for the truly mentally impaired offender should not be sustained.

Other Discussion Materials

Paul H. Robinson & John M. Darley, Study 12: Insanity
Justice, Liability & Blame 128-135 (1995)

...Within the legal system, mental disease or defect can affect a person's criminal liability either (1) by negating (i.e., making it impossible for the prosecution to prove) a culpable state of mind that is required by the definition of the offense charged or (2) by satisfying the conditions of a general insanity defense.... In this study, we test the goodness of fit between community standards and the provisions of the general insanity defense.

[The authors review the differences among the various insanity defense formulations.]

These distinctions — cognitive versus control, and complete loss versus substantial impairment of function — represent the major distinctions among the most common American formulations of the insanity defense....

The insanity study sought to determine whether the subjects would give a general defense because of a person's insanity, whether they recognize the validity of the cognitive versus control distinction that the doctrine uses, and which of the tests, if any, best reflects their views. In the core of the [test scenario] story we presented to subjects an individual characterized with various details that suggest insanity (different in each variation).[1] The person then is described as picking up an object that is nearby and hitting another person with it, killing that other person....

---

1. The scenarios read:

   Scenario (4): High Control, Low Cognitive. Stanley Charlson has been twice committed to a mental hospital, each following an attempt to disfigure or mutilate himself. On the first occasion, he stuck his hand into a fire in a fireplace and held it there; on the second, he cut his left shin repeatedly with a large bread knife. On both occasions, his injuries would have been life-threatening had he not been stopped by others who happened onto the scene. Other than these two episodes, Stanley is able to function and has many friends and a good relationship with his family. On a Sunday afternoon he goes to visit his parents and his younger brother, Peter, who lives with them. The back room windows of their house overlook a shallow river. Stanley calls Peter from the front room to look at a boat traveling down the river. While the boy is looking out of the window, Stanley picks up a wooden mallet and strikes the boy twice on the head, killing him instantly. When his mother enters the room, he is standing over the boy, with the mallet still in his hand and a horrified look on his face. He can give no explanation to his mother as to why he did what he did, saying simply that "something came over me and made me do it." When the police arrive, they find him huddled in the corner of the back room. He is transported to the local county hospital for treatment. In interviews with doctors and private talks with his mother, he describes that at the time he hit Peter on the head he was well aware of what he was doing and that it was wrong but felt subject to an overwhelming compulsion that "took control of his body," and compelled him to do what he did, although he has no idea why. Court-appointed psychiatrists testify that at the time of his conduct causing Peter's death he was mentally ill, suffering from severe impulse control disorder.

   Scenario (5): High Control, Low Cognitive. [See the "Michael's Madness" Problem, above, for the text of this scenario.]

...The cases and the way they are perceived are shown in Table 5.1.

The cases are numbered as they will appear in the next table, which is why the numbers run from 4-7 rather than begin with 1. The first two columns, (a) and (b), show the subjects' ratings of the degree to which the perpetrator suffers from a substantial or complete control dysfunction. The right hand three columns, (c), (d), and (e), report their perceptions of the degree of cognitive dysfunction. The questions on cognitive dysfunction are more numerous because, as we noted about cognitive dysfunction, the legal doctrine distinguishes between cognitive dysfunction of two sorts: first, one may be unaware of the nature of one's conduct (unaware that the thing one is hitting is a person) and second, even if one is aware of the nature of the conduct, one may be unaware of the wrongfulness of the conduct (unaware that hitting another is wrongful). Therefore we included questions about both of these sorts of dysfunction.

The results indicate that respondents are well able to distinguish cognitive from control dysfunction, a fact that lends some support for the use of this distinction by the doctrine....

Before we leave Table 5.1, one more result is worth interpreting. The two different aspects of cognitive dysfunction have a complex relation with each other. As we said above, one can be aware of the nature of one's conduct, but unaware of the wrongfulness of the conduct. It looks like this is the way that our subjects treat this situation, as the doctrine suggests. Scenario (7) is perceived by them as being a case in which the person is aware of the nature of his conduct, column (d), but unaware of its wrongfulness, column (e). As column (c) shows, they agree that this individual has a substantial degree of cognitive impairment. Note that if one is

---

Scenario (6): Medium Control, High Cognitive. Mrs. Jeanne Cogdon lives with her husband Frank and her daughter Pat, age 15. Mrs. Cogdon suffered a severely traumatic experience when she became lost during a camping trip two years earlier. She was found after six days, suffering from exposure, disorientation, and severe depression. Since that time, she has been seeing a psychiatrist, who is treating her for post-traumatic stress disorder. On this particular night, she goes to bed at 10:30 p.m. as usual and at 1:30 a.m. she awakes in order to check on her daughter, Pat. She sees Pat and becomes terrified because she thinks she is seeing Pat being attacked by moles. She screams "the moles are going to get us. They are attacking Pat!" Jeanne attempts to protect Pat by picking up a hockey stick and striking Pat's bed several times including one blow to Pat's head that kills her. When Jeanne's husband arrives she is striking at different parts of Pat's desktop although the desktop is actually empty. She yells to her husband, "you've got to help, the moles are hurting Pat." Her husband tells her to put the stick down, and she does. Psychiatrists testify that she was hallucinating at the time of the killing, as a result of post-traumatic stress disorder.

Scenario (7): Low Control, High Cognitive. Jeffrey stays in his room most of the time, with the shades pulled and the lights out. Every month he must go to the hospital for counseling with a psychiatrist. The trips are very stressful for Jeffrey, who becomes more agitated as the day for his monthly trip approaches. He is afraid that someone "will get him," he tells his mother and is upset with the hospital for making him go. She tries to assure him that everything will be fine, and that he should leave for the bus immediately. Jeffrey leaves the house, walking quickly, heading for the bus stop three blocks away. Two women and a young man are already at the stop waiting for the bus. Although the young man has done nothing, Jeffrey becomes frightened and feels physically threatened by him. He finds a stone and hides it in his pocket in order to defend himself. Jeffrey waits to board after the other people but the young man, who is ahead of him in line, steps out of line and bends to one knee to tie his shoe. The young man stands up just as Jeffrey passes him. Jeffrey, imagining that the man is about to attack him, reacts by hitting the youth in the face with the rock that he had hidden in his pocket. As the young man staggers, Jeffrey hits him again on the side of the head, killing him. Jeffrey turns and runs but several passengers tackle him and hold him until police arrive. Court-appointed psychiatrists testify that at the time of his conduct causing the young man's death, Jeffrey was suffering from severe paranoid schizophrenia.

Table 5.1 **Respondents' Perceptions of Cognitive and Control Dysfunctions**

	Control Dysfunction			Cognitive Dysfunction	
	(a)	(b)	(c)	(d) Unaware of Nature of Conduct	(e) Unaware of Wrongfulness
Suggested Scenario Label	Substantial	Complete	Substantial		
4. High control, low cognitive	7.58	7.39	3.05	2.76	2.71
5. High control, low cognitive	7.29	6.61	2.95	2.50	2.74
6. Medium control, high cognitive	4.47	4.74	7.68	7.97	7.58
7. Low control, high cognitive	3.79	3.89	6.82	3.29	6.68

The questions asked whether the respondent 1 = "strongly disagreed," 5 = was "unsure," or 9 = "strongly agreed," that the actor had a substantial or complete control or cognitive dysfunction.

Table 5.2 **Liability as Related to Insanity**

	(a)	(b) % No Liability (N)	(c) % Civil Commitment
Suggested Label	Liability[a]		
Control Conditions:			
1. Murder	10.42	0	
2. Self-defense	0.11	79	
3. Mistaken identify	7.79	0	
Experimental Conditions:			
4. High control, low cognitive	1.89 (19%–8.29)	81	81
5. High control, low cognitive	3.00 (34%–9.25)	86	86
6. Medium control, high cognitive	0.64 (8%–5.67)	92	92
7. Low control, high cognitive	1.65 (16%–9.00)	84	84

Liability Scale: N = No criminal Liability, 0 = Liability but no punishment, 1 = 1 day, 2 = 2 weeks, 3 = 2 months, 4 = 6 months, 5 = 1 year, 6 = 3 years, 7 = 7 years, 8 = 15 years, 9 = 30 years, 10 = life, and 11 = death.
[a]Civil commitment cases are included as 0 in calculating these means. The numbers in parentheses indicate the percentage of respondents who assigned criminal liability and, of those, the average liability they assigned.

unaware of the nature of one's conduct that one will of course be unaware of its wrongfulness, but not the reverse. The categories—aware of nature of conduct and wrongfulness—are serial in relation rather than alternative....

[In Table 5.2], the usual liability results are shown in columns (a) and (b), and there is one additional result in column (a) that we will explain in a moment. Before we examine the liability ratings for the mental illness cases, a note on the comparison cases is in order. The comparison cases are shown in rows (1), (2), and (3). The case in row (1) involves a person who, because he is angry at another, goes to that person's house and bludgeons him to death, a straightforward murder, and we notice, from column (a), that it commands a sentence of somewhere between life imprisonment and the death penalty. Row (2) shows the liability assigned to a convenience store owner who defends himself from a knife-carrying robber by pulling a nightstick from under the counter and striking the robber, who is lunging at him with a knife. The robber is killed. This seems a straightforward case of self-defense to us, and judging by their liability assignments, to our respondents as well. The third comparison case, row (3), involves again a convenience store owner who chases a robber and misidentifies another individual as that robber. The misidentified individual and the owner get into a fight, the owner uses the nightstick that he is carrying, and the misidentified individual eventually dies of his injuries. The liability assigned to this case is high [but not as high as the unmistaken murder]. This provides an indication of the respondents' views about the wrongfulness of a mistake as to what the person thinks is justified force. The subjects' response is notable because the mistake is in some sense similar to the sorts of mistakes that the mentally dysfunctional persons make in the test cases.

Column (c)...in this table gives the percentage of subjects who assign civil commitment to the perpetrator....We gave them this option as a way of assuring that those who are concerned about community safety more than anything else would feel that the civil commitment system would provide this assurance and that they need not impose criminal liability on someone who they thought might not deserve it in order to assure the community's safety. The ability to specify not just civil commitment but also a term of years thus makes the civil option equally effective at protecting the community as the criminal option did. Thus, those who give the criminal option would be those who are doing so because they believe that the person really deserves the condemnation and punishment of criminal conviction.

Notice that many of our subjects choose this civil commitment option; the percentages tabled in column (c) are 66% or higher.

The first result to notice from these various liability judgement comparisons is the global one. Perpetrators who are judged to be suffering from a high degree of dysfunction, whether that dysfunction is of the cognitive or conduct control sort, are normally not assigned criminal liability. In other words, our subjects do grant validity to a defense of insanity, and sharply reduce the liability assigned to a person who commits a crime while mentally ill; in making this judgement they are in general accord with the way that the criminal codes treat such cases. Typically, more than 70% of our respondents assign no criminal liability to such cases.

This result has special implications for the current controversy over whether the insanity defense should excuse only for cognitive dysfunction or whether control dysfunction also should provide a defense....In scenario (4), which is perceived as showing high control and low cognitive dysfunction, 81% of the respondents impose no criminal liability (in scenario (5), similarly perceived, 66%). Scenario (7), perceived as the reverse, low control and high cognitive, has about the same percentages of respondents giving no criminal liability, 84%. This suggests that *both* cognitive and control dysfunctions can support an insanity defense. This conclusion is supported as well by the results in scenario (6). Where *medium control* and high cognitive are perceived, 92% give the defense, noticeably more than the 84% who give the defense in scenario (7) for *low control* and high cognitive. Control dysfunction can support a defense; the greater the perceived control dysfunction the greater the likelihood of a defense. Of course, these respondents do judge that *civil* confinement is appropriate for the insane individual; they do not wish to release him into the community. Indeed, were we to table the length of the period of confinement recommended by the respondents, without respect to whether it was civil or criminal confinement, we would see that the time period of incarceration recommended was reasonably constant across cases. Our respondents seem to be making a complex judgement here. As is reasonably well understood in legal circles, there are a number of reasons why one incarcerates a person: because the person is blameworthy and deserves the sentence is one; to incapacitate the person so no further crimes will be committed is another.... What our respondents wish to happen, given the alternatives presented to them, is to punish the non-insane with a prison sentence and to incapacitate the insane for a long period of time, in a place that, within our system, may look remarkably like a prison.

Return now to the criminal liabilities assigned to the cases in which we depicted possibly insane persons bringing about death. Column (a) shows the criminal liabilities assigned, and we can now explain the numbers shown in parentheses in that column. The number not in parentheses ... is the average liability assigned by all respondents, treating those who assigned no liability, no liability or punishment, or civil commitment, as assigning a criminal liability of zero.

The other tabled number, in parentheses, shows the average criminal liability assigned *by those who assigned criminal liability*. (To make the reader's task easier, we have actually tabled two numbers. The first is the percentage of respondents who assigned criminal liability. The second is the average liability assigned by those persons. So, for instance, reading (4) we see that 19% of the people assigned criminal liability in that scenario, and their average liability was 8.29).... What the parenthetical number reveals is that those subjects, a minority of respondents in each case, who don't exculpate the offender for reasons of insanity, judge that quite high sentences are appropriate. And notice that this is true for all of the insanity cases shown in rows (4) through (7). Even within this minority group, however, liability differences can be seen to exist. Also, slightly fewer respondents assign criminal liability to the two high cognitive dysfunction cases than the two high control dysfunction cases. Further research will need to be done to determine the persistence and importance of these differences, and the degree to which they will transcend the specifics of the scenarios that we wrote to create each case.

Disability Excuses

The previous section, concerning insanity, offers a case study of the principles of exculpation for disability excuses. Involuntary intoxication and duress, as well as the involuntary act excuse contained in the voluntary act requirement, also are classic disability excuses. Defendants have pressed for the recognition of other excuses, some of which would seem to satisfy the principles of excuse, while others do not.

◆ THE CASE OF PATTY HEARST

Patty Hearst is a nineteen-year old art history major at the University of California at Berkeley. She lives in an apartment close to campus with her fiancé, Steven Weed, and finally feels happy. Hearst, always mature and independent, coaxed Weed into dating her while she was attending the small, elite Crystal Springs School for Girls, close to her parents' California home. She graduated early and, much in love, had her parents hire Weed as her full-time math tutor. They moved in together during Hearst's first year of college at Menlo Park, where she finished in the top of her class. After Weed was accepted into Berkeley's Ph.D. program in Philosophy, Hearst decided to enroll there as well. She had become quite interested in art history while at Menlo Park, and Berkeley seemed like an ideal place to continue her studies.

Hearst is just now getting into the swing of college. She took the Fall semester off and worked in the stationery section of a department store (her first job). She is enjoying her quiet domestic life. Weed does the cleaning; she does the cooking. Her chief aspiration in life is having a collie, a station wagon, and two children. Such goals are quite tame for the granddaughter of William Randolph Hearst, a member of one of the most influential families in California and the world. But most people who meet Patty Hearst find her to be quite different from the affected elitist that her name might imply. Her faculty adviser at Crystal Springs describes her as "delightful" and "unpretentious. [She] never rode on the laurels of her family name." Hearst feels comfortable with her casual lifestyle

Figure 104 **Party Hearst, 1973**

(F.B.I.)

but still uncomfortable about her family and their wealth. Her recent engagement has improved her familial relationships. Her usually overbearing, politically far-right mother has often been disappointed with Hearst and her liberal, unrefined ways. But that has changed now that they are shopping for china, silver, and crystal, and planning a big society wedding.

On February 2, 1974, Hearst goes through her usual routine. She and Weed are quite domestic, often staying in for the evening, cooking, reading, and talking. Their quiet evening is interrupted by a knock on the door. Two people, acting strange and fidgety, say they were told the apartment is going up for rent and ask whether they can see the inside. Weed replies that there has been a mistake and turns them away. Both Hearst and Weed are mildly shaken by the strange visitors. The next evening, Hearst is again disturbed when a stranger calls, persistently asking for Mary.

Two days later, Weed has an evening class, then walks home as usual. Hearst is waiting and they have dinner. They settle down to watch the television program *Star Trek*, followed by *Mission: Impossible*. Their domestic scene is interrupted for the third evening in a row by a sharp knock on the door. Annoyed, Weed goes to answer. Two shabbily dressed people are outside, asking to use their phone. Moments later, the visitors push open the door and barge in, followed by two men. Weed is beaten, tied up, and dragged into the living room. Hearst tries to fight the intruders before being overwhelmed. When the intruders notice that Weed is still struggling, they hit him with a rifle butt several times. Hearst, dressed only in her bathrobe, screams, cries, and pleads with her captors to let her go. She is dragged outside and thrown into the trunk of a car.

When the police arrive, they question the neighbors. From the cyanide-tipped bullets that were left at the scene, they determine that the infamous Symbionese Liberation Army is behind the kidnapping. The SLA has become well known for its killing of Dr. Marcus Foster, the African-American superintendent of schools for Oakland County. They are reputed to be dangerously driven by their far-far-left, slightly illogical politics, mixing Marxist theory with violent activism. (Most of the members come from upper middle-class backgrounds.)

Three days after the kidnapping, SLA leader Donald DeFreeze releases a communique. They declare that Hearst is a prisoner of war and is being ransomed

Figure 105 **Patricia Hearst's grandfather, William Randolph Hearst, 1935**

(AP)

Figure 106 **Patricia Hearst and Steven Weed's apartment on Benvenue Avenue in Berkeley**

(San Francisco Examiner, Florence Fang)

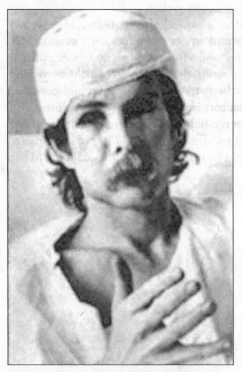

Figure 107 **Steven Weed, Hearst's boyfriend, in the hospital after the kidnapping**

(San Francisco Examiner, Florence Fang)

for Joseph Remiro and Russell Little, two men held in Foster's death. There is a tape of Hearst, saying that she is being well treated and in accordance with the Geneva Convention prisoner-of-war guidelines. The SLA calls for a good faith gesture, requiring the Hearst family to distribute $70 worth of food to every needy Californian. Hearst's father distributes $2 million worth of food and makes arrangements for another $4 million distribution.

Hearst is kept captive and isolated in a stuffy bedroom closet all day long except for brief trips to the bathroom. There is a single bare bulb in the hot, windowless room. She is blindfolded at all times. Since her kidnapping, Hearst has been threatened with death, taunted, ruthlessly interrogated, and terrorized by the constant sounds of cleaning and loading weapons. She is also raped by two of the SLA members. The leader, DeFreeze, comes into the closet to

Figure 108 **General Field Marshal Cinque Mtume, aka Donald DeFreeze**

(F.B.I.)

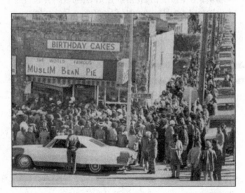

Figure 109 **Lines of people waiting to receive food from the giveaway sponsored by the Hearst family in response to SLA demands**

(UPI)

chide her for not cooperating with the "sisters." As he begins to talk to her, he grabs her pelvic region and breasts. He returns later and forces her to have sex with him.

Then William Wolfe, another SLA member, visits her in her closet and rapes her. Hearst feels helpless and afraid, and unable to put up much of a fight. Her captors tell her that her parents are bourgeois pigs who have abandoned her and that she has no hope of survival. They say that when and if the F.B.I. raids the house, they will not be concerned about her getting killed in the exchange of gunfire. Hearst vacillates between defending her parents and feeling as if they do not care about her predicament. As a result of her treatment and fears, Hearst is having difficulty eating.

After a month in captivity, Hearst is a physical and emotional wreck. She cannot walk at all and can only stand briefly before collapsing. She finds that she is gradually becoming sympathetic to the SLA mission and position. Her captors latch onto this new sentiment and encourage her SLA education, inviting her to attend meetings and giving her reading materials (on poverty, injustice, inequality, and the

evils of the Hearst family). After being isolated from all outside human contact, Hearst is buoyed by now being hugged and called "sister" by the SLA members.

On April 3, 1974, two months after being kidnapped, Hearst declares that she is joining the SLA. In a tape released to the public, Hearst says that she has taken the

Figure 110 **Closet where Hearst was held**

(Bob McLeod, San Francisco Examiner)

[handwritten margin note:] Hearst joins SLA 2 mon. later

name "Tania" after one of Che Guevera's comrades. She derides her father, saying that his attempts to meet the SLA demands were futile and weak. She now thinks that revolutionary action is the only way to make a difference. She says that she can never go back to her old life now that she is aware of the world's inequities. In addition to the tape, the SLA releases a poster depicting Hearst dressed in a jumpsuit and beret, crouching with a gun in front of a seven-headed cobra, the SLA symbol. Public and police sentiment turns against Hearst, but her

Figure 111 **Hearst posing before a SLA banner, 1974**
(Bettmann/Corbis)

parents maintain that she has been brainwashed by the group.

On April 15th, "Tania" accompanies her new comrades to the Hibernia Bank in San Francisco. They park illegally in a bus zone and approach the bank with Tania in the rear, equipped with a cut-down carbine. There are eighteen employees and six customers inside the bank on this sunny morning. The SLA women, wearing three-quarter length pea coats, dark flared pants, and hiking boots, force the people to the ground and keep them under control. Witnesses note that

Figure 112 **The Hibernia Bank in the Sunset District of San Francisco, 1976**
(AP)

the group acts like commandos, with each person assigned a discrete task. They are so well orchestrated that there is little need for communication among them during the robbery.

As she has been instructed, Tania announces that she is Patty Hearst. She threatens people if they do not stay horizontal on the floor. Upstairs, the bank manager is in the break room when he notices what is going on below. He activates the silent alarm, which in turn activates the security video cameras. Just before the robbery is completed, an SLA woman shoots two customers who walk into the midst of the robbery and try to leave again. (They will recover from their injuries.) The group then escapes with more than $10,000 and dump their getaway cars at an elementary school.

The F.B.I. arrives on the scene and recognizes Hearst on the security tapes. News of Hearst's role in the robbery reaches her family, who have retreated to

Figure 113 **Patty Hearst holding gun inside the Hibernia Bank, 1974**
(AP)

Desi Arnaz's home in Mexico. They are horrified, and assert that she was coerced and brainwashed. The F.B.I. Director says that, for the time being, they will assume Hearst is a coercion victim. However, the Attorney General says Hearst is now nothing more than a common criminal. The Bureau, however, wishes to arrest her only as a material witness. Media stories show no sympathy. The F.B.I. issues a wanted poster that becomes an immediate collectors' item and is offered for sale at alternative lifestyle stores in the Bay Area.

The next Wednesday, April 24th, Hearst issues a statement claiming that she willingly participated in the robbery and that she received one-ninth of the profits, just as did every other SLA participant. She also criticizes her parents and her former boyfriend, Steven Weed. After this statement, the SLA disappears from view, leaving their current hide-out and moving to 1808 Oakdale Street. On May 10th, the SLA decides that San Francisco is no longer a safe place and move to the anonymity of Los Angeles.

On May 15th, Hearst is waiting for two SLA members, Emily and Bill Harris, in a car outside of Mel's Sporting Goods Store. The proprietor catches Bill attempting to steal a bandolier. He confronts Harris as Harris tries to leave the premises. A struggle ensues. Hearst fires cover shots from across the street to facilitate the Harrises' escape. Twenty-seven slugs slam into the storefront; three hit an adjoining building. The trio drive away and, a few blocks later, hijack a van belonging to Tom Matthews, a high school student from Lynwood. He stays in the van and spends the next day and a half

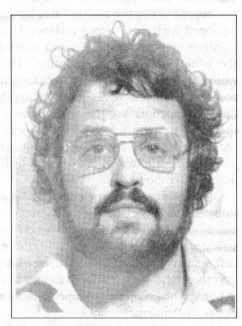

Figure 114 **William Harris**
(San Mateo County jail)

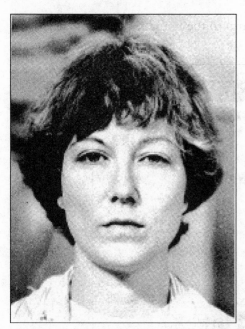

Figure 115 **Emily Harris**

(San Mateo County jail)

Figure 116 **Secluded Pennsylvania farmhouse where the SLA took refuge, 1975**

(AP)

Figure 117 **Hideout in Sacramento where the SLA took refuge, 1975**

(AP)

with Hearst, Bill, and Emily. Hearst tells Tom that she was not coerced into robbing the Hibernia Bank. (Hearst later says she told Tom this information because the Harrises were there.) During their time together, Tania pats Tom's head, telling him that he will be okay. They drop him off at his house in time for his upcoming ball game and even offer him gas money for his troubles. They do not return to the SLA safehouse.

The other SLA members evacuate their safehouse and find another refuge nearby. Police track them there and, after a shootout, all eight SLA members are dead. Patty and the Harrises watch the events unfold on television. They leave Los Angeles for the Bay Area and then travel, separately, across the country, meeting up in New York City. Together, they head to Pennsylvania for the summer.

In September 1974, Patty makes her way to Las Vegas and then to Sacramento. The Harrises arrive a few days later, and the SLA (with some new recruits) becomes active again. On January 31st, Patty registers for classes at Sacramento City College under the assumed name of Sue Hendricks. In late May, Hearst moves to the Mission District. She shares an apartment at 625 Morse Street with other SLA members until September 18, 1975, when the F.B.I. finally catches up with her. By this point, the federal government has spent more than $3.5 million and twenty months tracking her.

When Agent Tom Padden crashes through the door shouting "F.B.I. freeze," Hearst is in the process of packing a loaded .38 caliber Smith and Wesson handgun and has twenty-three bullets in her purse. After the arrest,

Hearst asks Agent Padden if she can return to the house to change, as her alarm caused her to wet her pants.

Figure 118 **F.B.I. Wanted poster for Hearst**
(F.B.I.)

1. Relying only on your own intuitions of justice, what liability and punishment, if any, does Patty Hearst deserve?

N	0	1	2	3	4	5	6	7	8	9	10	11
☐	☐	☐	☐	☐	☐	☐	☐	☐	☐	☐	☐	☐
no liability	liability but no punishment	1 day	2 wks	2 mo	6 mo	1 yr	3 yrs	7 yrs	15 yrs	30 yrs	life imprison-ment	No punish-ment but civil preventive detention for as long as she is dangerous

2. What liability, if any, under the then-existing statutes?
3. What liability, if any, under the Model Penal Code?

■ THE LAW

United States Code
Title 18 (1974)

Section 2113. Bank Robbery and Incidental Crimes

(a) Whoever, by force and violence, or by intimidation, takes, or attempts to take, from the person or presence of another any property or money or any other thing of value belonging to, or in the care, custody, control, management, or possession of, any bank, credit union, or any savings and loan association; or

Whoever enters or attempts to enter any bank, credit union, or any savings and loan association, or any building used in whole or in part as a bank, credit union, or any savings and loan association, or building, or part thereof, so used, any felony affecting such bank, credit union, or any savings and loan association and in violation of any statute of the United States, or any larceny—

Shall be fined not more than $5,000 or imprisoned not more than twenty years, or both.

(b) Whoever takes and carries away, with intent to steal or purloin, any property or money or any other thing of value exceeding $100 belonging to, or in the care, custody, control, management, or possession of any bank, credit union, or any savings and loan association, shall be fined not more than $5,000 or imprisoned not more than ten years, or both.

Whoever takes and carries away, with intent to steal or purloin, any property or money or any other thing of value not exceeding $100 belonging to, or in the care, custody, control, management, or possession of any bank, credit union, or any savings and loan association, shall be fined not more than $1,000 or imprisoned not more than one year, or both.

(c) Whoever receives, possesses, conceals, stores, barters, sells or disposes of, any property of money or other thing of value knowing the same to have been taken from a bank, credit union, or any savings and loan association, in violation of subsection (b) of this section shall be subject to the punishment provided by said subsection (b) for the taker.

(d) Whoever, in commission, or in attempting to commit, any offense defined in subsections (a) and (b) of this section, assaults any person, or puts in jeopardy the life of any person by the use of a dangerous weapon or device, shall be fined not more than $10,000 or imprisoned not more than twenty-five years, or both.

(e) Whoever, in committing any offense defined in this section, or in avoiding or attempting to avoid apprehension for the commission of such offense, kills any person, or forces any person to accompany him without the consent of such person, shall be imprisoned not less than ten years, or punished by death if the verdict of the jury shall so direct.

(f) As used in this section the term "bank" means any member of the Federal Reserve System, and any bank, banking association, trust company, savings bank, or other banking institution organized or operating under the laws of the United States, and any bank the deposits of which are insured by the Federal Deposit Insurance Corporation.

(g) As used in this section the term "savings and loan association" means any federal savings and loan association and any "insured institution" as defined in section 401 of the National Housing Act, as amended, and any "Federal credit union" as defined in section 2 of the Federal Credit Union Act.

(h) As used in this section the term "credit union" means any federal credit union and any State-chartered credit union the accounts of which are insured by the Administrator of the National Credit Union Administration.

Section 924. [Use of a Firearm in Commission of a Felony;] Penalties

(a) . . .

(c) Whoever —

(1) uses a firearm to commit any felony for which he may be prosecuted in a court of the United States, or

(2) carries a firearm unlawfully during the commission of any felony for which he may be prosecuted in a court of the United States.

shall, in addition to the punishment provided for the commission of such felony, be sentenced to a term of imprisonment for not less that one year nor more than ten years. In the case of his second or subsequent conviction under this subsection, such person shall be sentenced to a term of imprisonment for not less than two nor more than twenty-five years and, notwithstanding any other provision of law, the court shall not suspend the sentence in the case of a second or subsequent conviction of such person or give him a probationary sentence, nor shall the term of imprisonment imposed under this subsection run concurrently with any term of imprisonment imposed for the commission of such felony.

United States v. Gordon
526 F.2d 406 (9th Cir. 1975)

The defendant was convicted of possession and sale of amphetamine tablets, despite his claim of a duress defense arising from his belief that his life and the lives of his friends would be in danger if he did not complete the sale. The court of appeals applied the definition of duress, first appearing in *Shannon v. United States*, 76 F.2d 490, 493 (10th Cir. 1935), that "[c]oercion which will excuse the commission of a criminal act must be immediate and of such nature as to induce a well-grounded apprehension of death or serious bodily injury if the act is not done. One who has full opportunity to avoid the act without danger of that kind cannot invoke the doctrine of coercion. . . . For a defendant to success-fully urge duress as a defense, he must show that the threat and the fear which the threat caused were immediate and involved death or serious bodily injury. He must also show that the fear was well-grounded and that there was no reasonable opportunity to escape." The court ultimately found that his situation lacked in immediacy because the threats were over long-distance telephone calls by persons who were hundreds of miles away and that he held an opportunity to escape, as "[a]venues of escape were always available.... If they had not been selling drugs, they could have sought police protection."

D'Aquino v. United States
192 F.2d 338 (9th Cir. 1951)

The defendant was an American citizen of Japanese ancestry who was charged with treason for allegedly broadcasting over the radio from Japan during World War II. She claimed a defense of duress based on her fears that she would be harmed during her residency in Japan if she did not provide public support for their cause. However, the court held that the elements of duress would not be satisfied by her circumstances. She was not a military prisoner, for which there might have been an exception, and as such, was held to the standard that "in order to excuse a criminal act on the ground of coercion, compulsion or necessity, one must have acted under the apprehension of immediate and impending death or of serious and immediate bodily harm. Fear of injury to one's property or remote bodily harm do not excuse an offense." Further, the court noted:

> We know of no rule that would permit one who is under the protection of an enemy to claim immunity from prosecution for treason merely by setting up a claim of mental fear of possible future action on the part of the enemy. We think that the citizen owing allegiance to the United States must manifest a determination to resist commands and orders until such time as he is faced with the alternative of immediate injury or death. Were any other rule to be applied, traitors in the enemy country would by that fact alone be shielded from any requirement of resistance. The person claiming the defense of coercion and duress must be a person whose resistance has brought him to the last ditch.

Model Penal Code
(Official Draft 1962)

Section 2.08. Intoxication

(1) Except as provided in Subsection (4) of this Section, intoxication of the actor is not a defense unless it negatives an element of the offense.

(2) When recklessness establishes an element of the offense, if the actor, due to self-induced intoxication, is unaware of a risk of which he would have been aware had he been sober, such unawareness is immaterial.

(3) Intoxication does not, in itself, constitute mental disease within the meaning of Section 4.01.

(4) Intoxication which (a) is not self-induced or (b) is pathological is an affirmative defense if by reason of such intoxication the actor at the time of his conduct lacks substantial capacity either to appreciate its criminality [wrongfulness] or to conform his conduct to the requirements of law.

(5) Definitions. In this Section unless a different meaning plainly is required:

(a) "intoxication" means a disturbance of mental or physical capacities resulting from the introduction of substances into the body;

(b) "self-induced intoxication" means intoxication caused by substances which the actor knowingly introduces into his body, the tendency of which to cause intoxication he knows or ought to know, unless he introduces them pursuant to medical advice or under such circumstances as would afford a defense to a charge of crime;

(c) "pathological intoxication" means intoxication grossly excessive in degree, given the amount of the intoxicant, to which the actor does not know he is susceptible.

Section 2.09. Duress

(1) It is an affirmative defense that the actor engaged in the conduct charged to constitute an offense because he was coerced to do so by the use of, or a threat to use, unlawful force against his person or the person of another, which a person of reasonable firmness in his situation would have been unable to resist.

(2) The defense provided by this Section is unavailable if the actor recklessly placed himself in a situation in which it was probable that he would be subjected to duress. The defense is also unavailable if he was negligent in placing himself in such a situation, whenever negligence suffices to establish culpability for the offense charged.

(3) It is not a defense that a woman acted on the command of her husband, unless she acted under such coercion as would establish a defense under this Section. [The presumption that a woman, acting in the presence of her husband, is coerced is abolished.]

(4) When the conduct of the actor would otherwise be justifiable under Section 3.02, this Section does not preclude such defense.

▲ PROBLEM
Arthur's Adventure

Arthur, who just turned eighteen years old, is a shy, five-foot ten-inch overweight boy who lives with his mother in Winituck, Delaware. He has never been good at sports or anything else involving people, but is an astonishingly successful writer of romance novels. He has never traveled outside his small town but he sets his stories in exciting locations around the world by using his imagination and reading travel books. His writing has just won him the Romance Writers' Guild's "Sweet Tear" Award for the best newcomer in the business, and he is headed for his first trip out of Winituck, on a train to Philadelphia, where he is to receive his award at a Guild banquet dinner.

The Guild has reserved a room for Arthur at a local hotel. Feeling excited about his adventure, Arthur decides to experience the subway on his way to the banquet. In his black and pink formals, he stands out among the other passengers waiting for the train and is a target of ridicule by some local eleven-year old boys. "Where you goin', fat boy?," asks one of the boys. Arthur stares down at the white knuckles on his folded hands. Perhaps they will leave him alone if he doesn't respond. "I'm talkin' to you, blimpo!," the boy insists. Perhaps he can just stand up slowly and walk away, Arthur thinks. "I think fat boy is scared, and he hasn't even met my friend Bob," the boy says to the others. He pulls a one-inch pen knife from his pocket and shows it to Arthur. "Meet Bob," he says. Arthur's eyes tear up, bringing howls of laughter from the boys. "Bob wants to take us to the movies but he's got no money. He wants you to go over to that newsstand, take the money from the register when the old man isn't looking, and bring it here." Arthur is shaking visibly but walks to the newsstand. He sees the boys watching him. Still shaking, he leans across the counter and takes the bills from the register. At that moment the old man turns and grabs Arthur by the sleeve. Arthur pulls loose and pulls the old man off balance as he does. He runs toward the stairs and throws the money at the boys as he passes, knocking down several people as he runs. He reaches the exit turnstile and tries to jump over, but gets only inches off the ground. A few minutes later, a police officer arrives to pull Arthur off the turnstile, where he has become stuck.

Between sobs, Arthur tells his story. The officer is sympathetic but the old man and one of the persons knocked down on the stairs are seriously injured. Arthur is charged with two counts of bodily injury and one count of theft. Does he have a defense?

● OVERVIEW OF DISABILITY EXCUSES

Common Structure of Disability Excuses   One traditional disability excuse, insanity, is discussed in the previous Section. Others include subnormality, involuntary intoxication, immaturity, and duress. With a few important variations, each defense reflects the same internal structure as insanity, requiring that a disability cause an excusing condition. In each instance, however, the disability requirement is different and a different combination of excusing conditions is recognized.

SUBNORMALITY, INVOLUNTARY INTOXICATION & ADDICTION

In the excuse of subnormality, low intelligence is the disability. It frequently is treated as a form of "mental defect" under the insanity defense and typically requires the same cognitive dysfunction excusing conditions as are required for insanity. The involuntary intoxication excuse has a disability of intoxication and typically the same excusing conditions as the insanity defense, a cognitive or a control dysfunction. That is, an actor's involuntary intoxication provides an excuse if it causes the same level of dysfunction required by the jurisdiction's insanity defense (McNaghten test, McNaghten-plus-irresistible-impulse test, or ALI test, for example). *Voluntary* intoxication, even when severe enough to cause an excusing condition, will not provide an excuse defense.[1] Addiction is sometimes offered as a defense to crime. Addiction is a physiologically confirmable abnormal state — it may qualify as a disability — but frequently does not cause excusing conditions sufficient to render an actor blameless. Compare this to instances in which long-term addiction causes mental illness. In such a case, an actor may have a defense, under the standard insanity defense, not because of the actor's addiction but because of the mental illness that it has caused. (Addiction has another role distinct from that as a claimed defense to a crime: It sometimes is offered as a ground for claiming that the actor's intoxication is *involuntary*.)

Disability Without Excusing Condition The involuntary intoxication defense illustrates the importance of the excusing condition and the normative assessment that it embodies. As with insanity, it is not enough that the actor suffers the disability required for the defense; that is, it is not enough that the actor is involuntarily intoxicated. To merit an excuse, the disability must cause sufficient dysfunction that the actor could not reasonably have been expected to have avoided the violation. In *State v. Mriglot,* for example, the defendant sought an instruction on involuntary intoxication as a defense to his forgery conviction that would excuse him if the jury found that he had been "involuntarily *under the influence* [of] or *affected* by the use of liquor or drugs."[2] The court rejected defendant's instruction. Even if the defendant would not have committed the offense *but for* the involuntary intoxication, the court concluded, he would have no defense unless the involuntary intoxication caused sufficient dysfunction to render him blameless for the offense.

Obligation to Overcome Disability *Mriglot* illustrates a key point in the theory and operation of excuses. There will be cases, like *Mriglot,* in which an actor would not have committed an offense but for a disability that the actor suffers through no fault of his own. One can understand such a person's claim for excuse. If the actor would not have committed the offense "but for" the disability, the disability seems causally responsible for the offense. Undoubtedly this was the appeal of the *Durham* "product" test for insanity, where the defendant was excused if the offense was the product of the mental illness.[3] The argument must be rejected, however, as it was when *Durham* was overruled in *Brawner,* in part because it does not correspond to our notions of assessing blameworthiness. The fact is that each of us suffers temptations and impulses to break the law, but each of us is obliged to resist those temptations and remain law-abiding. It may well be unfair in a sense that an involuntarily intoxicated or mentally ill actor suffers a

---

1. See, e.g., Model Penal Code § 2.08(4)&(5), which requires both involuntary intoxication and resulting dysfunction similar to insanity.

2. 15 Wash. App. 446, 550 P.2d 17, 17-18 (1976) (emphasis in original).

3. See Section 22 Overview.

greater burden of resisting temptations and compulsions toward a violation, a burden that she would not have but for her disability. In each instance, however, the law nonetheless expects the actor to try to remain law-abiding, and exculpates only if the effect of the disability was sufficiently strong that the actor could not reasonably have been expected to have successfully avoided the violation.

Excuses as Embodying Community Norms   The point here is that the blamelessness recognized in an excuse defense does not derive from the existence of an actor's disability or even from the fact that the disability may influence the actor toward the violation. Our conclusion of blamelessness comes from a finding that *the actor could not reasonably have been expected to have done otherwise.* In control dysfunction cases, this requires a finding that the actor made *enough* of an effort to resist the compulsion. In cognitive dysfunction cases, it requires that the actor was *sufficiently* confused in his thinking, and therefore unsure about the nature or legality of his conduct, that he is not to be blamed for the violation. That an actor was unfairly burdened in having to resist or avoid committing an offense will not excuse him if, with reasonable effort, he could have successfully avoided the violation.

Articulating Conditions of Excuse   If there is a general explanation of excuses, it is this: our judgement that the actor could not reasonably have been expected to have done otherwise. This alone, of course, is too vague and general a standard to be of practical value. What is it that is reasonably expected in each of the variety of circumstances that can give rise to a conclusion of blamelessness? The challenge of criminal law theory and doctrine is to formulate rules that gives decision makers some help and guidance in reaching this complex judgment. At a minimum this requires that the law identify for the decision maker the circumstances and conditions that are likely to shape our expectations of an actor. The current formulations of disability excuses typically use the requirements of (1) a recognized disability (2) causing a recognized excusing condition. The challenge to current theorists is to articulate more precisely the requirements of excuse, or to show that no greater articulation is possible.

IMMATURITY

The immaturity excuse, sometimes called the infancy defense, is conceptually similar to the standard disability excuse requirements: a disability causing an excusing condition. But, in application, these requirements typically are conclusively presumed to be satisfied when the actor is below a set chronological age. All actors below a specified cutoff age are conclusively presumed to be immature and all those above are presumed mature. Further, current defense formulations irrebuttably presume that, where such presumed disability of immaturity exists, it is of such a nature and degree as to cause an adequate excusing condition.

Errors in Presumption of Maturity   Such an age cutoff formulation makes it easy to apply the defense, but it results in a failure to excuse an older actor who is as immature as a typical under-age actor and for whom we have reduced normative expectations. In *State v. Jamison,* for example, the defendant was denied an immaturity defense despite his "mental" age of 11.7 years, because his chronological age of seventeen put him over the statutory age cutoff for the immaturity defense.[1] Arthur, in the Problem hypothetical in this Section, has just

---

1. 23 Wash. App. 454, 597 P.2d 424, 428 (1980), aff'd, 96 Wash. 2d 794, 613 P.2d 776 (1979). In some jurisdictions, the insanity defense is formulated broadly enough to provide a defense in such a case. Model Penal Code § 4.01, for example, uses the phrase "mental disease *or defect.*" While a mentally

turned eighteen but does not have the maturity (in some respects) that the average eighteen-year old has, even an eighteen-year old from Winituck. If Arthur were so immature that we could not reasonably have expected him to have avoided the violation, should he nonetheless be irrebuttably presumed to be mature, and thus liable, because he exceeds a given chronological age?

Errors in Presumption of Immaturity A chronological age cutoff also creates the converse problem of understating our normative expectations for the fully mature but underage actor. As long as an actor's chronological age is less than the statutory cutoff age, the actor gets the excuse. This is the case even if the actor's level of maturity is such that the actor reasonably *could* have been expected to have avoided the violation. Application of the defense is reduced to disputes over timing. In *Parker v. State,* for example, the defendant noted that he committed the offense at 9:45 a.m. on his birthday, but that he was not born until 12:50 p.m. of his birthday. Thus, he argued, he had not yet reached the cutoff age.[1]

Rebuttable Presumption Alternative Objective, easy-to-apply criteria are always a virtue. In the realm of excuses, however, where the goal is to capture accurately a complex judgment of blameworthiness, subjective and judgemental criteria frequently are needed. In the case of the immaturity excuse, an approach more consistent with its goal would be a defense that looked to the actor's actual degree of immaturity. If a concession to easier application is needed, it can be achieved through rebuttable presumptions rather than the irrebuttable presumptions contained in most current formulations. That is, an actor below a given age might be presumed immature unless the prosecution proves otherwise. An actor above a given age might be presumed mature unless the defense proves otherwise. There is precedent for such a rebuttable presumption approach both in state codes and at common law.[2] To rebut the presumption, the party should have to prove (or disprove) not only the disability of being abnormally immature, but also that the effect of such immaturity was to cause an excusing condition sufficient to render the actor blameless for the offense charged. (Many jurisdictions have a system of two cutoff ages, where there is discretion as to whether a defendant between the two ages will be treated as underage—for example, Model Penal Code section 4.10—but this determination is not made on an assessment of actual

---

retarded actor may be excused under this formulation, a defense still may not be available to the actor who is immature for other reasons, such as having had a childhood of isolation. Developmental retardation is not likely to be seen as a form of mental disease or defect.

1. 61 Md. App. 35, 37, 484 A.2d 1020, 1021 (1984). The court in *Parker* rejected the defendant's claim, holding that the defense should be applied according to the defendant's birth *day*, not his birth *hour*. Of course, this hardly alters the arbitrariness of the defense or the irrationality of its results. Under the court's rule, Parker would have had the defense if he had committed the offense nine hours and forty-six minutes earlier or if he had been born eleven hours and eleven minutes later.

2. In several states, the fact that the defendant is younger than a specified age creates only a rebuttable presumption of immaturity. See Ariz. Rev. Stat. Ann. § 13-501 (1978) (under 14); Cal. Penal Code § 26(one) (1988) (under 14); Nev. Rev. Stat. §§ 194.010(1)-(2), 193.210 (1977) (between ages 8 and 14); Okla. Stat. Ann. tit. 21, § 152(1)-(2) (1983) (between ages 7 and 14); S.D. Codified Laws Ann. § 22-3-1(1)-(2) (Cum. Supp. 1987) (between ages 10 and 14); Wash. Rev. Code Ann. § 9A.04.050 (1977) (between ages 8 and 12). This also was the approach of the common law rule. Children under seven were given a defense; children over seven but under twelve (or fourteen) were entitled to a presumption of immaturity but the presumption could be rebutted. See 4 William Blackstone, Commentaries on the Laws of England 23 (1769); 1 Sir Matthew Hale, History of the Pleas of the Crown 22 (1778).

immaturity or blameworthiness but on other criteria, such as susceptibility to rehabilitation or the availability of a suitable rehabilitation program.)

Immaturity as Determining Only Proper Court The potentially erroneous irrebuttable presumptions inherent in current immaturity defenses might be justified by noting that a successful "defense" does not release a defendant; the defense only transfers jurisdiction to the juvenile court. Therefore, we need not worry that blameworthy offenders are going free under the defense. But this argument is flawed in two respects. First, it is not always true that blameworthy offenders receiving the defense are simply transferred to juvenile court custody for confinement. The criteria for juvenile detention may not be tied to matters of blameworthiness.[1] Thus, a blameless juvenile may be confined and a blameworthy juvenile may be released.

Problem of Immaturity Defense as Jurisdictional The jurisdictional quality of the "defense" also creates difficulties in court. Its practical effect is that, once allocated to an adult court, no further claim of an immaturity excuse is available to a defendant. Where the statutory cutoff age is 16 or higher, this may be a problem only in the unusual case, but under the current trend of lowering the cutoff age to 12 or less in some jurisdictions,[2] there is an increased danger that a defendant's immaturity will undercut his blameworthiness but that the issue will be ignored. At the very least, where an actor's immaturity is an issue, it ought to be an issue within the jury's consideration, yet the current approach provides no immaturity defense in the adult court. Even if a cutoff age is to be used to select the court of jurisdiction, an immaturity defense ought to be available that allows a jury to excuse an actor whose immaturity satisfies the traditional conditions of excuse.

DURESS

The duress excuse illustrates another variation in the formulation of disability excuses. Like the conclusive presumption of the immaturity defense, the structure of the duress defense is a variation that has its roots in the practical necessity of the situation. The defense has a disability requirement: The actor must have committed the offense while under *coercion* to do so.[3] The defense does not require, however, that the coercion cause in the actor a "substantial lack of capacity to conform his conduct to the requirements of law," or other similar description of the degree of control impairment that the excusing conditions for insanity or involuntary intoxication require. Instead, the duress defense requires that the actor's disability, the coercion, come from a particular cause: a threat of force that "a person of reasonable firmness in the actor's situation would have been unable to resist."

Coercion as Weak Disability No other disability excuse requires that the disability come from a particular cause. Any drug of any amount can give rise to an involuntary intoxication defense, for example, as long as its intoxicating effect on the actor causes the degree of impairment called for by the excusing condition.

---

1. For example, many state statutes focus on an offender's dangerousness. Ala. Code § 12-15-71.1 (1992); Ky. Rev. Stat. Ann. § 645.180 (1992); N.C. Gen. Stat. § 7A-574 (1989); Utah Code Ann. § 78-3a-30 (1992).

2. See, e.g., Oreg. Rev. Stat. § 161.290; Ga. Code Ann. § 16-3-1.

3. See, e.g., Model Penal Code § 2.09(1).

But the objective limit on the *cause* of the coercion in the duress defense should be no surprise. It reflects the weakness of coercion in satisfying the functions of a disability requirement. A state of coercion is not as easy to document as the presence of alcohol or drugs in the blood, for example. Nor is coercion likely to manifest itself in continuing abnormalities or in abnormalities other than the offense conduct, as mental illness would. Coercion is a product of the actor's immediate external conditions and may disappear without trace when the threatening conditions disappear. For all of these reasons, the coercion by itself does a poor job at serving the functions of a disability: It does little to signal the actor as abnormal or different from the rest of the population and also does little to provide an obvious and continuing cause to which to shift the blame for the violation.

Substituting Requirement of Serious Threat   The effectiveness of coercion as a disability can be buttressed, however, by requiring that the coercion come from a clear threat that a person of reasonable firmness would be unable to resist. Such a threat is objectively confirmable and sets the actor apart from others. Further, by requiring a sufficiently extreme threat, the presence of an adequate excusing condition can be presumed. If a person of reasonable firmness would have been unable to resist the coercion of the threat, then generally the actor cannot reasonably have been expected to resist. In duress, the jury is invited to make its normative judgement through this cause-of-the-disability requirement rather than through an independent excusing condition.

Potential Harshness of Objective Standard   A danger of such an objective cause-of-the-coercion requirement is that it may be too harsh. It may fail to excuse an actor that the community does not expect to be able to meet the standard of the person of reasonable firmness. The subnormal actor, for example, may be particularly susceptible to coercion, especially if the coercion plays on the actor's ignorance in order to exaggerate the degree of the threat. Arthur does not appear to be a "person of reasonable firmness." He is a good person in many ways but, given his age, experience, and temperament, he seems to have less ability to resist the coercion applied than the reasonable person would. Is he to be denied a defense even if we are persuaded that it was truly beyond his abilities to resist the coercion?

Person of Reasonable Firmness "in Actor's Situation"   The Model Penal Code duress formulation addresses this potential problem by permitting a court to take into account an actor's individual circumstances and characteristics through a partial individualization of the reasonable person standard. The device used in duress is the same as that used to partially individualize the reasonable person standard in negligence, recklessness, and extreme emotional disturbance. The seriousness of the threat is assessed against the kind of threat that would coerce "a person of reasonable firmness *in [the actor's] situation*."[1] A judge may use this language as authority to take account of an actor's immaturity or subnormality, for example. Would the person of reasonable firmness, suffering from such a condition, have been unable to resist? If the reasonable person standard were individualized in Arthur's case, Arthur would get the defense if an otherwise

---

1. Model Penal Code § 2.09(1) (emphasis added).

reasonable person with Arthur's shyness and inexperience would have been similarly unable to resist the coercion. Like in other instances, however, the Code's Commentary gives little guidance as to the characteristics or circumstances that ought to be permitted as individualizations of the reasonable person standard. Judges are left wide discretion to determine the issue *ad hoc*.

Dangers and Difficulties of Individualization As is the case wherever this partial individualization mechanism is used, its weakness is the lack of principled guidance in determining which characteristics or circumstances of the actor ought to modify the reasonable person standard. (Without limitation, a completely individualized reasonable person standard becomes a completely subjective standard, which would be too lenient and would excuse blameworthy actors.) Arthur's immaturity, inexperience, and temperament all contribute to his timidity. Are they all appropriate characteristics with which the reasonable person standard should be individualized? We may be particularly tempted to take into account individual characteristics that are both highly influential of an actor's conduct and clearly beyond his control. Arthur's immaturity due to his age of eighteen may be a candidate. His inexperience is closely related: If he had greater exposure to the experiences of life, he might have been less vulnerable. It would hurt Arthur's case, however, if other eighteen-year olds from Winituck who have been similarly sheltered would have been able to resist the coercion. Arthur's temperament, on the other hand, seems something more of his own making (although some mental health experts are likely to argue that this too is a product of his genetics and environment and is not within his control). Further complicating the individualizing task is the fact that characteristics like immaturity, inexperience, and temperament are in fact general terms that refer to a host of more specific individual abilities and tendencies. The characteristics may overlap; each may include within its meaning the same relevant characteristic, such as the ability to evaluate accurately the true extent of risk in a threat. Which specific characteristics of an actor ought to be taken into account in judging the actor's blameworthiness? As we have learned in other contexts, criminal law theory does not yet have an answer. Until it does, the issue is left to the intuitive judgement of judges and juries. Given the legality principle interests in articulating the rules of liability, this is tolerable only because no better approach is apparent. Arthur's fate, therefore, lies in the judge's and jury's normative assessment of his degree of blameworthiness.

▲ PROBLEM
The Brothers' Brawl

The Motan brothers, Acker and Ed, have a reputation for being a bit wild. Their wildness has given them near-celebrity status in some quarters, and they are happy to cultivate the image. They stop in at one of their favorite bars, The Wheel, and some "fans" buy them a round of beers. After they guzzle them down, a woman in the group reveals that their drinks were spiked with a "gorilla" drug.

"Watch out, everybody! You're going to get a show tonight!," she shouts to the crowd. Acker is feeling very strange, excited, and very aggressive. He starts dancing on the table. Ed joins in and before long both are kicking drinks and throwing pitchers of beer. Jote, a man in the group who usually is a fan of their antics, takes offense and begins to scream at them. As a brawl begins, the bar's bouncer moves toward the group. At six-feet six-inches and 250 pounds, his size is enough to make the Motan brothers quiet down. Jote, however, turns his anger toward the bouncer and is quickly ejected. After a few more beers, the brothers leave for another favorite bar but find Jote waiting for them outside. He is highly belligerent and vocal. His shouting draws a crowd from inside the bar. The brothers decide to beat him senseless for his remarks but then spot a patrol car across the street. They point it out to Jote, but he is undeterred. When Jote begins telling the assembled "fans" that the brothers are too "wimpy" and "yellow" to fight, the brothers conclude that they have no choice but to hurt him. They take turns punching him while the other holds him, but after a minute or two, the police intervene and arrest all three for their brawling.

Tired of the Motan brothers' relentless brawling, the prosecutor wants prison terms, but his case is complicated by the blood-test reports from the hospital. Acker and Jote (who mistakenly got the drug dose intended for Ed) had a level of Skopezine that would create uncontrollable feelings of aggression in the average person. In addition, the medical authorities explain that a belief that one has been subjected to an aggression-inducing drug, as Ed believed, could cause a loosening of psychological restraints to aggression that otherwise might prevent such conduct. Jote is tried first and is acquitted under the involuntary intoxication doctrine. Should both brothers also be excused?

▲ PROBLEM
Hypnotizing Bunny

Bunny shares a cell with Lane, who is larger and more aggressive. They have developed a close relationship in which Lane is dominant. The relationship is built in part on Lane's frequent sessions of hypnotizing Bunny. The sessions began as simple entertainment, as a means of killing time, but have taken on considerable importance. Lane followed the instructions in a book he had ordered through the mail found that he could indeed put Bunny into a hypnotic trance. He sometimes demonstrates his ability to other inmates by having Bunny cut himself. He also has Bunny climb up on the stairway railing and attempt to jump over, but Lane grabs him each time just before he is about to jump. Because Bunny works in the super-intendent's office, Lane decides he can put his power to good use by having Bunny steal keys and help him escape. Bunny steals the keys, as Lane has directed him to do under hypnosis, but both are caught soon after they leave the prison grounds.

Bunny claims an excuse under the involuntary act defense on grounds that his theft and escape were the product of a hypnotic suggestion by Lane. The

testimony of the expert witnesses is conflicting. All agree that Bunny was hypno-
tized and that Lane apparently did give Bunny the hypnotic suggestions that he
claims. Bunny's expert testifies that Bunny would not have stolen the keys or
escaped from prison but for Lane's hypnotic suggestion. The State's witness
testifies that the hypnotic suggestion may have created some mild motivation
toward performing as requested—Bunny would have felt very anxious for a
time if he had not complied—but that such was only a minor influence on
Bunny's conduct in stealing the keys and escaping. Will Bunny get a defense?
Should he?

▲ PROBLEM
Who Is Timothy Drum?

When he is six years old, Timothy Drum's parents join an "experimental
community" of 25 people who live together in an old warehouse. They lead an
unconventional life, try to avoid society's rules, and impose no rules or restrictions on their children. Timothy and his older brothers begin to follow a pied
piper of the community's children, a man named Donald (Toad) Starr. Toad
fawns over Timothy in particular. As if courting him, he gives Timothy presents
and is extremely attentive. Timothy is eight when his parents break up. He and
his two older brothers move in with Toad, who has moved into an old bus in a
field several miles from the community. Toad becomes sexually active with
Timothy and his two older brothers. Physical force is rarely used; generally the
boys are psychologically pressured and occasionally denied food until they cooperate. Because of Toad's sexual preference for younger boys, he concentrates his
sexual and emotional attention on Timothy. The older boys eventually break
with Toad and go out on their own, but Timothy remains. Toad preaches a
radical form of child rearing in which sexual relations between children and
adults is a good thing.

By age sixteen Timothy has long since lost the need for Toad's coaching to
participate in sexual activities. He helps Toad kidnap a thirteen-year old boy
named Vincento Lon. Vincento is sexually abused by Toad and, at Toad's request,
by Timothy, during which Toad watches and takes video movies. Over the next
two years, Vincento comes to participate in these sexual activities without coaching, as Timothy had come to do several years before. Two years after Vincento is
kidnapped, Toad conceives a plan to kidnap a young girl, whom he will impreg-
nate (he believes this is possible as young as eight or nine) and will have her
become "the perfect mother" as she raises a child under his radical theory of
parenting. Timothy and Vincento help Toad kidnap a three-year old girl named
Betsey Wynn. For eight months, the four live out of a converted bread truck.
Toad, Timothy, and Vincento take turns abusing Betsey.

On February 23, 1988, in Sacramento, California, a suspicious shopper
opens the back door of a truck parked in the shopping mall's parking lot. She

finds Vincento lying with Betsey, both naked from the waist down. The police are notified. They arrest Toad and Timothy when they return to the truck. Toad is charged with 121 counts of kidnapping, false imprisonment, lewd conduct, sodomy, rape, oral copulation, and assault. Timothy is charged with 93 similar counts, and Vincento with 23. Psychiatrists hired by defense counsel find no mental illness in any of the three defendants.*

▲ PROBLEM: PEOPLE v. KIMURA
"A 'Cultural Defense' at Issue in Trial"
(Philadelphia Inquirer, September 1, 1985)

Los Angeles—When 32-year-old Fumiko Kimura decided to kill herself—decided to walk into the icy cold Pacific Ocean to escape her humiliation and shame—she was essentially alone. She had no close friends, no job and a second husband who had just admitted he'd been cheating on her for three years. When she walked into the ocean one blustery January day, she did it quietly, clutching her two beloved children to her breast, trying to escape without bothering anyone. It was the way she would have done it in Japan.

Seven months later, as she sits in a Los Angeles women's jail awaiting trial on charges of first-degree murder, Kimura, ironically, is alone no longer.

Suddenly—too late—she has "friends." She has a husband who visits her every day. She receives hundreds of letters from strangers in Japan and around the United States. She has become a symbol to the Los Angeles Japanese-American and immigrant community, a challenge for attorneys and a cause celebre in the Japanese press.

But she does not have what she wants most—her children.

After 15 minutes of gulping down salt water and holding her children's heads under water, Kimura was pulled out by two college students. She survived. Her children, 4-year-old son Kazutaka and 6-month-old daughter Yuri, did not.

If she goes to trial Oct. 21, as scheduled, Kimura will face the death penalty. But attorneys for both sides are trying to reach an agreement that would prevent the case from reaching trial.

Kimura's case raises the issue of whether one's cultural background can be used as a defense for having committed acts that may be typical in the homeland but illegal in the United States. In Los Angeles, where the influx of several hundred thousand Asians during the last 10 years has brought their numbers to 15 percent of the city's population, the problem is especially acute.

No one doubts that Kimura, despondent over her marriage, was doing what she thought best. Oyako-shinju, or parent-child suicide, occurs about once a day

---

* Editor's Note—The facts of this hypothetical are loosely based on the case of Luis Reynaldo (Tree Frog) Johnson and Alex Cabarga. See San Francisco Chronicle, Aug. 5, 1984, at 9.

in Japan and is considered honorable, although not legal. A parent who survives usually is put on probation or given a light sentence.

A parent who left the children behind would be fiercely criticized. Not only would leaving the children put a burden on someone else or force the children to fend for themselves, but it would strap them with a legacy of shame and possibly discrimination for having had a parent who committed suicide.

But if the American judicial system were to make allowances for all the foreign practices brought here by immigrants, were to allow ignorance to be an excuse, the "cultural defense" would become a buzzword for chaos and crime, say some opponents of the concept.

But in Kimura's case, the cultural influence cannot be ignored. The problem is how much weight to give it.

"It's not the same situation as when a woman kills her kids because she's tired of having them around," said Deputy District Attorney Lauren Weis. "The jury must decide: Is she a criminal who is a danger to society, to herself, to other kids in the future?"

"The cultural aspect comes into it, but there are so many different cultures here, you can't really start letting people off for that sort of thing," she said. "Kimura was living in America. She can't forget that."

Weis, who noted that she had not heard of another oyako-shinju case in the United States, said she was not eager to try Kimura and would be willing to enter into plea-bargaining. She is waiting for proof that Kimura was mentally unstable at the time of the suicide attempt.

If there was nothing mentally wrong with Kimura, Weis said, the state cannot afford to go easy on her.

"We'd be saying to everyone of Japanese culture that it's OK to go out and kill your children, when it's not," she said. "I want a good psychiatric report that we can hang our hat on."

Kimura stands charged of first-degree murder with the special circumstances of multiple deaths. If special circumstances are proved, the state could seek the death penalty.

If defense attorneys can prove that Kimura was mentally disturbed, however, the charge could be reduced to manslaughter—which implies that there was no intent to commit murder—the special circumstances would be thrown out, and the death penalty would be out of range.

The jury could seek a sentence as light as several years' probation and psychiatric treatment.

Los Angeles attorney Ben Takahashi, who has written about the case for a Japanese newspaper, said a similar story would not be big news—"maybe five or six lines"—in Japan. "Any punishment would be light," he said, "because everyone would understand why the parent had committed oyako-shinju."

● OVERVIEW OF PROBLEMATIC EXCUSES

Pedagogical Value of Problematic Excuses   This Overview section considers several excuses that have been offered and rejected by the criminal law: chromosomal abnormality, brainwashing, cultural indoctrination, and "rotten social background." Studying these excuses sharpens our understanding of present theory and doctrine and, on occasion, illustrates its weaknesses. To explain why an excuse should not be given, especially in a situation where we feel some sympathy for the actor, sometimes requires us to examine more carefully, and to articulate with greater clarity, the reasons why we do give an excuse and the conditions that we insist on. Not infrequently, the study of problematic excuses reveals fundamental assumptions that we make about human nature and exculpation that are not otherwise apparent.

Chromosomal and Physiological Abnormalities   Chromosomal abnormality is sometimes offered as an excuse because some studies suggest a causal connection between one's genetic composition and a predisposition toward violence. Other studies suggest that physiological abnormalities, such as abnormalities in brain chemistry, predispose a person toward violence. Some writers conclude that if an abnormality, such as the XYY chromosomal pattern occurring in some males, involuntarily causes an actor to be more aggressive, the actor ought to be excused when such aggression appears as criminal conduct. But recent evidence suggests some doubt as to the strength of effect of such chromosomal or physiological abnormalities.

Perfect Disability Element   The appeal of recognizing chromosomal or physiological abnormality as the basis for excuse is understandable. The disability, the XYY pattern or the physiological misfunctioning, is easily shown to be abnormal. It is objectively manifested and is confirmable through scientific tests. Unlike most forms of mental illness, here clinicians can point to laboratory tests, not just therapists' judgements, to support the claimed abnormality. Further, especially in the case of chromosomal abnormality, it is beyond question that the abnormality is not the fault of the actor; unlike intoxication, where it is always a possibility that the actor voluntarily caused it. As disabilities, such abnormalities combine the best of traditional disability excuses: the involuntariness of mental illness and the scientific confirmability of intoxication.

Unproven Dysfunction   While such abnormalities have many qualities that make them attractive as disabilities, the effect of such abnormalities in causing excusing conditions is unclear. Most XYY males do not violate the law. Even if one assumes that the abnormality creates some predisposition toward violent conduct, a predisposition, even an involuntarily acquired one, does not excuse. As illustrated by the *Mriglot* case in the context of involuntary intoxication, and by the rejection of the *Durham* "product" test in insanity, it is not enough that the actor would not have committed the offense but for the involuntary intoxication or mental illness. The dysfunctional effect must be of such a degree that the actor could not reasonably have been expected to have avoided the violation. Even the strongest claims of researchers do not suggest that either the XYY chromosomal abnormality or most physiological abnormalities cause such a level of dysfunction. For this reason, these dysfunctions are rarely grounds for a successful defense.

see Patty Hearst

Brainwashing   "Brainwashing," sometimes called "coercive persuasion," "coercive indoctrination," or "thought reform," may be the most interesting of problematic excuses. It challenges many basic assumptions of excuse theory and, if recognized as a defense, arguably could lead to recognition of such interesting doctrines as a cultural defense or a defense for a "rotten social background." In some ways, brainwashing presents the reverse case from chromosomal and physiological abnormalities: Brainwashing may cause excusing conditions, at least in one sense, but no apparent disability exists in another sense.

Excuses During Brainwashing Process   Isolation, close control, physiological debilitation, threats, and psychological manipulation are all part of the classic brainwashing process. Under the right conditions, these qualify an actor for a duress defense. They also might produce effects that could qualify an actor for a temporary insanity defense. If an actor commits an offense as a direct result of the pressures common in the brainwashing process or as a result of mental illness caused by the process, he may be able to rely on one of those traditional disability excuses.

Excuses After Brainwashing   The difficulty in coping with brainwashing as a defense arises where a brainwashed actor commits an offense *after* the coercive brainwashing process is complete. A successful process may leave the person normal in every traditional sense, neither mentally ill nor subject to continuing duress or coercion. Yet the actor may hold a different set of beliefs and values than she did before the process. When such a person who holds these different (perhaps radical) beliefs and values commits an offense in furtherance of those beliefs and values, the person does not satisfy the disability or excusing condition of any traditional excuse. No coercion or mental illness exists—having radical beliefs or values is not a mental illness. (If it were, most radical terrorists would have an insanity defense simply because their conduct is a product of their radical beliefs.)

Accountability for One's Beliefs and Values   While the brainwashed actor presently suffers neither coercion nor mental illness, the actor's choices nonetheless have been highly influenced by others, and against his will, through the coercive indoctrination that the actor experienced. For that reason, it seems awkward to hold such an actor accountable for conduct in the same way as someone who has (more) freely chosen or developed his own beliefs and values. But the law presumes that each person is accountable for one's own personality, including one's beliefs and values. There simply is no mechanism under current doctrine for rebutting this presumption. This tension is the subject of the Section's Discussion Materials below.

Domination and Indoctrination   The reason for the law's adherence to this potentially inaccurate and unfair presumption may lie in part with the increasing difficulties that the law would encounter if it admitted that a person might not be accountable for her values and beliefs. Consider, for example, the most appealing case for such an excuse in the brainwashed POW who is indoctrinated to believe that his former country is condemnable. The evidence suggests that the ability of an experienced indoctrinator with complete control over every aspect of a prisoner's existence is quite powerful with many kinds of individuals, and that demonstrated level of success reinforces the propriety of an excuse because there will be some persons who could not reasonably have been expected to resist the indoctrination and any criminal conduct it logically compels. But if we were to give a defense in such a case, may we meaningfully distinguish Timothy Drum and Vincento Lon from the POW? If so, how? Both Timothy and Vincento were dominated and indoctrinated by Toad. Both can claim that it was involuntary: Timothy because he was eight years old and psychologically pressured; Vincento because he was thirteen years old and kidnapped. Because Timothy and Vincento were not coerced to engage in the conduct constituting the offense in a way that would satisfy a duress defense, neither is eligible for an excuse under traditional excuse doctrine. Yet it could be argued that they are not responsible for the perverted beliefs and values that Toad's indoctrination has instilled in them or for the offenses that resulted from these beliefs and values.

Timothy's Indoctrination vs. POW Brainwashing   While Timothy Drum's indoctrination by Toad may not have been as hostile as that of the classic brainwashing of a POW by a captor, Timothy, at age eight, did not make a meaningful choice to undergo such domination and indoctrination. Indeed, one could argue that both the length of the indoctrination process and Timothy's particular susceptibility (by virtue of his immaturity) made his indoctrination more powerful and more complete than that of a POW. Thus, one might argue, he is less accountable for the resulting effects. Yet Timothy's case seems less attractive for an excuse than the POW case in this respect: At no single point was Timothy as severely mistreated or coerced as the POW, who may have been regularly tortured, for example. Nor does Timothy attempt to resist the indoctrination as the typical POW does, although this may simply be a manifestation of his greater vulnerability. How shall we resolve these conflicting points? The POW case seems a more extreme and abnormal process than does Timothy's indoctrination, but Timothy's situation suggests greater vulnerability. Should the excuse depend more on the abnormality of the past treatment or the subjective effect of the indoctrination process?

Timothy's Indoctrination vs. Vincento's   Consider the difference between the situations of Timothy and of Vincento. Timothy's indoctrination seems more "voluntary," in that he chose to follow Toad. Vincento, in contrast, was kidnapped. On the other hand, at age eight, Timothy was more vulnerable to the indoctrination than Vincento, who was thirteen when kidnapped. It also appears that Vincento may have "come along" somewhat more quickly than Timothy did. Again, however, which of these apparently conflicting factors is more significant: greater objective coerciveness or greater subjective vulnerability? Without a clear theory for excusing conduct after brainwashing or indoctrination, the criteria for such an excuse is unclear.

Cultural Indoctrination   If one is tempted to give Timothy or Vincento a defense, one might be tempted as well to give a defense to actors who commit crimes because of cultural indoctrination. Recall *People v. Kimura,* for example, described in the Problem Case above. The defendant's act of drowning her two small dependent children at the time she attempts to kill herself is condemned in the United States, but such Oyako-shinju, or parent-child suicide, occurs about once a day in Japan and is considered honorable, albeit illegal.[1] Should Kimura get

---

1. That Oyako-shinju is not legal in Japan undercuts the force of many of Kimura's arguments.

a defense or mitigation because she was following one of the traditions of her culture?

Timothy & POW vs. Kimura   In many respects, the *Kimura* case exaggerates factors at play in Timothy's case. While Kimura's indoctrination is less abnormal than Timothy's — a large population share her cultural values and traditions — her indoctrinating environment is even more pervasive than Timothy's. The length of this cultural indoctrination is for most people a lifetime. There is no "getting away from it," as Timothy could have done (or as a POW might escape or hope to escape). Timothy is confronted with an outside world that is different from, and in conflict with, that which Toad presents, yet Timothy chooses to stay with Toad. Most of us have little or no ability to choose our cultural environment. Indeed, much of the power of Kimura's indoctrination derives from the fact that initially (when Kimura lived in Japan) the values represented the *norm,* not an abnormality.

Cultural Norms as Most Coercive Indoctrinators   The normative aspect of Kimura's indoctrination highlights a natural point of conflict in these cases. Excuses are made available only in the abnormal and unusual case; this is a central role of the disability requirement. Yet in the context of accountability for one's beliefs and values, the more pervasive the norm and the larger the group, the more "coercive" the indoctrination and arguably the stronger the excusing condition. The pressures on Kimura are all the more powerful because they are long-term and because they are subtle, they do not call for resistance. For Kimura, the overwhelming influence and legitimacy of the culture powers the indoctrination. Is abnormality or normality in the indoctrinating circumstances the more compelling ground for viewing the indoctrination as grounds for excuse?

Kimura as Relative Abnormality   One could dismiss the difficulties with *Kimura* by concluding that Kimura is indeed abnormal and unusual, as traditionally required for an excuse, in the sense that she has beliefs and values that are abnormal in the United States. Thus, as in the case of the POW, the abnormal yet forceful conditions of her indoctrination may be recognized to support an excuse, or at least as much of an excuse as is recognized for the POW. This opportunity to avoid the problem is not available, however, in the somewhat analogous case of the claimed "rotten social background" defense.

"Rotten Social Background" Defense   In *United States v. Alexander,*[1] excerpted in the Discussion Materials below, the defendants shot and killed several marine officer candidates visiting Washington, D.C., who where wearing their dress-white uniforms. After one of the marines used a racial epithet, the defendants pulled guns and began shooting, although the marines were neither armed nor physically threatening to the defendants. Defense counsel argued that defendant Murdock "did not have control of his conduct," and that the reason for that lack of control was a deep-seated emotional disorder rooted in his "rotten social background." Murdock was not claimed to be mentally ill. His "rotten social background," rather than mental illness, is said to have caused his conduct by creating a tendency to overreact to perceived threats and by creating in him feelings of racial oppression that, in turn, led to racial hatred.

---

1. 471 F.2d 923 (D.C. Cir. 1973).

"Rotten Social Background" as Coercive Indoctrination   As with *Kimura*, the indoctrination mechanism in *Alexander* seems quite powerful. Most of Murdock's daily existence was subject to his ghetto environment. He was not responsible for being born into such a situation. He had no obvious or easy means of escaping from it. On the other hand, not all people who live in a ghetto become criminals (but, then, neither do all POWs become traitors, nor do all Japanese people who commit suicide kill their soon-to-be-orphaned children). That is, even admitting that Murdock's environment significantly influenced the development of his personality, the strength of its causal contribution to the offense at hand is unclear.

Problem of "Normal" Coercive Indoctrination   Murdock's situation is not as abnormal as that of the brainwashed POW or the dominated and indoctrinated Timothy. His "rotten social background" is one he shares with a significant portion of the population. It is more akin to Kimura's situation (yet cannot be said to be abnormal in the United States, as one might say of Kimura). Indeed, one may claim that having a rotten social background is not necessarily limited to being poor and deprived of material goods. A middle- or upper-class upbringing in a family devoid of emotional support and meaningful interpersonal relationships may be as traumatic as ghetto life in some respects. Such an upbringing may be its own form of a rotten social background. In the end, the difficulty with the "rotten social background" defense is that it proves too much. To give an excuse for a rotten social background is to give an excuse to many, if not most, offenders, and that result does not reflect the community's normative expectations.

Lesson of Durham *and* Alexander   This is not to deny that many people may well commit crimes because of their rotten social background. A rotten social background may well be the but-for cause of many crimes; there might be many fewer violations if all people had pleasant and supportive social backgrounds. But such a but-for causal connection is not adequate for an excuse. Yet the adequacy of a but-for causal connection appears to be an underlying assumption of the dissent in *Alexander*, which argued in support of a rotten-social-background defense that such a cause was sufficient for an excuse. It should be no surprise, then, to find that the author of the court's opinion in *Durham* and of the dissenting view in *Alexander* are one and the same: Judge Bazelon. It is the same misunderstanding of the requirements of excuse that produces both opinions. One could conceive of a criminal law that did not claim to be guided by notions of moral blameworthiness or to express moral condemnation (although it is unclear why one would have a "criminal" system distinct from a civil system if this were the case). But, as long as criminal law purports to be a system that takes into account and expresses moral condemnation, it may excuse only according to rules that mirror the principles of blamelessness. The larger the number of people who share the actor's "disability" but are able to remain law-abiding, the more difficult it will be for the actor to argue persuasively that he could not reasonably have been expected to do the same.

Indoctrination and Excuse Theory   To merit excuse, an actor must show that her disability so significantly reduced the capacity to avoid the violation that the actor cannot reasonably have been expected to have acted otherwise. Murdock and Kimura will have a difficult time making this showing, given the large number of similarly situated people who have successfully avoided violations like theirs. The brainwashed POW and the indoctrinated Timothy and Vincento may have a better chance to make this claim, but they too must be prepared to explain why, when the coercive pressure of the indoctrination process subsided, they did not "get themselves back on track." A citizen's obligation to avoid violations of the law might be viewed as including not only an obligation to resist temptations and pressures toward violation, but also an obligation to shape, or reshape, one's character or values as needed to avoid violation of society's prohibitions. Were standard excuse theory used, and a "coercive indoctrination" defense recognized, the POW and Timothy and Vincento would qualify only if they could persuade a jury that they could not reasonably have been expected to have gotten themselves back on track.

● DISCUSSION MATERIALS

Should the Criminal Law Recognize an Excuse Defense for a Person Who Commits an Offense Because Coercively Indoctrinated with Values and Beliefs That Make the Person Want to Do So?

The brief Robinson excerpt gives some background on the various indoctrination techniques employed by the Communist Chinese during the Korean War and their sometimes powerful effects. The next three articles provide a dialogue of sorts between Richard Delgado and Joshua Dressler, arguing, respectively, for and against a defense for the coercively persuaded defendant, comparing and contrasting it with the excuse defenses of insanity and duress. In *United States v. Alexander*, highlighted in the Overview section, Chief Justice Bazelon's excerpted dissent takes the coercive indoctrination defense one step further, perhaps down the slippery slope, arguing for one's "rotten social background" as a defense; the majority opinion rejects the proposed defense and affirms the conviction.

Paul H. Robinson, Are We Responsible for Who We Are? The Case of Richard R. Tenneson
Criminal Law Case Studies 124, 125-126 (2d ed. 2002)

In the aftermath of the revolution in China, the Communists developed considerable expertise in what is now called "coercive indoctrination." Their methods have been studied by Westerners and their effectiveness proven. In fact, after the experience in Korea, the United States military changed its policy to no longer expect POW's to give only name, rank, and serial number, as the Geneva convention provides. The human psyche is too vulnerable, they concluded, to resist indoctrination by an experienced captor. The military services began giving special training to those in danger of capture to help them resist indoctrination. But early forms of the training, which give trainees a brief taste of the Communist Chinese methods, are discontinued when it becomes apparent they are counterproductive, causing trainees to fear the power and inevitability of the indoctrination process.

The Communist Chinese coercive indoctrination techniques do not rely on physical beatings or torture. Such methods were used crudely by the Viet Cong against some POW's in Vietnam, but are judged counterproductive to effective coercive indoctrination because they trigger undesirable resistance by the subject. Nor does effective coercive indoctrination use drugs or hypnosis, as a popular 1962 American movie, *The Manchurian Candidate*, suggests. Torture or drugs may be used to obtain a confession or some other single propaganda performance, but to produce a fully indoctrinated true believer requires a more subtle process of several stages.

The indoctrinator first must establish isolation and control of the subject — isolation from other persons and information, and control over the prisoner's body and environment. These conditions then allow implementation of the two-stage program: destruction of the previously existing self, and construction of a new self with new beliefs and values.

The destruction stage follows several avenues: (a) systematic physiological debilitation, commonly by means of inadequate diet, insufficient sleep, and poor sanitation; (b) creation of constant background anxiety, including implied threats of injury or death by a seemingly all-powerful captor (often with occasional periods of leniency, to create expectations that can be dashed, thereby reinforcing the subject's helplessness and the captor's power); (c) degradation of the subject's pre-existing self, including at later stages the use of peer pressure among indoctrinees, often applied through ritual "struggle" sessions; and (d) required performance of symbolic acts of self-betrayal, betrayal of group norms, and public confession. . . .

The construction stage is more prosaic. Once the subject is psychologically broken, he is built up again in the form that the captor desires through the alleviation of physical stress and deprivation and offerings of emotional support tied to the subject's appreciation of the rightness of the indoctrinator's views. The result is a true believer. While physical or psychological duress may be used during the indoctrination process, once the process is complete, the subject has internalized the captor's values and beliefs. His statements and conduct thereafter are guided by the coercively-induced beliefs and values, but are not themselves coerced. Focusing only on the present, one would say that the "brainwashed" subject's beliefs and values are as much his own as our beliefs and values are our own.

In milder form, the techniques of coercive indoctrination are used in cults, which even in their less coercive form have the power to take over lives and even produce mass suicides, for example, Jonestown and Heaven's Gate. One may have thought it peculiar for a leader to move an entire cult from San Francisco to Guyana, but shifting members to a faraway jungle is an ingenious means for inexpensive complete isolation and dependency.

The psychological dynamics behind the indoctrination power of the captor is sufficiently great that a captor can have an effect almost without effort or intention. The "Stockholm Syndrome" is named for a 1973 episode in which four hostages of bank robbers bonded with their captives during six days in captivity, coming to conclude that the captors actually were protecting them from the police. A 1982 study reports that Stockholm Syndrome develops in half of all victims of hostage cases, even though captors rarely plan such an effect.

Richard Delgado, Ascription of Criminal States of Mind: Toward a Defense Theory for the Coercively Persuaded ("Brainwashed") Defendant
63 Minnesota Law Review 1, 1-11 (1978)

[C]ommentators who have considered the problem of the coercively persuaded defendant have concluded, largely on an analysis of the Patricia Hearst case, that no legal defense is available to such an individual. If they are correct, their conclusion is a troubling one, for it means denying a defense to a class of defendants who are, by ordinary moral intuitions, often more victims than perpetrators.

Consider a hypothetical individual captured by an outlaw gang and subjected to lengthy thought reform techniques, beginning with threats and terror, and continuing with isolation, starvation, sleep deprivation, and guilt manipulation carried out by seemingly all-powerful captors. At various intervals in the process, that individual's captors demand that he perform criminal acts for their benefit. Under traditional criminal defense theories, exculpation would be available for those crimes the victim commits during the initial stages of captivity, when classic duress and coercion exist, but not during the latter stages, when such overt coercion no longer is necessary for the captors to maintain control. Such a result is surely wrong. The breakdown of the victim's identity and will in the latter stages of the coercive persuasion process destroys the very mechanisms by which he might have offered resistance. Thus, acquiescence is rendered more certain than in the early stages when simple duress is applied. A person under direct threats of death will rarely cling to even deeply held beliefs. Rarer still is the individual who can resist protracted, unremitting, coercive thought reform techniques.

Consideration of theories traditionally believed to justify punishment also suggests that coercive persuasion should be taken into account in assessing a defendant's criminal guilt. . . .

Past experience demonstrates that most such victims, once removed from the coercive environment, soon lose their inculcated responses and return to their former modes of thinking and acting. This return often is accompanied by expressions of anger, in which the former captive accuses his captors of the "rape" of his mind and personality. Punishment of such individuals does little to promote the rationales of the criminal justice system.

If punishment of the coercively persuaded defendant conflicts with both basic intuitions and the justifications advanced for invocation of criminal punishment, yet cannot be avoided under any existing defense theory, it becomes necessary to fashion a new theory of defense. Occam's razor[1] dictates that any

---

1. Attributed to William of Occam, the principle — that entities should not be multiplied beyond necessity — urges that the simplest possible rule or theory be adopted that is consistent with the facts or phenomena to be explained. See, e.g., Russell, A History of Western Philosophy 472 (Essandess paperback ed. 1945).

such new defense should constitute, insofar as is possible, a logical extension of existing concepts of act, intent, and blame. The actus reus of defendants who have undergone coercive persuasion is undisputed, they apparently are neither insane, coerced, nor acting under diminished capacity, and yet they seem less than fully responsible for their acts. This is so because the coercively persuaded defendant's choice to act criminally was not freely made and, indeed, appears to be not his choice at all. Traditional mens rea analysis has inquired only whether a defendant who committed an allegedly criminal act possessed the requisite state of criminal mind at the time of the act. In the case of the coercively persuaded defendant, it is appropriate to ask also whether the intent the actor possessed can properly be said to be his own.

The victim of thought reform typically commits criminal acts fully aware of their wrongfulness. He acts consciously, even enthusiastically, and without overt coercion. Yet, in an important sense, the guilty mind with which he acts is not his own. Rather, his mental state is more appropriately ascribed to the captors who instilled it in him for their own purposes. . . .

[While a coercive indoctrination defense] is difficult to reduce to a precise set of necessary and sufficient conditions, there are factors which, in combination, warrant its application. These include:

a. *The defendant's mental state results from unusual or abnormal influences,* including drugs, hypnosis, prolonged confinement, physiological depletion, and deliberate manipulation of guilt, terror, and anxiety. These are not the mechanisms of ordinary attitudinal change, and a finding that they were instrumental in bringing about the criminal act suggests that the mens rea with which the victim acted was not his own.

b. *The induced mental state represents a sharp departure from the individual's ordinary mode of thinking.* The more gradual the change, the more likely it is to be found to be the product of education, maturation, or other ordinary processes which do not call for exculpation. In some instances, the changes induced may be so great as to suggest that the individual has undergone a change of identity. A defense based on ownership and ascription of mens rea does not require that a defendant be so transformed, however. Rather, exculpation from criminal liability is appropriate whenever a defendant's state of mind with reference to a particular criminal act is found to be implanted, inauthentic, and not of his own choosing.

c. *The state is one that is imposed on the subject,* rather than self-induced or consciously selected. Most victims of coercive persuasion, like Cardinal Mindszenty or the American prisoners of war, will be found to have resisted the process, at least initially. In other cases, for example those involving religious cults, the voluntary quality of the joining process may be placed in question by the employment of deception in luring potential converts to initial meetings, after which thought reform techniques are brought to bear. Resistance or deception suggest that the resulting condition of psychological servitude was not freely chosen by the victim. The Manson women, by contrast, appeared to have elected to voluntarily become members of the group, and to undergo a lengthy process of initiation and indoctrination without protest. In such a case, a legal defense based on transferred mens rea should not be available. By analogy to voluntary intoxication, the victim can be blamed for his own condition. If his mental processes have been altered in such a way as to make it more likely that he will commit crimes, his initial choice to undergo such changes was made with a free will. This choice is itself blameworthy, rendering the actor an appropriate object of punishment.

   d. *The criminal acts benefit the captors.* Since ordinary human motivation is self-seeking, a showing that an individual engaged in behavior that could only benefit another suggests the presence of abnormal influence. This is particularly true when the actions induced are dangerous and are ones the individual showed no interest in performing before falling under the control of the captors.

   e. *The actor, when apprised of the manner in which he came to hold his beliefs, rejects them and sees them as inauthentic or foreign.* If, after having been acquainted with the details of his own treatment by the captors, including their motivation in subjecting him to it, he rejects his affiliation with them (and does so genuinely, and not simply to escape punishment), it seems reasonable to conclude that the mental state was not his own, but wrongfully implanted or superimposed.

   f. *The actor evidences symptoms typical of the coercively persuaded personality,* including flattened affect, reduced cognitive flexibility, drastic alteration of values, and extreme dissociation.

Where all or many of these factors are present, a defense should lie; where few are present, it may properly be denied. Even with these criteria, some cases will be difficult. Nevertheless, as in cases involving duress, insanity, or diminished capacity, final judgment should be entrusted to the collective moral sense of the jury. In coercive persuasion, a number of symptoms and causes must be weighed. Just as no clear lines separate those who are sane from those who are not, so here the jury must decide where on a continuum of responsibility a particular defendant lies. But this is scarcely a new problem. Innumerable situations require that the jury members evaluate the evidence before them and apply a general standard to the case at hand.

Joshua Dressler, Professor Delgado's "Brainwashing" Defense: Courting a Determinist Legal System

63 Minnesota Law Review 335, 335-336, 339-340, 351-360 (1979)

Introduction

   In 1951, journalist Edward Hunter wrote a book describing "brainwashing," a process of abrupt attitudinal change that was used in the People's Republic of China. At that time, the United States was involved in a "hot" war with the Communist government of North Korea and "cold" war with the ideology of Marxism. This situation caused both the unfamiliar term and the concept underlying it — that people can have their life-long values involuntarily and suddenly change — to become the subjects of widespread general interest and copious scientific literature. Except for some interest engendered by military court martial proceedings against American prisoners of war, however, brainwashing was largely ignored in legal circles until recently, when kidnaping victim Patricia Hearst was prosecuted for joining her captors in a bank robbery.

   The absence of debate within the legal community is unfortunate, because the subject of coercive persuasion raises more than esoteric questions. Its consideration leads to fundamental philosophical quandaries concerning the continued viability of the concept of free will, one of the basic premises of our substantive criminal justice system.

Nor can it any longer be said that the issue of coercive persuasion, and the related debate regarding free will, are of mere academic interest. The likelihood that a defense based on coercive persuasion will be raised in the future is great. Prosecution following "terrorist" kidnaping is but one situation raising the issue. Another is in connection with certain religious cults that allegedly not only coercively indoctrinate new members to their religious views but also indoctrinate them to commit fraudulent acts. In response to the conversion techniques adopted by the cults, parents and professional deprogrammers have imprisoned cultists in order to reverse this influence. The propriety of both the original coercive persuasion and subsequent deprogramming has already been litigated in criminal cases, actions in intentional tort, civil rights actions, and competency and conservatorship hearings. Arguments based loosely on coercive persuasion have also been made in trials that did not involve cultists. . . .

Criticism of Delgado's Thesis

Professor Delgado presents a case that, on first view, is appealing. He provides a defense for people with whom he, and many others, obviously sympathize. At the same time, he assures us that such a result can be reached without radical changes in criminal law doctrine. Thus, reformers can appear humane while causing ripples, not waves, in the criminal law system.

Unfortunately, a careful review of substantive criminal law and current jurisprudential doctrine demonstrates that Delgado's claim is not on solid ground. A fundamental premise of the criminal law, and that which distinguishes the criminal sanction from the civil, is that societal condemnation of the violator of societal norms, or at least of his actions, is a necessary, although not sufficient, condition to punishing the offender. The criminal sanction is applied only when the actor is deserving of punishment. Delgado's defense, however, fails to properly identify those people whom society currently believes are blameworthy (deserving of condemnation) and those who are not. Second, because he fails to frame a defense that has sufficiently clear and just limits to make it susceptible of administration, his defense necessitates embracing a determinist view of society. . . .

Excuses

[Two] societal standards of blameworthiness against which Delgado's coercive persuasion defense may be measured are the currently recognized excuses of insanity and duress. As with the mens rea and actus reus requirements, these excuses condition criminal responsibility on the presence or absence of meaningful choice. Insanity involves an internal circumstance — disease of the mind — that substantially or totally impairs the actor's cognitive capability. He must either be unaware of what he has done, or unaware of the wrongfulness of his conduct; alternatively, the disease must substantially impair his volitional capabilities, so that he cannot effectively control his conduct. Under these circumstances, talk of choice is meaningless. A person has no choice when disease causes him to lose all touch with reality or to be unable to conform to reality. Thus, blameworthiness is absent when insanity is proven.

Duress involves an external circumstance — an imminent threat of death or great bodily harm to the individual or a family member — that severely limits the actor's choice. Choice is greater in a case of duress than in a case of insanity, because the actor comprehends the alternatives and has the ability to not respond illegally. Nonetheless, practical choice is eliminated by the deadly threat. Again, the actor is blameless.

The case for exculpating the coercively persuaded defendant in the manner suggested by Delgado is far less compelling. First, he goes so far as to permit the defense not only in cases in which the person is indoctrinated to commit crimes but also in cases in which the defendant is the victim solely of attitudinal indoctrination and is free to choose the means by which to further his new ideology. As a result, Delgado would exculpate obviously morally blameworthy persons. . . .

The only way, then, in which Delgado's defense could be framed so as to avoid exculpating morally blameworthy actors is if it applies only to cases involving crime indoctrination. . . . Even so narrowed, the case for those coercively persuaded to commit crimes is less compelling than for those entitled to current excuses. Compared to the insane individual, the coercively persuaded actor's choices are far more substantial, and hence his blameworthiness commensurately greater. Since, as Delgado concedes, the coercively persuaded actor is aware of the wrongfulness of his action, choice is cognitively present. Delgado does not suggest that the actor is volitionally incapable of conforming his conduct to the law.

The case for the coercively persuaded defendant is also weaker than that of one acting under duress. A loaded and cocked gun pressed to one's head presents more substantial loss of choice, and a clearer example of blamelessness, than do the conditions undergone by religious cultists or Patricia Hearst. In the latter type of case, the person may experience a harsh environment, and thus have limited choice, but the residual options cannot be equated to the alternatives available to an actor under threat of immediate death.

Adequate Limitations

Even if Delgado could show that some coercively persuaded actors should be considered blameless, his defense would still be open to challenge on the ground that it does not impose clear and just limitations on the excuse's applicability. This failure forces society to choose between two alternatives, both of which are antithetical to current concepts of criminal responsibility. It must either allow some morally blameworthy actors to be excused, while not excusing some morally blameless actors, or accept a theory of criminal responsibility that embraces a determinist view of society.

Existing excuses are framed in a narrow and a relatively clear fashion so as to enable the trier of fact to make an uncomplicated moral judgment. . . .

Delgado argues, however, that suitable line drawing is possible with his defense. He notes that there are certain external manifestations of coercive persuasion that will aid in identifying when it is appropriate to apply the defense. First, coercively persuaded individuals exhibit dissociation, memory loss, confusion, and the like; second, there will be external evidence of imprisonment, isolation, sensory deprivation, interrogation, physiological depletion, and terror. The defense can be limited, Delgado claims, to cases involving such evidence.

Not even these external manifestations provide assurance that only blameless actors will be excused, however. One can easily envision a not-so-unlikely hypothetical situation that exemplifies the problem: A prison inmate is put in solitary confinement in a small dank, dark cell and fed little or nothing for an extended period of time. Upon his release from solitary confinement, he immediately comes under the influence of a fellow prisoner who speaks to him about a prison "religion" calling for the murder of guards. Would Delgado, or society, permit a coercive persuasion defense if the prisoner kills a guard? Although the factors for the defense arguably are present, it is unlikely that society would permit the prisoner's acquittal.

If Delgado requires that these external manifestations be present before applying the defense, his proposal may be criticized for an entirely different reason. It seems morally unexceptionable that excuses should be framed so that equal cases are treated equally. Indeed, Delgado asserts that a defense should not sacrifice individuals "for the sake of preserving an artificial conceptual simplicity." His defense, however, is far guiltier of artificial simplicity than is present law, because it fails to treat morally equal cases equally.

As discussed earlier, duress and insanity are limited to cases of substantial choice reduction. Society excuses the actor when substantial choice reduction is caused by a disease or defect, or by a lethal threat. No doubt certain mental conditions less substantial than disease and certain nonlethal threats also cause diminution, albeit of lesser degree, of the actor's available choices. Society has chosen, however, to limit the excuses to the more severe situations in the belief that extension to other cases might make the excuses limitless. A line has therefore been drawn: exculpation is permitted only for "diseases" and "imminent lethal threats" because society has found that choice is substantially limited in such cases, and not so in lesser situations. Such line drawing, while somewhat artificial, is at least fair because it separates the strong cases from the weak.

Delgado replaces this scheme with an artificiality far worse. He separates potentially *equal* cases from one another, so that defendants with arguably similar moral claims are treated unequally. He would excuse a defendant who is the victim of "abnormal influences," such as physical depletion, prolonged isolation, and interrogation, but would deny the defense to a person who presents some of the same symptoms of choice reduction, but whose symptoms are not the result of abnormal influences. Conditions such as life-long poverty, drug addiction, a broken home, peer group pressure, and lowered self-esteem might demonstrate that a ghetto inhabitant's choice in committing a criminal act was also substantially reduced, yet Delgado's defense would not apply.

Delgado offers no cogent explanation why one should prefer the artificial simplicity of his proposal over the present law of excuses. The morally relevant factor is choice reduction, not exposure to "abnormal influences." If one draws the line as he does, exculpating one form of choice reduction and ignoring others, one is obliged to explain why cases potentially equal on their face receive unequal treatment.

Delgado's defense, then, not only exculpates those who are blameworthy according to current standards and creates a test that is vague and difficult to apply, it also advocates the drawing of a new, morally doubtful line between criminal responsibility and blamelessness. There are only two ways to avoid such an unfair result: either reaffirm current law, which is strict but clear, or enlarge the coercive persuasion defense to include within its possible reach the full panoply of environmental influences. Such a defense would apply whenever the *conditions*, not merely threats or abnormal influences, affecting the actor were so great that a person of ordinary firmness in the actor's situation would have committed the crime. With the adoption of this test, however, determinists virtually win their case. Abundant scientific evidence demonstrates that the ordinary person will reject his preexisting moral values to obey antisocial orders even under comparatively noncoercive circumstances. The person of "ordinary firmness" is not very firm. Likewise, credible evidence shows that factors external to the actor serve as powerful influences, if not determinants, in a person's behavior. For example, parents who batter their children usually were battered in their youth; children of alcoholics are significantly more likely to have serious social problems than are those of nonalcoholic parents; juvenile prostitutes often are victims of physical and sexual abuse at home; some children can be made more susceptible to committing violent acts by the media; and, of course, the bitterness and conditions of ghetto life are conducive to crime. In short, if a defense based on reduced choice is to be created that treats equal cases equally, it must permit persons to present their entire life histories as part of a "blamelessness" defense to a crime.

Thus, we face a quandary: either we leave the law as it is, or we permit a defense which, if applied to all equal cases, would allow "morally blameless" but possibly dangerous persons back into society. If the latter path is followed, of course, society would have little choice but to throw away current jurisprudential underpinnings and incarcerate people on solely utilitarian grounds. Such a result may appear to some to be logical, even appropriate, but it is certainly revolutionary. Delgado, and other advocates of a coercive persuasion defense, should acknowledge that this is the real choice.

Richard Delgado, A Response to Professor Dressler
63 Minnesota Law Review 361-365 (1979)

In his reply article, Professor Dressler takes me to task for proposing a defense based, as he sees it, on no more than that the mental state of a defendant is "inculcated by another person." Such a defense is untenable, Dressler writes, even if limited to cases in which criminal intent is transplanted by force. Declaring that "[a]ll ideas and intents originate outside the individual," he asserts that the coercive persuasion defense I have proposed "unacceptably blur[s] concepts of moral and legal responsibility."

Dressler's argument constitutes a convincing refutation — but not of my position, for I have not advocated a defense predicated merely on the happenstance of another human being's somehow participating in the formation of the defendant's mens rea. The test is much narrower: Defendants are exculpated only if their behavioral and mentational patterns have been forcibly altered through terror, confinement, physical and psychological debilitation, and assaults on the self. It must be shown that these forces were applied over extended periods by persons who possessed life-and-death power over their victims and total control of their environment. Specifically excluded are criminal acts resulting from ordinary solicitation, voluntary membership in a criminal subculture, whole-life conditioning, or simply giving in to temptation. Dressler is wrong, then, in assuming that the defense would be available to anyone whose acts are influenced, however minimally, by external forces....

Dressler...argues that...my proposal should be rejected because, compared to the benchmark defenses of duress and insanity, the moral case for exculpating coercively persuaded actors is weak. This is so, he says, because the coercively persuaded person suffers less choice reduction than the victim of duress or the defendant who is insane. I acknowledge that the brainwashed victim retains some degree of choice; so do many who are presently classified as insane. What I dispute is that the coercively persuaded actor's choice is his own. One who undergoes thought reform is often more deserving of a defense than the individual who acts while insane or under duress. Persons who are insane may have earlier participated in their becoming insane. People are sometimes able to resist direct threats of death. In both these cases, moreover, there is at least the sense that one's self is involved. In coercive persuasion, it is the very self that is suppressed — if not demolished.

As a final line of attack, Dressler asserts that my defense lacks boundaries, that it is both underinclusive and overinclusive. It is overinclusive, he says, because it lacks the clear lines of such "medical model" defenses as insanity and diminished capacity, or the objective quality of a physical threat, as in coercion. As such, the defense will be unable to differentiate between individuals who have undergone coercive persuasion, and hence deserve a defense, and those who have not.

Dressler's faith in the medical model may be misplaced. At least with regard to insanity, the medical approach has come under withering attack for promising more than it can deliver. Moreover, to the extent that medical or psychological testimony might be helpful to the court in a case of coercive persuasion, it will be readily available; the main works in the area of coercive persuasion have been produced by psychiatrists and psychologists. Perhaps more importantly, cases of thought reform will often be recognizable without expert testimony. Those who have known the victim prior to his coercive persuasion will be able to testify to drastic changes, readily observable by lay persons. Often, such changes will be so unmistakable that even without medical testimony the finder of fact may conclude that coercive persuasion has occurred. The danger of overinclusiveness, then, is certainly no greater than with other mental defenses such as insanity, duress, or diminished capacity. In all likelihood it is considerably less.

Dressler's assertion of underinclusiveness is based on the assumption that the defense would be denied to persons, such as ghetto dwellers, who suffer extreme deprivation and poverty and whose choice, he believes, is reduced to as great a degree as is that of the coercively persuaded. He fails to differentiate, however, between two distinct types of choice reduction. The first is simple choice reduction — a narrowing of the alternatives available to an actor with unimpaired capacity to choose among them. A second variety works through curtailment of the victim's *capacity* to choose. We exonerate persons in this latter category because their mechanisms of self-determination are so impaired that it is unreasonable to hold them responsible for their acts. Insanity, involuntary intoxication, and my proposed coercive persuasion defense fall into this category, whereas ghetto dwellers exhibit only simple choice reduction. Most ghetto crime takes place because of socioeconomic reduction of opportunity. Ghetto residents, in general, do not become insane or suffer diminished capacity; nor are they brainwashed or victims of thought reform. They may commit antisocial acts out of anger or desperation, or as political gestures. We may feel pity, anger at the conditions that caused such responses, or, if hardhearted, we may condemn them for not choosing starvation over crime. But our response, I suggest, is not that such persons are coercively persuaded — acting with superimposed mens rea....

... Surely, one significant collateral benefit of allowing a coercive persuasion defense is that it fosters public discussion of the extent to which totalistic forces and groups operate in our society, and of the effect their operations should have on criminal responsibility. We should not deny ourselves this benefit.

Other Discussion Materials

United States v. Alexander

United States Court of Appeals, District of Columbia Circuit
as amended, 471 F.2d 923 (1972)

Bazelon, Chief Judge (dissenting):

The Evidence Presented at Trial

Five United States Marine Lieutenants — Ellsworth Kramer, Thaddeus Lesnick, William King, Frank Marasco, and Daniel LeGear — attended a dinner at the Marine Corps Base in Quantico, Virginia, on the evening of June 4, 1968, in celebration of their near-completion of basic officers' training. After dinner, they drove to Washington, arriving about midnight, still wearing their formal dress white uniforms. They stopped for about an hour-and-a-half at a nightclub, where they each had a drink. They were well-behaved and "conducted themselves like gentlemen." At the nightclub they met Barbara Kelly, a good friend of Lieutenant Kramer. They accompanied her to her apartment, which she shared with another young woman, and visited there with the two women until about 2:40 a.m. When the five Marines departed, Miss Kelly accompanied them, intending to return to the nightclub to meet another friend. Along the way, they decided to stop at a hamburger shop to get some coffee and sandwiches before the trip back to Quantico. The six of them entered the shop, stood by the take-out counter, and ordered their food. They noticed three Negro males sitting at the other end of the counter. As described by Lieutenant Kramer, "[T]heir hair was in Afro-bush cut, wearing medallions, jersey knit shirts, sport jackets.... [T]hey were what I consider in eccentric dress." The three men were Alexander, Murdock, and Cornelius Frazier. The critical events which subsequently took place in the restaurant were described by the four survivors of the Marine group and by Murdock and Frazier. Alexander chose not to take the stand.

According to the prosecution witnesses, Lieutenant Kramer realized that appellant Alexander was staring at him, and he returned the stare. "[I]t was on the order of a Mexican stand-off type thing where you just keep staring at one another for an indefinite period of time." No words were exchanged between the two men, and Lieutenant Kramer soon turned and faced the counter. Shortly thereafter Frazier, Murdock, and Alexander got up from where they were sitting and walked to the door behind the Marines. Murdock and Frazier left the shop, but Alexander stopped in the doorway. He tapped Lieutenant Kramer on the shoulder. When the Marine turned around, Alexander poked his uniform name tag and said, "You want to talk about it more? You want to come outside and talk about it more?" When Lieutenant Kramer replied, "Yes, I am ready to come out" or "Yes, I guess so," Alexander added, "I am going to make you a Little Red Ridinghood." At this point, Lieutenant King stepped up beside Lieutenant Kramer and made a remark variously reported by the prosecution witnesses as "What you God-damn niggers want?", "What do you want, you nigger?", "What do you want, dirty nigger bastard?", and "Get out of here nigger." Thereupon Alexander abruptly drew a long-barrelled .38 caliber revolver, cocked it, and pointed it at the group or directly into Lieutenant King's chest, saying, "I will show you what I want," or "This is what I want."

The Marines possessed no weapons whatsoever and, according to their testimony, were not advancing toward Alexander. As they stood there, shocked at the sight of the gun, Murdock reentered the shop at Alexander's left and rear, and drew a short-barrelled .38 caliber revolver. A series of shots suddenly rang out, and the Marines and Miss Kelly fell or dived to the floor. None attempted to retaliate because they all were taking cover and trying to get out of the line of fire. Alexander and Murdock withdrew from the shop, but one of them stuck his arm back into the shop and attempted — unsuccessfully — to fire his weapon several times more. Only Lieutenant Kramer attempted to identify this man, and he said it was Murdock.

Lieutenants King and Lesnick were mortally wounded in the fusillade; they died within minutes. Lieutenant Kramer was wounded in the head, but he remained conscious, as did Miss Kelly, who had been shot in the hip. Only Lieutenants LeGear and Marasco were not hit.

Alexander, Murdock, and Frazier fled to Alexander's automobile and drove off rapidly in the wrong direction on a one-way street. Alexander was driving, and as the car drove off, Murdock fired three more shots from the window of the car, at the door of the hamburger shop, and at people in the street. A nearby scout car raced after the fleeing car and stopped them within a few blocks. Two revolvers were recovered from the front floorboard of Alexander's automobile. . . .

The Hearing on Criminal Responsibility

. . . [I]n the charge to the jury [at a bifurcated insanity trial for Murdock], the court used language that seemed to tell the jury to disregard a portion of the evidence that was critical to Murdock's theory of the case.

The court has concluded, for the reasons set forth in Judge McGowan's separate opinion, that the record does not call for reversal [because of the jury charge]. Because the author of this opinion is persuaded that there is substantial merit [to defendant Murdock's claim], the author's views are set forth below. . . .

Instructions to the Jury

I turn . . . to what I regard as a serious error in the jury charge on the issue of criminal responsibility. In order to put the problem in perspective, it will be necessary to review the testimony in some detail.

1. Murdock relied primarily on the testimony of Dr. Williams, a board-certified psychiatrist, and professor at Howard University Medical School.

Dr. Williams had examined Murdock on two occasions during his confinement in St. Elizabeths Hospital [for psychiatric evaluation upon his plea of insanity]. According to the testimony of Dr. Williams, Murdock was strongly delusional, though not hallucinating or psychotic; he was greatly preoccupied with the unfair treatment of Negroes in this country, and the idea that racial war was inevitable. He showed compulsiveness in his behavior, emotional immaturity, and some psychopathic traits. Since his emotional difficulties were closely tied to his sense of racial oppression, it is probable that when the Marine in the Little Tavern called him a "black bastard" Murdock had an irresistible impulse to shoot. His emotional disorder had its roots in his childhood, in the Watts section of Los Angeles; particularly important was the fact that his father had deserted his mother, and he grew up in a large family with little money and little love or attention.

Dr. Williams stated firmly that in his view Murdock was suffering from an abnormal mental condition that substantially impaired his behavior controls. But he stated just as firmly that the condition did not amount to a mental illness....

Counsel's strategy was to bypass the troublesome term "mental illness," and invite the jury to focus directly on the legal definition of that term. He conceded to the jury that Murdock "did not have a mental disease in the classic sense," i.e., he did not have a psychosis. But, counsel argued, the expert testimony showed that at the critical moment Murdock did not have control of his conduct, and the reason for that lack of control was a deepseated emotional disorder that was rooted in his "rotten social background." Accordingly, he asked the trial court to omit the term "mental disease or defect" from the jury instructions. I think his proposal was ingenious; the trial court might well have framed a suitable instruction asking the jury to consider whether Murdock's act was the product, not of "mental illness," but of an "abnormal condition of the mind that substantially affects mental or emotional processes and substantially impairs behavior controls."

While the trial court denied the requested instruction, we cannot say that ruling was error. The judge carefully instructed the jury to resolve the question of mental illness in accordance with its legal definition; he told them they were not bound by medical conclusions as to what is or is not a mental disease, and he told them to ignore defense counsel's concession that Murdock was without mental disease. In this respect the instructions conform to the requirements set forth in our cases.

But the judge injected into the instructions a special note of caution, in response to the testimony and argument presented in this case. He told the jury:

> We are not concerned with a question of whether or not a man had a rotten social background. We are concerned with the question of his criminal responsibility. That is to say, whether he had an abnormal condition of the mind that affected his emotional and behavioral processes at the time of the offense.

Defense counsel had objected to that instruction before it was given, because his theory of the case was that Murdock had an abnormal mental condition caused in part by his "rotten social background." The trial court overruled his objection, deeming the instruction necessary to counteract what he saw as an attempt by defense counsel to appeal to the jurors on the basis of sympathy, or passion, or prejudice.

It may well be that the trial judge was motivated by a reasonable fear that the jury would reach its decision on the basis not of the law but of sympathy for the victims of a racist society. Nevertheless, I think that the quoted instruction was reversible error. It had the effect of telling the jury to disregard the testimony relating to Murdock's social and economic background and to consider only the testimony framed in terms of "illness." Such an instruction is contrary to law, and it clearly undermined Murdock's approach to the insanity defense in this case. For Murdock's strategy had two parts: first, he sought to convince the jury to disregard Dr. Williams' finding of no "mental illness," and then he sought to persuade them to find mental illness in the legal sense of the term. The jury could hardly consider the issue of mental illness without considering Murdock's background, in view of the fact that all the witnesses traced such disabilities as they found at least in part to his background.

No matter what the trial judge intended, his instruction may have deprived Murdock of a fair trial on the issue of responsibility. But even if that instruction had not been offered, Murdock could argue that he was denied a fair opportunity to present his particular responsibility defense — a defense not clearly grounded on any medically recognized "mental disease or defect." While the language of our responsibility test theoretically leaves room for such a defense, our experience reveals that in practice it imposes illogical constraints on the flow of information to the jury and also on the breadth of the jury's inquiry. Our test demands an "abnormal condition of the mind," and that term carries implications that may mislead counsel, the court, and the jury.

McDonald defined mental illness for purposes of the responsibility defense as an abnormal condition of the mind that "substantially affects mental or emotional processes and substantially impairs behavior controls." The thrust of Murdock's defense was that the environment in which he was raised — his "rotten social background" — conditioned him to respond to certain stimuli in a manner most of us would consider flagrantly inappropriate. Because of his early conditioning, he argued, he was denied any meaningful choice when the racial insult triggered the explosion in the restaurant. He asked the jury to conclude that his "rotten social background," and the resulting impairment of mental or emotional processes and behavior controls, ruled his violent reaction in the same manner that the behavior of a paranoid schizophrenic may be ruled by his "mental condition." Whether this impairment amounted to an "abnormal condition of the mind" is, in my opinion, at best an academic question. But the consequences we predicate on the answer may be very meaningful indeed.

We have never said that an exculpatory mental illness must be reflected in some organic or pathological condition. Nor have we enshrined psychosis as a prerequisite of the defense. But our experience has made it clear that the terms we use — "mental disease or defect" and "abnormal condition of the mind" — carry a distinct flavor of pathology. And they deflect attention from the crucial, functional question — did the defendant lack the ability to make any meaningful choice of action — to an artificial and misleading excursion into the thicket of psychiatric diagnosis and nomenclature. . . .

[W]e sacrifice a great deal by discouraging Murdock's responsibility defense. If we could remove the practical impediments to the free flow of information we might begin to learn something about the causes of crime. We might discover, for example, that there is a significant causal relationship between violent criminal behavior and a "rotten social background." That realization would require us to consider, for example, whether income redistribution and social reconstruction are indispensable first steps toward solving the problem of violent crime.

. . . It is a critical responsibility of courts, legislatures and commentators to undertake a purposive analysis of the responsibility defense, instead of merely paying it lip-service in deference to its historical significance and our "liberal" consciences. Under each of the prevailing tests of criminal responsibility, the operation of the defense has been haphazard, perfunctory, and virtually inexplicable. If we cannot overcome the irrational operation of the defense, we may have no honest choice but to abandon it and hold all persons criminally responsible for their action.

McGowan, Circuit Judge [writing for the majority]:

The tragic and senseless events giving rise to these appeals are a recurring byproduct of a society which, unable as yet to eliminate explosive racial tensions, appears equally paralyzed to deny easy access to guns. Cultural infantilism of this kind inevitably exacts a high price, which in this instance was paid by the two young officers who were killed. The ultimate responsibility for their deaths reaches far beyond these appellants.

As courts, however, we administer a system of justice which is limited in its reach. We deal only with those formally accused under laws which define criminal accountability narrowly. Our function on these appeals is to determine whether appellants had a fair opportunity to defend themselves, and were tried and sentenced according to law. . . .

Judge Bazelon . . . finds reversal to be compelled by reason of a statement made to the jury by the court in the course of its instructions. The bare words used are not a faulty statement of the law. They remind the jury that the issue before them for decision is not one of the shortcomings of society generally, but rather that of appellant Murdock's criminal responsibility for the illegal acts of which he had earlier been found guilty; and, the court added in the next breath, that issue turns on "whether [appellant] had an abnormal condition of the mind that affected his emotional and behavioral processes at the time of the offense." This last is, of course, an unexceptionable statement of what we have declared to be the law in this jurisdiction. . . .

[Affirmed.]

NONEXCULPATORY DEFENSES GENERALLY

● **OVERVIEW OF NONEXCULPATORY DEFENSES GENERALLY**

Examples of Nonexculpatory Defenses   "Nonexculpatory defenses" include statutes of limitation; diplomatic immunity; judicial, legislative, and executive immunities; immunity after compelled testimony or pursuant to a plea agreement; and incompetency to stand trial. Each of these forms of immunity furthers an important societal interest, respectively: reciprocal protection of our diplomats abroad, protection of government officials from personal liability arising from their official duties, the need to compel incriminating testimony from some offenders in order to successfully prosecute others, and the avoidance of the costs and risks of trials through inducement of plea agreements. The last defense, incompetency, is based primarily on concerns of fairness to the defendant. It prohibits trial unless the defendant has "an adequate ability to consult with his lawyer and to understand the proceedings against him."

Constitutional Defenses   Overriding nonexculpatory public policy interests also serve as the basis for many constitutional defenses. The Double Jeopardy Clause of the Fifth Amendment, for example, may foreclose the trial of even a blameworthy and convictable offender by barring the state from making a second attempt to convict him. Notions of procedural fairness are said to demand that the state not subject a defendant to the embarrassment, expense, and ordeal of trial more than once nor compel him to live in a continuing state of anxiety and insecurity. Dismissals based on the operation of the exclusionary rule or on prosecutorial misconduct also may be nonexculpatory in nature, especially if the dismissals are unrelated to the reliability of the evidence of the fact-finding process. The public policies served by nonexculpatory defenses may be as broad as protecting all members of society from unlawful searches or may focus on assuring fairness in the treatment of individual defendants.

Distinguished from Justifications   The balancing of competing interests that underlie nonexculpatory defenses should be distinguished from the balancing that occurs in justification defenses. In the latter, the harm done by defendant's act is weighed against the harm avoided or the benefit gained from that conduct. The actor whose conduct causes no *net* societal harm or evil is given a justification defense. In nonexculpatory defenses, the defendant's conduct neither creates a societal benefit nor avoids a societal harm; the defendant may well be fully blameworthy. The societal benefit that the defense seeks to promote arises not from the actor's conduct but from forgoing his conviction. Thus the defendant escapes liability despite his potential blameworthiness.

Detrimental Effects of Nonexculpatory Defenses   It should be clear that the criminal justice system incurs a cost each time a nonexculpatory defense is permitted. Recognizing such defenses undermines the purposes for which criminal liability is imposed. Acquitting blameworthy offenders, who admittedly have caused the harm or evil prohibited by the criminal law, undercuts the aims of special and general deterrence; the offender's acquittal shows others (and herself) that it is possible to culpably violate the criminal law without suffering the threatened sanction. In addition, such defenses may deprive the criminal justice system of authority to incapacitate or rehabilitate a dangeruous offender, thereby increasing the likelihood of future offenses. Finally, nonexculpatory defenses permit blameworthy offenders to escape the punishment they deserve, frustrating justice and undercutting the moral credibility of the criminal law.

24

Entrapment

Justifications and excuses exculpate. A third group of general defenses—nonexculpatory defenses—give a defense not because the person is blameless but because by forgoing prosecution or punishment some other important societal interest is thought to be advanced.

◆ THE CASE OF JOHN DELOREAN

John Zachary DeLorean is born on January 6, 1925, on Detroit's Near Eastside. He is the oldest of Zachary and Kathryn DeLorean's four boys. His father is a hard-drinking French Alsatian who works off and on for Ford. His mother is a factory worker with an Eastern European heritage. DeLorean's commitment to work hard yields early success; for example, he attends a better high school after winning a clarinet scholarship. He follows his father's interest and begins work in the car industry and is quickly recognized as a brilliant engineer. Although some people consider him brusque and erratic, he seems to know what people want and swiftly moves up the ranks of Detroit's elite.

DeLorean becomes one of GM's youngest division managers and is subsequently put in charge of Pontiac. In the 1970s, however, DeLorean and GM's administration increasingly clash over his attitude, the company's structure, and even his style of dress—sideburns and bell-bottoms, rather than blue suits. People say that he has "gone Hollywood" because of his frequent business travels to California, which have brought him in contact with new social circles and pleasant sunny weather. By 1973, he has divorced two wives, the second a 20-year old, and marries his third, fashion

Figure 119 **John DeLorean in his high-rise Manhattan office**

(Anthony Howarth)

model Christina Ferrare, in Los Angeles. A few months before his third marriage, he loses a $650,000 annual salary when GM asks him to resign. He announces that he will start his own company and build a luxury car that will be more fuel-efficient and have more safety features than any other on the market. The car also will have "gull-wing" doors that open from the top.

DeLorean knows that the endeavor will not be easy. He belatedly tries to block the publication of his exposé on the problems at GM, fearing that the book could have a detrimental effect on his new car project. However, when he is unsuccessful at persuading the publisher to hold the book's release, and it quickly sells out its first 600,000 copies, DeLorean immediately shifts gears and supports the book, claiming that he might "give [any money he receives from it] to some charity."

Although DeLorean is an advocate for several charities and a vocal proponent of civil rights, he gives people reason to question his motives when it comes to money. For example, an inventor, Peter Avrea, claims that DeLorean cheated him out of hundreds of thousands of dollars when DeLorean did not maintain the patents he was hired to protect. A couple claim that they lost a ranch he sold them because he failed to inform them of a large existing mortgage on the property. A Wichita car dealer claims that DeLorean ruined his dealership and stole his gull-winged Mercedes 300SL to use as a "model." The accusations seem to have never bothered DeLorean.

In 1977, he establishes the DeLorean Motor Company. He locates its production plant in Dunmurry, Northern Ireland, an area desperately in need of jobs, in exchange for $134.1 million in financing from the British government. DeLorean is able to start the company without much of his own money by obtaining investments from other Americans, such as Sammy Davis, Jr., who see DeLorean's company as a good tax shelter.

The company's first model, the DMC-12, is plagued with design problems from the start. Time and fiscal constraints created by technical conflicts between engineers that DeLorean had wooed away from GM and his new partners from Lotus make it impossible to incorporate into its design many of the innovations that DeLorean had hoped for. Critics suggest that the DMC-12 is quite different from the small, safety-motivated car DeLorean has been hyping for five years. Beyond failing to satisfy critics, the DMC-12's design problems contribute to the company's chronic cash-flow difficulties. DeLorean personally adds to the company's cash-flow problems by using its assets to make private purchases, such as a small Nevada-based snowmobile company and art for his New York office.

When first released, the stainless-steel DMC-12 sells well, but a slowdown in the luxury-car market concerns some at the company. They see the market for an expensive monochrome, non-convertible two-seater as limited, especially when it is priced higher than a comparable Porsche or Mercedes. Moreover, the cars have mechanical problems.

Figure 120 **DeLorean seated inside the DMC-12 model of his car at Earl's Court Motor Fair in London in 1981**

(Hulton-Deutsch Collection/Corbis)

Johnny Carson, the company's official spokesman, has his car break down within just a few miles. The company rushes over a new part, but that too breaks. On another occasion, a man climbs into a display model at the Cleveland Museum and is trapped when the doors will not open.

In 1980, after providing an additional $33 million in loans, the British government announces that DeLorean's company will receive no further government support. The following year, in October 1981, Prime Minister Margaret Thatcher orders a police investigation of the company's finances after a disgruntled former employee provides company memorandums and files suggesting both mismanagement of the company's finances and that DeLorean's personal investment in the company is much less than his deal with the government requires.

Meanwhile, the company's cars continue to suffer from mechanical problems, and by late November, the company has recalled most of the 2,000 DMC-12s on the road. After the British government refuses to provide additional loans, DeLorean authorizes the firing of almost half of his company's 2,600-person workforce in January 1982. The government begins a review to determine the company's likelihood of survival.

DeLorean initially reacts to the review meetings by asking Sir Cork, a respected financier, for advice on how to sue the British government for "war damages and criminal damages and breach of contract and other things." He drops the effort after being advised against it. By February, the company is in receivership — tantamount to declaring bankruptcy — and is placed under the total control of the appointed Sir Cork. During an interview, DeLorean responds that he is "delighted at the outcome," explaining that the government now has to deal with the company's debt problem.

In May 1982, the British government announces that it is closing the plant by the end of the month. Within hours of the announcement, DeLorean releases a statement that he has new backers who will provide the $37 million necessary to keep the plant open. He keeps the sources secret, describing them only as "an individual and a bank." Having heard vague promises of funding from unknown sources before, those closest to him are skeptical.

DeLorean is now seemingly out of ideas but recalls conversations he has had with a former neighbor, James Timothy Hoffman. They know each other through their sons, and have discussed in general terms their respective business troubles. Several days earlier, Hoffman had tried to reach DeLorean.

Hoffman did not find his success in the business world but rather in drug trafficking, which by the early 1980s is a very lucrative venture. The Drug Enforcement Agency (DEA) estimates that during that period more than $30 billion are spent yearly on cocaine alone. In 1981, the F.B.I. arrests the 40-year old Hoffman, who agrees to act as a government informant in exchange for a reduced sentence, and since January 1982 has been an F.B.I. informant.

When DeLorean calls, Hoffman mentions that he has made money smuggling drugs from Colombia and Thailand. On July 11, the two meet at the Marriott in Newport Beach, California. DeLorean raises the idea of arranging a drug deal. The following day, after Hoffman informs his contacts about DeLorean's suggestion to sell drugs, the F.B.I. opens an official file on DeLorean.

On July 13, in the first of many videotaped conversations, DeLorean explains to Hoffman that his company has $40 million in cars but no cash, and he would like to

proceed with the proposition they discussed. During the meeting, an F.B.I. camera, hidden underneath the table, records DeLorean's shoes, trouser legs, and muffled voice explaining that his tax man can reconstruct records to make anything look legitimate. Hoffman explains to DeLorean that they can channel the profits from the cocaine sales through Eureka Federal Savings, in San Carlos, California, to make the transaction appear legal.

DeLorean comments that he does not really care what the money's source is — drugs, organized crime, anything — so long as it eventually filters through a recognized financial institution.

On September 4, DeLorean meets with Hoffman in Washington, D.C. At this meeting, which the F.B.I. is again secretly videotaping, they specifically discuss the importation of heroin and cocaine as a way for DeLorean to generate capital; the drug deal could raise the estimated $40 million he needs to save his company. DeLorean agrees to provide $1.8 million in funding for the deal. Hoffman reassures him that he will not be easily connected to the transaction but warns DeLorean that, once they start, he better have a good reason not to follow through with the plan. Hoffman also reminds DeLorean, however, not to take part in anything with which he is uncomfortable. "I won't be mad, I won't be hurt, I won't be anything. If you can get the money somewhere else and it's better circumstances, I'd say do it," Hoffman says. Although he appreciates the option to withdraw, DeLorean tells him, "I want to proceed."

During his meetings with Hoffman and his associates, DeLorean makes a vague claim that he has a tight relationship with the Irish Republican Army (IRA) and warns that drug dealers should be warned not to mess with him. (When this claim becomes known, the United States government takes it quite seriously and conducts an investigation, but is unable to confirm or deny the claim. Upon hearing the claim later, the I.R.A. strongly denies any connection to DeLorean. In Belfast, it issues a statement: "In Ireland, we treat as an offense anyone who falsely uses the name of the Irish Republican Army to impress people, abuse people, or extricate themselves from situations of their own making.... We do not take lightly Mr. DeLorean's lies, nor will we forget them should he ever bump into us.")

On September 8, DeLorean travels to San Carlos, California, and meets the drug dealers' crooked banker, James Benedict (F.B.I. agent Benedict Tisa). Benedict outlines a plan to hire William Hetrick, a 50-year old pilot, who is "very successful for bringing in cocaine." The F.B.I. suspects that Hetrick, who maintains a lifestyle beyond the means of a flight operator with no clients, is one of southern California's major cocaine traffickers but have been unsuccessful in catching him.

Being unwilling to risk his own money, DeLorean calls Benedict a week later to tell him that the $1.8 million he promised is unavailable because his I.R.A. contact has made it impossible for him to get access to the money. Benedict does not hide his disappointment. He tells DeLorean that he is letting them down.

On September 17, DeLorean calls Benedict again to inform him that he has found another way to get the money needed for the deal and is ready to make the arrangements with pilot Hetrick. The three meet together on September 20 at the Bel Air Sands Hotel to discuss DeLorean's new plan. Eleven days later, at the Bonaventure Hotel in Washington, D.C., Hoffman introduces DeLorean to the bearded Mafia kingpin, Mr. Vicenza (DEA agent Valenstra). While eating lunch, Vicenza discusses rates of return on investment with DeLorean, estimating that DeLorean could have $10 million within 48 hours "from that particular cocaine purchase."

Trying to finalize the deal, DeLorean offers Vicenza a 50% ownership stake in his company as collateral if Vicenza will purchase the cocaine with his money. (In a September 29 letter, DeLorean signs over 500 shares of DeLorean Motor Company stock to Vicenza, and 5,000 to Benedict, which according to later estimates is his entire voting block in the company.) From the table, DeLorean calls pilot Hetrick and says awkwardly, "They'd like to go ahead with those monkeys [code for kilo of cocaine] you had up in San Francisco." They agree to meet in Los Angeles after the drugs have been flown in.

On Monday, October 18, the F.B.I. arrests Hetrick and his assistant, Steven Arrington, at the Los Angeles airport with more than 60 pounds of cocaine, worth about $24 million. Meanwhile, Hoffman calls DeLorean, who arranges to fly to Los Angeles the next morning, October 19.

While DeLorean is en route to Los Angeles, the British government announces that it is permanently closing his company's plant. Both are unaware that a legitimate banker has been desperately trying to contact DeLorean's office with loan papers for his signature that could provide the funds necessary to salvage his company. She is told that he is unreachable because he is in flight to Los Angeles.

Upon arrival, DeLorean goes to Room 501 of the airport's Bel Air Sands Hotel. The room is being audio- and videotaped. DeLorean enters the room to see an open suitcase with 60 pounds of cocaine worth $24 million. Picking up one of the bags, DeLorean says it is better than gold. "Just in the nick of time," he beams. They pass glasses of champagne around and DeLorean toasts, "A lot of success for everyone."

Figure 122 **The DA's evidence against John DeLorean**

(AP)

A knock at the door interrupts the celebration. Agent Jerry West enters, announcing, "I'm with the F.B.I. You are under arrest for narcotics law violations."

1. Relying only on your own intuitions of justice, what liability and punishment, if any, does John DeLorean deserve?

N	0	1	2	3	4	5	6	7	8	9	10	11
☐	☐	☐	☐	☐	☐	☐	☐	☐	☐	☐	☐	☐
no liability	liability but no punishment	1 day	2 wks	2 mo	6 mo	1 yr	3 yrs	7 yrs	15 yrs	30 yrs	life imprison- ment	death

2. What liability, if any, under the then-existing statutes?
3. What liability, if any, under the Model Penal Code?

■ THE LAW

United States Code
(1982)

Title 21. Food and Drugs

Chapter 13. Drug Abuse Prevention and Control
Subchapter I. Control and Enforcement

Section 802. Definitions

As used in this subchapter: . . .

(4) The term "Drug Enforcement Administration" means the Drug Enforcement Administration in the Department of Justice.

(5) The term "control" means to add a drug or other substance, or immediate precursor, included in schedule I, II, III, IV or V of part B of this subchapter, whether by transfer from another schedule or otherwise.

(6) The term "controlled substance" means a drug or other substance, or immediate precursor, included in schedule I, II, III, IV or V of part B of this subchapter. The term does not include distilled spirits, wine, malt beverages, or tobacco, as those terms are defined or used in subtitle E of the Internal Revenue Code of 1954.

(7) The term "counterfeit substance" means a controlled substance which, or the container or labeling of which, without authorization, bears the trademark, trade name, or other identifying mark, imprint, number, or device, or any likeness thereof, or a manufacturer, distributor, or dispenser other than the person or persons who in fact manufactured, distributed, or dispensed such substance and which thereby falsely purports or is

represented to be the product of, or to have been distributed by, such other manufacturer, distributor, or dispenser.

(8) The terms "deliver" or "delivery" mean the actual, constructive, or attempted transfer of a controlled substance, whether there exists an agency relationship.

(9) The term "depressant or stimulant substance" means—

(A) a drug which contains any quantity of (i) barbituric acid or any of the slats of barbituric acid; or (ii) any derivative of barbituric acid which has been designated by the Secretary as habit forming under section 352(d) of this title; or

(B) a drug which contains any quantity of (i) amphetamine or any or its optimal isomers; (ii) any slat of amphetamine or any slat of an optical isomer of amphetamine; or (iii) any substance which the Attorney General, after investigation, has been found to be, and by regulation designated as, habit forming because of its stimulant effect on the central nervous system; or

(C) lysergic acid diethylamide; or

(D) any drug which contains any quantity of a substance which the Attorney General, after investigation, has found to have, and by regulation designated as having, a potential for abuse because of its depressant or stimulant effect on the central nervous system or its hallucinogenic effect.

(10) The term "dispense" means to deliver a controlled substance to an ultimate user or research subject by, or pursuant to the lawful order of, a practitioner, including the prescribing and administering of a controlled substance and the packaging, labeling or compounding necessary to prepare the substance for such delivery. The term "dispenser" means a practitioner who so delivers a controlled substance to an ultimate user or research subject.

(11) The term "distribute" means to deliver (other than by administrating or dispensing) a controlled substance. The term "distributor" means a person who so delivers a controlled substance.

(12) The term "drug" has the meaning given that term by section 321(g)(1) of this title.

(13) The term "felony" means any Federal or State offense classified by applicable Federal or State law as a felony....

(16) The term "narcotic drug" means any of the following, whether produced directly or indirectly by extraction from substances of vegetable origin, or independently by means of chemical synthesis, or by a combination of extraction and chemical synthesis:

(A) Opium, coca leaves, and opiates.

(B) A compound, manufacture, salt, derivative, or preparation of opium, coca leaves, or opiates.

(C) A substance (and any compound manufacture, salt, derivative, or preparation thereof) which is chemically identical with any of the substances referred to in clause (A) or (B).

Such term does not include decocainized coca leaves or extracts of coca leaves which extracts do not contain cocaine or ecgonine.

(17) The term "opiate" means any drug or other substance having an addiction-forming or addiction-sustaining liability similar to morphine or being capable of having such addiction-forming or addiction-sustaining liability....

Section 841. Prohibited Acts

(a) Unlawful acts: Except as authorized by this subchapter, it shall be unlawful for any person knowingly or intentionally —

(1) to manufacture, distribute, or dispense, or possess with intent to manufacture, distribute, or dispense, a controlled substance; or

(2) to create, distribute, or dispense, or possess with intent to distribute or dispense, a counterfeit substance.

(b) Penalties: Except as otherwise provided in section 845 of this title, any person who violates subsection (a) of this section shall be sentenced as follows:

(1)(A) In the case of a controlled substance in schedule I or II which is a narcotic drug, such person shall be sentenced to a term of imprisonment of not more than 15 years, a fine of not more than $25,000, or both. If any person commits such violation after one or more prior convictions of him for an offense punishable under this paragraph, or for a felony under any other provision of this subchapter of subchapter II of this chapter or other law of the United States relating to narcotic drugs, marihuana, or depressant or stimulant substances, have become final, such person shall be sentenced to a term of imprisonment of not more than 30 years, a fine of not more than $50,000, or both. Any sentence imposing a term of imprisonment under this paragraph shall, in the absence of such prior conviction, impose a special parole term of at least 3 years in addition to such term of imprisonment and shall, if there was such a prior conviction, impose a special parole term of as least 6 years in addition to such term of imprisonment.

(B) In the case of a controlled substance in schedule I or II which is not a narcotic drug or in the case of any controlled substance in schedule III, such person shall, except as provided in paragraphs (4), (5) and (6) of this subsection, be sentenced to a term of imprisonment of not more than 5 years, a fine of not more than $15,000, or both. If any person commits such a violation after one or more prior convictions of him for an offense punishable under this paragraph, or for a felony under any other provision of this subchapter or subchapter II of this chapter of other law of the United States relating to narcotic drugs, marihuana, or depressant or stimulant substances, have become final, such person shall be sentenced to a term of imprisonment of not more than 10 years, a fine of not more than $30,000, or both. Any sentence imposing a term of imprisonment under this paragraph shall, in the absence of such a prior conviction, impose a special parole term of at least 2 years in addition to such term of imprisonment and shall, if there was such a prior conviction, impose a special parole term of at least 4 years in addition to such term of imprisonment....

Section 843. Prohibited Acts C

. . .

(b) Communication facility. It shall be unlawful for any person knowingly or intentionally to use any communication facility in committing or in causing or facilitating the commission of any act or acts constituting a felony under any provision of this subchapter. . . . Each separate use of a communication facility shall be a separate offense under this subsection. For purposes of this subsection, the term "communication facility" means any and all public and private instrumentalities used or useful in the transmission of writing, signs, signals, pictures, or sounds of all kinds and includes mail, telephone, wire, radio, and all other means of communication.

Section 846. Attempt and Conspiracy

Any person who attempts or conspires to commit any offenses defined in this subchapter is punishable by imprisonment or fine or both which may not exceed the maximum punishment prescribed by the offense, the commission of which was the object of the attempt or conspiracy.

Section 847. Additional Penalties

Any penalty imposed for violation of this subchapter shall be in addition to, and not in lieu of, any civil or administrative penalty or sanction authorized by law.

Title 18. Crimes and Criminal Procedure
Part I. Crimes
Chapter 95. Racketeering

Section 1952. Interstate and Foreign Travel or Transportation an Aid of Racketeering Enterprises

(a) Whoever travels in interstate or foreign commerce or uses any facility in interstate or foreign travel, including the mail, with intent to —

(1) distribute the proceeds of any unlawful activity; or

(2) commit any crime of violence to further any unlawful activity; or

(3) otherwise promote, manage, establish, carry on, or facilitate the promotion, management, establishment, or carrying on, of any unlawful activity,

and thereafter performs or attempts to perform any of the acts specified in subparagraph (1), (2), and (3), shall be fined not more than $10,000 or imprisoned for not more than five years, or both.

(b) As used in this section "unlawful activity" means (1) any business enterprise involving gambling, liquor on which the Federal excise tax has not been paid, narcotics or controlled substances, . . . or prosecution offenses in violation of the laws of the State in which they are committed or of the United States or (2) extortion, bribery, or arson in violation of the laws of the State in which committed or of the United States.

(c) Investigations of violations under this section involving liquor shall be conducted under the supervision of the Secretary of the Treasury.

Chapter 96. Racketeer-Influenced and Corrupt Organizations

Section 1961. Definitions

As used in this chapter —

(1) "racketeering activity" means (A) any act or threat involving murder, kidnapping, gambling, arson, robbery, bribery, extortion, or dealing in narcotic or other dangerous drugs, which is punishable under State law and punishable by imprisonment for more than one year; (B) any act which is indictable under any of the following provisions of title 18, United States Code: Section 201 (relating to bribery), section 224 (relating to sports bribery), section 471, 472, and 473 (relating to counterfeiting), section 569 (relating to theft from interstate shipment) if the act indictable under section 659 is felonious, section 664 (relating to embezzlement from pension and welfare funds, sections 891-894 (relating to extortionate credit transactions), section 1084 (relating to the transmission of gambling information), section 1341 (relating to wire fraud), section 1503 (relating to obstruction of justice), section 1510 (relating to obstruction of criminal investigations), section 1511 (relating to the obstruction of State or local enforcement), section 1951 (relating to interference with commerce, robbery, or extortion), section 1952 (relating to racketeering), section 1953 (relating to interstate transportation of wagering paraphernalia), section 1954 (relating to unlawful welfare fund payments), section 1955 (relating to the prohibition of illegal gambling businesses), sections 2314 and 2315 (relating to interstate transportation of stolen property), section 2341-2346 (relating to trafficking in contraband cigarettes), sections 2421-2424 (relating to white slave traffic), (C) any act which is indictable under title 29, United States Code, section 186 (dealing with restrictions on payments and loans to labor organizations) or section 501(c) (relating to embezzlement from union funds), or (D) any offense involving fraud connected with a case under title 11, fraud in the sale of securities, or the felonious manufacture, importation, receiving, concealment, buying, selling, or otherwise dealing with narcotic or other dangerous drugs, punishable under any law of the United States;

(2) "State" means any State of the United States, District of Columbia, the Commonwealth of Puerto Rico, any territory or possession of the United States, any political subdivision, or any department, agency, or instrumentality thereof;

(3) "person" includes any individual or entity capable of holding a legal or beneficial interest in property;

(4) "enterprise" includes any individual, partnership, corporation, association, or other legal entity, and any union or group of individuals associated in fact although not a legal entity;

(5) "pattern of racketeering activity" requires at least two acts of racketeering activity, one of which occurred after the effective date of this chapter and the last of which occurred within ten years (excluding any period of imprisonment) after the commission of a prior act of racketeering activity; . . .

Section 1962. Prohibited activities

(a) It shall be unlawful for any person who has received any income derived, directly or indirectly, from a pattern of racketeering activity or through collection of an unlawful debt in which such person has participated as a principal within the meaning of section 2, title 18, United States Code, to use or invest, directly or indirectly, any part of such income, or the proceeds of such income, in acquisition of any interest in, or the establishment or operation of, any enterprise which is engaged in, or the activity of which affect, interstate or foreign commerce. A purchase of securities on the open market for purposes of investment, and without the intention of controlling or participating in the control of the issuer, or of assisting another to do so, shall not be unlawful under this subsection if the securities of the issuer held by the purchaser, the members of his immediate family, and his or their accomplices in any pattern of racketeering activity or the collection of an unlawful debt after such purchase do not amount in the aggregate to one percent of the outstanding securities of any one class, and do not confer, either in law or in fact, the power to elect one or more directors of the issuer.

(b) It shall be unlawful for any person through a pattern of racketeering activity or through collection of an unlawful debt to acquire or maintain, directly or indirectly, any interest in or control of any enterprise which is engaged in, or the activities of which affect, interstate or foreign commerce.

(c) It shall be unlawful for any person employed by or associated with any enterprise engaged in, or the activities of which affect, interstate or foreign commerce, to conduct or participate, directly or indirectly, in the conduct of such enterprise's affairs through a pattern of racketeering activity or collection of unlawful debt.

(d) It shall be unlawful for any person to conspire to violate any of the provisions of subsections (a), (b), or (c) of this section.

Section 1963. Criminal penalties

(a) Whoever violates any provision of section 1962 of this chapter shall be fined not more than $25,000 or imprisoned not more than twenty years, or both, and shall forfeit to the United States (1) any interest he has acquired or maintained in violation of section 1962, and (2) any interest in, security in, claim against, or property or contractual right of any kind affording a source of influence over, any

enterprise which he has established, operated, controlled, conducted, or participated in the conduct of, in violation of section 1962.

(b) In any action brought by the United States under this section, the
district courts of the United States shall have jurisdiction to enter such restraining orders or prohibitions, or to take such other actions, including, but not
limited to, the acceptance of satisfactory performance bonds, in connection with
any property or other subject to forfeiture under this section, as it shall deem
proper.

(c) Upon conviction of a person under this section, the court shall authorize
the Attorney General to seize all property or other interest declared forfeited
under this section upon such terms and conditions as the court shall deem proper.
If property right or other interest is not exercisable or transferable for value by the
United States, it shall expire, and shall not revert to the convicted person. All
provisions of law relating to the disposition of property, or the proceeds from the
sale thereof, or the remission or mitigation of forfeitures for violation of the
customs laws, and the compromise of claims and the award of compensation to
informers in respect of such forfeitures incurred, or alleged to have been incurred,
under the provisions of this section, insofar as applicable and not inconsistent with
the provisions hereof. Such duties as are imposed upon the collector of customs or
any other person with respect to the disposition or property under the customs
laws shall be performed under this chapter by the Attorney General. The United
States shall dispose of all such property as soon as commercially feasible, making
due provision for the rights of innocent persons.

Grimm v. United States
156 U.S. 604 (1895)

Defendant was indicted for mailing letters in violation of Rev. St. §3893,
which provided that lewd pictures, books or pamphlets, and information on how
to receive them, could not be sent through the mail. He had responded to a letter
requesting the quantity and price of lewd pictures, which came from a government
agent using a fictitious name. The Court affirmed his indictment and denied his
defense of entrapment. The Court held that "[t]he law was actually violated by the
defendant; he placed letters in the post office which conveyed information as to
where obscene matter could be obtained . . . with a view of giving such information. . . . The fact that the person who wrote under these assumed names and
received his letters was a government detective in no manner detracts from his
guilt."

Sorrells v. United States
287 U.S. 435 (1932)

Nearly forty years after *Grimm,* the Court had moved away from it and had
found a rationale to provide a defense of entrapment. In *Sorrells,* the defendant
was convicted of possessing and selling one-half gallon of whiskey in violation of
the National Prohibition Act, and argued that he was entrapped by a prohibition

agent. The agent testified that on July 13, 1930, he visited the defendant's home with three of the defendant's acquaintances for a couple of hours, and at least three times, asked the defendant to procure him some whiskey. The government admitted that "[t]here was no evidence that the defendant had ever possessed or sold any intoxicating liquor prior to the transaction in question." The Court held that the defense of entrapment was available to the defendant in such circumstances. It stated that "[i]t is clear that the evidence was sufficient to warrant a finding that the act for which defendant was prosecuted was instigated by the prohibition agent, that it was the creature of his purpose . . . and that the agent lured defendant, otherwise innocent, to its commission by repeated and persistent solicitation. . . . Such a gross abuse of authority given for the purpose of detecting and punishing crime, and not for the making of criminals, deserves the severest condemnation." In support for its new rule, the Court found that "the weight of authority in the lower federal courts is decidedly in favor of . . . the defense of entrapment [being] available." To set limitations on its use, the Court held that "[t]he defense is available, not in the view that the accused though guilty may go free, but that the government cannot be permitted to contend that he is guilty of a crime where the government officials are the instigators of his conduct." At the same time, the defendant's intent must be investigated to determine the applicability of the defense, for "if the defendant seeks acquittal by reason of entrapment he cannot complain of an appropriate and searching inquiry into his own conduct and predisposition as bearing upon that issue."

(Roberts, concurrence.) "There is common agreement that where a law officer envisages a crime, plans it, and activates its commission by one not theretofore intending its perpetration, for the sole purpose of obtaining a victim through indictment, conviction and sentence, the consummation of so revolting a plan ought not to be permitted by any self-respecting tribunal. . . . The enforcement of this policy calls upon the court [as opposed to the jury], in every instance where alleged entrapment of a defendant is brought to its notice, to ascertain the facts, to appraise their effect upon the administration of justice, and to make such order with respect to the further prosecution of the cause as the circumstances require." The Court's opinion weighs the intent of the accused against that of the government agents. Instead, "[t]he applicable principle is that courts must be closed to the trial of a crime instigated by the government's own agents. No other issue, no comparison of equities as between the guilty official and the guilty defendant, has any place in the enforcement of this overruling principle of public policy."

Hampton v. United States
425 U.S. 484 (1976)

The defendant was convicted of distributing heroin. He invited a DEA informant to produce buyers, who turned out to be undercover officers. The defendant argued that, while his disposition might normally exclude him from an entrapment defense, his case fit the potential exception noted in *Russell*, in which the officers' conduct was "so outrageous . . . [as to] bar the government from . . . obtain[ing] a conviction." However, the Court rejected his argument and found that the defendant's case differed from *Russell* only in degree, and that "in each case the Government agents were acting in concert with the defendant, and in each case either the jury found or the defendant conceded that he was predisposed to commit the crime for which he was convicted. The Court reaffirmed that the defendant's predisposition to commit the crime "rendered this defense unavailable to him."

(Brennan, dissent.) The court should "refuse to convict an entrapped defendant, not because his conduct falls outside the proscription of the statute, but because, even if his guilt be admitted, the methods employed on behalf of the Government to bring about conviction cannot be countenanced." Instead, the court has adopted a "subjective" approach to the defense of entrapment that focuses on the "conduct and propensities of the particular defendant in each case and, in the absence of a conclusive showing, permits the jury to determine as a question of fact the defendant's "predisposition" to the crime. This jury determination produces an improper weighing of the defendant's intent against that of the government agent, when the propensities and predisposition of a specific defendant should not be at issue. Therefore, if the police conduct "falls below standards, to which common feelings respond, for the proper use of governmental power," the determination of the "lawfulness of the Government's conduct must be made — as it is on all questions involving the legality of law enforcement methods — by the trial judge, not the jury."

Model Penal Code
(Official Draft 1962)

Section 2.13. Entrapment

(1) A public law enforcement official or a person acting in cooperation with such an official perpetrates an entrapment if for the purpose of obtaining evidence of the commission of an offense, he induces or encourages another person to engage in conduct constituting such offense by either:

> (a) making knowingly false representations designed to induce the belief that such conduct is not prohibited; or

> (b) employing methods of persuasion or inducement which create a substantial risk that such an offense will be committed by persons other than those who are ready to commit it.

(2) Except as provided in Subsection (3) of this Section, a person prosecuted for an offense shall be acquitted if he proves by a preponderance of evidence that his conduct occurred in response to an entrapment. The issue of entrapment shall be tried by the Court in the absence of the jury.

(3) The defense afforded by this Section is unavailable when causing or threatening bodily injury is an element of the offense charged and the prosecution is based on conduct causing or threatening such injury to a person other than the person perpetrating the entrapment.

● OVERVIEW OF ENTRAPMENT

Variations in Formulation   Where a police officer or agent has some hand in having an actor commit an offense, the actor may be entitled to an entrapment defense. The United States is one of the few countries in the world that recognizes such a defense and, within the United States, jurisdictions disagree over how the defense should be formulated. The two most common forms of the defense are called the "objective" (police misconduct) formulation and the "subjective" (predisposition) formulation. The apparent terms of the disagreement concern how much the defense should focus on the impropriety of the *police conduct* and how much it should focus on the *defendant's predisposition* to commit the offense. Which of these two should be the focus of the defense may depend on what it is that we seek to achieve in recognizing an entrapment defense. Whether the criminal law should recognize any form of entrapment defense is the subject of the Discussion Materials below.

Objective Formulation   "Objective" formulations of the entrapment defense focus on the impropriety of the police conduct. Model Penal Code section 2.13, for example, defines entrapping conduct as conduct that "creates a substantial risk that such an offense will be committed by persons other than those who are ready to commit it."[1] There is no requirement that the defendant actually be a person "other than those ready to commit it." Indeed, it does not even require that the defendant be "induced" by the police conduct. The Code requires only that the defendant's offense be "in response to" the police conduct.[2] Thus, even if an actor were uninfluenced by the entrapping police conduct, he would have a defense under the Model Penal Code if the police conduct were judged to be improper inducement under the standard quoted above.

Subjective Formulation   "Subjective" formulations of the entrapment defense focus on the degree to which the entrapping conduct, rather than the actor's own choice, is responsible for commission of the offense. The Delaware statute, for example, permits an entrapment defense only if the defendant is "induced" to commit an offense that he (the defendant) "is not otherwise disposed" to commit.[3] Under this formulation, the defense is given "because the wrongdoing of the officer originates the idea of the crime and then induces the other person to [commit the offense] when the other person is not otherwise disposed to do so."

Evidence of Predisposition   Under a subjective formulation, the primary focus is the defendant's "predisposition" to commit the offense. Evidence of predisposition is not necessarily limited to the defendant's conduct *prior* to the entrapping conduct. In *Harrison v. State*, for example, the defendant, a prison guard, agrees to smuggle marijuana to a prisoner who is acting as an agent for the

---

1. Model Penal Code § 2.13(1)(b). An officer also entraps if he "[makes] knowingly false representations designed to induce the belief that such conduct is not prohibited." Id. at § 2.13(1)(a).
2. Model Penal Code § 2.13(2).
3. Del. Code Ann. tit. 11, § 432.

police.[1] The defendant is denied an entrapment defense, although it is clear that she had never smuggled drugs into prison before and would not have done so on this occasion but for the inducement of the police agent. The court explains that highly relevant evidence of the defendant's predisposition to commit the offense may come from how the defendant responds to the police inducement. In *Harrison,* the defendant took an active role in planning the smuggling once she was approached, then failed to take any of several opportunities to withdraw, and committed two offenses a month apart. In contrast, in *Jacobson v. United States,* the defendant ordered two *Bare Boys* magazines from a bookstore at a time when it was lawful to do so.[2] Subsequent federal legislation made it illegal to receive through the mails sexually explicit depictions of children. Federal agents acting through several fictitious organizations, finding defendant's name on the bookstore mailing list, tried to induce defendant to order more illegal magazines. After being on the government's mailing lists for a period of two and one-half years, and after receiving correspondence decrying censorship and calling for lobbying to prevent it, defendant was sent a catalogue from which he ordered a magazine. He was arrested on its delivery. A search of his home revealed no other relevant materials other than the original *Bare Boys* magazine and the subsequent material sent to him by the government. The Supreme Court reversed the conviction, finding that on this evidence a reasonable jury could not have found beyond a reasonable doubt that the defendant was predisposed to commit the offense.

Federal Position   Competition between the objective and the subjective formulations can be seen in the United States Supreme Court cases formulating the federal entrapment defense. (There is no federal entrapment statute.) In *Sorrells v. United States,* the Supreme Court adopted the subjective view that the entrapment defense is intended to prevent conviction of "otherwise innocent" individuals who have been lured into the commission of a crime that they had no predisposition to commit.[3] It has been noted that the opinion "left no doubt that the gravamen of the defense of entrapment was not the propriety of the conduct of the government agents but rather the subjective guilt of the defendant, that is, his predisposition to commit the offense."[4] A long line of cases have upheld this characterization of the defense. On the other hand, an equally long line of concurrences and dissents, beginning with the concurrence of Justice Roberts in *Sorrells,* have opposed this view. Justice Roberts argued that the basis of the entrapment defense is a public policy requirement that the integrity of the judicial process ought not be sullied by the use of improper police conduct to procure convictions. Under this rationale, the defendant's predisposition is immaterial; the only relevant question is the degree to which the police have overstepped the bounds of appropriate behavior.

"Due Process" Defense   Authority exists for a "due process" defense independent of the entrapment defense. Based as it is on constitutional grounds, it preempts whatever statutory formulation of the entrapment defense a state's

---

1. 442 A.2d 1377, 1379-1380 (Del. 1982).
2. 112 S. Ct. 1535 (1992).
3. 287 U.S. 435, 442, 53 S. Ct. 210, 212-213, 77 L. Ed. 413, 417 (1932).
4. S. Rep. No. 95-605, Part I, 95th Cong., 1st Sess. 111 (1977) (federal).

legislature may have adopted. It will most often have effect in jurisdictions that adopt the subjective formulation of entrapment, because it is this formulation that bars the defense for improper police conduct if the defendant is predisposed, no matter how shocking the police conduct may be. The "due process" defense is given because — echoing the arguments of the *Sorrells* dissent and the *Hampton* concurrence — it would compromise the dignity of the courts and violate the defendant's right to due process to allow such police conduct to support a conviction. The test for such a "due process" defense is not whether the police conduct induced this defendant or might have induced an innocent person, as all but the most objective formulations of the entrapment defense require. Rather, the defense is given if the conduct offends "the canons of fundamental fairness, shocking to the universal sense of justice." With a "due process" defense clearly available, there may be less need for the objective formulations of the entrapment defense; many of the cases given a defense under the objective formulation that are not given a defense under the subjective formulation are cases that may be given a "due process" defense.

Entrapment as Nonexculpatory vs. Excuse An objective formulation of the entrapment defense, as well as the "due process" defense, are clearly nonexculpatory defenses; they use the threat of acquittal of the defendant as a means of deterring improper police conduct. The blameworthiness of the defendant is not relevant. A subjective (predisposition) formulation might appear, in contrast, to be an excuse, similar to duress, that exculpates the defendant because he is coerced to commit an offense. More careful analysis, however, suggests that such a characterization is unfounded. The subjective formulation of the entrapment defense does not satisfy the traditional requirements for an excuse. The "induced" requirement in entrapment is analogous to the coercion requirement in duress but, as you will recall, a duress defense is not given simply because an actor was subject to coercion, just as an insanity defense is not given simply because the actor has some mental illness. An excuse requires that the disability be sufficiently strong in its effects that one could not reasonably have expected the actor to have avoided the violation.

Inducement vs. Duress In the context of a duress excuse, a defense is permitted only if the coercion was such that "a person of reasonable firmness would have been unable to resist." Nothing in the entrapment defense, even in the subjective formulation, ensures that the defense will be given only if such an overwhelming degree of coercion is present. The subjective formulation at most requires a showing that the actor would not have committed the offense *but for* the officer's inducement. But, as the laws of insanity and involuntary intoxication teach, a but-for causal connection between a disability and the offense is not enough to render the actor blameless. Any ambiguity as to the true nature of the entrapment defense should have disappeared with the rejection of *Durham*'s "product test." (Recall this discussion in the context of the insanity defense in Section 22 and the disability excuses in Section 23.)

Inducement by Private Citizen If the subjective formulation represented a true excuse based on the pressure brought to bear on the defendant, there would be no reason to limit the defense to cases of inducement by government agents. If a private citizen induced the offense through entrapment, and such inducement was sufficient to render the defendant blameless, then private entrapment logically would be recognized as a defense. Private entrapment, however, generally is not a defense. In *United States v. Perl*,[1] for example, defendant Dr. Perl was induced by a private citizen to commit minor acts of terrorism to help the plight of Soviet Jews. After the inducement, the private citizen turned Dr. Perl in to the police. The court denied an entrapment defense. It reasoned that Dr. Perl may well have been induced to commit the offense, but forgoing his conviction would do nothing toward deterring improper police conduct. One must conclude that the subjective formulation of entrapment, like the objective formulation, operates as a nonexculpatory defense, albeit one that lets off fewer offenders. By excluding predisposed offenders from the defense, it allows conviction of the more dangerous offenders, but continues somewhat to deter improper police conduct.

Offenses Excluded from Defense   The nonexculpatory public policies underlying the entrapment defense also manifest themselves in the defense's specific exclusion of certain serious offenses. The Model Penal Code, for example, makes its entrapment defense "unavailable" for offenses in which "causing or threatening bodily injury is an element."[2] A true excuse would have no such exclusion of classes of offenses. The duress defense, for example, remains available for offenses that cause or threaten bodily injury. But, in attempting to deter improper police conduct, it is reasonable for a jurisdiction to conclude that acquitting violent offenders is too high a price to pay for the deterrence of overreaching police entrapment.

Mixed Rationales   To summarize, some reduced blameworthiness may be present where an actor is induced to commit an offense, at least where the actor is not otherwise predisposed to do so. But such inducement alone, without a showing that the actor could not reasonably have been expected to avoid the violation, is insufficient to justify an excuse. Nor does the reduced blameworthiness from inducement explain why only police officers or agents can trigger the defense. In reality, the primary reasons for the defense are nonexculpatory interests of deterrence and estoppel: deterrence of improper police inducement and avoiding the apparent unfairness of allowing the government to induce an offense and then prosecute it. Given the nonexculpatory status of an entrapment defense, it seems most appropriate that the judge determine the defense before trial, rather than a jury at trial, as is sometimes done. Certainly a "not guilty" verdict for entrapment is misleading to the extent that it suggests that the defendant has engaged in no wrongdoing or is blameless for doing so.

---

1. 584 F.2d 1316 (4th Cir. 1978).
2. Model Penal Code § 2.13(3).

   It will not seem generally unfair to punish someone who has caused or threatened bodily injury to another, even though he was induced to his action by law enforcement officials. It is unlikely that a law-abiding person could be persuaded by any tactics to engage in such behavior, and a person who can be persuaded to cause such injury presents a danger that the public cannot safely disregard.

Model Penal Code § 2.13 comment at 420 (1985).

▲ PROBLEM
JJ's Out

JJ has a string of arrests and convictions for various drug offenses. Recently out of prison, he is anxious to get back into the drug business because the money is so good. He decides to work for another dealer while he reestablishes his connections. Garrett, an undercover narcotics agent, hears about JJ and works out a plan to catch him dealing. He approaches JJ and after some preliminary conversation and asks him if he wants a job. JJ replies, "Sounds good, but I don't even know you. How do I know you're not a cop?" Garrett assures JJ that he is not a cop and invites him to a party the following evening. For the party, Garrett hires JJ's ex-girlfriend, a prostitute, who left JJ after his last arrest. Garrett hopes that the party and the ex-girlfriend will remind JJ of the "good life" and that he will then be willing to take the risk of working with Garrett. On instructions from Garrett, JJ's ex-girlfriend has intercourse with JJ and tells him that if he starts working for Garrett, they can get back together again. At the end of the night, JJ agrees to work for Garrett.

Garrett arranges for JJ to deliver eight ounces of cocaine the following day. At the delivery point, JJ is arrested by drug enforcement officers. He is charged with possession of cocaine with intent to distribute. He offers an entrapment defense. Will he get it?

● DISCUSSION MATERIALS
Should the Criminal Law Recognize an Entrapment Defense?

The Model Penal Code Commentary at the start of these materials provides the rationale for recognizing an objective formulation of the entrapment defense and reviews how the defense is formulated in various jurisdictions. In contrast, Louis Seidman offers a methodical counter-argument to each justification offered for the defense and calls into question the logic and necessity of the doctrine in the American criminal law system. Last, Andrew Ashworth reviews a British proposal favoring the creation of an entrapment *offense*, comparing this with alternative methods of controlling undesirable law enforcement conduct — such as exclusion of evidence, mitigation of sentence, and an entrapment defense — and explaining why each of these were rejected by the Royal Commission.

Model Penal Code Section 2.13 Commentary
Official Draft and Revised Comments 406-408, 411-415 (1985)

Rationale for Defense. The defense of entrapment presents a fundamental policy choice of difficult dimensions. On the one hand, the defendant whose crime results from an entrapment is neither less reprehensible or dangerous, nor more reformable or deterrable, than other defendants who are properly convicted. Defendants who are aided, solicited, deceived or persuaded by police officials stand in the same moral position as those who are aided, solicited, deceived or persuaded by other persons; yet no one suggests a general defense for the latter. Thus, there is substantial reason to record convictions and take normal correctional measures in cases of defendants whose crimes are included by the police.

On the other hand, the harm done by increasing the risk of offending on the part of the innocent is great. Some persons will thus turn to crime and risk the pain of punishment in response to the call of law enforcement. Moreover, when officers are engaged in persuading citizens to commit criminal acts, they are absent from their proper task of apprehending those offenders who act without such encouragement. Such tactics spread suspicion in the community and can easily be employed as the expression of personal malice on the part of a police officer. Perhaps most important of all, however, is the injury to the reputation of law enforcement institutions that follows the employment of methods shocking to the moral standards of the community.

It is therefore the attempt to deter wrongful conduct on the part of the government that provides the justification for the defense of entrapment, not the innocence of the defendant. The extraordinary measure of freeing a defendant to deter the police is taken for several reasons. No other effective remedy to discourage the police is available as a practical matter; the ordinary civil or criminal sanctions are inadequate to prevent overreaching in the use of police instigation, persuasion or deceit.... Furthermore, the chief aims of the criminal law are to prevent people from engaging in socially harmful conduct and to instruct them in the basic requirements of good citizenship. It is consistent with these purposes to recognize a defense based upon those unsavory police methods that have the effect of fostering criminality.

This section is therefore concerned with those cases in which a crime has been committed but its commission has been induced by overzealous law enforcement. In such situations, the defense of entrapment has been almost universally recognized in the United States, though statements denying that it is recognized have occasionally been made. The defense has commonly been the product of judicial decision rather than statute....

The Code's Standard. The original draft of the Code's entrapment defense presented alternatives designed to conform to ... two positions.... The formulation that was adopted represents an objective standard.... The main criterion for evaluating the propriety of police methods is, therefore, the likely effect of such methods on law-abiding persons, and the propensities of the particular defendant are irrelevant.

Subsection (1)(a) makes the defense applicable whenever the government agents have knowingly made false representations designed to induce the belief that defendant's conduct was not prohibited. (This defense is supplemental to whatever defense may be available under Section 2.04.) The subsection represents a judgment both that this kind of police conduct is not appropriate, and that it is generally likely to induce persons to commit crimes when they would not otherwise do so. Thus, no evaluation of this kind of technique is required in particular cases.

The Institute was persuaded to adopt the "objective" approach of Subsection (1)(b) in preference to the "subjective" approach of *Sorrells* and *Sherman* for a number of reasons. First, if the defense is available only to those who are "innocent," its full deterrent effect is undermined. Police conduct toward a particular defendant may be seriously objectionable even though he entertained a purpose to commit crime prior to any inducement by officials. Law enforcement officers may feel free to employ forbidden methods if the "innocent" are to be freed but the habitual offenders, in whom they have greater interest, will nevertheless be punished.

Second, the very notion that certain police conduct may be improper in relation to the "innocent" (nonpredisposed), but acceptable when addressed to the "guilty" (predisposed), seems incompatible with the ideal of equality before the law.... Furthermore, to permit the use against a previously convicted person of police measures not permitted against the rest of society is to fix a permanent status of criminality on these persons against the hopes of enlightened penology.

Finally, the practical effect of the subjective approach is to lose sight in litigation of the main issue that should be before the court. The primary justification for the defense, as noted above, is to discourage unsavory police tactics; the defendant is just as guilty, with or without the entrapment. Yet as the defense has been actually litigated in many cases using the majority position of *Sorrells* and *Sherman*, investigation into the character of the defendant has often obscured the important task of judging the quality of the police behavior. The emphasis of courtroom inquiry is thus turned from the character of police conduct to the history of the accused and his immediate reaction to the enticement.

Those in the Institute who supported the alternative subjective approach did so mainly on two grounds. In their judgment, the greatest vice in entrapment cases inheres in police behavior that leads the previously innocent to crime. It is therefore a sensible judgment to limit the defense to that situation. Moreover, defendants who are predisposed to commit crime are largely the professionals, who constitute the greatest crime problem. Freeing them in order to discipline the police was thought too great a price. When officers deal with the criminally disposed, they may find it necessary to employ methods that would be quite out of place if directed to the "innocent." Thus, it was believed, they should be entitled to do.

Developments Since Promulgation of the Code

... Some jurisdictions have followed the Model Code in making entrapment a matter of statutory formulation, but others have left the matter to judicial decision. The recently enacted and proposed codes that deal with entrapment are about equally divided between those that adopt the subjective approach of *Sorrells* and *Sherman* and those that follow the Model Code's objective approach and designated as the crucial consideration whether the police methods used would be likely to induce law-abiding persons to engage in criminal activity. A few also indicate specifically that the defense may be successfully invoked whenever government agents knowingly falsely represent that illegal behavior is lawful. In states where the law of entrapment is still governed exclusively by judicial decision, the courts remain divided between the subjective and objective approaches.

Louis Michael Seidman, The Supreme Court, Entrapment, and Our Criminal Justice Dilemma

5 The Supreme Court Review 111, 127-133, 135-137, 139-142, 145-146 (1981)

Rationales for the Entrapment Defense

I have argued that the entrapment defense serves to shield defendants from punishment when their crimes are induced by government agents and when their general character, life-style, or nature is not "criminal." What remains to be considered are the reasons why we have such a doctrine....

... Sometimes, the Justices suggest that the defense is necessary because the entrapped defendant is in some sense "innocent" and unworthy of punishment. At other times, the Court suggests that the defense is unrelated to the defendant's guilt, but is instead necessary either to deter the police from engaging in objectionable behavior or to preserve the integrity of the courts. In fact, as others have demonstrated, the version of the defense actually fashioned by the Court is supported by neither of these arguments. It can hardly be maintained that entrapment doctrine is necessary to vindicate the innocent, so long as we continue to treat as guilty nondisposed defendants induced to commit crime by private, rather than by governmental, temptors. Because governmental conduct is a necessary predicate for the defense, it might therefore be thought that we allow a defendant to raise it in order to deter such conduct. But the defense is also inconsistent with this goal, since its success is unrelated to the wrongfulness of the government's actions.

Entrapment doctrine thus represents neither a consistent judgment as to the culpability of entrapped defendants nor an effective strategy for deterring unwanted police behavior. Although this simple observation has dominated academic discussion of the defense, the point should not be overstated. If that were all there were to the matter, entrapment would be no different from a score of other uneasy compromises in the law. The fact that such a compromise is not fully justified by any of the competing theories motivating it should neither surprise nor puzzle us.

But that is far from all there is to the matter. What should surprise and puzzle us is that each of these competing theories is itself incoherent. Moreover, while some anomalies result from the way the Court has defined predisposition and the special version of the entrapment defense it has thereby created, the problems are mostly intrinsic to the defense and cannot be remedied however it is reformulated.

A. The Culpability Theory

... [I]f a nondisposed defendant induced to commit a crime by another is "innocent," he should not be punished. But why should such a defendant be viewed as innocent? Ordinarily, one would expect to look to the statutory definition of a particular crime to discover the boundaries between guilt and innocence. Perhaps in response to this expectation, the Supreme Court has always treated the entrapment defense as somehow implicit in federal statutory law. But it is painfully obvious that the statutory basis for the defense is wholly fictional. An entrapped defendant has, by definition, committed an act made criminal by positive law, and he has done so with the requisite state of mind. One looks in vain through the United States Code for any indication that Congress meant to condition culpability on the defendant's predisposition, however that term is defined. Indeed, Congress has consistently declined to codify any of the versions of the entrapment defense presented to it.

It is, of course, true that the criminal law has traditionally recognized a series of defenses to what would otherwise be criminal acts, and that not all of these have been codified. In general, such defenses fall into two categories: claims such as duress, necessity, and self-defense, relating to external pressures brought to bear on the defendant; and claims such as insanity, infancy, and mistake, relating to the defendant's internal thought processes. Regardless of the categorization, each defense proceeds from the premise that a defendant should not be blamed for an act when he has done what we want him to do under the circumstances, in which case we say that he is justified, or when he lacked meaningful freedom to act differently, in which case we say that he is excused.

Superficially, the entrapment defense might be thought quite consistent with these firmly established limits on culpability. Indeed, the doctrine seems to fit comfortably in both the external and internal categories: it looks, on the one hand, to external pressure which in some sense explains or mitigates the defendant's conduct, and, on the other, to the defendant's innocent state of mind prior to committing the offense. Upon closer analysis, however, entrapment doctrine is consistent with neither type of defense.

1. External Pressure. The Court has occasionally suggested that we have an entrapment defense to prevent the punishment of a person whose conduct is the product of external forces. When the defendant is not predisposed, the argument goes, the government inducement in effect creates a crime in order to punish it. In the words of Justice Hughes, it is improper for the government "to punish [a person otherwise innocent] for an alleged offense which is the product of the creative activity of its own officials."

It is true, of course, that when a government agent entraps a defendant, the agent may cause a crime to be committed in the "but for" sense. Depending on the facts, it may be unwise on policy grounds for the government to pursue this course. But it is far from clear why this type of government causation should be thought to bear on culpability. As noted above, entrapment doctrine presently requires the acquittal of a nondisposed defendant regardless of the attractiveness of the inducement. Thus, the doctrine exculpates a defendant who succumbs to a temptation that a person of reasonable moral fortitude would easily spurn. It is hard to imagine a culpability principle which requires the acquittal of such a defendant....

2. Internal Behavior Controls. If one could show that nondisposed defendants were somehow congenitally less capable of resisting criminal offers, this might be a basis for exculpating them, since it would be unfair to hold such defendants to a standard devised for those better equipped to resist pressure. The Supreme Court's repeated references to victims of entrapment as "innocent" might be read as endorsing such a view.

But this defense of entrapment doctrine...founders on the Court's definition of "predisposition." There is no reason to suppose that a person lacking a criminal disposition or character is less able to control his behavior and, therefore, is less culpable. Indeed, from a culpability perspective, the predisposition requirement is perverse. An individual with an ordinary, "upstanding" life-style has presumably been thoroughly socialized to resist deviant behavior. The very reason we are surprised when such an individual commits a crime is because we "expect more" of him than of a person leading a dissolute life.

The argument cannot be salvaged by redefining "predisposed" to focus on the danger posed by the defendant. There is no culpability reason to acquit a defendant simply because he responded to an inducement unlikely to be replicated and therefore posed little danger. The culpability question is not *whether* the defendant is likely to commit a crime, but *why* he is likely to commit it. A defendant likely to respond to a small inducement may be disposed toward crime precisely because of a weakness in his behavior controls which reduces his culpability. Conversely, a defendant responding to only very large inducements may be able to resist smaller ones because of behavior controls which make him fully responsible for his conduct.

B. The Government Deterrence Theory

The inability to formulate a convincing argument that an entrapped defendant should be considered "innocent" strongly suggests that the defense does not in fact exist for his protection. If entrapment doctrine results in the release of culpable defendants, this must be because this cost is thought worth bearing to mold government conduct in desirable ways. . . .

[T]his view of entrapment is not easy to square with the actual defense, because the ability of the prosecution to convict the defendant does not depend on the wrongfulness *vel non** of its conduct. But even if the defense were reformulated so as to meet this objection, its proponents would still have the burden of demonstrating why the government conduct should be deemed wrongful.

Several arguments can be quickly dismissed. First, it might be asserted that the offering of inducements by government agents is undesirable because such conduct creates the risk that innocent people will be corrupted. But this argument obviously depends upon the characterization of those responding to the inducements as innocent — a characterization which is untenable. . . .

A more troubling argument against pursuit of an entrapment strategy is that it stimulates antisocial conduct that would not otherwise occur and, therefore, serves no legitimate end. . . .

The observation that entrapment creates crime hardly ends the analysis, however. It is also true that we would have no prison breaks if we tore down penitentiaries, and that assaults on policemen would decline dramatically if officers were kept off the streets. Obviously, the question is not whether a particular law enforcement strategy creates crime, but whether it creates more crime than it prevents. The question is hard with respect to entrapment, because, while the strategy unquestionably creates crime, it may also be an effective tool for stopping it.

Entrapment may reduce crime in two ways. First, it serves as a means of identifying and incapacitating dangerous individuals likely to commit crime in the future if not apprehended. Indeed, in the case of "victimless" crime, where the technique is most often utilized, entrapment may be the only effective means of apprehending law violators. . . .

---

* Editor's Note — "or not."

Second, even if the entrapped defendant is not dangerous, his incarceration may nonetheless reduce crime by deterring others. Potential criminals who know that police are utilizing an entrapment policy will realize that there is greater risk that they will be apprehended and so will be less tempted to commit crime. Put in concrete terms, the few well-publicized cases of Arab sheikhs who turned out to be F.B.I. agents are likely to make members of Congress think twice before accepting a bribe.

Unfortunately, these observations leave us with an uncomfortable sense of indeterminacy as to the utility of the entrapment strategy. About all that can be said is that the strategy creates some crime, stops other crime, and that it is hard to generalize about which effect is predominant. To be sure, there may be certain forms of entrapment that are likely to be inefficient. For example, when government agents engage in very harmful conduct to detect very minor offenses, the strategy is difficult to defend. Most of us would agree that narcotics agents should not commit murders to preserve their cover when investigating marijuana offenses. This observation explains the dicta, now supported by a majority of the Court, establishing due process limits on the extent to which government agents can engage in antisocial conduct in order to fight crime. . . . But the existence of these constitutional limits does not explain the need for an additional entrapment defense in situations where government agents have not imposed severe social costs. . . .

There is . . . one distinction between an entrapment strategy and other uses of law enforcement resources. Entrapment might be thought especially dangerous, because it places in the hands of the executive power to make criminals. If the government can offer inducements that no one would refuse, it can pick and choose the persons who will obey the law. The risk that this power might be used to punish disfavored groups is obvious.

I suspect that this fear of the government's power to create criminals provides the ultimate answer to the entrapment puzzle. It is not an obvious answer, however. It will not do to claim that entrapment is necessary to prevent the executive from engaging in selective application of the criminal sanction, because within broad limits, we tolerate precisely this risk when the universe of potential criminals consists solely of persons acting without government inducement. When the government chooses which shoplifters, pickpockets, and drug users to prosecute and to jail, we regularly rely upon political checks to guard against abuse. Why do these checks become suddenly inadequate when the class of potential criminals is broader?

Other Discussion Materials

Andrew J. Ashworth, Defences of General Application: The Law Commission's Report No. 83: (3) Entrapment
[1978] Criminal Law Review 137-138

In this section of their Report the Law Commission might have been expected to examine the arguments for and against a defence of entrapment. Instead, they focus on the different issue of *controlling* undesirable practices in law enforcement, and conclude by proposing the creation of a new offence of entrapping someone into committing a crime. Thus the Law Commission begin by setting themselves the question, "can entrapment be controlled satisfactorily at the trial stage?" and they discuss the exclusionary discretion, the defence of entrapment and mitigation of sentence in terms of their effectiveness in controlling objectionable practices. The judicial discretion to exclude unfairly obtained evidence is regarded as neither effective (since the discretionary element might lead to uncertainty and inconsistency) nor appropriate (the Law Commission argue that there is a distinction between unfairness in obtaining evidence of a crime which has already been committed and unfairness in contributing to the actual commission of a crime, and that the exclusionary discretion properly applies only to the former). Mitigation of sentence is likewise dismissed as "no sufficient disincentive to the continuance of objectionable practices," and is inappropriate since it does not strike at the errant trapper. The Commission also doubt whether a defence of entrapment could be an effective control on undesirable practices, since it would succeed only rarely, and they add that the drafting of a satisfactory defence would present great difficulty.

Having concluded that entrapment cannot be satisfactorily controlled at the trial stage, the Commission go on to consider and to dismiss administrative control by regulations and disciplinary proceedings for breach, and the prosecution of trappers as secondary parties to the crimes they incite. They argue that the most appropriate method of control might be a special offence of entrapment, with proceedings instituted only with the consent of the Director of Public Prosecutions. The provision should "in essence make it an offence to take the initiative in inciting or persuading someone into committing or attempting to commit a crime even though it was intended that the completion of the offence should be prevented or that its effect should be nullified." The definition of such an offence would depend on the types of practice agreed to be undesirable, and the Law Commission propose to hold further consultations on the matter....

...We have noted the Commission's argument that a defence would be ineffective in preventing entrapment, but general defences are usually justified in terms of the defendant's culpability or "responsibility." Only one paragraph of the report is addressed to the question whether entrapment may so affect an accused's culpability as to justify a complete defence to criminal liability, and the Commission's negative conclusion is supported by three reasons: (i) entrapment does not affect either the *actus reus* or the *mens rea* of the crime committed; (ii) defendants are sometimes induced by "fellow criminals" to commit crimes, and the fact that the inducement comes from an *agent provocateur* "corresponds with no moral distinction in [the defendant's] behaviour"; and (iii) where there is an element of entrapment, its effect on culpability can adequately be taken into account by the court when sentencing.*

---

* Editor's Note—Subsequent to this article, the United Kingdom enacted two important pieces of legislation: the Police and Criminal Evidence Act 1984 and the Human Rights Act 1998. In *Regina v. Looseley*, the House of Lords reviewed the doctrine of entrapment, relying in large part on these statutes. Lord Nicholls concluded, "although entrapment is not a substantive defense, English law has now developed remedies in respect to entrapment: the court may stay the relevant criminal proceedings [where needed to insure a defendant the right to a fair trial embodied in Article 6 of the Human Rights Act], and the court may exclude evidence pursuant to section 78 [of the Police and Criminal Evidence Act, which authorizes exclusion when "the admission of the evidence would have such an adverse effect on the fairness of the proceedings that the court ought not to admit it"].... Of these two remedies the grant of a stay, rather than the exclusion of evidence at the trial, should normally be regarded as the appropriate response in a case of entrapment." [2002] 1 Cr. App. R. 29.

PART VII

CHANGING PATTERNS OF CRIMINALITY

The interaction between the criminal law and social norms is complex. Changing social norms have brought waves of criminal law reform to many areas, including redefining sexual assault, increasing the severity of domestic violence offenses, decriminalizing same-sex intercourse, and aggravating hate-motivated crimes. The law-norms interaction can work in the other way as well, with criminal law helping to bring about changes in social norms. Indeed, it is probably rare that the two do not simultaneously stimulate one another in mutual support. Where the criminal law gets too far ahead of norms, it tends to be undercut, as happened with Prohibition. Where norms get too far ahead of criminal law, the law loses credibility, as being out of date and out of step.

But this interdependence creates a peculiar paradox: Law can most effectively change social norms if it has earned a reputation for moral authority with the community, but such moral authority is likely only if the law does not stray too far from existing norms. The result of this dynamic may be two important limitations on law: It can be an effective partner in changing norms but cannot do it alone, and it cannot go too far ahead of existing norms too fast. It is as if the law must earn its moral credibility before it can spend it, which counsels both conscientious efforts to build moral credibility and thoughtfulness in decisions to spend it.

The dynamic is apparent in the two areas of reform that are the subject of the following Sections. Sexual offense reforms, the subject of Section 25, reflect changing norms but also an attempt to change norms further. They are calculated to make people think differently about what is and is not acceptable conduct. Hate crimes, the subject of Section 26, similarly reflect both an increased sensitivity to the dangers of bigotry and an attempt to create a still greater public awareness of those dangers.

SECTION 25

Rape

◆ THE CASE OF ERIC STEVEN CARLSON

It is January 2000, in Grand Haven, Michigan, a small community on the edge of Lake Michigan. Eric Carlson is an eleventh-grader who is about to turn seventeen years old. He has asked one of the girls in his class, "Jane," who is seventeen, if she wants to go for a ride with him. Although they have attended the same school for two years, Carlson only knows her through their mutual friend, Amy, whom he dated a few times several months ago.

Jane considers Carlson an acquaintance and is familiar with him only through Amy. Jane also knows that Amy was upset after she last went out with Carlson. Amy says he would not take "no" for an answer and raped her. Jane nonetheless agrees to go out with him.

Carlson picks her up in the afternoon and they drive to the parking lot of Meijer's—a large grocery store. They sit for awhile in the front bucket seats talking and writing notes to each other. Things eventually escalate sexually and they begin kissing and groping one another; consensually, he digitally penetrates her and she manually masturbates him. She describes it later as they "made out and stuff."

On January 23, about two weeks later, Carlson calls her "to hang out" again. She agrees and he picks her up; she is wearing jeans and a long-sleeve shirt. They drive around a little before ending up in the YMCA parking lot. They quickly resume the activities as before, kissing and "stuff"; Jane allows Carlson to unbutton her jeans and to digitally penetrate her. Carlson then tells her that he wants to have intercourse. She says no. He asks her why not, and she says that she does not want to. (She has had sex before, in her last relationship, in August.)

Figure 123 **Lot where Carlson and Jane parked.**

Figure 124 **Grand Haven High School**

Now completely undressed, they continue groping one another. Carlson continues asking if she wants to have sex; he even asks to just stick his penis in once. She eventually tires of his asking and just stops answering. He leans over her, but she does not react. He then climbs on top of her and "penetrates her." He asks whether she is enjoying it; she again tells him that she does not want to "do it," but he continues anyway. She is unsure how to react, but she does not resist physically or push him away. After about five minutes, he stops and they put their clothes on. They stop at a gas station when she asks for a drink. Although she is not interested in talking, there is some forced conversation. He asks if she wants to go home and she replies, "I don't care." He then asks whether she still wants to go out with him. She does not respond.

The next day, she writes Carlson a note, sometimes addressing him in the note by his nickname, "Beeker," and sometimes as "sweetie," as she does with most people. Handing it to him personally, the note explains that she does not want a relationship and asks whether this will make him mad. She also writes that he owes her a note in response.

The same day she tells Amy what happened. Amy says that it was rape, and again alleges that Carlson raped her. When Jane remembers that Carlson was not wearing a condom, she becomes worried about being pregnant or having contracted a sexually transmitted disease.

She subsequently talks to the school counselor about the incident, who has her report it to the Ottawa County Sheriff's Department. Deputy Sarah Flick interviews Jane and three other students who claim that Carlson also sexually assaulted them. On February 9, Flick interviews Carlson. With his attorney, Philip Sielski, present, Carlson voluntarily surrenders himself to the authorities on March 10.

1. Relying only on your own intuitions of justice, what liability and punishment, if any, does Eric Carlson deserve, based on the incident with Jane?

N	0	1	2	3	4	5	6	7	8	9	10	11
☐	☐	☐	☐	☐	☐	☐	☐	☐	☐	☐	☐	☐
no liability	liability but no punishment	1 day	2 wks	2 mo	6 mo	1 yr	3 yrs	7 yrs	15 yrs	30 yrs	life imprison-ment	death

2. What liability, if any, under the then-existing statutes?
3. What liability, if any, under the Model Penal Code?

■ **THE LAW**

Michigan Statutes Annotated
(2000)

Title 28. Crimes

Part Two. Substantive Criminal Law
Chapter 286a. Penal Code
Chapter LXXVI. Criminal Sexual Conduct

Section 520a. Definitions

As used in sections 520a to 520-I:

(a) "Actor" means a person accused of criminal sexual conduct. . . .

(c) "Intimate parts" includes the primary genital area, groin, inner thigh, buttock, or breast of a human being. . . .

(i) "Physically helpless" means that a person is unconscious, asleep, or for any other reason is physically unable to communicate unwillingness to an act.

(j) "Personal injury" means bodily injury, disfigurement, mental anguish, chronic pain, pregnancy, disease, or loss or impairment of a sexual or reproductive organ.

(k) "Sexual contact" includes the intentional touching of the victim's or actor's intimate parts or the intentional touching of the clothing covering the immediate area of the victim's or actor's intimate parts, if that intentional touching can reasonably be construed as being for the purpose of sexual arousal or gratification.

(l) "Sexual penetration" means sexual intercourse, cunnilingus, fellatio, anal intercourse, or any other intrusion, however slight, of any part of a person's body or of any object into the genital or anal openings of another person's body, but emission of semen is not required.

(m) "Victim" means the person alleging to have been subjected to criminal sexual conduct.

Section 520b. Criminal Sexual Conduct in First Degree

(1) A person is guilty of criminal sexual conduct in the first degree if he or she engages in sexual penetration with another person and if any of the following circumstances exists:

(a) That other person is under 13 years of age.

(b) That other person is at least 13 but less than 16 years of age and any of the following:

(i) The actor is a member of the same household as the victim.

(ii) The actor is related to the victim by blood or affinity to the fourth degree.

(iii) The actor is in a position of authority over the victim and used this authority to coerce the victim to submit.

(c) Sexual penetration occurs under circumstances involving the commission of any other felony.

(d) The actor is aided or abetted by 1 or more other persons and either of the following circumstances exists:

(i) The actor knows or has reason to know that the victim is mentally incapable, mentally incapacitated, or physically helpless.

(ii) The actor uses force or coercion to accomplish the sexual penetration. Force or coercion includes but is not limited to any of the circumstances listed in subdivision (f)(i) to (v).

(e) The actor is armed with a weapon or any article used or fashioned in a manner to lead the victim to reasonably believe it to be a weapon.

(f) The actor causes personal injury to the victim and force or coercion is used to accomplish sexual penetration. Force or coercion includes but is not limited to any of the following circumstances:

(i) When the actor overcomes the victim through the actual application of physical force or physical violence.

(ii) When the actor coerces the victim to submit by threatening to use force or violence on the victim, and the victim believes that the actor has the present ability to execute these threats.

(iii) When the actor coerces the victim to submit by threatening to retaliate in the future against the victim, or any other person, and the victim believes that the actor has the ability to execute this threat. As used in this subdivision, "to retaliate" includes threats of physical punishment, kidnapping, or extortion.

(iv) When the actor engages in the medical treatment or examination of the victim in a manner or for purposes which are medically recognized as unethical or unacceptable.

(v) When the actor, through concealment or by the element of surprise, is able to overcome the victim.

(g) The actor causes personal injury to the victim, and the actor knows or has reason to know that the victim is mentally incapable, mentally incapacitated, or physically helpless.

(h) That other person is mentally incapable, mentally disabled, mentally incapacitated, or physically helpless, and any of the following:

(i) The actor is related to the victim by blood or affinity to the fourth degree.

(ii) The actor is in a position of authority over the victim and used this authority to coerce the victim to submit.

(2) Criminal sexual conduct in the first degree is a felony punishable by imprisonment in the state prison for life or for any term of years.

Section 520c. Criminal Sexual Conduct in Second Degree

(1) A person is guilty of criminal sexual conduct in the second degree if the person engages in sexual contact with another person and if any of the following circumstances exists:

(a) That other person is under 13 years of age.

(b) That other person is at least 13 but less than 16 years of age and any of the following:

(i) The actor is a member of the same household as the victim.

(ii) The actor is related by blood or affinity to the fourth degree to the victim.

(iii) The actor is in a position of authority over the victim and the actor used this authority to coerce the victim to submit.

(c) Sexual contact occurs under circumstances involving the commission of any other felony.

(d) The actor is aided or abetted by 1 or more other persons and either of the following circumstances exists:

(i) The actor knows or has reason to know that the victim is mentally incapable, mentally incapacitated, or physically helpless.

(ii) The actor uses force or coercion to accomplish the sexual contact. Force or coercion includes but is not limited to any of the circumstances listed in sections 520b(1)(f)(i) to (v).

(e) The actor is armed with a weapon, or any article used or fashioned in a manner to lead a person to reasonably believe it to be a weapon.

(f) The actor causes personal injury to the victim and force or coercion is used to accomplish the sexual contact. Force or coercion includes but is not limited to any of the circumstances listed in section 520b(1)(f)(i) to (v).

(g) The actor causes personal injury to the victim and the actor knows or has reason to know that the victim is mentally incapable, mentally incapacitated, or physically helpless.

(h) That other person is mentally incapable, mentally disabled, mentally incapacitated, or physically helpless, and any of the following:

(i) The actor is related to the victim by blood or affinity to the fourth degree.

(ii) The actor is in a position of authority over the victim and used this authority to coerce the victim to submit.

(2) Criminal sexual conduct in the second degree is a felony punishable by imprisonment for not more than 15 years.

Section 520d. Criminal Sexual Conduct in the Third Degree; Felony

(1) A person is guilty of criminal sexual conduct in the third degree if the person engages in sexual penetration with another person and if any of the following circumstances exist:

(a) That other person is at least 13 years of age and under 16 years of age.

(b) Force or coercion is used to accomplish the sexual penetration. Force or coercion includes but is not limited to any of the circumstances listed in section 520b(1)(f)(i) to (v).

(c) The actor knows or has reason to know that the victim is mentally incapable, mentally incapacitated, or physically helpless.

(d) That other person is related to the actor by blood or affinity to the third degree and the sexual penetration occurs under circumstances not otherwise prohibited by this chapter. It is an affirmative defense to a prosecution under this subdivision that the other person was in a position of authority over the defendant and used this authority to coerce the defendant to violate this subdivision. The defendant has the burden of proving this defense by a preponderance of the evidence. This subdivision does not apply if both persons are lawfully married to each other at the time of the alleged violation.

(2) Criminal sexual conduct in the third degree is a felony punishable by imprisonment for not more than 15 years.

Section 520e. Criminal Sexual Conduct in the Fourth Degree; Misdemeanor

(1) A person is guilty of criminal sexual conduct in the fourth degree if he or she engages in sexual contact with another person and if any of the following circumstances exist:

(a) That other person is at least 13 years of age and under 16 years of age, and the actor is 5 or more years older than that other person.

(b) Force or coercion is used to accomplish the sexual contact. Force or coercion includes but is not limited to any of the following circumstances:

(i) When the actor overcomes the victim through the actual application of physical force or physical violence.

(ii) When the actor coerces the victim to submit by threatening to use force or violence on the victim, and the victim believes that the actor has the present ability to execute these threats.

(iii) When the actor coerces the victim to submit by threatening to retaliate in the future against the victim, or any other person, and the victim believes that the actor has the ability to execute this threat. As used in this subdivision, "to retaliate" includes threats of physical punishment, kidnapping, or extortion.

(iv) When the actor engages in the medical treatment or examination of the victim in a manner or for purposes which are medically recognized as unethical or unacceptable.

(v) When the actor achieves the sexual contact through concealment or by the element of surprise.

(c) The actor knows or has reason to know that the victim is mentally incapable, mentally incapacitated, or physically helpless.

(d) That other person is under the jurisdiction of the department of corrections and the actor is an employee or a contractual employee of, or a volunteer with, the department of corrections who knows that the other person is under the jurisdiction of the department of corrections.

(e) That other person is a prisoner or probationer under the jurisdiction of a county for purposes of imprisonment or a work program or other probationary program and the actor is an employee or a contractual employee of or a volunteer with the county who knows that the other person is under the county's jurisdiction.

(f) The actor knows or has reason to know that the juvenile division of the probate court, the circuit court, or the recorder's court of the city of Detroit has detained the victim in a facility while the victim is awaiting a trial or hearing, or committed the victim to a facility as a result of the victim having been found responsible for committing an act that would be a crime if committed by an adult, and the actor is an employee or contractual employee of, or a volunteer with, the facility in which the victim is detained or to which the victim was committed.

(g) That other person is related to the actor by blood or affinity to the third degree and the sexual contact occurs under circumstances not otherwise prohibited by this chapter. It is an affirmative defense to a prosecution under this subdivision that the other person was in a position of authority over the defendant and used this authority to coerce the defendant to violate this subdivision. The defendant has the burden of proving this defense by a preponderance of the evidence. This subdivision does not apply if both persons are lawfully married to each other at the time of the alleged violation.

(2) Criminal sexual conduct in the fourth degree is a misdemeanor punishable by imprisonment for not more than 2 years or a fine of not more than $500.00, or both.

Section 520i. Resistance by Victim

A victim need not resist the actor in prosecution under sections 520b to 520g.

Section 520j. Admissibility of Evidence

(1) Evidence of specific instances of the victim's sexual conduct, opinion evidence of the victim's sexual conduct, and reputation evidence of the victim's sexual conduct shall not be admitted under sections 520b to 520g unless and only to the extent that the judge finds that the following proposed evidence is material to a fact at issue in the case and that its inflammatory or prejudicial nature does not outweigh its probative value:

(a) Evidence of the victim's past sexual conduct with the actor.

(b) Evidence of specific instances of sexual activity showing the source or origin of semen, pregnancy, or disease.

Section 750.81. Assault and Assault and Battery; Domestic Assault

(1) Except as otherwise provided in this section, a person who assaults or assaults and batters an individual, if no other punishment is prescribed by law, is guilty of a misdemeanor punishable by imprisonment for not more than 93 days or a fine of not more than $500.00, or both.

(2) Except as provided in subsection (3) or (4), an individual who assaults or assaults and batters his or her spouse or former spouse, an individual with whom he or she has or has had a dating relationship, an individual with whom he or she has had a child in common, or a resident or former resident of his or her household, is guilty of a misdemeanor punishable by imprisonment for not more than 93 days or a fine of not more than $500.00, or both.

(3) An individual who commits an assault or an assault and battery in violation of subsection (2), and who has previously been convicted of assaulting or assaulting and battering his or her spouse or former spouse, an individual with whom he or she has or has had a dating relationship, an individual with whom he or she has had a child in common, or a resident or former resident of his or her household, under any of the following, may be punished by imprisonment for not more than 1 year or a fine of not more than $1,000.00, or both:

(a) This section or an ordinance of a political subdivision of this state substantially corresponding to this section.

(b) Section 81a, 82, 83, 84, or 86.

(c) A law of another state or an ordinance of a political subdivision of another state substantially corresponding to this section or section 81a, 82, 83, 84, or 86.

(4) An individual who commits an assault or an assault and battery in violation of subsection (2), and who has 2 or more previous convictions for assaulting or assaulting and battering his or her spouse or former spouse, an individual with whom he or she has or has had a dating relationship, an individual with whom he or she has had a child in common, or a resident or former resident of his or her household, under any of the following, is guilty of a felony punishable by imprisonment for not more than 2 years or a fine of not more than $2,500.00, or both:

(a) This section or an ordinance of a political subdivision of this state substantially corresponding to this section.

(b) Section 81a, 82, 83, 84, or 86.

(c) A law of another state or an ordinance of a political subdivision of another state substantially corresponding to this section or section 81a, 82, 83, 84, or 86.

(5) This section does not apply to an individual using necessary reasonable physical force in compliance with section 1312 of the revised school code, 1976 PA 451, MCL 380.1312.

(6) As used in this section, "dating relationship" means frequent, intimate associations primarily characterized by the expectation of affectional involvement. This term does not include a casual relationship or an ordinary fraternization between 2 individuals in a business or social context.

Section 750.87. Assault with Intent to Commit Felony Not Otherwise Punished

Any person who shall assault another, with intent to commit any burglary, or any other felony, the punishment of which assault is not otherwise in this act prescribed, shall be guilty of a felony, punishable by imprisonment in the state prison not more than 10 years, or by fine of not more than 5,000 dollars.

Section 750.520g. Assault with Intent to Commit Criminal Sexual Conduct

(1) Assault with intent to commit criminal sexual conduct involving sexual penetration shall be a felony punishable by imprisonment for not more than 10 years.

(2) Assault with intent to commit criminal sexual conduct in the second degree is a felony punishable by imprisonment for not more than 5 years. . . .

People v. Premo
540 N.W.2d 715 (Mich. Ct. App. 1995)

The defendant was charged with three counts of fourth degree criminal sexual conduct and moved to quash the information. The district court denied the motion and the appeals court affirmed. Defendant contended that pinching the victims' buttocks, the alleged unlawful sexual conduct, is insufficient to satisfy the requirement that force or coercion be used to accomplish the sexual contact. The court held that "Defendant's pinching of the victims' buttocks satisfies the force element of the statute because the act of pinching requires the actual application of physical force. The definition of the term 'force' includes, among other things, 'strength or power exerted upon an object.' We believe that the act of pinching is an act of physical force because it requires a person to exert strength or power on another person" (Quoting *The Random House College Dictionary: Revised Edition*). Alternatively, the court found the acts to be by coercion because the defendant was the teacher and the victims were his students.

People v. Berlin
507 N.W.2d 816 (Mich. Ct. App. 1993)

Defendant gynecologist was charged with fourth-degree criminal sexual conduct when, after examining a patient, he took her hand and placed it on his crotch over his clothes. She quickly removed her hand. The patient testified that the defendant "took her hand and placed it on his crotch. She stated that he did not grab it or pull it and that he did not hurt her. She also testified that he did not resist at all when she pulled her hand away and that he did not threaten her." Given the ordinary meaning of the words "force or coercion," and the legislature's exclusion of the concealment or surprise provision from the fourth-degree criminal sexual conduct statute, the Court of Appeals held that the force or coercion required for such an offense was absent.

People v. Jansson
323 N.W.2d 508 (Mich. Ct. App. 1982)

The defendant was convicted of third-degree criminal sexual conduct. On appeal, he asserted that, "because there was no indication in the record that the complainant advised or communicated to the defendant that she did not wish to engage in sexual intercourse, the defendant did not know that the sexual relations were nonconsensual and, therefore, could not have intended to engage in those relations by force or coercion. Without some manifestation of the complainant's unwillingness to engage in sexual relations . . . [the] defendant could not have known of her nonconsent and, therefore, may . . . have assumed that signs of physical resistance by the complainant were . . . 'the final token manifestations of modesty.'" The court held that "[a]lthough consent . . . precludes conviction of criminal sexual conduct in the third degree by force or coercion, the prosecution is not required to prove nonconsent as an independent element of the offense. If the prosecution offers evidence to establish that an act of sexual penetration was accomplished by force or coercion, that evidence necessarily tends to establish that the act was nonconsensual."

People v. Hale
370 N.W.2d 382 (Mich. Ct. App. 1985)

The defendant was convicted of third-degree criminal sexual conduct. He appealed his conviction based on the instruction regarding consent that was given to the jury. The jury was instructed: "If the evidence does not convince you beyond a reasonable doubt that the sexual acts complained of were not consented to, then the defendant is not guilty of the crime." The defendant claimed that "the instruction was inadequate because it predicated criminal responsibility on the victim's subjective consent rather than on defendant's reasonable belief that the victim consented." He argued that the court should have instructed the jury that "if a defendant entertains a reasonable and bona fide belief that a prosecutrix voluntarily consented to engage in sexual intercourse, the jury should find the defendant not guilty. The appeals court rejected this standard for consent, noting that "no

Michigan case law requires the trial court to define consent in terms of a defendant's reasonable and honest belief."

People v. Lardie & Hudick
452 Mich. 231, 239, 551 N.W.2d 656, 660 (1996)

"In order to determine whether a statute imposes strict liability or requires proof of a mens rea, that is, a guilty mind, this Court first examines the statute itself and seeks to determine the Legislature's intent. In interpreting a statute in which the Legislature has not expressly included language indicating that fault is a necessary element of a crime, this Court must focus on whether the Legislature nevertheless intended to require some fault as a predicate to finding guilt. . . .

"Criminal intent is ordinarily an element of a crime even where the crime is created by statute. Statutes that create strict liability for all of their elements are not favored. Nevertheless, a state may decide under its police power that certain acts or omissions are to be punished irrespective of the actor's intent. Many of the crimes that impose strict liability have been termed 'public welfare regulation.' Chief Justice Thomas Cooley succinctly described the general rule that a criminal statute requires a mens rea:

> I agree that as a rule there can be no crime without a criminal intent; but this is not by any means a universal rule. One may be guilty of the high crime of manslaughter when his only fault is gross negligence; and there are many other cases where mere neglect may be highly criminal. Many statutes which are in the nature of police regulations . . . impose criminal penalties irrespective of any intent to violate them; the purpose being to require a degree of diligence for the protection of the public which shall render violation impossible."

Model Penal Code
(Official Draft 1962)

Section 213.1. Rape and Related Offenses

(1) Rape. A male who has sexual intercourse with a female not his wife is guilty of rape if:

(a) he compels her to submit by force or by threat of imminent death, serious bodily injury, extreme pain or kidnapping, to be inflicted on anyone; or

(b) he has substantially impaired her power to appraise or control her conduct by administering or employing without her knowledge drugs, intoxicants or other means for the purpose of preventing resistance; or

(c) the female is unconscious; or

(d) the female is less than 10 years old. Rape is a felony of the second degree unless (i) in the course thereof the actor inflicts serious bodily injury upon anyone, or (ii) the victim was not a voluntary social companion of the actor upon the occasion of the crime and had not previously permitted him sexual liberties, in which cases the offense is a felony of the first degree.

(2) Gross Sexual Imposition. A male who has sexual intercourse with a female not his wife commits a felony of the third degree if:

(a) he compels her to submit by any threat that would prevent resistance by a woman of ordinary resolution; or

(b) he knows that she suffers from a mental disease or defect which renders her incapable of appraising the nature of her conduct; or

(c) he knows that she is unaware that a sexual act is being committed upon her or that she submits because she mistakenly supposes that he is her husband.

Section 213.2. Deviate Sexual Intercourse by Force or Imposition

(1) By Force or Its Equivalent. A person who engages in deviate sexual intercourse with another person, or who causes another to engage in deviate sexual intercourse, commits a felony of the second degree if:

(a) he compels the other person to participate by force or by threat of imminent death, serious bodily injury, extreme pain or kidnapping, to be inflicted on anyone; or

(b) he has substantially impaired the other person's power to appraise or control his conduct, by administering or employing without the knowledge of the other person drugs, intoxicants or other means for the purpose of preventing resistance; or

(c) the other person is unconscious; or

(d) the other person is less than 10 years old.

(2) By Other Imposition. A person who engages in deviate sexual intercourse with another person, or who causes another to engage in deviate sexual intercourse, commits a felony of the third degree if:

(a) he compels the other person to participate by any threat that would prevent resistance by a person of ordinary resolution; or

(b) he knows that the other person suffers from a mental disease or defect which renders him incapable of appraising the nature of his conduct; or

(c) he knows that the other person submits because he is unaware that a sexual act is being committed upon him.

Section 213.4. Sexual Assault

A person who has sexual contact with another not his spouse, or causes such other to have sexual contact with him, is guilty of sexual assault, a misdemeanor, if:

(1) he knows that the contact is offensive to the other person; or

(2) he knows that the other person suffers from a mental disease or defect which renders him or her incapable of appraising the nature of his or her conduct; or

(3) he knows that the other person is unaware that a sexual act is being committed; or

(4) the other person is less than 10 years old; or

(5) he has substantially impaired the other person's power to appraise or control his or her conduct, by administering or employing without the other's knowledge drugs, intoxicants or other means for the purpose of preventing resistance; or

(6) the other person is less than [16] years old and the actor is at least [4] years older than the other person; or

(7) the other person is less than 21 years old and the actor is his guardian or otherwise responsible for general supervision of his welfare; or

(8) the other person is in custody of law or detained in a hospital or other institution and the actor has supervisory or disciplinary authority over him. Sexual contact is any touching of the sexual or other intimate parts of the person for the purpose of arousing or gratifying sexual desire.

Section 213.6. Provisions Generally Applicable to Article 213

(1) Mistake as to Age. Whenever in this Article the criminality of conduct depends on a child's being below the age of 10, it is no defense that the actor did not know the child's age, or reasonably believed the child to be older than 10. When criminality depends on the child's being below a critical age other than 10, it is a defense for the actor to prove by a preponderance of the evidence that he reasonably believed the child to be above the critical age.

(2) Spouse Relationships. Whenever in this Article the definition of an offense excludes conduct with a spouse, the exclusion shall be deemed to extend to persons living as man and wife, regardless of the legal status of their relationship. The exclusion shall be inoperative as respects spouses living apart under a decree of judicial separation. Where the definition of an offense excludes conduct with a spouse or conduct by a woman, this shall not preclude conviction of a spouse or woman as accomplice in a sexual act which he or she causes another person, not within the exclusion, to perform.

(3) Sexually Promiscuous Complainants. It is a defense to prosecution under Section 213.3 and paragraphs (6), (7) and (8) of Section 213.4 for the actor to prove by a preponderance of the evidence that the alleged victim had, prior to the time of the offense charged, engaged promiscuously in sexual relations with others.

(4) Prompt Complaint. No prosecution may be instituted or maintained under this Article unless the alleged offense was brought to the notice of public authority within [3] months of its occurrence or, where the alleged victim was less than [16] years old or otherwise incompetent to make complaint, within [3] months after a parent, guardian or other competent person specially interested in the victim learns of the offense.

(5) Testimony of Complainants. No person shall be convicted of any felony under this Article upon the uncorroborated testimony of the alleged victim. Corroboration may be circumstantial. In any prosecution before a jury for an offense under this Article, the jury shall be instructed to evaluate the testimony of a victim or complaining witness with special care in view of the emotional involvement of the witness and the difficulty of determining the truth with respect to alleged sexual activities carried out in private.

Section 213.0 Definitions

In this Article, unless a different meaning plainly is required:
(1) the definitions given in Section 210.0 apply;
(2) "Sexual intercourse" includes intercourse per os or per anum, with some penetration however slight; emission is not required;
(3) "Deviate sexual intercourse" means sexual intercourse per os or per anum between human beings who are not husband and wife, and any form of sexual intercourse with an animal.

Section 211.1. Assault

(1) Simple Assault. A person is guilty of assault if he:
(a) attempts to cause or purposely, knowingly or recklessly causes bodily injury to another; or
(b) negligently causes bodily injury to another with a deadly weapon; or
(c) attempts by physical menace to put another in fear of imminent serious bodily injury. Simple assault is a misdemeanor unless committed in a fight or scuffle entered into by mutual consent, in which case it is a petty misdemeanor.

(2) Aggravated Assault. A person is guilty of aggravated assault if he:
(a) attempts to cause serious bodily injury to another, or causes such injury purposely, knowingly or recklessly under circumstances manifesting extreme indifference to the value of human life; or
(b) attempts to cause or purposely or knowingly causes bodily injury to another with a deadly weapon. Aggravated assault under paragraph (a) is a felony of the second degree; aggravated assault under paragraph (b) is a felony of the third degree.

Section 2.11. Consent

(1) In General. The consent of the victim to conduct charged to constitute an offense or to the result thereof is a defense if such consent negatives an element of the offense or precludes the infliction of the harm or evil sought to be prevented by the law defining the offense.

(2) Consent to Bodily Injury. When conduct is charged to constitute an offense because it causes or threatens bodily injury, consent to such conduct or to the infliction of such injury is a defense if:
(a) the bodily injury consented to or threatened by the conduct consented to is not serious; or
(b) the conduct and the injury are reasonably foreseeable hazards of joint participation in a lawful athletic contest or competitive sport or other concerted activity not forbidden by law; or
(c) the consent establishes a justification for the conduct under Article 3 of the Code.

(3) Ineffective Consent. Unless otherwise provided by the Code or by the law defining the offense, assent does not constitute consent if:

(a) it is given by a person who is legally incompetent to authorize the conduct charged to constitute the offense; or

(b) it is given by a person who by reason of youth, mental disease or defect or intoxication is manifestly unable or known by the actor to be unable to make a reasonable judgment as to the nature or harmfulness of the conduct charged to constitute the offense; or

(c) it is given by a person whose improvident consent is sought to be prevented by the law defining the offense; or

(d) it is induced by force, duress or deception of a kind sought to be prevented by the law defining the offense.

● OVERVIEW OF RAPE

Every jurisdiction recognizes rape as a criminal offense, but the contours of the law are far from settled. In part, this state of flux is due to society's changing understanding of the nature of the crime. In the following overview, Margaret Gordon and Stephanie Riger analyze the frequency of under-reported rapes and the cause for this phenomenon, exploring specifically the prevalence of date rape and campus rape. Wayne LaFave's article traces the traditional approach to rape law and the requirements and attitudes that are reflected therein, providing a look at the issues addressed and action taken in recent reform initiatives.

Margaret T. Gordon & Stephanie Riger, The Female Fear: The Social Cost of Rape
2, 26-28, 32-36 (1991)

Most women experience fear of rape as a nagging, gnawing sense that something awful could happen, an angst that keeps them from doing things they want or need to do, or from doing them at the time or in the way they might otherwise do. Women's fear of rape is a sense that one must always be on guard, vigilant and alert, a feeling that causes a woman to tighten with anxiety if someone is walking too closely behind her, especially at night. . . . It is worse than fear of other crimes because women know they are held responsible for avoiding rape, and should they be victimized, they know they are likely to be blamed. . . .

[I]n 1986 there were 90,434 forcible rapes reported by police across the country to the F.B.I., representing an increase of 3.2 percent over 1985 and a rate of 73 per 100,000 women. . . .

Analyses of how UCR (Uniform Crime Reports) data are gathered and compiled (by the F.B.I.) have indicated errors of omission and commission, most of which lead to the under-representation of the actual rate of rape.... [The authors discuss the shortcomings of UCR data.]

These findings and others gave rise to the National Crime Surveys (also often referred to as the victimization surveys) now regularly conducted in conjunction with the U.S. Census. [R]apes reported to surveyors in 1986 yield a rate of about 140 per 100,000 women... a rate [double] that indicated by the UCR data....

Perhaps the greatest source of error in the reported rate of rape is the non-reported incidents. This "doubly dark" figure of crime, which is reported *neither* to the police *nor* to a victimization survey interviewer, remains elusive. Research indicates that rapes by known assailants are particularly likely to go unreported, resulting in a serious underestimation of the extent of violence against women....

When women living in [three] selected cities were asked in telephone interviews if they had ever been raped *or* sexually assaulted *at some time during their lives,* 2 percent said yes. That is a rate of 2,000 per 100,000, much higher than either yearly UCR or survey rates for these cities. But when women were asked the same question in person, the figures were even more startling. Eleven percent (or 11,000 in 100,000) said they had been raped or sexually assaulted. These rates are surprisingly high and help to underscore the problems with any of the figures now available....

While stranger rapes may constitute people's image of what is typical, acquaintance rapes or nonstranger rapes are an increasingly large proportion of actual rapes and now account for 55 to 60 percent of rapes reported to police....

But the words "nonstranger" or "acquaintance" cover a wide range of types of relationships. [One] type of acquaintance rape is referred to as date rape; this occurs when the victim initially is willing to be in the company of a man who then becomes violent toward her. For several reasons, many of these rapes are not reported.... Although the victim may have resisted and been forced, she herself may not recognize it as rape *because* she was on a date.... Most important, date-rape victims often feel they won't be believed or will be perceived as having "asked for it" — by the police, the courts, and everyone else and, therefore, there is no point in reporting it....

A special form of date rape is being increasingly reported on college campuses. In what may have become a typical campus rape, a young woman is assaulted by a young man she has met (often the same evening) at a party on campus. She may have danced with him, gone for a walk with him, gone to his room, or allowed him to walk her to her room. Many campus rapes seem to involve the use of excessive amounts of alcohol by one or both persons involved. One victim of campus rape blamed herself because she was drunk. When a faculty member reminded her that it is a crime to rape, but not a crime to get drunk, the coed decided to file charges. Experts in this field say, "Clearly, among college students sexual aggression is rare among strangers and common among acquaintances"....

[R]esearchers argue that campus rape may be so prevalent because of norms in our society that condone sexual violence. People are conditioned to accept sexual roles in which male aggression is an acceptable part of our modern courtship culture. According to this line of reasoning, campus rapists are ordinary males operating in an ordinary social context, not even knowing they are doing something wrong, let alone against the law.

Wayne R. LaFave, Rape — Overview; Act and Mental State
§ 7.18 Substantive Criminal Law 752-756 (3d ed. 2000)

This section concerns the controversial subject of rape, defined at common law as "the carnal knowledge of a woman forcibly and against her will." This definition suggests that a proper parsing of the crime of rape would be into (i) a specified act , i.e., "carnal knowledge," (ii) brought about by a specified means of imposition, i.e., "forcibly," and (iii) in circumstances where the woman had a particular state of mind concerning the perpetration of that act by those means, i.e., "against her will." But it is a bit more complicated than that. For one thing, there is the question of whether the *defendant's* state of mind, not specifically addressed in that definition, is relevant, considering that some mental state is required for most offenses, especially those this serious....

(a) The Traditional Approach: An Overview.... The traditional approach refers to the approach generally followed prior to the reforms undertaken in relatively recent years, and reflects primarily but not exclusively substantive and procedural principles received in this country as part of the common law. The most noteworthy features of this traditional approach . . . are these: (1) The physical act necessary for rape, usually referred to as "carnal knowledge," was penetration of the female sex organ by the male organ. (2) With rare exception, the necessary manner of commission of this act was "forcibly," which ordinarily required resort to force or threat of force above and beyond that inherent in the penetration. (3) Limited alternatives to force were recognized, namely, resort to fraud so extreme that the woman either did not know she was engaging in intercourse or did not know the intercourse was not with her husband, or to administration of drugs or intoxicants depriving the woman of the ability to resist. (4) The penetration also had to be against the will of the victim, and the need to establish such nonconsent often necessitated proof of the victim's continued physical resistance to the man's advances or a showing of force or threats to such a degree as to make such resistance unavailing. (5) Consent was conclusively presumed when a man engaged in intercourse with his wife. (6) No manifestation or refusal of consent was necessary when the female was under ten years of age and thus deemed incapable of consent as a matter of law, or when she was so incapacitated as to be unable to give consent. (7) The defendant's mental state at the time of the intercourse was generally deemed irrelevant, so that inquiry into whether he mistakenly believed the woman consented and on that basis should be exonerated was typically foreclosed. (8) Absence of a prompt complaint about an alleged rape was admissible as evidence that the later complaint was not genuine. (9) Some jurisdictions required that the victim's testimony be corroborated by other evidence. (10) Prior sexual conduct of the complainant was admissible in a rape prosecution as evidence of consent and to impeach the complainant's credibility. (11) Many jurisdictions used cautionary jury instructions warning that the offense was easily charged but hard to disprove and that consequently the victim's testimony required especially close scrutiny. (12) The crime of rape was at one time punishable by death in about half the states, and by extended prison terms in the others, but the number authorizing capital punishment ultimately dropped to just a few, and later the Supreme Court held such punishment unconstitutional in rape cases.

(b) The Impetus for Reform. One of the most frequently encountered quotations on the subject of rape, indeed, "one of the most oft-quoted passages in our jurisprudence" on any subject, originated with Lord Chief Justice Matthew Hale of England back in the seventeenth century: "rape . . . is an accusation easily to be made and hard to be proved, and harder to be defended by the party accused, tho never so innocent." The longstanding prevalence of that attitude doubtless accounts not only for the narrow and curious fashion in which the crime of rape came to be defined, but also for the array of procedural and evidentiary rules that are both unique to and inimical to rape prosecutions. This concern with false accusations is manifested in a variety of ways, including the usual requirement that force or threat of force must be shown, that nonconsent must ordinarily be manifested by physical resistance, that the victim's testimony must be corroborated, and that the prior sexual conduct of the complainant may be inquired into fully.

In more recent times, many have seen the aforementioned requirements in a quite different light, as a result of which "rape has increasingly become a topic of controversy . . . captur[ing] the public imagination." Those seeking redefinition of the crime of rape and reform of evidentiary and procedural impediments have frequently and vigorously put forward another proposition sharply contradictory to Hale's assertion: "In a rape case it is the victim, not the defendant, who is on trial." Critics of the status quo "argued that this focus on the victim was unique to rape law," and contended that traditional rape law negatively affected both victims of rape and the outcome of rape cases. They charged that the rules of evidence unique to rape caused pervasive skepticism of rape victims' claims and allowed criminal justice officials to use legally irrelevant assessments of the victim's character, behavior, and relationship with the defendant in processing and disposing of rape cases. Critics further suggested that traditional rape law was at least partially responsible for the unwillingness of victims to report rape, as well as low rates of arrest, prosecution, and conviction for rape. They argued, in short, that traditional rape law made it "easy to commit rape and get away with it."

Those pragmatic concerns were the primary motivation of victims' rights and "law and order" groups, while some feminist groups instead saw the consequences of rape law reform as being "largely symbolic and ideological — to educate the public about the seriousness of all forms of sexual assault, to reduce the stigma experienced by victims of rape, and to neutralize rape myth stereotypes."

Certainly one basic concern by many feminists and others seeking law reform in this area was that distinctions drawn in the substantive and procedural law regarding the crime of rape reflected perspectives about the crime that had no contemporary legitimacy. Some of these distinctions, most especially the marital exemption rule, reflected the ancient notion that rape was a property crime and that violation was the property right of the woman's father or husband. Another take on the situation was that many rape doctrines reflected not so much a special hostility toward women by the law, but rather the law's hostility toward those seeking to be excused from criminal liability, which the rape complainant ordinarily was back when rape resided alongside adultery and fornication as criminal offenses. But that, of course, is another circumstance lacking contemporary relevance given the virtual disappearance of the latter offenses from the law. A variety of more modern justifications for the crime of rape were put forward, which explains why it is said that rape "is now viewed simultaneously as a crime of violence, a sex crime, and a privacy offense." It seems fair to say, however, that today the crime of rape is properly classified . . . as a crime against the person, one which hopefully "protects the female's freedom of choice and punishes unwanted and coerced intimacy."

(c) The Modern Approach: An Overview. As a consequence of reforms undertaken in recent years, what might be called the modern approach to the crime of rape looks considerably different from the traditional approach of years past. This is not to suggest that all needed reforms have been accomplished in all jurisdictions, for this is not the case. Nor is it to suggest that in those many states where a full range of reform legislation has been adopted that all of the problems previously identified have been fully solved. In part this is attributable to the fact that the problem has never been entirely "the words of the statutes," but has also involved the general understanding in our society regarding such concepts as "consent," "will" and "force," which doubtless is changing, albeit at a somewhat slower pace.

The modern approach to rape has these features . . . : (1) The newer statutes are often drawn in gender-neutral terms and cover not only genital copulation but also anal and oral copulation and, sometimes, digital and mechanical penetration as well. (2) There is a trend toward recognition of a broader range of impositions as a basis for finding coercive conduct by the defendant, including other types of fraud and also certain nonphysical coercion. (3) The requirements regarding physical resistance manifesting nonconsent have been lessened in some jurisdictions, while elsewhere there is movement toward more ready recognition that verbal resistance (if not absence of affirmative consent) should suffice. (4) The marital exemption has been removed in most states and substantially limited in others. (5) Protection of younger females has been extended by raising the age for so-called "statutory rape," where no showing of nonconsent is necessary. (6) There is somewhat greater recognition that the defendant's mental state is not always irrelevant, and that some mistaken beliefs in consent are a basis for exoneration. (7) The concept of a "prompt" complaint has been considerably broadened, and the fact of such a complaint is now admissible in support of the prosecution's case. (8) Most jurisdictions have abolished any requirement that the victim's testimony be corroborated. (9) So-called rape shield laws have been enacted everywhere and bar admission of the complainant's prior sexual conduct in most instances. (10) Cautionary instructions calling upon the jury to give special scrutiny to the victim's testimony have been largely abandoned. (11) The great majority of states now divide the offense into degrees, taking into account the severity of the injury and the seriousness of the imposition employed.

▲ PROBLEM
Bob and Linda

Steve and Bob, both over six feet tall and powerfully built, are teammates on the football team and good friends. After a game, Steve and Bob's locker-room chatter turns to Linda. Bob and Linda have been dating ever since Linda broke up with Steve. Bob explains how very much he likes Linda. Steve agrees; Linda was great to date and a lot of fun. "Great in bed, isn't she?," Steve asks. Bob looks sheepish and does not respond. Steve laughs. "So you haven't been to bed with her. I'm not surprised. Linda is a real nice girl. I had to push her into it a little the first time but she really loved it and never gave me a rest after that." Bob winces inside. He doesn't like thinking about Steve and Linda together and he isn't the type to push.

Bob is serious about Linda and that night plans to suggest that they move in together. He picks up Linda at her apartment. They have a quick bite to eat, go to a movie, and then to Bob's apartment, where they talk for several hours. Bob tells Linda of his feelings for her and asks whether she would like it if they moved in together next week. Linda says she would like that, and Bob is thrilled. They hug and kiss and Bob begins fondling Linda, who responds by caressing Bob. They both slide to a reclining position on the couch, with Bob on top. Bob begins to unbutton Linda's blouse. "Let's make love," he says. Linda keeps hugging and caressing Bob but whispers in his ear, "That's a nice idea, but I don't know if we should. Why don't we wait until next week?" Bob whispers back, "I love you so much. I just can't wait." He undoes his own pants and takes them off. Linda continues to rub his back from a reclining position as he does so. Bob then pulls Linda's dress up and pulls her underpants down and off. "I'm not sure that this is a good idea, Bob," Linda says. "Let's wait till next week." Bob lies on Linda and has intercourse with her. Linda lies still and does not move. When Bob gets off her, Linda stands up, puts her underpants on, and says in a quiet voice, "I really didn't want to do that now, Bob. Why couldn't you have waited till next week?" Bob is surprised to see that Linda is angry with him. "I'm sorry. I thought you really wanted to." "You thought wrong," says Linda with obvious irritation. "I guess I just got carried away," Bob responds, afraid that he has hurt Linda. "I'm sorry. I promise it won't happen again." "I'm not sure that I want to have to worry about that," Linda responds. "I have to think more about whether we should move in together." She insists that Bob drive her home immediately.

Bob is heartbroken. He is angry with himself for not paying more attention to Linda's feelings and hopes that she will give him another chance to show that he loves her very much and wouldn't intentionally hurt her in any way. He feels worse when Linda stops by the following day to tell him that she has decided not to move in with him. He sees Linda in classes during the next few weeks, but she declines his invitations to go out. Three weeks after their date, police knock at Bob's door and take him into custody. He learns at the police station that Linda has accused him of rape. Is he criminally liable?

⊛ DISCUSSION MATERIALS

Should Rape Liability Be Allowed in the Absence of Force or Threat of Force? Should It Be Allowed Upon Use of Nonphysical Coercion to Gain Acquiescence?

The materials begin with a stirring article by Susan Ager exploring the gray line between rape and defeated submission, and describing some of the traditional reasons why people submit to sex even when they would prefer not. Stephen Schulhofer traces the development of the force requirement, its construction and evidentiary requirement, and the trends that are emerging today in many jurisdictions that relax or eliminate the requirement. David Bryden argues the benefits of the "force and resistance requirement," noting the various functions it performs, its similarity to other criminal law requirements, and the problems with looking only to consent given the unique character of sex as a criminal offense. The Wisconsin statute provides an illustration of such an unconsented-to intercourse offense. Finally, the excerpt from Catharine MacKinnon's campus rally speech puts the case for aggressive criminalization and urges a view of rape based on the victim's sense of violation rather than the aggressor's use of force.

In addition to the materials below, recall the Discussion Materials in Section 5 (Culpability and Mistake) concerning the kind of mistake as to consent, if any, that should be permitted as a defense to rape.

Susan Ager, The Incident
Detroit Free Press Magazine 17 (March 22, 1992)

We were alone beneath the stars, high in the mountains, miles from the nearest light, our sleeping bags unrolled on the ground, weary from a long drive and anticipating sleep. Or so I thought.

We were not lovers, merely acquaintances. We worked together. We respected each other. He owned a few acres in the mountains, and I admired that back-to-the-land streak in anyone. So we agreed to make this weekend camping trip together to his patch of earth.

A few days earlier, oh so briefly, I thought about saying something. Issuing a "don't-get-any-ideas" warning. But I didn't. I thought he'd feel insulted.

He did not worry so much about my feelings.

For hours on that starlit night he pestered me. Stroked me. Whispered to me first, then argues, then whines: "Oh, come on. You'll love it. Why'd you come up here with me then? Just once. It's such a beautiful night. You'll enjoy it, really. Come on. Please?"

I didn't scream, because there was no one to hear. I didn't fight, because there was nowhere to run. It was his car, and he had the keys. Instead, I curled up. I buried my head against my chest while he touched me. I slapped blindly at his touches, as if I were batting away mosquitos.

Because this happened more than a decade ago, I can't remember with precision how long he continued. I wore no watch that night.

All I know is that he went on forever. Unrelenting.

Finally, weary and weepy, I gave up. I remember the sting of my tears rolling down my cheeks and into my ears as I lay on my back and he moaned.

Then, I fell instantly into sleep, as if from the top of a mountain.

Our weekend ended early, because I was sullen and that made him angry. There was nothing to say on the long ride home.

I never called what happened that night "rape." I still don't.

But it wasn't bliss, either.

I wonder why it has no names. Because it happens all the time: Men push. We submit.

No violence, no shouting, no cries of "rape" afterwards. Just sadness and defeat.

How many of us women have watched this sort of thing happen to us, as if we were outside our bodies, in the 30 years since a confluence of factors made sexual interaction easier, at least practically speaking?

That night in the mountains I surrendered for one reason: I was tired and wanted to escape.

But we surrender for reasons besides fatigue.

- Duty: Some women may feel an obligation to reward men who've been particularly kind, or patient, or ardent. Other women may feel an obligation to be a good-and-ready wife.
- Ambiguity: Part of us wants sex, and the other part is wary. And as the train is moving toward the station, so to speak, we're still not sure. We may surrender at the same moment that we conclude, "No, this is stupid." Some men claim not to understand this. But most women know there is a vast geography of shifting sentiment between Yes and No.
- Hope: Sometimes we surrender because our disinterest might turn into delight. A friend calls this the "No-but-I-could-be-convinced" approach. Sometimes it works. Often it doesn't, and we wonder why we gave in.

We make these excuses for our surrenders, but that's no consolation for the vanquished.

Years after that night in the mountains, I'm surprised to find how angry I am about it. Angrier than I was then. At both him and me, and the games people play.

Now, wiser and less polite, I would not whimper but shout! Not for help, but for my own integrity — to let him know how I felt about his boorish presumptions.

I would surrender only if he held me down and forced me to. And then I could call it rape.

Stephen J. Schulhofer, Rape: Legal Aspects
Encyclopedia of Crime and Justice 1306-1309 (2d ed. 2002)

Force and resistance. Under the traditional definition, a rape conviction requires proof that the sexual act was committed "forcibly and against [the victim's] will". Thus, there must be *both* force and lack of consent....

The rationale for requiring proof of force is not self-evident, since many think that intercourse without consent should be an offense whether or not force was used. One rationale for the force requirement is that rape is considered a crime of violence, and penalties are severe. But this explanation implies that nonconsensual intercourse should qualify as a lesser offense, just as it is a crime to take property without consent by force (robbery) or without force (theft). But nonconsensual intercourse without force traditionally was not an offense at all, and this is still true in most states. Legally, force remains essential to distinguish criminal misconduct from permissible behavior.

The need for proof of force is sometimes explained on the ground that consent is too amorphous in sexual matters; it is argued that in the absence of force, genuine nonconsent is difficult to distinguish from "reluctant submission" or even from coy but voluntary participation. Others, however, argue that "reluctant submission" involves a harm the law should not ignore and that consent to sex is no more difficult to determine than consent in other important matters. Most fundamentally, critics of the force requirement argue that the law should protect not only physical safety but also sexual autonomy — the right to choose whether and when to be sexually intimate with another person. That right is denied not only by physical force but also by nonviolent actions that interfere with freely given consent.

These arguments for abolishing the force requirement have begun to make headway. Several states now punish all cases of intercourse without consent and treat force merely as a factor that aggravates the severity of the offense. But this remains a minority view, accepted in less than a dozen states. In most states force remains an essential element of the offense.

As traditionally interpreted, the force requirement could be met only by acts or threats of physical violence. In addition, as a corollary of the force requirement, the prosecution had to prove that the victim resisted. Absent resistance, courts assumed that the victim freely chose to acquiesce. One court, reflecting the view of early-twentieth-century judges, stated, a woman "is equipped to interpose most effective obstacles by means of hands and limbs and pelvic muscles. Indeed, medical writers insist that these obstacles are practically insuperable in the absence of more than the usual relative disproportion of age and strength between man and woman."

Under the traditional resistance standard, courts required that the victim resist "to the utmost." Convictions were therefore difficult to obtain even in cases of extreme abuse. In addition, the resistance rule in effect required the victim to fight her aggressor, even when that response could expose her to great danger.

Beginning in the 1950s courts and legislatures began to relax the resistance requirement, recognizing that resistance should not be required where it would be dangerous or futile. Today, most states still require resistance, but the requirement is less rigid than in the past. Courts require "reasonable" resistance, sometimes described as "resistance of a type reasonably to be expected from a person who genuinely refuses to participate in sexual intercourse" or as "a genuine physical effort to resist as judged by the circumstances."

Many states, taking the next step, have in theory abolished the resistance requirement. In these jurisdictions, however, the prosecution still must prove actual or threatened force. As a result, the resistance requirement often resurfaces in practice, because it is difficult to show that a defendant compelled submission by force, unless there is evidence that the victim physically resisted his advances. Evidence of resistance also remains important because some jurors still believe that a woman who only protests verbally, not physically, is not really unwilling.

With or without a resistance requirement, nearly all states require proof of "force," understood to mean that the defendant compelled submission by physically overpowering the victim or by threatening to inflict bodily injury. Current interpretations of the force requirement are more flexible than in the past. Courts once insisted, in most cases, on proof of extreme brutality or an explicit threat of physical harm. . . . Today, courts are more willing to find implicit threats sufficient. And even without an implicit threat, a complainant's fear can satisfy the force requirement, provided the fear is "reasonably grounded."

But nearly all courts insist that the injury feared must involve bodily harm; coercion by threats to inflict nonphysical injury is generally considered insufficient. In *State v. Thomson,* 792 P.2d 1103 (Mont. 1990), a high school principal allegedly compelled a student to submit to intercourse by threatening to prevent her from graduating. The court held that this threat, though clearly coercive, did not make the principal guilty of rape because he had not threatened any *physical* harm.

A few states have modified the strict rule that force must involve physical violence. The Pennsylvania Supreme Court has held that force includes "[any] superior force — physical, moral, psychological, or intellectual — [used] to compel a person to do a thing against that person's volition." This approach avoids the narrow strictures of the physical force requirement. But as it leaves unclear the line between compulsion and legitimate persuasion, there is concern about its potential vagueness. The Model Penal Code expands the concept of force in a less amorphous manner, permitting a conviction for "gross sexual imposition" when a man compels a woman to submit "by any threat that would prevent resistance by a woman of ordinary resolution" (Model Penal Code § 213.1(2)(a)).

The New Jersey Supreme Court has held that the force requirement can be met by the physical actions intrinsic to intercourse, whenever the complainant does not consent (*In re M.T.S.,* 609 A.2d 1266 (N.J. 1992)). This approach in effect eliminates force altogether and makes nonconsent sufficient to establish the offense. As a matter of statutory interpretation, this outcome is awkward because it equates violent and nonviolent rape for grading purposes and has the effect of imposing a high mandatory minimum sentence for both. Grading problems aside, *M.T.S.* achieves a significant result by criminalizing all intercourse without consent. Several states arrive at a similar outcome, with more tailored grading of penalties, through statutory reforms that require force for the most serious form of rape but create a lesser offense for nonconsensual intercourse without force.

To the extent that the criminal law should protect women and men not only from physical abuse but from all interference with sexual autonomy, this last approach seems best suited to a modern law of rape. Critics of this approach argue that nonviolent interference with autonomy is not sufficiently serious to warrant criminal sanctions, or that there is excessive danger of erroneous results when nonconsent alone is sufficient for conviction. Current law is far from static, with a slow but steady evolution in the direction of relaxing or eliminating the requirement of physical force.

David P. Bryden, Redefining Rape
3 Buffalo Criminal Law Review 317, 373-385 (2000)

Legitimate Functions of the Requirement

The Equal Treatment Function

To the extent that it reflects the average jury's attitude, the FRR [Force and Resistance Requirement] helps to assure equal treatment of similar defendants. If juries usually acquit defendants in a given set of circumstances, a legal rule that requires them to do so at least has the virtue of promoting equal treatment of defendants by controlling aberrant juries, however unwise the rule may be in other respects.

There is overwhelming evidence that, at least until recently, juries have often been highly lenient toward men accused of acquaintance rape, even in cases in which the victim claimed to have resisted strenuously. Although we lack empirical studies of the issue, perhaps juries will only rarely convict without evidence of force, even in jurisdictions that have abolished the FRR. On that admittedly speculative assumption, to allow conviction of a man who did not employ force, as that term has been defined in rape law, might in practice serve only to legitimize discrimination against an occasional unlucky defendant — perhaps a member of a minority group accused of raping a white woman, or someone who "looks like a rapist," or who has an incompetent lawyer, or an atypically pro-feminist jury.

Admittedly, even without the FRR courts would still reverse convictions when they thought that the evidence of nonconsent was too skimpy. But what if the evidence of subjective nonconsent (and mens rea) is legally adequate, yet the appellate court knows that the great majority of juries would have acquitted the defendant?

Even if jurors harbor no improper prejudices, a subjective consent test would be an invitation to inconsistent verdicts. To one jury, the woman's failure to offer physical resistance might be indicative of consent. To another jury, her verbal resistance or equivocation might suffice to demonstrate nonconsent. Whether juries would in fact behave less consistently under a subjective standard is uncertain, but it is at least a danger.

Standing alone, these problems may not be a sufficient justification for the FRR, especially now that evolving public attitudes apparently have reduced jurors' anti-victim biases. But equal treatment is only one of several functions of the FRR.

The Grading Function

In addition to drawing lines between lawful and unlawful conduct, the definitions of crimes determine the maximum penalty for which each convicted criminal is eligible. Although it is now unconstitutional to execute rapists, rape is still one of the most heinous and severely punished offenses. This is partly because it is a crime of violence: No nonviolent crime is punished as severely on average as forcible rape. Assuming that some new types of nonforcible sexual offenses should be established, the maximum penalty for these offenses should be lower than for forcible rape.

If the criminal code contains modern provisions establishing degrees of rape, nonforcible rapists can be convicted of a lesser offense, with a lighter maximum penalty. In defining such a crime, a court or legislature could abolish the FRR without creating a risk of excessive penalties. But in some states there are no degrees of rape. In those states, abolition of the FRR would lump together forcible and nonforcible offenders. Without corresponding changes in the sentencing structure, which of course are beyond the power of a court, this would create the possibility of excessive sentences for the nonforcible rapes. Admittedly, this problem is not novel. Moreover, it is not a reason for permanent retention of the FRR. But it is a reason, in some states, for dealing with the problem by comprehensive legislation, rather than by a premature judicial decision abolishing the FRR.

The Bright Line Function

Citizens need to know, approximately, the boundary between lawful and unlawful conduct. This is especially true of a serious crime like rape. Physical force marks the well-known bright line between seduction and rape. That purpose would be defeated if the only force required by the courts were the "force" that is inherent in intercourse. It would also be defeated by a wholly subjective definition of nonconsent. Courts could say, of course, that the man is guilty if the woman did not consent and he knew it. This would create a bright line of sorts, but the question would remain: When is he supposed to know it? Without an answer to that question, the line between lawful and unlawful behavior would be obscure and subject to the vagaries of aberrant juries.

The Corroborative Function

Another function of the FRR is to corroborate other evidence that the victim did not consent, and that the perpetrator had a culpable mens rea. Of course, we are not speaking here of the notorious "corroboration rule," a discarded evidentiary rule that required corroboration that the putative victim had been raped. Instead, we are dealing with a substantive rule (the FRR) that was shaped, like many rules (substantive as well as evidentiary, criminal as well as civil) by a judicial desire to control juries. If rape were defined simply as nonconsensual intercourse, then the physical act of rape would be indistinguishable from ordinary intercourse; criminality would turn on the parties' subjective states of mind. Interpreted subjectively, the concepts of consent to sex, and of intentional (or reckless) rape, are loaded with ambiguities and factfinding difficulties. Whatever its other vices, the FRR has reduced the danger of erroneous convictions by requiring objective evidence of the victim's nonconsent and the perpetrator's intention to have nonconsensual intercourse. (Whether this benefit has come at too high a price is another question.)

If the rule is to perform this corroborative function, courts must require more force than is customary in consensual sex:

> Rape is the only form of violent criminal assault in which the physical act accomplished by the offender . . . is an act which may, under other circumstances, be desirable to the victim. This unique feature of the offense necessitates the drawing of a line between forcible rape on the one hand and reluctant submission on the other, between true aggression and desired

intimacy. The difficulty of drawing this line is compounded by the fact that there often will be no witness to the event other than the participants and that their perceptions may change over time. The trial may turn as much on an assessment of the motives of the victim as of the actor.

To speak of a need for corroboration is to imply that some rape complainants are untrustworthy. Feminists are understandably suspicious of any such implication. The conventional scholarly wisdom today is that false reports of rape are no more common than for any other crime. But even on that assumption, it is difficult to tell whether, as some allege, the FRR reflects an inordinate and discriminatory suspicion of acquaintance rape accusations. Rules with a corroborative function are common in the criminal law. Some corroborative rules restrict defenses; others require extra proof of guilt. The common thread running through all these corroborative rules is not so much distrust of crime victims as distrust of the abilities of jurors to resolve certain types of issues.

For example, in the law of criminal attempts, some courts are reluctant to uphold convictions without objective evidence that corroborates the defendant's criminal intent.... The Model Penal Code requires that the "substantial step" toward commission of a crime, which is the act element of a criminal attempt, be corroborative of the actor's criminal intention. Without such corroboration, one cannot be convicted of a criminal attempt under the Code, even if there is proof beyond a reasonable doubt both that the defendant had a criminal purpose and that he engaged in seemingly innocent acts that were a substantial step in the execution of that purpose.

The same corroboration problem occurs in cases where the defendant is charged as an accessory in a crime committed by another. Some authorities indicate that knowing assistance to a criminal suffices to establish accessorial liability; others require a "purpose" to assist the principal. Where the alleged accessory is a supplier of goods, courts sometimes resolve the purpose issue by focusing on whether the goods can be used for lawful as well as unlawful purposes. In principle, this inquiry is irrelevant: If his purpose was to assist a crime, the defendant's culpability is not diminished by the fact that the goods have some lawful uses. But the lack of lawful uses for the goods is corroborative evidence that the accused indeed had a criminal purpose....

Another example is the duress defense. Although the precise limits of freedom of the will are unknown, no one claims that effective coercion necessarily requires a threat that would cause a reasonable person to fear physical harm. Yet most courts limit the duress defense to such threats. In part, this limitation reflects a reluctance to excuse crime. But a corroborative rationale is also plausible: The universal fear of bodily injury corroborates the defendant's claim of duress, obviating the need for difficult subjective appraisals.

A similar motivation is at least one of the reasons for judicial rejection of broad definitions of insanity, in favor of narrower tests such as the M'Naghten rule. Ultimately, the rationale of the insanity defense is that the defendant lacked freedom of will, yet in all states the legal standard is at least somewhat narrower than that. In other words, courts do not allow juries to determine the ultimate question directly. In this respect, insanity rules are analogous to the FRR, which also (in effect) prevents juries from directly resolving the consent issue.

As these examples illustrate, corroborative rules are ad hoc efforts to remedy real or imagined weaknesses in the fact-finding process. They exist because judges sometimes do not trust juries to resolve a question that is in principle critical to a defendant's guilt, without the assistance of the corroborative evidence required by the rule. The reasons for this mistrust are speculative and perhaps various. In any event, the point is not that all corroborative rules are wise, but rather that the judicial desire for corroborative evidence is evident in many contexts, not just rape.

To the extent that a rule's justifications are corroborative, principled objections miss the point. Corroborative rules are not dictated by general jurisprudential principles; on the contrary, one sign that a rule's purpose may be corroborative is its inconsistency with, or apparent superfluity in light of, some substantive principle. That is the price of any corroborative rule.

In general, courts trust juries to decide the facts; as exceptions to this practice, all corroborative rules, even when weighed on their own terms, are at best debatable. The same commonsensical arguments that may seem to justify a corroborative rule can be turned against it: Aren't juries able to recognize such obvious realities as the evidentiary value of force? Why tie their hands in the cases, perhaps rare, where force is absent but they are certain beyond a reasonable doubt both that the woman did not consent and that the man knew it? Although this argument is plausible, few legal scholars consistently disapprove of corroborative rules.

Given the role of force in corroborating the man's intentions, the FRR and the mens rea of rape should be evaluated together. If the defendant used considerable force, his claim of a mistake will almost always be implausible. Consequently, in jurisdictions with a FRR it probably makes little practical difference whether courts treat rape as an intentional crime or, at the other extreme, a strict liability crime. But if the FRR is abolished, the physical act of rape will not necessarily differ from ordinary sex; the proper characterization will turn on the parties' intentions. Claims of mistake will be more plausible, and courts may become more receptive to those claims. Intentionally or not, a severe approach toward one element of the crime may beget a lenient approach toward another element.

The Rubicon Function

In legal discourse, one either consents or doesn't consent; equivocation is not a legal category. But consent, as a legal construct, is not synonymous with subjective desire, which is often equivocal. One may desire something in one sense but not in another. For example, one with no physical desire for sex may nevertheless accede to a companion's wishes in order to preserve a relationship, to make a loved one happy, to avoid a scene, or because one is weary of the ordeal of refusal and recrimination. On any given occasion, some combination of these ulterior motives may or may not outweigh one's purely sexual feelings, which of course may also be mixed. Conversely, one's affirmative sexual feelings may be outweighed by negative, ulterior feelings ("he's married," "it's too soon," etc.). Frequently, the affirmative and negative feelings are, for a time, in equipoise, or in flux.

Given the many possible combinations of mixed desires, the law's yes/no answer to the question, "Did she consent to have sex?" is, as a description of subjective desire, grossly simplistic: Yes/no answers do not take account of mixed or half-conscious feelings. No purely subjective approach to consent can solve this problem.

In everyday life, we recognize that "actions speak louder than words." When we act, or fail to act, our shadowy and conflicting feelings coalesce into meaningful intentions. [A man] wants to lose weight, but feels tired at the end of the day. Does he want to exercise? He may think he knows the answer to that question, but on many evenings not even he can be certain until he either steps on the treadmill or goes to bed.

Partly in recognition of this psychological reality, courts have created various behavioral gauges of desire. For example, to make a legally effective gift of personal property, the actor's donative intent does not suffice. Absent a deed of gift, the donor must deliver the property to the donee. As circumstantial evidence of intent, delivery has a corroborative function. But the delivery requirement is also based on a psychological insight: Sometimes, at least, one does not truly know one's intentions until the time comes to cross the Rubicon. Action is the crucible of intention.

In some types of situations, there is not even a scintilla juris* during which the actor has a subjective intention. A batter swings at a low, inside pitch. One can imagine a robotic jurisprudent trying to figure out the batter's intentions. Did he think that the ball was in the strike zone? Or did he realize it was not, but think that he could hit it anyway? Did he apprehend the risk that he had misjudged the pitch? These questions are, of course, ridiculous. As the ball approaches the plate, a batter isn't thinking, at least not in the same sense as one thinks about whether to go to the store; he reacts instinctively. A batter's behavior is not just more important than his subjective intent, and not just easier to ascertain. Sometimes behavior is all there is.

The same is often true of consent to sex. Ambivalence, sudden decisions, and changes of mind are all extremely common. Even at the moment of decision, one's feelings may be conflicted. One sometimes responds impulsively, rather than by forming a conscious intention and then carrying it out. In some cases, even an omniscient factfinder could not describe the woman's subjective state of mind as either "consent" or "nonconsent." Even if the law does not prescribe it, the fact finder must rely on some sort of external standard.

An external standard is also valuable in ascertaining the man's intentions. No doubt some men consciously decide to overpower their unwilling partners; others consciously try to avoid compulsion. But surely there are some acquaintance rapists—perhaps many—whose mental states do not correspond to a simple dichotomy between intentional and unintentional sexual compulsion. They are pursuing their sexual objectives, not (or at least not necessarily) deliberating about the degree to which, or the sense in which, their companions voluntarily consent—indeed, that lack of reflection may be part of the problem. For such men, intention and action are one: When the woman resists, they either overpower her and at that moment become "intentional" rapists, or they desist.

The legitimate functions of the FRR suffice, at least, to distinguish acquaintance rape from other crimes to which consent is a defense. For example, none of the purposes of the FRR would be substantially served by a similar requirement in

---

* Editor's Note—In property law, "a spark of right or interest."

the law of nonsexual assault and battery. (If Jones is beating up Smith, Smith's failure to resist is not suggestive of possible consent.) Likewise, in the classic types of theft cases a FRR would be pointless. The perpetrator usually is either armed (like many stranger rapists), or takes the property by stealth, when the owner is absent or sleeping. The act of theft, unlike the act of intercourse, usually bespeaks criminality; we would laugh if a robber or a burglar said that he thought his victim was consenting. It would be less laughable, but still usually implausible, if a man claimed that his acquaintance had given him his wallet full of cash, identification, and credit cards. In contrast, the mere act of intercourse is as consistent with consensual as with nonconsensual sex. Indeed, since women usually resist unwanted advances, one normally assumes that intercourse is consensual unless the woman is offering at least verbal resistance. In short, the difficulties of drawing a boundary between consensual and nonconsensual events, and of ascertaining whether the defendant deliberately or negligently crossed that boundary, are far greater in the context of sex with an acquaintance than in such fields as transfers of property, stranger rapes, and nonsexual assaults.

Other Discussion Materials

Wisconsin Statutes

Section 940.225. Sexual Assault

(1) First Degree Sexual Assault. Whoever does any of the following is guilty of a Class B felony:

(a) Has sexual contact or sexual intercourse with another person without consent of that person and causes pregnancy or great bodily harm to that person.

(b) Has sexual contact or sexual intercourse with another person without consent of that person by use or threat of use of a dangerous weapon or any article used or fashioned in a manner to lead the victim reasonably to believe it to be a dangerous weapon.

(c) Is aided or abetted by one or more other persons and has sexual contact or sexual intercourse with another person without consent of that person by use or threat of force or violence.

(2) Second Degree Sexual Assault. Whoever does any of the following is guilty of a Class C felony:

(a) Has sexual contact or sexual intercourse with another person without consent of that person by use or threat of force or violence.

(b) Has sexual contact or sexual intercourse with another person without consent of that person and causes injury, illness, disease or impairment of a sexual or reproductive organ, or mental anguish requiring psychiatric care for the victim.

(c) Has sexual contact or sexual intercourse with a person who suffers from a mental illness or deficiency which renders that person temporarily or permanently incapable of appraising the person's conduct, and the defendant knows of such condition.

(cm) Has sexual contact or sexual intercourse with a person who is under the influence of an intoxicant to a degree which renders that person incapable of appraising the person's conduct, and the defendant knows of such condition.

(d) Has sexual contact or sexual intercourse with a person who the defendant knows is unconscious....

(f) Is aided or abetted by one or more other persons and has sexual contact or sexual intercourse with another person without the consent of that person.

(g) Is an employee of a facility or program under § 940.295(2)(b), (c), (h) or (k) and has sexual contact or sexual intercourse with a person who is a patient or resident of the facility or program.

(3) Third Degree Sexual Assault. Whoever has sexual intercourse with a person without the consent of that person is guilty of a Class D felony.* Whoever has sexual contact in the manner described in sub. (5)(b)2 with a person without the consent of that person is guilty of a Class D felony.

(3m) Fourth Degree Sexual Assault. Except as provided in sub. (3), whoever has sexual contact with a person without the consent of that person is guilty of a Class A misdemeanor.

(4) Consent. "Consent", as used in this section, means words or overt actions by a person who is competent to give informed consent indicating a freely given agreement to have sexual intercourse or sexual contact. Consent is not an issue in alleged violations of sub. (2)(c), (cm), (d) and (g). The following persons are presumed incapable of consent but the presumption may be rebutted by competent evidence, subject to the provisions of § 972.11(2):

(a)...

(b) A person suffering from a mental illness or defect which impairs capacity to appraise personal conduct.

(c) A person who is unconscious or for any other reason is physically unable to communicate unwillingness to an act.

(5) Definitions. In this section:

(ag) "Inpatient facility" has the meaning designated in § 51.01(10).

(ai) "Intoxicant" means any controlled substance, controlled substance analog or other drug, any combination of a controlled substance, controlled substance analog or other drug or any combination of an alcohol beverage and a controlled substance, controlled substance analog or other drug. "Intoxicant" does not include any alcohol beverage.

---

* Editor's Note — In *State v. Seeley*, 295 N.W.2d 226 (Table), 97 Wis. 2d 755, 1980 WL 99222 (Wis. App. 1980) (unpublished), in affirming a conviction for third-degree sexual assault, the court, citing *Gates v. State*, 91 Wis. 2d 512, 283 N.W.2d 474 (Ct. App. 1979), rejects the defendant's objection to the following jury instruction:

The second element requires that...[the prosecutrix] did not consent to the sexual intercourse. Consent means words or overt actions by a person indicating a freely given agreement to have sexual intercourse.

If you find beyond a reasonable doubt that the defendant had sexual intercourse with...[the prosecutrix] without consent as consent has been defined for you, then knowledge by the defendant of the lack of consent is not material, and the mistake regarding consent is not a defense.

(am) "Patient" means any person who does any of the following:

1. Receives care or treatment from a facility or program under § 940.295(2)(b), (c), (h) or (k), from an employee of a facility or program or from a person providing services under contract with a facility or program.

2. Arrives at a facility or program under § 940.295(2)(b), (c), (h) or (k) for the purpose of receiving care or treatment from a facility or program under § 940.295(2)(b), (c), (h) or (k), from an employee of a facility or program under § 940.295(2)(b), (c), (h) or (k), or from a person providing services under contract with a facility or program under § 940.295(2)(b), (c), (h) or (k).

(ar) "Resident" means any person who resides in a facility under § 940.295(2)(b), (c), (h) or (k).

(b) "Sexual contact" means any of the following:

1. Intentional touching by the complainant or defendant, either directly or through clothing by the use of any body part or object, of the complainant's or defendant's intimate parts if that intentional touching is either for the purpose of sexually degrading; or for the purpose of sexually humiliating the complainant or sexually arousing or gratifying the defendant or if the touching contains the elements of actual or attempted battery under § 940.19(1).

2. Intentional penile ejaculation of ejaculate or intentional emission of urine or feces by the defendant upon any part of the body clothed or unclothed of the complainant if that ejaculation or emission is either for the purpose of sexually degrading or sexually humiliating the complainant or for the purpose of sexually arousing or gratifying the defendant.

(c) "Sexual intercourse" includes the meaning assigned under § 939.22(36) as well as cunnilingus, fellatio or anal intercourse between persons or any other intrusion, however slight, of any part of a person's body or of any object into the genital or anal opening either by the defendant or upon the defendant's instruction. The emission of semen is not required.

(d) "State treatment facility" has the meaning designated in § 51.01(15).

(6) Marriage Not a Bar to Prosecution. A defendant shall not be presumed to be incapable of violating this section because of marriage to the complainant.

(7) Death of Victim. This section applies whether a victim is dead or alive at the time of the sexual contact or sexual intercourse.

939.22. Words and Phrases Defined

. . .

(48) "Without consent" means no consent in fact or that consent is given for one of the following reasons:

(a) Because the actor put the victim in fear by the use or threat of imminent use of physical violence on the victim, or on a person in the victim's presence, or on a member of the victim's immediate family; or

(b) Because the actor purports to be acting under legal authority; or

(c) Because the victim does not understand the nature of the thing to which the victim consents, either by reason of ignorance or mistake of fact or of law other than criminal law or by reason of youth or defective mental condition, whether permanent or temporary.

939.43. Mistake

(1) An honest error, whether of fact or of law other than criminal law, is a defense if it negatives the existence of a state of mind essential to the crime.

(2) A mistake as to the age of a minor or as to the existence or constitutionality of the section under which the actor is prosecuted or the scope or meaning of the terms used in that section is not a defense.

Catharine MacKinnon, A Rally Against Rape
Feminism Unmodified 81-83 (1987)

[This talk was given at White Plaza, Stanford University, Stanford, California, November 16, 1981, where several hundred students gathered to grieve and protest a series of rapes reported on campus.]

... Politically, I call it rape whenever a woman has sex and feels violated. You might think that's too broad. I'm not talking about sending all of you men to jail for that. I'm talking about attempting to change the nature of the relations between women and men by having women ask ourselves, "Did I feel violated?" To me, part of the culture of sexual inequality that makes women not report rape is that the definition of rape is not based on our sense of our violation.

I think it's fairly common, and is increasingly known to be common, for men to seek sexual access to women in ways that we find coercive and unwanted. On those occasions the amount and kind of force are only matters of degree. The problem is that rapes do not tend to be reported or prosecuted or sanctioned based on the force that was used; not based on how coercive it was and not based on how violated the woman feels; instead they are based on how intimate she is with the person who did it. This is why most women think we won't be believed in reporting the most common rapes, that is, rapes by people we know. As a result, I agree with what people have been saying, that rape is everyone's problem. But that doesn't mean that it's men's problem and women's problem in the same way.

To men I want to say: have you ever had sex with a woman when she didn't want it? Were you and are you really careful to find out? Is it enough that you say to yourself now, "I don't know"? Are you really afraid that nothing will happen between you and a woman if you don't make it happen? Are you afraid of our rage today? That we will turn it against you? Is there perhaps a reason for your fear? I think you need to remember that we love you. And that as a result it's often very unclear to us why you are so urgent. It's unclear to us why you are so pressured in seeking sexual access to us. We want you not to denigrate us if we refuse. We want you to support us, to listen to us, and to back off a little. Maybe to back off a lot. And we also want you to realize that supporting us is not the same as taking over either our injuries or our pleasure.

To women I want to say: What do you really want? Do you feel that you have the conditions under which you can ask yourself that question? If you feel that you are going to be raped when you say no, how do you know that you really want sex when you say yes? Do you feel responsible for men's sexual feelings about you? What about their responsibility for yours, including your lack of them? I also want to say that women need self-protection; we do not need more paranoia. The Stanford police tell us, "A little fear is a good thing right now." I think we do not need more fear. We need to make fear unnecessary....

Hate Crimes

◆ **THE CASE OF TODD MITCHELL**

It is October 7, 1989, in Kenosha, Wisconsin, an industrial community of 80,000 just north of the Illinois border. The city's population is 90% white and counts among its numbers many German, Irish, and Polish immigrants. Over the past decade, however, its minority population has increased, with African-Americans now accounting for 3%. For the most part, the different ethnic groups seem to live together comfortably, without the kind of racial problems that exist in larger communities. Like other midwestern factory towns, Kenosha has suffered economically with the decline of the American auto industry. Two years ago, the American Motor Company went out of business, and more recently a Chrysler plant closed, which have served to exacerbate the city's economic problems of high unemployment and empty industrial parks.

On Forty-fifth Street, near the defunct American Motor Company plant, a group of African-American teenagers are sitting in the hallway of an apartment complex, drinking wine and beer and talking. Many have criminal histories for offenses such as battery, disorderly conduct, and shoplifting. Some are also members of either the Vice Lords or the Disciples, which are both street gangs that first appeared in the early 1980s. Officials consider these "spin-off gangs" to be growing and potentially dangerous imports from Chicago, but estimate that presently there are only about twenty to thirty hard-core gang members in the city.

After awhile, the group's conversation turns to the recently released movie, *Mississippi Burning*, which a number of them have seen. It is a fictionalized account of an F.B.I. investigation into the disappearance of three civil rights workers, two white, one black, in Jessup County, Mississippi. In particular, several in the group are upset by one scene in particular. In the movie, evening services are

Figure 125 **Todd Mitchell at his trial in December 1989**

(Kenosha News)

just concluding with a hymn when trucks of hooded Ku Klux Klan men pull up and surround the exit of the church. The men and women of the congregation pause momentarily, but begin to run when the Klansmen firebomb the church. Many of the Klansmen start chasing down people and beating those they catch. While the violence is swirling about, one boy stops to stare at the church and drops to his knees to pray. One of the hooded men approaches the boy and kicks him hard in the face and stomach, warning him that things will not change. As the boy curls up in pain, the man kicks him one last time before striding away.

Discussing the scene makes the teenagers increasingly angry. Some of them have now moved outside and continue to talk and drink. After they have been talking for about forty-five minutes, nineteen-year old Todd Mitchell and his younger brother, Jermaine, who are also African-American and live nearby on Forty-third Avenue, join them.

The older Mitchell brother remains generally quiet during the discussion of the movie, but grows enraged listening to the description of the firebombing scene. Seeing that the discussion angers everyone, Mitchell asks, "Do you all feel hyped up to move on some white people?" Looking across the street, he spots Gregory Reddick, a white fourteen-year old, walking home to Fifty-second Avenue from a nearby pizza parlor. Several in the group attend Bullen Junior High with Reddick, but nobody recognizes him. Mitchell turns to the group and says, "There goes a white boy. Go get him!"

Figure 126 **Intersection of 40th Avenue and 45th Street. Mitchell and the others were gathered in front of the apartment complex on the left**

(Kenosha Joint Services)

Pointing left and right to signal that they should encircle him, Mitchell counts to three, and ten of them take off after Reddick. Knocking him to the ground, they kick, punch, and stomp on him for about five minutes. The beating leaves Reddick unconscious on the ground. One attacker thinks he is dead. Another takes Reddick's British Knight sneakers, a status symbol to some in the neighborhood, and shows them off around the apartment complex. Throughout the attack, Mitchell watches from across the street.

Mitchell then flags down a police officer and shows him where Reddick lies. Emergency officials rush Reddick to St. Catherine's Hospital, where he remains comatose for four days.

Doctors fear that his brain damage may become permanent.

Under then-existing Wisconsin law, prosecutors can seek a higher penalty for an offender who "intentionally selects" a person because of his or her "race, religion, color, disability, sexual orientation, national origin, or ancestry."

Figure 127 **Viewpoint** Mitchell and the others would have had while standing in front of the apartment complex and looking across the street to where Reddick was walking

(Kenosha Joint Services)

1. Relying only on your own intuitions of justice, what liability and punishment, if any, does Todd Mitchell deserve, if he had done what he did with no racially related motivation? Assume the victim was African-American and assume his motivation was simply a dislike for the victim.

   Now consider, and indicate below, what *additional liability and punishment above and beyond this amount,* if any, Todd Mitchell deserves on the actual facts of this case.

N	0	1	2	3	4	5	6	7	8	9	10	11
☐	☐	☐	☐	☐	☐	☐	☐	☐	☐	☐	☐	☐
no liability	liability but no punishment	1 day	2 wks	2 mo	6 mo	1 yr	3 yrs	7 yrs	15 yrs	30 yrs	life imprison-ment	death

2. What additional liability, if any, under the then-existing statutes?
3. What additional liability, if any, under the Model Penal Code?

■ THE LAW

Wisconsin Statutes
(1989)

Criminal Code

Section 940.19. Battery; Aggravated Battery

(1) Whoever causes bodily harm to another by an act done with intent to cause bodily harm to that person or another without the consent of the person so harmed is guilty of a Class A misdemeanor.

(1m) Whoever causes great bodily harm to another by an act done with intent to cause bodily harm to that person or another without the consent of the person so harmed is guilty of a Class E felony.

(2) Whoever causes great bodily harm to another by an act done with intent to cause great bodily harm to that person or another with or without the consent of the person so harmed is guilty of a Class C felony.

(3) Whoever intentionally causes bodily harm to another by conduct which creates a high probability of great bodily harm is guilty of a Class E felony. A rebuttable presumption of conduct creating a substantial risk of great bodily harm arises:

   (a) If the person harmed is 62 years of age or older; or

   (b) If the person harmed has a physical disability, whether congenital or acquired by accident, injury or disease, which is discernible by an ordinary person viewing the physically disabled person.

Section 939.22. Words and Phrases Defined

In chs. 939 to 948 and 951, the following words and phrases have the designated meanings unless the context of a specific section manifestly requires a different construction of the word of phrase as defined in § 948.01 for purposes of ch. 948:...

   (4) "Bodily harm" means physical pain or injury, illness, or any impairment of physical condition....

   (14) "Great bodily harm" means bodily injury which creates a substantial risk of death, or which causes serious permanent disfigurement, or which causes a permanent or protracted loss or impairment of the function of any bodily member or organ or other serious bodily injury....

Section 943.32. Robbery

(1) Whoever, with intent to steal, takes property from the person or presence of the owner by either of the following means is guilty of a Class C felony:

   (a) By using force against the person of the owner with intent thereby to overcome his physical resistance or physical power of resistance to the taking or carrying away of the property; or

(b) By threatening the imminent use of force against the person of the owner or of another who is present with intent thereby to compel the owner to acquiesce in the taking or carrying away of the property.

(2) Whoever violates sub. (1) by use or threat of use of a dangerous weapon or any article used or fashioned in a manner to lead the victim reasonably to believe that it is a dangerous weapon is guilty of a Class B felony.

(3) In this section "owner" means a person in possession of property whether his possession is lawful or unlawful.

Section 939.05. Parties to Crime

(1) Whoever is concerned in the commission of a crime is a principal and may be charged with and convicted of the commission of the crime although he did not directly commit it and although the person who directly committed it has not been convicted or has been convicted of some other degree of the crime or of some other crime based on the same act.

(2) A person is concerned in the commission of the crime if he:

(a) Directly commits the crime; or

(b) Intentionally aids and abets the commission of it; or

(c) Is a party to a conspiracy with another to commit it or advises, hires, counsels or otherwise procures another to commit it.

Such a party is also concerned in the commission of any other crime which is committed in pursuance of the intended crime and which under the circumstances is a natural and probable consequence of the intended crime. This paragraph does not apply to a person who voluntarily changes his mind and no longer desires that the crime be committed and notifies the other parties concerned of his withdrawal within a reasonable time before the commission of the crime so as to allow the others also to withdraw.

Section 939.645. Penalty; Crimes Committed Against Certain People or Property

(1) If a person does all of the following, the penalties for the underlying crime are increased as provided in sub. (2):

(a) Commits a crime under chs. 939 to 948.

(b) Intentionally selects the person against whom the crime under par. (a) is committed or selects the property which is damaged or otherwise affected by the crime under par. (a) because of the race, religion, color, disability, sexual orientation, national origin or ancestry of that person or the owner or occupant of that property.

(2) (a) If the crime committed under sub. (1) is ordinarily a misdemeanor other than a Class A misdemeanor, the revised maximum fine is $10,000 and the revised maximum period of imprisonment is one year in the county jail.

(b) If the crime committed under sub. (1) is ordinarily a Class A misdemeanor, the penalty increase under this section changes the status of the crime to a felony and the revised maximum fine is $10,000 and the revised maximum period of imprisonment is 2 years.

(c) If the crime committed under sub. (1) is a felony, the maximum fine prescribed by law for the crime may be increased by not more than $5,000 and the maximum period of imprisonment prescribed by law for the crime may be increased by not more than 5 years.

(3) This section provides for the enhancement of the penalties applicable for the underlying crime. The court shall direct that the trier of fact find a special verdict as to all of the issues specified in sub. (1).

(4) This section does not apply to any crime if proof of race, religion, color, disability, sexual orientation, national origin or ancestry is required for a conviction for that crime.

Section 939.23. Criminal Intent

(1) When criminal intent is an element of a crime in chs. 939 to 951, such intent is indicated by the term "intentionally", the phrase "with intent to", the phrase "with intent that", or some form of the verbs "know" or "believe".

(2) "Know" requires only that the actor believes that the specified fact exists.

(3) "Intentionally" means that the actor either has a purpose to do the thing or cause the result specified, or is aware that his or her conduct is practically certain to cause that result. In addition, except as provided in sub. (6), the actor must have knowledge of those facts which are necessary to make his or her conduct criminal and which are set forth after the word "intentionally".

(4) "With intent to" or "with intent that" means that the actor either has a purpose to do the thing or cause the result specified, or is aware that his or her conduct is practically certain to cause that result.

(5) Criminal intent does not require proof of knowledge of the existence or constitutionality of the section under which he is prosecuted or the scope or meaning of the terms used in that section.

(6) Criminal intent does not require proof of knowledge of the age of a minor even though age is a material element in the crime in question.

Section 939.24. Criminal Recklessness

(1) In this section, "criminal recklessness" means that the actor creates an unreasonable and substantial risk of death or great bodily harm to another human being and the actor is aware of that risk.

(2) If criminal recklessness is an element of a crime in chs. 939 to 951, the recklessness is indicated by the term "reckless" or "recklessly".

(3) A voluntarily produced intoxicated or drugged condition is not a defense to liability for criminal recklessness if, had the actor not been in that condition, he or she would have been aware of creating an unreasonable and substantial risk of death or great bodily harm to another human being.

Section 939.25. Criminal Negligence

(1) In this section, "criminal negligence" means ordinary negligence to a high degree, consisting of conduct which the actor should realize creates a substantial and unreasonable risk of death or great bodily harm to another.

(2) If criminal negligence is an element of a crime in chs. 939 to 951 or § 346.62, the negligence is indicated by the term "negligent".

● OVERVIEW OF HATE CRIMES

When an actor commits an offense against a person that is motivated by bias rooted in the person's membership in a certain kind of group, a hate crime dictates more liability than would have been imposed without the prejudicial motivation. The limits of these laws are, however, still being defined. The following article by James Jacobs and Kimberly Potter explores the rationales behind hate crime laws and the debate over their scope. The authors survey the various state positions and address what offenses and biases are covered, the extent to which the biases must be manifest in order to incur liability, and the relationship between hate crime laws and the Civil Rights Act.

James B. Jacobs & Kimberly Potter, Hate Crime Laws
Hate Crimes: Criminal Law & Identity Politics 29-44 (1998)

> [O]ur single most effective weapon is the law. I implore you to support the Bias
> Related Violence and Intimidation Act I have proposed, and make it clear to the
> people of this state that behaviour based on bias will not be ignored or tolerated.
>
> —Letter from New York State Governor Mario M. Cuomo
> to the New York State Legislature, August 16, 1991

By 1995, the federal government, thirty-seven states, and the District of Columbia had passed hate crime laws that fall into four categories: (1) sentence enhancements; (2) substantive crimes; (3) civil rights statutes; and (4) reporting statutes. The diversity of these laws demonstrates the plasticity of the hate crime concept.

Sentence Enhancements

The majority of hate crime statutes are of the sentence enhancement type. Typically, these laws bump up the penalty for a particular crime when the offender's motivation is an officially designated prejudice. The Montana and Alabama sentence enhancement statutes are typical. Montana provides that

> a person who has been found guilty of any offense . . . that was committed because
> of the victim's race, creed, religion, color, national origin, or involvement in

> civil rights or human rights activities . . . *in addition to* the punishment
> provided for commission of the offense, *may be* sentenced to a term of
> imprisonment of not less than two years or more than 10 years.

Alabama provides a mandatory minimum sentence for violent crimes motivated by
an officially designated bias.

> On a conviction of a Class A felony that was found to have been motivated by
> the victim's actual or perceived race, color, religion, national origin, ethnicity,
> or physical or mental disability, the sentence shall not be less than 15 years.

The size of the penalty enhancement varies from state to state. In Vermont, a
hate crime is subject to *double* the maximum prison term. Under Florida's
enhancement provision, the maximum possible sentence is tripled. The hate
crime statute challenged before the Supreme Court in *Wisconsin v. Mitchell*
provided for a two-year maximum prison term for aggravated battery, but if the
perpetrator was motivated by bias, the maximum punishment jumped to seven
years.

On the federal level, the Violent Crime Control and Law Enforcement Act of
1994 mandated that the U.S. Sentencing Guidelines provide a sentence enhancement of three "offense levels" above the base level for the underlying federal
offense, if the sentencing court finds

> beyond a reasonable doubt that the defendant intentionally selected any victim
> or any property as the object of the offense because of the actual or perceived
> race, color, religion, national origin, ethnicity, gender [but not in the case of a
> sexual offense], disability, or sexual orientation of any person.

Applying the Sentencing Guidelines in the case of an aggravated assault, for
example, the ordinary base level offense score of 15 is increased to 18, elevating
the sentencing range from 18-24 months to 27-33 months.

The Enumerated Prejudices

The various state substantive and sentence enhancement hate crime laws
differ from one another with respect to which prejudices transform ordinary crime
into hate crime. All hate crime laws are designed to punish criminals motivated by
prejudice based on race, color, religion, and national origin, but all uniformity
ends there. Only eighteen states and the District of Columbia include gender
and/or sexual orientation bias as hate crime triggers. Prejudice against Native
Americans, immigrants, the physically and mentally handicapped, union members,
nonunion members, right-to-life and pro-choice groups are included in some hate
crime laws. Vermont's law applies to offenders motivated by prejudice against
service in the armed forces. Montana condemns prejudice against "involvement in
civil rights or human rights activities." The District of Columbia statute is the
most inclusive; in addition to race, color, religion, national origin, gender, and
sexual orientation, it prohibits targeting an individual or group by reason of
physical disability, age, personal appearance, family responsibility, marital status,
political affiliation, and matriculation.

Predicate Offenses

State hate crime laws also differ with respect to which predicate offenses, when motivated by prejudice, qualify as hate crimes. The Anti-Defamation League (ADL) model statute, which many states used as a prototype for their statutes, covers only harassment or intimidation. By contrast, in Pennsylvania, Vermont, and Alabama, *any offense* is a hate crime if the offender was motivated by race, religion, national origin, or other selected prejudices. The Alabama statute, which covers all misdemeanors and felonies:

> The purpose of this section is to impose additional penalties where it is shown that a perpetrator committing the underlying offense was motivated by the victim's actual or perceived race, color, religion, national origin, ethnicity, or physical or mental disability.

Other states limit hate crimes to certain predicate offenses. Some states reserve hate crime designation for low-level offenses, such as harassment, menacing, or criminal mischief. The Ohio hate crime statute covers only menacing, aggravated menacing, criminal damage or endangering, criminal mischief, and phone harassment. Similarly, in New Jersey, only simple assault, aggravated assault, harassment, and vandalism can be classified as hate crimes. New York has a single hate crime offense—aggravated harassment. Illinois designates nine predicate offenses: assault, battery, aggravated assault, misdemeanor theft, criminal trespass to residence, misdemeanor criminal damage to property, criminal trespass to vehicle, criminal trespass to real property, and mob action. Washington, D.C., includes arson, assault, burglary, injury to property, kidnaping, manslaughter, murder, rape, robbery, theft, or unlawful entry as possible hate crimes.

Defining and Proving Prejudiced Motivation

Most state hate crime laws do not use the word "motivation," rather, they prohibit *choosing* the victim "by reason of" or "because of" certain characteristics. Other states prohibit choosing the victim "maliciously and with specific intent."

The hate crime statutes differ on whether the offender's prejudice has to be "manifest" in the commission of the crime itself, or whether prejudice can be based on character evidence and evidence of the defendant's actions or words prior to the crime. In Washington, D.C., an ordinary crime becomes a hate crime when the conduct "*demonstrates* an accused's prejudice." Florida requires that the crime "evidences prejudice." One would think that what has to be demonstrated is (1) that the defendant harbors prejudiced beliefs, and (2) that this particular crime, in the way it was committed, demonstrates or reaffirms the existence of such prejudice.

But some juries and/or courts, perhaps hostile to the idea of hate crimes or wary of applying the statutes in an unconstitutional manner, seem to require that the crime demonstrate hard core prejudice.

In interpreting Florida's hate crime statute, which requires that the crime "evidences prejudice," the Florida Supreme Court held that

> [t]he statute requires that it is the commission of the crime that must evidence the prejudice; the fact that racial prejudice may be exhibited during the commission of the crime is itself insufficient.

The court explained that the statute was not meant to cover disputes, such as arguments over a parking space, which escalate into fist fights accompanied by racial or other slurs. If that restricted interpretation of hate crime law prevailed, hate crime laws would be reserved for hard core ideologues like neo-Nazis and thus rarely used.

Other states, such as Wisconsin and California, deal with the motivation element by requiring that the offender have "intentionally selected" the victim "because of" or "by reason of" race, color, religion, and so forth. Read literally, this type of statute would not require proof of *prejudice*, but merely color consciousness in the selection of a victim. For example, it would be a hate crime for a white defendant to attack and rob only Asian women because he perceived them as more vulnerable and less likely to resist. The defendant, although not prejudiced against Asians, would be a hate criminal for selecting the victim by reason of race. However, it is doubtful that prosecutors and judges would interpret the hate crime statute this way, because they recognize the legislative intent to penalize prejudice. Despite differences in the language used to set forth motivation requirements (manifest, evidences, motivated in whole, or in part, because of, etc.), the majority of courts hold that prejudice must be a *substantial* motivating factor.

In Pittsburgh, Pennsylvania, Emmitt Harris, a black male, and Matthew Chapman, a white male, were throwing trash in a dumpster behind the deli where Harris worked. The defendant, Theresa Ferino, a white woman whom Harris and Chapman knew as a deli customer, walked up the alley to the rear of the deli, pointed a gun at Harris and Chapman, and stated, "I'm going to kill, you fucking nigger." Ferino fired the gun in the direction of both Harris and Chapman, but injured no one. The state supreme court, in less than straightforward language, reversed the conviction for ethnic intimidation on the grounds that

> the singularity of the act committed by the [defendant], directed as it was against both Harris [a black man] and his companion (a Caucasian), the antecedent of which was neither a harsh word, gesture nor conduct exhibited between the victim and the [defendant], we do not believe rises to the proof-level sufficient to constitute a contravention of the ethnic intimidation statute.

In other words, use of the word "nigger," plus the firing of the gun, was not sufficient to sustain a hate crime conviction, when a second possible victim was someone of the same race as the defendant.

Substantive Offenses

ADL Model Hate Crime Law

Some hate crime statutes define new substantive offenses. They redefine conduct that is already criminal as a new crime or as an aggravated form of an existing crime. The ADL model statutes, which many states have adopted, provide for new substantive offenses of "intimidation" and "institutional vandalism."

> A person commits the crime of intimidation if, by reason of the actual or perceived race, color, religion, national origin or sexual orientation of another individual or group of individuals, he violates Section ____ of the Penal Code (insert provision for criminal trespass, criminal mischief, harassment, menacing, assault and/or appropriate statutorily proscribed criminal conduct).
>
> Intimidation is a ____ misdemeanor/felony (the degree of liability should be at least one degree more serious than that imposed for commission of the offense).

Intimidation, a new substantive offense, recriminalizes several existing low-level offenses, in effect *enhancing the maximum possible sentence* when the offender is motivated by one of the enumerated biases. Whether a hate crime law takes the form of a new substantive offense, or a sentence enhancement, the end result is the same—a more severe punishment. Hate crime laws in general, and this statute in particular, do not seem aimed at the archetypical racists, anti-Semites, misogynists, and homophobes. Instead, they seem aimed at the ad hoc disputes, arguments, and fights that frequently erupt in a multiracial, multiethnic, multireligious society. The following [cases are] typical:

- In 1989, David Wyant and his wife, both white, were playing loud music at their campsite in Ohio's Alum Creek State Park. Two black campers at the adjoining campsite, Jerry White and Patricia McGowan, complained to park officials. When asked by park officials to turn off the music, Wyant complied, but fifteen minutes later turned on the radio again. White and McGowan then overheard Wyant shouting that "[w]e didn't have this problem until those niggers moved in next to us. I ought to shoot that black motherfucker. I ought to kick his black ass." Wyant was convicted of ethnic intimidation, a fourth degree felony, and sentenced to one and one-half years imprisonment, *triple* the maximum sentence for the underlying offense of aggravated menacing, a first degree misdemeanor, with a sentence range of 0–6 months imprisonment or a fine.
- In 1991, a white police officer, Stephen Keyes, responded to a domestic disturbance call at the Florida home of Michael Hamm, an African-American. When Officer Keyes attempted to arrest him, Hamm shouted, "I'll shoot you white cracker motherfucker." Believing that Hamm was armed, Keyes radioed for back-up. In the meantime, Hamm escaped, but was later apprehended. No gun was found. Hamm was charged with aggravated assault for "evidenc[ing] prejudice based on race, color, [etc.]." All charges were later dropped because there was not enough evidence (primarily, the lack of a weapon) that Hamm intended to assault Officer Keyes.
- In 1994, Herbert Cohen accompanied Denise Avard to Richard Stalder's Florida home to retrieve Avard's earrings; allegedly, Avard had some sort of dispute with Stalder. Stalder pushed Cohen and called him a "Jew boy," "Jewish lawyer," "you fat Jewish lawyer, get off my property," "Jewish kike, come on Jewish lawyer . . . I'm going to kick your ass." Stalder was charged with battery subject to a hate crime sentence enhancement.

ADL Model Institutional Vandalism Statute

The ADL recommends a second substantive hate crime statute for the destruction of property that belongs to religious groups. Its "Institutional Vandalism" law provides:

> A person commits the crime of institutional vandalism by knowingly vandalizing, defacing or otherwise damaging:
>
> i. Any church, synagogue, or other building, structure or place used for religious worship or other religious purposes;
>
> ii. Any cemetery, mortuary or other facility used for the purpose of burial or memorializing the dead;
>
> iii. Any school, educational facility or community center;
>
> iv. The grounds adjacent to, and owned or rented by any institution, facility, building, structure or place described in subsections (i), (ii), or (iii) above.

This statute increases penalties for vandalism of sacred buildings. "It is critical...that the enhanced penalties be sufficiently severe for the new statute to have its desired deterrent impact."

Some states combine the ADL intimidation and institutional vandalism model statutes. For example, Connecticut's hate crime statute provides:

> A person is guilty of intimidation based on bigotry or bias if such person maliciously, and with specific intent to intimidate or harass another person because of such other person's race, religion, ethnicity or sexual orientation does any of the following: (1) causes physical contact with such other person; (2) damages, destroys or defaces any real or personal property of such other person; or (3) threatens, by word or act, to do an act described in subdivision (1) or (2).

Under this statute, a hate crime prosecution could be brought if an offender spray paints anti-gay graffiti on the facade of a gay bar, but not if the offender spray paints misogynistic graffiti on *Ms. Magazine*'s headquarters. While both hypothetical acts of vandalism express prejudice, gender-based prejudice is not covered by Connecticut's statute. In contrast, the Alaska and Michigan hate crime laws would produce the opposite result; the definition of hate crime includes gender bias, but not sexual orientation bias.

In New York, the substantive hate crime statute is called "aggravated harassment." It provides:

> A person is guilty of aggravated harassment...when with intent to harass, annoy, threaten, or alarm another person, he: Strikes, shoves, kicks, or otherwise subjects another person to physical contact, or attempts to threaten to do the same, because of the race, color, religion or national origin of such person.

Essentially, when a crime is motivated by bias, the defendant is charged with the underlying crime, assault for example, plus an added count of aggravated harassment. If convicted of aggravated harassment, the defendant faces a significantly more severe sentence. For example, in *People v. Grupe,* the defendant was convicted of aggravated harassment for striking a Jewish man while shouting anti-Semitic epithets, such as "Is that the best you can do? I'll show you Jew bastard."

The maximum sentence under the aggravated harassment statute is one year imprisonment, whereas the maximum sentence for the same conduct, absent the anti-Semitic epithets, is 15 days imprisonment. Such significant differences in sentencing based on the words uttered during the crime have led some critics to call hate crime statutes "thought crime laws."

The Federal Civil Rights Acts

Some commentators refer to the federal criminal civil rights laws as hate crime statutes. However, they are actually quite different in intent, formulation, and operation — especially the post-Civil War statutes. They do not deconstruct criminal law into various offender/victim configurations based upon race, religion, sexual orientation, and the like; neither do they politicize "the crime problem" in the manner of the contemporary state hate crime laws.

Post-Civil War Rights Acts

After the Civil War, in many places within the former Confederacy, local law enforcement agencies would not prosecute crimes committed by whites against blacks, nor would local governments permit blacks to exercise rights guaranteed by the Fourteenth Amendment. So, Congress passed laws to authorize federal prosecution of the Ku Klux Klan and others, including law enforcement and government officials, who denied the newly freed slaves their civil rights. The authority for these statutes was Congress's power to enforce the Thirteenth and Fourteenth Amendments.

The federal statutes did not aim to enhance punishment or to *recriminalize* conduct already covered by criminal law. At the time, these statutes provided the only de facto law enforcement option. If local law enforcement officers had investigated and prosecuted those who victimized the former slaves, there would have been no need for the federal laws. The federal criminal civil rights statutes are not directed exclusively at hate crimes (although they can be used for that purpose), but at what law professor Frederick Lawrence calls "rights interference crimes." The civil rights statutes and hate crime laws both respond to issues of race and discrimination, but any similarity ends there. The civil rights statutes are not framed in terms of identity politics and group rights, but in terms of everyone's *individual* civil rights.

The first of the two post-Civil War statutes, 18 United States Code § 241, provides punishment for conspiracies to violate federally guaranteed rights. It provides that

> [i]f two or more persons conspire to injure, oppress, threaten, or intimidate any person . . . in the free exercise or enjoyment of any right or privilege secured to him by the Constitution or laws of the United States . . . or;
>
> If two or more persons go in disguise on the highway [i.e., the Ku Klux Klan], or on the premises of another, with intent to prevent or hinder [the] free exercise or enjoyment of any right or privilege so secured . . . [t]hey shall be fined not more than $10,000, or imprisoned not more than 10 years or both. . . .

The second post-Civil War statute, 18 U.S.C. § 242, is explicitly concerned with federal, state, or local government officials who deprive private citizens of their federally guaranteed rights on the basis of certain characteristics. Its purpose is to guarantee even-handed, color-blind law enforcement:

> Whoever, under color of any law, ... willfully subjects any person ... to the deprivation of any rights, privileges, or immunities secured or protected by the Constitution or laws of the United States, or to different punishments, pains, or penalties, on account of such person being an alien, or by reason of his color, or race, than are prescribed for the punishment of citizens, shall be fined ... or imprisoned. ...

Neither of these statutes was meant to single out the prejudices of common criminals for special condemnation and more severe punishment; rather, their purpose was to ensure that laws were enforced equally on behalf of all victims, no matter what race, and against all offenders, whatever their race, prejudice, or criminal motivation. Unlike modern-day state hate crime statutes, which cover only those victims who fall within the groups listed in the hate crime statute, the post-Civil War statutes apply to everyone.

Sections 241 and 242 have been used to prosecute a wide variety of conduct, including ballot tampering, extortion by a public defender, unlawful searches, obstruction of federal witness's testimony, and the abuse of a state hospital patient by hospital staff. When the federal civil rights statutes have been used to prosecute cases of racially motivated violence, the crimes have almost always been committed "under color of law" as, for example, the 1964 murders by Mississippi police of civil rights workers Michael Henry Schwerner, James Early Chaney, and Andrew Goodman, or the 1992 attack of black motorist Rodney King by a group of Los Angeles police officers.

The 1968 Civil Rights Act

Passed as part of the Civil Rights Act of 1968, 18 United States Code § 245, might be considered a precursor to the modern state hate crime laws. Indeed, § 245 was one component of the legislation that marks the beginning of the modern civil rights movement. Entitled "Federally Protected Activities," § 245 was designed to provide a remedy for the violence resulting from opposition to civil rights marches, voter registration drives and other voting issues, enrollment of black students in formerly all-white schools and universities, and efforts to abolish Jim Crow laws.

The first subsection of Section 245 mirrors §§ 241 and 242 by specifically enumerating federal activities, the enjoyment of which the Act seeks to protect against infringement by anybody for any reason. The second subsection specifically protects a broad category of "state and local activities" from interference motivated by certain prejudices. It protects participants in state and local activities from victimization based on race, color, religion, and national origin. The prosecution must prove that the defendant, motivated by bias, attacked a victim who was participating in a state or local activity. The offender's prejudice need not have been the sole motivating factor. Subsection (b)(2) provides that

> Whoever, whether or not acting under color of law, by force or threat of force willfully injures, intimidates or interferes with, or attempts to interfere with ... any person because of his race, color, religion, or national origin and because he is or has been ... enrolling in or attending a public school or

university; participating in any benefit, program, service or facility provided by a state or local government; applying or working for any state or local government or private employer; serving as a juror; traveling in or using any facility of interstate commerce, or using any vehicle, terminal, or facility of any common carrier; or using any public facility, such as a bar, restaurant, store, hotel, movie theater, or stadium shall be punished.... [The statute provides a range of different punishments depending on the conduct, whether firearms or explosives are used, and the degree of injury to victims.]

Perhaps because of its complexity and abstruseness, this statute has rarely been used. The Department of Justice estimates that it "seeks indictments [for violations of §§ 241, 242, and 245] in 50-60 cases per year." These statutes were never intended, and have never served, as all-purpose federal hate crime statutes. Rather, they function as insurance which can be called upon if, for discriminatory or other improper reasons, state and local law enforcement officers fail to prosecute violations of civil rights.

At least ten states have civil rights-type statutes, patterned on the federal laws. These statutes are quite justifiably referred to as hate crime laws, since they aim at criminals who are prejudiced. West Virginia's statute, titled "Prohibiting Violations of an Individual's Civil Rights," provides:

> All persons within the boundaries of the state of West Virginia have the right to be free from any violence, or intimidation by threat of violence, committed against their persons or property because of their race, sex, color, religion, ancestry, national origin, political affiliation, or sex.
>
> If any person does by force or threat of force, willfully injure, intimidate or interfere with, or attempt to injure, intimidate or interfere with, or oppress or threaten any other person in the free exercise or enjoyment of any right or privilege secured to him or her by the Constitution or laws of the state of West Virginia or ... of the United States, because of such other person's race, color, religion, ancestry, national origin, political affiliation, or sex, he or she shall be guilty of a felony, and upon conviction, shall be fined not more than five thousand dollars or imprisoned not more than ten years or both.

Conclusion

In the mid-1980s, Congress and a majority of state legislatures passed hate crime laws that do not criminalize previously *noncriminal* behavior, but enhance punishment for conduct that was already a crime. The well-known federal criminal civil rights statutes are often assumed to be the model for these new laws, but they are quite different. They do not recriminalize prohibited behavior, enhance sentences, or designate a finite list of prejudices. They protect the federal, constitutional, and statutory rights of all citizens by making it a criminal offense to interfere with those rights. They provide federal insurance that crime will be prosecuted if state and local law enforcement authorities default in carrying out their responsibilities.

There are significant differences in the ways that federal and state legislatures define hate crimes. A number of states, following the ADL's lead, treat hate crime as a low-level offense, such as intimidation or harassment. Other states have more general hate crime laws and sentence enhancements that mandate higher sentences for most or all crimes when motivated by prejudice. The statutes also differ as to which prejudices transform ordinary crime into hate crime and as to whether those prejudices must be manifest in the criminal conduct itself or can be proved by evidence concerning the defendant's beliefs, opinion, and character. The diversity of hate crime laws means that we cannot assume that people are talking about the same thing when they discuss "hate crime" or that hate crime reports and statistics from one jurisdiction can be compared with reports and statistics from other jurisdictions.

◉ DISCUSSION MATERIALS

Should the Criminal Law Impose Additional Liability and Punishment For an Offense That Is Motivated by Hatred Toward an Identifiable Group?

The Lawrence excerpt below sets out the consequentialist and non-consequentialist justifications for adopting hate crime laws and argues that increased punishment is an appropriate response. In contrast, Susan Gellman's article questions the constitutionality of laws like those upheld in the *Mitchell* case above, and claims that these laws infringe on first amendment rights and fail to meet their intended goals. She offers alternative formulations and norm-changing proposals that purport to better serve the objective.

Frederick M. Lawrence, Punishing Hate: Bias Crimes Under American Law
58-63, 161-163, 167-169 (1999)

The Relative Seriousness of Bias Crimes

Reconsideration of the Unique Harm Caused by Bias Crimes

The seriousness of a crime . . . is a function of the offender's culpability and the harm caused. It follows, therefore, that the relative seriousness of bias crimes and parallel crimes will also turn on the culpability and harm associated with each. . . .

. . . To establish a bias crime, the prosecution must prove . . . that the accused was motivated by bias in the commission of the parallel crime. Under both federal and state law, the burden is on the prosecution to show motivation. This proof would be necessary whether we are applying the racial animus model or the discriminatory selection model of bias crimes. Under the racial animus model, the offender must have purposefully acted in furtherance of his hostility toward the target group. Under the discriminatory selection model, the offender must have purposefully selected the victim on the basis of his perceived membership in the target group. Under either model, nothing short of this *mens rea* of *purpose* will constitute the requisite culpability for the second tier of a bias crime. Unless the perpetrator was motivated to cause harm to another because of the victim's race, the crime is clearly not a bias crime.

The culpability associated with the commission of parallel crimes and bias crimes is thus identical in terms of *what* the offender did and differs only in respect to *why* the offender did so. The relevance of this difference to the calculation of crime seriousness depends upon the reason that the culpability itself is relevant to crime seriousness.

Why is it that intentional murder ought to be punished more severely than the negligent killer? The result of the conduct of each is the death of the victim; they differ only as to their culpability. To the consequentialist, the murderer is punished more because he was more likely to cause death than was the negligent killer, or because the social value of his activity resulting in death was less relative to the chance of death. If this is the role of culpability in the calculation of crime seriousness, then the culpability associated with bias crimes makes these crimes more severe than parallel crimes. Bias crime offenders are more likely to cause harm than are those who commit the same crimes without bias motivation. [B]ias crimes generally are not more likely to be assaults than are parallel crimes, and bias-motivated assaults are far more likely to be brutal. Moreover, the social value of activity resulting in bias crimes is far less than even the antisocial behavior that results in the parallel crime.

An alternative explanation for punishing the murderer more severely than the negligent killer is that his act of intentionally killing is more blameworthy. If culpability is relevant to crime seriousness because it bears on blameworthiness, then the argument that the culpability associated with bias crimes makes these crimes more serious than parallel crimes is as compelling as it was for the consequentialist. The motivation of the bias crime offender violates the equality principle, one of the most deeply held tenets in our legal system and our culture. To the extent that crime seriousness is designed to capture a deontological concept of blameworthiness, bias crimes are more serious than other crimes. The rhetoric surrounding the enactment of bias crime laws suggests that most supporters of such legislation espouse a thoroughly deontological justification for the punishment of racially motivated violence.

This trend is well illustrated by an unusual punishment for bias crimes proposed in Marlborough, Massachusetts. The Marlborough city council unanimously approved an ordinance that would deny public services, such as local licenses, library cards, or even trash removal, to those convicted of bias crimes. Supporters of the ordinance drew upon the community's disdain for the racial prejudice demonstrated by the bias criminal rather than the harm caused by the criminal's conduct.

Culpability analysis, therefore, advances the argument for the relatively greater seriousness of bias crimes. The argument is equally supported by culpability theory based upon consequentialist and nonconsequentialist justifications for punishment.

A harms-based analysis also demonstrates that bias crimes are more serious than parallel crimes, regardless of the theory of punishment we assume. Under an ex ante analysis, the question is whether the rational person would risk a parallel crime before he would risk a bias crime. For several reasons, the answer is almost certainly yes. Consider first the context of vandalism. The parallel crime arising out of the defacement of a building or home is primarily a nuisance to the victim. The loss is insurable and, if not insured, is suffered in terms of time or money or both. However, if that vandalism is bias motivated, the defacement might take the form of swastikas on the home of a Jewish family or racist graffiti on the home of an African-American family. The harm here is not a mere nuisance. The potential for deep psychological harm, and the feelings of threat discussed earlier, exceed the harm ordinarily experienced by vandalism victims. No one can buy insurance to cover these additional harms.

The case of an electrical fire that destroyed a Boston-area synagogue provides the framework for a useful hypothetical example of the rational person's relative willingness to bear the risk of parallel vandalism versus bias-motivated vandalism. In the short period immediately after the fire, prior to the determination of the cause, there was widespread concern that the fire was the result of bias-motivated arson. The news that it was not was met with great relief. Part of this relief may be attributed to the fact that the fire had occurred accidentally and was not the result of arson, bias motivated or otherwise. But this explanation does not capture the entire reaction, part of which is attributable to the fact that anti-Semitism was ruled out as a cause. Had the fire been caused by foul play without bias motivation—for example, by pecuniarily motivated arson without any trace of anti-Semitism—surely the reaction of both victims and the general community would have exceeded the reaction that would have followed an accidental fire, but would not have been as great as if the cause were determined to have been religiously motivated. Faced with the choice between racist and nonracist vandalism, the rational person would risk the parallel crime before risking the more personally threatening bias crime with its longer-lasting effects.

This analysis applies to attacks against persons just as it does to those against property. In the parallel crime of assault, the perpetrator generally selects the victim (1) randomly or for no particularly conscious reason, (2) for a reason that has nothing to do with the victim's personal identity, such as the perpetrator's perceiving that the victim is carrying money, or (3) for a reason relating to personal animosity between the perpetrator and the victim. A random assault or mugging leaves a victim with, at least, a sense of being unfortunate and, at most, a sense of heightened vulnerability. An assault as a result of personal animosity causes, at most, a focused fear or anger directed at the perpetrator. Unlike a parallel assault, a bias-motivated assault is neither random nor directed at the victim as an individual, and this selection and the message it carries cause all the harms discussed earlier. The perpetrator selects the victim because of some immutable characteristic, actual or perceived. As unpleasant as a parallel assault is, the rational person would still risk being victimized in that manner before he would risk the unique humiliation of a bias-motivated assault.

An ex post analysis provides further clarity and support for this conclusion. A living standard analysis focuses on depth of injury caused by a crime to interests of physical safety, material possessions, personal dignity, and autonomy. Recall that when we compare a parallel crime with a bias crime, we are comparing the same crime with the addition of the perpetrator's bias motivation. The parallel assault crime and the bias assault crime will cause roughly similar injuries to the physical safety and material possessions of the victim. But the bias crime victim's injury to autonomy—in terms of his sense of control over his life—and to his personal dignity will exceed that inflicted upon the parallel assault victim. This is clear from the far greater occurrence of depression, withdrawal, anxiety, and feelings of helplessness and isolation among bias crime victims than is ordinarily experienced by assault victims.

Moreover, in order to assess completely the impact of bias crimes on living standards, we must look beyond the individual victims of these crimes. Here, too, we see a far greater societal injury caused by bias crimes than by parallel crimes. A parallel crime may cause concern or even sorrow among certain members of the victim's community, but it would be unusual for that impact to reach a level at which it would negatively affect their living standard. By contrast, bias crimes spread fear and intimidation beyond the immediate victims to those who share only racial characteristics with the victims. Members of the target group suffer injuries similar to those felt by the direct victim of the actual crime. Unlike the sympathetic nonvictims of a parallel crime, members of the target community will suffer a living standard loss in terms of a threat to dignity and autonomy and a perceived threat to physical safety. Bias crimes, therefore, cause a greater harm to a society's collective living standard than do parallel crimes.

A bias crime, as a matter of culpability or harm — and whether analyzed under retributive or consequentialist justifications for punishment — is more serious than the relevant parallel crime. Bias crimes thus warrant enhanced criminal punishment....

Why Punish Hate?

> Let us dedicate ourselves to what the Greeks wrote so many years ago: to tame the savageness of man and to make gentle the life of this world. Let us dedicate ourselves to that, and say a prayer for our country and for our people.
>
> Robert F. Kennedy, April 4, 1968

The last several decades have seen a dramatic increase in the awareness of bias crimes — both by the public generally and by the legal culture in particular — and the need for a legal response. We need look no further than the marked rise in the number of bias crime laws.

These developments, however, can obscure the controversy that often surrounds the debate over the enactment of a bias crime law. For example, during the debate over Arizona's bias crime law, enacted in 1997, one legislator objected on the grounds that "I still don't believe that a crime against one person is any more heinous than the same crime against someone else." Another put the matter more bluntly: "a few Jews" in the legislature were making the issue "emotional and divisive." Acrimony has surrounded the debate over many state laws. Is it really worth it?

This question is not entirely rhetorical. Obviously, the entire thrust of the preceding chapters argues that bias crime laws are justifiable and constitutional. But to a large extent, I have assumed the need to punish hate as my starting point. The implicit premise of the task has been to provide justifications for the punishment of racially motivated violence in criminal law doctrine, and to square this punishment with free expression doctrine.

Before concluding, it is wise to step back from this assumption, to ask not merely whether it is justified to punish hate, but whether it is *necessary* to punish hate. A state may do so — but should it? . . .

The answer is that it is well worthwhile to have laws that expressly punish racially motivated violence. In order to see why, we must return to the general justifications for punishment, and now augment that discussion with a consideration of the expressive value of punishment, or what is sometimes known as the denunciation theory of punishment. The expressive value of punishment allows us to say not only that bias crime laws are warranted, but they are essential.

The Expressive Value of Punishing Bias Crimes

. . . What happens when proposed bias crime legislation becomes law? This act of law-making constitutes a societal condemnation of racism, religious intolerance, and other forms of bigotry that are covered by that law. Moreover, every act of condemnation is dialectically twinning with an act of expression of values — in Durkheim's terms, social cohesion. Punishment not only signals the border between that which is permitted and that which is proscribed, but also denounces that which is rejected and announces that which is embraced. Because racial harmony and equality are among the highest values held in our society, crimes that violate these values should be punished and must be punished specifically as bias crimes. Similarly, bias crimes must be punished more harshly than crimes that, although otherwise similar, do not violate these values. Moreover, racial harmony and equality are not values that exist only, or even primarily, in an abstract sense. The particular biases that are implicated by bias crimes are connected with a real, extended history of grave injustices to the victim groups, resulting in enormous suffering and loss. In many ways these injustices, and their legacies, persist.

What happens if bias crimes are not expressly punished in a criminal justice system, or, if expressly punished, are not punished more harshly than parallel crimes? Here, too, a message is expressed by the legislation, a message that racial harmony and equality are not among the highest values held by the community. Put differently, it is impossible for the punishment choices made by the society *not* to express societal values. There is no neutral position, no middle ground. The only question is the content of that expression and the resulting statement of those values.

Two cases, one of which involves the debate over a bias crime law, illustrate the point. Consider first the case of the creation of a legal holiday to commemorate the birth of Dr. Martin Luther King, Jr. Once the idea of such a holiday gained widespread attention, the federal government and most states created Martin Luther King Day within a relatively short period of time. It was impossible, however, for a state to take "no position" on the holiday. Several states, including South Carolina, Arizona, New Hampshire, North Carolina, and Texas, did not immediately adopt the holiday. These states were perceived as rejecting the values associated with Dr. King, which were to be commemorated by the holiday marking his birthday. Civil rights groups brought pressure against these states with economic boycotts and the like. Once ignited, the debate over Martin Luther

King Day thus became one in which there was no neutral position. The lack of legislation was a rejection of the holiday and the values with which it was associated.

The second case concerns the debate in 1997 over a bias crime law in Georgia, the site of one of the most acrimonious legislative battles over such legislation. The tension surrounding the debate was heightened by the bombing that year of a lesbian nightclub in Atlanta. Ultimately, the legislation failed to reach the floor of the Georgia legislature for a vote. As with Martin Luther King Day, there was no middle position for Georgia to adopt. Either a bias crime law would be established, with the attending expression of certain values, or it would not, with a rejection of these values and an expression of other, antithetical values. The values expressed by the rejection of the law are aptly caught by the unusually blunt view of one Georgia legislator: "What's the big deal about a few swastikas on a synagogue?" Others derided the legislation as the "Queer Bill."

Thus far we have considered the enactment of a bias crime law to be a simply binary choice: a legislature enacts a bias crime law or it does not. To do so denounces racial hatred, and to fail to do so gives comfort to the racist. We can make a similar observation in the more subtle context of establishing grades of crimes and levels of criminal punishment. [Above] we discussed the ways in which both retributive and consequentialist theories of punishment embraced a concept of proportionality. Now we can see that expressive punishment theory does as well. Conduct that is more offensive to society should receive relatively greater punishment than that which is less offensive. We would be shocked if a legislature punished shoplifting equally with aggravated assault. We might disagree as to whether one was punished excessively or the other insufficiently, but we would agree that these crimes ought not to be treated identically. Society's most cherished values will be reflected in the criminal law by applying the harshest penalties to those crimes that violate these values. There will certainly be lesser penalties for those crimes that in some respects are similar but do not violate these values. The hierarchy of societal values involved in criminal conduct will thus be reflected by the lesser crime's status as a lesser offense included within the more serious crime.

The enshrinement of racial harmony and equality among our highest values not only calls for independent punishment of racially motivated violence as a bias crime and not merely as a parallel crime; it also calls for enhanced punishment of bias crimes over parallel crimes. If bias crimes are not punished more harshly than parallel crimes, the implicit message expressed by the criminal justice system is that racial harmony and equality are not among the highest values in our society. If a racially motivated assault is punished identically to a parallel assault, the racial motivation of the bias crime is rendered largely irrelevant and thus not part of that which is condemned. The individual victim, the target community, and indeed the society at large thus suffer the twin insults akin to those suffered by the narrator of Ralph Ellison's *Invisible Man*. Not only has the crime itself occurred, but the underlying hatred of the crime is invisible to the eyes of the legal system. The punishment of bias crimes as argued for in this book, therefore, is necessary for the full expression of commitment to American values of equality of treatment and opportunity.

Susan Gellman, Hate Crime Laws Are Thought Crime Laws
1992/1993 Annual Survey of American Law 509, 509-513, 518-;520, 528-531

Introduction

"Hate crime" laws are a response to the demand that government "Do Something!" about bigotry generally and bias crime specifically. This is a commendable goal, and one that ought to generate creative, constitutional, and effective ideas. Unfortunately, the penalty-enhancement hate crime laws some jurisdictions have adopted are "all sizzle and no steak." They simply do not accomplish their objectives, and succeed only in creating additional problems. Furthermore, even when they are upheld as constitutional, they are damaging to constitutional values.

This is why it is so distressing to see organizations and individuals who are knowledgeable and concerned about the First Amendment willing to accept the narrow interpretation of the First Amendment that is necessary to defend these hate crime laws. Practitioners must acknowledge and accept the Supreme Court's decision in *State v. Mitchell* finding Wisconsin's hate crime law constitutional. Nevertheless, we may well question the soundness of the Court's reasoning.

The *Mitchell* statute was upheld as constitutional; it is well-intentioned and is better than most in some ways. But the most that can be said about even the law upheld in *Mitchell*—certainly one of the best of its type—is that it is just barely constitutional. The *Mitchell* decision is no shining moment in First Amendment law; in fact, the statute was a successful attempt to circumvent the First Amendment to reach a desired result, not an attempt to strengthen it. It is worrisome that those who are ordinarily so protective of the First Amendment are satisfied with *minimal* constitutional compliance, instead of insisting on approaches that afford *maximum* protection to First Amendment values. Certainly, the goals of these laws are appealing. But it ill becomes those concerned with civil liberties and civil rights to be enthusiastic about what amounts to an end run around First Amendment values. Furthermore, as Professor Jacobs points out, the laws do little, if anything, to accomplish these goals. There are numerous alternative approaches that do not focus on motives, and that would also serve these goals better than enhancement or bump-up type hate crimes laws....

I. What *Mitchell* Doesn't Say

A. There's More Than One Way to Skin This Cat: Alternatives to Hate Crime Enhancement Laws

Discussion of hate crime laws often assumes that these laws are urgently needed because they are the only way to serve important social goals. In fact, not only are they not the only way, they are far from the best way. To begin with, noncriminal approaches are more likely to serve those goals than the punishment of selected motives. Realistically, only a major commitment to education and social and economic programs, which can alleviate the conditions of ignorance, frustration and despair that breed bias and crime, can be expected to make any significant progress toward discouraging bias crimes. Short of that, bias-crime-conscious victim assistance, police awareness training, and preventive measures such as community education and conscientious allocation of police protection are more likely to have measurable effects than hate crime laws. The reporting and statistical requirements adopted by many jurisdictions may or may not be useful. Even the symbolic function of hate crime laws is better achieved by other forms of governmental action, such as incentives for, recognition of, and the official practice of tolerance and pluralism. It is both futile and cynical for government to try to make a symbolic statement by punishing private persons' homophobic motives, while at the same time making the opposite statement by having sodomy laws, or by refusing to consider sexual orientation a "suspect classification" for equal protection purposes.

Even if a legislature determines that only some sort of penalty enhancement will do, the content- and viewpoint-specific approach is unnecessary, because many neutral enhancement factors would serve the same interests. For example, penalties could be enhanced where:

1. The offender acted with the specific intent to create (or with knowledge that he was likely to create) terror within a definable community.
2. The offender acted with specific intent to create (or with knowledge that he was likely to create) a threat of further crime.
3. The offender knew or should have known that a victim was particularly susceptible to the criminal conduct.
4. The offender, in the commission of the offense, intended to inflict serious emotional distress.
5. The commission of the offense created serious psychological harm (comparable to "serious physical harm" specifications that enhance penalties).
6. The offender acted with specific intent to interfere with another's exercise of constitutional or statutory rights, or another's enjoyment of or access to public facilities, or another's enjoyment of equal opportunity.

Each of these formulas is content- and viewpoint-neutral, and each alone or in conjunction with others would reach all the conduct contemplated by hate crimes laws. In fact, the federal sentencing guidelines upon which the third example above is based have already been used to enhance penalties for cross-burning offenses.

Indeed, these effects-centered approaches are better tailored to serve the government's asserted interest (which, after all, is claimed to focus on effects, not motives). The Wisconsin statute upheld in *Mitchell*, for example, was defended as punishing not bigotry, but the special harms to the victim and others created by "intentional selection of the victim" because of ethnicity. It therefore would apply where a victim is selected because of race, in a situation that has nothing to do with bigotry and creates no risk of the special harms which are said to justify the extra punishment. For example, A goes to her car and sees that the windshield has been smashed. A bystander tells her that the deed was done just a few seconds ago, by an Asian, B, whom she then assaults. A's selection of B was based upon his ethnicity, although it was significant only for identification, not for bias. Nevertheless, the law applies even though none of its purposes are implicated. If it doesn't, then the law demonstrably *is* punishing bigotry, not "intentional selection." At the same time, suppose C, motivated purely by bigotry and with specific intent to create fear and terror in the African-American community, assaults D, a white civil rights activist. C is not guilty under the Wisconsin statute, because D was not selected because of his race, but because of his identification with the civil rights movement.

These results do not make sense. C's actions were intentionally likely to create the racist shock waves the law seeks to prevent and punish; A's were not. The government's interest in preventing and punishing the specific harms and effects associated with hate crimes is not served by exposing A to an extra five years imprisonment, while not reaching C at all.

So why would a legislature insist on a motive-specific, "bump-up" type hate crime law? They do have some advantages over other approaches — for the legislature, anyway. They are quick, they are easy, they get great media coverage, they offend no important constituencies, and they cost nothing. They also punish bigotry, a purpose their proponents deny but which explains why none of the neutral alternatives is satisfactory. . . .

B. Now You See It, Now You Don't: Are Hate Crime Laws About Punishing Bigotry?

Proponents of hate crime laws are hard to pin down on whether the state's interest underlying those laws has anything to do with bigotry. They deny (as they must, to avoid running afoul of the First Amendment) that the government interest underlying these laws has anything to do with suppression of bigotry itself, or of bigoted thought, opinion, or messages. In support of this defense, they assert that these laws do not actually require proof of a *negative* race-related motive. A positive or neutral race-related motive (whatever that could be) will also trigger the statute.

However, when stating the government interest that justifies these laws, proponents assert that bias-motivated crime creates different and worse effects than other crime, has an impact on the victim's entire group, and sends a message of hatred. It is hard to imagine that these are the results of any race-related motive other than bigotry. Moreover, when opponents point out that neutral laws would address these effects even better, the response is that neutral laws fail to send a message of governmental disapproval of bigotry.

It is inconsistent to argue that hate crime laws are not directed at bigotry in one step of the strict scrutiny analysis (assertion of a legitimate and compelling state interest), and then to argue that these laws are directed specifically at bigotry at another step (wherein the state must show that neutral alternatives would not adequately serve the state's interest). But proponents of hate crime laws are forced into playing this shell game, with bigotry as the "pea," because a law specifically punishing bigotry is unconstitutional, and a law punishing all crimes with an ethnic element (even where none of the effects caused by a bias element occurs, is intended, or is foreseeable) is pointless.

The *Mitchell* Court said that "the Wisconsin statute singles out for enhancement bias-inspired conduct because this conduct is thought to inflict greater individual and societal harm. For example, according to the State and its amici, bias-motivated crimes are more likely to provoke retaliatory crimes, inflict distinct emotional harms on their victims, and incite community unrest." However, fears of responsive violence do not justify content- and viewpoint-based restrictions. Motives, like all First Amendment activity, cannot be regulated on the basis of conclusory and speculative assertions of possible future harm. Even statistical evidence of the likelihood of that harm actually occurring would not permit regulation on the basis of content: pornography and even the Super Bowl have been statistically linked to increases in violence against women, but that does not justify their prohibition or punishment.

Moreover, even if it could be reasonably assumed that crimes motivated by bias are more provocative than crimes motivated by greed or need, it cannot similarly be assumed that crimes motivated by one of the subjects enumerated in hate crime laws are more provocative of retaliation or imitation than crimes motivated by politics, gender, abortion, or antiwar sentiment. Nor is there any reason to believe that offenders motivated by ethnic bias are more likely to repeat than offenders who selected their victims "because of" other reasons such as politics or abortion or, for that matter, greed. It is reasonable to assume, in fact, that the defendants in *United States v. O'Brien, Texas v. Johnson, United States v. Eichman,* and *Bray v. Alexandria Women's Health Clinic,* all of whom deliberately acted to make public statements, would be at least as likely as Todd Mitchell, who acted spontaneously, to engage in similar conduct again and to feel no remorse for their actions.

As for the "distinct emotional harms" cause by bias-motivated crimes, the Court in *R.A.V.* stated that these consist of the impact of the defendant's beliefs and the offensiveness of their communication. This harm may well be both real and significant, but in *R.A.V.* the Court had acknowledged that the beliefs and their communications are still squarely within the protection of the First Amendment:

> What makes the anger, fear, sense of dishonor, etc. produced by the violation of this ordinance distinct from the anger, fear, sense of dishonor, etc. produced by other fighting words is nothing other than the fact that it is caused by a distinctive idea, conveyed by a distinctive message. The First Amendment cannot be evaded that easily.

Thus, even if the injuries suffered by the victim or others from hate crimes are "distinct" from the injuries caused by crimes with other motives, the essence of that distinction is something that the government has no power to punish.

Indeed, if government can point to the harmful effects of "a distinctive idea" as a compelling state interest justifying punishment of motives, there is no reason it could not point to those same harmful effects to justify punishing bigoted books, marches, speeches, and associations as well. Nazi demonstrations in Skokie or distribution of *Mein Kampf* would have effects at least as terrifying and widespread as would a battery in which the victim was selected "because of" her being Jewish.

The Satanic Verses causes "special harms" that *A Child's Garden of Verses* does not; *The Last Temptation of Christ* spread resentment that *E.T.* did not; Robert Mapplethorpe's art is more upsetting than Norman Rockwell's; a speech by Louis Farrakhan is more likely to provoke retaliation than a speech by Bill Cosby. Government has the same compelling interest in redressing the same "special harm" irrespective of how it is caused. A state may not constitutionally enact a law stating that "No person shall publish a book that he knows or should know is likely to create the same types of harms as are created by a violation of the statute upheld in *Mitchell,*" although its interest would be identical by definition. Understandable and even commendable as this interest may be, it cannot justify a law treating bigoted books differently from other books because the former create special harms. For the same reason, it does not justify hate crime laws, which treat bigoted crimes differently from other crimes because they do exactly the same thing. . . .

III. What *Mitchell* Could Not Reach: Policy Concerns

A. Encouragement of Other Bad Legislation

Punishment of thought may not seem too terrible when the thought punished is as widely abhorred as bigotry. But proponents of hate crime laws cannot build fail-safe laws that grant government the power to punish motives only when the motives relate to bigotry. Power to punish some motives is power to punish all motives.

If it is constitutional for the government to add penalties for motives related to race and religion, then it is constitutional for government to add penalties for motives relating to Communism, environmental concerns, labor, or anything else. A legislature in a pro-choice jurisdiction might upgrade offenses committed with an *anti*-abortion motive ("by reason of protection of the unborn").

Unfortunately, this is no fanciful hypothetical. In the wake of the recent shootings of abortionists in Pensacola, Mobile, and Wichita, activists on both sides of the abortion debate have been calling for the law to recognize the offenders' anti-abortion motives. Some pro-choice advocates have demanded the enactment of a special trespass offense for abortion clinics, and some pro-life advocates have called for a "justifiable homicide" defense for those motivated by the defense of "innocent boys and girls."

It can get even worse. If the government has the power to *increase* penalties for motives it *does not* like, it also has the power to *decrease* or even eliminate penalties for motives it *does* like. A homophobic legislature could take an offense for which the penalty is three years, upgrade it to eight years if the offender was motivated by race, and *downgrade* it to six months (or even zero) if the offender was motivated by sexual orientation. Preposterous? Sure — but again, quite possible. A bill passed by a broad margin in the Louisiana House of Representatives that would have reduced penalties for battery from six months prison time and a fine of $500, to no prison time and only a $25 fine, *if* the battery was motivated by the victim's having burned an American flag.

Our criminal laws and social policies should not be dictated by which side of a controversy has more clout nor the imminency of the next election. In the case of hate crime laws, the obvious and widespread appeal of the proponents' views makes it seem harmless to punish bigotry-related motives. Unfortunately, viewpoints are more likely to be written into law for the number of votes they represent than for their merit or fairness. In the case of bigotry we may feel popularity and merit coincide; in other areas they will not, but popularity will still carry the day if permitted. That is why we have the Bill of Rights: to protect the individual from the overbearing will — well-intentioned or not — of the majority. Carving out exceptions to please the majority defeats the purpose.

B. Discouragement of Good Legislation

Criminal statutes are poorly suited as tools for creating a tolerant society. Anti-social behavior (criminal or not) seems to thrive in communities where it is tolerated — not in the sense that it is condoned, but where it has become so commonplace that it has lost its power to shock. This seems to be true of many kinds of behaviors, including littering, substance abuse, domestic violence, and owning assault weapons. These things are illegal in all communities, and they also may be equally disapproved of by the majority in all communities. But in some communities these things are still shocking; in others, they are not. People still disapprove, but they have learned to accept the behavior as a fact of life; wrong but not a taboo.

Community taboos prevent anti-social behavior better than criminal penalties do. All the "anti-hate" laws in the world won't stop people from believing and expressing bigoted views as well as would a general understanding that their own communities reject bigotry and reject the bigots themselves. The law cannot make hatred shocking nor bigots pariahs; only the community, over time, can do that. Perhaps this is an endorsement of pressure to conform to political correctness. Still, there is a world of difference between social pressure and government force for the same ends.

C. Disproportionate Enforcement Against Minorities

Hate crime laws invite disproportionate enforcement against minority group members. In December 1993, Klanwatch, a project of the Southern Poverty Law Center whose hate crime data tracking system is considered one of the most reliable available, reported that "[h]ate violence committed by blacks in the United States is 'escalating at an alarming rate.'" Forty-one percent of all racially motivated murders so far that year had been committed by blacks, or blacks had been arrested as suspects. The figure was 46% for 1991-1993, although Klanwatch had documented only one racially motivated murder committed by a black in 1990 and none in 1989.

F.B.I. statistics showed the same trend. Pursuant to the Hate Crime Statistics Act of 1990, the F.B.I. released statistics for the first time in February 1993. The data, supplied by 2,771 law enforcement agencies in 32 states, disclosed that members of minority groups are being charged with "hate crimes" in numbers far in excess of their proportion to the population.

Conclusion

Proponents of hate crime laws surely have the finest of intentions. People of good will everywhere share the vision of a society free from the curses of bigotry, hate, and violence. However, an incursion into liberty is no less prohibited when employed in the name of good than when employed in the name of evil, and is no less dangerous.

One generation's faith in its own good intentions and judgment must not blind it to the reality that the license it grants to itself today will someday be inherited by others, perhaps less committed to the ideas of brotherhood and tolerance. Had a hate crime law been in force in Alabama in 1964 when Dr. Martin Luther King, Jr. held a civil rights demonstration without complying with a permit law, he could have been subject to drastically greater penalties.

Moreover, if our ultimate goal is not just to redress the criminal fruits of intolerance, but to eliminate intolerance altogether, our best hope lies outside of laws like these. In *Texas v. Johnson* the Supreme Court said: "We do not consecrate the flag by punishing its desecration, for in doing so we dilute the freedom that this cherished emblem represents." So it is with hate crime laws: we will not cure bigotry by punishing it, nor teach tolerance by being intolerant. Locking up or silencing the bigots among us will bring only the illusion of mutual acceptance and respect.

Fortunately, government need not choose between punishing thought of which it disapproves on the one hand, and standing silently by while people suffer on the other. Government is free to espouse the ideals of mutual tolerance and even to punish those who, in rejecting those ideals, hurt others. It must simply do so in a way that is as faithful to our commitment to liberty as it is to our aspirations to equality.

PROVING CRIMES

PART

PROVING CRIMES

Proving Crimes

■ THE LAW

Model Penal Code
(Official Draft 1962)

Section 1.12. Proof Beyond a Reasonable Doubt; Affirmative Defenses; Burden of Proving Fact When Not an Element of an Offense; Presumptions

(1) No person may be convicted of an offense unless each element of such offense is proved beyond a reasonable doubt. In the absence of such proof, the innocence of the defendant is assumed.

(2) Subsection (1) of this Section does not:

(a) require the disproof of an affirmative defense unless and until there is evidence supporting such defense; or

(b) apply to any defense which the Code or another statute plainly requires the defendant to prove by a preponderance of evidence.

(3) A ground of defense is affirmative, within the meaning of Subsection (2)(a) of this Section, when:

(a) it arises under a section of the Code which so provides; or

(b) it relates to an offense defined by a statute other than the Code and such statute so provides; or

(c) it involves a matter of excuse or justification peculiarly within the knowledge of the defendant on which he can fairly be required to adduce supporting evidence.

(4) When the application of the Code depends upon the finding of a fact which is not an element of an offense, unless the Code otherwise provides:

(a) the burden of proving the fact is on the prosecution or defendant, depending on whose interest or contention will be furthered if the finding should be made; and

(b) the fact must be proved to the satisfaction of the Court or jury, as the case may be.

(5) When the Code establishes a presumption with respect to any fact which is an element of an offense, it has the following consequences:

(a) when there is evidence of the facts which give rise to the presumption, the issue of the existence of the presumed fact must be submitted to the jury, unless the Court is satisfied that the evidence as a whole clearly negatives the presumed fact; and

(b) when the issue of the existence of the presumed fact is submitted to the jury, the Court shall charge that while the presumed fact must, on all the evidence, be proved beyond a reasonable doubt, the law declares that the jury may regard the facts giving rise to the presumption as sufficient evidence of the presumed fact.

(6) A presumption not established by the Code or inconsistent with it has the consequences otherwise accorded it by law.

● OVERVIEW OF PROVING CRIMES

Requirements and Limitations for Proving a Crime: Burdens of Proof Each jurisdiction sets rules for establishing which party in a criminal case has the burden of proving which issues. In addition, the federal Constitution has been interpreted to impose some restrictions on how a state may allocate the burdens of proof. Three distinct burdens of proof are involved: the burden of pleading, the burden of production, and the burden of persuasion.

Burden of Pleading The party that has the *burden of pleading* on an issue, or "burden of going forward," as it is sometimes called, has the burden of raising that issue. Little evidence is required. The state has the burden of pleading on all elements of the offense definition, but the defendant frequently is given the burden of raising issues of defense, even if such defenses operate by negating an offense element. For example, the defendant may have the burden of raising the issue of his mental illness even if its claimed effect is to negate a required offense culpability element. Once the burden of pleading is satisfied, it is then for the party having the burden of production to introduce sufficient evidence to satisfy its burden.

Burden of Production *The burden of production* establishes the quantum of evidence that a party must present on an issue to get that issue to the jury. The prosecution has the burden of production for all elements of the offense definition as well as any issues raised by the defendant that suggest the absence of a required element—that is, "absent element" defenses. Thus, if the defendant offers an alibi or claims a mistake or mental illness negating an offense element, the prosecution nonetheless must establish that, notwithstanding the evidence of alibi, mistake, or mental illness, sufficient evidence exists to satisfy its burden of production that the offense element exists. The defendant may be given the burden of production on issues of defense other than those relating to offense elements.

Failure to Satisfy Burden of Production   If the prosecution fails to meet its burden of production on an offense element, the trial judge enters a verdict of acquittal. If the prosecution fails to meet its burden of production to disprove a defense, the jury will be instructed on the defense. (Of course, if the prosecution also has the burden of persuasion to disprove the defense, the court may enter a judgement of acquittal on the theory that if the prosecution cannot meet its burden of production, it would be unable to meet its more demanding burden of persuasion.) If the defense fails to meet its burden of production on a defense issue, the jury will not be given an instruction to consider that defense.

Burden of Production vs. Pleading   The burden of production must be distinguished from the *burden of pleading,* discussed above. The burden of pleading simply imposes an obligation on the burdened party to raise the issue. The burden of production imposes a standard of evidence that must be met if the burdened party is to be successful in having the issue presented to or withheld from the jury, as the case may be. The burden of pleading is simply the first step in the evidentiary battle. Where the defense meets its burden of pleading for a defense, for example, subsequent evidence by the prosecution may so discredit the defense's initial claim as to leave the defense in the same position with regard to the burden of production that it was in before it presented its initial evidence suggesting the defense. Unless the defense presents further evidence, it will not satisfy its burden of production, and the claimed defense will not be presented to the jury.

Evidence Required to Satisfy Burden of Production   The amount of evidence required to satisfy a burden of production typically is stated in vague terms and is likely to vary from jurisdiction to jurisdiction. Such tests, contained as they are in statutes or court rules of procedure, generally do not have constitutional status. However, the Supreme Court has provided what is in effect a constitutional ~~Supreme~~ minimum standard for the burden of production for the prosecution. In *Jackson v.* ~~Ct. Std~~ *Virginia,* the Supreme Court set a constitutional standard for reviewing the insufficiency of evidence to support a conviction.[1] A conviction must be reversed if it is found that, on the record of evidence adduced at the trial, taken in the light most favorable to the prosecution, no rational trier of fact could have found proof of guilt beyond a reasonable doubt. If a conviction will be reversed as a violation of due process absent this amount of evidence, it would seem to follow that a trial court should not allow a case to go to the jury if this amount of evidence has not been adduced at trial.

Model Penal Code's Burden of Production   In civil practice, each party carries the burden of production for those issues from which the party will benefit. Thus, the defendant typically has the burden of production for all defenses. This tends to be true in criminal trials as well, but many jurisdictions follow the Model Penal Code in allocating the burden of production on many defense issues to the

---

1. 443 U.S. 307, 99 S. Ct. 2781, 61 L. Ed. 2d 560 (1979) (defendant, convicted of first degree murder, challenged jury finding of premeditation beyond reasonable doubt).

prosecution, even though it is not constitutionally required. Where this occurs, the prosecution must introduce sufficient evidence to *disprove* the defense. Where the burden is not met, the trial court will not let the case go to the jury and will, instead, enter a judgement of acquittal. Under the Model Penal Code, the defendant bears the burden of production only for defenses that are denoted "affirmative defenses." "[D]isproof of an affirmative defense [by the state is not required] *unless and until there is evidence supporting such defense....*"[1] Note that no set quantum of evidence is required of the defendant, but "evidence" presumably means something more than an unsubstantiated claim.[2] The Code also provides:

> A ground of defense is affirmative ... when:
> (a) it arises under a section of the Code which so provides; or
> (b) it relates to an offense defined by a statute other than the Code and such statute so provides; or
> (c) it involves a matter of excuse or justification peculiarly within the knowledge of the defendant on which he can fairly be required to adduce supporting evidence.[3]

General defenses labeled as "affirmative" in the Model Penal Code include the involuntary intoxication excuse, duress, military orders, all justification defenses, insanity, and renunciation.[4]

Burden of Persuasion Once the case reaches the jury, the burden of persuasion tells the jury how they should decide if they are unpersuaded on an issue. The jury is instructed that it is their obligation to acquit the defendant if the state has not met its burden of persuasion. The defendant also is to be acquitted if she satisfies the burden of persuasion on any defense. Typically, the state must prove all elements of the offense beyond a reasonable doubt. When the defendant is given a burden of persuasion it typically requires only "proof by a preponderance of the evidence" or, at most, "proof by clear and convincing evidence."

Constitutional Restrictions in Allocating Burden of Persuasion The federal Constitution limits the issues on which the defendant may be given the burden of persuasion. *In re Winship* held that the prosecution must prove beyond a reasonable doubt "every fact necessary to constitute the crime with which [the defendant] is charged."[5] In *Mullaney v. Wilbur,* this was held to include *disproving* the defendant's claim of provocation; provocation under the Maine murder statute was seen as inconsistent with the required element of malice aforethought.[6] In *Patterson v. New York,* however, the Court held that the state need

---

1. Model Penal Code § 1.12(2)(a) (emphasis added).

2. The Commentary states the drafters' preference for leaving this "quantum" vague in the code. They "thought it the wiser course to leave this question to the courts." Model Penal Code § 1.12 comment 3 at 193 (1985).

3. Model Penal Code § 1.12(3).

4. Model Penal Code §§ 2.08(4), 2.09(1), 2.10, 3.01, 4.03(1), 5.01(3), 5.02(3), 5.03(6). Specific offenses also contain affirmative defenses. See, e.g., id. §§ 212.4(1), 212.5(1), 220.1(1), 221.1(1), 221.2(3), 221.3(3), 223.4, 223.9, 224.6.

5. 397 U.S. 358, 364, 90 S. Ct. 1068, 1072, 25 L. Ed. 2d 368, 375 (1970) (in juvenile delinquency proceeding for 12-year old charged with stealing, child entitled, as matter of due process, to have case against him proven beyond reasonable doubt).

6. 421 U.S. 684, 95 S. Ct. 1881, 44 L. Ed. 2d 508 (1975).

not carry the burden of persuasion on disproving the defendant's claim of extreme emotional disturbance. A modern, expanded form of the provocation mitigation, New York's "extreme emotional disturbance" doctrine was defined not as something negating a required offense element, but rather as providing an independent doctrine of mitigation.[1] Earlier cases held, and *Patterson* confirmed, that the burden of persuasion also may be constitutionally allocated to the defendant for a defense of insanity.[2] Aside from these, the Court has not fully clarified the criteria to be used in assessing whether an issue is sufficiently like an offense element to require the prosecution to carry the burden of persuasion on it, or whether it is sufficiently like the defense of insanity or the mitigation of extreme emotional disturbance to allow allocation to the defendant.

Model Penal Code's Burden of Persuasion   The Model Penal Code, as noted above, allocates the burden of persuasion to the prosecution on most issues, including defenses, even though such allocation is not constitutionally required. The Code provides:

> No person may be convicted of an offense unless each element of such offense is proved beyond a reasonable doubt. In the absence of such proof, the innocence of the defendant is assumed.[3]

The code then defines "element of an offense" very broadly to include the absence of most general defenses:

> "element of an offense" means (i) such conduct or (ii) such attendant circumstances or (iii) such a result of conduct as
> > (a) is included in the description of the forbidden conduct in the definition of the offense; or
> > (b) establishes the required kind of culpability; or
> > (c) negatives an excuse or justification for such conduct; or
> > (d) negatives a defense under the statute of limitations; or
> > (e) establishes jurisdiction or venue;[4] . . .

The only exception to the prosecution's burden of persuasion is "any defense which the Code or another statute plainly requires the defendant to prove by a preponderance of evidence."[5] The defenses for which the Code allocates the burden of persuasion to the defendant include the general mistake of law defense for unavailable law and reliance upon official misstatement, the due diligence defense to liability of an organization, and entrapment.[6] For the few facts that

---

1. 432 U.S. 197, 97 S. Ct. 2319, 53 L. Ed. 2d 281 (1977).

2. Leland v. Oregon, 343 U.S. 790, 72 S. Ct. 1002, 96 L. Ed. 1302 (1952); Rivera v. Delaware, 429 U.S. 877, 97 S. Ct. 226, 50 L. Ed. 2d 160 (1976); Patterson, 432 U.S. at 204, 97 S. Ct. at 2324, 53 L. Ed. 2d at 288 (1977).

3. Model Penal Code § 1.12(1).

4. Model Penal Code § 1.13(9).

5. Model Penal Code § 1.12(2)(b).

6. Model Penal Code §§ 2.04(4), 2.07(5), 2.13(2). Some offenses also include defenses for which the defendant has the burden of persuasion. See, e.g., id. §§ 5.07, 213.6(1), 213.6(3), 223.1(2)(b), 224.6(3), 224.7.

do not fall under the Code's broad meaning of the phrase "element of an offense," the allocation of the burden of persuasion is governed as follows:

When the application of the Code depends upon the finding of a fact which is not an element of an offense, unless the Code otherwise provides:

(a) the burden of proving the fact is on the prosecution or defendant, depending on whose interest or contention will be furthered if the finding should be made; and

(b) the fact must be proved to the satisfaction of the Court or jury, as the case may be.[1]

Most states do not follow the Model Penal Code on these issues. Most define "elements of an offense" in a more common-sense way to include just the elements of the offense definition, and are more likely to put the burden of persuasion for a general defense on the defendant.

Mandatory Presumptions   Where a jury is instructed to presume the satisfaction of a required element from the presence of a different, proven fact, the effect of the instruction may be similar to shifting the burden of persuasion to the defendant. The use of such presumptions, therefore, has come under constitutional limitation. For example, murder may require proof of an intention to kill, but if the jury is instructed that "the law presumes that a person intends the ordinary consequences of his voluntary acts," the prosecution may in effect be relieved of its constitutional obligation, imposed in *Winship,* to prove the defendant's intention to kill beyond a reasonable doubt. It is for this reason that such a presumption was held unconstitutional in *Sandstrom v. Montana.*[2] These presumptions are called *mandatory* presumptions because they *direct,* or might be interpreted by a jury as directing, the jury to find the presumed fact if the proven fact is present.

Permissive Inferences   Only mandatory presumptions have been held unconstitutional. It is not improper to instruct a jury that the law *allows* the jury to presume one fact on proof of another fact. Such a rule commonly is called a *permissive inference.* Thus a jury properly may be instructed that it is permitted to presume, if it so chooses, that a prohibited weapon in a vehicle was possessed by the person in the vehicle. This means that the jury may be instructed that it is allowed to presume that the person in the car possessed the weapon based solely on the fact that the prosecution proved the fact that the weapon was present in the car. Permissible inferences are constitutional, however, only if in practice the fact to be presumed more likely than not follows from the fact proven.[3] It is likely that a person in a car containing a weapon possesses that weapon; it is not, however, more likely than not that a person who, for instance, bumps someone into the street from a crowded crosswalk, causing him to be struck and killed intended to kill that person.

---

1. Model Penal Code § 1.12(4).

2. 442 U.S. 510, 99 S. Ct. 2450, 61 L. Ed. 2d 39 (1979).

3. County Court of Ulster County v. Allen, 442 U.S. 140, 157, 99 S. Ct. 2213, 2225, 60 L. Ed. 2d 777, 792 (1979) (possession of firearm in automobile statutorily presumed to be evidence of its illegal possession by all occupants).

Model Penal Code's Use of Presumptions The Model Penal Code's treatment of presumptions does two things: (a) it creates a rebuttable presumption that a party has satisfied its burden of production on a presumed fact where there is evidence of the proven fact; and (b) it creates a permissive inference that may help a party satisfy its burden of persuasion. The relevant section provides:

When the Code establishes a presumption with respect to any fact which is an element of an offense, it has the following consequences:

(a) when there is evidence of the facts which give rise to the presumption, the issue of the existence of the presumed fact must be submitted to the jury, unless the Court is satisfied that the evidence as a whole clearly negatives the presumed fact; and

(b) when the issue of the existence of the presumed fact is submitted to the jury, the Court shall charge that while the presumed fact must, on all the evidence, be proved beyond a reasonable doubt, the law declares that the jury may regard the facts giving rise to the presumption as sufficient evidence of the presumed fact.

A presumption not established by the Code or inconsistent with it has the consequences otherwise accorded it by law.[1]

Thus the Code's use of presumptions is constitutional even under the most recent cases, decided more than seventeen years after the Code was drafted.

---

1. Model Penal Code § 1.12(5) & (6).

ADVANCED ISSUES

APPENDIX A: SECTION 3

Theories of Punishment

ADVANCED ISSUES

Notes on Hybrid Distributive Principles

Resolving Conflicts Among Distributive Principles If there is the greatest utility in a desert distribution, then no conflict exists between retributivist and utilitarian goals. But if one does not accept the notion that a desert distribution provides the greatest utility (as the traditional utilitarian view does not), then conflicts between the two kinds of distributive principles are inevitable. The previous discussion illustrates potential conflicts. If there are conflicts among distributive principles, then how are these conflicts to be resolved? When one distributive principle suggests one degree of liability and punishment for an offender or suggests one rule or policy but other principles suggest a different degree of liability and punishment or a different rule or policy, how does one choose between the conflicting principles?

"Familiar Litany" of Little Help Most criminal codes and criminal law courses offer the "familiar litany" of the purposes of criminal law sanctions — just punishment, deterrence, incapacitation of the dangerous, and rehabilitation. This is the approach the Model Penal Code takes.[1] We train and direct our lawyers, judges, and legislators to use these purposes as guiding principles for the distribution of criminal sanctions. But the list, by itself, gives judges, legislators, and sentencing-guideline drafters no guidance in what to do when two or more purposes on the list conflict.

Inconsistency in Selecting Distributive Principle In the absence of a guiding principle for resolving conflicts, there is little surprise that the resulting choices are somewhat inconsistent. For example, most state criminal codes maintain an insanity defense because it exculpates the blameless (and thus furthers just punishment), even though abolishing the defense might more effectively

---

1. See Model Penal Code § 1.02(1) ("the general purposes of the provisions governing the definition of offenses").

incapacitate the dangerous. Yet the same codes sacrifice just punishment in favor of increasing deterrence when they recognize strict liability. At the same time, codes frequently decrease the deterrent threat—such as, for example, in cases of provocation—because of the offender's reduced blameworthiness, instead of increasing the threatened sanction when the temptation or inclination is greater, as a deterrence principle suggests. Such inconsistencies indicate that code drafters are choosing to further different purposes in different contexts. At best, the reason for their selection among the conflicting principles in any given instance are unclear. At worst, it may lead to arbitrariness or prejudice.

Unprincipled Sentencing The potential for arbitrariness and prejudice is greatest where the selection of distributive principle concerns just a specific case, as in sentencing, rather than a rule that affects a class of cases, as in code or guideline drafting. For example, while rehabilitation might be the best means of avoiding future crime by a young addict who is caught selling drugs to support his habit, a judge rationally might decide to impose a long prison term in order to further general deterrent interests. The same judge, when faced with a young bank teller who embezzled money from her cash drawer, might decide, under an incapacitative theory, to sacrifice the general deterrent value of a long prison term and put the offender on probation—she is no longer dangerous because she will never again be placed in a position of trust. The judge has chosen to follow one distributive principle in one case but another principle in another case, yet we do not know the grounds for the judge's selection. While each of the sentences has a plausible justification, the selection of one justification over others is a hidden and unguided exercise of discretion that creates the opportunity for arbitrary or biased decision making. Without a principle governing when one sentencing purpose is to be followed at the expense of another, judges are free to choose whatever purpose justifies the sentence that they may desire for other, unspoken, reasons.

Absence of Principle as Useful Flexibility Why do we not insist that code and sentencing-guideline drafters adopt, and that judges follow, a statement of the inter-relationship among purposes that will guide the choice among conflicting purposes? A cynic may conclude that the ability to pick at will from the "familiar litany" of "the purposes" is a convenient means of rationalizing results for which the decision maker has other undisclosed reasons. This suspicion—that "the purposes" are popular as a method of justification precisely *because* they offer hidden flexibility—is fueled by the almost universal failure to articulate a guiding principle. The Model Penal Code, for example, lists the traditional purposes and directs judges to use them in interpreting the provisions of the Code and in fashioning sentences under the Code. But the Code provides no more guidance in cases of conflict than to urge, in the Commentaries, that the purposes be "just[ly] harmonize[d]." Other writers suggest that the competing interests are to be "balance[d],"[1] "blend[ed],"[2]

1. Stanley A. Cohen, An Introduction to the Theory, Justifications and Modern Manifestations of Criminal Punishment, 27 McGill L.J. 73, 81 (1981).

2. Solicitor General, Report of the Canadian Committee on Corrections—Toward Unity: Criminal Justice and Corrections 188 (1969) (known as the Duimet Report).

"accommodate[d]," [1] "taken account of," [2] or "deal[t] with [such that] the public interest will be served." [3] In other words, all would preserve the unchecked discretion of judges and sentencing-guideline drafters to pick among conflicting distributive principles.

Defining Hybrid Distributive Principles   Whether the flexibility of rationalization offered by "the purposes" has been used for conscious manipulation or is the result of inadvertent vagueness, a rational and principled system for the distribution of criminal sanctions is needed. If multiple principles are to be relied on, a principled system must define the interrelationship among the principles; that is, it must fully articulate a hybrid distributive principle. There are two sorts of challenges in defining a hybrid distributive principle; one somewhat easier than the other. Can one define the interrelationship of different utilitarian distributive principles? And can one define the interrelationship of utilitarian and retributivist principles? [4]

Defining a Utilitarian Hybrid   The first is the easier of the two. Assume that, from a general deterrence perspective, doctrinal formulation of sentence A costs 10 units to gain a benefit of 15 units, for a net societal benefit of 5; while formulation B costs 10 to save 10, for a net benefit of 0. In this situation, general deterrence as a distributive principle would prefer formulation A. Assume that incapacitation finds that formulation A costs 10 in order to avoid a harm of 5, for a net loss of 5, while formulation B costs 10 to avoid an injury of 15, for a net gain of 5. Thus incapacitation as the distributive principle prefers formulation B. This would be an instance where the two purposes conflict.

Summing Costs and Benefits   One might have a system that simply gives priority to one utilitarian mechanism over another, but the better approach would be to take account of the effect on both mechanisms. Because the two purposes have the same goal (efficient crime prevention) and thus have a single currency, the costs and benefits of each formulation for both mechanisms may be determined and compared in order to select the best formulation. Thus, if a formulation significantly increases the effectiveness of the incapacitation mechanism while, relative to an alternative formulation, only slightly hurting the general deterrence mechanism, then the difference between the effects of the two formulations may be enough to justify following the formulation preferred by the incapacitation mechanism. The example above might be represented by the following analysis:

---

1. Stanley A. Cohen at 73.
2. Herbert Wechsler, Sentencing, Corrections and the Model Penal Code, 109 U. Pa. L. Rev. 465, 468, (1961).
3. State v. Ivan, 33 N.J. 197, 201, 162 A.2d 851, 853 (1960) (Weintraub, C.J.).
4. See generally Paul H. Robinson, Hybrid Principles for the Distribution of Criminal Sanctions, 82 Nw. U.L. Rev. 19, 19-22, 28-35 (1987) (discussing variety of methods for creating hybrid distributive principles).

Formulation A		Formulation B	
Deterrence	−10	−10	
	+15	+10	
	+5	0	Deterrence prefers Formulation A
Incapacitation	−10	−10	
	+5	+15	
	−5	+5	Incapacitation prefers Formulation B
Combined Assessment	0	+5	Combined mechanisms prefer Formulation B

What A gains in deterrence, it loses in incapacitation. B, however, remains even in deterrence while gaining in incapacitation. Thus B has a positive net effect. By combining the costs and benefits of both mechanisms in this manner, one can determine that formulation B will best further the common goal of efficient crime prevention.

Utilitarian-Retributivist Hybrid   The same summing mechanism cannot be used to resolve conflicts between utilitarian and retributivist principles. The costs and benefits of efficient crime prevention have no relevance to the retributivist, who sees the punishment as an end in itself rather than as a means to another end, such as crime prevention. Where utilitarian and retributivist principles suggest different results, there is little that can be done. The system must commit itself to one as being dominant over the other. Of course, as discussed previously,[1] if a desert distribution is judged to be of greatest utility, then there will be few conflicts between the utilitarian and retributivist views.[2]

Liability and Amount vs. Method of Punishment   The traditional purposes are used to resolve a range of distinguishable issues in the distribution of sanctions: Who should be punished? How much punishment should they receive? How should the punishment be imposed? The first issue is essentially one of liability assignment—who should be held criminally liable? The second issue—how much punishment?—addresses both liability rules (that is, what grade or degree of offense is appropriate for certain conduct) and sentencing practice (for example, how long a sentence or how great a fine is appropriate in a particular case). Together, these two issues govern the quantitative distribution of punishment—who will receive how much. The third issue—how should punishment

---

1. See supra, "Utility of desert."
2. But recall that there will continue to be some utilitarian-retributivist conflicts because of the remaining disagreement over how one determines desert. See supra, "Community's vs. moral philosophy's perception of desert."

be imposed? — is distinguishable from the distribution of amount. Two offenders may merit the same *amount* of punishment, yet different *methods* of punishment may be suitable for imposing that amount.

Retributivist Amount and Utilitarian Method These three issues — how much, for whom, and what method — are not only functionally distinguishable, they also properly may be subject to different distributive principles. Effective crime control can be furthered through a variety of mechanisms — such as setting the amount or the method of punishment (by setting enforcement and prosecution patterns and expenditures). Satisfaction of desert concerns, in contrast, depends almost exclusively on the amount issue — who receives how much; the method issue (as well as the resource allocation issues) is generally not relevant. The desert requirement of a proper ordinal ranking of offenders by overall blameworthiness, for example, concerns the ranking of *amounts* of sanctions. As long as the ordinal ranking is correct, the *method* by which each amount is imposed is not relevant to desert.[1] Thus one could fully satisfy desert by having it determine how much punishment and for whom, having utilitarian concerns govern the method of sanction (and the allocation of resources).[2]

---

1. Thus, if spending one month in the state prison is the punitive equivalent to spending weekends in the local jail for five months, then desert is satisfied even if the more blameworthy offender gets probation, with a condition of seven months of weekends in jail, while the less blameworthy offender goes to prison for one month. For, in such a case, the probation sentence of seven months exceeds the punitive equivalent of one month in state prison. Such calculations, however, are possible only with a reliable table of punishment equivalencies. Empirical research has been done on perceptions of relative seriousness of punishments, but such work is still in its infancy. See Robert E. Harlow, John M. Darley, and Paul H. Robinson, The Severity of Intermediate Penal Sanctions: A Psychophysical Scaling Approach for Obtaining Community Perceptions, 11 Journal of Quantitative Criminology 71 (1995).

2. With a table of punishment equivalencies, one could construct a sentencing system that allowed independent determinations of the amount and method issues. The principles governing the "amount" issue could generate a total of "sanction units" due to an offender, which could then be allocated to a particular sanctioning method or combination of methods according to a different set of "method" principles. See Paul H. Robinson, Desert, Crime Control, Disparity, and Units of Punishment, in Penal Theory and Penal Practice (R.A. Duff, et al. eds., 1993).

APPENDIX A: SECTION 4

Culpability Requirements

ADVANCED ISSUES

Notes on Determining Offense Culpability Requirements

Culpability with Respect to Each Kind of Objective Element   The description of culpability levels in the Overview of this Section uses culpability as to causing a result to illustrate the differences between levels. Model Penal Code section 2.02(2), in fact, defines each of the four kinds of culpability in relation to each of the three kinds of objective elements: conduct, circumstance, and result. The following chart gives the section 2.02(2) definition for each variation provided by section 2.02(2):

Chart: Model Penal §2.02(2)
Culpability Definitions by Kind of Objective Element

A person acts [culpability level] with respect to [kind of objective element] when:

	Result	Circumstance	Conduct
Purposely	"it is his conscious object ... to cause such a result"	"he is a aware of such circumstances or hopes that they exist"	"it is his conscious object to engage in conduct of that nature"
Knowingly	"he is aware that it is practically certain that his conduct will cause such a result"	"he is aware ... that such circumstances exist"	"he is aware his conduct is of that nature"
Recklessly	"he consciously disregards a substantial and unjustifiable risk that the material element ... will result from his conduct"	"he consciously disregards a substantial and unjustifiable risk that the material element exists"	—
Negligently	"he should be aware of a substantial and unjustifiable risk that the material element ... will result from his conduct"	"he should be aware of a substantial and unjustifiable risk that the material element exists"	—

Failure to Define Recklessness and Negligence with Respect to Conduct The Code's precision does much to bring clarity to what previously had been a troubled area, but some peculiarities in the definitional scheme leave several ambiguities. For example, note that the Code does not expressly define "recklessness" and "negligence" with respect to a conduct element. One explanation for this failure is that the drafters determined that, as a practical matter, neither recklessness nor negligence as to conduct is likely to arise. That is, it is unlikely that a person would not at least *know* the nature of conduct that they were performing. The Model Penal Code Commentary notes that "[w]ith respect to each of [the] three types of elements, the draft attempts to define each of the kinds of culpability *that may arise*."[1] Other sections of the Commentary, however, might be interpreted to suggest that the drafters did contemplate the possibility of recklessness or negligence as to conduct. Indeed, certain Code offenses appear specifically to proscribe reckless conduct. For example, one who "recklessly tampers with tangible property of another so as to endanger person or property" commits criminal mischief.[2] Similarly, one who "purposely or recklessly . . . kills or injures any animal" is guilty of cruelty to animals.[3]

Interpretations of Culpability as to "Conduct" One might resolve this ambiguity in the Code's definitional scheme by reasoning that, because some culpability is required as to each element of an offense, and "recklessness" and "negligence" as to conduct are not defined, then "knowledge" — which is the minimum culpability that is defined with respect to conduct — should be required. This argument can be buttressed by referring to section 2.02(5), which states that "When recklessness suffices to establish an element, such element also is established if a person acts purposely or *knowingly*." Some jurisdictions specifically provide that while "reckless" is to be read in when an offense is silent as to the culpability required for a circumstance or result element (that is, "reckless" is implied by the absence of a specific culpability), "knowing" is read in for a conduct element.[4] Another approach may be for a court to define "recklessness" and "negligence" with respect to conduct by extrapolating from the definition of those terms that exist with regard to circumstance and result elements.

Narrow Interpretation of "Conduct" This ambiguity as to the definitions of "reckless" and "negligent" as to conduct may be insignificant if "conduct" elements are defined narrowly to include only literally the *conduct* (muscular movement) of the actor. Under this approach, culpability as to an actor's "conduct" is relevant in the rare case that he does not know that he is engaging in a muscular movement, and these instances are likely to be exempt from liability under the involuntary act defense. Culpability as to the *nature* of one's conduct, in the sense of culpability as to its circumstances and its results, would be represented by the culpability required as to the circumstance and result elements

---

1. Model Penal Code § 2.02 comment 2 at 124 (Tentative Draft No. 4, 1955) (emphasis added).

2. Model Penal Code § 220.3(1)(b) (1980). But see the alternative interpretation of such language discussed infra at "Combining conduct and result or conduct and circumstance," et seq.

3. Model Penal Code § 250.11.

4. See, e.g., S.1437, 95th Cong., 2d Sess. §§ 302(c), 303(b)(1) (1978) (recklessness as to conduct undefined; minimum state of mind that must be proved with respect to conduct is knowledge); see also Alaska Stat. §§ 11.81.610(b), .900(a)(2)–(4) (Supp. 1984).

of the offense. Thus the conduct of "obstructing a public roadway" would be understood to be conduct, whatever the particular actions might be, that caused the obstruction of (a result) a public roadway (a circumstance). The important culpability that might be in dispute at trial, then, is the actor's culpability as to causing the *result* of obstructing and his culpability as to the *circumstance* of it being a public roadway. Thus an actor's culpability as to his conduct itself, the actions he performed to cause the obstruction, are rarely an issue (and where they are — where, for example, he blocks the roadway because he faints in his tractor trailer — a general excuse defense arising from his involuntariness will govern the matter, not the offense culpability requirements).

Advantages of "Narrow" Definition of "Conduct"   This narrow interpretation of what constitutes a "conduct" element not only gives a clear definition, without need for judicial extrapolation, but also has the important advantage of maximizing the legislature's ability to provide a different culpability level for different elements of a single offense. To treat "conduct" as including the circumstances and results of one's conduct would be to treat the conduct (narrow sense) and the circumstances and results of the conduct as a single element. This would require that a single culpability level must apply to all. To strip the circumstances and results of conduct from the "conduct" element, on the other hand, and treat them as independent "circumstance" and "result" elements, is to create several elements and thereby allow different culpability as to different elements. These issues are discussed further in the next Section.

Asymmetry in Definition of "Purposely"   Another asymmetry revealed by the chart is found in the definition of "purposely" with respect to a circumstance element. Recall that the hallmark of purposeful culpability in the context of result elements is the actor's *conscious object* to cause that result; "knowing" as to a result requires only that the actor be aware that his conduct will cause the result, not that he desires or hopes that it will. "Purposely" as to a conduct element has an analogous meaning: It must be the actor's conscious object to engage in conduct of that nature. It is not enough that he is aware that his conduct is of that nature ("knowing" as to conduct). In the context of circumstance elements, however, "purposely" requires only that the actor "[be] *aware* of such circumstances or hope(s) that they exist." In other words, "purpose" as to a circumstance can be shown by proving no more than is required to show "knowing" as to a circumstance. The distinction between "purposely" and "knowingly" is thereby eliminated for circumstance elements. The Model Penal Code Commentary gives no explanation and, indeed, does not acknowledge the variation. One can only speculate that the drafters thought the purposeful-knowing distinction to be irrelevant in the context of culpability as to circumstances, as opposed to the context of result and conduct elements in which it is relevant.[1] The next Section examines how these and other ambiguities create significant difficulties in the operation of the Model Penal Code culpability scheme.

---

1. Knowledge that the requisite external circumstances exist is a common element of [purpose and knowledge]. But action is not purposive with respect to the nature or result of the actor's conduct unless it was his conscious object to perform an action of that nature or to cause such a result.

Model Penal Code § 2.02 comment 2 at 233 (1985).

Raimer Sets a Record Raimer works in the office of the university registrar to help pay his tuition. Anna, a student, asks for a copy of her official file. The photocopying machine in the office is not working at the moment, so Anna asks if she can take the file to copy it on another machine. Because Raimer is new, he is unsure of the office policy. He thinks it is probably all right and that he probably has the authority to let her do it. When Bob, another student who works in the office, returns from his coffee break and learns that Raimer has allowed Anna to take her file, he berates Raimer for what he says is Raimer's irresponsibility and his insensitivity to the importance of proper handling of the files. This is a serious matter, Bob explains, and shows Raimer a copy of the following criminal statute:

> *Tampering with Records.* A person commits a misdemeanor if, knowing that he has no privilege to do so, he falsifies, destroys, removes or conceals any writing or record, with purpose to deceive or injure anyone or to conceal any wrongdoing.[1]

Bob is usually pleasant, so Raimer is taken aback by Bob's sternness and haughty tone. To lighten the mood, Raimer looks up Bob's official grade file and changes As in criminal law and advanced criminal law classes to Fs. He shows Bob the new criminal law grade, and Bob launches into another lecture, including a description of how hard he worked to get Bs in his two criminal law courses. He insists that Raimer change his grade in criminal law back, which Raimer does. Raimer decides not to show Bob the second change he made — the one to the grade in advanced criminal law. After Bob leaves the room, Raimer changes that grade back as well. Raimer assumes that Bob knows what grades he got, especially given what an issue it apparently is with him. He concludes that the original As probably were an error and changes the joke F grades back to Bs.

A few moments later, Anna returns, very upset. She was on her way to photocopy her official file when a sudden gust of wind blew it out of her hand. She chased down as many sheets as she could but was only able to catch two and a half letters of recommendation. Raimer is concerned about losing his job. He asks Anna what her grades are, but she is able to remember only some of them. He nonetheless prepares a new file that will look like the old one, making up the grades that Anna cannot remember. Later that afternoon, Bob, who has taken to reviewing all of Raimer's work, notices the half letter of recommendation in Anna's file. Further investigation by the registrar, including questioning of Anna, reveals the full story of Anna's file and Bob's criminal law grades. (In fact, Bob had gotten an A in criminal law and advanced criminal law; Raimer simply misunderstood Bob.) Raimer is dismissed from his job and charged with four counts of violating the Tampering with Records statute: for causing Anna's file to be removed without authority; for altering Bob's criminal law grades as a joke; for changing Bob's criminal law grades "back" to Bs; and for fabricating a file for Anna. Is he liable?

Determining Culpability The previous Section introduces some of the Model Penal Code's significant innovations with regard to culpability requirements. This Section describes how these innovations are applied in practice. The ultimate goal of the Code is to provide for each offense a precise list of the culpability elements that must be proven to establish liability. Typically,

---

1. Model Penal Code § 224.4.

some of the culpability requirements for an offense are stated on the face of the offense definition. Other requirements must be determined by referring to other provisions in the Code.

Assuming Strict Liability from Absence of Culpability Requirement The absence of a specified culpability requirement in an offense definition does *not* mean that culpability is not required.[1] Modern codes permit strict liability in very limited instances — generally only for the least serious offenses, such as traffic violations. Model Penal Code sections 2.02(1) and 2.05, and similar provisions in state codes, are meant to require culpability for all elements of all offenses other than offenses classified as mere "violations." In some jurisdictions, when the drafters intend that culpability is not to be required, a phrase such as "in fact" is inserted at the appropriate place in the offense definition to signal the absence of a culpability requirement.[2]

Culpability Requirements Supplied by General Provision Where the offense definition does not explicitly provide a culpability requirement, Model Penal Code section 2.02(3) supplies one. Section 2.02(3) reads in a requirement of "reckless-ness" with respect to all circumstance and result elements and, because the Code fails to define "recklessness" as to conduct, is frequently interpreted to read in "knowing" with respect to all conduct elements. (This is discussed in greater detail later.) Consider, for example, the Model Penal Code's indecent exposure offense:

> A person commits a misdemeanor if, for the purpose of arousing or gratifying sexual desire..., he exposes his genitals under circumstances in which he knows his conduct is likely to cause affront or alarm.[3]

An application of section 2.02(3), reading in culpability requirements, results in the following complete offense definition:

> A person commits a misdemeanor if, for the *purpose* of arousing or gratifying sexual desire..., he [*knowingly* engages in conduct by which he *recklessly* causes the exposure of what he is aware of is a substantial risk (i.e., he is *reckless* as to the exposed parts being)] his genitals under circumstances in which he *knows* his conduct is likely to cause affront or alarm.

Reading in Recklessness Obviously, such an explicit statement generates a grammatically awkward definition. A general provision that reads in a fixed culp-ability can provide the necessary guidance while leaving offense definitions readable.[4] Such a general read-in-reckless provision also is useful because, as discussed in the next Section, recklessness generally is the minimum culpability required for criminal liability. Reading in "recklessness" when no culpability is stated articulates this norm. Special circumstances may lead code drafters to use a higher or a lower level in particular instances, but, absent special reasons,

---

1. Morrisette v. United States, 342 U.S. 246, 263, 72 S. Ct. 240, 250, 96 L. Ed. 288, 300, (1952) (absence of any intent element in statute prohibiting illegal conversion of United States property not to be construed as eliminating intent requirement).

2. Thus, "having intercourse with a person who is in fact under 14 years of age" would indicate that no culpability is required as to the fact that the sexual partner is under 14.

3. Model Penal Code § 213.5.

4. The practice seems particularly appropriate given that the culpability requirements read in to complete an offense definition frequently are less significant — e.g., less frequently at issue — than are the explicitly stated culpability elements.

recklessness will be the minimum culpability required. Thus a general provision such as Model Penal Code section 2.02(3) at once provides a comprehensive statement of all culpability requirements, a readable offense definition, and a standard minimum culpability of recklessness.

Providing Culpability Other than Recklessness Legislatures are free to deviate from the norm of recklessness in either of two ways. First, the legislature can explicitly provide a culpability requirement other than recklessness for a specific element of an offense definition. This is what the legislature has done in requiring "a purpose to arouse" and "know[ledge] [that the conduct] . . . is likely to affront" in the indecent exposure offense. In addition, a legislature can provide that a stated culpability requirement applies to more than a single element of the offense. This second alternative is provided in the Model Penal Code by section 2.02(4), which codifies a general rule of statutory construction requiring that a stated culpability term, which does not distinguish among the elements, be applied to all elements of the offense. Thus, where the offense of causing a suicide is defined to punish one who "purposely causes such suicide by force,"[1] the actor must be purposeful as to using force and as to the result of causing the suicide. Normal rules of statutory construction would undoubtedly generate the same result.

Tampering with Records Application of these Model Penal Code provisions to Raimer and the tampering-with-records statute suggests the following. On the face of the offense definition, the elements of "tampering with records" are:

Objective elements	Culpability requirements
(1) no privilege to do so	"Knowing" is expressly required.
(2) falsifies, destroys, removes, or conceals	(What culpability level applies?)
(3) a writing or record	(What culpability level applies?)
(4) — (There is no requirement that anyone actually be deceived.)	"Purpose to deceive" is expressly required.

"Knowing" is expressly provided as to "no privilege." It is unclear from the face of the offense definition what culpability level applies to the objective elements of "falsifies, etc." and "a writing or record." We can assume that some culpability level is required; strict liability is not to be presumed from the absence of a culpability requirement. Also explicitly required is the "purpose to deceive." Note that the corresponding objective element — that someone actually be deceived — is not required. Such a culpability element without a corresponding objective element is one of the things the common law called a "specific intent." To be liable for the offense of "assault with intent to rape," for example, the actor did not actually have to rape; he only had to intend to do so.

Raimer's Liability Under Model Penal Code sections 224.4 and 2.02(3), Raimer's liability for the four counts might be analyzed as follows:

> (Count 1) Raimer causes or permits Anna's record to be removed believing that he probably has the authority (privilege) to do so. That he believes he

---

1. Model Penal Code § 210.5(1).

probably has the authority suggests that Raimer is aware of a risk that he does not have the authority. But "knowing" is required as to lack of privilege. Thus Raimer is not liable for this count because he is only reckless as to lacking the privilege.

(Count 2) As a joke on Bob, Raimer changes Bob's grade card to show an F in criminal law and advanced criminal law and shows Bob the criminal law change. As to the change that he shows Bob, the "purpose to deceive" requirement probably is not satisfied, thus no liability. As to the advanced criminal law change that he does not show Bob, he may well have the purpose to deceive; he decides it best that Bob not know that he changed this other grade. But Raimer's intention to hide this change apparently emerged only after he showed the first grade to Bob; it did not exist at the time of his conduct in changing the grade. Thus there is no concurrence between his conduct and the required purpose to deceive.[1]

(Count 3) Raimer changes Bob's grades back to Bs because he erroneously believes that they were originally recorded incorrectly as As. Because of Bob's lecture, Raimer now knows that he has no authority to alter a grade, thus he satisfies the requirement of "knowing he has no privilege." Liability under the statute also requires a "purpose to deceive," which Raimer may not have. (But the prosecutor might argue that in changing the advanced criminal law grade "back" to a B, Raimer was trying to hide the fact that he had changed the grade in the first place, and thus has a purpose to deceive.) In any case, the offense requires culpability as to whether the change "falsifies" the record. One might conclude that Raimer is negligent as to whether his entry of Bs is a falsification of the record.[2] Would such negligence be sufficient for liability? While no culpability requirement is apparently provided on the face of the statute as to "falsifies," a requirement of recklessness is read in by section 2.02(3). Thus Raimer's defendant's negligence would not satisfy this recklessness requirement. (If a jury concludes that Raimer was aware of a risk that his changing the grades "back" to Bs was a falsification, then Raimer would be liable, provided that the other culpability requirements also are satisfied.)

(Count 4) To hide his earlier decision to let Anna take her file, and its disastrous consequences, Raimer fabricates a new file for Anna that he knows is inaccurate. He knows he has no authority to do so — his purpose is to deceive the people in the office — and he knows the record is false (only recklessness as to falsification is required). Under the above reading of the statute, Raimer will be liable for the fourth count, fabricating Anna's file.

Conflict and Inconsistency in Model Penal Code   The Model Penal Code culpability scheme is a great improvement over "the variety, disparity, and confusion" of judicial definitions of "the requisite but elusive mental element" that existed prior to the Code's advent.[3] As is frequently the case with reform, however, the Code makes great advances but inevitably has shortcomings. All jurisdictions that follow the Model Penal Code's culpability scheme face a variety of common difficulties. Some states have changed the Code's provisions to avoid some of the problems. Others have created additional difficulties by tinkering with the scheme's provisions without fully understanding the implications of their changes.

---

1. Recall the concurrence requirement discussed in the main text at "Concurrence requirement."

2. That is, he was not but should have been aware of a substantial risk that the grade was not incorrectly recorded.

3. Morrisette v. United States, 342 U.S. at 252, 72 S. Ct. at 244, 96 L. Ed. at 294.

Distinguishing Conduct, Circumstance, and Result Elements   One defect of the Code, already noted, is its failure to define the three categories of objective elements: conduct, circumstance, and result elements. For example, is "obstructs" a conduct or a result element? Does "insults another in a manner likely to provoke violent response" consist of a single conduct element or of one conduct element and one or more circumstance elements? Does "the death of another human being" consist of a single result element or of a result element and a circumstance element? The definition of the three categories of objective elements is important because the categories are used as terms of art in many places in the Code. For example, by the terms of section 2.03, the special requirements of causation must be satisfied where an offense contains a "result" element.[1]

Objective Element Categories and Culpability Requirements   Perhaps even more important, a precise definition of the "objective-element" categories is essential for proper application of the defined culpability terms. Recall the asymmetries in the Code's culpability definitions, discussed previously. To act "purposely" with respect to "conduct," or in causing "a result," an actor must have such conduct or result as his conscious object. But to act "purposely" with respect to "an attendant circumstance," an actor need only be aware of such circumstance, which is nothing more than what is required to prove "knowing" as to a circumstance. Recall also that "recklessness" and "negligence" are defined as to circumstance and result elements but are not defined as to conduct elements. Thus, if an element is categorized as a conduct element, there is some ambiguity as to what is to be required. Some jurisdictions would require that "knowing" be proven, for that is the lowest culpability with respect to conduct that is defined. Because of these asymmetries, the categorization of an objective element becomes essential in determining the precise culpability requirements that will apply.

Ambiguities from Failure to Define Categories   Consider the offense of theft by deception, which entails purposely obtaining another's property through deceit. A person "deceives" if he purposely "[c]reates or reinforces a false impression [as to value]."[2] One might argue that this requirement is a single elaborate conduct requirement: "creates or reinforces a false impression as to value." Or the prohibited conduct element might be "creates" or "reinforces" and the proscribed result might be interpreted as either (a) a false impression as to value (with no "attendant circumstance"), (b) a false impression (with value as a "circumstance"), or (c) an impression (with both falsity and value as "circumstances"). Selecting the proper interpretation requires a definition of what constitutes a "conduct," "circumstance," or "result," and the interpretation selected will determine the culpability required.

Implication of Ambiguities   Assume that a court applies section 2.02(4) to require that the stated culpability requirement, "purposely," apply to all elements

---

1. See Model Penal Code § 2.03 (defining necessary causal relationship between conduct and result elements). In addition, see id. § 5.01(1)(b) (providing special culpability requirements as to result element where attempt is charged), id. § 1.03(1)(a) (providing jurisdiction over offense if "result that is such an element [of offense] occurs within this state"), id. § 1.03(2) (excepting from (1)(a), supra, cases where "result occurs...only in another jurisdiction" where conduct is not offense).

2. Model Penal Code § 223.3(a).

of the offense of theft by deception. The actor's *conscious object* must then encompass all required conduct and results; but, because of the way "purposeful" as to a circumstance is defined, the actor need only be *aware* of the existence of a circumstance element. If the court applies interpretation (a) described above, the actor's *conscious object* must encompass every element of the offense because all elements are either conduct or results. If interpretation (b) is applied, however, the actor's *conscious object* must encompass only "creating" and a "false impression"; it need not be the actor's conscious object or hope — he need only be aware — that the false impression concerns "value." Finally, if the court applies interpretation (c), the actor's *conscious object* need only encompass "creating an impression"; he need only be *aware* of the fact that the impression is "false" and concerns "value." These differences create the potential to manipulate improperly a defendant's liability by altering the content of the categories "conduct," "result," and "circumstance," thereby altering the applicable culpability requirement.

Combining Conduct and Result or Conduct and Circumstance   Recall from section 3.1 that difficulties in distinguishing conduct, circumstance, and result elements also arise because most modern codes, including the Model Penal Code, use terms that combine conduct and a result as a single element or combine conduct and an attendant circumstance as a single element. Verbs like "damages," "obstructs," "destroys," "falsifies," "kills," and "desecrates" each combine both an act and a result of that act. Verbs like "compels"[1] combine conduct and circumstance elements. Such combinations create ambiguities and undermine consistency in the operation of the Code.

Implication of Combined Elements   Consider a statute that forbids "recklessly obstructing any highway."[2] What culpability should be required as to "obstructing"? A court might take any of three approaches. Because "obstructing" appears to be a conduct element and "recklessly" is not defined with respect to conduct, the court might determine that "knowing" is the appropriate culpability as to "obstructing" because it is the minimum culpability defined with respect to conduct. Or a court might attempt to define recklessness as to conduct and require that newly defined culpability. Given the enactment of a comprehensive culpability scheme, such a definition of culpability seems properly a legislative task. A third, and perhaps best, approach might be for a court to observe that the "obstructing" is a combination of separate conduct and result elements. "'Obstructs' means to *render impassable* without unreasonable inconvenience or hazard." In essence, the offense imposes liability when an actor engages in conduct by which he causes — that is, "renders" — any highway to be impassable. The stated culpability term "recklessly," under this approach, can be meaningfully read to apply to the result element of causing the highway to be impassable. The same term nonetheless could be interpreted to require "knowing" conduct because "knowing" is the minimum culpability defined as to conduct.

Proposed Revisions   The difficulties of the Model Penal Code scheme — arising from the failure to define the categories of objective elements and the use

---

1. Id. § 213.1(1)(a) (defining offense of rape). The term "compels" implies an unstated yet required circumstance element: lack of consent.

2. See, e.g., Model Penal Code § 250.7.

of terms that combine elements of different categories — can be avoided with a few revisions, most of which may be done through judicial interpretation of existing provisions. With revision, the Code's scheme can be made workable and can realize the full benefits of the insights and advances of the drafters. Here are some of the reforms that may be helpful.

Define Conduct Narrowly Define "conduct" elements literally, that is, narrowly, to mean pure conduct: bodily movement of the actor (which is the way Model Penal Code section 1.13 defines "act"). Thus, objective elements of an offense definition that might otherwise be classified as conduct elements, but which actually describe *characteristics* of the conduct, would be treated as separate circumstance or result elements. For example, the definition of harassment makes it an offense if an actor "insults... another in a manner likely to provoke violent... response." Under a narrow view of the conduct element, the required conduct is the simple act of speaking. The conduct's characteristics — its insulting character, its likelihood of provoking a violent response — would be treated as circumstance or result elements. Under this narrow view of conduct, the conduct element emerges as a relatively unspecific and unimportant aspect of an offense definition. In homicide, for example, the particular conduct that the actor engages in to cause the death of another human being does not matter. What matters is that the actor's conduct, of whatever nature, did cause the prohibited result. The most significant elements of an offense definition, then, typically are the circumstance and result elements.

Narrow Conduct Element as Act Requirement Such a narrowly defined conduct element continues adequately to serve the important purposes of the act requirement: to distinguish fantasy from intention and to exclude from liability intentions too irresolute ever to be carried out, to provide some minimal objective evidence confirming mens rea, and to set a minimal objective limit on the government's criminalization power. A narrow conduct element can improve on the act requirement function of providing a temporal point of reference for doctrines that need one, such as the concurrence requirement, statutes of limitation, and jurisdiction and venue. A broader definition of conduct makes application of these doctrines more difficult.

Distinguish Combined Elements As a corollary to this first revision, the legislature should redraft the language or, absent such redrafting, courts should distinguish the two aspects of the element in determining the culpability requirements whenever a single verb compounds a conduct element with a result element or with a circumstance element. By identifying the existence of a result element more clearly, this approach also identifies where the special requirements of causation apply.

Proposed Distinction Between Circumstance and Result Recall the problem of the Code's failure to define categories of objective elements: Is causing the "obstruction of a public highway" a single result element? Or is it a result element of causing an "obstruction" and a circumstance element of "a public highway"? A third proposal would resolve the problem by defining a "result" as a *circumstance changed by the actor*. All elements that did not fit this definition would be independent circumstance elements. In the short hypothetical above, the actor creates only the obstruction; he cannot create or alter the road's legal status as a "public highway." Thus, causing the "obstruction" would be a result element and "public highway" would be a circumstance element. To summarize, the conduct element in each offense is segregated, although it may be linguistically merged with other elements. It simply performs the function of the act requirement. Result elements are easy to identify as circumstances changed by the actor. All other elements are circumstance elements.

Culpability as to Conduct Similarly Narrow Another corollary to the narrow scope of the conduct element is that the culpability requirement accompanying the conduct element is given a similarly narrow meaning. If the conduct element encompasses only an actor's act and not the characteristics of the accompanying circumstances or the results of the act, the required culpability as to the conduct encompasses only the actor's mental state as to engaging in the bare act itself, not his mental state as to the circumstances or results of the conduct. As noted previously, any broader interpretation of conduct would make the culpability as to the conduct element all-encompassing. A requirement of "knowing" as to conduct, which would most frequently be required, would set "knowing" as the required culpability as to the pertinent attendant circumstances and the pertinent results of an actor's conduct. But to assume that the culpability required as to "conduct" controls the culpability as to the circumstances and results of the conduct as well, as the broader interpretation of conduct would do, is to undermine element analysis generally. Such an approach would short-circuit the Code's attempt to allow separate, and sometimes different, culpability requirements with respect to the circumstances and results of one's conduct.

Conduct Culpability Rarely an Issue Under the narrow definition of conduct, an actor's culpability as to his conduct — for example, being aware of the nature of one's conduct — rarely will be a matter of dispute; instead, his culpability as to the circumstances and result of his conduct will be of primary practical importance. Culpability as to conduct simply requires, for example, that an actor be aware that he is moving his trigger finger or swinging his arm. The only cases that would present an issue under the narrowly defined conduct element would involve an actor who suffers from a considerable and abnormal disability. Such abnormalities typically are given more detailed consideration under provisions governing the voluntariness requirement and excuse defenses. The culpability requirements of an offense definition, in contrast, operate primarily to assess the culpability of normal persons. The normal person typically desires to move his body in the way that he actually moves it and therefore satisfies the narrow culpability-as-to-conduct requirement. The narrow interpretation of conduct avoids the problems inherent in the drafters' failure to define recklessness and negligence as to conduct. An actor who is only "aware of a substantial risk" or is "unaware of a substantial risk" that he is moving his trigger finger or arm is an actor who will have an excuse defense. Thus, no definitions of recklessness or negligence as to conduct are necessary.

MPC § 2.02(4): Applying Stated Culpability to All Elements One final but important difficulty with the Model Penal Code scheme results from too broad a reading of section 2.02(4):

> *Prescribed Culpability Requirement Applies to All Material Elements.* When the law defining an offense prescribes the kind of culpability that is sufficient for the commission of an offense, without distinguishing among the material elements thereof, such provision shall apply to all the material elements of the offense, unless a contrary purpose plainly appears.

The Commentary describes this provision as one that will embody the most probable legislative intent.[1] The provision may be interpreted too broadly, however, to allow what may be an exceptional culpability requirement, such as purposeful, which is meant by the legislature to apply only to one element of the offense, to govern the culpability requirements of all other offense elements. In other instances, the provision may have the equally undesirable effect of having an unusually low culpability requirement, such as negligence, apply to all elements, when it was meant only to apply to one.

Too Literal Reading of § 2.02(4) Consider, for example, the offense of burglary. An actor commits burglary when he "enters a building or occupied structure . . . with purpose to commit a crime therein, unless the premises are at the time open to the public or the actor is licensed or privileged to enter."[2] As "purpose" is the only culpability element prescribed, and as no contrary legislative purpose plainly appears, a provision like Model Penal Code section 2.02(4) might be interpreted to require that an actor must not only have the purpose to commit a crime within, but also must be purposeful with respect to each element in order to be held liable for burglary. In other words, the actor must be aware of or believe or hope that *all the required circumstance* elements for burglary exist. He would escape liability if he thinks it likely, but is not certain and does not necessarily hope, that he is not "licensed or privileged to enter" or that he is entering a "building or occupied structure."[3] But burglary typically is understood to require purpose only as to the "intent to commit a crime therein." "Purpose" is an unusually stringent culpability requirement. There are few areas where legislatures want so demanding a requirement. Too broad a reading of section 2.02(4) allows the exceptional case where purpose is required to become the standard for all elements of the offense. An analogous difficulty arises with the use of negligence. Where only negligence is required as to an offense element, strict application of section 2.02(4) applies this stated culpability term to all elements,[4] although recklessness normally is the minimum culpability required.[5]

Workable Interpretation of § 2.02(4) A better reading of section 2.02(4) would apply its rule only to that part of the offense definition within the

---

1. Model Penal Code § 2.02 comment 6 at 245 (1985).

2. Model Penal Code § 221.1.

3. "Purposely" as to a circumstance requires either a hope *or awareness*; the latter requirement is no more than is required for "knowingly." See supra. Thus, "knowledge" as to a circumstance element — "aware of high probability of its existence," § 2.02(7) — satisfies the requirement but "recklessness" — "aware of a substantial risk," § 2.02(2)(c) — does not.

4. See, e.g., Model Penal Code § 210.4 ("Criminal homicide constitutes negligent homicide when it is committed negligently"); Model Penal Code § 211.1(1)(b) (person commits simple assault if "negligently causes bodily injury to another with a deadly weapon").

5. This is the point of having a section like Model Penal Code § 2.02(3) read in recklessness where no culpability is stated.

grammatical clause in which the stated term appears. This is consistent with the provision's direction that the rule applies only where the offense definition prescribes culpability, "without distinguishing among the material elements thereof." That is, grammatical structure may provide such distinction among elements. In the context of burglary, this interpretation would apply "purpose" only to "to commit a crime therein." The other elements of the offense would be governed by the other rules of construction; the culpability requirements would be derived either from other stated culpability terms or from section 2.02(3)'s reading in the standard "recklessness."

Interaction of §§ 2.02(3) & 2.02(4)   This discussion gives some guidance in suggesting rules for how Model Penal Code sections 2.02(3) and 2.02(4) ought to interact. Consider the definition of harassment:

> A person commits a petty misdemeanor if, with purpose to harass another, he … insults … another in a manner likely to provoke violent or disorderly response.[1]

Model Penal Code section 2.02(3) requires recklessness whenever an offense definition fails to specify the culpability with respect to a particular element. On the other hand, when the offense definition specifies a culpability element, without distinguishing among elements, section 2.02(4) requires that the stated culpability apply to all elements, unless a contrary purpose appears. If section 2.02(4) were applied to require the stated culpability of "purpose" to all elements, even those elements outside of its grammatical clause, the actor would have to be purposeful with respect to all elements — for example, it must be his conscious object to "insult another" and his conscious object that the insult be "likely to provoke violent or disorderly response." Yet, as noted above, purpose is a special and very demanding culpability requirement, while recklessness is well-established as the "norm" for criminal liability. If section 2.02(3) is applied to all elements outside the grammatical clause in which "purpose" appears, the defendant must be purposeful only as to harassing another, and need only be reckless with respect to all other elements. The section 2.02(3) recklessness requirement should be preferred. Section 2.02(4) admittedly should apply to the entire grammatical clause in which it appears, but it should apply outside that clause only when the placement and effect of the stated culpability term suggest that it is intended to govern culpability requirements outside of the clause.

Two Stated Culpability Terms   Another piece of evidence suggesting a restrictive interpretation of section 2.02(4) is illustrated by the offense of Tampering with Records, the offense with which Raimer is charged. The definition contains two stated culpability requirements on its face. A broad interpretation of section 2.02(4) — which would have a stated term apply beyond its grammatical clause — presents the issue of which of the two terms should be applied to the elements outside of the two clauses, such as "falsifies" or "renames." The broad interpretation seems to assume that an offense definition will have only one stated culpability requirement. That this offense has two stated terms itself suggests a need for care in the interpretation of section 2.02(4). It seems safe to assume that

---

1. Model Penal Code § 250.4(2).

each of the two requirements are intended to apply at least within the grammatical clause in which each appears. Thus, "knowing" is still required as to "no privilege," and a "purpose to deceive" is still required. But which of these stated terms, if either, will apply to the element outside of these two phrases? The best approach is to leave these other elements to the operation of section 2.02(3)'s reading of a requirement of recklessness.

More on Raimer's Records The proper interpretation of Model Penal Code section 2.02(4) can be examined in the context of Raimer's liability. What result if a broad reading of section 2.02(4) were used to determine the culpability requirements of Tampering with Records? Under a broad reading of section 2.02(4), what is the culpability required as to "falsifies," which is outside of both of the clauses in which the stated culpability terms of "knowing" and "purposeful" appear? Reconsider Raimer's liability for Counts 3 and 4, this time taking into account possible interpretations of section 2.02(4):

> (Count 3) Recall that Raimer changes Bob's grades back to Bs because he erroneously believes that they were originally recorded incorrectly as As. Earlier we assumed that Raimer was negligent as to whether his entry of Bs "falsifies" the record. This time, assume Raimer is reckless as to whether his conduct "falsifies" the record. That is, assume that he is aware of a substantial risk that the Bs he is entering might be incorrect. If section 2.02(4) controls, which would require either knowing or purposeful as to falsifying, the culpability requirement is not satisfied and Raimer still has no liability; his recklessness is insufficient. If section 2.02(4) is limited in application to the grammatical clauses in which the stated culpability terms appear, and section 2.02(3) is relied upon to read in a recklessness for elements outside of those clauses, Raimer's recklessness is sufficient.[1] (However, recall that even if Raimer satisfies the culpability, as to falsification, he nonetheless may claim that he had no "purpose to deceive" with regard to the first grade.)
>
> (Count 4) Recall that to hide his earlier decision to let Anna take her file, and its disastrous consequences, Raimer fabricates a new file for Anna that he knows is inaccurate. He knows he has no authority to do so; his purpose is to deceive the people in the office, and he knows the record is false. Under a narrow interpretation of section 2.02(4), Raimer is liable for the fourth count, fabricating Anna's file, because he satisfies section 2.02(3)'s requirement that he be at least reckless as to falsifying. Under a broad reading of 2.02(4), however, the result is unclear. It depends upon whether the stated purposeful requirement or the stated knowing requirement is applied to the falsification element. Raimer knows that his conduct will falsify the record. Is he "purposeful" as to such falsification? No; he would prefer to reproduce Anna's record accurately. Thus, Raimer's liability will depend upon which of the two stated terms applies to the element of falsification: If purpose is required, he is not liable; If only knowing is required, he is liable.

---

1. It would suffice, however, only if (a) "falsifies" is judged a conduct element and recklessness is interpreted as being applicable to a conduct element or (b) as proposed above, "falsifies" is judged to be a combined conduct/result element ("engages in conduct by which he causes the record to be made false"), so that the definition of recklessness can be applied to the result of "causing the record to be made false." The alternative is that "falsifies" is judged a conduct element and "knowing" is the lowest culpability defined as to conduct, thus "knowing" might be required, and Raimer's recklessness would be insufficient.

Aside from the obvious difficulty in the unresolved conflict between the two stated terms, the case illustrates the dangers of a broad reading of 2.02(4) in spreading a purpose requirement too broadly. It would be seem odd that an actor who *knew* he had no authority to change a record, *knew* he was falsifying the record, and had the *purpose* to deceive others by his conduct would nonetheless have no liability for the offense (because he did not have the falsification itself as his purpose). Application of section 2.02(3) to the falsification element would require only recklessness (or possibly knowing[1]).

Proposed Interpretation of §§ 2.02(3) & 2.02(4)   The better interpretation of section 2.02(4), as noted above, is to view it as requiring that a stated culpability term apply to the grammatical clause in which it appears unless the context demonstrates that it is intended to apply to other, subsequent clauses as well. Section 2.02(3) is best interpreted as supplying the culpability requirements to any elements to which section 2.02(4) does not apply. For example, in the absence of legislative direction to the contrary, recklessness would be required as to the circumstance element of "an unlicensed or unprivileged entry" in burglary. This interpretation of section 2.02(4) is not inconsistent with its language, which requires application of stated culpability only when such culpability is provided "without distinguishing among the material elements thereof." The interpretation rests on an assumption that, when a stated culpability is placed within a grammatical clause, such placement distinguishes the elements within the clause from those without. This use of section 2.02(3) to fill in any gaps after application of section 2.02(4) is consistent with the Model Penal Code's view that the culpability level of recklessness should be applied when the required culpability is unstated, a view that is supported by the fact that recklessness generally is accepted as the appropriate norm for imposing criminal liability.

Application to Homicide   In many offenses, section 2.02(3) will have no application. Consider homicide, for example.

> A person is guilty of criminal homicide if he purposely, knowingly, recklessly or negligently causes the death of another human being.

The different degrees of homicide are then identified as dependent upon the actor's level of culpability: Purposefully or knowingly causing the death is murder, recklessly is manslaughter, and negligently is negligent homicide.[2] Even under the more limited application of section 2.02(4), the culpability stated in homicide is likely to apply to both offense elements, causing death and the victim being a "human being." Because the offense is defined in a single clause, the stated culpability requirement would apply to all elements, including the circumstance element of "human being." Thus, if "human being" were defined for homicide purposes to include a "viable fetus," the doctor who purposely kills a fetus and is reckless as to its being a viable fetus would be liable for manslaughter, but not for murder.

---

1. Recall the ambiguity as to whether "falsifies" is a conduct element, for which the lowest defined culpability is "knowing," or a combined conduct and result element, where "recklessness" would be required as to the result of "causing to be made false."

2. See Model Penal Code §§ 210.2, 210.3, and 210.4.

Proposals Affecting Drafting Technique Not Content   Note that the interpretations of sections 2.02(3) and 2.02(4) proposed here are not designed either
to raise or to lower the culpability requirements of offense definitions. They are,
rather, designed to create a system in which the legislature can effectively,
easily, and clearly define the culpability requirements it desires. If a culpability
requirement other than recklessness is to apply to a particular element, the
legislature need only state such culpability requirement in the offense definition.
If the legislature desires the stated requirement to apply to more than one
element, it can achieve this by its choice of placement of the stated culpability
term within the offense definition. The legislature can provide an explicit culpability requirement to apply to particular elements (those within the clause)
without fear that the requirement will be interpreted to apply more broadly than
intended.

APPENDIX A: SECTION 5

Culpability and Mistake

ADVANCED ISSUES

Flow Chart of Functions of Criminal Law

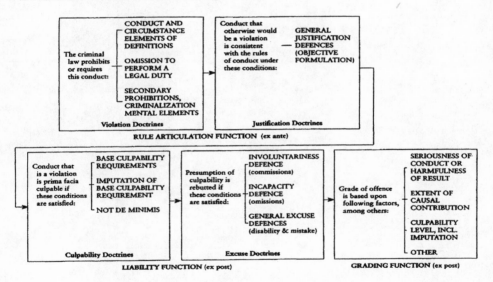

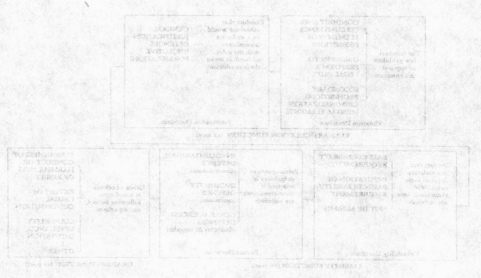

Culpability and Mistake

ADVANCED ISSUES

Flow Chart of Functions of Criminal Law

APPENDIX A: SECTION 6

Homicide: Doctrines
of Aggravation

ADVANCED ISSUES

California Penal Code §§ 187, 188, 189, 192
Homicide Offenses

Section 187. Murder Defined; Death of Fetus

(a) Murder is the unlawful killing of a human being, or a fetus, with malice aforethought....

Section 188. Malice, Express Malice, and Implied Malice Defined

Such malice may be express or implied. It is express when there is manifested a deliberate intention unlawfully to take away the life of a fellow creature. It is implied, when no considerable provocation appears, or when the circumstances attending the killing show an abandoned and malignant heart.

When it is shown that the killing resulted from the intentional doing of an act with express or implied malice as defined above, no other mental state need be shown to establish the mental state of malice aforethought. Neither an awareness of the obligation to act within the general body of laws regulating society nor acting despite such awareness is included within the definition of malice.

Section 189. Murder; Degrees

All murder which is perpetrated by means of a destructive device or explosive, knowing use of ammunition designed primarily to penetrate metal or armor, poison, lying in wait, torture, or by any other kind of willful, deliberate, and premeditated killing, or which is committed in the perpetration of, or attempt to perpetrate, arson, rape, robbery, burglary, mayhem, or any act punishable under

Section 288 [lewd or lascivious acts with child under age 14], is murder of the first degree; and all other kinds of murders are of the second degree.

As used in this section, "destructive device" shall mean any destructive device as defined in Section 12301, and "explosive" shall mean any explosive as defined in Section 12000 of the Health and Safety Code.

To prove the killing was "deliberate and premeditated," it shall not be necessary to prove the defendant maturely and meaningfully reflected upon the gravity of his or her act.

Section 192. Manslaughter; Voluntary, Involuntary, and Vehicular, Construction of Section

Manslaughter is the unlawful killing of a human being without malice. It is of three kinds:

1. Voluntary—upon a sudden quarrel or heat of passion.

2. Involuntary—in the commission of an unlawful act, not amounting to felony; or in the commission of a lawful act which might produce death, in an unlawful manner, or without due caution and circumspection; provided that this subdivision shall not apply to acts committed in the driving of a vehicle.

APPENDIX A: SECTION 7

Death Penalty

ADVANCED ISSUES

Elizabeth Rapaport, The Death Penalty and Gender Discrimination
25 Law and Society Review 369, 380-382 (1991)

The *Rapaport* excerpt in Section 7 continues:

At least three counterarguments are likely to be leveled at the feminist critique of the exclusion of the worst domestic homicides from among the most severely punished crimes. A consideration of their merits reveals the essentially ideological origin of the current moral grading of homicide offenses.

1. The most plausible defense for the relative leniency of our response to domestic murder takes the following form: It is a generalization of Wolfgang's theory of victim-precipitated homicide. If acquaintances, friends, and most especially family members quarrel and a homicide ensues, we are disposed to view the victim as sharing some responsibility with his or her killer for the killing—whether or not the provocation would be considered legally sufficient to reduce the charge from murder to manslaughter. The victim is regarded as having assumed a measure of the risk of victimization simply by remaining in an intimate relationship with the killer whom he or she may have known to be disposed to violence. We assume that the victim possessed some degree of control over the circumstances of his or her victimization, which puts the homicide in a less frightening light and diminishes the degree of punishment that appears appropriate.

There is a fatal objection to this theory: It is unable to account for the lesser opprobrium ascribed to the killing of a young child. Nor can it account for the relative leniency of response to the murder of an adult who is psychologically or otherwise dependent on his or her killer, as may be the case with a battered spouse.

2. The feminist critique of capital statutes offered here could also be accused of failing to respect the theory of relative culpability inherent in our law of homicide. Our law of homicide regards the unprovoked and calculated killer, the cold-blooded killer, as more reprehensible than the hot-blooded killer. Therefore, it may be said, because family murders are paradigms of hot-blooded crime, they ought not to be dealt with as harshly as cold-blooded, predatory murder.

However, it must be noted that ever since the introduction of degrees of murder, first-degree murder has included, in addition to deliberate and premeditated murder, felony murder. Conviction for felony murder does not require that the offender killed intentionally, much less with deliberation and premeditation. Felony murderers are not held capitally responsible for their actions because their crimes were cold-blooded in the sense that they were deliberate or premeditated. Our society places the full measure of the risk of a victim's death on the one who would use violence for a predatory end. Similarly, if we chose to do so, our traditional law of homicide offers no conceptual barrier to treating child abuse or spouse abuse as a felony capable of sustaining a capital sentence if a fatality results from it. To do so would be to make the moral and ideological choice to place the risk of a victim's death on someone using violence in the interests of domestic tyranny.

3. The feminist critic could also be taxed for failing to appreciate that cold-blooded killings are more apt to be subjected to the death penalty because cold-blooded killing is more susceptible to deterrence through severity of sanction than hot-blooded crime. I will not comment here on the vexing and contested question of whether the death penalty does in fact possess deterrent value. Suffice it to say that other kinds of murder now deemed capital are not obviously more or less susceptible to deterrence through severity of sanction than murder in the course of felonious domestic violence. Killing in the course of an armed robbery or killing a peace officer to avoid arrest are capital crimes that may not be either planned or coolly executed; they may be the product of panic, confusion, or lack of self-control. If such potential offenders are deterrable, deterrence presumably often takes the form of dissuading them from predatory crime rather than self-mastery in the midst of commission of felonies. By parity of reasoning, if we choose to, we could similarly attempt to deter severe family abuse by putting potential abusers on notice that society regards killing in the course of aggravated and habitual domestic abuse as among the most reprehensible forms of killing.

My purpose in offering a feminist critique of our capital punishment system is not in fact to advocate capital punishment for domestic murder. Nor would I wish to endorse the view that criminal law is the best, or the only, or an adequate, tool for dealing with all facets of the problem of domestic violence. My purpose rather is to expose the ideological biases of the status quo in which domestic homicide is treated, invidiously, as almost always less reprehensible than predatory murder. The logic of the argument suggests that egregious cases of domestic murder should be among the most severely condemned crimes and therefore eligible for the heaviest sanctions, whatever these may be. Such an allocation of penalties would use the law of homicide in the inculcation of new social values and the concomitant guiding of conduct.

It may well be that the underevaluation of the heinousness of domestic murder is the most serious form of gender discrimination to be discovered in our capital punishment system. In the present state of our knowledge, I have tried to show, we have no credible evidence that women are spared the death penalty in circumstances where it would be pronounced on men. The gender composition of death row rather appears to reflect differences between the kinds of homicides men and women commit. Additionally, there is some evidence that the admissions standards for death row may be somewhat different for the two sexes. Although women are indeed sent to death row for crimes that lead men to the same fate, a strikingly high percentage of the women on death row, unlike the men, killed family or intimates. The question of the death penalty and gender discrimination, then, appears to be fundamentally a question of social ideology. Women are doubly disserved by the current climate of belief and policy. First, women are disserved by the misleading or false belief that we are spared the most extreme criminal sanction because of our sex. Second, the criminal law is not being mobilized to sufficiently discredit, discourage, and sanction crimes of domestic oppression from which women and children suffer disproportionately.

Causation

ADVANCED ISSUES RELATING TO CAUSATION

Notes on Causation

[The persons referred to are the characters in the "Manny the Master" Problem Case in the main text.]

Multiple Causes We may tend to think that the number of possible causes depends on the facts of the case. Where the actor shoots the victim in the head, we say the gunshot is the cause of death. In the more complicated case of Baylor's death, we may say that the cause is either Manny's push or Baylor's curiosity or possibly both. Thus, more complicated cases like Baylor's seem to raise the issue of multiple causes. In fact, every result is necessarily the product of many causes, some acting immediately on and some acting long before the present result. The train was as necessary as Baylor's curiosity to bring about the death. If the local bar had not closed early, there would not have been as many people on the platform at the time, and Baylor would not have had to lean out as he did to see and would not have been hit. By closing early, the bar owner caused the death, then, in a factual cause sense. Technically, every causation case is a multiple cause case. It is not an academic question to ask how the doctrine is to determine the causal accountability of one particular cause among multiple causes of a result. The proximate cause requirement is highly useful in this effort. The bar owner's conduct in closing early is clearly so remote from Baylor's death that it ought not be seen as a proximate cause, and the owner ought not be liable for murder even if he somehow hoped that closing early might cause Baylor's death.[1]

Imputing Another's Causal Conduct It should be noted that the doctrine sometimes avoids the problem of determining which of multiple causes is

---

1. Or consider the actor who shoots at but misses his intended victim, who flees to escape the attack and four blocks later is struck and killed by a falling piano that breaks loose from its rope as it is being hoisted to a third-floor apartment. The actor's shot is a "but for" cause of the death; the deceased would not have been under the piano at the moment it fell *but for* the shot that caused him to flee. But the actor's missed shot would be judged by most people to be too remote and accidental a cause to have a just bearing on the actor's liability for the death caused by the piano. The actor's shot in the falling-piano hypothetical creates no injury that by itself would cause death. Rather, the effect of the actor's shot in the piano hypothetical is to trigger another action (flight of the intended victim), which in turn leads to the death. It is this serial effect of the causes that creates the potential proximate-cause remoteness issues.

accountable for a result by treating the multiple causes as a single cause. This occurs most often where the two causes spring from accomplices or co-conspirators who are legally accountable for each other's conduct, as noted previously. In *Henderson v. State*, for example, the defendant father stabbed the deceased during a struggle. The son then shot and killed the victim.[1] The father might argue that, even if the stab wound was lethal, his conduct was not a but-for cause of the resulting death, that the victim would have died when he did from the gunshot even without the father's stab wound. But if the father and son were accomplices, the court observes, the father is legally accountable for the conduct of the son and it does not matter whether the father's conduct alone was a necessary cause.

"Combined Effect" Analysis   Some jurisdictions recognize a second kind of situation in which the conduct of two actors may be combined and treated as one. In *Henderson*, for example, the court concluded that, even if the father and son were not accomplices, their independent conduct ought to be treated as one causal force if the two forces combined in their effect. Thus, the father was to be held for the death if the stab wound that he inflicted had combined in effect with the gunshot by his son. If this doctrine were simply an application of the but-for test, it would be unobjectionable. That is, if the two causes were said to combine and were to be treated as one whenever neither alone would have been lethal, then each in fact is necessary for the result and therefore is a but-for cause.

Dangers of "Combined Effect"   Unfortunately, by thinking in terms of "combined effects," courts sometimes apply the doctrine too broadly. In *Henderson*, for example, if the father's stabbing of the victim were *not* necessary for the resulting death, then the father's conduct should not be taken to be a factual cause of the death, even if its effect combined in some way with that of the son's shooting of the victim. For another example, assume that Squeeze's poison had caused Baylor to become dizzy and thus made it that much more sure that Manny would be successful in pushing Baylor in front of the train. If Baylor would have been killed at the same time even without the dizziness from Squeeze's poison, then Squeeze's conduct is not a but-for cause, even though a court might say that its effect combined with Manny's push. "Combined effect" analysis tends to be used by courts when it is unclear whether the defendant's cause was necessary for the result or was just a contributing but non-necessary factor. Would the son have successfully shot the victim even without the father's stabbing? Would Manny's push have made Baylor fall even without the dizziness from Squeeze's poison? These may be difficult factual questions for a jury to resolve. But if a necessary cause really is a requirement for establishing causation, then the state should have to prove this element beyond a reasonable doubt, as the state must prove every other offense element. To resort to "combined effect" analysis is to release the state from this burden and to substitute a lesser requirement of showing merely that the defendant's conduct contributed in some way to the result.

Serial vs. Intersecting Causes   Multiple causes may interact with one another in any number of ways. The train, Manny's push, Baylor's curiosity, the early closing of the local bar, and many other circumstances came together at the

---

1. 11 Ala. App. 37, 41-42, 65 So. 721, 722-723 (1914).

moment before Baylor's death. Each represents an independent chain of events that intersects at that moment. And each of these intersecting chains of events has many links, a serial dimension in which each link has a causal connection with the links before and after. Kenny "The Hat" is a cause of Baylor's death, it might be said, by motivating Manny to do his pushing. Kenny's contract is not a cause independent of Manny's push in the same way that the train and Manny's push are independent. The contract stands in serial relation to Manny's push; the train intersects with the push. (There is nothing in the legal doctrine that requires this conceptualization of causation problems, but many people find it useful to think about the problem in this way.) In sorting out which causes will come within the realm of legal causal accountability, the doctrine must address two distinguishable questions. Which of the intersecting causal chains are eligible for causal account-ability? And how far back along a causal chain, the serial dimension, should accountability extend?

Assessing Serial Dimension with Proximate Cause Test The proximate cause test is the law's device for assessing the reach of accountability along the serial dimension. If Manny had successfully pushed Baylor in front of the train, his push clearly would be judged a proximate cause of the death. Kenny's contract, which motivated Manny, probably would be considered a sufficiently proximate cause as well. But the informant's report of the investigation, which motivated Kenny's contract, might be judged too remote to be a proximate cause, even if it were given with the intention that it would cause Kenny to have Baylor killed. The problem of serial causes is particularly troublesome when one of the links in the causal chain is another person. *Root* and *Lassiter*, discussed below, illustrate the difficulties.

Assessing Accountability Among Intersecting Causes In addition to the issue of how far causal accountability travels down the chain of serial causes, the law must identify which among the many intersecting causal chains are eligible for being held accountable for the result. The law does this through the factual cause requirement, most commonly by using the necessary cause test. Only those conditions that are necessary for the result are judged to be factual causes of the result. The necessary-cause test is as clear and precise in application as the prox-imate cause test is judgmental and vague. A different sort of difficulty attends it: It tends to exclude from causal accountability at least two kinds of cases that some people think ought to be included: simultaneous sufficient causes, as in *Jones*, below, and intervening sufficient causes, as in *Wood*, above.

Necessary-Cause Test and Simultaneous Sufficient Causes In *Jones v. Com-monwealth*, two actors simultaneously shot the deceased and inflicted similar chest wounds.[1] Either shot was itself sufficient to cause death, thus each actor can (correctly) claim that his conduct was not a necessary cause of the death. That is, each can claim that his shot did not satisfy the "but for" requirement; the deceased would have died when he did (from the other actor's shot) even if the actor had not shot. Under a necessary cause test, then, both actors would escape liability. Most people find this result to be unacceptable. Similarly, the court in *Jones* imposed liability despite the failure of the necessary-cause test. Most courts and legislatures appear to agree with this result. The escape from accountability

---

1. 281 S.W.2d 920 (Ky. 1955).

permitted by the simultaneous-sufficient-cause flaw in the necessary cause test sometimes is avoided through enactment of a special statutory provision, such as that in subsection (4) of the causation provision quoted in the hypothetical at the beginning of this Section.

Necessary-Cause Test and Intervening Sufficient Cause   There is less agreement, however, as to the impropriety of a second peculiarity in application of the necessary-cause test. In intervening sufficient cause cases, an actor's conduct may be sufficient to cause the prohibited result, yet the actor may nonetheless escape liability if a subsequent sufficient cause intervenes to cause the earlier result. Recall that this is the situation with Squeeze's poisoning of Baylor. While Baylor would have died from the poison within 45 minutes, he was killed by earlier events. Because Squeeze's poisoning was not necessary for the death by train, she will escape liability for the death. (Thus, if the death is judged too remote or accidental in relation to Manny's push, no one will be liable for Baylor's death.) In *State v. Wood*, the defendant shot the deceased, inflicting a lethal wound. Before the deceased could die from the defendant's shot, however, he was killed by a subsequent lethal shot from another actor.[1] Because the defendant's earlier conduct was not necessary to cause the death, it did not satisfy the "but for" test. The court in *Wood* reversed the defendant's conviction on this ground.

Accountability Dependent on Sufficiency of Other Cause   The result in *Wood* is criticized by some, but is for the most part a popular view and one that most criminal codes would provide. The criticism comes from the result's illustration of an effect of the necessary-cause test that in broad outline may seem unsettling: An actor's liability depends not on the sufficiency of his own conduct to cause the result, but rather on *the sufficiency of the other cause(s)*. Indeed, it is this same effect that leads to the troubling result in *Jones*, the simultaneous-sufficient-cause case. The two tables in the footnote illustrate the application of the necessary-cause test for homicide in these two kinds of cases.[2] Note that in

---

1. 53 Vt. 558 (1881).
2.

Table: Causal Accountability of Actors Under the Necessary Cause Test Where Simultaneous Causes Result in Homicide

		Cause B	
		Lethal	Non-lethal
Cause A:	Lethal	A—no causation B—no causation (The situation in *Jones*)	A—causation B—no causation
	Non-lethal	A—no causation B—causation	A&B—causation

Table: Causal Accountability of Actor Under Necessary Cause Test Where an Sufficient Cause Results in Homicide

		Intervening Cause	
		Lethal	Non-lethal
Actor's (Prior) Cause:	Lethal	no causation (The situation in *Wood*)	causation
	Non-lethal	no causation	causation

each instance an actor's conduct will be accountable for the death if *the other cause* is non-lethal, and the actor will not be accountable if *the other cause* is lethal. This is true without regard to whether the actor's cause is itself lethal or non-lethal. This effect — having an actor's accountability depend on the nature of another's conduct and not on his own — may seem contrary to basic notions of accountability.

Sufficient-Cause Test This troubling effect of the necessary-cause test might lead one to examine alternative formulations of a test for factual cause. A sufficient-cause test, for example, would have the actor's accountability for a result depend on the nature of his own conduct rather than on that of another. An actor would be accountable for a result whenever his conduct was sufficient *in itself* to cause that result. Such a test would give different results than the necessary-cause test in two respects. First, it would hold accountable both of two simultaneous sufficient causes (as in the *Jones* case). This change seems clearly preferable to that generated by the necessary-cause test, which would hold neither accountable. Second, a sufficient-cause test would hold accountable a sufficient cause where the necessary-cause test would "cut off" accountability due to an intervening sufficient cause (as in the *Wood* case). This effect is somewhat more controversial. Many people feel that Wood should not be criminally liable for the death. While his conduct would have caused the death absent the intervening cause, it did not in fact cause the death, they would say. The view is little more than the expression of intuition, but it is an intuition that is strongly held, and the proximate cause requirement is essentially just an expression of the community's intuition on causal accountability. That is, it is the necessary-cause test, not the sufficient-cause test, that is said to match the community's view of causal accountability most effectively, despite its peculiar effects.

ADVANCED ISSUES RELATING TO THE SIGNIFICANCE OF RESULTING HARM

Sanford H. Kadish, The Criminal Law and the Luck of the Draw
84 Journal of Criminal Law and Criminology 679, 684-695 (1994)

I turn now to arguments designed to justify the harm doctrine in terms of the principle of desert. They all strike me the way one philosopher found metaphysics — "the finding of bad reasons for what we believe upon instinct." One argument proceeds as follows: our prevailing punishment practice with respect to results is no different than a penal lottery in which the amount of punishment for a crime depends on some such chance event as the drawing of long and short straws. To appreciate this, the argument goes, we need to cease thinking of the lesser punishment for failing to complete the crime as attributable to lesser guilt, and think of it merely as the chance event that determines the losers and winners of the lottery. Thought of as a penal lottery, then, there is no unfairness, for in leaving punishment to chance all attempters are treated alike. They all, in effect, draw straws. If they draw the short straw (that is, they succeed) they get the greater punishment. If they draw the long straw (that is, they fail) they get lesser punishment. There is no unfairness in treating the winners better than the losers so long as the lottery is unrigged.

But even unrigged, the basic injustice of a lottery in allocating punishment remains: to allow one of two offenders equally deserving of punishment to receive less punishment if she wins a lottery detaches punishment from desert. It would be the same if we allowed every equally guilty offender a throw of the dice — a throw of six or less and we halve the punishment. The two offenders end up being punished differently even though they are identical in every non-arbitrary sense. That is what is crucial, not the fact that they both had an equal chance of getting a lesser punishment when they threw the dice.

One might object that while punishing a person more than he deserves is unjust, punishing him less because he lucked out is not. Of course, the offender who lucked out can't complain. But the one who got what would otherwise be his just punishment may well complain, as any child knows who sees his sibling spanked once while he is spanked twice for the same offense. You wouldn't convince the child he wasn't unfairly treated by explaining to him that you left it to chance and he lost. He'd feel wronged, and rightly so. The parent's punishment action was arbitrary, in the sense that punishment of the children was left to chance, and thus forfeited any claim that the child should respect it as fair punishment.

A different defense of the harm doctrine rests on the judgment that given two people who try to do a harm or to risk it, the one who succeeds becomes a worse person than the one who fails, and thus deserves more punishment. So it has been argued that "in doing something evil one becomes something evil," and the one who fails to kill does not become what success in killing would have made him — an attempted murderer is not a murderer.

I do understand how most people would have heavier hearts if their blow had killed another than if it luckily only wounded. But I rather think they'd be kidding themselves to think themselves better persons because their victim happened to have a good constitution or a good doctor. Even if I'm wrong, though, I don't see how the difference warrants a difference in punishment. The principle of proportional punishment requires that the amount of punishment should bear some relation to the degree of blameworthiness of the defendants' actions, not to what they think of themselves or to what they have become in some existential sense.

Finally, I will mention two recent efforts to bring our intuitions about the harm doctrine into harmony with our reason. The first draws upon the recently popular retributive justification of punishment that views punishing the offender as restoring the imbalance of benefits and burdens created by the crime. There is, of course, one readily understandable imbalance produced by most crimes: the criminal profits from a loss he imposes on the victim — he steals or damages the victim's property, he causes the victim to suffer an economic loss, or he injures him physically. If punishment can justifiably be seen as somehow restoring the victim's loss, then less punishment for an attempt, where the victim has suffered no (or, arguably less) loss, could make sense. It is hard to see, however, how inflicting pain on the criminal restores anything — certainly it doesn't restore the victim to his property or compensate him for his economic loss or for his medical expenses and pain and suffering. And even if it somehow did, in the unpalatable sense that the victim received a restorative amount of pleasure from the offender's suffering, it is not the morality of retributive punishment that would have been demonstrated, but the desirability of satisfying the vengeful feelings of the victim, which is not the same thing.

However, the image of righting the imbalance is more often construed by those who use it in a different way—not as compensating the victim for physical injury or economic loss, but rather as depriving the offender of an unfair advantage; namely, the advantage of releasing himself from restraints the rest of us accept to allow the social enterprise to go forward. Punishment of the wrongdoer, then, deprives him of the parasitic advantage he has taken, somewhat analogously to the way a penalty in a competitive game is designed to negate any advantage gained by unsporting conduct. Using this as a justification for retributive punishment, Michael Davis has fashioned an ingenious argument to justify a lesser punishment for attempt. He draws an analogy to an imagined auction of licenses that permit the holder to act free of social restraints. Such an auction would reveal that a license to fail is worth less than a license to succeed, because people would naturally bid less for it. One who succeeds in committing a crime has unfairly imposed on the rest of us to the extent of the value of the license to succeed, while one who fails has imposed on us to the lesser extent of the value of a license to try and fail. Less is needed in the latter case, therefore, to rectify the unfairness.

There are many intriguing questions that may be pursued in connection with the working of this hypothetical auction, but my basic disquiet with Davis' argument arises from the premise on which it rests. For the psychoanalyst, it is plausible to conceive of people as spurred on by their deepest urges to ravage and plunder their neighbors, but held in check by social and legal constraints. On this view, presumably, the law-abiding have this grievance against the law-defying: "We played by the rules and held ourselves back from larceny, assault, rape and so forth. But you disregarded the implicitly agreed-on rules and did what the rest might have wanted to do. For taking this unfair advantage of the rest of us it is only right that you should be penalized."

As I said, this is the explanation some psychoanalysts give for the prevalence of the retributive urge. However, the contention that in punishing the criminal we are only cancelling the advantage the offender took of the rest of us in not restraining his anti-social impulses, as the rest of us do most of the time, seems an unlikely moral justification. No doubt there are some crimes for which this analysis is apt—for example, those in which the offender and others are indeed competing to win some goal, such as business people bidding for a contract. The one who cheats by finding out what the others have bid in order to be sure he submits the winning bid does derive precisely the kind of unfair advantage that Davis has in mind. The same can be said of income tax evasion. But, it seems unrealistic and demeaning to the rest of us to treat all crimes in this manner. What the law-abiding feel when they read of a child abduction, a rape, a murder, a vicious assault, is not that the offender has gotten an unfair advantage over them for which he should be penalized (and penalized proportionately to the price a license to commit these crimes would fetch at an auction). It is the evil of the offender and the harm he has imposed on the victim which moves them, not their own loss. So the theory of punishment as restoration of the unfair advantage the offender has taken of the rest of us ultimately fails, as does the notion of auctioned licenses which rests on it.

The second recent effort to justify the harm doctrine comes from R.A. Duff. He suggests that in punishing an attempt less than a completed crime the law serves to communicate to the offender that, although subjectively he is as culpable as one who does the harm, in fact all should be grateful that the harm he intended did not come to pass. The lesser punishment communicates the law's judgment that a worse state of affairs would have existed if the offender had achieved his objective — in other words, things are not as bad as they might have been. Perhaps the force of this argument turns on Duff's theory of justified punishment as communication directed towards the offender's repentance, but I find it hard to accept that we need the lesser punishment to keep us (and the offender) aware, for example, that things would be worse if the attempted rapist had succeeded in raping his victim.

Attempt Liability

ADVANCED ISSUES

Notes on the Culpability Requirements of Attempt Liability

No Elevation of Culpability as to Circumstance Under the narrow interpretation of "purposeful," the culpability required as to a circumstance is the same as that required for the substantive offense. The actor who is interrupted before he can complete a statutory rape would be liable for attempted statutory rape although he did not desire or know for certain that his partner was underage. In *State v. Galan*, for example, the defendant was charged with attempted trafficking in stolen property. The substantive offense required only recklessness as to the property being stolen, but the defendant claimed that the indictment was defective because "an attempt . . . requires a specific intent which is incompatible with a reckless state of mind."[1] The attempt statute was similar to the Model Penal Code provision (except for the substitution of the term "intentional" for "purposeful," a common lexical alteration). The court concluded:

> A common sense reading of the provision leads to the conclusion that the words *intentionally engages in conduct* refers [sic], in this case, to the actions that make up trafficking like buying property . . . and that the words *acting with the kind of culpability otherwise required for the commission of an offense* requires [sic] only that the acts be accompanied by a reckless state of mind as to the circumstances attending the status of the property. A contrary conclusion would mean that the words *acting with the kind of culpability otherwise required for the commission of an offense* are superfluous.[2]

The court goes on to quote the Model Penal Code Commentary, which confirms that, in the drafters' view, the actor's "purpose" need not encompass all the surrounding circumstances included in the definition of the substantive offense. As to these circumstances, it is sufficient that the actor has the culpability that is

---

1. 134 Ariz. 590, 590, 658 P.2d 243, 244 (Ariz. Ct. App. 1982).
2. Id. at 591-592, 658 P.2d at 244-245 (emphasis in original).

required for commission of the substantive offense.[1] This is the accepted view under modern statutes.

Culpability as to Result Under Code   The modern treatment of culpability as to a result is less clear. The Model Penal Code generally follows the common law rule in elevating the culpability required as to a result element.

> The general principle is...that the actor must affirmatively desire...to cause the result that will constitute the principal offense.[2]

This is said to follow from the common law's rule that attempt is a specific intent offense. In this respect, the code drafters appear to adopt the broad interpretation of section 5.01 discussed above. The drafters fear that punishing attempted recklessness or negligence would unduly extend criminal liability. Some coverage, such as recklessly creating a risk of death, is provided by the offense of reckless endangerment.[3] Thus, the drafters apparently wish the *purpose* and *knowing* requirements in the subsections to 5.01(1) to be interpreted as applying not only to the offense *conduct* that would constitute the offense, but also to a *result* element of the offense (but not to any *circumstance* elements). There seems little on the face of the statute that would suggest such an interpretation; it gives no hint that the "purposely" requirement applies to result elements but not circumstance elements.

Elevation Only to Knowing for Completed Conduct   The Code creates an exception to its requirement that the actor act "purposely" as to a result. Where the actor completes the conduct needed to cause the result, yet the result does not occur, section 5.01(1)(b) requires only a "belief" (knowing) as to the result:

> [W]hen causing a particular *result* is an element of the crime, [the actor is liable if he] does or omits to do anything with the purpose of causing or *with the belief* that it will cause such result without further conduct on his part.[4]

Such a rule is justified, in the drafters' view, because

> the manifestation of the actor's dangerousness is just as great — or very nearly as great — as in the case of purposive conduct. In both instances a deliberate choice is made to bring about the consequence forbidden by the criminal laws, and the actor has done all within his power to cause this result to occur.[5]

Some cases have reached the same conclusion, including a number of cases interpreting the common law's specific intent requirement to be satisfied by such a belief that the result will occur.[6] English law no longer requires a desire

---

1. "[W]ith respect to the circumstances under which a crime must be committed, the culpability otherwise required for commission of the crime is also applicable to the attempt." Model Penal Code § 5.01 explanatory note at 297 (1985).

2. Model Penal Code § 5.01 comment at 301 (1985).

3. Model Penal Code § 5.01 comment at 303-304 (1985).

4. Model Penal Code § 5.01(1)(b) (emphasis added). The Code's Commentary notes:

> Thus when the charge is attempted murder or assault with intent to kill, it is error to permit conviction on a finding of reckless disregard for human life or intent to inflict grievous bodily harm.

Model Penal Code § 5.01 comment at 306-307 (1985).

5. Model Penal Code § 5.01 comment at 305 (1985).

6. See, e.g., State v. Krovarz, 697 P.2d 378, 383 (Colo. 1985) (defendant convicted of attempted aggravated robbery on court's determination that "culpable mental state of knowledge suffices to support criminal attempt liability").

to cause the result (purpose); it requires only a belief that the conduct will cause the result. Under this approach, however, recklessness as to a result remains inadequate for attempt liability, even if such would be adequate for the substantive offense.

Case for Expanding Lower Culpability Beyond Completed Conduct The Code's exception to the purpose requirement—requiring elevation only to knowing—applies only where the actor has completed all of his conduct. The actor who sets the bomb knowing it will kill persons in the building but not wanting to kill such persons will be liable for attempted murder if the bomb malfunctions when triggered and does not explode. But if the bomb is fully functional and the actor is caught a moment before flipping the switch, he cannot be held liable for attempted murder under the Code. Because he has not completed all of the conduct required to constitute the substantive offense, he will fall under the *purpose* requirement of subsection 5.01(1)(c) rather than the *belief* requirement of subsection 5.01(1)(b). His belief in the practical certainty that his conduct will cause death is insufficient; it must be his conscious object to cause death. One may wonder whether the Code is wise to limit the instances where knowledge is sufficient, under subsection 5.01(1)(b), to cases of completed conduct. It is unclear why the bomber should have no liability for attempted murder because the police are lucky enough to stop him a moment before he detonates a bomb that would have killed the people in the building.[1]

Case for No Elevation as to Result Some jurisdictions would suggest that the larger difficulty with the Code's formulation is that it elevates culpability as to a result at all. Some statutory formulations drop the Model Penal Code's *purpose* or *belief* language, leaving only the requirement that the actor be "acting with the kind of culpability otherwise required for commission of the offense."[2] Under this approach, the "purpose" requirement in attempt would be the purpose to engage in the conduct necessary to commit the substantive offense. This purpose requirement certainly would be easy to prove in cases where the conduct is complete, cases under subsections (1)(a) and (1)(b) of the Code, but would be a more difficult issue, yet one of paramount importance, where the actor's conduct is incomplete, under subsection (1)(c). Under this approach, an actor could be charged with attempted statutory rape, for example, which might require only negligence or even strict liability as to the circumstance element of the partner's age. Similarly, an actor could be charged with attempted reckless endangerment, which would require purpose as to engaging in the conduct constituting the offense of endangerment but only recklessness as to creating a risk of death. Thus, an actor caught as he is about to dump toxic chemicals next to a school yard, aware that they might cause the death of one or more of the school children, could be held liable for attempted reckless endangerment because he purposely engages in conduct that he knows will create a risk of death.

"Accidental Attempt" vs. Attempt to Cause an "Accident" The drafters defend the Code's position by arguing that a general rule punishing attempts to

---

1. The Code's provision can give results similar to the "last proximate act" test, which was universally rejected as inadequate.
2. Model Penal Code § 5.01(1).

create risks would be unduly broad. But such liability is naturally limited to those few instances in which the code creates a substantive offense that punishes an actor for causing a specified risk.[1] It is true that there can be no such thing as an "accidental attempt," in the sense that to "attempt" an offense one must intend to complete the conduct that would constitute that offense. There is, however, such a thing as an attempt to cause an "accident," in the sense of an attempt to engage in conduct that creates, or would create, the opportunity for an "accident." As long as the law is careful to require that the actor's conscious object is to engage in *the conduct constituting the offense*, there seems little reason that attempts to create risks and attempts that create risks ought not to be punished.

Table: Summary of the Requirements of Attempt Liability

The doctrinal requirements for attempt liability may be summarized as follows:

Objective Requirements	Culpability Requirements
Conduct constituting substantive offense: Not required, instead: CL — proximity & res ipsa loquitur tests MPC — substantial step test	*Culpability as to conduct constituting substantive offense:* CL & MPC — purposeful
Result elements of substantive offense: CL & MPC — not required (nor is factual impossibility of it occurring a defense)	*Culpability as to result elements of substantive offense:* CL — elevate to purposeful MPC — elevate to purposeful, but only to knowing if conduct complete Other (e.g., Utah) — as required by substantive offense; do not elevate
Circumstance elements of substantive offense: CL — required (legal impossibility is a defense) MPC — not required (legal impossibility is not a defense)	*Culpability as to circumstance elements of substantive offense:* CL — elevate to purposeful MPC — as required by substantive offense; do not elevate (per commentary)

MPC = Model Penal Code
CL = Common Law

Problem: Gambling Life

Bertie Graham works at a convalescent hospital for cardiac patients. She has recently learned that her friend Iva, who also works at the hospital, made some extra money by selling the heart medication of the patient she cares for, substituting aspirin. Bertie would like to do the same but is concerned that she might get caught and held criminally liable if her patient dies from an attack

---

1. Result elements typically appear only in homicide, personal injury, and property damage offenses.

because the medication is not immediately available. Iva explains that on many occasions when patients take the medication, they are not really having an attack. Bertie decides to make the substitution.

After Bertie acquires the aspirin that she plans to substitute and changes the label to look like heart medicine but before she can make the switch, a patient dies from an attack and the authorities discover that the patient's medication had been switched. The offending employee, Jenkins, is found and charged with manslaughter (reckless homicide). Later that day, Iva's patient dies from a heart attack. All medication bottles are seized and a review uncovers several more medication switches. To Iva's surprise and confusion, her patient's medication is found to be heart medication, not the aspirin she thought she had substituted. Those employees who made medication switches are charged with endangerment (recklessly creating a risk of death to another). In the hopes of getting better treatment from prosecutors, Iva turns in Bertie, who admits to investigators that she planned to make the switch later that day. What, if anything, are Iva and Bertie liable for?

APPENDIX A: SECTION 11

Impossibility

ADVANCED ISSUES

Notes on Impossibility

Dangerousness Rationale for Subjective Criminality The rationale for the defense for an inherently unlikely attempt logically follows from the rationale of the Model Penal Code drafters in rejecting a defense for legal impossibility: The actor who attempts an offense generally has demonstrated his dangerousness, even if actual commission of the offense is impossible. In those rare cases where neither the method of attempt nor the actor is dangerous, the Code's rationale for liability evaporates and a defense becomes appropriate. Most of the Code's changes from common law rules—in the context of attempt, its rejection of a legal impossibility defense and its switch from a proximity to a substantial step test—are consistent with such a focus on the dangerousness of the offender. The attempter caught short of dangerous proximity and the legally impossible attempter ought to be liable, the Code drafters can argue, because both are dangerous. The Code's grading of an attempt equal to the substantive offense reflects a similar view: Whether the attempter was successful or unsuccessful, she has demonstrated dangerousness. The shift from the common law's bilateral agreement requirement in conspiracy to a unilateral agreement requirement also is consistent with a dangerousness focus. An actor demonstrates dangerousness by agreeing with an apparent co-conspirator to commit an offense, whether or not the co-conspirator is really agreeing back.

Dangerousness vs. Blameworthiness as Rationale Yet it does not follow that a shift to subjectivist criminality, as reflected in the illustrations above, is necessarily due to adoption of dangerousness as the central criterion for criminal liability. A subjective view of criminality is useful not only to identify dangerous offenders but also to identify blameworthy offenders. The substantial-step test for attempt, the rejection of a defense for legal impossibility, and the unilateral view of agreement in conspiracy all do as good a job, or better, than their common law counterparts in identifying an actor who is blameworthy in a subjective, individual sense. The attempter who has passed a substantial step but has not yet reached a point of adequate proximity nonetheless is blameworthy because he has shown a willingness to act on an intention to break the law. The actor who mistakenly believes the circumstances are such that her conduct constitutes an offense is blameworthy because this demonstrates a willingness to commit such an offense. The actor who mistakenly thinks he is conspiring with another to commit an offense is blameworthy for the same reason. The denial of a defense by modern codes in each of these cases avoids the escape from liability of one who may not have caused the substantive harm or created the social disruption that the common law required to justify inchoate liability but who nonetheless is morally blameworthy for attempting, or conspiring to commit, an offense.

Inherently Unlikely Defense as Manifestation of Dangerousness-Subjectivism It is not surprising that the dangerousness and blameworthiness rationales frequently generate similar results. Dangerous people commonly do blameworthy things. Many blameworthy people are likely to do something unlawful in the future. This is not always the case, however. The inherently unlikely attempter may not be dangerous in the future, but nonetheless may be blameworthy for his past attempt. The actor's conduct, in light of her *belief* that the voodoo pins will work, is enough to demonstrate her intention and willingness to kill. The Model Penal Code's recognition of a defense for an inherently unlikely attempt gives evidence, on the face of the Code, that the Code's subjectivist view of criminality is based on dangerousness rather than blameworthiness. A jurisdiction that adopts a subjectivist view of criminality because it best furthers the blameworthiness rationale might adopt most of the Code's subjectivist changes to common law but reject the Code's "inherently unlikely" defense.

Blameworthiness-Subjectivism Permitting Mitigation but Not Defense One could argue that a mitigation , if not a defense, for an inherently unlikely attempt is appropriate even under a blameworthiness rationale. Many things, in addition to an actor's subjective culpability, may affect an actor's blameworthiness: the extent of the harm caused, the seriousness of the evil committed, the degree of the danger created. A blameworthiness rationale does not rely exclusively on subjective criteria. Thus, an inherently unlikely attempt, where there is no danger of a resulting harm or evil, might be judged less blameworthy, all other things being equal, than a feasible attempt, just as an unsuccessful attempt to kill may be judged less blameworthy than a successful attempt. The first pair of cases are distinguished from one another by the creation of a risk of death; the second pair are distinguished by a resulting death. This kind of analysis suggests that some mitigation in liability beyond that for the normal attempt may be appropriate for an inherently unlikely attempt, but a complete defense would be inconsistent with the actor's demonstrated blameworthiness.

Problem: The Crays Go to Church

The Cray brothers, Lynch, Morse, and Nick, have hit on a great target for a robbery: the church collection monies. After reconnoitering, they determine that security is almost nonexistent. They decide to wait until the church is empty, then two of them will stand lookout, one at each end, while the other ducks into the minister's office and jimmies open the desk drawer where the money is kept.

Each of the brothers disguises his appearance, and the brothers go to the church after the very lucrative Easter service is over. As they are waiting for the church to clear, Morse begins to have second thoughts. He reminds the others that the church helped them when they needed it, and so forth, until Lynch finally blows up. "If you're chicken, just leave!" he says through clenched teeth, attempting to whisper. "I'm going to leave, but I want you guys to come too." "No way," Lynch responds. Nick speaks up, "Look, Lynch. If Morse takes off, we can't do this job without getting caught. We need three people" "If you're chicken too, Nick, just take off with Morse" Morse and Nick get up to leave. After a word whispered between them, they each grab one of Lynch's arms and drag him out of the church. Their commotion draws a good deal of attention. When they get outside, they drop Lynch and the three scatter in different directions.

Twenty minutes later, after the church is quiet again, Lynch returns. He is still steaming about what his brothers did to him. He decides to show them that he can pull off the job by himself. When he sees his chance, he slips in, steals the money, and makes it safely home. But then he begins to think. Perhaps Morse is right about the church money. After some thought, he decides to return the money before it is missed. He sneaks back into the church and replaces the money in the minister's drawer. As he is coming out of the office, he runs into a policeman who had been called about the original commotion. An investigation turns up witnesses to both the original fiasco and Lynch's subsequent conduct. Lynch is charged with theft of over $1,000. Morse and Nick are identified and arrested and charged as accomplices in the theft (based on their help in reconnoitering the scene, etc.). All three also are charged with conspiracy to commit the theft. All three plead renunciation as a defense to all charges. Morse and Nick also are charged with complicity in the theft. They plead termination as a defense. Who will be held liable for what?

Notes on Renunciation and Termination

Completed Offense   If you steal a classmate's notes, suffer an attack of conscience, and return them before your classmate is injured by, or even knows of, their absence, you nonetheless are liable for theft. Generally, once the elements of a substantive offense are satisfied, the offense cannot be "undone." No jurisdiction will give Lynch a defense to the theft charge. That he returned the money on his own may be seen by some sentencing judges as reducing his deserved sentence, but it will not provide a defense or mitigation of his liability.

Common Law Incentives to Stop Offense   The common law and some current codes take this same view of inchoate offenses. The offense is complete and irrevocable the moment the actor satisfies the elements of the inchoate offense.[1]

---

1. See, e.g., Blaylock v. State, 598 P.2d 251 (Okla. Crim. App. 1979) (because defendant met with undercover agents posing as hitmen to plan death of colleague, defendant guilty of conspiracy, even though plan not carried out); Rollin M. Perkins & R. Boyce, Criminal Law 654-658 (1982). English law still does not recognize a renunciation defense to inchoate liability. See Andrew Ashworth, Principles of Criminal Law 436, 464 (2d ed. 1995).

The common law had no need for a renunciation defense in order to encourage potential offenders to stop short of the offense. When criminal liability for an attempt attaches late in the process between preparation and commission, such as with the common law's proximity tests, the actor has an incentive to stop in his planned offense, because by doing so he avoids all liability. Even after the point where conduct becomes a criminal attempt, after the point of proximity, the actor's incentive to stop remains right up to the point of actual commission, because the completed offense typically is graded more seriously than an inchoate offense. By stopping, the actor might not be able to avoid all liability, but can limit it.

Modern Absence of Incentives to Stop   By its formulation and grading of attempt (and other inchoate offenses), the Model Penal Code takes away the incentive to stop that exists under common law. Because the Code generally grades inchoate offense the same as the completed offense,[1] an actor has no incentive to stop once his conduct has become a criminal attempt. In addition, the Code moves the point at which conduct becomes criminal to an earlier point in the process, from proximity to the offense to a "substantial step" toward commission.[2] Early in the process, then, liability attaches that is equal to that for the completed offenses. Thus, at an early stage, an actor would have every reason to continue with the offense because commission would not increase liability. In this situation, the Code could not afford not to have a renunciation defense.

Blameworthiness Rationale for Defense   If providing an incentive to stop were the only rationale for the defense, one might wonder whether a mitigation, rather than a complete defense, would be adequate. Some liability might be useful, one might observe, because one who tries but renounces might nonetheless be dangerous. One can argue for a complete defense, however, on desert grounds. That is, the actor's presumed willingness to commit the substantive offense is a central modern rationale for punishing inchoate offenses. The willingness shows the actor to be blameworthy (and dangerous). Where an actor voluntarily and completely renounces before commission of the offense, it reveals that the initial conclusion about the actor's willingness to commit the offense was wrong.

"Complete and Voluntary"   This culpability-undercutting rationale justifies a defense, however, only if the defense is limited to instances where the actor renounces commission for the sole reason that her intention is not (and presumably never was) sufficiently resolute. The rationale would not support a defense where the actor stops because of changed conditions or new information, for example, which make the offense look more difficult or less profitable than initially supposed. The Model Penal Code definition of voluntary and complete renunciation provides appropriate limitations:

> Within the meaning of this Article, renunciation of criminal purpose is not voluntary if it is motivated, in whole or in part, by circumstances, not present or apparent at the inception of the actor's course of conduct, which increase the probability of detection or apprehension or which make more difficult the accomplishment of the criminal purpose. Renunciation is not complete if it is motivated by a decision to postpone the criminal conduct until a more

---

1. Model Penal Code § 5.05(1).
2. Model Penal Code § 5.01(1)(c).

advantageous time or to transfer the criminal effort to another but similar objective or victim.[1]

Under this test, Morse's renunciation is "complete and voluntary." Nick's is not, for it is motivated by a fear of getting caught because of Morse's withdrawal.

Defense Excluded for Completed Conduct The blameworthiness rationale for the defense does not apply where, from the actor's view, the offense is complete, such as in cases of legal impossibility. In such cases, the actor has demonstrated the willingness to complete the offense. Nor is there a reason to provide an incentive to stop before completion of the offense in such completed offense cases. The Model Penal Code appropriately excludes a renunciation defense in such cases by barring the defense for an offense under section 5.01(1)(a), where the actor has engaged in conduct "which would constitute the crime if the attendant circumstances were as he believes them to be." One may wonder, however, whether the defense also should be barred for a prosecution under section 5.01(1)(b), where the actor believes that his conduct will cause a required result (will cause death, in a homicide offense, for example) "without further conduct on his part." These too are instances where the actor has shown his willingness to commit the offense. As with subsection (1)(a) cases, the subsection (1)(b) actor thinks he has done everything needed to complete the offense. The Code permits a defense in the latter cases, despite the actor's demonstrated willingness to commit the offense, because the drafters wish to provide an incentive for the actor to prevent the harmful result that has not yet occurred.[2] Where the harm remains a threat and can be avoided, the incentive may be useful. (In section (1)(a) cases, of course, the offense never can occur.) This may offer another illustration of the drafters' greater attention to utilitarian concerns. The drafters' decision to allow a renunciation defense to provide an incentive to avoid the harm, despite the actor's demonstrated willingness to commit the offense, is another example that utilitarian concerns trump desert concerns in their minds. A purer focus on blameworthiness would suggest a renunciation defense for a true renunciation in which the actor had made all reasonable efforts to avoid the harm. More on this in a moment.

Requirement of Offense Prevention It is not enough under the Code for the actor completely and voluntarily to renounce her criminal purpose. She must, in addition, prevent the commission of the offense.[3] The attempter must abandon her attempt "or otherwise prevent its commission."[4] The renouncing conspirator

---

1. Model Penal Code § 5.01(4).

2. [One] reason for allowing renunciation of criminal purpose as a defense to an attempt charge is to

provide actors with a motive for desisting from their criminal designs, thereby diminishing the risk that the substantive crime will be committed. While under the proposed subsection such encouragement is held out at all stages of the criminal effort, its significance becomes greatest as the actor nears his criminal objective and the risk that the crime will be completed is correspondingly high. At the very point where abandonment least influences a judgment as to the dangerousness of the actor—where the last proximate act has been committed but the resulting crime can still be avoided—the inducement to desist stemming from the abandonment defense achieves its greatest value.

Model Penal Code § 5.01 comment 359 (1985).

3. See Model Penal Code §§ 5.02(3), 5.03(6).

4. Model Penal Code § 5.01(4) (tense changed).

must "thwart the success of the conspiracy."[1] The renouncing solicitor must "persuade [the perpetrator] not to [commit the offense] or otherwise prevent commission of the crime."[2] Under the Code, then, while Morse may get a renunciation defense to his own attempted theft, he might not get a renunciation defense to conspiracy to commit theft because he did not prevent Lynch's commission of the theft. Although his renunciation was complete and voluntary, his efforts to thwart the success of the conspiracy were unsuccessful.[3] That Morse withdrew from the conspiracy before the offense does not provide a defense to conspiracy; it serves only to cut off his own liability for the collateral consequences of any continuing conspiracy.[4]

Blameworthiness vs. Crime Prevention Rationales   The prevention requirement illustrates the Code's use of the renunciation defense, not only as a means to exculpate actors who do not have an adequately resolute intent, but also as a device to encourage desistance. If the renunciation defense rationale were purely a rebuttal of an earlier appearance of blameworthiness, a voluntary and complete renunciation alone would be adequate for the defense. One might require proper *effort* to prevent the offense, which would confirm that the actor has truly repudiated the offense plan. But to require actual prevention of the offense, no matter how heroic the effort to prevent, is to risk holding liable an actor, like Morse, who truly has renounced but, because of the particular circumstances, is unable to prevent commission. The Code drafters' view of crime prevention as the primary distributive principle for liability has been confirmed in other instances. Recall that the Code recognizes an inherently unlikely defense to inchoate offenses, for example. Indeed, recall that the Code's attraction to subjective culpability is based primarily upon a dangerousness rationale rather than a blameworthiness rationale.

Renunciation Under Blameworthiness Rationale   If a jurisdiction has blameworthiness as its primary distributive principle for liability, rather than crime prevention, it is likely to reject the Code's limitations on the renunciation defense. That is, it would require complete and voluntary renunciation and possibly reasonable efforts to prevent commission of the offense. It would not require actual prevention of the offense. (A blameworthiness rationale might suggest, however, that complete and voluntary renunciation provide a mitigation, rather than a complete defense.) Under a pure blameworthiness rationale, Morse might well be allowed a defense to conspiracy. He could argue that he could not reasonably have known that Lynch would sneak back into the church twenty minutes after the commotion involved in dragging him out.

Termination of Complicity   It may seem odd that while the Code requires actual offense prevention for a defense to inchoate liability, it does not require

---

1. Model Penal Code § 5.03(6) (tense changed).
2. Model Penal Code § 5.02(3) (tense changed).
3. Morse might be able to argue that Lynch's subsequent theft offense was not the same offense as that which was the objective of the conspiracy. The success of this argument may depend on whether the jurisdiction is more interested in exculpating blameless actors under the renunciation defense than in upholding a rule that creates the strongest incentives for renouncing conspirators to prevent the offense by former co-conspirators. See next two paragraphs of text discussion.
4. Model Penal Code § 5.03(7).

actual prevention for a termination defense to complicity. The Code provides a defense to the withdrawing accomplice if

> he terminates his complicity prior to the commission of the offense and
> (i) wholly deprives [his complicity] of effectiveness in the commission of the offense; or
> (ii) gives timely warning to the law enforcement authorities *or otherwise makes proper effort* to prevent the commission of the offense.[1]

The accomplice need only take out what he put into the offense or make "proper effort" to prevent commission; he need not actually prevent the offense. Thus, Morse and Nick would each have a defense to complicity in theft under the Code. Both made proper effort to prevent the offense by dragging Lynch from the church.

Complicity as Quasi-Inchoate   Why should there be a defense to complicity, which is substantive liability, for an actor who terminates? Is not the normal rule that a substantive offense cannot be undone once the offense is complete? While this is true, the use of such a defense for complicity recognizes that complicity, during the time before the perpetrator completes the offense, is a form of inchoate liability for the accomplice. Like that of a co-conspirator, the accomplice's conduct before the offense is in the nature of preparation. Indeed, the Code makes special provision for complicity to be treated as an attempt where the perpetrator does not ultimately commit the offense.[2] From that perspective, a renunciation-like defense for the accomplice seems appropriate.

No Prevention Requirement for Termination Defense   The Code requires prevention of the substantive offense for a renunciation defense to conspiracy and solicitation. It does this in order to maximize the incentive to prevent commission. One may wonder, then, why the Code does not apply the same reasoning to the termination of complicity defense. Indeed, why not require the accomplice actually to prevent the offense in order to earn a termination defense? The Code at first may seem to have things backwards. Complicity, as a source of full substantive liability, ought to have a more demanding requirement for a renunciation-like defense, if any at all; normally, one cannot escape liability for a substantive offense once the elements are satisfied. Inchoate offenses, one might argue, ought to have a less demanding defense, based as they are on the actor's subjective culpability, which is undercut by his renunciation. For the same reasons, one might also criticize the Code's complicity termination defense in that it fails to require that the termination be complete and voluntary, as is required for the comparable renunciation defense to inchoate liability. But these criticisms miss the point that the issue for the termination defense to complicity typically is only a grading judgment: whether the actor is to suffer full substantive liability or reduced inchoate liability. Even if an actor escapes full liability because he "terminates his complicity" and "makes proper effort to prevent the offense," he nonetheless may be liable for inchoate liability. To escape inchoate liability, as well, and to get a complete defense, he must satisfy the more demanding requirements of the

---

1. Model Penal Code § 2.06(6)(c) (emphasis added).
2. Model Penal Code § 5.01(3).

renunciation defense. (Of course, this rationale makes sense only if inchoate and substantive offenses are graded differently. Under the Model Penal Code scheme, without the grading distinction, the explanation for the termination-renunciation difference is less clear.)

Liability for Lynch, Morse, and Nick?   Let us summarize our liability conclusions. Even though Lynch's renunciation may be complete and voluntary, he will not get a defense to the completed theft offense. Morse and Nick, charged as accomplices to Lynch's theft because they helped him reconnoiter the scene and so forth, will get a termination defense to complicity because they terminated their complicity and made proper effort to prevent the offense, albeit unsuccessfully. Morse and Nick are likely to remain liable for conspiracy, however, if the jurisdiction, like the Model Penal Code, requires that the actor successfully prevent the offense in order to get a renunciation defense to conspiracy liability. (A blameworthiness rationale for the renunciation defense, which would require only a proper effort to prevent the offense, would give Morse a defense to conspiracy, but not Nick.) Morse will get a renunciation (and termination) defense to a charge of complicity in an attempt; Nick may get a termination defense to such complicity, even though he does not satisfy the requirements for a renunciation defense.[1]

"Abandonment" and "Withdrawal"   Courts and legislatures do not uniformly use the terms "renunciation" and "termination" to refer to the defenses discussed here. The terms "abandonment" and "withdrawal" also have been used from time to time. In modern codes, however, "renunciation" generally is preferred when referring to the defense to inchoate liability because the term carries with it the connotation of a change of attitude, a repudiation. Terms like "abandonment" and "withdrawal" suggest simply that the actor has stopped the planned conduct. Thus, the words might be appropriate to refer to the complicity defense, or to the even less demanding doctrine (usually called "withdrawal") that determines when an actor is no longer part of a conspiracy. The latter doctrine is not a defense to liability at all; it only has the effect of cutting off the collateral consequences that flow from being a member of a conspiracy.[2]

---

1. Where § 5.01(3) is relied on as the grounds for inchoate liability for an accomplice in a failed offense, the provision would seem to give a complete defense to such inchoate liability on proof of the requirements of a termination defense to complicity. That is, if the actor satisfies the requirements of a termination defense, he has a defense to complicity liability, and such liability is a precondition to attempt liability under § 5.01(3).

2. For example, after an effective "withdrawal" or "abandonment" of this sort, subsequent hearsay statements are not admissible, the statute of limitations begins running as to the actor, subsequent offenses are not attributable to the actor under the Pinkerton Rule, and so on.

Conspiracy

ADVANCED ISSUES

Note, Conspiracy: Statutory Reform Since the Model Penal Code

75 Columbia Law Review 1122-1125, 1129-1130, 1145-1147, 1153-1154, 1158-1160, 1164-1165, 1188 (1975)

Conspiracy is a crime with a long, and not always illustrious, history. From its common law origins as a retaliatory weapon for an individual subjected to false arrest and prosecution at the instance of another to its present status as a favorite tool of federal prosecutors in the war against organized crime, conspiracy has been subject to frequent and severe criticism. The suspicion is strong that the underlying source of this continuing dissatisfaction is a widespread and deep-seated aversion to the punishment of mere evil intent. Conspiracy, even in its modern formulations, advances the moment of criminal guilt and permissible official intervention to a point considerably earlier than that allowed by the law of attempt. While such a result may be justified by the need to protect society, it poses significant dangers to the preservation of personal rights and liberties. These dangers stem partially from the definition of the conspiracy offense, and partially from the procedural features of a conspiracy prosecution. Reduced to their least common denominator, the vast majority of statutes define conspiracy as an agreement to commit a crime. The nebulous concept of agreement is thus characterized as the essential element of the conspiracy offense. Since agreement is ordinarily not susceptible of direct proof, jury verdicts in conspiracy cases frequently turn on inferences draw from equivocal or inconclusive conduct by defendants. Moreover, the potential for unjust convictions is magnified by a series of procedural peculiarities connected with conspiracy trials. Liberal joinder, venue, and statute of limitations rules, along with the co-conspirators' hearsay exception, open several avenues of possible abuse. In particular, where numerous alleged co-conspirators are tied together, juries may be unable to evaluate independently the evidence against each individual defendant. Guilt by association is therefore a serious threat.

The difficult task of achieving an appropriate balance between the desire to afford adequate opportunity for early law enforcement efforts and the obligation to safeguard constitutional freedoms was essayed by the drafters of the American Law Institute's Model Penal Code (MPC) in the late 1950's. The product of their deliberations, promulgated in 1962, has since served as the basis for revision of conspiracy statutes in numerous jurisdictions....

II. The Objectives of Criminal Conspiracy

A major failing of conventional, i.e., pre-reform, conspiracy statutes involves their vague and overbroad specification of the objectives of a criminal agreement. A typical formulation makes it a crime to agree "to commit any act injurious to the public health, to public morals, or to pervert or obstruct justice, or the due administration of the laws." Though a number of these unsatisfactory statutes remain in force today, the legislative trend is clearly in the direction of major reform suggested by the MPC. Stated simply, the ALI drafters refused to approve the imposition of criminal sanctions on agreements directed toward the performance of conduct which, if achieved, would not itself constitute a penal violation. With only one exception, each new statute, adopted or proposed, has reflected this conclusion by making criminal only those conspiracies whose objective is the commission of a crime (or, in some states, an offense) as defined elsewhere in the jurisdiction's penal code....

IV. Culpability

A. Some General Observations

But for the language of both versions of the proposed Federal Criminal Code, the proper statutory treatment of the culpability standard to be utilized in conspiracy prosecutions would be reasonably well settled. Under the MPC, no person may be convicted of conspiracy unless he acts with the purpose of promoting or facilitating commission of the object crime. This fundamental MPC innovation has been accepted by 35 of 43 states which have undertaken to modernize their penal laws. Moreover, the group following the MPC line includes not only the larger, more influential states, but also, with the exception of North Dakota, all the states which have demonstrated their intention to enact a relatively thorough codification of the conspiracy offense. Only minor variations in terminology distinguish the culpability formulations of these jurisdictions.

The requirement that one accused of conspiracy must be shown to have intended the substantive offense he has allegedly agreed to commit has two important implications. First, it successfully divorces the culpability with respect to the object crime which is necessary for conspiracy from the culpability sufficient for the object crime itself. Specific intent to engage in certain conduct or to produce a certain result is essential to a conspiracy conviction, though simple knowledge or belief that such conduct or result will or may ensue may be an adequate basis for guilt of the substantive offense. Second, the MPC's purpose formula serves to mitigate some of the potential abuses inherent in statutory reliance on the vague agreement concept for the definition of conspiracy. The comparative ease with which agreement may be established has occasioned frequent criticism. The MPC hoped to allay some of these misgivings by insisting on proof that the particular defendant on trial for conspiracy intended to advance the object crime. . . .

V. The Overt Act

Some dispute exists among the states over whether an overt act in pursuance of an agreement to commit a crime should be a prerequisite for a conspiracy conviction. Though such an act was not necessary at common law, two-thirds of the jurisdictions which have revised or are considering revision of their conspiracy statutes have elected to impose such an additional requirement before an agreement to commit any offense will be proscribed. Another five states, choosing to follow the MPC pattern, insist on an overt act in all cases other than those involving agreements to commit a first or second degree felony (or one of a similar list of serious crimes). Maine, Ohio, Washington, and Vermont, all members of the former group, set even stricter standards than the rest of the majority. Statutes in these states permit conspiracy convictions only where a "*substantial step*" has been taken in furtherance of the conspiracy. Under the laws recently adopted in Ohio and proposed in Vermont, an act, to qualify as "substantial," must be "of such character as to manifest a purpose on the part of the actor that the object of the conspiracy should be completed." Maine's new conspiracy provision further narrows the definition of "substantial step," demanding "conduct which, under the circumstances in which it occurs, is *strongly corroborative* of the firmness of the actor's intent to complete commission of the crime," and adding that "speech alone may not constitute a substantial step." This language greatly resembles that found in Maine's attempt section, and indicates that Maine may be tending toward the elimination of all conspiracy liability where a substantive offense has not been at least attempted. Such a development may also be favored by Washington, which uses the phrase "substantial step" without definition in both its conspiracy and its attempt provisions. At the opposite extreme, eight states have decided, for one reason or another, to preserve the common law scheme on this issue, and so require no overt act whatever. Under such statutes, the crime of conspiracy is complete when the agreement is formed. . . .

VI. The Party and Object Dimensions

Ascertaining the dimensions of a criminal conspiracy, as to both parties and objectives, is perhaps the most complex and the most common of all the tasks presented by conspiracy litigation. The difficulty and recurrence of this problem mirror the great import assigned to its solution in determining the answers to numerous other questions confronting the courts in conspiracy cases. For example, in jurisdictions demanding an overt act, the satisfaction of that requirement may depend on whether a particular individual may legitimately be classified as defendant's co-conspirator.

Generally speaking, current case law, in measuring the party dimensions of a criminal conspiracy, focuses on the "over-all operation," viewed from a pragmatic standpoint. This approach is typified by the leading case of *United States v. Bruno*, in which the Second Circuit held that narcotics smugglers, middlemen, and two groups of retailers, one in New York and the other in Texas and Louisiana, could all be properly joined in one large conspiracy. The MPC's proposed method for identifying the participants in a single conspiracy is more technical, and directly derived from the definition of the inchoate offense. Observe first that, under MPC § 5.03(1), agreement may be inferred from behavior and surrounding circumstances even in the absence of proof of direct contact or communication between alleged conspirators. However, such an inference becomes increasingly strained when evidence of mutual cooperation is weak, and personal connections are not easily visible. MPC § 5.03(2) therefore provides that if a conspirator *knows* that his co-conspirator "*has conspired* with another person or persons to commit the *same* crime," then he is guilty of conspiring to commit. . . .

VII. Duration — The Time Dimension

The duration of a criminal agreement is important primarily for statute of limitations purposes. The MPC essentially codifies existing case law on the subject. According to MPC § 5.03(7)(a), "conspiracy is a continuing course of conduct which terminates when the crime or crimes which are its object are committed or the agreement that they be committed is abandoned by the defendant and by those with whom he conspired." Perhaps because prior decisions have left the key issues reasonably well settled, most state statutes say nothing about conspiracy's time dimension. Eleven states include provisions which track the MPC language, while Maine, North Dakota, Massachusetts, Vermont, and H.R. 333 add "frustration" to "success" and "abandonment" in the catalog of means by which a conspiracy may reach its conclusion. This latter modification seems reasonable, unless frustration is too broadly defined. Where circumstances simply make the criminal object slightly more difficult to achieve, a conspiracy should not be regarded as terminated. On the other hand, when an intended victim permanently relocates in a distant land or when new security procedures are instituted which make effective implementation of a criminal plan virtually impossible, a permissible inference might be drawn that a conspiracy no longer continues. Of course, evidence would be required to the effect that the conspirators were aware of the relevant developments and that they had not transferred their criminal purpose to another object. In point of fact, the leading case cited in support of the "frustration" alternative involved parties to a criminal agreement already in custody, and thus left little doubt that the participants would proceed no further. . . .

XI. Conclusion

The MPC has clearly had a deep and pervasive influence on conspiracy laws in the United States. Three leading reforms advocated by the ALI have achieved widespread adoption. They are: (i) limitation of the objectives of a criminal agreement to statutorily defined crimes; (ii) description of conspiracy as a unilateral offense; and (iii) requirement of specific intent to promote or facilitate the commission of a crime in order to sustain a conspiracy charge. The renunciation defense has been somewhat less successful, but, perhaps as a consolation, eight states have proposed what may be an improvement on the MPC formula. Making the least inroads have been the MPC provisions on the party, object, and time dimensions of the conspiracy offense. In light of the considerable opportunities for abuse on such issues, further reform efforts might well be concentrated in this field. Finally, the majority of jurisdictions have partially endorsed the MPC grading scheme, acknowledging the wisdom of tying conspiracy penalties to those assigned to related substantive crimes, but retreating from total similarity between such penalties. They have thus evidenced a persistent concern for the actual outcome of conspiratorial efforts as a factor determining appropriate penal treatment. However theoretically unjustifiable this departure may be, it probably enjoys a strong basis in practical realities and community sentiment.

Further Notes on Conspiracy Culpability Requirements

Questioning Code's Rationale for Elevation   While there is a surface appeal to the Code's rationale in increasing the required culpability as to a result (and, perhaps, as to a circumstance) to offset the minimal conduct required, one may wonder whether the Code's reasoning is sound. Why exactly should the preparatory nature of conspiracy require higher culpability? If the sliding scale is appropriate for result elements, why is it not equally appropriate for circumstance elements? The concern about the preparatory nature of conspiracy is presumably twofold: First, the more preliminary the conduct, the more ambiguous it may be that it is in fact conduct toward a criminal end. Second, the more preliminary the conduct, the less clear it may be that the actor actually intends to carry through to the completed offense. As to the first, one could argue that conspiracy presents a stronger case than many attempts for showing unequivocal criminal intent. The agreement requires that the actor agree that a criminal offense be committed. This leaves little room for ambiguity about whether the intended objective is criminal. A substantial-step attempt carries no such evidence of criminal intent on its face. As to the second concern, that the actor may not actually intend to carry the plan to conclusion, the requirement of the actor's purpose to promote the *conduct constituting the offense* would seem to provide adequate confirmation. Once it is proven that it is the actor's *purpose to carry through with the offense conduct*, why is it not adequate for liability to prove the culpability of the substantive offense as to circumstance and result elements? Note as well that the renunciation defense is available to conspiracy and will give a defense to those with an intention too equivocal to carry through with the offense.

Legalize Conspiracies to Create Risks?   The peculiarity of the Code's position is apparent from the results it generates. Assume two actors agree that one will dump toxic waste down a bore hole leading to an abandoned mine shaft. They are aware of a substantial risk that such conduct will create a risk of catastrophe. On learning of their plan, police arrest them before they are able to carry out their agreement and charge them with conspiracy to risk a catastrophe, under a provision like Model Penal Code section 220.2(2). The offense requires that an actor recklessly create a risk of catastrophe. These are essentially the facts in *Commonwealth v. Scatera*.[1] The defendants have the required culpable state of mind for the offense, but their conduct has not progressed beyond their agreement and an overt act. The Code would bar conviction, requiring that the actors be purposeful as to creating a risk of catastrophe. But why should liability be barred? Why is it not enough that these actors were purposeful as to engaging in the conduct constituting

---

1. 332 Pa. Super. 415, 481 A.2d 855 (1984), rev'd, 508 Pa. 512, 498 A.2d 1314 (1985).

the offense — dumping toxic waste into the bore hole — with the culpability required by the offense for creating a risk of catastrophe? To put the problem in the context of Abe and Ben, assume both Abe and Ben were discovered immediately after contacting the scrap dealer and that the evidence of their intention is clear. Their agreement is to do something that is clearly criminal and dangerous to human life, yet the Code would bar conspiracy liability for even the most minor offense, even endangerment, a misdemeanor.[1] While their proven purpose was to engage in conduct that they *knew* created a risk of death, the Code finds this inadequate for liability because causing the risk of death is not their *purpose*.[2]

Common Law Rationale Inapplicable   The Code's view may be shaped in part by the common law's position that conspiracy, like attempt, is a "specific intent" offense. But the rule made more sense at common law than it does for the Code. Common law relied on any number of evidentiary presumptions to prove culpable state of mind — for example, a person is presumed to intend the natural and probable consequences of his acts. In this environment, a true danger existed that, if the conduct requirement was minimal, the innocent person might well be convicted of an offense that he did not intend. The Code, of course, does away with such evidentiary presumptions and requires proof beyond a reasonable doubt of all required culpable states of mind.

Alternative Interpretation: Purposeful Only as to Offense Conduct   A better interpretation of the Code's "purpose" requirement, one that is consistent with the drafters' proposed interpretation of similar language in other contexts, is to require only that it be the actor's purpose that the *conduct constituting the object offense* be performed. That is, it must be the actor's conscious object and desire that one of the conspirators engage in the *conduct* that would constitute the object offense. It is suggested that this is the useful point that can be gleaned from the common law maxim that conspiracy is a specific intent offense. An actor ought not be liable for conspiracy to commit an offense unless the actor truly intends to conspire and intends that the conduct constituting the offense be committed. This interpretation of the purposeful requirement does not demand that the actor be purposeful as to the results or circumstances required by the substantive offense. It suffices for liability that the actor have the culpability as to these elements that is required by the substantive offense. This more narrow interpretation of the "purpose" requirement generates different results. On the facts in *Beccia*, for example, the defendant need only intend that he or the other conspirator set the fire, but he need not intend that the fire destroy or damage the building. He need only be reckless as to that result, as required by the substantive offense of third-degree arson. Under this interpretation, if Abe and Ben are caught after contacting the scrap dealer, they could be held liable for conspiracy to endanger.

Code's Failure to Justify Exclusions from Liability   It is true that conspiracy can punish very preliminary conduct. This justifies requiring proof beyond a reasonable doubt that it was the actor's purpose to promote the conduct constituting

---

1. See Model Penal Code § 211.1.

2. The Commentary suggests that purpose is not necessarily required for offense conduct that creates a risk, such as reckless driving. Model Penal Code § 5.03 comment at 408 (1985). But this exception does not apply where the creation of risk is an explicit element of the offense, as is the case for the general risk creation offenses of endangerment (§ 211.2) and risking catastrophe (§ 220.2).

the object offense — starting the fire, selling defective detectors, or having inter-course with a child under ten. The preliminary nature of the conduct otherwise might raise questions about whether the actor really intends to go further than talking and intends that the offense be completed. It remains unclear, however, why the preliminary nature of conspiracy means that all culpability elements, even those as to results and circumstances, must be elevated. Why would the Code drafters think it appropriate to exclude from liability the actor who agrees with another that one of them shall engage in conduct that they know creates a criminal risk (selling defective detectors), or engage in conduct that they know risks being criminal (having intercourse with a partner who might be underage)? It seems difficult to conceive of rational arguments to suggest that such an actor is not blameworthy or dangerous and should not be subject to police intervention.

Code's Inconsistency in Treatment of Conspiracy vs. Complicity   An entirely different basis for challenging the Code's elevation requirement in conspiracy concerns the apparent inconsistency with its failure to elevate the culpability requirements of complicity. The Code does not elevate the culpability require-ments in complicity, although the same preliminary conduct, an agreement, can be the basis for liability of either conspiracy or complicity. Assume an actor agrees to aid another in the commission of an offense. That agreement is sufficient for conspiracy liability, but only if the actor has the required elevated culpability. The same agreement is sufficient for complicity for the full substantive offense *without elevated culpability*, even if the actor does nothing more than agree. Why? If the culpability required for the substantive offense is adequate for full substantive liability of complicity, ought it not also be adequate for the inchoate liability of conspiracy, especially given that the conduct performed by the actor is the same in either case?

MPC § 5.01(3) Undercutting Elevation of Culpability   The inconsistency between the Code's treatment of complicity and conspiracy has immediate prac-tical implications. Model Penal Code section 5.01(3) provides:

> *Conduct Designed to Aid Another in Commission of a Crime.* A person who engages in conduct designed to aid another to commit a crime which would establish his complicity under Section 2.06 if the crime were committed by such other person, is guilty of an attempt to commit the crime, although the crime is not committed or attempted by such other person.

Where a conspirator's agreement is to "agree to aid" a co-conspirator in the commission of the offense, such agreement is adequate for complicity liability under section 2.06.[1] Thus, the same agreement gives rise to attempt liability under section 5.01(3) if the offense is not committed. This overlap between conspiracy and attempt under section 5.01(3) is not in itself troubling; it simply creates an alternative basis for inchoate liability for such conspirators. In reality, its effect is profound, because complicity does not require the elevation to purposeful of culpability as to a result that conspiracy does. Thus, such a conspirator *can* be held liable for an inchoate offense under section 5.01(3) without a showing of any greater culpability as to a result than that required by the substantive offense (and

---

1. See Model Penal Code § 2.06(3)(a)(ii).

therefore required for complicity liability under section 2.06). It may well be that the drafters did not foresee this effect of section 5.01(3) and did not intend it, for it can undercut the elevation of culpability required for conspiracy that is, as the Commentary makes clear, the drafters' intent. (Section 5.01(3) has the same effect in undercutting the elevation of culpability provided in the inchoate offense of solicitation; every instance of solicitation constitutes complicity if the offense is committed.)

Table: Summary of Conspiracy Requirements

The requirements for conspiracy liability may be summarized as follows:

The defendant must satisfy these requirements:

Objective Requirements	Culpability Requirements
Conduct constituting substantive offense: Not required, instead: CL & MPC — actor must agree with another that one of them will engage in the conduct that would constitute the substantive offense	*Culpability as to conduct constituting substantive offense:* CL & MPC § 5.03(1) — "purpose of promoting or facilitating" the offense
Result elements of substantive offense: CL & MPC — not required (nor is factual impossibility of it occurring a defense)	*Culpability as to result elements of substantive offense:* CL — elevate to purposeful MPC — elevate to purposeful Other (e.g., *Feola* reasoning) — as required by substantive offense; do not elevate
Circumstance elements of substantive offense: CL — required (legal impossibility is a defense) MPC — not required (legal impossibility is not a defense)	*Culpability as to circumstance elements of substantive offense:* CL — elevate to purposeful MPC — perhaps do not elevate, left to "interpretation" (per commentary) Other (e.g., *Feola*) — as required by substantive offense; do not elevate

The co-conspirator must satisfy these requirements:

Objective Requirements	Culpability Requirements
Agreement requirement: CL — at least one other conspirator must actually agree (bilateral agreement: "two or more persons agree to . . ."); MPC — no conspirator need agree (unilateral agreement; defendant "agrees . . . that one of them . . .")	*Intent to agree:* CL — Bilateral requires that co-conspirator intend to agree back MPC — Unilateral does not *Unconvictable co-conspirator defense:* CL — requires that co-conspirator satisfy all elements of conspiracy and has no defense MPC § 5.04(1)
Overt act requirement: CL & MPC § 5.03(5) — act in pursuance of conspiracy by any conspirator	

MPC = Model Penal Code
CL = Common Law

Problem: Selling Death

New national regulations requiring smoke detectors have just gone into effect. Because of anticipated enforcement difficulties, the authorities undertake a major advertising campaign announcing serious fines for any house or apartment dweller caught without the required number of detectors. Hans and Fri have seized on this as an opportunity to make some easy money. They plan to purchase several thousand unfinished smoke detectors from a scrap dealer. The detectors appear complete and the warning buzzer sounds when tested but the detection circuitry has not been installed. Hans and Fri estimate that they can make several thousand dollars each week selling their defective units door to door. When Hans calls the scrap dealer and confirms that the dealer has the units, the dealer becomes suspicious. He notifies the police, who trace the call back to Hans and Fri. Only Fri is at home when the police arrive; Hans is out purchasing a supply of the defective detectors. Under questioning Fri reveals their plan. On his return, Hans notices the police presence and keeps driving.

The next day Hans begins selling the faulty detectors. Business is even better than expected. Two weeks later, as a result of two non-functional detectors that Hans sold, a fire in a local rowhouse kills a mother and her child. The fire investigation reveals the defective detectors and ties them to the scheme by Fri and Hans. On a tip, police learn that Hans is a frequent customer at a local bar. An undercover officer approaches him and, presenting himself as a longtime con man, he suggests that Hans let him join the sales operation for half of the profit from his sales. Hans is happy to have a new partner. The next morning, Hans and the officer work together selling detectors so that Hans can show his new partner the ropes. As they work, they talk about many things, including the fire deaths from earlier sales. The officer then arrests Hans. The defective detectors sold that morning are retrieved for evidence. What can Hans be held liable for? What can Fri be convicted of?

Notes on Collateral Consequences of Conspiracy

Collateral Consequences In many cases, the procedural effects of a conspiracy charge are of greater importance than the penalty for a conspiracy conviction. These effects typically benefit the state more than the defendant and make conspiracy an attractive offense to prosecutors. For example, the Sixth Amendment and many state constitutions require that a defendant be tried in the district where the crime is committed. In conspiracy prosecutions, this is interpreted to mean in any district where an overt act is performed by any one of the conspirators. Especially in larger conspiracies, this gives the prosecution considerable choice in selecting a district in which to bring the prosecution. A prosecution for the conspiracy described above could be brought in either New York City or Newark. While a defendant generally may request a trial separate from other offenders, defendants charged in a single conspiracy may be indicted and tried together. Such joint trials may provide judicial and prosecutorial economy, but they may disadvantage defendants in several ways. Defendants may be required to share peremptory challenges of jurors, thus each defendant may have fewer to use than if tried alone. Defendants may find it more difficult to have the jury focus on the special facts and circumstances of the individual defendant's situation.

Defense counsel also may be concerned about a tendency of juries to apply damaging evidence to all defendants unless a defendant can affirmatively explain why it is inapplicable to her. Finally, hearsay generally is not admissible in a criminal prosecution, but an exception is made for statements made by a conspirator during or in furtherance of the conspiracy. Such hearsay statements are admissible against all co-conspirators. Thus, the larger and longer the conspiracy, the more statements by more conspirators that are admissible against all conspirators.

Pinkerton Doctrine: Conspiracy as Complicity One additional collateral effect of conspiracy is the practice in some jurisdictions that allows conspiracy to be treated as a form of complicity. The Pinkerton Doctrine, as this frequently is called, holds that a conspirator is liable for substantive offenses committed by other conspirators in furtherance of the conspiracy.[1] There is no requirement that the other conspirators satisfy the culpability requirements of the offense committed; only the conspirator committing the offense need satisfy the elements of the offense. Thus, all conspirators of DeSaco at the time of the shooting of the guard would be liable with him for murder, even though they had agreed that no firearms would be used. It is this potential of the rule to hold an actor liable for crimes of another beyond those agreed to and beyond the bounds of normal complicity liability that has led to criticism of the Pinkerton Doctrine. The Model Penal Code does not adopt the rule. An actor may be held liable as an accomplice under the Code if he "aids or *agrees*... to aid such other person in planning or committing [an offense],"[2] but such complicity liability requires proof of the normal requirements of complicity, including "the purpose of promoting or facilitating the commission of the offense."[3]

Scope and Duration Each of these collateral consequences applies only within the time period and scope of the conspiracy. A co-conspirator's overt act, incriminating statement, or substantive offense will not trigger the relevant collateral consequences if, at the time of the act, statement, or offense, the conspiracy has ended, has not yet begun, or the actor is no longer a member or has not yet become a member. Thus, the rules governing the scope and duration of a conspiracy are critical in determining whether and to what extent these collateral consequences will have effect. The "scope" of a conspiracy concerns: Who does the conspiracy include? Is a conspiracy among many deemed one large conspiracy or two or more smaller ones? The issues relating to the "duration" of a conspiracy include: When did the conspiracy begin? When did it end?

Multiple Objectives One difficulty in determining the scope of a conspiracy arises where a conspiracy has multiple objectives. While there is some disagreement on the issue, a conspiracy with multiple objectives nonetheless is treated as a single conspiracy. Thus, while the conspiracy described above includes both a kidnapping and a bank robbery, under this ruling it can only be charged as one conspiracy. Such a rule is consistent with the view that conspiracy is a harm in itself, not just an inchoate form of liability. If the harm is the criminal combination

---

1. See Pinkerton v. United States, 328 U.S. 640, 66 S. Ct. 1180, 90 L. Ed. 1489 (1946).
2. Model Penal Code § 2.06(3)(a)(ii).
3. Model Penal Code § 2.06(3)(a).

or agreement, then one agreement means one harm. The rule was adopted by the Model Penal Code,[1] but its rationale in that context is less clear. The Code treats conspiracy only as an inchoate form of liability, like attempt, not as a harm in itself for group criminality. One can have two attempt convictions where a scheme involves an attempt of two different offenses—for example, the murder of two victims or attempted murder and attempted robbery of the same victim. One may wonder why it is not similarly appropriate to have two convictions for conspiracy to murder or convictions for both conspiracy to murder and conspiracy to rob, although both offenses arise from a single agreement. Under the Code, if the conspirators are caught before commission, they cannot be convicted of both conspiracy to kidnap and conspiracy to rob the bank. Yet it is not clear why this is the proper result. (If the hypothetical bank robbery conspirators are caught after commission, they can be convicted of both offenses. They cannot be convicted of conspiracy under the Code because, as an inchoate offense, conspiracy is subsumed into the completed offense.)

Scope of a Single Conspiracy Complications in determining the scope of a conspiracy also arise where members of the group have entered into agreements with some members but not others. For example, DeSaco has agreed with Krule (and Hardler), but only Krule has agreed with Morris. Is the entire group a single large conspiracy? Or is it a collection of smaller, overlapping conspiracies?

"Chains" and "Wheels" A single conspiracy traditionally was one in which all conspirators shared a "community of interest" or purpose. In *United States v. Bruno*,[2] for example, a drug distribution scheme involved smugglers, middlemen, and retailers, many of whom did not know the identities of the others in the scheme. The court held, however, that they need not know the identities of the others as long as they knew the existence of the others and the success of the conspiracy depended on all. The "chain" structure among conspirators in *Bruno* was distinguished from the "wheel" structure in *Kotteakos v. United States*,[3] where each conspirator dealt with a single central conspirator. Each of several applicants conspired with one Brown to obtain a fraudulent loan under the National Housing Act. Without a "rim" on the wheel, the court held, there was no "community of interest" and thus no single conspiracy but rather multiple conspiracies between the hub and each spoke. It seems likely that a court would find that DeSaco and Morris shared a "community of interest," unlike the spokes of the wheel in *Kotteakos*.

Subjective View of Scope The Model Penal Code adopts a rule that permits a defendant to be a conspirator with another person if he knows that such other person has agreed with a person with whom the defendant has conspired.[4] This subjective view of the scope of a conspiracy means that the "scope" may be different for each member. Such is consistent with the Code's subjective view of criminality manifested in other contexts, such as attempts, impossibility, and the agreement requirement in conspiracy. Such a subjective scope does complicate the

---

1. Model Penal Code § 5.03(3).
2. 105 F.2d 921 (2d Cir. 1939), rev'd on other grounds, 308 U.S. 287, 50 S. Ct. 198, 84 L. Ed. 257.
3. 328 U.S. 750, 66 S. Ct. 1239, 90 L. Ed. 1557 (1946).
4. Model Penal Code § 5.03(2).

application of collateral consequences, however. A consequence may apply to one conspirator but not to another, because one may be a member of the other's conspiracy but not visa versa. From DeSaco's view, Morris is a co-conspirator under the Code because he knows that a substitute for Handler was to be arranged. Whether DeSaco is a co-conspirator of Morris, from Morris' view, will depend on whether Krule told Morris that another person was involved.

Duration A conspiracy begins for each conspirator with that person's agreement that the object offense be committed. Thus, Morris is free from the collateral consequences of conspiracy that rest on overt acts before he joined. A conspiracy ends for a conspirator when the object of the conspiracy is completed or when the actor withdraws from the conspiracy. One conspirator may end the conspiracy as to himself by withdrawing, even though the conspiracy may continue as to others who have not withdrawn. Thus, Handler's withdrawal does not alter the existence or effects of the conspiracy for those remaining. Unlike renunciation, which provides a defense to conspiracy liability, withdrawal simply ends the actor's participation in the conspiracy and thus ends for him the collateral effects that would arise from continuing membership. For example, Handler's withdrawal bars his liability under *Pinkerton* for the subsequent substantive murder committed by DeSaco. It also triggers the running of the statute of limitations as to him but it does not trigger it for the others. He remains liable for the offense of conspiracy.

Requirements for Withdrawal Withdrawal, sometimes called abandonment, typically has less demanding requirements than does renunciation. Effective withdrawal traditionally required an affirmative act of disassociation: a decision and announcement that one will no longer participate may be enough if accompanied by conduct inconsistent with continued membership. To be effective, the withdrawal must be communicated to all conspirators and must be made in time for the others to abandon the conspiracy. The Model Penal Code takes a similar approach. It is adequate under the Code that the actor advise his co-conspirators of his withdrawal or that he advise law enforcement authorities of the conspiracy and his participation.[1] It seems likely that Handler's conduct is adequate to be an effective withdrawal. Thus, the statute of limitations has run out for him.

Presumed Abandonment Where conspirators do not declare withdrawal or abandonment but simply become inactive, abandonment of the conspiracy by all members sometimes may be presumed. The Model Penal Code claims to adopt the rule of the *Grunewald* case, which provides that a conspiracy is presumed to have been abandoned after the period of limitation has passed with no overt act by any conspirator.[2] Thus, the statute of limitations has run for the hypothetical participants in the robbery, unless their meetings are taken as additional overt acts that each extend the conspiracy. But, in *Grunewald,* the Court makes clear that one cannot assume a continuing conspiracy to conceal simply from evidence that the conspiracy was kept secret.[3] Something more than mere overt

---

1. Model Penal Code § 5.03(7)(c).
2. Model Penal Code § 5.03(7)(b).
3. Grunewald v. United States, 353 U.S. 391, 77 S. Ct. 963, 1 L. Ed. 2d 931 (1957).

acts to conceal the past offense must be shown if the original conspiracy is to be extended in duration.[1] Of course, if the jurisdiction adopts the Pinkerton Doctrine, all conspirators will be liable for the murder, which has no statute of limitations.

Problem: Bank Robbery with a Sub

DeSaco, Krule, and Handler meet in New York City to plan the robbery of a bank across the river in Newark, New Jersey. It is agreed that Handler will kidnap the bank manager and bring him to the back door of the bank, where Krule will take him inside to open the vault. DeSaco is responsible for overpowering the guard, tying him up, and standing lookout during the robbery. All agree that no firearms will be used so that there will be no danger that anyone will be seriously injured.

The preparations, including a planned visit to the bank, go according to plan until Handler telephones Krule the day before to tell him that he will not be able to participate. His mother is coming to town for a few days and he wants to spend the time with her. Krule calls DeSaco and they decide to go ahead as scheduled but Krule will come up with someone to do Handler's job. Krule then calls Morris and arranges with him to sub for Handler.

When they pull the job, Morris does a fine job as a last-minute replacement, but DeSaco screws up. DeSaco brings a gun and shoots the guard to avoid having to wrestle with him; the guard dies from the gunshot. In this jurisdiction, the statute of limitations for bank robbery, kidnapping, and conspiracy is five years; murder has no limitation period. The three members who participated in the robbery meet annually to discuss the running of the statute of limitations and other matters relating to how best to avoid being caught. Five years and one day after the robbery they are all arrested and charged with murder, kidnapping, bank robbery, and conspiracy. Are they liable?

Problem: Bongo Sam Blows It

Phinimin violently opposes the draft. After participating in many protests, to no avail, he decides that more direct action is needed. He searches the protest meetings for a fellow draft opponent who has a background in chemistry and electronics. Cocker seems to fit the bill. Phinimin asks Cocker to use his expertise to build a bomb to blow up the local Selective Service office. Cocker refuses.

Phinimin subsequently finds Bongo Sam, who also has the necessary expertise. He approaches Bongo and Bongo agrees but is unenthusiastic about the project because he does not want to kill the office's night watchman in the process. Phinimin explains that he too would prefer that the watchman not be killed but persuades Bongo of the need to sacrifice the watchman for the greater cause.

---

1. The robbery conspirators may argue that their meetings, if anything, are a separate conspiracy to hide the earlier offenses. They do not extend the duration of the original conspiracy to rob. Under the Model Penal Code, however, such problems of distinguishing conspiracies to keep prior offenses secret from an extension of the original conspiracy rarely arise because once the object is committed the conspiracy to commit that offense is subsumed by the prosecution for the object offense.

Bongo constructs the bomb and plants it in the Selective Service office but is surprised and disappointed when the bomb does not detonate as planned. It is found, and an investigation traces it back to Bongo. Bongo is arrested and charged with attempted murder of the night watchman and attempted arson. He confesses and reveals Phinimin's involvement. An investigation of Phinimin reveals his earlier overture to Cocker. Phinimin is arrested and charged with two counts each of solicitation to commit murder and solicitation to commit arson. Is he liable?

APPENDIX A: SECTION 13

Voluntary Intoxication

ADVANCED ISSUES

Current Indiana Statutes

Indiana Code § 35-41-2-5. Intoxication

Intoxication is not a defense in a prosecution for an offense and may not be taken into consideration in determining the existence of a mental state that is an element of the offense unless the defendant meets the requirements of IC 35-41-3-5.

Indiana Code § 35-41-3-5. Intoxication

It is a defense that the person who engaged in the prohibited conduct did so while he was intoxicated, only if the intoxication resulted from the introduction of a substance into his body:

(1) without his consent; or
(2) when he did not know that the substance might cause intoxication.

Sanchez v. State of Indiana
749 N.E.2d 509 (Ind. 2001)

The court notes that in 1996, the United States Supreme Court held, in *Montana v. Egelhoff*, 518 U.S. 37 (1996), that the Fourteenth Amendment Due Process Clause is not offended by a statute that bars the use of evidence of voluntary intoxication to negate a culpable state of mind required by an offense definition. In response, the Indiana legislature enacted Section 35-41-2-5. Relying on *Egelhoff* as to the federal constitution and reaching a similar conclusion with regard to their state constitution, the court held *Terry v. State* to no longer be good law and the new statute constitutional. [In *Egelhoff*, a plurality of the Court concluded that due process is offended only if an exclusion of evidence "offends some principle of justice so rooted in the traditions and conscience of our people as to be ranked as fundamental."]

Complicity

ADVANCED ISSUES

Notes on Complicity Culpability Requirements

Culpability as to Assistance vs. as to Offense Elements In *State v. Etzweiler*, the defendant gives his car keys to Bailey, a fellow worker, who he knows is intoxicated. Ten minutes later, Bailey collides with another car and kills two people, for which he is charged with manslaughter.[1] As a factual matter, Etzweiler might be *purposeful as to assisting* Bailey in Bailey's *conduct* constituting the offense (driving); that is, it was his purpose to give Bailey his car keys and to have Bailey drive his car. Yet Etzweiler might only be *negligent* as to whether his conduct assists Bailey *in causing the deaths*. While it was his conscious object (that is, purpose) to let Bailey drive his car, he was not, but should have been, aware of a substantial risk (that is, negligent) that letting Bailey drive his car while intoxicated would cause another's death.

Purpose of Facilitating Commission of Offense Neither the majority nor the dissent in *Etzweiler* disagrees with the empirical claim that an actor can have a different culpability as to assisting the perpetrator's conduct that constitutes the offense than culpability as to the offense elements, such as causing death. Their disagreement concerns whether the statute requires (and should require) a different level of culpability as to these matters. The New Hampshire statute at issue tracks Model Penal Code section 2.06, which required that the accomplice assist the perpetrator, "with the purpose of promoting or facilitating the commission of the offense."[2] The majority concludes that this means that, to be liable as an accomplice, an actor must be purposeful not only as to assisting the perpetrator's conduct but also as to all elements of the object offense. Thus, they conclude, while perpetrator Bailey might be liable for *recklessly* causing the deaths, Etzweiler, as an accomplice, can have no liability unless he was *purposeful* as to causing the deaths. In giving his keys to Bailey, it must be his conscious object that Bailey kill another person.

---

1. 125 N.H. 57, 480 A.2d 870 (1984).
2. N.H. Rev. Stat. Ann. § 626:8 (1981).

Elevating All Culpability Elements Such a view—that all culpability requirements of the object offense are elevated to purposeful in setting the requirements for accomplice liability—obviously reduces the possibility of imposing accomplice liability. The view is all the more dramatic in its effect because "purposeful" is such a demanding culpability level. An accomplice frequently may *know* of the circumstances and results of a perpetrator's planned conduct but not be purposeful as to them. In fact, purposeful is such a demanding level of culpability that even the offense of murder does not require purpose; it requires only that the perpetrator *know* his conduct will cause a death. The terrorist is liable for murder if he blows up the embassy knowing that the blast will kill a night watchman, even though he may hope that the night watchman will go on break before the explosion and not be killed; he is knowing, but not purposeful, as to the killing. Under the majority view in *Etzweiler*, if an accomplice of the terrorist similarly *knows* that the bombing will cause the watchman's death but does not necessarily desire it, the accomplice will escape complicity liability in the killing. Under this view, if Yetsil purposely stands watch for Bib at John's house and at the time is aware of a substantial risk (reckless) that Bib will kill John, he nonetheless has no complicity in the homicide. He can be an accomplice in the homicide only if it is his conscious object to assist in causing John's death.

No Elevation as to Result Under MPC It is perhaps for these reasons that the Model Penal Code expressly provides that the "purpose" requirement does not apply to a result element of the offense. Section 2.06(4) provides that an accomplice need only have "the kind of culpability, if any, with respect to [a] result that is sufficient for the commission of the offense." In other words, if charged with negligent homicide under a complicity theory, Etzweiler need only be shown to have been negligent as to causing a death when he gave his keys to Bailey. This was the view of the dissent in *Etzweiler*, which cites language in the New Hampshire statute parallel to the Model Penal Code language just quoted. The nonelevation of culpability as to a result is not only a more accurate reading of the statute, it is also a sounder policy. Under this view, Yetsil's purposeful assistance, with recklessness as to John's death, would not bar complicity liability. The degree of his complicity liability would be a function of the level of his culpability. That he is only reckless as to the killing means that, unlike Bib, he is liable only for manslaughter, not murder. If, at the time of his assistance, he knew Bib would kill John, or desired it, he would be liable for murder.

Culpability as to Circumstance Element The culpability required of an accomplice as to a circumstance element under the Code is less clear. That the Code specifically provides for no elevation of culpability as to a result element might be interpreted as an expression of legislative intent to have circumstance elements treated differently from result elements—that is, elevated to purposeful. On the other hand, the policy arguments against elevation of culpability as to a result are equally applicable to circumstance elements.[1] For example, assume that, when Yetsil purposely assists Bib by standing guard, he is aware of a substantial risk (reckless) that Susan is underage. Under this view, although statutory rape

---

1. Some courts have held there to be no elevation as to a circumstance element. See, e.g., United States v. Corbin Farm Service, 444 F. Supp. 510 (E.D. Cal. 1978) (requiring defendant have same knowledge as principal as to poisoning endangered water fowl).

requires of the perpetrator only negligence as to age (or may have no culpability requirement in some jurisdictions),[1] Yetsil would have no complicity liability because he is not purposeful as to her age. That he has a higher culpability as to age than the offense requires is not enough for complicity if for complicity the culpability required as to circumstance is elevated to purposeful. The Model Penal Code refuses to take a position on the issue, leaving it to judges to sort out case by case.[2] Whatever one thinks is the proper view, elevation or no elevation, this failure to take a position seems grossly insensitive to the demands of the legality principle.

Complicity Liability for Offenses Other than Those Planned Some courts permit an accomplice to be held liable for offenses beyond those for which the accomplice satisfies the required culpability. An accomplice may be liable for any offense that was the natural and probable consequence of the offense for which the defendant is an accomplice. In *People v. Luparello*, for example, the defendant had enlisted his friends to compel one Martin to tell them where to find Luparello's former lover, who had left him.[3] Luparello was convicted of murder when, in his absence, his friends shot and killed Martin in trying to get the requested information. The court held that an actor may be liable "not only for the offense he intended to facilitate or encourage, but also [for] any reasonably foreseeable offense committed by the person he aids and abets." The complicity aspect of the felony-murder rule is a specific application of this doctrine of holding accomplices liable for any foreseeable offense committed by a principal. While the felony-murder rule remains popular, this foreseeable-offense extension of the complicity doctrine is clearly a minority view, with good reason. It imposes liability beyond that which the actor's blameworthiness can justify.

Summary of Complicity Requirements The better view is that the "purpose" requirement in complicity requires only that the accomplice purposely *assist* the perpetrator's *conduct*, not that all offense elements be elevated to purposeful. The culpability requirements of the substantive offense, as to both result and circumstance elements, ought to be the culpability required for complicity in that offense. These, then, are the elements of complicity that the *accomplice* must satisfy: assisting the perpetrator (or, under the Model Penal Code, attempting or agreeing to assist), with the purpose to assist the perpetrator in his conduct that in

---

1. See, e.g., Model Penal Code § 213.3(1)(a) (offense to have intercourse with person under sixteen if more than four years older); id. § 213.6(1) (mistake defense to statutory rape charge unavailable even if mistake as to age reasonable); Fla. Stat. Ann. § 794.021 (1976) (rejects defense of reasonable mistake of age); N.J. Stat. Ann. § 2C:14-5(c) (imposes strict liability with respect to element of age in statutory rape).

2. In explaining the phrase "purpose to promote or facilitate" in the context of conspiracy, the Commentary addresses the impact of that phrase on the actor's culpability as to the circumstance elements of the substantive crime promoted. It concludes that "*as in the section on complicity*," the draft "does not attempt to solve the problem by explicit formulation...." Model Penal Code § 5.03 comment at 413 (1985) (emphasis added). On the other hand, in discussing the provision that requires the accomplice to have the culpability with respect to the result that is required by the substantive offense, the Commentary states that: "This formulation serves, it is submitted, to combine the policy that accomplices are equally accountable within the range of their complicity with the policies embodied in the definitions of particular crimes." Model Penal Code § 2.04(4) (currently § 2.06(4)) comment at 34 (Tentative Draft No. 1, 1953) (emphasis added). This might be taken as an argument for no elevation as to circumstance elements. But the revised Commentary rewrites this sentence expressly to apply only to "crimes defined according to results." Model Penal Code § 2.06 comment at 321 (1985).

3. 187 Cal. App. 3d 410, 231 Cal. Rptr. 832 (1986).

fact constitutes the offense, and with the culpability as to the circumstance and result elements of the offense as required by the offense definition (or, under some interpretations, purposeful as to circumstance (or as to all) elements). In addition, complicity liability also may require that the *perpetrator* satisfy some offense elements.

Elements Satisfied by Perpetrator for Liability of Accomplice To summarize what has been said, the common law and modern codes require that, for the accomplice to be held liable, the perpetrator must actually commit the offense, at least to the extent of satisfying the objective requirements of the offense. The Model Penal Code presents this requirement in section 2.06(7) when it requires "proof of commission of the offense." The common law also requires that the perpetrator satisfy the culpability requirements of the offense and that the perpetrator have no general defense. In keeping with its subjective view of criminality, the Model Penal Code rejects such a defense and bases liability instead on the accomplice's conduct and culpable state of mind. Thus, under the Code, if Yetsil knows and hopes Susan is underage, he could be liable for statutory rape even though the person he assists is not liable because that person reasonably believes that Susan is over the required age.

Table: Summary of Requirements for Complicity Liability

The requirements for a defendant's liability for an offense as an accomplice may be summarized as follows:

The defendant must satisfy these requirements:

Objective Requirements	Culpability Requirements
Conduct: CL—assist (or encourage) MPC—aid or agree or attempt to aid	*Culpability as to aiding perpetrator's conduct constituting object offense:* CL & MPC—"purpose of promoting or facilitating the commission of the offense" (§ 2.06(3)(a)) *Culpability as to result elements of object offense:* CL—elevate to purposeful MPC—do not elevate (§ 2.06(4)) *Culpability as to circumstance elements of object offense:* CL—elevate to purposeful MPC—unclear; probably left to "interpretation," as in conspiracy

The perpetrator must satisfy these requirements:

Objective Requirements	Culpability Requirements
CL—objective elements of object offense MPC—same ("on proof of commission of the offense," § 2.06(7))	CL—culpability requirements of object offense MPC—none (§ 2.06(7) rejects unconvictable perpetrator defense)

MPC = Model Penal Code
CL = Common Law

Notes on the Requirements for Liability for Causing Crime by an Innocent

Innocent or Irresponsible Person The person engaging in the conduct constituting the offense may be "innocent or irresponsible" for any number of reasons. It may be that the perpetrator is innocent because she does not satisfy the culpability requirements of the offense, as, for instance, when the actor asks another to retrieve her yellow umbrella from the coatroom, knowing that she does not own a yellow umbrella. The person taking the umbrella may satisfy the objective elements of theft but does not have the culpability required, because he believes instead that the umbrella's owner has requested the taking. Or the innocent person may have a justification or an excuse. In *State v. Dowell*, for example, the defendant compelled another man at gunpoint to attempt to rape the defendant's wife.[1] The coerced man would have an excuse, a duress defense, in most jurisdictions, yet the defendant nonetheless may be liable for causing the rape. In *Bailey v. Commonwealth*, the defendant tricked the deceased and the police into a confrontation during which the police justifiably shot the deceased.[2] While the police conduct is entirely justified, Bailey nonetheless is liable for the homicide, because he caused the police to act by causing the conditions giving rise to the need for their justified conduct.

Objective Requirement The objective requirement for liability for causing crime by an innocent is considerably more demanding than that for complicity. The actor must do more than assist in some way or attempt to assist; he must "cause" the innocent person to commit the offense. The nature of this causation requirement is defined in the Code's section on causation. This means that the actor's conduct must be a necessary ("but for") cause of the innocent actor's conduct constituting the offense.[3] It also means that the result must not be "too remote or accidental" (and some states' codes add "not too dependent upon another's volitional act") "to have a [just] bearing on the actor's liability or on the gravity of his offense."

Innocents as Mere Instruments The necessary-cause requirement does not explicitly require that the actor be the moving force in the offense; but where the "perpetrator" is innocent, it is common that one who is a necessary cause of the conduct is the instigator. Indeed, in some cases, the role of the actor is so prominent that the case is prosecuted without reference to the causing-crime-by-an-innocent doctrine. Instead, the actor is treated as the principal and the innocent party is treated as simply an "instrument" of the actor, much like a mechanical weapon or device. While this may seem natural enough in many cases, it is undesirable as a general practice because it short-circuits the special requirements contained in both the doctrine of causing crime by an innocent and the doctrine of causation.

Culpability Requirements The culpability requirements for causing crime by an innocent are more explicit than those for complicity. For the offense of

---

1. 106 N.C. 722, 11 S.E. 525 (1890).
2. 229 Va. 258, 329 S.E.2d 37 (1985).
3. See, e.g., Model Penal Code § 2.03(2)(b) & (3)(b); N.J. Stat. Ann. § 2C:2-3 (1982); 18 Pa. Cons. Stat. Ann. tit. § 303 (1983); Tenn. Code Ann. § 407 (1986).

causing crime by an innocent, the Model Penal Code requires that the actor have "the kind of culpability that is sufficient for the commission of the offense."[1] Thus, one may be liable, under this theory of liability, for negligent homicide or statutory rape, both of which require less than "purpose" as to a result and circumstance element, respectively. Recall the ambiguity under complicity theory as to whether such liability is permissible — there is confusion as to whether the culpability elements of the object offense are all elevated to "purposeful" for the accomplice although they may be only "negligent" for the perpetrator. The absence of an elevation requirement for causing crime by an innocent might be used as additional evidence to support the "no-elevation" interpretation of the complicity statute. If elevation is not necessary for imputation of the conduct of an innocent, one might argue, why should elevation be necessary for imputation of the conduct of a fellow criminal?

Offense Analysis Revisited While the culpability requirements for causing crime by an innocent seem clear in comparison to the murky picture in complicity, the language of the provision is not without ambiguity. That the drafters spoke in the singular — "the *kind* of culpability that *is* sufficient for the commission of the offense" — might suggest that they envision a single culpability level for each offense. The same phrase is used in other parts of the Code where the implication is even stronger.[2] Such a reference is a throwback to "offense analysis," yet offense analysis is repudiated by the Code in favor of "element analysis." Section 2.02(1) provides that "a person is not guilty of an offense unless he acted purposely, knowingly, recklessly or negligently . . . with respect *to each material element* of the offense." Thus, under the Code's element analysis system, an offense may require a different culpability level as to each separate element of the same offense. There seems little difficulty in this instance in concluding that the "causing crime by an innocent" language of section 2.06(2)(a) is intended by the drafters to mean that such liability requires that the actor satisfy each of the culpability requirements — each culpability requirement as to each objective element — of the object offense. Despite its misleading language, then, the causing-crime-by-an-innocent doctrine is consistent with the code's overarching scheme of element analysis.

Culpability as to Causing Innocent to Act vs. Object Offense Recall that in complicity there exist two distinct kinds of culpability requirements: culpability as to assisting the perpetrator in his conduct that in fact constitutes the offense, and culpability as to the elements of the object offense. An actor's culpability as to these two kinds of issues might be different. Thus, Etzweiler might be purposeful as to assisting his drunken friend to drive his car when he gives him the keys, but he might simultaneously be only negligent as to that conduct helping to bring about the death of another motorist. Similarly, in cases of causing crime by an innocent, an actor may have one level of culpability as to causing the innocent person to act and a different level of culpability as to the elements of the object offense. An actor might be "purposeful" in causing his severely retarded brother to shoot a hunting rifle, but may be only reckless as to the conduct causing the death of another person who is accidentally shot.

---

1. Model Penal Code § 2.06(2)(a).
2. See, e.g., Model Penal Code §§ 3.02(2), 3.09(2).

Variable vs. Fixed Culpability as to Causing The Model Penal Code provision defining liability for causing crime by an innocent, quoted above, is silent regarding what culpability is required as to "causing" the innocent to engage in the conduct constituting the offense. One interpretation of the provision is that the drafters intend the culpability as to "causing" the offense conduct to be "the kind of culpability that is sufficient for the commission of the offense." But, as noted above, such an interpretation makes the false "offense analysis" assumption that each offense has only a single culpability level. One approach may be to set a fixed, minimum level of culpability as to causing the innocent person to act. One might argue that the causing-crime-by-an-innocent provision is silent on the culpability required as to causing the innocent person to act, arguing that strict liability should not be assumed; thus one can use Model Penal Code section 2.02(3) to read in a minimum requirement of "recklessness." If the offense contains a single, stated culpability level, another approach may be to apply this stated culpability level, through application of Model Penal Code section 2.02(4), to all of the offense elements.

Case for Recklessness as to Causing Innocent Though "recklessness" is considerably lower than the "purpose" required in the analogous context in complicity, it might be an appropriate level here, where the actor is the chief instigator and is a necessary ("but for") cause of the innocent's criminal conduct. By contrast, the actor in complicity need only assist or attempt or agree to assist the perpetrator in some way. In other words, the high culpability requirement in complicity might be appropriate given complicity's minimal or non-existent causal contribution requirement. A high culpability requirement, one might argue, is an appropriate counterbalance to a low causal contribution requirement. Where the causal contribution requirement is high, however, as in causing crime by an innocent, in which the actor's conduct must be a necessary cause of the offense conduct, a lower culpability requirement as to causing the offense conduct may be appropriate. In both instances, the actor must also satisfy all of the culpability requirements of the object offense.

Requirements of Innocent Person for Liability of Instigator As with complicity, the actor's liability in causing crime by an innocent depends on the innocent person actually engaging in the conduct constituting the offense. These requirements reflect the traditional view that full substantive liability is not appropriate unless the harm or evil of the offense actually occurs. In this respect, complicity and causing crime by an innocent are similar. Note, however, that an actor who is unsuccessful in attempting to cause an innocent to commit a crime is not liable for the full offense if the innocent nonetheless commits the offense (on the urging of another instigator, for example). In this respect, complicity and causing crime by an innocent under the Model Penal Code are different. Recall that complicity under the Code imposed full liability even when the accomplice failed in his attempt to assist the perpetrator. One might wonder whether the Code should, in a similar manner, hold an actor liable if he unsuccessfully attempts to cause an innocent to commit an offense. The drafters may simply be assuming that in causing crime by an innocent, because the culpable actor is the moving force, it is not likely that the offense conduct in fact will be performed if the actor is unsuccessful in causing the innocent to perform the offense conduct. If such is the case, then refusing to hold an actor liable for an unsuccessful attempt to cause an innocent to commit an offense is not logically inconsistent with the rules governing complicity. Unsuccessful complicity may not avoid an offense, but unsuccessful instigation generally will.

Table: Summary of Requirements for Causing Crime by an Innocent

The requirements for a defendant's liability for causing crime by an innocent may be summarized as follows:

The defendant must satisfy these requirements:

Objective Requirements	Culpability Requirements
Conduct: CL & MPC—cause an innocent or irresponsible person to engage in the conduct constituting the offense (MPC § 2.06(2)(a)); "cause" is defined by the normal requirements of causation	*Culpability as to causing person to perform conduct constituting object offense:* CL & MPC—unspecified; recklessness read in by MPC § 2.02(3)?
	Culpability as to elements of object offense: CL & MPC—as required by the substantive offense ("acting with the kind of culpability that is sufficient for the commission of the offense," MPC § 2.06(2)(a))

The *"perpetrator"* must satisfy these requirements:

Objective Requirements	Culpability Requirements
CL & MPC—objective elements of offense	CL & MPC—none (person performing offense conduct is "innocent or irresponsible," MPC § 2.06(2)(a))

MPC = Model Penal Code
CL = Common Law

Problem: The Egg Hunt

Walker lives in an apartment at Cottage 12 of Southbury Training School. His charges are severely retarded men. "Pop," as he is called by his charges, shaves the men, helps them dress and shower, and generally supervises their activities. They are gentle people but their retardation sometimes creates difficult situations. The "boys," as the staff call them, have recently taken to collecting anything small and shiny, which they call "eggs." A recent visitor became frightened when her car was surrounded by a group of men three-deep, pressing their faces against the glass, pointing at the chrome dials on her console, and shouting "Egg! Egg!" The boys' interest in shiny objects is not accidental. Walker has cultivated it as a means of motivating them to steal silverware from the large restaurant where many of them work during the day as dishwashers.

Attie Winter, the housemother at Cottage 20, disapproves of the way Walker runs his cottage. In her view, the strip-baseball and tackle-badminton games, which Walker allows and the boys love, breed bad habits. Attie suspects Walker has the boys doing even more objectionable things but cannot prove it. Walker knows of Attie's attempts to have him fired. He decides that a little intimidation may be helpful. During lunch and again at dinner, he describes in detail to the boys Mom Winter's beautiful necklace of small silver eggs. After the boys have gone to bed, Walker leaves to meet a friend for drinks at a nearby bar, as he frequently does. The night janitor is under instructions to call the central office if any problem arises. Walker leaves the front door to the dormitory unlocked with the expectation that the boys will take the opportunity to sneak past the sleeping night janitor and head for Cottage 20 to find Mom Winter's necklace and no doubt scare her plenty in the process.

Half way to the bar, Walker remembers that he has forgotten to lock his room where his loaded gun is stored. He has let the boys play cops and robbers with his gun when it was unloaded. They might think to take it with them when they go to Cottage 20 on their "egg hunt." After debating with himself, he concludes that it is more likely that they will not think of it. As it happens, the boys have been calculating their attack on Cottage 20 ever since lunch. They notice immediately when Walker does not lock the dormitory door and his room. After waiting until they are sure he will not soon be returning, they take his gun and head en masse in search of the now-legendary necklace. They confront Mom Winter. When she resists turning over her necklaces, they "shoot" her. To their horror, she falls to the floor bleeding. Walker is fired from his position when an investigation reveals his part in the affair. He is charged with the silverware thefts and with the murder of Attie Winter. Is Walker liable?

Corporate Criminality

ADVANCED ISSUES

Problem: Collapse at Kalahoo No. 3

Burt Richards is operator of Kalahoo Mine, a small incorporated mining operation. Earl Single is his mining foreman. Mine inspectors frequently cite Kalahoo for safety violations but none serious enough to cause them to close the mine. On this day, Single, who is paid under a bonus system based on tonnage mined, insists on skipping the normal shoring procedures in order to meet the bonus quota by the end of the month. Several of the miners object but are threatened with dismissal if they refuse to go along. Several hours later, an unshored section of Tunnel No. 3 collapses. Seven of the miners are hurt in the collapse; two are killed, one of them foreman Single. Richards is charged with two counts of manslaughter for failing to assure compliance with mining safety rules knowing that such failure created a risk of cave-in and serious injury or death. Richards argues that he always instructed Single to comply with mining safety rules and, beyond that, he left mine operations to foreman Single. Like most owner-operators, he rarely visits the mining operations himself. He points out that Single was fully qualified and certified for the position for which he was hired. Is Richards liable for two counts of manslaughter?

APPENDIX A: SECTION 18

Defensive Force Justifications

ADVANCED ISSUES

Notes on the Unknowingly Justified Actor

Biker's Break   Ranger Yardley, 70, retired from service several years ago but still hangs around the station. He helped lay out the fireroads that crisscross the Pine Barrens. At the moment, both crews at the station are out on small fire calls. Yardley is alone. The Southwest Tower signals: "Class 4 fire...burn all of A-11...Atsion endangered." Yardley calls the crews, but they are too far from road A-11 to get there before the blaze. He jumps in the flame truck, used to burn firebreaks to stop advancing forest fires, and heads out on his own. With no firefighting crews within reach, there will be no stopping the fire if it gets across A-11. He starts at the north end of A-11 and prepares to lay a strip of burning kerosene beside the road as he drives. But then he starts to feel faint, his chest starts to hurt, and he can't breath. He jumps from the truck to the ground, gasping for air, and heads back in the direction he came, staggering and incoherent.

Lorenzo and Katherine keep an eye out for rangers. Motorcycles aren't permitted on the Pine Barrens' fireroads, but it's a great ride. They spot a flame truck up ahead and pull up in the bush. After a few minutes they realize that no rangers are around and the truck even has its flame going! "Maybe the rangers are in the woods taking a whiz," Lorenzo suggests. "Talk about great rides!," blurts Katherine, as she jumps off the bike and heads for the truck cab. With Lorenzo alongside on the bike watching for rangers, Katherine roars off, spreading fire as she goes. When the road ends at the state highway, Katherine dumps the truck, jumps on with Lorenzo, and they're off down the highway. To Katherine, it was her best ride ever, and both are screaming and laughing, until a highway patrolman pulls them over and arrests them both for a third degree felony, causing a catastrophe. Lorenzo argues the point. "Don't you know about the forest fire, man? We just saved Atsion. You should be giving us a medal." Katherine is shocked. "Are you kidding?," she asks Lorenzo before Lorenzo can signal her not to talk in front of the trooper. Investigation shows that many people would have died but for Katherine and Lorenzo's burning of A-11 and that Lorenzo realized the situation at the time they took the truck, but Katherine did not. Do Lorenzo and Katherine get a justification defense?

Current Law   Recall from the previous Section that the Model Penal Code gives a justification defense to an actor who "believes" that her conduct is justified. Katherine's conduct saved many lives, but at the time she drove the truck she did not "believe" that justifying circumstances existed. Such "believes" language has the effect of denying a defense to the unknowingly justified actor, because she does not "believe" her conduct is justified. Other authorities, of which there are few, are split on the issue. Some permit a defense to the unknowingly justified actor; others do not. There also is disagreement as to which theory is intuitively preferred.

"Deeds" vs. "Reasons" Theory of Justification   The issue of the unknowingly justified actor is of special significance because it forces an inquiry into the basic nature of justification defenses. If the theory of a justification defense is the avoidance of a greater harm, then the defense should focus on purely objective criteria — the balance of conflicting interests — and an unknowingly justified actor, such as Katherine, should have a justification defense to liability for the full substantive offense, despite her ignorance. If the theory of justifications is that an actor is blameless because, whatever the ultimate effect, she has tried to act in a proper way, then the defense should focus on the actor's state of mind — the purpose of her conduct. Under this approach, Lorenzo might be justified — he knew of the justifying circumstances — but Katherine is not. The "deeds" theory justifies *conduct*; the "reasons" theory holds the *actor* justified because of her justificatory purpose. These alternative theories of justification are evident in the discussion in the Section 20 overview concerning mistaken justification, when it compares "objective" and "subjective" formulations of justification defenses. A "deeds" theory generates an objectively defined justification; a "reasons" theory generates a subjectively defined justification.

"Deeds" Theory of Justification   Under a "deeds" theory of justification, the primary role of justification defenses is to fill out the rules of conduct in guiding future behavior. A defense is given whenever the harm or evil of the offense charged has been outweighed by the harm avoided by the conduct. By analogy, we do not hold an actor liable for an offense simply because the actor mistakenly believes that she has committed an offense. Liability and ensuing punishment for the substantive offense require that the harm or evil of the offense in fact occur. Absent this, only attempt liability is appropriate. So, too, with the unknowingly justified actor. Both Lorenzo and Katherine can argue that they are entitled to a lesser evils defense under a "deeds" theory.

Liability for Impossible Attempt   Because an unknowingly justified actor is permitted a justification defense to the offense charged, under the "deeds" theory, it does not follow that she will escape all liability. A majority of jurisdictions follow the Model Penal Code in imposing liability on an actor who mistakenly believes the circumstances exist that make her conduct an offense. The actor may be liable under the Model Penal Code attempt provision, for example, if she "purposely engages in conduct which would constitute the crime if the attendant circumstances were as [s]he believes them to be."[1] Attempt liability acknowledges that

---

1. Model Penal Code § 5.01(1)(a).

the harm or evil of the offense has not occurred. It bases liability instead on the actor's demonstrated willingness to act in a way that she believes constitutes an offense. Such attempt liability seems well suited for the unknowingly justified actor who has not caused a net harm but mistakenly believes that she has.[1] Because Katherine mistakenly believed she was causing an unjustified harm, she would be liable for an attempt to cause such harm under the Model Penal Code's impossible attempt provision.

"Reasons" Theory of Justification Under a "reasons" theory of justification, an unknowingly justified actor gets no justification defense and therefore is liable for the full offense, even though her conduct is objectively justified and in fact avoids a greater harm. Under this view, the existence of the justifying circumstances and the harm avoided is irrelevant in assessing the actor's liability. Katherine gets no defense because her conduct is not properly motivated. Her mistaken belief (that she is not justified) is used to impose full liability for the substantive offense, not just attempt liability.

Justificatory Purpose vs. Knowledge One complication in the "reasons" theory of justification comes from the reliance on an actor's motivation as a foundation for the offense. Fletcher, for example, claims the rule to be that "actors may avail themselves of justifications only if they act with a *justificatory intent.*"[2] As Greenawalt expresses the theory: "[J]ustified action is morally proper action. [T]o be justified is to have sound, good reasons for what one does. . . ."[3] It is the actor's reasons or motive for the conduct that supports the defense. This rationale for the defense would seem to require that the person act for the justificatory *purpose*, not just with knowledge of the justifying circumstances. This means that, not only should Katherine be denied a defense, so also should Lorenzo if it is shown that he knew of the justifying circumstances but had been joy-riding rather than saving the town as his purpose. That Lorenzo gets the defense under the Model Penal Code suggests that the Code is inconsistent with the rationale for the "reasons" theory. If the defense's rationale is the actor's proper purpose, then the defense should require that the actor have acted for the justifying purpose.

Resisting Unknowingly Justified Actor Another complication for the "reasons" theory is the effect it has for persons who resist or assist the unknowingly justified actor. Under a "reasons" theory, because the unknowingly justified actor is not justified, that actor's conduct may be lawfully resisted. Thus, for example, if a land owner wished to resist the firebreak burning of his property out of pure selfishness, the Code would allow him lawfully to resist Katherine's burning *even though he knows of the forest fire and the circumstances that justify the burning.* Because Katherine's lack of "belief" in the justifying circumstances denies her a justification defense, her conduct is "unlawful" and therefore triggers a defense of property by the landowner under Model Penal Code section 3.06(1)(a).

---

1. Of course, a minority of jurisdictions reject the propriety of punishing impossible attempts, of which the unknowingly justified actor is an example. In these jurisdictions, attempt liability would not be available.

2. George P. Fletcher, Rethinking Criminal Law 557 (1978).

3. Kent Greenawalt, The Perplexing Borders of Justification and Excuse, 84 Colum. L. Rev. 1897, 1903 (1984).

Model Penal Code section 3.11(1) defines "unlawful" force as: "force...
which...would constitute [an] offense...except for a defense...not amounting
to a privilege to use the force."[1] Katherine has no defense for her burning of the
landowner's property; she will in fact be held fully liable for it. Thus, her burning is
"unlawful" and the owner lawfully can resist it under the Code, even though he
knows of the justifying facts! Even the contorted definition of "unlawful" force in
section 3.11(1) does not save the Code from improper results. Under a "deeds"
theory, in contrast, the unknowingly justified actor's conduct remains justified,
thus no one lawfully may interfere with the justified conduct. The selfish property
owner who knows of the justifying circumstances could not lawfully resist Katherine's burning of the firebreak.

Assisting Unknowingly Justified Actor   A similar difficulty arises under the
"reasons" theory for those who assist the unknowingly justified actor. An anomalous situation arises in which, of two people engaging in the same conduct at the
same time, one is justified and one is not. Ranger Yardley's conduct and Lorenzo's
conduct in assisting Katherine will be judged to be justified under a subjective
("believes") view, while Katherine's conduct, which is the same as that of Yardley
and Lorenzo, will be held unjustified. Under an objective "deeds" theory, in
contrast, the unknowingly justified actor remains justified and anyone lawfully
may assist. If one person is justified in performing the conduct, then all persons
performing the same conduct or assisting it will similarly be justified.

"Reasons" Theory Difficulties Beyond Liability Results   In addition to the
problematic performance of the subjective "reasons" theory with regard to liability results, that theory ought to be rejected on independent grounds because it
obscures and confuses the analysis of justification cases. As discussed previously
the "deeds" theory is preferable because it makes the important distinction
between mistaken and actual justification and highlights the conceptual and
functional identity of mistaken justification as an excuse. Making the distinction
between actual and mistaken justification is particularly important to the law's
obligation to communicate its rules of conduct to the public that is bound by
those rules. By including both mistaken and actual justification within the single
term "justified," a "reasons" conceptualization invites the public to misconstrue a
finding of "justified" due to a mistaken belief in justification to mean truly justified
in the sense of being within the rules of proper conduct to be condoned here and
in the future. The reverse confusion can also occur. A finding of "justified" based
on a finding that conduct is proper and condoned may be misinterpreted as a
finding that the conduct actually is disapproved but the actor is excused.
A "deeds" theory, in contrast, uses every case adjudication to tell the community
which conduct is approved ("justified") and which is disapproved even though the
offender at hand may not be punished for it ("excused"). The "deeds" theory of
justification, then, is to be preferred because it is the only theory that gives proper
liability results, the only theory whose conceptualization accurately describes the
important similarities and differences between the doctrines, and the only theory
that educates the public as to the proper rules of conduct.

---

1. Recall the contorted nature of this definition, required to prevent improper results by the "reasons"
theory in the context of mistaken justification.

Mistake Excuses

LAW (SUBSEQUENT)

United States v. Ehrlichman
376 F. Supp. 29 (D.D.C. 1974)

The defendants were indicted for conspiring to contravene a psychiatrist's Fourth Amendment rights by entering his offices without a warrant to obtain a patient's medical records. They sought pre-trial discovery with respect to alleged national security of their case. The defendants contended that "even if the break-in was illegal, they lacked the specific intent necessary to violate section 241 because they reasonably believed that they had been authorized to enter and search Dr. Fielding's office." The district court granted their discovery request but held that "it is well established that a mistake of law is no defense in a conspiracy case to the knowing performance of acts which, like the unauthorized entry and search at issue here, are malum in se." Unlike an exception that "resulted from good faith reliance on a court order . . . or upon the legal advice of an executive officer charged with interpreting or enforcing the law in question . . . [t]his principle . . . cannot be stretched to encompass a mistake based upon the assurances of an alleged co-conspirator with regard to the criminality of acts that are malum in se."

APPENDIX A: SECTION 24

Entrapment

ADVANCED ISSUES

Notes on Limiting the Detrimental Effects of Nonexculpatory Defenses

Minimizing the Detrimental Effects Reforms to the current system could reduce the detrimental effects of nonexculpatory defenses without abolishing the defenses. For example, while permitting an acquittal, the system nonetheless could make clear its condemnation of the conduct and the actor. A special verdict of "guilty but not punishable" might do this. Certainly, the verdict of "not guilty" exacerbates the detrimental effects of nonexculpatory acquittals because it misleads the public into thinking that no wrong was done. Minimizing the detrimental effects of nonexculpatory acquittals depends in part on public awareness of the special nature of nonexculpatory defenses, yet at present there seems little public appreciation that nonexculpatory defenses are different and still less awareness of which are defenses of this sort.

Less Strict Adherence to Legality Principle The special nature of nonexculpatory defenses also suggests that less strict adherence to the legality principle might be in order. Recall that the legality principle is meant to assure, among other things, that an actor has the opportunity for notice of the rules governing liability. Such potential for notice is desirable because an actor cannot conform his conduct to the requirements of law if those requirements are not made available to him. In the case of nonexculpatory defenses, where the conduct may be deplored and sought to be deterred, vagueness and ambiguity in the defenses may serve the useful purpose of deterring undesirable conduct. This deterrence must be distinguished from the undesirable "chilling effect" of vague offense definitions. Here, the prohibited conduct is clearly defined; only the limits of the nonexculpatory defense are vague. Thus, the immune foreign embassy attache may behave himself if he is unsure whether he is covered by diplomatic immunity. The corrupt congressman may decline to exercise improper influence if he is not sure whether his legislative immunity extends to such impropriety. One can argue that such offenders have little grounds to complain of the vagueness or ambiguity of the defense or to insist on a favorable construction, for they had notice that their conduct is prohibited.

Mistake as to Nonexculpatory Defense   For these same reasons, there seems little reason to provide a defense to an actor who calculates his conduct to take advantage of a nonexculpatory defense but who is mistaken, even reasonably mistaken, as to the conditions of the defense. The better rule provides that an actor who acts under a belief that he has a nonexculpatory defense acts at his peril. If the requirements for the defense in fact are not satisfied — the attache is not immune, legislative immunity does not extend to the contemplated crime, or the statute of limitations in fact has not fully run — then the public policy interests that normally would support the defense are not served and no defense ought to be permitted.

Resisting Aggressor with Nonexculpatory Defense   Defensive force justifications generally give an actor a right to resist physical aggression against his person and to interfere when aggression is directed against another person or against one's property. But this right should and in many instances does in current law depend on whether the aggressor's conduct is lawful or unlawful. If the aggression is not unlawful, such as when an officer makes a lawful arrest, generally there is no right to resist or interfere. When the aggressor's conduct is not unlawful because he has a nonexculpatory defense, however, resistance and interference should be permitted, even encouraged. The immune diplomat may escape conviction for an unjustified and unexcused attack, but it hardly follows that the victim is bound to submit or the observer to acquiesce.

Collateral Consequences of Conviction   Conviction for a criminal offense typically risks not only punishment, such as through imprisonment, fine, or probation, but also risks a host of other civil disabilities. An offender may lose many of his basic rights and privileges: citizenship; employment opportunities in licensed and unlicensed occupations; the capacity to litigate, to testify, and to serve as a juror or as a court-appointed fiduciary; voting, parental, and marital rights; and the rights to hold public office, to carry a firearm, to inherit, and to receive insurance, pension, and workmen's compensation benefits. The offender also may incur forfeiture, civil restraint and injunction, civil liability, and civil commitment. Further, the conviction may be used to impeach an offender in a subsequent trial where the offender is a witness or a defendant-witness, and to aggravate the sentence for a subsequent offense.

Collateral Consequences of Nonexculpatory Acquittal   Given the disfavored nature of nonexculpatory defenses, some of these collateral consequences might appropriately be retained if the acquittal derives from a nonexculpatory defense. Even if the offender is not to be punished for his past violation, ought not society be able to protect itself from new violations? Some precedent exists for this. The criminal diplomat can be expelled from the country. The incompetent defendant can be incarcerated until his trial is possible. Collateral consequences are retained frequently where an offender is pardoned. In most cases, however, offenders acquitted under a nonexculpatory defense escape all penalties and disabilities. Assume a guilty defendant's case is dismissed because of police or prosecutorial misconduct. Presumably it has been concluded that allowing such an offender to escape the primary consequences of conviction — the condemnation of conviction and the restraint of imprisonment or supervision — is an acceptable cost of furthering the important societal interest in deterring such official misconduct.

But is it equally clear that the interest in deterring such official misconduct also outweighs the benefits of all collateral consequences that might have attached to the conviction? Should the corrupt official be able to keep his public office? Should the child molester retain his license to drive a school bus? Should the rapist be permitted to escape sentencing as a repeat offender after a subsequent rape? Should the con man escape impeachment as a prosecution witness in a subsequent capital offense trial?

Competing Interests in Collateral Consequences The nonexculpatory acquittee may be by all standards blameworthy, and there may be nothing in his character or conduct to suggest that he deserves to escape conviction. It is the *societal* interests that justify an acquittal under a nonexculpatory defense. Just as society may choose to adopt a nonexculpatory defense because of the balance of competing societal interests, so may society properly modify or limit the defense or its consequences as it sees fit. Thus, a nonexculpatory defense might result in exemption from custodial or supervisory sanctions yet might permit the imposition of collateral consequences that are, on balance, too important to society's protection to be ignored. In other words, the public policy nature of nonexculpatory defenses means that the scope and effect of the defense ought to be a matter of balancing the competing societal interests. Because the interests supporting a nonexculpatory defense are enough to permit the offender to escape conviction itself, it does not follow that the interests necessarily support the offender escaping all collateral consequences that might accompany conviction. Collateral consequences often can provide the most critical protections for society, sometimes with modest infringement of an offender's interests.

Identifying Nonexculpatory Dismissals The greatest practical hurdle to maintaining collateral consequences is in identifying cases of nonexculpatory acquittals of blameworthy offenders. Many nonexculpatory defenses bar prosecution, thus no authoritative determination of blameworthiness is readily available. Double jeopardy, diplomatic immunity, and incompetency by their terms bar trial of the defendant. Other nonexculpatory defenses, such as the statute of limitations and the immunities (judicial, legislative, executive, testimonial, and plea bargaining) often are litigated before trial. The difficulty can be solved easily enough through a change in procedural rules. If the prosecution intends to seek the imposition of some of the collateral consequences of conviction despite a nonexculpatory dismissal, determination of the nonexculpatory defense could be delayed until after a determination of guilt. Alternatively, the issues of blameworthiness could be litigated at a proceeding concerning the imposition of the collateral consequences. Whether the additional expenditure of resources would be worth the effort may depend on how great a threat the defendant would continue to present if no collateral consequences were imposed.

MODEL PENAL CODE
SELECTED PROVISIONS

TABLE OF CONTENTS

Part I. General Provisions

Article 1. Preliminary

Article 2. General Principles of Liability

Article 3. General Principles of Justification

Article 4. Responsibility

Part II. Definition of Specific Crimes

Offenses Involving Danger to the Person

Article 210. Criminal Homicide

Article 211. Assault; Reckless Endangering; Threats

Article 212. Kidnapping and Related Offenses; Coercion

Article 213. Sexual Offenses

Offenses Against Property

Article 220. Arson, Criminal Mischief, and Other Property Destruction

Article 221. Burglary and Other Criminal Intrusion

Article 222. Robbery

Article 223. Theft and Related Offenses

Article 224. Forgery and Fraudulent Practices

Offenses Against the Family

Article 230. Offenses Against the Family

Offenses Against Public Administration

Article 240. Bribery and Corrupt Influence

Article 241. Perjury and Other Falsification in Official Matters

Article 242. Obstructing Governmental Operations; Escapes

Article 243. Abuse of Office

Offenses Against Public Order and Decency

Article 250. Riot, Disorderly Conduct, and Related Offenses

Article 251. Public Indecency

Model Penal Code Selected Provisions
[Copyright 1962 by The American Law Institute]

Part I. General Provisions

Article 1. Preliminary

Section 1.01. Title and Effective Date.

(1) This Act is called the Penal and Correctional Code and may be cited as P.C.C. It shall become effective on

(2) Except as provided in Subsections (3) and (4) of this Section, the Code does not apply to offenses committed prior to its effective date and prosecutions for such offenses shall be governed by the prior law, which is continued in effect for that purpose, as if this Code were not in force. For the purposes of this Section, an offense was committed prior to the effective date of the Code if any of the elements of the offense occurred prior thereto.

(3) In any case pending on or after the effective date of the Code, involving an offense committed prior to such date:

(a) procedural provisions of the Code shall govern, insofar as they are justly applicable and their application does not introduce confusion or delay;

(b) provisions of the Code according a defense or mitigation shall apply, with the consent of the defendant;

(c) the Court, with the consent of the defendant, may impose sentence under the provisions of the Code applicable to the offense and the offender.

(4) Provisions of the Code governing the treatment and the release or discharge of prisoners, probationers and parolees shall apply to persons under sentence for offenses committed prior to the effective date of the Code, except that the minimum or maximum period of their detention or supervision shall in no case be increased.

Section 1.02. Purposes; Principles of Construction.

(1) The general purposes of the provisions governing the definition of offenses are:

(a) to forbid and prevent conduct that unjustifiably and inexcusably inflicts or threatens substantial harm to individual or public interests;

(b) to subject to public control persons whose conduct indicates that they are disposed to commit crimes;

(c) to safeguard conduct that is without fault from condemnation as criminal;

(d) to give fair warning of the nature of the conduct declared to constitute an offense;

(e) to differentiate on reasonable grounds between serious and minor offenses.

(2) The general purposes of the provisions governing the sentencing and treatment of offenders are:

(a) to prevent the commission of offenses;

(b) to promote the correction and rehabilitation of offenders;

(c) to safeguard offenders against excessive, disproportionate or arbitrary punishment;

(d) to give fair warning of the nature of the sentences that may be imposed on conviction of an offense;

(e) to differentiate among offenders with a view to a just individualization in their treatment;

(f) to define, coordinate and harmonize the powers, duties and functions of the courts and of administrative officers and agencies responsible for dealing with offenders;

(g) to advance the use of generally accepted scientific methods and knowledge in the sentencing and treatment of offenders;

(h) to integrate responsibility for the administration of the correctional system in a State Department of Correction [or other single department or agency].

(3) The provisions of the Code shall be construed according to the fair import of their terms but when the language is susceptible of differing constructions it shall be interpreted to further the general purposes stated in this Section and the special purposes of the particular provision involved. The discretionary powers conferred by the Code shall be exercised in accordance with the criteria stated in the Code and, insofar as such criteria are not decisive, to further the general purposes stated in this Section.

Section 1.03. Territorial Applicability.

(1) Except as otherwise provided in this Section, a person may be convicted under the law of this State of an offense committed by his own conduct or the conduct of another for which he is legally accountable if:

(a) either the conduct which is an element of the offense or the result which is such an element occurs within this State; or

(b) conduct occurring outside the State is sufficient under the law of this State to constitute an attempt to commit an offense within the State; or

(c) conduct occurring outside the State is sufficient under the law of this State to constitute a conspiracy to commit an offense within the State and an overt act in furtherance of such conspiracy occurs within the State; or

(d) conduct occurring within the State establishes complicity in the commission of, or an attempt, solicitation or conspiracy to commit, an offense in another jurisdiction which also is an offense under the law of this State; or

(e) the offense consists of the omission to perform a legal duty imposed by the law of the State with respect to domicile, residence or a relationship to a person, thing or transaction in the State; or

(f) the offense is based on a statute of this State which expressly prohibits conduct outside the State, when the conduct bears a reasonable relation to a legitimate interest of this State and the actor knows or should know that his conduct is likely to affect that interest.

(2) Subsection (1)(a) does not apply when either causing a specified result or a purpose to cause or danger of causing such a result is an element of an offense and the result occurs or is designed or likely to occur only in another jurisdiction where the conduct charged would not constitute an offense, unless a legislative purpose plainly appears to declare the conduct criminal regardless of the place of the result.

(3) Subsection (1)(a) does not apply when causing a particular result is an element of an offense and the result is caused by conduct occurring outside the State which would not constitute an offense if the result had occurred there, unless the actor purposely or knowingly caused the result within the State.

(4) When the offense is homicide, either the death of the victim or the bodily impact causing death constitutes a "result," within the meaning of Subsection (1)(a) and if the body of a homicide victim is found within the State, it is presumed that such result occurred within the State.

(5) This State includes the land and water and the air space above such land and water with respect to which the State has legislative jurisdiction.

Section 1.04. Classes of Crimes; Violations.

(1) An offense defined by this Code or by any other statute of this State, for which a sentence of [death or of] imprisonment is authorized, constitutes a crime. Crimes are classified as felonies, misdemeanors or petty misdemeanors.

(2) A crime is a felony if it is so designated in this Code or if persons convicted thereof may be sentenced [to death or] to imprisonment for a term which, apart from an extended term, is in excess of one year.

(3) A crime is a misdemeanor if it is so designated in this Code or in a statute other than this Code enacted subsequent thereto.

(4) A crime is a petty misdemeanor if it is so designated in this Code or in a statute other than this Code enacted subsequent thereto or if it is defined by a statute other than this Code which now provides that persons convicted thereof may be sentenced to imprisonment for a term of which the maximum is less than one year.

(5) An offense defined by this Code or by any other statute of this State constitutes a violation if it is so designated in this Code or in the law defining the offense or if no other sentence than a fine, or fine and forfeiture or other civil penalty is authorized upon conviction or if it is defined by a statute other than this Code which now provides that the offense shall not constitute a crime. A violation does not constitute a crime and conviction of a violation shall not give rise to any disability or legal disadvantage based on conviction of a criminal offense.

(6) Any offense declared by law to constitute a crime, without specification of the grade thereof or of the sentence authorized upon conviction, is a misdemeanor.

(7) An offense defined by any statute of this State other than this Code shall be classified as provided in this Section and the sentence that may be imposed upon conviction thereof shall hereafter be governed by this Code.

Section 1.05. All Offenses Defined by Statute; Application of General Provisions of the Code.

(1) No conduct constitutes an offense unless it is a crime or violation under this Code or another statute of this State.

(2) The provisions of Part I of the Code are applicable to offenses defined by other statutes, unless the Code otherwise provides.

(3) This Section does not affect the power of a court to punish for contempt or to employ any sanction authorized by law for the enforcement of an order or a civil judgment or decree.

Section 1.06. Time Limitations.

(1) A prosecution for murder may be commenced at any time.

(2) Except as otherwise provided in this Section, prosecutions for other offenses are subject to the following periods of limitation:

(a) a prosecution for a felony of the first degree must be commenced within six years after it is committed;

(b) a prosecution for any other felony must be commenced within three years after it is committed;

(c) a prosecution for a misdemeanor must be commenced within two years after it is committed;

(d) a prosecution for a petty misdemeanor or a violation must be commenced within six months after it is committed.

(3) If the period prescribed in Subsection (2) has expired, a prosecution may nevertheless be commenced for:

(a) any offense a material element of which is either fraud or a breach of fiduciary obligation within one year after discovery of the offense by an aggrieved party or by a person who has a legal duty to represent an aggrieved party and who is himself not a party to the offense, but in no case shall this provision extend the period of limitation otherwise applicable by more than three years; and

(b) any offense based upon misconduct in office by a public officer or employee at any time when the defendant is in public office or employment or within two years thereafter, but in no case shall this provision extend the period of limitation otherwise applicable by more than three years.

(4) An offense is committed either when every element occurs, or, if a legislative purpose to prohibit a continuing course of conduct plainly appears, at the time when the course of conduct or the defendant's complicity therein is terminated. Time starts to run on the day after the offense is committed.

(5) A prosecution is commenced either when an indictment is found [or an information filed] or when a warrant or other process is issued, provided that such warrant or process is executed without unreasonable delay.

(6) The period of limitation does not run:

(a) during any time when the accused is continuously absent from the State or has no reasonably ascertainable place of abode or work within the State, but in no case shall this provision extend the period of limitation otherwise applicable by more than three years; or

(b) during any time when a prosecution against the accused for the same conduct is pending in this State.

Section 1.07. Method of Prosecution When Conduct Constitutes More Than One Offense.

(1) Prosecution for Multiple Offenses; Limitation on Convictions. When the same conduct of a defendant may establish the commission of more than one offense, the defendant may be prosecuted for each such offense. He may not, however, be convicted of more than one offense if:

(a) one offense is included in the other, as defined in Subsection (4) of this Section; or

(b) one offense consists only of a conspiracy or other form of preparation to commit the other; or

(c) inconsistent findings of fact are required to establish the commission of the offenses; or

(d) the offenses differ only in that one is defined to prohibit a designated kind of conduct generally and the other to prohibit a specific instance of such conduct; or

(e) the offense is defined as a continuing course of conduct and the defendant's course of conduct was uninterrupted, unless the law provides that specific periods of such conduct constitute separate offenses.

(2) Limitation on Separate Trials for Multiple Offenses. Except as provided in Subsection (3) of this Section, a defendant shall not be subject to separate trials for multiple offenses based on the same conduct or arising from the same criminal episode, if such offenses are known to the appropriate prosecuting officer at the time of the commencement of the first trial and are within the jurisdiction of a single court.

(3) Authority of Court to Order Separate Trials. When a defendant is charged with two or more offenses based on the same conduct or arising from the same criminal episode, the Court, on application of the prosecuting attorney or of the defendant, may order any such charge to be tried separately, if it is satisfied that justice so requires.

(4) Conviction of Included Offense Permitted. A defendant may be convicted of an offense included in an offense charged in the indictment [or the information]. An offense is so included when:

(a) it is established by proof of the same or less than all the facts required to establish the commission of the offense charged; or

(b) it consists of an attempt or solicitation to commit the offense charged or to commit an offense otherwise included therein; or

(c) it differs from the offense charged only in the respect that a less serious injury or risk of injury to the same person, property or public interest or a lesser kind of culpability suffices to establish its commission.

(5) Submission of Included Offense to Jury. The Court shall not be obligated to charge the jury with respect to an included offense unless there is a rational basis for a verdict acquitting the defendant of the offense charged and convicting him of the included offense.

Section 1.08. When Prosecution Barred by Former Prosecution for the Same Offense.

When a prosecution is for a violation of the same provision of the statutes and is based upon the same facts as a former prosecution, it is barred by such former prosecution under the following circumstances:

(1) The former prosecution resulted in an acquittal. There is an acquittal if the prosecution resulted in a finding of not guilty by the trier of fact or in a determination that there was insufficient evidence to warrant a conviction. A finding of guilty of a lesser included offense is an acquittal of the greater inclusive offense, although the conviction is subsequently set aside.

(2) The former prosecution was terminated, after the information had been filed or the indictment found, by a final order or judgment for the defendant, which has not been set aside, reversed, or vacated and which necessarily required a determination inconsistent with a fact or a legal proposition that must be established for conviction of the offense.

(3) The former prosecution resulted in a conviction. There is a conviction if the prosecution resulted in a judgment of conviction which has not been reversed or vacated, a verdict of guilty which has not been set aside and which is capable of supporting a judgment, or a plea of guilty accepted by the Court. In the latter two cases failure to enter judgment must be for a reason other than a motion of the defendant.

(4) The former prosecution was improperly terminated. Except as provided in this Subsection, there is an improper termination of a prosecution if the termination is for reasons not amounting to an acquittal, and it takes place after the first witness is sworn but before verdict. Termination under any of the following circumstances is not improper:

(a) The defendant consents to the termination or waives, by motion to dismiss or otherwise, his right to object to the termination.

(b) The trial court finds that the termination is necessary because:

(1) it is physically impossible to proceed with the trial in conformity with law; or

(2) there is a legal defect in the proceedings which would make any judgment entered upon a verdict reversible as a matter of law; or

(3) prejudicial conduct, in or outside the courtroom, makes it impossible to proceed with the trial without injustice to either the defendant or the State; or

(4) the jury is unable to agree upon a verdict; or

(5) false statements of a juror on voir dire prevent a fair trial.

Section 1.09. When Prosecution Barred by Former Prosecution for Different Offense.

Although a prosecution is for a violation of a different provision of the statutes than a former prosecution or is based on different facts, it is barred by such former prosecution under the following circumstances:

(1) The former prosecution resulted in an acquittal or in a conviction as defined in Section 1.08 and the subsequent prosecution is for:

(a) any offense of which the defendant could have been convicted on the first prosecution; or

(b) any offense for which the defendant should have been tried on the first prosecution under Section 1.07, unless the Court ordered a separate trial of the charge of such offense; or

(c) the same conduct, unless (i) the offense of which the defendant was formerly convicted or acquitted and the offense for which he is subsequently prosecuted each requires proof of a fact not required by the other and the law defining each of such offenses is intended to prevent a substantially different harm or evil, or (ii) the second offense was not consummated when the former trial began.

(2) The former prosecution was terminated, after the information was filed or the indictment found, by an acquittal or by a final order or judgment for the defendant which has not been set aside, reversed or vacated and which acquittal, final order or judgment necessarily required a determination inconsistent with a fact which must be established for conviction of the second offense.

(3) The former prosecution was improperly terminated, as improper termination is defined in Section 1.08, and the subsequent prosecution is for an offense of which the defendant could have been convicted had the former prosecution not been improperly terminated.

Section 1.10. Former Prosecution in Another Jurisdiction: When a Bar.

When conduct constitutes an offense within the concurrent jurisdiction of this State and of the United States or another State, a prosecution in any such other jurisdiction is a bar to a subsequent prosecution in this State under the following circumstances:

(1) The first prosecution resulted in an acquittal or in a conviction as defined in Section 1.08 and the subsequent prosecution is based on the same conduct, unless (a) the offense of which the defendant was formerly convicted or acquitted and the offense for which he is subsequently prosecuted each requires proof of a fact not required by the other and the law defining each of such offenses is intended to prevent a substantially different harm or evil or (b) the second offense was not consummated when the former trial began; or

(2) The former prosecution was terminated, after the information was filed or the indictment found, by an acquittal or by a final order or judgment for the defendant which has not been set aside, reversed or vacated and

which acquittal, final order or judgment necessarily required a determination inconsistent with a fact which must be established for conviction of the offense of which the defendant is subsequently prosecuted.

Section 1.11. Former Prosecution Before Court Lacking Jurisdiction or When Fraudulently Procured by the Defendant.

A prosecution is not a bar within the meaning of Sections 1.08, 1.09 and 1.10 under any of the following circumstances:

(1) The former prosecution was before a court which lacked jurisdiction over the defendant or the offense; or

(2) The former prosecution was procured by the defendant without the knowledge of the appropriate prosecuting officer and with the purpose of avoiding the sentence which might otherwise be imposed; or

(3) The former prosecution resulted in a judgment of conviction which was held invalid in a subsequent proceeding on a writ of habeas corpus, coram nobis or similar process.

Section 1.12. Proof Beyond a Reasonable Doubt; Affirmative Defenses; Burden of Proving Fact When Not an Element of an Offense; Presumptions.

(1) No person may be convicted of an offense unless each element of such offense is proved beyond a reasonable doubt. In the absence of such proof, the innocence of the defendant is assumed.

(2) Subsection (1) of this Section does not:

(a) require the disproof of an affirmative defense unless and until there is evidence supporting such defense; or

(b) apply to any defense which the Code or another statute plainly requires the defendant to prove by a preponderance of evidence.

(3) A ground of defense is affirmative, within the meaning of Subsection (2)(a) of this Section, when:

(a) it arises under a section of the Code which so provides; or

(b) it relates to an offense defined by a statute other than the Code and such statute so provides; or

(c) it involves a matter of excuse or justification peculiarly within the knowledge of the defendant on which he can fairly be required to adduce supporting evidence.

(4) When the application of the Code depends upon the finding of a fact which is not an element of an offense, unless the Code otherwise provides:

(a) the burden of proving the fact is on the prosecution or defendant, depending on whose interest or contention will be furthered if the finding should be made; and

(b) the fact must be proved to the satisfaction of the Court or jury, as the case may be.

(5) When the Code establishes a presumption with respect to any fact which is an element of an offense, it has the following consequences:

(a) when there is evidence of the facts which give rise to the presumption, the issue of the existence of the presumed fact must be submitted to the jury, unless the Court is satisfied that the evidence as a whole clearly negatives the presumed fact; and

(b) when the issue of the existence of the presumed fact is submitted to the jury, the Court shall charge that while the presumed fact must, on all the evidence, be proved beyond a reasonable doubt, the law declares that the jury may regard the facts giving rise to the presumption as sufficient evidence of the presumed fact.

(6) A presumption not established by the Code or inconsistent with it has the consequences otherwise accorded it by law.

Section 1.13. General Definitions.

In this Code, unless a different meaning plainly is required:

(1) "statute" includes the Constitution and a local law or ordinance of a political subdivision of the State;

(2) "act" or "action" means a bodily movement whether voluntary or involuntary;

(3) "voluntary" has the meaning specified in Section 2.01;

(4) "omission" means a failure to act;

(5) "conduct" means an action or omission and its accompanying state of mind, or, where relevant, a series of acts and omissions;

(6) "actor" includes, where relevant, a person guilty of an omission;

(7) "acted" includes, where relevant, "omitted to act";

(8) "person," "he" and "actor" include any natural person and, where relevant, a corporation or an unincorporated association;

(9) "element of an offense" means (i) such conduct or (ii) such attendant circumstances or (iii) such a result of conduct as

(a) is included in the description of the forbidden conduct in the definition of the offense; or

(b) establishes the required kind of culpability; or

(c) negatives an excuse or justification for such conduct; or

(d) negatives a defense under the statute of limitations; or

(e) establishes jurisdiction or venue;

(10) "material element of an offense" means an element that does not relate exclusively to the statute of limitations, jurisdiction, venue or to any other matter similarly unconnected with (i) the harm or evil, incident to conduct, sought to be prevented by the law defining the offense, or (ii) the existence of a justification or excuse for such conduct;

(11) "purposely" has the meaning specified in Section 2.02 and equivalent terms such as "with purpose," "designed" or "with design" have the same meaning;

(12) "intentionally" or "with intent" means purposely;

(13) "knowingly" has the meaning specified in Section 2.02 and equivalent terms such as "knowing" or "with knowledge" have the same meaning;

(14) "recklessly" has the meaning specified in Section 2.02 and equivalent terms such as "recklessness" or "with recklessness" have the same meaning;

(15) "negligently" has the meaning specified in Section 2.02 and equivalent terms such as "negligence" or "with negligence" have the same meaning;

(16) "reasonably believes" or "reasonable belief" designates a belief which the actor is not reckless or negligent in holding.

Article 2. General Principles of Liability.

Section 2.01. Requirement of Voluntary Act; Omission as Basis of Liability; Possession as an Act.

(1) A person is not guilty of an offense unless his liability is based on conduct which includes a voluntary act or the omission to perform an act of which he is physically capable.

(2) The following are not voluntary acts within the meaning of this Section:

(a) a reflex or convulsion;

(b) a bodily movement during unconsciousness or sleep;

(c) conduct during hypnosis or resulting from hypnotic suggestion;

(d) a bodily movement that otherwise is not a product of the effort or determination of the actor, either conscious or habitual.

(3) Liability for the commission of an offense may not be based on an omission unaccompanied by action unless:

(a) the omission is expressly made sufficient by the law defining the offense; or

(b) a duty to perform the omitted act is otherwise imposed by law.

(4) Possession is an act, within the meaning of this Section, if the possessor knowingly procured or received the thing possessed or was aware of his control thereof for a sufficient period to have been able to terminate his possession.

Section 2.02. General Requirements of Culpability.

(1) Minimum Requirements of Culpability. Except as provided in Section 2.05, a person is not guilty of an offense unless he acted purposely, knowingly, recklessly or negligently, as the law may require, with respect to each material element of the offense.

(2) Kinds of Culpability Defined.

(a) Purposely. A person acts purposely with respect to a material element of an offense when:

(i) if the element involves the nature of his conduct or a result thereof, it is his conscious object to engage in conduct of that nature or to cause such a result; and

(ii) if the element involves the attendant circumstances, he is aware of the existence of such circumstances or he believes or hopes that they exist.

(b) Knowingly. A person acts knowingly with respect to a material element of an offense when:

(i) if the element involves the nature of his conduct or the attendant circumstances, he is aware that his conduct is of that nature or that such circumstances exist; and

(ii) if the element involves a result of his conduct, he is aware that it is practically certain that his conduct will cause such a result.

(c) Recklessly. A person acts recklessly with respect to a material element of an offense when he consciously disregards a substantial and unjustifiable risk that the material element exists or will result from his conduct. The risk must be of such a nature and degree that, considering the nature and purpose of the actor's conduct and the circumstances known to him, its disregard involves a gross deviation from the standard of conduct that a law-abiding person would observe in the actor's situation.

(d) Negligently. A person acts negligently with respect to a material element of an offense when he should be aware of a substantial and unjustifiable risk that the material element exists or will result from his conduct. The risk must be of such a nature and degree that the actor's failure to perceive it, considering the nature and purpose of his conduct and the circumstances known to him, involves a gross deviation from the standard of care that a reasonable person would observe in the actor's situation.

(3) Culpability Required Unless Otherwise Provided. When the culpability sufficient to establish a material element of an offense is not prescribed by law, such element is established if a person acts purposely, knowingly or recklessly with respect thereto.

(4) Prescribed Culpability Requirement Applies to All Material Elements. When the law defining an offense prescribes the kind of culpability that is sufficient for the commission of an offense, without distinguishing among the material elements thereof, such provision shall apply to all the material elements of the offense, unless a contrary purpose plainly appears.

(5) Substitutes for Negligence, Recklessness and Knowledge. When the law provides that negligence suffices to establish an element of an offense, such element also is established if a person acts purposely, knowingly or recklessly. When recklessness suffices to establish an element, such element also is established if a person acts purposely or knowingly. When acting knowingly suffices to establish an element, such element also is established if a person acts purposely.

(6) Requirement of Purpose Satisfied if Purpose Is Conditional. When a particular purpose is an element of an offense, the element is established although such purpose is conditional, unless the condition negatives the harm or evil sought to be prevented by the law defining the offense.

(7) Requirement of Knowledge Satisfied by Knowledge of High Probability. When knowledge of the existence of a particular fact is an element of an offense, such knowledge is established if a person is aware of a high probability of its existence, unless he actually believes that it does not exist.

(8) Requirement of Wilfulness Satisfied by Acting Knowingly. A requirement that an offense be committed wilfully is satisfied if a person acts knowingly

with respect to the material elements of the offense, unless a purpose to impose further requirements appears.

(9) Culpability as to Illegality of Conduct. Neither knowledge nor recklessness or negligence as to whether conduct constitutes an offense or as to the existence, meaning or application of the law determining the elements of an offense is an element of such offense, unless the definition of the offense or the Code so provides.

(10) Culpability as Determinant of Grade of Offense. When the grade or degree of an offense depends on whether the offense is committed purposely, knowingly, recklessly or negligently, its grade or degree shall be the lowest for which the determinative kind of culpability is established with respect to any material element of the offense.

Section 2.03. Causal Relationship Between Conduct and Result; Divergence Between Result Designed or Contemplated and Actual Result or Between Probable and Actual Result.

(1) Conduct is the cause of a result when:

(a) it is an antecedent but for which the result in question would not have occurred; and

(b) the relationship between the conduct and result satisfies any additional causal requirements imposed by the Code or by the law defining the offense.

(2) When purposely or knowingly causing a particular result is an element of an offense, the element is not established if the actual result is not within the purpose or the contemplation of the actor unless:

(a) the actual result differs from that designed or contemplated, as the case may be, only in the respect that a different person or different property is injured or affected or that the injury or harm designed or contemplated would have been more serious or more extensive than that caused; or

(b) the actual result involves the same kind of injury or harm as that designed or contemplated and is not too remote or accidental in its occurrence to have a [just] bearing on the actor's liability or on the gravity of his offense.

(3) When recklessly or negligently causing a particular result is an element of an offense, the element is not established if the actual result is not within the risk of which the actor is aware or, in the case of negligence, of which he should be aware unless:

(a) the actual result differs from the probable result only in the respect that a different person or different property is injured or affected or that the probable injury or harm would have been more serious or more extensive than that caused; or

(b) the actual result involves the same kind of injury or harm as the probable result and is not too remote or accidental in its occurrence to have a [just] bearing on the actor's liability or on the gravity of his offense.

(4) When causing a particular result is a material element of an offense for which absolute liability is imposed by law, the element is not established unless the actual result is a probable consequence of the actor's conduct.

Section 2.04. Ignorance or Mistake.

(1) Ignorance or mistake as to a matter of fact or law is a defense if:

(a) the ignorance or mistake negatives the purpose, knowledge, belief, recklessness or negligence required to establish a material element of the offense; or

(b) the law provides that the state of mind established by such ignorance or mistake constitutes a defense.

(2) Although ignorance or mistake would otherwise afford a defense to the offense charged, the defense is not available if the defendant would be guilty of another offense had the situation been as he supposed. In such case, however, the ignorance or mistake of the defendant shall reduce the grade and degree of the offense of which he may be convicted to those of the offense of which he would be guilty had the situation been as he supposed.

(3) A belief that conduct does not legally constitute an offense is a defense to a prosecution for that offense based upon such conduct when:

(a) the statute or other enactment defining the offense is not known to the actor and has not been published or otherwise reasonably made available prior to the conduct alleged; or

(b) he acts in reasonable reliance upon an official statement of the law, afterward determined to be invalid or erroneous, contained in (i) a statute or other enactment; (ii) a judicial decision, opinion or judgment; (iii) an administrative order or grant of permission; or (iv) an official interpretation of the public officer or body charged by law with responsibility for the interpretation, administration or enforcement of the law defining the offense.

(4) The defendant must prove a defense arising under Subsection (3) of this Section by a preponderance of evidence.

Section 2.05. When Culpability Requirements Are Inapplicable to Violations and to Offenses Defined by Other Statutes; Effect of Absolute Liability in Reducing Grade of Offense to Violation.

(1) The requirements of culpability prescribed by Sections 2.01 and 2.02 do not apply to:

(a) offenses which constitute violations, unless the requirement involved is included in the definition of the offense or the Court determines that its application is consistent with effective enforcement of the law defining the offense; or

(b) offenses defined by statutes other than the Code, insofar as a legislative purpose to impose absolute liability for such offenses or with respect to any material element thereof plainly appears.

(2) Notwithstanding any other provision of existing law and unless a subsequent statute otherwise provides:

(a) when absolute liability is imposed with respect to any material element of an offense defined by a statute other than the Code and a conviction is based upon such liability, the offense constitutes a violation; and

(b) although absolute liability is imposed by law with respect to one or more of the material elements of an offense defined by a statute other than the Code, the culpable commission of the offense may be charged and proved, in which event negligence with respect to such elements constitutes sufficient culpability and the classification of the offense and the sentence that may be imposed therefor upon conviction are determined by Section 1.04 and Article 6 of the Code.

Section 2.06. Liability for Conduct of Another; Complicity.

(1) A person is guilty of an offense if it is committed by his own conduct or by the conduct of another person for which he is legally accountable, or both.

(2) A person is legally accountable for the conduct of another person when:

(a) acting with the kind of culpability that is sufficient for the commission of the offense, he causes an innocent or irresponsible person to engage in such conduct; or

(b) he is made accountable for the conduct of such other person by the Code or by the law defining the offense; or

(c) he is an accomplice of such other person in the commission of the offense.

(3) A person is an accomplice of another person in the commission of an offense if:

(a) with the purpose of promoting or facilitating the commission of the offense, he

(i) solicits such other person to commit it; or

(ii) aids or agrees or attempts to aid such other person in planning or committing it; or

(iii) having a legal duty to prevent the commission of the offense, fails to make proper effort so to do; or

(b) his conduct is expressly declared by law to establish his complicity.

(4) When causing a particular result is an element of an offense, an accomplice in the conduct causing such result is an accomplice in the commission of that offense, if he acts with the kind of culpability, if any, with respect to that result that is sufficient for the commission of the offense.

(5) A person who is legally incapable of committing a particular offense himself may be guilty thereof if it is committed by the conduct of another person for which he is legally accountable, unless such liability is inconsistent with the purpose of the provision establishing his incapacity.

(6) Unless otherwise provided by the Code or by the law defining the offense, a person is not an accomplice in an offense committed by another person if:

(a) he is a victim of that offense; or

(b) the offense is so defined that his conduct is inevitably incident to its commission; or

(c) he terminates his complicity prior to the commission of the offense and

(i) wholly deprives it of effectiveness in the commission of the offense; or

(ii) gives timely warning to the law enforcement authorities or otherwise makes proper effort to prevent the commission of the offense.

(7) An accomplice may be convicted on proof of the commission of the offense and of his complicity therein, though the person claimed to have committed the offense has not been prosecuted or convicted or has been convicted of a different offense or degree of offense or has an immunity to prosecution or conviction or has been acquitted.

Section 2.07. Liability of Corporations, Unincorporated Associations and Persons Acting, or Under a Duty to Act, in Their Behalf.

(1) A corporation may be convicted of the commission of an offense if:

(a) the offense is a violation or the offense is defined by a statute other than the Code in which a legislative purpose to impose liability on corporations plainly appears and the conduct is performed by an agent of the corporation acting in behalf of the corporation within the scope of his office or employment, except that if the law defining the offense designates the agents for whose conduct the corporation is accountable or the circumstances under which it is accountable, such provisions shall apply; or

(b) the offense consists of an omission to discharge a specific duty of affirmative performance imposed on corporations by law; or

(c) the commission of the offense was authorized, requested, commanded, performed or recklessly tolerated by the board of directors or by a high managerial agent acting in behalf of the corporation within the scope of his office or employment.

(2) When absolute liability is imposed for the commission of an offense, a legislative purpose to impose liability on a corporation shall be assumed, unless the contrary plainly appears.

(3) An unincorporated association may be convicted of the commission of an offense if:

(a) the offense is defined by a statute other than the Code which expressly provides for the liability of such an association and the conduct is performed by an agent of the association acting in behalf of the association within the scope of his office or employment, except that if the law defining the offense designates the agents for whose conduct the association is accountable or the circumstances under which it is accountable, such provisions shall apply; or

(b) the offense consists of an omission to discharge a specific duty of affirmative performance imposed on associations by law.

(4) As used in this Section:

(a) "corporation" does not include an entity organized as or by a governmental agency for the execution of a governmental program;

(b) "agent" means any director, officer, servant, employee or other person authorized to act in behalf of the corporation or association and, in the case of an unincorporated association, a member of such association;

(c) "high managerial agent" means an officer of a corporation or an unincorporated association, or, in the case of a partnership, a partner, or any other agent of a corporation or association having duties of such responsibility that his conduct may fairly be assumed to represent the policy of the corporation or association.

(5) In any prosecution of a corporation or an unincorporated association for the commission of an offense included within the terms of Subsection (1)(a) or Subsection (3)(a) of this Section, other than an offense for which absolute liability has been imposed, it shall be a defense if the defendant proves by a preponderance of evidence that the high managerial agent having supervisory responsibility over the subject matter of the offense employed due diligence to prevent its commission. This paragraph shall not apply if it is plainly inconsistent with the legislative purpose in defining the particular offense.

(6) (a) A person is legally accountable for any conduct he performs or causes to be performed in the name of the corporation or an unincorporated association or in its behalf to the same extent as if it were performed in his own name or behalf.

(b) Whenever a duty to act is imposed by law upon a corporation or an unincorporated association, any agent of the corporation or association having primary responsibility for the discharge of the duty is legally accountable for a reckless omission to perform the required act to the same extent as if the duty were imposed by law directly upon himself.

(c) When a person is convicted of an offense by reason of his legal accountability for the conduct of a corporation or an unincorporated association, he is subject to the sentence authorized by law when a natural person is convicted of an offense of the grade and the degree involved.

Section 2.08. Intoxication.

(1) Except as provided in Subsection (4) of this Section, intoxication of the actor is not a defense unless it negatives an element of the offense.

(2) When recklessness establishes an element of the offense, if the actor, due to self-induced intoxication, is unaware of a risk of which he would have been aware had he been sober, such unawareness is immaterial.

(3) Intoxication does not, in itself, constitute mental disease within the meaning of Section 4.01.

(4) Intoxication which (a) is not self-induced or (b) is pathological is an affirmative defense if by reason of such intoxication the actor at the time of his conduct lacks substantial capacity either to appreciate its criminality [wrongfulness] or to conform his conduct to the requirements of law.

(5) Definitions. In this Section unless a different meaning plainly is required:

(a) "intoxication" means a disturbance of mental or physical capacities resulting from the introduction of substances into the body;

(b) "self-induced intoxication" means intoxication caused by substances which the actor knowingly introduces into his body, the tendency of which to cause intoxication he knows or ought to know, unless he introduces them pursuant to medical advice or under such circumstances as would afford a defense to a charge of crime;

(c) "pathological intoxication" means intoxication grossly excessive in degree, given the amount of the intoxicant, to which the actor does not know he is susceptible.

Section 2.09. Duress.

(1) It is an affirmative defense that the actor engaged in the conduct charged to constitute an offense because he was coerced to do so by the use of, or a threat to use, unlawful force against his person or the person of another, which a person of reasonable firmness in his situation would have been unable to resist.

(2) The defense provided by this Section is unavailable if the actor recklessly placed himself in a situation in which it was probable that he would be subjected to duress. The defense is also unavailable if he was negligent in placing himself in such a situation, whenever negligence suffices to establish culpability for the offense charged.

(3) It is not a defense that a woman acted on the command of her husband, unless she acted under such coercion as would establish a defense under this Section. [The presumption that a woman, acting in the presence of her husband, is coerced is abolished.]

(4) When the conduct of the actor would otherwise be justifiable under Section 3.02, this Section does not preclude such defense.

Section 2.10. Military Orders.

It is an affirmative defense that the actor, in engaging in the conduct charged to constitute an offense, does no more than execute an order of his superior in the armed services which he does not know to be unlawful.

Section 2.11. Consent.

(1) In General. The consent of the victim to conduct charged to constitute an offense or to the result thereof is a defense if such consent negatives an element

of the offense or precludes the infliction of the harm or evil sought to be prevented by the law defining the offense.

(2) Consent to Bodily Injury. When conduct is charged to constitute an offense because it causes or threatens bodily injury, consent to such conduct or to the infliction of such injury is a defense if:

(a) the bodily injury consented to or threatened by the conduct consented to is not serious; or

(b) the conduct and the injury are reasonably foreseeable hazards of joint participation in a lawful athletic contest or competitive sport or other concerted activity not forbidden by law; or

(c) the consent establishes a justification for the conduct under Article 3 of the Code.

(3) Ineffective Consent. Unless otherwise provided by the Code or by the law defining the offense, assent does not constitute consent if:

(a) it is given by a person who is legally incompetent to authorize the conduct charged to constitute the offense; or

(b) it is given by a person who by reason of youth, mental disease or defect or intoxication is manifestly unable or known by the actor to be unable to make a reasonable judgment as to the nature or harmfulness of the conduct charged to constitute the offense; or

(c) it is given by a person whose improvident consent is sought to be prevented by the law defining the offense; or

(d) it is induced by force, duress or deception of a kind sought to be prevented by the law defining the offense.

Section 2.12. De Minimis Infractions.

The Court shall dismiss a prosecution if, having regard to the nature of the conduct charged to constitute an offense and the nature of the attendant circumstances, it finds that the defendant's conduct:

(1) was within a customary license or tolerance, neither expressly negatived by the person whose interest was infringed nor inconsistent with the purpose of the law defining the offense; or

(2) did not actually cause or threaten the harm or evil sought to be prevented by the law defining the offense or did so only to an extent too trivial to warrant the condemnation of conviction; or

(3) presents such other extenuations that it cannot reasonably be regarded as envisaged by the legislature in forbidding the offense. The Court shall not dismiss a prosecution under Subsection (3) of this Section without filing a written statement of its reasons.

Section 2.13. Entrapment.

(1) A public law enforcement official or a person acting in cooperation with such an official perpetrates an entrapment if for the purpose of obtaining evidence

of the commission of an offense, he induces or encourages another person to engage in conduct constituting such offense by either:

> (a) making knowingly false representations designed to induce the belief that such conduct is not prohibited; or

> (b) employing methods of persuasion or inducement which create a substantial risk that such an offense will be committed by persons other than those who are ready to commit it.

(2) Except as provided in Subsection (3) of this Section, a person prosecuted for an offense shall be acquitted if he proves by a preponderance of evidence that his conduct occurred in response to an entrapment. The issue of entrapment shall be tried by the Court in the absence of the jury.

(3) The defense afforded by this Section is unavailable when causing or threatening bodily injury is an element of the offense charged and the prosecution is based on conduct causing or threatening such injury to a person other than the person perpetrating the entrapment.

Article 3. General Principles of Justification.

Section 3.01. Justification an Affirmative Defense; Civil Remedies Unaffected.

(1) In any prosecution based on conduct which is justifiable under this Article, justification is an affirmative defense.

(2) The fact that conduct is justifiable under this Article does not abolish or impair any remedy for such conduct which is available in any civil action.

Section 3.02. Justification Generally: Choice of Evils.

(1) Conduct which the actor believes to be necessary to avoid a harm or evil to himself or to another is justifiable, provided that:

> (a) the harm or evil sought to be avoided by such conduct is greater than that sought to be prevented by the law defining the offense charged; and

> (b) neither the Code nor other law defining the offense provides exceptions or defenses dealing with the specific situation involved; and

> (c) a legislative purpose to exclude the justification claimed does not otherwise plainly appear.

(2) When the actor was reckless or negligent in bringing about the situation requiring a choice of harms or evils or in appraising the necessity for his conduct, the justification afforded by this Section is unavailable in a prosecution for any offense for which recklessness or negligence, as the case may be, suffices to establish culpability.

Section 3.03. Execution of Public Duty.

(1) Except as provided in Subsection (2) of this Section, conduct is justifiable when it is required or authorized by:

> (a) the law defining the duties or functions of a public officer or the assistance to be rendered to such officer in the performance of his duties; or

(b) the law governing the execution of legal process; or

(c) the judgment or order of a competent court or tribunal; or

(d) the law governing the armed services or the lawful conduct of war; or

(e) any other provision of law imposing a public duty.

(2) The other sections of this Article apply to:

(a) the use of force upon or toward the person of another for any of the purposes dealt with in such sections; and

(b) the use of deadly force for any purpose, unless the use of such force is otherwise expressly authorized by law or occurs in the lawful conduct of war.

(3) The justification afforded by Subsection (1) of this Section applies:

(a) when the actor believes his conduct to be required or authorized by the judgment or direction of a competent court or tribunal or in the lawful execution of legal process, notwithstanding lack of jurisdiction of the court or defect in the legal process; and

(b) when the actor believes his conduct to be required or authorized to assist a public officer in the performance of his duties, notwithstanding that the officer exceeded his legal authority.

Section 3.04. Use of Force in Self-Protection.

(1) Use of Force Justifiable for Protection of the Person. Subject to the provisions of this Section and of Section 3.09, the use of force upon or toward another person is justifiable when the actor believes that such force is immediately necessary for the purpose of protecting himself against the use of unlawful force by such other person on the present occasion.

(2) Limitations on Justifying Necessity for Use of Force.

(a) The use of force is not justifiable under this Section:

(i) to resist an arrest which the actor knows is being made by a peace officer, although the arrest is unlawful; or

(ii) to resist force used by the occupier or possessor of property or by another person on his behalf, where the actor knows that the person using the force is doing so under a claim of right to protect the property, except that this limitation shall not apply if:

(1) the actor is a public officer acting in the performance of his duties or a person lawfully assisting him therein or a person making or assisting in a lawful arrest; or

(2) the actor has been unlawfully dispossessed of the property and is making a re-entry or recaption justified by Section 3.06; or

(3) the actor believes that such force is necessary to protect himself against death or serious bodily harm.

(b) The use of deadly force is not justifiable under this Section unless the actor believes that such force is necessary to protect himself against death, serious bodily harm, kidnapping or sexual intercourse compelled by force or threat; nor is it justifiable if:

(i) the actor, with the purpose of causing death or serious bodily harm, provoked the use of force against himself in the same encounter; or

(ii) the actor knows that he can avoid the necessity of using such force with complete safety by retreating or by surrendering possession of a thing to a person asserting a claim of right thereto or by complying with a demand that he abstain from any action which he has no duty to take, except that:

(1) the actor is not obliged to retreat from his dwelling or place of work, unless he was the initial aggressor or is assailed in his place of work by another person whose place of work the actor knows it to be; and

(2) a public officer justified in using force in the performance of his duties or a person justified in using force in his assistance or a person justified in using force in making an arrest or preventing an escape is not obliged to desist from efforts to perform such duty, effect such arrest or prevent such escape because of resistance or threatened resistance by or on behalf of the person against whom such action is directed.

(c) Except as required by paragraphs (a) and (b) of this Subsection, a person employing protective force may estimate the necessity thereof under the circumstances as he believes them to be when the force is used, without retreating, surrendering possession, doing any other act which he has no legal duty to do or abstaining from any lawful action.

(3) Use of Confinement as Protective Force. The justification afforded by this Section extends to the use of confinement as protective force only if the actor takes all reasonable measures to terminate the confinement as soon as he knows that he safely can, unless the person confined has been arrested on a charge of crime.

Section 3.05. Use of Force for the Protection of Other Persons.

(1) Subject to the provisions of this Section and of Section 3.09, the use of force upon or toward the person of another is justifiable to protect a third person when:

(a) the actor would be justified under Section 3.04 in using such force to protect himself against the injury he believes to be threatened to the person whom he seeks to protect; and

(b) under the circumstances as the actor believes them to be, the person whom he seeks to protect would be justified in using such protective force; and

(c) the actor believes that his intervention is necessary for the protection of such other person.

(2) Notwithstanding Subsection (1) of this Section:

(a) when the actor would be obliged under Section 3.04 to retreat, to surrender the possession of a thing or to comply with a demand before using force in self-protection, he is not obliged to do so before using force for the protection of another person, unless he knows that he can thereby secure the complete safety of such other person; and

(b) when the person whom the actor seeks to protect would be obliged under Section 3.04 to retreat, to surrender the possession of a thing or to comply with a demand if he knew that he could obtain complete safety by so doing, the actor is obliged to try to cause him to do so before using force in his protection if the actor knows that he can obtain complete safety in that way; and

(c) neither the actor nor the person whom he seeks to protect is obliged to retreat when in the other's dwelling or place of work to any greater extent than in his own.

Section 3.06. Use of Force for the Protection of Property.

(1) Use of Force Justifiable for Protection of Property. Subject to the provisions of this Section and of Section 3.09, the use of force upon or toward the person of another is justifiable when the actor believes that such force is immediately necessary:

(a) to prevent or terminate an unlawful entry or other trespass upon land or a trespass against or the unlawful carrying away of tangible, movable property, provided that such land or movable property is, or is believed by the actor to be, in his possession or in the possession of another person for whose protection he acts; or

(b) to effect an entry or re-entry upon land or to retake tangible movable property, provided that the actor believes that he or the person by whose authority he acts or a person from whom he or such other person derives title was unlawfully dispossessed of such land or movable property and is entitled to possession, and provided, further, that:

(i) the force is used immediately or on fresh pursuit after such dispossession; or

(ii) the actor believes that the person against whom he uses force has no claim of right to the possession of the property and, in the case of land, the circumstances, as the actor believes them to be, are of such urgency that it would be an exceptional hardship to postpone the entry or re-entry until a court order is obtained.

(2) Meaning of Possession. For the purposes of Subsection (1) of this Section:

(a) a person who has parted with the custody of property to another who refuses to restore it to him is no longer in possession, unless the property is movable and was and still is located on land in his possession;

(b) a person who has been dispossessed of land does not regain possession thereof merely by setting foot thereon;

(c) a person who has a license to use or occupy real property is deemed to be in possession thereof except against the licensor acting under claim of right.

(3) Limitations on Justifiable Use of Force.

(a) Request to Desist. The use of force is justifiable under this Section only if the actor first requests the person against whom such force is used to desist from his interference with the property, unless the actor believes that:

(i) such request would be useless; or

(ii) it would be dangerous to himself or another person to make the request; or

(iii) substantial harm will be done to the physical condition of the property which is sought to be protected before the request can effectively be made.

(b) Exclusion of Trespasser. The use of force to prevent or terminate a trespass is not justifiable under this Section if the actor knows that the exclusion of the trespasser will expose him to substantial danger of serious bodily harm.

(c) Resistance of Lawful Re-entry or Recaption. The use of force to prevent an entry or re-entry upon land or the recaption of movable property is not justifiable under this Section, although the actor believes that such re-entry or recaption is unlawful, if:

(i) the re-entry or recaption is made by or on behalf of a person who was actually dispossessed of the property; and

(ii) it is otherwise justifiable under paragraph (1)(b) of this Section.

(d) Use of Deadly Force. The use of deadly force is not justifiable under this Section unless the actor believes that:

(i) the person against whom the force is used is attempting to dispossess him of his dwelling otherwise than under a claim of right to its possession; or

(ii) the person against whom the force is used is attempting to commit or consummate arson, burglary, robbery or other felonious theft or property destruction and either:

(1) has employed or threatened deadly force against or in the presence of the actor; or

(2) the use of force other than deadly force to prevent the commission or the consummation of the crime would expose the actor or another in his presence to substantial danger of serious bodily harm.

(4) Use of Confinement as Protective Force. The justification afforded by this Section extends to the use of confinement as protective force only if the actor takes all reasonable measures to terminate the confinement as soon as he knows that he can do so with safety to the property, unless the person confined has been arrested on a charge of crime.

(5) Use of Device to Protect Property. The justification afforded by this Section extends to the use of a device for the purpose of protecting property only if:

(a) the device is not designed to cause or known to create a substantial risk of causing death or serious bodily harm; and

(b) the use of the particular device to protect the property from entry or trespass is reasonable under the circumstances, as the actor believes them to be; and

(c) the device is one customarily used for such a purpose or reasonable care is taken to make known to probable intruders the fact that it is used.

(6) Use of Force to Pass Wrongful Obstructor. The use of force to pass a person whom the actor believes to be purposely or knowingly and unjustifiably obstructing the actor from going to a place to which he may lawfully go is justifiable, provided that:

(a) the actor believes that the person against whom he uses force has no claim of right to obstruct the actor; and

(b) the actor is not being obstructed from entry or movement on land which he knows to be in the possession or custody of the person obstructing him, or in the possession or custody of another person by whose authority the obstructor acts, unless the circumstances, as the actor believes them to be, are of such urgency that it would not be reasonable to postpone the entry or movement on such land until a court order is obtained; and

(c) the force used is not greater than would be justifiable if the person obstructing the actor were using force against him to prevent his passage.

Section 3.07. Use of Force in Law Enforcement.

(1) Use of Force Justifiable to Effect an Arrest. Subject to the provisions of this Section and of Section 3.09, the use of force upon or toward the person of another is justifiable when the actor is making or assisting in making an arrest and the actor believes that such force is immediately necessary to effect a lawful arrest.

(2) Limitations on the Use of Force.

(a) The use of force is not justifiable under this Section unless:

(i) the actor makes known the purpose of the arrest or believes that it is otherwise known by or cannot reasonably be made known to the person to be arrested; and

(ii) when the arrest is made under a warrant, the warrant is valid or believed by the actor to be valid.

(b) The use of deadly force is not justifiable under this Section unless:

(i) the arrest is for a felony; and

(ii) the person effecting the arrest is authorized to act as a peace officer or is assisting a person whom he believes to be authorized to act as a peace officer; and

(iii) the actor believes that the force employed creates no substantial risk of injury to innocent persons; and

(iv) the actor believes that:

(1) the crime for which the arrest is made involved conduct including the use or threatened use of deadly force; or

(2) there is a substantial risk that the person to be arrested will cause death or serious bodily harm if his apprehension is delayed.

(3) Use of Force to Prevent Escape from Custody. The use of force to prevent the escape of an arrested person from custody is justifiable when the force could justifiably have been employed to effect the arrest under which the person is in custody, except that a guard or other person authorized to act as a peace officer is justified in using any force, including deadly force, which he believes to be immediately necessary to prevent the escape of a person from a jail, prison, or other institution for the detention of persons charged with or convicted of a crime.

(4) Use of Force by Private Person Assisting an Unlawful Arrest.

(a) A private person who is summoned by a peace officer to assist in effecting an unlawful arrest is justified in using any force which he would be justified in using if the arrest were lawful, provided that he does not believe the arrest is unlawful.

(b) A private person who assists another private person in effecting an unlawful arrest, or who, not being summoned, assists a peace officer in effecting an unlawful arrest, is justified in using any force which he would be justified in using if the arrest were lawful, provided that (i) he believes the arrest is lawful, and (ii) the arrest would be lawful if the facts were as he believes them to be.

(5) Use of Force to Prevent Suicide or the Commission of a Crime.

(a) The use of force upon or toward the person of another is justifiable when the actor believes that such force is immediately necessary to prevent such other person from committing suicide, inflicting serious bodily harm upon himself, committing or consummating the commission of a crime involving or threatening bodily harm, damage to or loss of property or a breach of the peace, except that:

(i) any limitations imposed by the other provisions of this Article on the justifiable use of force in self-protection, for the protection of others, the protection of property, the effectuation of an arrest or the prevention of an escape from custody shall apply notwithstanding the criminality of the conduct against which such force is used; and

(ii) the use of deadly force is not in any event justifiable under this Subsection unless:

(1) the actor believes that there is a substantial risk that the person whom he seeks to prevent from committing a crime will cause death or serious bodily harm to another unless the commission or the consummation of the crime is prevented and that the use of such force presents no substantial risk of injury to innocent persons; or

(2) the actor believes that the use of such force is necessary to suppress a riot or mutiny after the rioters or mutineers have been ordered to disperse and warned, in any particular manner that the law may require, that such force will be used if they do not obey.

(b) The justification afforded by this Subsection extends to the use of confinement as preventive force only if the actor takes all reasonable measures to terminate the confinement as soon as he knows that he safely can, unless the person confined has been arrested on a charge of crime.

Section 3.08. Use of Force by Persons with Special Responsibility for Care, Discipline or Safety of Others.

The use of force upon or toward the person of another is justifiable if:

(1) the actor is the parent or guardian or other person similarly responsible for the general care and supervision of a minor or a person acting at the request of such parent, guardian or other responsible person and:

(a) the force is used for the purpose of safeguarding or promoting the welfare of the minor, including the prevention or punishment of his misconduct; and

(b) the force used is not designed to cause or known to create a substantial risk of causing death, serious bodily harm, disfigurement, extreme pain or mental distress or gross degradation; or

(2) the actor is a teacher or a person otherwise entrusted with the care or supervision for a special purpose of a minor and:

(a) the actor believes that the force used is necessary to further such special purpose, including the maintenance of reasonable discipline in a school, class or other group, and that the use of such force is consistent with the welfare of the minor; and

(b) the degree of force, if it had been used by the parent or guardian of the minor, would not be unjustifiable under Subsection (1)(b) of this Section; or

(3) the actor is the guardian or other person similarly responsible for the general care and supervision of an incompetent person; and:

(a) the force is used for the purpose of safeguarding or promoting the welfare of the incompetent person, including the prevention of his misconduct, or, when such incompetent person is in a hospital or other institution for his care and custody, for the maintenance of reasonable discipline in such institution; and

(b) the force used is not designed to cause or known to create a substantial risk of causing death, serious bodily harm, disfigurement, extreme or unnecessary pain, mental distress, or humiliation; or

(4) the actor is a doctor or other therapist or a person assisting him at his direction, and:

(a) the force is used for the purpose of administering a recognized form of treatment which the actor believes to be adapted to promoting the physical or mental health of the patient; and

(b) the treatment is administered with the consent of the patient or, if the patient is a minor or an incompetent person, with the consent of his parent or guardian or other person legally competent to consent in his behalf, or the treatment is administered in an emergency when the actor believes that no one competent to consent can be consulted and that a reasonable person, wishing to safeguard the welfare of the patient, would consent; or

(5) the actor is a warden or other authorized official of a correctional institution, and:

(a) he believes that the force used is necessary for the purpose of enforcing the lawful rules or procedures of the institution, unless his belief in the lawfulness of the rule or procedure sought to be enforced is erroneous and his error is due to ignorance or mistake as to the provisions of the Code, any other provision of the criminal law or the law governing the administration of the institution; and

(b) the nature or degree of force used is not forbidden by Article 303 or 304 of the Code; and

(c) if deadly force is used, its use is otherwise justifiable under this Article; or

(6) the actor is a person responsible for the safety of a vessel or an aircraft or a person acting at his direction, and

(a) he believes that the force used is necessary to prevent interference with the operation of the vessel or aircraft or obstruction of the execution of a lawful order, unless his belief in the lawfulness of the order is erroneous and his error is due to ignorance or mistake as to the law defining his authority; and

(b) if deadly force is used, its use is otherwise justifiable under this Article; or

(7) the actor is a person who is authorized or required by law to maintain order or decorum in a vehicle, train or other carrier or in a place where others are assembled, and:

(a) he believes that the force used is necessary for such purpose; and

(b) the force used is not designed to cause or known to create a substantial risk of causing death, bodily harm, or extreme mental distress.

Section 3.09. Mistake of Law as to Unlawfulness of Force or Legality of Arrest; Reckless or Negligent Use of Otherwise Justifiable Force; Reckless or Negligent Injury or Risk of Injury to Innocent Persons.

(1) The justification afforded by Sections 3.04 to 3.07, inclusive, is unavailable when:

(a) the actor's belief in the unlawfulness of the force or conduct against which he employs protective force or his belief in the lawfulness of an arrest which he endeavors to effect by force is erroneous; and

(b) his error is due to ignorance or mistake as to the provisions of the Code, any other provision of the criminal law or the law governing the legality of an arrest or search.

(2) When the actor believes that the use of force upon or toward the person of another is necessary for any of the purposes for which such belief would establish a justification under Sections 3.03 to 3.08 but the actor is reckless or negligent in having such belief or in acquiring or failing to acquire any knowledge or belief which is material to the justiciability of his use of force, the justification afforded by those Sections is unavailable in a prosecution for an offense for which recklessness or negligence, as the case may be, suffices to establish culpability.

(3) When the actor is justified under Sections 3.03 to 3.08 in using force upon or toward the person of another but he recklessly or negligently injures or creates a risk of injury to innocent persons, the justification afforded by those Sections is unavailable in a prosecution for such recklessness or negligence towards innocent persons.

Section 3.10. Justification in Property Crimes.

Conduct involving the appropriation, seizure or destruction of, damage to, intrusion on or interference with property is justifiable under circumstances which would establish a defense of privilege in a civil action based thereon, unless:

(1) the Code or the law defining the offense deals with the specific situation involved; or

(2) a legislative purpose to exclude the justification claimed otherwise plainly appears.

Section 3.11. Definitions.

In this Article, unless a different meaning plainly is required:

(1) "unlawful force" means force, including confinement, which is employed without the consent of the person against whom it is directed and the employment of which constitutes an offense or actionable tort or would constitute such offense or tort except for a defense (such as the absence of intent, negligence, or mental capacity; duress; youth; or diplomatic status) not amounting to a privilege to use the force. Assent constitutes consent, within the meaning of this Section, whether or not it otherwise is legally effective, except assent to the infliction of death or serious bodily harm.

(2) "deadly force" means force which the actor uses with the purpose of causing or which he knows to create a substantial risk of causing death or serious bodily harm. Purposely firing a firearm in the direction of another person or at a vehicle in which another person is believed to be constitutes deadly force. A threat to cause death or serious bodily harm, by the production of a weapon or other-wise, so long as the actor's purpose is limited to creating an apprehension that he will use deadly force if necessary, does not constitute deadly force;

(3) "dwelling" means any building or structure, though movable or temporary, or a portion thereof, which is for the time being the actor's home or place of lodging.

Article 4. Responsibility.

Section 4.01. Mental Disease or Defect Excluding Responsibility.

(1) A person is not responsible for criminal conduct if at the time of such conduct as a result of mental disease or defect he lacks substantial capacity either to appreciate the criminality [wrongfulness] of his conduct or to conform his conduct to the requirements of law.

(2) As used in this Article, the terms "mental disease or defect" do not include an abnormality manifested only by repeated criminal or otherwise anti-social conduct.

Section 4.02. Evidence of Mental Disease or Defect Admissible When Relevant to Element of the Offense; [Mental Disease or Defect Impairing Capacity as Ground for Mitigation of Punishment in Capital Cases].

(1) Evidence that the defendant suffered from a mental disease or defect is admissible whenever it is relevant to prove that the defendant did or did not have a state of mind which is an element of the offense.

[(2) Whenever the jury or the Court is authorized to determine or to recommend whether or not the defendant shall be sentenced to death or imprisonment upon conviction, evidence that the capacity of the defendant to appreciate the criminality [wrongfulness] of his conduct or to conform his conduct to the requirements of law was impaired as a result of mental disease or defect is admissible in favor of sentence of imprisonment.]

Section 4.03. Mental Disease or Defect Excluding Responsibility Is Affirmative Defense; Requirement of Notice; Form of Verdict and Judgment When Finding of Irresponsibility Is Made.

(1) Mental disease or defect excluding responsibility is an affirmative defense.

(2) Evidence of mental disease or defect excluding responsibility is not admissible unless the defendant, at the time of entering his plea of not guilty or within ten days thereafter or at such later time as the Court may for good cause permit, files a written notice of his purpose to rely on such defense.

(3) When the defendant is acquitted on the ground of mental disease or defect excluding responsibility, the verdict and the judgment shall so state.

Section 4.04. Mental Disease or Defect Excluding Fitness to Proceed.

No person who as a result of mental disease or defect lacks capacity to understand the proceedings against him or to assist in his own defense shall be tried, convicted or sentenced for the commission of an offense so long as such incapacity endures.

Section 4.05. Psychiatric Examination of Defendant with Respect to Mental Disease or Defect.

(1) Whenever the defendant has filed a notice of intention to rely on the defense of mental disease or defect excluding responsibility, or there is reason to

doubt his fitness to proceed, or reason to believe that mental disease or defect of the defendant will otherwise become an issue in the cause, the Court shall appoint at least one qualified psychiatrist or shall request the Superintendent of the Hospital to designate at least one qualified psychiatrist, which designation may be or include himself, to examine and report upon the mental condition of the defendant. The Court may order the defendant to be committed to a hospital or other suitable facility for the purpose of the examination for a period of not exceeding sixty days or such longer period as the Court determines to be necessary for the purpose and may direct that a qualified psychiatrist retained by the defendant be permitted to witness and participate in the examination.

(2) In such examination any method may be employed which is accepted by the medical profession for the examination of those alleged to be suffering from mental disease or defect.

(3) The report of the examination shall include the following: (a) a description of the nature of the examination; (b) a diagnosis of the mental condition of the defendant; (c) if the defendant suffers from a mental disease or defect, an opinion as to his capacity to understand the proceedings against him and to assist in his own defense; (d) when a notice of intention to rely on the defense of irresponsibility has been filed, an opinion as to the extent, if any, to which the capacity of the defendant to appreciate the criminality [wrongfulness] of his conduct or to conform his conduct to the requirements of law was impaired at the time of the criminal conduct charged; and (e) when directed by the Court, an opinion as to the capacity of the defendant to have a particular state of mind which is an element of the offense charged.

If the examination cannot be conducted by reason of the unwillingness of the defendant to participate therein, the report shall so state and shall include, if possible, an opinion as to whether such unwillingness of the defendant was the result of mental disease or defect.

The report of the examination shall be filed [in triplicate] with the clerk of the Court, who shall cause copies to be delivered to the district attorney and to counsel for the defendant.

Section 4.06. Determination of Fitness to Proceed; Effect of Finding of Unfitness; Proceedings if Fitness Is Regained; [Post-Commitment Hearing].

(1) When the defendant's fitness to proceed is drawn in question, the issue shall be determined by the Court. If neither the prosecuting attorney nor counsel for the defendant contests the finding of the report filed pursuant to Section 4.05, the Court may make the determination on the basis of such report. If the finding is contested, the Court shall hold a hearing on the issue. If the report is received in evidence upon such hearing, the party who contests the finding thereof shall have the right to summon and to cross-examine the psychiatrists who joined in the report and to offer evidence upon the issue.

(2) If the Court determines that the defendant lacks fitness to proceed, the proceeding against him shall be suspended, except as provided in Subsection (3) [Subsections (3) and (4)] of this Section, and the Court shall commit him to the

custody of the Commissioner of Mental Hygiene [Public Health or Correction] to be placed in an appropriate institution of the Department of Mental Hygiene [Public Health or Correction] for so long as such unfitness shall endure. When the Court, on its own motion or upon the application of the Commissioner of Mental Hygiene [Public Health or Correction] or the prosecuting attorney, determines, after a hearing if a hearing is requested, that the defendant has regained fitness to proceed, the proceeding shall be resumed. If, however, the Court is of the view that so much time has elapsed since the commitment of the defendant that it would be unjust to resume the criminal proceeding, the Court may dismiss the charge and may order the defendant to be discharged or, subject to the law governing the civil commitment of persons suffering from mental disease or defect, order the defendant to be committed to an appropriate institution of the Department of Mental Hygiene [Public Health].

(3) The fact that the defendant's unfit to proceed does not preclude any legal objection to the prosecution which is susceptible of fair determination prior to trial and without the personal participation of the defendant. [Alternative: (3) At any time within ninety days after commitment as provided in Subsection (2) of this Section, or at any later time with permission of the Court granted for good cause, the defendant or his counsel or the Commissioner of Mental Hygiene [Public Health or Correction] may apply for a special post-commitment hearing. If the application is made by or on behalf of a defendant not represented by counsel, he shall be afforded a reasonable opportunity to obtain counsel, and if he lacks funds to do so, counsel shall be assigned by the Court. The application shall be granted only if the counsel for the defendant satisfies the Court by affidavit or otherwise that as an attorney he has reasonable grounds for a good faith belief that his client has, on the facts and the law, a defense to the charge other than mental disease or defect excluding responsibility.]

[(4) If the motion for a special post-commitment hearing is granted, the hearing shall be by the Court without a jury. No evidence shall be offered at the hearing by either party on the issue of mental disease or defect as a defense to, or in mitigation of, the crime charged. After hearing, the Court may in an appropriate case quash the indictment or other charge, or find it to be defective or insufficient, or determine that it is not proved beyond a reasonable doubt by the evidence, or otherwise terminate the proceedings on the evidence or the law. In any such case, unless all defects in the proceedings are promptly cured, the Court shall terminate the commitment ordered under Subsection (2) of this Section and order the defendant to be discharged or, subject to the law governing the civil commitment of persons suffering from mental disease or defect, order the defendant to be committed to an appropriate institution of the Department of Mental Hygiene [Public Health].]

Section 4.07. Determination of Irresponsibility on Basis of Report; Access to Defendant by Psychiatrist of His Own Choice; Form of Expert Testimony When Issue of Responsibility Is Tried.

(1) If the report filed pursuant to Section 4.05 finds that the defendant at the time of the criminal conduct charged suffered from a mental disease or defect

which substantially impaired his capacity to appreciate the criminality [wrongfulness] of his conduct or to conform his conduct to the requirements of law, and the Court, after a hearing if a hearing is requested by the prosecuting attorney or the defendant, is satisfied that such impairment was sufficient to exclude responsibility, the Court on motion of the defendant shall enter judgment of acquittal on the ground of mental disease or defect excluding responsibility.

(2) When, notwithstanding the report filed pursuant to Section 4.05, the defendant wishes to be examined by a qualified psychiatrist or other expert of his own choice, such examiner shall be permitted to have reasonable access to the defendant for the purposes of such examination.

(3) Upon the trial, the psychiatrists who reported pursuant to Section 4.05 may be called as witnesses by the prosecution, the defendant or the Court. If the issue is being tried before a jury, the jury may be informed that the psychiatrists were designated by the Court or by the Superintendent of the _____ Hospital at the request of the Court, as the case may be. If called by the Court, the witness shall be subject to cross-examination by the prosecution and by the defendant. Both the prosecution and the defendant may summon any other qualified psychiatrist or other expert to testify, but no one who has not examined the defendant shall be competent to testify to an expert opinion with respect to the mental condition or responsibility of the defendant, as distinguished from the validity of the procedure followed by, or the general scientific propositions stated by, another witness.

(4) When a psychiatrist or other expert who has examined the defendant testifies concerning his mental condition, he shall be permitted to make a statement as to the nature of his examination, his diagnosis of the mental condition of the defendant at the time of the commission of the offense charged and his opinion as to the extent, if any, to which the capacity of the defendant to appreciate the criminality [wrongfulness] of his conduct or to conform his conduct to the requirements of law or to have a particular state of mind which is an element of the offense charged was impaired as a result of mental disease or defect at that time. He shall be permitted to make any explanation reasonably serving to clarify his diagnosis and opinion and may be cross-examined as to any matter bearing on his competency or credibility or the validity of his diagnosis or opinion.

Section 4.08. Legal Effect of Acquittal on the Ground of Mental Disease or Defect Excluding Responsibility; Commitment; Release or Discharge.

(1) When a defendant is acquitted on the ground of mental disease or defect excluding responsibility, the Court shall order him to be committed to the custody of the Commissioner of Mental Hygiene [Public Health] to be placed in an appropriate institution for custody, care and treatment.

(2) If the Commissioner of Mental Hygiene [Public Health] is of the view that a person committed to his custody, pursuant to paragraph (1) of this Section, may be discharged or released on condition without danger to himself or to others, he shall make application for the discharge or release of such person in a report to the Court by which such person was committed and shall transmit a copy

of such application and report to the prosecuting attorney of the county [parish] from which the defendant was committed. The Court shall thereupon appoint at least two qualified psychiatrists to examine such person and to report within sixty days, or such longer period as the Court determines to be necessary for the purpose, their opinion as to his mental condition. To facilitate such examination and the proceedings thereon, the Court may cause such person to be confined in any institution located near the place where the Court sits, which may hereafter be designated by the Commissioner of Mental Hygiene [Public Health] as suitable for the temporary detention of irresponsible persons.

(3) If the Court is satisfied by the report filed pursuant to paragraph (2) of this Section and such testimony of the reporting psychiatrists as the Court deems necessary that the committed person may be discharged or released on condition without danger to himself or others, the Court shall order his discharge or his release on such conditions as the Court determines to be necessary. If the Court is not so satisfied, it shall promptly order a hearing to determine whether such person may safely be discharged or released. Any such hearing shall be deemed a civil proceeding and the burden shall be upon the committed person to prove that he may safely be discharged or released. According to the determination of the Court upon the hearing, the committed person shall thereupon be discharged or released on such conditions as the Court determines to be necessary, or shall be recommitted to the custody of the Commissioner of Mental Hygiene [Public Health], subject to discharge or release only in accordance with the procedure prescribed above for a first hearing.

(4) If, within [five] years after the conditional release of a committed person, the Court shall determine, after hearing evidence, that the conditions of release have not been fulfilled and that for the safety of such person or for the safety of others his conditional release should be revoked, the Court shall forthwith order him to be recommitted to the Commissioner of Mental Hygiene [Public Health], subject to discharge or release only in accordance with the procedure prescribed above for a first hearing.

(5) A committed person may make application for his discharge or release to the Court by which he was committed, and the procedure to be followed upon such application shall be the same as that prescribed above in the case of an application by the Commissioner of Mental Hygiene [Public Health]. However, no such application by a committed person need be considered until he has been confined for a period of not less than [six months] from the date of the order of commitment, and if the determination of the Court be adverse to the application, such person shall not be permitted to file a further application until [one year] has elapsed from the date of any preceding hearing on an application for his release or discharge.

Section 4.09. Statements for Purposes of Examination or Treatment Inadmissible Except on Issue of Mental Condition.

A statement made by a person subjected to psychiatric examination or treatment pursuant to Sections 4.05, 4.06 or 4.08 for the purposes of such examination or treatment shall not be admissible in evidence against him in any criminal proceeding on any issue other than that of his mental condition but it shall be admissible upon that issue, whether or not it would otherwise be deemed a privileged communication[, unless such statement constitutes an admission of guilt of the crime charged].

Section 4.10. Immaturity Excluding Criminal Convictions; Transfer of Proceedings to Juvenile Court.

(1) A person shall not be tried for or convicted of an offense if:

(a) at the time of the conduct charged to constitute the offense he was less than sixteen years of age[, in which case the Juvenile Court shall have exclusive jurisdiction*]; or

(b) at the time of the conduct charged to constitute the offense he was sixteen or seventeen years of age, unless:

(i) the Juvenile Court has no jurisdiction over him, or,

(ii) the Juvenile Court has entered an order waiving jurisdiction and consenting to the institution of criminal proceedings against him.

(2) No court shall have jurisdiction to try or convict a person of an offense if criminal proceedings against him are barred by Subsection (1) of this Section. When it appears that a person charged with the commission of an offense may be of such an age that criminal proceedings may be barred under Subsection (1) of this Section, the Court shall hold a hearing thereon, and the burden shall be on the prosecution to establish to the satisfaction of the Court that the criminal proceeding is not barred upon such grounds. If the Court determines that the proceeding is barred, custody of the person charged shall be surrendered to the Juvenile Court, and the case, including all papers and processes relating thereto, shall be transferred.

Article 5. Inchoate Crimes.

Section 5.01. Criminal Attempt.

(1) Definition of Attempt. A person is guilty of an attempt to commit a crime if, acting with the kind of culpability otherwise required for commission of the crime, he:

(a) purposely engages in conduct which would constitute the crime if the attendant circumstances were as he believes them to be; or

(b) when causing a particular result is an element of the crime, does or omits to do anything with the purpose of causing or with the belief that it will cause such result without further conduct on his part; or

(c) purposely does or omits to do anything which, under the circumstances as he believes them to be, is an act or omission constituting a substantial step in a course of conduct planned to culminate in his commission of the crime.

[* The bracketed words are unnecessary if the Juvenile Court Act so provides or is amended accordingly.]

(2) Conduct Which May Be Held Substantial Step Under Subsection (1)(c). Conduct shall not be held to constitute a substantial step under Subsection (1)(c) of this Section unless it is strongly corroborative of the actor's criminal purpose. Without negativing the sufficiency of other conduct, the following, if strongly corroborative of the actor's criminal purpose, shall not be held insufficient as a matter of law:

(a) lying in wait, searching for or following the contemplated victim of the crime;

(b) enticing or seeking to entice the contemplated victim of the crime to go to the place contemplated for its commission;

(c) reconnoitering the place contemplated for the commission of the crime;

(d) unlawful entry of a structure, vehicle or enclosure in which it is contemplated that the crime will be committed;

(e) possession of materials to be employed in the commission of the crime, which are specially designed for such unlawful use or which can serve no lawful purpose of the actor under the circumstances;

(f) possession, collection or fabrication of materials to be employed in the commission of the crime, at or near the place contemplated for its commission, where such possession, collection or fabrication serves no lawful purpose of the actor under the circumstances;

(g) soliciting an innocent agent to engage in conduct constituting an element of the crime.

(3) Conduct Designed to Aid Another in Commission of a Crime. A person who engages in conduct designed to aid another to commit a crime which would establish his complicity under Section 2.06 if the crime were committed by such other person, is guilty of an attempt to commit the crime, although the crime is not committed or attempted by such other person.

(4) Renunciation of Criminal Purpose. When the actor's conduct would otherwise constitute an attempt under Subsection (1)(b) or (1)(c) of this Section, it is an affirmative defense that he abandoned his effort to commit the crime or otherwise prevented its commission, under circumstances manifesting a complete and voluntary renunciation of his criminal purpose. The establishment of such defense does not, however, affect the liability of an accomplice who did not join in such abandonment or prevention. Within the meaning of this Article, renunciation of criminal purpose is not voluntary if it is motivated, in whole or in part, by circumstances, not present or apparent at the inception of the actor's course of conduct, which increase the probability of detection or apprehension or which make more difficult the accomplishment of the criminal purpose. Renunciation is not complete if it is motivated by a decision to postpone the criminal conduct until a more advantageous time or to transfer the criminal effort to another but similar objective or victim.

Section 5.02. Criminal Solicitation.

(1) Definition of Solicitation. A person is guilty of solicitation to commit a crime if with the purpose of promoting or facilitating its commission he commands, encourages or requests another person to engage in specific conduct which would

constitute such crime or an attempt to commit such crime or which would establish his complicity in its commission or attempted commission.

(2) Uncommunicated Solicitation. It is immaterial under Subsection (1) of this Section that the actor fails to communicate with the person he solicits to commit a crime if his conduct was designed to effect such communication.

(3) Renunciation of Criminal Purpose. It is an affirmative defense that the actor, after soliciting another person to commit a crime, persuaded him not to do so or otherwise prevented the commission of the crime, under circumstances manifesting a complete and voluntary renunciation of his criminal purpose.

Section 5.03. Criminal Conspiracy.

(1) Definition of Conspiracy. A person is guilty of conspiracy with another person or persons to commit a crime if with the purpose of promoting or facilitating its commission he:

(a) agrees with such other person or persons that they or one or more of them will engage in conduct which constitutes such crime or an attempt or solicitation to commit such crime; or

(b) agrees to aid such other person or persons in the planning or commission of such crime or of an attempt or solicitation to commit such crime.

(2) Scope of Conspiratorial Relationship. If a person guilty of conspiracy, as defined by Subsection (1) of this Section, knows that a person with whom he conspires to commit a crime has conspired with another person or persons to commit the same crime, he is guilty of conspiring with such other person or persons, whether or not he knows their identity, to commit such crime.

(3) Conspiracy With Multiple Criminal Objectives. If a person conspires to commit a number of crimes, he is guilty of only one conspiracy so long as such multiple crimes are the object of the same agreement or continuous conspiratorial relationship.

(4) Joinder and Venue in Conspiracy Prosecutions.

(a) Subject to the provisions of paragraph (b) of this Subsection, two or more persons charged with criminal conspiracy may be prosecuted jointly if:

(i) they are charged with conspiring with one another; or

(ii) the conspiracies alleged, whether they have the same or different parties, are so related that they constitute different aspects of a scheme of organized criminal conduct.

(b) In any joint prosecution under paragraph (a) of this Subsection:

(i) no defendant shall be charged with a conspiracy in any county [parish or district] other than one in which he entered into such conspiracy or in which an overt act pursuant to such conspiracy was done by him or by a person with whom he conspired; and

(ii) neither the liability of any defendant nor the admissibility against him of evidence of acts or declarations of another shall be enlarged by such joinder; and

(iii) the Court shall order a severance or take a special verdict as to any defendant who so requests, if it deems it necessary or appropriate to promote the fair determination of his guilt or innocence, and shall take any other proper measures to protect the fairness of the trial.

(5) Overt Act. No person may be convicted of conspiracy to commit a crime, other than a felony of the first or second degree, unless an overt act in pursuance of such conspiracy is alleged and proved to have been done by him or by a person with whom he conspired.

(6) Renunciation of Criminal Purpose. It is an affirmative defense that the actor, after conspiring to commit a crime, thwarted the success of the conspiracy, under circumstances manifesting a complete and voluntary renunciation of his criminal purpose.

(7) Duration of Conspiracy. For purposes of Section 1.06(4):

(a) conspiracy is a continuing course of conduct which terminates when the crime or crimes which are its object are committed or the agreement that they be committed is abandoned by the defendant and by those with whom he conspired; and

(b) such abandonment is presumed if neither the defendant nor anyone with whom he conspired does any overt act in pursuance of the conspiracy during the applicable period of limitation; and

(c) if an individual abandons the agreement, the conspiracy is terminated as to him only if and when he advises those with whom he conspired of his abandonment or he informs the law enforcement authorities of the existence of the conspiracy and of his participation therein.

Section 5.04. Incapacity, Irresponsibility or Immunity of Party to Solicitation or Conspiracy.

(1) Except as provided in Subsection (2) of this Section, it is immaterial to the liability of a person who solicits or conspires with another to commit a crime that:

(a) he or the person whom he solicits or with whom he conspires does not occupy a particular position or have a particular characteristic which is an element of such crime, if he believes that one of them does; or

(b) the person whom he solicits or with whom he conspires is irresponsible or has an immunity to prosecution or conviction for the commission of the crime.

(2) It is a defense to a charge of solicitation or conspiracy to commit a crime that if the criminal object were achieved, the actor would not be guilty of a crime under the law defining the offense or as an accomplice under Section 2.06(5) or 2.06(6)(a) or (b).

Section 5.05. Grading of Criminal Attempt, Solicitation and Conspiracy; Mitigation in Cases of Lesser Danger; Multiple Convictions Barred.

(1) Grading. Except as otherwise provided in this Section, attempt, solicitation and conspiracy are crimes of the same grade and degree as the most serious

offense which is attempted or solicited or is an object of the conspiracy. An attempt, solicitation or conspiracy to commit a [capital crime or a] felony of the first degree is a felony of the second degree.

(2) Mitigation. If the particular conduct charged to constitute a criminal attempt, solicitation or conspiracy is so inherently unlikely to result or culminate in the commission of a crime that neither such conduct nor the actor presents a public danger warranting the grading of such offense under this Section, the Court shall exercise its power under Section 6.12 to enter judgment and impose sentence for a crime of lower grade or degree or, in extreme cases, may dismiss the prosecution.

(3) Multiple Convictions. A person may not be convicted of more than one offense defined by this Article for conduct designed to commit or to culminate in the commission of the same crime.

Section 5.06. Possessing Instruments of Crime; Weapons.

(1) Criminal Instruments Generally. A person commits a misdemeanor if he possesses any instrument of crime with purpose to employ it criminally. "Instrument of crime" means:

(a) anything specially made or specially adapted for criminal use; or

(b) anything commonly used for criminal purposes and possessed by the actor under circumstances which do not negative unlawful purpose.

(2) Presumption of Criminal Purpose from Possession of Weapon. If a person possesses a firearm or other weapon on or about his person, in a vehicle occupied by him, or otherwise readily available for use, it is presumed that he had the purpose to employ it criminally, unless:

(a) the weapon is possessed in the actor's home or place of business;

(b) the actor is licensed or otherwise authorized by law to possess such weapon; or

(c) the weapon is of a type commonly used in lawful sport.

"Weapon" means anything readily capable of lethal use and possessed under circumstances not manifestly appropriate for lawful uses which it may have; the term includes a firearm which is not loaded or lacks a clip or other component to render it immediately operable, and components which can readily be assembled into a weapon.

(3) Presumptions as to Possession of Criminal Instruments in Automobiles. Where a weapon or other instrument of crime is found in an automobile, it shall be presumed to be in the possession of the occupant if there is but one. If there is more than one occupant, it shall be presumed to be in the possession of all, except under the following circumstances:

(a) where it is found upon the person of one of the occupants;

(b) where the automobile is not a stolen one and the weapon or instrument is found out of view in a glove compartment, car trunk, or other enclosed customary depository, in which case it shall be presumed to be in the possession of the occupant or occupants who own or have authority to operate the automobile;

(c) in the case of a taxicab, a weapon or instrument found in the passengers' portion of the vehicle shall be presumed to be in the possession of all the passengers, if there are any, and, if not, in the possession of the driver.

Section 5.07. Prohibited Offensive Weapons.

A person commits a misdemeanor if, except as authorized by law, he makes, repairs, sells, or otherwise deals in, uses, or possesses any offensive weapon. "Offensive weapon" means any bomb, machine gun, sawed-off shotgun, firearm specially made or specially adapted for concealment or silent discharge, any blackjack, sandbag, metal knuckles, dagger, or other implement for the infliction of serious bodily injury which serves no common lawful purpose. It is a defense under this Section for the defendant to prove by a preponderance of evidence that he possessed or dealt with the weapon solely as a curio or in a dramatic performance, or that he possessed it briefly in consequence of having found it or taken it from an aggressor, or under circumstances similarly negativing any purpose or likelihood that the weapon would be used unlawfully. The presumptions provided in Section 5.06(3) are applicable to prosecutions under this Section.

Article 6. Authorized Disposition of Offenders.

Section 6.01. Degrees of Felonies.

(1) Felonies defined by this Code are classified, for the purpose of sentence, into three degrees, as follows:
(a) felonies of the first degree;
(b) felonies of the second degree;
(c) felonies of the third degree. A felony is of the first or second degree when it is so designated by the Code. A crime declared to be a felony, without specification of degree, is of the third degree.
(2) Notwithstanding any other provision of law, a felony defined by any statute of this State other than this Code shall constitute for the purpose of sentence a felony of the third degree.

Section 6.02. Sentence in Accordance with Code; Authorized Dispositions.

(1) No person convicted of an offense shall be sentenced otherwise than in accordance with this Article.
[(2) The Court shall sentence a person who has been convicted of murder to death or imprisonment, in accordance with Section 210.6.]
(3) Except as provided in Subsection (2) of this Section and subject to the applicable provisions of the Code, the Court may suspend the imposition of sentence on a person who has been convicted of a crime, may order him to be

committed in lieu of sentence, in accordance with Section 6.13, or may sentence him as follows:

(a) to pay a fine authorized by Section 6.03; or

(b) to be placed on probation [, and, in the case of a person convicted of a felony or misdemeanor to imprisonment for a term fixed by the Court not exceeding thirty days to be served as a condition of probation]; or

(c) to imprisonment for a term authorized by Sections 6.05, 6.06, 6.07, 6.08, 6.09, or 7.06; or

(d) to fine and probation or fine and imprisonment, but not to probation and imprisonment[, except as authorized in paragraph (b) of this Subsection].

(4) The Court may suspend the imposition of sentence on a person who has been convicted of a violation or may sentence him to pay a fine authorized by Section 6.03.

(5) This Article does not deprive the Court of any authority conferred by law to decree a forfeiture of property, suspend or cancel a license, remove a person from office, or impose any other civil penalty. Such a judgment or order may be included in the sentence.

Section 6.03. Fines.

A person who has been convicted of an offense may be sentenced to pay a fine not exceeding:

(1) $10,000, when the conviction is of a felony of the first or second degree;

(2) $5,000, when the conviction is of a felony of the third degree;

(3) $1,000, when the conviction is of a misdemeanor;

(4) $500, when the conviction is of a petty misdemeanor or a violation;

(5) any higher amount equal to double the pecuniary gain derived from the offense by the offender;

(6) any higher amount specifically authorized by statute.

Section 6.04. Penalties Against Corporations and Unincorporated Association; Forfeiture of Corporate Charter or Revocation of Certificate Authorizing Foreign Corporation to Do Business in the State.

(1) The Court may suspend the sentence of a corporation or an unincorporated association which has been convicted of an offense or may sentence it to pay a fine authorized by Section 6.03.

(2) (a) The [prosecuting attorney] is authorized to institute civil proceedings in the appropriate court of general jurisdiction to forfeit the charter of a corporation organized under the laws of this State or to revoke the certificate authorizing a foreign corporation to conduct business in this State. The Court may order the charter forfeited or the certificate revoked upon finding (i) that the board of

directors or a high managerial agent acting in behalf of the corporation has, in conducting the corporation's affairs, purposely engaged in a persistent course of criminal conduct and (ii) that for the prevention of future criminal conduct of the same character, the public interest requires the charter of the corporation to be forfeited and the corporation to be dissolved or the certificate to be revoked.

(b) When a corporation is convicted of a crime or a high managerial agent of a corporation, as defined in Section 2.07, is convicted of a crime committed in the conduct of the affairs of the corporation, the Court, in sentencing the corporation or the agent, may direct the [prosecuting attorney] to institute proceedings authorized by paragraph (a) of this Subsection.

(c) The proceedings authorized by paragraph (a) of this Subsection shall be conducted in accordance with the procedures authorized by law for the involuntary dissolution of a corporation or the revocation of the certificate authorizing a foreign corporation to conduct business in this State. Such proceedings shall be deemed additional to any other proceedings authorized by law for the purpose of forfeiting the charter of a corporation or revoking the certificate of a foreign corporation.

Section 6.05. Young Adult Offenders.

(1) Specialized Correctional Treatment. A young adult offender is a person convicted of a crime who, at the time of sentencing, is sixteen but less than twenty-two years of age. A young adult offender who is sentenced to a term of imprisonment which may exceed thirty days [alternatives: (1) ninety days; (2) one year] shall be committed to the custody of the Division of Young Adult Correction of the Department of Correction, and shall receive, as far as practicable, such special and individualized correctional and rehabilitative treatment as may be appropriate to his needs.

(2) Special Term. A young adult offender convicted of a felony may, in lieu of any other sentence of imprisonment authorized by this Article, be sentenced to a special term of imprisonment without a minimum and with a maximum of four years, regardless of the degree of the felony involved, if the Court is of the opinion that such special term is adequate for his correction and rehabilitation and will not jeopardize the protection of the public.

[(3) Removal of Disabilities; Vacation of Conviction.

(a) In sentencing a young adult offender to the special term provided by this Section or to any sentence other than one of imprisonment, the Court may order that so long as he is not convicted of another felony, the judgment shall not constitute a conviction for the purposes of any disqualification or disability imposed by law upon conviction of a crime.

(b) When any young adult offender is unconditionally discharged from probation or parole before the expiration of the maximum term thereof, the Court may enter an order vacating the judgment of conviction.]

[(4) Commitment for Observation. If, after pre-sentence investigation, the Court desires additional information concerning a young adult offender before imposing sentence, it may order that he be committed, for a period not exceeding ninety days, to the custody of the Division of Young Adult Correction of the

Department of Correction for observation and study at an appropriate reception or classification center. Such Division of the Department of Correction and the [Young Adult Division of the] Board of Parole shall advise the Court of their findings and recommendations on or before the expiration of such ninety-day period.]

Section 6.06. Sentence of Imprisonment for Felony; Ordinary Terms.

A person who has been convicted of a felony may be sentenced to imprisonment, as follows:

(1) in the case of a felony of the first degree, for a term the minimum of which shall be fixed by the Court at not less than one year nor more than ten years, and the maximum of which shall be life imprisonment;

(2) in the case of a felony of the second degree, for a term the minimum of which shall be fixed by the Court at not less than one year nor more than three years, and the maximum of which shall be ten years;

(3) in the case of a felony of the third degree, for a term the minimum of which shall be fixed by the Court at not less than one year nor more than two years, and the maximum of which shall be five years.

Alternate Section 6.06. Sentence of Imprisonment for Felony; Ordinary Terms.

A person who has been convicted of a felony may be sentenced to imprisonment, as follows:

(1) in the case of a felony of the first degree, for a term the minimum of which shall be fixed by the Court at not less than one year nor more than ten years, and the maximum at not more than twenty years or at life imprisonment;

(2) in the case of a felony of the second degree, for a term the minimum of which shall be fixed by the Court at not less than one year nor more than three years, and the maximum at not more than ten years;

(3) in the case of a felony of the third degree, for a term the minimum of which shall be fixed by the Court at not less than one year nor more than two years, and the maximum at not more than five years. No sentence shall be imposed under this Section of which the minimum is longer than one-half the maximum, or, when the maximum is life imprisonment, longer than ten years.

Section 6.07. Sentence of Imprisonment for Felony; Extended Terms.

In the cases designated in Section 7.03, a person who has been convicted of a felony may be sentenced to an extended term of imprisonment, as follows:

(1) in the case of a felony of the first degree, for a term the minimum of which shall be fixed by the Court at not less than five years nor more than ten years, and the maximum of which shall be life imprisonment;

(2) in the case of a felony of the second degree, for a term the minimum of which shall be fixed by the Court at not less than one year nor more than five years,

and the maximum of which shall be fixed by the Court at not less than ten years nor more than twenty years;

(3) in the case of a felony of the third degree, for a term the minimum of which shall be fixed by the Court at not less than one year nor more than three years, and the maximum of which shall be fixed by the Court at not less than five years nor more than ten years.

Section 6.08. Sentence of Imprisonment for Misdemeanors and Petty Misdemeanors; Ordinary Terms.

A person who has been convicted of a misdemeanor or a petty misdemeanor may be sentenced to imprisonment for a definite term which shall be fixed by the Court and shall not exceed one year in the case of a misdemeanor or thirty days in the case of a petty misdemeanor.

Section 6.09. Sentence of Imprisonment for Misdemeanors and Petty Misdemeanors; Extended Terms.

(1) In the cases designated in Section 7.04, a person who has been convicted of a misdemeanor or a petty misdemeanor may be sentenced to an extended term of imprisonment, as follows:

(a) in the case of a misdemeanor, for a term the minimum of which shall be fixed by the Court at not more than one year and the maximum of which shall be three years;

(b) in the case of a petty misdemeanor, for a term the minimum of which shall be fixed by the Court at not more than six months and the maximum of which shall be two years.

(2) No such sentence for an extended term shall be imposed unless:

(a) the Director of Correction has certified that there is an institution in the Department of Correction, or in a county, city [or other appropriate political subdivision of the State] which is appropriate for the detention and correctional treatment of such misdemeanants or petty misdemeanants, and that such institution is available to receive such commitments; and

(b) the [Board of Parole] [Parole Administrator] has certified that the Board of Parole is able to visit such institution and to assume responsibility for the release of such prisoners on parole and for their parole supervision.

Section 6.10. First Release of All Offenders on Parole; Sentence of Imprisonment Includes Separate Parole Term; Length of Parole Term; Length of Recommitment and Re-parole After Revocation of Parole; Final Unconditional Release.

(1) First Release of All Offenders on Parole. An offender sentenced to an indefinite term of imprisonment in excess of one year under Section 6.05, 6.06,

6.07, 6.09 or 7.06 shall be released conditionally on parole at or before the expiration of the maximum of such term, in accordance with Article 305.

(2) Sentence of Imprisonment Includes Separate Parole Term; Length of Parole Term. A sentence to an indefinite term of imprisonment in excess of one year under Section 6.05, 6.06, 6.07, 6.09 or 7.06 includes as a separate portion of the sentence a term of parole or of recommitment for violation of the conditions of parole which governs the duration of parole or recommitment after the offender's first conditional release on parole. The minimum of such term is one year and the maximum is five years, unless the sentence was imposed under Section 6.05(2) or Section 6.09, in which case the maximum is two years.

(3) Length of Recommitment and Re-Parole After Revocation of Parole. If an offender is recommitted upon revocation of his parole, the term of further imprisonment upon such recommitment and of any subsequent re-parole or recommitment under the same sentence shall be fixed by the Board of Parole but shall not exceed in aggregate length the unserved balance of the maximum parole term provided by Subsection (2) of this Section.

(4) Final Unconditional Release. When the maximum of his parole term has expired or he has been sooner discharged from parole under Section 305.12, an offender shall be deemed to have served his sentence and shall be released unconditionally.

Section 6.11. Place of Imprisonment.

(1) When a person is sentenced to imprisonment for an indefinite term with a maximum in excess of one year, the Court shall commit him to the custody of the Department of Correction [or other single department or agency] for the term of his sentence and until release in accordance with law.

(2) When a person is sentenced to imprisonment for a definite term, the Court shall designate the institution or agency to which he is committed for the term of his sentence and until released in accordance with law.

Section 6.12. Reduction of Conviction by Court to Lesser Degree of Felony or to Misdemeanor.

If, when a person has been convicted of a felony, the Court, having regard to the nature and circumstances of the crime and to the history and character of the defendant, is of the view that it would be unduly harsh to sentence the offender in accordance with the Code, the Court may enter judgment of conviction for a lesser degree of felony or for a misdemeanor and impose sentence accordingly.

Section 6.13. Civil Commitment in Lieu of Prosecution or of Sentence.

(1) When a person prosecuted for a [felony of the third degree,] misdemeanor or petty misdemeanor is a chronic alcoholic, narcotic addict [or prostitute] or person suffering from mental abnormality and the Court is authorized by law to

order the civil commitment of such person to a hospital or other institution for medical, psychiatric or other rehabilitative treatment, the Court may order such commitment and dismiss the prosecution. The order of commitment may be made after conviction, in which event the Court may set aside the verdict or judgment of conviction and dismiss the prosecution.

(2) The Court shall not make an order under Subsection (1) of this Section unless it is of the view that it will substantially further the rehabilitation of the defendant and will not jeopardize the protection of the public.

Article 7. Authority of Court in Sentencing.

Section 7.01. Criteria for Withholding Sentence of Imprisonment and for Placing Defendant on Probation.

(1) The Court shall deal with a person who has been convicted of a crime without imposing sentence of imprisonment unless, having regard to the nature and circumstances of the crime and the history, character and condition of the defendant, it is of the opinion that his imprisonment is necessary for protection of the public because:

(a) there is undue risk that during the period of a suspended sentence or probation the defendant will commit another crime; or

(b) the defendant is in need of correctional treatment that can be provided most effectively by his commitment to an institution; or

(c) a lesser sentence will depreciate the seriousness of the defendant's crime.

(2) The following grounds, while not controlling the discretion of the Court, shall be accorded weight in favor of withholding sentence of imprisonment:

(a) the defendant's criminal conduct neither caused nor threatened serious harm;

(b) the defendant did not contemplate that his criminal conduct would cause or threaten serious harm;

(c) the defendant acted under a strong provocation;

(d) there were substantial grounds tending to excuse or justify the defendant's criminal conduct, though failing to establish a defense;

(e) the victim of the defendant's criminal conduct induced or facilitated its commission;

(f) the defendant has compensated or will compensate the victim of his criminal conduct for the damage or injury that he sustained;

(g) the defendant has no history of prior delinquency or criminal activity or has led a law-abiding life for a substantial period of time before the commission of the present crime;

(h) the defendant's criminal conduct was the result of circumstances unlikely to recur;

(i) the character and attitudes of the defendant indicate that he is unlikely to commit another crime;

(j) the defendant is particularly likely to respond affirmatively to probationary treatment;

(k) the imprisonment of the defendant would entail excessive hardship to himself or his dependents.

(3) When a person who has been convicted of a crime is not sentenced to imprisonment, the Court shall place him on probation if he is in need of the supervision, guidance, assistance or direction that the probation service can provide.

Section 7.02. Criteria for Imposing Fines.

(1) The Court shall not sentence a defendant only to pay a fine, when any other disposition is authorized by law, unless having regard to the nature and circumstances of the crime and to the history and character of the defendant, it is of the opinion that the fine alone suffices for protection of the public.

(2) The Court shall not sentence a defendant to pay a fine in addition to a sentence of imprisonment or probation unless:

(a) the defendant has derived a pecuniary gain from the crime; or

(b) the Court is of opinion that a fine is specially adapted to deterrence of the crime involved or to the correction of the offender.

(3) The Court shall not sentence a defendant to pay a fine unless:

(a) the defendant is or will be able to pay the fine; and

(b) the fine will not prevent the defendant from making restitution or reparation to the victim of the crime.

(4) In determining the amount and method of payment of a fine, the Court shall take into account the financial resources of the defendant and the nature of the burden that its payment will impose.

Section 7.03. Criteria for Sentence of Extended Term of Imprisonment; Felonies.

The Court may sentence a person who has been convicted of a felony to an extended term of imprisonment if it finds one or more of the grounds specified in this Section. The finding of the Court shall be incorporated in the record.

(1) The defendant is a persistent offender whose commitment for an extended term is necessary for protection of the public. The Court shall not make such a finding unless the defendant is over twenty-one years of age and has previously been convicted of two felonies or of one felony and two misdemeanors, committed at different times when he was over [insert Juvenile Court age] years of age.

(2) The defendant is a professional criminal whose commitment for an extended term is necessary for protection of the public. The Court shall not make such a finding unless the defendant is over twenty-one years of age and:

(a) the circumstances of the crime show that the defendant has knowingly devoted himself to criminal activity as a major source of livelihood; or

(b) the defendant has substantial income or resources not explained to be derived from a source other than criminal activity.

(3) The defendant is a dangerous, mentally abnormal person whose commitment for an extended term is necessary for protection of the public. The Court shall not make such a finding unless the defendant has been subjected to a psychiatric examination resulting in the conclusions that his mental condition is gravely abnormal; that his criminal conduct has been characterized by a pattern of repetitive or compulsive behavior or by persistent aggressive behavior with heedless indifference to consequences; and that such condition makes him a serious danger to others.

(4) The defendant is a multiple offender whose criminality was so extensive that a sentence of imprisonment for an extended term is warranted. The Court shall not make such a finding unless:

 (a) the defendant is being sentenced for two or more felonies, or is already under sentence of imprisonment for felony, and the sentences of imprisonment involved will run concurrently under Section 7.06; or

 (b) the defendant admits in open court the commission of one or more other felonies and asks that they be taken into account when he is sentenced; and

 (c) the longest sentences of imprisonment authorized for each of the defendant's crimes, including admitted crimes taken into account, if made to run consecutively would exceed in length the minimum and maximum of the extended term imposed.

Section 7.04. Criteria for Sentence of Extended Term of Imprisonment; Misdemeanors and Petty Misdemeanors.

The Court may sentence a person who has been convicted of a misdemeanor or petty misdemeanor to an extended term of imprisonment if it finds one or more of the grounds specified in this Section. The finding of the Court shall be incorporated in the record.

(1) The defendant is a persistent offender whose commitment for an extended term is necessary for protection of the public. The Court shall not make such a finding unless the defendant has previously been convicted of two crimes, committed at different times when he was over [insert Juvenile Court age] years of age.

(2) The defendant is a professional criminal whose commitment for an extended term is necessary for protection of the public. The Court shall not make such a finding unless:

 (a) the circumstances of the crime show that the defendant has knowingly devoted himself to criminal activity as a major source of livelihood; or

 (b) the defendant has substantial income or resources not explained to be derived from a source other than criminal activity.

(3) The defendant is a chronic alcoholic, narcotic addict, prostitute or person of abnormal mental condition who requires rehabilitative treatment for a substantial period of time. The Court shall not make such a finding unless, with respect to the particular category to which the defendant belongs, the Director of Correction has certified that there is a specialized institution or facility which is satisfactory for the rehabilitative treatment of such persons and which otherwise meets the requirements of Section 6.09, Subsection (2).

(4) The defendant is a multiple offender whose criminality was so extensive that a sentence of imprisonment for an extended term is warranted. The Court shall not make such a finding unless:

(a) the defendant is being sentenced for a number of misdemeanors or petty misdemeanors or is already under sentence of imprisonment for crimes of such grades, or admits in open court the commission of one or more such crimes and asks that they be taken into account when he is sentenced; and

(b) maximum fixed sentences of imprisonment for each of the defendant's crimes, including admitted crimes taken into account, if made to run consecutively, would exceed in length the maximum period of the extended term imposed.

Section 7.05. Former Conviction in Another Jurisdiction; Definition and Proof of Conviction; Sentence Taking Into Account Admitted Crimes Bars Subsequent Conviction for Such Crimes.

(1) For purposes of paragraph (1) of Section 7.03 or 7.04, a conviction of the commission of a crime in another jurisdiction shall constitute a previous conviction. Such conviction shall be deemed to have been of a felony if sentence of death or of imprisonment in excess of one year was authorized under the law of such other jurisdiction, of a misdemeanor if sentence of imprisonment in excess of thirty days but not in excess of a year was authorized and of a petty misdemeanor if sentence of imprisonment for not more than thirty days was authorized.

(2) An adjudication by a court of competent jurisdiction that the defendant committed a crime constitutes a conviction for purposes of Sections 7.03 to 7.05 inclusive, although sentence or the execution thereof was suspended, provided that the time to appeal has expired and that the defendant was not pardoned on the ground of innocence.

(3) Prior conviction may be proved by any evidence, including fingerprint records made in connection with arrest, conviction or imprisonment, that reasonably satisfies the Court that the defendant was convicted.

(4) When the defendant has asked that other crimes admitted in open court be taken into account when he is sentenced and the Court has not rejected such request, the sentence shall bar the prosecution or conviction of the defendant in this State for any such admitted crime.

Section 7.06. Multiple Sentences; Concurrent and Consecutive Terms.

(1) Sentences of Imprisonment for More Than One Crime. When multiple sentences of imprisonment are imposed on a defendant for more than one crime, including a crime for which a previous suspended sentence or sentence of probation has been revoked, such multiple sentences shall run concurrently or consecutively as the Court determines at the time of sentence, except that:

(a) a definite and an indefinite term shall run concurrently and both sentences shall be satisfied by service of the indefinite term; and

(b) the aggregate of consecutive definite terms shall not exceed one year; and

(c) the aggregate of consecutive indefinite terms shall not exceed in minimum or maximum length the longest extended term authorized for the highest grade and degree of crime for which any of the sentences was imposed; and

(d) not more than one sentence for an extended term shall be imposed.

(2) Sentences of Imprisonment Imposed at Different Times. When a defendant who has previously been sentenced to imprisonment is subsequently sentenced to another term for a crime committed prior to the former sentence, other than a crime committed while in custody:

(a) the multiple sentences imposed shall so far as possible conform to Subsection (1) of this Section; and

(b) whether the Court determines that the terms shall run concurrently or consecutively, the defendant shall be credited with time served in imprisonment on the prior sentence in determining the permissible aggregate length of the term or terms remaining to be served; and

(c) when a new sentence is imposed on a prisoner who is on parole, the balance of the parole term on the former sentence shall be deemed to run during the period of the new imprisonment.

(3) Sentence of Imprisonment for Crime Committed While on Parole. When a defendant is sentenced to imprisonment for a crime committed while on parole in this State, such term of imprisonment and any period of re-imprisonment that the Board of Parole may require the defendant to serve upon the revocation of his parole shall run concurrently, unless the Court orders them to run consecutively.

(4) Multiple Sentences of Imprisonment in Other Cases. Except as otherwise provided in this Section, multiple terms of imprisonment shall run concurrently or consecutively as the Court determines when the second or subsequent sentence is imposed.

(5) Calculation of Concurrent and Consecutive Terms of Imprisonment.

(a) When indefinite terms run concurrently, the shorter minimum terms merge in and are satisfied by serving the longest minimum term and the shorter maximum terms merge in and are satisfied by discharge of the longest maximum term.

(b) When indefinite terms run consecutively, the minimum terms are added to arrive at an aggregate minimum to be served equal to the sum of all minimum terms and the maximum terms are added to arrive at an aggregate maximum equal to the sum of all maximum terms.

(c) When a definite and an indefinite term run consecutively, the period of the definite term is added to both the minimum and maximum of the indefinite term and both sentences are satisfied by serving the indefinite term.

(6) Suspension of Sentence or Probation and Imprisonment; Multiple Terms of Suspension and Probation. When a defendant is sentenced for more than one offense or a defendant already under sentence is sentenced for another offense committed prior to the former sentence:

(a) the Court shall not sentence to probation a defendant who is under sentence of imprisonment [with more than thirty days to run] or impose a sentence of probation and a sentence of imprisonment[, except as authorized by Section 6.02(3)(b)]; and

(b) multiple periods of suspension or probation shall run concurrently from the date of the first such disposition; and

(c) when a sentence of imprisonment is imposed for an indefinite term, the service of such sentence shall satisfy a suspended sentence on another count or a prior suspended sentence or sentence to probation; and

(d) when a sentence of imprisonment is imposed for a definite term, the period of a suspended sentence on another count or a prior suspended sentence or sentence to probation shall run during the period of such imprisonment.

(7) Offense Committed While Under Suspension of Sentence or Probation. When a defendant is convicted of an offense committed while under suspension of sentence or on probation and such suspension or probation is not revoked:

(a) if the defendant is sentenced to imprisonment for an indefinite term, the service of such sentence shall satisfy the prior suspended sentence or sentence to probation; and

(b) if the defendant is sentenced to imprisonment for a definite term, the period of the suspension or probation shall not run during the period of such imprisonment; and

(c) if sentence is suspended or the defendant is sentenced to probation, the period of such suspension or probation shall run concurrently with or consecutively to the remainder of the prior periods, as the Court determines at the time of sentence.

Section 7.07. Procedure on Sentence; Pre-sentence Investigation and Report; Remand for Psychiatric Examination; Transmission of Records to Department of Correction.

(1) The Court shall not impose sentence without first ordering a pre-sentence investigation of the defendant and according due consideration to a written report of such investigation where:

(a) the defendant has been convicted of a felony; or

(b) the defendant is less than twenty-two years of age and has been convicted of a crime; or

(c) the defendant will be [placed on probation or] sentenced to imprisonment for an extended term.

(2) The Court may order a pre-sentence investigation in any other case.

(3) The pre-sentence investigation shall include an analysis of the circumstances attending the commission of the crime, the defendant's history of delinquency or criminality, physical and mental condition, family situation and background, economic status, education, occupation and personal habits and any other matters that the probation officer deems relevant or the Court directs to be included.

(4) Before imposing sentence, the Court may order the defendant to submit to psychiatric observation and examination for a period of not exceeding sixty days or such longer period as the Court determines to be necessary for the purpose. The defendant may be remanded for this purpose to any available clinic or mental hospital or the Court may appoint a qualified psychiatrist to make the examination. The report of the examination shall be submitted to the Court.

(5) Before imposing sentence, the Court shall advise the defendant or his counsel of the factual contents and the conclusions of any pre-sentence investigation or psychiatric examination and afford fair opportunity, if the defendant so requests, to controvert them. The sources of confidential information need not, however, be disclosed.

(6) The Court shall not impose a sentence of imprisonment for an extended term unless the ground therefor has been established at a hearing after the conviction of the defendant and on written notice to him of the ground proposed. Subject to the limitation of Subsection (5) of this Section, the defendant shall have the right to hear and controvert the evidence against him and to offer evidence upon the issue.

(7) If the defendant is sentenced to imprisonment, a copy of the report of any pre-sentence investigation or psychiatric examination shall be transmitted forthwith to the Department of Correction [or other state department or agency] or, when the defendant is committed to the custody of specific institution, to such institution.

Section 7.08. Commitment for Observation; Sentence of Imprisonment for Felony Deemed Tentative for Period of One Year; Re-sentence on Petition of Commissioner of Correction.

(1) If, after pre-sentence investigation, the Court desires additional information concerning an offender convicted of a felony or misdemeanor before imposing sentence, it may order that he be committed, for a period not exceeding ninety days, to the custody of the Department of Correction, or, in the case of a young adult offender, to the custody of the Division of Young Adult Correction, for observation and study at an appropriate reception or classification center. The Department and the Board of Parole, or the Young Adult Divisions thereof, shall advise the Court of their findings and recommendations on or before the expiration of such ninety-day period. If the offender is thereafter sentenced to imprisonment, the period of such commitment for observation shall be deducted from the maximum term and from the minimum, if any, of such sentence.

(2) When a person has been sentenced to imprisonment upon conviction of a felony, whether for an ordinary or extended term, the sentence shall be deemed tentative, to the extent provided in this Section, for the period of one year following the date when the offender is received in custody by the Department of Correction [or other state department or agency].

(3) If, as a result of the examination and classification by the Department of Correction [or other state department or agency] of a person under sentence of imprisonment upon conviction of a felony, the Commissioner of Correction

[or other department head] is satisfied that the sentence of the Court may have been based upon a misapprehension as to the history, character or physical or mental condition of the offender, the Commissioner, during the period when the offender's sentence is deemed tentative under Subsection (2) of this Section shall file in the sentencing Court a petition to re-sentence the offender. The petition shall set forth the information as to the offender that is deemed to warrant his re-sentence and may include a recommendation as to the sentence to be imposed.

(4) The Court may dismiss a petition filed under Subsection (3) of this Section without a hearing if it deems the information set forth insufficient to warrant reconsideration of the sentence. If the Court is of the view that the petition warrants such reconsideration, a copy of the petition shall be served on the offender, who shall have the right to be heard on the issue and to be represented by counsel.

(5) When the Court grants a petition filed under Subsection (3) of this Section, it shall re-sentence the offender and may impose any sentence that might have been imposed originally for the felony of which the defendant was convicted. The period of his imprisonment prior to re-sentence and any reduction for good behavior to which he is entitled shall be applied in satisfaction of the final sentence.

(6) For all purposes other than this Section, a sentence of imprisonment has the same finality when it is imposed that it would have if this Section were not in force.

(7) Nothing in this Section shall alter the remedies provided by law for vacating or correcting an illegal sentence.

Section 7.09. Credit for Time of Detention Prior to Sentence; Credit for Imprisonment Under Earlier Sentence for the Same Crime.

(1) When a defendant who is sentenced to imprisonment has previously been detained in any state or local correctional or other institution following his [conviction of] [arrest for] the crime for which such sentence is imposed, such period of detention following his [conviction] [arrest] shall be deducted from the maximum term, and from the minimum, if any, of such sentence. The officer having custody of the defendant shall furnish a certificate to the Court at the time of sentence, showing the length of such detention of the defendant prior to sentence in any state or local correctional or other institution, and the certificate shall be annexed to the official records of the defendant's commitment.

(2) When a judgment of conviction is vacated and a new sentence is thereafter imposed upon the defendant for the same crime, the period of detention and imprisonment theretofore served shall be deducted from the maximum term, and from the minimum, if any, of the new sentence. The officer having custody of the defendant shall furnish a certificate to the Court at the time of sentence, showing the period of imprisonment served under the original sentence, and the certificate shall be annexed to the official records of the defendant's new commitment.

Part II. Definition of Specific Crimes
Offenses Involving Danger to the Person
Article 210. Criminal Homicide

Section 210.0. Definitions.

In Articles 210-213, unless a different meaning plainly is required:

(1) "human being" means a person who has been born and is alive;

(2) "bodily injury" means physical pain, illness or any impairment of physical condition;

(3) "serious bodily injury" means bodily injury which creates a substantial risk of death or which causes serious, permanent disfigurement, or protracted loss or impairment of the function of any bodily member or organ;

(4) "deadly weapon" means any firearm, or other weapon, device, instrument, material or substance, whether animate or inanimate, which in the manner it is used or is intended to be used is known to be capable of producing death or serious bodily injury.

Section 210.1. Criminal Homicide.

(1) A person is guilty of criminal homicide if he purposely, knowingly, recklessly or negligently causes the death of another human being.

(2) Criminal homicide is murder, manslaughter or negligent homicide.

Section 210.2. Murder.

(1) Except as provided in Section 210.3(1)(b), criminal homicide constitutes murder when:

(a) it is committed purposely or knowingly; or

(b) it is committed recklessly under circumstances manifesting extreme indifference to the value of human life. Such recklessness and indifference are presumed if the actor is engaged or is an accomplice in the commission of, or an attempt to commit, or flight after committing or attempting to commit robbery, rape or deviate sexual intercourse by force or threat of force, arson, burglary, kidnapping or felonious escape.

(2) Murder is a felony of the first degree [but a person convicted of murder may be sentenced to death, as provided in Section 210.6].

Section 210.3. Manslaughter.

(1) Criminal homicide constitutes manslaughter when:

(a) it is committed recklessly; or

(b) a homicide which would otherwise be murder is committed under the influence of extreme mental or emotional disturbance for which there is reasonable explanation or excuse. The reasonableness of such explanation or excuse shall be determined from the viewpoint of a person in the actor's situation under the circumstances as he believes them to be.

(2) Manslaughter is a felony of the second degree.

Section 210.4. Negligent Homicide.

(1) Criminal homicide constitutes negligent homicide when it is committed negligently.

(2) Negligent homicide is a felony of the third degree.

Section 210.5. Causing or Aiding Suicide.

(1) Causing Suicide as Criminal Homicide. A person may be convicted of criminal homicide for causing another to commit suicide only if he purposely causes such suicide by force, duress or deception.

(2) Aiding or Soliciting Suicide as an Independent Offense. A person who purposely aids or solicits another to commit suicide is guilty of a felony of the second degree if his conduct causes such suicide or an attempted suicide, and otherwise of a misdemeanor.

[Section 210.6. Sentence of Death for Murder; Further Proceedings to Determine Sentence.]

(1) Death Sentence Excluded. When a defendant is found guilty of murder, the Court shall impose sentence for a felony of the first degree if it is satisfied that:

(a) none of the aggravating circumstances enumerated in Subsection (3) of this Section was established by the evidence at the trial or will be established if further proceedings are initiated under Subsection (2) of this Section; or

(b) substantial mitigating circumstances, established by the evidence at the trial, call for leniency; or

(c) the defendant, with the consent of the prosecuting attorney and the approval of the Court, pleaded guilty to murder as a felony of the first degree; or

(d) the defendant was under 18 years of age at the time of the commission of the crime; or

(e) the defendant's physical or mental condition calls for leniency; or

(f) although the evidence suffices to sustain the verdict, it does not foreclose all doubt respecting the defendant's guilt.

(2) Determination by Court or by Court and Jury. Unless the Court imposes sentence under Subsection (1) of this Section, it shall conduct a separate proceeding to determine whether the defendant should be sentenced for a felony of the

first degree or sentenced to death. The proceeding shall be conducted before the Court alone if the defendant was convicted by a Court sitting without a jury or upon his plea of guilty or if the prosecuting attorney and the defendant waive a jury with respect to sentence. In other cases it shall be conducted before the Court sitting with the jury which determined the defendant's guilt or, if the Court for good cause shown discharges that jury, with a new jury empaneled for the purpose.

In the proceeding, evidence may be presented as to any matter that the Court deems relevant to sentence, including but not limited to the nature and circumstances of the crime, the defendant's character, background, history, mental and physical condition and any of the aggravating or mitigating circumstances enumerated in Subsections (3) and (4) of this Section. Any such evidence, not legally privileged, which the Court deems to have probative force, may be received, regardless of its admissibility under the exclusionary rules of evidence, provided that the defendant's counsel is accorded a fair opportunity to rebut such evidence. The prosecuting attorney and the defendant or his counsel shall be permitted to present argument for or against sentence of death.

The determination whether sentence of death shall be imposed shall be in the discretion of the Court, except that when the proceeding is conducted before the Court sitting with a jury, the Court shall not impose sentence of death unless it submits to the jury the issue whether the defendant should be sentenced to death or to imprisonment and the jury returns a verdict that the sentence should be death. If the jury is unable to reach a unanimous verdict, the Court shall dismiss the jury and impose sentence for a felony of the first degree.

The Court, in exercising its discretion as to sentence, and the jury, in determining upon its verdict, shall take into account the aggravating and mitigating circumstances enumerated in Subsections (3) and (4) and any other facts that it deems relevant, but it shall not impose or recommend sentence of death unless it finds one of the aggravating circumstances enumerated in Subsection (3) and further finds that there are no mitigating circumstances sufficiently substantial to call for leniency. When the issue is submitted to the jury, the Court shall so instruct and also shall inform the jury of the nature of the sentence of imprisonment that may be imposed, including its implication with respect to possible release upon parole, if the jury verdict is against sentence of death.

Alternative formulation of Subsection (2):

(2) Determination by Court. Unless the Court imposes sentence under Subsection (1) of this Section, it shall conduct a separate proceeding to determine whether the defendant should be sentenced for a felony of the first degree or sentenced to death. In the proceeding, the Court, in accordance with Section 7.07, shall consider the report of the pre-sentence investigation and, if a psychiatric examination has been ordered, the report of such examination. In addition, evidence may be presented as to any matter that the Court deems relevant to sentence, including but not limited to the nature and circumstances of the crime, the defendant's character, background, history, mental and physical condition and any of the aggravating or mitigating circumstances enumerated in Subsections (3) and (4) of this Section. Any such evidence, not legally privileged, which the Court

deems to have probative force, may be received, regardless of its admissibility under the exclusionary rules of evidence, provided that the defendant's counsel is accorded a fair opportunity to rebut such evidence. The prosecuting attorney and the defendant or his counsel shall be permitted to present argument for or against sentence of death.

The determination whether sentence of death shall be imposed shall be in the discretion of the Court. In exercising such discretion, the Court shall take into account the aggravating and mitigating circumstances enumerated in Subsections (3) and (4) and any other facts that it deems relevant but shall not impose sentence of death unless it finds one of the aggravating circumstances enumerated in Subsection (3) and further finds that there are no mitigating circumstances sufficiently substantial to call for leniency.

(3) Aggravating Circumstances.

(a) The murder was committed by a convict under sentence of imprisonment.

(b) The defendant was previously convicted of another murder or of a felony involving the use or threat of violence to the person.

(c) At the time the murder was committed the defendant also committed another murder.

(d) The defendant knowingly created a great risk of death to many persons.

(e) The murder was committed while the defendant was engaged or was an accomplice in the commission of, or an attempt to commit, or flight after committing or attempting to commit robbery, rape or deviate sexual intercourse by force or threat of force, arson, burglary or kidnapping.

(f) The murder was committed for the purpose of avoiding or preventing a lawful arrest or effecting an escape from lawful custody.

(g) The murder was committed for pecuniary gain.

(h) The murder was especially heinous, atrocious or cruel, manifesting exceptional depravity.

(4) Mitigating Circumstances.

(a) The defendant has no significant history of prior criminal activity.

(b) The murder was committed while the defendant was under the influence of extreme mental or emotional disturbance.

(c) The victim was a participant in the defendant's homicidal conduct or consented to the homicidal act.

(d) The murder was committed under circumstances which the defendant believed to provide a moral justification or extenuation for his conduct.

(e) The defendant was an accomplice in a murder committed by another person and his participation in the homicidal act was relatively minor.

(f) The defendant acted under duress or under the domination of another person.

(g) At the time of the murder, the capacity of the defendant to appreciate the criminality [wrongfulness] of his conduct or to conform his conduct to the requirements of law was impaired as a result of mental disease or defect or intoxication.

(h) The youth of the defendant at the time of the crime.

Article 211. Assault; Reckless Endangering; Threats.

Section 211.0. Definitions.

In this Article, the definitions given in Section 210.0 apply unless a different meaning plainly is required.

Section 211.1. Assault.

(1) Simple Assault. A person is guilty of assault if he:

(a) attempts to cause or purposely, knowingly or recklessly causes bodily injury to another; or

(b) negligently causes bodily injury to another with a deadly weapon; or

(c) attempts by physical menace to put another in fear of imminent serious bodily injury. Simple assault is a misdemeanor unless committed in a fight or scuffle entered into by mutual consent, in which case it is a petty misdemeanor.

(2) Aggravated Assault. A person is guilty of aggravated assault if he:

(a) attempts to cause serious bodily injury to another, or causes such injury purposely, knowingly or recklessly under circumstances manifesting extreme indifference to the value of human life; or

(b) attempts to cause or purposely or knowingly causes bodily injury to another with a deadly weapon. Aggravated assault under paragraph (a) is a felony of the second degree; aggravated assault under paragraph (b) is a felony of the third degree.

Section 211.2. Recklessly Endangering Another Person.

A person commits a misdemeanor if he recklessly engages in conduct which places or may place another person in danger of death or serious bodily injury. Recklessness and danger shall be presumed where a person knowingly points a firearm at or in the direction of another, whether or not the actor believed the firearm to be loaded.

Section 211.3. Terroristic Threats.

A person is guilty of a felony of the third degree if he threatens to commit any crime of violence with purpose to terrorize another or to cause evacuation of a building, place of assembly, or facility of public transportation, or otherwise to cause serious public inconvenience, or in reckless disregard of the risk of causing such terror or inconvenience.

Article 212. Kidnapping and Related Offenses; Coercion.

Section 212.0. Definitions.

In this Article, the definitions given in Section 210.0 apply unless a different meaning plainly is required.

Section 212.1. Kidnapping.

A person is guilty of kidnapping if he unlawfully removes another from his place of residence or business, or a substantial distance from the vicinity where he is found, or if he unlawfully confines another for a substantial period in a place of isolation, with any of the following purposes:

(a) to hold for ransom or reward, or as a shield or hostage; or

(b) to facilitate commission of any felony or flight thereafter; or

(c) to inflict bodily injury on or to terrorize the victim or another; or

(d) to interfere with the performance of any governmental or political function. Kidnapping is a felony of the first degree unless the actor voluntarily releases the victim alive and in a safe place prior to trial, in which case it is a felony of the second degree. A removal or confinement is unlawful within the meaning of this Section if it is accomplished by force, threat or deception, or, in the case of a person who is under the age of 14 or incompetent, if it is accomplished without the consent of a parent, guardian or other person responsible for general supervision of his welfare.

Section 212.2. Felonious Restraint.

A person commits a felony of the third degree if he knowingly:

(a) restrains another unlawfully in circumstances exposing him to risk of serious bodily injury; or

(b) holds another in a condition of involuntary servitude.

Section 212.3. False Imprisonment.

A person commits a misdemeanor if he knowingly restrains another unlawfully so as to interfere substantially with his liberty.

Section 212.4. Interference with Custody.

(1) Custody of Children. A person commits an offense if he knowingly or recklessly takes or entices any child under the age of 18 from the custody of its parent, guardian or other lawful custodian, when he has no privilege to do so. It is an affirmative defense that:

(a) the actor believed that his action was necessary to preserve the child from danger to its welfare; or

(b) the child, being at the time not less than 14 years old, was taken away at its own instigation without enticement and without purpose to commit a criminal offense with or against the child. Proof that the child was below the critical age gives rise to a presumption that the actor knew the child's age or acted in reckless disregard thereof. The offense is a misdemeanor unless the actor, not being a parent or person in equivalent relation to the child, acted with knowledge that his conduct would cause serious alarm for the child's safety, or in reckless disregard of a likelihood of causing such alarm, in which case the offense is a felony of the third degree.

(2) Custody of Committed Persons. A person is guilty of a misdemeanor if he knowingly or recklessly takes or entices any committed person away from lawful custody when he is not privileged to do so. "Committed person" means, in addition to anyone committed under judicial warrant, any orphan, neglected or delinquent child, mentally defective or insane person, or other dependent or incompetent person entrusted to another's custody by or through a recognized social agency or otherwise by authority of law.

Section 212.5. Criminal Coercion.

(1) Offense Defined. A person is guilty of criminal coercion if, with purpose unlawfully to restrict another's freedom of action to his detriment, he threatens to:

  (a) commit any criminal offense; or

  (b) accuse anyone of a criminal offense; or

  (c) expose any secret tending to subject any person to hatred, contempt or ridicule, or to impair his credit or business repute; or (d) take or withhold action as an official, or cause an official to take or withhold action. It is an affirmative defense to prosecution based on paragraphs (b), (c) or (d) that the actor believed the accusation or secret to be true or the proposed official action justified and that his purpose was limited to compelling the other to behave in a way reasonably related to the circumstances which were the subject of the accusation, exposure or proposed official action, as by desisting from further misbehavior, making good a wrong done, refraining from taking any action or responsibility for which the actor believes the other disqualified.

(2) Grading. Criminal coercion is a misdemeanor unless the threat is to commit a felony or the actor's purpose is felonious, in which cases the offense is a felony of the third degree.

Article 213. Sexual Offenses.

Section 213.0. Definitions.

In this Article, unless a different meaning plainly is required:

(1) the definitions given in Section 210.0 apply;

(2) "Sexual intercourse" includes intercourse per os or per anum, with some penetration however slight; emission is not required;

(3) "Deviate sexual intercourse" means sexual intercourse per os or per anum between human beings who are not husband and wife, and any form of sexual intercourse with an animal.

Section 213.1. Rape and Related Offenses.

(1) Rape. A male who has sexual intercourse with a female not his wife is guilty of rape if:

  (a) he compels her to submit by force or by threat of imminent death, serious bodily injury, extreme pain or kidnapping, to be inflicted on anyone; or

(b) he has substantially impaired her power to appraise or control her conduct by administering or employing without her knowledge drugs, intoxicants or other means for the purpose of preventing resistance; or

(c) the female is unconscious; or

(d) the female is less than 10 years old. Rape is a felony of the second degree unless (i) in the course thereof the actor inflicts serious bodily injury upon anyone, or (ii) the victim was not a voluntary social companion of the actor upon the occasion of the crime and had not previously permitted him sexual liberties, in which cases the offense is a felony of the first degree.

(2) Gross Sexual Imposition. A male who has sexual intercourse with a female not his wife commits a felony of the third degree if:

(a) he compels her to submit by any threat that would prevent resistance by a woman of ordinary resolution; or

(b) he knows that she suffers from a mental disease or defect which renders her incapable of appraising the nature of her conduct; or

(c) he knows that she is unaware that a sexual act is being committed upon her or that she submits because she mistakenly supposes that he is her husband.

Section 213.2. Deviate Sexual Intercourse by Force or Imposition.

(1) By Force or Its Equivalent. A person who engages in deviate sexual intercourse with another person, or who causes another to engage in deviate sexual intercourse, commits a felony of the second degree if:

(a) he compels the other person to participate by force or by threat of imminent death, serious bodily injury, extreme pain or kidnapping, to be inflicted on anyone; or

(b) he has substantially impaired the other person's power to appraise or control his conduct, by administering or employing without the knowledge of the other person drugs, intoxicants or other means for the purpose of preventing resistance; or

(c) the other person is unconscious; or

(d) the other person is less than 10 years old.

(2) By Other Imposition. A person who engages in deviate sexual intercourse with another person, or who causes another to engage in deviate sexual intercourse, commits a felony of the third degree if:

(a) he compels the other person to participate by any threat that would prevent resistance by a person of ordinary resolution; or

(b) he knows that the other person suffers from a mental disease or defect which renders him incapable of appraising the nature of his conduct; or

(c) he knows that the other person submits because he is unaware that a sexual act is being committed upon him.

Section 213.3. Corruption of Minors and Seduction.

(1) Offense Defined. A male who has sexual intercourse with a female not his wife, or any person who engages in deviate sexual intercourse or causes another to engage in deviate sexual intercourse, is guilty of an offense if:

(a) the other person is less than [16] years old and the actor is at least [4] years older than the other person; or

(b) the other person is less than 21 years old and the actor is his guardian or otherwise responsible for general supervision of his welfare; or

(c) the other person is in custody of law or detained in a hospital or other institution and the actor has supervisory or disciplinary authority over him; or

(d) the other person is a female who is induced to participate by a promise of marriage which the actor does not mean to perform.

(2) Grading. An offense under paragraph (a) of Subsection (1) is a felony of the third degree. Otherwise an offense under this section is a misdemeanor.

Section 213.4. Sexual Assault.

A person who has sexual contact with another not his spouse, or causes such other to have sexual contact with him, is guilty of sexual assault, a misdemeanor, if:

(1) he knows that the contact is offensive to the other person; or

(2) he knows that the other person suffers from a mental disease or defect which renders him or her incapable of appraising the nature of his or her conduct; or

(3) he knows that the other person is unaware that a sexual act is being committed; or

(4) the other person is less than 10 years old; or

(5) he has substantially impaired the other person's power to appraise or control his or her conduct, by administering or employing without the other's knowledge drugs, intoxicants or other means for the purpose of preventing resistance; or

(6) the other person is less than [16] years old and the actor is at least [4] years older than the other person; or

(7) the other person is less than 21 years old and the actor is his guardian or otherwise responsible for general supervision of his welfare; or

(8) the other person is in custody of law or detained in a hospital or other institution and the actor has supervisory or disciplinary authority over him. Sexual contact is any touching of the sexual or other intimate parts of the person for the purpose of arousing or gratifying sexual desire.

Section 213.5. Indecent Exposure.

A person commits a misdemeanor if, for the purpose of arousing or gratifying sexual desire of himself or of any person other than his spouse, he exposes his genitals under circumstances in which he knows his conduct is likely to cause affront or alarm.

Section 213.6. Provisions Generally Applicable to Article 213.

(1) Mistake as to Age. Whenever in this Article the criminality of conduct depends on a child's being below the age of 10, it is no defense that the actor did not know the child's age, or reasonably believed the child to be older than 10. When criminality depends on the child's being below a critical age other than 10, it is a defense for the actor to prove by a preponderance of the evidence that he reasonably believed the child to be above the critical age.

(2) Spouse Relationships. Whenever in this Article the definition of an offense excludes conduct with a spouse, the exclusion shall be deemed to extend to persons living as man and wife, regardless of the legal status of their relationship. The exclusion shall be inoperative as respects spouses living apart under a decree of judicial separation. Where the definition of an offense excludes conduct with a spouse or conduct by a woman, this shall not preclude conviction of a spouse or woman as accomplice in a sexual act which he or she causes another person, not within the exclusion, to perform.

(3) Sexually Promiscuous Complainants. It is a defense to prosecution under Section 213.3 and paragraphs (6), (7) and (8) of Section 213.4 for the actor to prove by a preponderance of the evidence that the alleged victim had, prior to the time of the offense charged, engaged promiscuously in sexual relations with others.

(4) Prompt Complaint. No prosecution may be instituted or maintained under this Article unless the alleged offense was brought to the notice of public authority within [3] months of its occurrence or, where the alleged victim was less than [16] years old or otherwise incompetent to make complaint, within [3] months after a parent, guardian or other competent person specially interested in the victim learns of the offense.

(5) Testimony of Complainants. No person shall be convicted of any felony under this Article upon the uncorroborated testimony of the alleged victim. Corroboration may be circumstantial. In any prosecution before a jury for an offense under this Article, the jury shall be instructed to evaluate the testimony of a victim or complaining witness with special care in view of the emotional involvement of the witness and the difficulty of determining the truth with respect to alleged sexual activities carried out in private.

Offenses Against Property.

Article 220. Arson, Criminal Mischief, and Other Property Destruction.

Section 220.1. Arson and Related Offenses.

(1) Arson. A person is guilty of arson, a felony of the second degree, if he starts a fire or causes an explosion with the purpose of:

    (a) destroying a building or occupied structure of another; or

    (b) destroying or damaging any property, whether his own or another's, to collect insurance for such loss. It shall be an affirmative defense to prosecution under this paragraph that the actor's conduct did not recklessly endanger any building or occupied structure of another or place any other person in danger of death or bodily injury.

(2) Reckless Burning or Exploding. A person commits a felony of the third degree if he purposely starts a fire or causes an explosion, whether on his own property or another's, and thereby recklessly:

(a) places another person in danger of death or bodily injury; or

(b) places a building or occupied structure of another in danger of damage or destruction.

(3) Failure to Control or Report Dangerous Fire. A person who knows that a fire is endangering life or a substantial amount of property of another and fails to take reasonable measures to put out or control the fire, when he can do so without substantial risk to himself, or to give a prompt fire alarm, commits a misdemeanor if:

(a) he knows that he is under an official, contractual, or other legal duty to prevent or combat the fire; or

(b) the fire was started, albeit lawfully, by him or with his assent, or on property in his custody or control.

(4) Definitions. "Occupied structure" means any structure, vehicle or place adapted for overnight accommodation of persons, or for carrying on business therein, whether or not a person is actually present. Property is that of another, for the purposes of this section, if anyone other than the actor has a possessory or proprietary interest therein. If a building or structure is divided into separately occupied units, any unit not occupied by the actor is an occupied structure of another.

Section 220.2. Causing or Risking Catastrophe.

(1) Causing Catastrophe. A person who causes a catastrophe by explosion, fire, flood, avalanche, collapse of building, release of poison gas, radioactive material or other harmful or destructive force or substance, or by any other means of causing potentially widespread injury or damage, commits a felony of the second degree if he does so purposely or knowingly, or a felony of the third degree if he does so recklessly.

(2) Risking Catastrophe. A person is guilty of a misdemeanor if he recklessly creates a risk of catastrophe in the employment of fire, explosives or other dangerous means listed in Subsection (1).

(3) Failure to Prevent Catastrophe. A person who knowingly or recklessly fails to take reasonable measures to prevent or mitigate a catastrophe commits a misdemeanor if:

(a) he knows that he is under an official, contractual or other legal duty to take such measures; or

(b) he did or assented to the act causing or threatening the catastrophe.

Section 220.3. Criminal Mischief.

(1) Offense Defined. A person is guilty of criminal mischief if he:

(a) damages tangible property of another purposely, recklessly, or by negligence in the employment of fire, explosives, or other dangerous means listed in Section 220.2(1); or

(b) purposely or recklessly tampers with tangible property of another so as to endanger person or property; or

(c) purposely or recklessly causes another to suffer pecuniary loss by deception or threat.

(2) Grading. Criminal mischief is a felony of the third degree if the actor purposely causes pecuniary loss in excess of $5,000, or a substantial interruption or impairment of public communication, transportation, supply of water, gas or power, or other public service. It is a misdemeanor if the actor purposely causes pecuniary loss in excess of $100, or a petty misdemeanor if he purposely or recklessly causes pecuniary loss in excess of $25. Otherwise criminal mischief is a violation.

Article 221. Burglary and Other Criminal Intrusion.

Section 221.0. Definitions.

In this Article, unless a different meaning plainly is required:

(1) "occupied structure" means any structure, vehicle or place adapted for overnight accommodation of persons, or for carrying on business therein, whether or not a person is actually present.

(2) "night" means the period between thirty minutes past sunset and thirty minutes before sunrise.

Section 221.1. Burglary.

(1) Burglary Defined. A person is guilty of burglary if he enters a building or occupied structure, or separately secured or occupied portion thereof, with purpose to commit a crime therein, unless the premises are at the time open to the public or the actor is licensed or privileged to enter. It is an affirmative defense to prosecution for burglary that the building or structure was abandoned.

(2) Grading. Burglary is a felony of the second degree if it is perpetrated in the dwelling of another at night, or if, in the course of committing the offense, the actor:

(a) purposely, knowingly or recklessly inflicts or attempts to inflict bodily injury on anyone; or

(b) is armed with explosives or a deadly weapon. Otherwise, burglary is a felony of the third degree. An act shall be deemed "in the course of committing" an offense if it occurs in an attempt to commit the offense or in flight after the attempt or commission.

(3) Multiple Convictions. A person may not be convicted both for burglary and for the offense which it was his purpose to commit after the burglarious entry or for an attempt to commit that offense, unless the additional offense constitutes a felony of the first or second degree.

Section 221.2. Criminal Trespass.

(1) Buildings and Occupied Structures. A person commits an offense if, knowing that he is not licensed or privileged to do so, he enters or surreptitiously remains in any building or occupied structure, or separately secured or occupied portion thereof. An offense under this Subsection is a misdemeanor if it is committed in a dwelling at night. Otherwise it is a petty misdemeanor.

(2) Defiant Trespasser. A person commits an offense if, knowing that he is not licensed or privileged to do so, he enters or remains in any place as to which notice against trespass is given by:

(a) actual communication to the actor; or

(b) posting in a manner prescribed by law or reasonably likely to come to the attention of intruders; or

(c) fencing or other enclosure manifestly designed to exclude intruders. An offense under this Subsection constitutes a petty misdemeanor if the offender defies an order to leave personally communicated to him by the owner of the premises or other authorized person. Otherwise it is a violation.

(3) Defenses. It is an affirmative defense to prosecution under this Section that:

(a) a building or occupied structure involved in an offense under Subsection (1) was abandoned; or

(b) the premises were at the time open to members of the public and the actor complied with all lawful conditions imposed on access to or remaining in the premises; or

(c) the actor reasonably believed that the owner of the premises, or other person empowered to license access thereto, would have licensed him to enter or remain.

Article 222. Robbery.

Section 222.1. Robbery.

(1) Robbery Defined. A person is guilty of robbery if, in the course of committing a theft, he:

(a) inflicts serious bodily injury upon another; or

(b) threatens another with or purposely puts him in fear of immediate serious bodily injury; or

(c) commits or threatens immediately to commit any felony of the first or second degree. An act shall be deemed "in the course of committing a theft" if it occurs in an attempt to commit theft or in flight after the attempt or commission.

(2) Grading. Robbery is a felony of the second degree, except that it is a felony of the first degree if in the course of committing the theft the actor attempts to kill anyone, or purposely inflicts or attempts to inflict serious bodily injury.

Article 223. Theft and Related Offenses.

Section 223.0. Definitions.

In this Article, unless a different meaning plainly is required:

(1) "deprive" means:

(a) to withhold property of another permanently or for so extended a period as to appropriate a major portion of its economic value, or with intent to restore only upon payment of reward or other compensation; or

(b) to dispose of the property so as to make it unlikely that the owner will recover it.

(2) "financial institution" means a bank, insurance company, credit union, building and loan association, investment trust or other organization held out to the public as a place of deposit of funds or medium of savings or collective investment.

(3) "government" means the United States, any State, county, municipality, or other political unit, or any department, agency or subdivision of any of the foregoing, or any corporation or other association carrying out the functions of government.

(4) "movable property" means property the location of which can be changed, including things growing on, affixed to, or found in land, and documents although the rights represented thereby have no physical location. "Immovable property" is all other property.

(5) "obtain" means:

(a) in relation to property, to bring about a transfer or purported transfer of a legal interest in the property, whether to the obtainer or another; or

(b) in relation to labor or service, to secure performance thereof.

(6) "property" means anything of value, including real estate, tangible and intangible personal property, contract rights, choses-in-action and other interests in or claims to wealth, admission or transportation tickets, captured or domestic animals, food and drink, electric or other power.

(7) "property of another" includes property in which any person other than the actor has an interest which the actor is not privileged to infringe, regardless of the fact that the actor also has an interest in the property and regardless of the fact that the other person might be precluded from civil recovery because the property was used in an unlawful transaction or was subject to forfeiture as contraband. Property in possession of the actor shall not be deemed property of another who has only a security interest therein, even if legal title is in the creditor pursuant to a conditional sales contract or other security agreement.

Section 223.1. Consolidation of Theft Offenses; Grading; Provisions Applicable to Theft Generally.

(1) Consolidation of Theft Offenses. Conduct denominated theft in this Article constitutes a single offense. An accusation of theft may be supported by evidence that it was committed in any manner that would be theft under this Article, notwithstanding the specification of a different manner in the indictment or information, subject only to the power of the Court to ensure fair trial by granting a continuance or other appropriate relief where the conduct of the defense would be prejudiced by lack of fair notice or by surprise.

(2) Grading of Theft Offenses.

(a) Theft constitutes a felony of the third degree if the amount involved exceeds $500, or if the property stolen is a firearm, automobile, airplane, motorcycle, motorboat, or other motor-propelled vehicle, or in the case of theft by receiving stolen property, if the receiver is in the business of buying or selling stolen property.

(b) Theft not within the preceding paragraph constitutes a misdemeanor, except that if the property was not taken from the person or by threat, or in breach of a fiduciary obligation, and the actor proves by a preponderance of the evidence that the amount involved was less than $50, the offense constitutes a petty misdemeanor.

(c) The amount involved in a theft shall be deemed to be the highest value, by any reasonable standard, of the property or services which the actor stole or attempted to steal. Amounts involved in thefts committed pursuant to one scheme or course of conduct, whether from the same person or several persons, may be aggregated in determining the grade of the offense.

(3) Claim of Right. It is an affirmative defense to prosecution for theft that the actor:

(a) was unaware that the property or service was that of another; or

(b) acted under an honest claim of right to the property or service involved or that he had a right to acquire or dispose of it as he did; or

(c) took property exposed for sale, intending to purchase and pay for it promptly, or reasonably believing that the owner, if present, would have consented.

(4) Theft from Spouse. It is no defense that theft was from the actor's spouse, except that misappropriation of household and personal effects, or other property normally accessible to both spouses, is theft only if it occurs after the parties have ceased living together.

Section 223.2. Theft by Unlawful Taking or Disposition.

(1) Movable Property. A person is guilty of theft if he unlawfully takes, or exercises unlawful control over, movable property of another with purpose to deprive him thereof.

(2) Immovable Property. A person is guilty of theft if he unlawfully transfers immovable property of another or any interest therein with purpose to benefit himself or another not entitled thereto.

Section 223.3. Theft by Deception.

A person is guilty of theft if he purposely obtains property of another by deception. A person deceives if he purposely:

(1) creates or reinforces a false impression, including false impressions as to law, value, intention or other state of mind; but deception as to a person's intention to perform a promise shall not be inferred from the fact alone that he did not subsequently perform the promise; or

(2) prevents another from acquiring information which would affect his judgment of a transaction; or

(3) fails to correct a false impression which the deceiver previously created or reinforced, or which the deceiver knows to be influencing another to whom he stands in a fiduciary or confidential relationship; or

(4) fails to disclose a known lien, adverse claim or other legal impediment to the enjoyment of property which he transfers or encumbers in consideration for the property obtained, whether such impediment is or is not valid, or is or is not a matter of official record.

The term "deceive" does not, however, include falsity as to matters having no pecuniary significance, or puffing by statements unlikely to deceive ordinary persons in the group addressed.

Section 223.4. Theft by Extortion.

A person is guilty of theft if he purposely obtains property of another by threatening to:

(1) inflict bodily injury on anyone or commit any other criminal offense; or

(2) accuse anyone of a criminal offense; or

(3) expose any secret tending to subject any person to hatred, contempt or ridicule, or to impair his credit or business repute; or

(4) take or withhold action as an official, or cause an official to take or withhold action; or

(5) bring about or continue a strike, boycott or other collective unofficial action, if the property is not demanded or received for the benefit of the group in whose interest the actor purports to act; or

(6) testify or provide information or withhold testimony or information with respect to another's legal claim or defense; or

(7) inflict any other harm which would not benefit the actor. It is an affirmative defense to prosecution based on paragraphs (2), (3) or (4) that the property obtained by threat of accusation, exposure, lawsuit or other invocation of official action was honestly claimed as restitution or indemnification for harm done in the circumstances to which such accusation, exposure, lawsuit or other official action relates, or as compensation for property or lawful services.

Section 223.5. Theft of Property Lost, Mislaid, or Delivered by Mistake.

A person who comes into control of property of another that he knows to have been lost, mislaid, or delivered under a mistake as to the nature or amount of the property or the identity of the recipient is guilty of theft if, with purpose to deprive the owner thereof, he fails to take reasonable measures to restore the property to a person entitled to have it.

Section 223.6. Receiving Stolen Property.

(1) Receiving. A person is guilty of theft if he purposely receives, retains, or disposes of movable property of another knowing that it has been stolen, or believing that it has probably been stolen, unless the property is received, retained, or disposed with purpose to restore it to the owner. "Receiving" means acquiring possession, control or title, or lending on the security of the property.

(2) Presumption of Knowledge. The requisite knowledge or belief is presumed in the case of a dealer who:

(a) is found in possession or control of property stolen from two or more persons on separate occasions; or

(b) has received stolen property in another transaction within the year preceding the transaction charged; or

(c) being a dealer in property of the sort received, acquires it for a consideration which he knows is far below its reasonable value.

"Dealer" means a person in the business of buying or selling goods including a pawnbroker.

Section 223.7. Theft of Services.

(1) A person is guilty of theft is he purposely obtains services which he knows are available only for compensation, by deception or threat, or by false token or other means to avoid payment for the service. "Services" includes labor, professional service, transportation, telephone or other public service, accommodation in hotels, restaurants or elsewhere, admission to exhibitions, use of vehicles or other movable property. Where compensation for service is ordinarily paid immediately upon the rendering of such service, as in the case of hotels and restaurants, refusal to pay or absconding without payment or offer to pay gives rise to a presumption that the service was obtained by deception as to intention to pay.

(2) A person commits theft if, having control over the disposition of services of others, to which he is not entitled, he knowingly diverts such services to his own benefit or to the benefit of another not entitled thereto.

Section 223.8. Theft by Failure to Make Required Disposition of Funds Received.

A person who purposely obtains property upon agreement, or subject to a known legal obligation, to make specified payment or other disposition, whether from such property or its proceeds or from his own property to be reserved in equivalent amount, is guilty of theft if he deals with the property obtained as his own and fails to make the required payment or disposition. The foregoing applies notwithstanding that it may be impossible to identify particular property as belonging to the victim at the time of the actor's failure to make the required payment or disposition. An officer or employee of the government or of a financial institution is presumed: (i) to know any legal obligation relevant to his criminal liability under this Section, and (ii) to have dealt with the property as his own if he fails to pay or account upon lawful demand, or if an audit reveals a shortage or falsification of accounts.

Section 223.9. Unauthorized Use of Automobiles and Other Vehicles.

A person commits a misdemeanor if he operates another's automobile, airplane, motorcycle, motorboat, or other motor-propelled vehicle without consent of the owner. It is an affirmative defense to prosecution under this Section that the actor reasonably believed that the owner would have consented to the operation had he known of it.

Article 224. Forgery and Fraudulent Practices.

Section 224.0. Definitions.

In this Article, the definitions given in Section 223.0 apply unless a different meaning plainly is required.

Section 224.1. Forgery.

(1) Definition. A person is guilty of forgery if, with purpose to defraud or injure anyone, or with knowledge that he is facilitating a fraud or injury to be perpetrated by anyone, the actor:

(a) alters any writing of another without his authority; or

(b) makes, completes, executes, authenticates, issues or transfers any writing so that it purports to be the act of another who did not authorize that act, or to have been executed at a time or place or in a numbered sequence other than was in fact the case, or to be a copy of an original when no such original existed; or

(c) utters any writing which he knows to be forged in a manner specified in paragraphs (a) or (b). "Writing" includes printing or any other method of recording information, money, coins, tokens, stamps, seals, credit cards, badges, trade-marks, and other symbols of value, right, privilege, or identification.

(2) Grading. Forgery is a felony of the second degree if the writing is or purports to be part of an issue of money, securities, postage or revenue stamps, or other instruments issued by the government, or part of an issue of stock, bonds or other instruments representing interests in or claims against any property or enterprise. Forgery is a felony of the third degree if the writing is or purports to be a will, deed, contract, release, commercial instrument, or other document evidencing, creating, transferring, altering, terminating, or otherwise affecting legal relations. Otherwise forgery is a misdemeanor.

Section 224.2. Simulating Objects of Antiquity, Rarity, Etc.

A person commits a misdemeanor if, with purpose to defraud anyone or with knowledge that he is facilitating a fraud to be perpetrated by anyone, he makes, alters or utters any object so that it appears to have value because of antiquity, rarity, source, or authorship which it does not possess.

Section 224.3. Fraudulent Destruction, Removal or Concealment of Recordable Instruments.

A person commits a felony of the third degree if, with purpose to deceive or injure anyone, he destroys, removes or conceals any will, deed, mortgage, security instrument or other writing for which the law provides public recording.

Section 224.4. Tampering with Records.

A person commits a misdemeanor if, knowing that he has no privilege to do so, he falsifies, destroys, removes or conceals any writing or record, with purpose to deceive or injure anyone or to conceal any wrongdoing.

Section 224.5. Bad Checks.

A person who issues or passes a check or similar sight order for the payment of money, knowing that it will not be honored by the drawee, commits a misdemeanor. For the purposes of this Section as well as in any prosecution for theft committed by means of a bad check, an issuer is presumed to know that the check or order (other than a postdated check or order) would not be paid, if:

(1) the issuer had no account with the drawee at the time the check or order was issued; or

(2) payment was refused by the drawee for lack of funds, upon presentation within 30 days after issue, and the issuer failed to make good within 10 days after receiving notice of that refusal.

Section 224.6. Credit Cards.

A person commits an offense if he uses a credit card for the purpose of obtaining property or services with knowledge that:

(1) the card is stolen or forged; or

(2) the card has been revoked or cancelled; or

(3) for any other reason his use of the card is unauthorized by the issuer.

It is an affirmative defense to prosecution under paragraph (3) if the actor proves by a preponderance of the evidence that he had the purpose and ability to meet all obligations to the issuer arising out of his use of the card. "Credit card" means a writing or other evidence of an undertaking to pay for property or services delivered or rendered to or upon the order of a designated person or bearer. An offense under this Section is a felony of the third degree if the value of the property or services secured or sought to be secured by means of the credit card exceeds $500; otherwise it is a misdemeanor.

Section 224.7. Deceptive Business Practices.

A person commits a misdemeanor if in the course of business he:

(1) uses or possesses for use a false weight or measure, or any other device for falsely determining or recording any quality or quantity; or

(2) sells, offers or exposes for sale, or delivers less than the represented quantity of any commodity or service; or

(3) takes or attempts to take more than the represented quantity of any commodity or service when as buyer he furnishes the weight or measure; or

(4) sells, offers or exposes for sale adulterated or mislabeled commodities. "Adulterated" means varying from the standard of composition or quality prescribed by or pursuant to any statute providing criminal penalties for such variance, or set by established commercial usage. "Mislabeled" means varying from the standard of truth or disclosure in labeling prescribed by or pursuant to any statute providing criminal penalties for such variance, or set by established commercial usage; or

(5) makes a false or misleading statement in any advertisement addressed to the public or to a substantial segment thereof for the purpose of promoting the purchase or sale of property or services; or

(6) makes a false or misleading written statement for the purpose of obtaining property or credit; or

(7) makes a false or misleading written statement for the purpose of promoting the sale of securities, or omits information required by law to be disclosed in written documents relating to securities. It is an affirmative defense to prosecution under this Section if the defendant proves by a preponderance of the evidence that his conduct was not knowingly or recklessly deceptive.

Section 224.8. Commercial Bribery and Breach of Duty to Act Disinterestedly.

(1) A person commits a misdemeanor if he solicits, accepts or agrees to accept any benefit as consideration for knowingly violating or agreeing to violate a duty of fidelity to which he is subject as:

(a) partner, agent or employee of another;

(b) trustee, guardian, or other fiduciary;

(c) lawyer, physician, accountant, appraiser, or other professional adviser or informant;

(d) officer, director, manager or other participant in the direction of the affairs of an incorporated or unincorporated association; or

(e) arbitrator or other purportedly disinterested adjudicator or referee.

(2) A person who holds himself out to the public as being engaged in the business of making disinterested selection, appraisal, or criticism of commodities or services commits a misdemeanor if he solicits, accepts or agrees to accept any benefit to influence his selection, appraisal or criticism.

(3) A person commits a misdemeanor if he confers, or offers or agrees to confer, any benefit the acceptance of which would be criminal under this Section.

Section 224.9. Rigging Publicly Exhibited Contest.

(1) A person commits a misdemeanor if, with purpose to prevent a publicly exhibited contest from being conducted in accordance with the rules and usages purporting to govern it, he:

(a) confers or offers or agrees to confer any benefit upon, or threatens any injury to a participant, official or other person associated with the contest or exhibition; or

(b) tampers with any person, animal or thing.

(2) Soliciting or Accepting Benefit for Rigging. A person commits a misdemeanor if he knowingly solicits, accepts or agrees to accept any benefit the giving of which would be criminal under Subsection (1).

(3) Participation in Rigged Contest. A person commits a misdemeanor if he knowingly engages in, sponsors, produces, judges, or otherwise participates in a publicly exhibited contest knowing that the contest is not being conducted in compliance with the rules and usages purporting to govern it, by reason of conduct which would be criminal under this Section.

Section 224.10. Defrauding Secured Creditors.

A person commits a misdemeanor if he destroys, removes, conceals, encumbers, transfers or otherwise deals with property subject to a security interest with purpose to hinder enforcement of that interest.

Section 224.11. Fraud in Insolvency.

A person commits a misdemeanor if, knowing that proceedings have been or are about to be instituted for the appointment of a receiver or other person entitled to administer property for the benefit of creditors, or that any other composition or liquidation for the benefit of creditors has been or is about to made, he:

(1) destroys, removes, conceals, encumbers, transfers, or otherwise deals with any property with purpose to defeat or obstruct the claim of any creditor, or otherwise to obstruct the operation of any law relating to administration of property for the benefit of creditors; or

(2) knowingly falsifies any writing or record relating to the property; or

(3) knowingly misrepresents or refuses to disclose to a receiver or other person entitled to administer property for the benefit of creditors, the existence, amount or location of the property, or any other information which the actor could be legally required to furnish in relation to such administration.

Section 224.12. Receiving Deposits in a Failing Financial Institution.

An officer, manager or other person directing or participating in the direction of a financial institution commits a misdemeanor if he receives or permits the receipt of a deposit, premium payment or other investment in the institution knowing that:

(1) due to financial difficulties the institution is about to suspend operations or go into receivership or reorganization; and

(2) the person making the deposit or other payment is unaware of the precarious situation of the institution.

Section 224.13. Misapplication of Entrusted Property and Property of Government or Financial Institution.

A person commits an offense if he applies or disposes of property that has been entrusted to him as a fiduciary, or property of the government or of a financial institution, in a manner which he knows is unlawful and involves substantial risk of loss or detriment to the owner of the property or to a person for whose benefit the property was entrusted. The offense is a misdemeanor if the amount involved exceeds $50; otherwise it is a petty misdemeanor. "Fiduciary" includes trustee, guardian, executor, administrator, receiver and any person carrying on fiduciary functions on behalf of a corporation or other organization which is a fiduciary.

Section 224.14. Securing Execution of Documents by Deception.

A person commits a misdemeanor if by deception he causes another to execute any instrument affecting or purporting to affect or likely to affect the pecuniary interest of any person.

Offenses Against the Family

Article 230. Offenses Against the Family.

Section 230.1. Bigamy and Polygamy.

(1) Bigamy. A married person is guilty of bigamy, a misdemeanor, if he contracts or purports to contract another marriage, unless at the time of the subsequent marriage:

> (a) the actor believes that the prior spouse is dead; or
>
> (b) the actor and the prior spouse have been living apart for five consecutive years throughout which the prior spouse was not known by the actor to be alive; or
>
> (c) a Court has entered a judgment purporting to terminate or annul any prior disqualifying marriage, and the actor does not know that judgment to be invalid; or
>
> (d) the actor reasonably believes that he is legally eligible to remarry.

(2) Polygamy. A person is guilty of polygamy, a felony of the third degree, if he marries or cohabits with more than one spouse at a time in purported exercise of the right of plural marriage. The offense is a continuing one until all cohabitation and claim of marriage with more than one spouse terminates. This section does not apply to parties to a polygamous marriage, lawful in the country of which they are residents or nationals, while they are in transit through or temporarily visiting this State.

(3) Other Party to Bigamous or Polygamous Marriage. A person is guilty of bigamy or polygamy, as the case may be, if he contracts or purports to contract marriage with another knowing that the other is thereby committing bigamy or polygamy.

Section 230.2. Incest.

A person is guilty of incest, a felony of the third degree, if he knowingly marries or cohabits or has sexual intercourse with an ancestor or descendant, a brother or sister of the whole or half blood [or an uncle, aunt, nephew or niece of the whole blood]. "Cohabit" means to live together under the representation or appearance of being married. The relationships referred to herein include blood relationships without regard to legitimacy, and relationship of parent and child by adoption.

Section 230.3. Abortion.

(1) Unjustified Abortion. A person who purposely and unjustifiably terminates the pregnancy of another otherwise than by a live birth commits a felony of the third degree or, where the pregnancy has continued beyond the twenty-sixth week, a felony of the second degree.

(2) Justifiable Abortion. A licensed physician is justified in terminating a pregnancy if he believes there is substantial risk that continuance of the pregnancy would gravely impair the physical or mental health of the mother or that the child would be born with grave physical or mental defect, or that the pregnancy resulted from rape, incest, or other felonious intercourse. All illicit intercourse with a girl below the age of 16 shall be deemed felonious for purposes of this subsection. Justifiable abortions shall be performed only in a licensed hospital except in case of emergency when hospital facilities are unavailable. [Additional exceptions from the requirement of hospitalization may be incorporated here to take account of situations in sparsely settled areas where hospitals are not generally accessible.]

(3) Physicians' Certificates; Presumption from Non-Compliance. No abortion shall be performed unless two physicians, one of whom may be the person performing the abortion, shall have certified in writing the circumstances which they believe to justify the abortion. Such certificate shall be submitted before the abortion to the hospital where it is to be performed and, in the case of abortion following felonious intercourse, to the prosecuting attorney or the police. Failure to comply with any of the requirements of this Subsection gives rise to a presumption that the abortion was unjustified.

(4) Self-Abortion. A woman whose pregnancy has continued beyond the twenty-sixth week commits a felony of the third degree if she purposely terminates her own pregnancy otherwise than by a live birth, or if she uses instruments, drugs or violence upon herself for that purpose. Except as justified under Subsection (2), a person who induces or knowingly aids a woman to use instruments, drugs or violence upon herself for the purpose of terminating her pregnancy otherwise than by a live birth commits a felony of the third degree whether or not the pregnancy has continued beyond the twenty-sixth week.

(5) Pretended Abortion. A person commits a felony of the third degree if, representing that it is his purpose to perform an abortion, he does an act adapted to cause abortion in a pregnant woman although the woman is in fact not pregnant, or the actor does not believe she is. A person charged with unjustified abortion under Subsection (1) or an attempt to commit that offense may be convicted thereof upon proof of conduct prohibited by this Subsection.

(6) Distribution of Abortifacients. A person who sells, offers to sell, possesses with intent to sell, advertises, or displays for sale anything specially designed to

terminate a pregnancy, or held out by the actor as useful for that purpose, commits a misdemeanor, unless:

      (a) the sale, offer or display is to a physician or druggist or to an intermediary in a chain of distribution to physicians or druggists; or

      (b) the sale is made upon prescription or order of a physician; or

      (c) the possession is with intent to sell as authorized in paragraphs (a) and (b); or

      (d) the advertising is addressed to persons named in paragraph (a) and confined to trade or professional channels not likely to reach the general public.

(7) Section Inapplicable to Prevention of Pregnancy. Nothing in this Section shall be deemed applicable to the prescription, administration or distribution of drugs or other substances for avoiding pregnancy, whether by preventing implantation of a fertilized ovum or by any other method that operates before, at or immediately after fertilization.

Section 230.4. Endangering Welfare of Children.

    A parent, guardian, or other person supervising the welfare of a child under 18 commits a misdemeanor if he knowingly endangers the child's welfare by violating a duty of care, protection or support.

Section 230.5. Persistent Non-Support.

    A person commits a misdemeanor if he persistently fails to provide support which he can provide and which he knows he is legally obliged to provide to a spouse, child or other dependent.

Offenses Against Public Administration

Article 240. Bribery and Corrupt Influence.

Section 240.0. Definitions.

    In Articles 240-243, unless a different meaning plainly is required:

(1) "benefit" means gain or advantage, or anything regarded by the beneficiary as gain or advantage, including benefit to any other person or entity in whose welfare he is interested, but not an advantage promised generally to a group or class of voters as a consequence of public measures which a candidate engages to support or oppose;

(2) "government" includes any branch, subdivision or agency of the government of the State or any locality within it;

(3) "harm" means loss, disadvantage or injury, or anything so regarded by the person affected, including loss, disadvantage or injury to any other person or entity in whose welfare he is interested;

(4) "official proceeding" means a proceeding heard or which may be heard before any legislative, judicial, administrative or other governmental agency or official authorized to take evidence under oath, including any referee, hearing examiner, commissioner, notary or other person taking testimony or deposition in connection with any such proceeding;

(5) "party official" means a person who holds an elective or appointive post in a political party in the United States by virtue of which he directs or conducts, or participates in directing or conducting party affairs at any level of responsibility;

(6) "pecuniary benefit" is benefit in the form of money, property, commercial interests or anything else the primary significance of which is economic gain;

(7) "public servant" means any officer or employee of government, including legislators and judges, and any person participating as juror, advisor, consultant or otherwise, in performing a governmental function; but the term does not include witnesses;

(8) "administrative proceeding" means any proceeding, other than a judicial proceeding, the outcome of which is required to be based on a record or documentation prescribed by law, or in which law or regulation is particularized in application to individuals.

Section 240.1. Bribery in Official and Political Matters.

A person is guilty of bribery, a felony of the third degree, if he offers, confers or agrees to confer upon another, or solicits, accepts or agrees to accept from another:

(1) any pecuniary benefit as consideration for the recipient's decision, opinion, recommendation, vote or other exercise of discretion as a public servant, party official or voter; or

(2) any benefit as consideration for the recipient's decision, vote, recommendation or other exercise of official discretion in a judicial or administrative proceeding; or

(3) any benefit as consideration for a violation of a known legal duty as public servant or party official. It is no defense to prosecution under this section that a person whom the actor sought to influence was not qualified to act in the desired way whether because he had not yet assumed office, or lacked jurisdiction, or for any other reason.

Section 240.2. Threats and Other Improper Influence in Official and Political Matters.

(1) Offenses Defined. A person commits an offense if he:

(a) threatens unlawful harm to any person with purpose to influence his decision, opinion, recommendation, vote or other exercise of discretion as a public servant, party official or voter; or

(b) threatens harm to any public servant with purpose to influence his decision, opinion, recommendation, vote or other exercise of discretion in a judicial or administrative proceeding; or

(c) threatens harm to any public servant or party official with purpose to influence him to violate his known legal duty; or

(d) privately addresses to any public servant who has or will have an official discretion in a judicial or administrative proceeding any representation, entreaty, argument or other communication with purpose to influence the outcome on the basis of considerations other than those authorized by law. It is no defense to prosecution under this Section that a person whom the actor sought to influence was not qualified to act in the desired way, whether because he had not yet assumed office, or lacked jurisdiction, or for any other reason.

(2) Grading. An offense under this Section is a misdemeanor unless the actor threatened to commit a crime or made a threat with purpose to influence a judicial or administrative proceeding, in which cases the offense is a felony of the third degree.

Section 240.3. Compensation for Past Official Action.

A person commits a misdemeanor if he solicits, accepts or agrees to accept any pecuniary benefit as compensation for having, as public servant, given a decision, opinion, recommendation or vote favorable to another, or for having otherwise exercised a discretion in his favor, or for having violated his duty. A person commits a misdemeanor if he offers, confers or agrees to confer compensation acceptance of which is prohibited by this Section.

Section 240.4. Retaliation for Past Official Action.

A person commits a misdemeanor if he harms another by any unlawful act in retaliation for anything lawfully done by the latter in the capacity of public servant.

Section 240.5. Gifts to Public Servants by Persons Subject to Their Jurisdiction.

(1) Regulatory and Law Enforcement Officials. No public servant in any department or agency exercising regulatory functions, or conducting inspections or investigations, or carrying on civil or criminal litigation on behalf of the government, or having custody of prisoners, shall solicit, accept or agree to accept any pecuniary benefit from a person known to be subject to such regulation, inspection, investigation or custody, or against whom such litigation is known to be pending or contemplated.

(2) Officials Concerned with Government Contracts and Pecuniary Transactions. No public servant having any discretionary function to perform in connection with contracts, purchases, payments, claims or other pecuniary transactions of the government shall solicit, accept or agree to accept any pecuniary benefit from any person known to be interested in or likely to become interested in any such contract, purchase, payment, claim or transaction.

(3) Judicial and Administrative Officials. No public servant having judicial or administrative authority and no public servant employed by or in a court or other tribunal having such authority, or participating in the enforcement of its decisions, shall solicit, accept or agree to accept any pecuniary benefit from a person known to be interested in or likely to become interested in any matter before such public servant or a tribunal with which he is associated.

(4) Legislative Officials. No legislator or public servant employed by the legislature or by any committee or agency thereof shall solicit, accept or agree to accept any pecuniary benefit from any person known to be interested in a bill, transaction or proceeding, pending or contemplated, before the legislature or any committee or agency thereof.

(5) Exceptions. This Section shall not apply to:

(a) fees prescribed by law to be received by a public servant, or any other benefit for which the recipient gives legitimate consideration or to which he is otherwise legally entitled; or

(b) gifts or other benefits conferred on account of kinship or other personal, professional or business relationship independent of the official status of the receiver; or

(c) trivial benefits incidental to personal, professional or business contacts and involving no substantial risk of undermining official impartiality.

(6) Offering Benefits Prohibited. No person shall knowingly confer, or offer or agree to confer, any benefit prohibited by the foregoing Subsections.

(7) Grade of Offense. An offense under this Section is a misdemeanor.

Section 240.6. Compensating Public Servant for Assisting Private Interests in Relation to Matters Before Him.

(1) Receiving Compensation. A public servant commits a misdemeanor if he solicits, accepts or agrees to accept compensation for advice or other assistance in preparing or promoting a bill, contract, claim, or other transaction or proposal as to which he knows that he has or is likely to have an official discretion to exercise.

(2) Paying Compensation. A person commits a misdemeanor if he pays or offers or agrees to pay compensation to a public servant with knowledge that acceptance by the public servant is unlawful.

Section 240.7. Selling Political Endorsement; Special Influence.

(1) Selling Political Endorsement. A person commits a misdemeanor if he solicits, receives, agrees to receive, or agrees that any political party or other person shall receive, any pecuniary benefit as consideration for approval or disapproval of an appointment or advancement in public service, or for approval or disapproval of any person or transaction for any benefit conferred by an official or agency of government. "Approval" includes recommendation, failure to disapprove, or any other manifestation of favor or acquiescence. "Disapproval" includes failure to approve, or any other manifestation of disfavor or nonacquiescence.

(2) Other Trading in Special Influence. A person commits a misdemeanor if he solicits, receives or agrees to receive any pecuniary benefit as consideration for exerting special influence upon a public servant or procuring another to do so. "Special influence" means power to influence through kinship, friendship or other relationship, apart from the merits of the transaction.

(3) Paying for Endorsement or Special Influence. A person commits a misdemeanor if he offers, confers or agrees to confer any pecuniary benefit receipt of which is prohibited by this Section.

Article 241. Perjury and Other Falsification in Official Matters.

Section 241.0. Definitions.

In this Article, unless a different meaning plainly is required:

(1) the definitions given in Section 240.0 apply; and

(2) "statement" means any representation, but includes a representation of opinion, belief or other state of mind only if the representation clearly relates to state of mind apart from or in addition to any facts which are the subject of the representation.

Section 241.1. Perjury.

(1) Offense Defined. A person is guilty of perjury, a felony of the third degree, if in any official proceeding he makes a false statement under oath or equivalent affirmation, or swears or affirms the truth of a statement previously made, when the statement is material and he does not believe it to be true.

(2) Materiality. Falsification is material, regardless of the admissibility of the statement under rules of evidence, if it could have affected the course or outcome of the proceeding. It is no defense that the declarant mistakenly believed the falsification to be immaterial. Whether a falsification is material in a given factual situation is a question of law.

(3) Irregularities No Defense. It is not a defense to prosecution under this Section that the oath or affirmation was administered or taken in an irregular manner or that the declarant was not competent to make the statement. A document purporting to be made upon oath or affirmation at any time when the actor presents it as being so verified shall be deemed to have been duly sworn or affirmed.

(4) Retraction. No person shall be guilty of an offense under this Section if he retracted the falsification in the course of the proceeding in which it was made before it became manifest that the falsification was or would be exposed and before the falsification substantially affected the proceeding.

(5) Inconsistent Statements. Where the defendant made inconsistent statements under oath or equivalent affirmation, both having been made within the period of the statute of limitations, the prosecution may proceed by setting forth the inconsistent statements in a single count alleging in the alternative that one or the other was false and not believed by the defendant. In such case it shall not be necessary for the prosecution to prove which statement was false but only that one or the other was false and not believed by the defendant to be true.

(6) Corroboration. No person shall be convicted of an offense under this Section where proof of falsity rests solely upon contradiction by testimony of a single person other than the defendant.

Section 241.2. False Swearing.

(1) False Swearing in Official Matters. A person who makes a false statement under oath or equivalent affirmation, or swears or affirms the truth of such a statement previously made, when he does not believe the statement to be true, is guilty of a misdemeanor if:

    (a) the falsification occurs in an official proceeding; or

    (b) the falsification is intended to mislead a public servant in performing his official function.

(2) Other False Swearing. A person who makes a false statement under oath or equivalent affirmation, or swears or affirms the truth of such a statement previously made, when he does not believe the statement to be true, is guilty of a petty misdemeanor, if the statement is one which is required by law to be sworn or affirmed before a notary or other person authorized to administer oaths.

(3) Perjury Provisions Applicable. Subsections (3) to (6) of Section 241.1 apply to the present Section.

Section 241.3. Unsworn Falsification to Authorities.

(1) In General. A person commits a misdemeanor if, with purpose to mislead a public servant in performing his official function, he:

    (a) makes any written false statement which he does not believe to be true; or

    (b) purposely creates a false impression in a written application for any pecuniary or other benefit, by omitting information necessary to prevent statements therein from being misleading; or

    (c) submits or invites reliance on any writing which he knows to be forged, altered or otherwise lacking in authenticity; or

    (d) submits or invites reliance on any sample, specimen, map, boundary-mark, or other object which he knows to be false.

(2) Statements "Under Penalty." A person commits a petty misdemeanor if he makes a written false statement which he does not believe to be true, on or pursuant to a form bearing notice, authorized by law, to the effect that false statements made therein are punishable.

(3) Perjury Provisions Applicable. Subsections (3) to (6) of Section 241.1 apply to the present section.

Section 241.4. False Alarms to Agencies of Public Safety.

A person who knowingly causes a false alarm of fire or other emergency to be transmitted to or within any organization, official or volunteer, for dealing with emergencies involving danger to life or property commits a misdemeanor.

Section 241.5. False Reports to Law Enforcement Authorities.

(1) Falsely Incriminating Another. A person who knowingly gives false information to any law enforcement officer with purpose to implicate another commits a misdemeanor.

(2) Fictitious Reports. A person commits a petty misdemeanor if he:

(a) reports to law enforcement authorities an offense or other incident within their concern knowing that it did not occur; or

(b) pretends to furnish such authorities with information relating to an offense or incident when he knows he has no information relating to such offense or incident.

Section 241.6. Tampering with Witnesses and Informants; Retaliation Against Them.

(1) Tampering. A person commits an offense if, believing that an official proceeding or investigation is pending or about to be instituted, he attempts to induce or otherwise cause a witness or informant to:

(a) testify or inform falsely; or

(b) withhold any testimony, information, document or thing; or

(c) elude legal process summoning him to testify or supply evidence; or

(d) absent himself from any proceeding or investigation to which he has been legally summoned. The offense is a felony of the third degree if the actor employs force, deception, threat or offer of pecuniary benefit. Otherwise it is a misdemeanor.

(2) Retaliation Against Witness or Informant. A person commits a misdemeanor if he harms another by any unlawful act in retaliation for anything lawfully done in the capacity of witness or informant.

(3) Witness or Informant Taking Bribe. A person commits a felony of the third degree if he solicits, accepts or agrees to accept any benefit in consideration of his doing any of the things specified in clauses (a) to (d) of Subsection (1).

Section 241.7. Tampering with or Fabricating Physical Evidence.

A person commits a misdemeanor if, believing that an official proceeding or investigation is pending or about to be instituted, he:

(1) alters, destroys, conceals or removes any record, document or thing with purpose to impair its verity or availability in such proceeding or investigation; or

(2) makes, presents or uses any record, document or thing knowing it to be false and with purpose to mislead a public servant who is or may be engaged in such proceeding or investigation.

Section 241.8. Tampering with Public Records or Information.

(1) Offense Defined. A person commits an offense if he:

(a) knowingly makes a false entry in, or false alteration of, any record, document or thing belonging to, or received or kept by, the government for information or record, or required by law to be kept by others for information of the government; or

(b) makes, presents or uses any record, document or thing knowing it to be false, and with purpose that it be taken as a genuine part of information or records referred to in paragraph (a); or

(c) purposely and unlawfully destroys, conceals, removes or otherwise impairs the verity or availability of any such record, document or thing.

(2) Grading. An offense under this Section is a misdemeanor unless the actor's purpose is to defraud or injure anyone, in which case the offense is a felony of the third degree.

Section 241.9. Impersonating a Public Servant.

A person commits a misdemeanor if he falsely pretends to hold a position in the public service with purpose to induce another to submit to such pretended official authority or otherwise to act in reliance upo that pretense to his prejudice.

Article 242. Obstructing Governmental Operations; Escapes.

Section 242.0. Definitions.

In this Article, unless another meaning plainly is required, the definitions given in Section 240.0 apply.

Section 242.1. Obstructing Administration of Law or Other Governmental Function.

A person commits a misdemeanor if he purposely obstructs, impairs or perverts the administration of law or other governmental function by force, violence, physical interference or obstacle, breach of official duty, or any other unlawful act, except that this Section does not apply to flight by a person charged with crime, refusal to submit to arrest, failure to perform a legal duty other than an official duty, or any other means of avoiding compliance with law without affirmative interference with governmental functions.

Section 242.2. Resisting Arrest or Other Law Enforcement.

A person commits a misdemeanor if, for the purpose of preventing a public servant from effecting a lawful arrest or discharging any other duty, the person creates a substantial risk of bodily injury to the public servant or anyone else, or employs means justifying or requiring substantial force to overcome the resistance.

Section 242.3. Hindering Apprehension or Prosecution.

A person commits an offense if, with purpose to hinder the apprehension, prosecution, conviction or punishment of another for crime, he:

(1) harbors or conceals the other; or

(2) provides or aids in providing a weapon, transportation, disguise or other means of avoiding apprehension or effecting escape; or

(3) conceals or destroys evidence of the crime, or tampers with a witness, informant, document or other source of information, regardless of its admissibility in evidence; or

(4) warns the other of impending discovery or apprehension, except that this paragraph does not apply to a warning given in connection with an effort to bring another into compliance with law; or

(5) volunteers false information to a law enforcement officer. The offense is a felony of the third degree if the conduct which the actor knows has been charged or is liable to be charged against the person aided would constitute a felony of the first or second degree. Otherwise it is a misdemeanor.

Section 242.4. Aiding Consummation of Crime.

A person commits an offense if he purposely aids another to accomplish an unlawful object of a crime, as by safeguarding the proceeds thereof or converting the proceeds into negotiable funds. The offense is a felony of the third degree if the principal offense was a felony of the first or second degree. Otherwise it is a misdemeanor.

Section 242.5. Compounding.

A person commits a misdemeanor if he accepts or agrees to accept any pecuniary benefit in consideration of refraining from reporting to law enforcement authorities the commission or suspected commission of any offense or information relating to an offense. It is an affirmative defense to prosecution under this Section that the pecuniary benefit did not exceed an amount which the actor believed to be due as restitution or indemnification for harm caused by the offense.

Section 242.6. Escape.

(1) Escape. A person commits an offense if he unlawfully removes himself from official detention or fails to return to official detention following temporary leave granted for a specific purpose or limited period. "Official detention" means arrest, detention in any facility for custody of persons under charge or conviction of crime or alleged or found to be delinquent, detention for extradition or deportation, or any other detention for law enforcement purposes; but "official detention" does not include supervision of probation or parole, or constraint incidental to release on bail.

(2) Permitting or Facilitating Escape. A public servant concerned in detention commits an offense if he knowingly or recklessly permits an escape. Any person who knowingly causes or facilitates an escape commits an offense.

(3) Effect of Legal Irregularity in Detention. Irregularity in bringing about or maintaining detention, or lack of jurisdiction of the committing or detaining authority, shall not be a defense to prosecution under this Section if the escape is

from a prison or other custodial facility or from detention pursuant to commitment by official proceedings. In the case of other detentions, irregularity or lack of jurisdiction shall be a defense only if:

    (a) the escape involved no substantial risk of harm to the person or property of anyone other than the detainee; or

    (b) the detaining authority did not act in good faith under color of law.

(4) Grading of Offenses. An offense under this Section is a felony of the third degree where:

    (a) the actor was under arrest for or detained on a charge of felony or following conviction of crime; or

    (b) the actor employs force, threat, deadly weapon or other dangerous instrumentality to effect the escape; or

    (c) a public servant concerned in detention of persons convicted of crime purposely facilitates or permits an escape from a detention facility. Otherwise an offense under this section is a misdemeanor.

Section 242.7. Implements for Escape; Other Contraband.

(1) Escape Implements. A person commits a misdemeanor if he unlawfully introduces within a detention facility, or unlawfully provides an inmate with, any weapon, tool or other thing which may be useful for escape. An inmate commits a misdemeanor if he unlawfully procures, makes, or otherwise provides himself with, or has in his possession, any such implement of escape. "Unlawfully" means surreptitiously or contrary to law, regulation or order of the detaining authority.

(2) Other Contraband. A person commits a petty misdemeanor if he provides an inmate with anything which the actor knows it is unlawful for the inmate to possess.

Section 242.8. Bail Jumping; Default in Required Appearance.

A person set at liberty by court order, with or without bail, upon condition that he will subsequently appear at a specified time and place, commits a misdemeanor if, without lawful excuse, he fails to appear at that time and place. The offense constitutes a felony of the third degree where the required appearance was to answer to a charge of felony, or for disposition of any such charge, and the actor took flight or went into hiding to avoid apprehension, trial or punishment. This Section does not apply to obligations to appear incident to release under suspended sentence or on probation or parole.

Article 243. Abuse of Office.

Section 243.0. Definitions.

In this Article, unless a different meaning plainly is required, the definitions given in Section 240.0 apply.

Section 243.1. Official Oppression.

A person acting or purporting to act in an official capacity or taking advantage of such actual or purported capacity commits a misdemeanor if, knowing that his conduct is illegal, he:

(1) subjects another to arrest, detention, search, seizure, mistreatment, dispossession, assessment, lien or other infringement of personal or property rights; or

(2) denies or impedes another in the exercise or enjoyment of any right, privilege, power or immunity.

Section 243.2. Speculating or Wagering on Official Action or Information.

A public servant commits a misdemeanor if, in contemplation of official action by himself or by a governmental unit with which he is associated, or in reliance on information to which he has access in his official capacity and which has not been made public, he:

(1) acquires a pecuniary interest in any property, transaction or enterprise which may be affected by such information or official action; or

(2) speculates or wagers on the basis of such information or official action; or

(3) aids another to do any of the foregoing.

Offenses Against Public Order and Decency
Article 250. Riot, Disorderly Conduct, and Related Offenses.

Section 250.1. Riot; Failure to Disperse.

(1) Riot. A person is guilty of riot, a felony of the third degree, if he participates with [two] or more others in a course of disorderly conduct:

(a) with purpose to commit or facilitate the commission of a felony or misdemeanor;

(b) with purpose to prevent or coerce official action; or

(c) when the actor or any other participant to the knowledge of the actor uses or plans to use a firearm or other deadly weapon.

(2) Failure of Disorderly Persons to Disperse Upon Official Order. Where [three] or more persons are participating in a course of disorderly conduct likely to cause substantial harm or serious inconvenience, annoyance or alarm, a peace officer or other public servant engaged in executing or enforcing the law may order the participants and others in the immediate vicinity to disperse. A person who refuses or knowingly fails to obey such an order commits a misdemeanor.

Section 250.2. Disorderly Conduct.

(1) Offense Defined. A person is guilty of disorderly conduct if, with purpose to cause public inconvenience, annoyance or alarm, or recklessly creating a risk thereof, he:

(a) engages in fighting or threatening, or in violent or tumultuous behavior; or

(b) makes unreasonable noise or offensively coarse utterance, gesture or display, or addresses abusive language to any person present; or

(c) creates a hazardous or physically offensive condition by any act which serves no legitimate purpose of the actor.

"Public" means affecting or likely to affect persons in a place to which the public or a substantial group has access; among the places included are highways, transport facilities, schools, prisons, apartment houses, places of business or amusement, or any neighborhood.

(2) Grading. An offense under this section is a petty misdemeanor if the actor's purpose is to cause substantial harm or serious inconvenience, or if he persists in disorderly conduct after reasonable warning or request to desist. Otherwise disorderly conduct is a violation.

Section 250.3. False Public Alarms.

A person is guilty of a misdemeanor if he initiates or circulates a report or warning of an impending bombing or other crime or catastrophe, knowing that the report or warning is false or baseless and that it is likely to cause evacuation of a building, place of assembly, or facility of public transport, or to cause public inconvenience or alarm.

Section 250.4. Harassment.

A person commits a petty misdemeanor if, with purpose to harass another, he:

(1) makes a telephone call without purpose of legitimate communication; or

(2) insults, taunts or challenges another in a manner likely to provoke violent or disorderly response; or

(3) makes repeated communications anonymously or at extremely inconvenient hours, or in offensively coarse language; or

(4) subjects another to an offensive touching; or

(5) engages in any other course of alarming conduct serving no legitimate purpose of the actor.

Section 250.5. Public Drunkenness; Drug Incapacitation.

A person is guilty of an offense if he appears in any public place manifestly under the influence of alcohol, narcotics or other drug, not therapeutically administered, to the degree that he may endanger himself or other persons or property, or annoy persons in his vicinity. An offense under this Section constitutes a petty misdemeanor if the actor has been convicted hereunder twice before within a period of one year. Otherwise the offense constitutes a violation.

Section 250.6. Loitering or Prowling.

A person commits a violation if he loiters or prowls in a place, at a time, or in a manner not usual for law-abiding individuals under circumstances that warrant alarm for the safety of persons or property in the vicinity. Among the circumstances which may be considered in determining whether such alarm is warranted is the fact that the actor takes flight upon appearance of a peace officer, refuses to identify himself, or manifestly endeavors to conceal himself or any object. Unless flight by the actor or other circumstance makes it impracticable, a peace officer shall prior to any arrest for an offense under this section afford the actor an opportunity to dispel any alarm which would otherwise be warranted, by requesting him to identify himself and explain his presence and conduct. No person shall be convicted of an offense under this Section if the peace officer did not comply with the preceding sentence, or if it appears at trial that the explanation given by the actor was true and, if believed by the peace officer at the time, would have dispelled the alarm.

Section 250.7. Obstructing Highways and Other Public Passages.

(1) A person, who, having no legal privilege to do so, purposely or recklessly obstructs any highway or other public passage, whether alone or with others, commits a violation, or, in case he persists after warning by a law officer, a petty misdemeanor. "Obstructs" means renders impassable without unreasonable inconvenience or hazard. No person shall be deemed guilty of recklessly obstructing in violation of this Subsection solely because of a gathering of persons to hear him speak or otherwise communicate, or solely because of being a member of such a gathering.

(2) A person in a gathering commits a violation if he refuses to obey a reasonable official request or order to move:

(a) to prevent obstruction of a highway or other public passage; or

(b) to maintain public safety by dispersing those gathered in dangerous proximity to a fire or other hazard.

An order to move, addressed to a person whose speech or other lawful behavior attracts an obstructing audience, shall not be deemed reasonable if the obstruction can be readily remedied by police control of the size or location of the gathering.

Section 250.8. Disrupting Meetings and Processions.

A person commits a misdemeanor if, with purpose to prevent or disrupt a lawful meeting, procession or gathering, he does any act tending to obstruct or interfere with it physically, or makes any utterance, gesture or display designed to outrage the sensibilities of the group.

Section 250.9. Desecration of Venerated Objects.

A person commits a misdemeanor if he purposely desecrates any public monument or structure, or place of worship or burial, or if he purposely desecrates the national flag or any other object of veneration by the public or a substantial segment thereof in any public place. "Desecrate" means defacing, damaging, polluting or otherwise physically mistreating in a way that the actor knows will outrage the sensibilities of persons likely to observe or discover his action.

Section 250.10. Abuse of Corpse.

Except as authorized by law, a person who treats a corpse in a way that he knows would outrage ordinary family sensibilities commits a misdemeanor.

Section 250.11. Cruelty to Animals.

A person commits a misdemeanor if he purposely or recklessly:
(1) subjects any animal to cruel mistreatment; or
(2) subjects any animal in his custody to cruel neglect; or
(3) kills or injures any animal belonging to another without legal privilege or consent of the owner.
Subsections (1) and (2) shall not be deemed applicable to accepted veterinary practices and activities carried on for scientific research.

Section 250.12. Violation of Privacy.

(1) Unlawful Eavesdropping or Surveillance. A person commits a misdemeanor if, except as authorized by law, he:

(a) trespasses on property with purpose to subject anyone to eavesdropping or other surveillance in a private place; or

(b) installs in any private place, without the consent of the person or persons entitled to privacy there, any device for observing, photographing, recording, amplifying or broadcasting sounds or events in such place, or uses any such unauthorized installation; or

(c) installs or uses outside a private place any device for hearing, recording, amplifying or broadcasting sounds originating in such place which would not ordinarily be audible or comprehensible outside, without the consent of the person or persons entitled to privacy there.

"Private place" means a place where one may reasonably expect to be safe from casual or hostile intrusion or surveillance, but does not include a place to which the public or a substantial group thereof has access.

(2) Other Breach of Privacy of Messages. A person commits a misdemeanor if, except as authorized by law, he:

(a) intercepts without the consent of the sender or receiver a message by telephone, telegraph, letter or other means of communicating privately; but this paragraph does not extend to (i) overhearing of messages through a regularly installed instrument on a telephone party line or on an extension, or (ii) interception by the telephone company or subscriber incident to enforcement of regulations limiting use of the facilities or incident to other normal operation and use; or

(b) divulges without the consent of the sender or receiver the existence or contents of any such message if the actor knows that the message was illegally intercepted, or if he learned of the message in the course of employment with an agency engaged in transmitting it.

Article 251. Public Indecency.

Section 251.1. Open Lewdness.

A person commits a petty misdemeanor if he does any lewd act which he knows is likely to be observed by others who would be affronted or alarmed.

Section 251.2. Prostitution and Related Offenses.

(1) Prostitution. A person is guilty of prostitution, a petty misdemeanor, if he or she:

(a) is an inmate of a house of prostitution or otherwise engages in sexual activity as a business; or

(b) loiters in or within view of any public place for the purpose of being hired to engage in sexual activity.

"Sexual activity" includes homosexual and other deviate sexual relations. A "house of prostitution" is any place where prostitution or promotion of prostitution is regularly carried on by one person under the control, management or supervision of another. An "inmate" is a person who engages in prostitution in or through the agency of a house of prostitution. "Public place" means any place to which the public or any substantial group thereof has access.

(2) Promoting Prostitution. A person who knowingly promotes prostitution of another commits a misdemeanor or felony as provided in Subsection (3). The following acts shall, without limitation of the foregoing, constitute promoting prostitution:

(a) owning, controlling, managing, supervising or otherwise keeping, alone or in association with others, a house of prostitution or a prostitution business; or

(b) procuring an inmate for a house of prostitution or a place in a house of prostitution for one who would be an inmate; or

(c) encouraging, inducing, or otherwise purposely causing another to become or remain a prostitute; or

(d) soliciting a person to patronize a prostitute; or

(e) procuring a prostitute for a patron; or

(f) transporting a person into or within this state with purpose to promote that person's engaging in prostitution, or procuring or paying for transportation with that purpose; or

(g) leasing or otherwise permitting a place controlled by the actor, alone or in association with others, to be regularly used for prostitution or the promotion of prostitution, or failure to make reasonable effort to abate such use by ejecting the tenant, notifying law enforcement authorities, or other legally available means; or

(h) soliciting, receiving, or agreeing to receive any benefit for doing or agreeing to do anything forbidden by this Subsection.

(3) Grading of Offenses Under Subsection (2). An offense under Subsection (2) constitutes a felony of the third degree if:

(a) the offense falls within paragraph (a), (b) or (c) of Subsection (2); or

(b) the actor compels another to engage in or promote prostitution; or

(c) the actor promotes prostitution of a child under 16, whether or not he is aware of the child's age; or

(d) the actor promotes prostitution of his wife, child, ward or any person for whose care, protection or support he is responsible. Otherwise the offense is a misdemeanor.

(4) Presumption from Living off Prostitutes. A person, other than the prostitute or the prostitute's minor child or other legal dependent incapable of self-support, who is supported in whole or substantial part by the proceeds of prostitution is presumed to be knowingly promoting prostitution in violation of Subsection (2).

(5) Patronizing Prostitutes. A person commits a violation if he hires a prostitute to engage in sexual activity with him, or if he enters or remains in a house of prostitution for the purpose of engaging in sexual activity.

(6) Evidence. On the issue whether a place is a house of prostitution the following shall be admissible evidence: its general repute; the repute of the persons who reside in or frequent the place; the frequency, timing and duration of visits by non-residents. Testimony of a person against his spouse shall be admissible to prove offenses under this Section.

Section 251.3. Loitering to Solicit Deviate Sexual Relations.

A person is guilty of a petty misdemeanor if he loiters in or near any public place for the purpose of soliciting or being solicited to engage in deviate sexual relations.

Section 251.4. Obscenity.

(1) Obscene Defined. Material is obscene if, considered as a whole, its predominant appeal is to prurient interest, that is, a shameful or morbid interest, in nudity, sex or excretion, and if in addition it goes substantially beyond customary limits of candor in describing or representing such matters. Predominant appeal shall be judged with reference to ordinary adults unless it appears from

the character of the material or the circumstances of its dissemination to be designed for children or other specially susceptible audience. Undeveloped photographs, molds, printing plates, and the like, shall be deemed obscene notwithstanding that processing or other acts may be required to make the obscenity patent or to disseminate it.

(2) Offenses. Subject to the affirmative defense provided in Subsection (3), a person commits a misdemeanor if he knowingly or recklessly:

(a) sells, delivers or provides, or offers or agrees to sell, deliver or provide, any obscene writing, picture, record or other representation or embodiment of the obscene; or

(b) presents or directs an obscene play, dance or performance, or participates in that portion thereof which makes it obscene; or

(c) publishes, exhibits or otherwise makes available any obscene material; or

(d) possesses any obscene material for purposes of sale or other commercial dissemination; or

(e) sells, advertises or otherwise commercially disseminates material, whether or not obscene, by representing or suggesting that it is obscene.

A person who disseminates or possesses obscene material in the course of his business is presumed to do so knowingly or recklessly.

(3) Justifiable and Non-Commercial Private Dissemination. It is an affirmative defense to prosecution under this Section that dissemination was restricted to:

(a) institutions or persons having scientific, educational, governmental or other similar justification for possessing obscene material; or

(b) non-commercial dissemination to personal associates of the actor.

(4) Evidence; Adjudication of Obscenity. In any prosecution under this Section evidence shall be admissible to show:

(a) the character of the audience for which the material was designed or to which it was directed;

(b) what the predominant appeal of the material would be for ordinary adults or any special audience to which it was directed, and what effect, if any, it would probably have on conduct of such people;

(c) artistic, literary, scientific, educational or other merits of the material;

(d) the degree of public acceptance of the material in the United States;

(e) appeal to prurient interest, or absence thereof, in advertising or other promotion of the material; and

(f) the good repute of the author, creator, publisher or other person from whom the material originated.

Expert testimony and testimony of the author, creator, publisher or other person from whom the material originated, relating to factors entering into the determination of the issue of obscenity, shall be admissible. The Court shall dismiss a prosecution for obscenity if it is satisfied that the material is not obscene.

Table of Authors

Table of Model Penal Code References

Index

Mental disease or defect (*continued*)
  as negating element of offense, 272
  constitutionality of excluding admission of, 272
  defined, 699
Mentes reae, *see* Mens rea
Mfume, Kweisi, 241
Michael M. v. Superior Court of Sonoma County, 144
Michigan Penal Code, 133-136, 801-807
Military orders, reliance upon unlawful, 661
Mississippi Burning, 833
Mississippi Code, Title 97, Crimes, 349-352
Mistake, *see also* General mistake defense, Mistake negating culpability element, Mistake as to justification, Mistake of law
  at common law, 181-182
  exculpatory vs. inculpatory, 181
  general vs. specific intent offenses and, 182
  mistake excuses vs. disability excuses, 658
  types of mistake excuses compared, 661
  vs. accident, 181
  umbrella analogies, 180-181
Mistake negating culpability requirement
  generally, 160-186
  as to circumstance vs. result element, 181
  cf. law of mistake, 148
  for rape, 196-197
  mistake as to criminality of conduct, 186
  negating negligence, 183
  negating recklessness, 182-183
  negligent mistake, 183
  reckless mistake, 183
  rule of logical evidence, 182
  strict liability, 183
Mistake as to justification
  generally, 638-645
  ambiguity of acquittals, 641
  arguments against granting a defense for reasonable mistakes, 647-649
  arguments against subjectively defined justifications, 643
  arguments for granting a defense for reasonable mistakes, 645-646, 646, 649-650
  arguments supporting subjectively defined justifications, 642-643
  as excuse vs. subjective formulation, 638-639
  culpability and, 643-645
  empirical studies of community views, 650-656
  examples of objectively defined justifications, 641-642
  objective vs. subjective formulation, 641-643

privileged vs. unprivileged justification, 640-641
problems with subjective formulation, 643
reasons vs. deeds theory of justification, 639-640, 650-651
standard of reasonableness, 644-645
Mistake of law excuse
  generally, 672-674
  arguments against, 676, 680-682
  arguments in favor of, 677-680, 682-683
  as negating element of offense, 185
  estoppel rationale, 674
  in common law, 185
  in modern codes, 185
  law enforcement and, 677
  mixed fact/law mistake, 185
  New Jersey's reasonable mistake of law excuse, 674
  potential for odd results, 680-683
  rationales for, 676
  reliance upon official misstatement, 674
  unavailable law, 674
Mitchell, Wisconsin v., 854-860
Mitigation, *see* Homicide mitigations
Mixed fact/law mistake, *see* Mistake of law
Model Penal Code, *see also* Table of codes
  drafting of, 25
  homicide aggravations, 269-271
  difficulties with defensive force justifications, 579
  discussion of deadly force, 588-589
  format of, 25
  general part of criminal code, 28
  imaginary offenses, 361
  impossibility defense, 359
  inherently unlikely attempt, 361-362
  limitations on use of deadly force, 587-588
  reform, 24
  special part of criminal code, 28
  subjectivization of justification defenses, 614
Moral luck, 309
Morales, City of Chicago vs., 63-69
Morgan, Director of Prosecution v., 189, 190
Mubarak, Hosni, 371, 374-375

Necessary cause requirement, for causing crime by an innocent, 947
Necessary cause test, *see also* Factual cause requirement
  intervening sufficient cause and, 908
  simultaneous sufficient causes and, 907-908
Necessity, *see* Lesser evils defense
Necessity requirement
  defensive force justifications, 580